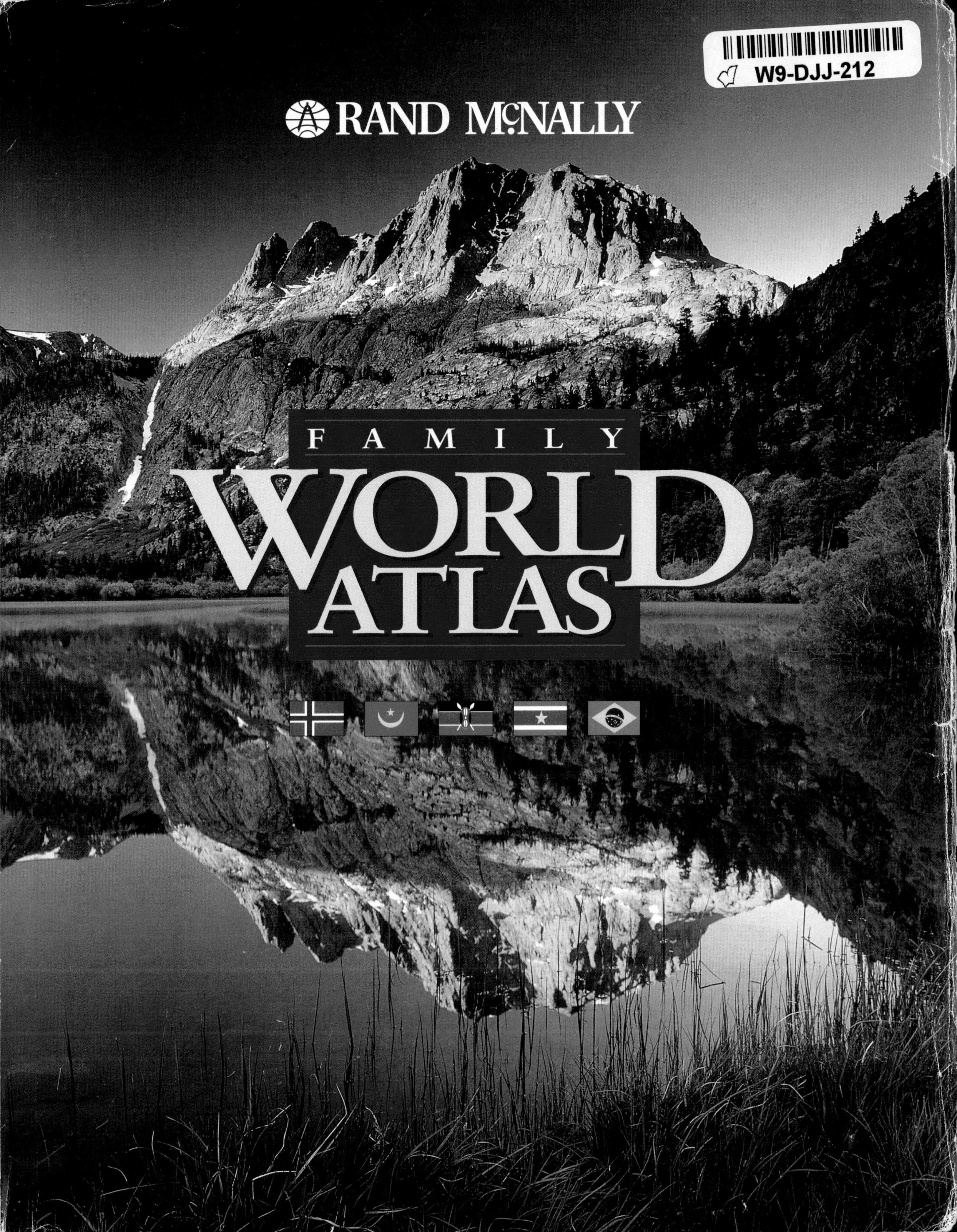

RAND McNALLY

FAMILY WORLD ATLAS

Using the Atlas .... I-3 – I-4
Flags of Nations .... I-5 – I-7
Table of Nations I-8
Reference Maps .... 1 – 128
Map Symbols and Index Map 1
World .... 2 – 3
Europe .... 4 – 5
Scandinavia 6
British Isles 7
Central Europe .... 8 – 9
France and the Alps .... 10 – 11
Spain and Portugal .... 12 – 13
Italy .... 14 – 15
Southeastern Europe .... 16 – 17
Baltic and Moscow Regions .... 18 – 19
Asia .... 20 – 21
Northwest Asia .... 22 – 23
Northeast Asia .... 24 – 25
China, Japan, and Korea .... 26 – 27
Eastern and Southeastern China .... 28 – 29
Japan .... 30 – 31
Southeastern Asia .... 32 – 33
Myanmar, Thailand, and Indochina .... 34 – 35
India and Pakistan 36
Southern India and Sri Lanka 37
Northern India and Pakistan .... 38 – 39
Eastern Mediterranean Lands 40
Africa 41
Northern Africa .... 42 – 43
Southern Africa .... 44 – 45
Eastern Africa and Middle East 46
Antarctica 47
Pacific Ocean .... 48 – 49
Australia .... 50 – 51
New Zealand 52
South America 53
Northern South America .... 54 – 55
Southern South America 56
Southeastern Brazil 57
Colombia, Ecuador, Venezuela, and Guyana .... 58 – 59
Atlantic Ocean 60
North America 61
Mexico .... 62 – 63
Central America and the Caribbean .... 64 – 65
Canada .... 66 – 67
Alberta 68
British Columbia 69
Manitoba 70
New Brunswick, Nova Scotia, and Prince Edward Island 71
Newfoundland 72
Ontario 73
Quebec 74
Saskatchewan 75
United States of America .... 76 – 77

Alabama 78	Louisiana........95	Ohio 112
Alaska 79	Maine 96	Oklahoma 113
Arizona 80	Maryland 97	Oregon 114
Arkansas 81	Massachusetts ..98	Pennsylvania ..115
California 82	Michigan 99	Rhode Island..116
Colorado 83	Minnesota 100	SouthCarolina 117
Connecticut 84	Mississippi 101	South Dakota 118
Delaware 85	Missouri 102	Tennessee 119
Florida 86	Montana 103	Texas............120
Georgia 87	Nebraska 104	Utah 121
Hawaii 88	Nevada 105	Vermont 122
Idaho 89	New Hampshire 106	Virginia 123
Illinois 90	New Jersey 107	Washington ...124
Indiana 91	New Mexico ..108	West Virginia .125
Iowa 92	New York 109	Wisconsin 126
Kansas.............93	NorthCarolina 110	Wyoming 127
Kentucky 94	North Dakota 111	

North Polar Regions 128
Index to Reference Maps .... 129 – 192

Published and printed in the United States

Library of Congress Cataloging-in-Publication Data

Rand McNally & Company.
Family world atlas
p. cm.
At head of title: *Rand McNally.*
Includes index.
ISBN 0-528-83673-0
(1. Atlas .) I. Title. II. Title: Rand McNally family world atlas.
G1021.R170 1994 <C&M> 93-48823
912--dc20 CIP
MAP

MAPS AND ATLASES

Satellite images of the world (figure 1) constantly give us views of the shape and size of the earth. It is hard, therefore, to imagine how difficult it once was to ascertain the look of our planet. Yet from early history we have evidence of humans trying to work out what the world actually looked like.

Twenty-five hundred years ago, on a tiny clay tablet the size of a hand, the Babylonians inscribed the earth as a flat disk (figure 2) with Babylon at the center. The section of the Cantino map of 1502 (figure 3) is an example of a *portolan* chart used to chart the newly discovered Americas. The maps in this atlas show the detail and accuracy that cartographers are now able to achieve.

FIGURE 1

FIGURE 2

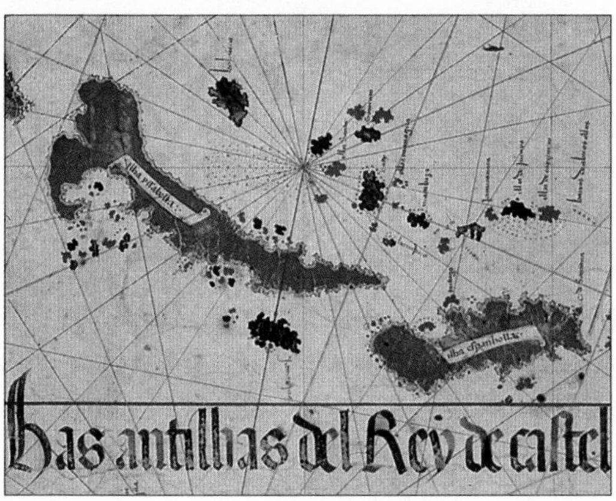

FIGURE 3

In 1589 Gerardus Mercator used the word "atlas" to describe a collection of maps. Atlases now bring together not only a variety of maps, but an assortment of tables and other reference material as well. They have become a unique and indispensable reference for graphically defining the world and answering the question, "Where?" With them, routes between places are traced, trips planned, distances measured, places imagined, and our earth visualized.

SEQUENCE OF THE MAPS

The world is made up of seven major landmasses: the continents of Europe, Asia, Africa, Antarctica, Australia, South America, and North America. The maps in this atlas follow this continental sequence. To allow for the inclusion of detail, each continent is broken down into a series of regional maps, and this grouping is arranged so that as consecutive pages are turned, a successive part of the continent is shown. Larger-scale maps are used for regions of greater detail or for areas of global significance.

GETTING THE INFORMATION

To realize the potential of an atlas the user must be able to:

1. Find places on the maps
2. Measure distances
3. Determine directions
4. Understand map symbols

FINDING PLACES

One of the most common and important tasks facilitated by an atlas is finding the location of a place in the world. A river's name in a book, a city mentioned in the news, or a vacation spot may prompt your need to know where the place is located. The illustrations and text below explain how to find Yangon (Rangoon), Myanmar(Burma).

Yancheng, China	B9	28
Yandoon, Mya.	F3	34
Yangjiang, China	G9	26
Yangon (Rangoon), Mya.	B2	32
Yangquan, China	D9	26
Yangtze see Chang, stm., China .	E10	26
Yangzhou, China	C8	28

FIGURE 4

1. Look up the place-name in the index at the back of the atlas. Yangon, Myanmar can be found on the map on page 32, and it can be located on the map by the letter-number key B2 (figure 4). If you know the general area in which a place is found, you may turn directly to the appropriate map and use the special marginal index.

2. Turn to the map of Southeastern Asia found on page 32. Note that the letters A through H and the numbers 1 through 11 appear in the margins of the map.

3. To find Yangon on the map, place your left index finger on B and your right index finger on 2. Move your left finger across the map and your right finger down the map. Your fingers will meet in the area in which Yangon is located (figure 5).

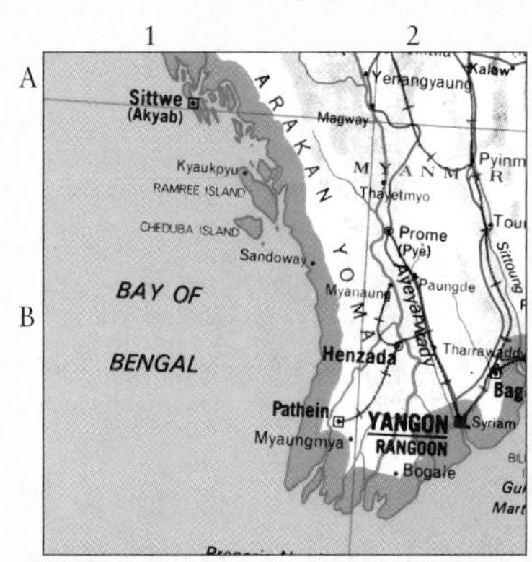

FIGURE 5

MEASURING DISTANCES

When planning trips, determining the distance between two places is essential, and an atlas can help in travel preparation. For instance, to determine the approximate distance between Paris and Rouen, France, follow these three steps:

1. Lay a slip of paper on the map on page 10 so that its edge touches the two cities. Adjust the paper so one corner touches Rouen. Mark the paper directly at the spot where Paris is located (figure 6).

2. Place the paper along the scale of miles beneath the map. Position the corner at 0 and line up the edge of the paper along the scale. The pencil mark on the paper indicates Rouen is between 50 and 100 miles from Paris (figure 7).

3. To find the exact distance, move the paper to the left so that the pencil mark is at 100 on the scale. The corner of the paper stands on the fourth 5-mile unit on the scale. This means that the two towns are 50 plus 20, or 70 miles apart (figure 8).

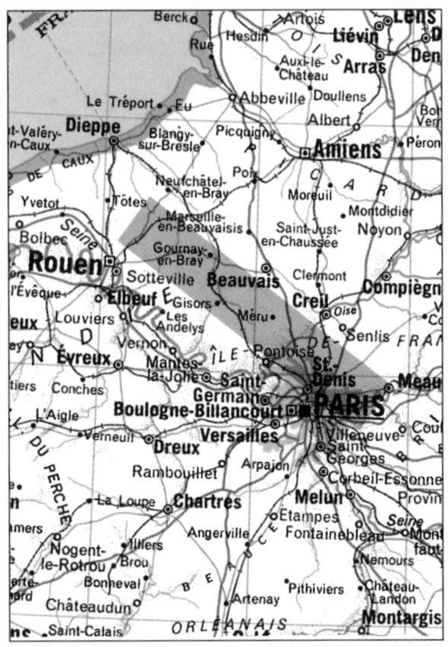

FIGURE 6

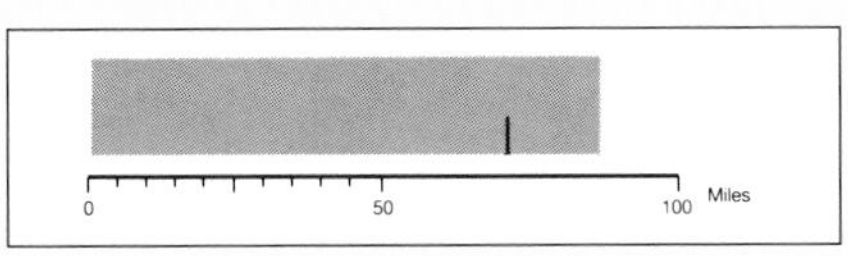

FIGURE 7

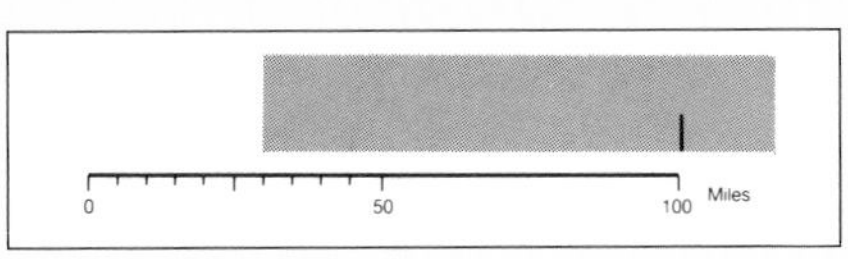

FIGURE 8

DETERMINING DIRECTIONS

Most of the maps in the atlas are drawn so that when oriented for normal reading, north is at the top of the map, south is at the bottom, west is at the left, and east is at the right. Most maps have a series of lines drawn across them–the lines of *latitude* and *longitude*. Lines of latitude, or *parallels* of latitude, are drawn east and west. Lines of longitude, or *meridians* of longitude, are drawn north and south (figure 9).

Parallels and meridians appear as either curved or straight lines. For example, in the section of the map of Europe (figure 10) the parallels of latitude appear as curved lines. The meridians of longitude are straight lines that come together toward the top of the map. Latitude and longitude lines help locate places on maps. Parallels of latitude are numbered in degrees north and south of the *Equator*. Meridians of longitude are numbered in degrees east and west of a line called the *Prime Meridian*, running through Greenwich, England, near London. Any place on earth can be located by the latitude and longitude lines running through it.

FIGURE 9

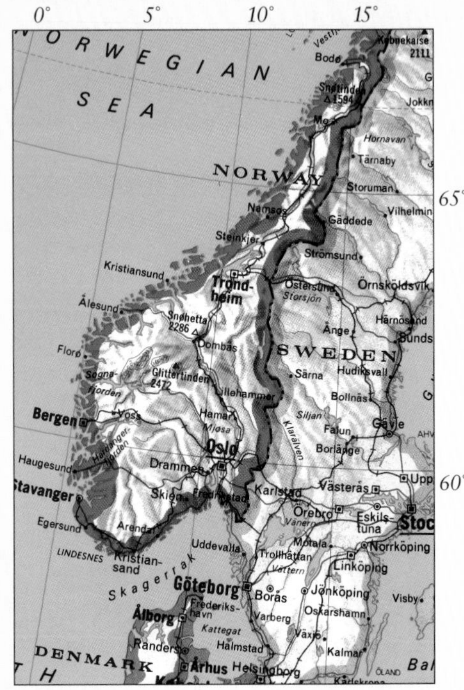

FIGURE 10

To determine directions or locations on the map, you must use the parallels and meridians. For example, suppose you want to know which is farther north, Bergen, Norway, or Norrköping, Sweden. The map (figure 10) shows that Norrköping is south of the 60° parallel of latitude and Bergen is north of it. Bergen is farther north than Norrköping. By looking at the meridians of longitude, you can determine which city is farther east. Bergen is approximately 5° east of the 0° meridian (Prime Meridian), and Norrköping is more than 15° east of it. Norrköping is farther east than Bergen.

UNDERSTANDING MAP SYMBOLS

In a very real sense, the whole map is a symbol, representing the world or a part of it. It is a reduced representation of the earth; each of the world's features – cities, rivers, etc. – is represented on the map by a symbol.

Symbols seldom look like the feature they represent and therefore must be identified and interpreted. The Map Symbols page in this atlas identifies the symbols used on the maps.

FLAGS OF NATIONS

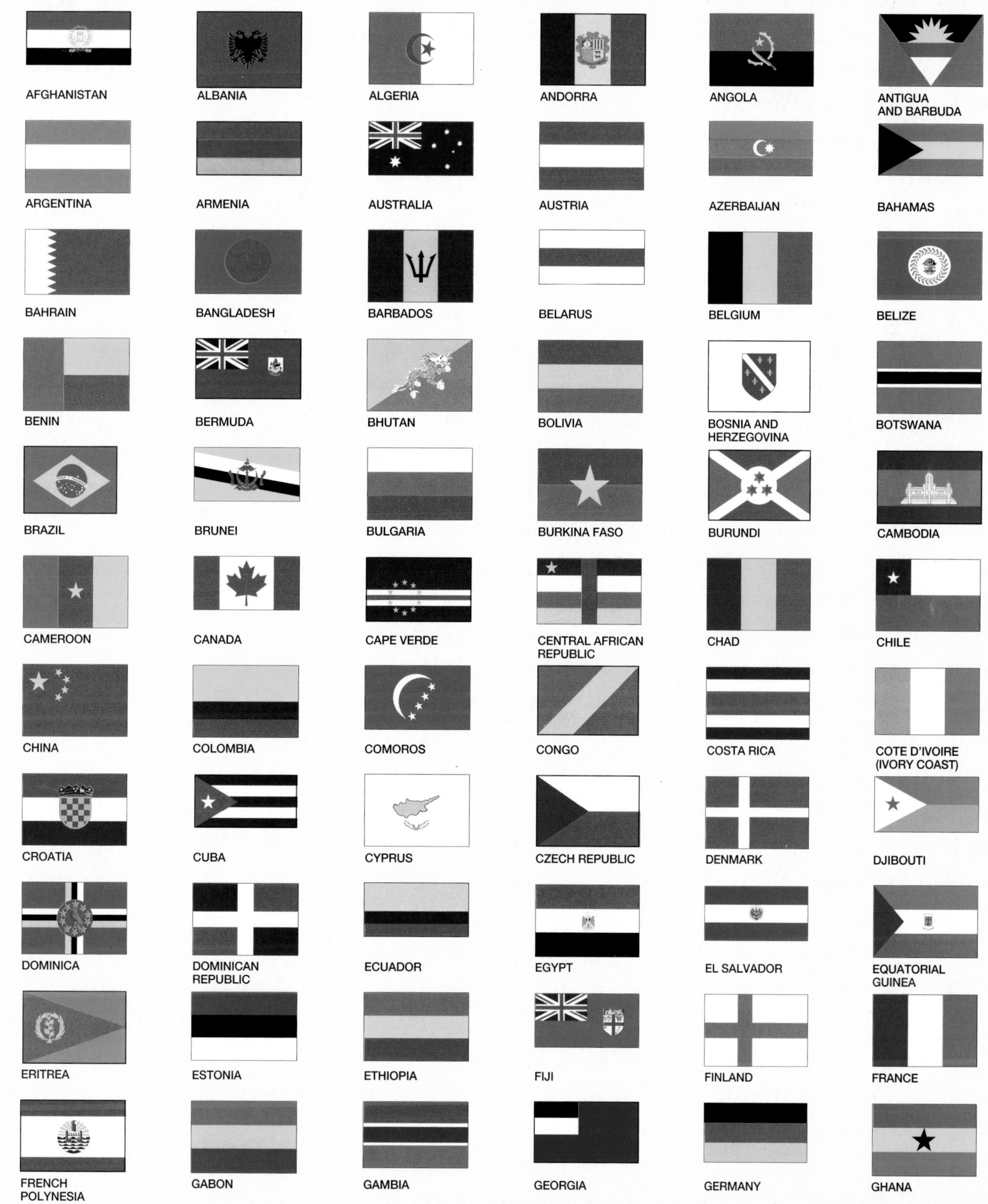

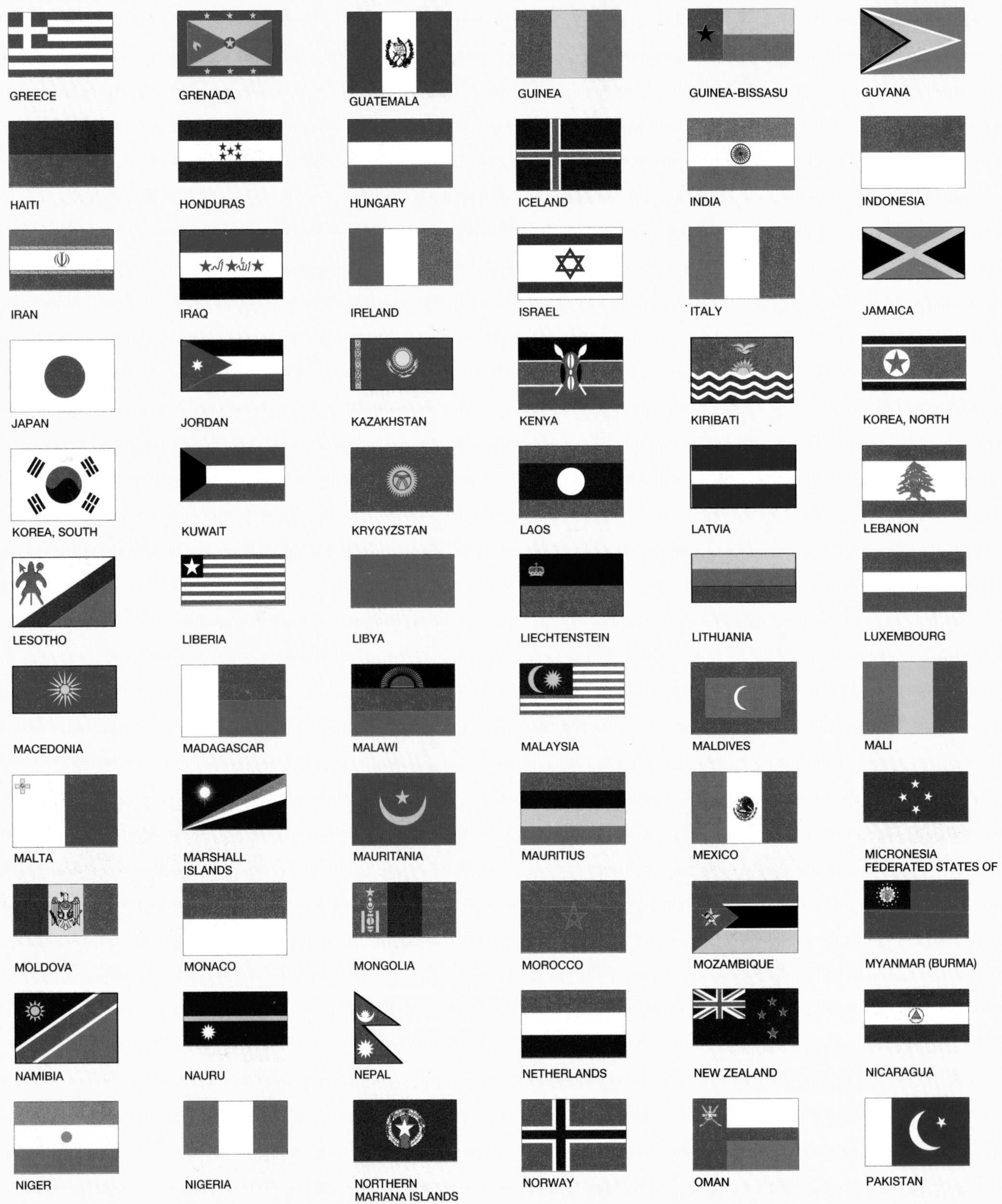

GREECE, GRENADA, GUATEMALA, GUINEA, GUINEA-BISSASU, GUYANA

HAITI, HONDURAS, HUNGARY, ICELAND, INDIA, INDONESIA

IRAN, IRAQ, IRELAND, ISRAEL, ITALY, JAMAICA

JAPAN, JORDAN, KAZAKHSTAN, KENYA, KIRIBATI, KOREA, NORTH

KOREA, SOUTH, KUWAIT, KRYGYZSTAN, LAOS, LATVIA, LEBANON

LESOTHO, LIBERIA, LIBYA, LIECHTENSTEIN, LITHUANIA, LUXEMBOURG

MACEDONIA, MADAGASCAR, MALAWI, MALAYSIA, MALDIVES, MALI

MALTA, MARSHALL ISLANDS, MAURITANIA, MAURITIUS, MEXICO, MICRONESIA FEDERATED STATES OF

MOLDOVA, MONACO, MONGOLIA, MOROCCO, MOZAMBIQUE, MYANMAR (BURMA)

NAMIBIA, NAURU, NEPAL, NETHERLANDS, NEW ZEALAND, NICARAGUA

NIGER, NIGERIA, NORTHERN MARIANA ISLANDS, NORWAY, OMAN, PAKISTAN

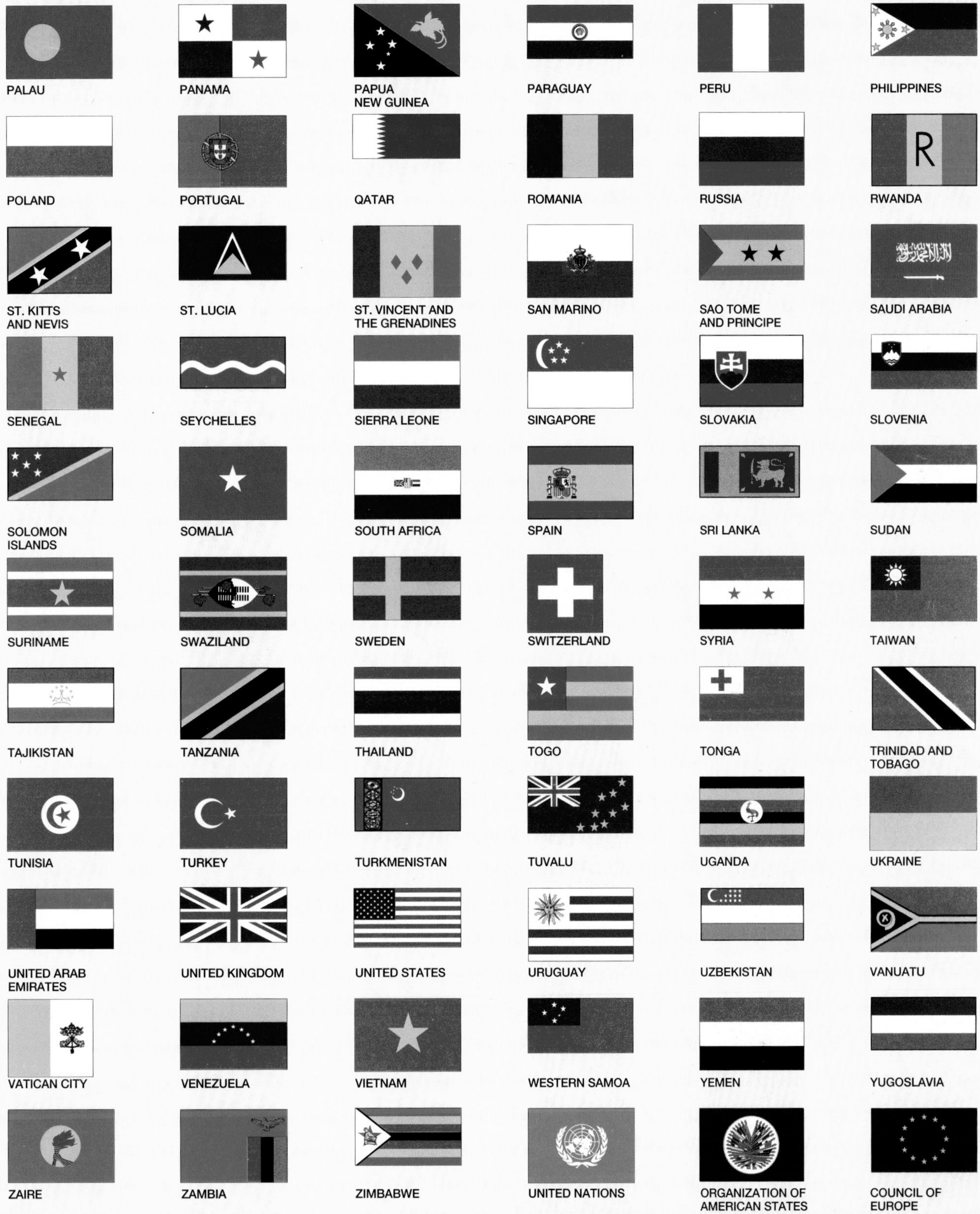
PALAU
PANAMA
PAPUA NEW GUINEA
PARAGUAY
PERU
PHILIPPINES
POLAND
PORTUGAL
QATAR
ROMANIA
RUSSIA
RWANDA
R
ST. KITTS AND NEVIS
ST. LUCIA
ST. VINCENT AND THE GRENADINES
SAN MARINO
SAO TOME AND PRINCIPE
SAUDI ARABIA
SENEGAL
SEYCHELLES
SIERRA LEONE
SINGAPORE
SLOVAKIA
SLOVENIA
SOLOMON ISLANDS
SOMALIA
SOUTH AFRICA
SPAIN
SRI LANKA
SUDAN
SURINAME
SWAZILAND
SWEDEN
SWITZERLAND
SYRIA
TAIWAN
TAJIKISTAN
TANZANIA
THAILAND
TOGO
TONGA
TRINIDAD AND TOBAGO
TUNISIA
TURKEY
TURKMENISTAN
TUVALU
UGANDA
UKRAINE
UNITED ARAB EMIRATES
UNITED KINGDOM
UNITED STATES
URUGUAY
UZBEKISTAN
VANUATU
VATICAN CITY
VENEZUELA
VIETNAM
WESTERN SAMOA
YEMEN
YUGOSLAVIA
ZAIRE
ZAMBIA
ZIMBABWE
UNITED NATIONS
ORGANIZATION OF AMERICAN STATES
COUNCIL OF EUROPE

TABLE OF NATIONS

Region or Political Division	Area in sq. miles	Estimated Population	Pop. per sq. mi.
* Afghanistan	251,826	16,290,000	65
* Albania	11,100	3,305,000	298
* Algeria	919,595	26,925,000	29
American Samoa	77	52,000	675
Andorra	175	56,000	320
* Angola	481,354	10,735,000	22
Anguilla	35	7,000	200
Antarctica	5,400,000	(1)	*
* Antigua and Barbuda	171	77,000	450
* Argentina	1,073,519	32,950,000	31
* Armenia	11,506	3,429,000	298
Aruba	75	65,000	867
* Australia	2,966,155	16,965,000	5.7
* Austria	32,377	7,899,000	244
* Azerbaijan	33,436	7,510,000	225
* Bahamas	5,382	265,000	49
* Bahrain	267	561,000	2,101
* Bangladesh	55,598	120,850,000	2,174
* Barbados	166	258,000	1,554
* Belarus	80,155	10,400,000	130
* Belgium	11,783	10,030,000	851
* Belize	8,866	186,000	21
* Benin	43,475	5,083,000	117
Bermuda	21	60,000	2,857
* Bhutan	17,954	1,680,000	94
* Bolivia	424,165	7,411,000	17
* Bosnia and Herzegovina	19,741	4,375,000	222
* Botswana	224,711	1,379,000	6.1
* Brazil	3,286,500	159,630,000	49
British Indian Ocean Territory	23	(1)	*
* Brunei	2,226	273,000	123
* Bulgaria	42,823	8,842,000	206
* Burkina Faso	105,869	9,808,000	93
* Burundi	10,745	6,118,000	569
* Cambodia	69,898	8,928,000	128
* Cameroon	183,569	12,875,000	70
* Canada	3,849,674	30,530,000	7.9
* Cape Verde	1,557	404,000	259
Cayman Islands	100	29,000	290
* Central African Republic	240,535	3,068,000	13
* Chad	495,755	5,297,000	11
* Chile	292,135	13,635,000	47
* China (excl. Taiwan)	3,689,631	1,179,030,000	320
Christmas Island	52	900	17
Cocos (Keeling) Islands	5.4	500	93
* Colombia	440,831	34,640,000	79
* Comoros (excl. Mayotte)	863	503,000	583
* Congo	132,047	2,413,000	18
Cook Islands	91	18,000	198
* Costa Rica	19,730	3,225,000	163
* Cote d'Ivoire (Ivory Coast)	124,518	13,765,000	111
* Croatia	21,829	4,793,000	220
* Cuba	42,804	10,900,000	255
* Cyprus (excl. North Cyprus)	2,276	527,000	232
* Cyprus, North (2)	1,295	193,000	149
* Czech Republic	30,450	10,335,000	339
* Denmark	16,638	5,169,000	311
* Dijbouti	8,958	396,000	44
* Dominica	305	88,000	289
* Dominican Republic	18,704	7,591,000	406
* Ecuador	109,484	11,055,000	101
* Egypt	386,662	57,050,000	148
* El Salvador	8,124	5,635,000	694
* Equatorial Guinea	10,831	394,000	36
Eritrea	36,170	3,425,000	95
* Estonia	17,413	1,613,000	93
* Ethiopia	446,953	51,715,000	116
Faeroe Islands	540	49,000	91
Falkland Islands (3)	4,700	2,100	0.4
* Fiji	7,056	754,000	107
* Finland	130,559	5,074,000	39
* France (excl. Overseas Departments)	211,208	57,570,000	273
French Guiana	35,135	131,000	3.7
French Polynesia	1,359	208,000	153
* Gabon	103,347	1,115,000	11
* Gambia	4,127	916,000	222
Georgia	26,911	5,593,000	208
* Germany	137,822	80,590,000	585
* Ghana	92,098	16,445,000	179
Gibraltar	2.3	32,000	13,913
* Greece	50,949	10,075,000	198
Greenland	840,004	57,000	0.1
* Grenada	133	97,000	729
Guadeloupe (incl. Dependencies)	687	413,000	601
Guam	209	143,000	684
* Guatemala	42,042	9,705,000	231
Guernsey (incl. Dependencies)	30	58,000	1,933
* Guinea	94,926	7,726,000	81
* Guinea-Bissau	13,948	1,060,000	76
* Guyana	83,000	737,000	8.9
* Haiti	10,714	6,509,000	608
* Honduras	43,277	5,164,000	119
Hong Kong	414	5,580,000	13,478
* Hungary	35,920	10,305,000	287
* Iceland	36,769	260,000	6.5
* India (incl. part of Jammu & Kashmir)	1,237,062	873,850,000	706
* Indonesia	752,410	186,180,000	247
* Iran	632,457	60,500,000	96
* Iraq	169,235	18,815,000	111
* Ireland	27,137	3,525,000	130
Isle of Man	221	70,000	317
* Israel (excl. Occupied Area)	8,019	4,593,000	573
Israel Occupied Areas (4)	2,947	2,461,000	835
* Italy	116,324	56,550,000	486
* Jamaica	4,244	2,412,000	568
* Japan	145,870	124,710,000	855
Jersey	45	85,000	1,889
* Jordan	35,135	3,632,000	103
* Kazakhstan	1,049,156	17,190,000	16
* Kenya	224,961	26,635,000	118
Kiribati	313	76,000	243
* Korea, North	46,540	22,450,000	482
* Korea, South	38,230	43,660,000	1,142
* Kuwait	6,880	2,388,000	347
* Kyrgyzstan	76,641	4,613,000	60
* Laos	91,429	4,507,000	49
* Latvia	24,595	2,737,000	111
* Lebanon	4,015	3,467,000	864
* Lesotho	11,720	1,873,000	160
* Liberia	38,250	2,869,000	75
* Libya	679,362	4,552,000	6.7
* Liechtenstein	62	30,000	484
* Lithuania	25,174	3,804,000	151
* Luxemborg	998	392,000	393
Macau	6.6	477,000	72,273
Macedonia	9,928	2,179,000	219
* Madagascar	226,658	12,800,000	56
* Malawi	45,747	9,691,000	212
* Malaysia	129,251	18,630,000	144
* Maldives	115	235,000	2,043
* Mali	482,077	8,754,000	18
* Malta	122	360,000	2,951
* Marshall Islands	70	51,000	729
Martinique	425	372,000	875
* Mauritania	395,956	2,092,000	5.3
* Mauritius (incl. Dependencies)	788	1,096,000	1,391
Mayotte (5)	144	89,000	618
* Mexico	759,534	86,170,000	113
* Micronesia, Federated States of	271	117,000	432
Midway Islands	2.0	500	250
* Moldova	13,012	4,474,000	344
Monaco	0.7	31,000	44,286
* Mongolia	604,829	2,336,000	3.9
Montserrat	39	13,000	333
* Morocco	172,414	27,005,000	157
* Mozambique	308,642	15,795,000	51
* Myanmar (Burma)	261,228	43,070,000	165
* Namibia	318,252	1,626,000	5.1
Nauru	8.1	10,000	1,235
* Nepal	56,827	20,325,000	358
* Netherlands	16,164	15,190,000	940
Netherlands Antilles	309	191,000	618
New Caledonia	7,358	177,000	24
* New Zealand	104,454	3,477,000	33
* Nicaragua	50,054	3,932,000	79
* Niger	489,191	8,198,000	17
* Nigeria	356,669	91,700,000	257
Niue	100	1,700	17
Norfolk Island	14	2,600	186
Northern Mariana Islands	184	48,000	261
* Norway (incl. Svalbard and Jan Mayen)	149,412	4,308,000	29
* Oman	82,030	1,617,000	20
* Pakistan (incl. part of Jammu & Kashmir)	339,732	123,490,000	363
Palau (Belau)	196	16,000	82
* Panama	29,157	2,555,000	88
* Papua New Guinea	178,704	3,737,000	21
* Paraguay	157,048	5,003,000	32
* Peru	496,225	22,995,000	46
* Philippines	115,831	65,500,000	565
Pitcairn (incl. Dependencies)	19	50	2.6
* Poland	120,728	38,330,000	317
* Portugal	35,516	10,660,000	300
Puerto Rico	3,515	3,594,000	1,022
* Qatar	4,412	492,000	112
Reunion	969	633,000	653
* Romania	91,699	23,200,000	253
* Russia	6,592,849	150,500,000	23
* Rwanda	10,169	7,573,000	745
St. Helena (incl. Dependencies)	121	7,000	58
* St. Kitts and Nevis	104	40,000	385
* St. Lucia	238	153,000	643
St. Pierre and Miquelon	93	7,000	75
* St. Vincent and the Grenadines	150	116,000	773
* San Marino	24	23,000	958
* Sao Tome and Principe	372	134,000	360
* Saudi Arabia	830,000	15,985,000	19
* Senegal	75,951	7,849,000	103
* Seychelles	175	70,000	400
* Sierra Leone	27,925	4,424,000	158
* Singapore	246	2,812,000	11,431
* Slovakia	18,933	5,287,000	279
* Slovenia	7,819	1,965,000	251
* Solomon Islands	10,954	366,000	33
* Somalia	246,201	6,000,000	24
* South Africa	433,246	33,017,000	76
* Spain	194,885	39,155,000	201
Spanish North Africa (6)	12	144,000	12,000
* Sri Lanka	24,962	17,740,000	711
* Sudan	967,500	28,760,000	30
* Suriname	63,251	413,000	6.5
* Swaziland	6,704	925,000	138
* Sweden	173,732	8,619,000	50
Switzerland	15,943	6,848,000	430
* Syria	71,498	14,070,000	197
Taiwan	13,900	20,985,000	1,510
* Tajikistan	55,251	5,765,000	104
* Tanzania	364,900	28,265,000	77
* Thailand	198,115	58,030,000	293
* Togo	21,925	4,030,000	184
Tokelau Islands	4.6	1,800	391
Tonga	288	103,000	358
* Trinidad and Tobago	1,980	1,307,000	660
* Tunisia	63,170	8,495,000	134
* Turkey	300,948	58,620,000	195
* Turkmenistan	188,456	3,884,000	21
Turks & Caicos Islands	193	13,000	67
Tuvalu	10	10,000	1,000
* Uganda	93,104	17,410,000	187
* Ukraine	233,090	51,990,000	223
* United Arab Emirates	32,278	2,590,000	80
* United Kingdom	94,269	57,890,000	614
* United States	3,787,425	256,420,000	68
* Uruguay	68,500	3,151,000	46
* Uzbekistan	172,742	21,885,000	127
* Vanuatu	4,707	157,000	33
Vatican City	0.2	800	4,000
* Venezuela	352,145	19,085,000	54
* Vietnam	127,428	69,650,000	547
Virgin Islands (U.S.)	133	104,000	782
Virgin Islands, British	59	13,000	220
Wake Island	3	200	67
Wallis and Futuna	98	17,000	173
Western Sahara	102,703	200,000	1.9
* Western Samoa	1,093	197,000	180
* Yemen	203,850	12,215,000	60
Yugoslavia	39,449	10,670,000	270
* Zaire	905,446	39,750,000	44
* Zambia	290,586	8,475,000	29
* Zimbabwe	150,873	10,000,000	66
WORLD	57,900,000	5,477,000,000	95

* Member of the United Nations (1993). (1) No permanent population. (2) North Cyrus unilaterally declared its independence from Cyprus in 1983. (3) Claimed by Argentina (4) Includes West Bank, Golan Heights, and Gaza Strip. (5) Claimed by Comoros. (6) Comprises Ceuta, Melilla, and several small islands.

Map Symbols and Index Map

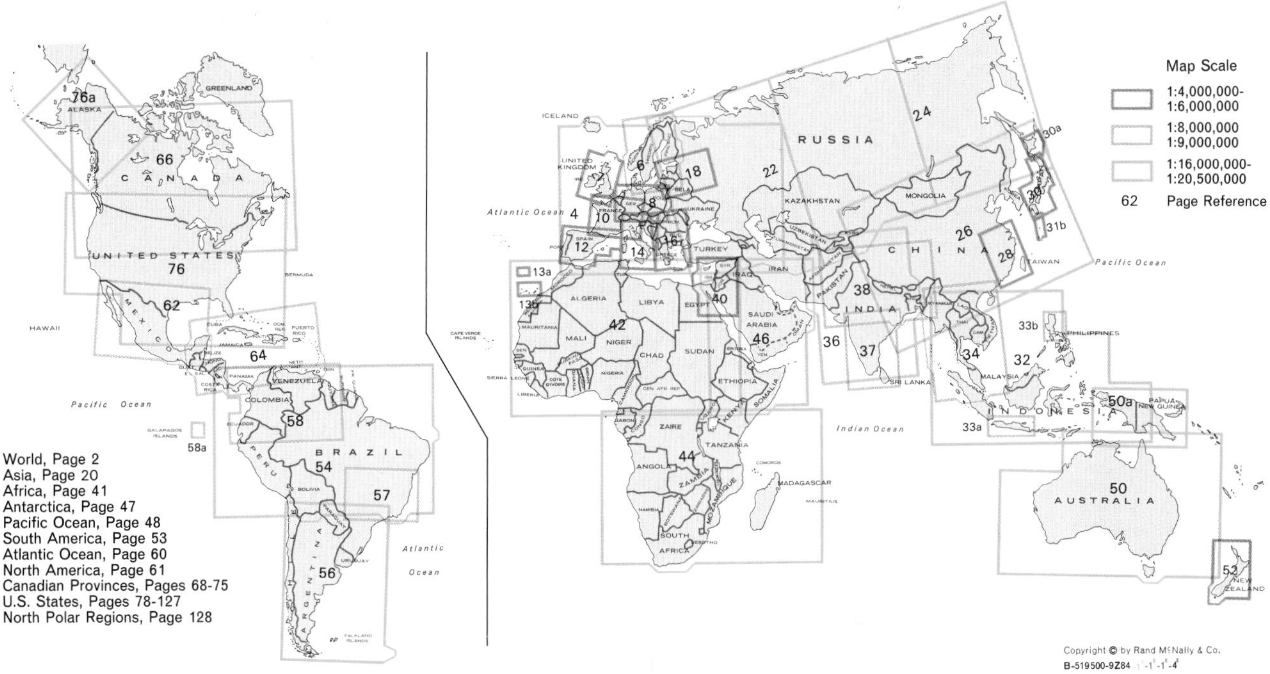

World, Page 2
Asia, Page 20
Africa, Page 41
Antarctica, Page 47
Pacific Ocean, Page 48
South America, Page 53
Atlantic Ocean, Page 60
North America, Page 61
Canadian Provinces, Pages 68-75
U.S. States, Pages 78-127
North Polar Regions, Page 128

World Maps Symbols

Inhabited Localities

The size of type indicates the relative economic and political importance of the locality

Écommoy **Lisieux** **Rouen**

Trouville **Orléans** **PARIS**

Bi'r Safājah ° Oasis

Alternate Names

MOSKVA
MOSCOW English or second official language names are shown in reduced size lettering

Basel
Bâle

Volgograd **(Stalingrad)** Historical or other alternates in the local language are shown in parentheses

Urban Area (Area of continuous industrial, commercial, and residential development)

Capitals of Political Units

BUDAPEST Independent Nation

Cayenne Dependency (Colony, protectorate, etc.)

Recife State, Province, County, Oblast, etc.

Political Boundaries

International (First-order political unit)

Demarcated and Undemarcated

Disputed de jure

Indefinite or Undefined

Demarcation Line

Internal

State, Province, etc. (Second-order political unit)

MURCIA Historical Region (No boundaries indicated)

GALAPAGOS (Ecuador) Administering Country

Transportation

Primary Road

Secondary Road

Minor Road, Trail

Railway

Canal du Midi Navigable Canal

Bridge

Tunnel

TO MALMÖ Ferry

Hydrographic Features

Shoreline

Undefined or Fluctuating Shoreline

Amur River, Stream

Intermittent Stream

Rapids, Falls

Irrigation or Drainage Canal

Reef

The Everglades Swamp

RIMO GLACIER Glacier

L. Victoria Lake, Reservoir

Tuz Gölü Salt Lake

Intermittent Lake, Reservoir

Dry Lake Bed

(395) Lake Surface Elevation

Topographic Features

Matterhorn △ 4478 Elevation Above Sea Level

76 ▽ Elevation Below Sea Level

Mount Cook ▲ 3764 Highest Elevation in Country

133 ▼ Lowest Elevation in Country

Khyber Pass 1067 Mountain Pass

Elevations are given in meters.
The highest and lowest elevations in a continent are underlined

Sand Area

Lava

Salt Flat

State, Province Maps Symbols

Capital

County Seat

Military Installation

Point of Interest

Mountain Peak

International Boundary

State, Province Boundary

County Boundary

Railroad

Road

Urban Area

ARCTIC OCEAN
GREENLAND (Den.)
Beaufort Sea
VICTORIA ISLAND
BAFFIN ISLAND
Baffin Bay
UNITED STATES
Arctic Circle
Mount McKinley 6194
Anchorage
Yellowknife
Godthåb
Reykjavík
ICELAND
FAEROE ISLANDS (Den.)
Bering Sea
Gulf of Alaska
Juneau
Hudson Bay
ROCKY MOUNTAINS
C A N A D A
ALEUTIAN ISLANDS
Vancouver
Seattle
Winnipeg
NEWFOUNDLAND
IRELAND
LONDON
Saint Lawrence
Montréal
Toronto
DETROIT
NORTH AMERICA
CHICAGO
NEW YORK
Washington
APPALACHIAN MOUNTAINS
Denver
St. Louis
ATLANTIC OCEAN
PORTUGAL
Madrid
SPAIN
P A C I F I C
SAN FRANCISCO
UNITED STATES
AÇORES AZORES (Port.)
LOS ANGELES
Phoenix
Mississippi
Atlanta
ARQUIPÉLAGO DA MADEIRA (Port.)
Casablanca
MOROCCO
MIDWAY ISLANDS (U.S.)
O C E A N
Houston
New Orleans
BERMUDA (U.K.)
ISLAS CANARIAS CANARY ISLANDS (Sp.)
HAWAIIAN ISLANDS (U.S.)
Honolulu
Gulf of Mexico
Monterrey
Miami
BAHAMAS
WESTERN SAHARA
Tropic of Cancer
MEXICO
La Habana
CUBA
MAURITANIA
Guadalajara
CIUDAD DE MÉXICO
BELIZE
JAMAICA
HAITI
DOMINICAN REPUBLIC
PUERTO RICO (U.S.)
GUADELOUPE (Fr.)
MARTINIQUE (Fr.)
CAPE VERDE
SENEGAL
GAMBIA
GUINEA-BISSAU
GUATEMALA
HONDURAS
Caribbean Sea
EL SALVADOR
NICARAGUA
TRINIDAD AND TOBAGO
CLIPPERTON (Fr.)
COSTA RICA
Panamá
PANAMA
Caracas
VENEZUELA
GUYANA
SURINAME
FRENCH GUIANA
GUINEA
SIERRA LEONE
LIBERIA
Santa Fe de Bogotá
COLOMBIA
Quito
ECUADOR
Equator
ARCHIPIÉLAGO DE COLÓN GALAPAGOS ISLANDS (Ec.)
Manaus
Amazon
Belém
Fortaleza
PERU
ANDES
B R A Z I L
Recife
TOKELAU ISLANDS (N.Z.)
ÎLES MARQUISES
WALLIS AND FUTUNA (Fr.)
W. SAMOA
AM. SAMOA
Lima
SOUTH AMERICA
Salvador
FIJI
La Paz
BOLIVIA
Brasília
NIUE (N.Z.)
COOK ISLANDS (N.Z.)
FRENCH POLYNESIA
TONGA
Tropic of Capricorn
PARAGUAY
SÃO PAULO
RIO DE JANEIRO
PITCAIRN (U.K.)
Antofagasta
Asunción
ISLA DE PASCUA EASTER ISLAND (Chile)
CHILE
Pôrto Alegre
Córdoba
URUGUAY
International Date Line
Santiago
BUENOS AIRES
Montevideo
P A C I F I C
Co. Aconcagua 6959
ARGENTINA
CHATHAM ISLAND (N.Z.)
O C E A N
FALKLAND ISLANDS (U.K.)
Punta Arenas
SOUTH GEORGIA (Falk. Is.)
CABO DE HORNOS CAPE HORN
SOUTH ORKNEY ISLANDS (B.A.T.)
Antarctic Circle
Bellingshausen Sea
Weddell Sea
Ross Sea
Vinson Massif 4897
A N T A R

14 30° 15 45° 16 60° 17 75° 18 90° 19 105° 20 120° 21 135° 22 150° 23 165° 24 180°
90°
ARCTIC OCEAN
A
ZEML'A FRANCA-IOSIFA
NOVOSIBIRSKIJE OSTROVA
SVALBARD (Nor.)
Barents Sea
NOVAJA ZEML'A
Karskoje More
More Laptevych
75°
Noril'sk
Jenisej
Lena
Arctic Circle
B
Anadyr'
NORWAY
SWEDEN
FINLAND
Helsinki
Oslo
Stockholm
SANKT-PETERBURG
Archangel'sk
URAL'SKIJE
GORY
Ob'
Jakutsk
60°
R U S S I A
Sea of Okhotsk
Bering Sea
ALEUTIAN IS. (U.S.)
C
EST.
LAT.
LITH.
BELA.
MOSKVA
Nižnij Novgorod
Jekaterinburg
Novosibirsk
Ozero Bajkal
OSTROV SACHALIN
Petropavlovsk-Kamčatskij
GERMANY
POLAND
E U R O P E
Kyyiv
UKRAINE
MOLD.
ROM.
AUS.
HUNG.
SLVK.
SWITZ.
SLO.
CRO.
BOS.
ALPS
ITALY
BUL.
ALB.
GREECE
Roma
Karaganda
K A Z A K H S T A N
A S I A
ALTAI
MONGOLIA
Harbin
45°
Volga
Caspian Sea
Gora El'brus 5633
Black Sea
GEOR.
ARM.
AZER.
Aral Sea
UZBEK.
TURKMENISTAN
Taškent
KYRG.
TAJIK.
GOBI
BEIJING
PEKING
Sea of Japan
KOREA
SOUL
JAPAN
ŌSAKA
TŌKYŌ
International Date Line
D
İstanbul
TURKEY
Mediterranean Sea
MALTA
TUNISIA
SYRIA
LEB.
ISRAEL
JORDAN
IRAQ
Tehrān
IRAN
AFGHANISTAN
C H I N A
Yellow Sea
Xi'an
Wuhan
SHANGHAI
Chongqing
30°
LIBYA
AL-QĀHIRAH
CAIRO
EGYPT
KUWAIT
PAKISTAN
DELHI
NEPAL
HIMALAYAS
Mount Everest 8848
BHU.
BNGL.
CALCUTTA
Karāchi
Tropic of Cancer
QATAR
UNITED ARAB EMIRATES
SAUDI ARABIA
OMAN
Red Sea
PACIFIC OCEAN
Guangzhou
HONG KONG (U.K.)
TAIWAN
E
A F R I C A
NIGER
CHAD
Nile
Al-Kharṭūm
SUDAN
ERITREA
YEMEN
Adan
DJIBOUTI
ETHIOPIA
SOMALIA
INDIA
BOMBAY
Bay of Bengal
Arabian Sea
MYANMAR (BURMA)
LAOS
THAILAND
Krung Thep
Bangkok
CAMB.
VIETNAM
South China Sea
Philippine Sea
MANILA
PHILIPPINES
GUAM (U.S.)
WAKE ISLAND (U.S.)
15°
MICRONESIA
NIGERIA
Lagos
CAMEROON
CEN. AFR. REP.
Madras
SRI LANKA
Colombo
BRUNEI
MALAYSIA
Singapore
F
EQUATORIAL GUINEA
GABON
CONGO
UGANDA
KENYA
Lake Victoria
Nairobi
Kilimanjaro 5895
Muqdisho
MALDIVES
Equator
SUMATERA
BORNEO
SULAWESI
KIRIBATI
0°
RWANDA
BURUNDI
ZAIRE
Kinshasa
Congo
TANZANIA
SEYCHELLES
CHAGOS ARCHIPELAGO (B.I.O.T.)
JAKARTA
JAWA
INDONESIA
IRIAN JAYA
PAPUA NEW GUINEA
NEW GUINEA
SOLOMON ISLANDS
TUVALU
G
Luanda
ANGOLA
ZAMBIA
MALAWI
MOZAMBIQUE
Mozambique Channel
INDIAN OCEAN
CHRISTMAS ISLAND (Austl.)
TIMOR
Port Moresby
MELANESIA
VANUATU
ZIMBABWE
MADAGASCAR
MAURITIUS
REUNION (Fr.)
Tropic of Capricorn
Cairns
Coral Sea
NEW CALEDONIA (Fr.)
FIJI
H
NAMIBIA
BOTSWANA
Johannesburg
SWAZILAND
LESOTHO
Durban
SOUTH AFRICA
Cape Town
CAPE OF GOOD HOPE
AUSTRALIA
Brisbane
Perth
Sydney
Mount Kosciusko 2230
Melbourne
Tasman Sea
NEW ZEALAND
Wellington
TASMANIA
I
ILES KERGUELEN (F.S.A.T.)
45°
J
60°
Antarctic Circle
K
ENDERBY LAND
WILKES LAND
75°
Copyright © by Rand McNally & Co.
Map prepared by Rand McNally & Co.
C-510000-264
L
A N T A R C T I C A
Kilometers 0 1000 2000 3000 Km.
Miles 0 1000 2000 3000 Mi.
Robinson Projection

Europe

ALBANIA.................... G11
Amsterdam, 6,965,000 ('89) (1,860,000★) ....E 8
ANDORRA...................G 8
Antwerpen, 497,748 ('87) (1,100,000★) ....E 8
Athínai (Athens), 885,737 ('81) (3,027,331★) ... H12
AUSTRIA.................... F10
Barcelona, 1,714,355 ('88) (4,040,000★) .... G 8
BELARUS....................E13
Belfast, 303,800 ('87) (685,000★) ....E 6
BELGIUM....................E 8
Beograd (Belgrade), 1,130,000 ('87) (1,400,000★) G12
Berlin, 3,352,848 ('89) (3,825,000★) E10
Bern, 134,393 ('90) (298,800★) ....F 9
Birmingham, 1,013,995 ('81) (2,675,000★) ....E 7
Bonn, 282,190 ('89) (570,000★) ....E 9
BOSNIA AND HERZEGOVINA........G11
Bratislava, 444,482 ('91)..........................F11
Bremen, 535,058 ('89) (800,000★) ....E 9
Bruxelles, 136,920 ('87) (2,385,000★) ....E 8
București, 1,989,823 ('86) (2,275,000★) G13
Budapest, 2,016,132 ('90) (2,565,000★) F11
BULGARIA.................. G12
Cardiff, 262,313 ('81) (625,000★) ....E 7
CROATIA....................F11
CZECH REPUBLIC......F11
DENMARK.................D 9
Dnipropetrovsk, 1,179,000 ('89) (1,600,000★) F14
Donets'k, 1,110,000 ('89) (2,200,000★) F15
Dresden, 518,057 ('89) (670,000★) E10
Dublin, 502,749 ('86) (1,140,000★) ....E 6
Düsseldorf, 569,641 ('89) (1,190,000★) ....E 9
Edinburgh, 433,200 ('89) (630,000★) ....D 7
Essen, 620,594 ('89) (4,950,000★) ....E 9
ESTONIA....................D12
FAEROE ISLANDS......C 6
FINLAND....................C13
Firenze, 425,835 ('87) (640,000★) G10
FRANCE..................... F 8
Frankfurt, 625,258 ('89) (1,855,000★) ....E 9
Gdańsk, 461,500 ('89) (909,000★) E11
Genève (Geneva), 165,404 ('90) (460,000★) ....F 9
Genova, 727,427 ('87) (805,000★) .... G 9
GERMANY................. E10
Gibraltar, 30,077 ('88). H 6
Glasgow, 695,630 ('89) (1,800,000★) ....D 7
GREECE..................... H12
GUERNSEY................ F 7
Hamburg, 1,603,070 ('89) (2,225,000★) ....E 9
Helsinki, 490,034 ('88) (1,040,000★) C12
HUNGARY.................. F11
ICELAND..................... B 4
IRELAND..................... E 6
ISLE OF MAN.............E 7
İstanbul, 6,748,435 ('90) (7,000,000★) G13
ITALY..........................G10
JERSEY.......................F 7
Katowice, 365,800 ('89) (2,778,000★) E11
Kazan', 1,094,000 ('89) (1,140,000★) D17
Kharkiv, 1,611,000 ('89) (1,940,000★) F15
København, 466,723 ('90) (1,685,000★) D10
Köln, 937,482 ('89) (1,760,000★) ....E 9
Kraków, 743,700 ('89) (828,000★) E11
Kyyiv (Kiev), 2,587,000 ('89) (2,900,000★) ... E14
LATVIA...................... D12
Leipzig, 545,307 ('89) (700,000★) E10
Leningrad *see* Sankt-Peterburg..................D14
LIECHTENSTEIN.........F 9
Ljubljana, 233,200 ('87) (316,607▲) F10
Lisboa, 807,167 ('81) (2,250,000★) ....H 6

★ Population of metropolitan area, including suburbs.

Barents Sea
Beloje More
White Sea
Murmansk
Archangel'sk
Severodvinsk
FINLAND
Helsinki
SANKT-PETERBURG ST. PETERSBURG (LENINGRAD)
ESTONIA
Tallinn
LATVIA
Riga
LITHUANIA
Vilnius
BELARUS
Minsk
MOSCOW MOSKVA
RUSSIA
Nižnij Novgorod
Kazan'
Samara
Saratov
Volgograd (Stalingrad)
Perm'
Jekaterinburg
Čel'abinsk
URAL'SKIJE GORY
URAL MOUNTAINS
ZAPADNO-SIBIRSKAJA NIZMENNOST'
KAZAKHSTAN
UKRAINE
KYYIV
Kharkiv
Odesa
DONETS'K
Rostov-na-Donu
MOLDOVA
Chişinău
ROMANIA
Bucureşti
BULGARIA
Sofija
BLACK SEA
Sea of Azov
CASPIAN SEA
Aral Sea
CAUCASUS
GEORGIA
Tbilisi
ARMENIA
Jerevan
AZERBAIJAN
Baku
TURKMENISTAN
UZBEK.
TURKEY
Ankara
İstanbul
İzmir
ASIA MINOR
GREECE
Athínai Athens
Thessaloníki
CYPRUS
NORTH CYPRUS
SYRIA
IRAQ
Baghdād
IRAN
TEHRĀN
MESOPOTAMIA
Miller Oblated Stereographic Projection

LITHUANIA..................D12
Liverpool, 538,809 ('81) (1,525,000★) ....E 7
Łódź, 851,500 ('89) (1,061,000★) E11
London, 6,574,009 ('81) (11,100,000★) ....E 7
LUXEMBOURG............F 9
Lyon, 413,095 ('82) (1,275,000★) ....F 8
MACEDONIA..............G12
Madrid, 3,102,846 ('88) (4,650,000★) .... G 7
MALTA........................H10
Manchester, 437,612 ('81) (2,775,000★) ....E 7
Marseille, 874,436 ('82) (1,225,000★) .... G 9
Milano, 1,495,260 ('87) (3,750,000★) ....F 9
Minsk, 1,589,000 ('89) (1,650,000★) E13
MOLDOVA...................F13
MONACO.................... G 9
Moskva (Moscow), 8,769,000 ('89) (13,100,000★) D15
München, 1,211,617 ('89) (1,955,000★) F10
Napoli, 1,204,211 ('87) (2,875,000★) G10
NETHERLANDS..........E 9
Nižnij Novgorod (Gor'kij), 1,438,000 ('89) (2,025,000★) D16
NORWAY.................... C 9
Nürnberg, 480,078 ('89) (1,030,000★) F10
Odesa, 1,115,000 ('89) (1,185,000★) F14
Oslo, 452,415 ('87) (720,000★) D10
Paris, 2,078,900 ('87) (9,775,000★) ....F 8
POLAND......................E11
Porto, 327,368 ('81) (1,225,000★) .... G 6
PORTUGAL................G 6
Praha, 1,215,656 ('90) (1,325,000★) E10
Reykjavík, 93,425 ('87) (137,941★) ....C 3
Rīga, 915,000 ('89) (1,005,000★) D12
Roma, 2,815,457 ('87) (3,175,000★) G10
ROMANIA....................F12
Rostov-na-Donu, 1,020,000 ('89) (1,165,000★) F15
Rotterdam, 576,300 ('89) (1,110,000★) ....E 8
RUSSIA........................D16
Samara, 1,257,000 ('89) (1,505,000★) E18
Sankt-Peterburg, 4,456,000 ('89) (5,825,000★) D14
SAN MARINO............. G10
Sarajevo, 341,200 ('87) (479,688▲) G11
Saratov, 905,000 ('89) (1,155,000★) E17
Sevilla, 663,132 ('88) (945,000★) ....H 6
's-Gravenhage (The Hague), 443,900 ('89) (770,000★) ....E 8
Skopje, 444,900 ('87) (547,214▲) G12
SLOVAKIA...................F11
SLOVENIA...................F10
Sofija, 1,119,152 ('86) (1,205,000★) G12
SPAIN..........................H 7
Stockholm, 672,187 ('90) (1,449,972★) D11
SWEDEN.....................C11
SWITZERLAND........... F 9
Tallinn, 482,000...........D12
Thessaloníki, 406,413 ('81) (706,180★) G12
Tiranë, 255,700 ('87).. G11
Torino, 1,035,565 ('87) (1,550,000★) ....F 9
UKRAINE.....................F14
UNITED KINGDOM......E 7
Valencia, 743,933 ('88) (1,270,000★) ....H 7
Valletta, 9,210 ('89) (215,000★) H10
Vilnius, 582,000...........E12
Warszawa, 1,651,200 ('89) (2,323,000★) ... E12
Wien (Vienna), 1,482,800 ('88) (1,875,000★) F11
YUGOSLAVIA............. G11
Zagreb, 697,925 ('87)..F11
Zürich, 342,861 ('90) (860,000★) ....F 9

Scandinavia

Denmark

1990 ESTIMATE

Ålborg, 114,000 (155,019▲) .... H 7
Århus, 202,300 (261,437▲) .... H 8
Copenhagen *see* København .... I 9
København (Copenhagen), 466,723 (1,685,000★) ...... I 9
Odense, 140,100 (176,133▲) .... I 8

Finland

1988 ESTIMATE

Helsinki (Helsingfors), 490,034 (1,040,000★) F15
Lahti, 74,300 (108,000★) F15
Oulu, 98,582 (121,000★) D15
Tampere, 170,533 (241,000★) F14
Turku (Åbo), 160,456 (228,000★) F14

Norway

1987 ESTIMATE

Bergen, 209,320 (239,000★) .... F 5
Hammerfest, 7,208('83) A14
Oslo, 452,415 (720,000★) ...... G 8
Stavanger, 94,200 (132,000★)('85) ... G 5
Trondheim, 135,010 .. E 8

Sweden

1990 ESTIMATE

Göteborg (Gothenburg), 431,840 (710,894★) H 8
Helsingborg, 108,359 H 9
Jönköping, 110,860 .. H10
Linköping, 120,562 .. G10
Malmö, 232,908 (445,000★) .... I 9
Norrköping, 119,921 G11
Örebro, 120,353 .... G10
Stockholm, 672,187 (1,449,972★) G12
Uppsala, 164,754 .... G11
Västerås, 118,386 .. G11

★ Population of metropolitan area, including suburbs.
▲ Population of entire district, including rural area.

Kilometers 0 100 200 300 Km.
Miles 0 100 200 300 Mi.

1:8 000 000

British Isles

Ireland
1986 CENSUS

Cork, 133,271 (173,694★) . . . . . . J 4
Dublin (Baile Átha Cliath), 502,749 (1,140,000★) . . . . H 6
Galway, 47,104 . . . . H 3
Limerick, 56,279 (76,557★) . . . . I 4
Waterford, 39,529 (41,054★) . . . . I 5

Isle of Man
1986 CENSUS

Douglas, 20,368 (28,500★) . . . . . . G 8

United Kingdom
England
1981 CENSUS

Birmingham, 1,013,995 (2,675,000★) I11
Blackpool, 146,297 (280,000★) . . . . . . H 9
Bournemouth, 142,829 (315,000★) K11
Bradford, 293,336 . . H11
Brighton, 134,581 (420,000★) K12
Bristol, 413,861 (630,000★) J10
Coventry, 318,718 (645,000★) I11
Derby, 218,026 (275,000★) I11
Kingston upon Hull, 322,144 (350,000★) H12
Leeds, 445,242 (1,540,000★) H11
Leicester, 324,394 (495,000★) I11
Liverpool, 538,809 (1,525,000★) H10
London, 6,574,009 (11,100,000★) J12
Manchester, 437,612 (2,775,000★) H10
Newcastle upon Tyne, 199,064 (1,300,000★) G11
Nottingham, 273,300 (655,000★) I11
Oxford, 113,847 (230,000★) J11
Plymouth, 238,583 (290,000★) . . . . . . K 8
Portsmouth, 174,218 (485,000★) K11
Preston, 166,675 (250,000★) H10
Reading, 194,727 (200,000★) J12
Sheffield, 470,685 (710,000★) H11
Southampton, 211,321 (415,000★) K11
Southend-on-Sea, 155,720 . . . . J13
Stoke-on-Trent, 272,446 (440,000★) H10
Sunderland, 195,064 G11
Teesside, 158,516 (580,000★) G11
Wolverhampton, 263,501 . . . . I10

Northern Ireland
1987 ESTIMATE

Bangor, 70,700 . . . . G 7
Belfast, 303,800 (685,000★) . . . . . . G 7
Londonderry, 97,500 (97,200★) . . . . . . G 5
Newtownabbey, 72,300 . . . . G 7

Scotland
1989 ESTIMATE

Aberdeen, 210,700 . . D10
Dundee, 172,540 . . . . E 9
Edinburgh, 433,200 (630,000★) . . . . . . F 9
Glasgow, 695,630 (1,800,000★) . . . . F 8
Greenock, 58,436 (101,000★)('81) . . F 8
Inverness, 38,204('81) D 8
Paisley, 84,330('81) . . F 8

Wales
1981 CENSUS

Cardiff, 262,313 (625,000★) . . . . . . J 9
Newport, 115,896 (310,000★) . . . . . . J 9
Swansea, 172,433 (275,000★) . . . . . . J 9

★ Population of metropolitan area, including suburbs.

Central Europe

Austria

1981 CENSUS

Graz, 243,166 (325,000★)........H15

Innsbruck, 117,287 (185,000★)........H11

Linz, 199,910 (335,000★) G14

Salzburg, 139,426 (220,000★)........H13

Vienna *see* Wien G16

Villach, 52,692 (65,000★) I13

Wien (Vienna), 1,482,800 (1,875,000★)('88) .. G16

Belgium

1987 ESTIMATE

Antwerpen (Antwerp), 479,748 (1,100,000★)......D 4

Brugge, 117,755 (223,000★)........D 3

Bruxelles (Brussel), 136,920 (2,385,000★)......E 4

Charleroi, 209,395 (480,000★)........E 4

Gent (Gand), 233,856 (465,000★)........D 3

Hasselt, 65,563 (290,000★)........E 5

Liège, 200,891 (750,000★)........E 5

Mons, 89,697 (242,000★)........E 3

Czech Republic

1990 ESTIMATE

Brno, 392,285 (450,000★)........F16

Hradec Králové, 101,302 (113,000★)........E15

Liberec, 104,256 (175,000★)........E15

Olomouc, 107,044 (126,000★)........F17

Ostrava, 331,557 (760,000★)........F18

Plzeň, 175,038 (210,000★)........F13

Praha (Prague), 1,215,656 (1,325,000★)...... E14

Ústí nad Labem, 106,499 (115,000★)........E14

Germany

1989 ESTIMATE

Aachen, 233,255 (535,000★)........E 6

Augsburg, 247,731 (405,000★) G10

Berlin, 3,352,848 (3,825,000★)......C13

Bielefeld, 311,946 (515,000★)........C 8

Bochum, 389,087 .. D 7

Bonn, 282,190 (570,000★)........E 7

Braunschweig, 253,794 (330,000★)........C10

Bremen, 535,058 (800,000★)........B 8

Bremerhaven, 126,934 (190,000★)........B 8

Chemnitz, 311,765 (450,000★)........E12

Cologne *see* Köln .... E 6

Dortmund, 587,328 .. D 7

Dresden, 518,057 (670,000★)........D13

Duisburg, 527,447 .. D 6

Düsseldorf, 569,641 (1,190,000★)......D 6

Erfurt, 220,016 ...... E11

Essen, 620,594 (4,950,000★)......D 7

Frankfurt am Main, 625,258 (1,855,000★)......E 8

Gelsenkirchen, 287,255 ....D 7

Hagen, 210,640 .... D 7

Halle, 236,044 (475,000★)........D11

Hamburg, 1,603,070 (2,225,000★)......B 9

Hannover, 498,495 (1,000,000★)......C 9

Karlsruhe, 265,100 (485,000★)........F 8

Kiel, 240,675 (335,000★)........A10

Köln (Cologne), 937,482 (1,760,000★)......E 6

Leipzig, 545,307 (700,000★)........D12

Lübeck, 210,681 (260,000★)........B10

Magdeburg, 290,579 (400,000★)........C11

★ Population of metropolitan area, including suburbs.

Mannheim, 300,468 (1,400,000★) . . . . . . F 8
Mönchengladbach, 252,910 (410,000★) D 6
München (Munich), 1,211,617 (1,955,000★) G11
Münster, 248,919 . . . . D 7
Nürnberg, 480,078 (1,030,000★) F11
Potsdam, 142,862 . . C13
Rostock, 253,990 . . . . A12
Saarbrücken, 188,467 (385,000★) . . . . F 6
Stuttgart, 562,658 (1,925,000★) . . . . . . G 9
Wiesbaden, 254,209 (795,000★) . . . . E 8
Wuppertal, 371,283 (830,000★) . . . . D 7

Hungary

1990 ESTIMATE

Budapest, 2,016,132 (2,565,000★) H19
Debrecen, 212,247 . . H21
Miskolc, 196,449 . . . . G20
Pécs, 170,119 . . . . . . I18
Szeged, 175,338 . . . . I20
Szombathely, 85,418 H16

Liechtenstein

1990 ESTIMATE

Vaduz, 4,874 . . . . . . H 9

Luxembourg

1985 ESTIMATE

Luxembourg, 76,130 (136,000★) . . . . F 6

Netherlands

1989 ESTIMATE

Amsterdam, 6,965,000 (1,860,000★) . . . . . . C 4
Eindhoven, 190,700 (379,377★) . . . . D 5
Groningen, 167,800 (206,781★) . . . . B 6
Rotterdam, 576,300 (1,110,000★) . . . . . . D 4
's-Gravenhage (The Hague), 443,900 (770,000★) . . . . C 4
Tilburg, 155,100 (224,934★) . . . . D 5
Utrecht, 230,700 (518,779★) . . . . C 5

Poland

1989 ESTIMATE

Białystok, 263,900 . . B23
Bydgoszcz, 377,900 B18
Gdańsk (Danzig), 461,500 (909,000★) A18
Gdynia, 250,200 . . . . A18
Katowice, 365,800 (2,778,000★) E19
Kielce, 211,100 . . . . . . E20
Kraków, 743,700 (828,000★) E19
łódź, 851,500 (1,061,000★) D19
Lublin, 339,500 (389,000★) D22
Poznań, 586,500 (672,000★) C16
Radom, 223,600 . . . . D21
Szczecin (Stettin), 409,500 (449,000★) B14
Toruń, 199,600 . . . . . . B18
Wałbrzych (Waldenburg), 141,400 (207,000★) E16
Warszawa (Warsaw), 1,651,200 (2,323,000★) C21
Wrocław (Breslau), 637,400 . . . . D17

Slovakia

1990 ESTIMATE

Bratislava, 442,999 . . G17
Košice, 237,099 . . . . G21

France and the Alps

France

1982 CENSUS

Aix-en-Provence, 121,327 (126,552★) I12
Alès, 43,268 (70,180★) H11
Amiens, 131,332 (154,498★)........C 9
Angers, 136,038 (195,859★)........E 6
Angoulême, 46,197 (103,552★) ...... G 7
Bayonne, 41,381 (127,477★) .... I 5
Belfort, 51,206 (76,221★) E13
Besançon, 113,283 (120,772★)........E13
Béziers, 76,647 (81,347★) I10
Bordeaux, 208,159 (640,012★)........H 6
Boulogne-Billancourt, 102,582 .... D 9
Boulogne-sur-Mer, 47,653 (98,566★) .... B 8
Brest, 156,060 (201,145★)........D 2
Brive-la-Gaillarde, 51,511 (64,301★) .... G 8
Caen, 114,068 (183,526★)........C 6
Calais, 76,527 (100,823★)........B 8
Cannes, 72,259 (295,525★) I14
Chalon-sur-Saône, 56,194 (78,064★) F11
Chambéry, 53,427 (96,163★) G12
Cherbourg, 28,442 (85,485★) .... C 5
Cholet, 55,524 ...... E 6
Clermont-Ferrand, 147,361 (256,189★) G10
Compiègne, 40,384 (62,778★) .... C 9
Creil, 34,709 (82,505★) .... C 9
Dieppe, 35,957 (41,812★) .... C 8
Dijon, 140,942 (215,865★)........E12
Douai, 42,576 (202,366★)........B10
Dunkerque, 73,120 (195,705★)........A 9
Fontainebleau, 15,679 (35,629★) .... D 9
Grenoble, 156,637 (392,021★) G12
La Rochelle, 75,840 (102,143★)........F 5
Laval, 50,360 (55,984★) .... D 6
Le Havre, 199,388 (254,595★)........C 7
Le Mans, 147,697 (191,080★)........D 7
Lens, 38,244 (327,383★)........B 9
Lille, 168,424 (1,020,000★)...... B10
Limoges, 140,400 (171,689★) ...... G 8
Lorient, 62,554 (104,025★)........E 3
Lourdes, 17,425...... I 6
Lyon, 413,095 (1,275,000★)...... G11
Mâcon, 38,404 (47,274★) F11
Marseille, 874,436 (1,225,000★) J12
Maubeuge, 36,061 (105,714★)........B10
Meaux, 45,005 (55,797★) .... D 9
Melun, 35,005 (82,479★) .... D 9
Metz, 114,232 (186,437★)........C13
Montbéliard, 31,836 (128,194★)........E13
Montluçon, 49,912 (67,963★) .... F 9
Montpellier, 197,231 (221,307★) I10
Mulhouse, 112,157 (220,613★)........E14
Nancy, 96,317 (306,982★)........D13
Nantes, 240,539 (464,857★)........E 5
Nevers, 43,013 (59,274★) E10
Nice, 337,085 (449,496★) I14
Nîmes, 124,220 (132,343★) I11
Niort, 58,203 (61,959★) .... F 6

Kilometers 0 50 100 150 Km.
Miles 0 50 100 150 Mi.
1:4 000 000

Orléans, 102,710 (220,478★) . . . . E 8
Paris, 2,078,900 (9,775,000★)('87) . . D 9
Pau, 83,790 (131,265★) . . . . I 6
Perpignan, 111,669 (137,915★) . . . . J 9
Poitiers, 79,350 (103,204★) . . . . F 7
Quimper, 56,907 . . . . D 2
Reims, 194,656 (199,388★) C11
Rennes, 117,234 (234,418★) . . . . D 5
Roanne, 48,705 (81,786★) F11
Roubaix, 101,602 . . . . B10
Rouen, 101,945 (379,879★) . . . . C 8
Saint-Brieuc, 48,563 (83,900★) . . . . D 4
Saint-Denis, 90,829 . . D 9
Saint-Étienne, 204,955 (317,228★) G11
Saint-Germain, 38,499 D 9
Saint-Malo, 46,347 . . D 4
Saint-Nazaire, 68,348 (130,271★) . . . . E 4
Saint-Quentin, 63,567 (71,887★) C10
Saint-Tropez, 4,961 (6,213▲) I13
Sedan, 23,477 (30,871★) C11
Strasbourg, 248,712 (400,000★) D14
Toulon, 179,423 (410,393★) I12
Toulouse, 347,995 (541,271★) . . . . I 8
Tourcoing, 96,908 . . B10
Tours, 132,209 (262,786★) . . . . E 7
Troyes, 63,581 (125,240★) D11
Valence, 66,356 (106,041★) H11
Valenciennes, 40,275 (349,505★) B10
Verdun, 21,516 (26,944★) C12
Versailles, 91,494 . . . . D 9
Vichy, 30,527 (63,501★) F10
Villeurbanne, 115,960 G11

Guernsey
1986 CENSUS
Saint Peter Port, 16,085 (36,000★) . . . . C 4

Jersey
1986 CENSUS
Saint Helier, 27,083 (46,500★) . . . . C 4

Liechtenstein
1990 ESTIMATE
Vaduz, 4,874 . . . . E16

Luxembourg
1985 ESTIMATE
Luxembourg, 76,130 (136,000★) C13

Monaco
1982 CENSUS
Monaco, 27,063 (87,000★) I14

Switzerland
1990 ESTIMATE
Basel (Bâle), 169,587 (575,000★) E14
Bern (Berne), 134,393 (298,800★) F14
Fribourg (Freiburg), 33,962 (56,800★) F14
Genève, 165,404 (460,000★) F13
Lausanne, 122,600 (259,900★) F13
Luzern, 59,115 (159,500★) E15
Neuchâtel, 32,509 (65,900★) F13
Sankt Gallen, 73,191 (125,000★) E16
Sankt Moritz, 5,335('87) F16
Schaffhausen, 33,956 (53,000★) E15
Thun, 37,707 (77,200★) F14
Winterthur, 85,174 (107,400★) E15
Zürich, 342,861 (860,000★) E15

★ Population of metropolitan area, including suburbs.
▲ Population of entire district, including rural area.

Spain and Portugal

Andorra
1986 CENSUS
Andorra, 18,463 .... C13

Gibraltar
1988 ESTIMATE
Gibraltar, 30,077 .... I 6

Portugal
1981 CENSUS
Almada, 42,607 .... G 2
Barreiro, 50,863 .... G 2
Beja, 19,643 .... G 4
Braga, 63,033 ...... D 3
Coimbra, 74,616 .... E 3
Covilhã, 21,807 ...... E 4
Évora, 34,851 ...... G 4
Faro, 27,974 .... H 4
Funchal, 44,111 .... m21
Guimarães, 21,947 .. D 3
Lisboa (Lisbon), 807,167 (2,250,000★) ...... G 2
Montijo, 23,017 ...... G 3
Porto, 327,368 (1,225,000★) ...... D 3
Póvoa de Varzim, 23,729 .... D 3
Santarém, 19,761 ... F 3
Setúbal, 77,885 .... G 3
Vila do Conde, 20,613 D 3
Vila Nova de Gaia, 62,469 .... D 3

Spain
1988 ESTIMATE
Albacete, 125,997 .. G10
Alcalá de Guadaira, 50,935 .... H 6
Alcalá de Henares, 150,021 .... E 8
Alcantarilla, 28,279 .. H10
Alcázar de San Juan, 26,258 .... F 8
Alcira, 40,575 ...... F11
Alcoy, 66,074 ...... G11
Algeciras, 99,528 .... I 6
Alicante, 261,051 .... G11
Almendralejo, 25,352 G 5
Almería, 157,644 .... I 9
Andújar, 32,300 (37,020▲) .... G 7
Antequera, 32,200 (41,284▲) .... H 7
Aranjuez, 37,694 .... E 8
Arcos de la Frontera, 19,600 (27,311▲) .. I 6
Arrecife, 36,297 ...... p27
Ávila, 45,092 .... E 7
Avilés, 87,811 (131,000★) .... B 6
Badajoz, 106,400 (122,407▲) ...... G 5
Badalona, 225,229 .. D14
Barcelona, 1,714,355 (4,040,000★) D14
Baza, 20,910 ...... H 9
Bilbao, 384,733 (985,000★) .... B 9
Burgos, 160,561 .... C 8
Burjasot, 35,011 .... F11
Cáceres, 71,598 .... F 5
Cádiz, 156,591 (240,000★) .... I 5
Cartagena, 70,000 (172,710▲) H11
Castellón de la Plana, 131,809 .... F11
Chiclana de la Frontera, 43,157 .... I 5
Ciudad Real, 56,300 G 8
Córdoba, 302,301 .. H 7
Coria del Río, 21,844 H 5
Cuenca, 42,222 ...... E 9
Don Benito, 24,500 (29,324▲) .... G 6
Durango, 27,425 .... B 9
Écija, 30,900 (35,836▲) .... H 6
Éibar, 34,355 ...... B 9
Elche, 158,300 (180,256▲) G11
Elda, 56,756 .... G11
El Ferrol del Caudillo, 86,503 (129,000★) B 3
El Puerto de Santa María, 49,900 (62,285▲) .. I 5
Gandía, 46,100 (52,646▲) G11
Gavá, 34,613 ...... D14
Gerona, 30,900 (68,902▲) D14
Getafe, 135,367 .... E 8
Gijón, 262,156 ...... B 6
Granada, 263,334 .... H 8
Granollers, 49,045 .. D14
Guadalajara, 61,309 .. E 8
Hospitalet, 278,449 .. D14
Huelva, 137,826 .... H 5
Huesca, 41,841 ...... C11
Irún, 54,886 .... B10
Jaén, 106,435 ...... H 8

★ Population of metropolitan area, including suburbs.
▲ Population of entire district, including rural area.

Játiva, 23,755 ...... G11
Jerez de la Frontera, 156,200 (183,007▲) I 5
La Coruña, 248,862 .. B 3
La Línea, 60,956 .... I 6
Las Palmas de Gran Canaria, 319,000 (366,347▲) p25
León, 136,558 (159,000★) .... C 6
Lérida, 91,500 (109,795▲) D12
Linares, 58,622 ...... G 8
Logroño, 119,038 .... C 9
Lorca, 26,700 (66,437▲) H10
Los Palacios y Villafranca, 28,798 .... H 6
Lugo, 68,700 (78,795▲) .... B 4
Madrid, 3,102,846 (4,650,000★) ...... E 8
Málaga, 574,456 .... I 7
Manresa, 65,607 .... D13
Mataró, 100,817 .... D14
Mérida, 52,368 ...... G 5
Miranda de Ebro, 36,201 .... C 9
Morón de la Frontera, 29,048 .... H 6
Motril, 38,600 (45,901▲) .... I 8
Murcia, 149,800 (314,124▲) H10
Onteniente, 29,591 .. G11
Orense, 106,042 .... C 4
Oviedo, 168,900 (190,073▲) .... B 6
Palencia, 76,692 .... C 7
Palma [de Mallorca], 249,000 (314,608▲) F14
Pamplona, 180,598 .. C10
Plasencia, 33,613 .... E 5
Ponferrada, 33,900 (59,868▲) .... C 5
Pontevedra, 40,500 (68,223▲) .... C 3
Portugalete, 57,813 .. B 8
Prat de Llobregat, 64,193 .... D14
Puertollano, 52,284 .. G 7
Reus, 83,800 ...... D13
Sabadell, 189,489 .... D14
Sagunto, 19,600 (56,551▲) F11
Salamanca, 159,342 .. E 6
San Fernando, 81,975 I 5
Sanlúcar de Barrameda, 38,100 (54,690▲) .. I 5
San Sebastián, 177,622 (285,000★) B10
Santa Cruz de Tenerife, 215,228 .... p24
Santander, 166,800 (190,795▲) .... B 8
Santiago de Compostela, 68,800 (88,110▲) .. C 3
San Vicente de Baracaldo, 113,502 .... B 9
Segovia, 54,402 .... E 7
Sevilla, 663,132 (945,000★) .... H 6
Soria, 31,926 ...... D 9
Sueca, 24,667 ...... F11
Talavera de la Reina, 68,158 .... F 7
Tarragona, 63,500 (109,586▲) D13
Tarrasa, 161,410 .... D14
Teruel, 28,029 ...... E10
Toledo, 59,551 ...... F 7
Tomelloso, 28,386 .. F 9
Torrelavega, 28,900 (59,601▲) .... B 7
Torrente, 55,751 .... F11
Tudela, 26,618 ...... C10
Úbeda, 31,179 ...... G 8
Utrera, 36,300 (41,902▲) .... H 6
Valdepeñas, 25,568 .. G 8
Valencia, 743,933 (1,270,000★) F11
Valladolid, 331,461 .. D 7
Vall de Uxó, 27,853 .. F11
Vélez-Málaga, 32,200 (51,132▲) .... I 7
Vich, 28,873 .... D14
Vigo, 179,500 (271,128▲) .... C 3
Villanueva y Geltrú, 46,364 .... D13
Vitoria, 204,264 .... C 9
Zamora, 62,047 ...... D 6
Zaragoza, 582,239 .. D11

Spanish North Africa

1988 ESTIMATE

Ceuta, 67,188 ...... J 6
Melilla, 55,717 ...... J 9

Bosnia and Herzegovina
1987 ESTIMATE

Banja Luka, 130,900 (193,890▲) E12
Mostar, 47,606('71) F12
Sarajevo, 341,200 (479,688▲) F13
Tuzla, 67,300 (129,967▲) E13
Zenica, 67,500 (144,869▲) E12

Croatia
1987 ESTIMATE

Osijek, 106,800 (162,490▲)('87) D13
Rijeka, 166,400 (199,282▲)('87) .... D 9
Sisak, 38,421('71) D11
Split, 191,074('87) F11
Zadar, 43,187('71) E10
Zagreb, 697,925('87) .. D10

Italy
1987 ESTIMATE

Acireale, 46,997 ...... L10
Agrigento, 41,200 (54,600▲) .... L 8
Alcamo, 43,072 ...... L 7
Alessandria, 76,100 (96,014▲) .... E 3
Altamura, 54,784 ...... I11
Ancona, 104,409 ...... F 8
Andria, 88,348 .... H11
Anzio, 30,806 .... H 7
Arezzo, 74,200 (91,681▲) .... F 6
Asti, 63,600 (75,459▲) E 3
Avellino, 56,407 .... I 9
Bagheria, 43,725 ...... K 8
Bari, 362,524 (475,000★) H11
Barletta, 86,954 ...... H11
Benevento, 54,400 (65,661▲) .... H 9
Bergamo, 118,959 (345,000★) .... D 4
Bisceglie, 47,771 ...... H11
Bologna, 432,406 (525,000★) .... E 6
Bolzano (Bozen), 101,515 .... C 6
Brescia, 199,286 ...... D 5
Brindisi, 92,280 .... I12
Busto Arsizio, 78,056 . . D 3
Cagliari, 220,574 (305,000★) .... J 4
Caltanissetta, 62,352 .. L 9
Carrara, 69,229 .... E 5
Caserta, 65,974 ...... H 9
Castellammare [di Stabia], 68,491 .... I 9
Catania, 372,486 (550,000★) L10
Catanzaro, 102,558 .... K11
Cerignola, 53,463 .... H10
Cesena, 72,600 (90,012▲) .... E 7
Civitavecchia, 50,806 .. G 6
Como, 91,738 (165,000★) .... D 4
Cosenza, 106,026 (150,000★) J11
Cremona, 76,979 ...... D 5
Ferrara, 113,300 (143,950▲) .... E 6
Firenze (Florence), 425,835 (640,000★) .... F 6
Foggia, 155,051 ...... H10
Forlì, 91,200 (110,482▲) E 7
Gela, 79,378 .... L 9
Genova (Genoa), 727,427 (805,000★) .... E 3
Grosseto, 56,400 (70,592▲) .... G 6
Iesi, 40,855 .... F 8
Imola, 48,200 (61,587▲) E 6
Imperia, 41,481 ...... F 3
La Spezia, 108,937 (185,000★) .... E 4

★ Population of metropolitan area, including suburbs. ▲ Population of entire district, including rural area.

Kilometers 0 50 100 150 Km.
Miles 0 50 100 150 Mi.

1:4 000 000

Latina, 67,800 (98,479▲) . . . . H 7
Lecce, 100,981 . . . . I13
Livorno (Leghorn), 174,065 . . . . F 5
Lucca, 88,024 . . . . F 5
Manfredonia, 57,707 . . H10
Marsala, 80,468 . . . . L 7
Massa, 66,872 (145,000★) . . . . E 5
Messina, 268,896 . . . . K10
Mestre, 189,700 . . . . D 7
Milano (Milan), 1,495,260 (3,750,000★) . . . . D 4
Modena, 176,880 . . . . E 5
Molfetta, 64,519 . . . . H11
Monza, 122,064 . . . . D 4
Napoli (Naples), 1,204,211 (2,875,000★) . . . . I 9
Novara, 102,742 . . . . D 3
Padova, 225,769 (270,000★) . . . . D 6
Palermo, 723,732 . . . . K 8
Parma, 175,842 . . . . E 5
Pavia, 82,065 . . . . D 4
Perugia, 106,700 (146,713▲) . . . . F 7
Pesaro, 78,700 (90,336▲) . . . . F 7
Pescara, 131,027 . . . . G 9
Piacenza, 105,626 . . . . D 4
Pisa, 104,384 . . . . F 5
Pistoia, 76,800 (90,689▲) . . . . F 5
Pozzuoli, 65,000 . . . . I 9
Prato, 164,595 (215,000★) . . . . F 6
Ragusa, 67,748 . . . . M 9
Ravenna, 86,500 (136,016▲) . . . . E 7
Reggio di Calabria, 178,821 . . . . K10
Reggio nell'Emilia, 107,300 (130,086▲) . . E 5
Rimini, 114,600 (130,698▲) . . . . E 7
Roma (Rome), 2,815,457 (3,175,000★) . . . . H 7
Salerno, 154,848 (250,000★) . . . . I 9
San Remo, 60,797 . . . . F 2
Sassari, 120,152 . . . . I 3
Siracusa, 122,857 . . . . L10
Taranto, 244,997 . . . . I12
Terni, 94,500 (111,157▲) . . . . G 7
Torino (Turin), 1,035,565 (1,550,000★) . . . . D 2
Trento, 81,500 (100,202▲) . . . . C 6
Treviso, 85,083 . . . . D 7
Trieste, 239,031 . . . . D 8
Udine, 100,211 (126,000★) . . . . C 8
Varese, 88,353 . . . . D 3
Venezia (Venice), 88,700 (420,000★) . . . . D 7
Verona, 259,151 . . . . D 6
Vicenza, 110,449 . . . . D 6

Malta
1989 ESTIMATE

Valletta, 9,210 (215,000★) . . . . N 9

San Marino
1988 ESTIMATE

San Marino, 2,777 . . . . F 7

Slovenia
1987 ESTIMATE

Ljubljana, 233,200 (316,607▲)('87) . . . . C 9
Maribor, 107,400 (187,651▲)('87) C10

Vatican City
1988 ESTIMATE

Vatican City, 766 . . . . H 7

Albania
1987 ESTIMATE

Berat, 40,500 . . . . I 3
Durrës, 78,700 . . . . . . H 3
Elbasan, 78,300 . . . . . . H 4
Fier, 40,300('83) . . . . . . I 3
Korçë, 61,500 . . . . I 4
Shkodër, 76,300 . . . . G 3
Tiranë, 255,700 . . . . . . H 3
Vlorë, 67,700 . . . . I 3

Bosnia and Herzegovina
1987 ESTIMATE

Sarajevo, 341,200 (479,688▲) . . . . F 2
Zenica, 67,500 (144,869▲) . . . . E 1

Bulgaria
1986 ESTIMATE

Burgas, 186,369 . . . . G11
Dobrič, 110,471 . . . . . . F11
Gabrovo, 81,688 . . . . G 9
Haskovo, 89,273 . . . . H 9
Jambol, 92,321 . . . . . . G10
Pernik, 96,277 . . . . . . G 7
Pleven, 132,206 . . . . . . F 8
Plovdiv, 349,148 . . . . G 8
Ruse, 186,428 . . . . . . F 9
Sliven, 104,345 . . . . . . G10
Sofia *see* Sofija . . . . . . G 7
Sofija (Sofia), 1,119,152 (1,205,000★) . . . . . . G 7
Stara Zagora, 153,538 G 9
Šumen, 102,886 . . . . . . F10
Varna, 303,071 . . . . . . F11
Veliko Tărnovo, 70,610 F 9
Vidin, 63,813 . . . . F 6
Vraca, 77,934 . . . . . . F 7

Greece
1981 CENSUS

Agrínion, 35,774 (45,087★) . . . . K 5
Athínai (Athens), 885,737 (3,027,331★) . . . . . . L 7
Iráklion, 102,398 (110,958★) . . . . N 9
Kalámai, 42,075 (43,235★) . . . . L 6
Kavála, 56,375 . . . . . . I 8
Kérkira (Corfu), 33,561 J 3
Khaniá, 47,451 (61,976★) . . . . N 8
Lárisa, 102,048 . . . . . . J 6
Pátrai, 142,163 (154,596★) . . . . K 5
Piraiévs (Piraeus), 196,389 . . . . L 7
Ródhos (Rhodes), 40,392 . . . . M12
Thessaloníki (Salonika), 406,413 (706,180★) . . I 6
Vólos, 71,378 (107,407★) . . . . J 6

Macedonia
1987 ESTIMATE

Skopje, 444,900 (547,214▲) . . . . H 5

Moldova
1989 CENSUS

Bălţi, 159,000 . . . . . . B11
Chişinău, 665,000 . . . . B12
Rîbniţa, 58,000('87) . . B13
Tighina, 130,000 . . . . C13
Tiraspol, 182,000 . . . . C13

Romania
1986 ESTIMATE

Arad, 187,744 . . . . . . C 5
Bacău, 179,877 . . . . . . C10
Baia Mare, 139,704 . . B 7
Brăila, 235,620 . . . . . . D11
Braşov, 351,493 . . . . D 9

★ Population of metropolitan area, including suburbs. ▲ Population of entire district, including rural area.

1 : 4 000 000

Bucureşti (Bucharest), 1,989,823 (2,275,000★) E10
Buzău, 136,080 . . . . . . D10
Cluj-Napoca, 310,017 . . C 7
Constanţa, 327,676 . . E12
Craiova, 281,044 . . . . E 7
Galaţi, 295,372 . . . . . . D12
Iaşi, 313,060 . . . . B11
Oradea, 213,846 . . . . B 5
Ploieşti, 234,886 (310,000★) E10
Satu Mare, 130,082 . . B 6
Sibiu, 177,511 . . . . . . D 8
Târgu Mureş, 158,998 C 8
Timişoara, 325,272 . . . . D 5

Turkey
1990 CENSUS

Bursa, 838,323 . . . . . . I13
Denizli, 203,130 . . . . . . L13
İstanbul, 6,748,435 (7,000,000★) H12
İzmir, 2,553,209 (1,620,000★) K11
Manisa, 158,283 . . . . K11
Ödemiş, 511,110 . . . . K11

Yugoslavia
1987 ESTIMATE

Beograd (Belgrade), 1,130,000 (1,400,000★) . . . . . . E 4
Niš, 168,400 (240,219▲) F 5
Novi Sad, 176,000 (266,772▲) . . . . D 3
Pančevo, 62,700 . . . . E 4
Podgorica, 82,500 (145,163▲) . . . . G 3
Priština, 125,400 (244,830▲) . . . . G 5
Subotica, 100,500 (153,306▲) . . . . C 3
Zrenjanin, 65,400 (140,009▲) . . . . D 4

Baltic and Moscow Regions

Belarus
1989 CENSUS
Baranoviči, 159,000 . . H 9
Bobrujsk, 223,000 . . H12
Borisov, 144,000 . . . . G11
Brest, 258,000 . . . . . . I 6
Gomel', 500,000 . . . . . .I14
Grodno, 270,000 . . . . H 6
Lida, 81,000('87) . . . . H 8
Minsk, 1,589,000
(1,650,000★) H10
Mogil'ov, 356,000 . . . H13
Molodečno,
87,000('87) . . . . . . G 9
Novopolock,
90,000('87) F11
Orša, 123,000 . . . . . . G13
Pinsk, 119,000 . . . . . . I 9
Polock, 80,000('87) . . F11
Rečica, 71,000('87) . . I13
Sluck, 55,000('87) . . H10
Svetlogorsk,
68,000('87) . . . . . . G 3
Vitebsk, 350,000 . . . . F13
Žlobin, 52,000('87) I13

Estonia
1989 CENSUS
Kohtla-Järve,
78,000('87) B10
Narva, 81,000('87) . . B11
Pärnu, 53,000('87) . . C 7
Tallinn, 482,000 . . . . B 7
Tartu, 114,000 . . . . . . C 9

Latvia
1989 CENSUS
Daugavpils, 127,000 . . F 9
Jelgava, 72,000('87) . . E 6
Jūrmala, 65,000('87) . . E 6
Liepāja, 114,000 . . . . E 4
Rēzekne, 35,620('79) E10
Rīga, 915,000
(1,005,000★) . . . . . . E 7
Ventspils, 52,000('87) D 4

Lithuania
1989 CENSUS
Kaunas, 423,000 . . . . G 6
Klaipėda (Memel),
204,000 . . . . F 4
Panevėžys, 126,000 . . F 7
Šiauliai, 145,000 . . . . F 6
Vilnius, 582,000 . . . . G 8

Russia
1989 CENSUS
Aleksandrov,
66,000('87) E21
Aleksin, 72,000('87) . . G20
Balachna, 35,359('79) E26
Balašicha, 136,000 . . F20
Bežeck, 30,711('79) . . D19
Bor, 65,000('87) E27
Boroviči, 64,000('87) C16
Br'ansk, 452,000 . . . . H17
Čechov, 57,000('87) . . F20
Čerepovec, 310,000 . . B20
Čern'achovsk,
36,361('79) . . . . . . G 4
Chimki, 133,000 . . . . F20
Dmitrov, 64,000('87) . . E20
Domodedovo,
51,000('87) F20
Dubna, 64,000('87) . . E20
Dzeržinsk, 285,000 . . E26
Elektrostal', 153,000 . . F21
Furmanov, 44,430('79)D24
Gatčina, 81,000('87) . . B13
Gorki *see* Nižnij
Novgorod E27
Gr'azi, 41,082('79) I22
Gus'-Chrustal'nyj,
75,000('87) F23
Ivanovo, 481,000 . . . . D23
Jarcevo, 40,908('79) . . F15
Jaroslavl', 633,000 . . D22
Jefremov, 58,000('87) H21
Jegorjevsk,
73,000('87) F22

★ Population of metropolitan area, including suburbs.

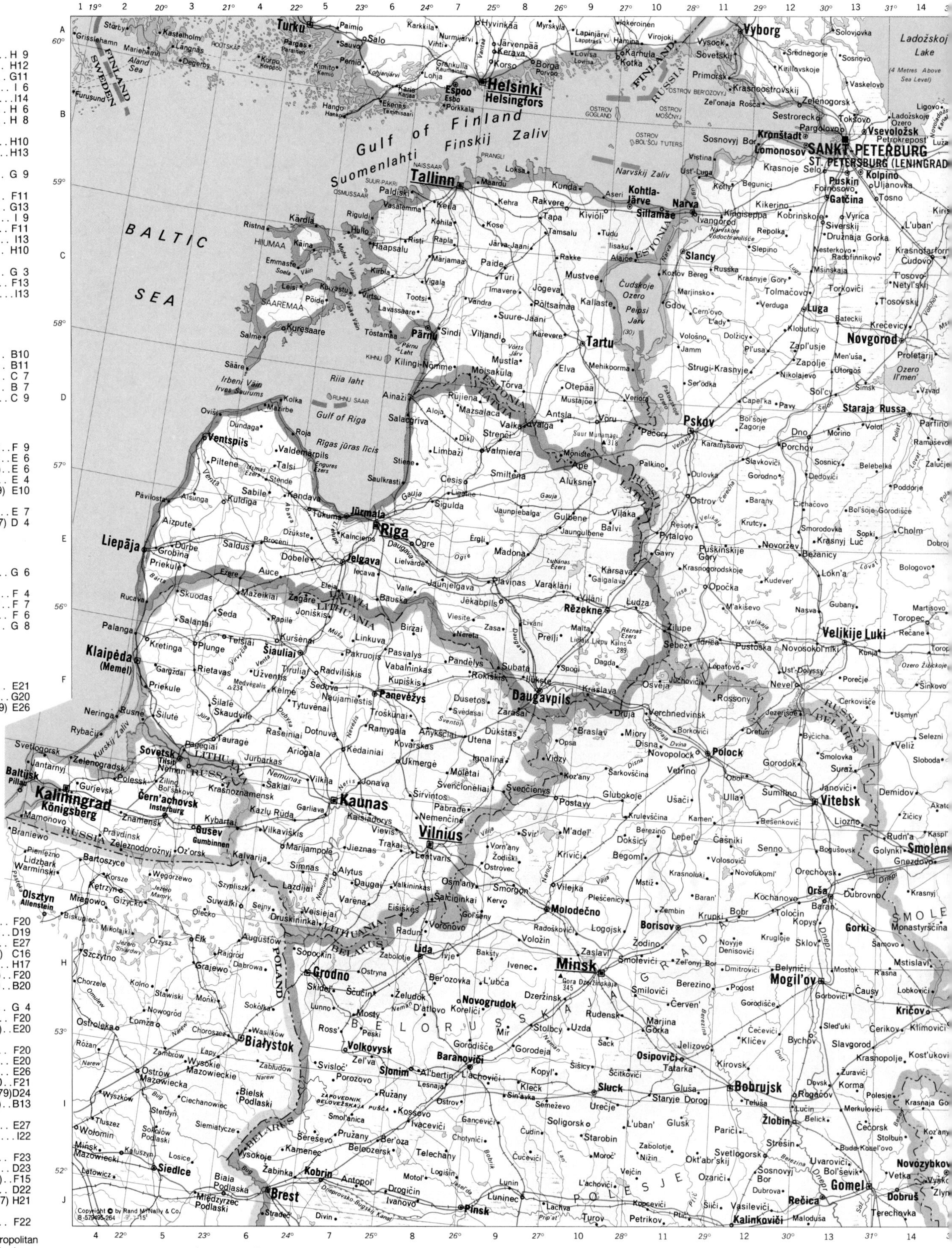

Kilometers 0 50 100 150 Km.
Miles 0 50 100 150 Mi.

1:4 000 000

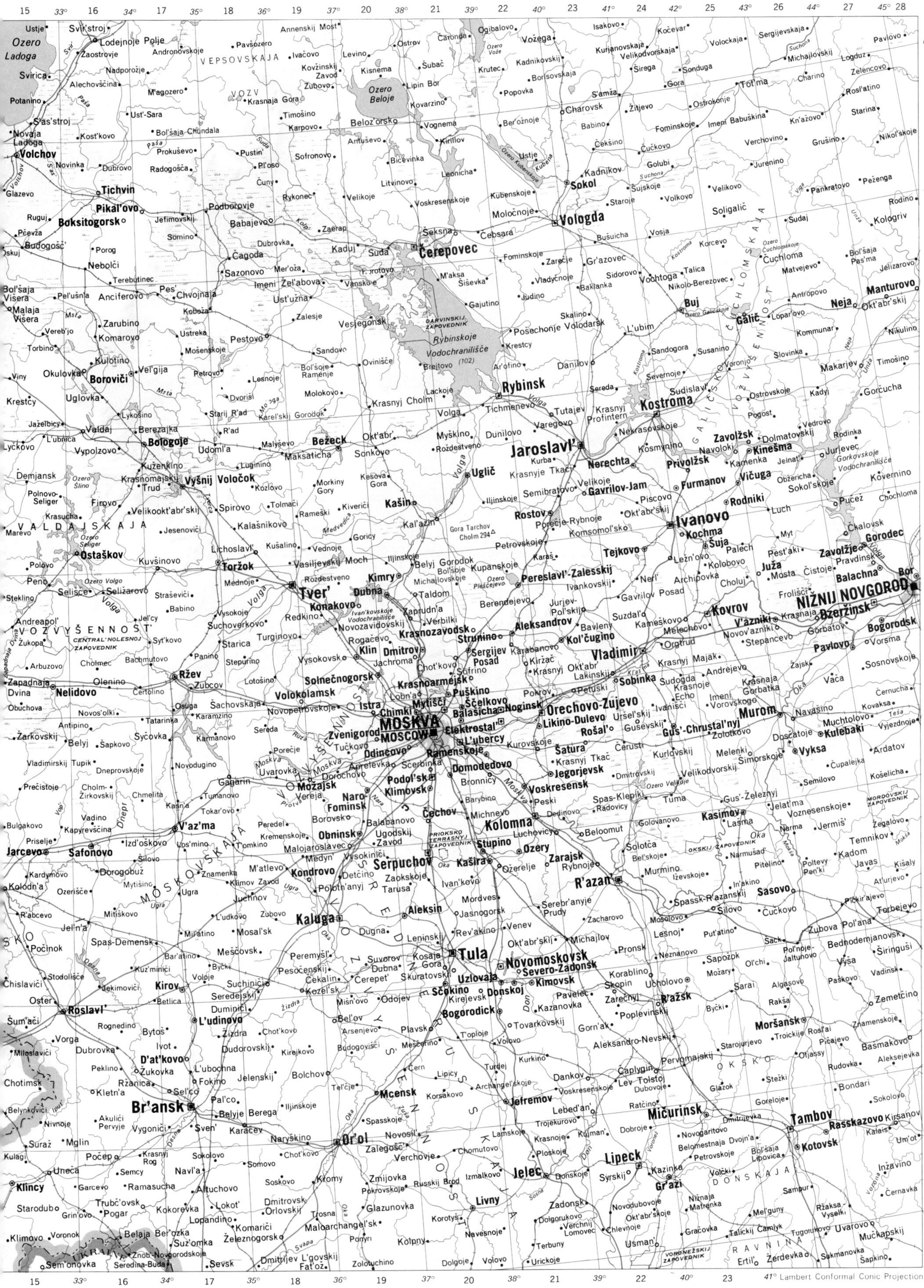

Jelec, 120,000 ...... I21
Kaliningrad (Königsberg), 401,000 .... G 3
Kaluga, 312,000 .... G19
Kasimov, 33,993('79) G24
Kašira, 43,867('79) .. G21
Kimovsk, 42,163('79) H21
Kimry, 61,000('87) .. E20
Kinešma, 105,000 .... D25
Klimovsk, 57,000('87) F20
Klin, 95,000('87) E19
Klincy, 72,000('87) I15
Kol'čugino, 43,686('79) E22
Kolomna, 162,000 .... F21
Kolpino, 142,000 .... B13
Konakovo, 37,087('79)E19
Kostroma, 278,000 .. D23
Kotovsk, 36,000('74) .. I24
Kovrov, 160,000 .... E24
Kronštadt, 40,102('79)B12
Kulebaki, 48,302('79) F25
Leningrad *see* Sankt-Peterburg B13
Lipeck, 450,000 ...... I22
Livny, 51,000('87) I20
Lomonosov, 43,514('79) B12
L'ubercy, 165,000 .... F20
L'udinovo, 40,339('79)H17
Luga, 37,680('79) C12
Mcensk, 42,306('79) H19
Mičurinsk, 109,000 .... I23
Moršansk, 51,000('87)H24
Moskva (Moscow), 8,769,000 (13,100,000★) F20
Murom, 124,000 .... F25
Mytišči, 154,000 .... F20
Naro-Fominsk, 60,000('87) F19
Nižnij Novgorod (Gorki), 1,438,000 (2,025,000★) E27
Novgorod, 229,000 ... C14
Novomoskovsk, 146,000 (365,000★) G21
Novozybkov, 41,344('79) I14
Obninsk, 100,000 .... F19
Odincovo, 125,000 .. F20
Orechovo-Zujevo, 137,000 (205,000★) F21
Or'ol, 337,000 ...... I19
Pavlovo, 72,000('87) .. F26
Podol'sk, 210,000 .... F20
Pskov, 204,000 ...... D11
Puškin, 97,000('87) .. B13
Puškino, 74,000('87) E20
Ramenskoje, 86,000('87) F21
Rasskazovo, 43,227('79) I24
R'azan', 515,000 .... G22
R'ažsk, 26,000('74) .. H23
Roslavl', 61,000('87) H15
Rybinsk, 252,000 .... C21
Rževٍ, 70,000('87) E17
Safonovo, 56,000('87) F16
Sankt-Peterburg (Saint Petersburg), 4,456,000 (5,825,000★) B13
Ščelkovo, 109,000 .. F21
Ščokino, 70,000('87) .. G20
Sergijev Podad, 115,000 .... E21
Serpuchov, 144,000 .. G20
Slancy, 42,253('79) .. B11
Smolensk, 341,000 .. G15
Sokol, 45,424('79) .. B23
Solnečnogorsk, 53,000('87) E19
Sovetsk (Tilsit), 40,091('79) ...... F 4
Stupino, 73,000('87) G21
Šuja, 72,000('87) E24
Tambov, 305,000 .... I24
Tichvin, 70,000('87) .. B16
Toržok, 51,000('87) .. D17
Tula, 540,000 (640,000★) G20
Tver', 451,000 ...... E18
Uglič, 39,872('79) D21
Uzlovaja, 63,000('87) H21
V'az'ma, 57,000('87) F17
V'azniki, 45,916('79) .. E25
Velikije Luki, 114,000 E13
Vičuga, 51,000('87) .. D24
Vladimir, 350,000 .... E23
Volchov, 51,000('87) B15
Vologda, 283,000 .... B22
Voskresensk, 80,000('87) F21
Vyborg, 81,000('87) .. A11
Vyksa, 60,000('87) .. F25
Vyšnij Voloćok, 70,000('87) D17

'Adan, 176,100 ('84) (318,000★) ....H 7
AFGHANISTAN...........F 9
Ahmadābād, 2,059,725 ('81) (2,400,000★) .. G10
Al Baṣrah, 616,700 ('85)..........................F 7
Al-Kuwayt, 44.335 ('85) (1,375,000★) ....G 7
Alma-Ata, 1,128,000 ('89) (1,190,000★) E10
Al-Madīnah, 290,000 ('80)......................... G 6
'Ammān, 936,300 ('89) (1,450,000★) ....F 6
Ankara, 2,553,209 ('90) (2,670,000★) ....F 6
ARMENIA..................... F 7
Ar-Riyāḍ, 1,250,000 ('80)......................... G 7
Aščhabad, 398,000 ('89)..........................F 8
AZERBAIJAN.............. E 7
Baghdād, 3,841,268 ('87)..........................F 7
Baku, 1,150,000 ('89) (2,020,000★) ....E 7
Bangalore, 2,476,355 ('81) (2,950,000★) H10
Bangkok see Krung Thep H13
BANGLADESH............G12
Batumi, 136,000 ('89)..E 7
Bayrūt, 509,000 ('82) (1,675,000★) ....F 6
Beijing (Peking), 6,710,000 ('88) (6,450,000★) F14
BHUTAN......................G12
Biškek, 616,000 ('89).. E10
Bombay, 8,243,405 ('81) (9,950,000★) H10
BRUNEI.........................I14
Calcutta, 3,305,006 ('81) (11,100,000★) H11
CAMBODIA.................H13
Canton see Guangzhou G14
Celinograd, 277,000 ('89)......................... D10
Chabarovsk, 601,000 ('89)..........................E16
Changchun, 1,822,000 ('88) (2,000,000▲) ...E15
Changsha, 1,230,000 ('88)......................... G14
Chengdu, 1,884,000 ('88) (2,960,000▲) F13
CHINA..........................F12
Chongqing (Chungking), 2,502,000 ('88) (2,890,000▲) G13
Čita, 366,000 ('89)...... D14
Colombo, 683,000 ('86) (2,050,000★) I10
CYPRUS..................... F 6
CYPRUS, NORTH........F 6
Dacca see Dhaka G12
Dalian, 2,280,000 ('88) F15
Damascus see Dimashq .... F 6
Da Nang, 318,653 ('79).......................... H13
Delhi, 4,884,234 ('81) (7,200,000★) G10
Dhaka (Dacca), 2,365,695 ('81) (3,430,312★) .. G12
Dimashq (Damascus), 1,326,000 ('88) (1,950,000★) .... F 6
Dušanbe, 595,000 ('89)..........................F 9
Eṣfahān, 986,753 ('86) (1,175,000★) .... F 8
Frunze see Biškek E10
Fukuoka, 1,160,440 ('85) (1,750,000★) F16
Fuzhou, 910,000 ('88) (1,240,000▲) G14
George Town, 248,241 ('80) (495,000★) I13
GEORGIA..................... E 7
Guangzhou (Canton), 3,100,000 ('88) (3,420,000▲) G14
Hakodate, 319,194 ('85)..........................E17
Ha Noi, 1,089,000 ('89) (1,500,000★) G13
Harbin, 2,710,000 ('88)..........................E15
Herāt, 177,300 ('88).... F 9
Hiroshima, 1,044,118 ('85) (1,575,000★) F16
HONG KONG.............. G14
Hyderābād, 2,187,262 ('81) (2,750,000★) .. H10
INDIA.......................... G10
INDONESIA................. I13
IRAN........................... F 8
IRAQ........................... F 7
Irkutsk, 626,000 ('89)..D13
Islāmābād, 204,364 ('81)..........................F10
ISRAEL........................F 6
izmir, 2,553,209 ('90) (1,620,000★) .... F 5
Jakutsk, 187,000 ('89).......... C15
JAPAN........................F16
Jekateringbug, 1,367,000 ('89) (1,620,000★) ....D 9
Jerevan, 1,199,000 ('89) (1,315,000★) .... E 7
Jerusalem see Yerushalayim ....F 6
Jiddah, 1,300,000 ('80)......................... G 6
Jinan, 1,546,000 ('88) (2,140,000▲) F14
JORDAN...................... F 6
Kābol (Kabul), 1,424,400 ('88)..........................F 9
Kānpur, 1,481,789 ('81) (1,875,000★) G11
Karāchi, 4,901,627 ('81) (5,300,000★) ....G 9
Kashi, 146,300 ('86) (194,500▲) F10
Kaṭhmāṇḍau, 235,160 ('81) (320,000★) G11
KAZAKHSTAN.............E 9
Kermān, 257,284 ('86)............F 8
Konsomol'sk-na-Amure, 315,000 ('89)........... D16
KOREA, NORTH..........E15
KOREA, SOUTH.........F15
Krasnojarsk, 912,000 ('89)........................ D12
Krung Thep (Bangkok), 5,716,779 ('88) (6,450,000★) H13
Kuala Lumpur, 919,610 ('80) (1,475,000★) I13
Kuching, 72,555 ('80)... I14

ARABIAN SEA
INDIAN OCEAN
SAUDI ARABIA
IRAN
IRAQ
INDIA
KAZAKHSTAN
AFGHANISTAN
PAKISTAN
OMAN
YEMEN
TURKEY
CAUCASUS
Black Sea
Caspian Sea
Red Sea
Gulf of Aden
Persian Gulf
Baltic Sea
North Sea
Barents Sea
Gulf of Bothnia
MOSKVA
SANKT-PETERBURG
ISTANBUL
ANKARA
BAGHDAD
TEHRĀN
KARĀCHI
DELHI
BOMBAY
MADRAS
BANGALORE
Colombo
SRI LANKA
MALDIVES
Equator
Tropic of Cancer
Arctic Circle
Copyright © by Rand McNally & Co.
A-519695-286
Miles 0 200 400 600 800 1000 Mi.
Kilometers 0 400 800 1200 1600 Km.
1:40 000 000

Kunming, 1,310,000 ('88) (1,550,000▲) G13
KUWAIT .... G 7
Kyōto, 1,479,218 ('85).........F16
KYRGYZSTAN........... E10
Kyzyl, 80,000 ('87)...... D12
Lahore, 2,707,215 ('81) (3,025,000★) F10
Lanzhou, 1,297,000 ('88) (1,420,000▲) F13
LAOS H13
LEBANON ....F 6
Lhasa, 84,400 ('86) (107,700▲) G12
MACAU....................... G14
Madras, 3,276,622 ('81) (4,475,000★) H11
Makkah, 550,000 ('80).......... G 6
MALAYSIA I13
MALDIVES....................I10
Mandalay, 532,949 ('83).......................... G12
Manila, 1,587,000 ('90) (6,800,000★) H15
Mashhad, 1,463,508 ('86)......................... F 8
Masqaṭ, 50,000 ('81)...G 8
Mawlamyine, 219,961 ('83)........................ H12
MONGOLIA E13
MYANMAR G12
Nāgpur, 1,219,461 ('81) (1,302,066★) G10
Nanjing, 2,390,000 ('88).........................F14
NEPAL G11
New Delhi, 273,036 ('81).......................... G10
Novosibirsk, 1,436,000 ('89) (1,600,000★) .. D11
Ochotsk, 9,000.......... D17
OMAN......................... G 8
Omsk, 1,148,000 ('89) (1,175,000★) D10
Ōsaka, 2,636,249 ('85) (1,645,000★) F16
PAKISTAN....................G 9
Patna, 776,371 ('81) (1,025,000★) G11
Peking see Beijing F14
Peshāwar, 506,896 ('81) (566,248★) F10
Petropavlovsk-Kamčatskij, 269,000 ('89).......... D18
PHILIPPINES...............H15
Phnum Penh, 700,000 ('86)......................... H13
Pyŏngyang, 1,283,000 ('81) (1,600,000★) ...F15
QATAR........................G 8
Qingdao (Tsingtao), 1,300,000 ('88).........F15
Quetta, 244,842 ('81) (285,719★) .... F 9
Quezon City, 1,632,000 ('90)......................... H15
Rangoon see Yangon H12
Rāwalpindi, 457,091 ('81) (1,040,000★) F10
RUSSIA D10
Saigon see Thanh Pho Ho Chi Minh H13
Samarkand, 366,000 ('89).......................... F 9
Ṣan'ā', 427,150 ('86)...H 7
SAUDI ARABIA.......... G 7
Semipalatinsk, 334,000 ('89)......................... D11
Sendai, 700,254 ('85) (1,175,000★) F17
Shanghai, 7,220,000 ('88) (9,300,000★) F15
Shenyang (Mukden), 3,910,000 ('88) (4,370,000▲) E15
Shīrāz, 848,289 ('86)...G 8
SINGAPORE.................I13
Sŏul, 10,522,000 ('89) (15,850,000★) F15
SRI LANKA..................I11
Srīnagar, 594,775 ('81) (606,002★) F10
SYRIA..........................F 6
Tabrīz, 971,482 ('86)... F 7
T'aipei, 2,637,100 ('88) (6,130,000★) G15
TAIWAN.....................G15
Taiyuan, 1,700,000 ('88) (1,980,000▲) F14
TAJIKISTAN................F10
Taškent, 2,073,000 ('89) (2,325,000★) ....E 9
Tbilisi, 1,260,000 ('89) (1,460,000★) ....E 7
Tehrān, 6,042,584 ('86) (7,500,000★) .... F 8
THAILAND................. H13
Thanh Pho Ho Chi Minh (Saigon), 3,169,000 ('89) (3,100,000★) H13
Tianjin (Tientsin), 4,950,000 ('88) (5,540,000▲) F14
Tobol'sk, 82,000 ('87)............ D 9
Tōkyō, 8,354,615 ('85) (27,700,000★) F16
Tomsk, 502,000 ('89)..D11
TURKEY.......................F 6
TURKMENISTAN.........F 9
Ulaanbaatar, 548,400 ('89).........................E13
UNITED ARAB EMIRATES............. G 8
Ürümqi, 1,060,000 ('88).........................E11
UZBEKISTAN............. E 9
Vārānasi, 708,647 ('81) (925,000★) G11
Verchojansk, 1,400..... C16
Viangchan, 377,409 ('85)......................... H13
VIETNAM................... H13
Vladivostok, 648,000 ('89).........................E16
Wuhan, 3,570,000 ('88).........................F14
Xiamen, 343,700 ('86) (546,400▲) G14
Xi'an, 2,210,000 ('88) (2,580,000▲) F13
Yangon (Rangoon), 2,705,039 ('83) (2,800,000★) H12
YEMEN.......................H 7
Yerevan see Jerevan ..E 7
Yerushalayim (Jerusalem), 493,500 ('89) (530,000★) .... F 6
Yokohama, 2,992,926 ('85).........................F16
Zhangjiakou, 500,000 ('88) (640,000▲) E14

★ Population of metropolitan area, including suburbs.
▲ Population of entire district, including rural area.

Northwest Asia

Armenia
1989 CENSUS
Jerevan, 1,199,000 (1,315,000★) . . . . . . I 6

Azerbaijan
1989 CENSUS
Baku, 1,150,000 (2,020,000★) . . . . . . I 7
Gjandža, 278,000 . . . . I 7
Sumgait, 231,000 . . . . I 7

Belarus
1989 CENSUS
Brest, 258,000 . . . . . . G 2
Gomel', 500,000 . . . . G 4
Grodno, 270,000 . . . . G 2
Minsk, 1,589,000 (1,650,000★) . . . . . . G 3
Mogil'ov, 356,000 . . . G 4
Vitebsk, 350,000 . . . . F 4

Estonia
1989 CENSUS
Tallinn, 482,000 . . . . . . F 2

Georgia
1989 CENSUS
Kutaisi, 235,000 . . . . . . I 6
Tbilisi, 1,260,000 (1,460,000★) . . . . . . I 6

Kazakhstan
1989 CENSUS
Akt'ubinsk, 253,000 . . G 9
Alma-Ata, 1,128,000 (1,190,000★) I13
Celinograd, 277,000 . . G12
Čimkent, 393,000 . . . . I11
Džambul, 307,000 . . . . I12
Karaganda, 614,000 . . H12
Pavlodar, 331,000 . . G13
Petropavlovsk, 241,000 . . . . G11
Semipalatinsk, 334,000 . . . . G14
Temirtau, 212,000 . . . G12
Ural'sk, 200,000 . . . G 8
Ust'-Kamenogorsk, 324,000 . . . . H14

Kyrgyzstan
1989 CENSUS
Biškek, 616,000 . . . . . . I12
Oš, 213,000 . . . . I12

Latvia
1989 CENSUS
Rīga, 915,000 (1,005,000★) . . . . . . F 2

Lithuania
1989 CENSUS
Kaunas, 423,000 . . . . G 2
Klaipėda, 204,000 . . . . F 2
Vilnius, 582,000 . . . . . . F 3

Moldova
1989 CENSUS
Bălţi, 131,000('81) . . H 3
Chişinău, 665,000 . . . . H 3
Tiraspol, 182,000 . . . . H 3

Russia
1989 CENSUS
Archangel'sk, 416,000 E 6
Astrachan', 509,000 . . H 7
Belgorod, 300,000 . . G 5
Br'ansk, 452,000 . . . . G 4
Čeboksary, 420,000 . . F 7
Čel'abinsk, 1,143,000 (1,325,000★) F10
Čerepovec, 310,000 . . F 5
Gor'kij see Nižnij Novgorod . . . . F 6
Groznyj, 401,000 . . . . I 7
Ivanovo, 481,000 . . . . F 6
Iževsk, 635,000 . . . . . . F 8
Jaroslavl', 633,000 . . F 5
Jekaterinburg (Sverdlovsk), 1,367,000 (1,620,000★) F10
Kaliningrad, 401,000 G 2
Kaluga, 312,000 . . . . G 5
Kazan', 1,094,000 (1,140,000★) . . . . . . F 7
Kirov, 441,000 . . . . . . F 7
Krasnodar, 620,000 . . H 5
Kurgan, 356,000 . . . . F11
Kursk, 424,000 . . . . . . G 5
Leningrad see Sankt-Peterburg . . F 4
Lipeck, 450,000 . . . . G 5
Machačkala, 315,000 . . I 7
Magnitogorsk, 440,000 . . . . G 9

★ Population of metropolitan area, including suburbs.

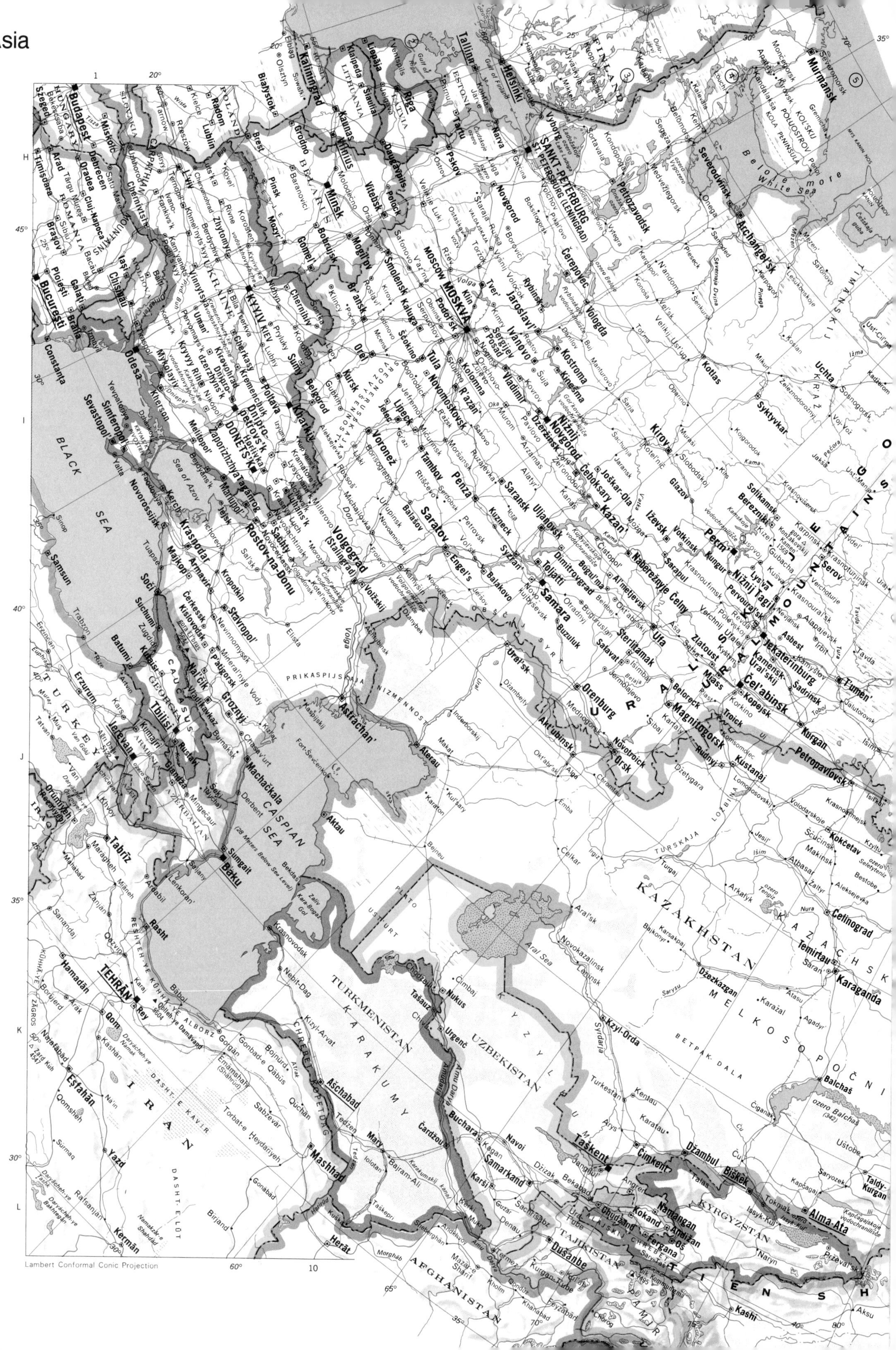

Moskva (Moscow), 8,769,000 (13,100,000★) .... F 5
Murmansk, 468,000 .. D 4
Naberežnyje Čelny, 501,000 .... F 8
Nižnij Novgorod (Gor'kij), 1,438,000 (2,025,000★) ...... F 6
Nižnij Tagil, 440,000 .. F 9
Orel, 337,000 ...... G 5
Orenburg, 547,000 .. G 9
Orsk, 271,000 ...... G 9
Penza, 543,000 .... G 7
Perm', 1,091,000 (1,160,000★) ...... F 9
Petrozavodsk, 270,000 .... E 4
R'azan', 515,000 .... G 5
Rostov-na-Donu, 1,020,000 (1,165,000★) ...... H 5
Samara, 1,257,000 (1,505,000★) ...... G 8
Sankt-Peterburg (St. Petersburg), 4,456,000 (5,825,000★) ...... F 4
Saransk, 312,000 .... G 7
Saratov, 905,000 (1,155,000★) ...... G 7
Smolensk, 341,000 .. G 4
Soči, 337,000 .... I 5
Stalingrad *see* Volgograd .... H 6
Stavropol', 318,000 .. H 6
Sverdlovsk *see* Jekaterinburg F10
Syktyvkar, 233,000 .. E 8
Taganrog, 291,000 .. H 5
Tambov, 305,000 .... G 6
Toljatti, 630,000 .... G 7
Tula, 540,000 (640,000★) ...... G 5
Tver' (Kalinin), 451,000 .... F 5
Ufa, 1,083,000 (1,100,000★) ...... G 9
Uljanovsk, 625,000 .. G 7
Vladikavkaz, 300,000 .. I 6
Vladimir, 350,000 .... F 6
Volgograd (Stalingrad), 999,000 (1,360,000★) ...... H 6
Vologda, 283,000 .... F 5
Volžskij, 269,000 .... H 6
Voronež, 887,000 .... G 5

Tajikistan

1989 CENSUS

Dušanbe, 595,000 .... J11

Turkmenistan

1989 CENSUS

Aščhabad, 398,000 .. J 9

Ukraine

1989 CENSUS

Cherkasy, 290,000 .. H 4
Chernihiv, 296,000 .. G 4
Dniprodzerzhynsk, 282,000 .... H 4
Dnipropetrovsk, 1,179,000 (1,600,000★) ...... H 4
Donets'k, 1,110,000 (2,200,000★) ...... H 5
Horlivka, 337,000 (710,000★) .... H 5
Kharkiv, 1,611,000 (1,940,000★) ...... G 5
Kherson, 355,000 .... H 4
Kryvyy Rih, 713,000 .. H 4
Kyyiv (Kiev), 2,587,000 (2,900,000★) ...... G 4
Luhansk, 497,000 .... H 5
L'viv, 790,000 ...... H 2
Mariupol' (Ždanov), 517,000 .... H 5
Mykolayiv, 503,000 .. H 4
Odesa, 1,115,000 (1,185,000★) ...... H 4
Poltava, 315,000 .... H 4
Sevastopol', 356,000 .. I 4
Simferopol', 344,000 .. I 4
Sumy, 291,000 ...... G 4
Vinnytsya, 374,000 .. H 3
Yalta, 89,000('87) .... I 4
Zaporizhzhya, 884,000 .... H 5
Zhytomyr, 292,000 .. G 3

Uzbekistan

1989 CENSUS

Andižan, 293,000 .... I12
Buchara, 224,000 .... J10
Fergana, 200,000 .... I12
Namangan, 308,000 .. I12
Samarkand, 366,000 .. J11
Taškent, 2,073,000 (2,325,000★) I11

Northeast Asia

Russia

1989 CENSUS

Abakan, 154,000 .... G12
Ačinsk, 122,000 .... F12
Alapajevsk, 51,000('87) ...... F 6
Aldan, 20,000('74) .. F19
Alejsk, 31,390('79) .. G10
Aleksandrovsk-Sachalinskij, 20,000('74) G22
Angarsk, 266,000 .... G14
Anžero-Sudžensk, 108,000 .... F11
Arsenjev, 67,000('87) .. I20
Art'om, 73,000('87) .. I20
Art'omovsk, 17,000('79) G12
Asbest, 83,000('87) .. F 6
Asino, 31,329('79) ... F11
Balej, 25,000('79) G17
Barabinsk, 35,035('79) F 9
Barnaul, 602,000 (665,000★) G10
Belogorsk, 71,000('87) G19
Belovo, 118,000('87) G11
Berdsk, 77,000('87) .. G10
Berezniki, 201,000 .. F 5
Bijsk, 233,000 ...... G11
Bikin, 18,000('79) H20
Birobidžan, 82,000('87) H20
Blagoveščensk, 206,000 .... G19
Bogotol, 29,000('79) .. F11
Bolotnoje, 20,000('79) F10
Bratsk, 255,000 .... F14
Čel'abinsk, 1,143,000 (1,325,000★) ...... F 6
Čeremchovo, 73,000('87) G14
Černogorsk, 80,000('87) G12
Chabarovsk, 601,000 H21
Chanty-Mansijsk, 27,961('79) ...... E 7
Cholmsk, 50,000('87) H22
Čita, 366,000 ...... G16
Čusovoj, 59,000('87) F 5
Dudinka, 23,000('74) D11
Gorno-Altajsk, 39,917('79) G11
Gubacha, 32,461('79) F 5
Gusinoozersk, 18,000('79) G15
Igarka, 16,918('79) .. D11
Inta, 58,000('87) .... D 6
Irbit, 53,000('87) .... F 6
Irkutsk, 626,000 .... G14
Iskitim, 69,000('87) .. G10
Issyk-Kul', 64,000('87) I 9
Jakutsk, 187,000 .... E19
Jekaterinburg, 1,367,000 (1,620,000★) ...... F 6
Jenisejsk, 22,000('79) F12
Jurga, 92,000('87) .. F10
Južno-Sachalinsk, 157,000 .... H22
Kamen'-na-Obi, 40,684('79) G10
Kamensk-Ural'skij, 209,000 .... F 6
Kansk, 110,000 ...... F13
Karpinsk, 36,569('79) F 6
Kemerovo, 520,000 .. F11
Kirensk, 16,000('74) .. F15
Kisel'ovsk, 128,000 .. G11
Kizel, 40,157('79) .... F 5
Kolpaševo, 27,000('79) F10
Komsomol'sk-na-Amure, 315,000 .... G21
Kopejsk, 99,000('87) F 6
Korkino, 63,000('81) G 6
Korsakov, 43,348('79) H22
Krasnojarsk, 912,000 F12

★ Population of metropolitan area, including suburbs.

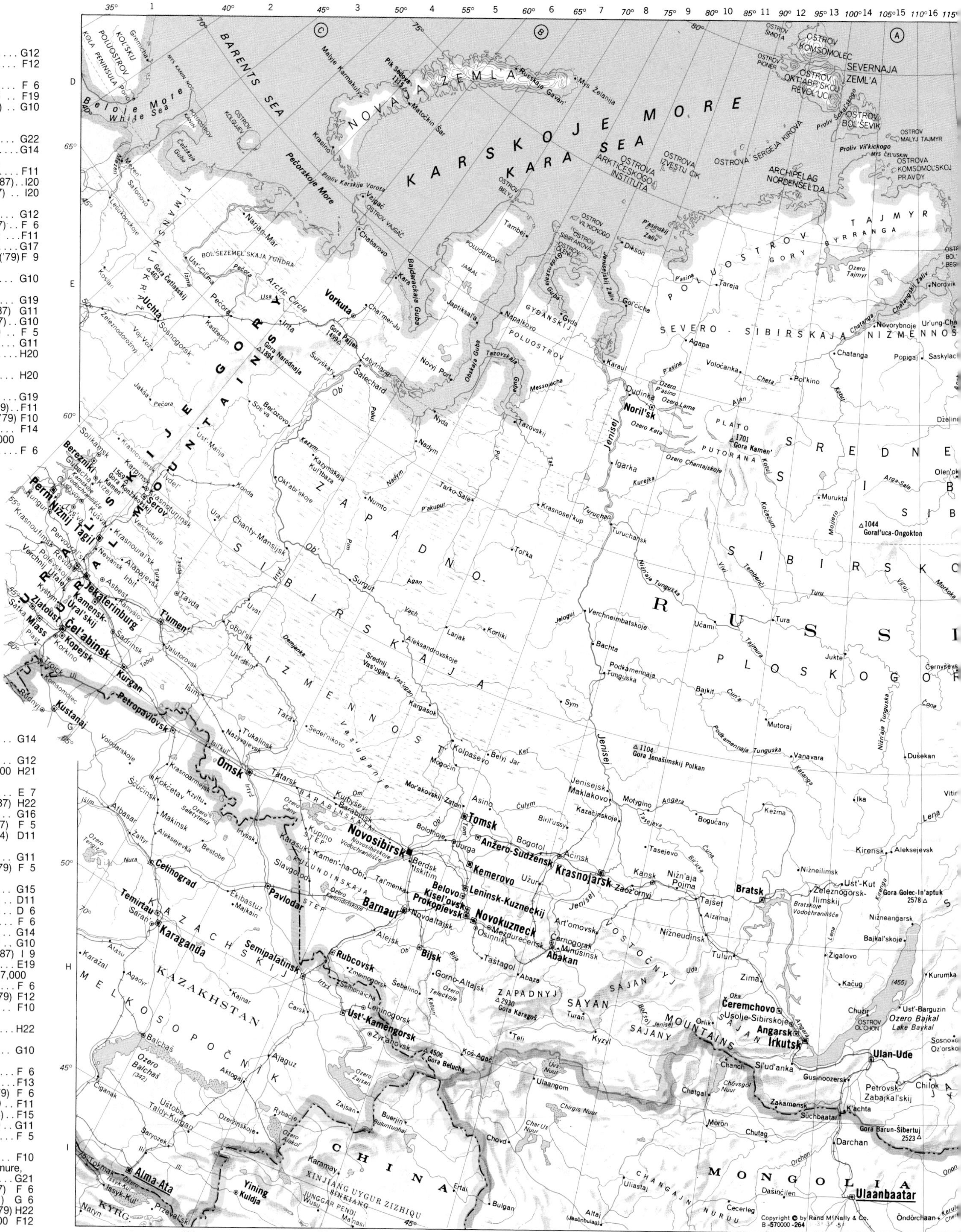

Kilometers 0 200 400 600 Km.
Miles 0 200 400 600 Mi.

1 : 16 000 000

Krasnoturjinsk, 66,000('87) ...... F 6
Krasnoufimsk, 40,027('79) ...... F 5
Krasnoural'sk, 38,212('79) ...... F 6
Kujbyšev, 51,000('87) F 9
Kungur, 83,000('87) .. F 5
Kupino, 19,000('79) .. G 9
Kurgan, 356,000 .... F 7
Kušva, 43,089('79) .. F 5
Kyštym, 39,701('79) .. F 6
Kyzyl, 80,000('87) .. G12
Leninsk-Kuzneckij, 165,000 .... G11
Lensk, 23,500('79) .. E16
Lesozavodsk, 38,573('79) H20
Lys'va, 77,000('87) .. F 5
Magadan, 152,000 .. F24
Meždurečensk, 107,000 .... G11
Miass, 168,000 ...... G 6
Minusinsk, 72,000('87) G12
Mirnyj, 30,500('79) .. E16
Mogoča, 19,000('74) G17
Nachodka, 165,000 .. I20
Narjan-Mar, 18,000('74) ...... D 4
Nevjansk, 31,946('79) F 6
Nikolajevsk-na-Amure, 33,795('79) G22
Nižneudinsk, 40,902('79) G13
Nižnij Tagil, 440,000 .. F 5
Noril'sk, 174,000 .... D11
Novoaltajsk, 51,000('87) G10
Novokuzneck, 600,000 .... G11
Novosibirsk, 1,436,000 (1,600,000★) F10
Ocha, 33,761('79) .. G22
Omsk, 1,148,000 (1,175,000★) ...... F 8
Osinniki, 63,000('87) G11
Pečora, 58,000('81) .. D 5
Perm', 1,091,000 (1,160,000★) ...... F 5
Pervoural'sk, 142,000 F 5
Petropavlovsk-Kamčatskij, 269,000 .... G25
Petrovsk-Zabajkal'skij, 30,000('74) G15
Polevskoj, 71,000('87) F 6
Poronajsk, 24,000('74) H22
Prokopjevsk, 274,000 (410,000★) G11
Rajčichinsk, 27,000('79) H19
Revda, 66,000('87) .. F 5
Rubcovsk, 172,000 .. G10
Šadrinsk, 87,000('87) F 6
Salechard, 26,000('74) D 7
Satka, 46,202('79) .. F 5
Serov, 104,000 ...... F 6
Slavgorod, 33,000('74) ...... G 9
Sl'ud'anka, 21,000('74) G14
Solikamsk, 110,000 .. F 5
Sovetskaja Gavan', 31,000('74) H22
Spassk-Dal'nij, 60,000('87) I20
Sučan, 45,628('79) I20
Surgut, 248,000 .... E 8
Sverdlovsk *see* Jekaterinburg ...... F 6
Svobodnyj, 78,000('87) G19
Tajšet, 36,254('79) .. F13
Tal'menka, 22,000('79) G10
Tara, 24,000('74) .... F 8
Taštagol, 23,000('79) G11
Tatarsk, 29,190('79) .. F 9
Tavda, 46,115('79) .. F 7
Tobol'sk, 82,000('87) F 7
Tomsk, 502,000 .... F10
Troick, 91,000('87) .. G 6
Tulun, 56,000('87) .. G14
T'umen', 477,000 .... F 7
Tyndinskij, 56,000('85) F18
Uchta, 111,000 ...... E 4
Uglegorsk, 18,000('79) H22
Ulan-Ude, 353,000 .. G15
Usolje-Sibirskoje, 107,000 .... G14
Ussurijsk, 162,000 .... I20
Ust'-Kut, 58,000('87) F15
Užur, 22,000('79) F11
V'azemskij, 19,000('79) H20
Vladivostok, 648,000 .. I20
Vorkuta, 116,000 .... D 6
Zaoz'ornyj, 26,000('79) F12
Zeja, 24,000('74) G19
Železnogorsk-Ilimskij, 30,000('79) F14
Zima, 51,000('87) G14
Zlatoust, 208,000 .... F 5

China, Japan, and Korea

Bhutan

1982 ESTIMATE

Thimphu, 12,000 .... F 4

China

1988 ESTIMATE

Andong, 579,800('86) C11
Anshan, 1,330,000 .. C11
Bangbu, 403,900
(612,600▲)('86) E10
Baoding, 423,200
(535,100▲)('86) D10
Baotou, 1,130,000 .. C 8
Beijing (Peking), 6,710,000
(6,450,000★) D10
Benxi, 860,000 ...... C11
Canton *see*
Guangzhou ...... G 9
Changchun, 1,822,000
(2,000,000▲) C12
Changsha, 1,230,000 F 9
Changzhou,
522,700('86) E10
Chengdu, 1,884,000
(2,960,000▲) ...... E 7
Chongqing, 2,502,000
(2,890,000▲) ...... F 8
Dalian, 2,280,000 .... D11
Datong, 810,000
(1,040,000▲) ...... C 9
Fushun, 1,290,000 .. C11
Fuzhou, 910,000
(1,240,000▲) F10
Guangzhou (Canton),
3,100,000
(3,420,000▲) ...... G 9
Guiyang, 1,030,000
(1,430,000▲) ...... F 8
Handan, 870,000
(1,030,000▲) ...... D 9
Hanzhou, 1,290,000 E 11
Harbin, 2,710,000 .... B12
Hefei, 740,000
(930,000▲) E10
Hegang, 588,300('86) B13
Hengyang, 419,200
(601,300▲)('86) .... F 9
Hohhot, 670,000
(830,000▲) .... C 9
Huainan, 700,000
(1,110,000▲) E10
Huangshi,
451,900('86) E10
Jilin, 1,200,000 ...... C12
Jinan (Tsinan), 1,546,000
(2,140,000▲) D10
Jinzhou, 710,000
(810,000▲) C11
Jixi, 700,000
(820,000▲) B13
Kaifeng, 458,800
(629,100▲)('86) .... E 9
Kunming, 1,310,000
(1,550,000▲) ...... F 7
Lanzhou, 1,297,000
(1,420,000▲) ...... D 7
Lasa (Lhasa), 84,400
(107,700▲)('86) .... F 5
Liuzhou, 680,000 .... G 8
Luoyang, 760,000
(1,090,000▲) ...... E 9
Mudanjiang, 650,000 C12
Nanchang, 1,090,000
(1,260,000▲) F10
Nanjing, 2,390,000 .. E10
Nanning, 720,000
(1,000,000▲) ...... G 8
Ningbo, 570,000
(1,050,000▲) F11
Peking *see* Beijing .. D10
Qingdao (Tsingtao),
1,300,000 .... D11
Shanghai, 7,220,000
(9,300,000★) E11
Shantou (Swatow),
560,000 (790,000▲) G10
Shenyang (Mukden),
3,910,000
(4,370,000▲) C11
Shijiazhuang,
1,220,000 .... D 9
Suzhou, 740,000 .... E11
Taiyuan, 1,700,000
(1,980,000▲) ...... D 9
Tangshan, 1,080,000
(1,440,000▲) D10
Tianjin (Tientsin),
4,950,000
(5,540,000▲) D10
Ürümqi, 1,060,000 .. C 4
Wenzhou, 372,200
(530,600▲)('86) F11
Wuhan, 3,570,000 .. E 9
Wuhu, 396,000
(502,200▲)('86) E10
Wuxi, 880,000 ...... E11
Xi'an (Sian), 2,210,000
(2,580,000▲) ...... E 8
Xining, 620,000 ...... D 7
Xuzhou, 860,000 .... E10
Zhangjiakou (Kalgan),
500,000 (640,000▲) C 9

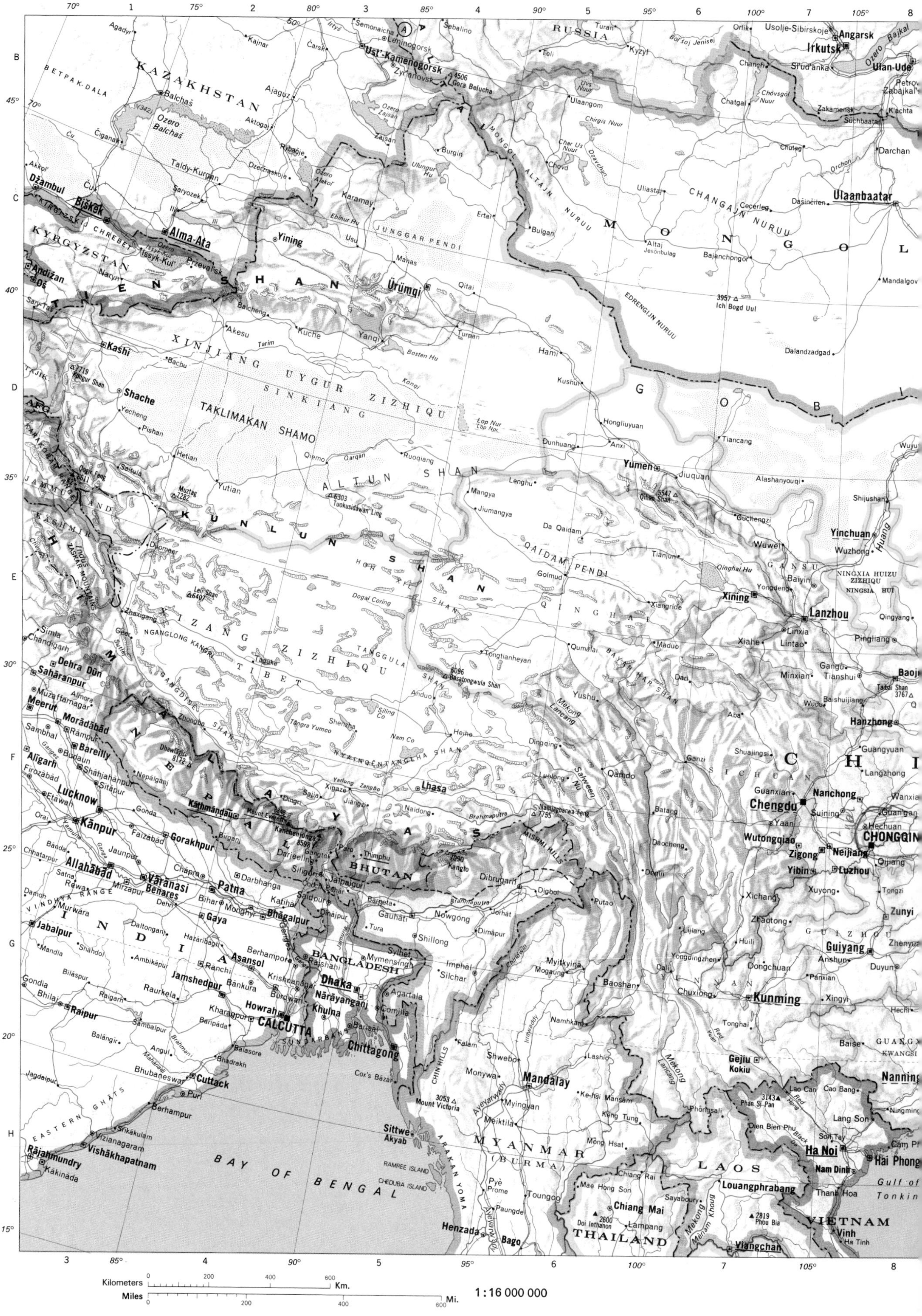

Zhengzhou, 1,150,000 (1,580,000▲) . . . . . E 9
Zibo, 840,000 (2,370,000▲) D10

Hong Kong
1986 CENSUS
Kowloon (Jiulong), 774,781 . . . . G 9
Victoria (Xianggang), 1,175,860 (4,770,000★) . . . . . G 9

Japan
1985 CENSUS
Asahikawa, 363,631 . . C15
Chiba, 788,930 . . . . . D15
Fukuoka, 1,160,440 (1,750,000★) E13
Hakodate, 319,194 . . C15
Hamamatsu, 514,118 E14
Himeji, 452,917 (660,000★) E13
Hiroshima, 1,044,118 (1,575,000★) E13
Kagoshima, 530,502 . . E13
Kanazawa, 430,481 . . D14
Kitakyūshū, 1,056,402 (1,525,000★) E13
Kōbe, 1,410,834 . . . . E14
Kumamoto, 555,719 . . E13
Kurashiki, 413,632 . . E13
Kyōto, 1,479,218 . . . . D14
Matsuyama, 426,658 E13
Nagasaki, 449,382 . . E12
Nagoya, 2,116,381 (4,800,000★) D14
Niigata, 475,630 . . . . D14
Okayama, 572,479 . . E13
Ōsaka, 2,636,249 (16,450,000★) E14
Sapporo, 1,542,979 (1,900,000★) C15
Sendai, 700,254 (1,175,000★) D15
Shizuoka, 468,362 (975,000★) E14
Tōkyō, 8,354,615 (27,700,000★) D14
Utsunomiya, 405,375 D14
Yokohama, 2,992,926 D14

Korea, North
1981 ESTIMATE
Ch'ŏngjin, 490,000 . . C12
Kaesŏng, 259,000 . . D12
Namp'o, 241,000 . . . . D12
P'yŏngyang, 1,283,000 (1,600,000★) D12
Sinŭiju, 305,000 . . . . C11
Wŏnsan, 398,000 . . . . D12

Korea, South
1989 ESTIMATE
Chŏnju, 426,473('85) D12
Inch'ŏn, 1,628,000 . . D12
Kwangju, 1,165,000 . . D12
Masan, 448,746 (625,000★)('85) D12
Pusan, 3,773,000 (3,800,000★) D12
Soŭl (Seoul), 10,522,000 (15,850,000★) D12
Taegu, 2,207,000 . . . . D12
Taejŏn, 1,041,000 . . D12

Macau
1987 ESTIMATE
Macau (Aomen), 429,000 . . . . G 9

Mongolia
1989 ESTIMATE
Ulaanbaatar (Ulan Bator), 548,400 . . . . B 8

Nepal
1981 CENSUS
Kāṭhmāṇḍau (Kathmandu), 235,160 (320,000★) . . . . F 4

Taiwan
1988 ESTIMATE
Kaohsiung, 1,342,797 (1,845,000★) G11
T'aichung, 715,107 . . G11
T'ainan, 656,927 . . . . G11
T'aipei, 2,637,100 (6,130,000★) F11

★ Population of metropolitan area, including suburbs.
▲ Population of entire district, including rural area.

Eastern and Southeastern China

China

1986 ESTIMATE

Anlu, 35,199('85) . . . . . D 2
Anqing, 213,200 (433,900▲) . . . . E 6
Baoying, 50,479('85) . . B 8
Bengbu, 403,900 (612,600▲) . . . . C 6
Binhai (Dongkan), 37,565('85) . . . . A 8
Boxian, 63,222('85) . . . . B 4
Canton *see* Guangzhou L 2
Changsha, 1,230,000('88) . . . . . . G 1
Changshu, 281,300 (998,000▲) . . . . D 9
Changzhou (Changchow), 522,700 . . . . D 8
Chaoan, 265,400 (1,214,500▲) . . . . L 5
Chaoxian, 116,800 (739,500▲) . . . . D 6
Chezhou, 143,500 (191,900▲) . . . . J 1
Chuxian, 113,300 (365,000▲) . . . . C 7
Dinghai, 50,161('85) . . E11
Dingshan, 46,373('85) . . D 8
Dongguan, 254,900 (1,208,500▲) . . . . L 2
Echeng, 217,400 (938,000▲) . . . . E 3
Foshan, 243,500 (312,700▲) . . . . L 2
Fuyang, 143,400 (195,200▲) . . . . C 4
Fuzhou, 106,700 (171,800▲) . . . . G 5
Fuzhou (Foochow), 910,000 (1,240,000▲)('88) . . . . I 8
Ganzhou, 191,600 (346,000▲) . . . . J 3
Gaoyou, 57,844('85) . . C 8
Guangzhou (Canton), 3,100,000 (3,420,000▲)('88) . . . L 2
Hangzhou (Hangchow), 1,290,000('88) . . . . . . E 9
Hefei, 740,000 (930,000▲)('88) . . . . D 6
Huainan, 700,000 (1,110,000▲)('88) . . . . C 6
Huaiyin, 201,700 (382,500▲) . . . . B 8
Huanggang, 65,961('82) E 3
Huangshi, 451,900 . . . . E 4
Huiyang (Huizhou), 117,000 (182,100▲) . . . . L 3
Huzhou, 208,500 (964,400▲) . . . . E 9
Jian, 132,200 (184,300▲) . . . . H 3
Jiangmen, 168,800 (231,700▲) . . . . M 2
Jiangyin, 66,476('85) . . D 9
Jiaxing, 210,200 (686,500▲) . . . . E 9
Jieyang, 98,531('85) . . L 5
Jingdezhen (Kingtechen), 304,000 (569,700▲) . . F 6
Jinhua, 147,800 (799,900▲) . . . . F 8
Jiujiang, 248,500 (382,300▲) . . . . F 4
Lanxi, 70,500 (606,800▲) . . . . F 8
Lechang, 56,913 . . . . . . J 2
Liling, 107,100 (856,300▲) . . . . H 2
Linhai, 52,653('85) G10
Liuan, 122,600 (163,400▲) . . . . D 5
Longyan, 114,500 (378,500▲) . . . . J 6
Luohe, 102,300 (159,100▲) . . . . B 3
Maanshan, 258,900 (367,000▲) . . . . D 7
Meixian, 169,100 (740,600▲) . . . . K 5
Nanchang, 1,090,000 (1,260,000)('88) . . . . G 4
Nanjing (Nanking), 2,390,000('88) . . . . . . C 7

★ Population of metropolitan area, including suburbs. ▲ Population of entire district, including rural area.

Kilometers 0 50 100 150 Km.

Miles 0 50 100 150 Mi.

1:4 000 000

Nanping, 157,100 (420,800▲) .... I 7
Nantong, 308,800 (411,000▲) .... C 9
Nanyang, 199,400 (294,800▲) .... B 1
Ningbo, 570,000 (1,050,000▲)('88).... F10
Pingxiang, 368,700 (1,286,700▲) ...... H 2
Quanzhou, 157,000 (436,000▲) .... K 7

Shanghai, 7,220,000 (9,300,000★)('88).... D10
Shantou (Swatow), 560,000 (790,000▲)('88) .... L 5
Shaoguan, 363,100 (344,892▲) .... K 2
Shaoxing, 167,100 (250,900▲) .... E 9
Suixian, 187,700 (1,281,600▲) ...... D 2
Suzhou (Soochow), 740,000('88)........D 9

Tongling, 182,900 (216,400▲) .... E 6
Wenzhou, 372,200 (530,600▲) .... G 9
Wuhan, 3,570,000('88) E 3
Wuhu, 396,000 (502,200▲) .... D 7
Wusong, 64,017('82) .. D10
Wuxi (Wuhsi), 880,000('88)........D 9
Xiamen (Amoy), 343,700 (546,400▲) .... K 7

Xiangcheng, 363,200 (819,900▲) .... B 2
Xiangtan, 389,500 (511,100▲) .... H 1
Xinyang, 169,100 (234,200▲) .... C 3
Xuchang, 167,800 (247,200▲) .... A 2
Xuzhou (Süchow), 860,000('88)........A 6
Yancheng, 258,400 (1,251,400▲) ...... B 9

Yangzhou, 321,500 (417,300▲) .... C 8
Yanling, 52,679('82) .. C 8
Yueyang, 239,500 (411,300▲) .... F 2
Yuyao, 169,700 (772,700▲) E10
Zhangzhou (Longxi), 159,400 (310,400▲) K 6
Zhenjiang, 412,400 .... C 8
Zhongshan, 238,700 (1,059,700▲) ...... M 2

Zhuzhou, 344,800 (499,600▲) .... H 2

Hong Kong
1986 CENSUS

Kowloon (Jiulong), 774,781 .... M 3
Victoria (Xianggang), 1,175,860 (4,770,000★) ...... M 3

Macau
1987 ESTIMATE

Macau (Aomen), 429,000 .... M 2

Taiwan
1988 ESTIMATE

Changhua, 158,400 (206,603▲) .... K 9
Chiai, 254,875 .... L 9
Chilung, 348,541 ...... J10
Hsinchu, 309,899 .... K 9
Kaohsiung, 1,342,797 (1,845,000★) ...... M 9
Kaohsiunghsien, 276,259 .... M 9
P'ingtung, 167,600 (204,990▲) .... M 9
T'ainan, 656,927 ...... L 9
T'aipei, 2,637,100 (6,130,000★)........J10
T'aipeihsien, 506,220 .. J10

Japan

1985 CENSUS

Aizu-wakamatsu, 118,140 .... E12
Akashi, 263,363 ..... H 7
Akita, 296,400 .... C13
Amagasaki, 509,115 .. H 8
Aomori, 294,045 ..... B13
Asahikawa, 363,631 .. p20
Ashikaga, 167,656 .... F12
Beppu, 134,775 ...... I 4
Chiba, 788,930 ...... G13
Chigasaki, 185,030 .... G12
Chōshi, 87,883 ...... G13
Fuji, 214,448 (370,000★) G11
Fujinomiya, 112,642 .. G11
Fujisawa, 328,387 .... G12
Fukui, 250,261 .... F 9
Fukuoka, 1,160,440 (1,750,000★) .... I 3
Fukushima, 270,762 .. E13
Fukuyama, 360,261 .. H 6
Funabashi, 506,966 .. G13
Gifu, 411,743 .... G 9
Hachinohe, 241,430 .. B14
Hachiōji, 426,654 .... G12
Hakodate, 319,194 .... r18
Hamamatsu, 514,118 .. H10
Handa, 92,883 .... H 9
Higashiōsaka, 522,805 H 8
Hikone, 94,204 ...... G 9
Himeji, 452,917 (660,000★) .... H 7
Hiratsuka, 229,990 .... G12
Hirosaki, 134,800 (176,082▲) B13
Hiroshima, 1,044,118 (1,575,000★) ...... H 5
Hitachi, 206,074 ...... F13
Hōfu, 118,067 .... H 4
Ichinomiya, 257,388 .. G 9
Iizuka, 81,868 (110,000★) .... I 3
Imabari, 125,115 ...... H 6
Ise, 105,455 .... H 9
Isesaki, 112,459 ...... F12
Ishinomaki, 122,674 .. D14
Iwaki (Taira), 350,569 .. E13
Iwakuni, 111,833 ...... H 5
Kagoshima, 530,502 .. K 3
Kakogawa, 227,311 .. H 7
Kamaishi, 60,007 ...... C14
Kamakura, 175,495 .... G12
Kanazawa, 430,481 .... F 9
Kariya, 112,403 ...... H 9
Kashiwa, 273,128 .... G12
Kasugai, 256,990 .... G 9
Kawagoe, 285,437 .... G12
Kawaguchi, 403,015 .. G12
Kawasaki, 1,088,624 .. G12
Kiryū, 131,267 .... F12
Kishiwada, 185,731 .... H 8
Kitakyūshū, 1,056,402 (1,525,000★) .... I 3
Kitami, 107,281 ...... p21
Kōbe, 1,410,834 ...... H 8
Kōchi, 312,241 .... I 6
Kōfu, 202,405 .... G11
Komatsu, 106,041 .... F 9
Kōriyama, 301,673 .... E13
Kumagaya, 143,496 .. F12
Kumamoto, 555,719 .. J 3
Kurashiki, 413,632 .... H 6
Kure, 226,488 .... H 5
Kurume, 222,847 ...... I 3
Kushiro, 214,541 ...... q22
Kyōto, 1,479,218 ...... G 8
Maebashi, 277,319 .... F12
Maizuru, 98,775 ...... G 8
Matsudo, 427,473 .... G12
Matsue, 140,005 ...... G 6
Matsumoto, 197,340 .. F10
Matsusaka, 116,886 .. H 9
Matsuyama, 426,658 .. I 5
Mito, 228,985 .... F13
Miyazaki, 279,114 .... K 4
Morioka, 235,469 .... C14
Muroran, 136,208 (195,000★) q18
Nagahama, 55,531 .... G 9
Nagano, 336,973 ...... F11
Nagaoka, 183,756 .... E11
Nagasaki, 449,382 .... J 2

★ Population of metropolitan area, including suburbs. ▲ Population of entire district, including rural area.

Kilometers 0 50 100 150 Km.
Miles 0 50 100 150 Mi.
1:4 000 000

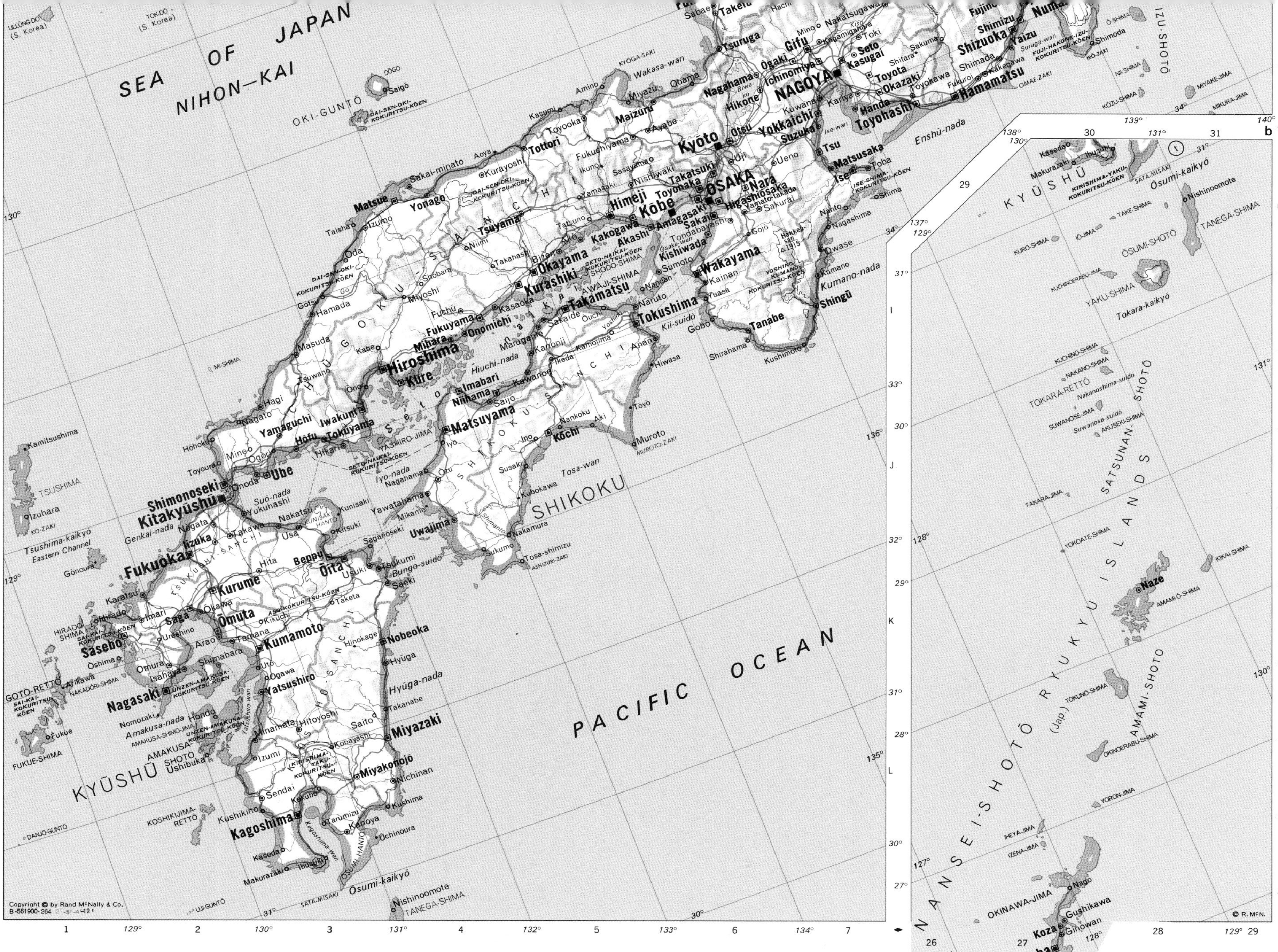

Nagoya, 2,116,381 (4,800,000★) ...... G 9
Naha, 303,674 .... y27
Nara, 327,702 .... H 8
Niigata, 475,630 ...... E12
Niihama, 132,184 ...... I 6
Nobeoka, 136,381 .... J 4
Numazu, 210,490 (495,000★) G11
Obihiro, 162,932 ...... q21
Odawara, 185,941 .... G12
Ōgaki, 145,910 ...... G 9
Ōita, 390,096 .... I 4
Okayama, 572,479 .... H 6
Okazaki, 284,996 .... H10
Ōmiya, 373,022 ...... G12
Ōmuta, 159,424 (225,000★) .... I 3
Onomichi, 100,640 .... H 6
Ōsaka, 2,636,249 (16,450,000★) .... H 8
Ōta, 133,670 .... F12
Otaru, 172,486 .... p19
Ōtsu, 234,551 .... G 8
Oyama, 113,100 (134,242▲) F12
Saga, 168,252 .... I 3
Sagamihara, 482,778 .. G12
Sakai, 818,271 ...... H 8
Sakata, 101,392 ...... D12
Sanjō, 86,325 .... E11
Sapporo, 1,542,979 (1,900,000★) p19
Sasebo, 250,633 ...... I 2
Sendai, 700,254 (1,175,000★) D13
Seto, 124,623 .... G10
Shimizu, 242,166 .... G11
Shimonoseki, 269,169 .. I 3
Shizuoka, 468,362 (975,000★) H11
Suzuka, 164,936 ...... H 9
Tachikawa, 146,523 .. G12
Takamatsu, 326,999 .. H 7
Takaoka, 175,780 (220,000★) F10
Takasaki, 231,766 .... F12
Takatsuki, 348,784 .... H 8
Tokushima, 257,884 .. H 7
Tokuyama, 112,638 (250,000★) .... H 4
Tōkyō, 8,354,615 (27,700,000★) G12
Tomakomai, 158,061 .. q19
Tottori, 137,060 ...... G 7
Toyama, 314,111 ...... F10
Toyohashi, 322,142 .... H10
Toyonaka, 413,213 .... H 8
Toyota, 308,111 ...... G10
Tsu, 150,690 .... H 9
Ube, 174,855 (230,000★) I 4
Ueda, 116,178 .... F11
Uji, 165,411 .... H 8
Utsunomiya, 405,375 .. F12
Wakayama, 401,352 (495,000★) .... H 8
Yamagata, 245,158 .... D13
Yamaguchi, 124,213 .. H 4
Yokkaichi, 263,001 .... H 9
Yokohama, 2,992,926 G12
Yokosuka, 427,116 .... G12
Yonago, 131,792 ...... G 6

Southeastern Asia

Brunei
1981 CENSUS
Bandar Seri Begawan, 22,777 (64,000★) . . E 5

Cambodia
1986 ESTIMATE
Phnum Pénh, 700,000 C 3

Indonesia
1980 CENSUS
Ambon, 111,914 (207,702▲). . . . . F 8
Balikpapan, 208,040 (279,852▲). . . . . F 6
Bandung, 1,633,000 (1,800,000★)('85) . . m13
Banjarmasin, 424,000('83) . . . . . . F 5
Banjuwangi, 90,378 . . n17
Blitar, 78,503 (100,000★). n16
Bogor, 246,946 (560,000★) m13
Cilacap, 127,017 . . . . m14
Cirebon, 223,504 (275,000★) m14
Denpasar, 159,233 . . G 6
Dili, 6,890 (67,039▲) G 8
Garut, 145,624. . . . . .m13
Jakarta, 9,200,000 (10,000,000★)('89) m13
Jambi, 155,761 (230,046▲). . . . . F 3
Jember, 171,284 . . . . n16
Kediri, 176,261 (221,830▲) m16
Kudus, 154,478 . . . . m15
Kupang, 84,587 . . . . H 7
Madiun, 150,562 (180,000★) m15
Magelang, 123,358 (160,000★) m15
Malang, 547,000('83) m16
Manado, 217,091 . . . . E 7
Medan, 2,110,000('85) E 2
Padang, 405,600 (657,000▲)('83) . . . . F 3
Pakanbaru, 186,199 . . E 3
Palembang, 874,000('83) . . . . . . F 3
Pangkalpinang, 90,078 F 4
Pasuruan, 95,864 (125,000★) m16
Pekalongan, 132,413 (260,000★) m14
Pemalang, 72,663 . . m14
Pematangsiantar, 150,296 (175,000★). . . . . E 2
Pontianak, 343,000('83) . . . . . . F 4
Probolinggo, 100,296 m16
Purwokerto, 143,787 m14
Salatiga, 85,740 . . . . m15
Samarinda, 182,473 (264,012▲). . . . . F 6
Semarang, 1,206,000('83) m15
Sukabumi, 109,898 (225,000★) m13
Surabaya, 2,345,000('85) m16
Surakarta, 491,000 (575,000★)('83). . . .m15
Tanjungkarang-Telukbetung, 284,167 (375,000★). k12
Tasikmalaya, 192,267 m14
Tegal, 131,440 (340,000★) m14
Tual, 7,833 . . . . G 9
Tulungagung, 91,585 n15
Ujungpandang, 841,000('83) . . . . . . G 6
Yogyakarta, 421,000 (510,000★)('83). . . .m15

Laos
1975 ESTIMATE
Louangphrabang, 46,000 . . . . B 3
Paksé, 47,000 . . . . . . B 4
Savannakhet, 53,000 B 3
Viangchan, 377,409('85) . . . . . . B 3

Malaysia
1980 CENSUS
Alor Setar, 69,435 . . D 3
George Town (Pinang), 248,241 (495,000★) D 3
Ipoh, 293,849 . . . . . . E 3
Johor Baharu, 246,395 . . . . E 3
Kelang, 192,080 . . . . E 3
Kota Baharu, 167,872 D 3
Kuala Lumpur, 919,610 (1,475,000★) . . . . . . E 3
Kuala Terengganu, 180,296 . . . . D 3
Kuantan, 131,547 . . . . E 3

Kuching, 72,555 .... E 5
Melaka, 87,494 ...... E 3
Sandakan, 70,420 .. D 6
Seremban, 132,911 .. E 3
Sibu, 85,231 .... E 5

Myanmar

1983 CENSUS

Bago, 150,528 ...... B 2
Henzada, 82,005 .... B 2
Mandalay, 532,949 .. A 2
Mawlamyine, 219,961 B 2
Monywa, 106,843 .... A 2
Pathein, 144,096 .... B 1
Pyè (Prome), 83,332 .. B 2
Sittwe (Akyab), 107,621 .... A 1
Yangon (Rangoon), 2,705,039 (2,800,000★) ...... B 2

Philippines

1990 CENSUS

Angeles, 236,000 .... q19
Bacolod, 364,000 .... C 7
Baguio, 183,000 .... p19
Batangas, 31,600 (184,000▲) r19
Cabanatuan, 75,700 (173,000▲) q19
Cavite, 92,000 (175,000★) q19
Cebu, 610,000 (720,000★) .... C 7
Cotabato, 127,000 .. D 7
Dagupan, 122,000 .. p19
Davao, 569,300 (850,000▲) .... D 8
Dumaguete, 80,000 .. D 7
Iloilo, 311,000 ...... C 7
Legaspi, 63,000 (121,000▲) r20
Lipa, 30,000 (160,000▲) r19
Lucena, 151,000 .... r19
Malalos, 95,699('80) .. q19
Manila, 1,587,000 (6,800,000★) q19
Naga, 115,000 ...... r20
Pasig, 318,853('84) .. q19
Puerto Princesa, 52,000 (92,000▲) .... D 6
Quezon City, 1,632,000 .... q19
San Fernando, 110,891('80) q19
San Pablo, 83,900 (161,000▲) q19
Tarlac, 38,205 (175,691▲)('80) q19
Zamboanga, 107,000 (444,000▲) .... D 7

Singapore

1989 ESTIMATE

Singapore, 2,685,400 (3,025,000★) ...... E 3

Thailand

1988 ESTIMATE

Bangkok *see* Krung Thep .... C 3
Chiang Mai, 164,030 B 2
Hat Yai, 138,046 .... D 3
Khon Kaen, 131,340 B 3
Krung Thep (Bangkok), 5,716,779 (6,450,000★) ...... C 3
Nakhon Ratchasima, 204,982 .... C 3
Nakhon Sawan, 105,220 .... B 3
Nakhon Si Thammarat, 72,407 .... D 2
Phitsanulok, 77,675 .. B 3
Songkhla, 84,433 .... D 3
Ubon Ratchathani, 100,374 .... B 3
Udon Thani, 81,202 .. B 3

Vietnam

1979 CENSUS

Can Tho, 182,856 .. C 4
Da Nang, 318,653 .. B 4
Hai Phong, 456,000 (1,279,067▲)('89) .. A 4
Ha Noi, 1,089,000 (1,500,000★)('89) .. A 4
Hue, 165,710 ...... B 4
My Tho, 101,493 .... C 4
Nam Dinh, 160,179 .. A 4
Nha Trang, 172,663 .. C 4
Phan Thiet, 75,241 .. C 4
Qui Nhon, 127,211 .. C 4
Rach Gia, 81,075 .... C 4
Saigon *see* Thanh Pho Ho Chi Minh .... C 4
Thanh Pho Ho Chi Minh (Saigon), 3,169,000 (3,300,000★)('89) .. C 4
Vinh, 159,753 ...... B 4

★ Population of metropolitan area, including suburbs.
▲ Population of entire district, including rural area.

Myanmar, Thailand, and Indochina

Cambodia
1986 ESTIMATE

Bătdâmbâng, 38,780('62) . . . . H 7
Kâmpóng Cham, 35,000('71) . . . . H 8
Kâmpóng Saôm, 53,000('81) . . . . I 7
Phnum Pénh (Phnom Penh), 700,000 . . . . I 8

Indonesia
1980 CENSUS

Banda Aceh, 71,868 . . L 3
Binjai, 71,444 . . . . M 5
Bukittinggi, 55,577 (70,691▲) . . . . O 6
Medan, 2,110,000('85) M 5
Padang, 405,600 (657,000▲)('83) . . . . O 6
Padangsidempuan, 56,984 . . . . N 5
Payakumbuh, 24,567 (78,789▲) . . . . O 6
Pekanbaru, 186,199 . . N 6
Pematangsiantar, 150,296 (175,000★) . . . . M 5
Rantauprapat, 25,043 M 5
Sibolga, 59,466 . . . . . . N 5
Singkawang, 58,693 . . N10
Tanjungpinang, 36,999 N 8
Tarutung, 5,522 . . . . . . M 5
Tebingtinggi, 69,569 (92,068▲) . . . . M 5

Laos
1975 ESTIMATE

Louangphrabang, 46,000 . . . . E 7
Pakxé, 47,000 . . . . G 8
Savannakhet, 53,000 . . F 8
Viangchan, 377,409('85) F 7

Malaysia
1980 CENSUS

Batu Pahat, 64,727 . . . . N 7
Butterworth, 77,982 . . L 6
George Town (Pinang), 248,241 (495,000★) . . L 6
Ipoh, 293,849 . . . . L 6
Johor Baharu, 246,395 N 7
Kelang, 192,080 . . . . . . M 6
Kota Baharu, 167,872 . . K 7
Kuala Lumpur, 919,610 (1,475,000★) . . . . . . M 6
Kuala Terengganu, 180,296 . . . . L 7
Kuantan, 131,547 . . . . M 7
Kuching, 72,555 . . . . . . N11
Melaka, 87,494 . . . . . . M 7
Muar, 65,151 . . . . M 7
Seremban, 132,911 . . M 6
Taiping, 146,000 . . . . . . L 6

Myanmar
1983 CENSUS

Bago, 150,528 . . . . F 4
Chauk, 51,437 . . . . D 3
Dawei, 69,882 . . . . G 5
Henzada, 82,005 . . . . . . F 3
Mandalay, 532,949 . . . . C 4
Mawlamyine (Moulmein), 219,961 . . . . F 4
Maymyo, 63,782 . . . . . . C 4
Meiktila, 96,496 . . . . . . D 3
Mergui (Myeik), 88,600 H 5
Monywa, 106,843 . . . . C 3
Myingyan, 77,060 . . . . D 3
Myitkyinā, 56,427 . . . . B 4
Pakokku, 71,860 . . . . . D 3
Pathein, 144,096 . . . . . . F 3
Pyè (Prome), 83,332 . . E 3
Rangoon *see* Yangon . . F 4
Sittwe (Akyab), 107,621 D 2
Thaton, 61,790 . . . . F 4
Toungoo, 65,861 . . . . . . E 4
Yangon (Rangoon), 2,705,039 (2,800,000★) . . . . F 4
Yenangyaung, 62,582 . . D 3

★ Population of metropolitan area, including suburbs. ▲ Population of entire district, including rural area.

Singapore
1989 ESTIMATE

Singapore, 2,685,400 (3,025,000★) . . . . . . N 7

Thailand
1988 ESTIMATE

Bangkok *see* Krung Thep . . . . H 6
Chiang Mai, 164,030 . . E 5
Hat Yai, 138,046 . . . . . . K 6
Khon Kaen, 131,340 . . F 7
Krung Thep (Bangkok), 5,716,779 (6,450,000★) . . . . . . H 6
Nakhon Ratchasima, 204,982 . . . . G 7
Nakhon Sawan, 105,220 . . . . G 6
Songkhla, 84,433 . . . . K 6
Ubon Ratchathani, 100,374 . . . . G 8

Vietnam
1979 CENSUS

Bien Hoa, 187,254 . . . . I 9
Can Tho, 182,856 . . . . . . I 8
Da Nang, 318,653 . . . . F10
Hai Phong, 456,000 (1,279,067▲)('89) . . . D 9
Ha Noi, 1,089,000 (1,500,000★)('89) . . . D 8
Hon Gai, 114,573 . . . . D 9
Hue, 165,710 . . . . F 9
Long Xuyen, 112,485 . . I 8
Nam Dinh, 160,179 . . . . D 9
Nha Trang, 172,663 . . H10
Qui Nhon, 127,211 . . . . H10
Rach Gia, 81,075 . . . . . . I 8
Saigon *see* Thanh Pho Ho Chi Minh . . . . I 9
Thai Nguyen, 138,023 D 8
Thanh Pho Ho Chi Minh (Saigon), 3,169,000 (3,300,000★)('89) . . . . I 9
Vinh, 159,753 . . . . E 8

India and Pakistan

Afghanistan
1988 ESTIMATE
Herāt, 177,300 . . . . . . C 1
Kābol, 1,424,400 . . . . C 2

Bangladesh
1981 CENSUS
Chittagong, 980,000
(1,391,877★) . . . . . . E 7
Dhaka, 2,365,695
(3,430,312★) . . . . . . E 7
Nārāyanganj, 405,562 E 7

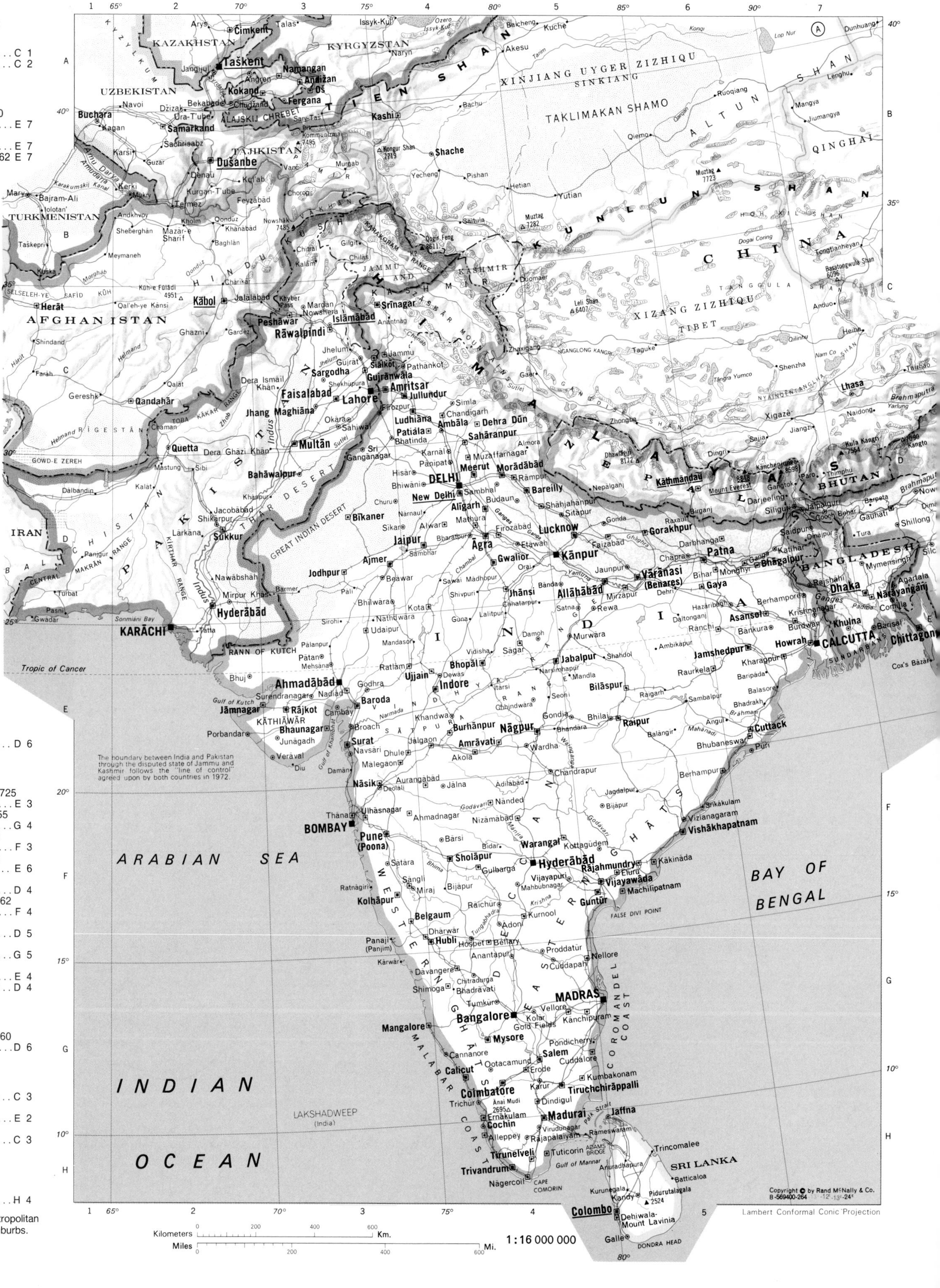

Bhutan
1982 ESTIMATE
Thimphu, 12,000 . . . . D 6

India
1981 CENSUS
Ahmadābād, 2,059,725
(2,400,000★) . . . . . . E 3
Bangalore, 2,476,355
(2,950,000★) . . . . . . G 4
Bombay, 8,243,405
(9,950,000★) . . . . . . F 3
Calcutta, 3,305,006
(11,100,000★) . . . . E 6
Delhi, 4,884,234
(7,200,000★) . . . . . . D 4
Hyderābād, 2,187,262
(2,750,000★) . . . . . . F 4
Kānpur, 1,481,789
(1,875,000★) . . . . . . D 5
Madras, 3,276,622
(4,475,000★) . . . . . . G 5
Nāgpur, 1,219,461
(1,302,066★) . . . . . . E 4
New Delhi, 273,036 . . D 4

Nepal
1981 CENSUS
Kāthmāndau, 235,160
(320,000★) . . . . D 6

Pakistan
1981 CENSUS
Islāmābād, 204,364 . . C 3
Karāchi, 4,901,627
(5,300,000★) . . . . . . E 2
Lahore, 2,707,215
(3,025,000★) . . . . . . C 3

Sri Lanka
1986 ESTIMATE
Colombo, 683,000
(2,050,000★) . . . . . . H 4

★ Population of metropolitan area, including suburbs.

India

1981 CENSUS

Akola, 225,412 . . . . . . B 4
Amrāvati, 261,404 . . B 4
Aurangābād, 284,607 (316,421★) . . . . C 3
Bangalore, 2,476,355 (2,950,000★) . . . . . . F 4
Baroda, 734,473 (744,881★) . . . . A 2
Belgaum, 274,430 (300,372★) . . . . E 3
Bhāvnagar, 307,121 (308,642★) . . . . B 2
Bhilai, 290,090 (490,214★) . . . . B 6
Bhubaneswar, 219,211 . . . . B 8
Bombay, 8,243,405 (9,950,000★) . . . . . . C 2
Calicut, 394,447 (546,058★) . . . . . . G 3
Cochin, 513,249 (685,836★) . . . . H 4
Coimbatore, 704,514 (965,000★) . . . . . . G 4
Cuttack, 269,950 (327,412★) . . . . B 8
Dhule, 210,759 . . . . . . B 3
Gulbarga, 221,325 . . D 4
Guntūr, 367,699 . . . . D 6
Hubli, 527,108 . . . . . . E 3
Hyderābād, 2,187,262 (2,750,000★) . . . . . . D 5
Indore, 829,327 (850,000★) . . . . A 3
Kolhāpur, 340,625 (351,392★) . . . . D 3
Madras, 3,276,622 (4,475,000★) . . . . . . F 6
Madurai, 820,891 (960,000★) . . . . H 5
Mālegaon, 245,883 . . B 3
Mysore, 441,754 (479,081★) . . . . F 4
Nāgpur, 1,219,461 (1,302,066★) . . . . . . B 5
Nāsik, 262,428 (429,034★) . . . . C 2
Nellore, 237,065 . . . . E 5
Pondicherry, 162,636 (251,420★) . . . . . . G 5
Pune (Poona), 1,203,351 (1,775,000★) . . . . . . C 2
Raipur, 338,245 . . . . B 6
Salem, 361,394 (518,615★) . . . . . . G 5
Sholāpur, 511,103 (514,860★) . . . . D 3
Surat, 776,583 (913,806★) . . . . B 2
Thāna, 309,897 . . . . C 2
Tiruchchirāppalli, 362,045 (609,548★) . . . . . . G 5
Trivandrum, 483,086 (520,125★) . . . . H 4
Ulhāsnagar, 273,668 C 2
Vijayawāda, 454,577 (543,008★) . . . . D 6
Vishākhapatnam, 565,321 (603,630★) . . . . D 7
Warangal, 335,150 . . C 5

Sri Lanka

1986 ESTIMATE

Colombo, 683,000 (2,050,000★) . . . . . . I 5
Dehiwala-Mount Lavinia, 191,000 . . . . I 5
Kandy, 130,000 . . . . . . I 6
Kotte, 104,000 . . . . . . I 5

★ Population of metropolitan area, including suburbs.

Northern India and Pakistan

Afghanistan

1981 ESTIMATE

Baghlān, 41,000('82) B 3
Ghaznī, 31,196 . . . . . . D 3
Jalālābād, 58,000('82) C 4
Kābol, 1,424,400('88) C 3
Khānābād, 27,482 . . B 3
Kholm, 28,788 . . . . . . B 2
Mazār-e Sharīf,
130,600('88) . . . . . . B 2
Meymaneh, 39,218 . . C 1
Qandahār,
225,500('88) . . . . . . E 1
Sheberghān, 19,475 . . B 1

Bangladesh

1981 CENSUS

Barisāl, 172,905 . . . . . . I14
Brāhmanbāria, 87,570 I14
Chittagong, 980,000
(1,391,877★) I14
Comilla, 184,132 . . . . I14
Dhaka, 2,365,695
(3,430,312★) I14
Jessore, 148,927 . . . . I13
Khulna, 648,359 . . . . . . I13
Mymensingh, 190,991 H14
Nārāyanganj, 405,562 I14
Pābna, 109,065 . . . . H13
Rājshāhi, 253,740 . . . . H13
Rangpur, 153,174 . . . . H13
Saidpur, 126,608 . . . . H13
Sirājganj, 106,774 . . . . H13
Sylhet, 168,371 . . . . H14

Bhutan

1982 ESTIMATE

Thimphu, 12,000 . . . . G13

India

1981 CENSUS

Āgra, 694,191
(747,318★) . . . . . . G 8
Ahmadābād, 2,059,725
(2,400,000★) . . . . . . I 5
Ajmer, 375,593 . . . . . . G 6
Alīgarh, 320,861 . . . . G 8
Allāhābād, 616,051
(650,070★) . . . . H 9
Alwar, 145,795 . . . . . . G 7
Amritsar, 594,844 . . . . E 6
Asansol, 183,375
(1,050,000★) I12
Bareilly, 386,734
(449,425★) . . . . F 8
Baroda, 734,473
(744,881★) . . . . I 5
Bhāgalpur, 225,062 . . H12
Bhātpāra, 260,761 . . . . I13
Bhāvnagar, 307,121
(308,642★) . . . . J 5
Bhilai, 290,090
(490,214★) . . . . J 9
Bhopāl, 671,018 . . . . . . I 7
Bhubaneswar, 219,211J11
Bīkaner, 253,174
(287,712★) . . . . F 5
Calcutta, 3,305,006
(11,100,000★) I13
Chandīgarh, 373,789
(422,841★) . . . . E 7
Cuttack, 269,950
(327,412★) J11
Dehra Dūn, 211,416
(293,010★) . . . . E 8
Delhi, 4,884,234
(7,200,000★) . . . . . . F 7
Durgāpur, 311,798 . . . . I12
Gaya, 247,075 . . . . . . H11
Ghāziābād, 271,730
(287,170★) . . . . F 7
Gorakhpur, 290,814
(307,501★) G10
Gwalior, 539,015
(555,862★) . . . . . . G 8
Howrah, 744,429 . . . . I13
Indore, 829,327
(850,000★) . . . . I 6
Jabalpur, 614,162
(757,303★) . . . . I 8
Jaipur, 977,165
(1,025,000★) . . . . . . G 6
Jammu, 206,135
(223,361★) . . . . D 6
Jāmnagar, 277,615
(317,362★) . . . . I 4
Jamshedpur, 438,385
(669,580★) I12
Jhānsi, 246,172
(284,141★) . . . . H 8
Jodhpur, 506,345 . . . . G 5
Jullundur, 408,186
(441,552★) . . . . E 6
Kānpur, 1,481,789
(1,875,000★) . . . . . . G 9
Kota, 358,241 . . . . . . H 6
Lucknow, 895,721
(1,060,000★) . . . . . . G 9
Ludhiāna, 607,052 . . E 6
Mathura, 147,493
(160,995★) . . . . . . G 7

★ Population of metropolitan area, including suburbs.

Kilometers 0 100 200 300 Km.
Miles 0 100 200 300 Mi.
1:8 000 000

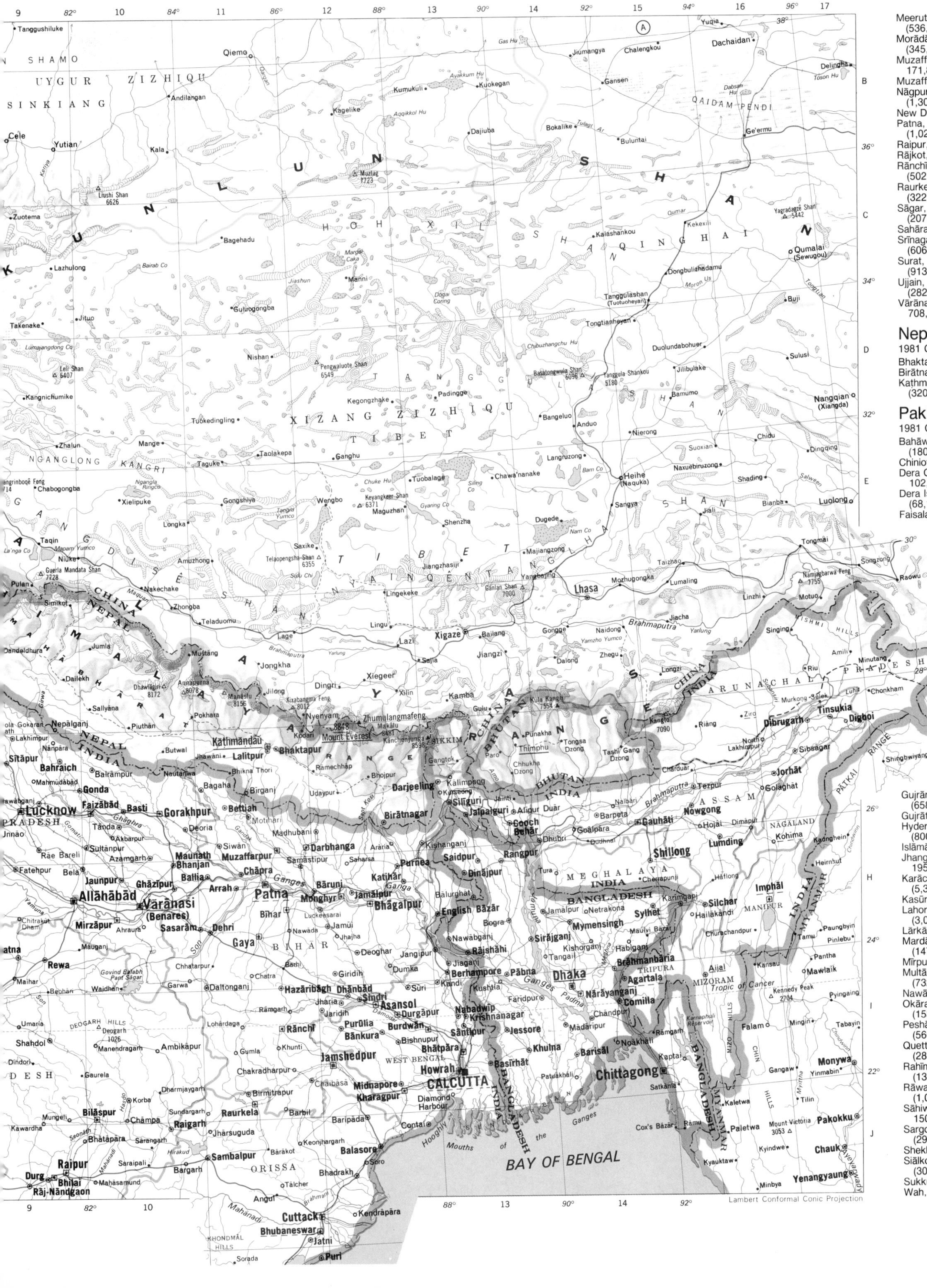

Meerut, 417,395 (536,615★) . . . . F 7
Morādābād, 330,051 (345,350★) . . . . F 8
Muzaffarnagar, 171,816 . . . . F 7
Muzaffarpur, 190,416 G11
Nāgpur, 1,219,461 (1,302,066★) . . . . . J 8
New Delhi, 273,036 . . F 7
Patna, 776,371 (1,025,000★) H11
Raipur, 338,245 . . . . . J 9
Rājkot, 445,076 . . . . . I 4
Rānchī, 489,626 (502,771★) I11
Raurkela, 206,821 (322,610★) I11
Sāgar, 160,392 (207,479★) . . . . I 8
Sahāranpur, 295,355 F 7
Srīnagar, 594,775 (606,002★) . . . . C 6
Surat, 776,583 (913,806★) . . . . J 5
Ujjain, 278,454 (282,203★) . . . . I 6
Vārānasi (Benares), 708,647 (925,000★) H10

Nepal

1981 CENSUS

Bhaktapur, 48,472 . . G11
Birātnagar, 93,544 . . G12
Kathmāndau, 235,160 (320,000★) G11

Pakistan

1981 CENSUS

Bahāwalpur, 152,009 (180,263★) . . . . F 4
Chiniot, 105,559 . . . . E 5
Dera Ghāzi Khān, 102,007 . . . . E 4
Dera Ismāīl Khān, 64,358 (68,145★) . . . . E 4
Faisalabad, 1,104,209 E 5
Gujrānwāla, 600,993 (658,753★) . . . . D 6
Gujrāt, 155,058 . . . . . . D 6
Hyderābād, 702,539 (800,000★) . . . . H 3
Islāmābād, 204,364 . . D 5
Jhang Maghiāna, 195,558 . . . . E 5
Karāchi, 4,901,627 (5,300,000★) . . . . . . H 2
Kasūr, 155,523 . . . . . . E 6
Lahore, 2,707,215 (3,025,000★) . . . . . . E 6
Lārkāna, 123,890 . . . . G 3
Mardān, 141,842 (147,977★) . . . . C 5
Mīrpur Khās, 124,371 H 3
Multān, 696,316 (732,070★) . . . . E 4
Nawābshāh, 102,139 G 3
Okāra, 127,455 (153,483★) . . . . E 5
Peshāwar, 506,896 (566,248★) . . . . C 4
Quetta, 244,842 (285,719★) . . . . E 2
Rahīmyār Khān, 119,036 (132,635★) . . . . F 4
Rāwalpindi, 457,091 (1,040,000★) . . . . . D 5
Sāhīwāl (Montgomery), 150,954 . . . . E 5
Sargodha, 231,895 (291,362★) . . . . D 5
Shekhūpura, 141,168 E 5
Siālkot, 258,147 (302,009★) . . . . D 6
Sukkur, 190,551 . . . . G 3
Wah, 122,335 . . . . . . D 5

Eastern Mediterranean Lands

Cyprus
1982 CENSUS
Lemesós (Limassol), 74,782 (107,161★) B 3
Nicosia, 48,221 (185,000★) . . . . . . B 3

Cyprus, North
1985 ESTIMATE
Nicosia, 37,400 . . . . B 3

Egypt
1986 CENSUS
Al-Iskandarīyah (Alexandria), 2,917,327 (3,350,000★) . . . . D 1
Al-Ismā'īlīyah (Ismailia), 212,567 (235,000★) D 3
Al-Jīzah (Giza), 1,870,508 . . . . . . D 2
Al-Qāhirah (Cairo), 6,052,836 (9,300,000★) . . . . D 2
As-Suways (Suez), 326,820 . . . . E 3
Asyūt, 273,191 . . . . F 2
Būr Sa'īd (Port Said), 399,793 . . . . D 3
Cairo *see* Al-Qāhirah D 2
Ṭanṭā, 334,505 . . . . D 2

Israel
1989 ESTIMATE
Be'er Sheva', 113,200 D 4
Ḥefa (Haifa), 222,600 (435,000★) . . . . . . C 4
Jerusalem *see* Yerushalayim . . . . D 4
Tel Aviv-Yafo, 317,800 (1,735,000★) . . . . C 4
Yerushalayim (Jerusalem), 493,500 (530,000★) D 4

Israeli Occupied Territories
1971 ESTIMATE
Ghazzah (Gaza), 118,272('67) . . . . D 4
Nābulus, 64,000 . . . . C 4

Jordan
1989 ESTIMATE
'Ammān, 936,300 (1,450,000★) . . . . D 4
Az-Zarqā', 318,055 . . C 5
Irbid, 167,785 . . . . . . C 4

Lebanon
1982 ESTIMATE
Bayrūt (Beirut), 509,000 (1,675,000★) . . . . C 4
Ṭarābulus (Tripoli), 198,000 . . . . B 4

Saudi Arabia
1980 ESTIMATE
Al-Madīnah (Medina), 290,000 . . . . G 6

Syria
1988 ESTIMATE
Al-Lādhiqīyah (Latakia), 249,000 . . . . B 4
Al-Qāmishlī, 126,236 A 7
Dayr az-Zawr, 112,000 . . . . B 7
Dimashq (Damascus), 1,326,000 (1,950,000★) . . . . C 5
Ḥalab (Aleppo), 1,261,000 (1,275,000★) . . . . A 5
Ḥamāh, 222,000 . . . . B 5
Ḥimṣ (Homs), 447,000 B 5

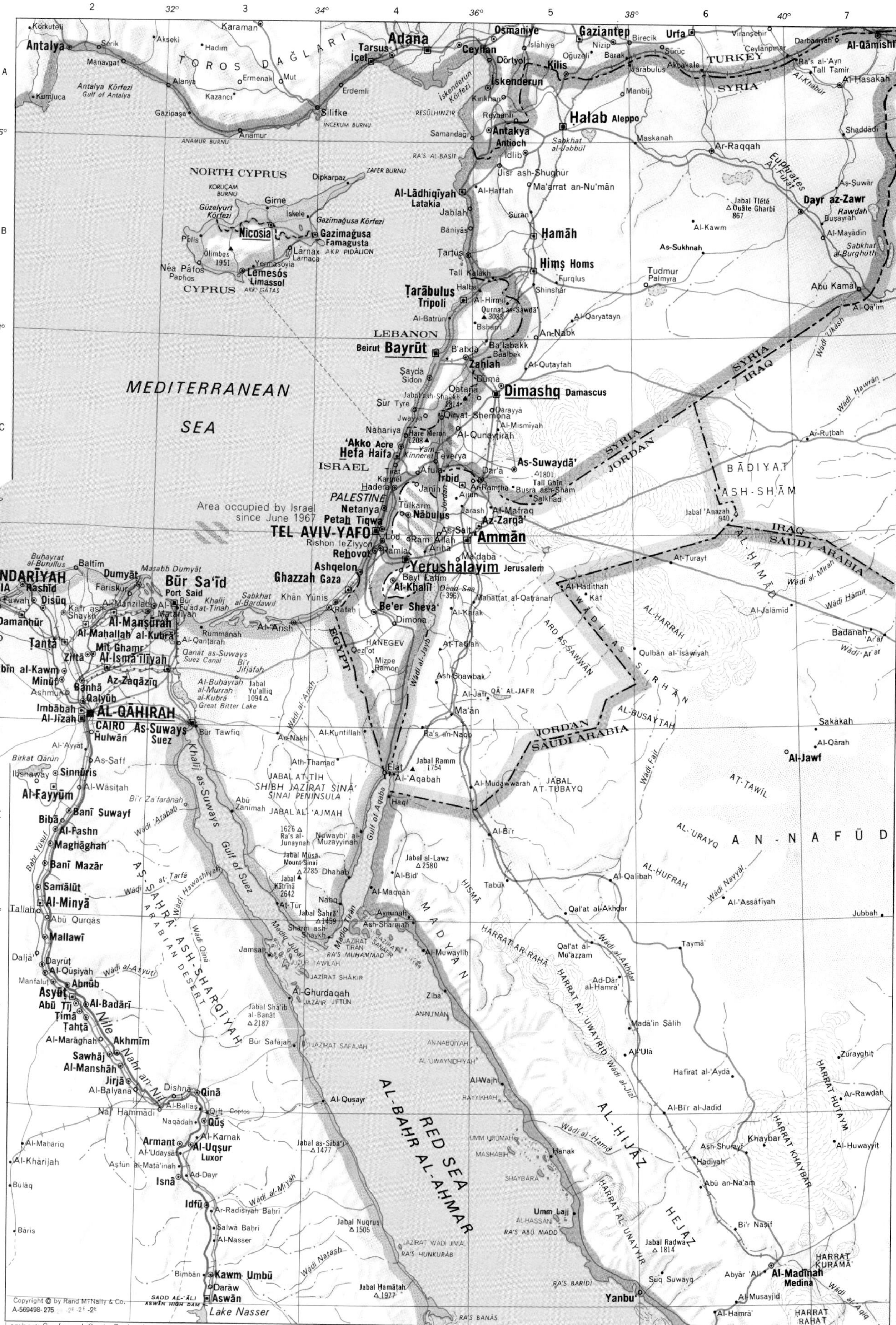

Kilometers 0 100 200 300 Km.
Miles 0 100 200 300 Mi.
1 : 6 000 000

★ Population of metropolitan area, including suburbs.

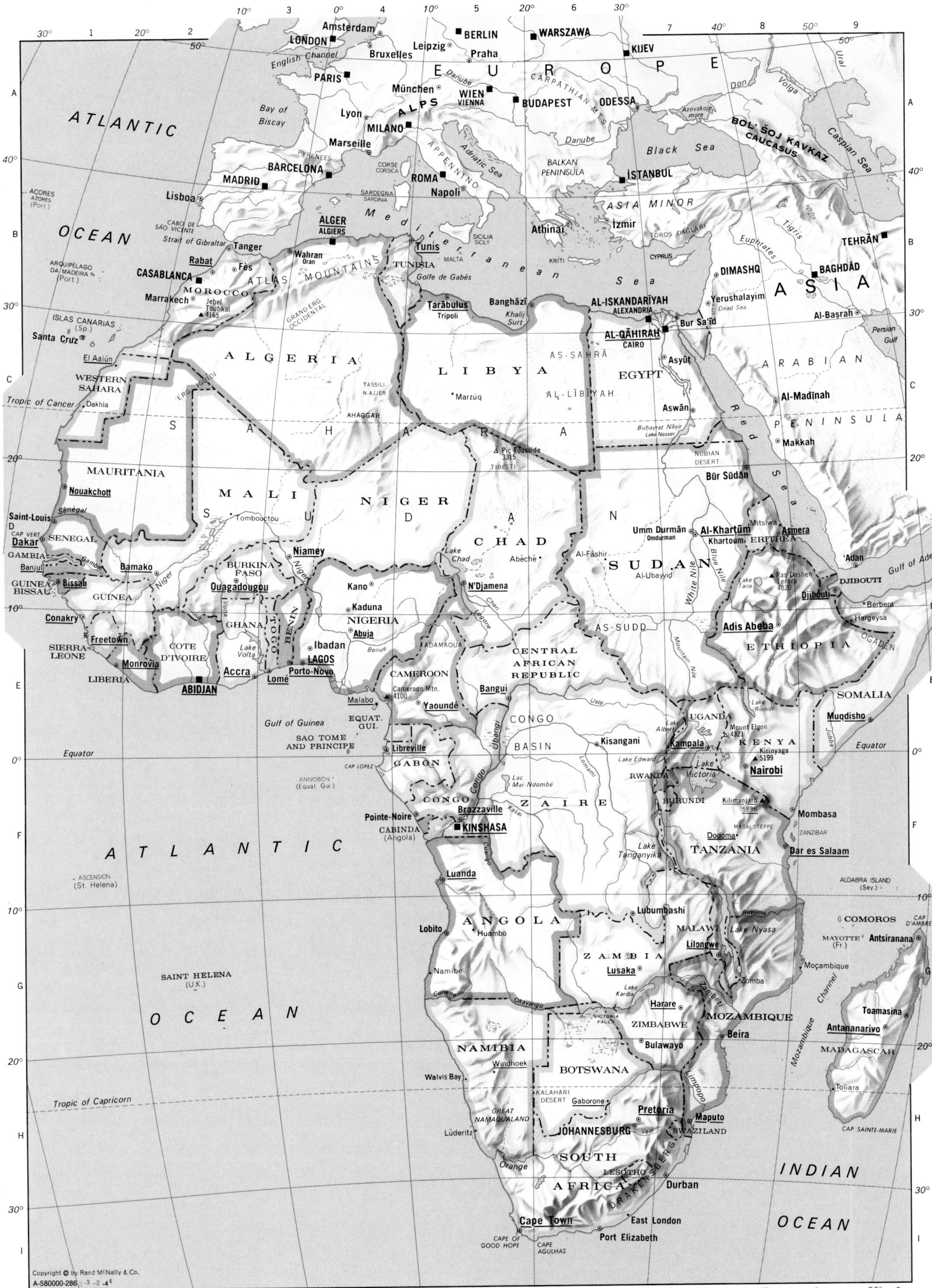

Lambert Azimuthal Equal Area Projection

Miles 0 200 400 600 800 1000 Mi.
Kilometers 0 400 800 1200 1600 Km.

1:40 000 000

Abidjan, 1,950,000 ('83)....E 3
Accra, 859,640 ('84) (1,250,000★)....E 3
Adis Abeba (Addis Ababa), 1,686,300 ('88) (1,500,000★)....E 7
Alger (Algiers), 1,507,241 ('87) (2,547,983★)...B 4
ALGERIA....C 4
Al-Iskandarīyah (Alexandria), 2,917,327 ('86) (3,350,000★)....B 6
Al-Kharṭūm (Khartoum), 476,218 ('83) (1,450,000★)....D 7
Al-Qāhirah (Cairo), 6,052,836 ('86) (9,300,000★)....B 7
ANGOLA....G 5
BENIN....E 4
BOTSWANA....H 6
Brazzaville, 585,812 ('84)....F 5
BURKINA FASO....D 3
BURUNDI....F 6
CAMEROON....E 5
Cape Town, 776,617 ('85) (1,790,000★)....I 5
Casablanca, 2,139,204 ('82) (2,475,000★)...B 3
CENTRAL AFRICAN REPUBLIC....E 5
CHAD....D 5
COMOROS....G 8
CONGO....F 5
COTE D'IVOIRE....E 3
Dakar, 1,447,642 ('88) D 2
Dar es Salaam, 1,300,000 ('84)....F 7
DJIBOUTI....D 8
EGYPT....C 6
EQUATORIAL GUINEA....E 4
ERITREA....D 7
ETHIOPIA....E 7
GABON....F 5
GAMBIA....D 2
GHANA....E 3
GUINEA....D 2
GUINEA-BISSAU....D 2
Johannesburg, 632,369 ('85) (3,650,000★)....H 6
Kampala, 1,008,707 ('90)....E 7
KENYA....E 7
Kinshasa (Léopoldville), 3,000,000 ('86)....F 5
Lagos, 1,213,000 ('87)· (3,800,000★)....E 4
LESOTHO....H 6
LIBERIA....E 3
LIBYA....C 5
MADAGASCAR....G 8
MALAWI....G 7
MALI....D 3
Maputo (Lourenço Marques), 1,069,727 ('89)....H 7
MAURITANIA....D 2
MOROCCO....B 3
MOZAMBIQUE....G 7
Nairobi, 1,505,000 ('90)....F 7
NAMIBIA....H 5
NIGER....D 4
NIGERIA....E 4
RWANDA....F 6
SAO TOME AND PRINCIPE....E 4
SENEGAL....D 2
SIERRA LEONE....E 2
SOMALIA....E 8
SOUTH AFRICA....I 6
SUDAN....D 6
SWAZILAND....H 7
TANZANIA....F 7
Tarābulus (Tripoli), 990,697 ('84)....B 5
TOGO....E 4
Tunis, 596,654 ('84) (1,225,000★)....B 5
TUNISIA....B 4
UGANDA....E 7
WESTERN SAHARA...C 2
ZAIRE....F 6
ZAMBIA....G 6
ZIMBABWE....G 6

★ Population of metropolitan area, including suburbs.

Northern Africa

Algeria
1987 CENSUS
Alger (Algiers), 1,507,241 (2,547,983★) . . . . . A 6
Annaba (Bône), 305,526 . . . . A 7
Batna, 181,601 . . . . . A 7
Blida, 170,935 . . . . . A 6
Constantine (Qacentina), 440,842 . . . . A 7
Oran (Wahran), 628,558 . . . . A 5
Sidi bel Abbès, 152,778 . . . . A 5
Skikda, 128,747 . . . . A 7

Benin
1984 ESTIMATE
Cotonou, 478,000 . . G 6
Porto-Novo, 164,000 G 6

Burkina Faso
1985 ESTIMATE
Bobo Dioulasso, 228,668 . . . . F 5
Ouagadougou, 441,514 . . . . F 5

Cameroon
1986 ESTIMATE
Douala, 1,029,731 . . H 7
Yaoundé, 653,670 . . H 8

Central African Republic
1984 ESTIMATE
Bangui, 473,817 . . . . H 9

Chad
1979 ESTIMATE
N'Djamena (Fort-Lamy), 303,000 . . . . F 9

Cote d'Ivoire
1983 ESTIMATE
Abidjan, 1,950,000 . . G 5
Bouaké, 275,000 . . . . G 4
Yamoussoukro, 80,000 . . . . G 4

Egypt
1986 CENSUS
Al-Fayyūm, 212,523 . . C12
Al-Iskandarīyah (Alexandria), 2,917,327 (3,350,000★) B11
Al-Manṣūrah, 316,870 (375,000★) B12
Al-Qāhirah (Cairo), 6,052,836 (9,300,000★) B12
Al-Uqṣur (Luxor), 125,404 . . . . C12
As-Suways (Suez), 326,820 . . . . C12
Aswān, 191,461 . . . . D12
Asyūṭ, 273,191 . . . . . . C12
Banī Suwayf, 151,813 C12
Būr Sa'īd (Port Said), 399,793 . . . . B12
Cairo *see* Al-Qāhirah B12
Qinā, 119,794 . . . . . . C12
Ṭanṭā, 334,505 . . . . . . B12

Equatorial Guinea
1983 CENSUS
Malabo, 31,630 . . . . . . H 7

Gambia
1983 CENSUS
Banjul, 44,536 (95,000★) . . . . F 2

Ghana
1984 CENSUS
Accra, 859,640 (1,250,000★) . . . . . . G 5
Cape Coast, 86,620 . . G 5
Kumasi, 348,880 (600,000★) . . . . . . G 5
Sekondi-Takoradi, 93,882 . . . . H 5
Tamale, 136,828 (168,091★) . . . . . . G 5

Guinea
1986 ESTIMATE
Conakry, 800,000 . . . G 3
Kankan, 100,000 . . . . F 4

Guinea-Bissau
1988 ESTIMATE
Bissau, 125,000 . . . . F 2

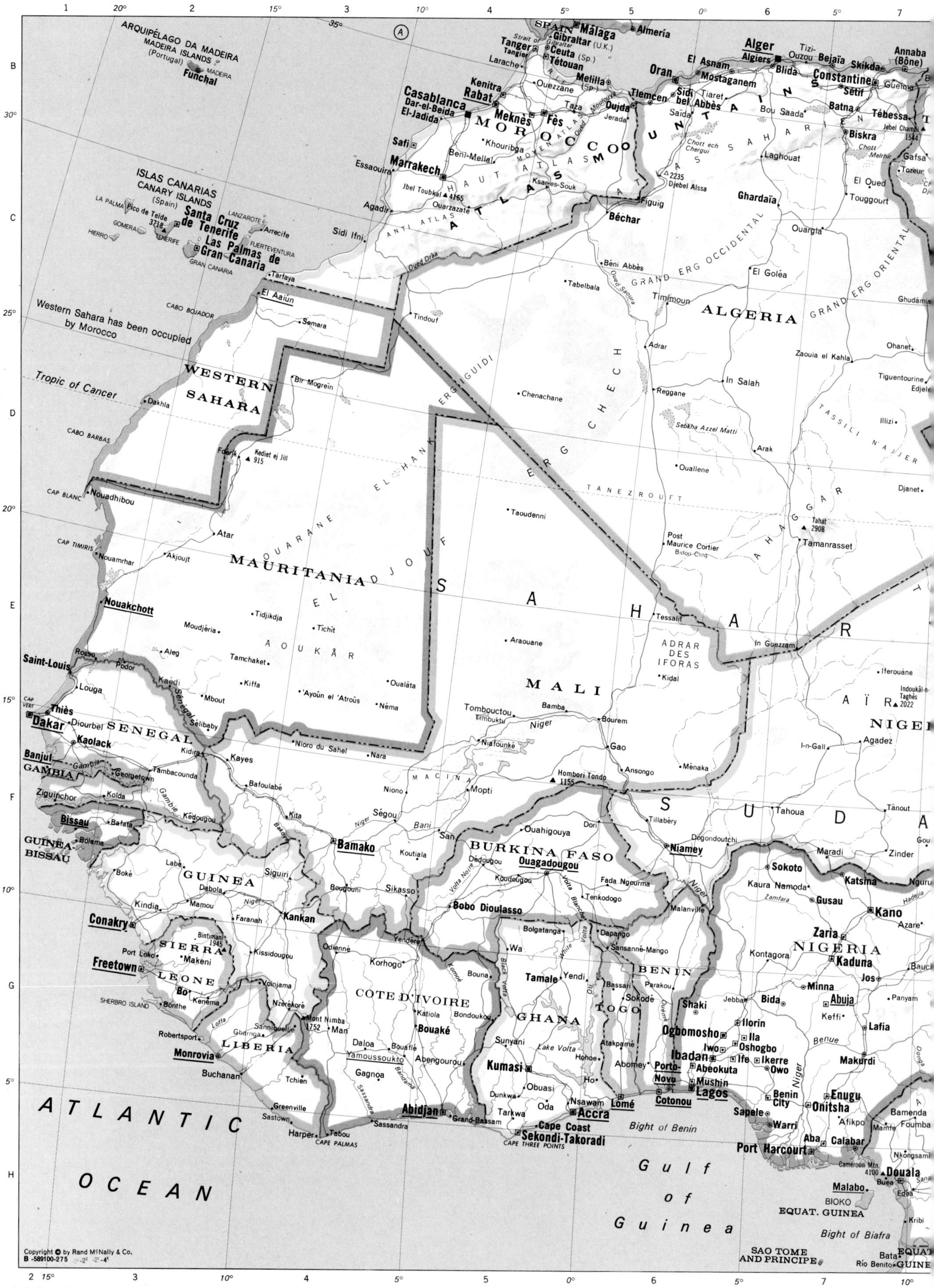

★ Population of metropolitan area, including suburbs.

Kilometers 0 200 400 600 Km.
Miles 0 200 400 600 Mi.
1:16 000 000

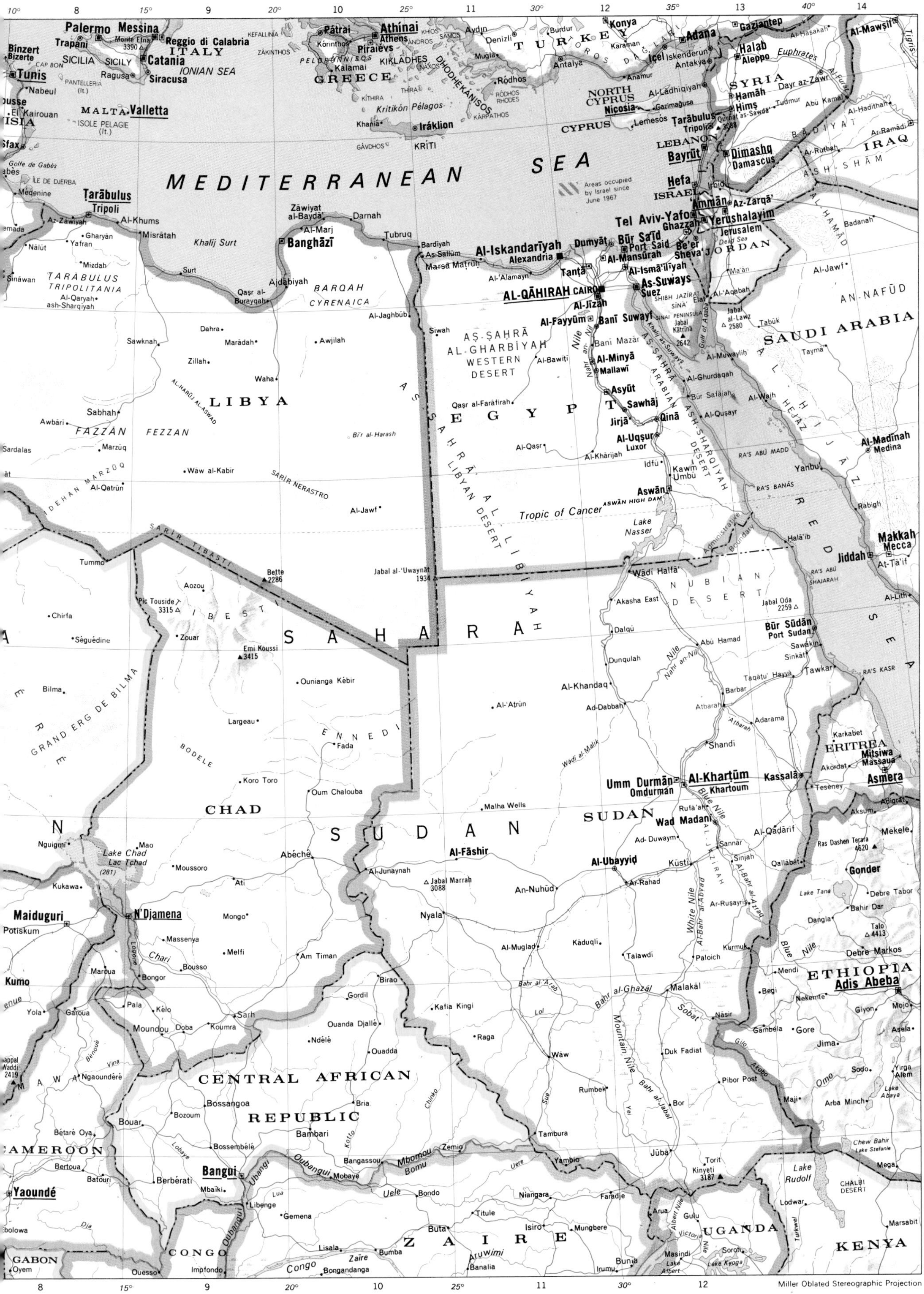

Liberia
1986 ESTIMATE
Monrovia, 465,000 . . G 3

Libya
1984 CENSUS
Banghāzī, 435,886 . . B10
Tarābulus (Tripoli), 990,697 . . . . B 8
Tripoli *see* Ṭarābulus B 8

Mali
1987 CENSUS
Bamako, 646,163 . . . . F 4
Tombouctou (Timbuktu), 31,925 . . . . E 5

Mauritania
1987 ESTIMATE
Nouakchott, 285,000 E 2

Morocco
1982 CENSUS
Casablanca (Dar-el-Beida), 2,139,204 (2,475,000★) . . . . . . B 4
Fès, 448,823 (535,000★) . . . . B 5
Marrakech, 439,728 (535,000★) . . . . B 4
Meknès, 319,783 (375,000★) . . . . B 4
Oujda, 260,082 . . . . . . B 5
Rabat, 518,616 (980,000★) . . . . B 4
Safi, 197,309 . . . . . . B 4
Tanger (Tangier), 266,346 (370,000★) . . . . A 4

Niger
1988 ESTIMATE
Niamey, 398,265 . . . . F 6

Nigeria
1987 ESTIMATE
Abeokuta, 341,300 . . G 6
Abuja, 150,000('93) . . G 7
Benin City, 183,200 . . G 7
Enugu, 252,500 . . . . G 7
Ibadan, 1,144,000 . . G 6
Ilorin, 380,000 . . . . . . G 6
Iwo, 289,100 . . . . G 6
Kaduna, 273,200 . . . . F 7
Kano, 538,300 . . . . . . F 7
Lagos, 1,213,000 (3,800,000★) . . . . . . G 6
Maiduguri, 255,100 . . F 8
Ogbomosho, 582,900 G 6
Onitsha, 298,200 . . . . G 7
Oshogbo, 380,800 . . G 6
Port Harcourt, 327,300 . . . . H 7
Zaria, 302,800 . . . . . . F 7

Senegal
1988 CENSUS
Dakar, 1,447,642 . . . . F 2
Saint-Louis, 160,689 E 2

Sierra Leone
1985 CENSUS
Freetown, 469,776 (525,000★) . . . . . . G 3

Sudan
1983 CENSUS
Al-Kharṭūm (Khartoum), 476,218 (1,450,000★) E12
Al-Ubayyid, 140,000 . . F12
Būr Sūdān (Port Sudan), 206,727 . . . . E13
Khartoum *see* Al-Khartūm E12
Umm Durmān (Omdurman), 526,287 . . . . E12

Togo
1984 ESTIMATE
Lomé, 400,000 . . . . . . G 6

Tunisia
1984 CENSUS
Bizerte, 94,509 . . . . . . A 7
Sfax, 231,911 (310,000★) . . . . B 8
Tunis, 596,654 (1,225,000★) . . . . . . A 8

Western Sahara
1982 CENSUS
El Aaiún, 93,875 . . . . C 3

Angola
1983 ESTIMATE
Benguela, 155,000 . . D 2
Huambo, 203,000 . . D 3
Lobito, 150,000 . . . . D 2
Luanda, 1,459,900('89) . . . . C 2
Namibe, 100,000('81) E 2

Botswana
1987 ESTIMATE
Gaborone, 107,677 . . F 5

Burundi
1986 ESTIMATE
Bujumbura, 273,000 B 5

Comoros
1990 ESTIMATE
Moroni, 23,432 . . . . D 8

Congo
1984 CENSUS
Brazzaville, 585,812 B 3
Pointe-Noire, 294,203 B 2

Gabon
1985 ESTIMATE
Libreville, 235,700 . . A 1
Port-Gentil, 124,400 . . B 1

Kenya
1990 ESTIMATE
Mombasa, 537,000 . . B 7
Nairobi, 1,505,000 . . B 7
Nakuru, 101,700('84) B 7

Lesotho
1986 CENSUS
Maseru, 109,382 . . . . G 5

Madagascar
1984 ESTIMATE
Antananarivo, 663,000('85) . . . . E 9
Antsiranana, 100,000 D 9
Fianarantsoa, 130,000 F 9
Mahajanga, 85,000 . . E 9
Toamasina, 100,000 E 9

Malawi
1987 CENSUS
Blantyre, 331,588 . . E 7
Lilongwe, 233,973 . . D 6
Zomba, 42,878 . . . . E 7

Mauritius
1987 ESTIMATE
Port Louis, 139,730 (420,000★) F11

Mayotte
1985 ESTIMATE
Dzaoudzi, 5,865 (6,979★) . . . . D 9

Mozambique
1989 ESTIMATE
Beira, 291,604 . . . . . . E 6
Maputo (Lourenço Marques), 1,069,727 . . . . . . G 6
Xai-Xai, 51,620('86) . . G 6

Namibia
1988 ESTIMATE
Windhoek, 114,500 . . F 3

Reunion
1982 CENSUS
Saint-Denis, 84,400 (109,072▲) F11

Rwanda
1983 ESTIMATE
Kigali, 181,600 . . . . B 6

Sao Tome and Principe
1970 CENSUS
São Tomé, 17,380 . . A 1

Seychelles
1984 ESTIMATE
Victoria, 23,000 . . . . B11

★ Population of metropolitan area, including suburbs.
▲ Population of entire district, including rural area.

Somalia
1984 ESTIMATE

Kismayu, 70,000 . . . . B 8

South Africa
1985 CENSUS

Bloemfontein, 104,381 (235,000★) . . . . . . G 5
Cape Town (Kaapstad), 776,617 (1,790,000★) . . . . H 3
Durban, 634,301 (1,550,000★) . . . . G 6
East London (Oos-Londen), 85,699 (320,000★) . . . . . . H 5
Germiston, 116,718 . . G 5
Johannesburg, 632,369 (3,650,000★) . . . . G 5
Kimberley, 74,061 (145,000★) . . . . . . G 4
King William's Town, 16,123 (48,300★) . . H 5
Klerksdorp, 48,947 (205,000★) . . . . . . G 5
Ladysmith, 25,102 (31,670★) . . . . . . G 5
Pietermaritzburg, 133,809 (230,000★) . . . . . . G 6
Port Elizabeth, 272,844 (690,000★) . . . . . . H 5
Potchefstroom, 43,766 (78,865★) . . . . . . G 5
Pretoria, 443,059 (960,000★) . . . . . . G 5
Springs, 68,235 . . . . G 5
Uitenhage, 54,987 . . H 5
Vereeniging, 60,584 (525,000★) . . . . . . G 5
Welkom, 54,488 (215,000★) . . . . . . G 5

Swaziland
1986 CENSUS

Mbabane, 38,290 . . G 6

Tanzania
1984 ESTIMATE

Arusha, 69,000 . . . . B 7
Dar es Salaam, 1,300,000 . . . . . . C 7
Dodoma, 54,000('84) C 7
Tanga, 121,000 . . . . C 7
Zanzibar, 133,000('85)C 7

Uganda
1990 ESTIMATE

Kampala, 1,008,707 . . A 6

Zaire
1984 CENSUS

Boma, 88,556 . . . . . . C 2
Bukavu, 171,064 . . . . B 5
Kalemie (Albertville), 70,694 . . . . C 5
Kananga (Luluabourg), 290,898 . . . . C 4
Kikwit, 146,784 . . . . C 3
Kinshasa (Léopoldville), 3,000,000('86) . . . . B 3
Kisangani (Stanleyville), 282,650 . . . . A 5
Kolwezi, 201,382 . . . . D 5
Likasi (Jadotville), 194,465 . . . . D 5
Lubumbashi (Élisabethville), 543,268 . . . . D 5
Matadi, 144,742 . . . . C 2
Mbandaka (Coquilhatville), 125,263 . . . . A 3
Mbuji-Mayi (Bakwanga), 423,363 . . . . C 4

Zambia
1980 CENSUS

Chingola, 130,872 . . D 5
Kabwe (Broken Hill), 127,420 . . . . D 5
Kitwe, 207,500 (283,962★) . . . . . . D 5
Livingstone, 61,296 . . E 5
Luanshya, 61,600 (113,422★) . . . . . . D 5
Lusaka, 535,830 . . . . E 5
Mufulira, 77,100 (138,824★) . . . . . . D 5
Ndola, 250,490 . . . . D 5

Zimbabwe
1983 ESTIMATE

Bulawayo, 429,000 . . F 5
Harare, 681,000 (890,000★) . . . . . . E 6

Eastern Africa and Middle East

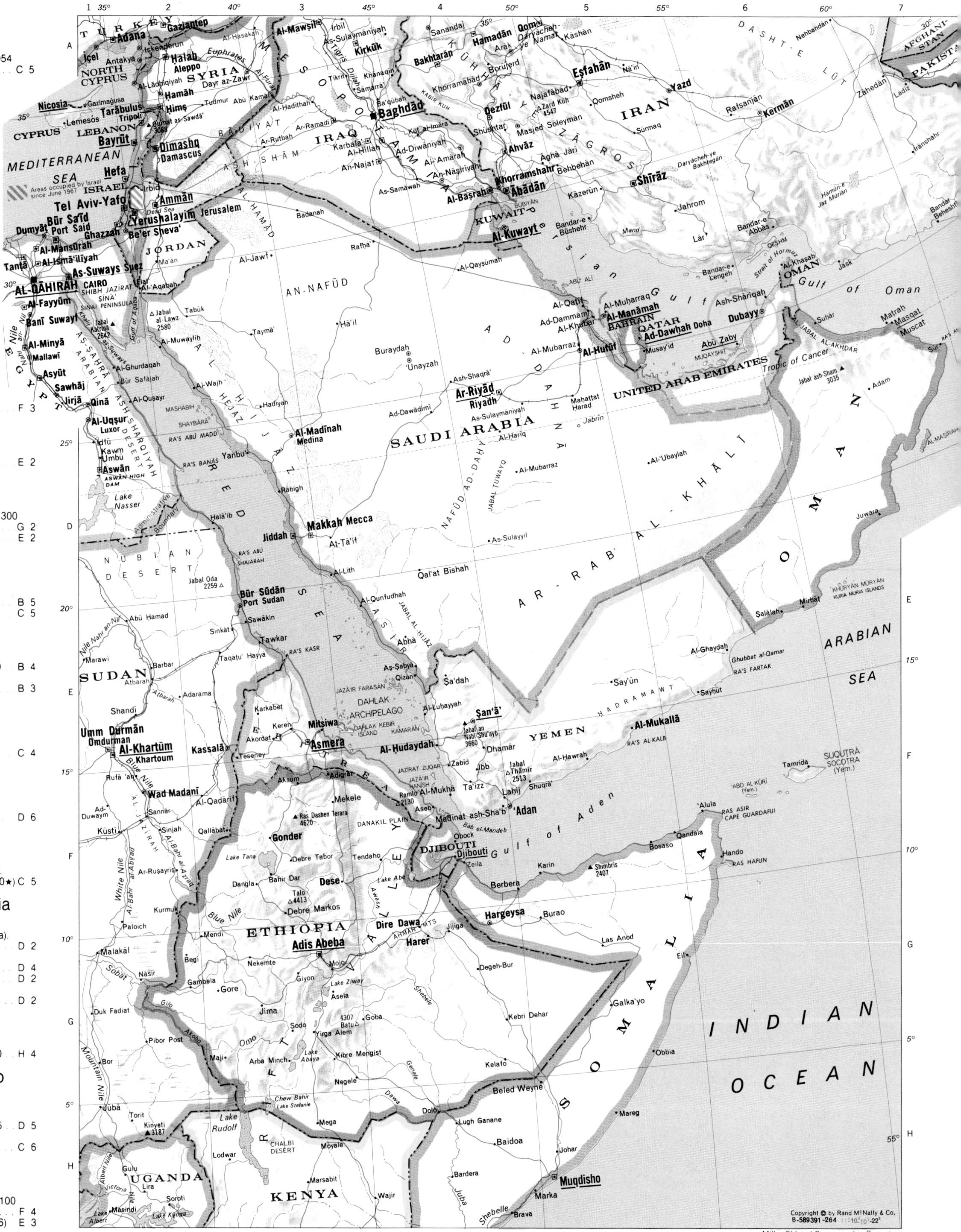

Miller Oblated Stereographic Projection

Kilometers 0 200 400 600 Km.

Miles 0 200 400 600 Mi.

1:16 000 000

Bahrain

1981 CENSUS

Al-Manāmah, 115,054 (224,643★) . . . . . . C 5

Djibouti

1976 ESTIMATE

Djibouti, 120,000 . . . . . . F 3

Eritrea

1988 ESTIMATE

Asmara, 319,353 . . . . E 2

Ethiopia

1988 ESTIMATE

Adis Abeba, 1,686,300 (1,500,000★) . . . . G 2

Asmera, 319,353 . . . . E 2

Iran

1986 CENSUS

Esfahān, 986,753 (1,175,000★) . . . . B 5

Shīrāz, 848,289 . . . . C 5

Iraq

1985 ESTIMATE

Al-Basrah, 616,700 . . B 4

Baghdād, 3,841,268('87) . . . B 3

Kuwait

1985 CENSUS

Al-Kuwayt, 44,335 (1,375,000★) . . . . C 4

Oman

1981 ESTIMATE

Masqat (Muscat), 50,000 . . . . D 6

Qatar

1986 CENSUS

Ad-Dawhah (Doha), 217,294 (310,000★) C 5

Saudi Arabia

1980 ESTIMATE

Al-Madīnah (Medina), 290,000 . . . . D 2

Ar-Riyāḍ (Riyadh), 1,250,000 . . . . . D 4

Jiddah, 1,300,000 . . D 2

Makkah (Mecca), 550,000 . . . . D 2

Somalia

1984 ESTIMATE

Muqdisho, 600,000 . . H 4

United Arab Emirates

1980 CENSUS

Abū Ẓaby, 242,975 . . D 5

Dubayy (Dubai), 265,702 . . . . C 6

Yemen

1984 ESTIMATE

'Adan (Aden), 176,100 (318,000★) . . . . . . F 4

San'ā', 427,150('86) E 3

★ Population of metropolitan area, including suburbs.

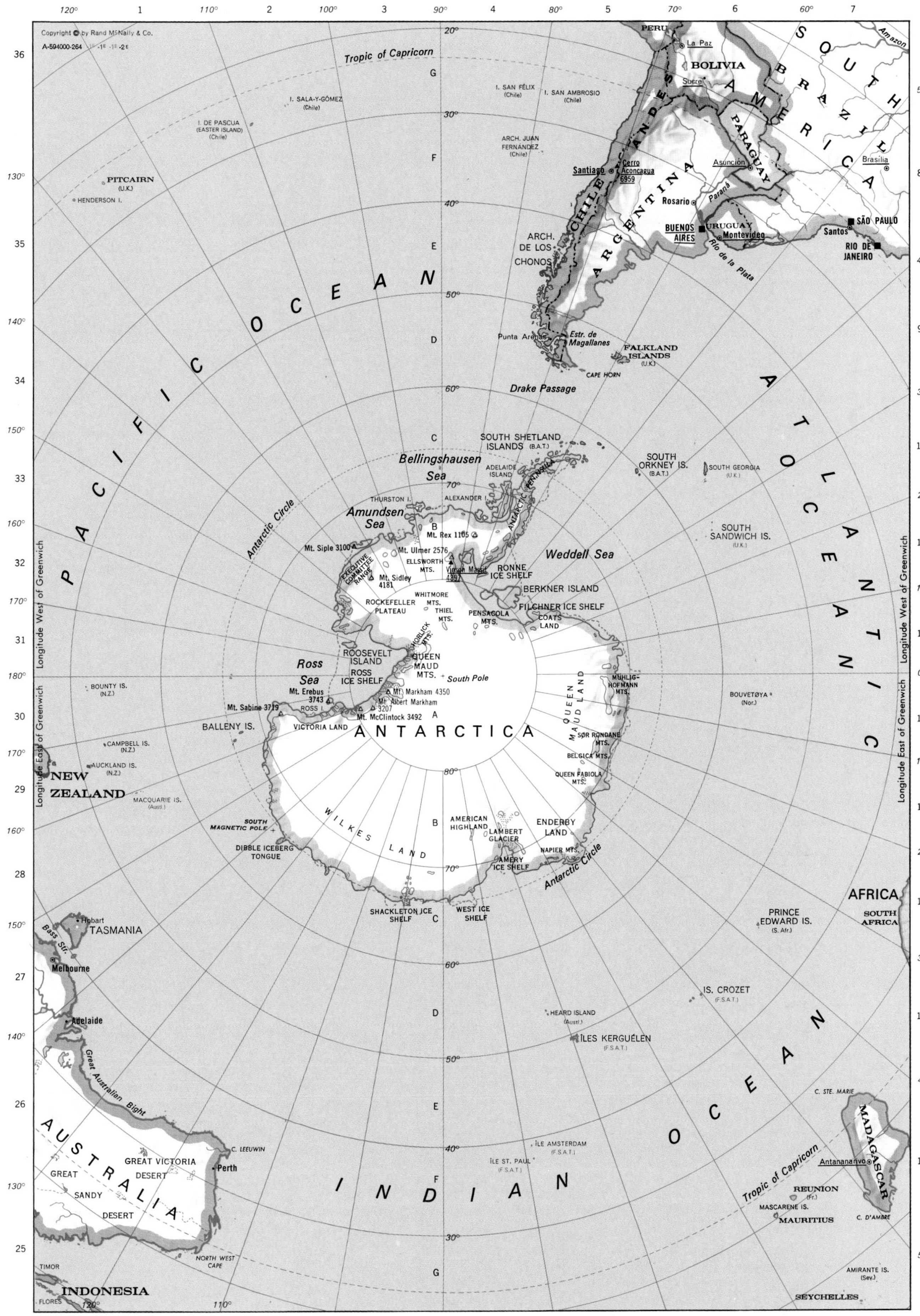

Kilometers 0 500 1000 1500 2000 Km.
Miles 0 500 1000 1500 2000 Mi.

1:60 000 000

Antarctica

Adelaide Island . . . . C 5
Albert Markham, Mount A29
Alexander Island . . . . B 5
American Highland . . B21
Amery Ice Shelf C20
Amsterdam, Île (island) F20
Amundsen Sea . . . . B 1
Antarctic Circle C34
Antarctic Peninsula . . B 6
Auckland Islands D29
Balleny Islands C29
Belgica Mountains . . B16
Bellingshausen Sea . . C 3
Berkner Island . . . . . . B 8
Bounty Islands D30
Bouvetøya (island) . . D13
Campbell Islands D29
Coats Land (region) . . B10
Crozet, Îles (islands) . . E18
Dibble Iceberg Tongue C26
Drake Passage . . . . D 5
Ellsworth Mountains B 3
Enderby Land (region) B18
Erebus, Mount B29
Executive Committee Range B35
Filchner Ice Shelf . . . . B 9
Heard Island D20
Horlick Mountains . . A35
Kerguélen, Îles (islands) E19
Lambert Glacier B20
Macquarie Islands . . D28
Markham, Mount A29
McClintock, Mount . . A28
Mühlighofmann Mountains B13
Napier Mountains . . C18
Pensacola Mountains A 7
Prince Edward Islands E16
Queen Fabiola Mountains B16
Queen Maud Land (region) B14
Queen Maud Mountains A33
Rex, Mount . . . . B 5
Rockefeller Plateau . . A35
Ronne Ice Shelf . . . . B 7
Roosevelt Island B32
Ross Ice Shelf A30
Ross Island B29
Ross Sea B31
Sabine, Mount B29
Saint Paul, Île (island) F21
Shackleton Ice Shelf C22
Sidley, Mount B36
Siple, Mount B36
Sør Rondane Mountains B15
South Georgia (island) . . . . D 9
South Magnetic Pole C26
South Orkney Islands . . . . D 8
South Pole . . . . A 1
South Sandwich Islands D10
South Shetland Islands . . . . C 5
Thiel Mountains . . . . A 3
Thurston Island . . . . B 2
Ulmer, Mount . . . . . . B 4
Victoria Land (region) B28
Vinson Massif (mountain) . . . . . . B 4
Weddell Sea . . . . . . B 8
West Ice Shelf C21
Whitmore Mountains A 2
Wilkes Land (region) B25

Pacific Ocean

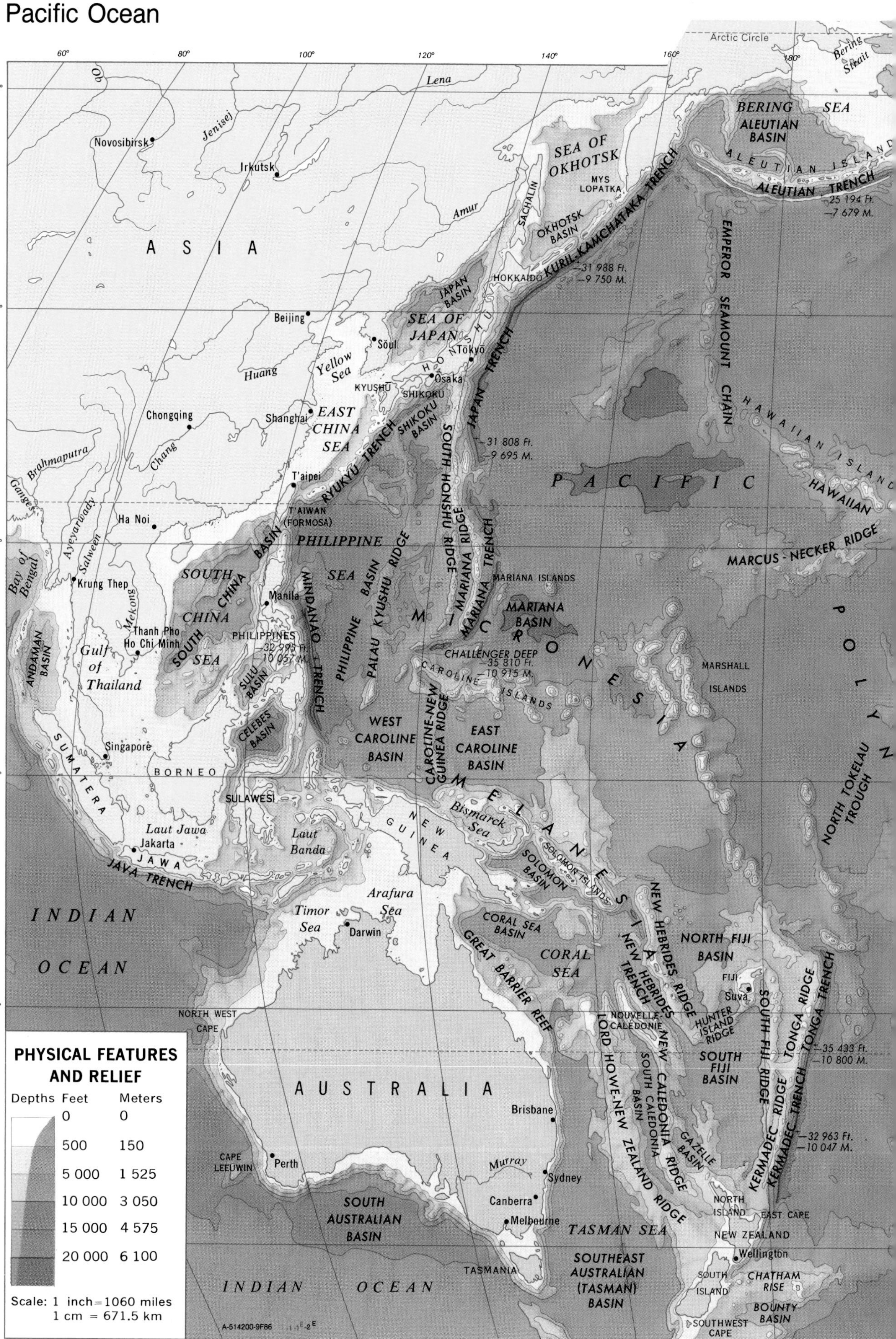

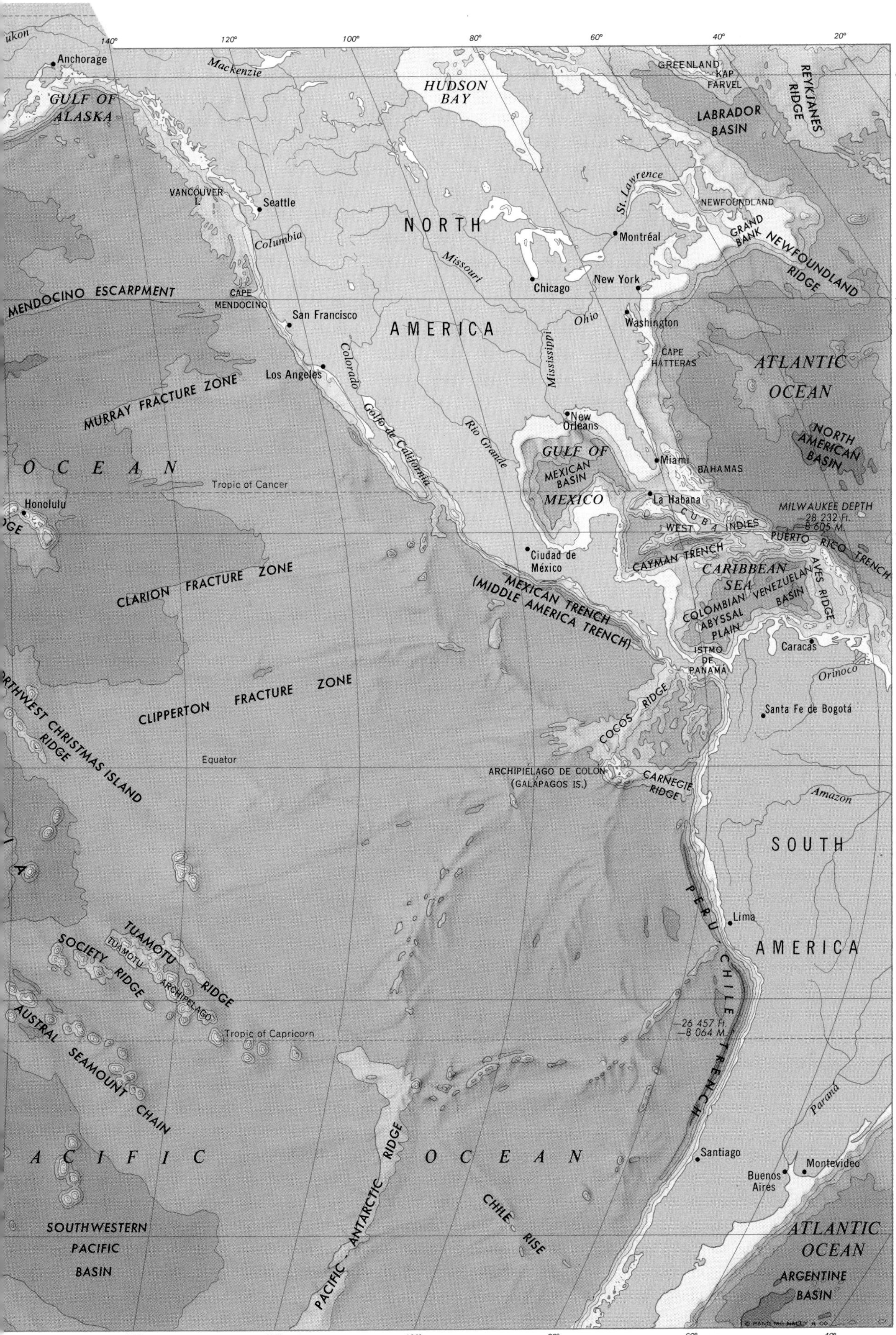

Anchorage
Mackenzie
HUDSON BAY
GREENLAND
KAP FARVEL
REYKJANES RIDGE
GULF OF ALASKA
LABRADOR BASIN
St. Lawrence
NEWFOUNDLAND
VANCOUVER I.
Seattle
NORTH
Montréal
GRAND BANK
NEWFOUNDLAND RIDGE
Columbia
Missouri
Chicago
New York
MENDOCINO ESCARPMENT
CAPE MENDOCINO
San Francisco
Ohio
Washington
AMERICA
Colorado
Mississippi
CAPE HATTERAS
ATLANTIC OCEAN
Los Angeles
MURRAY FRACTURE ZONE
Golfo de California
New Orleans
Rio Grande
NORTH AMERICAN BASIN
GULF OF MEXICO
MEXICAN BASIN
Miami
BAHAMAS
OCEAN
Tropic of Cancer
La Habana
Honolulu
CUBA
WEST INDIES
MILWAUKEE DEPTH
−28 232 Ft.
−8 605 M.
PUERTO RICO TRENCH
Ciudad de México
CAYMAN TRENCH
CARIBBEAN SEA
CLARION FRACTURE ZONE
MEXICAN TRENCH
(MIDDLE AMERICA TRENCH)
COLOMBIAN ABYSSAL PLAIN
VENEZUELAN BASIN
AVES RIDGE
Caracas
ISTMO DE PANAMA
Orinoco
CLIPPERTON FRACTURE ZONE
NORTHWEST CHRISTMAS ISLAND RIDGE
COCOS RIDGE
Santa Fe de Bogotá
Equator
ARCHIPIÉLAGO DE COLON
(GALÁPAGOS IS.)
CARNEGIE RIDGE
Amazon
SOUTH
PERU-CHILE TRENCH
Lima
AMERICA
TUAMOTU RIDGE
TUAMOTU ARCHIPELAGO
SOCIETY RIDGE
AUSTRAL SEAMOUNT CHAIN
−26 457 Ft.
−8 064 M.
Tropic of Capricorn
Paraná
PACIFIC OCEAN
PACIFIC ANTARCTIC RIDGE
Santiago
Montevideo
Buenos Aires
CHILE RISE
SOUTHWESTERN PACIFIC BASIN
ATLANTIC OCEAN
ARGENTINE BASIN
© RAND McNALLY & CO.

Australia

Australia

1989 ESTIMATE

Adelaide, 12,340 (1,036,747★) . . . . . . F 7
Albany, 14,958 . . . . . G 3
Albury, 40,730 (66,530★) . . . . G 9
Alice Springs, 23,600 . . . . D 6
Ararat, 8,015('86) . . . . G 8
Armidale, 21,600 . . . . F10
Augusta, 933('86) . . . . F 3
Ballarat, 36,680 (80,090★) . . . . G 8
Barcaldine, 1,427('86) . . . . D 9
Bendigo, 32,050 (67,920★) . . . . G 8
Blackall, 1,497('86) . . D 9
Bombala, 1,458('86) . . G 9
Bordertown, 2,318('86) . . . . G 8
Bourke, 3,018('86) . . F 9
Bowen, 7,705('86) . . C 9
Brisbane, 744,828 (1,273,511★) E10
Broken Hill, 22,550 . . F 8
Broome, 5,778('86) . . C 4
Bunbury, 26,398 . . . . F 3
Bundaberg, 33,024 (45,161★) D10
Burketown, 232('86) . . . . C 7
Burnie, 20,665('86) . . H 9
Busselton, 7,784('86) . . . . F 3
Cairns, 42,839 (80,875★) . . . . C 9
Camooweal, 315('86) . . . . C 7
Canberra, 247,194 (271,362★)('86) . . . . G 9
Carnarvon, 6,847('86) . . . . D 2
Ceduna, 2,877('86) . . F 6
Cessnock, 43,870 . . . . F10
Charleville, 3,588('86) . . . . E 9
Charters Towers, 7,208('86) . . . . D 9
Cloncurry, 2,297('86) . . . . D 8
Coffs Harbour, 47,890 . . . . F10
Cooktown, 964('86) . . C 9
Coolgardie, 989('86) . . F 4
Cooma, 7,406('86) . . G 9
Croydon, 229('86) . . C 8
Cunnamulla, 1,697('86) . . . . E 9
Dampier, 2,201('86) . . D 3
Darwin, 63,900 (72,937★) . . . . B 6
Derby, 3,258('86) . . . . C 4
Devonport, 25,370 . . H 9
Dongara, 1,496('86) . . E 2
Dubbo, 32,230 . . . . . . F 9
Elizabeth, 29,998 . . . . F 7
Emerald, 5,982('86) . . D 9
Esperance, 6,440('86) . . . . F 4
Geelong, 13,190 (148,980★) . . . . . . G 8
Geraldton, 20,968 . . . . E 2
Gladstone, 22,033('86) D10
Glen Innes, 5,971('86) E10
Goondiwindi, 4,103('86) E10
Goulburn, 21,580 . . . . F 9
Grafton, 15,890 . . . . . . E10
Griffith, 13,630('86) . . F 9
Gympie, 10,772('86) . . E10
Halls Creek, 1,182('86) . . . . C 5
Hay, 2,961('86) . . . . . . F 8
Hobart, 47,280 (181,210★) . . . . H 9
Home Hill, 3,286('86) . . . . C 9
Horsham, 12,850 . . . . G 8
Hughenden, 1,791('86) . . . . D 8
Ingham, 5,202('86) . . C 9
Inverell, 9,693('86) . . E10
Ipswich, 75,283 . . . . . . E10
Kalgoorlie, 26,813 . . . . F 4
Kingaroy, 6,362('86) . . E10
Launceston, 32,150 (92,350★) . . . . H 9
Leonora, 1,004('86) . . E 4
Lismore, 39,450 . . . . E10
Longreach, 3,159('86) . . . . D 8
Mackay, 22,583 (50,885★) . . . . D 9
Maitland, 47,280 . . . . F10
Marble Bar, 332('86) D 3
Mareeba, 6,614('86) . . C 9
Marree, 300('76) . . . . E 7
Meekatharra, 1,018('86) . . . . E 3

★ Population of metropolitan area, including suburbs.

Melbourne, 55,300 (3,039,100★) ...... G 8
Mildura, 20,512('86) .. F 8
Mitchell, 1,212('86) .. E 9
Moora, 1,469('86) .... F 3
Moree, 10,215('86) .. E 9
Morwell, 16,880 .... G 9
Mount Gambier, 22,194 (27,228★) .... G 8
Mount Isa, 24,023 .. D 7
Mount Magnet, 1,000('86) .... E 3
Mullewa, 758('86) .... E 3
Murwillumbah, 7,678('86) E10
Nambour, 9,579('86) E10
Naracoorte, 4,636('86) .... G 8
Newcastle, 130,940 (425,610★) F10
New Norfolk, 6,152('86) .... H 9
Normanton, 1,109('86) .... C 8
Norseman, 1,775('86) .... F 4
Northam, 6,377('86) .. F 3
Nyngan, 2,502('86) .. F 9
Onslow, 750('86) .... D 3
Oodnadatta, 200('76) E 7
Orange, 32,980 ...... F 9
Pemberton, 802('86) .. F 3
Perth, 82,413 (1,158,387★) ...... F 3
Peterborough, 2,239('86) .... F 7
Port Augusta, 15,752 .... F 7
Port Hedland, 13,069('86) ...... D 3
Port Lincoln, 12,941 .. F 7
Port Macquarie, 22,884('86) F10
Port Pirie, 15,210 .... F 7
Quilpie, 780('86) .... E 8
Ravensthorpe, 299('86) .... F 3
Richmond, 704('86) .. D 8
Rockhampton, 58,890 (61,694★) D10
Roebourne, 1,269('86) .... D 3
Roma, 6,069('86) .... E 9
Saint George, 2,323('86) .... E 9
Sale, 13,800 .... G 9
Shepparton, 26,420 (39,700★) .... G 9
Smithton, 3,414('86) .. H 9
Southern Cross, 898('86) .... F 3
Swan Hill, 8,831('86) .... G 8
Sydney, 9,800 (3,623,550★) F10
Tamworth, 34,430 .. F10
Taree, 38,760 ...... F10
Tennant Creek, 3,503('86) .... C 6
Tenterfield, 3,370('86) E10
Theodore, 576('86) .. D10
Toowoomba, 81,071 .... E10
Townsville, 83,339 (111,972★) .... C 9
Wagga Wagga, 52,180 .... G 9
Walgett, 2,151('86) .. E 9
Wangaratta, 16,320 .. G 9
Warrnambool, 24,480 .... G 8
Weipa, 2,406('86) .... B 8
Whyalla, 26,706 .... F 7
Wilcannia, 1,048('86) F 8
Wiluna, 279('86) .... E 4
Winton, 1,281('86) .. D 8
Wollongong, 174,770 (236,690★) F10
Woomera, 1,805('86) .... F 7
Wyndham, 1,329('86) .... C 5

Indonesia

1980 CENSUS

Jayapura, 60,641 .... k15
Kupang, 84,587 .... B 4
Sorong, 52,041 ...... k13

Papua New Guinea

1987 ESTIMATE

Lae, 79,600 .... m16
Madang, 24,700 .... m16
Port Moresby, 152,100 .... m16
Rabaul, 14,954('80) .. k17
Wewak, 23,200 ...... k15

New Zealand

New Zealand

1986 CENSUS

Alexandra, 4,842 . . . . F 2
Ashburton, 14,030 . . E 3
Auckland, 149,046
(850,000★) . . . . . . B 5
Blenheim, 18,308
(22,681★) . . . . . . D 4
Bluff, 2,537 . . . . G 2
Cambridge, 10,145 . . B 5
Christchurch, 168,200
(320,000★) . . . . . . E 4
Dannevirke, 5,873 . . D 6
Dargaville, 4,859 . . . . A 4
Devonport, 10,543 . . B 5
Dunedin, 76,964
(109,000★) . . . . . . F 3
Gisborne, 30,020
(32,238★) . . . . . . C 7
Gore, 8,594 (11,249★)G 2
Greymouth, 7,624
(11,261★) . . . . . . E 3
Hamilton, 94,511
(101,814★) . . . . . . B 5
Hastings, 37,658 . . . . C 6
Hawera, 4,151
(11,375★) . . . . . . C 5
Hokitika, 3,427 . . . . E 3
Huntly, 6,750 . . . . . . B 5
Invercargill, 48,197
(52,807★) . . . . . . G 2
Kaiapoi, 5,234 . . . . . . E 4
Kaikoura, 2,209 . . . . E 4
Levin, 15,368
(18,962★) . . . . . . D 5
Lower Hutt, 63,862 . . D 5
Masterton, 18,511
(20,145★) . . . . . . D 5
Milton, 2,154 . . . . . . G 2
Morrinsville, 5,281 . . B 5
Motueka, 5,052 . . . . D 4
Murapara, 2,566 . . . . C 6
Napier, 49,428
(107,060★) . . . . . . C 6
Nelson, 34,274
(44,593★) . . . . . . D 4
New Plymouth, 36,865
(47,384★) . . . . . . C 5
Oamaru, 12,652
(14,247★). . . . . F 3
Opotiki, 3,719 . . . . . . C 6
Otaki, 4,407 . . . . . . D 5
Palmerston North, 60,503
(67,405★) . . . . . . D 5
Picton, 4,129 . . . . . . D 5
Port Chalmers, 2,871 F 3
Pukekohe, 9,398
(13,823★) . . . . . . B 5
Queenstown, 3,659 . . F 2
Richmond, 7,204 . . . . D 4
Rotorua, 40,597
(52,001★) . . . . . . C 6
Stratford, 5,528 . . . . C 5
Taihape, 2,472 . . . . C 5
Takapuna, 69,419 . . B 5
Taumarunui, 6,387 . . C 5
Taupo, 15,873 . . . . C 6
Tauranga, 41,611
(59,435★) . . . . . . B 6
Te Awamutu, 8,096 . . C 5
Te Kuiti, 4,787 . . . . C 5
Thames, 6,461 . . . . B 5
Timaru, 27,757
(28,621★). . . . . F 3
Tokoroa, 17,628
(18,193★) . . . . . . C 5
Waihi, 3,679 . . . . . . B 5
Waimate, 3,250 . . . . F 3
Waipukurau, 3,862 . . D 6
Wairoa, 5,094 . . . . . . C 6
Waitara, 6,482 . . . . C 5
Waiuku, 4,357 . . . . . . B 5
Wanaka, 1,710 . . . . F 2
Wanganui, 38,084
(40,758★) . . . . . . C 5
Wellington, 137,495
(350,000★) . . . . . . D 5
Wellsford, 1,627 . . . . B 5
Westport, 4,660 . . . . D 3
Whakatane, 12,800
(15,954★) . . . . . . B 6
Whangarei, 40,179
(44,043★) . . . . . . A 5
Winton, 2,082 . . . . . . G 2

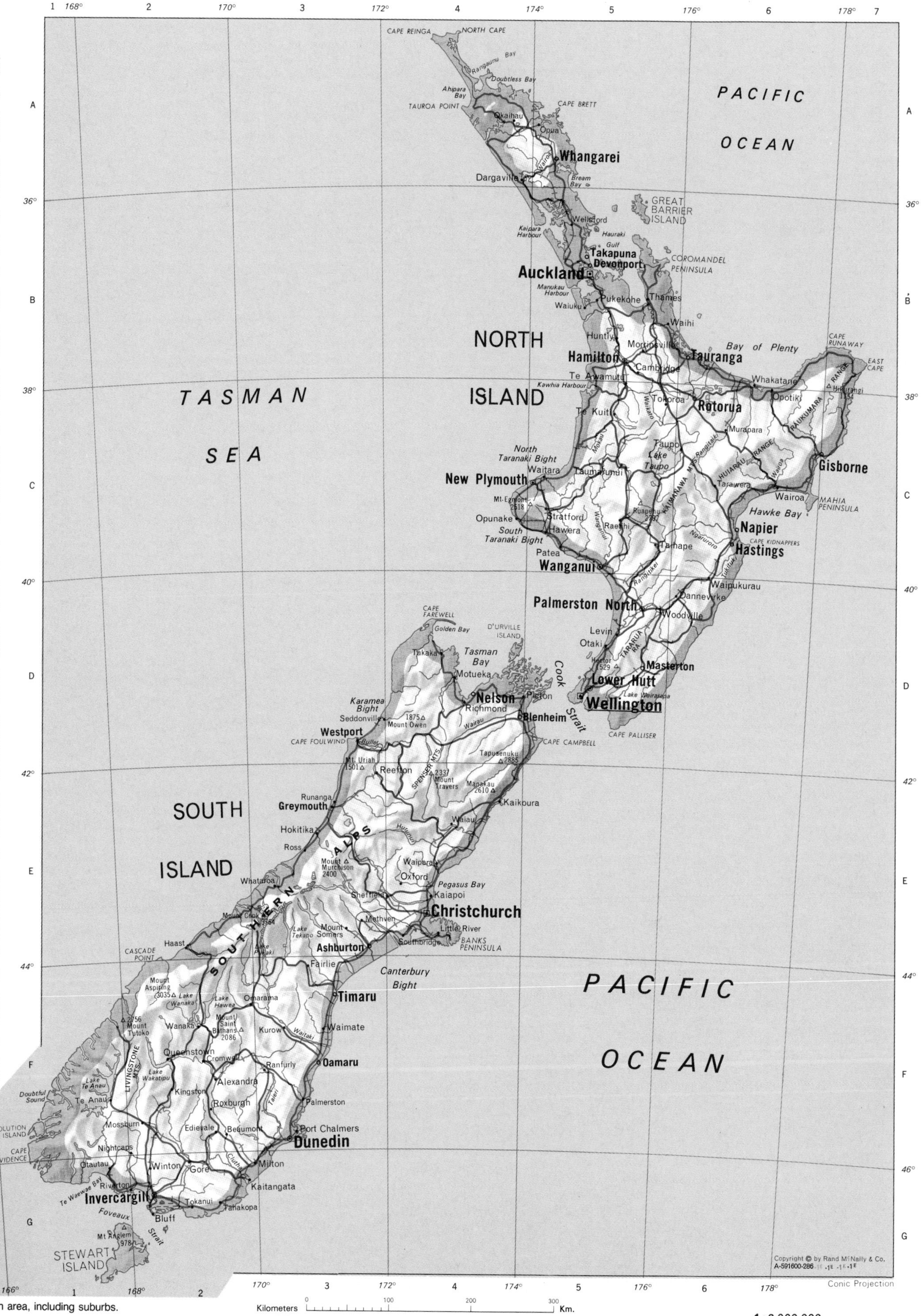

Kilometers 0 100 200 300 Km.
Miles 0 100 200 300 Mi.

1:6 000 000

★ Population of metropolitan area, including suburbs.

Lambert Azimuthal Equal Area Projection

Miles 0 200 400 600 800 1000 Mi.

Kilometers 0 400 800 1200 1600 Km.

1:40 000 000

- Antofagasta, 185,486 ('82)....F 3
- Arequipa, 108,023 ('81) (446,942★)....E 3
- **ARGENTINA**....G 4
- Asunción, 477,100 ('85) (700,000★)....F 5
- Barranquilla, 899,781 ('85) (1,140,000★)....B 3
- Belém, 1,116,578 ('85) (1,200,000★)....D 6
- Belo Horizonte, 2,114,429 ('85) (2,950,000★)....E 6
- Bogotá *see* Santa Fe de Bogotá....C 3
- **BOLIVIA**....E 4
- Brasília, 1,567,709 ('85)....E 6
- **BRAZIL**....E 5
- Buenos Aires, 2,922,829 ('80) (10,750,000★)....G 5
- Caracas, 1,816,901 ('81) (3,600,000★)....B 4
- Cartagena, 531,426 ('85)....B 3
- Cayenne, 38,091 ('82)....C 5
- Chiclayo, 213,095 ('81) (279,527★)....D 3
- **CHILE**....G 3
- Ciudad Bolívar, 182,941 ('81)....C 4
- **COLOMBIA**....C 3
- Concepción, 267,891 ('82) (675,000★)....G 3
- Cuzco, 89,563 ('81) (184,550★)....E 3
- **ECUADOR**....D 3
- **FALKLAND ISLANDS**....I 5
- Fortaleza, 1,582,414 ('85) (1,825,000★)....D 7
- **FRENCH GUIANA**....C 5
- Georgetown, 78,500 ('83) (188,000★)....C 5
- Guayaquil, 1,572,615 ('87) (1,580,000★)....D 3
- **GUYANA**....C 5
- Iquitos, 178,738 ('81)....D 3
- João Pessoa, 348,500 ('85) (550,000★)....D 7
- La Paz, 992,592 ('85)....E 4
- La Plata, 477,175 ('80)....G 5
- Lima, 371,122 ('81) (4,608,010★)....E 3
- Maceió, 482,195 ('85)....D 7
- Manaus, 809,914 ('85)....D 5
- Maracaibo, 890,643 ('81)....B 3
- Medellín, 1,468,089 ('85) (2,095,000★)....C 3
- Mendoza, 119,088 ('80) (650,000★)....G 4
- Montevideo, 1,251,647 ('85) (1,550,000★)....G 5
- Natal, 510,106 ('85)....D 7
- **PARAGUAY**....F 5
- Paramaribo, 241,000 ('88) (296,000★)....C 5
- **PERU**....E 3
- Porto Alegre, 1,272,121 ('85) (2,600,000★)....G 5
- Quito, 1,137,705 ('87) (1,300,000★)....D 3
- Recife, 1,287,623 ('85) (2,625,000★)....D 7
- Rio Branco, 109,800 ('85) (145,486▲)....D 4
- Rio de Janeiro, 5,603,388 ('85) (10,150,000★)....F 6
- Rosario, 938,120 ('80) (1,045,000★)....G 4
- Salta, 260,744 ('80)....F 4
- Salvador, 1,804,438 ('85) (2,050,000★)....E 7
- San Miguel de Tucumán, 392,888 ('80) (525,000★)....F 4
- Santa Fe, 292,165 ('80)....G 4
- Santa Fe de Bogotá, 3,982,941 ('85) (4,260,000★)....C 3
- Santiago, 232,667 ('82) (4,100,000★)....G 3
- Santos, 460,100 ('85) (1,065,000★)....F 6
- São Luís, 227,900 ('85) (600,000★)....D 6
- São Paulo, 10,063,110 ('85) (15,175,000★)....F 6
- Stanley, 1,200 ('86)....I 5
- Sucre, 86,609 ('85)....E 4
- **SURINAME**....C 5
- Teresina, 425,300 ('85) (525,000★)....D 6
- Trujillo, 202,469 ('81) (354,301★)....D 3
- **URUGUAY**....G 5
- Valparaíso, 265,355 ('82) (675,000★)....G 3
- **VENEZUELA**....C 4
- Vitória, 201,500 ('85) (735,000★)....F 6

★ Population of metropolitan area, including suburbs.
▲ Population of entire district, including rural area.

Northern South America

Bolivia
1985 ESTIMATE
Cochabamba, 317,251 G 5
La Paz, 992,592 .... G 5
Oruro, 178,393 ...... G 5
Potosí, 113,380 .... G 5
Santa Cruz, 441,717 G 6
Sucre, 86,609 ...... G 5

Brazil
1985 ESTIMATE
Anápolis, 225,840 .. G 9
Aracaju, 360,013 .... F11
Araçatuba, 129,304 .. H 8
Bauru, 220,105 ...... H 9
Belém, 1,116,578 (1,200,000★) ...... D 9
Belo Horizonte, 2,114,429 (2,950,000★) G10
Brasília, 1,567,709 .. G 9
Campina Grande, 279,929 .... E11
Campinas, 841,016 (1,125,000★) ...... H 9
Campo Grande, 384,398 .... H 8
Campos, 187,900 (366,716▲) H10
Caruaru, 152,100 (190,794▲) E11
Cuiabá, 220,400 (279,651▲) ...... G 7
Feira de Santana, 278,600 (355,201▲) F11
Fortaleza, 1,582,414 (1,825,000★) D11
Goiânia, 923,333 (990,000★) ...... G 9
Governador Valadares, 192,300 (216,957▲) G10
João Pessoa, 348,500 (550,000★) E12
Juàzeiro do Norte, 159,806 .... E11
Juiz de Fora, 349,720 H10
Jundiaí, 268,900 (313,652▲) .... H 9
Maceió, 482,195 .... E11
Manaus, 809,914 .... D 6
Montes Claros, 183,500 (214,472▲) G10
Natal, 510,106 ...... E11
Niterói, 441,684 .... H10
Petrolina, 92,100 (225,000★) E10
Petrópolis, 170,300 .. H10
Piracicaba, 211,000 (252,079▲) .... H 9
Porto Velho, 152,700 (202,011▲) .... E 6
Presidente Prudente, 155,883 .... H 8
Recife, 1,287,623 (2,625,000★) E12
Ribeirão Prêto, 383,125 .... H 9
Rio de Janeiro, 5,603,388 (10,150,000★) H10
Salvador, 1,804,438 (2,050,000★) F11
Santarém, 120,800 (226,618▲) .... D 8
Santos, 460,100 (1,065,000★) ...... H 9
São Carlos, 140,383 H 9
São José do Rio Prêto, 229,221 .... H 9
São Luís, 227,900 (600,000★) D10
São Paulo, 10,063,110 (15,175,000★) .... H 9
Sorocaba, 327,468 .. H 9
Teresina, 425,300 (525,000★) E10
Uberaba, 244,875 .... G 9
Uberlândia, 312,024 .. G 9
Vitória, 201,500 (735,000★) H10
Vitória da Conquista, 145,800 (198,150▲) F10
Volta Redonda, 219,267 (375,000★) H10

Colombia
1985 CENSUS
Armenia, 187,130 .... C 3
Barrancabermeja, 137,406 .... B 4
Barranquilla, 899,781 (1,140,000★) ...... A 4
Bogotá *see* Santa Fe de Bogotá .... C 4
Bucaramanga, 352,326 (550,000★) .... B 4
Buenaventura, 160,342 .... C 3
Buga, 82,992 ...... C 3
Cali, 1,350,565 (1,400,000★) ...... C 3
Cartagena, 531,426 .. A 3
Cúcuta, 379,478 (445,000★) .... B 4

- Ibagué, 292,965 .... C 3
- Manizales, 299,352 (330,000★)........ B 3
- Medellín, 1,468,089 (2,095,000★)...... B 3
- Montería, 157,466 .. B 3
- Neiva, 194,556 ...... C 3
- Palmira, 175,186 .... C 3
- Pasto, 197,407 ...... C 3
- Pereira, 233,271 (390,000★)........ C 3
- Popayán, 141,964 .. C 3
- Santa Fe de Bogotá, 3,982,941 (4,260,000★)...... C 4
- Santa Marta, 177,922 A 4
- Tuluá, 99,721 ...... C 3
- Valledupar, 142,771 .. A 4
- Villavicencio, 178,685 C 4

Ecuador

1987 ESTIMATE

- Ambato, 126,067 .... D 3
- Cuenca, 201,490 .... D 3
- Guayaquil, 1,572,615 (1,580,000★)...... D 3
- Machala, 144,396 .... D 3
- Manta, 135,990 .... D 2
- Portoviejo, 141,568 .. D 2
- Quito, 1,137,705 (1,300,000★)...... D 3

French Guiana

1982 CENSUS

- Cayenne, 38,091 .... C 8

Guyana

1983 ESTIMATE

- Georgetown, 78,500 (188,000★)........ B 7

Peru

1981 CENSUS

- Arequipa, 108,023 (446,942★) ...... G 4
- Ayacucho, 57,432 (69,533★) .... F 4
- Cajamarca, 62,259 .. E 3
- Callao, 264,133 ...... F 3
- Cerro de Pasco, 55,597 (66,373★) .... F 3
- Chiclayo, 213,095 (279,527★)........ E 3
- Chimbote, 223,341 .. E 3
- Cuzco, 89,563 (184,550★)........ F 4
- Huancayo, 84,845 (164,954★)........ F 3
- Huánuco, 61,812 .... E 3
- Ica, 114,786 .... F 3
- Iquitos, 178,738 .... D 4
- Lima, 371,122 (4,608,010★)...... F 3
- Piura, 144,609 (207,934★)........ E 2
- Sullana, 89,037 ...... D 2
- Tacna, 97,173 ...... G 4
- Trujillo, 202,469 (354,301★)........ E 3
- Tumbes, 47,936 .... D 2
- Vitarte, 145,504 .... F 3

Suriname

1988 ESTIMATE

- Paramaribo, 241,000 (296,000★)........ B 7

Venezuela

1981 CENSUS

- Acarigua, 91,662 .... B 5
- Barinas, 110,462 .... B 4
- Barquisimeto, 497,635 A 5
- Cabimas, 140,435 .. A 4
- Calabozo, 61,995 .... B 5
- Caracas, 1,816,901 (3,600,000★)...... A 5
- Ciudad Bolívar, 182,941 .... B 6
- Ciudad Guayana, 314,497 .... B 6
- Ciudad Ojeda, 83,565 A 4
- Cumaná, 179,814 .... A 6
- El Tigre, 73,595 .... B 6
- Maracaibo, 890,643 .. A 4
- Maracay, 322,560 .... A 5
- Maturín, 154,976 .... B 6
- Mérida, 143,209 .... B 4
- Puerto Cabello, 71,759 .... A 5
- Punto Fijo, 71,114 .. A 4
- San Cristóbal, 198,793 .... B 4
- Valencia, 616,224 .... A 5
- Valera, 102,068 .... B 4

★ Population of metropolitan area, including suburbs.
▲ Population of entire district, including rural area.

Southern South America

Argentina
1980 CENSUS

Avellaneda, 334,145 . . C 5
Bahía Blanca, 223,818 D 4
Buenos Aires, 2,922,829 (10,750,000★) . . . . C 5
Catamarca, 78,799 (90,000★) . . . . B 3
Comodoro Rivadavia, 96,817 . . . . F 3
Concordia, 94,222 . . C 5
Córdoba, 993,055 (1,070,000★) . . . . . . C 4
Corrientes, 180,612 . . B 5
La Plata, 477,175 . . . . C 5
Mar del Plata, 414,696 . . . . D 5
Mendoza, 119,088 (650,000★) . . . . C 3
Paraná, 161,638 . . . . C 4
Posadas, 143,889 . . . B 5
Río Cuarto, 110,254 . . C 4
Rosario, 938,120 (1,045,000★) . . . . . . C 4
Salta, 260,744 . . . . . . A 3
San Isidro, 289,170 . . C 5
San Juan, 118,046 (300,000★) . . . . C 3
San Miguel de Tucumán, 392,888 (525,000★) B 3
Santa Fe, 292,165 . . C 4
Santiago del Estero, 148,758 (200,000★) B 4

Brazil
1985 ESTIMATE

Bauru, 220,105 . . . . . . A 7
Blumenau, 192,074 . . B 7
Campinas, 841,016 (1,125,000★) . . . . . . A 7
Caxias do Sul, 266,809 . . . . B 6
Curitiba, 1,279,205 (1,700,000★) . . . . . . B 7
Florianópolis, 178,400 (365,000★) . . . . B 7
Joinvile, 302,877 . . . . B 7
Jundiaí, 268,900 (313,652▲) . . . . A 7
Londrina, 296,400 (346,676▲) . . . . A 6
Maringá, 196,871 . . . . A 6
Pelotas, 210,300 (277,730▲) . . . . C 6
Piracicaba, 211,000 (252,079▲) . . . . A 7
Ponta Grossa, 223,154 . . . . B 6
Porto Alegre, 1,272,121 (2,600,000★) . . . . . . C 6
Presidente Prudente, 155,883 . . . . A 6
Ribeirão Prêto, 383,125 . . . . A 7
Rio Grande, 164,221 C 6
Santa Maria, 163,900 (196,827▲) . . . . B 6
Santos, 460,100 (1,065,000★) . . . . . . A 7
São Carlos, 140,383 A 7
São Paulo, 10,063,110 (15,175,000★) . . . . A 7
Sorocaba, 327,468 . . A 7

Chile
1982 CENSUS

Antofagasta, 185,486 A 2
Chillán, 118,163 . . . . D 2
Concepción, 267,891 (675,000★) . . . . D 2
Osorno, 95,286 . . . . . . E 2
Punta Arenas, 95,332 G 2
Rancagua, 139,925 . . C 2
Santiago, 232,667 (4,100,000★) . . . . . . C 2
Talca, 128,544 . . . . . . C 2
Talcahuano, 202,368 D 2
Temuco, 157,297 . . . . D 2
Valdivia, 100,046 . . . . D 2
Valparaíso, 265,355 (675,000★) . . . . C 2
Viña del Mar, 244,899 C 2

Falkland Islands
1986 ESTIMATE

Stanley, 1,200 . . . . . . G 5

Paraguay
1985 ESTIMATE

Asunción, 477,100 (700,000★) . . . . B 5

Uruguay
1985 CENSUS

Montevideo, 1,251,647 (1,550,000★) . . . . . C 5
Paysandú, 76,191 . . . . . C 5
Salto, 80,823 . . . . . . C 5

★ Population of metropolitan area, including suburbs.
▲ Population of entire district, including rural area.

Kilometers 0 200 400 600 Km.
Miles 0 200 400 600 Mi.

1:16 000 000

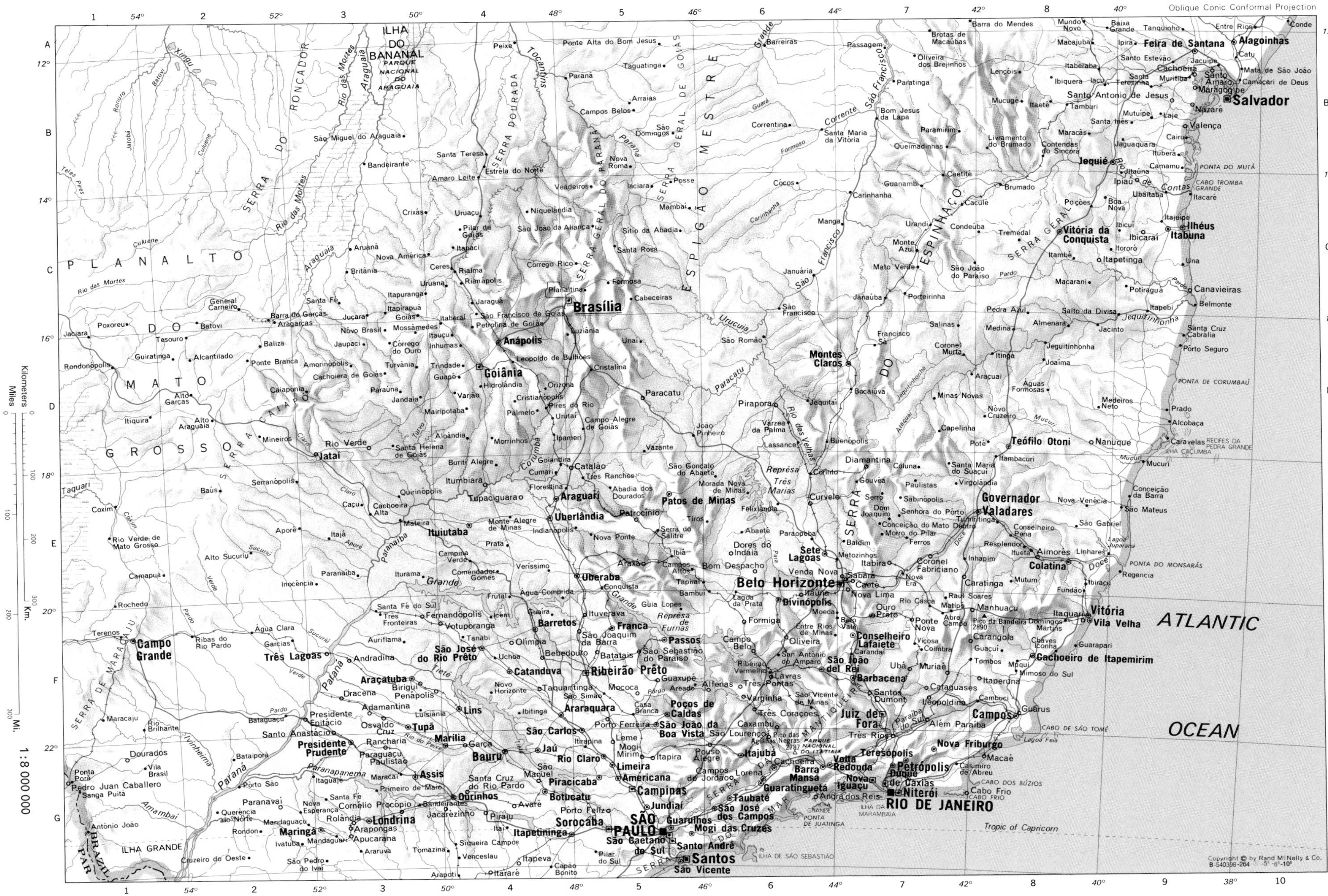

★ Population of metropolitan area, including suburbs. ▲ Population of entire district, including rural area.

Brazil

1985 ESTIMATE

Americana, 156,030 .. G 5
Anápolis, 225,840 .... D 4
Araçatuba, 129,304 .... F 3
Araraquara, 87,500 (145,042▲) .... F 4
Assis, 63,100 (74,238▲) G 3
Barbacena, 80,200 (99,337▲) .... F 7
Barra Mansa, 149,200 G 6
Bauru, 220,105 ...... G 4
Belo Horizonte, 2,114,429 (2,950,000★) ...... E 7
Brasília, 1,567,709 .... C 5
Cachoeiro de Itapemirim, 95,000 (138,156▲) .. F 8
Campinas, 841,016 (1,125,000★) ...... G 5
Campo Grande, 384,398 F 1
Campos, 187,900 (366,716▲) .... F 8
Conselheiro Lafaiete, 77,958 .... F 7
Divinópolis, 139,940 .. F 6
Duque de Caxias, 353,200 .... G 7
Feira de Santana, 278,600 (355,201▲) .... B 9
Franca, 182,820 ...... F 5
Goiânia, 923,333 (990,000★) .... D 4
Governador Valadares, 192,300 (216,957▲) .. E 8
Guarulhos, 571,700 .. G 5
Itabuna, 142,200 (167,543▲) .... C 9
Itajubá, 61,500 (69,675▲) .... G 6
Itapetininga, 76,700 (105,512▲) .... G 4
Itaquari, 163,900 ...... F 8
Juiz de Fora, 349,720 .. F 7
Jundiaí, 268,900 (313,652▲) .... G 5
Limeira, 186,986 ...... G 5
Londrina, 296,400 (346,676▲) .... G 3
Maringá, 196,871 .... G 3
Mogi das Cruzes, 144,800 .... G 5
Montes Claros, 183,500 (214,472▲) .... D 7
Niterói, 441,684 ...... G 7
Nova Friburgo, 103,500 (143,529▲) .... G 7
Nova Iguaçu, 592,800 G 7
Petrópolis, 170,300 .... G 7
Piracicaba, 211,000 (252,079▲) .... G 5
Poços de Caldas, 100,004 .... F 5
Presidente Prudente, 155,883 .... G 3
Ribeirão Prêto, 383,125 F 5
Rio Claro, 129,859 .... G 5
Rio de Janeiro, 5,603,388 (10,150,000★) ...... G 7
Salvador, 1,804,438 (2,050,000★) ...... B 9
Santo André, 635,129 G 5
Santos, 460,100 (1,065,000★) ...... G 5
São Caetano do Sul, 171,005 .... G 5
São Carlos, 140,383 .. G 5
São José do Rio Prêto, 229,221 .... F 4
São José dos Campos, 372,578 .... G 6
São Paulo, 10,063,110 (15,175,000★) ...... G 5
São Vicente, 239,778 .. G 5
Sete Lagoas, 121,418 .. E 6
Sorocaba, 327,468 .... G 5
Taubaté, 205,120 .... G 6
Uberaba, 244,875 .... E 5
Uberlândia, 312,024 .. E 4
Vitória, 201,500 (735,000★) .... F 8
Vitória da Conquista, 145,800 (198,150▲) C 8
Volta Redonda, 219,267 (375,000★) .... G 6

Colombia, Ecuador, Venezuela, and Guyana

Aruba
1987 ESTIMATE
Oranjestad, 19,800 . . A 7

Colombia
1985 CENSUS
Armenia, 187,130 . . . . E 5
Barrancabermeja, 137,406 . . . . D 6
Barranquilla, 899,781 (1,140,000★) . . . . . B 5
Bello, 212,861 . . . . . . D 5
Bogotá *see* Santa Fe de Bogotá . . . . E 5
Bucaramanga, 352,326 (550,000★) . . . . D 6
Buenaventura, 160,342 . . . . F 4
Buga, 82,992 . . . . F 4
Cali, 1,350,565 (1,400,000★) . . . . . F 4
Cartagena, 531,426 . . B 5
Cartago, 97,791 . . . . E 5
Ciénaga, 56,860 . . . . B 5
Cúcuta, 379,478 (445,000★) . . . . D 6
Duitama, 56,390 . . . . E 6
Envigado, 91,391 . . . . D 5
Espinal, 37,563 . . . . . . E 5
Facatativá, 44,331 . . E 5
Florencia, 66,430 . . . . G 5
Florida, 30,040 . . . . . . F 4
Floridablanca, 143,824 . . . . D 6
Girardot, 70,078 . . . . E 5
Ibagué, 292,965 . . . . E 5
Ipiales, 45,419 . . . . . . G 4
Itagüí, 137,623 . . . . . . D 5
La Dorada, 48,572 . . E 5
Magangué, 49,160 . . C 5
Manizales, 299,352 (330,000★) . . . . E 5
Medellín, 1,468,089 (2,095,000★) . . . . . . D 5
Montería, 157,466 . . C 5
Neiva, 194,556 . . . . . . F 5
Ocaña, 51,443 . . . . . . C 6
Palmira, 175,186 . . . . F 4
Pamplona, 34,213 . . . D 6
Pasto, 197,407 . . . . . . G 4
Pereira, 233,271 (390,000★) . . . . E 5
Planeta Rica, 24,238 C 5
Popayán, 141,964 . . . F 4
Puerto Berrío, 21,414 D 5
Quibdó, 47,950 . . . . . . E 4
Ríohacha, 46,667 . . . . B 6
Santa Fe de Bogotá, 3,982,941 (4,260,000★) . . . . . . E 5
Santa Marta, 177,922 . . . . B 5
Santa Rosa de Cabal, 37,112 . . . . E 5
Sincelejo, 120,537 . . C 5
Sogamoso, 64,437 . . E 6
Soledad, 165,791 . . . . B 5
Tuluá, 99,721 . . . . . . E 4
Tumaco, 45,456 . . . . G 3
Tunja, 93,792 . . . . . . E 6
Valledupar, 142,771 . . B 6
Villavicencio, 178,685 E 6
Zipaquirá, 45,676 . . . . E 5

Ecuador
1987 ESTIMATE
Alfaro, 51,023('82) . . . . I 3
Ambato, 126,067 . . . . H 3
Babahoyo, 42,266('82) . . . . . . H 3
Chone, 33,839('82) . . H 2
Cuenca, 201,490 . . . . I 3
Esmeraldas, 120,387 G 3
Guayaquil, 1,572,615 (1,580,000★) . . . . . . I 3
Ibarra, 53,428('82) . . G 3
Jipijapa, 27,146('82) . . H 2
Latacunga, 28,764('82) . . . . . . H 3
Loja, 71,652('82) . . . . J 3
Machala, 144,396 . . . . I 3
Manta, 135,990 . . . . H 2
Milagro, 102,884 . . . . I 3
Portoviejo, 141,568 . . H 2
Quevedo, 67,023('82) . . . . . . H 3
Quito, 1,137,705 (1,300,000★) . . . . . H 3
Riobamba, 75,455('82) . . . . . . H 3
Santo Domingo de los Colorados, 104,059 H 3
Tulcán, 30,985('82) . . G 4

Guyana
1983 ESTIMATE
Georgetown, 78,500 (188,000★) D13
New Amsterdam, 20,000('82) D14

★ Population of metropolitan area, including suburbs.

Kilometers 0 100 200 300 Km.
Miles 0 100 200 300 Mi.
1:8 000 000

Netherlands Antilles
1981 CENSUS

Willemstad, 31,883 (130,000★) . . . . A 8

Panama
1990 CENSUS

Colón, 54,469 (96,000★) . . . . C 3
David, 65,635 . . . . . . C 1
La Chorrera, 44,110 . . C 3
Panamá, 411,549 (770,000★) . . . . C 3
Puerto Armuelles, 12,562('80) . . . . . . C 1
Santiago, 43,678 . . . . C 2

Trinidad and Tobago
1990 CENSUS

Arima, 29,695 . . . . . . B12
Point Fortin, 6,538('80) B12
Port of Spain, 50,878 (370,000★) B12
San Fernando, 30,092 (75,000★) B12
Scarborough, 6,089('80) B12

Venezuela
1981 CENSUS

Acarigua, 91,662 . . . . C 8
Altagracia de Orituco, 31,582 . . . . C 9
Anaco, 43,607 . . . . . . C10
Araure, 41,747 . . . . . . C 8
Barcelona, 156,461 . . B10
Barinas, 110,462 . . . . C 7
Barquisimeto, 497,635 . . . . B 8
Cabimas, 140,435 . . B 7
Calabozo, 61,995 . . . . C 9
Cantaura, 21,236 . . . . C10
Caracas, 1,816,901 (3,600,000★) . . . . . . B 9
Caripito, 18,172 . . . . B11
Carora, 58,694 . . . . . . B 7
Carúpano, 64,579 . . . . B11
Ciudad Bolívar, 182,941 . . . . C11
Ciudad Guayana, 314,497 . . . . C11
Ciudad Ojeda (Lagunillas), 83,565 . . . . B 7
Coro, 96,339 . . . . B 8
Cumaná, 179,814 . . . . B10
El Tigre, 73,595 . . . . C10
El Tocuyo, 22,854 . . C 8
Guanare, 64,025 . . . . C 8
La Guaira, 21,815 . . . . B 9
Los Teques, 112,857 B 9
Machiques, 27,242 . . B 6
Maiquetía, 66,056 . . . . B 9
Maracaibo, 890,643 . . B 7
Maracay, 322,560 . . . . B 9
Maturín, 154,976 . . . . C11
Mérida, 143,209 . . . . C 7
Ocumare del Tuy, 40,666 . . . . B 9
Porlamar, 51,079 . . . . B11
Puerto Ayacucho, 28,248 . . . . E 9
Puerto Cabello, 71,759 . . . . B 8
Puerto la Cruz, 53,881 . . . . B10
Punto Fijo, 71,114 . . B 7
Rosario, 23,914 . . . . B 6
San Carlos, 37,892 . . C 8
San Carlos del Zulia, 31,437 . . . . C 7
San Cristóbal, 198,793 . . . . D 6
San Felipe, 57,526 . . B 8
San Fernando de Apure, 57,308 . . . . D 9
San José de Guanipa, 35,689 . . . . C10
San Juan de Colón, 23,447 . . . . C 6
San Juan de los Morros, 57,219 . . . . C 9
Tinaquillo, 28,168 . . . . C 8
Trujillo, 31,774 . . . . . . C 7
Tucupita, 27,299 . . . . C11
Upata, 33,238 . . . . . . C11
Valencia, 616,224 . . . . C 8
Valera, 102,068 . . . . C 7
Valle de la Pascua, 55,761 . . . . C 9
Yaritagua, 31,936 . . . . B 8
Zaraza, 24,562 . . . . . . C10

NORTH AMERICA
SOUTH AMERICA
AFRICA
EUROPE
ANTARCTICA
ATLANTIC OCEAN
PACIFIC OCEAN
Pacific Ocean
MID-ATLANTIC RIDGE
NORTH AMERICAN BASIN
CANARY BASIN
CAPE VERDE BASIN
GUIANA BASIN
BRAZIL BASIN
ANGOLA BASIN
CAPE BASIN
ARGENTINE BASIN
AGULHAS BASIN
WEST EUROPEAN BASIN
NEWFOUNDLAND BASIN
LABRADOR BASIN
NORWEGIAN BASIN
GREENLAND BASIN
IBERIAN ABYSSAL PLAIN
AZORES PLATEAU
AZORES-GIBRALTAR RIDGE
REYKJANES RIDGE
FAEROE PLATEAU
PUERTO RICO TRENCH
MILWAUKEE DEPTH 28 232 Ft. 8 605 M.
SIERRA LEONE RISE
SIERRA LEONE BASIN
GUINEA BASIN
GUINEA RIDGE
WALVIS RIDGE
CAPE RISE
BROMLEY PLATEAU
FALKLAND PLATEAU
SCOTIA RIDGE
S. SANDWICH TRENCH
W. SCOTIA BASIN
NORTHEASTERN GEORGIA RIDGE
WEST ATLANTIC-INDIAN BASIN
ATLANTIC-INDIAN RIDGE
SOUTHEAST PACIFIC BASIN
PERU-CHILE TRENCH
COCOS RIDGE
CARNEGIE RIDGE
COLOMBIAN ABYSSAL PLAIN
VENEZUELAN BASIN
BEATA RIDGE
AVES RIDGE
MEXICO BASIN
Caribbean Sea
Gulf of Mexico
Hudson Bay
North Sea
Baltic Sea
Black Sea
Mediterranean Sea
Gulf of Guinea
Weddell Sea
Drake Passage
SAHARA
Seattle
Chicago
Montréal
New York
Washington
New Orleans
Miami
La Habana
Caracas
Santa Fe de Bogotá
Lima
Recife
Rio de Janeiro
São Paulo
Buenos Aires
Santiago
London
Paris
Berlin
Stockholm
Sankt-Peterburg
Moskva
Madrid
Roma
İstanbul
El Djazair
Casablanca
Dakar
Lagos
Kinshasa
Cape Town
-26 457 Ft. -8 064 M.
27 318 Ft. 8 325 M.
PHYSICAL FEATURES AND RELIEF
Depths Feet Meters
0 0
500 150
5 000 1 525
10 000 3 050
15 000 4 575
20 000 6 100
Scale:
1 inch = 1 200 miles
1 cm = 760 km
A-513700-9F86
© RAND McNALLY & CO.

Lambert Azimuthal Equal Area Projection

Miles 0 200 400 600 800 1000 Mi.
Kilometers 0 400 800 1200 1600 Km.
1:40 000 000

Atlanta, 394,017 ('90)..F12
BAHAMAS..................G13
Baltimore, 736,014 ('90)..........................F13
BARBADOS................H14
BELIZE........................H12
Boston, 574,283 ('90). E13
Calgary, 636,104 ('86) (671,326★) ....D 9
CANADA......................D11
Chicago, 2,783,726 ('90)..........................E12
Ciudad de México (Mexico City), 8,831,079 ('80) (14,100,000★) H11
COSTA RICA.............H12
CUBA..........................G13
Dallas, 1,006,877 ('90) F11
Denver, 467,610 ('90)..F10
Detroit, 1,027,974 ('90)..........................E12
DOMINICAN REPUBLIC...............H13
EL SALVADOR...........H12
GREENLAND.............B16
Guadalajara, 1,626,152 ('80) (2,325,000★) .. H10
GUATEMALA.............H11
HAITI..........................H13
HONDURAS................H12
Houston, 1,630,553 ('90)..........................G11
JAMAICA....................H13
Kansas City, 435,146 ('90)..........................F11
La Habana (Havana), 2,036,800 ('87) (2,125,000★) G12
Los Angeles, 3,485,398 ('90)..........................F 9
Memphis, 610,337 ('90)..........................F11
MEXICO......................G10
Miami, 358,548 ('90)...G12
Milwaukee, 628,088 ('90)..........................E12
Minneapolis, 368,383 ('90)..........................E11
Montréal, 1,015,420 ('86) (2,921,357★) E13
New Orleans, 496,938 ('90)..........................G11
New York, 7,322,564 ('90)..........................E13
NICARAGUA...............H12
Ottawa, 300,763 ('86) (819,263★) E13
PANAMA.......................I13
Philadelphia, 1,585,577 ('90)..........................F13
Phoenix, 900,013 ('90) F 9
PUERTO RICO...........H14
San Antonio, 935,933 ('90)..........................G11
San Francisco, 723,959 ('90)..........................F 8
Santo Domingo, 1,313,172 ('81)..........................H13
Seattle, 516,259 ('90)..E 8
Toronto, 612,289 ('86) (3,427,168★) E13
TRINIDAD AND TOBAGO................H14
UNITED STATES........F11
Washington, 606,900 ('90)..........................F13

★ Population of metropolitan area, including suburbs.

Mexico

1980 CENSUS

Acámbaro, 38,224 . . G 9
Acapulco [de Juárez], 301,902 . . . . I10
Aguascalientes, 293,152 . . . . G 8
Ameca, 25,946 . . . . G 7
Apatzingán [de la Constitución], 55,522 . . . . H 8
Apizaco, 30,498 . . . . H10
Caborca, 33,696 . . . . B 3
Campeche, 128,434 H14
Celaya, 141,675 . . . . G 9
Chihuahua, 385,603 C 6
Chilpancingo [de los Bravos], 67,498 . . . . I10
Ciudad Acuña, 38,898 C 9
Ciudad Chetumal, 56,709 . . . . H15
Ciudad del Carmen, 72,489 . . . . H14
Ciudad de México (Mexico City), 8,831,079 (14,100,000★) H10
Ciudad de Valles, 65,609 . . . . G10
Ciudad Guzmán, 60,938 . . . . H 8
Ciudad Hidalgo, 32,311 . . . . H 9
Ciudad Juárez, 544,496 . . . . B 6
Ciudad Madero, 132,444 . . . . F11
Ciudad Mante, 70,647 F10
Ciudad Obregón, 165,572 . . . . D 5
Ciudad Victoria, 140,161 . . . . F10
Coatzacoalcos, 127,170 . . . . H12
Colima, 86,044 . . . . H 8
Córdoba, 99,972 . . . . H11
Cuernavaca, 192,770 H10
Culiacán, 304,826 . . E 6
Delicias, 65,504 . . . . C 7
Durango, 257,915 . . E 7
Empalme, 31,555 . . D 4
Ensenada, 120,483 . . B 1
Fresnillo, 56,066 . . . . F 8
Gómez Palacio, 116,967 . . . . E 8
Guadalajara, 1,626,152 (2,325,000★) . . . . G 8
Guadalupe, 370,524 . . E 9
Guanajuato, 48,981 . . G 9
Guaymas, 54,826 . . D 4
Hermosillo, 297,175 . . C 4
Hidalgo del Parral, 75,590 . . . . D 7
Iguala, 66,005 . . . . . . H10
Irapuato, 170,138 . . G 9
Jalapa Enríquez, 204,594 . . . . H11
Juchitán [de Zaragoza], 38,801 . . . . I12
La Barca, 20,889 . . G 8
Lagos de Moreno, 44,223 . . . . G 9
La Paz, 91,453 . . . . E 4
La Piedad [Cavadas], 47,441 . . . . G 8
León [de los Aldamas], 593,002 . . . . G 9
Los Mochis, 122,531 E 5
Manzanillo, 39,088 . . H 7
Matamoros, 188,745 E11
Matehuala, 41,550 . . F 9
Mazatlán, 199,830 . . F 6
Mérida, 400,142 . . . . G15
Mexicali, 341,559 (365,000★) . . . . . . A 2
Mexico City *see* Ciudad de México H10
Minatitlán, 106,765 . . I12
Monclova, 115,786 . . D 9
Montemorelos, 28,342 E10
Monterrey, 1,090,009 (2,015,000★) . . . . E 9
Morelia, 297,544 . . . . H 9
Navojoa, 62,901 . . . . D 5
Nogales, 65,603 . . . . B 4
Nueva Casas Grandes, 28,514 . . . . B 6
Nueva Rosita, 33,121 D 9
Nuevo Laredo, 201,731 . . . . D10
Oaxaca [de Juárez], 154,223 . . . . I11
Ocotlán, 48,931 . . . . G 8
Orizaba, 114,848 (215,000★) H11
Pachuca [de Soto], 110,351 . . . . G10
Papantla [de Olarte], 43,935 . . . . G11
Pátzcuaro, 32,902 . . H 9
Piedras Negras, 67,455 . . . . C 9
Poza Rica de Hidalgo, 166,799 . . . . G11

★ Population of metropolitan area, including suburbs.

Kilometers 0 100 200 300 Km.
Miles 0 100 200 300 Mi.
1 : 8 000 000

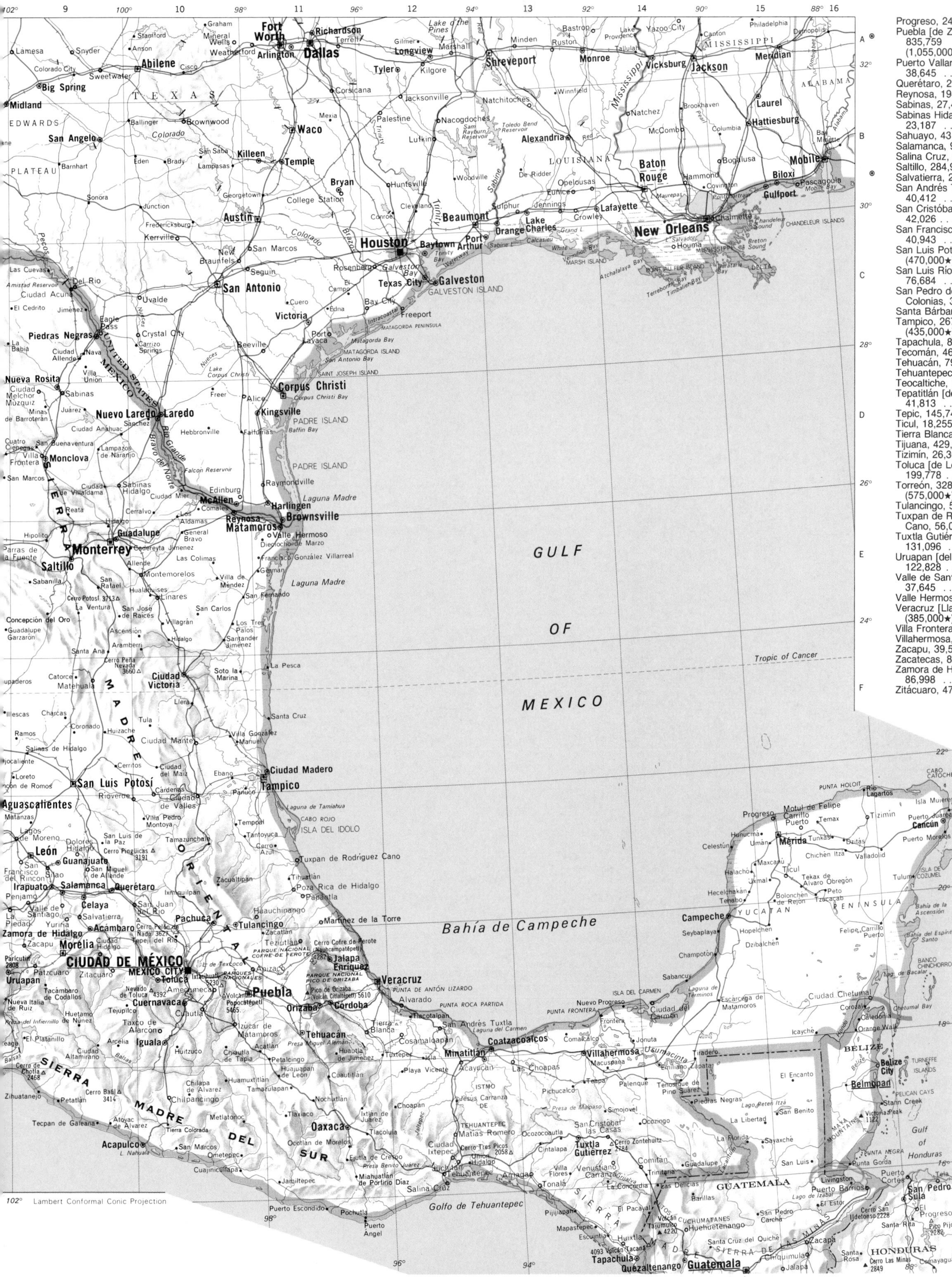

Progreso, 24,257 .. G15
Puebla [de Zaragoza], 835,759 (1,055,000★) H10
Puerto Vallarta, 38,645 .... G 7
Querétaro, 215,976 .. G 9
Reynosa, 194,693 .. D10
Sabinas, 27,413 .... D 9
Sabinas Hidalgo, 23,187 .... D 9
Sahuayo, 43,258 .... G 8
Salamanca, 96,703 .. G 9
Salina Cruz, 40,010 .. I12
Saltillo, 284,937 .... E 9
Salvatierra, 28,878 .. G 9
San Andrés Tuxtla, 40,412 .... H12
San Cristóbal las Casas, 42,026 .... I13
San Francisco del Rincón, 40,943 .... G 9
San Luis Potosí, 362,371 (470,000★) ...... F 9
San Luis Río Colorado, 76,684 ....A 2
San Pedro de las Colonias, 35,879 .. E 8
Santa Bárbara, 14,894D 7
Tampico, 267,957 (435,000★) F11
Tapachula, 85,766 .. J13
Tecomán, 46,371 .. H 8
Tehuacán, 79,547 .. H11
Tehuantepec, 22,019 I12
Teocaltiche, 16,559 .. G 8
Tepatitlán [de Morelos], 41,813 .... G 8
Tepic, 145,741 .... G 7
Ticul, 18,255 ...... G15
Tierra Blanca, 31,653 H11
Tijuana, 429,500 .... A 1
Tizimín, 26,305 .... G15
Toluca [de Lerdo], 199,778 .... H10
Torreón, 328,086 (575,000★) ...... E 8
Tulancingo, 53,400 .. G10
Tuxpan de Rodríguez Cano, 56,037 .... G11
Tuxtla Gutiérrez, 131,096 .... I13
Uruapan [del Progreso], 122,828 .... H 8
Valle de Santiago, 37,645 .... G 9
Valle Hermoso, 27,966E11
Veracruz [Llave], 284,822 (385,000★) H11
Villa Frontera, 32,568 D 9
Villahermosa, 158,216 I13
Zacapu, 39,570 .... H 9
Zacatecas, 80,088 .. F 8
Zamora de Hidalgo, 86,998 .... H 8
Zitácuaro, 47,520 .. H 9

Central America and the Caribbean

Antigua and Barbuda
1977 ESTIMATE
Saint Johns, 24,359 . . F17

Bahamas
1982 ESTIMATE
Nassau, 135,000 . . . . B 9

Barbados
1980 CENSUS
Bridgetown, 7,466 (115,000★) H18

Belize
1985 ESTIMATE
Belize City, 47,000 . . F 3
Belmopan, 4,500 . . . . F 3

Cayman Islands
1988 ESTIMATE
Georgetown, 13,700 E 7

Costa Rica
1988 ESTIMATE
Limón, 40,400 (62,600▲) . . . . I 6
San José, 278,600 (670,000★) . . . . . . J 5

Cuba
1987 ESTIMATE
Camagüey, 265,588 D 9
Guantánamo, 179,091 D10
Havana *see* La Habana . . . . C 6
Holguín, 199,861 . . . . D 9
La Habana (Havana), 2,036,800 (2,125,000★) . . . . C 6
Santa Clara, 182,349 C 8
Santiago de Cuba, 364,554 . . . . D10

Dominican Republic
1981 CENSUS
Santiago, 278,638 . . E 12
Santo Domingo, 1,313,172 . . . . . . E 13

El Salvador
1985 ESTIMATE
San Salvador, 462,652 (920,000★) . . . . . . H 3
Santa Ana, 137,879 . . H 3

Guadeloupe
1982 CENSUS
Basse-Terre, 13,656 (26,600★) F17

Guatemala
1989 ESTIMATE
Guatemala, 1,057,210 (1,400,000★) . . . . G 2

★ Population of metropolitan area, including suburbs.

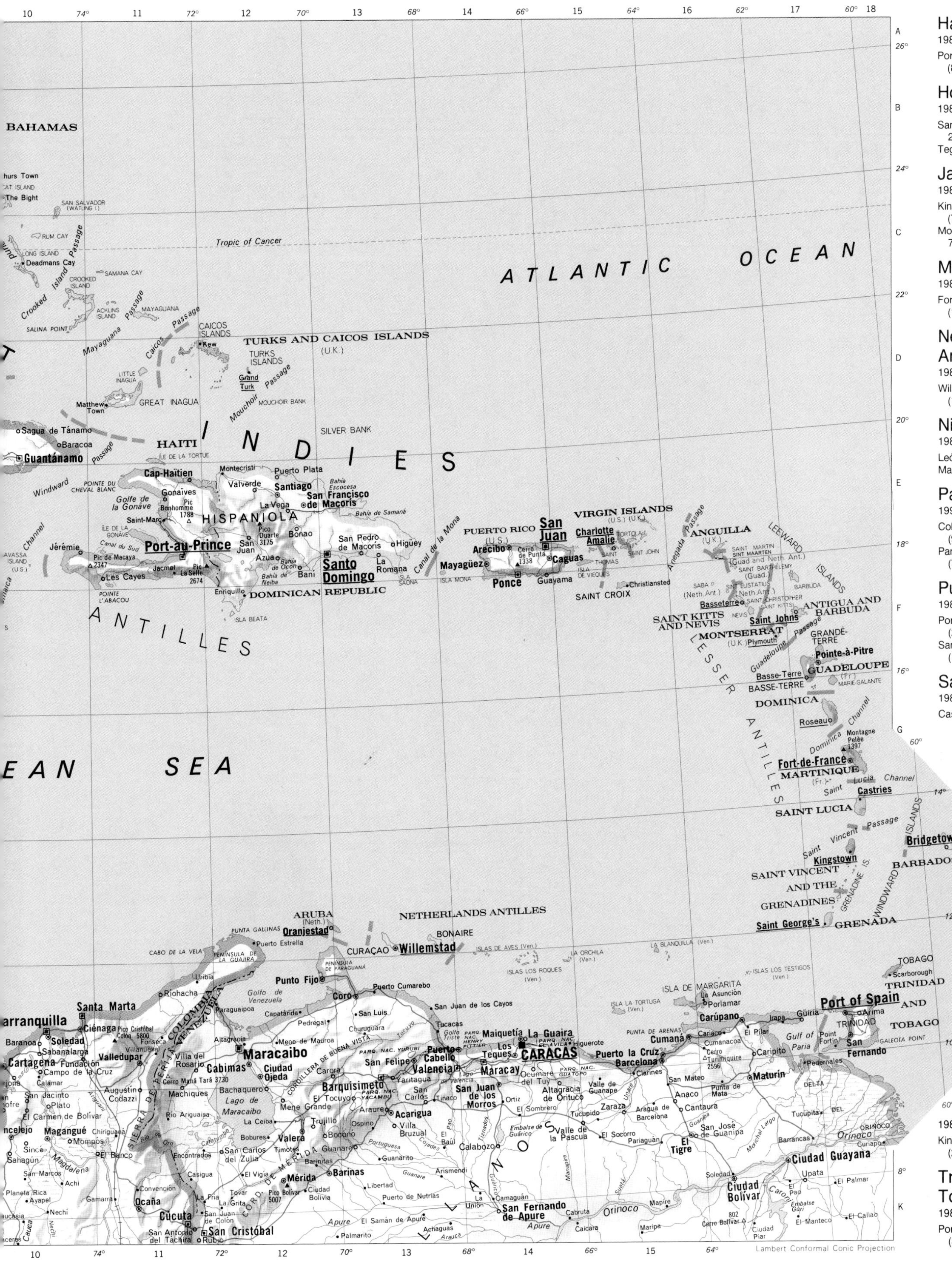

Haiti
1987 ESTIMATE

Port-au-Prince, 797,000 (880,000★) E11

Honduras
1988 CENSUS

San Pedro Sula, 279,356 .... G 4

Tegucigalpa, 551,606 G 4

Jamaica
1987 ESTIMATE

Kingston, 646,400 (770,000★) ...... E 9

Montego Bay, 70,265('82) ...... E 9

Martinique
1982 CENSUS

Fort-de-France, 99,844 (116,017★) G17

Netherlands Antilles
1981 CENSUS

Willemstad, 31,883 (130,000★)......H 13

Nicaragua
1985 ESTIMATE

León, 101,000......H 4

Managua, 682,000 . . H 4

Panama
1990 CENSUS

Colón, 54,469 (96,000★)........J 8

Panamá, 411,549 (770,000★) ...... J 8

Puerto Rico
1980 CENSUS

Ponce, 161,739 (232,551★) E14

San Juan, 424,600 (1,775,260★) E14

Saint Lucia
1987 ESTIMATE

Castries, 53,933 .... G17

Saint Vincent and the Grenadines
1987 ESTIMATE

Kingstown, 19,028 (28,936★) H17

Trinidad and Tobago
1988 ESTIMATE

Port of Spain, 59,200 (370,000★) I17

Canada

ALBERTA F10
Alma, 25,923 ('86) (29,977★) G18
Baie-Comeau, 26,244 ('86) (33,047★) G19
Banff, 4,208 ('81) .... F 9
Barrie, 48,287 ('86) (67,703★) H17
Bathurst, 14,683 ('86) (34,895★) G19
Belleville, 36,041 ('86) (87,530★) H17
Brandon, 38,708 ('86). G13
BRITISH COLUMBIA ... F 8
Brockville, 20,880 ('86) (37,115★) H17
Calgary, 636,104 ('86) (671,326★) F10
Cambridge, 79,920 ('86) H16
Campbell River, 15,370 ('81) .... F 7
Campbellton, 9,077 ('86) (17,418★) G19
CANADA D13
Charlottetown, 15,776 ('86) (53,868★) G20
Chatham, 42,211 ('86) H16
Chicoutimi, 61,083 ('86) (158,468★) G18
Chilliwack, 41,337 ('86) (50,288★) .... G 8
Churchill, 1,186 ('81) ... E14
Corner Brook, 22,719 ('86) (33,730★) G21
Cornwall, 46,425 ('86) (51,719★) G18
Dartmouth, 65,243 ('86) H20
Dawson Creek, 10,544 ('86) .... E 8
Dolbeau, 8,554 ('86) (15,288★) G18
Drummondville, 36,020 ('86) (56,283★) G18
Edmonton, 573,982 ('86) (785,465★) F10
Edmundston, 11,497 ('86) (22,614★) G19
Eskimo Point, 1,189 ('86) D14
Flin Flon, 7,591 ('86) (9,211★) F12
Fort McMurray, 34,949 ('86) (48,497★) E10
Fort Saint John, 13,355 ('86) .... E 8
Fredericton, 44,352 ('86) (65,768★) G19
Gander, 10,207 ('86) (10,899★) G22
Gaspé, 17,350 ('86) G20
Granby, 38,508 ('86) (51,176★) G18
Grande-Prairie, 26,471 ('86) .... E 9
Grand Falls, 9,121 ('86) (25,612★) G21
Guelph, 78,235 ('86) (85,962★) H16
Halifax, 113,577 ('86) (295,990★) H20
Hamilton, 306,728 ('86) (557,029★) H17
Happy Valley-Goose Bay, 7,248 ('86) F20
Hull, 58,722 ('86) G17
Inuvik, 3,389 ('86) .... C 6
Jasper, 3,269 ('81) .... F 9
Joliette, 16,845 ('86) (34,897★) G18
Jonquière, 58,467 ('86) G18
Kamloops, 61,773 ('86) .... F 8
Kelowna, 61,213 ('86) (89,730★) .... G 9
Kenora, 9,621 ('86) (15,456★) G14
Kirkland Lake, 11,604 ('86) G16
Kitchener, 150,604 ('86) (311,195★) H16
Kitimat, 11,196 ('86) .... F 7
Labrador City, 8,664 ('86) (11,301★) F19
La Tuque, 10,723 ('86) (13,468★) G18
Laval, 284,164 ('86) G18
Lethbridge, 58,841 ('86) G10
Lloydminster, 17,356 ('86) F11
London, 269,140 ('86) (342,302★) H16
MANITOBA F13
Matane, 13,243 ('86) (15,361★) G19
Medicine Hat, 41,804 ('86) (50,734★) F10
Midland, 12,092 ('86) (35,003★) H17
Moncton, 55,468 ('86) (102,084★) G20

★ Population of metropolitan area, including suburbs.

Montréal, 1,015,420 ('86) (2,921,357★) G18
Moose Jaw, 35,073 ('86) (37,219★) F11
Nanaimo, 49,029 ('86) (60,420★) .... G 8
NEW BRUNSWICK..... G19
NEWFOUNDLAND.......F21
New Glasgow, 10,022 ('86) (38,737★) G20
Niagara Falls, 72,107 ('86).......................... H17
North Bay, 50,623 ('86) (57,422★) G17
NORTHWEST TERRITORIES.......... C13
NOVA SCOTIA........... G20
ONTARIO.................... G16
Orillia, 24,077 ('86) (31,252★) H17
Oshawa, 123,651 ('86) (203,543★) H17
Ottawa, 300,763 ('86) (819,263★) G17
Owen Sound, 19,804 ('86) (27,364★) H16
Pembroke, 14,131 ('86) (22,560★) G17
Penticton, 23,588 ('86) (38,966★) .... G 9
Peterborough, 61,049 ('86) (87,083★) H17
Portage-la-Prairie, 13,198 ('86).......................... G13
Port Alberni, 18,241 ('86).......................... G 8
Prince Albert, 33,686 ('86) (40,841★) F11
PRINCE EDWARD ISLAND.................... G20
Prince George, 67,621 ('86)..........................F 8
Prince Rupert, 15,755 ('86) (17,581★) ....F 6
QUÉBEC.......................F18
Québec, 164,580 ('86) (603,267★) G18
Rankin Inlet, 1,374 ('86).......................... D14
Red Deer, 54,425 ('86)F10
Regina, 175,064 ('86) (186,521★) F12
Saint-Hyacinthe, 38,603 ('86) (48,303★) G18
Saint-Jérôme, 23,316 ('86) (44,048★) G18
Saint John, 76,831 ('86) (121,265★) G19
Saint John's, 96,216 ('86) (161,901★) G22
Sarnia, 49,033 ('86) (85,700★) H16
SASKATCHEWAN.......F11
Saskatoon, 177,641 ('86) (200,665★) F11
Sault Sainte Marie, 80,905 ('86) (84,617★) G16
Selkirk, 10,013 ('86).... F13
Sept-Îles (Seven Islands), 25,637 ('86) (28,050★) F19
Shawinigan, 21,470 ('86) (61,965★) G18
Sherbrooke, 74,438 ('86) (129,960★) G18
Sorel, 19,522 ('86) (46,096★) G18
Sudbury, 88,717 ('86) (148,877★) G16
Summerside, 8,020 ('86) (15,614★) G20
Swift Current, 15,666 ('86).............................F11
Sydney Mines, 8,063 ('86).......................... G20
Thetford Mines, 18,561 ('86) (31,940★) G18
Thunder Bay, 112,272 ('86) (122,217★) G15
Timmins, 46,657 ('86). G16
Toronto, 612,289 ('86) (3,427,168★) H17
Trail, 7,948 ('86) (20,257★) .... G 9
Trois-Rivières, 50,122 ('86) (128,888★) G18
Truro, 12,124 ('86) (41,516★).................... G20
Val-d'Or, 22,252 ('86) (27,178★) G17
Vancouver, 431,147 ('86) (1,380,729★) .... G 8
Victoria, 66,303 ('86) (255,547★) .... G 8
Whitehorse, 15,199 ('86).......................... D 5
Windsor, 193,111 ('86) (253,988★) H16
Winnipeg, 594,551 ('86) (625,304★) G13
Yellowknife, 11,753 ('86).......................... D10
YUKON........................D 5

Alberta

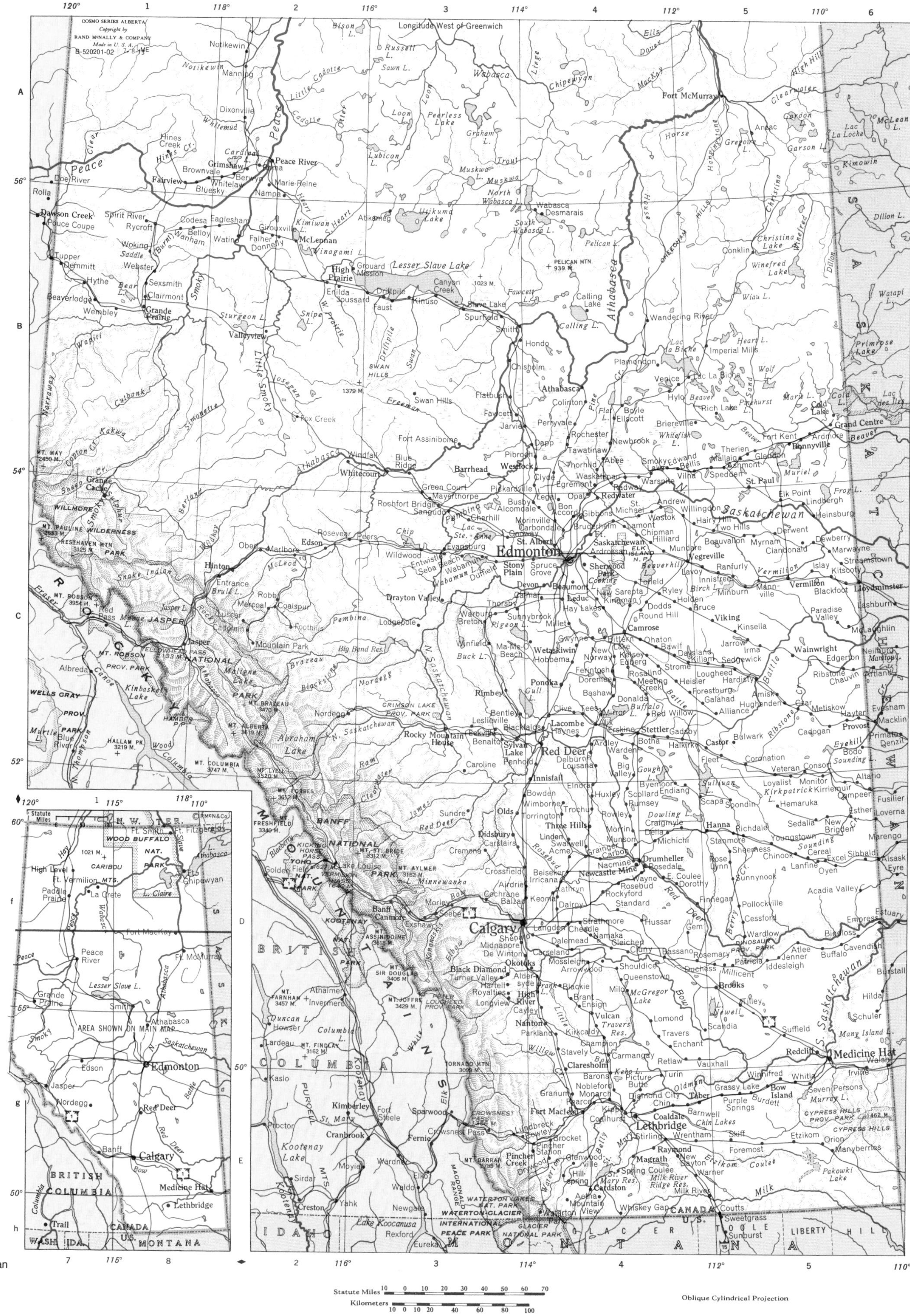

Alberta

1986 CENSUS

- Airdrie, 10,390 . . . . . . D 3
- Athabasca, 1,970 . . . . B 4
- Banff . . . . D 3
- Barrhead, 3,991 . . . . B 3
- Beaumont, 3,944 . . . . C 4
- Beaverlodge, 1,808 . . B 1
- Blackfalds, 1,688 . . . . C 4
- Bonnyville, 5,470 . . . . B 5
- Bow Island, 1,650 . . E 5
- Brooks, 9,464 . . . . . . D 5
- Calgary, 636,104 (671,326★) . . . . . . D 3
- Camrose, 12,968 . . . . C 4
- Canmore, 4,182 . . . . D 3
- Cardston, 3,497 . . . . E 4
- Carstairs, 1,629 . . . . D 3
- Claresholm, 3,382 . . D 4
- Coaldale, 4,796 . . . . E 4
- Cochrane, 4,190 . . . . D 3
- Cold Lake, 3,195 . . . . B 5
- Coronation, 1,310 . . C 5
- Crowsnest Pass, 6,912 . . . . E 3
- Devon, 3,691 . . . . . . C 4
- Didsbury, 3,184 . . . . D 3
- Drayton Valley, 5,290 C 3
- Drumheller, 6,366 . . D 4
- Edmonton, 573,982 (785,465★) . . . . . . C 4
- Edson, 7,323 . . . . . . C 2
- Fairview, 2,998 . . . . A 1
- Fort Chipewyan, 922 f 8
- Fort Macleod, 3,123 E 4
- Fort McMurray, 34,949 (48,497★) . . . . A 5
- Fort Saskatchewan, 11,983 . . . . C 4
- Fox Creek, 2,068 . . . B 2
- Gibbons, 2,335 . . . . C 4
- Grand Centre, 3,655 B 5
- Grande Cache, 3,646 C 1
- Grande Prairie, 26,471 . . . . B 1
- Grimshaw, 2,579 . . . A 2
- Hanna, 3,017 . . . . . . D 5
- High Level, 3,004 . . . F 7
- High Prairie, 2,817 . . B 2
- High River, 5,096 . . . D 4
- Hinton, 8,629 . . . . . . C 2
- Innisfail, 5,535 . . . . . C 4
- Jasper . . . . C 1
- Lac La Biche, 2,553 B 5
- Lacombe, 6,080 . . . . C 4
- La Crete, 689 . . . . . . f 7
- Lake Louise, 688 . . . . D 2
- Lamont, 1,576 . . . . . C 4
- Leduc, 13,126 . . . . . . C 4
- Lethbridge, 58,841 . . E 4
- Lloydminster, 17,354 C 5
- Magrath, 1,637 . . . . . E 4
- Medicine Hat, 41,804 (50,734★) . . . . D 5
- Morinville, 5,364 . . . . C 4
- Nordegg, 53 . . . . C 2
- Okotoks, 5,214 . . . . D 4
- Olds, 4,871 . . . . D 3
- Peace River, 6,288 . . A 2
- Penhold, 1,580 . . . . . C 4
- Picture Butte, 1,576 . . E 4
- Pincher Creek, 3,800 E 4
- Ponoka, 5,473 . . . . . . C 4
- Provost, 1,725 . . . . . . C 5
- Raymond, 2,957 . . . . E 4
- Redcliff, 3,834 . . . . . . D 5
- Red Deer, 54,425 . . C 4
- Redwater, 1,982 . . . . C 4
- Rimbey, 1,786 . . . . . . C 3
- Rocky Mountain House, 5,182 . . . . C 3
- Saint Albert, 36,710 . . C 4
- Saint Paul, 5,030 . . . . B 5
- Sherwood Park . . . . C 4
- Slave Lake, 5,429 . . B 3
- Smith, 251 . . . . B 3
- Spruce Grove, 11,918 C 4
- Stettler, 5,147 . . . . . . C 4
- Stony Plain, 5,802 . . C 3
- Strathmore, 3,544 . . D 4
- Sundre, 1,712 . . . . . . D 3
- Swan Hills, 2,403 . . . . B 3
- Sylvan Lake, 3,937 . . C 4
- Taber, 6,382 . . . . E 4
- Three Hills, 2,528 . . . . D 4
- Valleyview, 1,987 . . . . B 2
- Vegreville, 5,276 . . . . C 4
- Vermilion, 3,879 . . . . C 5
- Vulcan, 1,420 . . . . . . D 4
- Wainwright, 4,665 . . C 5
- Westlock, 4,532 . . . . B 4
- Wetaskiwin, 10,071 . . C 4
- Whitecourt, 5,737 . . B 3

★ Population of metropolitan area, including suburbs.

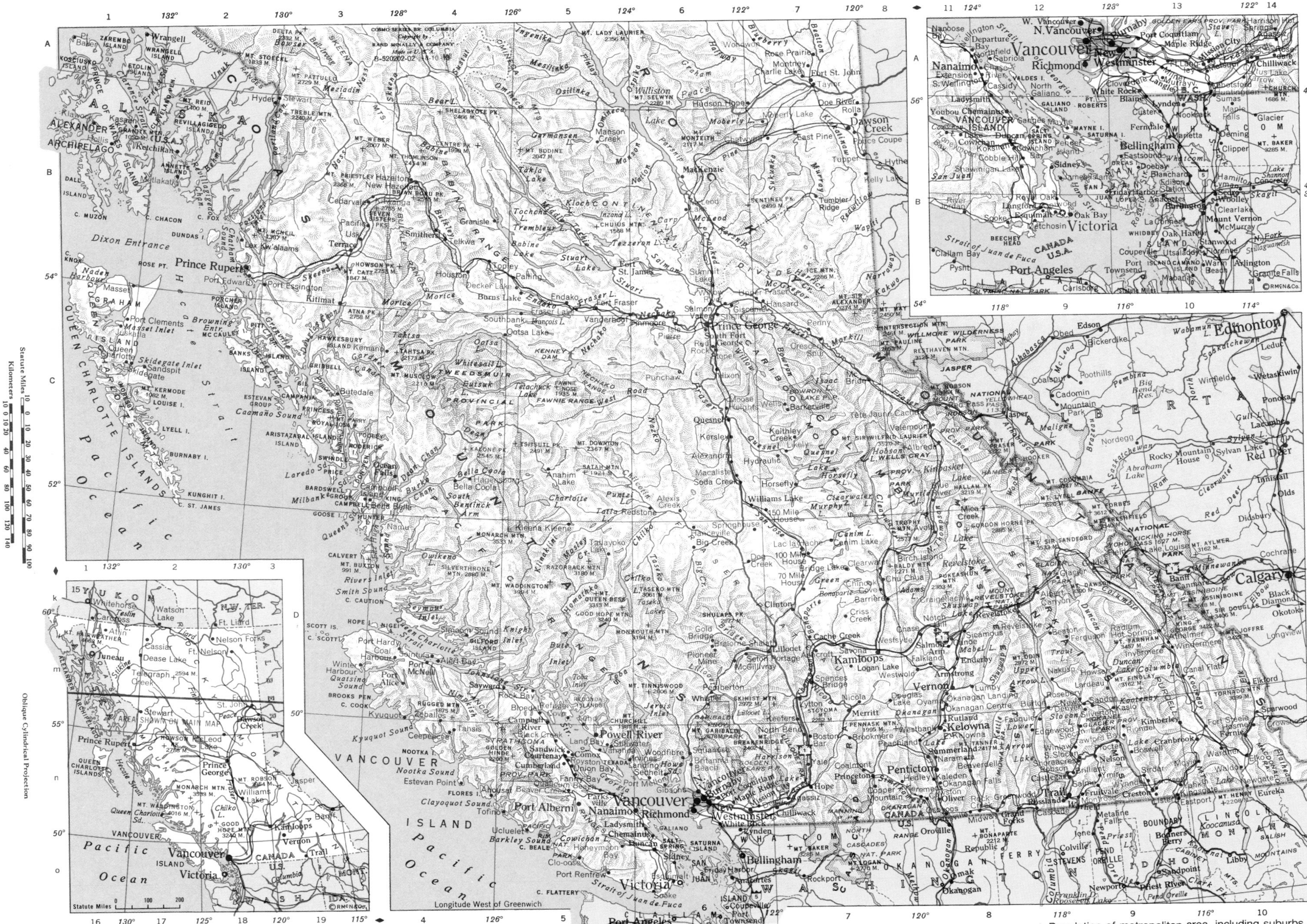

British Columbia

1986 CENSUS

Armstrong, 2,706 .... D 8
Ashcroft, 1,914 ...... D 7
Black Creek, 1,972 .... E 5
Burnaby, 145,161 .... E 6
Castlegar, 6,385 ...... E 9
Chetwynd, 2,774 ...... B 7
Chilliwack, 41,337 (50,288★) .... E 7
Clearwater, 1,375 .... D 7
Colwood, 11,546 ...... h12
Comox, 6,873 .... E 5
Courtenay, 9,631 (37,553★) .... E 5
Cranbrook, 15,893 .... E10
Creston, 4,098 .... E 9
Dawson Creek, 10,544 B 7
Duncan, 4,039 (24,062★) .... E 6
Elkford, 3,187 .... D10
Esquimalt, 15,972 .... E 6
Fernie, 5,188 .... E10
Fort Nelson, 3,729 .... m18
Fort Saint.John, 13,355 A 7
Gibsons, 2,675 ...... E 6
Golden, 3,584 .... D 9
Grand Forks, 3,282 .... E 8
Hope, 3,046 .... E 7
Kamloops, 61,773 .... D 7
Kelowna, 61,213 (89,730★) .... E 8
Kimberley, 6,732 ...... E 9
Kitimat, 11,196 ...... B 3
Ladysmith, 4,393 ...... E 6
Lake Cowichan, 2,170 .. g11
Langley, 16,557 ...... f13
MacKenzie, 5,542 .... B 6
Matsqui, 51,449 (88,420★) f13
Merritt, 6,180 .... D 7
Nanaimo, 49,029 (60,420★) .... E 5
Nelson, 8,113 .... E 9
New Westminster, 39,972 .... E 6
North Vancouver, 35,698 .... E 6
Oak Bay, 17,065 ...... h12
One Hundred Mile House, 1,692 .... D 7
Parksville, 5,828 ...... E 5
Penticton, 23,588 (38,966★) .... E 8
Port Alberni, 18,241 (26,134★) .... E 5
Port Coquitlam, 29,115 E 6
Powell River, 12,440 (18,374★) .... E 5
Prince George, 67,621 C 6
Prince Rupert, 15,755 (17,581★) .... B 2
Qualicum Beach, 3,410 E 5
Quesnel, 8,358 (23,264★) .... C 6
Revelstoke, 8,279 .... D 8
Richmond, 108,492 .... E 6
Rossland, 3,472 ...... E 9
Sidney, 8,982 .... E 6
Smithers, 4,713 ...... B 4
Sparwood, 4,540 ...... E10
Summerland, 7,755 .... E 8
Terrace, 10,532 (17,390★) .... B 3
Trail, 7,948 (20,257★) .. E 9
Tumbler Ridge, 4,540 .. B 7
Vancouver, 431,147 (1,380,729★) ...... E 6
Vanderhoof, 3,505 .... C 5
Vernon, 20,241 (42,802★) .... D 8
Victoria, 66,303 (255,547★) .... E 6
West Vancouver, 36,266 f12
White Rock, 14,387 .... E 6
Williams Lake, 10,280 (33,556★) .... C 6

★ Population of metropolitan area, including suburbs.

Manitoba

Manitoba

1986 CENSUS

Altona, 2,958 ...... E 3
Arborg, 1,018 ...... D 3
Ashern, 620 .... D 2
Beausejour, 2,535 .. D 3
Birch River, 509 .... C 1
Birtle, 850 .... D 1
Boissevain, 1,572 .... E 1
Brandon, 38,708 .... E 2
Camperville, 588 .... D 1
Carberry, 1,544 .... E 2
Carman, 2,500 ...... E 2
Churchill, 1,109 ...... f 9
Cranberry Portage, 849 .... B 1
Cross Lake, 580 .... B 3
Crystal City, 487 .... E 2
Dauphin, 8,875 .... D 1
Deloraine, 1,134 .... E 1
Duck Bay, 559 ...... C 1
Easterville, 675 .... C 2
East Selkirk, 572 .... D 3
Elkhorn, 534 .... E 1
Emerson, 725 ...... E 3
Erickson, 565 ...... D 2
Flin Flon, 7,591 (9,211★) .... B 1
Gilbert Plains, 816 .. D 1
Gillam, 1,909 ...... A 4
Gimli, 1,681 .... D 3
Gladstone, 951 ..... D 2
Glenboro, 719 ..... E 2
Grandview, 941 .... D 1
Gretna, 503 .... E 3
Grunthal, 639 ...... E 3
Hamiota, 815 ...... D 1
Hartney, 523 .... E 1
Killarney, 2,318 .... E 2
Lac du Bonnet, 1,021 D 3
Leaf Rapids, 1,950 .. A 1
Lorette, 1,169 ...... E 3
Lundar, 562 .... D 2
MacGregor, 854 .... E 2
Manitou, 856 ...... E 2
McCreary, 578 ...... D 2
Melita, 1,239 ...... E 1
Minitonas, 559 ...... C 1
Minnedosa, 2,520 .. D 2
Moose Lake, 541 .... C 1
Morden, 5,004 ...... E 2
Morris, 1,613 ...... E 3
Neepawa, 3,314 .... D 2
Niverville, 1,452 .... E 3
Norway House, 633 .. C 3
Notre Dame de Lourdes, 628 .... E 2
Pilot Mound, 819 .... E 2
Pine Falls, 831 ...... D 3
Plum Coulee, 677 .. E 3
Portage la Prairie, 13,198 .... E 2
Powerview, 724 .... D 3
Reston, 616 .... E 1
Rivers, 1,157 ...... D 1
Riverton, 635 ...... D 3
Roblin, 1,913 ...... D 1
Rossburn, 664 ...... D 1
Russell, 1,669 ...... D 1
Saint Adolphe, 1,059 E 3
Sainte Anne-des-Chênes, 1,402 .... E 3
Saint Claude, 610 .. E 2
Saint Jean Baptiste, 571 .... E 3
Saint Malo, 742 .... E 3
Saint Pierre-Jolys, 912 .... E 3
Sainte Rose du Lac, 1,030 .... D 2
Selkirk, 10,013 ...... D 3
Shoal Lake, 832 .... D 1
Snow Lake, 1,837 .. B 1
Somerset, 534 ...... E 2
Souris, 1,751 ...... E 1
South Indian Lake, 743 .... A 2
Steinbach, 7,473 .... E 3
Stonewall, 2,349 .... D 3
Swan River, 3,946 .. C 1
Teulon, 953 .... D 3
The Pas, 6,283 .... C 1
Thompson, 14,701 .. B 3
Treherne, 762 ...... E 2
Virden, 3,054 ...... E 1
Wabowden, 571 .... B 2
Wawanesa, 502 .... E 2
Winkler, 5,926 ...... E 3
Winnipeg, 594,551 (625,304★) ...... E 3
Winnipeg Beach, 548 D 3
Winnipegosis, 832 .. D 2

★ Population of metropolitan area, including suburbs.

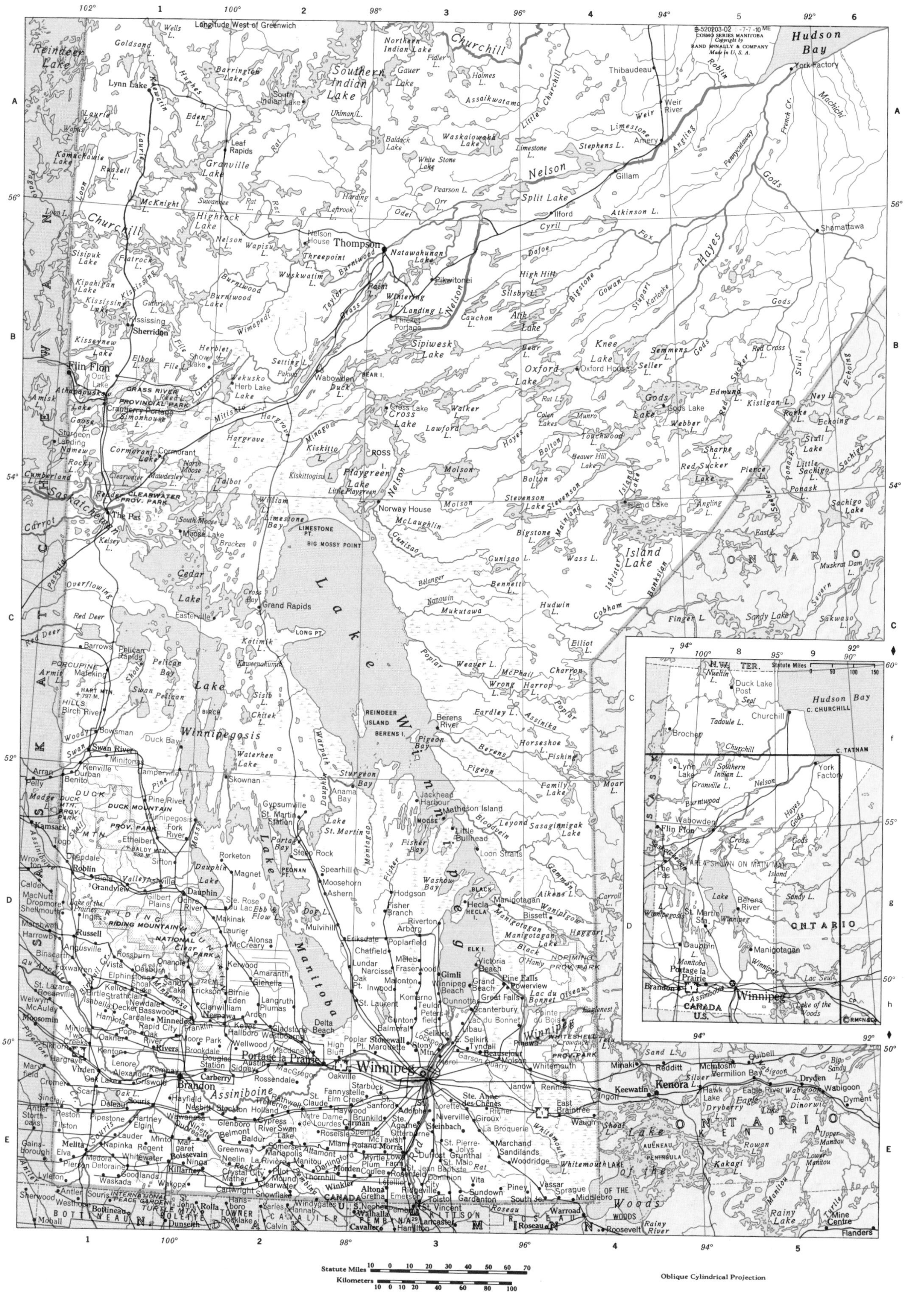

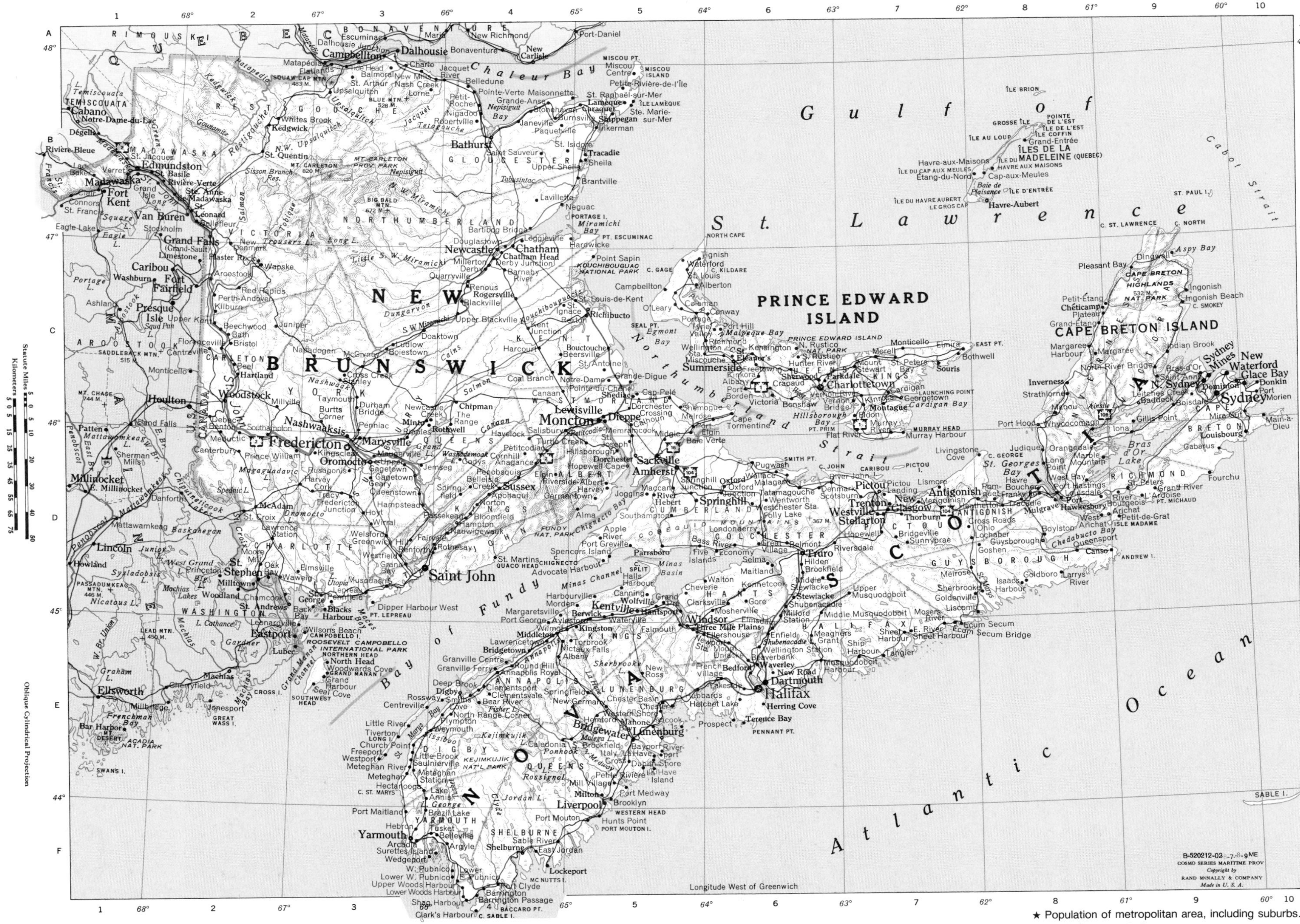

★ Population of metropolitan area, including suburbs.

New Brunswick

1986 CENSUS

Bathurst, 14,683 (34,895★)	B 4
Blacks Harbour, 1,224	D 3
Bouctouche, 2,420	C 5
Campbellton, 9,077 (17,418★)	A 3
Caraquet, 4,493	B 5
Chatham, 6,218	B 4
Dalhousie, 5,363	A 3
Dieppe, 9,084	C 5
Edmundston, 11,497 (22,614★)	B 1
Fairvale, 4,660	D 4
Fredericton, 44,352 (65,768★)	D 3
Grand Bay, 3,319	D 3
Grand Falls (Grand-Sault), 6,209	B 2
Hampton, 3,405	D 4
Minto, 3,197	C 3
Moncton, 55,468 (102,084★)	C 5
Newcastle, 5,804	C 4
Oromocto, 9,656	D 3
Sackville, 5,470	D 5
Saint Basile, 3,306	B 1
Saint Jacques, 2,310	B 1
Saint John, 76,381 (121,265★)	D 3
Saint Quentin, 2,264	B 2
Saint Stephen, 5,032	D 2
Shediac, 4,370	C 5
Shippegan, 2,801	B 5
Sussex, 4,114	D 4
Tracadie, 2,444	B 5
Woodstock, 4,549	C 2

Nova Scotia

1986 CENSUS

Amherst, 9,671	D 5
Antigonish, 5,291	D 8
Bedford, 8,010	E 6
Berwick, 2,058	D 5
Bridgewater, 6,617	E 5
Canso, 1,285	D 8
Chéticamp, 984	C 8
Dartmouth, 65,243	E 6
Digby, 2,525	E 4
Dominion, 2,754	C 9
Enfield, 1,775	E 6
Glace Bay, 20,467	C10
Halifax, 113,577 (295,990★)	E 6
Kentville, 5,208	D 5
Liverpool, 3,295	E 5
Lunenburg, 2,972	E 5
New Glasgow, 10,022 (38,737★)	D 7
New Waterford, 8,326	C 9
North Sydney, 7,472	C 9
Pictou, 4,413	D 7
Port Hawkesbury, 3,869	D 8
Springhill, 4,712	D 5
Stellarton, 5,259	D 7
Sydney, 27,754 (119,470★)	C 9
Sydney Mines, 8,063	C 9
Trenton, 3,083	D 7
Truro, 12,124 (41,516★)	D 6
Westville, 4,271	D 7
Windsor, 3,665	E 5
Wolfville, 3,277	D 5
Yarmouth, 7,617	F 3

Prince Edward Island

1986 CENSUS

Charlottetown, 15,776 (53,868★)	C 6
Parkdale, 2,065	C 6
Saint Eleanor's, 3,743	C 6
Sherwood, 5,769	C 6
Summerside, 8,020 (15,614★)	C 6

Newfoundland and Labrador

1986 CENSUS

Arnold's Cove, 1,117 E 4
Badger, 1,151 . . . . . . D 3
Baie Verte, 2,049 . . . . D 3
Bay Bulls, 1,114 . . . . E 5
Bay Roberts, 4,446 . . E 5
Bishop's Falls, 4,213 D 4
Bonavista, 4,605 . . . . D 5
Botwood, 3,916 . . . . . D 4
Buchans, 1,281 . . . . . D 3
Burgeo, 2,582 . . . . . . E 3
Burin, 2,892 . . . . E 4
Burnt Islands, 1,042 E 2
Carbonear, 5,337 (13,082★) . . . . E 5
Carmanville, 987 . . . . D 4
Cartwright, 674 . . . . B 3
Catalina, 1,211 . . . . . . D 5
Channel-Port-aux-Basques, 5,901 . . E 2
Clarenville, 2,967 . . . . D 4
Conception Bay South, 15,531 . . . . E 5
Corner Brook, 22,719 (33,730★) . . . . D 3
Cox's Cove, 999 . . . . D 2
Deer Lake, 4,233 . . . . D 3
Dunville, 1,833 . . . . . . E 5
Durrell, 1,060 . . . . . . D 4
Englee, 1,012 . . . . C 3
Fogo, 1,153 . . . . D 4
Fortune, 2,370 . . . . . . E 4
Gambo, 2,723 . . . . . . D 4
Gander, 10,207 . . . . D 4
Glenwood, 1,038 . . . . D 4
Glovertown, 2,184 . . D 4
Grand Bank, 3,732 . . E 4
Grand Falls, 9,121 (25,612★) . . . . D 4
Hampden, 875 . . . . . . D 3
Happy Valley-Goose Bay, 7,248 . . . . B 1
Harbour Breton, 2,432 . . . . E 4
Harbour Grace, 3,053 E 5
Hare Bay, 1,436 . . . . D 4
Hermitage, 831 . . . . E 4
Isle-aux-Morts, 1,203 E 2
Joe Batt's Arm [-Barr'd Islands-Shoal Bay], 1,232 . . . . D 4
King's Point, 923 . . . . D 3
Labrador City, 8,664 (11,301★) . . . . h 8
Lark Harbour, 829 . . D 2
La Scie, 1,429 . . . . . . D 4
Lawn, 1,015 . . . . E 4
Lewisporte, 3,978 . . D 4
Lourdes, 937 . . . . . . D 2
Marystown, 6,660 . . E 4
Milltown [-Head of Bay d'Espoir], 1,276 . . E 4
Mount Pearl, 20,293 E 5
Musgrave Harbour, 1,527 . . . . D 5
Nain, 1,018 . . . . g 9
New Harbour, 957 . . E 5
Norris Arm, 1,127 . . D 4
Norris Point, 1,010 . . D 3
Pasadena, 3,268 . . . . D 3
Placentia, 2,016 . . . . . E 5
Point Leamington, 850 . . . . D 4
Port au Port [West-Aguathuna-Felix Cove], 842 . . . . D 2
Pouch Cove, 1,576 . . E 5
Ramea, 1,380 . . . . . . E 3
Robert's Arm, 1,111 D 4
Rocky Harbour, 1,268 D 3
Roddickton, 1,223 . . C 3
Rose-Blanche [-Harbour le Cou], 967 . . . . E 2
Saint Alban's, 1,780 E 4
Saint Anthony, 3,182 C 4
Saint George's, 1,852 D 2
Saint John's, 96,216 (161,901★) . . . . . . E 5
Saint Lawrence, 1,841 . . . . E 4
Shoal Harbour, 1,049 D 4
Spaniard's Bay, 2,190 E 5
Springdale, 3,555 . . . . D 3
Stephenville, 7,994 . . D 2
Stephenville Crossing, 2,252 . . . . D 2
Summerford, 1,169 . . D 4
Torbay, 3,730 . . . . . . E 5
Trepassey, 1,460 . . . . E 5
Twillingate, 1,506 . . . . D 4
Upper Island Cove, 2,055 . . . . E 5
Victoria, 1,895 . . . . . . E 5
Wabana (Bell Island), 4,057 . . . . E 5
Wabush, 2,637 . . . . . . h 8
Wesleyville, 1,208 . . D 5
Whitbourne, 1,151 . . E 5
Windsor, 5,545 . . . . D 4
Witless Bay, 1,022 . . E 5

★ Population of metropolitan area, including suburbs.

Statute Miles 5 0 5 10 20 30 40 50 60
Kilometers 5 0 5 10 20 30 40 50 60 70 80

Lambert Conformal Conic Projection

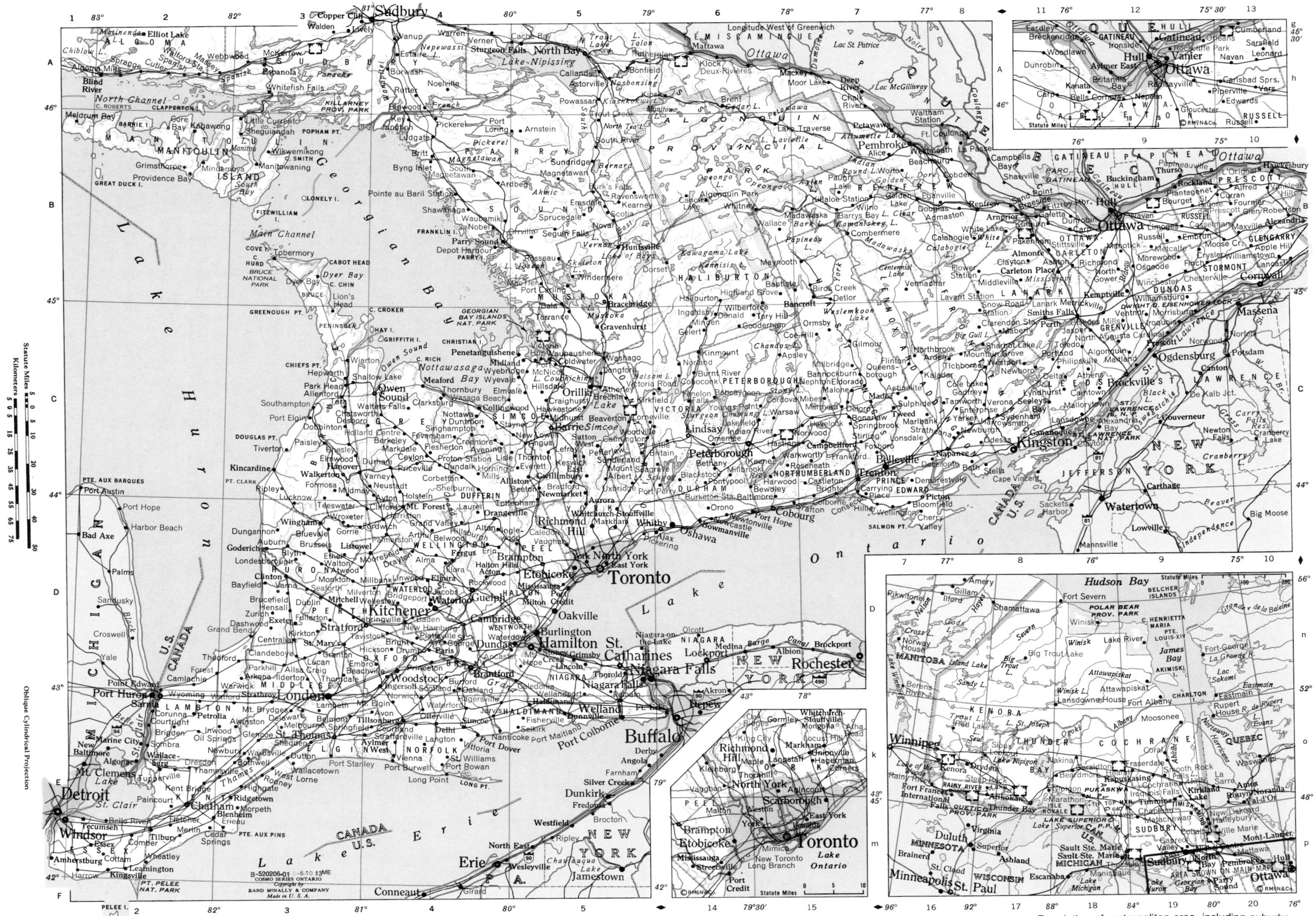

Ontario

1986 CENSUS

Ajax, 36,550 . . . . D 6
Barrie, 48,287
(67,703★) . . . . C 5
Belleville, 36,041
(87,530★) . . . . C 7
Brampton, 188,498 . . . . D 5
Brantford, 76,146
(90,521★) . . . . D 4
Brockville, 20,880
(37,115★) . . . . C 9
Burlington, 116,675 . . . . D 5
Caledon, 29,666 . . . . D 5
Cambridge, 79,920 . . . . D 4
Chatham, 42,211 . . . . . . E 2
Cornwall, 46,425
(51,719★) B10
East York, 101,085 . . . . D 5
Etobicoke, 302,973 . . . . D 5
Gloucester, 89,810 . . . . h12
Guelph, 78,235
(85,962★) . . . . D 4
Haileybury, 4,820
(14,781★) p20
Haldimand, 17,701 . . . . E 5
Halton Hills, 35,570 . . . . D 5
Hamilton, 306,728
(557,029★) . . . . D 5
Kanata, 27,519 . . . . . . B 9
Kingston, 55,050
(122,350★) . . . . C 8
Kitchener, 150,604
(311,195★) . . . . D 4
Lindsay, 14,455
(17,913★) . . . . C 6
London, 269,140
(342,302★) . . . . E 3
Markham, 114,597 . . . . D 5
Midland, 12,092
(35,003★) . . . . C 5
Milton, 32,037 . . . . D 5
Mississauga, 374,005 . . D 5
Nepean, 95,490 . . . . . . B 9
Newcastle, 34,073 . . . . D 6
Newmarket, 34,923 . . . . C 5
Niagara Falls, 72,107 . . D 5
North Bay, 50,623
(57,422★) . . . . A 5
North York, 556,297 . . D 5
Oakville, 87,107 . . . . . . D 5
Orillia, 24,077 (31,252★) C 5
Oshawa, 123,651
(203,543★) . . . . D 6
Ottawa, 300,763
(819,263★) . . . . B 9
Owen Sound, 19,804
(27,364★) . . . . C 4
Peterborough, 61,049
(87,083★) . . . . C 6
Pickering, 48,959 . . . . . D 5
Port Colborne, 18,281 . . E 5
Richmond Hill, 46,766 . . D 5
Saint Catharines, 123,455
(343,258★) . . . . D 5
Sarnia, 49,033
(85,700★) . . . . E 2
Sault Sainte Marie, 80,905
(84,617★) p18
Scarborough, 484,676 m15
Stoney Creek, 43,554 . . D 5
Stratford, 26,451 . . . . . . D 3
Sudbury, 88,717
(148,877★) . . . . A 4
Thunder Bay, 112,272
(122,217★) o17
Timmins, 46,657 . . . . . . o19
Toronto, 612,289
(3,427,168★) . . . . . . D 5
Vaughan, 65,058 . . . . . . D 5
Waterloo, 58,718 . . . . . . D 4
Welland, 45,054 . . . . . . E 5
Whitby, 45,819 . . . . D 6
Windsor, 193,111
(253,988★) . . . . E 1
Woodstock, 26,386 . . . . D 4
York, 135,401 . . . . D 5

★ Population of metropolitan area, including suburbs.

Quebec

1986 CENSUS

Alma, 25,923 (29,977★) A 6
Ancienne-Lorette, 13,747 C 6
Anjou, 36,916 p19
Aylmer East, 28,976 D 2
Baie-Comeau, 26,244 (33,047★) k13
Beaconsfield, 19,301 q19
Beauport, 62,869 n17
Boucherville, 31,116 D 4
Brossard, 57,441 q20
Cap-de-la-Madeleine, 32,800 C 5
Charlesbourg, 68,996 n17
Châteauguay, 37,865 D 4
Chicoutimi, 61,083 (158,468★) A 6
Drummondville, 36,020 (56,283★) D 5
Gaspé, 17,350 k14
Gatineau, 81,244 D 2
Granby, 38,508 (51,176★) D 5
Grand-Mère, 14,582 C 5
Hull, 58,722 D 2
Joliette, 16,845 (34,897★) C 4
Jonquière, 58,467 A 6
Lachine, 34,906 D 4
Lachute, 11,586 D 3
LaSalle, 75,621 q19
La Tuque, 10,723 (13,468★) B 5
Laval, 284,164 D 4
Lévis, 18,310 C 6
Longueuil, 125,441 D 4
Magog, 13,530 (18,738★) D 5
Mascouche, 21,285 D 4
Matane, 13,243 (15,361★) k13
Montréal, 1,015,420 (2,921,357★) D 4
Montréal-Nord, 90,303 p19
Outremont, 23,080 p19
Pierrefonds, 39,605 q19
Pointe-Claire, 26,026 D 4
Québec, 164,580 (603,267★) C 6
Repentigny, 40,778 D 4
Rimouski, 29,672 (46,210★) A 9
Rivière-du-Loup, 13,321 (22,471★) B 8
Rouyn, 17,319 (36,495★) k11
Saint-Eustache, 32,226 D 4
Sainte-Foy, 69,615 n17
Saint-Hubert, 66,218 q20
Saint-Hyacinthe, 38,603 (48,303★) D 5
Saint-Jean-sur-Richelieu, 34,745 (59,958★) D 4
Saint-Jérôme, 23,316 (44,048★) D 3
Saint-Laurent, 67,002 p19
Salaberry-de-Valleyfield, 27,942 (38,797★) D 3
Sept-Îles (Seven Islands), 25,637 (28,050★) h13
Shawinigan, 21,412 (61,965★) C 5
Sherbrooke, 74,438 (129,960★) D 6
Sorel, 19,522 (46,096★) C 4
Terrebonne, 31,310 D 4
Thetford Mines, 18,561 (31,940★) C 6
Trois-Rivières, 50,122 (128,888★) C 5
Verdun, 60,246 q19
Victoriaville, 21,587 (38,003★) C 6
Ville Saint-Georges, 11,723 (21,022★) C 7

★ Population of metropolitan area, including suburbs.

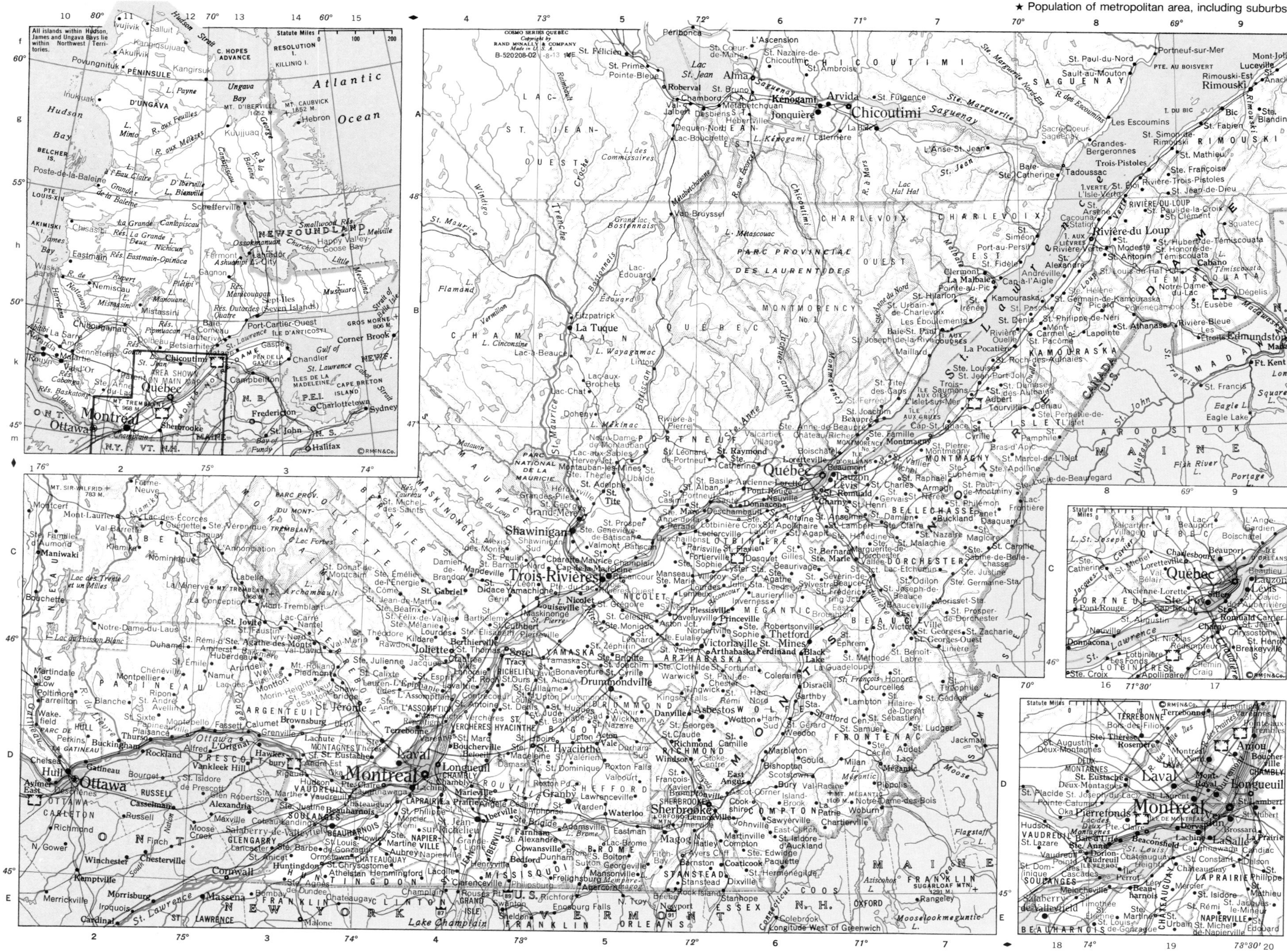

Statute Miles 5 0 5 10 20 30 40
Kilometers 5 0 5 15 25 35 45 55

Oblique Cylindrical Projection

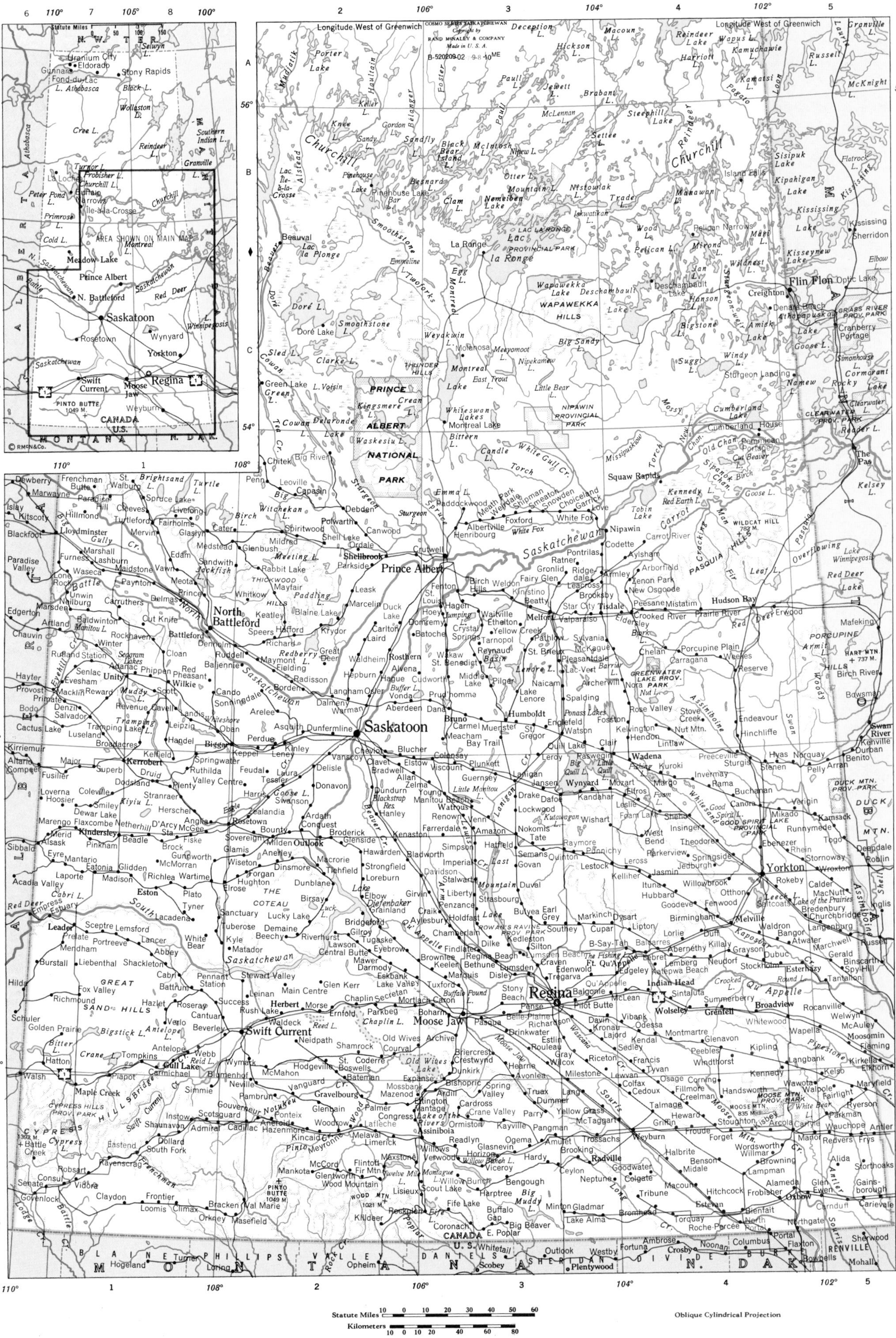

Saskatchewan

1986 CENSUS

Assiniboia, 3,001 .... H 2
Balgonie, 901 ...... G 3
Battleford, 3,833 .... E 1
Bienfait, 833........ H 4
Biggar, 2,626 ...... E 1
Birch Hills, 947...... E 3
Broadview, 837 .... G 4
Buffalo Narrows, 1,183 .... m 7
Canora, 2,602 ...... F 4
Carlyle, 1,172 ...... H 4
Carnduff, 1,090 .... H 5
Carrot River, 1,101 .. D 4
Churchbridge, 1,035 G 5
Coronach, 1,006 ..... H 3
Creighton, 1,620 .... C 5
Cudworth, 873 ...... E 3
Cumberland House, 862 .... D 4
Dalmeny, 1,328 .... E 2
Davidson, 1,183 ..... F 3
Delisle, 986 .... F 2
Esterhazy, 3,083 .... G 4
Estevan, 10,161 ..... H 4
Eston, 1,383 .... F 1
Foam Lake, 1,535 .. F 4
Fort Qu'Appelle, 1,915 .... G 4
Gravelbourg, 1,305 .. H 2
Grenfell, 1,274 ...... G 4
Gull Lake, 1,164 .... G 1
Herbert, 964 .... G 2
Hudson Bay, 2,133 .. E 4
Humboldt, 5,089 ..... E 3
Île-à-la-Crosse, 1,030 m 7
Indian Head, 1,886 .. G 4
Ituna, 902 .... F 4
Kamsack, 2,565 .... F 5
Kelvington, 1,084 .... E 4
Kerrobert, 1,288 ..... F 1
Kindersley, 4,912 .... F 1
Kipling, 1,033 ...... G 4
La Loche, 1,623 ..... m 7
Langenburg, 1,371 .. G 5
Langham, 1,193 ..... E 2
Lanigan, 1,698 ...... F 3
La Ronge, 2,696 .... B 3
Lashburn, 873 .... D 1
Leader, 1,130 .... G 1
Lloydminster (Alta. and Sask.), 17,356 .... D 1
Lumsden, 1,369 ..... G 3
Macklin, 1,131 ...... E 1
Maidstone, 1,112..... D 1
Maple Creek, 2,452.. H 1
Meadow Lake, 3,976 n 7
Melfort, 6,078 .... E 3
Melville, 5,123 ...... G 4
Moose Jaw, 35,073 (37,219★) .... G 3
Moosomin, 2,557.... G 5
Naicam, 902 .... E 3
Nipawin, 4,588 ...... D 4
North Battleford, 14,876 (18,709★) .... E 1
Outlook, 2,137 ...... F 2
Oxbow, 1,229 .... H 4
Pilot Butte, 1,387.... G 3
Porcupine Plain, 918 E 4
Preeceville, 1,272.... F 4
Prince Albert, 33,686 (40,841★) .... D 3
Radville, 960 .... H 3
Redvers, 924 .... H 5
Regina, 175,064 (186,521★) .... G 3
Rocanville, 920 ..... G 5
Rosetown, 2,663 .... F 1
Rosthern, 1,594 ..... E 2
Saskatoon, 177,641 (200,665★) .... E 2
Shaunavon, 2,153 .. H 1
Shellbrook, 1,238.... D 2
Spiritwood, 1,025 .. D 2
Strasbourg, 826 ..... F 3
Swift Current, 15,666 G 2
Tisdale, 3,184 .... E 3
Unity, 2,471 .... E 1
Wadena, 1,602...... F 4
Wakaw, 1,010 .... E 3
Warman, 2,455 ..... E 2
Watrous, 1,953 ..... F 3
Watson, 964 .... E 3
Weyburn, 10,153 .... H 4
Whitewood, 1,107 ... G 4
Wilkie, 1,526 .... E 1
Wolseley, 896 .... G 4
Wynyard, 2,079 ..... F 3
Yorkton, 15,574 (18,525★) .... F 4

★ Population of metropolitan area, including suburbs.

United States of America

Akron, 223,019 ('90)...C10
ALABAMA..................E 9
ALASKA....................M19
Albany, 101,082 ('90)..C12
Albuquerque, 384,736 ('90)......................... D 5
Amarillo, 157,615 ('90)D 6
Anchorage, 226,338 ('90).........................M20
Annapolis, 33,187 ('90)......................... D11
ARIZONA...................E 4
ARKANSAS................E 8
Atlanta, 394,017 ('90)..E10
Augusta, 21,325 ('90). C13
Austin, 465,622 ('90)...E 7
Baltimore, 736,014 ('90)......................... D11
Baton Rouge, 219,531 ('90).........................E 8
Billings, 81,151 ('90)....B 5
Birmingham, 265,968 ('90).........................E 9
Bismarck, 49,256 ('90)B 6
Boise, 125,738 ('90)....C 3
Boston, 574,283 ('90). C12
Buffalo, 328,123 ('90). C11
CALIFORNIA..............D 2
Carson City, 40,443 ('90)......................... D 3
Charleston, 57,287 ('90)......................... D10
Charleston, 80,414 ('90).........................E11
Charlotte, 395,934 ('90)......................... D10
Chattanooga, 152,466 ('90)......................... D 9
Cheyenne, 50,008 ('90)......................... C 6
Chicago, 2,783,726 ('90)......................... C 9
Cincinnati, 364,040 ('90)......................... D10
Cleveland, 505,616 ('90)......................... C10
COLORADO...............D 5
Colorado Springs, 281,140 ('90)......................... D 6
Columbia, 98,052 ('90)E10
Columbus, 178,681 ('90).........................E10
Columbus, 632,910 ('90)......................... D10
Concord, 36,006 ('90). C12
CONNECTICUT..........C12
Dallas, 1,006,877 ('90) E 7
DELAWARE...............D11
Denver, 467,610 ('90). D 6
Des Moines, 193,187 ('90)......................... C 8
Detroit, 1,027,974 ('90)......................... C10
Dover, 27,630 ('90).....D11
El Paso, 515,342 ('90).E 5
FLORIDA....................F10
Fort Wayne, 173,072 ('90)......................... C 9
Fort Worth, 447,619 ('90).........................E 7
Frankfort, 25,968 ('90)D10
Fresno, 354,202 ('90)..D 3
GEORGIA...................E10
Grand Rapids, 189,126 ('90)......................... C 9
Harrisburg, 52,376 ('90)......................... C11
Hartford, 139,739 ('90)......................... C12
Helena, 24,569 ('90)....B 4
Houston, 1,630,553 ('90).........................F 7
IDAHO.......................C 4
ILLINOIS....................C 9
INDIANA....................C 9
Indianapolis, 731,327 ('90)......................... D 9
IOWA.........................C 8
Jackson, 196,637 ('90)E 8
Jacksonville, 635,230 ('90).........................E10
Jefferson City, 35,481 ('90)......................... D 8
Juneau, 26,751 ('90)...N21
KANSAS....................D 7
Kansas City, 435,146 ('90)......................... D 8
KENTUCKY................D 9
Knoxville, 165,121 ('90)......................... D10
Las Vegas, 258,295 ('90)......................... D 3
Lincoln, 191,972 ('90)..C 7
Little Rock, 175,795 ('90).........................E 8
Los Angeles, 3,485,398 ('90).........................E 3
LOUISIANA.................E 8
Louisville, 269,063 ('90)......................... D 9
Madison, 191,262 ('90)......................... C 9
MAINE........................B13
MARYLAND...............D11

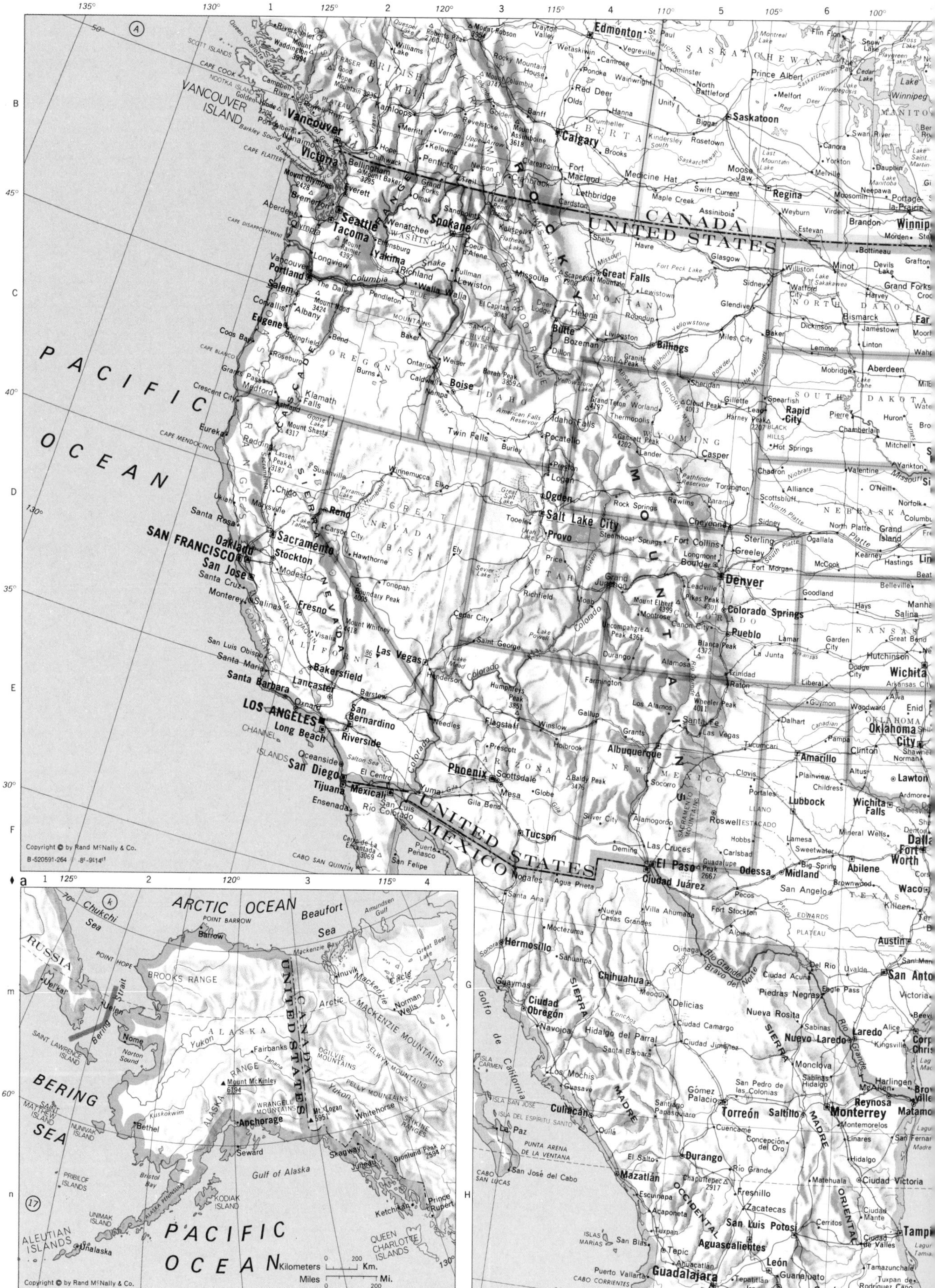

Kilometers 0 200 400 600 Km.
Miles 0 200 400 600 Mi.
1:16 000 000

MASSACHUSETTS.....C12
Memphis, 610,337 ('90)..........D 8
Miami, 358,548 ('90)....F10
MICHIGAN..........C10
Milwaukee, 628,088 ('90)..........C 9
Minneapolis, 368,383 ('90)..........C 8
MINNESOTA..........B 8
MISSISSIPPI..........E 9
MISSOURI..........D 8
Mobile, 196,278 ('90)...E 9
MONTANA..........B 5
Montgomery, 187,106 ('90)..........E 9
Montpelier, 8,247 ('90)C12
Nashville, 487,969 ('90)..........D 9
NEBRASKA..........C 7
NEVADA..........D 3
Newark, 275,221 ('90) C12
NEW HAMPSHIRE......C12
NEW JERSEY..........C12
NEW MEXICO..........E 5
New Orleans, 496,938 ('90)..........F 8
NEW YORK..........C11
New York, 7,322,564 ('90)..........C12
Norfolk, 261,229 ('90). D11
NORTH CAROLINA.....D11
NORTH DAKOTA........B 6
Oakland, 372,242 ('90)D 2
OHIO..........C10
OKLAHOMA..........D 7
Oklahoma City, 444,719 ('90)..........D 7
Olympia, 33,840 ('90)..B 2
Omaha, 335,795 ('90). C 7
OREGON..........C 2
PENNSYLVANIA.........C11
Philadelphia, 1,585,577 ('90)..........D11
Phoenix, 900,013 ('90) E 4
Pierre, 12,906 ('90)..... C 6
Pittsburgh, 369,879 ('90)..........C11
Portland, 64,358 ('90). C12
Providence, 160,728 ('90)..........C12
Raleigh, 207,951 ('90). D11
Rapid City, 54,523 ('90)..........C 6
Reno, 133,850 ('90).... D 3
RHODE ISLAND..........C12
Richmond, 203,056 ('90)..........D11
Rochester, 231,636 ('90)..........C11
Sacramento, 369,365 ('90)..........D 2
Saint Louis, 396,685 ('90)..........D 8
Saint Paul, 272,235 ('90)..........C 8
Saint Petersburg, 238,629 ('90)..........F10
Salem, 107,786 ('90)...C 2
Salt Lake City, 159,936 ('90)..........C 4
San Antonio, 935,933 ('90)..........F 7
San Diego, 1,110,549 ('90)..........E 3
San Francisco, 723,959 ('90)..........D 2
San Jose, 782,248 ('90)..........D 2
Santa Fe, 55,859 ('90) D 5
Savannah, 137,560 ('90)..........E10
Seattle, 516,259 ('90)..B 2
Shreveport, 198,525 ('90)..........E 8
SOUTH CAROLINA.....E10
SOUTH DAKOTA........C 7
Spokane, 177,196 ('90)..........B 3
Springfield, 105,227 ('90)..........D 9
Syracuse, 163,860 ('90)..........C11
Tacoma, 176,664 ('90)B 2
Tallahassee, 124,773 ('90)..........E10
Tampa, 280,015 ('90)..F10
TENNESSEE..........D 9
TEXAS..........E 7
Toledo, 332,943 ('90)..C10
Topeka, 119,883 ('90).D 7
Trenton, 88,675 ('90).. C12
Tulsa, 367,302 ('90).... D 7
UNITED STATES........D 7
UTAH..........D 4
VERMONT..........C12
VIRGINIA..........D11
WASHINGTON..........B 2
Washington, 606,900 ('90)..........D11
WEST VIRGINIA.........D10
Wichita, 304,011 ('90). D 7
WISCONSIN..........C 9
WYOMING..........C 5

Alabama

1990 CENSUS

Alabaster, 14,732 .. B 3
Albertville, 14,507 .. A 3
Alexander City, 14,917 .... C 4
Andalusia, 9,269 .... D 3
Anniston, 26,623 ... B 4
Arab, 6,321 .... A 3
Athens, 16,901 .... A 3
Atmore, 8,046 ...... D 2
Attalla, 6,859 ...... A 3
Auburn, 33,830 .... C 4
Bay Minette, 7,168 .. E 2
Bessemer, 33,497 .. B 3
Birmingham, 265,968 B 3
Bluff Park, 8,000('85) g 7
Boaz, 6,928 .... A 3
Brewton, 5,885 .... D 2
Center Point, 22,000('85) ...... f 7
Chickasaw, 6,649 .. E 1
Childersburg, 4,579 .. B 3
Clanton, 7,669 ...... C 3
Cullman, 13,367 .... A 3
Decatur, 48,761 .... A 3
Demopolis, 7,512.... C 2
Dothan, 53,589 .... D 4
Enterprise, 20,123 .. D 4
Eufaula, 13,220 .... D 4
Fairfield, 12,200 .. B 3
Fairhope, 8,485 .... E 2
Fayette, 4,909 ...... B 2
Florence, 36,426 .... A 2
Fort Payne, 11,838 .. A 4
Frisco City, 1,581 .. D 2
Fultondale, 6,400 .... f 7
Gadsden, 42,523 .... A 3
Gardendale, 9,251 .. B 3
Geneva, 4,681 ...... D 4
Greenville, 7,492 .... D 3
Guntersville, 7,038 .. A 3
Haleyville, 4,452 .... A 2
Hamilton, 5,787 .... A 2
Hartselle, 10,795 .... A 3
Homewood, 22,922 .. g 7
Hueytown, 15,280 .. g 6
Huntsville, 159,789 .. A 3
Irondale, 9,454 ...... f 7
Jackson, 5,819 ...... D 2
Jacksonville, 10,283 B 4
Jasper, 13,553 ...... B 2
Lanett, 8,985 ...... C 4
Leeds, 9,946 ...... B 3
Millbrook, 6,050 .... C 3
Mobile, 196,278 .... E 1
Monroeville, 6,993 .. D 2
Montgomery, 187,106 C 3
Moundville, 1,348.... C 2
Mountain Brook, 19,810 .... g 7
Muscle Shoals, 9,611 A 2
Northport, 17,366 .. B 2
Oneonta, 4,844 .... B 3
Opelika, 22,122 .... C 4
Opp, 6,985 .... D 3
Oxford, 9,362 ...... B 4
Ozark, 12,922 ...... D 4
Pelham, 9,765 ...... B 3
Pell City, 8,118 .... B 3
Phenix City, 25,312 .. C 4
Piedmont, 5,288 .... B 4
Pleasant Grove, 8,458 g 7
Prattville, 19,587 .... C 3
Prichard, 34,311 .... E 1
Rainbow City, 7,673 A 3
Roanoke, 6,362 .... B 4
Russellville, 7,812 .. A 2
Saraland, 11,751 .... E 1
Scottsboro, 13,786 .. A 3
Selma, 23,755 ...... C 2
Sheffield, 10,380 .... A 2
Spanish Fort, 3,415('80) .... E 2
Sylacauga, 12,520 .. B 3
Talladega, 18,175 .. B 3
Tallassee, 5,112 .... C 4
Tarrant, 8,046 ...... B 3
Theodore, 6,392('80) E 1
Tillmans Corner, 5,000('85) .... E 1
Troy, 13,051 ...... D 4
Tuscaloosa, 77,759 .. B 2
Tuscumbia, 8,413 .. A 2
Tuskegee, 12,257 .. C 4
Vestavia Hills, 19,749 g 7
Warrior, 3,280 ...... B 3
Wetumpka, 4,670 .. C 3

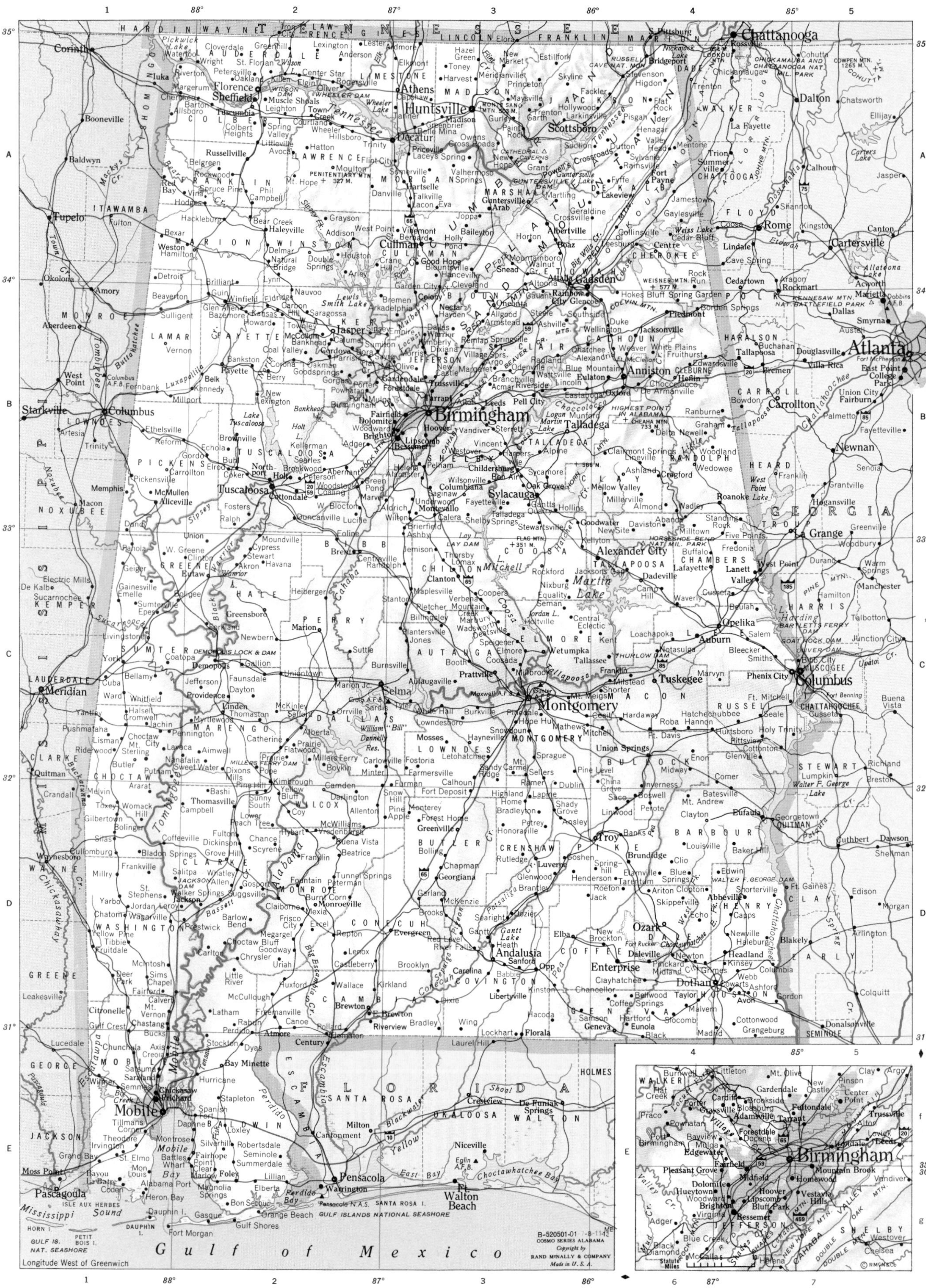

Statute Miles 5 0 5 10 20 30 40
Kilometers 5 0 5 15 25 35 45 55

Lambert Conformal Conic Projection

Alaska

1990 CENSUS

Akiachak, 400('83)	C 7
Alakanuk, 544	C 7
Anchorage, 226,338	C10
Anderson, 628	C10
Angoon, 638	D13
Aniak, 540	C 8
Barrow, 3,469	A 8
Bethel, 4,674	C 7
Big Delta, 285('80)	C10
Chevak, 598	C 6
Cold Bay, 148	E 7
College, 800('83)	B10
Cordova, 2,110	C10
Craig, 1,260	D13
Delta Junction, 652	C10
Dillingham, 2,017	D 8
Emmonak, 642	C 7
Fairbanks, 30,843	C10
Fort Yukon, 580	B10
Galena, 833	C 8
Gambell, 525	C 5
Glennallen, 511('80)	f19
Haines, 1,238	D12
Healy, 334('80)	C10
Homer, 3,660	D 9
Hoonah, 795	D12
Hooper Bay, 845	C 6
Hydaburg, 384	D13
Juneau, 26,751	D13
Kake, 700	D13
Kenai, 6,327	C 9
Ketchikan, 8,263	D13
Kiana, 385	B 7
King Cove, 451	E 7
King Salmon, 545('80)	D 8
Kipnuk, 371('80)	C 7
Klawock, 722	D13
Kodiak, 6,365	D 9
Kotlik, 461	C 7
Kotzebue, 2,751	B 7
Kwethluk, 558	C 7
Kwigillingok, 354('80)	D 7
Manokotak, 385	D 8
McGrath, 528	C 8
Metlakatla, 1,056('80)	D13
Mountain Village, 674	C 7
Nenana, 393	C10
Nikishka, 1,109('80)	g16
Ninilchik, 341('80)	C 9
Nome, 3,500	C 6
Noorvik, 531	B 7
Nulato, 359	C 8
Old Harbor, 284	D 9
Palmer, 2,866	C10
Petersburg, 3,207	D13
Pilot Station, 463	C 7
Point Hope, 639	B 6
Prudhoe Bay, 50('80)	A10
Quinhagak, 501	D 7
Saint Marys, 441	C 7
Saint Paul, 763	D 5
Sand Point, 878	D 7
Savoonga, 519	C 5
Selawik, 596	B 7
Seldovia, 316	D 9
Seward, 2,699	C10
Shishmaref, 456	B 6
Shungnak, 223	B 8
Sitka, 8,588	D12
Skagway, 692	D12
Soldotna, 3,482	g16
Stebbins, 400	C 7
Sterling, 919('80)	g16
Tanana, 345	B 9
Togiak, 613	D 7
Tok, 589('80)	C11
Tununak, 316	C 6
Unalakleet, 714	C 7
Unalaska, 3,089	E 6
Valdez, 4,068	C10
Wainwright, 492	A 8
Wasilla, 4,028	C10
Whittier, 243	C10
Wrangell, 2,479	D13
Yakutat, 534	D12

Arizona

1990 CENSUS

Ajo, 5,189('80) . . . . . E 3
Apache Junction, 18,100 . . . . m 9
Avondale, 16,169 . . . D 3
Bagdad, 2,331('80) . . C 2
Benson, 3,824 . . . . . F 5
Bisbee, 6,288 . . . . . . F 6
Black Canyon City, 850('86) . . . . C 3
Buckeye, 5,038 . . . . D 3
Bullhead City, 21,951 B 1
Camp Verde, 6,243 . . C 4
Casa Grande, 19,082 E 4
Casas Adobes, 12,155('86) . . . . . . E 5
Cashion, 3,014('80) . . m 8
Cave Creek, 2,925 . . D 4
Chandler, 90,533 . . . D 4
Chinle, 2,815('80) . . . A 6
Chino Valley, 4,837 . . C 3
Claypool, 2,362('80) D 5
Clifton, 2,840 . . . . . . D 6
Coolidge, 6,927 . . . . . E 4
Cottonwood, 5,918 . . C 3
Crane, 2,650('86) . . . . E 1
Douglas, 12,822 . . . . F 6
Eagar, 4,025 . . . . . . C 6
El Mirage, 5,001 . . . . k 8
Eloy, 7,211 . . . . E 4
Flagstaff, 45,857 . . . . B 4
Florence, 7,510 . . . . . D 4
Fort Defiance, 3,431('80) . . . . B 6
Ganado, 3,400('86) . . B 6
Gila Bend, 1,747 . . . . E 3
Gilbert, 29,188 . . . . . D 4
Glendale, 148,134 . . D 3
Globe, 6,062 . . . . . . D 5
Goodyear, 6,258 . . . . D 3
Grand Canyon, 1,348('80) . . . . A 3
Green Valley, 7,999('80) . . . . F 5
Guadalupe, 5,458 . . m 9
Holbrook, 4,686 . . . . C 5
Huachuca City, 1,782 F 5
Kayenta, 3,343('80) . . A 5
Kearny, 2,262 . . . . . . D 5
Kingman, 12,722 . . . . B 1
Lake Havasu City, 24,363 . . . . C 1
Lakeside-Pinetop, 2,422 . . . . C 6
Litchfield Park, 3,303 m 8
Mammoth, 1,845 . . . . E 5
Mesa, 288,091 . . . . . . D 4
Miami, 2,018 . . . . . . D 5
Nogales, 19,489 . . . . F 5
Oracle, 2,484('80) . . E 5
Page, 6,598 . . . . A 4
Paradise Valley, 11,671 . . . . k 9
Parker, 2,897 . . . . . . C 1
Payson, 8,377 . . . . . . C 4
Peoria, 50,618 . . . . . . D 3
Phoenix, 900,013 . . . D 3
Prescott, 26,455 . . . . C 3
Sacaton, 1,951('80) . . D 4
Safford, 7,359 . . . . . . E 6
Saint Johns, 3,294 . . C 6
San Carlos, 2,668('80) . . . . D 5
San Luis, 70('86) . . . . E 3
San Manuel, 5,443('80) . . . . E 5
Scottsdale, 130,069 D 4
Sedona, 7,720 . . . . . . C 4
Sells, 1,864('80) . . . . F 4
Show Low, 5,019 . . . C 5
Sierra Vista, 32,983 . . F 5
Snowflake, 3,679 . . . . C 5
Somerton, 5,282 . . . . E 1
South Tucson, 5,093 E 5
Sun City, 57,000 . . . . k 8
Superior, 3,468 . . . . . D 4
Surprise, 7,122 . . . . . k 8
Taylor, 2,418 . . . . . . C 5
Tempe, 141,865 . . . . D 4
Thatcher, 3,763 . . . . . E 6
Tolleson, 4,434 . . . . m 8
Tombstone, 1,220 . . F 5
Tuba City, 5,045('80) A 4
Tucson, 405,390 . . . . E 5
Twin Knolls, 5,210('86) . . . . m 9
Wickenburg, 4,515 . . D 3
Willcox, 3,122 . . . . . . E 6
Williams, 2,532 . . . . . B 3
Window Rock, 2,230('80) . . . . B 6
Winslow, 8,190 . . . . . C 5
Youngtown, 2,542 . . k 8
Yuma, 54,923 . . . . . . E 1

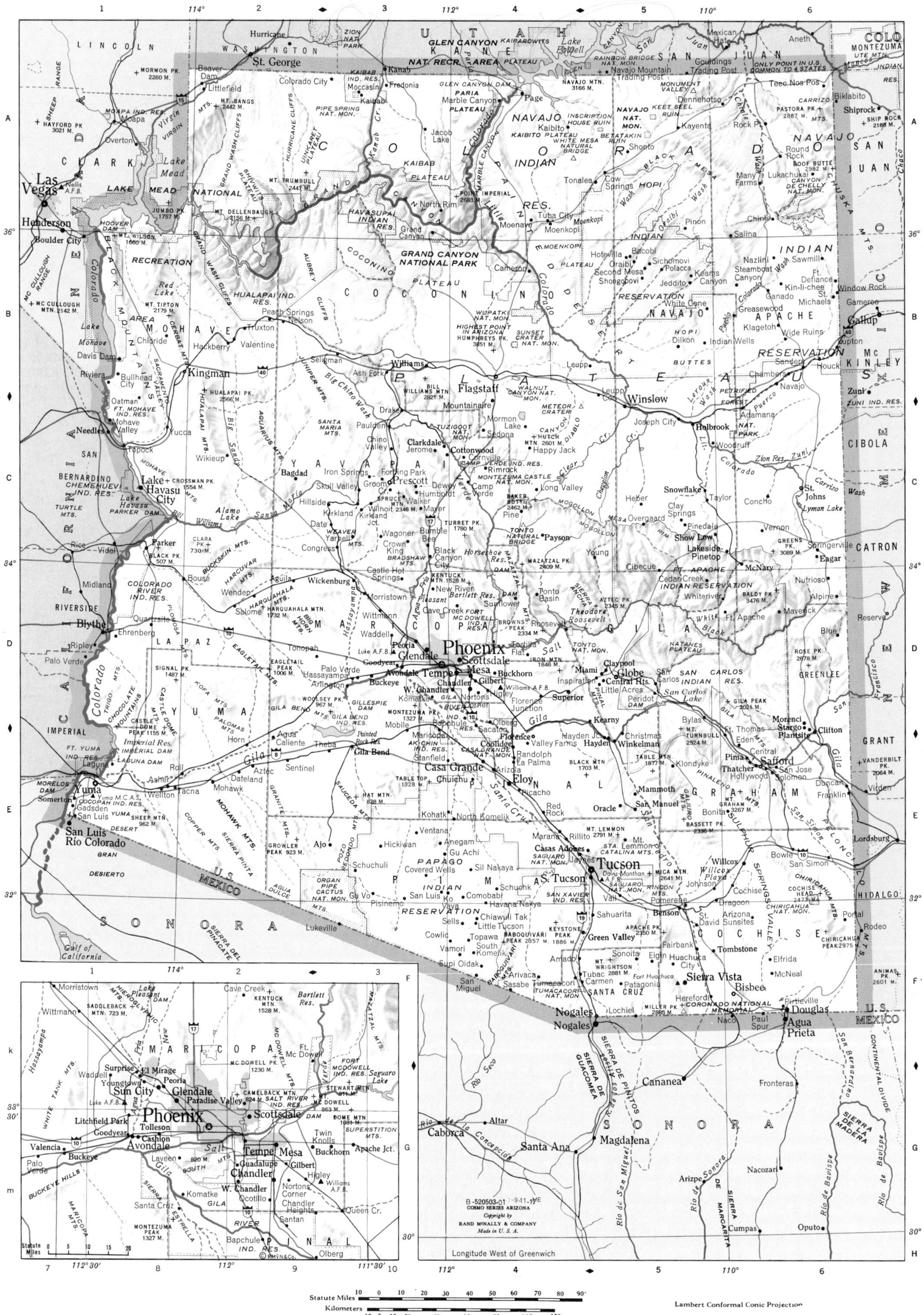

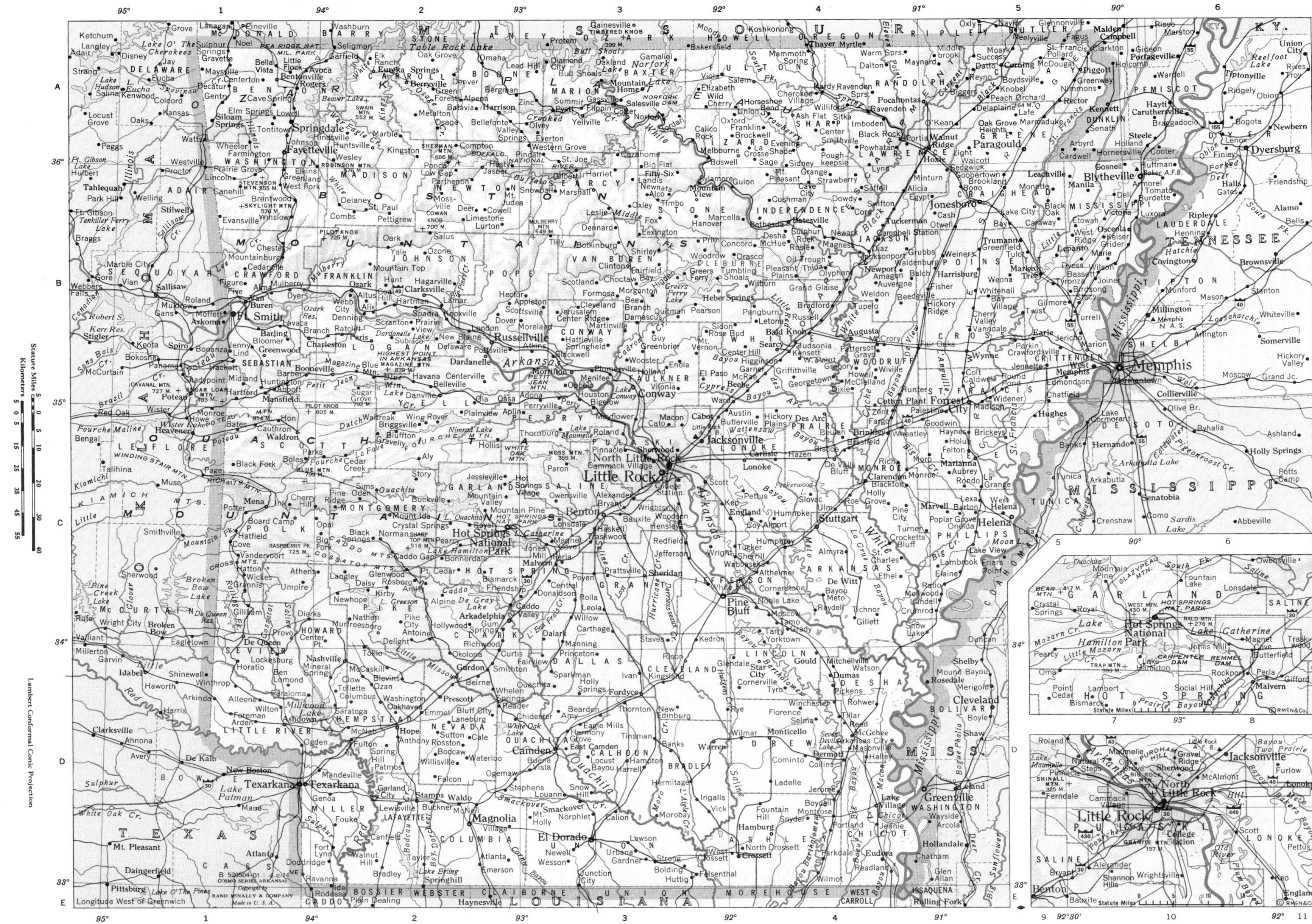

Arkansas

1990 CENSUS

Arkadelphia, 10,014 .. C 2
Ashdown, 5,150 ...... D 1
Bald Knob, 2,653 .... B 4
Barling, 4,078 .... B 1
Batesville, 9,187 ...... B 4
Beebe, 4,455 .... B 4
Benton, 18,177 ...... C 3
Bentonville, 11,257 .... A 1
Berryville, 3,212 ...... A 2
Blytheville, 22,906 .... B 6
Booneville, 3,804 ...... B 2
Brinkley, 4,234 .... C 4
Bryant, 5,269 .... C 3
Cabot, 8,319 .... C 3
Camden, 14,380 ...... D 3
Clarksville, 5,833 ...... B 2
Conway, 26,481 .... B 3
Corning, 3,323 .... A 5
Crossett, 6,282 .... D 4
Dardanelle, 3,722 .... B 2
De Queen, 4,633 ...... C 1
Dermott, 4,715 .... D 4
De Witt, 3,553 .... C 4
Dumas, 5,520 .... D 4
Earle, 3,393 .... B 5
El Dorado, 23,146 ..... D 3
Eudora, 3,155 .... D 4
Eureka Springs, 1,900 . A 2
Fayetteville, 42,099 .... A 1
Fordyce, 4,729 .... D 3
Forrest City, 13,364 .. B 5
Fort Smith, 72,798 .... B 1
Greenwood, 3,984 .... B 1
Harrisburg, 1,943 ..... B 5
Harrison, 9,922 ...... A 2
Heber Springs, 5,628 .. B 3
Helena, 7,491 .... C 5
Hope, 9,643 .... D 2
Hot Springs National Park, 32,462 .... C 2
Hoxie, 2,676 .... A 5
Jacksonville, 29,101 .. C 3
Jonesboro, 46,535 .... B 5
Lake Village, 2,791 .... D 4
Little Rock, 175,795 .. C 3
Lonoke, 4,022 .... C 4
Magnolia, 11,151 ...... D 2
Malvern, 9,256 .... C 3
Marianna, 5,910 .... C 5
Marked Tree, 3,100 .... B 5
McGehee, 4,997 ...... D 4
Mena, 5,475 .... C 1
Monticello, 8,116 ...... D 4
Morrilton, 6,551 .... B 3
Mountain Home, 9,027 A 3
Mountain View, 2,439 .. B 3
Nashville, 4,639 .... D 2
Newport, 7,459 .... B 4
North Little Rock, 61,741 .... C 3
Osceola, 8,930 .... B 6
Ozark, 3,330 .... B 2
Paragould, 18,540 .... A 5
Paris, 3,674 .... B 2
Piggott, 3,777 .... A 5
Pine Bluff, 57,140 .... C 3
Pocahontas, 6,151 ..... A 5
Prescott, 3,673 ...... D 2
Rogers, 24,692 .... A 1
Russellville, 21,260 .... B 2
Searcy, 15,180 .... B 4
Sherwood, 18,893 ..... C 3
Siloam Springs, 8,151 . A 1
Smackover, 2,232 ..... D 3
Springdale, 29,941 .... A 1
Stuttgart, 10,420 ...... C 4
Texarkana, 22,631 ..... D 1
Trumann, 6,304 .... B 5
Tuckerman, 2,020 .... B 4
Van Buren, 14,979 .... B 1
Walnut Ridge, 4,388 .. A 5
Warren, 6,455 .... D 3
West Helena, 9,695 .... C 5
West Memphis, 28,259 B 5
Wynne, 8,187 .... B 5

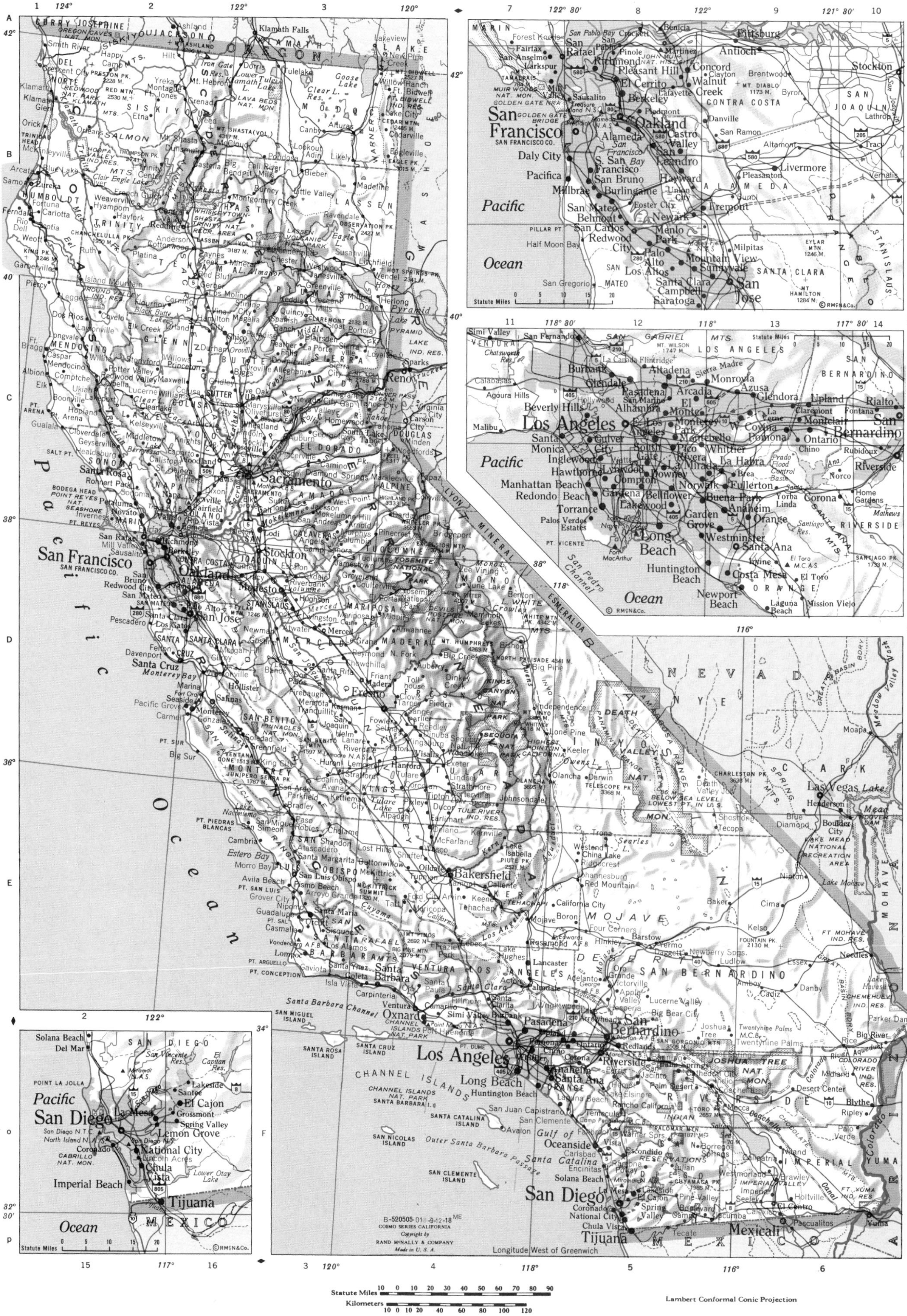

California

1990 CENSUS

Alameda, 76,459 . . . . h 8
Alhambra, 82,106 . . m12
Anaheim, 266,406 . . F 5
Antioch, 62,195 . . . . h 9
Bakersfield, 174,820 E 4
Berkeley, 102,724 . . D 2
Beverly Hills, 31,971 m12
Burbank, 93,643 . . . . E 4
Calexico, 18,633 . . . . F 6
Chico, 40,079 . . . . . . C 3
Chula Vista, 135,163 F 5
Compton, 90,454 . . . . n12
Concord, 111,348 . . h 8
Costa Mesa, 96,357 . . n13
Daly City, 92,311 . . . . h 8
Davis, 46,209 . . . . . . C 3
Downey, 91,444 . . . . n12
East Los Angeles, 126,379 . . . . m12
El Cajon, 88,693 . . . . F 5
El Centro, 31,384 . . . F 6
Escondido, 108,635 . . F 5
Eureka, 27,025 . . . . B 1
Fairfield, 77,211 . . . . C 2
Fremont, 173,339 . . D 2
Fresno, 354,202 . . . . D 4
Fullerton, 114,144 . . n13
Garden Grove, 143,050 . . . . n13
Glendale, 180,038 . . m12
Hayward, 111,498 . . h 8
Huntington Beach, 181,519 . . . . F 4
Indio, 36,793 . . . . . . F 5
Inglewood, 109,602 . . n12
Irvine, 110,330 . . . . . . n13
Lancaster, 97,291 . . E 4
Lompoc, 37,649 . . . . E 3
Long Beach, 429,433 F 4
Los Angeles, 3,485,398 . . . . E 4
Marysville, 12,324 . . C 3
Menlo Park, 28,040 . . k 8
Merced, 56,216 . . . . D 3
Modesto, 164,730 . . D 3
Monterey, 31,954 . . D 3
Napa, 61,842 . . . . . . C 2
Newport Beach, 66,643 . . . . n13
Norwalk, 94,279 . . . . n12
Oakland, 372,242 . . D 2
Oceanside, 128,398 . . F 5
Ontario, 133,179 . . . . E 5
Orange, 110,658 . . . . n13
Oxnard, 142,21 . . . . E 4
Palm Springs, 40,181 F 5
Palo Alto, 55,900 . . . D 2
Pasadena, 131,591 . . E 4
Pomona, 131,723 . . . E 5
Redding, 66,462 . . . . B 2
Redwood City, 66,072 . . . . D 2
Richmond, 87,425 . . D 2
Riverside, 226,505 . . F 5
Sacramento, 369,365 C 3
Salinas, 108,777 . . . . D 3
San Bernardino, 164,164 . . . . E 5
San Clemente, 41,100 F 5
San Diego, 1,110,549 F 5
San Francisco, 723,959 . . . . D 2
San Jose, 782,248 . . D 3
San Juan Capistrano, 26,183 . . . . F 5
San Luis Obispo, 41,958 . . . . E 3
San Mateo, 85,486 . . D 2
Santa Ana, 293,742 . . F 5
Santa Barbara, 85,571 . . . . E 4
Santa Clara, 93,613 D 2
Santa Cruz, 49,040 . . D 2
Santa Maria, 61,284 E 3
Santa Monica, 86,905 m12
Santa Rosa, 113,313 C 2
Simi Valley, 100,217 E 4
South Gate, 86,284 . . n12
South Lake Tahoe, 21,586 . . . . C 4
Stockton, 210,943 . . D 3
Sunnyvale, 117,229 . . k 8
Torrance, 133,107 . . n12
Tulare, 33,249 . . . . . . D 4
Turlock, 42,198 . . . . . D 3
Vallejo, 109,199 . . . . C 2
Ventura (San Buenaventura), 92,575 . . . . E 4
Visalia, 75,636 . . . . . . D 4
West Covina, 96,086 m13
Westminster, 78,118 n12
Whittier, 77,671 . . . . F 4
Yuba City, 27,437 . . . C 3

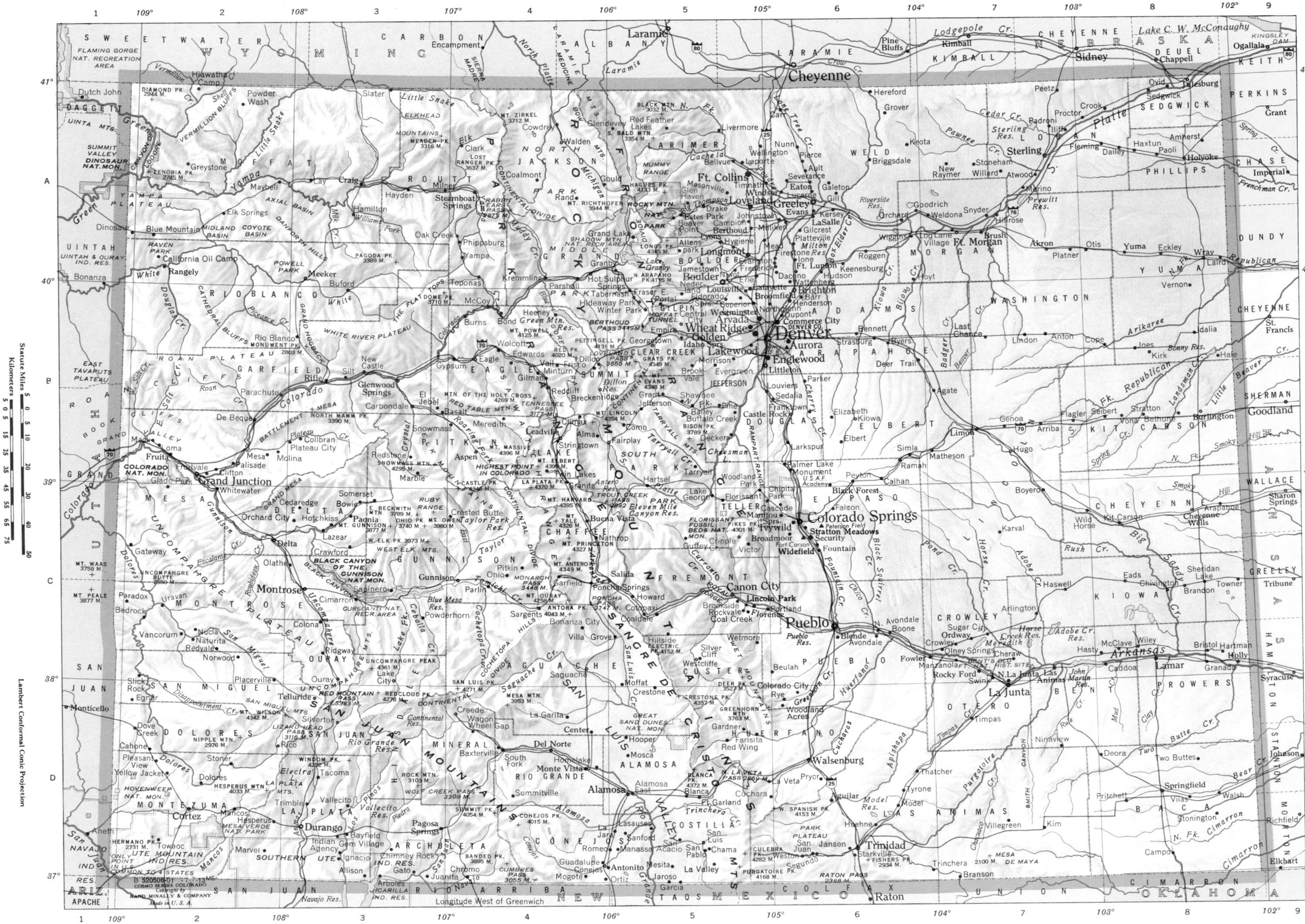

Colorado

1990 CENSUS

Place	Key
Alamosa, 7,579	D 5
Applewood, 8,130('85)	B 5
Arvada, 89,235	B 5
Aspen, 5,049	B 4
Aurora, 222,103	B 6
Berthoud, 2,990	A 5
Boulder, 83,312	A 5
Breckenridge, 1,285	B 4
Brighton, 14,203	B 6
Broomfield, 24,638	B 5
Brush, 4,165	A 7
Buena Vista, 1,752	C 4
Burlington, 2,941	B 8
Canon City, 12,687	C 5
Carbondale, 3,004	B 3
Castle Rock, 8,708	B 6
Central City, 335	B 5
Colorado Springs, 281,140	C 6
Commerce City, 16,466	B 6
Cortez, 7,284	D 2
Craig, 8,091	A 3
Dacono, 2,228	A 6
Delta, 3,789	C 2
Denver, 467,610	B 6
Durango, 12,430	D 3
Eaton, 1,959	A 6
Englewood, 29,387	B 6
Estes Park, 3,184	A 5
Evans, 5,877	A 6
Florence, 2,990	C 5
Fort Collins, 87,758	A 5
Fort Lupton, 5,159	A 6
Fort Morgan, 9,068	A 7
Fountain, 9,984	C 6
Fruita, 4,045	B 2
Glenwood Springs, 6,561	B 3
Golden, 13,116	B 5
Grand Junction, 29,034	B 2
Greeley, 60,536	A 6
Gunnison, 4,636	C 4
Holyoke, 1,931	A 8
Idaho Springs, 1,834	B 5
Julesburg, 1,295	A 8
Lafayette, 14,548	B 5
La Junta, 7,637	D 7
Lakewood, 126,481	B 5
Lamar, 8,343	C 8
La Salle, 1,783	A 6
Las Animas, 2,481	C 7
Leadville, 2,629	B 4
Limon, 1,831	B 7
Littleton, 33,685	B 6
Longmont, 51,555	A 5
Louisville, 12,361	B 5
Loveland, 37,352	A 5
Manitou Springs, 4,535	C 6
Meeker, 2,098	A 3
Monte Vista, 4,324	D 4
Montrose, 8,854	C 3
Northglenn, 27,195	B 6
Orchard City, 2,218	C 3
Ouray, 644	C 3
Pagosa Springs, 1,207	D 3
Pueblo, 98,640	C 6
Rangely, 2,278	A 2
Rifle, 4,636	B 3
Rocky Ford, 4,162	C 7
Salida, 4,737	C 5
Springfield, 1,475	D 8
Steamboat Springs, 6,695	A 4
Sterling, 10,362	A 7
Telluride, 1,309	D 3
Trinidad, 8,580	D 6
Vail, 3,659	B 4
Walsenburg, 3,300	D 6
Westminster, 74,625	B 5
Wheat Ridge, 29,419	B 5
Widefield, 12,112('85)	C 6
Windsor, 5,062	A 6
Woodland Park, 4,610	C 5
Wray, 1,998	A 8
Yuma, 2,719	A 8

Connecticut

1990 CENSUS

Ansonia, 18,403 . . . . . . D 3
Bethel, 8,755 (17,541▲) D 2
Bloomfield, 7,120
(19,483▲) . . . . B 5
Branford, 5,438
(27,603▲) . . . . D 4
Bridgeport, 141,686 . . E 3
Bristol, 60,640 . . . . C 4
Cheshire, 5,722
(25,684▲) . . . . D 4
Clinton, 11,195('87) . . . . D 5
Coventry, 3,769
(10,063▲) . . . . B 6
Danbury, 65,585 . . . . . . D 2
Danielson, 4,441 . . . . . . B 8
Derby, 12,199 . . . . D 3
East Hartford, 50,452 . . B 5
East Haven, 26,144 . . . D 4
Enfield, 8,454 (45,532▲) B 5
Fairfield, 52,400 . . . . . . E 2
Glastonbury, 7,049
(27,901▲) . . . . C 5
Greenwich, 58,000 . . . . E 1
Groton, 9,837 . . . . D 7
Hamden, 53,100 . . . . . . D 4
Hartford, 139,739 . . . . B 5
Harwinton, 3,293
(5,228▲) . . . . B 3
Jewett City, 3,349 . . . . C 8
Manchester, 51,000 . . B 5
Meriden, 59,479 . . . . . . C 4
Middlebury, 4,140
(6,145▲) . . . . C 3
Middletown, 42,762 . . . . C 5
Milford, 48,168 . . . . . . E 3
Mystic, 2,333('80) . . . . D 8
Naugatuck, 30,625 . . . . D 3
New Britain, 75,491 . . C 4
New Fairfield, 4,600
(12,911▲) . . . . D 2
New Haven, 130,474 . . D 4
Newington, 29,800 . . . . C 5
New London, 28,540 . . D 7
New Milford, 5,186
(23,629▲) . . . . C 2
North Branford, 6,600
(12,996▲) . . . . D 4
North Haven, 22,700 . . D 4
Norwalk, 78,331 . . . . . . E 2
Norwich, 37,391 . . . . . . C 7
Orange, 13,300 . . . . . . D 3
Putnam, 6,850 (9,031▲) B 8
Ridgefield, 6,066
(20,919▲) . . . . D 2
Shelton, 35,418 . . . . . . D 3
Simsbury, 5,488
(22,023▲) . . . . B 4
Southington, 40,700 . . C 4
South Windsor, 10,800
(22,090▲) . . . . B 5
Stafford Springs, 4,100 B 6
Stamford, 108,056 . . . . E 1
Stratford, 50,400 . . . . . E 3
Thomaston, 3,590
(6,947▲) . . . . C 3
Torrington, 33,687 . . . . B 3
Trumbull, 33,200 . . . . . E 3
Wallingford, 41,400 . . . D 4
Waterbury, 108,961 . . C 3
Watertown, 5,920
(20,456▲) . . . . C 3
West Hartford, 59,100 B 4
West Haven, 54,021 . . D 4
Westport, 25,300 . . . . . E 2
Wethersfield, 26,500 . . C 5
Willimantic, 14,600('87) C 7
Wilton, 7,200 (15,989▲) E 2
Windsor, 17,517
(27,817▲) . . . . B 5
Windsor Locks,
12,190('80) . . . . B 5
Wolcott, 6,070
(13,700▲) . . . . C 4
Woodbridge, 7,700
(7,924▲) . . . . D 3

▲ Population of entire town (township), including rural area.

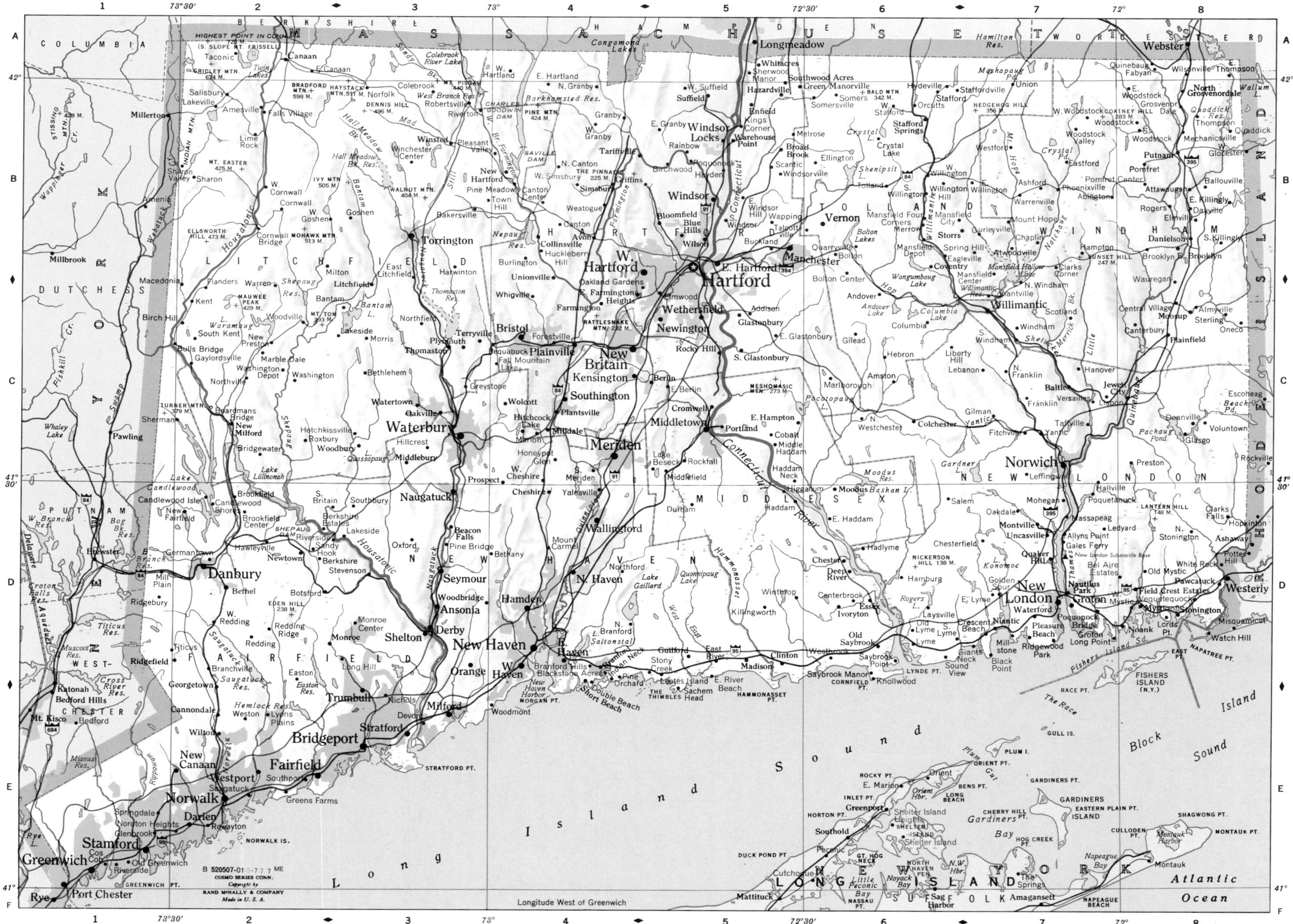

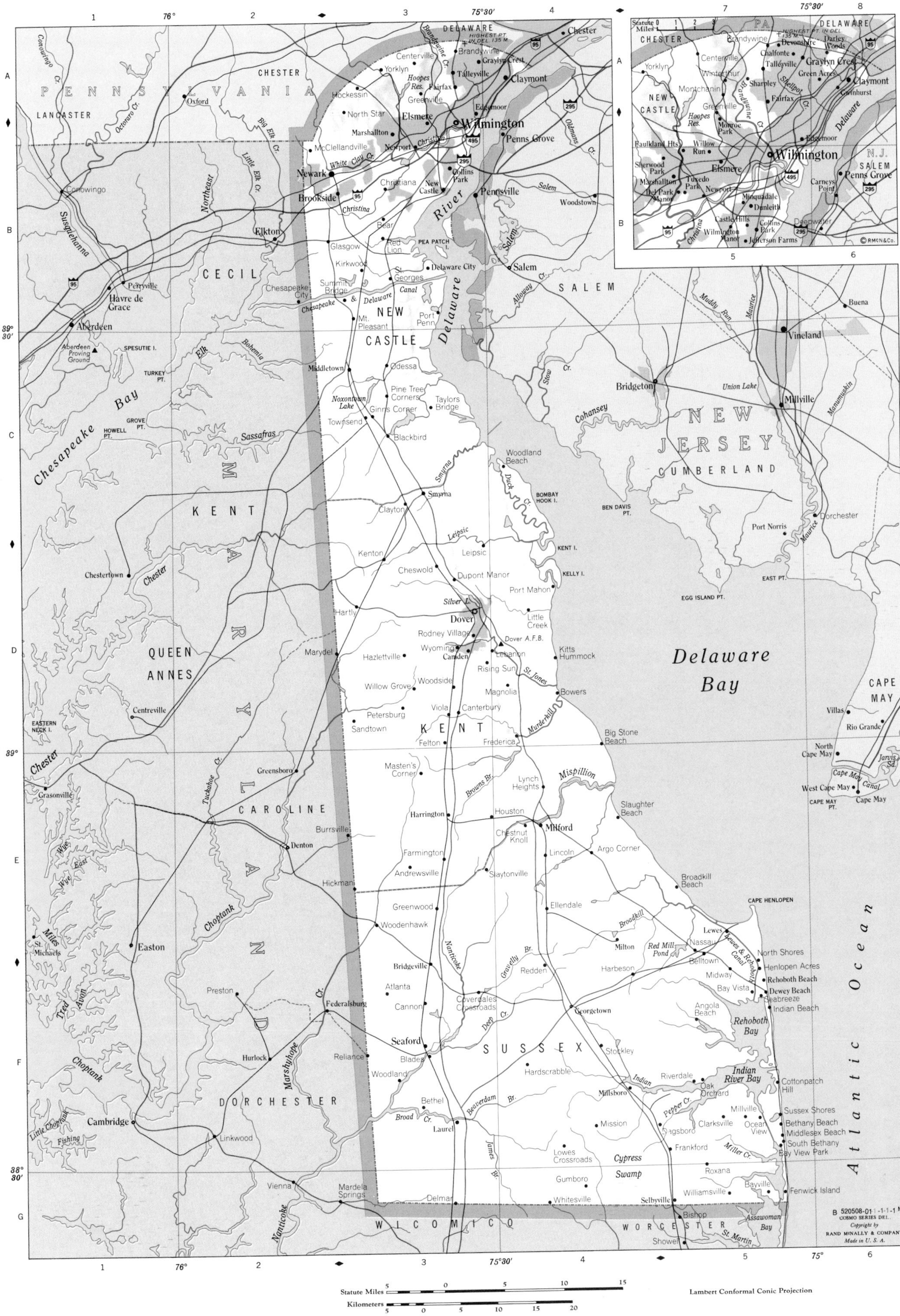

Delaware

1990 CENSUS

Bear, 1,200('88) .... B 3
Bethany Beach, 326 F 5
Blades, 834 .... F 3
Bridgeville, 1,210 .... F 3
Broadkill Beach, 390('88) .... E 5
Brookside, 7,450('88) B 3
Camden, 1,899 .... D 3
Canterbury, 500('88) D 3
Castle Hills, 1,475('88) i 7
Chalfonte, 1,740('88) h 7
Cheswold, 321 ...... D 3
Christiana, 500('88) .. B 3
Clarksville, 500('88) .. F 5
Claymont, 15,100('88) A 4
Clayton, 1,163 ...... C 3
Collins Park, 2,100('88) .... B 3
Dagsboro, 398 ...... F 5
Darley Woods, 1,220('88) .... h 8
Delaware City, 1,682 B 3
Delmar, 962 .... G 3
Del Park Manor, 1,550('88) .... i 7
Devonshire, 2,120('88) h 7
Dewey Beach, 204 .. F 5
Dover, 27,630 ...... D 3
Dunleith, 2,600('88) .. i 7
Dupont Manor, 1,059('80) .... D 3
Edgemoor, 5,400('88) A 3
Ellendale, 313 ...... E 4
Elsmere, 5,935 ...... B 3
Fairfax, 2,075('88) .. A 3
Faulkland Heights, 1,300('88) .... i 7
Felton, 683 .... D 3
Frankford, 591 ...... F 5
Frederica, 761 ...... D 4
Georgetown, 3,732 .. F 4
Graylyn Crest, 4,380('88) .... A 3
Green Acres, 1,140('88) .... h 8
Greenville, 800('88) .. a 3
Greenwood, 578 .... E 3
Gumboro, 200('88) .. g 4
Gwinhurst, 1,340('88) h 8
Harbeson, 500('88) .. f 4
Harrington, 2,311 .... E 8
Hockessin, 2,430('88) A 3
Houston, 487 ...... E 3
Jefferson Farms, 3,130('88) .... i 7
Kenton, 232 .... D 3
Kirkwood, 350('88) .. b 3
Laurel, 3,226 ...... F 3
Lebanon, 130('88) .. d 4
Leipsic, 236 .... D 3
Lewes, 2,295 ...... E 5
Lincoln, 500('88) .... e 4
Little Creek, 167 .... D 4
Marshallton, 1,765('88) .... B 3
Middletown, 3,834 .. C 3
Midway, 500('88) .... f 5
Milford, 6,040 ...... E 4
Millsboro, 1,643 .... F 4
Milton, 1,417 ...... E 4
Minquadale, 790('88) .. i 7
Monroe Park, 1,000('88) .... h 7
Montchanin, 500('88) h 7
Newark, 25,098 .... B 3
New Castle, 4,837 .. B 3
Newport, 1,240 .... B 3
North Star, 1,030('88) A 3
Oak Orchard, 350('88) f 5
Ocean View, 606 .... F 5
Odessa, 303 ...... C 3
Port Penn, 300('88) .. b 3
Rehoboth Beach, 1,234 .... F 5
Rising Sun, 540('88) D 3
Rodney Village, 1,100('88) .... D 3
Saint Georges, 500('88) .... B 3
Seabreeze, 350('88) .. F 5
Seaford, 5,689 ...... F 3
Selbyville, 1,335 .... G 5
Sharpley, 1,250('88) .. h 7
Sherwood Park, 2,000('88) .... i 7
Silview, 1,500('88) .. B 3
Smyrna, 5,231 ...... C 3
Talleyville, 6,880('80) A 3
Townsend, 322 .... C 3
Tuxedo Park, 1,300('88) .... i 7
Willow Run, 1,600('88) i 7
Wilmington, 71,529 .. B 3
Wilmington Manor, 1,235('88) .... i 7
Wyoming, 977 ...... D 3
Yorklyn, 600('88) .... A 3

Florida

1990 CENSUS

Altamonte Springs, 34,879 .... D 5
Bartow, 14,716 .... E 5
Belle Glade, 16,177 .. F 6
Boca Raton, 61,492 .. F 6
Boynton Beach, 46,194 .... F 6
Bradenton, 43,779 .. E 4
Brandon, 36,300 .... E 4
Brownsville, 18,058('80) s13
Cape Canaveral, 8,014 .... D 6
Cape Coral, 74,991 .. F 5
Carol City, 52,800 .. s13
Clearwater, 98,784 .. E 4
Cocoa, 17,722 ...... D 6
Coral Gables, 40,091 G 6
Cutler Ridge, 20,886('80) s13
Davie, 47,217 ...... F 6
Daytona Beach, 61,921 .... C 5
Deerfield Beach, 46,325 .... F 6
De Land, 16,491 .... C 5
Delray Beach, 47,181 F 6
Dunedin, 34,012 .... D 4
Fort Lauderdale, 149,377 .... F 6
Fort Myers, 45,206 .. F 5
Fort Pierce, 36,830 .. E 6
Fort Walton Beach, 21,471 .... u15
Gainesville, 84,770 .. C 4
Hallandale, 30,996 .. G 6
Hialeah, 188,004 .... G 6
Hollywood, 121,697 .. F 6
Homestead, 26,866 .. G 6
Jacksonville, 635,230 B 5
Kendall, 53,100 ...... s13
Key Largo, 7,447('80) G 6
Key West, 24,832 .. H 5
Kissimmee, 30,050 .. D 5
Lake City, 10,005 .. B 4
Lakeland, 70,576 .... D 5
Lake Worth, 28,564 .. F 6
Largo, 65,674 ...... E 4
Lauderdale Lakes, 27,341 .... r13
Lealman, 19,873('80) p10
Leesburg, 14,903 .... D 5
Leisure City, 17,905('80) s13
Margate, 42,985 .... F 6
Melbourne, 59,646 .. D 6
Merritt Island, 44,300 D 6
Miami, 358,548 .... G 6
Miami Beach, 92,639 G 6
Miramar, 40,663 .... s13
Naples, 19,505 ...... F 5
New Smyrna Beach, 16,543 .... C 6
North Fort Myers, 17,200('83) ...... F 5
North Miami, 49,998 G 6
North Miami Beach, 35,359 .... s13
Oakland Park, 26,326 r13
Ocala, 42,045 ...... C 4
Orlando, 164,693 .... D 5
Ormond Beach, 29,721 .... C 5
Palm Bay, 62,632 .. D 6
Panama City, 34,378 u16
Pembroke Pines, 65,452 .... r13
Pensacola, 58,165 .. u14
Pine Hills, 35,600 .... D 5
Pinellas Park, 43,426 E 4
Plantation, 66,692 .... r13
Plant City, 22,754 .. D 4
Pompano Beach, 72,411 .... F 6
Port Charlotte, 43,300 F 4
Port Orange, 35,317 C 6
Riviera Beach, 27,639 F 6
Saint Augustine, 11,692 .... C 5
Saint Petersburg, 238,629 .... E 4
Sanford, 32,387 .... D 5
Sarasota, 50,961 .... E 4
Sebring, 8,900 ...... E 5
South Miami Heights, 18,000('83) s13
Sweetwater Creek, 18,000('83) p10
Tallahassee, 124,773 B 2
Tampa, 280,015 .... E 4
Tarpon Springs, 17,906 .... D 4
Titusville, 39,394 .... D 6
Venice, 16,922 ...... E 4
Vero Beach, 17,350 .. E 6
West Palm Beach, 67,643 .... F 6
West Pensacola, 30,200 .... u14
Winter Haven, 24,725 D 5
Winter Park, 22,242 D 5

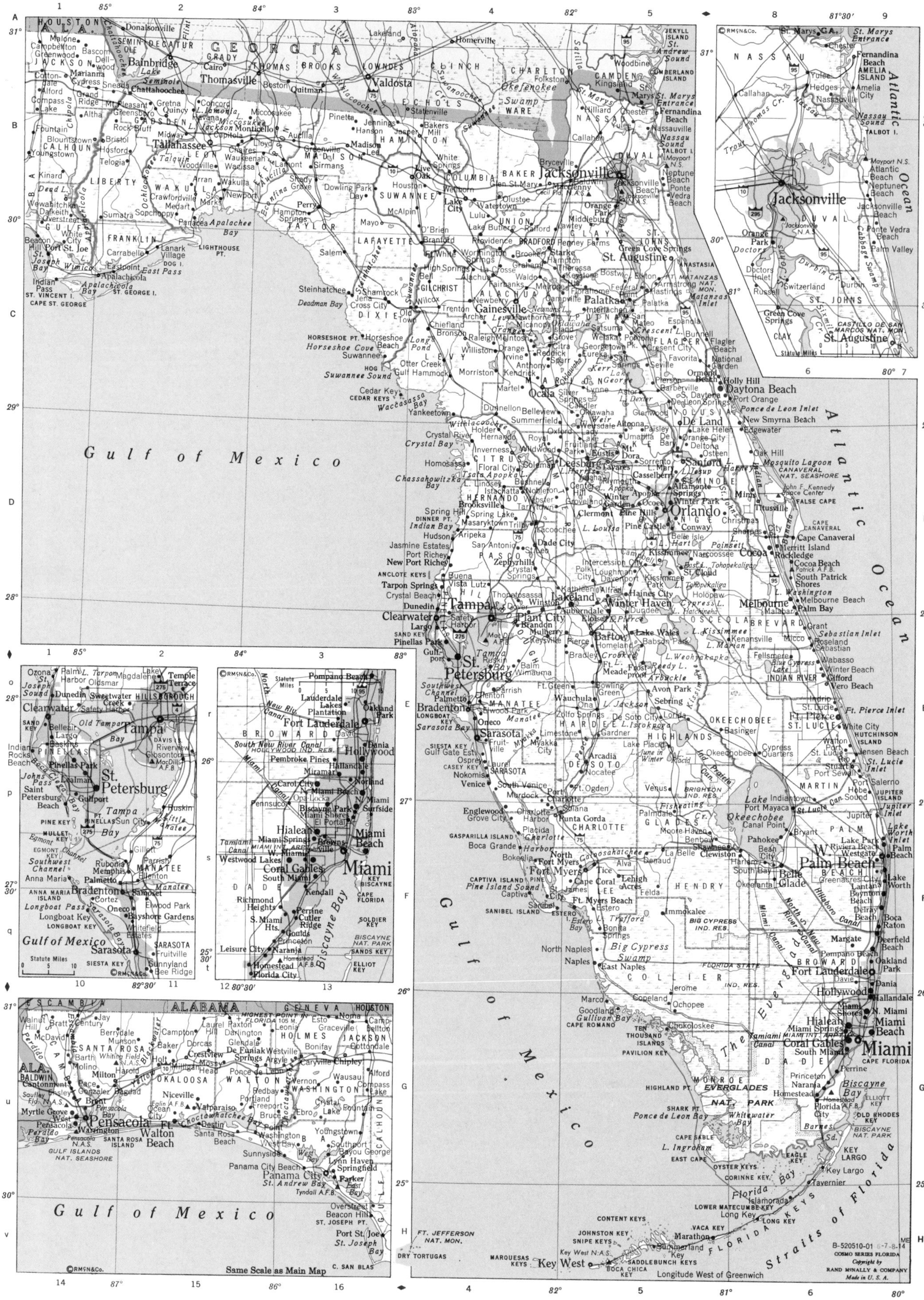

Statute Miles 5 0 5 10 20 30 40 50

Kilometers 5 0 5 15 25 35 45 55 65

Lambert Conformal Conic Projection

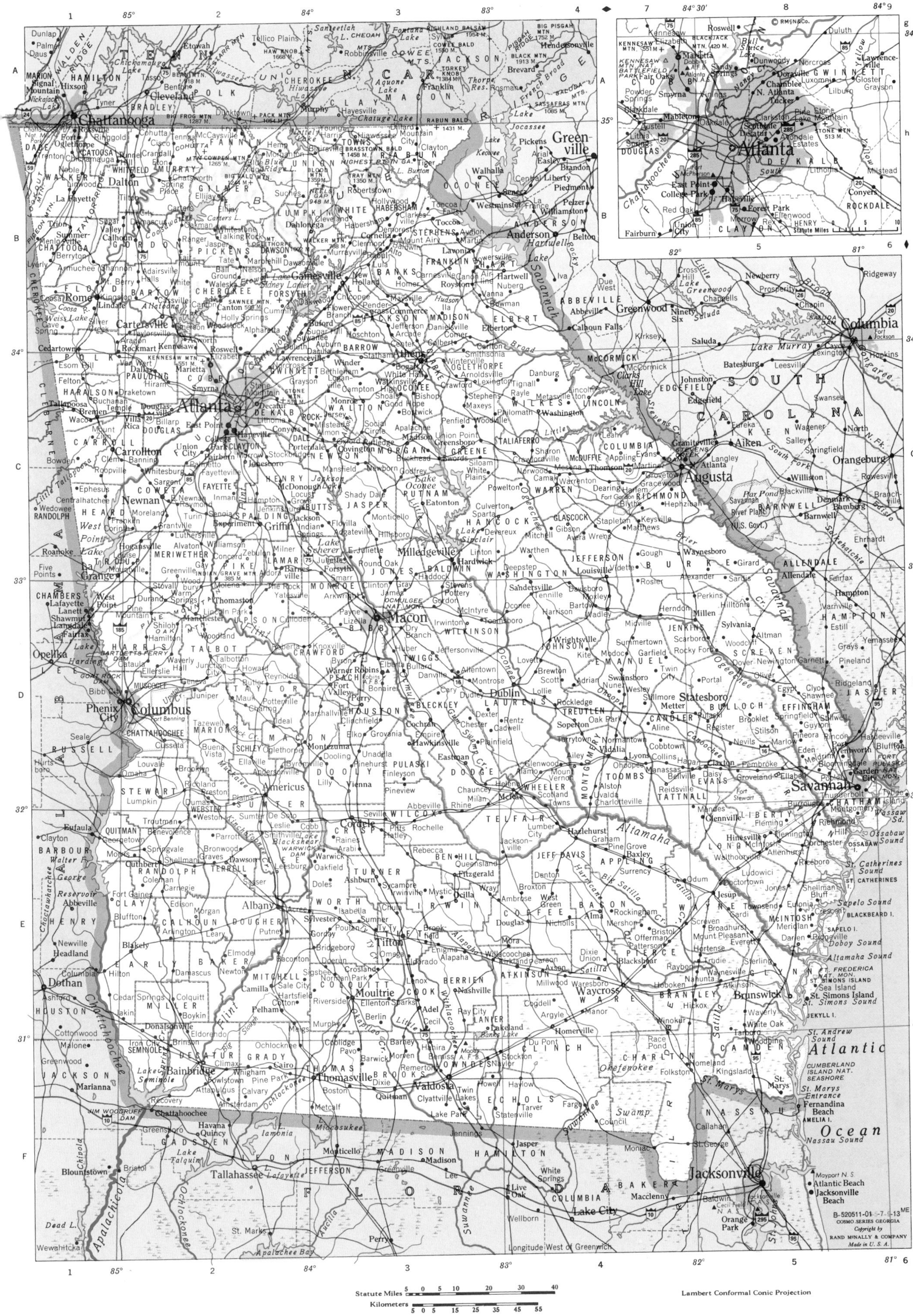

Georgia

1990 CENSUS

Adel, 5,093 . . . . E 3
Albany, 78,122 . . . . . . E 2
Americus, 16,512 . . . . D 2
Athens, 45,734 . . . . C 3
Atlanta, 394,017 . . . . C 2
Augusta, 44,639 . . . . C 5
Bainbridge, 10,712 . . F 2
Blakely, 5,595 . . . . . . E 2
Brunswick, 16,433 . . E 5
Buford, 8,771 . . . . . . B 2
Cairo, 9,035 . . . . F 2
Calhoun, 7,135 . . . . . B 2
Camilla, 5,008 . . . . . . E 2
Carrollton, 16,029 . . C 1
Cartersville, 12,035 . . B 2
Cedartown, 7,978 . . . B 1
Chamblee, 7,668 . . . . h 8
Cochran, 4,390 . . . . D 3
College Park, 20,457 C 2
Columbus, 178,681 . . D 2
Conyers, 7,380 . . . . C 2
Cordele, 10,321 . . . . E 3
Covington, 10,026 . . C 3
Dalton, 21,761 . . . . . B 2
Dawson, 5,295 . . . . . E 2
Decatur, 17,336 . . . . C 2
Dock Junction, 6,189('80) . . . . E 5
Doraville, 7,626 . . . . . h 8
Douglas, 10,464 . . . . E 4
Douglasville, 11,635 C 2
Dublin, 16,312 . . . . . . D 4
Dunwoody, 7,840('85) h 8
Eastman, 5,153 . . . . D 3
East Point, 34,402 . . C 2
Elberton, 5,682 . . . . B 4
Fair Oaks, 8,486('80) h 7
Fitzgerald, 8,612 . . . . E 3
Forest Park, 16,925 . . h 8
Fort Oglethorpe, 5,880 . . . . B 1
Fort Valley, 8,198 . . D 3
Gainesville, 17,885 . . B 3
Garden City, 7,410 . . D 5
Griffin, 21,347 . . . . . C 2
Hapeville, 5,483 . . . . C 2
Hardwick, 8,800('85) C 3
Hinesville, 21,603 . . . E 5
Jesup, 8,958 . . . . . . E 5
Kennesaw, 8,936 . . . . B 2
Lafayette, 6,313 . . . . B 1
La Grange, 25,597 . . C 1
Lawrenceville, 16,848 C 3
Lithia Springs, 9,145('80) . . . . h 7
Mableton, 21,390('85) h 7
Macon, 106,612 . . . . D 3
Marietta, 44,129 . . . . C 2
Martinez, 16,472('80) C 4
Milledgeville, 17,727 C 3
Monroe, 9,759 . . . . . . C 3
Moultrie, 14,865 . . . . E 3
Newnan, 12,497 . . . . C 2
North Atlanta, 21,340('85) . . . . . . h 8
North Druid Hills, 4,900('85) . . . . h 8
Pendley Hills, 5,400('85) . . . . h 8
Perry, 9,452 . . . . D 3
Quitman, 5,292 . . . . . . F 3
Rome, 30,326 . . . . . . B 1
Roswell, 47,923 . . . . B 2
Saint Simons Island, 6,566('80) . . . . E 5
Sandersville, 6,290 . . D 4
Sandy Springs, 21,120('85) . . . . . . h 8
Savannah, 137,560 . . D 5
Scottdale, 8,770('80) h 8
Smyrna, 30,981 . . . . C 2
Statesboro, 15,854 . . D 5
Stone Mountain, 6,494 . . . . C 2
Swainsboro, 7,361 . . D 4
Sylvester, 5,702 . . . . E 3
Thomaston, 9,127 . . D 2
Thomasville, 17,457 . . F 3
Thomson, 6,862 . . . . . C 4
Tifton, 14,215 . . . . . . E 3
Toccoa, 8,266 . . . . . . B 3
Tucker, 22,250('85) . . h 8
Union City, 8,375 . . . . C 2
Valdosta, 39,806 . . . . F 3
Vidalia, 11,078 . . . . . . D 4
Warner Robins, 43,726 . . . . D 3
Waycross, 16,410 . . E 4
Waynesboro, 5,701 . . C 4
Winder, 7,373 . . . . . . C 3

Hawaii

1990 CENSUS

Place	Key
Aiea, 8,906	B 4
Anahola, 1,181	A 2
Captain Cook, 2,595	D 6
Ewa, 3,780	B 3
Ewa Beach, 14,315	B 3
Halawa Heights, 7,000('83)	g10
Haleiwa, 2,442	B 3
Haliimaile, 841	C 5
Hana, 683	C 6
Hanamaulu, 3,611	B 2
Hanapepe, 1,395	B 2
Hauula, 3,479	B 4
Hawi, 924	C 6
Hilo, 37,808	D 6
Holualoa, 3,834	D 6
Honokaa, 2,186	C 6
Honolulu, 365,272	B 4
Honomu, 532	D 6
Kaaawa, 1,138	f10
Kahaluu, 3,068	g10
Kahuku, 2,063	B 4
Kahului, 16,889	C 5
Kailua, 36,818	B 4
Kailua Kona, 9,126	D 6
Kalaheo, 3,592	B 2
Kamuela (Waimea), 5,972	C 6
Kaneohe, 35,448	B 4
Kapaa, 8,149	A 2
Kapaau, 1,083	C 6
Kaumakani, 803	B 2
Kaunakakai, 2,658	B 4
Keaau, 1,584	D 6
Kealakekua, 1,453	D 6
Kealia, 700('83)	A 2
Kekaha, 3,506	B 2
Keokea, 900('83)	C 5
Kihei, 11,107	C 5
Kilauea, 1,685	A 2
Koloa, 1,791	B 2
Kula, 1,300('83)	C 5
Kurtistown, 910	D 6
Lahaina, 9,073	C 5
Laie, 5,577	B 4
Lanai City, 2,400	C 5
Lawai, 1,787	B 2
Lihue, 5,536	B 2
Lower Paia, 1,500('80)	C 5
Maili, 6,059	g 9
Makaha, 7,990	g 9
Makakilo City, 9,828	g 9
Makawao, 5,405	C 5
Makaweli, 565	B 2
Maunaloa, 405	B 4
Maunawili, 4,847	g10
Mililani Town, 29,359	g 9
Naalehu, 1,027	D 6
Nanakuli, 9,575	B 3
Paauilo, 620	C 6
Pacific Palisades, 10,000('83)	g10
Pahala, 1,520	D 6
Pahoa, 1,027	D 7
Paia, 2,091	C 5
Papaikou, 1,634	D 6
Pearl City, 30,993	B 4
Pepeekeo, 1,813	D 6
Poipu, 975	B 2
Puhi, 1,210	B 2
Pukalani, 5,879	C 5
Sunset Beach, 800('83)	f 9
Volcano, 1,516	D 6
Wahiawa, 17,386	B 3
Waialua, 3,943	B 3
Waianae, 8,758	B 3
Waikapu, 729	C 5
Wailua, 2,018	A 2
Wailuku, 10,688	C 5
Waimanalo, 3,508	B 4
Waimea, 600('83)	f 9
Waimea, 1,840	B 2
Waipahu, 31,435	B 3
Waipio Acres, 5,304	g 9
Whitmore Village, 3,373	f 9

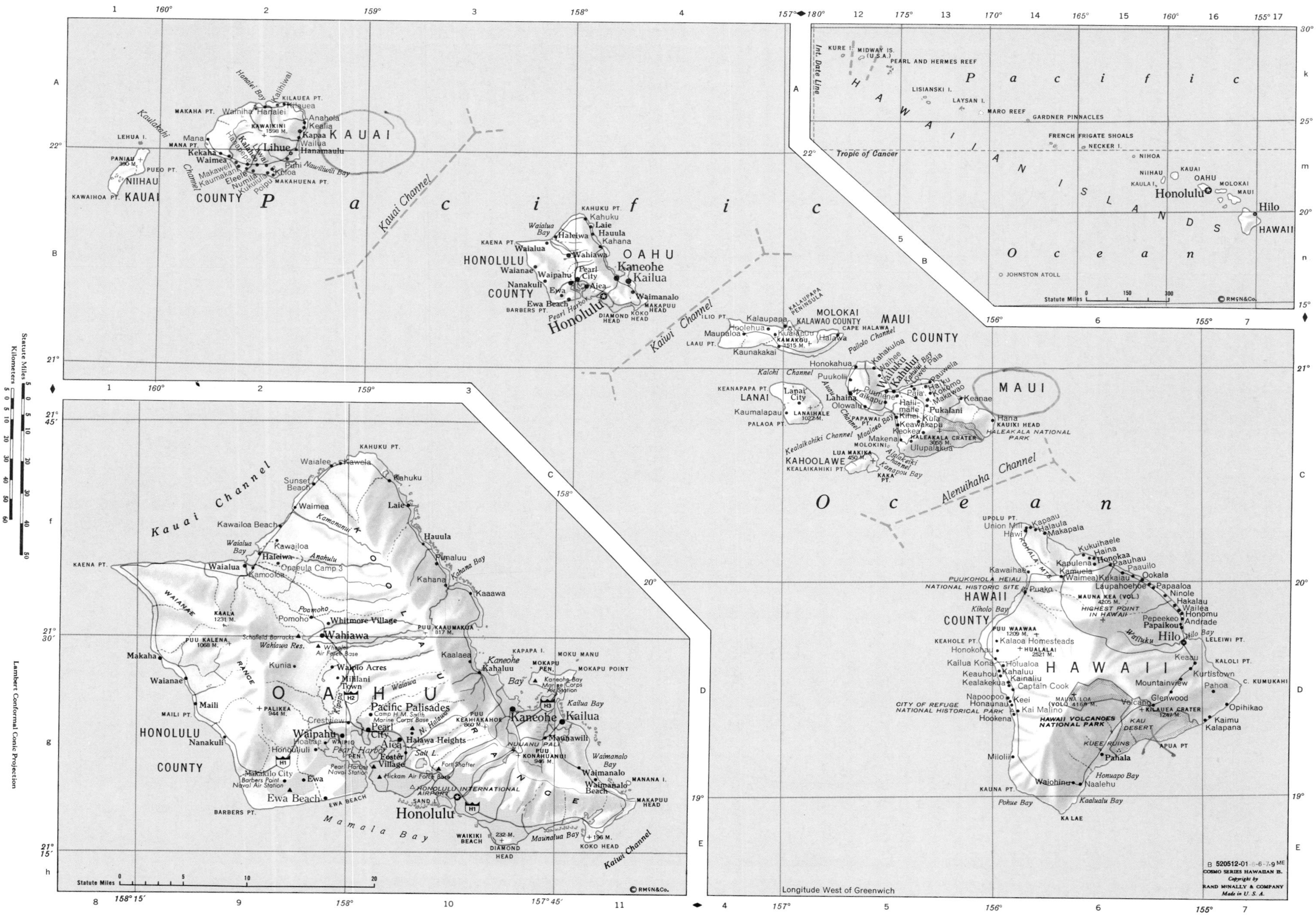

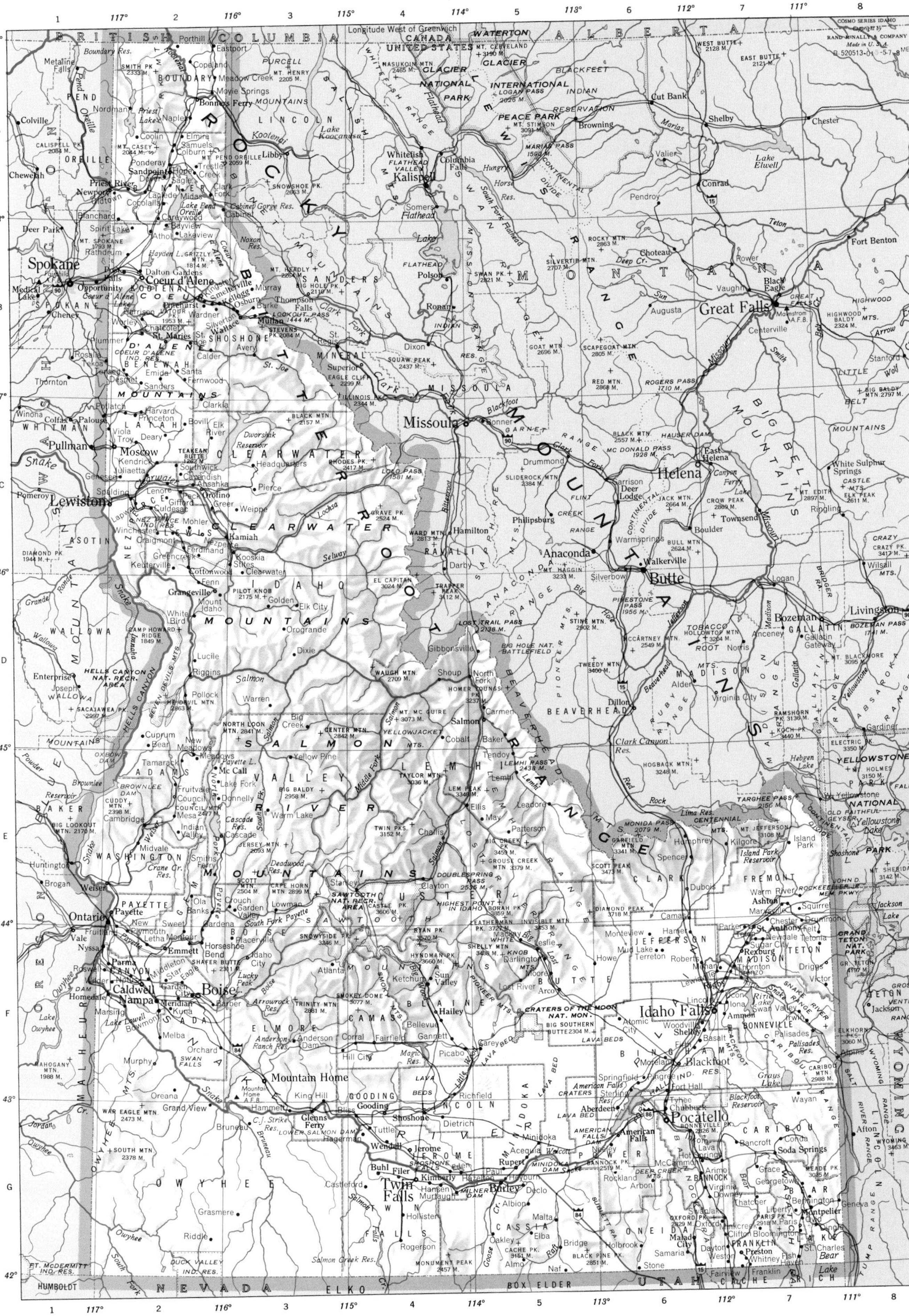

Statute Miles 5 0 5 10 20 30 40 50 60

Kilometers 5 0 5 15 25 35 45 55 65 75

Lambert Conformal Conic Projection

Idaho

1990 CENSUS

Aberdeen, 1,406 . . . . G 6
American Falls, 3,757 G 6
Ammon, 5,002 . . . . . F 7
Arco, 1,016 . . . . F 5
Ashton, 1,114 . . . . . . E 7
Bellevue, 1,275 . . . . . F 4
Blackfoot, 9,646 . . . . F 6
Boise, 125,738 . . . . . F 2
Bonners Ferry, 2,193 A 2
Buhl, 3,516 . . . . G 4
Burley, 8,702 . . . . . . G 5
Caldwell, 18,400 . . . . F 2
Cascade, 877 . . . . . . E 2
Chubbuck, 7,791 . . . . G 6
Coeur d'Alene, 24,563 . . . . B 2
Cottonwood, 822 . . . . C 2
Council, 831 . . . . E 2
Dalton Gardens, 1,951 . . . . B 2
Eagle, 3,327 . . . . F 2
Emmett, 4,601 . . . . . . F 2
Filer, 1,511 . . . . G 4
Fort Hall, 900('83) . . F 6
Fruitland, 2,400 . . . . F 2
Garden City, 6,369 . . F 2
Genesee, 725 . . . . . . C 2
Glenns Ferry, 1,304 . . G 3
Gooding, 2,820 . . . . G 4
Grace, 973 . . . . G 7
Grangeville, 3,226 . . D 2
Hailey, 3,687 . . . . . . F 4
Hansen, 848 . . . . . . G 4
Heyburn, 2,714 . . . . G 5
Homedale, 1,963 . . . . F 2
Idaho Falls, 43,929 . . F 6
Inkom, 769 . . . . G 6
Iona, 1,049 . . . . F 7
Jerome, 6,529 . . . . . . G 4
Kamiah, 1,157 . . . . . . C 2
Kellogg, 2,591 . . . . . B 2
Ketchum, 2,523 . . . . F 4
Kimberly, 2,367 . . . . G 4
Kingston, 1,000('83) B 2
Kuna, 1,955 . . . . F 2
Lapwai, 932 . . . . C 2
Lewiston, 28,082 . . . . C 1
Malad City, 1,946 . . G 6
Marsing, 798 . . . . . . F 2
McCall, 2,005 . . . . . . E 2
Meridian, 9,596 . . . . F 2
Middleton, 1,851 . . . . F 2
Montpelier, 2,656 . . . . G 7
Moscow, 18,519 . . . . C 2
Mountain Home, 7,913 . . . . F 3
Mullan, 821 . . . . B 3
Nampa, 28,365 . . . . . F 2
New Plymouth, 1,313 F 2
Orofino, 2,868 . . . . . C 2
Osburn, 1,579 . . . . . . B 3
Parma, 1,597 . . . . . . F 2
Paul, 901 . . . . G 5
Payette, 5,592 . . . . . E 2
Pierce, 746 . . . . C 3
Pocatello, 46,080 . . . G 6
Post Falls, 7,349 . . . . B 2
Potlatch, 790 . . . . . . C 2
Preston, 3,710 . . . . . . G 7
Priest River, 1,560 . . A 2
Rathdrum, 2,000 . . . . B 2
Rexburg, 14,302 . . . . F 7
Rigby, 2,681 . . . . F 7
Rupert, 5,455 . . . . . . G 5
Saint Anthony, 3,010 F 7
Saint Maries, 2,442 . . B 2
Salmon, 2,941 . . . . . . D 5
Sandpoint, 5,203 . . . . A 2
Shelley, 3,536 . . . . . . F 6
Shoshone, 1,249 . . . . G 4
Shoup, 10('83) . . . . . . D 4
Soda Springs, 3,111 G 7
Spirit Lake, 790 . . . . B 2
Sugar City, 1,275 . . . . F 7
Sun Valley, 938 . . . . F 4
Troy, 699 . . . . C 2
Twin Falls, 27,591 . . G 4
Ucon, 895 . . . . F 7
Wallace, 1,010 . . . . . . B 3
Weippe, 532 . . . . C 3
Weiser, 4,571 . . . . . . E 2
Wendell, 1,963 . . . . . . G 4
Wilder, 1,232 . . . . . . F 2

Illinois

1990 CENSUS

Addison, 32,058 .... k 8
Alton, 32,905 ...... E 3
Arlington Heights, 75,460 .... A 5
Aurora, 99,581 ...... B 5
Belleville, 42,785 ..... E 4
Berwyn, 45,426 .... k 9
Bloomington, 51,972 C 4
Bolingbrook, 40,843 .. k 8
Bourbonnais, 13,934 B 6
Brookfield, 18,876 .. k 9
Burbank, 27,600 ..... k 9
Cahokia, 17,550 .... E 3
Cairo, 4,846 .... F 4
Calumet City, 37,840 B 6
Canton, 13,922 .... C 3
Carbondale, 27,033 .. F 4
Centralia, 14,274 .... E 4
Champaign, 63,502 .. C 5
Charleston, 20,398 .. D 5
Chicago, 2,783,726 .. B 6
Chicago Heights, 33,072 .... B 6
Cicero, 67,436 ...... B 6
Danville, 33,828 .... C 6
Decatur, 83,885 .... D 5
De Kalb, 34,925 .... B 5
Des Plaines, 53,223 .. A 6
Dixon, 15,144 ...... B 4
Downers Grove, 46,858 .... B 5
East Saint Louis, 40,944 .... E 3
Elgin, 77,010 ...... A 5
Elk Grove Village, 33,429 .... h 9
Elmhurst, 42,029 .... B 6
Evanston, 73,233 .... A 6
Freeport, 25,840 .... A 4
Galena, 3,647 ...... A 3
Galesburg, 33,530 .. C 3
Glenview, 37,093 .... h 9
Granite City, 32,862 .. E 3
Gurnee, 13,701 .... h 9
Hanover Park, 32,895 k 8
Harvey, 29,771 .... B 6
Highland Park, 30,575 A 6
Hoffman Estates, 46,561 .... h 8
Jacksonville, 19,324 D 3
Joliet, 76,836 ...... B 5
Kankakee, 27,575 .. B 6
Kewanee, 12,969 .... B 4
Lake Forest, 17,836 A 6
Lansing, 28,086 .... B 6
La Salle, 9,717 ..... B 4
Lincoln, 15,418 ..... C 4
Lombard, 39,408 .... k 8
Macomb, 19,952 .... C 3
Marion, 14,545 ...... F 5
Mattoon, 18,441 .... D 5
Moline, 43,202 ...... B 3
Monmouth, 9,489 .. C 3
Mount Prospect, 53,170 .... A 6
Mount Vernon, 16,988 E 5
Naperville, 85,351 .. B 5
Nauvoo, 1,108 ...... C 2
Niles, 28,284 .... h 9
Normal, 40,023 .... C 5
Northbrook, 32,308 .. h 9
North Chicago, 34,978 .... A 6
Oak Lawn, 56,182 .. B 6
Oak Park, 53,648 .. B 6
Ottawa, 17,451 .... B 5
Palatine, 39,253 .... A 5
Park Ridge, 36,175 .. B 6
Pekin, 32,254 ...... C 4
Peoria, 113,504 .... C 4
Peru, 9,302 .... B 4
Pontiac, 11,428 .... C 5
Quincy, 39,681 ...... D 2
Rockford, 139,426 .. A 4
Rock Island, 40,552 .. B 3
Salem, 7,470 ...... E 5
Schaumburg, 68,586 h 8
Skokie, 59,432 ...... A 6
Springfield, 105,227 .. D 4
Sterling, 15,132 .... B 4
Streator, 14,121 .... B 5
Taylorville, 11,133 .. D 4
Tinley Park, 37,121 .. k 9
Urbana, 36,344 .... C 5
Vandalia, 6,114 .... E 4
Waukegan, 69,392 .. A 6
Wheaton, 51,464 .... B 5
Zion, 19,775 .... A 6

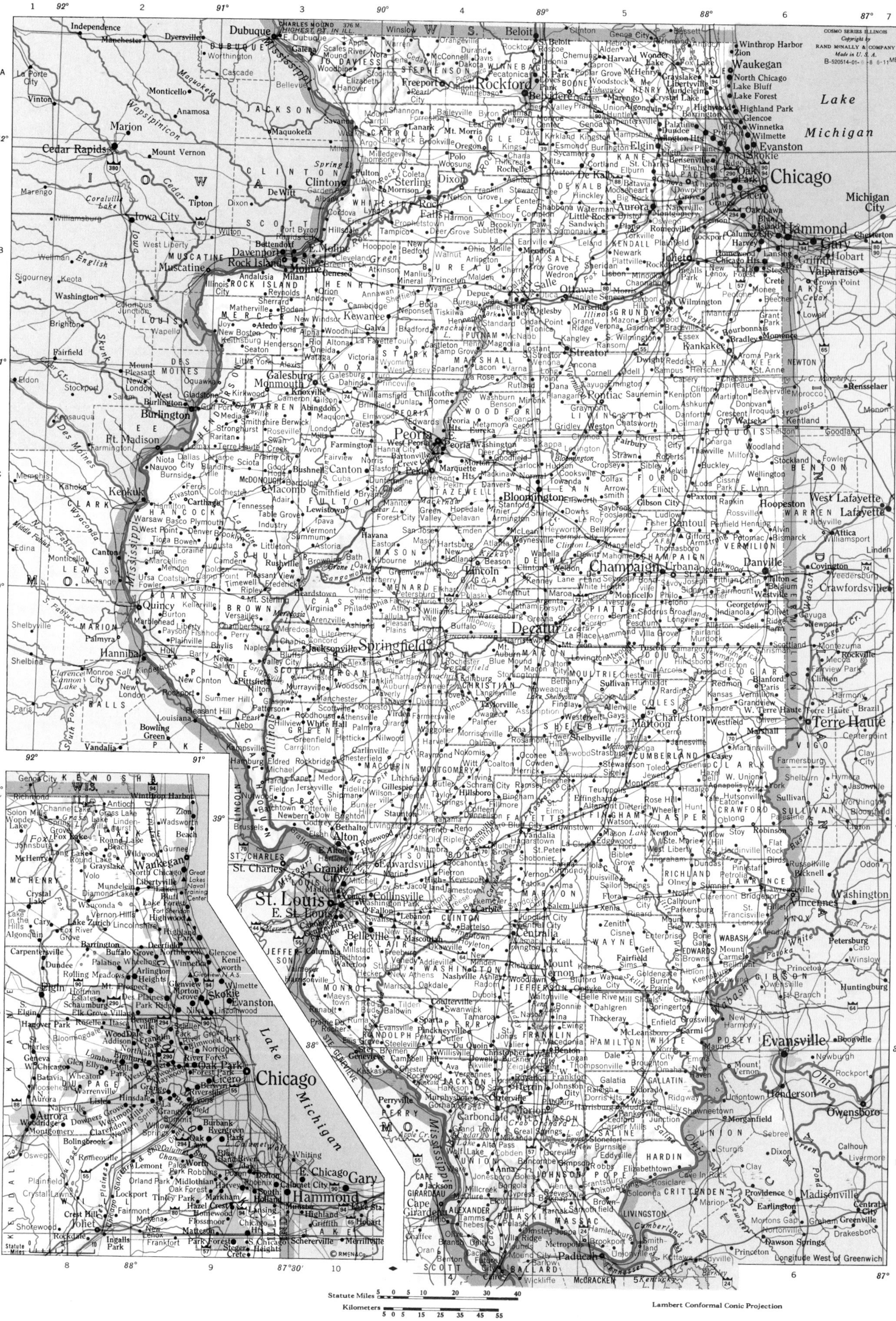

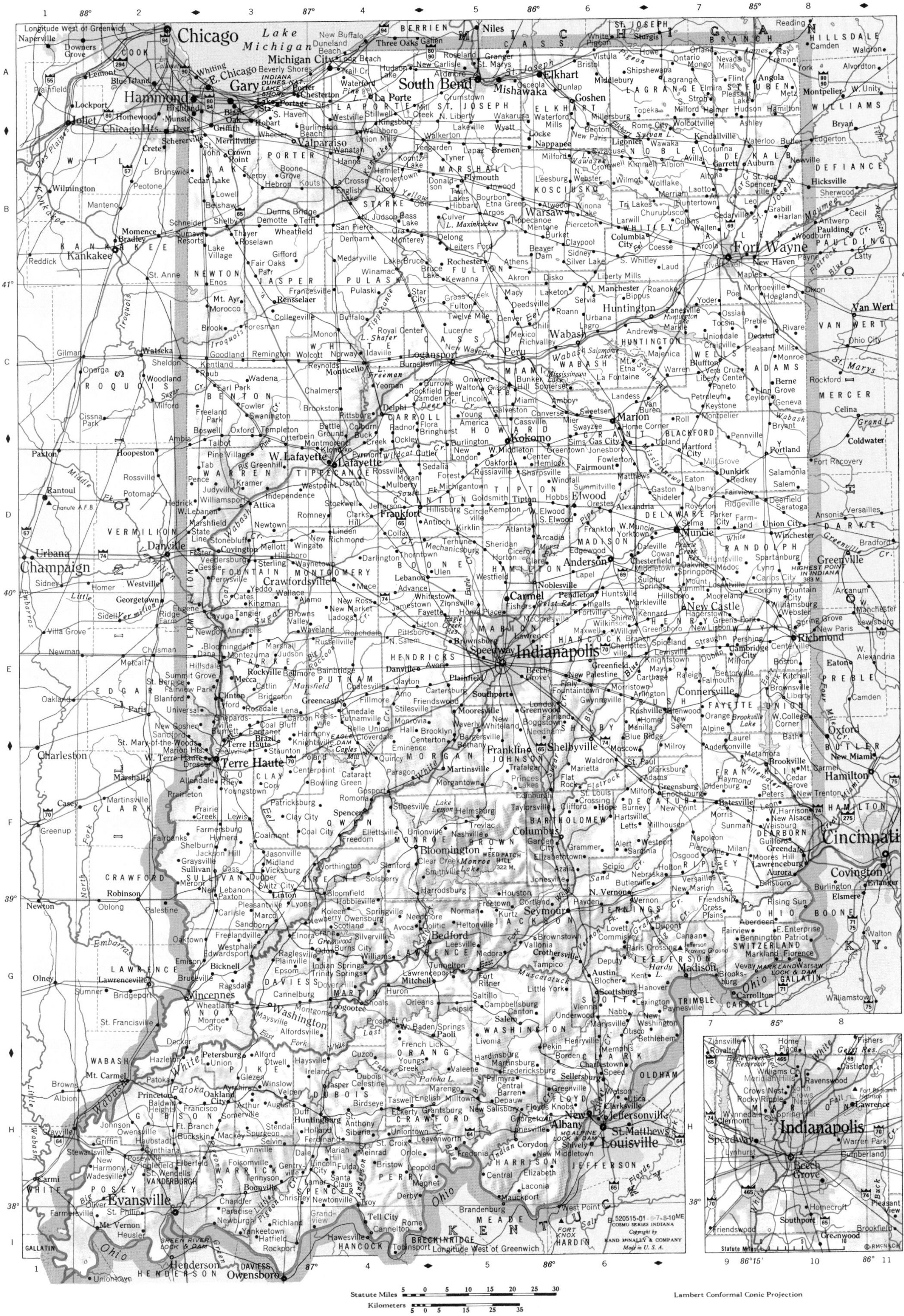

Indiana

1990 CENSUS

Anderson, 59,459 .. D 6
Auburn, 9,379 ...... B 7
Bedford, 13,817 .... G 5
Beech Grove, 13,383 E 5
Bloomington, 60,633 F 4
Bluffton, 9,020 ...... C 7
Boonville, 6,724 .... H 3
Brazil, 7,640 .... E 3
Brownsburg, 7,628 .. E 5
Carmel, 25,380 .... E 5
Cedar Lake, 8,885 .. B 3
Chesterton, 9,124 .. A 3
Clarksville, 19,833 .. H 6
Columbus, 31,802 .. F 6
Connersville, 15,550 E 7
Corydon, 2,661 .... H 5
Crawfordsville, 13,584 D 4
Crown Point, 17,728 B 3
Decatur, 8,644 ...... C 8
Dyer, 10,923 ...... A 2
East Chicago, 33,892 A 3
Elkhart, 43,627 .... A 6
Elwood, 9,494 ...... D 6
Evansville, 126,272 .. I 2
Fort Wayne, 173,072 B 7
Frankfort, 14,754 .... D 4
Franklin, 12,907 .... F 5
French Lick, 2,087 .. G 4
Gary, 116,646 ...... A 3
Gas City, 6,296 .... D 6
Goshen, 23,797 .... A 6
Greencastle, 8,984 .. E 4
Greenfield, 11,657 .. E 6
Greensburg, 9,286 .. F 7
Greenwood, 26,265 .. E 5
Griffith, 17,916 ...... A 3
Hammond, 84,236 .. A 2
Hartford City, 6,960 .. D 7
Highland, 23,696 .... A 3
Hobart, 21,822 ...... A 3
Huntington, 16,389 .. C 7
Indianapolis, 731,327 E 5
Jasper, 10,030 ...... H 4
Jeffersonville, 21,841 H 6
Kendallville, 7,773 .. B 7
Kokomo, 44,962 .... D 5
Lafayette, 43,764 .. D 4
Lake Station, 13,899 A 3
La Porte, 21,507 .... A 4
Lawrence, 26,763 .. E 5
Lebanon, 12,059 .... D 5
Linton, 5,814 ...... F 3
Logansport, 16,812 .. C 5
Madison, 12,006 .... G 7
Marion, 32,618 ...... C 6
Martinsville, 11,677 .. F 5
Merrillville, 27,257 .. B 3
Michigan City, 33,822 A 4
Mishawaka, 42,608 .. A 5
Mount Vernon, 7,217 I 2
Muncie, 71,035 .... D 7
Munster, 19,949 .... A 2
New Albany, 36,322 H 6
New Castle, 17,753 .. E 7
New Haven, 9,320 .. B 7
Noblesville, 17,655 .. D 6
Peru, 12,843 ...... C 5
Plainfield, 10,433 .... E 5
Plymouth, 8,303 .... B 5
Portage, 29,060 .... A 3
Portland, 6,483 .... D 8
Princeton, 8,127 .... H 2
Richmond, 38,705 .. E 8
Rockville, 2,706 .... E 3
Rushville, 5,533 .... E 7
Schererville, 19,926 .. B 3
Seymour, 15,576 .... G 6
Shelbyville, 15,336 .. F 6
South Bend, 105,511 A 5
South Haven, 6,679('80) .... A 3
Speedway, 13,092 .. E 5
Tell City, 8,088 ...... I 4
Terre Haute, 57,483 .. F 3
Valparaiso, 24,414 .. B 3
Vincennes, 19,859 .. G 2
Wabash, 12,127 .... C 6
Warsaw, 10,968 .... B 6
Washington, 10,838 G 3
West Lafayette, 25,907 .... D 4

Iowa

1990 CENSUS

Algona, 6,015	A 3
Altoona, 7,191	C 4
Amana, 540('87)	C 6
Ames, 47,198	B 4
Anamosa, 5,100	B 6
Ankeny, 18,482	C 4
Atlantic, 7,432	C 2
Bettendorf, 28,132	C 7
Boone, 12,392	B 4
Burlington, 27,208	D 6
Camanche, 4,436	C 7
Carroll, 9,579	B 3
Cedar Falls, 34,298	B 5
Cedar Rapids, 108,751	C 6
Centerville, 5,936	D 5
Chariton, 4,616	C 4
Charles City, 7,878	A 5
Cherokee, 6,026	B 2
Clarinda, 5,104	D 2
Clear Lake, 8,183	A 4
Clinton, 29,201	C 7
Clive, 7,462	e 8
Coralville, 10,347	C 6
Council Bluffs, 54,315	C 2
Creston, 7,911	C 3
Davenport, 95,333	C 7
Decorah, 8,063	A 6
Denison, 6,604	B 2
Des Moines, 193,187	C 4
Dubuque, 57,546	B 7
Estherville, 6,720	A 3
Evansdale, 4,638	B 5
Fairfield, 9,768	C 6
Forest City, 4,430	A 4
Fort Dodge, 25,894	B 3
Fort Madison, 11,618	D 6
Glenwood, 4,571	C 2
Grinnell, 8,902	C 5
Hampton, 4,133	B 4
Harlan, 5,148	C 2
Hiawatha, 4,986	B 6
Humboldt, 4,438	B 3
Independence, 5,972	B 6
Indianola, 11,340	C 4
Iowa City, 59,738	C 6
Iowa Falls, 5,424	B 4
Jefferson, 4,292	B 3
Keokuk, 12,451	D 6
Knoxville, 8,232	C 4
Le Mars, 8,454	B 1
Manchester, 5,137	B 6
Maquoketa, 6,111	B 7
Marion, 20,403	B 6
Marshalltown, 25,178	B 5
Mason City, 29,040	A 4
Mount Pleasant, 8,027	D 6
Muscatine, 22,881	C 6
Nevada, 6,009	B 4
New Hampton, 3,660	A 5
Newton, 14,789	C 4
Oelwein, 6,493	B 6
Orange City, 4,940	B 1
Oskaloosa, 10,632	C 5
Ottumwa, 24,488	C 5
Pella, 9,270	C 5
Perry, 6,652	C 3
Red Oak, 6,264	D 2
Sheldon, 4,937	A 2
Shenandoah, 5,572	D 2
Sioux Center, 5,074	A 1
Sioux City, 80,505	B 1
Spencer, 11,066	A 2
Spirit Lake, 3,871	A 2
Storm Lake, 8,769	B 2
Urbandale, 23,500	C 4
Vinton, 5,103	B 5
Washington, 7,074	C 6
Waterloo, 66,467	B 5
Waukon, 4,019	A 6
Waverly, 8,539	B 5
Webster City, 7,894	B 4
West Branch, 1,908	C 6
West Des Moines, 31,702	C 4
Windsor Heights, 5,190	e 8

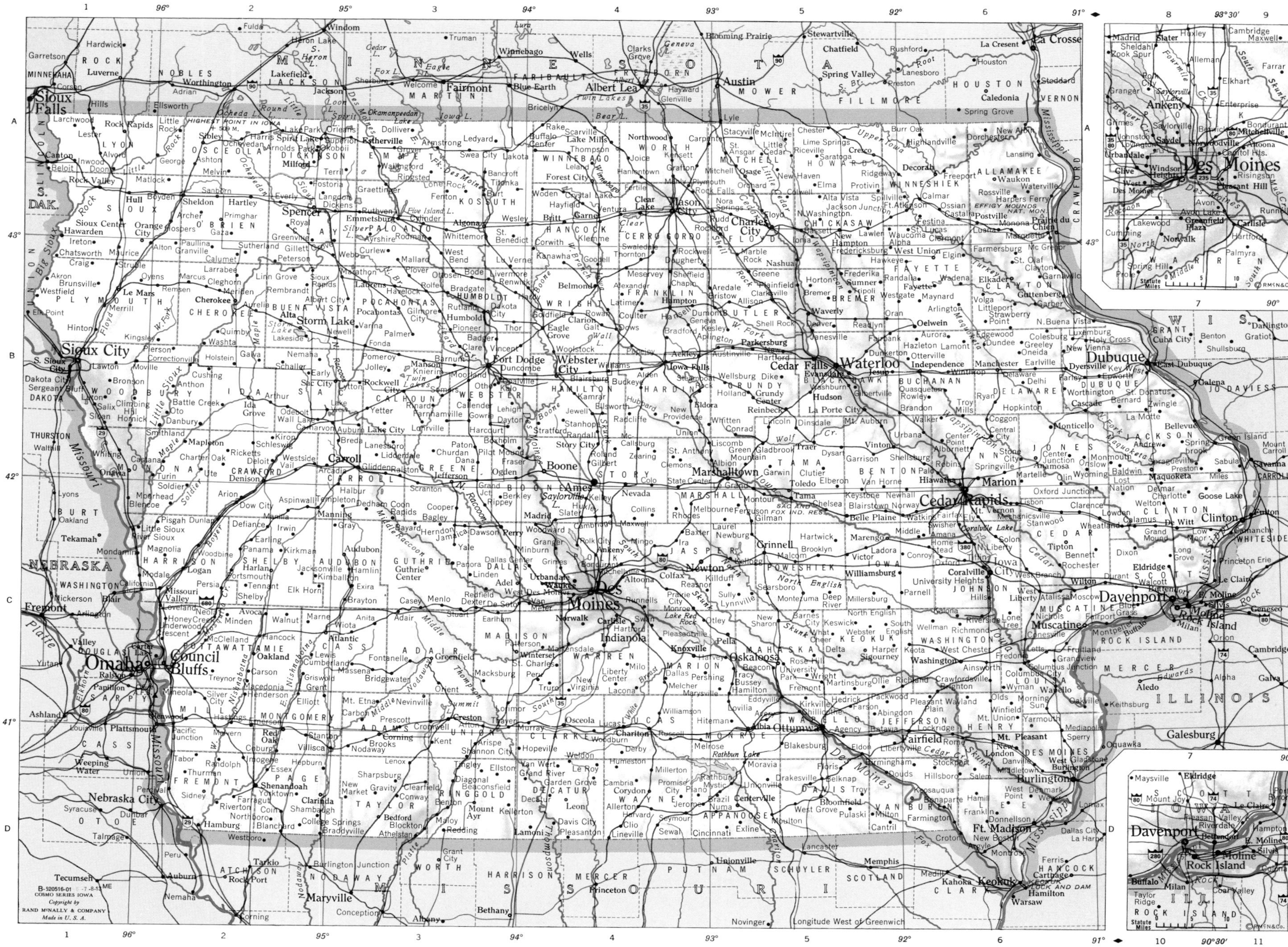

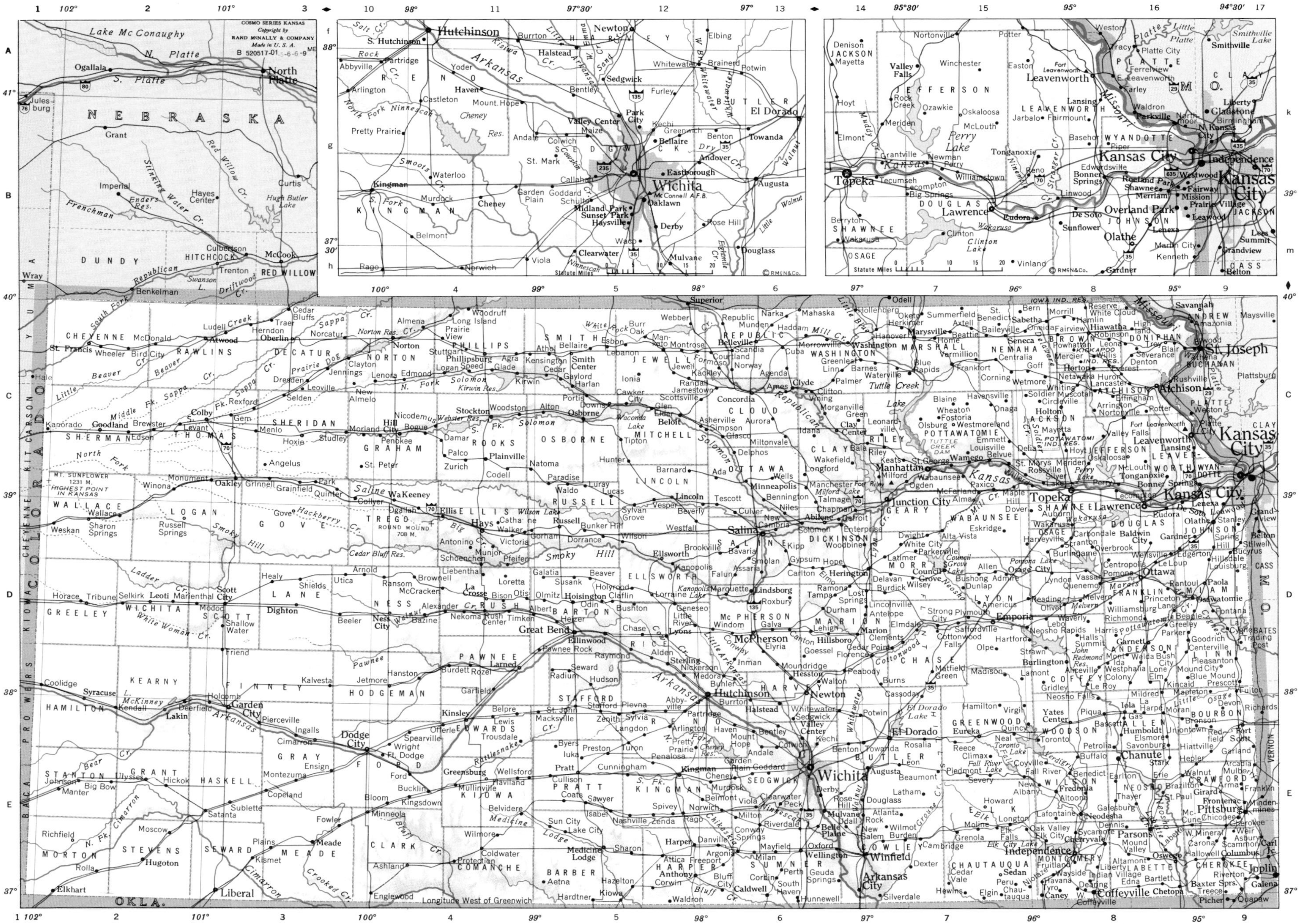

Kansas

1990 CENSUS

Abilene, 6,242	D 6
Andover, 4,047	g12
Arkansas City, 12,762	E 6
Atchison, 10,656	C 8
Augusta, 7,876	E 7
Baldwin City, 2,961	D 8
Baxter Springs, 4,351	E 9
Beloit, 4,066	C 5
Bonner Springs, 6,413	C 9
Burlington, 2,735	D 8
Chanute, 9,488	E 8
Clay Center, 4,613	C 6
Coffeyville, 12,917	E 8
Colby, 5,396	C 2
Columbus, 3,268	E 9
Concordia, 6,167	C 6
Derby, 14,699	E 6
Dodge City, 21,129	E 3
Edwardsville, 3,979	k16
El Dorado, 11,504	E 7
Emporia, 25,512	D 7
Eudora, 3,006	D 8
Eureka, 2,974	E 7
Fairway, 4,173	k16
Fort Scott, 8,362	E 9
Fredonia, 2,599	E 8
Galena, 3,308	E 9
Garden City, 24,097	E 3
Garnett, 3,210	D 8
Goodland, 4,983	C 2
Great Bend, 15,427	D 5
Hays, 17,767	D 4
Haysville, 8,364	g12
Herington, 2,685	D 7
Hiawatha, 3,603	C 8
Hoisington, 3,182	D 5
Holton, 3,196	C 8
Hugoton, 3,179	E 2
Hutchinson, 39,308	D 6
Independence, 9,942	E 8
Iola, 6,351	E 8
Junction City, 20,604	C 7
Kansas City, 149,767	C 9
Kingman, 3,196	E 5
Lansing, 7,120	C 9
Larned, 4,490	D 4
Lawrence, 65,608	D 8
Leavenworth, 38,495	C 9
Leawood, 19,693	D 9
Lenexa, 34,034	D 9
Liberal, 16,573	E 3
Lindsborg, 3,076	D 6
Lyons, 3,688	D 5
Manhattan, 37,712	C 7
Marysville, 3,359	C 7
McPherson, 12,422	D 6
Merriam, 11,821	k16
Mission, 9,504	m16
Mulvane, 4,674	E 6
Neodesha, 2,837	E 8
Newton, 16,700	D 6
Norton, 3,017	C 4
Olathe, 63,352	D 9
Osawatomie, 4,590	D 9
Ottawa, 10,667	D 8
Overland Park, 111,790	m16
Paola, 4,698	D 9
Park City, 5,050	g12
Parsons, 11,924	E 8
Phillipsburg, 2,828	C 4
Pittsburg, 17,775	E 9
Prairie Village, 23,186	m16
Pratt, 6,687	E 5
Roeland Park, 7,706	k16
Russell, 4,781	D 5
Salina, 42,303	D 6
Scott City, 3,785	D 3
Shawnee, 37,993	k16
Topeka, 119,883	C 8
Ulysses, 5,474	E 2
Valley Center, 3,624	E 6
Wamego, 3,706	C 7
Wellington, 8,411	E 6
Wichita, 304,011	E 6
Winfield, 11,931	E 7

Kentucky

1990 CENSUS

Alexandria, 5,592 . . . . B 5
Ashland, 23,622 . . . . . . B 7
Barbourville, 3,658 . . . D 6
Bardstown, 6,801 . . . . C 4
Bellevue, 6,997 . . . . . . h13
Benton, 3,899 . . . . f 9
Berea, 9,126 . . . . C 5
Bowling Green, 40,641 D 3
Campbellsville, 9,577 . . C 4
Carrollton, 3,715 . . . . . . B 4
Cave City, 1,953 . . . . . . C 4
Central City, 4,979 . . . . C 2
Columbia, 3,845 . . . . . . C 4
Corbin, 7,419 . . . . D 5
Covington, 43,264 . . . . . A 5
Cumberland, 3,112 . . . . . D 7
Cynthiana, 6,497 . . . . . . B 5
Danville, 12,420 . . . . . . C 5
Dayton, 6,576 . . . . h14
Edgewood, 8,143 . . . . . . h13
Elizabethtown, 18,167 C 4
Elsmere, 6,847 . . . . . . B 5
Erlanger, 15,979 . . . . . . A 5
Flatwoods, 7,799 . . . . . . B 7
Florence, 18,624 . . . . . . A 5
Fort Mitchell, 7,438 . . . . h13
Fort Thomas, 16,032 . . h14
Fort Wright, 6,570 . . . . . h13
Frankfort, 25,968 . . . . . . B 5
Franklin, 7,607 . . . . D 3
Georgetown, 11,414 . . B 5
Glasgow, 12,351 . . . . . . C 4
Greenville, 4,689 . . . . . . C 2
Harrodsburg, 7,335 . . . . C 5
Hazard, 5,416 . . . . C 6
Henderson, 25,945 . . . . C 2
Hopkinsville, 29,809 . . D 2
Independence, 10,444 . . B 5
Jeffersontown, 23,221 B 4
Lawrenceburg, 5,911 . . B 5
Lebanon, 5,695 . . . . . . C 4
Leitchfield, 4,965 . . . . . . C 3
Lexington, 225,366 . . . . B 5
London, 5,757 . . . . C 5
Louisville, 269,063 . . . . B 4
Ludlow, 4,736 . . . . h13
Madisonville, 16,200 . . . C 2
Mayfield, 9,935 . . . . f 9
Maysville, 7,169 . . . . B 6
Middlesboro, 11,328 . . . D 6
Monticello, 5,357 . . . . . . D 5
Morehead, 8,357 . . . . . . B 6
Morganfield, 3,776 . . . . C 2
Mount Sterling, 5,362 . . B 6
Mount Washington, 5,226 . . . . B 4
Murray, 14,439 . . . . f 9
Newport, 18,871 . . . . . . A 5
Nicholasville, 13,603 . . C 5
Owensboro, 53,549 . . . C 2
Paducah, 27,256 . . . . . . e 9
Paintsville, 4,354 . . . . . . C 7
Paris, 8,730 . . . . B 5
Pikeville, 6,324 . . . . . . C 7
Prestonsburg, 3,558 . . . . C 7
Princeton, 6,940 . . . . . . C 2
Providence, 4,123 . . . . . C 2
Radcliff, 19,772 . . . . C 4
Richmond, 21,155 . . . . . C 5
Russell, 4,014 . . . . B 7
Russellville, 7,454 . . . . D 3
Saint Matthews, 15,800 B 4
Scottsville, 4,278 . . . . . . D 3
Shelbyville, 6,238 . . . . . B 4
Shepherdsville, 4,805 . . C 4
Shively, 15,535 . . . . . . B 4
Somerset, 10,733 . . . . . . C 5
Taylor Mill, 5,530 . . . . . . k14
Tompkinsville, 2,861 . . D 4
Valley Station, 20,000('84) g11
Versailles, 7,269 . . . . . . B 5
Williamsburg, 5,493 . . . . D 5
Wilmore, 4,215 . . . . C 5
Winchester, 15,799 . . . . C 5

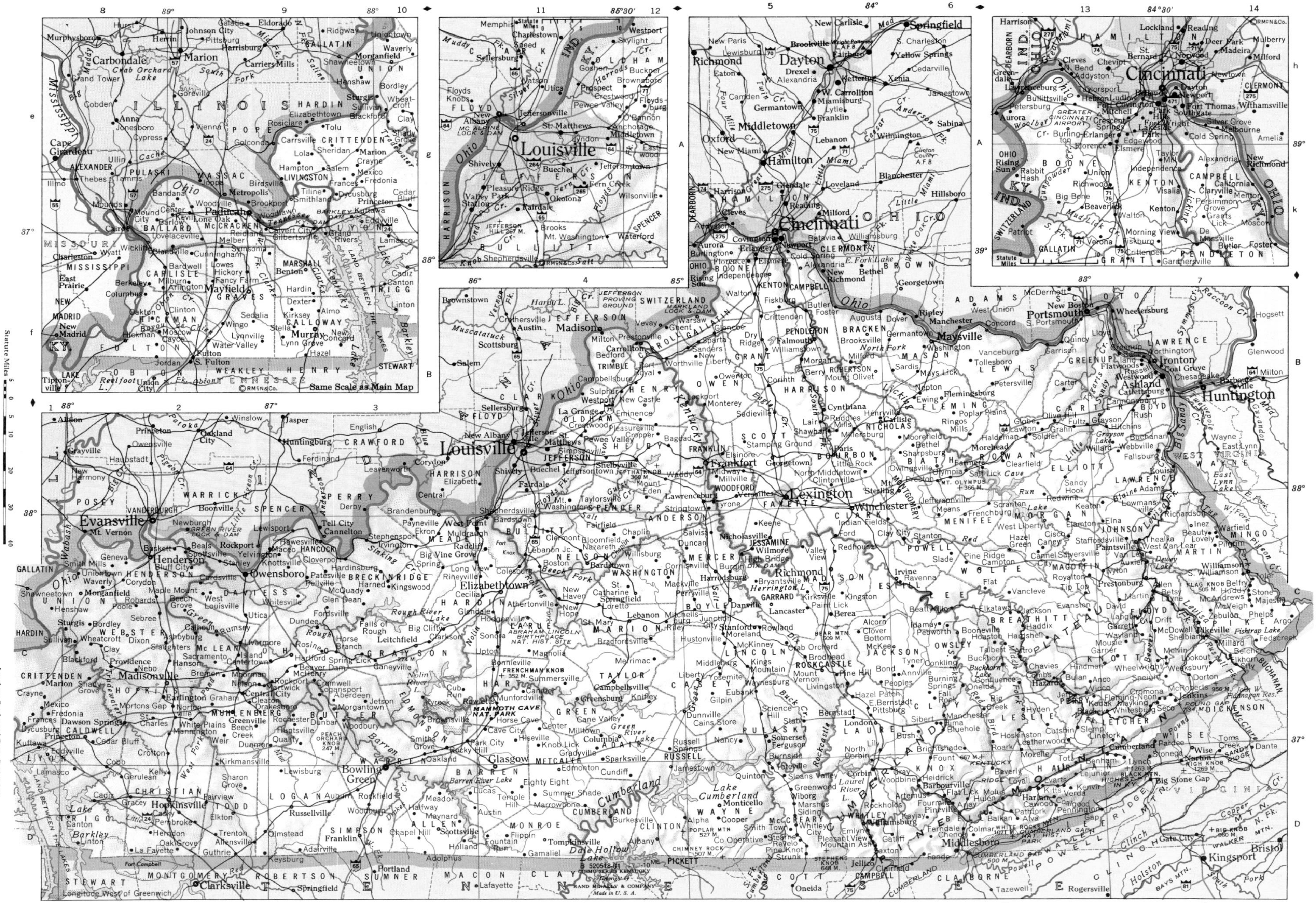

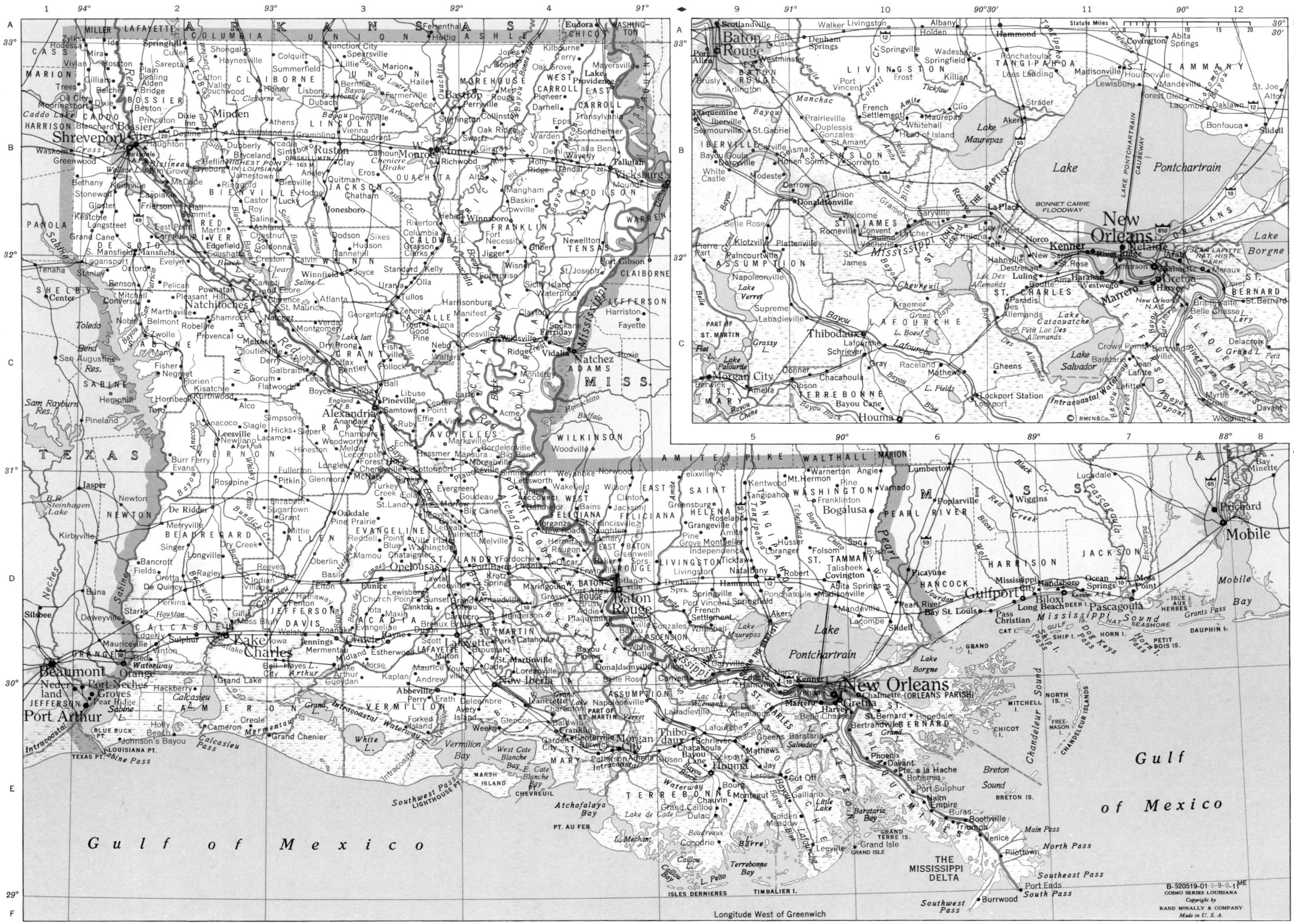

Statute Miles 5 0 5 10 20 30 40
Kilometers 5 0 5 15 25 35 45 55

Lambert Conformal Conic Projection

Louisiana

1990 CENSUS

Abbeville, 11,187 . . . . . . E 3
Alexandria, 49,188 . . . . C 3
Arabi, 10,248('80) k11
Baker, 13,233 . . . . D 4
Bastrop, 13,916 . . . . B 4
Baton Rouge, 219,531 D 4
Berwick, 4,375 . . . . E 4
Bogalusa, 14,280 . . . . D 6
Bossier City, 52,721 . . B 2
Breaux Bridge, 6,515 . . D 4
Bunkie, 5,044 . . . . D 3
Chalmette, 31,860 . . . . E 6
Church Point, 4,677 . . . D 3
Covington, 7,691 . . . . . . D 5
Crowley, 13,983 . . . . . . D 3
Cut Off, 5,049('80) . . . . E 5
Denham Springs, 8,381 D 5
De Ridder, 9,868 . . . . . . D 2
Donaldsonville, 7,949 . . D 4
Eunice, 11,162 . . . . D 3
Ferriday, 4,111 . . . . . . C 4
Franklin, 9,004 . . . . E 4
Gonzales, 7,003 . . . . D 5
Grambling, 5,484 . . . . . . B 3
Gretna, 17,208 . . . . E 5
Hammond, 15,871 . . . . . . D 5
Harahan, 9,927 . . . . . . k11
Harvey, 15,000 . . . . . . E 5
Houma, 96,982 . . . . E 5
Jeanerette, 6,205 . . . . . E 4
Jefferson, 15,550('80) . . k11
Jena, 2,626 . . . . C 3
Jennings, 11,305 . . . . . . D 3
Jonesboro, 4,305 . . . . B 3
Kaplan, 4,535 . . . . D 3
Kenner, 72,033 . . . . . . E 5
Lafayette, 94,440 . . . . . D 3
Lake Charles, 70,580 . . D 2
Lake Providence, 5,380 B 4
La Place, 16,112('80) . . . h11
Leesville, 7,638 . . . . . . C 2
Lutcher, 3,907 . . . . D 5
Mandeville, 7,083 . . . . D 5
Mansfield, 5,389 . . . . . . B 2
Marksville, 5,526 . . . . . . C 3
Marrero, 36,671 . . . . . . E 5
Metairie, 149,428 . . . . . k11
Minden, 13,661 . . . . B 2
Monroe, 54,909 . . . . . . B 3
Morgan City, 14,531 . . . . E 4
Moss Bluff, 7,004('80) D 2
Natchitoches, 16,609 . . C 2
New Iberia, 31,828 . . . . D 4
New Orleans, 496,938 E 5
Oakdale, 6,832 . . . . . . D 3
Opelousas, 18,151 . . . . D 3
Patterson, 4,736 . . . . . . E 4
Pineville, 12,251 . . . . . . C 3
Plaquemine, 7,186 . . . . . D 4
Ponchatoula, 5,425 . . . D 5
Port Allen, 6,277 . . . . . . D 4
Raceland, 6,302('80) . . E 5
Rayne, 8,502 . . . . D 3
Rayville, 4,411 . . . . B 4
Reserve, 7,288('80) h10
River Ridge, 17,146('80) k11
Ruston, 20,027 . . . . B 3
Saint Martinville, 7,137 D 4
Scotlandville, 15,113('80) . . . . D 4
Shreveport, 198,525 . . B 2
Slidell, 24,124 . . . . D 6
Springhill, 5,668 . . . . . . A 2
Sulphur, 20,125 . . . . D 2
Tallulah, 8,526 . . . . B 4
Thibodaux, 14,035 . . . . . . E 5
Vidalia, 4,953 . . . . C 4
Ville Platte, 9,037 . . . . . D 3
Violet, 6,000 . . . . k12
Westlake, 5,007 . . . . D 2
West Monroe, 14,096 . . B 3
Westwego, 11,218 . . . . . k11
Winnfield, 6,138 . . . . . . C 3
Winnsboro, 5,755 . . . . . . B 4
Zachary, 9,036 . . . . D 4

Maine

1990 CENSUS

Auburn, 24,309 .... D 2
Augusta, 21,325 .... D 3
Bangor, 33,181 .... D 4
Bar Harbor, 2,685 (4,443▲) .... D 4
Bath, 9,799 .... E 3
Belfast, 6,355 ...... D 3
Berwick, 2,378 (5,995▲) .... E 2
Biddeford, 20,710 .. E 2
Brewer, 9,021 ...... D 4
Bridgton, 1,639 (4,307▲) .... D 2
Brunswick, 10,990 (20,906▲) .... E 3
Bucksport, 2,853 (4,825▲) .... D 4
Calais, 3,963 ...... C 5
Camden, 3,743 (5,060▲) .... D 3
Caribou, 9,415 ...... B 5
Dexter, 3,118 (4,419▲) .... C 3
Dixfield, 1,725 (2,574▲) .... D 2
Dover-Foxcroft, 2,974 (4,657▲) .... C 3
Eastport, 1,965 .... D 6
Ellsworth, 5,975 .... D 4
Fairfield, 3,169 (6,718▲) .... D 3
Farmingdale, 2,014 (2,918▲) .... D 3
Farmington, 3,583 (7,436▲) .... D 2
Fort Fairfield, 2,282 (3,998▲) .... B 5
Fort Kent, 2,375 (4,268▲) .... A 4
Fryeburg, 1,644 (2,968▲) .... D 2
Gardiner, 6,746 .... D 3
Gorham, 4,052 (11,856▲) .... E 2
Hallowell, 2,534 .... D 3
Hampden, 2,300 (5,974▲) .... D 4
Houlton, 5,730 (6,613▲) .... B 5
Kennebunk, 3,294 (8,004▲) .... E 2
Kennebunkport, 1,685 (3,356▲) .... E 2
Kittery, 5,465 (9,372▲) .... E 2
Lewiston, 39,757 .... D 2
Lincoln, 3,524 (5,587▲) .... C 4
Livermore Falls, 2,441 (3,455▲) .... D 2
Madawaska, 4,165 (4,803▲) .... A 4
Madison, 2,788 (4,725▲) .... D 3
Mexico, 3,207 (3,344▲) .... D 2
Milford, 1,688 (2,884▲) .... D 4
Milo, 2,255 (2,600▲) C 4
Newport, 1,748 (3,036▲) .... D 3
Norway, 2,653 (4,754▲) .... D 2
Oakland, 3,387 (5,595▲) .... D 3
Old Town, 8,317 .... D 4
Pittsfield, 3,117 (4,190▲) .... D 3
Portland, 64,358 .... E 2
Presque Isle, 10,550 B 5
Richmond, 1,578 (3,072▲) .... D 3
Rockland, 7,972 .... D 3
Rumford, 6,256 (7,078▲) .... D 2
Saco, 15,181 ...... E 2
Sanford, 10,268 (20,463▲) .... E 2
Scarborough, 2,280 (12,518▲) .... E 2
Skowhegan, 6,517 (8,725▲) .... D 3
South Berwick, 2,120 (5,877▲) .... E 2
South Portland, 23,163 .... E 2
Thomaston, 2,348 (3,306▲) .... D 3
Topsham, 4,657 (8,746▲) .... E 3
Waterville, 17,173 .. D 3
Westbrook, 16,121 .. E 2
Wilton, 2,262 (4,242▲) .... D 2
Winslow, 5,903 (7,997▲) .... D 3
Winthrop, 3,264 (5,968▲) .... D 3
Yarmouth, 2,981 (7,862▲) .... E 2
York, 3,130 (9,818▲) E 2

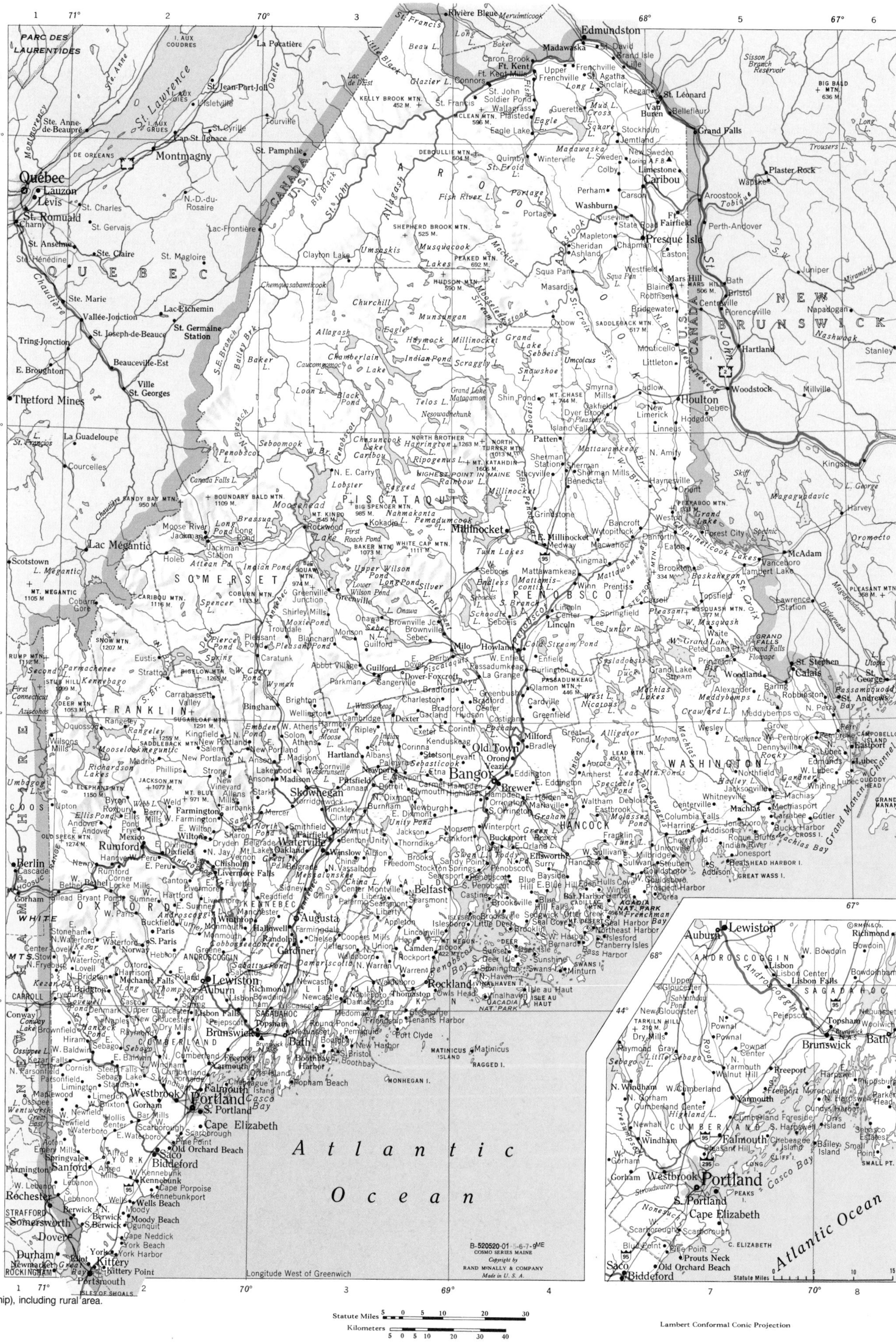

▲ Population of entire town (township), including rural area.

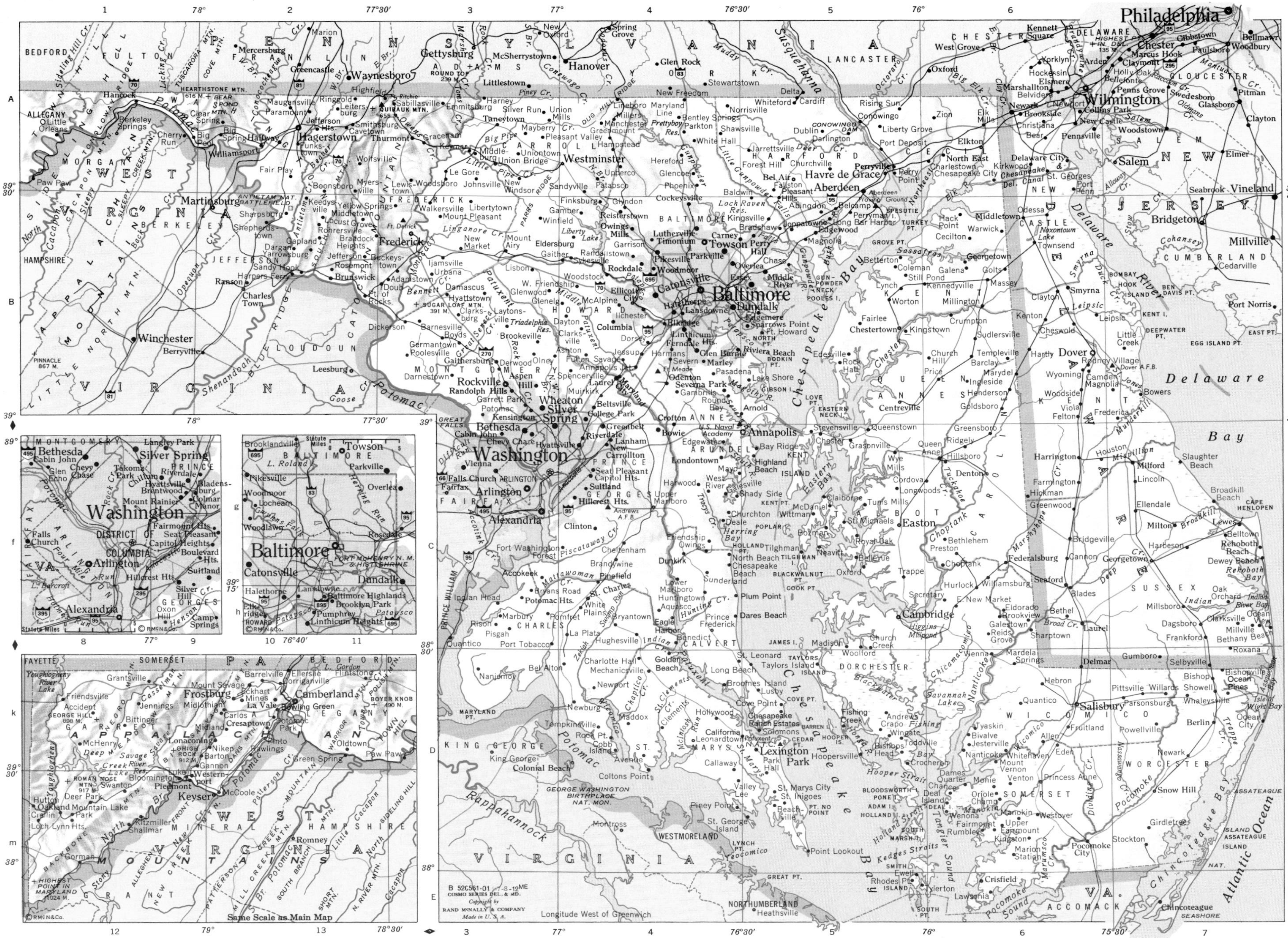

Lambert Conformal Conic Projection

Statute Miles 5 0 5 10 15 20

Kilometers 5 0 5 10 15 20 25 30

Maryland

1990 CENSUS

Aberdeen, 13,087 .... A 5
Annapolis, 33,187 .... C 5
Baltimore, 736,014 .... B 4
Bel Air, 8,860 .... A 5
Beltsville, 7,670('88) .. B 4
Bethesda, 62,936 .... C 3
Bladensburg, 8,064 .... f 9
Bowie, 37,589 .... C 4
Brunswick, 5,117...... B 2
Calverton, 7,649('80) .. B 4
Cambridge, 11,514 .... C 5
Catonsville, 35,200 .... B 4
Chevy Chase, 8,559 .... C 3
Chillum, 12,500('88) .... f 9
Clinton, 7,570('88) .... C 4
College Park, 21,927 .. C 4
Columbia, 75,883 ...... B 4
Crofton, 12,009('80) .. B 4
Cumberland, 23,706 .. k13
Dundalk, 65,800 ...... B 4
Easton, 9,372 .... C 5
Edgemere, 7,410('88) . B 5
Edgewood, 19,455('80) B 5
Elkton, 9,073 .... A 6
Essex, 40,872.......... B 5
Fallston, 5,572('80).... A 5
Frederick, 40,148 ...... B 3
Frostburg, 8,075 ...... k13
Gaithersburg, 39,542 .. B 3
Germantown, 760('88) B 3
Glen Burnie, 32,700 .. B 4
Greenbelt, 21,096 .... C 4
Hagerstown, 35,445 .. A 2
Halethorpe, 20,163 .... B 4
Halfway, 2,000('88).... A 2
Havre de Grace, 8,952 A 5
Hyattsville, 13,864 .... C 4
Langley Park, 9,150('88) f 9
Lanham, 5,000('88).... C 4
Lansdowne, 9,430('88) B 4
Laurel, 19,438 .... B 4
La Vale, 5,000('88) k13
Lutherville-Timonium,
16,871('80)............ B 4
Lynne Acres, 5,910('88) B 4
Middle River, 24,616 .. B 5
Mount Rainier, 7,954 .. f 9
Oakland, 1,741 ...... m12
Ocean City, 5,146 .... D 7
Odenton, 6,590('88) .. B 4
Olney, 9,500('88)...... B 3
Overlea, 3,320('88).... B 5
Owings Mills, 9,526('80) B 4
Oxon Hill, 3,730('88).... f 9
Parkville, 31,617 ...... B 4
Perry Hall, 10,285('88) B 5
Pikesville, 16,280...... B 4
Pocomoke City, 3,922..D 6
Potomac, 25,370...... B 3
Randallstown,
18,680('88) .... B 4
Reisterstown,
19,385('80) .... B 4
Rockville, 44,835...... B 3
Rosedale, 11,390('88) .. g11
Salisbury, 20,592........D 6
Seat Pleasant, 5,359 .. C 4
Severn, 20,147('80)....B 4
Severna Park,
21,253('80) .... B 4
Sharpsburg, 659 .... B 2
Silver Spring, 76,200 .. C 3
Snow Hill, 2,217 ...... D 7
Suitland, 35,400 ...... C 4
Takoma Park, 16,700 .. f 8
Towson, 49,445 ...... B 4
Westminster, 13,068 .. A 4
Wheaton, 58,300...... B 3
Woodmoor, 8,630('88) B 4

District of Columbia

1990 CENSUS

Washington, 606,900 .. C 3

Massachusetts

1990 CENSUS

Amherst, 17,773 (35,228▲) . . . . B 2
Arlington, 44,630 . . . . . B 5
Attleboro, 38,383 . . . . C 5
Belmont, 24,720 . . . . . . g11
Beverly, 38,195 . . . . . . A 6
Boston, 574,283 . . . . . . B 5
Braintree, 33,836 . . . . . B 5
Brockton, 92,788 . . . . . B 5
Brookline, 54,718 . . . . B 5
Burlington, 23,302 . . . . f11
Cambridge, 95,802 . . . . B 5
Chelmsford, 32,383 . . . A 5
Chelsea, 28,710 . . . . . . B 5
Chicopee, 56,632 . . . . B 2
Concord, 4,680 (17,076▲) . . . . B 5
Danvers, 24,174 . . . . . . A 6
Dedham, 23,782 . . . . . . B 5
Everett, 35,701 . . . . . . g11
Fall River, 92,703 . . . . C 5
Fitchburg, 41,194 . . . . A 4
Framingham, 64,989 . . B 5
Gardner, 20,125 . . . . . . A 4
Gloucester, 28,716 . . . . A 6
Greenfield, 14,198 (18,666▲) . . . . A 2
Haverhill, 51,418 . . . . . A 5
Holyoke, 43,704 . . . . . . B 2
Hyannis, 9,900 . . . . . . C 7
Lawrence, 70,207 . . . . A 5
Leominster, 38,145 . . . . A 4
Lexington, 28,974 . . . . B 5
Lowell, 103,439 . . . . . . A 5
Lynn, 81,245 . . . . B 6
Malden, 53,884 . . . . . . B 5
Marblehead, 20,126('80) B 6
Marlborough, 31,813 . . B 4
Medford, 57,407 . . . . . . B 5
Melrose, 28,150 . . . . . . B 5
Methuen, 40,300 . . . . . . A 5
Milford, 25,200 . . . . . . B 4
Milton, 25,725 . . . . B 5
Nantucket, 3,229 (6,012▲) . . . . D 7
Natick, 30,100 . . . . B 5
Needham, 27,557 . . . . . g11
New Bedford, 99,922 . . C 6
Newburyport, 16,317 . . A 6
Newton, 82,585 . . . . . . B 5
North Adams, 16,797 . . A 1
Northampton, 29,289 . . B 2
North Andover, 20,129('87) . . . . A 5
North Attleboro, 24,200 C 5
Norwood, 28,700 . . . . . B 5
Peabody, 47,039 . . . . . A 6
Pittsfield, 48,622 . . . . . B 1
Plymouth, 7,232 (45,608▲) . . . . C 6
Quincy, 84,985 . . . . . . B 5
Randolph, 30,093 . . . . B 5
Reading, 22,539 . . . . . . A 5
Revere, 42,786 . . . . . . g11
Salem, 38,091 . . . . A 6
Saugus, 25,549 . . . . . . B 5
Shrewsbury, 23,400 . . B 4
Somerville, 76,210 . . . . B 5
Springfield, 156,983 . . B 2
Stoneham, 22,203 . . . g11
Stoughton, 27,800 . . . . B 5
Taunton, 49,832 . . . . . . C 5
Vineyard Haven, 1,704('80) . . . . D 6
Wakefield, 24,825 . . . . B 5
Waltham, 57,878 . . . . . . B 5
Watertown, 33,284 . . . . g11
Wellesley, 26,615 . . . . B 5
Westfield, 38,372 . . . . B 2
West Springfield, 27,537 B 2
Weymouth, 54,063 . . . . B 6
Winchester, 20,701('80) g11
Winthrop, 19,294('80) . . B 6
Woburn, 35,943 . . . . . . B 5
Worcester, 169,759 . . . . B 4

▲ Population of entire town (township), including rural area.

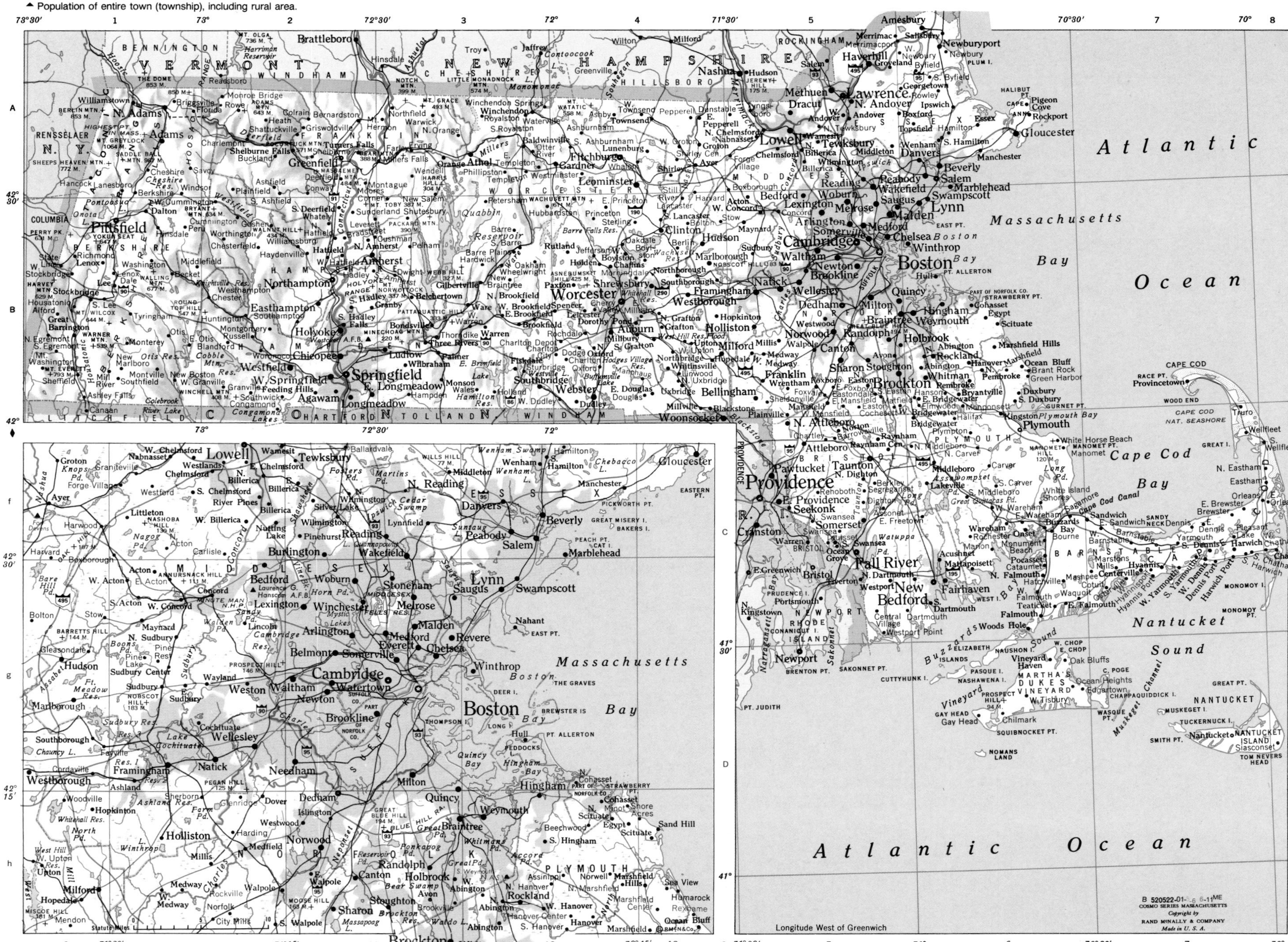

Statute Miles 5 0 5 10 15 20

Kilometers 5 0 5 10 15 20 25

Lambert Conformal Conic Projection

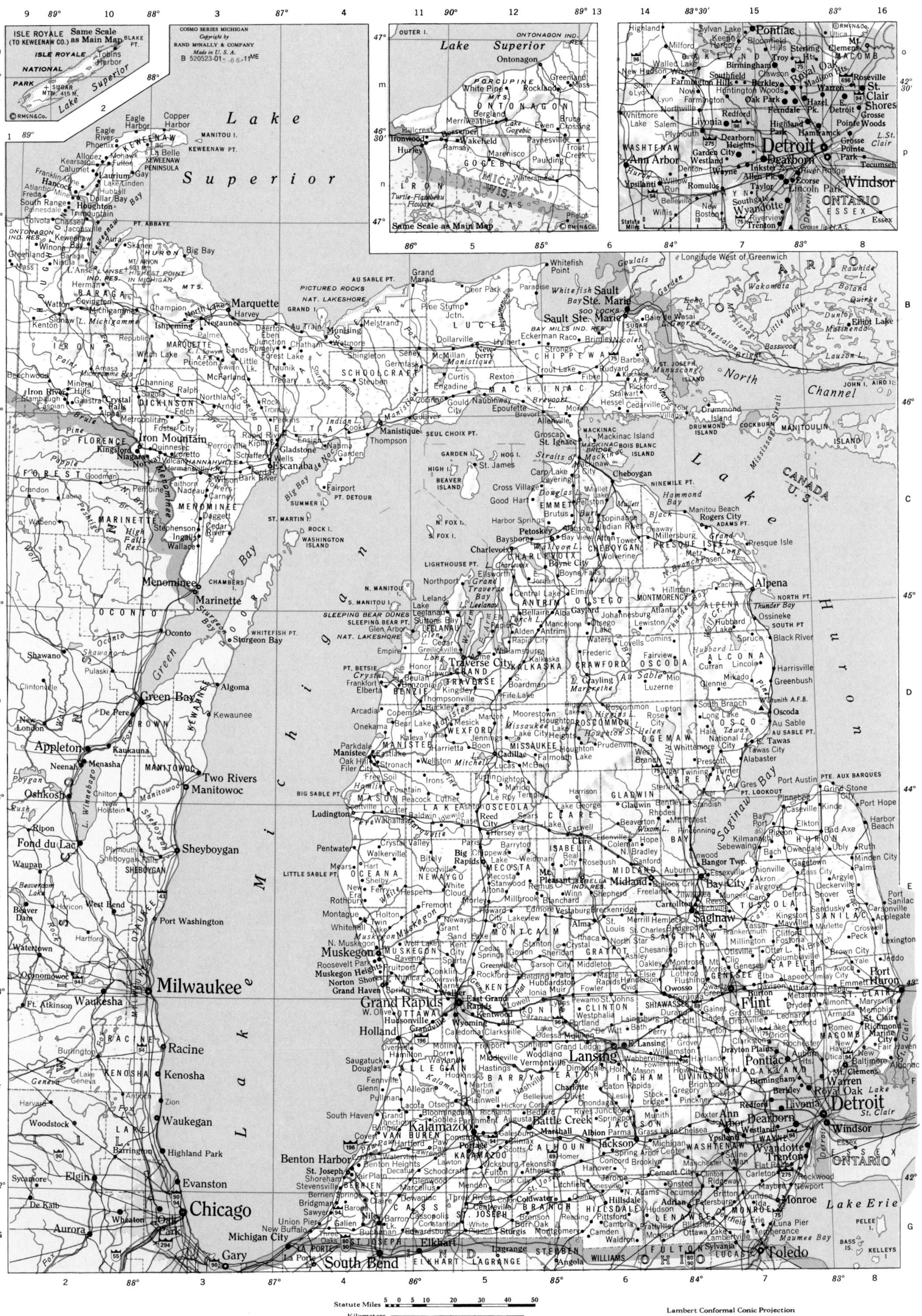

Statute Miles 5 0 5 10 20 30 40 50

Kilometers 5 0 5 15 25 35 45 55 65 75

Lambert Conformal Conic Projection

Michigan

1990 CENSUS

Adrian, 22,097 . . . . . . G 6
Albion, 10,066 . . . . . . F 6
Allen Park, 31,092 . . p15
Alpena, 11,354 . . . . . . C 7
Ann Arbor, 109,592 . . F 7
Auburn Heights, 17,076 . . . . F 7
Bangor Township, 17,494('88) . . . . . . E 7
Battle Creek, 53,540 F 5
Bay City, 38,936 . . . . E 7
Beecher, 17,178('80) E 7
Benton Harbor, 12,818 . . . . F 4
Berkley, 16,960 . . . . F 7
Big Rapids, 12,603 . . E 5
Birmingham, 19,997 . . F 7
Burton, 27,617 . . . . . . E 7
Cadillac, 10,104 . . . . D 5
Cheboygan, 4,999 . . C 6
Clawson, 13,874 . . . . o15
Coldwater, 9,607 . . . . G 5
Dearborn, 89,286 . . . . F 7
Dearborn Heights, 60,838 . . . . p15
Detroit, 1,027,974 . . F 7
Drayton Plains, 18,000('88) . . . . . . F 7
East Detroit, 35,283 . . p16
East Lansing, 50,677 F 6
Escanaba, 13,659 . . C 3
Farmington Hills, 74,652 . . . . o15
Ferndale, 25,084 . . . . P15
Flint, 140,761 . . . . . . E 7
Garden City, 31,846 . . p15
Grand Haven, 11,951 E 4
Grand Rapids, 189,126 . . . . F 5
Grosse Pointe Woods, 17,715 . . . . p16
Hamtramck, 18,372 . . p15
Hazel Park, 20,051 . . p15
Highland, 750('88) . . o14
Highland Park, 20,121 p15
Holland, 30,745 . . . . F 4
Houghton, 7,498 . . . . A 2
Inkster, 30,772 . . . . . . p15
Iron Mountain, 8,525 C 2
Ironwood, 6,849 . . . . n11
Jackson, 37,446 . . . . F 6
Kalamazoo, 80,277 . . F 5
Kentwood, 37,826 . . F 5
Lansing, 127,321 . . . . F 6
Lincoln Park, 41,832 p15
Livonia, 100,850 . . . . F 7
Ludington, 8,507 . . . . E 4
Mackinaw City, 875 . . C 6
Madison Heights, 32,196 . . . . o15
Manistee, 6,734 . . . . D 4
Marquette, 21,977 . . B 3
Menominee, 9,398 . . C 3
Midland, 38,053 . . . . E 6
Monroe, 22,902 . . . . G 7
Mount Clemens, 18,405 . . . . F 8
Mount Pleasant, 23,285 . . . . E 6
Muskegon, 40,283 . . E 4
Niles, 12,458 . . . . . . G 4
Norton Shores, 21,755 . . . . E 4
Novi, 32,998 . . . . p15
Oak Park, 30,462 . . . . p15
Owosso, 16,322 . . . . E 6
Petoskey, 6,056 . . . . C 6
Pontiac, 71,166 . . . . F 7
Portage, 41,042 . . . . F 5
Port Huron, 33,694 . . F 8
Redford, 54,387 . . . . F 7
Romulus, 22,897 . . . . p15
Roseville, 51,412 . . . . o16
Royal Oak, 65,410 . . F 7
Saginaw, 69,512 . . . . E 7
Saint Clair Shores, 68,107 . . . . p16
Sault Sainte Marie, 14,689 . . . . B 6
Southfield, 75,728 . . o15
Southgate, 30,771 . . p15
Sterling Heights, 117,810 . . . . o15
Sturgis, 10,130 . . . . G 5
Taylor, 70,811 . . . . . . p15
Traverse City, 15,155 D 5
Trenton, 20,586 . . . . F 7
Troy, 72,884 . . . . o15
Walker, 17,279 . . . . . . E 5
Warren, 144,864 . . . . F 7
Wayne, 19,899 . . . . . . p15
Westland, 84,724 . . . . F 7
Wyandotte, 30,938 . . F 7
Wyoming, 63,891 . . . . F 5
Ypsilanti, 24,846 . . . . F 7

Minnesota

1990 CENSUS

Albert Lea, 18,310 .. G 5
Alexandria, 7,838 .... E 3
Andover, 15,216 .... m12
Anoka, 17,192 ...... E 5
Apple Valley, 34,598 n12
Austin, 21,907 ...... G 6
Bemidji, 11,245 .... C 4
Blaine, 38,975 ...... m12
Bloomington, 86,335 F 5
Brainerd, 12,353 .... D 4
Brooklyn Center, 28,887 .... E 5
Brooklyn Park, 56,381 .... m12
Burnsville, 51,288 .... F 5
Champlin, 16,849 .. m12
Chisholm, 5,290 .... C 6
Cloquet, 10,885 .... D 6
Columbia Heights, 18,910 .... m12
Coon Rapids, 52,978 E 5
Cottage Grove, 22,935 .... n13
Crookston, 8,119 .... C 2
Crystal, 23,788 .... m12
Detroit Lakes, 6,635 D 3
Duluth, 85,493 ...... D 6
Eagan, 47,409 ...... n12
East Bethel, 8,050 .. E 5
East Grand Forks, 8,658 .... C 2
Eden Prairie, 39,311 .. n12
Edina, 46,070 ...... F 5
Ely, 3,968 .... C 7
Fairmont, 11,265 .... G 4
Faribault, 17,085 .... F 5
Fergus Falls, 12,362 D 2
Fridley, 28,335 ...... m12
Golden Valley, 20,971 n12
Grand Marais, 1,171 k 9
Grand Rapids, 7,976 C 5
Hastings, 15,445 .... F 6
Hibbing, 18,046 .... C 6
Hopkins, 16,534 .... n12
Hutchinson, 11,523 .. F 4
International Falls, 8,325 .... B 5
Inver Grove Heights, 22,477 .... n12
Lakeville, 24,854 .... F 5
Litchfield, 6,041 .... E 4
Little Falls, 7,232 .... E 4
Mankato, 31,477 .... F 5
Maple Grove, 38,736 m12
Maplewood, 30,954 .. n12
Marshall, 12,023 .... F 3
Minneapolis, 368,383 F 5
Minnetonka, 48,370 .. n12
Montevideo, 5,499 .. F 3
Moorhead, 32,295 .. D 2
Morris, 5,613 ...... E 3
Mound, 9,634 ...... n11
Mounds View, 12,541 m12
New Brighton, 22,207 m12
New Hope, 21,853 .. m12
New Ulm, 13,132 .... F 4
Northfield, 14,684 .. F 5
North Mankato, 10,164 .... F 4
North St. Paul, 12,376 .... m13
Owatonna, 19,386 .. F 5
Pipestone, 4,554 .... G 2
Plymouth, 50,889 .. m12
Prior Lake, 11,482 .. F 5
Ramsey, 12,408 .... E 5
Red Wing, 15,134 .. F 6
Redwood Falls, 4,859 F 3
Richfield, 35,710 .... F 5
Robbinsdale, 14,396 m12
Rochester, 70,745 .. F 6
Roseville, 33,485 .... m12
Saint Cloud, 48,812 .. E 4
Saint Louis Park, 43,787 .... n12
Saint Paul, 272,235 .. F 5
Saint Peter, 9,421 .. F 5
Shakopee, 11,739 .. F 5
Shoreview, 24,587 .. m12
South St. Paul, 20,197 .... n12
Stillwater, 13,882 .... E 6
Thief River Falls, 8,010 .... B 2
Virginia, 9,410 ...... C 6
Waseca, 8,385 ...... F 5
West Saint Paul, 19,248 .... n12
White Bear Lake, 24,704 .... E 5
Willmar, 17,531 .... E 3
Winona, 25,399 .... F 7
Woodbury, 20,075 .. F 6
Worthington, 9,977 .. G 3

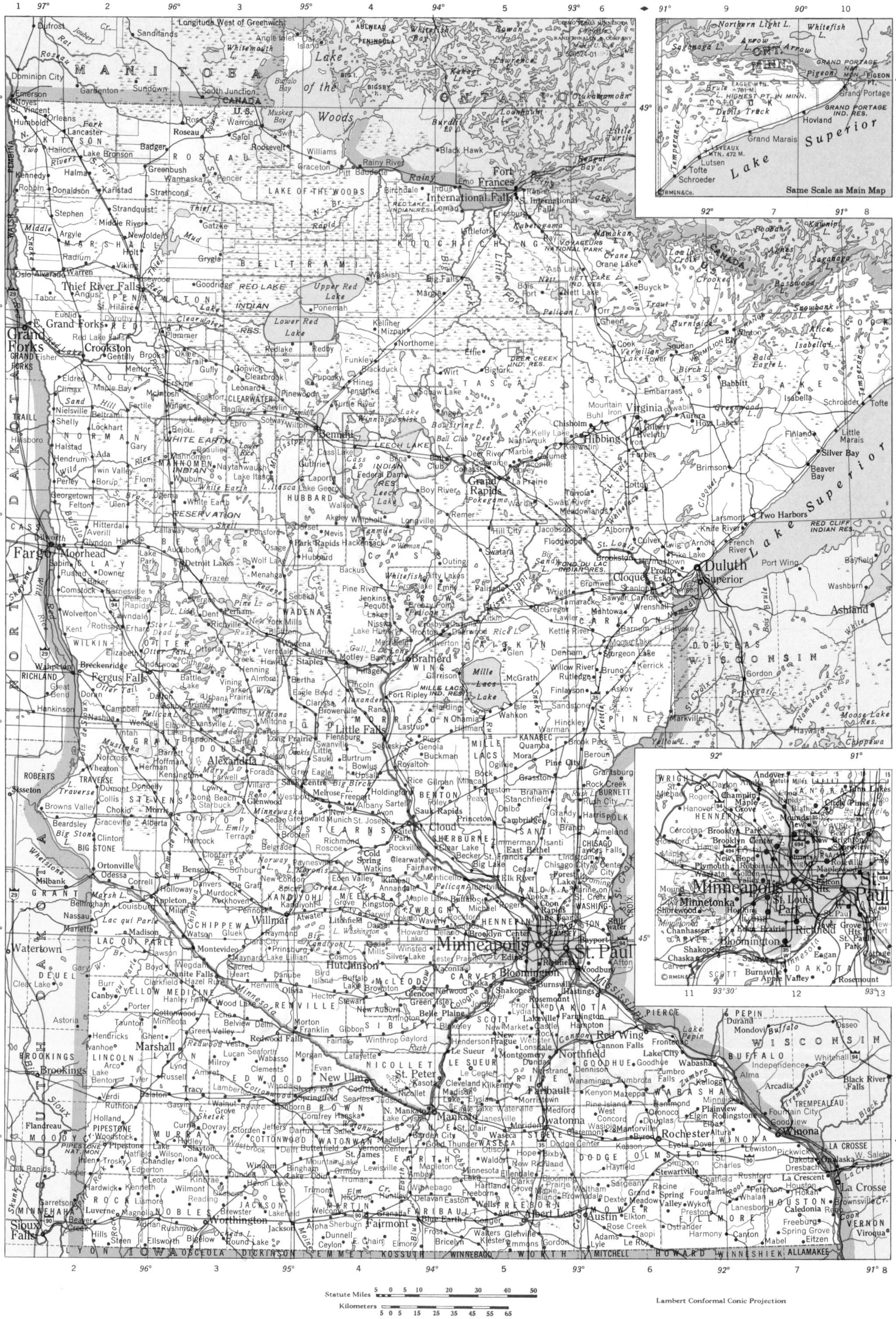

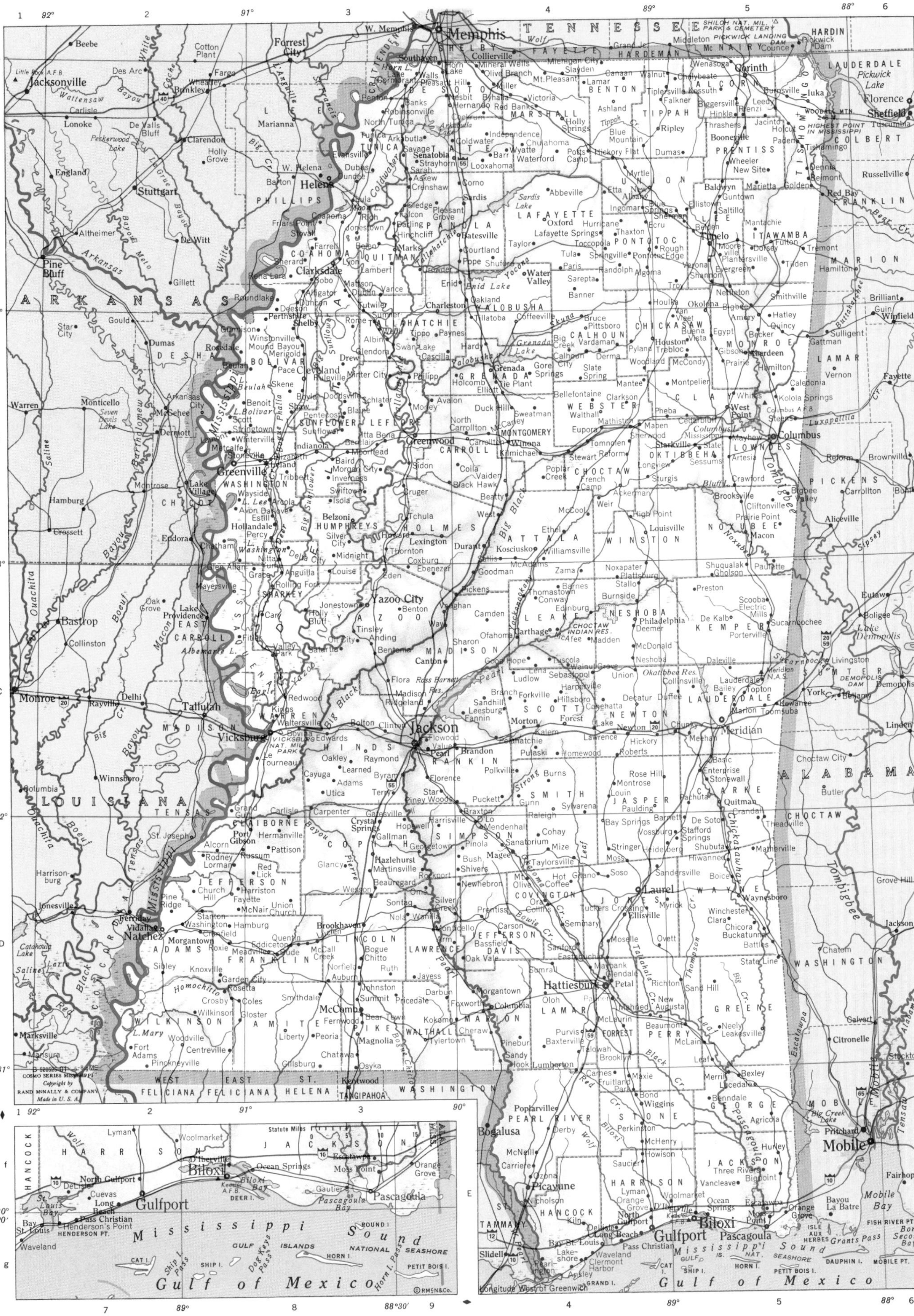

Statute Miles 5 0 5 10 20 30 40

Kilometers 5 0 5 15 25 35 45 55

Lambert Conformal Conic Projection

Mississippi

1990 CENSUS

Aberdeen, 6,837 .... B 5
Amory, 7,093 ...... B 5
Baldwyn, 3,204 .... A 5
Batesville, 6,403 .... A 4
Bay Saint Louis, 8,063 .... E 4
Belzoni, 2,536 ...... B 3
Biloxi, 46,319 ...... E 5
Booneville, 7,955 .... A 5
Brandon, 11,077 .... C 4
Brookhaven, 10,243 D 3
Canton, 10,062 .... C 3
Carthage, 3,819 .... C 4
Charleston, 2,328 .. A 3
Clarksdale, 19,717 .. A 3
Cleveland, 15,384 .. B 3
Clinton, 21,847 .... C 3
Columbia, 6,815 .... D 4
Columbus, 23,799 .. B 5
Corinth, 11,820 .... A 5
Crystal Springs, 5,643 D 3
D'Iberville, 6,566 .... E 5
Durant, 2,838 ...... B 4
Ellisville, 3,634 ...... D 4
Escatawpa, 5,367('80) E 5
Forest, 5,060 ...... C 4
Fulton, 3,387 ...... A 5
Gautier, 10,088 ...... f 8
Greenville, 45,226 .. B 2
Greenwood, 18,906 .. B 3
Grenada, 10,864 .... B 4
Gulfport, 40,775 .... E 4
Hattiesburg, 41,882 .. D 4
Hazlehurst, 4,221 .. D 3
Hernando, 3,125 .... A 4
Hollandale, 3,576 .... B 3
Holly Springs, 7,261 A 4
Horn Lake, 9,069 .... A 3
Houston, 3,903 .... B 4
Indianola, 11,809 .. B 3
Itta Bena, 2,377 .... B 3
Iuka, 3,122 .... A 5
Jackson, 196,637 .. C 3
Kosciusko, 6,986 .... B 4
Laurel, 18,827 ...... D 4
Leland, 6,366 ...... B 3
Lexington, 2,227 .... B 3
Long Beach, 15,804 .. g 7
Louisville, 7,169 .... B 4
Magee, 3,607 ...... D 4
McComb, 11,591 .... D 3
Meridian, 41,036 .... C 5
Mississippi State, 4,600('81) .... B 5
Morgantown, 3,288('80) .... D 2
Morton, 3,212 ...... C 4
Moss Point, 17,837 .. E 5
Mound Bayou, 2,222 B 3
Natchez, 19,460 .... D 2
New Albany, 6,775 .. A 4
Newton, 3,701 ...... C 4
North Gulfport, 6,660('80) .... E 4
Ocean Springs, 14,658 .... E 5
Okolona, 3,267 .... B 5
Orange Grove, 3,000('81) .... E 5
Oxford, 9,984 ...... A 4
Palmer, 2,765('80) .. D 4
Pascagoula, 25,899 .. E 5
Pass Christian, 5,557 E 4
Pearl, 19,588 ...... C 3
Petal, 7,883 .... D 4
Philadelphia, 6,758 .. C 4
Picayune, 10,633 .... E 4
Pontotoc, 4,570 .... A 4
Quitman, 2,736 .... C 5
Ridgeland, 11,714 .. C 3
Ripley, 5,371 ...... A 5
Rolling Fork, 2,444 .. C 3
Rosedale, 2,595 .... B 2
Ruleville, 3,245 ...... B 3
Senatobia, 4,772 .... A 4
Southaven, 17,949 .. A 3
Starkville, 18,458 .... B 5
Tupelo, 30,685 ...... A 5
Vicksburg, 20,908 .. C 3
Water Valley, 3,610 .. A 4
Waveland, 5,369 .... E 4
Waynesboro, 5,143 .. D 5
West Point, 8,489 .. B 5
Wiggins, 3,185 ...... E 4
Winona, 5,705 ...... B 4
Yazoo City, 12,427 .. C 3

Missouri

1990 CENSUS

Arnold, 18,828 . . . . C 7
Aurora, 6,459 . . . . E 4
Ballwin, 21,816 . . . . f12
Belton, 18,150 . . . . C 3
Berkeley, 12,450 . . . . f13
Blue Springs, 40,153 . . . h11
Bolivar, 6,845 . . . . D 4
Boonville, 7,095 . . . . . . C 5
Brentwood, 8,150 . . . . . . f13
Bridgeton, 17,779 . . . . C 7
Brookfield, 4,888 . . . . . . B 4
Cape Girardeau, 34,438 D 8
Carthage, 10,747 . . . . D 3
Caruthersville, 7,389 . . . E 8
Charleston, 5,085 . . . . E 8
Chillicothe, 8,804 . . . . . . B 4
Clayton, 13,874 . . . . . . C 7
Clinton, 8,703 . . . . C 4
Columbia, 69,101 . . . . C 5
De Soto, 5,993 . . . . . . C 7
Des Peres, 8,395 . . . . . . f13
Dexter, 7,559 . . . . E 8
Ellisville, 7,545 . . . . f12
Eureka, 4,683 . . . . f12
Excelsior Springs, 10,354 . . . . B 3
Farmington, 11,598 . . . . D 7
Ferguson, 22,286 . . . . C 7
Festus, 8,105 . . . . C 7
Florissant, 51,206 . . . . . . f13
Fulton, 10,033 . . . . C 6
Gladstone, 26,243 . . . . h10
Grandview, 24,967 . . . . C 3
Hannibal, 18,004 . . . . . . B 6
Harrisonville, 7,683 . . . . C 3
Independence, 112,301 B 3
Jackson, 9,256 . . . . D 8
Jefferson City, 35,481 C 5
Jennings, 15,905 . . . . . . f13
Joplin, 40,961 . . . . D 3
Kansas City, 435,146 . . B 3
Kennett, 10,941 . . . . . . E 7
Kirksville, 17,152 . . . . . . A 5
Kirkwood, 27,291 . . . . . . f13
Lebanon, 9,983 . . . . . . D 5
Lees Summit, 46,418 . . C 3
Liberty, 20,459 . . . . . . B 3
Macon, 5,571 . . . . B 5
Malden, 5,123 . . . . E 8
Manchester, 6,542 . . . . f12
Maplewood, 9,962 . . . . f13
Marshall, 12,711 . . . . . . B 4
Maryland Heights, 25,407 . . . . f13
Maryville, 10,663 . . . . . . A 3
Mexico, 11,290 . . . . . . B 6
Moberly, 12,839 . . . . . . B 5
Monett, 6,529 . . . . E 4
Neosho, 9,254 . . . . E 3
Nevada, 8,597 . . . . D 3
O'Fallon, 18,698 . . . . . . f12
Overland, 17,987 . . . . . . f13
Perryville, 6,933 . . . . . D 8
Pine Lawn, 5,092 . . . . . . f13
Poplar Bluff, 16,996 . . E 7
Raytown, 30,601 . . . . . . h11
Richmond Heights, 10,448 . . . . f13
Rolla, 14,090 . . . . D 6
Saint Charles, 54,555 . . C 7
Sainte Genevieve, 4,411 D 7
Saint Joseph, 71,852 . . B 3
Saint Louis, 396,685 . . C 7
Saint Peters, 45,779 . . C 7
Sedalia, 19,800 . . . . . . C 4
Sikeston, 17,641 . . . . . . E 8
Springfield, 140,494 . . D 4
Sullivan, 5,661 . . . . C 6
Trenton, 6,129 . . . . A 4
University City, 40,087 C 7
Warrensburg, 15,244 . . C 4
Washington, 10,704 . . C 6
Webb City, 7,449 . . . . . D 3
Webster Groves, 22,987 f13
West Plains, 8,913 . . . . E 6

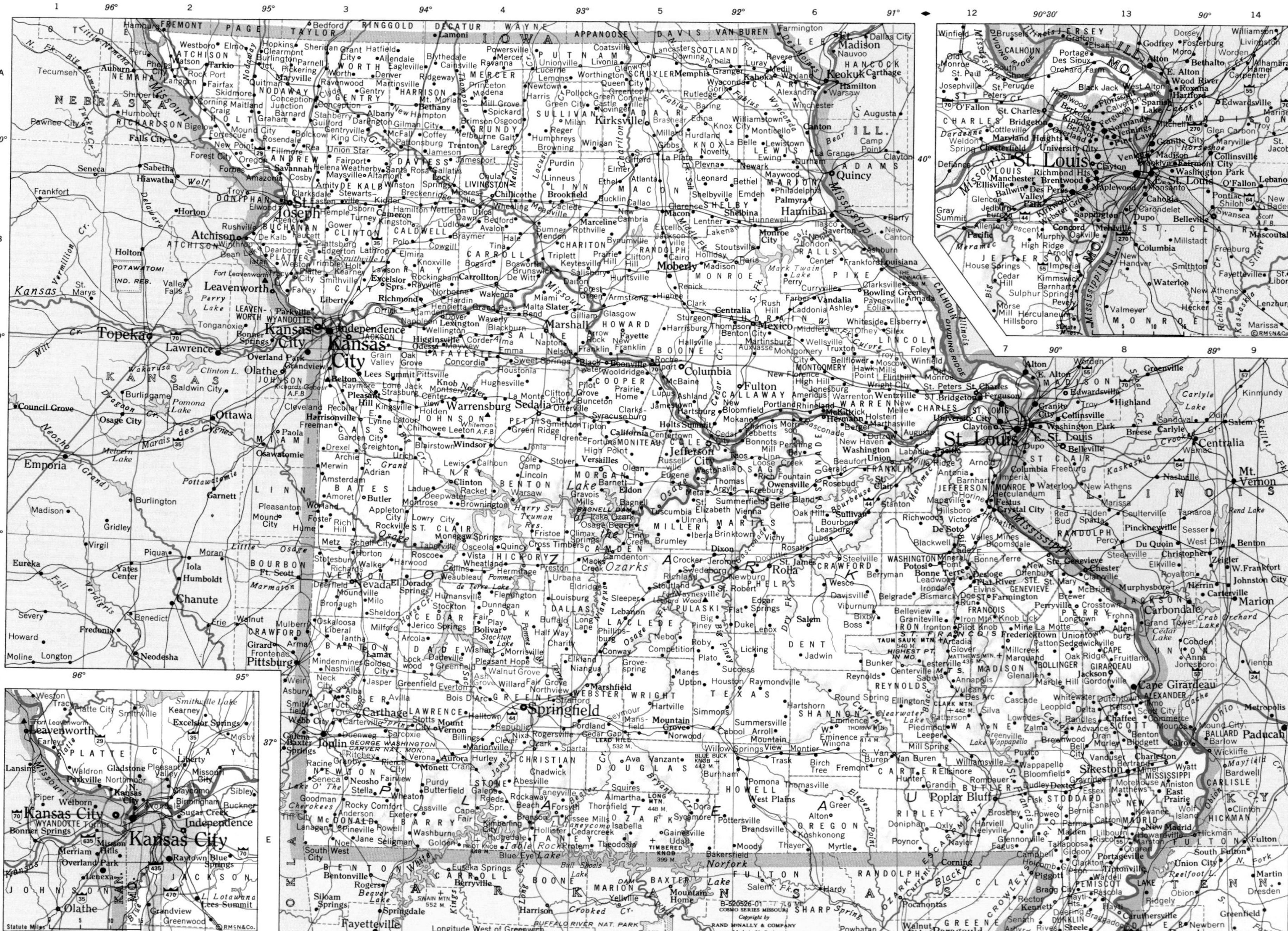

IOWA
NEBRASKA
KANSAS
ILLINOIS
KENTUCKY
TENNESSEE
ARKANSAS
OKLAHOMA
Kansas City
St. Louis
Springfield
Independence
St. Joseph
Columbia
Jefferson City
Topeka
Quincy
Hannibal
Joplin
Cape Girardeau
Paducah
Lake of the Ozarks
Mississippi
Missouri
Statute Miles 5 0 5 15 25 35 45
Kilometers 5 0 5 15 25 35 45 55 65
Longitude West of Greenwich
Lambert Conformal Conic Projection

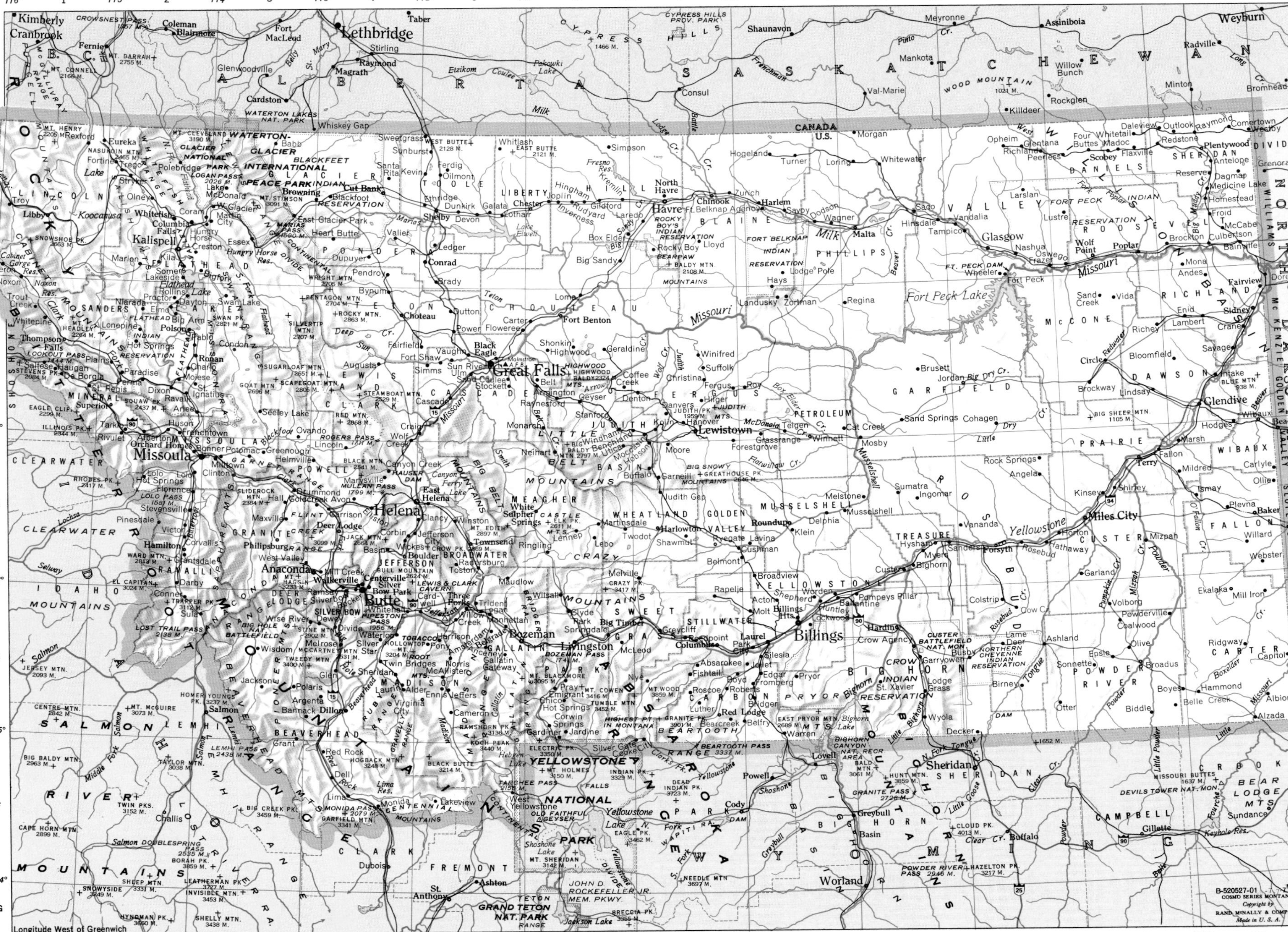

Statute Miles 10 0 10 20 30 40 50 60 70

Kilometers 10 0 10 30 50 70 90

Lambert Conformal Conic Projection

Montana

1990 CENSUS

Anaconda, 10,278 .... D 4
Baker, 1,818 .... D12
Belgrade, 3,411 .... E 5
Belt, 571 .... C 6
Bigfork, 1,080('80) .... B 2
Big Sandy, 740 .... B 6
Big Timber, 1,557 .... E 7
Billings, 81,151 .... E 8
Billings Heights, 8,480('80) .... E 8
Boulder, 1,316 .... D 4
Bozeman, 22,660 .... E 5
Bridger, 692 .... E 8
Broadus, 572 .... E11
Browning, 1,170 .... B 3
Butte, 33,336 .... E 4
Cascade, 729 .... C 5
Chester, 942 .... B 6
Chinook, 1,512 .... B 7
Choteau, 1,741 .... C 4
Circle, 805 .... C11
Colstrip, 1,476('80) E10
Columbia Falls, 2,942 .... B 2
Columbus, 1,573 .... E 7
Conrad, 2,891 .... B 5
Culbertson, 796 .... B12
Cut Bank, 3,329 .... B 4
Deer Lodge, 3,378 .... D 4
Dillon, 3,991 .... E 4
East Helena, 1,538 .... D 5
Ennis, 773 .... E 5
Eureka, 1,043 .... B 1
Fairview, 869 .... C12
Forsyth, 2,178 .... D10
Fort Benton, 1,660 .... C 6
Glasgow, 3,572 .... B10
Glendive, 4,802 .... C12
Great Falls, 55,097 .... C 5
Hamilton, 2,737 .... D 2
Hardin, 2,940 .... E 9
Harlem, 882 .... B 8
Harlowton, 1,049 .... D 7
Havre, 10,201 .... B 7
Helena, 24,569 .... D 4
Kalispell, 11,917 .... B 2
Laurel, 5,686 .... E 8
Lewistown, 6,051 .... C 7
Libby, 2,532 .... B 1
Livingston, 6,701 .... E 6
Lockwood, 2,300('89) .... E 8
Lolo, 2,418('80) .... D 2
Malta, 2,340 .... B 9
Manhattan, 1,034 .... E 5
Miles City, 8,461 .... D11
Missoula, 42,918 .... D 2
Orchard Homes, 4,500('89) .... D 2
Philipsburg, 925 .... D 3
Plains, 992 .... C 2
Plentywood, 2,136 .... B12
Polson, 3,283 .... C 2
Poplar, 881 .... B11
Red Lodge, 1,958 .... E 7
Ronan, 1,547 .... C 2
Roundup, 1,808 .... D 8
Saint Ignatius, 778 .... C 2
Scobey, 1,154 .... B11
Shelby, 2,763 .... B 5
Sidney, 5,217 .... C12
Stevensville, 1,221 .... D 2
Superior, 881 .... C 2
Terry, 659 .... D11
Thompson Falls, 1,319 .... C 1
Three Forks, 1,203 .... E 5
Townsend, 1,635 .... D 5
Troy, 953 .... B 1
Vaughn, 2,270('80) .... C 5
Walkerville, 605 .... D 4
West Yellowstone, 913 .... F 5
Whitefish, 4,368 .... B 2
Whitehall, 1,067 .... E 4
White Sulphur Springs, 963 .... D 6
Wibaux, 628 .... D12
Wolf Point, 2,880 .... B11

Nebraska

1990 CENSUS

Ainsworth, 1,870 . . . . . B 6
Albion, 1,916 . . . . C 7
Alliance, 9,765 . . . . B 3
Alma, 1,226 . . . . D 6
Ashland, 2,136 . . . . . . C 9
Atkinson, 1,380 . . . . . . B 7
Auburn, 3,443 . . . . D10
Aurora, 3,810 . . . . D 7
Bayard, 1,196 . . . . C 2
Beatrice, 12,354 . . . . . . D 9
Bellevue, 30,982 . . . . . . C10
Blair, 6,860 . . . . C 9
Bridgeport, 1,581 . . . . . C 2
Broken Bow, 3,778 . . . . . C 6
Central City, 2,868 . . . . . C 7
Chadron, 5,588 . . . . B 3
Columbus, 19,480 . . . . . . C 8
Cozad, 3,823 . . . . D 6
Creighton, 1,223 . . . . B 8
Crete, 4,841 . . . . D 9
Dakota City, 1,470 . . . . B 9
David City, 2,522 . . . . . . C 8
Elkhorn, 1,398 . . . . g12
Fairbury, 4,335 . . . . D 8
Falls City, 4,769 . . . . . . D10
Fremont, 23,680 . . . . C 9
Fullerton, 1,452 . . . . C 8
Geneva, 2,310 . . . . D 8
Gering, 7,946 . . . . C 2
Gibbon, 1,525 . . . . D 7
Gordon, 1,803 . . . . B 3
Gothenburg, 3,232 . . . . . D 5
Grand Island, 39,386 . . D 7
Gretna, 2,249 . . . . C 9
Hartington, 1,583 . . . . . B 8
Hastings, 22,837 . . . . . . D 7
Hebron, 1,765 . . . . D 8
Holdrege, 5,671 . . . . . . D 6
Imperial, 2,007 . . . . D 4
Kearney, 24,396 . . . . . . D 6
Kimball, 2,574 . . . . C 2
La Vista, 9,840 . . . . . . g12
Lexington, 6,601 . . . . . . D 6
Lincoln, 191,972 . . . . . . D 9
Loup City, 1,104 . . . . . . C 7
Madison, 2,135 . . . . C 8
McCook, 8,112 . . . . D 5
Milford, 1,886 . . . . D 8
Minden, 2,749 . . . . D 7
Mitchell, 1,743 . . . . C 2
Nebraska City, 6,547 . . D10
Neligh, 1,742 . . . . B 7
Norfolk, 21,476 . . . . . . B 8
North Bend, 1,249 . . . . . C 9
North Platte, 22,605 . . . C 5
Ogallala, 5,095 . . . . . . C 4
Omaha, 335,795 . . . . . . C10
O'Neill, 3,852 . . . . B 7
Ord, 2,481 . . . . C 7
Papillion, 10,372 . . . . . . C 9
Pierce, 1,615 . . . . B 8
Plainview, 1,333 . . . . . . B 8
Plattsmouth, 6,412 . . . . D10
Ralston, 6,236 . . . . g12
Saint Paul, 2,009 . . . . . . C 7
Schuyler, 4,052 . . . . C 8
Scottsbluff, 13,711 . . . . C 2
Seward, 5,634 . . . . D 8
Sidney, 5,959 . . . . C 3
South Sioux City, 9,677 B 9
Stanton, 1,549 . . . . C 8
Superior, 2,397 . . . . . . D 7
Sutton, 1,353 . . . . D 8
Syracuse, 1,646 . . . . . . D 9
Tecumseh, 1,702 . . . . . D 9
Tekamah, 1,852 . . . . . . C 9
Valentine, 2,826 . . . . . . B 5
Valley, 1,775 . . . . C 9
Wahoo, 3,681 . . . . C 9
Waverly, 1,869 . . . . D 9
Wayne, 5,142 . . . . B 8
West Point, 3,250 . . . . C 9
Wilber, 1,527 . . . . D 9
Wymore, 1,611 . . . . . . D 9
York, 7,884 . . . . D 8

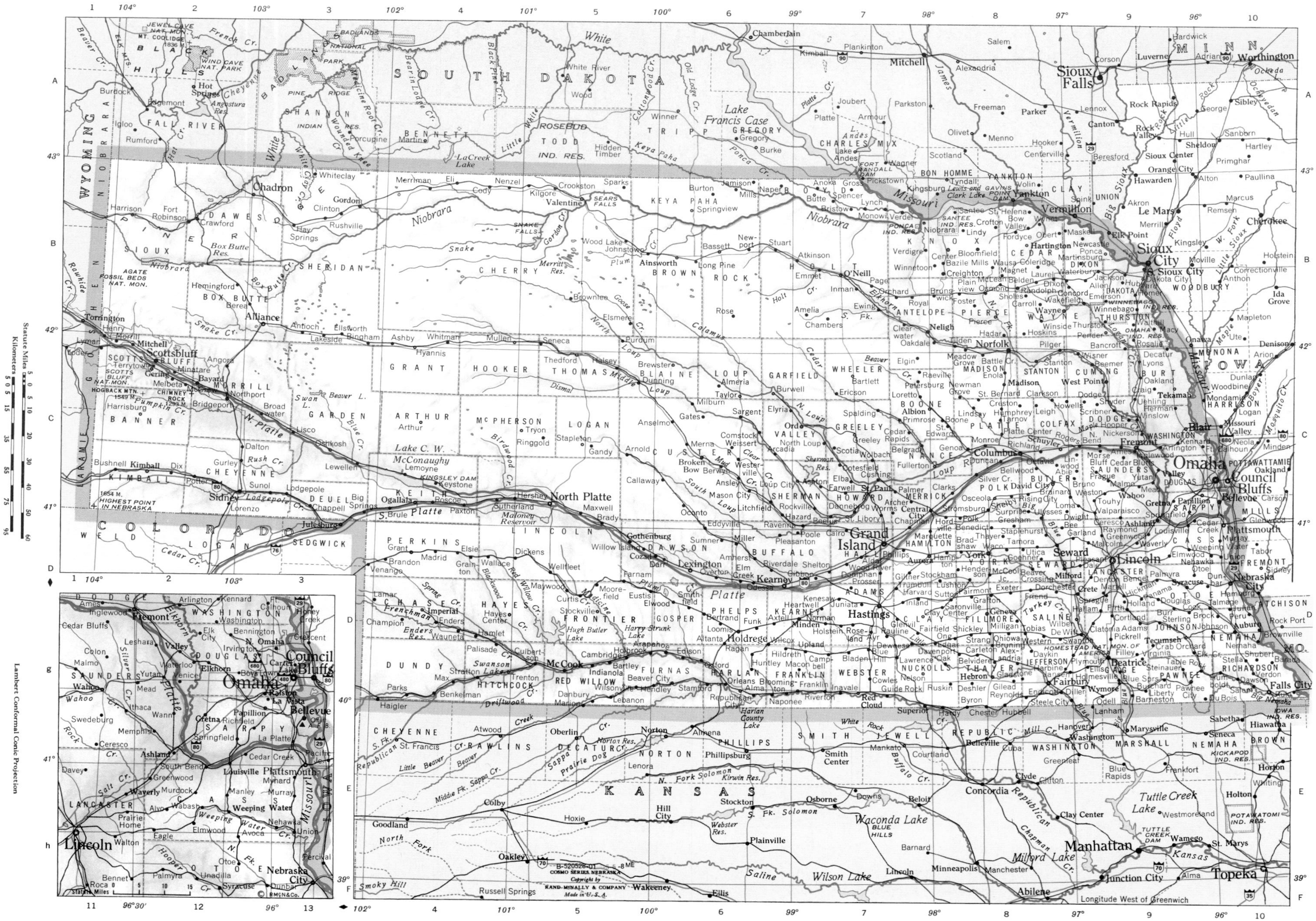

Lambert Conformal Conic Projection

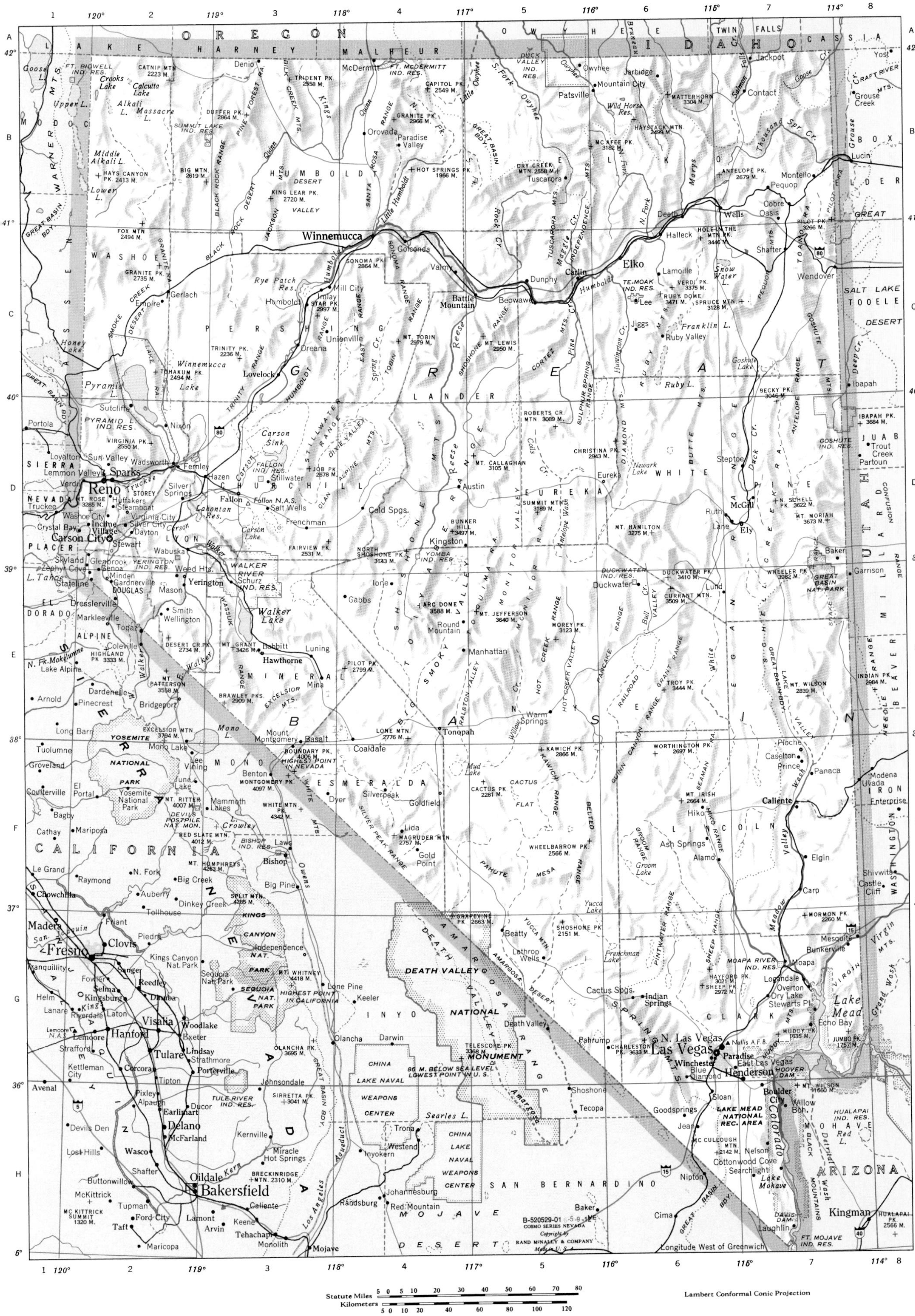

Nevada

1990 CENSUS

Alamo, 400('89) .... F 6
Austin, 370('89) .... D 4
Babbitt, 1,800('77) .. E 3
Battle Mountain, 2,749('80) .... C 5
Beatty, 1,200('89) .. G 5
Beowawe, 250('89) .. C 5
Blue Diamond, 420('89) .... G 6
Boulder City, 12,567 H 7
Bunkerville, 300('89) G 7
Caliente, 1,111 ...... F 7
Carlin, 2,220 .... C 5
Carson City, 40,443 D 2
Crystal Bay, 1,200('89) .... D 1
Dayton, 600('89) .... D 2
Dresslerville, 180('89) E 2
East Las Vegas, 6,449('80) .... G 6
Echo Bay, 120('89) .. G 7
Elko, 14,736 .... C 6
Ely, 4,756 .... D 7
Empire, 300('89) .... C 2
Eureka, 650('89) .... D 6
Fallon, 6,438 ...... D 3
Fernley, 1,680('89) .. D 2
Gabbs, 667 .... E 4
Gardnerville, 3,700('89) .... E 2
Genoa, 190('89) .... D 2
Gerlach, 200('89) .... C 2
Glenbrook, 400('89) .. D 2
Golconda, 200('89) .. C 4
Goldfield, 600('89) .. F 4
Goodsprings, 150('89) H 6
Hawthorne, 3,741('80) E 3
Henderson, 64,942 .. G 7
Huffakers, 150('77) .. D 2
Imlay, 250('89) ...... C 3
Incline Village, 4,500('89) .... D 2
Indian Springs, 1,200('89) .... G 6
Jackpot, 570('89) .... B 7
Jean, 150('89) ...... H 6
Lamoille, 110('89) .. C 6
Las Vegas, 258,295 G 6
Lathrop Wells, 350('89) .... G 5
Laughlin, 140('89) .. H 7
Lemmon Valley, 4,100('89) .... D 2
Logandale, 500('89) .. G 7
Lovelock, 2,069 .... C 3
Lund, 330('89) ...... E 6
Mason, 400('89) .... E 2
McDermitt, 250('89) .. B 4
McGill, 1,419('80) .... D 7
Mesquite, 1,871 .... G 7
Mina, 400('89) ...... E 3
Minden, 1,700('89) .. E 2
Montello, 200('89) .. B 7
Mountain City, 110('89) .... B 6
Nixon, 150('89) .... D 2
North Las Vegas, 47,707 .... G 6
Overton, 1,111('80) .. G 7
Owyhee, 790('89) .. B 5
Pahrump, 1,300('89) G 6
Panaca, 700('89) .... F 7
Paradise, 124,682 .. G 6
Paradise Valley, 150('89) .... B 4
Pioche, 830('89) .... F 7
Reno, 133,850 ...... D 2
Round Mountain, 210('89) .... E 4
Ruth, 550('89) ...... D 6
Schurz, 330('89) .... E 3
Searchlight, 430('89) H 7
Silver City, 100('89) .. D 2
Silverpeak, 190('89) .. F 4
Silver Springs, 420('89) .... D 2
Skyland, 660('89) .... D 2
Sparks, 53,367 .... D 2
Stateline, 1,500('89) .. E 2
Steamboat, 450('89) D 2
Sunrise Manor, 95,362 .... G 6
Sun Valley, 8,822('80) D 2
Tonopah, 1,952('80) E 4
Verdi, 1,140('89) .... D 2
Virginia City, 920('89) D 2
Wadsworth, 510('89) D 2
Washoe City, 400('89) D 2
Weed Heights, 230('89) .... E 2
Wellington, 280('89) .. E 2
Wells, 1,256 .... B 7
Winchester, 19,728('80) ...... G 6
Winnemucca, 6,134 .. C 4
Yerington, 2,367 .... E 2
Zephyr Cove, 1,700('89) .... E 2

New Hampshire

New Hampshire

1990 CENSUS

Alton, 975 (3,286▲) . . D 4
Amherst, 850 (9,068▲) . . . . E 3
Antrim, 1,142 (2,360▲) . . . . D 3
Ashland, 1,479 (1,915▲) . . . . C 3
Bedford, 1,400 (12,563▲) . . . . E 3
Berlin, 11,824 . . . . . . B 4
Bristol, 1,258 (2,537▲) . . . . C 3
Charlestown, 1,294 (4,630▲) . . . . D 2
Claremont, 13,902 . . D 2
Colebrook, 1,131 (2,444▲) . . . . g 7
Concord, 36,006 . . . . D 3
Conway, 1,781 (7,940▲) . . . . C 4
Derry, 12,248 (29,603▲) . . . . E 4
Dover, 25,042 . . . . . . D 5
Durham, 8,448 (11,818▲) . . . . D 5
Enfield, 1,581 (3,979▲) . . . . C 2
Epping, 1,384 (5,162▲) . . . . D 4
Exeter, 8,947 (12,481▲) . . . . E 5
Farmington, 3,284 (5,739▲) . . . . D 4
Franklin, 8,304 . . . . . . D 3
Goffstown, 2,700 (14,621▲) . . . . D 3
Gorham, 2,180 (3,173▲) . . . . B 4
Greenville, 1,447 (2,231▲) . . . . E 3
Hampton, 6,779 (12,278▲) . . . . E 5
Hanover, 6,861 (9,212▲) . . . . C 2
Henniker, 1,538 (4,151▲) . . . . D 3
Hinsdale, 1,546 (3,936▲) . . . . E 2
Hooksett, 1,868 (8,767▲) . . . . D 4
Hudson, 6,248 (19,530▲) . . . . E 4
Jaffrey, 2,684 (5,361▲) . . . . E 2
Keene, 22,430 . . . . . . E 2
Laconia, 15,743 . . . . C 4
Lancaster, 2,134 (3,522▲) . . . . B 3
Lebanon, 12,183 . . . . C 2
Lisbon, 1,151 (1,664▲) . . . . B 3
Littleton, 4,480 (5,827▲) . . . . B 3
Manchester, 99,567 . . E 4
Marlborough, 1,184 (1,927▲) . . . . E 2
Meredith, 1,202 (4,837▲) . . . . C 3
Merrimack, 1,300 (22,156▲) . . . . E 4
Milford, 6,269 (11,795▲) . . . . E 3
Milton, 1,000 (3,691▲) D 5
Nashua, 79,662 . . . . E 4
New London, 1,335 (3,180▲) . . . . D 3
Newmarket, 3,749 (7,157▲) . . . . D 5
Newport, 4,388 (6,110▲) . . . . D 2
Northfield, 1,375 (4,263▲) . . . . D 3
North Hampton, 1,000 (3,637▲) . . . . E 5
Peterborough, 2,100 (5,239▲) . . . . E 3
Pittsfield, 1,584 (3,701▲) . . . . D 4
Plaistow, 1,850 (7,316▲) . . . . E 4
Plymouth, 3,628 (5,811▲) . . . . C 3
Portsmouth, 25,925 . . D 5
Raymond, 1,192 (8,713▲) . . . . D 4
Rochester, 26,630 . . D 5
Rollinsford, 1,173 (2,645▲) . . . . D 5
Rye, 835 (4,612▲) . . D 5
Salem, 12,000 (25,746▲) . . . . E 4
Somersworth, 11,249 D 5
Tilton, 1,380 (3,240▲) D 3
Troy, 1,318 (2,097▲) E 2
Whitefield, 1,005 (1,909▲) . . . . B 3
Winchester, 1,732 (4,038▲) . . . . E 2
Wolfeboro, 2,000 (4,807▲) . . . . C 4

◄ Population of entire town (township), including rural area.

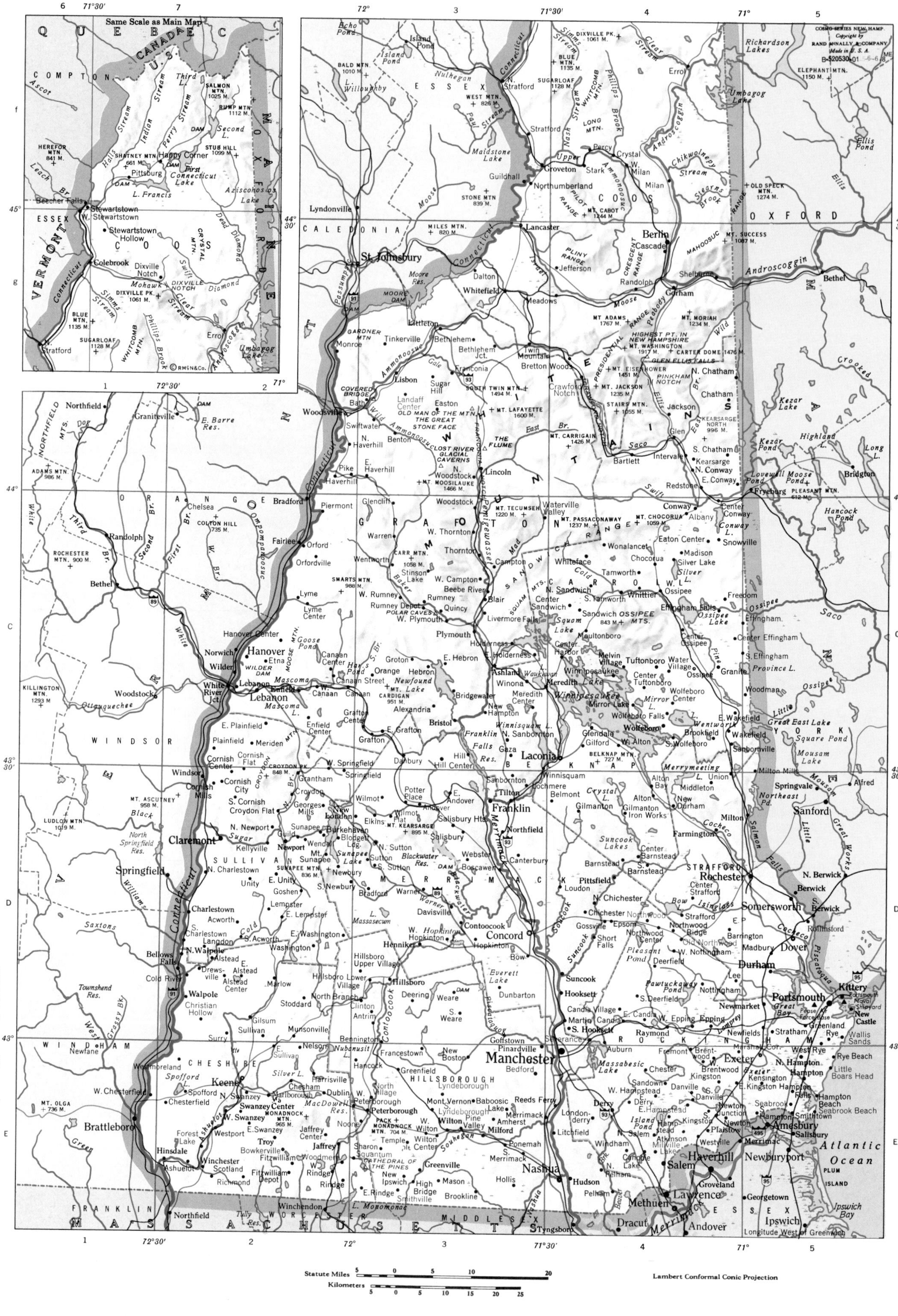

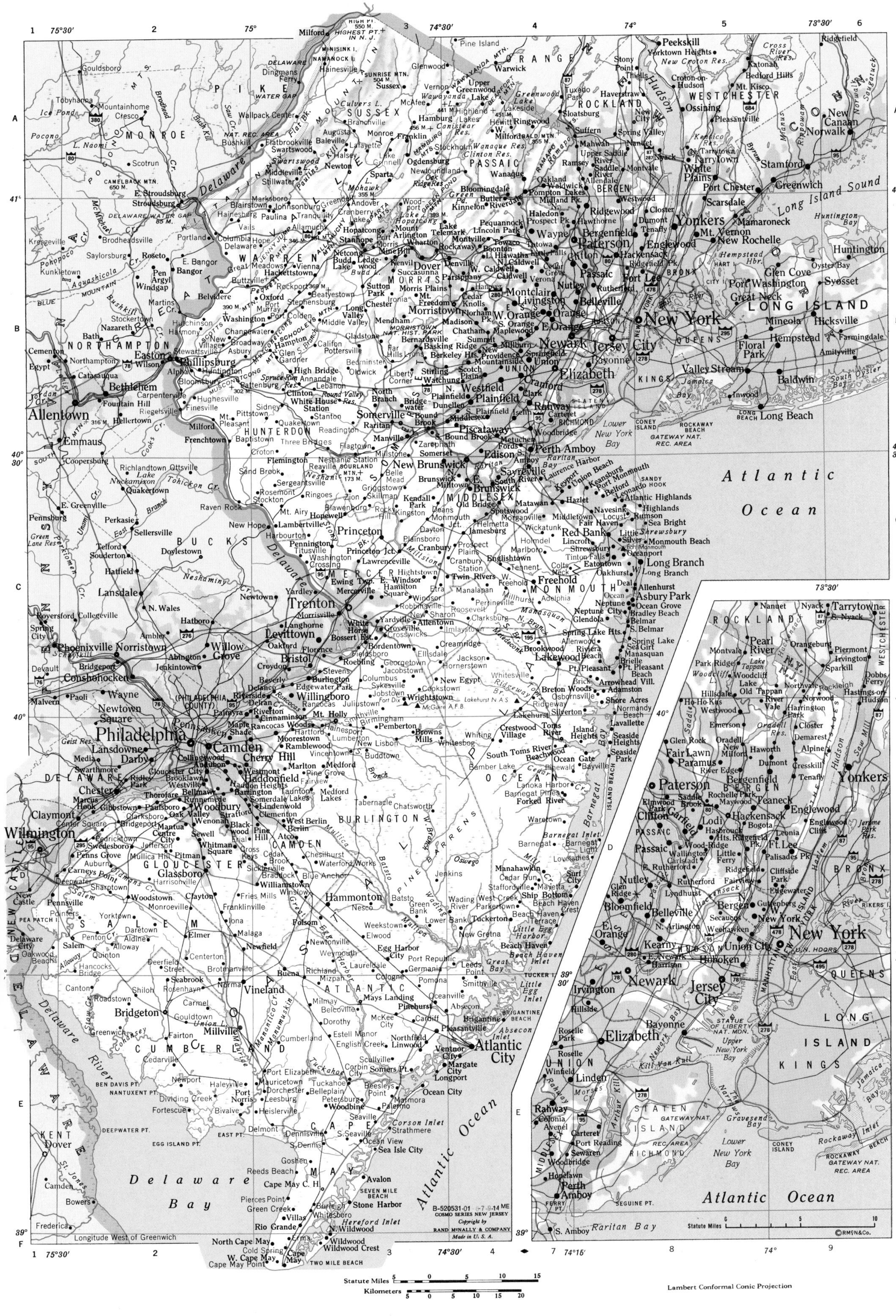

New Jersey

1990 CENSUS

Asbury Park, 16,799 C 4
Atlantic City, 37,986 E 4
Bayonne, 61,444 . . . . B 4
Belleville, 34,213 . . . . B 4
Bergenfield, 24,458 . . B 4
Bloomfield, 45,061 . . h 8
Brick [Township], 64,800('89) . . . . . . C 4
Bridgeton, 18,942 . . . E 2
Camden, 87,492 . . . . D 2
Cape May, 4,668 . . . . F 3
Carteret, 19,025 . . . . . B 4
Cherry Hill, 69,319 . . D 2
Cliffside Park, 20,393 h 9
Clifton, 71,742 . . . . . . B 4
Cranford, 22,624 . . . . B 4
Dover, 15,115 . . . . . . B 3
East Brunswick, 43,548 . . . . C 4
East Orange, 73,552 B 4
Edison, 88,680 . . . . . . B 4
Elizabeth, 110,002 . . B 4
Englewood, 24,850 . . B 5
Ewing Township, 34,185 . . . . C 3
Fair Lawn, 30,548 . . . h 8
Fort Lee, 31,997 . . . B 5
Freehold, 10,742 . . . . C 4
Garfield, 26,727 . . . . h 8
Glassboro, 15,614 . . D 2
Hackensack, 37,049 B 4
Hackettstown, 8,120 B 3
Hammonton, 12,208 D 3
Hazlet, 23,013('80) . . C 4
Hillside, 21,044 . . . . . . k 8
Hoboken, 33,397 . . . . k 8
Irvington, 59,774 . . . . k 8
Jersey City, 228,537 B 4
Kearny, 34,874 . . . . . . h 8
Lakewood, 26,095 . . C 4
Linden, 36,701 . . . . . . k 8
Livingston, 26,609 . . B 4
Lodi, 22,355 . . . . h 8
Long Branch, 28,658 C 5
Lyndhurst, 20,326('80)h 8
Maple Shade, 20,525('80) . . . . . . D 2
Maplewood, 21,756 . . B 4
Middletown, 21,300('85) . . . . . . C 4
Millburn, 18,630 . . . . B 4
Millville, 25,992 . . . . . . E 2
Montclair, 37,729 . . . . B 4
Morristown, 16,189 . . B 4
Neptune, 29,800 . . . . . C 4
Newark, 275,221 . . . . . B 4
New Brunswick, 41,711 . . . . C 4
North Bergen, 48,414 h 8
North Brunswick, 31,287 . . . . C 4
North Plainfield, 18,820 . . . . B 4
Nutley, 27,099 . . . . B 4
Ocean [Township], 24,700('86) . . . . . . C 4
Orange, 29,925 . . . . B 4
Paramus, 25,067 . . . . h 8
Passaic, 58,041 . . . . B 4
Paterson, 140,891 . . B 4
Pennsauken, 34,733 D 2
Pennsville, 12,467('80) . . . . . . D 1
Perth Amboy, 41,967 B 4
Phillipsburg, 15,757 . . B 2
Piscataway, 43,800 . . B 4
Plainfield, 46,567 . . . . B 4
Princeton, 12,016 . . C 3
Rahway, 25,325 . . . . B 4
Red Bank, 10,636 . . C 4
Ridgewood, 24,152 . . B 4
Roselle, 20,314 . . . . . k 7
Sayreville, 34,986 . . C 4
Scotch Plains, 20,774('80) . . . . . . B 4
Somerset, 21,731('80)B 3
Somerville, 11,632 . . B 3
South Plainfield, 20,489 . . . . B 4
Summit, 19,757 . . . . . B 4
Sussex, 2,201 . . . . A 3
Teaneck, 37,825 . . . . h 8
Trenton, 88,675 . . . . C 3
Union City, 58,012 . . h 8
Vineland, 54,780 . . . . E 2
Wayne, 47,025 . . . . . . B 4
Westfield, 28,870 . . . . B 4
West New York, 38,125 . . . . h 8
West Orange, 39,103 B 4
Willingboro, 36,291 . . C 3
Woodbine, 2,678 . . . . E 3
Woodbridge [Township], 95,100('86) . . . . . . B 4

New Mexico

1990 CENSUS

Alameda, 5,900('87) B 3
Alamogordo, 27,596 E 4
Albuquerque, 384,736 B 3
Anthony, 3,285('80) .. F 3
Armijo, 14,600('87) .. k 7
Artesia, 10,610 ..... E 5
Aztec, 5,479 .... A 2
Bayard, 2,598 ...... E 1
Belen, 6,547 .... C 3
Bernalillo, 5,960 .... B 3
Bloomfield, 5,214 ... A 2
Carlsbad, 24,952 .... E 5
Carrizozo, 1,075 .... D 4
Cedar Crest, 1,200('87) .... k 8
Central, 1,835 ...... E 1
Chama, 1,048 ...... A 3
Chimayo, 1,993('80) A 4
Clayton, 2,484 ..... A 6
Clovis, 30,954 ..... C 6
Crownpoint, 1,134('80) .... B 1
Deming, 10,970 .... E 2
Dona Ana, 950('87) .. E 3
Dulce, 1,648('80) ... A 2
Espanola, 8,389 .... B 3
Eunice, 2,676 ...... E 6
Farmington, 33,997 .. A 1
Five Points, 4,200('87) .... B 3
Fort Sumner, 1,269 .. C 5
Fort Wingate, 950('87) .... B 1
Gallup, 19,154 ...... B 1
Grants, 8,626 ...... B 2
Hagerman, 961 .... D 5
Hatch, 1,136 .... E 2
Hobbs, 29,115 ...... E 6
Hurley, 1,534 ...... E 1
Isleta, 1,246('80) ... C 3
Jal, 2,156 .... E 6
Jemez Pueblo, 1,503('80) .... B 3
Kirtland, 2,358('80) .. A 1
La Luz, 1,194('80) .. D 4
La Mesa, 900('87) .. E 3
Las Cruces, 62,126 . E 3
Las Vegas, 14,753 .. B 4
Lordsburg, 2,951 .... E 1
Los Alamos, 11,039('80) ...... B 3
Los Lunas, 6,013 .... C 3
Los Ranchos de Albuquerque, 3,955 B 3
Loving, 1,243 ...... E 5
Lovington, 9,322 .... E 6
Magdalena, 861 .... C 2
Mescalero, 1,259('80) D 4
Mesilla, 1,975 ...... E 3
Milan, 1,911 .... B 2
Moriarty, 1,399 .... C 3
Mountainair, 926 .... C 3
Mountain View, 2,300('87) .... C 3
Paradise Hills, 5,096('80) .... B 3
Portales, 10,690 .... C 6
Questa, 1,707 ...... A 4
Ranchos de Taos, 1,411('80) .... A 4
Raton, 7,372 ...... A 5
Rio Rancho, 32,505 .. B 3
Roswell, 44,654 .... D 5
Ruidoso, 4,600 .... D 4
Ruidoso Downs, 920 D 4
San Felipe Pueblo, 1,465('80) .... B 3
Santa Cruz, 975('87) B 3
Santa Fe, 55,859 .... B 4
Santa Rosa, 2,263 .. C 5
Santo Domingo Pueblo, 2,082('80) .... B 3
Shiprock, 7,237('80) A 1
Silver City, 10,683 .. E 1
Socorro, 8,159 ...... C 3
Springer, 1,262 .... A 5
Sunland Park, 8,179 F 3
Taos, 4,065 .... A 4
Taos Pueblo, 1,030('87) .... A 4
Tesuque, 1,014('80) B 4
Texico, 966 .... C 6
Thoreau, 1,099('80) .. B 1
Tierra Amarilla, 900('87) .... A 3
Tohatchi, 1,011('80) .. B 1
Truth or Consequences (Hot Springs), 6,221 D 2
Tucumcari, 6,831 .... B 6
Tularosa, 2,615 .... D 3
Tyrone, 950('87) .... E 1
University Park, 4,353('80) .... E 3
Zuni, 5,551('80) .... B 1

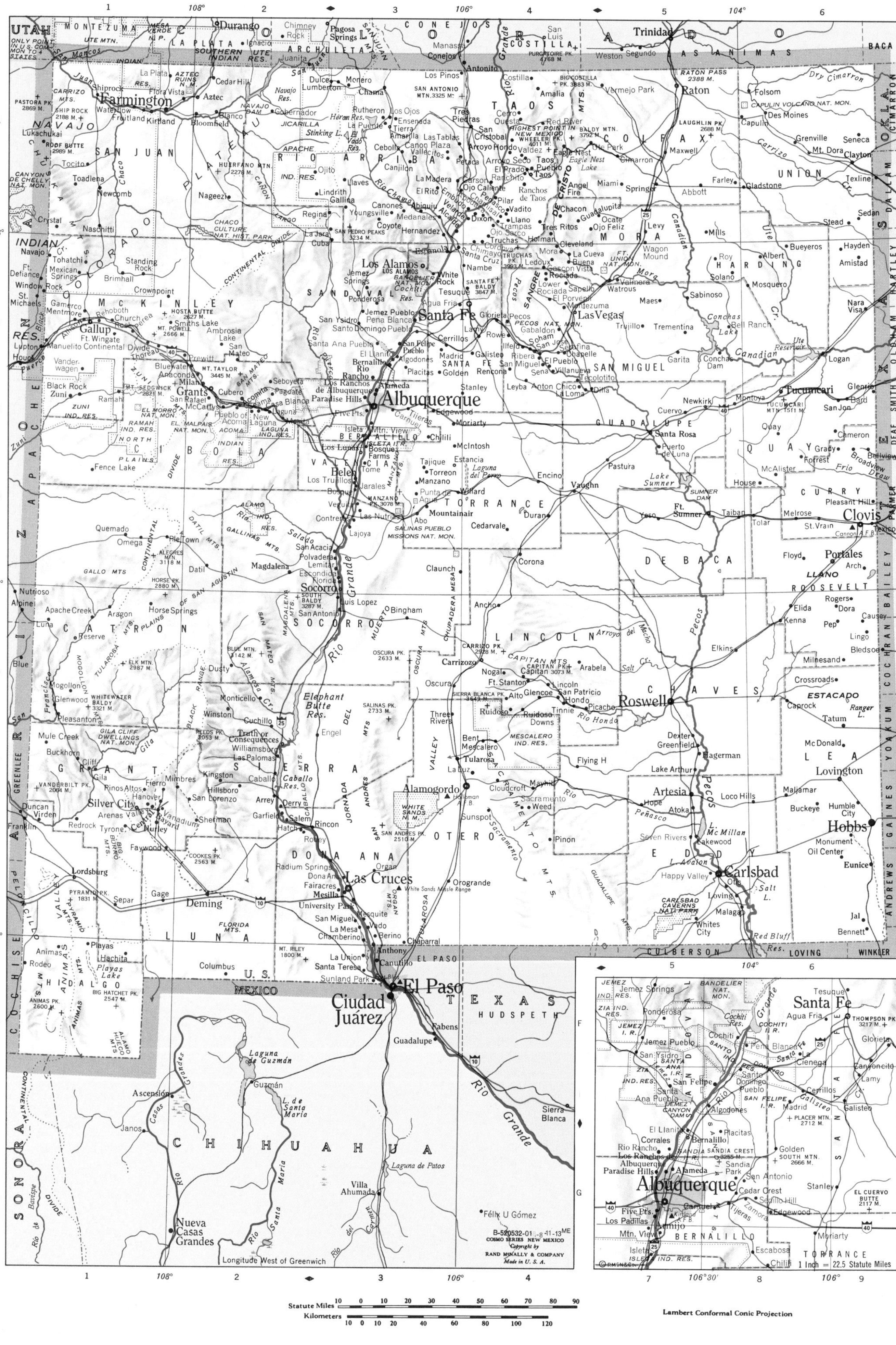

Lambert Conformal Conic Projection

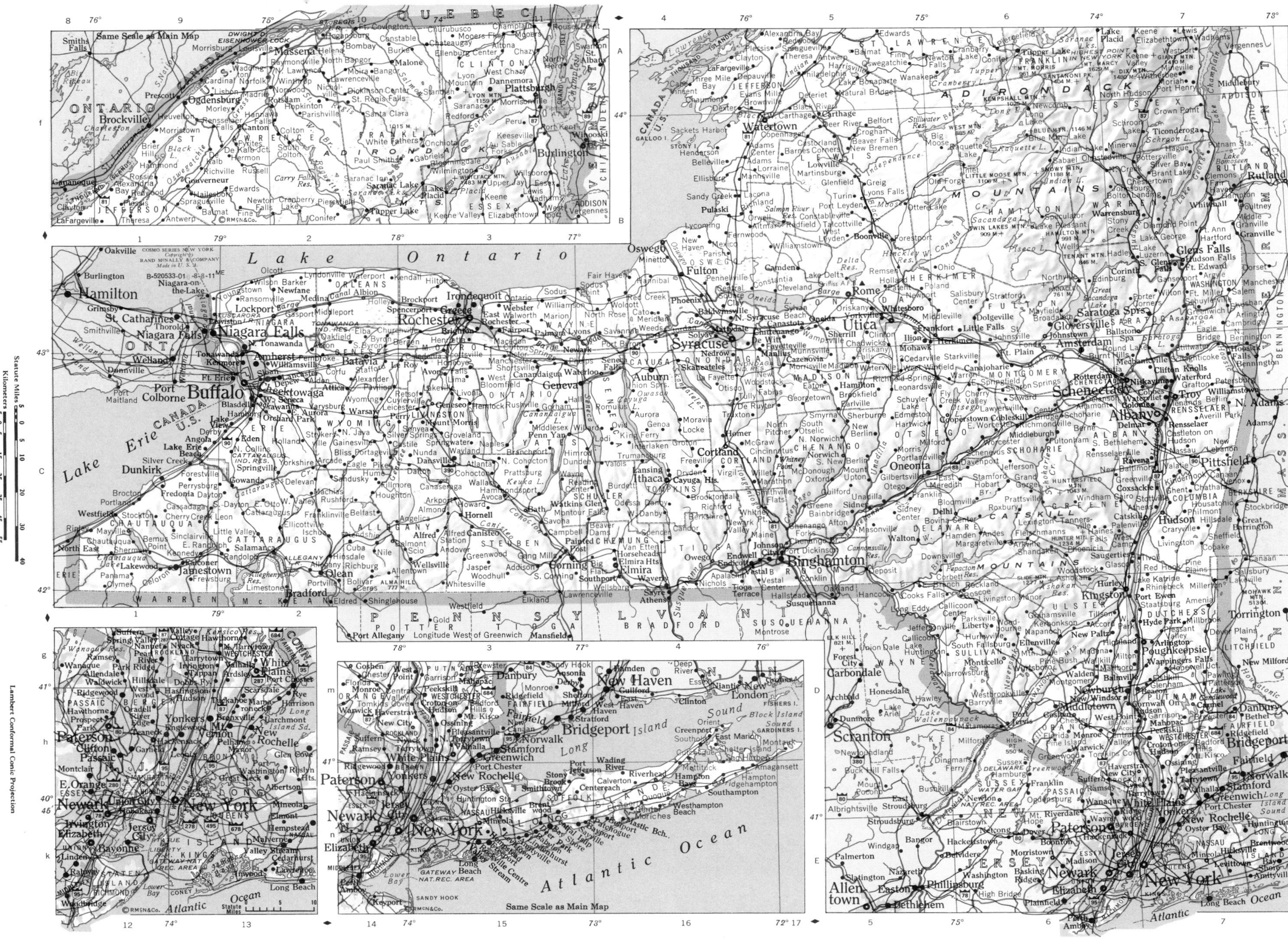

New York

1990 CENSUS

Albany, 101,082 . . . . . . C 7
Amherst, 45,600 . . . . . . C 2
Amityville, 9,286 . . . . . . E 7
Amsterdam, 20,714 . . . . C 6
Auburn, 31,258 . . . . . . C 4
Batavia, 16,310 . . . . . . C 2
Bay Shore, 33,000 . . . . E 7
Binghamton, 53,008 . . C 5
Brentwood, 45,218 . . . . E 7
Brighton, 34,455 . . . . . . B 3
Buffalo, 328,123 . . . . . . C 2
Centereach, 26,720 . . . . n15
Central Islip, 42,600 . . . . n15
Cheektowaga, 84,387 . . C 2
Cooperstown, 2,180 . . C 6
Corning, 11,938 . . . . . . C 3
Cortland, 19,801 . . . . . . C 4
Deer Park, 28,840 . . . . n15
Depew, 17,673 . . . . . . C 2
Dunkirk, 13,989 . . . . . . C 1
Elmira, 33,724 . . . . C 4
Elmont, 28,612 . . . . k13
Freeport, 39,894 . . . . . . n15
Fulton, 12,929 . . . . B 4
Gates, 30,000 . . . . B 3
Geneva, 14,143 . . . . . . C 4
Glen Cove, 24,149 . . . . . . h13
Glens Falls, 15,023 . . . . B 7
Gloversville, 16,656 . . . . B 6
Greece, 64,600 . . . . . . B 3
Harrison, 23,308 . . . . . . h13
Hempstead, 49,453 . . . . n15
Hicksville, 40,174 . . . . . . E 7
Hyde Park, 2,550('80) . . D 7
Irondequoit, 52,322 . . . . B 3
Ithaca, 29,541 . . . . C 4
Jamestown, 34,681 . . . . C 1
Kenmore, 17,180 . . . . . . C 2
Kingston, 23,095 . . . . . . D 6
Lackawanna, 20,585 . . C 2
Lake Placid, 2,485 . . . . A 7
Levittown, 53,286 . . . . E 7
Lindenhurst, 26,879 . . . . n15
Lockport, 24,426 . . . . . . B 2
Long Beach, 33,510 . . . . E 7
Massena, 11,719 . . . . . . f10
Middletown, 24,160 . . . . D 6
Mineola, 18,994 . . . . . . E 7
Mount Vernon, 67,153 . . h13
Newburgh, 26,454 . . . . D 6
New City, 33,673 . . . . D 6
New Rochelle, 67,265 . . E 7
New York, 7,322,564 . . E 7
Niagara Falls, 61,840 . . B 1
North Tonawanda, 34,989 . . . . B 2
Ogdensburg, 13,521 . . . . f 9
Olean, 16,946 . . . . C 2
Oneonta, 13,954 . . . . . . C 5
Ossining, 22,582 . . . . . . D 7
Oswego, 19,195 . . . . . . B 4
Palmyra, 3,566 . . . . . . B 3
Peekskill, 19,536 . . . . . . D 7
Plattsburgh, 21,255 . . . . f11
Port Chester, 24,728 . . E 7
Poughkeepsie, 28,844 D 7
Rochester, 231,636 . . . . B 3
Rockville Centre, 24,727 n15
Rome, 44,350 . . . . B 5
Rotterdam, 21,228 . . . . C 6
Saratoga Springs, 25,001 . . . . B 7
Schenectady, 65,566 . . C 7
Spring Valley, 21,802 . . g12
Syracuse, 163,860 . . . . B 4
Ticonderoga, 2,770 . . . . B 7
Tonawanda, 17,284 . . B 2
Troy, 54,269 . . . . C 7
Utica, 68,637 . . . . B 5
Valley Stream, 33,946 . . n15
Watertown, 29,429 . . . . B 5
West Point, 8,105('80) D 7
West Seneca, 47,866 . . C 2
White Plains, 48,718 . . D 7
Yonkers, 188,082 . . . . E 7

North Carolina

1990 CENSUS

- Ahoskie, 4,391 ... A 6
- Albemarle, 14,939 ... B 2
- Archdale, 6,913 ... B 3
- Asheboro, 16,362 ... B 3
- Asheville, 61,607 ... f10
- Bessemer City, 4,698 .. B 1
- Boone, 12,915 ... A 1
- Brevard, 5,388 ... f10
- Burlington, 39,498 ... A 3
- Carrboro, 11,553 ... B 3
- Cary, 43,858 ... B 4
- Chapel Hill, 38,719 ... B 3
- Charlotte, 395,934 ... B 2
- Cherryville, 4,756 ... B 1
- Clemmons, 6,020 ... A 2
- Clinton, 8,204 ... C 4
- Concord, 27,347 ... B 2
- Dunn, 8,336 ... B 4
- Durham, 136,611 ... B 4
- Eden, 15,238 ... A 3
- Edenton, 5,268 ... A 6
- Elizabeth City, 14,292 .. A 6
- Farmville, 4,392 ... B 5
- Fayetteville, 75,695 ... B 4
- Forest City, 7,475 ... B 1
- Garner, 14,967 ... B 4
- Gastonia, 54,732 ... B 1
- Goldsboro, 40,709 ... B 5
- Graham, 10,426 ... A 3
- Greensboro, 183,521 .. A 3
- Greenville, 44,972 ... B 5
- Hamlet, 6,196 ... C 3
- Havelock, 20,268 ... C 6
- Henderson, 15,655 ... A 4
- Hendersonville, 7,284 .. f10
- Hickory, 28,301 ... B 1
- High Point, 69,496 ... B 2
- Hope Mills, 8,184 ... C 4
- Jacksonville, 30,013 .. C 5
- Kannapolis, 29,696 ... B 2
- Kernersville, 10,836 ... A 2
- Kings Mountain, 8,763 B 1
- Kinston, 25,295 ... B 5
- Laurinburg, 11,643 ... C 3
- Lenoir, 14,192 ... B 1
- Lexington, 16,581 ... B 2
- Lincolnton, 6,847 ... B 1
- Lumberton, 18,601 ... C 3
- Matthews, 13,651 ... B 2
- Mint Hill, 11,567 ... B 2
- Monroe, 16,127 ... C 2
- Mooresville, 9,317 ... B 2
- Morehead City, 6,046 .. C 6
- Morganton, 15,085 ... B 1
- Mount Airy, 7,156 ... A 2
- Mount Olive, 4,582 ... B 4
- Nags Head, 1,838 ... B 7
- New Bern, 17,363 ... B 5
- Newton, 9,304 ... B 1
- Oxford, 7,913 ... A 4
- Plymouth, 4,328 ... B 6
- Raleigh, 207,951 ... B 4
- Reidsville, 12,183 ... A 3
- Roanoke Rapids, 15,722 ... A 5
- Rockingham, 9,399 ... C 3
- Rocky Mount, 48,997 .. B 5
- Roxboro, 7,332 ... A 4
- Salisbury, 23,087 ... B 2
- Sanford, 14,475 ... B 3
- Selma, 4,600 ... B 4
- Shelby, 14,669 ... B 1
- Smithfield, 7,540 ... B 4
- Southern Pines, 9,129 .. B 3
- Spring Lake, 7,524 ... B 4
- Statesville, 17,567 ... B 2
- Tarboro, 11,037 ... B 5
- Thomasville, 15,915 .. B 2
- Washington, 9,075 ... B 5
- Waynesville, 6,758 ... f10
- Whiteville, 5,078 ... C 4
- Williamston, 5,503 ... B 5
- Wilmington, 55,530 ... C 5
- Wilson, 36,930 ... B 5
- Winston-Salem, 143,485 A 2

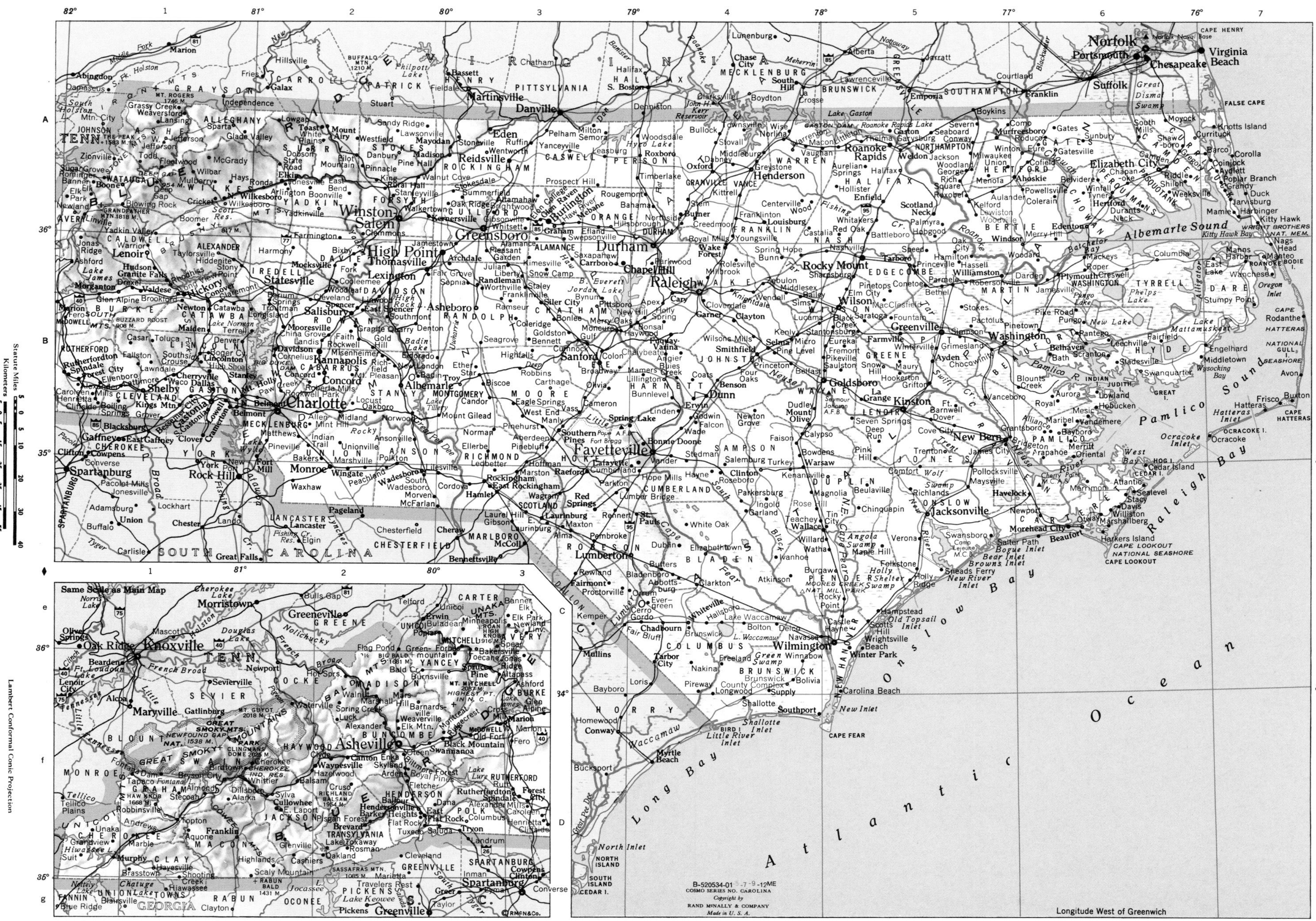

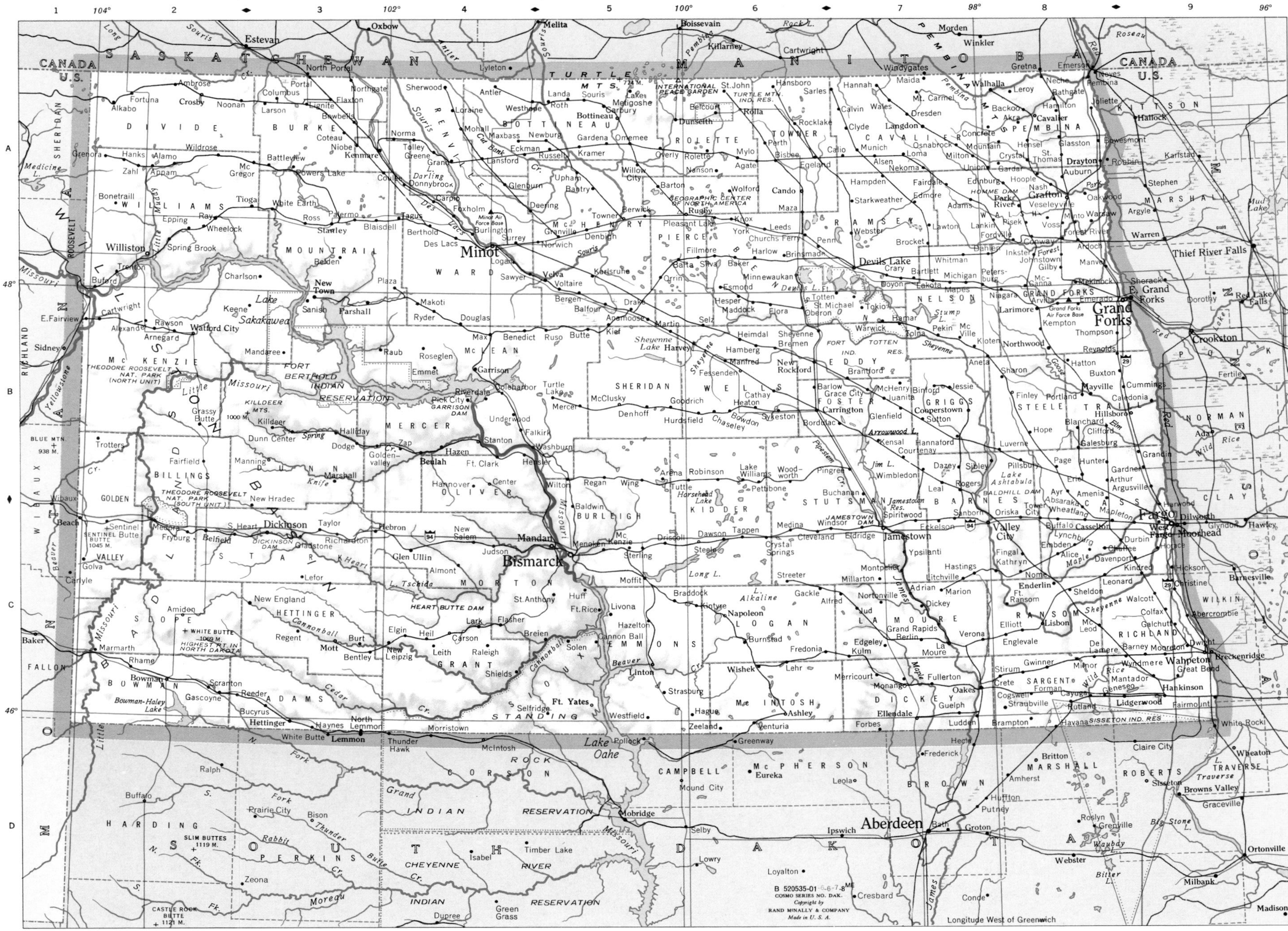

Statute Miles 5 0 5 10 20 30 40 50 60
Kilometers 5 0 5 15 25 35 45 55 65 75

Lambert Conformal Conic Projection

North Dakota

1990 CENSUS

Ashley, 1,052 . . . . C 6
Beach, 1,205 . . . . C 1
Belfield, 887 . . . . C 2
Beulah, 3,363 . . . . B 4
Bismarck, 49,256 . . . . C 5
Bottineau, 2,598 . . . . . . A 5
Bowman, 1,741 . . . . . . C 2
Burlington, 995 . . . . . . A 4
Cando, 1,564 . . . . A 6
Carrington, 2,267 . . . . B 6
Casselton, 1,601 . . . . . . C 8
Cavalier, 1,508 . . . . A 8
Center, 826 . . . . B 4
Cooperstown, 1,247 . . B 7
Crosby, 1,312 . . . . A 2
Devils Lake, 7,782 . . . . A 7
Dickinson, 16,097 . . . . . C 3
Drayton, 961 . . . . A 8
Dunseith, 723 . . . . A 5
Edgeley, 680 . . . . C 7
Elgin, 765 . . . . C 4
Ellendale, 1,798 . . . . . . C 7
Enderlin, 997 . . . . C 8
Fargo, 74,111 . . . . C 9
Fessenden, 655 . . . . . . B 6
Garrison, 1,530 . . . . . . B 4
Glen Ullin, 927 . . . . C 4
Grafton, 4,840 . . . . A 8
Grand Forks, 49,425 . . B 8
Gwinner, 585 . . . . C 8
Hankinson, 1,038 . . . . C 9
Harvey, 2,263 . . . . B 6
Hatton, 800 . . . . B 8
Hazen, 2,818 . . . . B 4
Hebron, 888 . . . . C 3
Hettinger, 1,574 . . . . . . D 3
Hillsboro, 1,488 . . . . B 8
Jamestown, 15,571 . . . . C 7
Kenmare, 1,214 . . . . A 3
Killdeer, 722 . . . . B 3
Lakota, 898 . . . . A 7
La Moure, 970 . . . . C 7
Langdon, 2,241 . . . . . . A 7
Larimore, 1,464 . . . . . . B 8
Lidgerwood, 799 . . . . . . C 8
Linton, 1,410 . . . . C 5
Lisbon, 2,177 . . . . C 8
Mandan, 15,177 . . . . . . C 5
Mayville, 2,092 . . . . B 8
Milnor, 651 . . . . C 8
Minot, 34,544 . . . . A 4
Mohall, 931 . . . . A 4
Mott, 1,019 . . . . C 3
Napoleon, 930 . . . . C 6
New England, 663 . . . . C 3
New Rockford, 1,604 . . B 6
New Salem, 909 . . . . . . C 4
New Town, 1,388 . . . . B 3
Northwood, 1,166 . . . . B 8
Oakes, 1,775 . . . . C 7
Park River, 1,725 . . . . A 8
Parshall, 943 . . . . B 3
Ray, 603 . . . . A 2
Richardton, 625 . . . . . . C 3
Rolla, 1,286 . . . . A 6
Rugby, 2,909 . . . . A 6
Stanley, 1,371 . . . . A 3
Steele, 762 . . . . C 6
Surrey, 856 . . . . A 4
Thompson, 930 . . . . . . B 8
Tioga, 1,278 . . . . A 3
Towner, 669 . . . . A 5
Turtle Lake, 681 . . . . . . B 5
Underwood, 976 . . . . . . B 4
Valley City, 7,163 . . . . C 8
Velva, 968 . . . . A 5
Wahpeton, 8,751 . . . . . C 9
Walhalla, 1,131 . . . . A 8
Washburn, 1,506 . . . . . . B 5
Watford City, 1,784 . . . B 2
West Fargo, 12,287 . . . C 9
Westhope, 578 . . . . A 4
Williston, 13,131 . . . . . . A 2
Wilton, 728 . . . . B 5
Wishek, 1,171 . . . . C 6

Ohio

1990 CENSUS

Akron, 223,019 . . . . . . A 4
Alliance, 23,376 . . . . . . B 4
Ashland, 20,079 . . . . . . B 3
Ashtabula, 21,633 . . . . A 5
Athens, 21,265 . . . . . . C 3
Austintown, 23,300 . . . . A 5
Barberton, 27,623 . . . . A 4
Beavercreek, 33,626 . . C 1
Bellefontaine, 12,142 . . B 2
Boardman, 38,596 . . . . A 5
Bowling Green, 28,176 A 2
Brook Park, 22,865 . . . . h 9
Brunswick, 28,230 . . . . A 4
Canton, 84,161 . . . . . . B 4
Chillicothe, 21,923 . . . . C 3
Cincinnati, 364,040 . . . . C 1
Cleveland, 505,616 . . . . A 4
Cleveland Heights,
  54,052 . . . . A 4
Columbus, 632,910 . . . . C 2
Cuyahoga Falls, 48,950 A 4
Dayton, 182,044 . . . . . . C 1
Defiance, 16,768 . . . . . . A 1
Delaware, 20,030 . . . . B 2
East Cleveland, 33,096 g 9
Eastlake, 21,161 . . . . . . A 4
East Liverpool, 13,654 B 5
Elyria, 56,746 . . . . A 3
Euclid, 54,875 . . . . A 4
Fairborn, 31,300 . . . . . . C 1
Fairfield, 39,729 . . . . . . n12
Findlay, 35,703 . . . . . . A 2
Fostoria, 14,983 . . . . . . A 2
Fremont, 17,648 . . . . . . A 2
Garfield Heights, 31,739 h 9
Greenville, 12,863 . . . . B 1
Hamilton, 61,368 . . . . . . C 1
Ironton, 12,751 . . . . . . D 3
Kent, 28,835 . . . . A 4
Kettering, 60,569 . . . . . . C 1
Lakewood, 59,718 . . . . A 4
Lancaster, 34,507 . . . . C 3
Lima, 45,549 . . . . B 1
Lorain, 71,245 . . . . A 3
Mansfield, 50,627 . . . . B 3
Maple Heights, 27,089 . . h 9
Marietta, 15,026 . . . . . . C 4
Marion, 34,075 . . . . . . B 2
Massillon, 31,007 . . . . B 4
Medina, 19,231 . . . . . . A 4
Mentor, 47,358 . . . . . . A 4
Middletown, 46,022 . . . . C 1
Mount Vernon, 14,550 B 3
Newark, 44,389 . . . . . . B 3
New Philadelphia,
  15,698 . . . . B 4
Niles, 21,128 . . . . A 5
North Olmsted, 34,204 h 9
Norwalk, 14,731 . . . . . . A 3
Norwood, 23,674 . . . . . . o13
Oxford, 18,937 . . . . . . C 1
Parma, 87,876 . . . . A 4
Parma Heights, 21,448 h 9
Piqua, 20,612 . . . . B 1
Portsmouth, 22,676 . . D 3
Reynoldsburg, 25,748 . . C 3
Salem, 12,233 . . . . B 5
Sandusky, 29,764 . . . . A 3
Shaker Heights, 30,831 A 4
South Euclid, 23,866 . . g 9
Springfield, 70,487 . . . . C 2
Steubenville, 22,125 . . B 5
Stow, 27,702 . . . . A 4
Strongsville, 35,308 . . . . A 4
Tiffin, 18,604 . . . . A 2
Toledo, 332,943 . . . . . . A 2
Upper Arlington, 34,128 B 2
Urbana, 11,353 . . . . . . B 2
Warren, 50,793 . . . . . . A 5
Westerville, 30,269 . . . . B 3
Whitehall, 20,572 . . . . m11
Wooster, 22,191 . . . . . . B 4
Xenia, 24,664 . . . . C 2
Youngstown, 95,732 . . A 5
Zanesville, 26,778 . . . . C 4

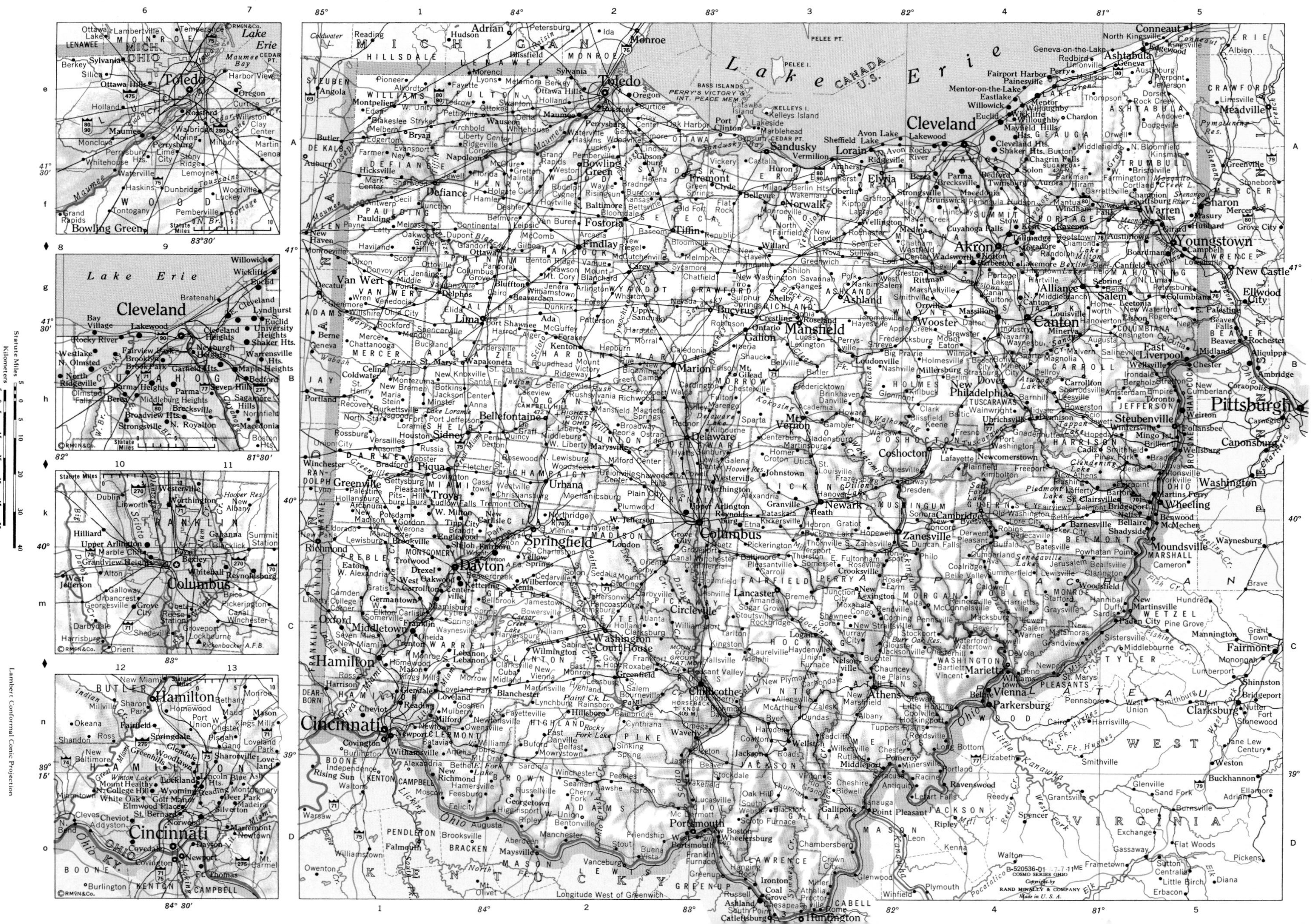

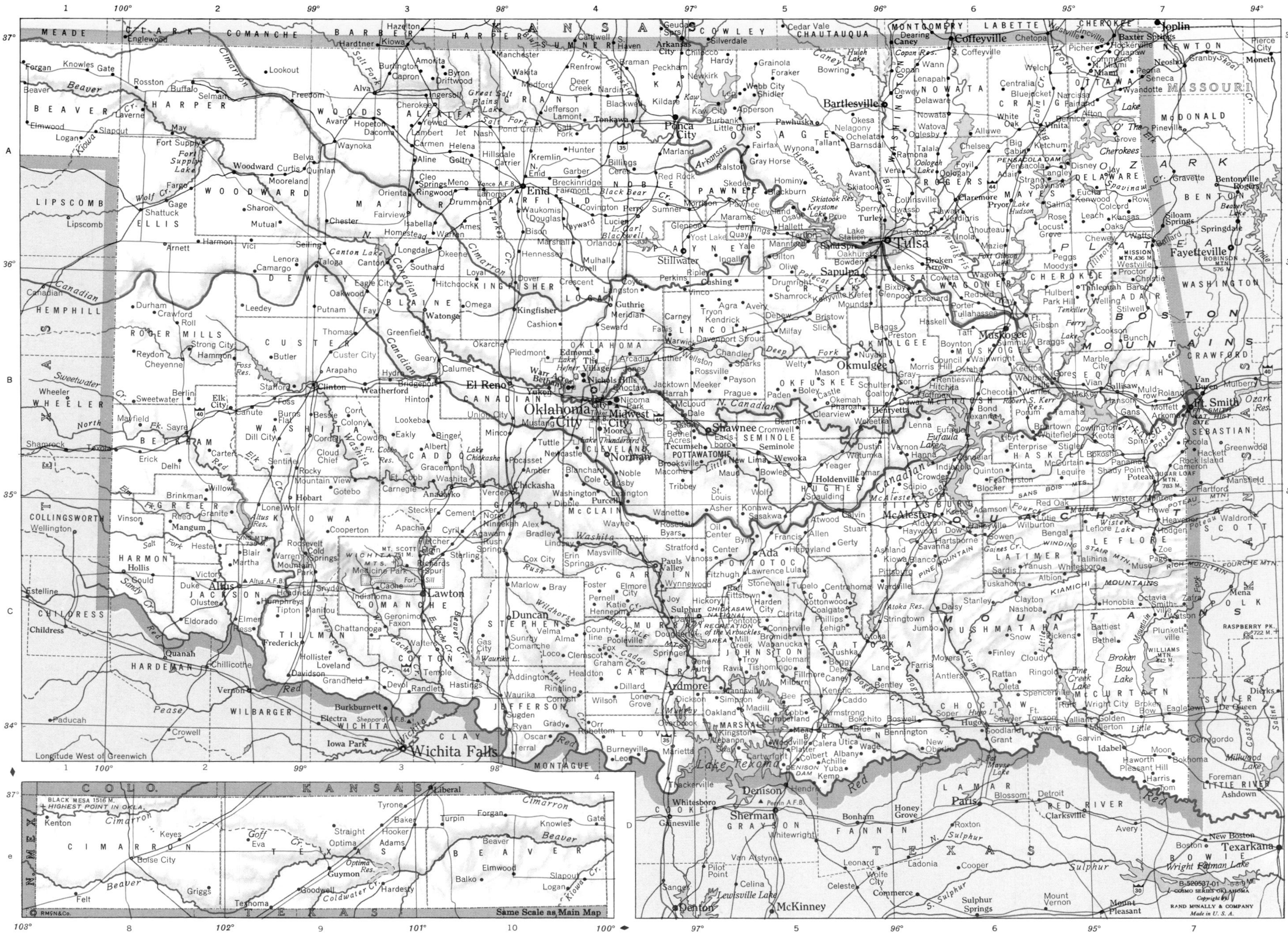

Statute Miles 5 0 5 10 20 30 40

Kilometers 5 0 5 15 25 35 45 55

Lambert Conformal Conic Projection

Oklahoma

1990 CENSUS

Ada, 15,820	C 5
Altus, 21,910	C 2
Alva, 5,495	A 3
Anadarko, 6,586	B 3
Ardmore, 23,079	C 4
Atoka, 3,298	C 5
Bartlesville, 34,256	A 6
Bethany, 20,075	B 4
Bixby, 9,502	B 6
Blackwell, 7,538	A 4
Bristow, 4,062	B 5
Broken Arrow, 58,043	A 6
Broken Bow, 3,961	C 7
Checotah, 3,290	B 6
Chickasha, 14,988	B 4
Choctaw, 8,545	B 4
Claremore, 13,280	A 6
Clinton, 9,298	B 3
Collinsville, 3,612	A 6
Coweta, 6,159	B 6
Cushing, 7,218	B 5
Del City, 23,928	B 4
Dewey, 3,326	A 6
Duncan, 21,732	C 4
Durant, 12,823	D 5
Edmond, 52,315	B 4
Elk City, 10,428	B 2
El Reno, 15,414	B 4
Enid, 45,309	A 4
Frederick, 5,221	C 2
Guthrie, 10,518	B 4
Guymon, 7,803	e 9
Harrah, 4,206	B 4
Henryetta, 5,872	B 6
Hobart, 4,305	B 2
Holdenville, 4,792	B 5
Hugo, 5,978	C 6
Idabel, 6,957	D 7
Jenks, 7,493	A 6
Kingfisher, 4,095	B 4
Lawton, 80,561	C 3
Lindsay, 2,947	C 4
Madill, 3,069	C 5
Mangum, 3,344	C 2
Marlow, 4,416	C 4
McAlester, 16,370	C 6
McLoud, 2,493	B 5
Miami, 13,142	A 7
Midwest City, 52,267	B 4
Moore, 40,318	B 4
Muskogee, 37,708	B 6
Mustang, 10,434	B 4
Nichols Hills, 4,020	B 4
Noble, 4,710	B 4
Norman, 80,071	B 4
Nowata, 3,896	A 6
Oklahoma City, 444,719	B 4
Okmulgee, 13,441	B 6
Owasso, 11,151	A 6
Pauls Valley, 6,150	C 4
Perry, 4,978	A 4
Ponca City, 26,359	A 4
Poteau, 7,210	B 7
Pryor, 8,327	A 6
Purcell, 4,784	B 4
Sallisaw, 7,122	B 7
Sand Springs, 15,346	A 5
Sapulpa, 18,074	B 5
Seminole, 7,071	B 5
Shawnee, 26,017	B 5
Skiatook, 4,910	A 5
Stillwater, 36,676	A 4
Sulphur, 4,824	C 5
Tahlequah, 10,398	B 7
Tecumseh, 5,750	B 5
The Village, 10,353	B 4
Tonkawa, 3,127	A 4
Tulsa, 367,302	A 6
Vinita, 5,804	A 6
Wagoner, 6,894	B 6
Warr Acres, 9,288	B 4
Weatherford, 10,124	B 3
Wewoka, 4,050	B 5
Woodward, 12,340	A 2
Yukon, 20,935	B 4

Oregon

1990 CENSUS

Albany, 29,462	C 3
Aloha, 10,000('82)	h12
Altamont, 19,805('80)	E 5
Ashland, 16,234	E 4
Astoria, 10,069	A 3
Baker, 9,140	C 9
Beaverton, 53,310	B 4
Bend, 20,469	C 5
Brookings, 4,400	E 2
Burns, 2,913	D 7
Canby, 8,983	B 4
Central Point, 7,509	E 4
Coos Bay, 15,076	D 2
Coquille, 4,121	D 2
Cornelius, 6,148	g11
Corvallis, 44,757	C 3
Cottage Grove, 7,402	D 3
Dallas, 9,422	C 3
Eugene, 112,669	C 3
Florence, 5,162	D 2
Forest Grove, 13,559	B 3
Gladstone, 10,152	B 4
Grants Pass, 17,488	E 3
Green, 3,897('80)	D 3
Gresham, 68,235	B 4
Hermiston, 10,040	B 7
Hillsboro, 37,520	B 4
Hood River, 4,632	B 5
Independence, 4,425	C 3
John Day, 1,836	C 8
Junction City, 3,670	C 3
Keizer, 21,884	C 3
Klamath Falls, 17,737	E 5
La Grande, 11,766	B 8
Lake Oswego, 30,576	B 4
Lakeview, 2,526	E 6
Lebanon, 10,950	C 4
Lincoln City, 5,892	C 3
McMinnville, 17,894	B 3
Medford, 46,951	E 4
Metzger, 5,544('80)	h12
Milton-Freewater, 5,533	B 8
Milwaukie, 18,692	B 4
Molalla, 3,651	B 4
Monmouth, 6,288	C 3
Mount Angel, 2,778	B 4
Myrtle Creek, 3,063	D 3
Myrtle Point, 2,712	D 2
Newberg, 13,086	B 4
Newport, 8,437	C 2
North Albany, 4,499('80)	k11
North Bend, 9,614	D 2
Nyssa, 2,629	D 9
Oak Grove, 11,640('80)	B 4
Oakridge, 3,063	D 4
Ontario, 9,392	C10
Oregon City, 14,698	B 4
Parkrose, 21,108('80)	B 4
Pendleton, 15,126	B 8
Portland, 437,319	B 4
Prineville, 5,355	C 6
Redmond, 7,163	C 5
Reedsport, 4,796	D 2
River Road, 10,370('80)	C 3
Roseburg, 17,032	D 3
Saint Helens, 7,535	B 4
Salem, 107,786	C 4
Sandy, 4,152	B 4
Scappoose, 3,529	B 4
Seaside, 5,359	B 3
Silverton, 5,635	C 4
Springfield, 44,683	C 4
Stayton, 5,011	C 4
Sutherlin, 5,020	D 3
Sweet Home, 6,850	C 4
The Dalles, 11,060	B 5
Tigard, 29,344	h12
Tillamook, 4,001	B 3
Toledo, 3,174	C 3
Tri City, 3,439('80)	E 3
Umatilla, 3,046	B 7
West Linn, 16,367	B 4
Wilsonville, 7,106	h12
Winston, 3,773	D 3
Woodburn, 13,404	B 4

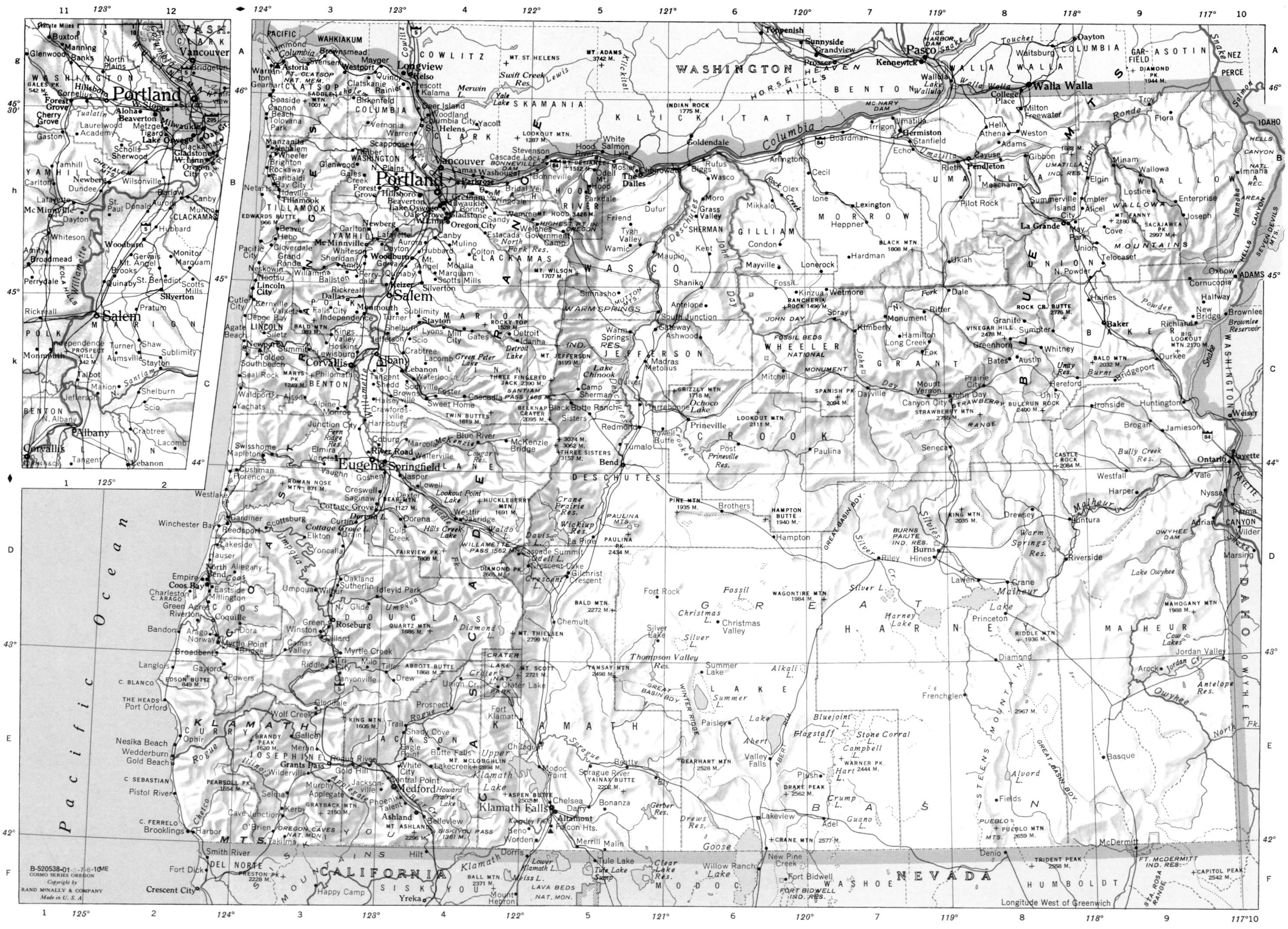

Statute Miles 0 5 10 20 30 40 50

Kilometers 0 5 15 25 35 45 55 65 75

Lambert Conformal Conic Projection

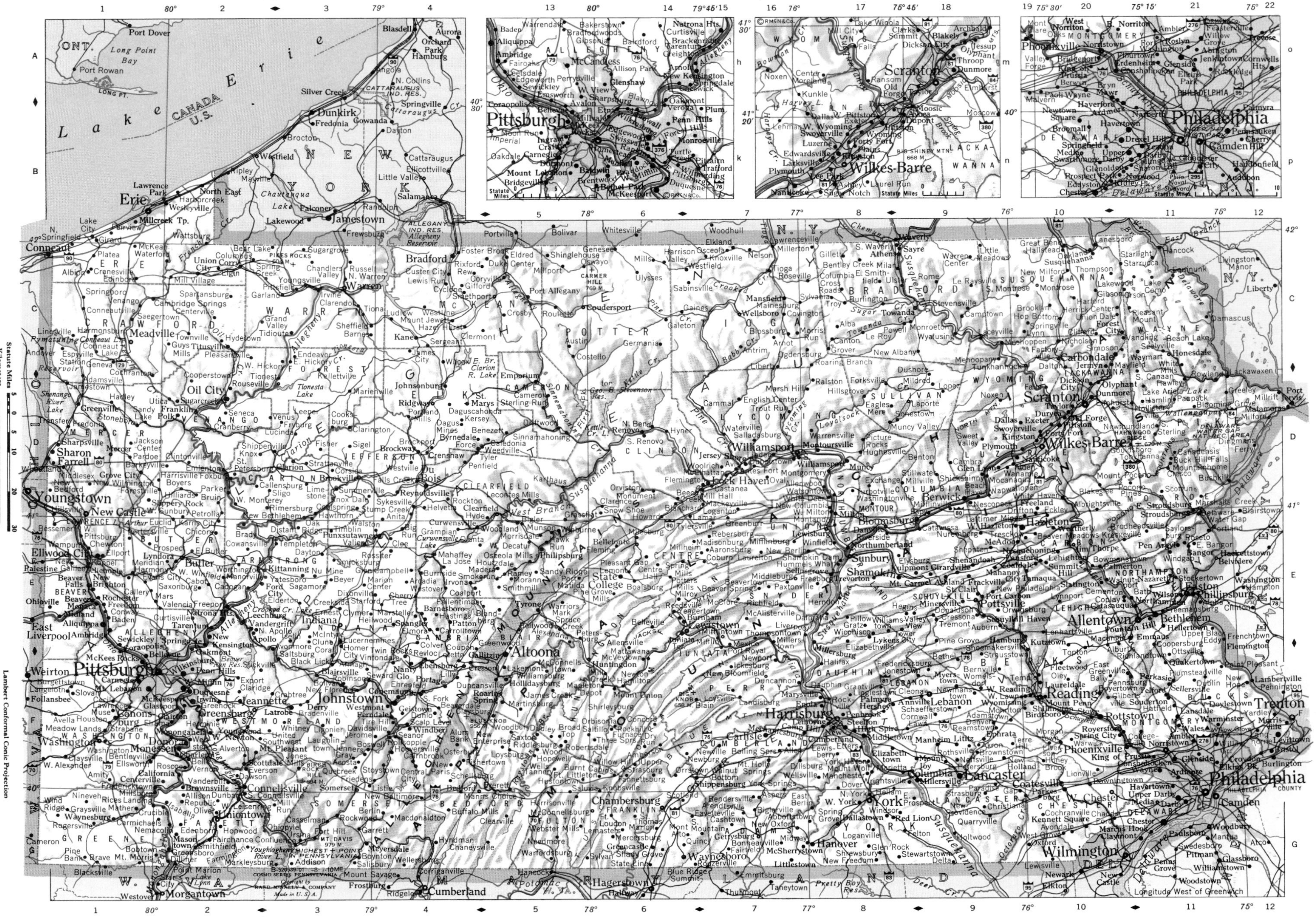

Pennsylvania

1990 CENSUS

Abington Township, 59,300 .... o21
Aliquippa, 13,374 .... E 1
Allentown, 105,090 .... E11
Altoona, 51,881 .... E 5
Baldwin, 21,923 .... k13
Beaver Falls, 10,687 .... E 1
Bethel Park, 33,823 ..... k14
Bethlehem, 71,428 .... E11
Bloomsburg, 12,439 ...... E 9
Bradford, 9,625 .... C 4
Brentwood, 10,823 .... k14
Broomall, 10,930 .... p20
Butler, 15,714 .... E 2
Carbondale, 10,664 ...... C10
Carlisle, 18,419 .... F 7
Chambersburg, 16,647 .... G 6
Chester, 41,856 .... G11
Clairton, 9,656 .... F 2
Coatesville, 11,038 ..... G10
Connellsville, 9,229 .... F 2
Du Bois, 8,286 .... D 4
Dunmore, 15,403 .... D10
Easton, 26,276 .... E11
Ephrata, 12,133 .... F 9
Erie, 108,718 .... B 1
Gettysburg, 7,025 .... G 7
Greensburg, 16,318 ...... F 2
Hanover, 14,399 .... G 8
Harrisburg, 52,376 ...... F 8
Haverford Township, 51,800 .... o20
Hazleton, 24,730 .... E10
Hershey, 13,249('80) .... F 8
Indiana, 15,174 .... E 3
Jeannette, 11,221 .... F 2
Johnstown, 28,134 .... F 4
Kingston, 14,507 .... D10
Lancaster, 55,551 .... F 9
Lansdale, 16,362 .... F11
Latrobe, 9,265 .... F 3
Lebanon, 24,800 .... F 9
Levittown, 17,420('84) .. F12
Lewistown, 9,341 .... E 6
Lock Haven, 9,230 .... D 7
McCandless, 28,781 ...... h13
McKeesport, 26,016 ...... F 2
Meadville, 14,318 .... C 1
Middletown, 9,254 .... F 8
Millcreek Township, 46,100 .... B 1
Monroeville, 29,169 ..... k14
Mount Lebanon, 33,362 ... F 1
Munhall, 13,158 .... k14
Nanticoke, 12,267 .... D10
Natrona Heights, 12,200 . E 2
New Castle, 28,334 ...... D 1
New Kensington, 15,894 .. E 2
Norristown, 30,749 ...... F11
Oil City, 11,949 .... D 2
Penn Hills, 51,430 ...... k14
Philadelphia, 1,585,577 . G11
Phoenixville, 15,066 .... F10
Pittsburgh, 369,879 ..... F 1
Plum, 25,609 .... k14
Pottstown, 21,831 .... F10
Pottsville, 16,603 ...... E 9
Punxsutawney, 6,782 ..... E 4
Reading, 78,380 .... F10
Scranton, 81,805 .... D10
Sharon, 17,493 .... D 1
Springfield, 24,160 ..... p20
State College, 38,923 ... E 6
Uniontown, 12,034 .... G 2
Upper Darby, 86,100 ..... G11
Warminster, 36,900 ...... F11
Warren, 11,122 .... C 3
Washington, 15,864 ...... F 1
Waynesboro, 9,578 .... G 6
West Chester, 18,041 .... G10
West Mifflin, 23,644 .... F 2
Wilkes-Barre, 47,523 .... D10
Wilkinsburg, 21,080 ..... F 2
Williamsport, 31,933 .... D 7
York, 42,192 .... G 8

Rhode Island

Rhode Island

1990 CENSUS

Abbott Run Valley, 1,050('87) . . . . B 4
Adamsville, 600('87) E 6
Albion, 1,600('87) . . B 4
Allenton, 600('87) . . . . E 4
Anthony, 2,980('87) . . D 3
Arnold Mills, 600('87) B 4
Ashton, 820('87) . . . . B 4
Barrington, 16,174('80) . . . . . . D 5
Berkeley, 830('87) . . B 4
Block Island, 620('87) h 7
Branch Village, 400('87) . . . . B 3
Bristol, 20,128('80) . . D 5
Burdickville, 500('87) F 2
Carolina, 650('87) . . . . F 2
Central Falls, 17,637 B 4
Charlestown, 1,500 (6,478▲) . . . . F 2
Chepachet, 900('87) B 2
Common Fence Point, 860('87) . . . . D 6
Coventry, 6,980 (31,083▲) . . . . D 3
Cranston, 76,060 . . . . C 4
Davisville, 500('87) . . E 4
Diamond Hill, 810('87) B 4
East Greenwich, 10,211('87) . . . . . . D 4
East Matunuck, 500('87) . . . . F 3
East Providence, 50,380 . . . . C 4
Esmond, 4,320('87) . . B 4
Forestdale, 530('87) B 3
Glendale, 700('87) . . B 2
Greenville, 7,576('80) C 3
Harmony, 820('87) . . B 3
Harris, 1,050('87) . . . . D 3
Hope, 270('87) . . . . . . D 3
Hopkinton, 550 (6,873▲) . . . . F 1
Island Park, 1,240('87) . . . . E 6
Jamestown, 4,040('87) . . . . F 5
Johnston, 26,800 . . . . C 4
Kenyon, 400('87) . . . . F 2
Kingston, 5,479('80) . . F 3
La Fayette, 640('87) E 4
Little Compton, 500 (3,339▲) . . . . E 6
Lonsdale, 3,850('87) B 4
Manville, 3,030('87) . . B 4
Mapleville, 1,300('87) B 2
Matunuck, 550('87) . . G 3
Middletown, 3,350 (19,460▲) . . . . E 5
Mount View, 610('87) D 4
Narragansett, 3,342 (14,985▲) . . . . F 4
Newport, 28,227 . . . . . F 5
North Kingstown, 2,750 (23,786▲) . . . . E 4
North Providence, 32,090 . . . . C 4
Oakland, 600('87) . . B 2
Pascoag, 3,807('80) B 2
Pawtucket, 72,644 . . C 4
Peace Dale, 3,100('87) . . . . F 3
Plum Beach, 400('87) E 4
Portsmouth, 3,540 (16,857▲) . . . . E 6
Primrose, 500('87) . . B 3
Providence, 160,728 C 4
Quidnessett, 3,300('87) . . . . E 4
Quidnick, 2,300('87) D 3
Quonochontaug, 1,500('87) . . . . G 2
Saunderstown, 400('87) . . . . E 4
Saylesville, 3,510('87) B 4
Shannock, 950('87) . . F 2
Shores Acres, 410('87) . . . . E 4
Slatersville, 2,330('87) A 3
South Hopkinton, 900('87) . . . . F 1
Tiverton, 7,653 (14,312▲) . . . . D 6
Union Village, 2,150('87) . . . . B 3
Usquepaug, 400('87) F 3
Valley Falls, 10,892('80) . . . . . . B 4
Wakefield, 3,450('87) F 3
Warren, 10,640('87) . . D 5
Warwick, 85,427 . . . . D 4
Westerly, 16,477 (21,605▲) . . . . F 1
West Kingston, 1,150('87) . . . . F 3
West Warwick, 29,268 . . . . D 3
Woonsocket, 43,877 A 3
Yorktown Manor, 2,520('87) . . . . C 3

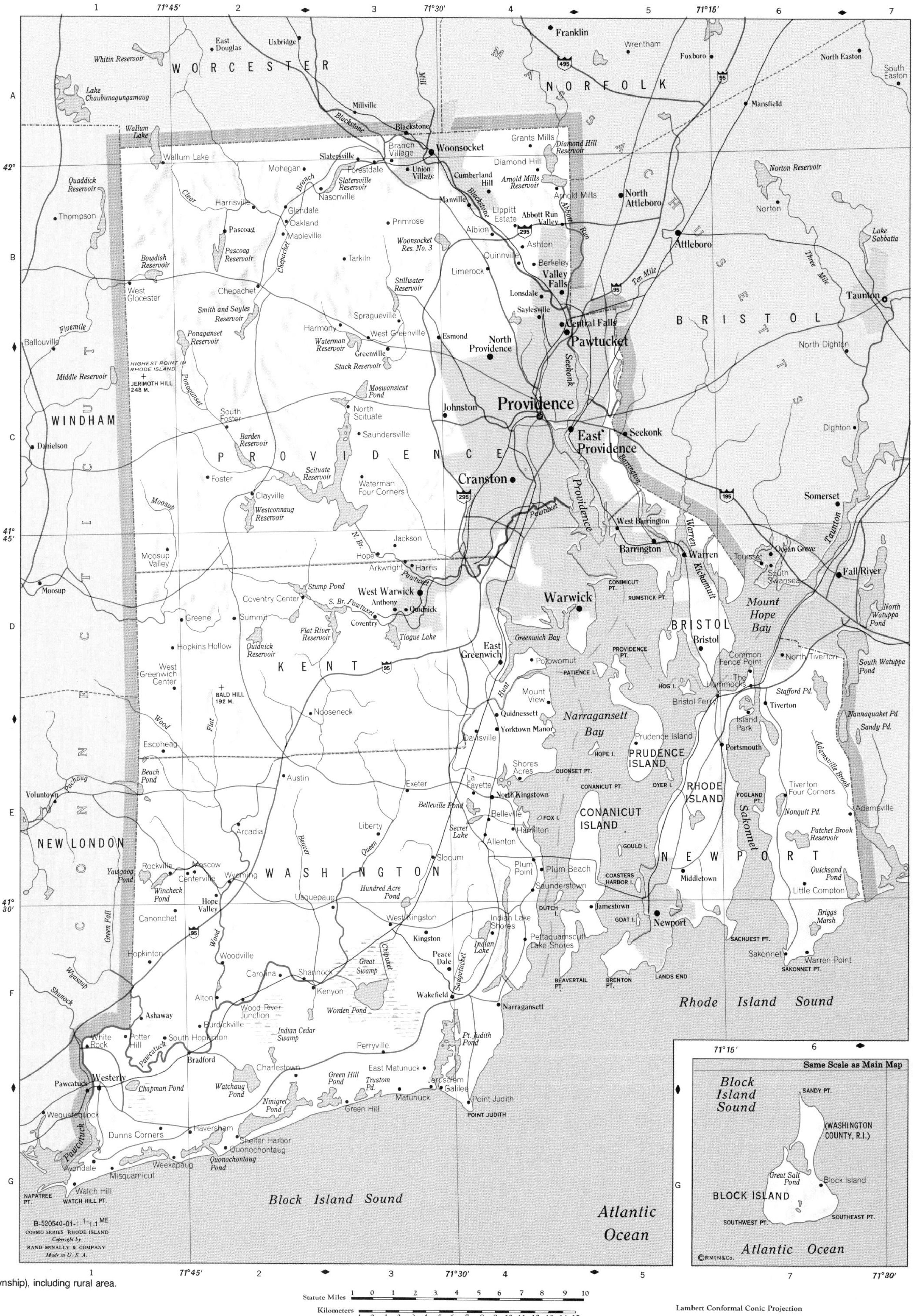

▲ Population of entire town (township), including rural area.

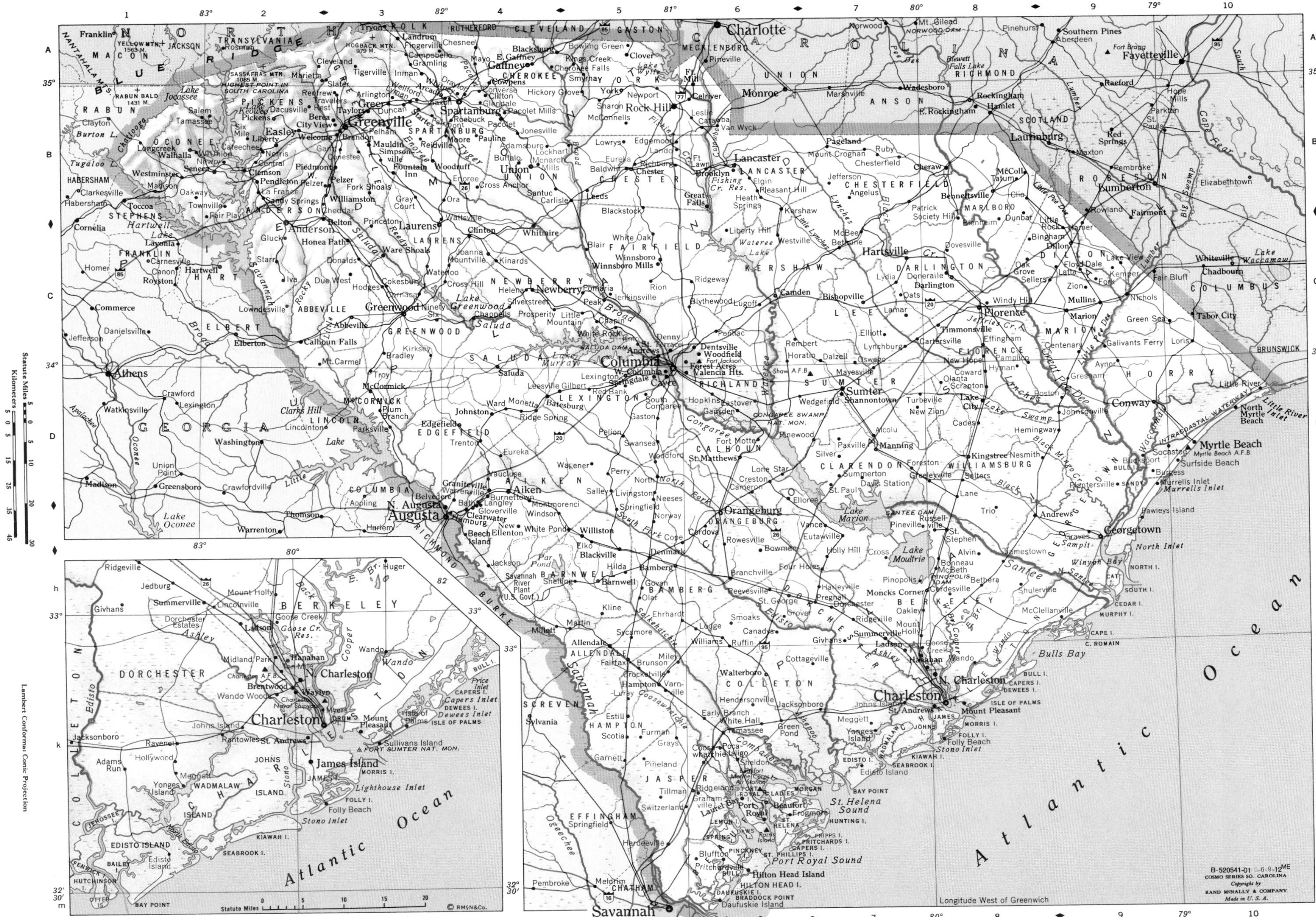

South Carolina

1990 CENSUS

Abbeville, 5,778 ...... C 3
Aiken, 19,872 .... D 4
Allendale, 4,410 ...... E 5
Anderson, 26,184 .... B 2
Bamberg, 3,843 .... E 5
Barnwell, 5,255 .... E 5
Batesburg, 4,082 ..... D 4
Beaufort, 9,576 .... G 6
Belton, 4,646 .... B 3
Bennettsville, 9,345 ... B 8
Bishopville, 3,560 .... C 7
Camden, 6,696 .... C 6
Cayce, 11,163 .... D 5
Charleston, 80,414 .... F 8
Cheraw, 5,505 .... B 8
Chester, 7,158 .... B 5
Clemson, 11,096 ...... B 2
Clinton, 7,987 .... C 4
Clover, 3,422 .... A 5
Columbia, 98,052 .... C 5
Conway, 9,819 .... D 9
Cowpens, 2,176 ...... A 4
Darlington, 7,311 ...... C 8
Denmark, 3,762 ...... E 5
Dillon, 6,829 .... C 9
Easley, 15,195 .... B 2
East Gaffney, 4,092('80) A 4
Florence, 29,813 ...... C 8
Forest Acres, 7,197 ... C 6
Fort Mill, 4,930 ...... A 6
Fountain Inn, 4,388 .... B 3
Gaffney, 13,145 ...... A 4
Georgetown, 9,517 .... E 9
Goose Creek, 24,692 .. F 7
Greenville, 58,282 .... B 3
Greenwood, 20,807 ... C 3
Greer, 10,322 .... B 3
Hanahan, 13,176 ...... F 7
Hartsville, 8,372 ...... C 7
Hilton Head Island, 23,694 .... G 6
Honea Path, 3,841 .... C 3
Irmo, 11,280 .... C 5
Isle of Palms, 3,680 .... k12
James Island, 24,124('80) k12
Kingstree, 3,858 ...... D 8
Ladson, 13,246('80) ... F 7
Lake City, 7,153 ...... D 8
Lancaster, 8,914 ...... B 6
Laurens, 9,694 .... C 3
Liberty, 3,228 .... B 2
Manning, 4,428 ...... D 7
Marion, 7,658 .... C 9
Mauldin, 11,587 ...... B 3
Moncks Corner, 5,607 E 7
Mount Pleasant, 30,108 F 8
Mullins, 5,910 .... C 9
Myrtle Beach, 24,848 .. D10
Newberry, 10,542 ..... C 4
North Augusta, 15,351 D 4
North Charleston, 70,218 .... F 8
North Myrtle Beach, 8,636 .... D10
Orangeburg, 13,739 .. E 6
Pickens, 3,042 .... B 2
Rock Hill, 41,643 ...... B 5
Saint Andrews, 9,908('80) .... F 7
Saint Andrews, 20,245('80) .... C 5
Seneca, 7,726 .... B 2
Simpsonville, 11,708 .. B 3
Spartanburg, 43,467 .. B 4
Summerville, 22,519 .. E 7
Sumter, 41,943 .... D 7
Union, 9,836 .... B 4
Walhalla, 3,755 ...... B 1
Walterboro, 5,492 .... F 6
West Columbia, 10,588 D 5
Williamston, 3,876 .... B 3
Williston, 3,099 .... E 5
Woodruff, 4,365 ...... B 3
York, 6,709 .... B 5

South Dakota

1990 CENSUS

Place, population	Key
Aberdeen, 24,927	B 7
Alcester, 843	D 9
Arlington, 908	C 8
Armour, 854	D 7
Belle Fourche, 4,335	C 2
Beresford, 1,849	D 9
Box Elder, 2,680	C 2
Brandon, 3,543	D 9
Britton, 1,394	B 8
Brookings, 16,270	C 9
Burke, 756	D 6
Canton, 2,787	D 9
Centerville, 887	D 9
Chamberlain, 2,347	D 6
Clark, 1,292	C 8
Clear Lake, 1,247	C 9
Custer, 1,741	D 2
Deadwood, 1,830	C 2
Dell Rapids, 2,484	D 9
De Smet, 1,172	C 8
Edgemont, 906	D 2
Elk Point, 1,423	E 9
Eureka, 1,197	B 6
Faulkton, 809	B 6
Flandreau, 2,311	C 9
Fort Pierre, 1,854	C 5
Freeman, 1,293	D 8
Garretson, 924	D 9
Gettysburg, 1,510	C 6
Gregory, 1,384	D 6
Groton, 1,196	B 7
Hartford, 1,262	D 9
Highmore, 835	C 6
Hot Springs, 4,325	D 2
Howard, 1,156	C 8
Huron, 12,448	C 7
Ipswich, 965	B 6
Kadoka, 736	D 4
Lake Andes, 846	D 7
Lake Preston, 663	C 8
Lead, 3,632	C 2
Lemmon, 1,614	B 3
Lennox, 1,767	D 9
Madison, 6,257	C 8
Marion, 831	D 8
Martin, 1,151	D 4
McLaughlin, 780	B 5
Menno, 768	D 8
Milbank, 3,879	B 9
Miller, 1,678	C 7
Mitchell, 13,798	D 7
Mobridge, 3,768	B 5
North Sioux City, 2,019	E 9
Onida, 761	C 5
Parker, 984	D 8
Parkston, 1,572	D 8
Philip, 1,077	C 4
Pierre, 12,906	C 5
Platte, 1,311	D 7
Presho, 654	D 5
Rapid City, 54,523	C 2
Redfield, 2,770	C 7
Saint Francis, 815	D 5
Salem, 1,289	D 8
Scotland, 968	D 8
Selby, 707	B 5
Sioux Falls, 100,814	D 9
Sisseton, 2,181	B 8
Spearfish, 6,966	C 2
Springfield, 834	E 8
Sturgis, 5,330	C 2
Tyndall, 1,201	E 8
Valley Springs, 739	D 9
Vermillion, 10,034	E 9
Volga, 1,263	C 9
Wagner, 1,462	D 7
Wall, 834	D 3
Watertown, 17,592	C 8
Webster, 2,017	B 8
Wessington Springs, 1,083	C 7
Whitewood, 891	C 2
Winner, 3,354	D 6
Woonsocket, 766	C 7
Yankton, 12,703	E 8

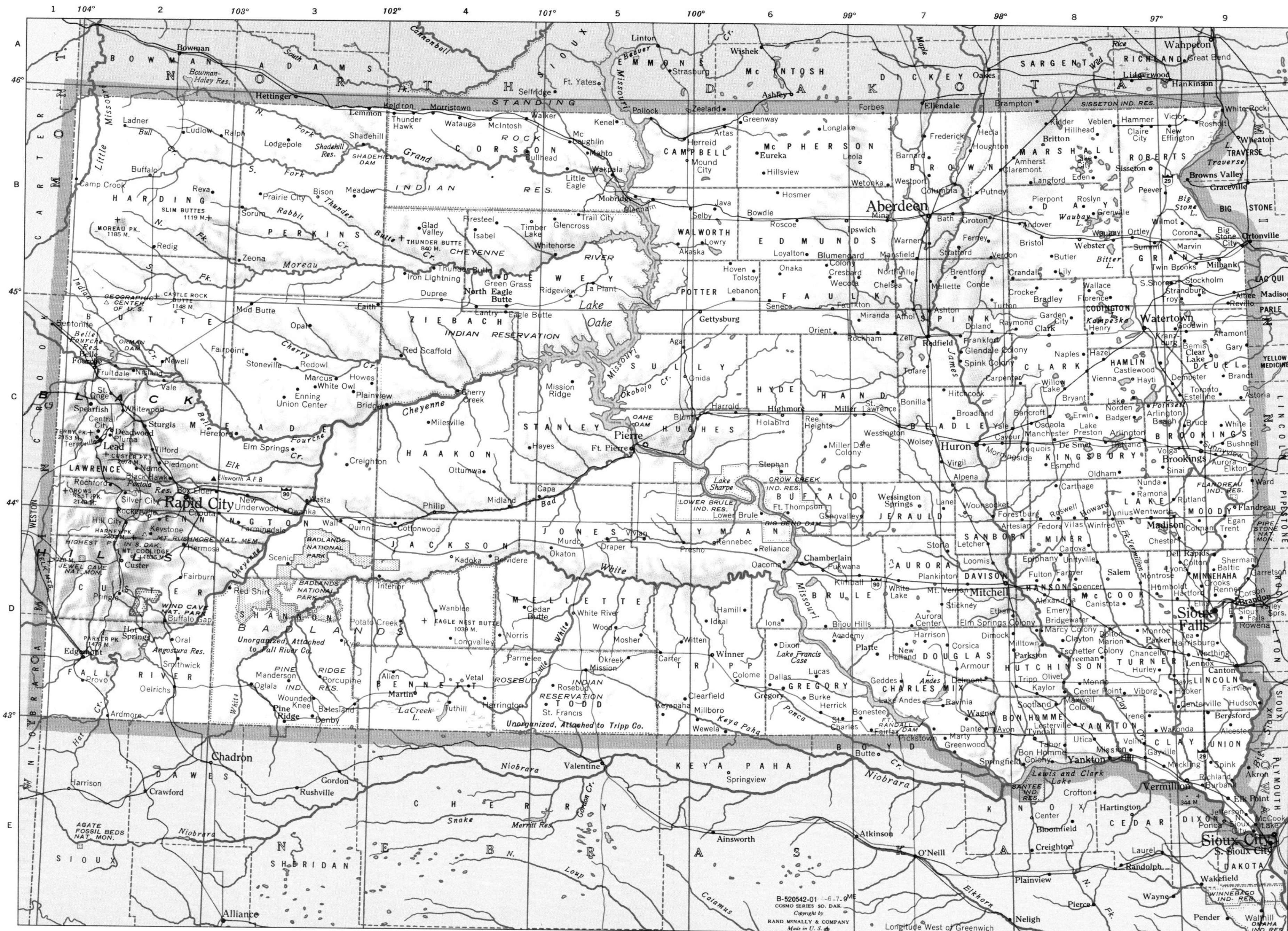

Statute Miles 0 5 10 20 30 40 50 60
Kilometers 5 0 5 15 25 35 45 55 65 75

Lambert Conformal Conic Projection

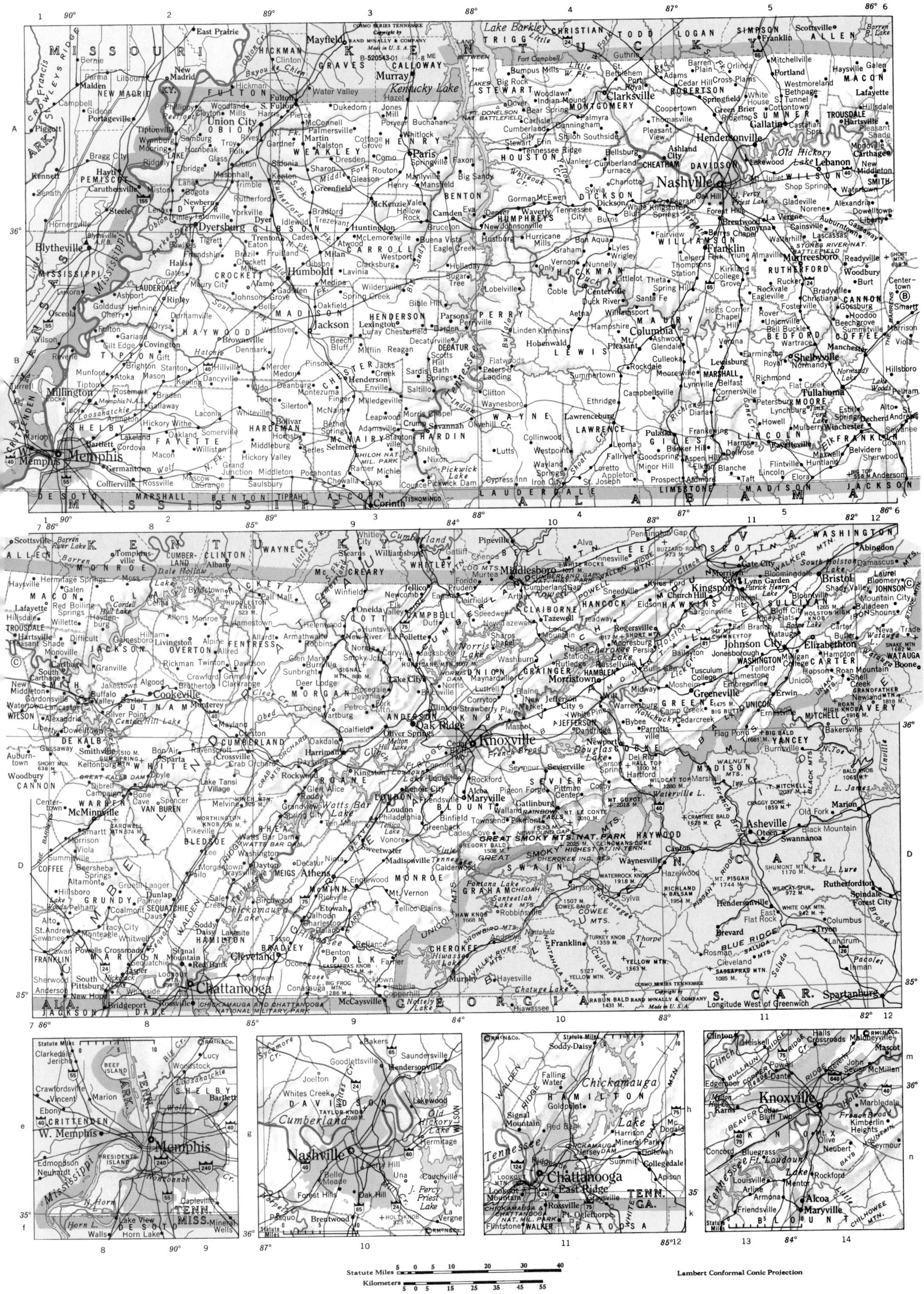

Tennessee

1990 CENSUS

Alcoa, 6,400 . . . . D10
Athens, 12,054 . . . . D 9
Bartlett, 26,989 . . . . B 2
Bloomingdale,
600('84) C11
Bolivar, 5,969 . . . . . . B 3
Brentwood, 16,392 . . A 5
Bristol, 23,421 . . . . . . C11
Brownsville, 10,019 . . B 2
Chattanooga, 152,466 D 8
Church Hill, 4,834 . . C11
Clarksville, 75,494 . . A 4
Cleveland, 30,354 . . D 9
Clinton, 8,972 . . . . . . C 9
Collegedale, 5,048 . . h11
Collierville, 14,427 . . B 2
Colonial Heights,
6,744('80) C11
Columbia, 28,583 . . . . B 4
Cookeville, 21,744 . . C 8
Covington, 7,487 . . . . B 2
Crossville, 6,930 . . . . D 8
Dayton, 5,671 . . . . . . D 8
Dickson, 8,791 . . . . . . A 4
Dyersburg, 16,317 . . A 2
East Ridge, 21,101 . . h11
Elizabethton, 11,931 C11
Erwin, 5,015 . . . . C11
Fayetteville, 6,921 . . B 5
Franklin, 20,098 . . . . B 5
Gallatin, 18,794 . . . . A 5
Gatlinburg, 3,417 . . . . D10
Germantown, 32,893 B 2
Goodlettsville, 11,219 g10
Greeneville, 13,532 . . C11
Harriman, 7,119 . . . . D 9
Harrison, 6,206('80) . . h11
Henderson, 4,760 . . B 3
Hendersonville,
32,188 . . . . A 5
Humboldt, 9,651 . . . . B 3
Huntingdon, 4,180 . . A 3
Jackson, 48,949 . . . . B 3
Jefferson City, 5,494 C10
Johnson City, 49,381 C11
Kingsport, 36,365 . . C11
Kingston, 4,552 . . . . D 9
Knoxville, 165,121 . . D10
La Follette, 7,192 . . . . C 9
La Vergne, 7,499 . . . . A 5
Lawrenceburg, 10,412 B 4
Lebanon, 15,208 . . . . A 5
Lenoir City, 6,147 . . D 9
Lewisburg, 9,879 . . . . B 5
Lexington, 5,810 . . . . B 3
Loudon, 4,026 . . . . . . D 9
Lynn Garden,
7,213('80) C11
Manchester, 7,709 . . B 5
Martin, 8,600 . . . . . . A 3
Maryville, 19,208 . . . . D10
McKenzie, 5,168 . . . . A 3
McMinnville, 11,194 . . D 8
Memphis, 610,337 . . B 1
Milan, 7,512 . . . . B 3
Millington, 17,866 . . B 2
Morristown, 21,385 . . C10
Murfreesboro, 44,922 B 5
Nashville, 487,969 . . A 5
Newport, 7,123 . . . . D10
Oak Ridge, 27,310 . . C 9
Oneida, 3,502 . . . . . . C 9
Paris, 9,332 . . . . A 3
Portland, 5,165 . . . . A 5
Powell, 7,220('80) . . m13
Pulaski, 7,895 . . . . . . B 4
Red Bank, 12,322 . . D 8
Ripley, 6,188 . . . . . . B 2
Rockwood, 5,348 . . D 9
Rogersville, 4,149 . . C10
Savannah, 6,547 . . . . B 3
Sevierville, 7,178 . . . . D10
Shelbyville, 14,049 . . B 5
Signal Mountain,
7,034 . . . . D 8
Smyrna, 13,647 . . . . B 5
Soddy-Daisy, 8,240 . . D 8
Sparta, 4,681 . . . . . . D 8
Springfield, 11,227 . . A 5
Sweetwater, 5,066 . . D 9
Trenton, 4,836 . . . . . . B 3
Tullahoma, 16,761 . . B 5
Union City, 10,513 . . A 2
Waverly, 3,925 . . . . . . A 4
Winchester, 6,305 . . B 5

Texas

1990 CENSUS

Abilene, 106,654 . . . . C 3
Alice, 19,788 . . . . . . F 3
Alvin, 19,220 . . . . . . E 5
Amarillo, 157,615 . . . B 2
Arlington, 261,721 . . n 9
Austin, 465,622 . . . . D 4
Bay City, 18,170 . . . . E 5
Baytown, 63,850 . . . . E 5
Beaumont, 114,323 . . D 5
Beeville, 13,547 . . . . E 4
Big Spring, 23,093 . . C 2
Borger, 15,675 . . . . . B 2
Brownsville, 98,962 . . G 4
Brownwood, 18,387 D 3
Bryan, 55,002 . . . . . . D 4
Cleburne, 22,205 . . . . C 4
College Station,
52,456 . . . . D 4
Conroe, 27,610 . . . . . D 5
Copperas Cove,
24,079 . . . . D 4
Corpus Christi,
257,453 . . . . F 4
Corsicana, 22,911 . . C 4
Dallas, 1,006,877 . . . . C 4
Del Rio, 30,705 . . . . E 2
Denison, 21,505 . . . . C 4
Denton, 66,270 . . . . C 4
Duncanville, 35,748 . . n10
Eagle Pass, 20,651 . . E 2
Edinburg, 29,885 . . . . F 3
El Paso, 515,342 . . . . o11
Farmers Branch,
24,250 . . . . n10
Fort Worth, 447,619 C 4
Galveston, 59,070 . . E 5
Garland, 180,650 . . . . n10
Grand Prairie, 99,616 n10
Greenville, 23,071 . . C 4
Harlingen, 48,735 . . . F 4
Hereford, 14,745 . . . . B 1
Houston, 1,630,553 . . E 5
Huntsville, 27,925 . . D 5
Irving, 155,037 . . . . . n10
Kerrville, 17,384 . . . D 3
Killeen, 63,535 . . . . . D 4
Kingsville, 25,276 . . . F 4
Lake Jackson, 22,776 E 5
La Porte, 27,910 . . . . r14
Laredo, 122,899 . . . . F 3
Lewisville, 46,521 . . C 4
Longview, 70,311 . . C 5
Lubbock, 186,206 . . C 2
Lufkin, 30,206 . . . . . D 5
Marshall, 23,682 . . . . C 5
McAllen, 84,021 . . . . F 3
Mesquite, 101,484 . . n10
Midland, 89,443 . . . . D 1
Mineral Wells, 14,870 C 3
Mission, 28,653 . . . . F 3
Missouri City, 36,176 r14
Nacogdoches, 30,872 D 5
New Braunfels,
27,334 . . . . E 3
North Richland Hills,
45,895 . . . . n 9
Odessa, 89,699 . . . . D 1
Orange, 19,381 . . . . D 6
Palestine, 18,042 . . . D 5
Pampa, 19,959 . . . . . B 2
Paris, 24,699 . . . . . . C 5
Pasadena, 119,363 . . r14
Pecos, 12,069 . . . . . . D 1
Pharr, 32,921 . . . . . . F 3
Plainview, 21,700 . . . B 2
Plano, 128,713 . . . . . C 4
Port Arthur, 58,724 . . E 6
Richardson, 74,840 . . n10
Rosenberg, 20,183 . . E 5
San Angelo, 84,474 . . D 2
San Antonio, 935,933 E 3
San Benito, 20,125 . . F 4
San Marcos, 28,743 E 4
Seguin, 18,853 . . . . . E 4
Sherman, 31,601 . . . . C 4
Temple, 46,109 . . . . D 4
Texarkana, 31,656 . . C 5
Texas City, 40,822 . . E 5
Tyler, 75,450 . . . . . . C 5
University Park,
22,259 . . . . n10
Uvalde, 14,729 . . . . . E 3
Victoria, 55,076 . . . . E 4
Waco, 103,590 . . . . D 4
Waxahachie, 18,168 C 4
Weslaco, 21,877 . . . . F 4
Wichita Falls, 96,259 C 3

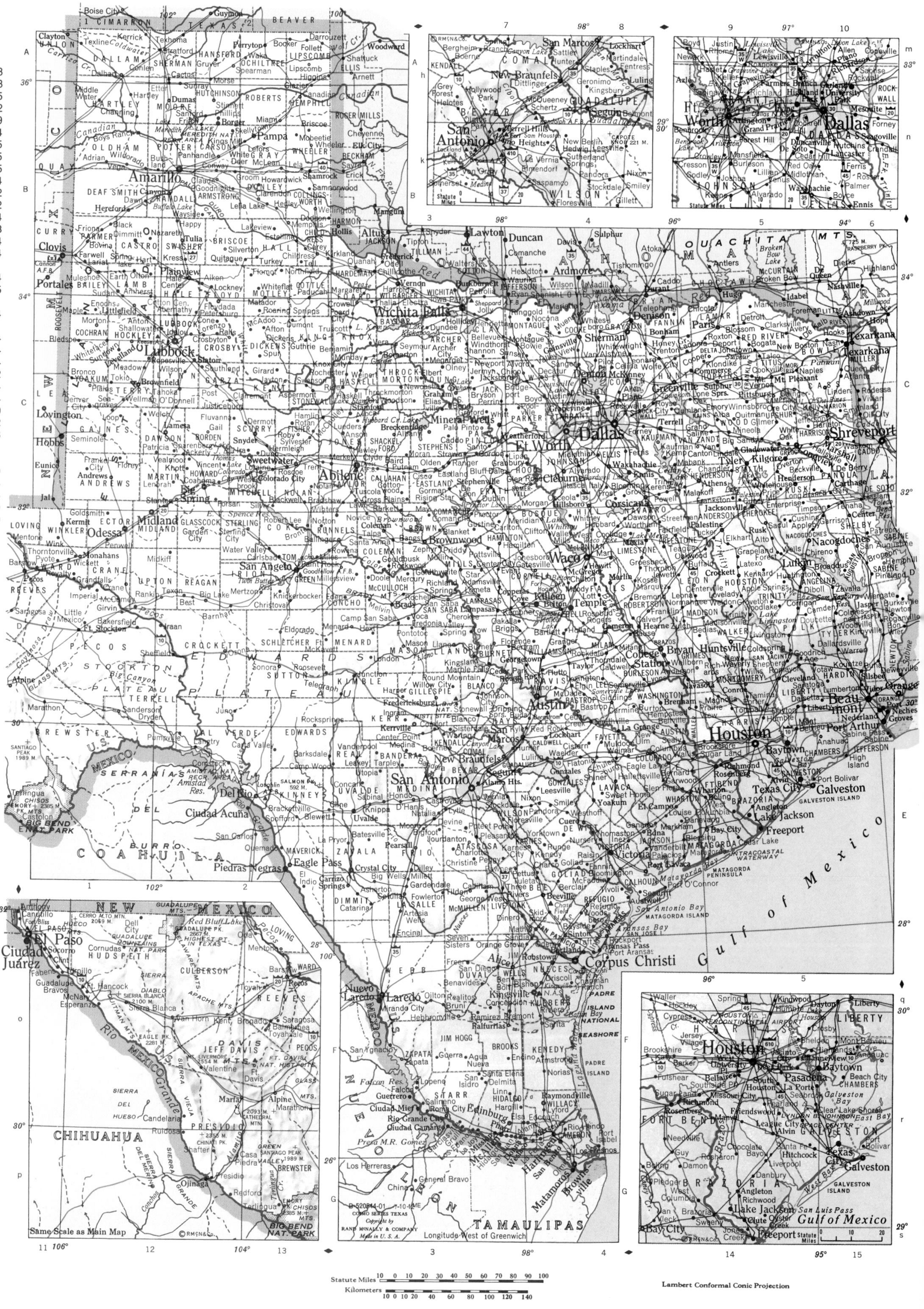

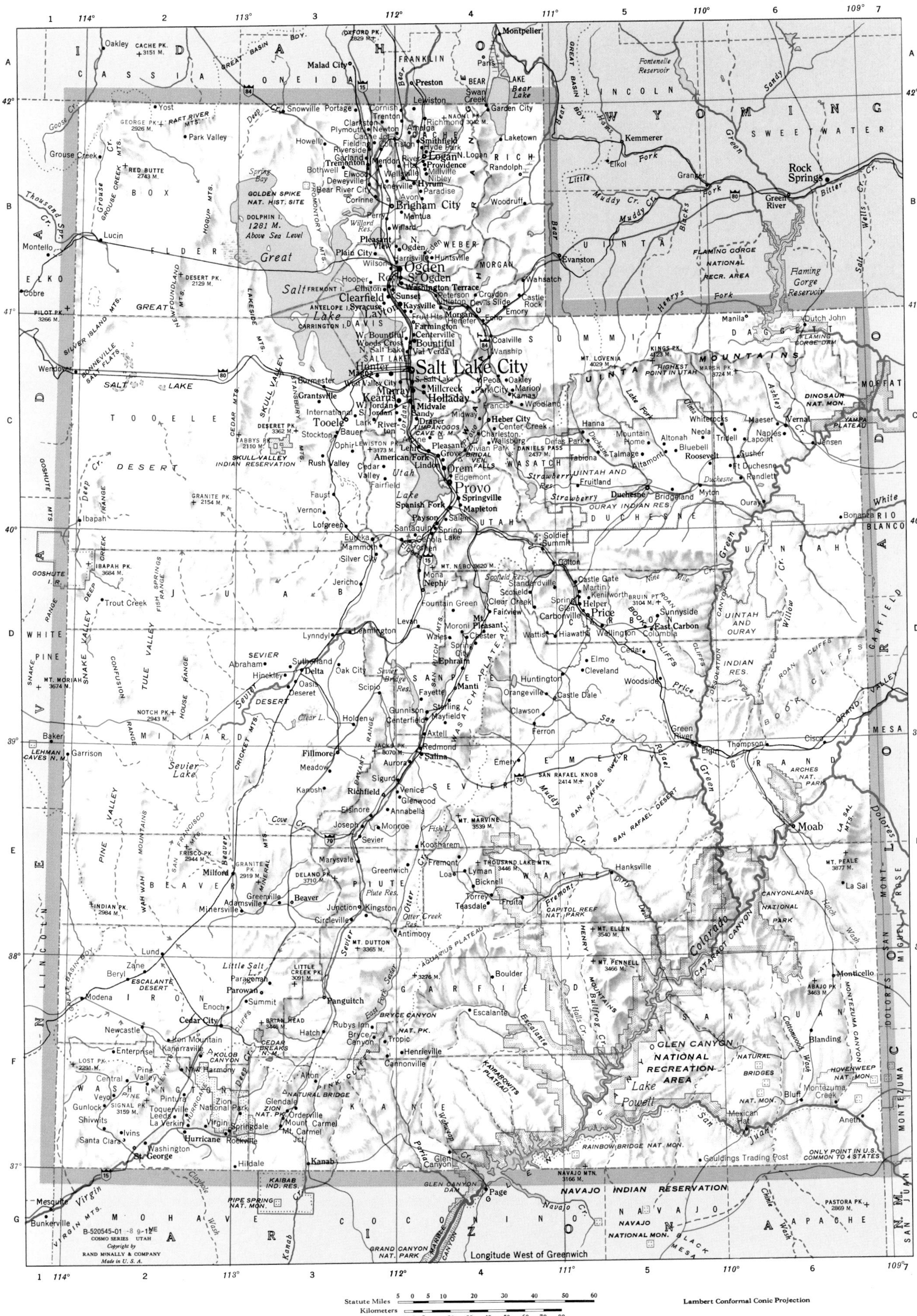

Utah

1990 CENSUS

Alpine, 3,492 . . . . . . C 4
American Fork, 15,696 . . . . C 4
Beaver, 1,998 . . . . . . E 3
Blanding, 3,162 . . . . F 6
Bountiful, 36,659 . . . . C 4
Brigham City, 15,644 B 3
Castle Dale, 1,704 . . D 4
Cedar City, 13,443 . . F 2
Centerville, 11,500 . . C 4
Clearfield, 21,435 . . . . B 3
Clinton, 7,945 . . . . . . B 3
Delta, 2,998 . . . . D 3
Draper, 7,257 . . . . . . C 4
Duchesne, 1,308 . . . . C 5
East Carbon, 1,270 . . D 5
Ephraim, 3,363 . . . . D 4
Farmington, 9,028 . . C 4
Ferron, 1,606 . . . . . . D 4
Fillmore, 1,956 . . . . . . E 3
Fruit Heights, 3,900 . . B 4
Grantsville, 4,500 . . . . C 3
Heber City, 4,782 . . C 4
Helper, 2,148 . . . . . . D 5
Holladay, 26,200 . . . . C 4
Huntington, 1,875 . . D 5
Hurricane, 3,915 . . . . F 2
Hyrum, 4,829 . . . . . . B 4
Kanab, 3,289 . . . . . . F 3
Kaysville, 13,961 . . . . B 4
Kearns, 17,000('80) . . C 4
Layton, 41,784 . . . . . . B 4
Lehi, 8,475 . . . . C 4
Lindon, 3,818 . . . . C 4
Logan, 32,762 . . . . . . B 4
Maeser, 1,850('80) . . C 6
Magna, 8,600('80) . . C 3
Manti, 2,268 . . . . D 4
Mapleton, 3,572 . . . . C 4
Midvale, 11,886 . . . . C 4
Millcreek, 28,500 . . . . C 4
Moab, 3,971 . . . . E 6
Monticello, 1,806 . . . . F 6
Morgan, 2,023 . . . . . . B 4
Mount Pleasant, 2,092 . . . . D 4
Murray, 31,282 . . . . C 4
Nephi, 3,515 . . . . D 4
North Logan, 3,768 . . B 4
North Ogden, 11,668 B 4
North Salt Lake, 6,474 . . . . C 4
Ogden, 63,909 . . . . . . B 4
Orem, 67,561 . . . . . . C 4
Panguitch, 1,444 . . . . F 3
Park City, 4,468 . . . . C 4
Parowan, 1,873 . . . . F 3
Payson, 9,510 . . . . . . C 4
Plain City, 2,722 . . . . B 3
Pleasant Grove, 13,476 . . . . C 4
Price, 8,712 . . . . D 5
Providence, 3,344 . . B 4
Provo, 86,835 . . . . . . C 4
Richfield, 5,593 . . . . E 3
Richmond, 1,955 . . . . B 4
Riverton, 11,261 . . . . C 4
Roosevelt, 3,915 . . . . C 5
Roy, 24,603 . . . . B 3
Saint George, 28,502 F 2
Salem, 2,284 . . . . . . C 4
Salina, 1,943 . . . . . . E 4
Salt Lake City, 159,936 . . . . C 4
Sandy, 75,058 . . . . C 4
Santaquin, 2,386 . . . . D 4
Smithfield, 5,566 . . . . B 4
South Jordan, 12,220 C 3
South Ogden, 12,105 B 4
Spanish Fork, 11,272 C 4
Springville, 13,950 . . C 4
Sunset, 5,128 . . . . . . B 4
Syracuse, 4,658 . . . . B 3
Tooele, 13,887 . . . . . . C 3
Tremonton, 4,264 . . B 3
Val Verda, 6,500('80) C 4
Vernal, 6,644 . . . . . . C 6
Washington, 4,198 . . F 2
Washington Terrace, 8,189 . . . . B 4
Wellsville, 2,206 . . . . B 4
Wendover, 1,127 . . . . C 1
West Bountiful, 4,477 C 4
West Jordan, 42,892 C 4
West Valley City, 86,976 . . . . C 4
Woods Cross, 5,384 C 4

Vermont

1990 CENSUS

Arlington, 700 (2,299▲) .... E 2
Barre, 9,482 .... C 4
Barton, 908 .... B 4
Bellows Falls, 3,313 .. E 4
Bennington, 9,349 (16,451▲) .... F 2
Bethel, 1,016 (1,866▲) .... D 3
Bradford, 672 ...... D 4
Brandon, 1,925 (4,223▲) .... D 2
Brattleboro, 8,596 (12,241▲) .... F 3
Bristol, 1,801 ...... C 2
Burlington, 39,127 .. C 2
Castleton, 600 (4,278▲) .... D 2
Chester, 550 (2,832▲) E 3
Chester Depot, 500 .. E 3
Derby Line, 855 .... A 4
Dorset, 550 (1,918▲) E 2
East Arlington, 600 .. E 2
East Barre, 700 .... C 4
East Middlebury, 500 D 2
East Montpelier, 600 (2,239▲) .... C 4
Enosburg Falls, 1,350 B 3
Essex, 800 (16,498▲) B 2
Essex Junction, 8,396 C 2
Fair Haven, 2,887 .. D 2
Forest Dale, 350 .... D 2
Gilman, 500 .... C 5
Graniteville, 500 .... C 4
Hardwick, 1,400 (2,964▲) .... B 4
Hartford, 500 (9,404▲) .... D 4
Hydeville, 450 ...... D 2
Jericho, 1,300 (4,302▲) .... B 3
Johnson, 1,470 ...... B 3
Ludlow, 1,123 ...... E 3
Lyndonville, 1,255 .. B 4
Manchester, 561 ..... E 2
Middlebury, 5,591 (8,034▲) .... C 2
Milton, 1,578 ...... B 2
Montpelier, 8,247 .... C 3
Morrisville, 1,984 .... B 3
Newport, 4,434 .... B 4
North Bennington, 1,520 .... F 2
North Clarendon, 500 D 3
Northfield, 1,889 .... C 3
Northfield Falls, 600 C 3
North Springfield, 750 E 3
North Troy, 723 .... B 4
Norwich, 1,000 (3,093▲) .... D 4
Orleans, 806 ...... B 4
Pittsford, 650 (2,919▲) .... D 2
Plainfield, 600 (1,302▲) .... C 4
Poultney, 1,731 .... D 2
Proctor, 1,979 ...... D 2
Proctorsville, 480 ... E 3
Putney, 1,100 (2,352▲) .... F 3
Quechee, 550 ...... D 4
Randolph, 2,200 (4,764▲) .... D 3
Richford, 1,425 .... B 3
Richmond, 650 (3,729▲) .... C 3
Riverton, 150 ...... C 3
Rochester, 500 (1,181▲) .... D 3
Rutland, 18,230 ..... D 3
Saint Albans, 7,339 .. B 2
Saint Johnsbury, 7,150 (7,608▲) .... C 4
Saxtons River, 541 .. E 3
Shaftsbury, 700 (3,368▲) .... E 2
South Burlington, 12,809 .... C 2
South Royalton, 700 D 3
Springfield, 5,603 (9,579▲) .... E 4
Stamford, 400 (773▲) F 2
Stowe, 450 .... C 3
Swanton, 2,360 ..... B 2
Vergennes, 2,578 .. C 2
Wallingford, 1,141 (2,184▲) .... E 3
Warren, 350 (1,172▲) C 3
Waterbury, 1,702 .... C 3
Waterbury Center, 500 .... C 3
Websterville, 600 .... C 4
West Pawlet, 350 .. E 2
West Rutland, 2,448 D 2
Williamstown, 650 (2,839▲) .... C 3
Wilmington, 550 (1,968▲) .... F 3
Windsor, 3,714 ...... E 4
Winooski, 6,649 .... C 2
Woodstock, 1,037 .. D 3

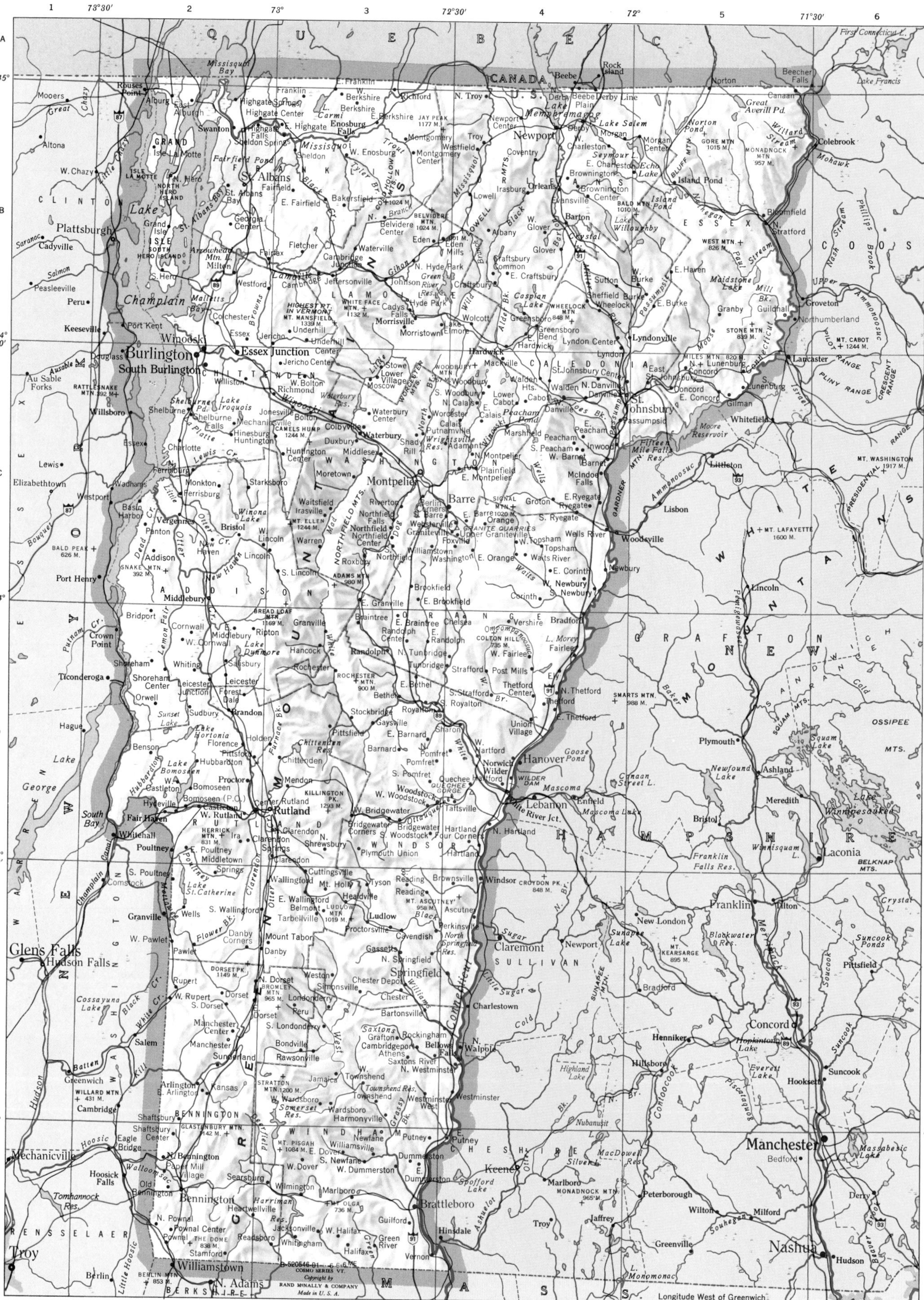

▲ Population of entire town (township), including rural area.

Statute Miles 5 0 5 10 20
Kilometers 5 0 5 10 15 20 25

Lambert Conformal Conic Projection

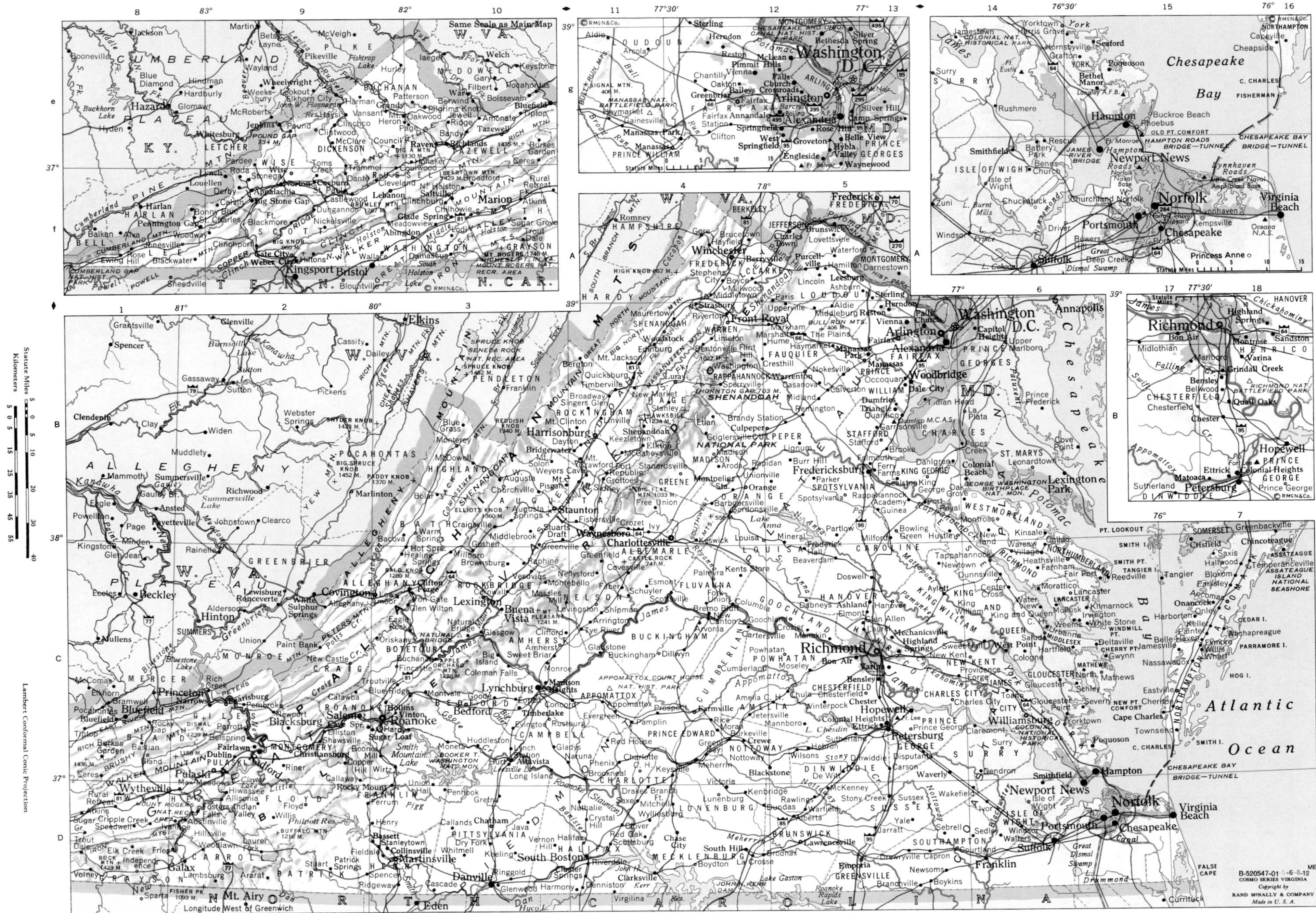

Virginia

1990 CENSUS

Alexandria, 111,183 .. B 5
Annandale, 38,000 .... g12
Appomattox, 1,707 .... C 4
Arlington, 170,936 .... B 5
Bedford, 6,073 ...... C 3
Big Stone Gap, 4,748 .. f 9
Blacksburg, 34,590 .... C 2
Bluefield, 5,363 ...... C 1
Bristol, 18,426 .... f 9
Buena Vista, 6,406 .... C 3
Cave Spring, 15,200 .. C 2
Charlottesville, 40,341 .. B 4
Chesapeake, 151,976 .. D 6
Chincoteague, 3,572 .. C 7
Christiansburg, 15,004 C 2
Clifton Forge, 4,679 .. C 3
Colonial Heights, 16,064 C 5
Covington, 6,991 ...... C 3
Culpeper, 8,581 ...... B 5
Dale City, 47,170 ...... B 5
Danville, 53,056 ...... D 3
Emporia, 5,306 ...... D 5
Engleside, 24,058('80) .. g12
Fairfax, 19,622 ...... B 5
Falls Church, 9,578 .... g12
Farmville, 6,046 ...... C 4
Franklin, 7,864 .... D 6
Fredericksburg, 19,027 B 5
Front Royal, 11,880 .. B 4
Galax, 6,670 .... D 2
Greenbriar, 6,200 ...... g12
Groveton, 6,300 ...... g12
Hampton, 133,793 .... C 6
Harrisonburg, 30,707 .. B 4
Herndon, 16,139 ...... B 5
Highland Springs, 4,230 C 5
Hollins, 12,295('80) .... C 3
Hopewell, 23,101 ...... C 5
Leesburg, 16,202 ...... A 5
Lexington, 6,959 ...... C 3
Lynchburg, 66,049 .... C 3
Madison Heights, 14,146('80) .... C 3
Manassas, 27,957 .... B 5
Manassas Park, 6,734 B 5
Marion, 6,630 .... f10
Martinsville, 16,162 .... D 3
McLean, 24,000 ...... g12
Mechanicsville, 2,969('80) .... C 5
Newport News, 170,045 D 6
Norfolk, 261,229 ...... D 6
Norton, 4,247 .... f 9
Oakton, 12,500 ...... g12
Petersburg, 38,386 .... C 5
Poquoson, 11,005 .... C 6
Portsmouth, 103,907 .. D 6
Pulaski, 9,985 .... C 2
Radford, 15,940 ...... C 2
Reston, 48,556 ...... B 5
Richlands, 4,456 ...... e10
Richmond, 203,056 .... C 5
Roanoke, 96,397 ...... C 3
Salem, 23,756 .... C 2
Shenandoah, 2,213 .... B 4
South Boston, 6,997 .. D 4
Springfield, 15,000 .... g12
Staunton, 24,461 ...... B 3
Sterling, 16,080('80) .. A 5
Suffolk, 52,141 ...... D 6
Sugar Loaf, 2,000 .... C 3
Tazewell, 4,176 ...... e10
Timberlake, 8,700 .... C 3
Vienna, 14,852 ...... B 5
Vinton, 7,665 .... C 3
Virginia Beach, 393,069 D 7
Waynesboro, 18,549 .. B 4
Waynewood, 5,000 .... g12
West Springfield, 18,000 g12
Williamsburg, 11,530 .. C 6
Winchester, 21,947 .... A 4
Woodbridge, 26,401 .. B 5
Wytheville, 8,038 ...... D 1
Yorktown, 270 .... C 6

Washington

1990 CENSUS

Aberdeen, 16,565 .... C 2
Anacortes, 11,451 .... A 3
Auburn, 33,102 ...... B 3
Bellevue, 86,874 ...... e11
Bellingham, 52,179 .... A 3
Bonney Lake, 7,494 .. B 3
Bothell, 12,345 ...... B 3
Bremerton, 38,142 .... B 3
Camas, 6,442 .... D 3
Centralia, 12,101 ...... C 3
Chehalis, 6,527 ...... C 3
Cheney, 7,723 .... B 8
Clarkston, 6,753 ...... C 8
College Place, 6,308 .. C 7
Colville, 4,360 .... A 8
Coulee Dam, 1,087 .... B 7
Des Moines, 17,283 .. B 3
Edmonds, 30,744 .... B 3
Ellensburg, 12,361 .... C 5
Enumclaw, 7,227 ..... B 4
Ephrata, 5,349 .... B 6
Everett, 69,961 ...... B 3
Ferndale, 5,398 ...... A 3
Fircrest, 5,258 .... f10
Goldendale, 3,319 .... D 5
Grandview, 7,169 .... C 6
Hoquiam, 8,972 ...... C 2
Issaquah, 7,786 ...... B 3
Kelso, 11,820 .... C 3
Kennewick, 42,155 .... C 6
Kent, 37,960 .... B 3
Kirkland, 40,052 ...... B 3
Lacey, 19,279 .... B 3
Lakewood Center, 62,000 .... B 3
Longview, 31,499 ...... C 3
Lynden, 5,709 .... A 3
Lynnwood, 28,695 .... B 3
Marysville, 10,328 .... A 3
Medical Lake, 3,664 .. B 8
Mercer Island, 20,816 .. B 3
Montesano, 3,064 .... C 2
Moses Lake, 11,235 .. B 6
Mount Vernon, 17,647 A 3
Oak Harbor, 17,176 .. A 3
Olympia, 33,840 ...... B 3
Omak, 4,117 .... A 6
Othello, 4,638 .... C 6
Parkland, 27,300 ...... f11
Parkwater, 4,300('91) .. g14
Pasco, 20,337 .... C 6
Port Angeles, 17,710 .. A 2
Port Orchard, 4,984 .. B 3
Port Townsend, 7,001 A 3
Prosser, 4,476 .... C 6
Pullman, 23,478 ...... C 8
Puyallup, 23,875 ...... B 3
Quincy, 3,738 .... B 6
Redmond, 35,800 .... e11
Renton, 41,688 ...... B 3
Richland, 32,315 ...... C 6
Richmond Beach, 6,700('91) .... B 3
Richmond Highlands, 27,900 .... B 3
Riverton Heights, 14,182 f11
Seattle, 516,259 ...... B 3
Sedro Woolley, 6,031 .. A 3
Selah, 5,113 .... C 5
Shelton, 7,241 .... B 2
Snohomish, 6,499 .... B 3
Spokane, 177,196 .... B 8
Steilacoom, 5,728 ...... f10
Sumner, 6,281 .... B 3
Sunnyside, 11,238 .... C 5
Tacoma, 176,664 .... B 3
Toppenish, 7,419 .... C 5
Tukwila, 11,874 ...... f11
Tumwater, 9,976 ...... B 3
Vancouver, 46,380 .... D 3
Walla Walla, 26,478 .. C 7
Wenatchee, 21,756 .... B 5
White Center, 18,000('91) e11
Yakima, 54,827 ...... C 5

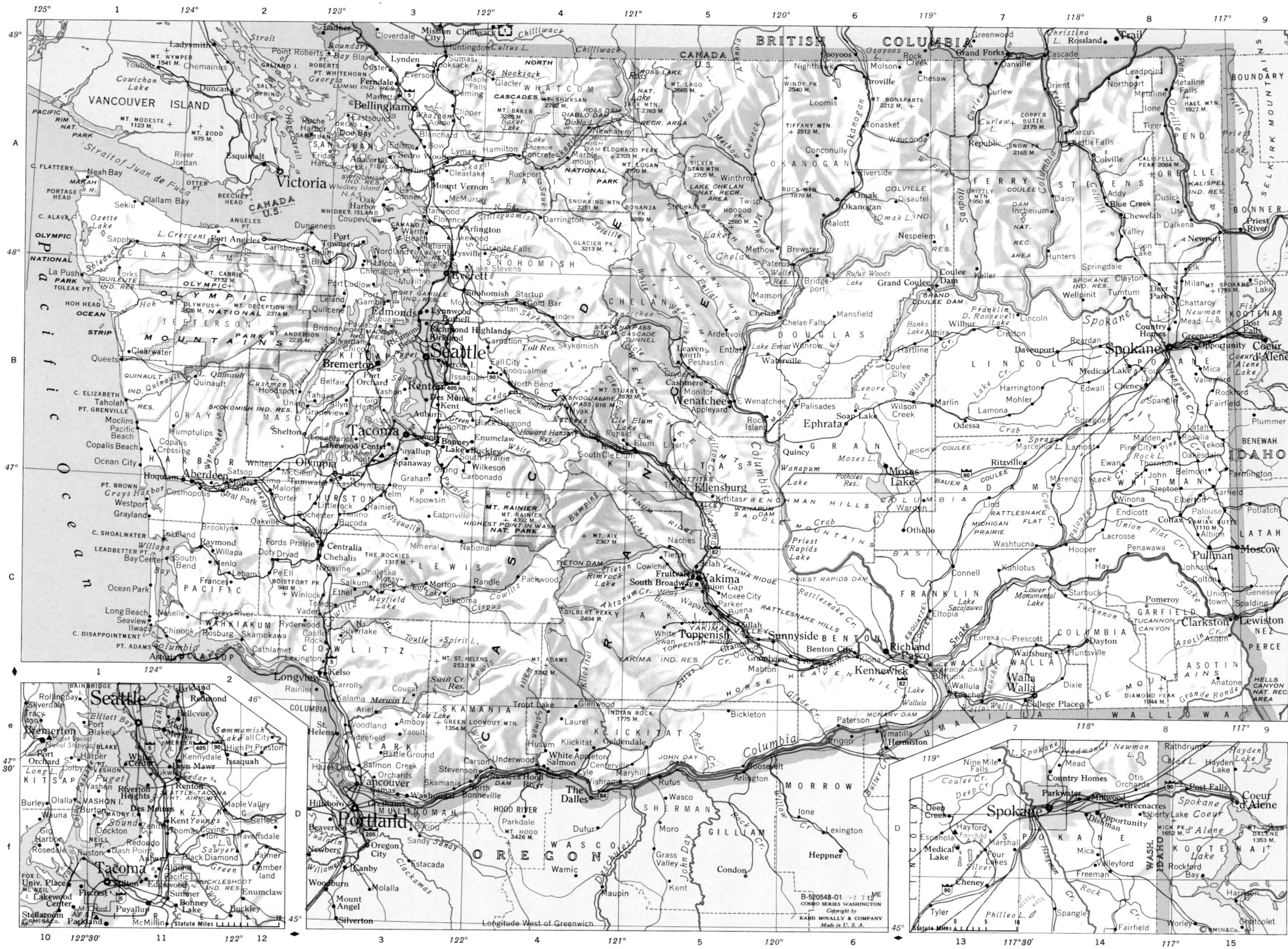

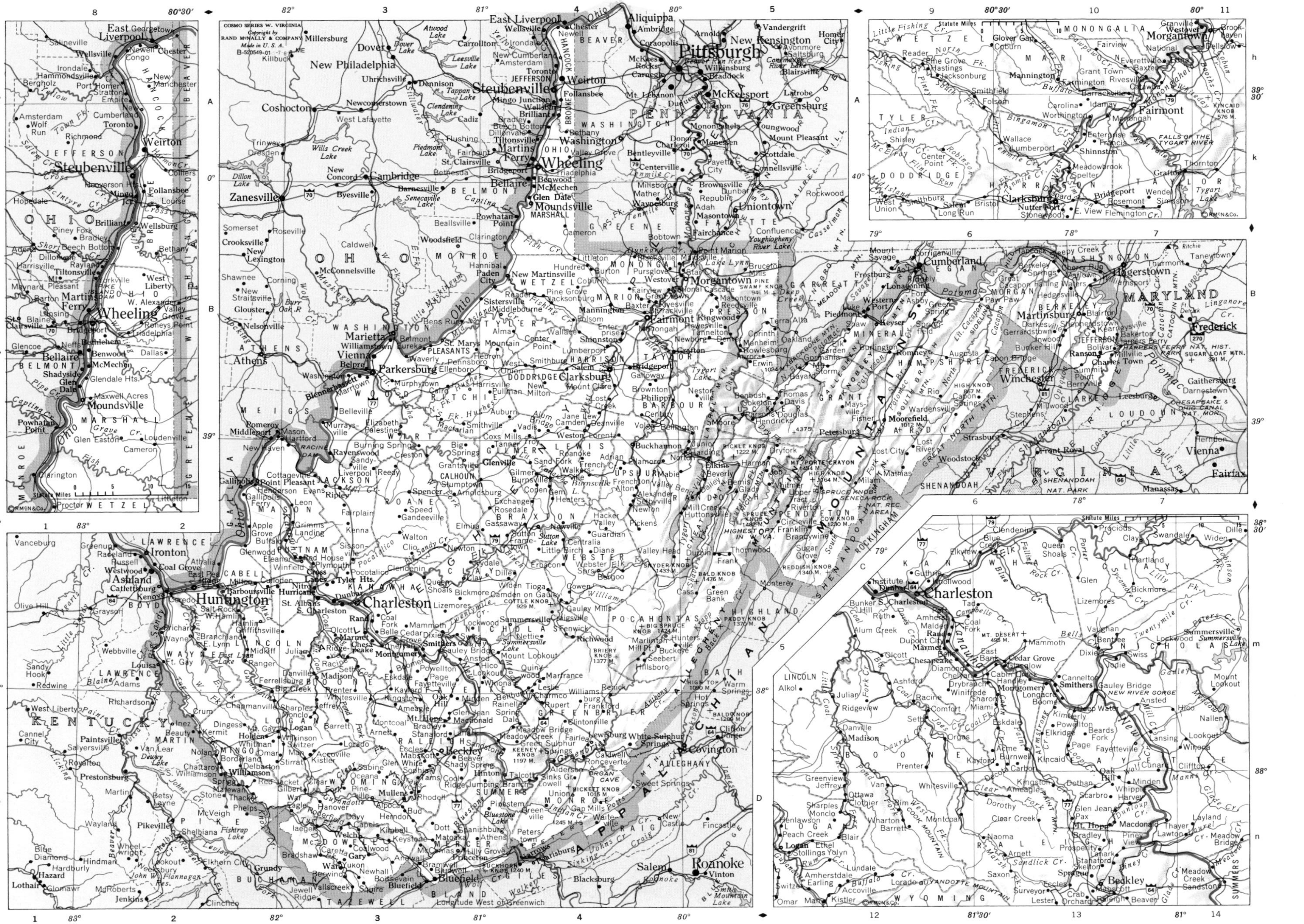

Statute Miles 5 0 5 10 20 30 40

Kilometers 5 0 5 15 25 35 45 55

Lambert Conformal Conic Projection

West Virginia

1990 CENSUS

Ansted, 1,643 . . . . C 3
Barboursville, 2,774 . . C 2
Beckley, 18,296 . . . . . D 3
Belington, 1,850 . . . . . B 5
Benwood, 1,669 . . . . . f 8
Bluefield, 12,756 . . . . D 3
Bridgeport, 6,739 . . . . B 4
Buckhannon, 5,909 . . . . C 4
Ceredo, 1,916 . . . . C 2
Charleston, 57,287 . . . . C 3
Charles Town, 3,122 . . B 7
Chesapeake, 1,896 . . . . C 3
Chester, 2,905 . . . . A 4
Clarksburg, 18,059 . . . . B 4
Dunbar, 8,697 . . . . C 3
Elkins, 7,420 . . . . C 5
Fairmont, 20,210 . . . . . B 4
Fayetteville, 2,182 . . . . C 3
Follansbee, 3,339 . . . . A 4
Gary, 1,355 . . . . D 3
Glenville, 1,923 . . . . . . C 4
Grafton, 5,524 . . . . B 4
Harpers Ferry, 308 . . . . B 7
Hinton, 3,433 . . . . D 4
Huntington, 54,844 . . . . C 2
Hurricane, 4,461 . . . . . C 2
Kenova, 3,748 . . . . C 2
Keyser, 5,870 . . . . B 6
Kingwood, 3,243 . . . . . . B 5
Lewisburg, 3,598 . . . . . . D 4
Logan, 2,206 . . . . D 3
Madison, 3,051 . . . . . . C 3
Mannington, 2,184 . . . . B 4
Marmet, 1,879 . . . . C 3
Martinsburg, 14,073 . . . B 7
McMechen, 2,130 . . . . . B 4
Milton, 2,242 . . . . C 2
Montgomery, 2,449 . . . . C 3
Moorefield, 2,148 . . . . . B 6
Morgantown, 25,879 . . . B 5
Moundsville, 10,753 . . . B 4
Mullens, 2,006 . . . . D 3
New Martinsville, 6,705 B 4
Nitro, 6,851 . . . . C 3
Nutter Fort, 1,819 . . . . k10
Oak Hill, 6,812 . . . . D 3
Oceana, 1,791 . . . . D 3
Paden City, 2,862 . . . . . B 4
Parkersburg, 33,862 . . . B 3
Parsons, 1,453 . . . . B 5
Petersburg, 2,360 . . . . . B 5
Philippi, 3,132 . . . . B 4
Point Pleasant, 4,996 . . C 2
Princeton, 7,043 . . . . . . D 3
Rainelle, 1,681 . . . . D 4
Rand, 2,400('86) . . . . . C 3
Ranson, 2,890 . . . . B 7
Ravenswood, 4,189 . . . . C 3
Richwood, 2,808 . . . . . . C 4
Ripley, 3,023 . . . . C 3
Romney, 1,966 . . . . B 6
Ronceverte, 1,754 . . . . D 4
Saint Albans, 11,194 . . C 3
Saint Marys, 2,148 . . . . B 3
Salem, 2,063 . . . . B 4
Shinnston, 2,543 . . . . . . B 4
Sistersville, 1,797 . . . . B 4
South Charleston,
13,645 . . . . C 3
Spencer, 2,279 . . . . . . C 3
Stonewood, 1,996 . . . . k10
Summersville, 2,906 . . . C 4
Terra Alta, 1,713 . . . . . B 5
Vienna, 10,862 . . . . . . B 3
War, 1,081 . . . . D 3
Weirton, 22,124 . . . . . . A 4
Welch, 3,028 . . . . D 3
Wellsburg, 3,385 . . . . . A 4
Weston, 4,994 . . . . B 4
Westover, 4,201 . . . . . . B 5
Wheeling, 34,882 . . . . . A 4
White Sulphur Springs,
2,779 . . . . D 4
Williamson, 4,154 . . . . D 2
Williamstown, 2,774 . . B 3

Wisconsin

1990 CENSUS

Allouez, 14,431 .... h 9
Antigo, 8,276 ...... C 4
Appleton, 65,695 .... D 5
Ashland, 8,695...... B 3
Ashwaubenon, 16,376 D 5
Baraboo, 9,203 .... E 4
Beaver Dam, 14,196 E 5
Beloit, 35,573 ...... F 4
Brookfield, 35,184 .. m11
Brown Deer, 12,236 m12
Burlington, 8,855 .... F 5
Cedarburg, 9,895 .... E 6
Chippewa Falls, 12,727 .... D 2
Cudahy, 18,659 ..... F 6
De Pere, 16,569 ..... D 5
Eau Claire, 56,856 .. D 2
Fond du Lac, 37,757 E 5
Fort Atkinson, 10,227 F 5
Franklin, 21,855 .... n11
Germantown, 13,658 E 5
Glendale, 14,088 .... m12
Grafton, 9,340 .... E 6
Green Bay, 96,466 .. D 6
Greendale, 15,128 .. F 6
Greenfield, 33,403 ... n11
Hayward, 1,897 ..... B 2
Howard, 9,874....... D 5
Hudson, 6,378 .... D 1
Janesville, 52,133.... F 4
Kaukauna, 11,982 .. D 5
Kenosha, 80,352 ..... F 6
La Crosse, 51,003 ... E 2
Lake Geneva, 5,979 .. F 5
Little Chute, 9,207 .. D 5
Madison, 191,262 ... E 4
Manitowoc, 32,520 .. D 6
Marinette, 11,843 ... C 6
Marshfield, 19,291 .. D 3
Menasha, 14,711 .... D 5
Menomonee Falls, 26,840 .... E 5
Menomonie, 13,547 .. D 2
Mequon, 18,885 ..... E 6
Merrill, 9,860 .... C 4
Middleton, 13,289 .. E 4
Milwaukee, 628,088 .. E 6
Monona, 8,637 .... E 4
Monroe, 10,241 ...... F 4
Muskego, 16,813 .... F 5
Neenah, 23,219 ..... D 5
New Berlin, 33,592 .. n11
New London, 6,658 .. D 5
Oak Creek, 19,513 .. n12
Oconomowoc, 10,993 E 5
Oconto, 4,474 .... D 6
Onalaska, 11,284 .... E 2
Oshkosh, 55,006 .... D 5
Park Falls, 3,104 .... C 3
Platteville, 9,708 ..... F 3
Portage, 8,640 .... E 4
Port Washington, 9,338 .... E 6
Prairie du Chien, 5,659 .... E 2
Racine, 84,298 .... F 6
Reedsburg, 5,834 ... E 3
Rhinelander, 7,427 ... C 4
Rice Lake, 7,998 .... C 2
River Falls, 10,610 .. D 1
Saint Francis, 9,245 .. n12
Shawano, 7,598 ..... D 5
Sheboygan, 49,676 .. E 6
Shorewood, 14,116 .. E 6
South Milwaukee, 20,958 .... F 6
Stevens Point, 23,006 D 4
Stoughton, 8,786 .... F 4
Sturgeon Bay, 9,176 D 6
Sun Prairie, 15,333 .. E 4
Superior, 27,134 ..... B 1
Tomah, 7,570 .... E 3
Two Rivers, 13,030 .. D 6
Watertown, 19,142 .. E 5
Waukesha, 56,958 .. F 5
Waupun, 8,207 ...... E 5
Wausau, 37,060 ..... D 4
Wauwatosa, 49,366 m12
West Allis, 63,221 .. m11
West Bend, 23,916 .. E 5
Weston, 8,775('80) .. D 4
Whitefish Bay, 14,272 m12
Whitewater, 12,636 .. F 5
Wisconsin Dells, 2,393 .... E 4
Wisconsin Rapids, 18,245 .... D 4

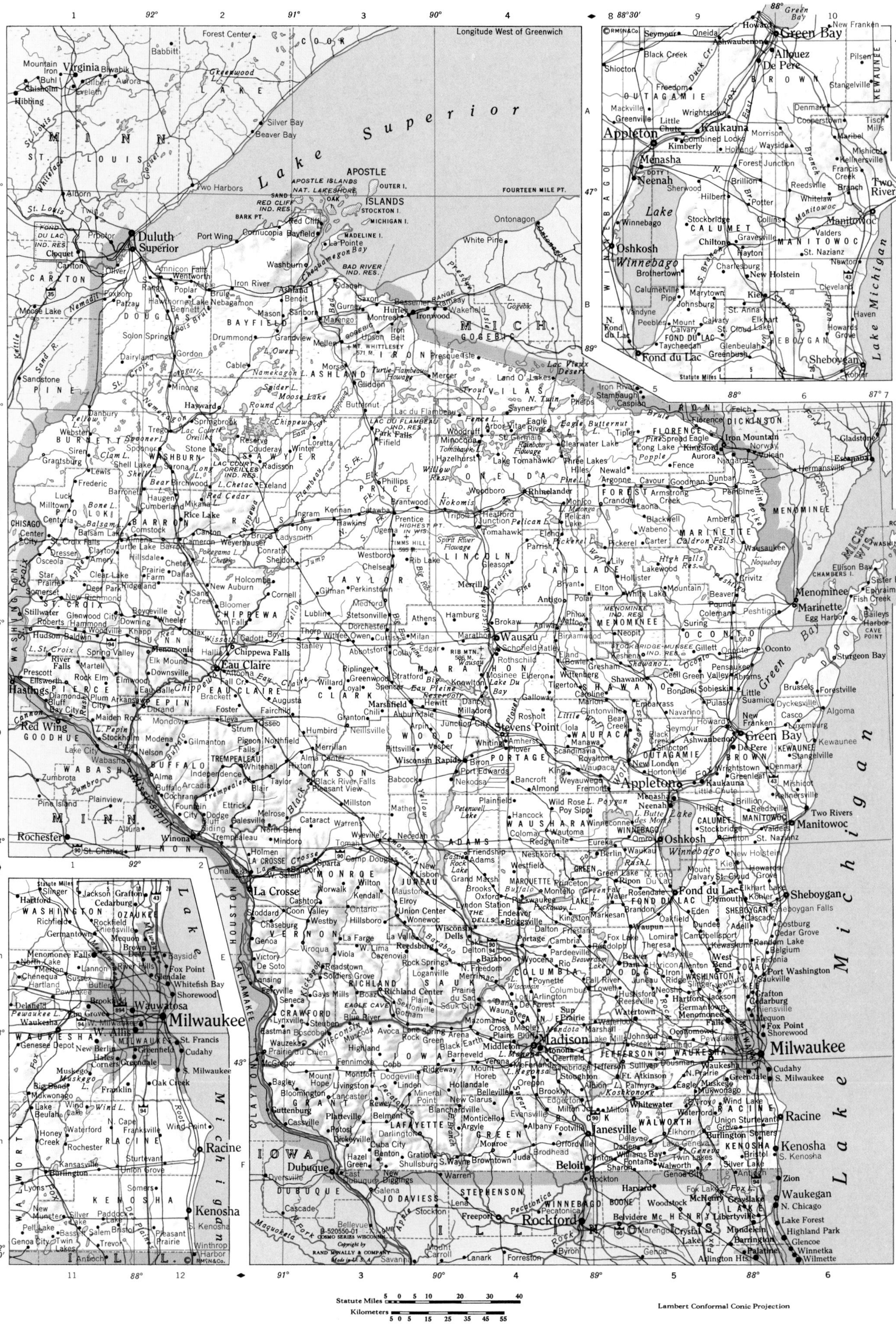

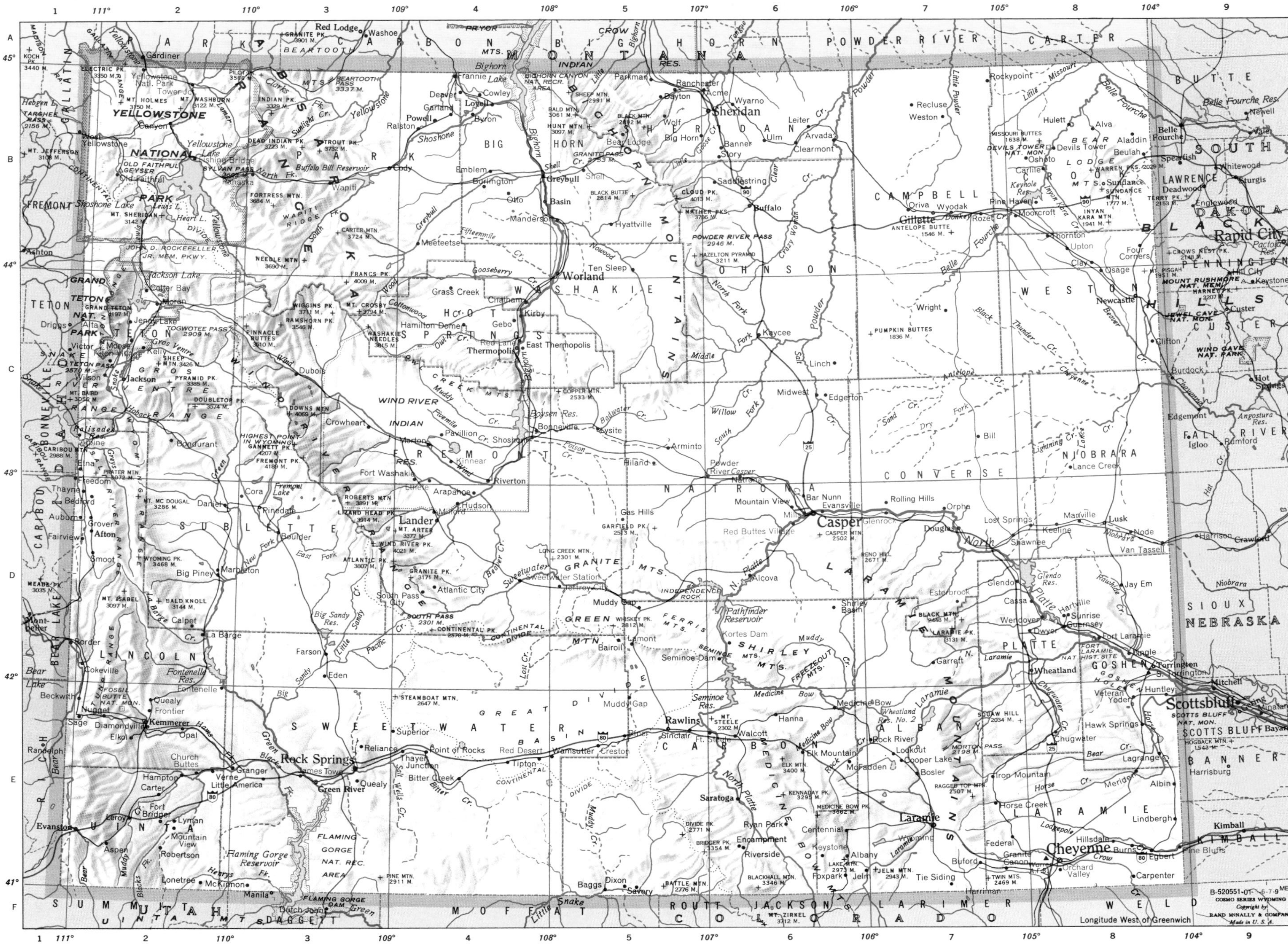

Statute Miles 5 0 5 10 20 30 40 50
Kilometers 5 0 5 15 25 35 45 55 65 75

Lambert Conformal Conic Projection

Wyoming

1990 CENSUS

- Afton, 1,394 . . . D 2
- Baggs, 272 . . . E 5
- Basin, 1,180 . . . B 4
- Big Piney, 454 . . . D 2
- Buffalo, 3,302 . . . B 6
- Burns, 254 . . . E 8
- Byron, 470 . . . B 4
- Casper, 46,742 . . . D 6
- Cheyenne, 50,008 . . . E 8
- Chugwater, 192 . . . E 8
- Cody, 7,897 . . . B 3
- Cokeville, 493 . . . D 2
- Cowley, 477 . . . B 4
- Dayton, 565 . . . B 5
- Diamondville, 864 . . . E 2
- Douglas, 5,076 . . . D 7
- Dubois, 895 . . . C 3
- Edgerton, 247 . . . C 6
- Elk Mountain, 174 . . . E 6
- Encampment, 490 . . . E 6
- Evanston, 10,903 . . . E 2
- Evansville, 1,403 . . . D 6
- Fort Laramie, 243 . . . D 8
- Freedom, 450('91) . . . D 2
- Gillette, 17,635 . . . B 7
- Glendo, 195 . . . D 7
- Glenrock, 2,153 . . . D 7
- Green River, 12,711 . . . E 3
- Greybull, 1,789 . . . B 4
- Guernsey, 1,155 . . . D 8
- Hanna, 1,076 . . . E 6
- Hudson, 392 . . . D 4
- Hulett, 429 . . . B 8
- Jackson, 4,472 . . . C 2
- James Town, 280('91) . . . E 3
- Kaycee, 256 . . . C 6
- Kemmerer, 3,020 . . . E 2
- La Barge, 493 . . . D 2
- Lander, 7,023 . . . D 4
- Laramie, 26,687 . . . E 7
- Lingle, 473 . . . D 8
- Lovell, 2,131 . . . B 4
- Lusk, 1,504 . . . D 8
- Lyman, 1,896 . . . E 2
- Marbleton, 634 . . . D 2
- Medicine Bow, 389 . . . E 6
- Meeteetse, 368 . . . B 4
- Midwest, 495 . . . C 6
- Mills, 1,574 . . . D 6
- Moorcroft, 768 . . . B 8
- Mountain View, 1,189 . . E 2
- Newcastle, 3,003 . . . C 8
- Osage, 350('91) . . . C 8
- Pine Bluffs, 1,054 . . . E 8
- Pinedale, 1,181 . . . D 3
- Powell, 5,292 . . . B 4
- Ranchester, 676 . . . B 5
- Rawlins, 9,380 . . . E 5
- Reliance, 500('91) . . . E 3
- Riverton, 9,202 . . . C 4
- Rock River, 190 . . . E 7
- Rock Springs, 19,050 . . E 3
- Saratoga, 1,969 . . . E 6
- Sheridan, 13,900 . . . B 6
- Shoshoni, 497 . . . C 4
- Sinclair, 500 . . . E 5
- South Torrington, 300('91) . . . D 8
- Story, 700('91) . . . B 6
- Sundance, 1,139 . . . B 8
- Superior, 273 . . . E 4
- Ten Sleep, 311 . . . B 5
- Teton Village, 250('91) C 2
- Thayne, 267 . . . D 1
- Thermopolis, 3,247 . . . C 4
- Torrington, 5,651 . . . D 8
- Upton, 980 . . . B 8
- Wamsutter, 240 . . . E 5
- West Laramie, 2,000('91) . . . E 7
- Wheatland, 3,271 . . . D 8
- Wilson, 500('91) . . . C 2
- Worland, 5,742 . . . B 5
- Yellowstone National Park, 400('91) . . . B 2

North Polar Regions

Anchorage, 226,338 ('90)........C27
Archangel'sk, 416,000 ('89)........C 8
BELGIUM........D12
Berlin, 3,352,848 ('89) (3,825,000★)........D11
CANADA........D22
Chicago, 2,783,726 ('90)........E21
CHINA........F 2
Churchill, 1,186 ('81)...D22
DENMARK........D11
Dublin, 502,749 ('86) (1,140,000★)........D13
Dutch Harbor, 20 ('81)D29
Edmonton, 573,982 ('86) (785,465★)........D24
ESTONIA........C10
FAEROE ISLANDS.....C13
Fairbanks, 30,843 ('90)........C27
FINLAND........C10
FRANCE........E12
Gander, 10,207 ('86) (10,899★)........E18
GERMANY........D11
Godthåb, 12,217 ('90).C18
GREENLAND........B17
Hammerfest, 7,208 ('83)........B10
Happy Valley-Goose Bay, 7,248 ('86)........D19
Helsinki, 490,034 ('88) (1,040,000★)........C10
ICELAND........C14
Igarka, 16,918 ('79).....C 4
IRELAND........D13
JAPAN........F35
Jekaterinburg, 1,367,000 ('89) (1,620,000★) .. D 6
Juneau, 26,751 ('90)...D26
Kijev (Kiev), 2,587,000 ('89) (2,900,000★) .. D 9
KOREA, NORTH........E36
KOREA, SOUTH........F36
LATVIA........C10
LITHUANIA........C10
Leningrad, 4,456,000 ('89) (5,825,000★)........D 9
LUXEMBOURG........E12
Magadan, 152,000 ('89)........D33
MONGOLIA........E 2
Moskva (Moscow), 8,769,000 ('89) (13,100,000★)........D 9
Murmansk, 468,000 ('89)........C 9
NETHERLANDS........D12
New York, 7,322,564 ('90)........E20
Nižnij Novgorod (Gorky), 1,438,000 ('89) (2,025,000★)........D 8
Nome, 3,500 ('90)......C29
Noril'sk, 174,000 ('89).C 4
NORWAY........C12
Novosibirsk, 1,436,000 ('89) (1,600,000★) .. D 4
Ōsaka, 2,636,249 ('85) (16,450,000★)........F35
Oslo, 452,415 ('87) (720,000★)........D11
Ottawa, 300,763 ('86) (819,263★)........E20
Paris, 2,078,900 ('87) (9,775,000★)........E12
POLAND........D11
Québec, 164,580 ('86) (603,267★)........E20
Reykjavík, 93,425 ('87) (137,941★)........C15
RUSSIA........C 4
Saint John's, 96,216 ('86) (161,901★)........E18
Sankt-Peterburg, 4,456,000 ('89) (5,825,000★)........D 9
Seattle, 516,259 ('90)..E25
Shenyang (Mukden), 3,910,000 ('88) (4,370,000▲)........E36
Sŏul (Seoul), 10,522,000 ('89) (15,850,000★) .F36
Stockholm, 672,187 ('90) (1,449,972★)........D11
SWEDEN........C11
Thule, 551 ('90)........B19
Tōkyō, 8,354,615 ('85) (27,700,000★)........F35
UKRAINE........E 9
Ulaanbaatar (Ulan Bator), 548,400 ('89)........E 2
UNITED KINGDOM.....D13
UNITED STATES........F22
Vancouver, 431,147 ('86) (1,380,729★)........E25
Vladivostok, 648,000 ('89)........E35
Vorkuta, 116,000 ('89) C 6
Warszawa, 1,651,200 ('89) (2,323,000★) .. D10
Winnipeg, 594,551 ('86) (625,304★)........E22

Kilometers 0 500 1000 1500 2000 Km.
Miles 0 500 1000 1500 2000 Mi.

1:60 000 000

★ Population of metropolitan area, including suburbs.
▲ Population of entire district, including rural area.

Index to World Reference Maps

Introduction to the Index

This universal index includes in a single alphabetical list approximately 38,000 names of features that appear on the reference maps. Each name is followed by the name of the country or continent in which it is located, a map-reference key and a page reference.

Names The names of cities appear in the index in regular type. The names of all other features appear in *italics*, followed by descriptive terms (hill, mtn., state) to indicate their nature.

Names that appear in shortened versions on the maps due to space limitations are spelled out in full in the index. The portions of these names omitted from the maps are enclosed in brackets — for example, Acapulco [de Juárez].

Abbreviations of names on the maps have been standardized as much as possible. Names that are abbreviated on the maps are generally spelled out in full in the index.

Country names and names of features that extend beyond the boundaries of one country are followed by the name of the continent in which each is located. Country designations follow the names of all other places in the index. The locations of places in the United States, Canada, and the United Kingdom are further defined by abbreviations that indicate the state, province, or political division in which each is located.

All abbreviations used in the index are defined in the List of Abbreviations below.

Alphabetization Names are alphabetized in the order of the letters of the English alphabet. Spanish *ll* and *ch*, for example, are not treated as distinct letters. Furthermore, diacritical marks are disregarded in alphabetization — German or Scandinavian *ä* or *ö* are treated as *a* or *o*.

The names of physical features may appear inverted, since they are always alphabetized under the proper, not the generic, part of the name, thus: 'Gibraltar, Strait of'. Otherwise every entry, whether consisting of one word or more, is alphabetized as a single continuous entity. 'Lakeland', for example, appears after 'La Crosse' and before 'La Salle'. Names beginning with articles (Le Havre, Den Helder, Al Manṣūrah) are not inverted. Names beginning 'St.', 'Ste.' and 'Sainte' are alphabetized as though spelled 'Saint'.

In the case of identical names, towns are listed first, then political divisions, then physical features. Entries that are completely identical are listed alphabetically by country name.

Map-Reference Keys and Page References The map-reference keys and page references are found in the last two columns of each entry.

Each map-reference key consists of a letter and number. The letters appear along the sides of the maps. Lowercase letters indicate reference to inset maps. Numbers appear across the tops and bottoms of the maps.

Map reference keys for point features, such as cities and mountain peaks, indicate the locations of the symbols. For extensive areal features, such as countries or mountain ranges, locations are given for the approximate centers of the features. Those for linear features, such as canals and rivers, are given for the locations of the names.

Names of some important places or features that are omitted from the maps due to space limitations are included in the index. Each of these places is identified by an asterisk (*) preceding the map-reference key.

The page number generally refers to the main map for the country in which the feature is located. Page references to two-page maps always refer to the left-hand page.

List of Abbreviations

Afg.	Afghanistan
Afr.	Africa
Ak., U.S.	Alaska, U.S.
Al., U.S.	Alabama, U.S.
Alb.	Albania
Alg.	Algeria
Alta., Can.	Alberta, Can.
Am. Sam.	American Samoa
anch.	anchorage
And.	Andorra
Ang.	Angola
Ant.	Antarctica
Antig.	Antigua and Barbuda
Ar., U.S.	Arkansas, U.S.
Arg.	Argentina
Arm.	Armenia
Aus.	Austria
Austl.	Australia
Az., U.S.	Arizona, U.S.
Azer.	Azerbaijan
b.	bay, gulf, inlet, lagoon
Bah.	Bahamas
Bahr.	Bahrain
Barb.	Barbados
B.A.T.	British Antarctic Territory
B.C., Can.	British Columbia, Can.
Bdi.	Burundi
Bel.	Belgium
Bela.	Belarus
Ber.	Bermuda
Bhu.	Bhutan
B.I.O.T.	British Indian Ocean Territory
Bngl.	Bangladesh
Bol.	Bolivia
Boph.	Bophuthatswana
Bos.	Bosnia and Herzegovina
Bots.	Botswana
Braz.	Brazil
Bru.	Brunei
Br. Vir. Is.	British Virgin Islands
Bul.	Bulgaria
Burkina	Burkina Faso
c.	cape, point
Ca., U.S.	California, U.S.
Cam.	Cameroon
Camb.	Cambodia
Can.	Canada
Cay. Is.	Cayman Islands
Cen. Afr. Rep.	Central African Republic
Christ. I.	Christmas Island
C. Iv.	Cote d'Ivoire
clf.	cliff, escarpment
co.	county, parish
Co., U.S.	Colorado, U.S.
Col.	Colombia
Com.	Comoros
cont.	continent
C.R.	Costa Rica
crat.	crater
Cro.	Croatia
Ct., U.S.	Connecticut, U.S.
ctry.	country
C.V.	Cape Verde
Cyp.	Cyprus
Czech.	Czech Republic
D.C., U.S.	District of Columbia, U.S.
De., U.S.	Delaware, U.S.
Den.	Denmark
dep.	dependency, colony
depr.	depression
dept.	department, district
des.	desert
Dji.	Djibouti
Dom.	Dominica
Dom. Rep.	Dominican Republic
Ec.	Ecuador
El Sal.	El Salvador
Eng., U.K.	England, U.K.
Eq. Gui.	Equatorial Guinea
Erit.	Eritrea
est.	estuary
Est.	Estonia
Eth.	Ethiopia
Eur.	Europe
Faer. Is.	Faeroe Islands
Falk. Is.	Falkland Islands
Fin.	Finland
Fl., U.S.	Florida, U.S.
for.	forest, moor
Fr.	France
Fr. Gu.	French Guiana
Fr. Poly.	French Polynesia
F.S.A.T.	French Southern and Antarctic Territory
Ga., U.S.	Georgia, U.S.
Gam.	Gambia
Geor.	Georgia
Ger.	Germany
Gib.	Gibraltar
Grc.	Greece
Gren.	Grenada
Grnld.	Greenland
Guad.	Guadeloupe
Guat.	Guatemala
Gui.	Guinea
Gui.-B.	Guinea-Bissau
Guy.	Guyana
Hi., U.S.	Hawaii, U.S.
hist.	historic site, ruins
hist. reg.	historic region
H.K.	Hong Kong
Hond.	Honduras
Hung.	Hungary
i.	island
Ia., U.S.	Iowa, U.S.
Ice.	Iceland
ice	ice feature, glacier
Id., U.S.	Idaho, U.S.
Il., U.S.	Illinois, U.S.
In., U.S.	Indiana, U.S.
Indon.	Indonesia
I. of Man	Isle of Man
Ire.	Ireland
is.	islands
Isr.	Israel
Isr. Occ.	Israeli Occupied Territories
Jam.	Jamaica
Jord.	Jordan
Kaz.	Kazakhstan
Kir.	Kiribati
Ks., U.S.	Kansas, U.S.
Kuw.	Kuwait
Ky., U.S.	Kentucky, U.S.
Kyrg.	Kyrgyzstan
l.	lake, pond
La., U.S.	Louisiana, U.S.
Lat.	Latvia
Leb.	Lebanon
Leso.	Lesotho
Lib.	Liberia
Liech.	Liechtenstein
Lith.	Lithuania
Lux.	Luxembourg
Ma., U.S.	Massachusetts, U.S.
Mac.	Macedonia
Madag.	Madagascar
Malay.	Malaysia
Mald.	Maldives
Man., Can.	Manitoba, Can.
Marsh. Is.	Marshall Islands
Mart.	Martinique
Maur.	Mauritania
May.	Mayotte
Md., U.S.	Maryland, U.S.
Me., U.S.	Maine, U.S.
Mex.	Mexico
Mi., U.S.	Michigan, U.S.
Micron.	Federated States of Micronesia
Mid. Is.	Midway Islands
mil.	military installation
Mn., U.S.	Minnesota, U.S.
Mo., U.S.	Missouri, U.S.
Mol.	Moldova
Mon.	Monaco
Mong.	Mongolia
Monts.	Montserrat
Mor.	Morocco
Moz.	Mozambique
Mrts.	Mauritius
Ms., U.S.	Mississippi, U.S.
Mt., U.S.	Montana, U.S.
mth.	river mouth or channel
mtn.	mountain
mts.	mountains
Mwi.	Malawi
Mya.	Myanmar
N.A.	North America
N.B., Can.	New Brunswick, Can.
N.C., U.S.	North Carolina, U.S.
N. Cal.	New Caledonia
N. Cyp.	North Cyprus
N.D., U.S.	North Dakota, U.S.
Ne., U.S.	Nebraska, U.S.
Neth.	Netherlands
Neth. Ant.	Netherlands Antilles
Newf., Can.	Newfoundland, Can.
N.H., U.S.	New Hampshire, U.S.
Nic.	Nicaragua
Nig.	Nigeria
N. Ire., U.K.	Northern Ireland, U.K.
N.J., U.S.	New Jersey, U.S.
N. Kor.	North Korea
N.M., U.S.	New Mexico, U.S.
N. Mar. Is.	Northern Mariana Islands
Nmb.	Namibia
Nor.	Norway
Norf. I.	Norfolk Island
N.S., Can.	Nova Scotia, Can.
Nv., U.S.	Nevada, U.S.
N.W. Ter., Can.	Northwest Territories, Can.
N.Y., U.S.	New York, U.S.
N.Z.	New Zealand
Oc.	Oceania
Oh., U.S.	Ohio, U.S.
Ok., U.S.	Oklahoma, U.S.
Ont., Can.	Ontario, Can.
Or., U.S.	Oregon, U.S.
Pa., U.S.	Pennsylvania, U.S.
Pak.	Pakistan
Pan.	Panama
Pap. N. Gui.	Papua New Guinea
Para.	Paraguay
P.E.I., Can.	Prince Edward Island, Can.
pen.	peninsula
Phil.	Philippines
Pit.	Pitcairn
pl.	plain, flat
plat.	plateau, highland
Pol.	Poland
Port.	Portugal
P.R.	Puerto Rico
prov.	province, region
Que., Can.	Quebec, Can.
reg.	physical region
res.	reservoir
Reu.	Reunion
rf.	reef, shoal
R.I., U.S.	Rhode Island, U.S.
Rom.	Romania
Rw.	Rwanda
S.A.	South America
S. Afr.	South Africa
Sask., Can.	Saskatchewan, Can.
Sau. Ar.	Saudi Arabia
S.C., U.S.	South Carolina, U.S.
sci.	scientific station
Scot., U.K.	Scotland, U.K.
S.D., U.S.	South Dakota, U.S.
Sen.	Senegal
Sey.	Seychelles
Sing.	Singapore
S. Kor.	South Korea
S.L.	Sierra Leone
Slo.	Slovenia
Slov.	Slovakia
S. Mar.	San Marino
Sol. Is.	Solomon Islands
Som.	Somalia
Sp. N. Afr.	Spanish North Africa
Sri L.	Sri Lanka
state	state, republic, canton
St. Hel.	St. Helena
St. K./N	St. Kitts and Nevis
St. Luc.	St. Lucia
stm.	stream (river, creek)
S. Tom./P.	Sao Tome and Principe
St. P./M.	St. Pierre and Miquelon
strt.	strait, channel, sound
St. Vin.	St. Vincent and the Grenadines
Sud.	Sudan
Sur.	Suriname
sw.	swamp, marsh
Swaz.	Swaziland
Swe.	Sweden
Switz.	Switzerland
Tai.	Taiwan
Taj.	Tajikistan
Tan.	Tanzania
T./C. Is.	Turks and Caicos Islands
ter.	territory
Thai.	Thailand
Tn., U.S.	Tennessee, U.S.
Tok.	Tokelau
Trin.	Trinidad and Tobago
Tun.	Tunisia
Tur.	Turkey
Turk.	Turkmenistan
Tx., U.S.	Texas, U.S.
U.A.E.	United Arab Emirates
Ug.	Uganda
U.K.	United Kingdom
Ukr.	Ukraine
Ur.	Uruguay
U.S.	United States
Ut., U.S.	Utah, U.S.
Uzb.	Uzbekistan
Va., U.S.	Virginia, U.S.
val.	valley, watercourse
Vat.	Vatican City
Ven.	Venezuela
Viet.	Vietnam
V.I.U.S.	Virgin Islands (U.S.)
vol.	volcano
Vt., U.S.	Vermont, U.S.
Wa., U.S.	Washington, U.S.
Wal./F.	Wallis and Futuna
Wi., U.S.	Wisconsin, U.S.
W. Sah.	Western Sahara
W. Sam.	Western Samoa
wtfl.	waterfall
W.V., U.S.	West Virginia, U.S.
Wy., U.S.	Wyoming, U.S.
Yugo.	Yugoslavia
Yukon, Can.	Yukon Territory, Can.
Zam.	Zambia
Zimb.	Zimbabwe

Index

A

Name	Map Ref	Page
Aachen, Ger.	E6	8
Aalen, Ger.	G10	8
Aalst, Bel.	E4	8
Äänekoski, Fin.	E15	6
Aarau, Switz.	E15	10
Aarschot, Bel.	E4	8
Aba, China	E7	26
Aba, Nig.	G7	42
Ābādān, Iran	B4	46
Abaeté, Braz.	E6	57
Abajo Peak, mtn., Ut., U.S.	F6	121
Abakan, Russia	G12	24
Abancay, Peru	F4	54
Abashiri, Japan	o22	30a
Abasolo, Mex.	E7	62
Abaya, Lake, l., Eth.	G2	46
Abaza, Russia	G12	24
Abbadia San Salvatore, Italy	G6	14
Abbaye, Point, c., Mi., U.S.	B2	99
Abbeville, Fr.	B8	10
Abbeville, Al., U.S.	D4	78
Abbeville, Ga., U.S.	E3	87
Abbeville, La., U.S.	E3	95
Abbeville, S.C., U.S.	C3	117
Abbeville, co., S.C., U.S.	C2	117
Abbotsford, Wi., U.S.	D3	126
Abbottābād, Pak.	C5	38
Abbott Butte, mtn., Or., U.S.	E4	114
Abbott Run, stm., U.S.	B4	116
Abbott Run Valley, R.I., U.S.	B4	116
'Abd al-Kūrī, i., Yemen	F5	46
Abe, Lake, l., Afr.	F3	46
Abéché, Chad	F10	42
Abéjar, Spain	D9	12
Abengourou, C. Iv.	G5	42
Abeokuta, Nig.	G6	42
Aberayron, Wales, U.K.	I8	7
Aberdeen, Scot., U.K.	D10	7
Aberdeen, Id., U.S.	G6	89
Aberdeen, Md., U.S.	A5	97
Aberdeen, Ms., U.S.	B5	101
Aberdeen, N.C., U.S.	B3	110
Aberdeen, Oh., U.S.	D2	112
Aberdeen, S.D., U.S.	B7	118
Aberdeen, Wa., U.S.	C2	124
Aberdeen Lake, l., N.W. Ter., Can.	D13	66
Aberdeen Proving Ground, mil., Md., U.S.	A5	97
Abernathy, Tx., U.S.	C2	120
Abert, Lake, l., Or., U.S.	E6	114
Abert Rim, clf, Or., U.S.	E6	114
Aberystwyth, Wales, U.K.	I8	7
Abhā, Sau. Ar.	E3	46
Abidjan, C. Iv.	G5	42
Abilene, Ks., U.S.	D6	93
Abilene, Tx., U.S.	C3	120
Abingdon, Il., U.S.	C3	90
Abingdon, Md., U.S.	B5	97
Abingdon, Va., U.S.	f10	123
Abington, Ma., U.S.	B6	98
Abington [Township], Pa., U.S.	o21	115
Abisko, Swe.	B12	6
Abita Springs, La., U.S.	D5	95
Abitibi, stm., Ont., Can.	o19	73
Abitibi, Lake, l., Can.	G17	66
Abohar, India	E6	38
Abomey, Benin	G6	42
Aborigen, Pik, mtn., Russia	E23	24
Abraham Lake, res., Alta., Can.	C2	68
Abraham Lincoln Birthplace National Historic Site, hist., Ky., U.S.	C4	94
Abrantes, Port.	F3	12
Absaroka Range, mts., U.S.	F7	127
Absarokee, Mt., U.S.	E7	103
Absecon, N.J., U.S.	E4	107
Absecon Inlet, b., N.J., U.S.	E4	107
Abū 'Alī, i., Sau. Ar.	C4	46
Abu Dhabi see Abū Ẓaby, U.A.E.	D5	46
Abū Ḥamad, Sudan	E12	42
Abuja, Nig.	G7	42
Abū Kamāl, Syria	B7	40
Abukuma-sanchi, mts., Japan	E13	30
Abū Madd, Ra's, c., Sau. Ar.	D2	46
Abunã, Braz.	E5	54
Abū Shajarah, Ra's, c., Sudan	D13	42
Abū Ẓaby, U.A.E.	D5	46
Academia, Oh., U.S.	B3	112
Acadia, co., La., U.S.	D3	95
Acadia National Park, Me., U.S.	D4	96
Acajutla, El Sal.	H3	64
Acámbaro, Mex.	G9	62
Acaponeta, Mex.	F7	62
Acapulco [de Juárez], Mex.	I10	62
Acaraí Mountains, mts., S.A.	C7	54
Acaraú, Braz.	D10	54
Acarigua, Ven.	C8	58
Acatlán [de Osorio], Mex.	H10	62
Acayucan, Mex.	I12	62
Accomack, co., Va., U.S.	C7	123
Accoville, W.V., U.S.	D3	125
Accra, Ghana	G5	42
Acerra, Italy	I9	14
Achaguas, Ven.	D8	58
Achalpur, India	B4	37
Acheng, China	B12	26
Achí, Col.	C5	58
Achill Island, i., Ire.	H2	7
Achtubinsk, Russia	H7	22
Ačinsk, Russia	F12	24
Acireale, Italy	L10	14
Ackerman, Ms., U.S.	B4	101
Ackley, Ia., U.S.	B4	92
Acklins Island, i., Bah.	C10	64
Acoma Indian Reservation, N.M., U.S.	C2	108
Aconcagua, Cerro, mtn., Arg.	C2	56
Açores (Azores), is., Port.	D11	2
Acquapendente, Italy	G6	14
Acqui Terme, Italy	E3	14
Acre, stm., S.A.	E5	54
Acri, Italy	J11	14
Acton, Ma., U.S.	B5	98
Acton Vale, Que., Can.	D5	74
Acushnet, Ma., U.S.	C6	98
Acworth, Ga., U.S.	B2	87
Ada, Mn., U.S.	C2	100
Ada, Oh., U.S.	B2	112
Ada, Ok., U.S.	C5	113
Ada, co., Id., U.S.	F2	89
Ada, Mount, mtn., Ak., U.S.	m22	79
Adair, Ia., U.S.	C3	92
Adair, Ok., U.S.	A6	113
Adair, co., Ia., U.S.	C3	92
Adair, co., Ky., U.S.	C4	94
Adair, co., Mo., U.S.	A5	102
Adair, co., Ok., U.S.	B7	113
Adair, Cape, c., N.W. Ter., Can.	B18	66
Adairsville, Ga., U.S.	B2	87
Adairville, Ky., U.S.	D3	94
Adak Island, i., Ak., U.S.	E4	79
Adak Naval Station, mil., Ak., U.S.	E4	79
Ādam, Oman	D6	46
Adamantina, Braz.	F3	57
Adamawa, mts., Afr.	G8	42
Adam Island, i., Md., U.S.	D5	97
Adams, Ma., U.S.	A1	98
Adams, Mn., U.S.	G6	100
Adams, N.Y., U.S.	B4	109
Adams, Wi., U.S.	E4	126
Adams, co., Co., U.S.	B6	83
Adams, co., Id., U.S.	E2	89
Adams, co., Il., U.S.	D2	90
Adams, co., In., U.S.	C8	91
Adams, co., Ia., U.S.	C3	92
Adams, co., Ms., U.S.	D2	101
Adams, co., Ne., U.S.	D7	104
Adams, co., N.D., U.S.	C3	111
Adams, co., Oh., U.S.	D2	112
Adams, co., Pa., U.S.	G7	115
Adams, co., Wa., U.S.	B7	124
Adams, co., Wi., U.S.	D4	126
Adams, Mount, mtn., N.H., U.S.	B4	106
Adams, Mount, mtn., Wa., U.S.	C4	124
Adams Bridge, rf., Asia	H5	37
Adams Point, c., Mi., U.S.	C7	99
Adams Run, S.C., U.S.	k11	117
Adamstown, Pa., U.S.	F9	115
Adamsville, Al., U.S.	f7	78
Adamsville, R.I., U.S.	E6	116
Adamsville, Tn., U.S.	B3	119
Adamsville Brook, stm., R.I., U.S.	E6	116
'Adan (Aden), Yemen	F4	46
Adana, Tur.	H15	4
Adapazarı, Tur.	G14	4
Adarama, Sudan	E12	42
Ad-Dabbah, Sudan	E12	42
Ad-Dahnā, des., Sau. Ar.	D4	46
Ad-Dammām, Sau. Ar.	C5	46
Ad-Dawādimī, Sau. Ar.	D3	46
Ad-Dawḥah (Doha), Qatar	C5	46
Addis, La., U.S.	D4	95
Addis Ababa see Adis Abeba, Eth.	G2	46
Addison, Al., U.S.	A2	78
Addison, Ct., U.S.	C5	84
Addison, Il., U.S.	k8	90
Addison, N.Y., U.S.	C3	109
Addison, co., Vt., U.S.	C2	122
Ad-Dīwānīyah, Iraq	B3	46
Ad-Duwaym, Sudan	F12	42
Addyston, Oh., U.S.	o12	112
Adel, Ga., U.S.	E3	87
Adel, Ia., U.S.	C3	92
Adelaide, Austl.	F7	50
Adelaide Peninsula, pen., N.W. Ter., Can.	C13	66
Adelanto, Ca., U.S.	E5	82
Aden, Gulf of, b.	F4	46
Aden see 'Adan, Yemen	F4	46
Adieu, Cape, c., Austl.	F6	50
Adige, stm., Italy	D7	14
Adigrat, Eth.	F2	46
Ādilābād, India	C5	37
Adimi, Russia	H21	24
Adirondack Mountains, mts., N.Y., U.S.	A6	109
Adis Abeba, Eth.	G2	46
Admiralty Bay, b., Ak., U.S.	A9	79
Admiralty Inlet, b., N.W. Ter., Can.	B15	66
Admiralty Island, i., Ak., U.S.	m22	79
Admiralty Islands, is., Pap. N. Gui.	k16	50a
Adobe Acres, N.M., U.S.	*B3	108
Adobe Creek Reservoir, res., Co., U.S.	C7	83
Adolfo López Mateos, Presa, res., Mex.	E6	62
Ādoni, India	E4	37
Adour, stm., Fr.	I7	10
Adra, Spain	I8	12
Adrano, Italy	L9	14
Adrar, Alg.	C5	42
Adria, Italy	D7	14
Adrian, Ga., U.S.	D4	87
Adrian, Mi., U.S.	G6	99
Adrian, Mn., U.S.	G3	100
Adrian, Mo., U.S.	C3	102
Adriatic Sea, Eur.	G11	4
Advance, Mo., U.S.	D8	102
Adyča, stm., Russia	D21	24
Aegean Sea	J8	16
Afars and Issas see Djibouti, ctry., Afr.	F3	46
Afghanistan, ctry., Asia	C1	36
Afikpo, Nig.	G7	42
Åfjord, Nor.	E8	6
Afmadu, Som.	A8	44
Afognak Island, i., Ak., U.S.	D9	79
Africa	D6	41
Afton, Ia., U.S.	C3	92
Afton, Mn., U.S.	F6	100
Afton, Ok., U.S.	A7	113
Afton, Wy., U.S.	D2	127
'Afula, Isr.	C4	40
Afyon, Tur.	H14	4
Agadez, Niger	E7	42
Agadir, Mor.	B4	42
Agalega Islands, is., Mrts.	D11	44
Agalta, Cordillera de, mts., Hond.	G5	64
Agapa, Russia	C11	24
Agartala, India	I14	38
Agate Fossil Beds National Monument, Ne., U.S.	B2	104
Agattu Island, i., Ak., U.S.	E2	79
Agawam, Ma., U.S.	B2	98
Agen, Fr.	H7	10
Agency, Ia., U.S.	D5	92
Agency, Mo., U.S.	B3	102
Āghā Jārī, Iran	B4	46
Agira, Italy	L9	14
Agnone, Italy	H9	14
Agoura Hills, Ca., U.S.	m11	82
Āgra, India	G8	38
Ágreda, Spain	D10	12
Ağrı Dağı (Mount Ararat), mtn., Tur.	H16	4
Agrigento, Italy	L8	14
Agrínion, Grc.	K5	16
Agropoli, Italy	I9	14
Agua Caliente, Mex.	F7	62
Agua Caliente Grande, Mex.	D5	62
Aguachica, Col.	C6	58
Água Clara, Braz.	F2	57
Agua Fria, N.M., U.S.	B3	108
Agua Fria, stm., Az., U.S.	D3	80
Agua Prieta, Mex.	B5	62
Aguascalientes, Mex.	G8	62
Águas Formosas, Braz.	D8	57
Águeda, Port.	E3	12
Aguila, Az., U.S.	D2	80
Aguilar, Spain	H7	12
Águilas, Spain	H10	12
Agulhas, Cape, c., S. Afr.	H3	44
Agustín Codazzi, Col.	B6	58
Agustín Codazzi, Col.	I11	64
Ahaggar, mts., Alg.	D7	42
Ahipara Bay, b., N.Z.	A4	52
Ahklun Mountains, mts., Ak., U.S.	D7	79
Ahlen, Ger.	D7	8
Ahmadābād, India	I5	38
Ahmadnagar, India	C3	37
Ahmadpur East, Pak.	F4	38
Ahmar Mountains, mts., Eth.	G3	46
Ahoskie, N.C., U.S.	A6	110
Ahtanum Creek, stm., Wa., U.S.	C5	124
Ahu, China	A7	28
Ahuacatlán, Mex.	G7	62
Ahvāz, Iran	B4	46
Ahvenanmaa (Åland), is., Fin.	F12	6
Aialik, Cape, c., Ak., U.S.	D10	79
Aichach, Ger.	G11	8
Aiea, Hi., U.S.	B4	88
Aihun, China	A12	26
Aijal, India	I15	38
Aiken, S.C., U.S.	D4	117
Aiken, co., S.C., U.S.	D4	117
Ailsa Craig, Ont., Can.	D3	73
Aim, Russia	F20	24
Aimorés, Braz.	E8	57
Ainslie Lake, l., N.S., Can.	C8	71
Ainsworth, Ne., U.S.	B6	104
Aipe, Col.	F5	58
Aïr, mts., Niger	E7	42
Airdrie, Alta., Can.	D3	68
Aire-sur-l'Adour, Fr.	I6	10
Air Force Island, i., N.W. Ter., Can.	C18	66
Air Park West, Ne., U.S.	*D9	104
Aisne, stm., Fr.	C10	10
Aïssa, Djebel, mtn., Alg.	B5	42
Aitape, Pap. N. Gui.	k15	50a
Aitkin, Mn., U.S.	D5	100
Aitkin, co., Mn., U.S.	D5	100
Aix, Mount, mtn., Wa., U.S.	C4	124
Aix-en-Provence, Fr.	I12	10
Aix-la-Chapelle see Aachen, Ger.	E6	8
Aix-les-Bains, Fr.	G12	10
Aizu-wakamatsu, Japan	E12	30
Ajaccio, Fr.	n23	11a
Ajaguz, Kaz.	H10	24
Ajan, Russia	F21	24
Ajan, stm., Russia	C13	24
Ajax, Ont., Can.	D6	73
Ajdābiyah, Libya	B10	42
Ajjer, Tassili n', plat., Alg.	C7	42
'Ajlūn, Jord.	C4	40
Ajmer, India	G6	38
Ajo, Az., U.S.	E3	80
Ajo, Cabo de, c., Spain	B8	12
Ajon, Ostrov, i., Russia	D27	24
Ajtos, Bul.	G11	16
Akademii, Zaliv, b., Russia	G21	24
Akaltara, India	A7	37
Akan, Japan	p22	30a
'Akasha East, Sudan	D12	42
Akashi, Japan	H7	30
Akçakale, Tur.	A6	40
Ak-Chin Indian Reservation, Az., U.S.	E3	80
Akesu, China	C3	26
Akharnaí, Grc.	K7	16
Akhisar, Tur.	H13	4
Akiachak, Ak., U.S.	C7	79
Akimiski Island, i., N.W. Ter., Can.	F16	66
Akita, Japan	C13	30
Akjoujt, Maur.	E3	42
'Akko (Acre), Isr.	C4	40
Aklavik, N.W. Ter., Can.	C6	66
Akō, Japan	H7	30
Akobo, stm., Afr.	G12	42
Akola, India	B4	37
Akordat, Erit.	E2	46
Akot, India	B4	37
Akpatok Island, i., N.W. Ter., Can.	D19	66
Akron, Co., U.S.	A7	83
Akron, In., U.S.	B5	91
Akron, Ia., U.S.	B1	92
Akron, N.Y., U.S.	B2	109
Akron, Oh., U.S.	A4	112
Akron, Pa., U.S.	F9	115
Aksaray, Tur.	H14	4
Akşehir, Tur.	H14	4
Aksum, Eth.	F2	46
Aktau, Kaz.	I8	22
Akt'ubinsk, Kaz.	G9	22
Akureyri, Ice.	B4	4
Ål, Nor.	F7	6
Alabama, state, U.S.	C3	78
Alabama, stm., Al., U.S.	D2	78
Alabaster, Al., U.S.	B3	78
Alachua, Fl., U.S.	C4	86
Alachua, co., Fl., U.S.	C4	86
Alagoinhas, Braz.	B9	57
Alagón, Spain	D10	12
Alajuela, C.R.	I5	64
Alakanuk, Ak., U.S.	C7	79
Alalakeiki Channel, strt., Hi., U.S.	C5	88
Al-'Alamayn, Egypt	B11	42
Alamance, co., N.C., U.S.	B3	110
Al-'Amārah, Iraq	B4	46
Alameda, Ca., U.S.	h8	82
Alameda, N.M., U.S.	B3	108
Alameda, co., Ca., U.S.	D3	82
Alameda Naval Air Station, mil., Ca., U.S.	h8	82
Alamito Creek, stm., Tx., U.S.	p12	120
Alamo, Ga., U.S.	D4	87
Alamo, Nv., U.S.	F6	105
Alamo, Tn., U.S.	B2	119
Alamo, Tx., U.S.	F3	120
Alamogordo, N.M., U.S.	E4	108
Alamo Heights, Tx., U.S.	E3	120
Alamo Hueco Mountains, mts., N.M., U.S.	F1	108
Alamo Indian Reservation, N.M., U.S.	C2	108
Alamo Lake, res., Az., U.S.	C2	80
Alamosa, Co., U.S.	D5	83
Alamosa, co., Co., U.S.	D5	83
Alamosa, stm., Co., U.S.	D4	83
Alamosa Creek, stm., N.M., U.S.	D2	108
Alamosa East, Co., U.S.	D5	83
Alanäs, Swe.	D10	6
Alanya, Tur.	A3	40
Alapaha, Ga., U.S.	E3	87
Alapaha, stm., U.S.	E3	87
Al-'Aqabah, Jord.	E4	40
Alaşehir, Tur.	K12	16
Alashanyouqi, China	C7	26
Alaska, state, U.S.	C9	79
Alaska, Gulf of, b., Ak., U.S.	D10	79
Alaska Peninsula, pen., Ak., U.S.	D8	79
Alaska Range, mts., Ak., U.S.	C9	79
Alassio, Italy	E3	14
Alatna, stm., Ak., U.S.	B9	79
Al-'Aṭrūn, Sudan	E11	42
Alava, Cape, c., Wa., U.S.	A1	124
Alazeja, stm., Russia	C24	24
Alba, Italy	E3	14
Albacete, Spain	G10	12
Alba de Tormes, Spain	E6	12
Albaida, Spain	G11	12
Albanel, Lac, l., Que., Can.	F18	66
Albania, ctry., Eur.	G11	4
Albano Laziale, Italy	H7	14
Albany, Austl.	G3	50
Albany, Ga., U.S.	E2	87
Albany, Il., U.S.	B3	90
Albany, In., U.S.	D7	91
Albany, Ky., U.S.	D4	94
Albany, La., U.S.	g10	95
Albany, Mn., U.S.	E4	100
Albany, Mo., U.S.	A3	102
Albany, N.Y., U.S.	C7	109
Albany, Or., U.S.	C3	114
Albany, Tx., U.S.	C3	120
Albany, Wi., U.S.	F4	126
Albany, co., N.Y., U.S.	C6	109
Albany, co., Wy., U.S.	E7	127
Albany, stm., Ont., Can.	o18	73
Al-Başrah, Iraq	B4	46
Albatross Bay, b., Austl.	B8	50
Al-Batrūn, Leb.	B4	40
Al-Bawīṭī, Egypt	C11	42
Albemarle, N.C., U.S.	B2	110
Albemarle, co., Va., U.S.	C4	123
Albemarle Lake, l., Ms., U.S.	C2	101
Albemarle Sound, strt., N.C., U.S.	A6	110
Albenga, Italy	E3	14
Albergaria-a-Velha, Port.	E3	12
Albert, Fr.	B9	10
Albert, Lake, l., Afr.	A6	44
Alberta, prov., Can.	C4	68
Alberta, Mount, mtn., Alta., Can.	C2	68
Albert City, Ia., U.S.	B3	92
Albert Lea, Mn., U.S.	G5	100
Albert Nile, stm., Ug.	H12	42
Alberton, P.E.I., Can.	C5	71
Albertson, N.Y., U.S.	k13	109
Albertville, Fr.	G13	10
Albertville, Al., U.S.	A3	78
Albertville, Mn., U.S.	E5	100
Albertville see Kalemie, Zaire	C5	44
Albi, Fr.	I9	10
Albia, Ia., U.S.	C5	92
Albino, Italy	D4	14
Albion, Il., U.S.	E5	90
Albion, In., U.S.	B7	91
Albion, Mi., U.S.	F6	99
Albion, Ne., U.S.	C7	104
Albion, N.Y., U.S.	B2	109
Albion, Pa., U.S.	C1	115
Albion, R.I., U.S.	B4	116
Albion, Wa., U.S.	C8	124
Alborán, Isla de, i., Spain	J8	12
Ålborg, Den.	H7	6
Alborz, Reshteh-ye Kūhhā-ye, mts., Iran	J8	22
Albufeira, Port.	H3	12
Albuñol, Spain	I8	12
Albuquerque, N.M., U.S.	B3	108
Alburquerque, Spain	F4	12
Alburtis, Pa., U.S.	F10	115
Albury, Austl.	G9	50
Alcácer do Sal, Port.	G3	12
Alcalá de Guadaira, Spain	H6	12
Alcalá de Henares, Spain	E8	12
Alcalá la Real, Spain	H8	12
Alcalde, N.M., U.S.	A3	108
Alcamo, Italy	L7	14
Alcañices, Spain	D5	12
Alcañiz, Spain	D11	12
Alcântara, Braz.	D10	54
Alcántara, Spain	F5	12
Alcantarilla, Spain	H10	12
Alcaraz, Spain	G9	12
Alcázar de San Juan, Spain	F8	12
Alcester, S.D., U.S.	D9	118
Alcira, Spain	F11	12
Alcoa, Tn., U.S.	D10	119
Alcobaça, Braz.	D9	57
Alcobaça, Port.	F3	12
Alcolu, S.C., U.S.	D7	117
Alcona, co., Mi., U.S.	D7	99
Alconchel, Spain	G4	12
Alcorn, co., Ms., U.S.	A5	101
Alcoy, Spain	G11	12
Aldabra Islands, atoll, Sey.	C9	44
Aldan, Russia	F19	24
Aldan, stm., Russia	E20	24
Aldanskoje Nagorje, plat., Russia	F19	24
Alden, Ia., U.S.	B4	92
Alden, Mn., U.S.	G5	100
Alden, N.Y., U.S.	C2	109
Alder Brook, stm., Vt., U.S.	B4	122
Aldershot, Eng., U.K.	J12	7
Alderson, W.V., U.S.	D4	125
Aldrich, Al., U.S.	B3	78
Aledo, Il., U.S.	B3	90
Aleg, Maur.	E3	42
Alegres Mountain, mtn., N.M., U.S.	C2	108
Alegrete, Braz.	B5	56
Alejsk, Russia	G10	24
Aleksandrov, Russia	E21	18
Aleksandrovsk-Sachalinskij, Russia	G22	24
Aleksejevsk, Russia	F15	24
Aleksin, Russia	G20	18
Além Paraíba, Braz.	F7	57
Alençon, Fr.	D7	10
Alenuihaha Channel, strt., Hi., U.S.	C5	88
Aleppo see Ḥalab, Syria	A5	40
Alert Bay, B.C., Can.	D4	69
Alès, Fr.	H11	10
Alessandria, Italy	E3	14
Ålessano, Italy	J13	14
Ålesund, Nor.	E6	6
Aleutian Islands, is., Ak., U.S.	E3	79
Aleutian Range, mts., Ak., U.S.	D9	79
Aleutka, Russia	H24	24
Alevina, Mys, c., Russia	F24	24
Alex, Ok., U.S.	C4	113
Alexander, co., Il., U.S.	F4	90
Alexander, co., N.C., U.S.	B1	110
Alexander, Lake, l., Mn., U.S.	D4	100
Alexander Archipelago, is., Ak., U.S.	D12	79
Alexander Bay, S. Afr.	G3	44
Alexander City, Al., U.S.	C4	78
Alexander Island, i., Ant.	B6	47
Alexandra, N.Z.	F2	52
Alexandretta, Gulf of see İskenderun Körfezi, b., Tur.	A4	40
Alexandria, Ont., Can.	B10	73
Alexandria, In., U.S.	D6	91
Alexandria, Ky., U.S.	B5	94
Alexandria, La., U.S.	C3	95
Alexandria, Mn., U.S.	E3	100
Alexandria, Tn., U.S.	A5	119
Alexandria, Va., U.S.	B5	123
Alexandria see Al-Iskandarīyah, Egypt	B11	42
Alexandroúpolis, Grc.	I9	16
Alexis, Il., U.S.	B3	90
Alfalfa, co., Ok., U.S.	A3	113
Alfaro, Ec.	I3	58
Alfaro, Spain	C10	12
Alfarrás, Spain	D12	12
Al-Fāshir, Sudan	F11	42
Al-Fayyūm, Egypt	C12	42
Alfeld, Ger.	D9	8
Alfenas, Braz.	F6	57
Alfred, Ont., Can.	B10	73
Alfred, N.Y., U.S.	C3	109
Algarve, hist. reg., Port.	H3	12
Algeciras, Spain	I6	12
Algemesí, Spain	F11	12
Alger (Algiers), Alg.	A6	42
Alger, Oh., U.S.	B2	112
Alger, co., Mi., U.S.	B4	99
Algeria, ctry., Afr.	C6	42
Al-Ghayḍah, Yemen	E5	46
Alghero, Italy	I3	14
Al-Ghurdaqah, Egypt	C12	42
Algiers see Alger, Alg.	A6	42
Algoma, Wi., U.S.	D6	126
Algona, Ia., U.S.	A3	92
Algona, Wa., U.S.	B3	124
Algonac, Mi., U.S.	F8	99
Algonquin, Il., U.S.	A5	90
Algonquin Provincial Park, Ont., Can.	B6	73
Algood, Tn., U.S.	C8	119
Algorta, Ur.	C5	56
Al-Ḥadīthah, Iraq	B3	46
Al-Haffah, Syria	B5	40
Al-Hamād, pl., Sau. Ar.	B2	46
Alhama de Granada, Spain	H8	12
Alhambra, Ca., U.S.	m12	82
Al-Ḥarīq, Sau. Ar.	D4	46
Al-Harūj al-Aswad, hills, Libya	C9	42
Al-Ḥasakah, Syria	A7	40
Alhaurín el Grande, Spain	I7	12
Al-Hawrah, Yemen	F4	46
Al-Hijāz (Hejaz), reg., Sau. Ar.	C2	46
Al-Hillah, Iraq	B3	46
Al-Hirmil, Leb.	B5	40
Al-Hudaydah, Yemen	F3	46
Al-Hufūf, Sau. Ar.	C4	46
Aliaga, Spain	E11	12
Alicante, Spain	G11	12
Alice, Tx., U.S.	F3	120
Alice Lake, l., Mn., U.S.	C7	100
Alice Springs, Austl.	D6	50
Aliceville, Al., U.S.	B1	78
Alīgarh, India	G8	38
Alijos, Escollos, Mex.	E2	62
Alingsås, Swe.	H9	6
Alīpur Duār, India	G13	38
Aliquippa, Pa., U.S.	E1	115
Al-Iskandarīyah (Alexandria), Egypt	B11	42
Al-Ismā'īlīyah, Egypt	B12	42
Aliwal North, S. Afr.	H5	44
Alix, Alta., Can.	C4	68
Al-Jabal al-Akhḍar, mts., Oman	D6	46
Al-Jafr, Jord.	D5	40
Al-Jaghbūb, Libya	C10	42

Name	Map Ref	Page
Al-Jawf, Libya	D10	42
Al-Jawf, Sau. Ar.	C2	46
Al-Jazīrah, reg., Sudan	F12	42
Aljezur, Port.	H3	12
Al-Jīzah, Egypt	B12	42
Al-Junaynah, Sudan	F10	42
Aljustrel, Port.	H3	12
Alkali Lake, l., Nv., U.S.	B2	105
Alkali Lake, l., Or., U.S.	E6	114
Alkaline Lake, l., N.D., U.S.	C6	111
Al-Karak, Jord.	D4	40
Al-Kawm, Syria	B6	40
Al-Khābūr, stm., Syria	A7	40
Al-Khalīl, Isr. Occ.	D4	40
Al-Khandaq, Sudan	E12	42
Al-Khārijah, Egypt	C12	42
Al-Kharṭūm (Khartoum), Sudan	E12	42
Al-Khaṣab, Oman	C6	46
Al-Khubar, Sau. Ar.	C5	46
Al-Khums, Libya	B8	42
Alkmaar, Neth.	C4	8
Al-Kuwayt, Kuw.	C4	46
Allach-Jun', Russia	E21	24
Al-Lādhiqīyah (Latakia), Syria	B4	40
Allagash, stm., Me., U.S.	B3	96
Allagash Lake, l., Me., U.S.	B3	96
Allāhābād, India	H9	38
Allamakee, co., Ia., U.S.	A6	92
Allan, Sask., Can.	F2	75
Allanche, Fr.	G9	10
Allanmyo, Mya.	E3	34
Allardt, Tn., U.S.	C9	119
Allatoona Lake, res., Ga., U.S.	B2	87
Allegan, Mi., U.S.	F5	99
Allegan, co., Mi., U.S.	F5	99
Allegany, N.Y., U.S.	C2	109
Allegany, co., Md., U.S.	k13	97
Allegany, co., N.Y., U.S.	C2	109
Allegany Indian Reservation, N.Y., U.S.	C2	109
Alleghany, co., N.C., U.S.	A1	110
Alleghany, co., Va., U.S.	C2	123
Allegheny, co., Pa., U.S.	E2	115
Allegheny, stm., U.S.	E2	115
Allegheny Reservoir, res., U.S.	B4	115
Allemands, Lac Des, l., La., U.S.	E5	95
Allen, Ok., U.S.	C5	113
Allen, co., In., U.S.	B7	91
Allen, co., Ks., U.S.	E8	93
Allen, co., Ky., U.S.	D3	94
Allen, co., La., U.S.	D3	95
Allen, co., Oh., U.S.	B1	112
Allen, Mount, mtn., Ak., U.S.	C11	79
Allendale, N.J., U.S.	A4	107
Allendale, S.C., U.S.	E5	117
Allendale, co., S.C., U.S.	F5	117
Allen Park, Mi., U.S.	p15	99
Allenton, R.I., U.S.	E4	116
Allenton, Wi., U.S.	E5	126
Allentown, Pa., U.S.	E11	115
Allentsteig, Aus.	G15	8
Alleppey, India	H4	37
Aller, stm., Ger.	C9	8
Allerton, Point, c., Ma., U.S.	B6	98
Allgäuer Alpen, mts., Eur.	H10	8
Alliance, Ne., U.S.	B3	104
Alliance, Oh., U.S.	B4	112
Alligator, stm., N.C., U.S.	B6	110
Alligator Lake, l., Me., U.S.	D4	96
Allison, Ia., U.S.	B5	92
Allison, Pa., U.S.	G2	115
Allison Park, Pa., U.S.	h14	115
Alliston [Beeton Tecumseth and Tottenham], Ont., Can.	C5	73
Al-Līth, Sau. Ar.	D3	46
Allouez, Wi., U.S.	h9	126
Alloway Creek, stm., N.J., U.S.	D2	107
Al-Luḥayyah, Yemen	E3	46
Allumette Lake, l., Can.	B7	73
Allyn, Wa., U.S.	B3	124
Alma, Que., Can.	A6	74
Alma, Ar., U.S.	B1	81
Alma, Ga., U.S.	E4	87
Alma, Ks., U.S.	C7	93
Alma, Mi., U.S.	E6	99
Alma, Ne., U.S.	D6	104
Alma, Wi., U.S.	D2	126
Alma-Ata, Kaz.	I9	24
Almada, Port.	G2	12
Al-Madīnah (Medina), Sau. Ar.	D2	46
Al-Mafraq, Jord.	C5	40
Almagro, Spain	G8	12
Al-Manāmah, Bahr.	C5	46
Almanor, Lake, l., Ca., U.S.	B3	82
Almansa, Spain	G10	12
Al-Manṣūrah, Egypt	B12	42
Al-Marj, Libya	B10	42
Almas, Pico das, mtn., Braz.	F10	54
Al-Maṣīrah, i., Oman	D6	46
Al-Mawṣil, Iraq	A3	46
Al-Mayādīn, Syria	B7	40
Almazán, Spain	D9	12
Almelo, Neth.	C6	8
Almenara, Braz.	D8	57
Almendralejo, Spain	G5	12
Almería, Spain	I9	12
Al'metjevsk, Russia	G8	22
Al-Minyā, Egypt	C12	42
Almirante, Pan.	J6	64
Al-Mismīyah, Syria	C5	40
Almodôvar, Port.	H3	12
Almodóvar del Campo, Spain	G7	12
Almont, Mi., U.S.	F7	99
Almonte, Ont., Can.	B8	73
Almonte, Spain	H5	12
Almora, India	F8	38
Al-Mubarraz, Sau. Ar.	C4	46
Al-Mubarraz, Sau. Ar.	D4	46
Al-Muglad, Sudan	F11	42
Al-Muḥarraq, Bahr.	C5	46
Al-Mukallā, Yemen	F4	46
Al-Mukhā, Yemen	F3	46
Al-Muwayliḥ, Sau. Ar.	C2	46
Alnwick, Eng., U.K.	F11	7
Aloândia, Braz.	D4	57
Aloha, Or., U.S.	h12	114
Alor, Pulau, i., Indon.	G7	32
Álora, Spain	I7	12
Alor Setar, Malay.	K6	34
Aloysius, Mount, mtn., Austl.	E5	50
Alpena, Mi., U.S.	C7	99
Alpena, co., Mi., U.S.	D7	99
Alpharetta, Ga., U.S.	B2	87
Alphonse Island, i., Sey.	C10	44
Alpiarça, Port.	F3	12
Alpine, Az., U.S.	D6	80
Alpine, Tx., U.S.	D1	120
Alpine, Ut., U.S.	C4	121
Alpine, co., Ca., U.S.	C4	82
Alps, mts., Eur.	F9	4
Al-Qaḍārif, Sudan	F13	42
Al-Qāhirah (Cairo), Egypt	B12	42
Al-Qāmishlī, Syria	A7	40
Al-Qaryah ash-Sharqīyah, Libya	B8	42
Al-Qaryatayn, Syria	B5	40
Al-Qaṣr, Egypt	C11	42
Al-Qaṭīf, Sau. Ar.	C4	46
Al-Qaṭrūn, Libya	D8	42
Al-Qayṣūmah, Sau. Ar.	C4	46
Al-Qunayṭirah, Syria	C4	40
Al-Qunfudhah, Sau. Ar.	E3	46
Al-Quṣayr, Egypt	C12	42
Al-Quṭayfah, Syria	C5	40
Alsace, hist. reg., Fr.	E14	10
Alsasua, Spain	C9	12
Alsfeld, Ger.	E9	8
Alta, Nor.	B14	6
Alta, Ia., U.S.	B2	92
Altadena, Ca., U.S.	m12	82
Altagracia, Ven.	B7	58
Altagracia de Orituco, Ven.	C9	58
Altai, mts., Asia	B4	26
Altaj (Jesönbulag), Mong.	B6	26
Altamaha, stm., Ga., U.S.	E4	87
Altamira, Braz.	D8	54
Altamont, Il., U.S.	D5	90
Altamont, Ks., U.S.	E8	93
Altamont, Or., U.S.	E5	114
Altamont, Tn., U.S.	D8	119
Altamonte Springs, Fl., U.S.	D5	86
Altamura, Italy	I11	14
Altar, Mex.	B4	62
Altar, Desierto de, des., Mex.	B3	62
Altata, Mex.	E6	62
Altavista, Va., U.S.	C3	123
Altdorf, Switz.	F15	10
Altenburg, Ger.	E12	8
Altheimer, Ar., U.S.	C4	81
Altiplano, plat., S.A.	G5	54
Alto, Ga., U.S.	B3	87
Alto, N.M., U.S.	D4	108
Alto Araguaia, Braz.	D2	57
Alton, Il., U.S.	E3	90
Alton, Ia., U.S.	B2	92
Alton, Mo., U.S.	E6	102
Alton, N.H., U.S.	D4	106
Altona, Man., Can.	E3	70
Alton Bay, N.H., U.S.	D4	106
Altoona, Al., U.S.	A3	78
Altoona, Fl., U.S.	D5	86
Altoona, Ia., U.S.	C4	92
Altoona, Pa., U.S.	E5	115
Altoona, Wi., U.S.	D2	126
Alto Parnaíba, Braz.	E9	54
Altötting, Ger.	G12	8
Altun Shan, mts., China	D4	26
Alturas, Ca., U.S.	B3	82
Altus, Ok., U.S.	C2	113
Altus Air Force Base, mil., Ok., U.S.	C2	113
Altus Reservoir, res., Ok., U.S.	C2	113
Al-'Ubaylah, Sau. Ar.	D5	46
Al-Ubayyiḍ, Sudan	F12	42
'Alula, Som.	F5	46
Alum Bank, Pa., U.S.	F4	115
Alum Creek, stm., Oh., U.S.	k11	112
Al-Uqṣur (Luxor), Egypt	C12	42
Alva, Fl., U.S.	F5	86
Alva, Ok., U.S.	A3	113
Alvarado, Mex.	H12	62
Alvarado, Tx., U.S.	C4	120
Álvaro Obregón, Presa, res., Mex.	D5	62
Älvdalen, Swe.	F10	6
Alvin, Tx., U.S.	E5	120
Alvinston, Ont., Can.	E3	73
Älvkarleby, Swe.	F11	6
Alvord Lake, l., Or., U.S.	E8	114
Älvsbyn, Swe.	D13	6
Al-Wajh, Sau. Ar.	C2	46
Alwar, India	G7	38
Alzamaj, Russia	F13	24
Ama, La., U.S.	k11	95
Amadeus, Lake, l., Austl.	D6	50
Amadjuak Lake, l., N.W. Ter., Can.	C18	66
Amador, co., Ca., U.S.	C3	82
Amagansett, N.Y., U.S.	n16	109
Amagasaki, Japan	H8	30
Amakusa-nada, Japan	J2	30
Amakusa-shotō, is., Japan	J3	30
Åmål, Swe.	G9	6
Amalāpuram, India	D7	37
Amalfi, Italy	I9	14
Amalner, India	J6	38
Amambaí, stm., Braz.	G1	57
Amambaí, Serra de, mts., S.A.	H7	54
Amami-Ō-shima, i., Japan	w29	31b
Amami-shotō, is., Japan	x29	31b
Amana, Ia., U.S.	C6	92
Amantea, Italy	J11	14
Amares, Port.	D3	12
Amargosa, stm., U.S.	D5	82
Amargosa Desert, des., U.S.	G5	105
Amargosa Range, mts., U.S.	G5	105
Amarillo, Tx., U.S.	B2	120
Amatignak Island, i., Ak., U.S.	E4	79
Amazon (Solimões) (Amazonas), stm., S.A.	D7	54
Ambāla, India	E7	38
Ambarčik, Russia	D26	24
Ambāsamudram, India	H4	37
Ambato, Ec.	H3	58
Ambatolampy, Madag.	E9	44
Ambatondrazaka, Madag.	E9	44
Amberg, Ger.	F11	8
Ambérieu-en-Bugey, Fr.	G1	10
Ambert, Fr.	G10	10
Ambikāpur, India	I10	38
Ambilobe, Madag.	D9	44
Amble, Eng., U.K.	F11	7
Ambler, Pa., U.S.	F11	115
Amboise, Fr.	E7	10
Ambon, Indon.	F8	32
Ambositra, Madag.	F9	44
Ambovombe, Madag.	G9	44
Amboy, Il., U.S.	B4	90
Ambre, Cap d', c., Madag.	D9	44
Ambridge, Pa., U.S.	E1	115
Ambrières, Fr.	D6	10
Ambriz, Ang.	C2	44
Āmbūr, India	F5	37
Amchitka Island, i., Ak., U.S.	E3	79
Amchitka Pass, strt., Ak., U.S.	E4	79
Ameca, Mex.	G7	62
Amecameca [de Juárez], Mex.	H10	62
Amelia, La., U.S.	E4	95
Amelia, Oh., U.S.	C1	112
Amelia, co., Va., U.S.	C4	123
Amelia Court House, Va., U.S.	C5	123
Amelia Island, i., Fl., U.S.	k9	86
American, stm., Ca., U.S.	C3	82
Americana, Braz.	G5	57
American Falls, Id., U.S.	G6	89
American Falls Dam, Id., U.S.	G6	89
American Falls Reservoir, res., Id., U.S.	F5	89
American Fork, Ut., U.S.	C4	121
American Highland, plat., Ant.	B20	47
American Samoa, dep., Oc.	G1	2
Americus, Ga., U.S.	D2	87
Americus, Ks., U.S.	D7	93
Amersfoort, Neth.	C5	8
Amery, Wi., U.S.	C1	126
Ames, Ia., U.S.	B4	92
Amesbury, Ma., U.S.	A6	98
Amfilokhía, Grc.	K5	16
Ámfissa, Grc.	K6	16
Amga, Russia	E20	24
Amga, stm., Russia	E20	24
Amgun', stm., Russia	G21	24
Amherst, Ma., U.S.	B2	98
Amherst, N.H., U.S.	E3	106
Amherst, N.Y., U.S.	C2	109
Amherst, Oh., U.S.	A3	112
Amherst, Va., U.S.	C3	123
Amherst, Wi., U.S.	D4	126
Amherst, co., Va., U.S.	C3	123
Amherstburg, Ont., Can.	E1	73
Amherstdale, W.V., U.S.	n12	125
Amiens, Fr.	C9	10
Amīndīvi Islands, is., India	G2	37
Amirante Islands, is., Sey.	C10	44
Amisk Lake, l., Sask., Can.	C4	75
Amistad National Recreation Area, Tx., U.S.	E2	120
Amistad Reservoir, res., N.A.	C9	62
Amite, La., U.S.	D5	95
Amite, co., Ms., U.S.	D3	101
Amite, stm., La., U.S.	D5	95
Amity, Or., U.S.	B3	114
Amityville, N.Y., U.S.	E7	109
Amlia Island, i., Ak., U.S.	E5	79
'Ammān, Jord.	D4	40
Ämmänsaari, Fin.	D17	6
Ammon, Id., U.S.	F7	89
Ammonoosuc, stm., N.H., U.S.	B3	106
Amo, stm., Asia	G13	38
Amory, Ms., U.S.	B5	101
Amos, Que., Can.	k11	74
Åmot, Nor.	G6	6
Amoy see Xiamen, China	K7	28
Amposta, Spain	E12	12
Amrāvati, India	B4	37
Amreli, India	J4	38
Amritsar, India	E6	38
Amroha, India	F8	38
Amsterdam, Neth.	C4	8
Amsterdam, N.Y., U.S.	C6	109
Amstetten, Aus.	G14	8
Am Timan, Chad	F10	42
Amu Darya (Amudarja), stm., Asia	I10	22
Amukta Pass, strt., Ak., U.S.	E5	79
Amundsen Gulf, b., N.W. Ter., Can.	B8	66
Amundsen Sea, Ant.	B1	47
Amuntai, Indon.	F6	32
Amur (Heilongjiang), stm., Asia	G21	24
An, Mya.	E3	34
Anabar, stm., Russia	C16	24
Anaco, Ven.	C10	58
Anacoco, La., U.S.	C2	95
Anaconda, Mt., U.S.	D4	103
Anaconda Range, mts., Mt., U.S.	E3	103
Anacortes, Wa., U.S.	A3	124
Anacostia, stm., U.S.	C4	97
Anacostia, Northwest Branch, stm., Md., U.S.	B3	97
Anadarko, Ok., U.S.	B3	113
Anadyr', Russia	E29	24
Anadyr', stm., Russia	E29	24
Anadyrskij Zaliv, b., Russia	E30	24
Anagni, Italy	H8	14
Anaheim, Ca., U.S.	F5	82
Anahola, Hi., U.S.	A2	88
Anahuac, Tx., U.S.	E5	120
Ānai Mudi, mtn., India	G4	37
Anakāpalle, India	D7	37
Analalava, Madag.	D9	44
Ana María, Golfo de, b., Cuba	D8	64
Anambas, Kepulauan, is., Indon.	M9	34
Anamosa, Ia., U.S.	B6	92
Anamur, Tur.	H14	4
Anamur Burnu, c., Tur.	A3	40
Anan, Japan	I7	30
Ānand, India	I5	38
Anantapur, India	E4	37
Anantnāg (Islāmābād), India	D6	38
Anápolis, Braz.	D4	57
Anastasia Island, i., Fl., U.S.	C5	86
Añatuya, Arg.	B4	56
'Anazah, Jabal, mtn., Asia	C6	40
Ancaster, Ont., Can.	D4	73
Ancha, Sierra, mts., Az., U.S.	D4	80
Anchang, China	E9	28
Anchorage, Ak., U.S.	C10	79
Anchorage, Ky., U.S.	g11	94
Anchor Point, Ak., U.S.	D9	79
Anchor Point, c., Ak., U.S.	h15	79
Ancienne-Lorette, Que., Can.	C6	74
Anclote Keys, is., Fl., U.S.	D4	86
Ancona, Italy	F8	14
Ancud, Chile	E2	56
Ancud, Golfo de, b., Chile	E2	56
Andalucía, hist. reg., Spain	H7	12
Andalusia, Al., U.S.	D3	78
Andalusia, Il., U.S.	B3	90
Andaman Islands, is., India	H2	34
Andaman Sea, Asia	I3	34
Andermatt, Switz.	F15	10
Andernach, Ger.	E7	8
Anderson, Ak., U.S.	C10	79
Anderson, Ca., U.S.	B2	82
Anderson, In., U.S.	D6	91
Anderson, Mo., U.S.	E3	102
Anderson, S.C., U.S.	B2	117
Anderson, co., Ks., U.S.	D8	93
Anderson, co., Ky., U.S.	C4	94
Anderson, co., S.C., U.S.	B2	117
Anderson, co., Tn., U.S.	C9	119
Anderson, co., Tx., U.S.	D5	120
Anderson, stm., N.W. Ter., Can.	C7	66
Anderson, stm., In., U.S.	H4	91
Anderson, Mount, mtn., Wa., U.S.	B2	124
Anderson Ranch Reservoir, res., Id., U.S.	F3	89
Andes, mts., S.A.	F4	53
Andes, Lake, l., S.D., U.S.	D7	118
Andhra Pradesh, state, India	D5	37
Andižan, Uzb.	I12	22
Andkhvoy, Afg.	B1	38
Andong, China	C11	26
Andong, S. Kor.	D12	26
Andorra, And.	C13	12
Andorra, ctry., Eur.	G8	4
Andover, Ks., U.S.	g12	93
Andover, Ma., U.S.	A5	98
Andover, Mn., U.S.	m12	100
Andover, Oh., U.S.	A5	112
Andover Lake, res., Ct., U.S.	C6	84
Andradina, Braz.	F3	57
Andreanof Islands, is., Ak., U.S.	E4	79
Andrew, co., Mo., U.S.	B3	102
Andrew Island, i., N.S., Can.	D9	71
Andrews, In., U.S.	C6	91
Andrews, N.C., U.S.	f9	110
Andrews, S.C., U.S.	E8	117
Andrews, Tx., U.S.	C1	120
Andrews, co., Tx., U.S.	C1	120
Andrews Air Force Base, mil., Md., U.S.	C4	97
Andria, Italy	H11	14
Androka, Madag.	G8	44
Ándros, i., Grc.	L8	16
Androscoggin, co., Me., U.S.	D2	96
Androscoggin, stm., Me., U.S.	D2	96
Androscoggin Lake, l., Me., U.S.	D2	96
Andros Island, i., Bah.	B8	64
Andros Town, Bah.	B9	64
Andújar, Spain	G7	12
Anduo, China	D14	38
Anegada Passage, strt., N.A.	E16	64
Anfeng, China	C9	28
Anfu, China	H3	28
Ang'angxi, China	B11	26
Angara, stm., Russia	F13	24
Angarsk, Russia	G14	24
Ånge, Swe.	E10	6
Ángel, Salto (Angel Falls), wtfl, Ven.	E11	58
Ángel de la Guarda, Isla, i., Mex.	C3	62
Angeles, Phil.	q19	32
Angeles Point, c., Wa., U.S.	A2	124
Angel Falls see Ángel, Salto, wtfl, Ven.	E11	58
Ängelholm, Swe.	H9	6
Angelina, co., Tx., U.S.	D5	120
Angels Camp, Ca., U.S.	C3	82
Angermünde, Ger.	B13	8
Angers, Fr.	E6	10
Angerville, Fr.	D8	10
Angicos, Braz.	E11	54
Angier, N.C., U.S.	B4	110
Ângk Tasaôm, Camb.	I8	34
Angleton, Tx., U.S.	E5	120
Angmagssalik, Grnld.	C25	66
Angol, Chile	D2	56
Angola, In., U.S.	A8	91
Angola, N.Y., U.S.	C1	109
Angola, ctry., Afr.	D3	44
Angola Swamp, sw., N.C., U.S.	C5	110
Angoon, Ak., U.S.	D13	79
Angostura Reservoir, res., S.D., U.S.	D2	118
Angoulême, Fr.	G7	10
Angra dos Reis, Braz.	G6	57
Anguilla, Ms., U.S.	C3	101
Anguilla, dep., N.A.	E16	64
Anguille, Cape, c., Newf., Can.	E2	72
Angul, India	J11	38
Anhai, China	K7	28
Anhui, prov., China	E10	26
Aniak, Ak., U.S.	C8	79
Animas, stm., U.S.	D3	83
Animas Mountains, mts., N.M., U.S.	F1	108
Animas Peak, mtn., N.M., U.S.	F2	108
Animas Valley, val., N.M., U.S.	F1	108
Anita, Ia., U.S.	C3	92
Anjār, India	I4	38
Anji, China	E8	28
Anjiang, China	F9	26
Anjou, Que., Can.	p19	74
Anjouan, i., Com.	D8	44
Ankang, China	E8	26
Ankara, Tur.	H14	4
Ankavandra, Madag.	E9	44
Ankazoabo, Madag.	F8	44
Ankazobe, Madag.	E9	44
Ankeny, Ia., U.S.	C4	92
Anklesvar, India	B2	37
Anlong, China	B8	34
Anlu, China	D2	28
Ann, Cape, c., Ma., U.S.	A6	98
Anna, Il., U.S.	F4	90
Anna, Oh., U.S.	B1	112
Anna, Lake, res., Va., U.S.	B5	123
Annaba (Bône), Alg.	A7	42
Annaberg-Buchholz, Ger.	E12	8
An-Nabk, Syria	B5	40
An-Nafūd, des., Sau. Ar.	C3	46
An-Najaf, Iraq	B3	46
Anna Maria, Fl., U.S.	p10	86
Anna Maria Island, i., Fl., U.S.	q10	86
Annandale, Mn., U.S.	E4	100
Annandale, Va., U.S.	g12	123
Annapolis, Md., U.S.	C5	97
Annapolis, stm., N.S., Can.	E4	71
Annapolis Junction, Md., U.S.	B4	97
Annapolis Royal, N.S., Can.	E4	71
Annapurna, mtn., Nepal	F10	38
Ann Arbor, Mi., U.S.	F7	99
Anna Regina, Guy.	D13	58
An-Nāṣirīyah, Iraq	B4	46
Annawan, Il., U.S.	B4	90
Anne Arundel, co., Md., U.S.	B4	97
Annecy, Fr.	G13	10
Annemasse, Fr.	F13	10
Annette, Ak., U.S.	n24	79
Anniston, Al., U.S.	B4	78
Annobón, i., Eq. Gui.	B1	44
Annonay, Fr.	G11	10
An-Nuhūd, Sudan	F11	42
Annville, Pa., U.S.	F8	115
Anoka, Mn., U.S.	E5	100
Anoka, co., Mn., U.S.	E5	100
Anqing, China	E6	28
Anren, China	I2	28
Ansbach, Ger.	F10	8
Anshan, China	C11	26
Anshun, China	A8	34
Anson, Me., U.S.	D3	96
Anson, Tx., U.S.	C3	120
Anson, co., N.C., U.S.	B2	110
Ansonia, Ct., U.S.	D3	84
Ansonia, Oh., U.S.	B1	112
Ansted, W.V., U.S.	C3	125
Antakya, Tur.	H15	4
Antalaha, Madag.	D10	44
Antalya, Tur.	H14	4
Antalya, Gulf of see Antalya Körfezi, b., Tur.	A2	40
Antalya Körfezi, b., Tur.	A2	40
Antananarivo, Madag.	E9	44
Antarctica	A18	47
Antarctic Peninsula, pen., Ant.	C6	47
Antelope, co., Ne., U.S.	B7	104
Antelope Creek, stm., Wy., U.S.	C7	127
Antelope Island, i., Ut., U.S.	B3	121
Antelope Peak, mtn., Nv., U.S.	B7	105
Antelope Range, mts., Nv., U.S.	D7	105
Antelope Reservoir, res., Or., U.S.	E9	114
Antelope Wash, val., Nv., U.S.	D5	105
Antequera, Spain	H7	12
Antero, Mount, mtn., Co., U.S.	C4	83
Antero Reservoir, res., Co., U.S.	C5	83
Anthon, Ia., U.S.	B2	92
Anthony, Fl., U.S.	C4	86
Anthony, Ks., U.S.	E5	93
Anthony, N.M., U.S.	F3	108
Anthony, R.I., U.S.	D3	116
Anthony, Tx., U.S.	o11	120
Anthony Creek, stm., W.V., U.S.	D4	125
Anti Atlas, mts., Mor.	B4	42
Antibes, Fr.	I14	10
Anticosti, Île d', i., Que., Can.	k14	74
Antietam National Battlefield, hist., Md., U.S.	B2	97
Antigo, Wi., U.S.	C4	126
Antigua and Barbuda, ctry., N.A.	F17	64
Antioch, Ca., U.S.	h9	82
Antioch, Il., U.S.	A5	90
Antioch see Antakya, Tur.	H15	4
Antisana, vol., Ec.	H3	58
Antlers, Ok., U.S.	C6	113
Antofagasta, Chile	A2	56
Antofalla, Salar de, pl., Arg.	B3	56
Anton, Tx., U.S.	C1	120
Antongila, Helodrano, b., Madag.	E9	44
António Enes, Moz.	E7	44
Antônio João, Braz.	G1	57
Antonito, Co., U.S.	D5	83
Antora Peak, mtn., Co., U.S.	C4	83
Antrim, N.H., U.S.	D3	106
Antrim, co., Mi., U.S.	C5	99
Antrodoco, Italy	G8	14
Antsirabe, Madag.	E9	44
Antsiranana, Madag.	D9	44
Antwerp, Oh., U.S.	A1	112
Antwerp see Antwerpen, Bel.	D4	8
Antwerpen (Antwerp), Bel.	D4	8
Anuradhapura, Sri L.	H6	37
Anxi, China	C6	26
Anxi, China	J7	28
Anyang, China	D9	26
Anyi, China	G4	28
Anyuan, China	H2	28
Anyuan, China	J4	28
Anžero-Sudžensk, Russia	F11	24
Anzio, Italy	H7	14
Anžu, Ostrova, is., Russia	B23	24
Aoiz, Spain	C10	12
Aomori, Japan	B13	30
Aóös (Vijosë), stm., Eur.	J4	16
Aôral, Phnum, mtn., Camb.	H8	34
Aosta, Italy	D2	14
Aoukâr, reg., Maur.	E4	42
Aozou, Chad	D9	42
Apache, Ok., U.S.	C3	113
Apache, co., Az., U.S.	B6	80
Apache Junction, Az., U.S.	m9	80
Apache Peak, mtn., Az., U.S.	F5	80
Apalachee Bay, b., Fl., U.S.	B2	86
Apalachicola, Fl., U.S.	C2	86
Apalachicola, stm., Fl., U.S.	B1	86
Apalachicola Bay, b., Fl., U.S.	C2	86
Apaporis, stm., S.A.	H7	58
Aparri, Phil.	B7	32
Apatzingán [de la Constitución], Mex.	H8	62
Apeldoorn, Neth.	C5	8
Apennines see Appennino, mts., Italy	F7	14

Name	Map Ref	Page
Apex, N.C., U.S.	B4	110
Apishapa, stm., Co., U.S.	D6	83
Apizaco, Mex.	H10	62
Aplington, Ia., U.S.	B5	92
Apo, Mount, mtn., Phil.	D8	32
Apolda, Ger.	D11	8
Apollo, Pa., U.S.	E2	115
Apopka, Fl., U.S.	D5	86
Apopka, Lake, l., Fl., U.S.	D5	86
Aporé, Braz.	E2	57
Apostle Islands, is., Wi., U.S.	A3	126
Apostle Islands National Lakeshore, Wi., U.S.	A3	126
Appalachia, Va., U.S.	f9	123
Appalachian Mountains, mts., N.A.	D10	76
Appanoose, co., Ia., U.S.	D5	92
Appennino (Apennines), mts., Italy	F7	14
Appiano, Italy	C6	14
Apple, stm., Wi., U.S.	C1	126
Apple Creek, Oh., U.S.	B4	112
Applegate, Or., U.S.	E3	114
Applegate, stm., Or., U.S.	E3	114
Appleton, Mn., U.S.	E2	100
Appleton, Wi., U.S.	D5	126
Appleton City, Mo., U.S.	C3	102
Apple Valley, Ca., U.S.	E5	82
Apple Valley, Mn., U.S.	n12	100
Applewood, Co., U.S.	*B5	83
Appleyard, Wa., U.S.	B5	124
Appling, co., Ga., U.S.	E4	87
Appomattox, Va., U.S.	C4	123
Appomattox, co., Va., U.S.	C4	123
Appomattox, stm., Va., U.S.	C4	123
Appomattox Court House National Historical Park, Va., U.S.	C4	123
Apua Point, c., Hi., U.S.	D6	88
Apucarana, Braz.	G3	57
Apure, stm., Ven.	D9	58
Apurímac, stm., Peru	F4	54
Aqaba, Gulf of, b.	E4	40
Āqcheh, Afg.	B2	38
Āq Koprūk, Afg.	B2	38
Aquarius Mountains, mts., Az., U.S.	C2	80
Aquidauana, Braz.	H7	54
Arab, Al., U.S.	A3	78
'Arab, Baḥr al-, stm., Sudan	G11	42
Arabelo, Ven.	E10	58
Arabi, La., U.S.	k11	95
Arabian Desert see Sharqīyah, Aṣ-Ṣaḥrā' al-, des., Egypt	C12	42
Arabian Sea	E17	2
Aracaju, Braz.	F11	54
Aracati, Braz.	D11	54
Araçatuba, Braz.	F3	57
Aracena, Spain	H5	12
Araçuaí, Braz.	D7	57
Arad, Rom.	C5	16
Arafura Sea	G9	32
Arago, Cape, c., Or., U.S.	D2	114
Aragon, Ga., U.S.	B1	87
Aragón, hist. reg., Spain	D11	12
Araguacema, Braz.	E9	54
Aragua de Barcelona, Ven.	C10	58
Araguari, Braz.	E4	57
Arak, Alg.	C6	42
Arāk, Iran	B4	46
Arakan Yoma, mts., Mya.	E3	34
Aral Sea, Asia	H10	22
Arambaza, Col.	I6	58
Aranda de Duero, Spain	D8	12
Arandas, Mex.	G8	62
Ārani, India	F5	37
Aran Island, i., Ire.	G4	7
Aran Islands, is., Ire.	H3	7
Aranjuez, Spain	E8	12
Aransas, co., Tx., U.S.	E4	120
Aransas Bay, b., Tx., U.S.	E4	120
Aransas Pass, Tx., U.S.	F4	120
Aranyaprathet, Thai.	H7	34
Arao, Japan	I3	30
Arapaho, Ok., U.S.	B3	113
Arapahoe, Ne., U.S.	D6	104
Arapahoe, co., Co., U.S.	B6	83
Arapiraca, Braz.	E11	54
Arapongas, Braz.	G3	57
Araraquara, Braz.	F4	57
Ararat, Austl.	G8	50
Ararat, Mount see Ağrı Dağı, mtn., Tur.	H16	4
Arauca, Col.	D7	58
Araure, Ven.	C8	58
Arāvalli Range, mts., India	H5	38
Araxá, Braz.	E5	57
Araya, Punta de, c., Ven.	B10	58
Arba Minch, Eth.	G2	46
Arbois, Fr.	F12	10
Arbon, Switz.	E16	10
Arborg, Man., Can.	D3	70
Arbroath, Scot., U.K.	E10	7
Arbuckle, Lake, l., Fl., U.S.	E5	86
Arbuckle Mountains, mts., Ok., U.S.	C4	113
Arbuckles, Lake of the, res., Ok., U.S.	C5	113
Arcachon, Fr.	H5	10
Arcade, Ca., U.S.	*C3	82
Arcade, Ga., U.S.	B3	87
Arcade, N.Y., U.S.	C2	109
Arcadia, Ca., U.S.	m12	82
Arcadia, Fl., U.S.	E5	86
Arcadia, In., U.S.	D5	91
Arcadia, La., U.S.	B3	95
Arcadia, Mo., U.S.	D7	102
Arcadia, S.C., U.S.	B4	117
Arcadia, Wi., U.S.	D2	126
Arcanum, Oh., U.S.	C1	112
Arcata, Ca., U.S.	B1	82
Arc Dome, mtn., Nv., U.S.	E4	105
Archangel'sk, Russia	E6	22
Archbald, Pa., U.S.	m18	115
Archbold, Oh., U.S.	A1	112
Archdale, N.C., U.S.	B3	110
Archer, Fl., U.S.	C4	86
Archer, co., Tx., U.S.	C3	120
Archer City, Tx., U.S.	C3	120
Arches National Park, Ut., U.S.	E6	121
Archidona, Spain	H7	12
Archie, Mo., U.S.	C3	102
Archuleta, co., Co., U.S.	D3	83
Arcis-sur-Aube, Fr.	D11	10
Arco, Id., U.S.	F5	89
Arco de Baúlhe, Port.	D4	12
Arcola, Il., U.S.	D5	90
Arcos de la Frontera, Spain	I6	12
Arctic Bay, N.W. Ter., Can.	B15	66
Arctic Ocean	A32	128
Arda, stm., Eur.	H9	16
Ardabīl, Iran	J7	22
Ardalstangen, Nor.	F6	6
Ardennes, reg., Eur.	E5	8
Ardlussa, Scot., U.K.	E7	7
Ardmore, Al., U.S.	A3	78
Ardmore, In., U.S.	A5	91
Ardmore, Ok., U.S.	C4	113
Ardmore, Tn., U.S.	B5	119
Ardsley, N.Y., U.S.	g13	109
Åre, Swe.	E9	6
Arecibo, P.R.	E14	64
Arena, Point, c., Ca., U.S.	C2	82
Arena, Punta, c., Mex.	F5	62
Arenac, co., Mi., U.S.	D7	99
Arenas de San Pedro, Spain	E6	12
Arendal, Nor.	G7	6
Arequipa, Peru	G4	54
Arès, Fr.	H5	10
Arévalo, Spain	D7	12
Arezzo, Italy	F6	14
Arganda, Spain	E8	12
Arga-Sala, stm., Russia	D15	24
Argelès-Gazost, Fr.	I7	10
Argenta, Italy	E6	14
Argenta, Il., U.S.	D5	90
Argentan, Fr.	D6	10
Argentat, Fr.	G8	10
Argentera, mtn., Italy	E2	14
Argentina, ctry., S.A.	C4	56
Argentino, Lago, l., Arg.	G2	56
Argenton-sur-Creuse, Fr.	F8	10
Argonne, reg., Fr.	C12	10
Árgos, Grc.	L6	16
Argos, In., U.S.	B5	91
Argostólion, Grc.	K4	16
Argun' (Ergun), stm., Asia	A11	26
Argyle, Mn., U.S.	B2	100
Argyle, Wi., U.S.	F4	126
Århus, Den.	H8	6
Ariano Irpino, Italy	H10	14
Arica, Chile	G4	54
Arica, Col.	I7	58
Arichat, N.S., Can.	D8	71
Arid, Cape, c., Austl.	F4	50
Arīḥā (Jericho), Jord.	D4	40
Arikaree, stm., U.S.	B8	83
Arima, Trin.	I17	64
Arinos, stm., Braz.	F7	54
Aripuanã, stm., Braz.	E7	54
Ariquemes, Braz.	E6	54
Arismendi, Ven.	C8	58
Aristazabal Island, i., B.C., Can.	C3	69
Ariton, Al., U.S.	D4	78
Arizona, state, U.S.	C4	80
Arizona Sunsites, Az., U.S.	F6	80
Arizpe, Mex.	B4	62
Arjay, Ky., U.S.	D6	94
Arjeplog, Swe.	C11	6
Arjona, Col.	B5	58
Arkabutla Lake, res., Ms., U.S.	A4	101
Arkadelphia, Ar., U.S.	C2	81
Arkansas, co., Ar., U.S.	C4	81
Arkansas, state, U.S.	C3	81
Arkansas, stm., U.S.	D8	76
Arkansas City, Ks., U.S.	E6	93
Arklow, Ire.	I6	7
Arkoma, Ok., U.S.	B7	113
Arkonam, India	F5	37
Arktičeskogo Instituta, Ostrova, is., Russia	B10	24
Arles, Fr.	I11	10
Arlington, Ga., U.S.	E2	87
Arlington, Ma., U.S.	B5	98
Arlington, Mn., U.S.	F4	100
Arlington, Ne., U.S.	C9	104
Arlington, N.Y., U.S.	D7	109
Arlington, N.C., U.S.	A2	110
Arlington, Oh., U.S.	B2	112
Arlington, S.C., U.S.	B3	117
Arlington, S.D., U.S.	C8	118
Arlington, Tn., U.S.	B2	119
Arlington, Tx., U.S.	n9	120
Arlington, Vt., U.S.	E2	122
Arlington, Va., U.S.	B5	123
Arlington, Wa., U.S.	A3	124
Arlington, co., Va., U.S.	g12	123
Arlington, Lake, res., Tx., U.S.	n9	120
Arlington Heights, Il., U.S.	A5	90
Arma, Ks., U.S.	E9	93
Armada, Mi., U.S.	F8	99
Armagh, Que., Can.	C7	74
Armavir, Russia	H6	22
Armenia, Col.	E5	58
Armenia, ctry., Asia	I6	22
Armentières, Fr.	B9	10
Armidale, Austl.	F10	50
Armijo, N.M., U.S.	k7	108
Armour, S.D., U.S.	D7	118
Armstrong, B.C., Can.	D8	69
Armstrong, Ia., U.S.	A3	92
Armstrong, co., Pa., U.S.	E2	115
Armstrong, co., Tx., U.S.	B2	120
Armstrong, Mount, mtn., Yukon, Can.	D6	66
Armstrong Creek, stm., W.V., U.S.	m13	125
Arnaudville, La., U.S.	D4	95
Arnedo, Spain	C9	12
Arnett, W.V., U.S.	D3	125
Arnhem, Neth.	D5	8
Arnhem, Cape, c., Austl.	B7	50
Arnhem Land, reg., Austl.	B6	50
Árnissa, Grc.	I5	16
Arno, stm., Italy	F5	14
Arnold, Mn., U.S.	D6	100
Arnold, Mo., U.S.	C7	102
Arnold, Ne., U.S.	C5	104
Arnold, Pa., U.S.	h14	115
Arnold Mills, R.I., U.S.	B4	116
Arnold Mills Reservoir, res., R.I., U.S.	B4	116
Arnold's Cove, Newf., Can.	E4	72
Arnolds Park, Ia., U.S.	A2	92
Arnprior, Ont., Can.	B8	73
Arnsberg, Ger.	D8	8
Arnstadt, Ger.	E10	8
Arona, Italy	D3	14
Aroostook, co., Me., U.S.	B4	96
Arpajon, Fr.	D9	10
Ar-Rab' al-Khālī, des., Asia	D5	46
Arrah, India	H11	38
Ar-Rahad, Sudan	F12	42
Ar-Ramadi, Iraq	B3	46
Ar-Ramthā, Jord.	C4	40
Arran, Island of, i., Scot., U.K.	F7	7
Ar-Raqqah, Syria	B6	40
Arras, Fr.	B9	10
Arrecife, Spain	C3	42
Arriaga, Mex.	I13	62
Ar-Riyāḍ (Riyadh), Sau. Ar.	D4	46
Arronches, Port.	F4	12
Arrowhead Mountain Lake, res., Vt., U.S.	B2	122
Arrowrock Reservoir, res., Id., U.S.	F3	89
Arrowwood Lake, res., N.D., U.S.	B7	111
Arroyo de la Luz, Spain	F5	12
Arroyo Grande, Ca., U.S.	E3	82
Ar-Ruṣayriṣ, Sudan	F12	42
Ar-Ruṭbah, Iraq	C7	40
Arsenjev, Russia	I20	24
Árta, Grc.	J4	16
Artá, Spain	F15	12
Artemisa, Cuba	C6	64
Artemus, Ky., U.S.	D6	94
Artenay, Fr.	D8	10
Arter, Mount, mtn., Wy., U.S.	D4	127
Artesia, N.M., U.S.	E5	108
Arthabaska, Que., Can.	C6	74
Arthur, Ont., Can.	D4	73
Arthur, Il., U.S.	D5	90
Arthur, co., Ne., U.S.	C4	104
Arthur, Lake, l., La., U.S.	D3	95
Arthur, Lake, res., Pa., U.S.	E1	115
Arthur Kill, stm., N.J., U.S.	k8	107
Arthurs Town, Bah.	B10	64
Artigas, Ur.	C5	56
Art'om, Russia	I20	24
Art'omovsk, Russia	G12	24
Artvin, Tur.	G16	4
Aru, Kepulauan, is., Indon.	G9	32
Arua, Ug.	H12	42
Aruanã, Braz.	C3	57
Aruba, dep., N.A.	H13	64
Arunachal Pradesh, ter., India	F16	38
Aruppukkottai, India	H5	37
Arusha, Tan.	B7	44
Aruwimi, stm., Zaire	A5	44
Arvada, Co., U.S.	B5	83
Arvi, India	B5	37
Arvidsjaur, Swe.	D12	6
Arvika, Swe.	G9	6
Arvin, Ca., U.S.	E4	82
Arvon, Mount, mtn., Mi., U.S.	B2	99
Arvonia, Va., U.S.	C4	123
Arzachena, Italy	H4	14
Arzignano, Italy	D6	14
Arzúa, Spain	C3	12
Asadābād, Afg.	C4	38
Asahi-dake, mtn., Japan	p20	30a
Asahikawa, Japan	p20	30a
Asansol, India	I12	38
Asbestos, Que., Can.	D6	74
Asbury Park, N.J., U.S.	C4	107
Ascensión, Mex.	E10	62
Ascension, co., La., U.S.	D5	95
Ascensión, Bahía de la, b., Mex.	H16	62
Aščhabad, Turk.	J9	22
Aschaffenburg, Ger.	F9	8
Aschersleben, Ger.	D11	8
Asciano, Italy	F6	14
Ascoli Piceno, Italy	G8	14
Ascoli Satriano, Italy	H10	14
Aseb, Erit.	F3	46
Åsele, Swe.	D11	6
Åsen, Nor.	E8	6
Asenovgrad, Bul.	G8	16
Ashaway, R.I., U.S.	F1	116
Ashburn, Ga., U.S.	E3	87
Ashburton, N.Z.	E3	52
Ashcroft, B.C., Can.	D7	69
Ashdown, Ar., U.S.	D1	81
Ashe, co., N.C., U.S.	A1	110
Asheboro, N.C., U.S.	B3	110
Ashepoo, stm., S.C., U.S.	F6	117
Ashern, Man., Can.	D2	70
Asherton, Tx., U.S.	E3	120
Asheville, N.C., U.S.	f10	110
Ash Flat, Ar., U.S.	A4	81
Ashford, Eng., U.K.	J13	7
Ashford, Al., U.S.	D4	78
Ashford, W.V., U.S.	m12	125
Ash Grove, Mo., U.S.	D4	102
Ashibetsu, Japan	p20	30a
Ashikaga, Japan	F12	30
Ashizuri-zaki, c., Japan	J6	30
Ashkhabad see Aščhabad, Turk.	J9	22
Ashland, Al., U.S.	B4	78
Ashland, Il., U.S.	D3	90
Ashland, Ks., U.S.	E4	93
Ashland, Ky., U.S.	B7	94
Ashland, Me., U.S.	B4	96
Ashland, Ma., U.S.	g10	98
Ashland, Mo., U.S.	C5	102
Ashland, Ne., U.S.	C9	104
Ashland, N.H., U.S.	C3	106
Ashland, Oh., U.S.	B3	112
Ashland, Or., U.S.	E4	114
Ashland, Pa., U.S.	E9	115
Ashland, Va., U.S.	C5	123
Ashland, Wi., U.S.	B3	126
Ashland, co., Oh., U.S.	B3	112
Ashland, co., Wi., U.S.	B3	126
Ashland, Mount, mtn., Or., U.S.	E4	114
Ashland City, Tn., U.S.	A4	119
Ashland Reservoir, res., Ma., U.S.	h10	98
Ashley, In., U.S.	A7	91
Ashley, N.D., U.S.	C6	111
Ashley, Oh., U.S.	B3	112
Ashley, Pa., U.S.	n17	115
Ashley, co., Ar., U.S.	D4	81
Ashley, stm., S.C., U.S.	F7	117
Ashley Creek, stm., Ut., U.S.	C6	121
Ashmore, Il., U.S.	D5	90
Ashokan Reservoir, res., N.Y., U.S.	D6	109
Ashqelon, Isr.	D4	40
Ash-Shaqrā', Sau. Ar.	C4	46
Ash-Shāriqah, U.A.E.	C6	46
Ash-Shawbak, Jord.	D4	40
Ashtabula, Oh., U.S.	A5	112
Ashtabula, co., Oh., U.S.	A5	112
Ashtabula, Lake, res., N.D., U.S.	B8	111
Ashton, Id., U.S.	E7	89
Ashton, Il., U.S.	B4	90
Ashton, Md., U.S.	B3	97
Ashton, R.I., U.S.	B4	116
Ashuanipi Lake, l., Newf., Can.	h8	72
Ashuelot, stm., N.H., U.S.	E2	106
Ashville, Al., U.S.	B3	78
Ashville, Oh., U.S.	C3	112
Ashwaubenon, Wi., U.S.	D5	126
Asia	D12	20
Asia, Kepulauan, is., Indon.	E9	32
Asia Minor, reg., Tur.	H14	4
Asino, Russia	F11	24
'Asīr, reg., Sau. Ar.	E3	46
Asir, Ras, c., Som.	F5	46
Askham, S. Afr.	G4	44
Askvoll, Nor.	F5	6
Asmara see Asmera, Erit.	E2	46
Asmera, Erit.	E2	46
Asotin, Wa., U.S.	C8	124
Asotin, co., Wa., U.S.	C8	124
Asotin Creek, stm., Wa., U.S.	C8	124
Aspang Markt, Aus.	H16	8
Aspen, Co., U.S.	B4	83
Aspen Butte, mtn., Or., U.S.	E4	114
Aspermont, Tx., U.S.	C2	120
Aspinwall, Pa., U.S.	k14	115
Aspiring, Mount, mtn., N.Z.	F2	52
Aspres-sur-Buëch, Fr.	H12	10
Aspy Bay, b., N.S., Can.	C9	71
Assabet, stm., Ma., U.S.	g9	98
Aṣ-Ṣabyā, Sau. Ar.	E3	46
As-Sallūm, Egypt	B11	42
As-Salṭ, Jord.	C4	40
Assam, state, India	G15	38
As-Samāwah, Iraq	B4	46
Assateague Island, i., U.S.	D7	97
Assateague Island National Seashore, U.S.	D7	97
Assawoman Bay, b., Md., U.S.	D7	97
Assen, Neth.	C6	8
Assiniboine, stm., Can.	E2	70
Assiniboine, Mount, mtn., Can.	D3	68
Assis, Braz.	G3	57
Assisi, Italy	F7	14
As-Sulaymānīyah, Iraq	A4	46
As-Sulaymānīyah, Sau. Ar.	D4	46
As-Sulayyil, Sau. Ar.	D4	46
Assumption, Il., U.S.	D4	90
Assumption, co., La., U.S.	E4	95
Assumption Island, i., Sey.	C9	44
Aṣ-Ṣuwār, Syria	B7	40
As-Suwaydā', Syria	C5	40
As-Suways (Suez), Egypt	C12	42
Asti, Italy	E3	14
Astorga, Spain	C5	12
Astoria, Il., U.S.	C3	90
Astoria, Or., U.S.	A3	114
Astove Island, i., Sey.	D9	44
Astrachan', Russia	H7	22
Astrakhan see Astrachan', Russia	H7	22
Astudillo, Spain	C7	12
Asunción, Para.	B5	56
Aswān, Egypt	D12	42
Aswān High Dam, Egypt	D12	42
Asyūṭ, Egypt	C12	42
Atacama, Desierto de, des., Chile	A3	56
Atacama, Puna de, plat., S.A.	A3	56
Atacama, Salar de, pl., Chile	A3	56
Ataco, Col.	F5	58
Atakpamé, Togo	G6	42
Atami, Japan	G12	30
Atar, Maur.	D3	42
Atascadero, Ca., U.S.	E3	82
Atascosa, co., Tx., U.S.	E3	120
'Aṭbarah, Sudan	E12	42
'Aṭbarah (Atbara), stm., Afr.	E12	42
Atchafalaya, stm., La., U.S.	D4	95
Atchafalaya Bay, b., La., U.S.	E4	95
Atchison, Ks., U.S.	C8	93
Atchison, co., Ks., U.S.	C8	93
Atchison, co., Mo., U.S.	A2	102
Ateca, Spain	D10	12
Aterau, Kaz.	H8	22
Athabasca, Alta., Can.	B4	68
Athabasca, stm., Alta., Can.	f8	68
Athabasca, Lake, l., Can.	m7	75
Athena, Or., U.S.	B8	114
Athenry, Ire.	H4	7
Athens, Ont., Can.	C9	73
Athens, Al., U.S.	A3	78
Athens, Ga., U.S.	C3	87
Athens, Il., U.S.	D4	90
Athens, Mi., U.S.	F5	99
Athens, N.Y., U.S.	C7	109
Athens, Oh., U.S.	C3	112
Athens, Pa., U.S.	C8	115
Athens, Tn., U.S.	D9	119
Athens, Tx., U.S.	C5	120
Athens, W.V., U.S.	D3	125
Athens, Wi., U.S.	C3	126
Athens, co., Oh., U.S.	C3	112
Athens see Athínai, Grc.	L7	16
Athínai (Athens), Grc.	L7	16
Athlone, Ire.	H5	7
Athol, Ma., U.S.	A3	98
Ati, Chad	F9	42
Atienza, Spain	D9	12
Atik Lake, l., Man., Can.	B4	70
Atikonak Lake, l., Newf., Can.	h8	72
Atka Island, i., Ak., U.S.	E5	79
Atkins, Ar., U.S.	B3	81
Atkins, Va., U.S.	D1	123
Atkinson, Il., U.S.	B3	90
Atkinson, Ne., U.S.	B7	104
Atkinson, N.H., U.S.	E4	106
Atkinson, co., Ga., U.S.	E4	87
Atlanta, Ga., U.S.	C2	87
Atlanta, Il., U.S.	C4	90
Atlanta, In., U.S.	D5	91
Atlanta, Mi., U.S.	C6	99
Atlanta, Tx., U.S.	C5	120
Atlantic, Ia., U.S.	C2	92
Atlantic, N.C., U.S.	C6	110
Atlantic, co., N.J., U.S.	E3	107
Atlantic Beach, Fl., U.S.	m9	86
Atlantic City, N.J., U.S.	E4	107
Atlantic Highlands, N.J., U.S.	C4	107
Atlantic Ocean	G11	2
Atlantic Peak, mtn., Wy., U.S.	D3	127
Atlas Mountains, mts., Afr.	B5	42
Atlas Saharien, mts., Alg.	B6	42
Atmore, Al., U.S.	D2	78
Atna Peak, mtn., B.C., Can.	C3	69
Atoka, Ok., U.S.	C5	113
Atoka, Tn., U.S.	B2	119
Atoka, co., Ok., U.S.	C5	113
Atoka Reservoir, res., Ok., U.S.	C5	113
Atotonilco el Alto, Mex.	G8	62
Atrato, stm., Col.	D4	58
Aṭ-Ṭafīlah, Jord.	D4	40
Aṭ-Ṭā'if, Sau. Ar.	D3	46
Attala, co., Ms., U.S.	B4	101
Attalla, Al., U.S.	A3	78
Attawapiskat, stm., Ont., Can.	n18	73
Attica, In., U.S.	D3	91
Attica, Ks., U.S.	E5	93
Attica, N.Y., U.S.	C2	109
Attica, Oh., U.S.	A3	112
Attleboro, Ma., U.S.	C5	98
Attopeu, Laos	G9	34
Attow, Ben, mtn., Scot., U.K.	D7	7
Attu Island, i., Ak., U.S.	E2	79
Āttūr, India	G5	37
Atwater, Ca., U.S.	D3	82
Atwater, Mn., U.S.	E4	100
Atwood, Ont., Can.	D3	73
Atwood, Il., U.S.	D5	90
Atwood, Ks., U.S.	C2	93
Atwood, Tn., U.S.	B3	119
Atwood Lake, res., Oh., U.S.	B4	112
Auau Channel, strt., Hi., U.S.	C5	88
Aubagne, Fr.	I12	10
Aube, stm., Fr.	D11	10
Auberry, Ca., U.S.	D4	82
Aubigny-sur-Nère, Fr.	E9	10
Aubin, Fr.	H9	10
Auburn, Al., U.S.	C4	78
Auburn, Ca., U.S.	C3	82
Auburn, Ga., U.S.	B3	87
Auburn, Il., U.S.	D4	90
Auburn, In., U.S.	B7	91
Auburn, Ks., U.S.	D8	93
Auburn, Ky., U.S.	D3	94
Auburn, Me., U.S.	D2	96
Auburn, Ma., U.S.	B4	98
Auburn, Mi., U.S.	E6	99
Auburn, Ne., U.S.	D10	104
Auburn, N.Y., U.S.	C4	109
Auburn, Wa., U.S.	B3	124
Auburndale, Fl., U.S.	D5	86
Auburn Heights, Mi., U.S.	F7	99
Aubusson, Fr.	G9	10
Auch, Fr.	I7	10
Aucilla, stm., Fl., U.S.	B3	86
Auckland, N.Z.	B5	52
Audincourt, Fr.	E13	10
Audrain, co., Mo., U.S.	B6	102
Audubon, Ia., U.S.	C3	92
Audubon, N.J., U.S.	D2	107
Audubon, co., Ia., U.S.	C2	92
Aue, Ger.	E12	8
Auglaize, co., Oh., U.S.	B1	112
Auglaize, stm., Oh., U.S.	A1	112
Au Gres, Mi., U.S.	D7	99
Augsburg, Ger.	G10	8
Augusta, Italy	L10	14
Augusta, Ar., U.S.	B4	81
Augusta, Ga., U.S.	C5	87
Augusta, Ks., U.S.	E7	93
Augusta, Ky., U.S.	B6	94
Augusta, Me., U.S.	D3	96
Augusta, Mi., U.S.	F5	99
Augusta, Wi., U.S.	D2	126
Augusta, co., Va., U.S.	B3	123
Augustus, Mount, mtn., Austl.	D3	50
Aulander, N.C., U.S.	A5	110
Auld, Lake, l., Austl.	D4	50
Aulneau Peninsula, pen., Ont., Can.	E4	70
Ault, Co., U.S.	A6	83
Aumont-Aubrac, Fr.	H10	10
Aumsville, Or., U.S.	k12	114
Aurangābād, India	C3	37
Auray, Fr.	E4	10
Aurelia, Ia., U.S.	B2	92
Aurich, Ger.	B7	8
Aurilândia, Braz.	F3	57
Aurillac, Fr.	H9	10
Aurora, Ont., Can.	C5	73
Aurora, Co., U.S.	B6	83
Aurora, Il., U.S.	B5	90
Aurora, In., U.S.	F8	91
Aurora, Mn., U.S.	C6	100
Aurora, Mo., U.S.	E4	102
Aurora, Ne., U.S.	D7	104
Aurora, Oh., U.S.	A4	112
Aurora, S.D., U.S.	C9	118
Aurora, Ut., U.S.	E4	121
Aurora, co., S.D., U.S.	D7	118
Aus, Nmb.	G3	44
Au Sable, Mi., U.S.	D7	99
Au Sable, stm., Mi., U.S.	D6	99
Ausable, stm., N.Y., U.S.	f11	109
Au Sable Forks, N.Y., U.S.	f11	109
Au Sable Point, c., Mi., U.S.	D7	99
Au Sable Point, c., Mi., U.S.	B4	99
Auschwitz see Oświęcim, Pol.	E19	8
Austell, Ga., U.S.	h7	87
Austin, In., U.S.	G6	91

Name — Map Ref — Page

Austin, Mn., U.S. G6 100
Austin, Nv., U.S. D4 105
Austin, Tx., U.S. D4 120
Austin, co., Tx., U.S. E4 120
Austin, Lake, l., Austl. E3 50
Austin Channel, strt., N.W. Ter., Can. A12 66
Austintown, Oh., U.S. A5 112
Austinville, Va., U.S. D2 123
Australia, ctry., Oc. D6 50
Australian Capital Territory, ter., Austl. G9 50
Austria, ctry., Eur. F10 4
Autauga, co., Al., U.S. C3 78
Autaugaville, Al., U.S. C3 78
Autlán de Navarro, Mex. H7 62
Autun, Fr. F11 10
Auxerre, Fr. E10 10
Auxier, Ky., U.S. C7 94
Auxi-le-Château, Fr. B9 10
Auxonne, Fr. E12 10
Auxvasse, Mo., U.S. B6 102
Auyán Tepuy, mtn., Ven. E11 58
Auzances, Fr. F9 10
Ava, Mo., U.S. E5 102
Avallon, Fr. E10 10
Avalon, Ca., U.S. F4 82
Avalon, Pa., U.S. h13 115
Avalon, Lake, res., N.M., U.S. E5 108
Avalon Peninsula, pen., Newf., Can. E5 72
Avaré, Braz. G4 57
Aveiro, Port. E3 12
Avella, Pa., U.S. F1 115
Avellaneda, Arg. C5 56
Avellino, Italy I9 14
Avenal, Ca., U.S. E3 82
Avery, co., N.C., U.S. e11 110
Aves, Islas de, is., Ven. A9 58
Avesnes, Fr. B10 10
Avesta, Swe. F11 6
Avezzano, Italy G8 14
Aviemore, Scot., U.K. D9 7
Avignon, Fr. I11 10
Ávila, Spain E7 12
Avilés, Spain B6 12
Avilla, In., U.S. B7 91
Avis, Pa., U.S. D7 115
Avispa, Cerro, mtn., Ven. G10 58
Aviston, Il., U.S. E4 90
Aviz, Port. F4 12
Avoca, Ia., U.S. C2 92
Avoca, Pa., U.S. m18 115
Avola, Italy M10 14
Avon, Ct., U.S. B4 84
Avon, Il., U.S. C3 90
Avon, Ma., U.S. B5 98
Avon, Mn., U.S. E4 100
Avon, N.Y., U.S. C3 109
Avon, Oh., U.S. A3 112
Avondale, Az., U.S. D3 80
Avondale, Co., U.S. C6 83
Avondale, Pa., U.S. G10 115
Avondale Estates, Ga., U.S. h8 87
Avon Lake, Ia., U.S. e8 92
Avon Lake, Oh., U.S. A3 112
Avonmore, Pa., U.S. E3 115
Avon Park, Fl., U.S. E5 86
Avoyelles, co., La., U.S. C3 95
Avranches, Fr. D5 10
Awaji-shima, i., Japan H7 30
Awash, stm., Eth. F3 46
Awbārī, Libya C8 42
Awe, Loch, l., Scot., U.K. E7 7
Awjilah, Libya C10 42
Axiós (Vardar), stm., Eur. I6 16
Axis, Al., U.S. E1 78
Axtell, Ne., U.S. D6 104
Ayabe, Japan G8 30
Ayacucho, Peru F4 54
Ayamonte, Spain H4 12
Ayapel, Col. C5 58
Ayaviri, Peru F4 54
Āybak, Afg. B3 38
Ayden, N.C., U.S. B5 110
Aydın, Tur. H13 4
Ayer, Ma., U.S. A4 98
Ayers Cliff, Que., Can. D5 74
Ayeyarwady (Irrawaddy), stm., Mya. G3 34
Áyion Óros, pen., Grc. I8 16
Áyios Nikólaos, Grc. N9 16
Aylesbury, Eng., U.K. J12 7
Aylesford, N.S., Can. D5 71
Aylmer, Mount, mtn., Alta., Can. D3 68
Aylmer East, Que., Can. D2 74
Aylmer Lake, l., N.W. Ter., Can. D11 66
Aylmer West, Ont., Can. E4 73
Ayora, Spain F10 12
'Ayoûn el 'Atroûs, Maur. E4 42
Ayr, Scot., U.K. F8 7
Ayre, Point of, c., I. of Man G8 7
Ayu, Kepulauan, is., Indon. E9 32
Ayvalık, Tur. J10 16
Azambuja, Port. F3 12
Azamgarh, India G10 38
Azare, Nig. F8 42
Azerbaijan, ctry., Asia I7 22
Aziscohos Lake, l., Me., U.S. C1 96
Azle, Tx., U.S. n9 120
Azogues, Ec. I3 58
Azores see Açores, is., Port. D11 2
Azov, Sea of, Eur. H5 22
Aztec, N.M., U.S. A2 108
Aztec Peak, mtn., Az., U.S. D5 80
Aztec Ruins National Monument, N.M., U.S. A1 108
Azua, Dom. Rep. E12 64
Azuaga, Spain G6 12
Azuero, Península de, pen., Pan. K7 64
Azul, Arg. D5 56
Azur, Côte d', Fr. I14 10
Azusa, Ca., U.S. m13 82
Az-Zaqāzīq, Egypt D2 40
Az-Zarqā', Jord. C5 40
Az-Zāwiyah, Libya B8 42
Azzel Matti, Sebkha, pl., Alg. C6 42

B

Ba, stm., Viet. H10 34
Babaeski, Tur. H11 16
Babahoyo, Ec. H3 58
Babar, Kepulauan, is., Indon. G8 32
Babb Creek, stm., Pa., U.S. C7 115
Babbitt, Mn., U.S. C7 100
Babbitt, Nv., U.S. E3 105
B'abdā, Leb. C4 40
Bāb el-Mandeb see Mandeb, Bāb el-, strt. F3 46
Babine, stm., B.C., Can. B4 69
Babine Lake, l., B.C., Can. B5 69
Babine Range, mts., B.C., Can. B4 69
Bābol, Iran J8 22
Baboquivari Mountains, mts., Az., U.S. F4 80
Baboquivari Peak, mtn., Az., U.S. F4 80
Babuyan Islands, is., Phil. B7 32
Babylon, N.Y., U.S. n15 109
Baca, co., Co., U.S. D8 83
Bacabal, Braz. D10 54
Bacan, Pulau, i., Indon. F8 32
Bacău, Rom. C10 16
Bac Can, Viet. C8 34
Bacerac, Mex. B5 62
Bachaquero, Ven. C7 58
Bachta, Russia E11 24
Bachu, China D2 26
Back, stm., N.W. Ter., Can. C13 66
Back, stm., S.C., U.S. h12 117
Backbone Mountain, mtn., U.S. m12 97
Backnang, Ger. G9 8
Bac Lieu, Viet. J8 34
Bac Ninh, Viet. D9 34
Bacolod, Phil. C7 32
Bacon, co., Ga., U.S. E4 87
Baconton, Ga., U.S. E2 87
Bacoor, Phil. q19 33b
Bad, stm., S.D., U.S. C5 118
Bad, stm., Wi., U.S. B3 126
Badagara, India G3 37
Badajia, China B9 28
Badajoz, Spain G5 12
Badalona, Spain D14 12
Badanah, Sau. Ar. B3 46
Bad Aussee, Aus. H13 8
Bad Axe, Mi., U.S. E8 99
Baddeck, N.S., Can. C9 71
Bad Doberan, Ger. A11 8
Bad Ems, Ger. E7 8
Baden, Aus. G16 8
Baden, Ont., Can. D4 73
Baden, Switz. E15 10
Baden, Pa., U.S. E1 115
Baden-Baden, Ger. G8 8
Badgastein, Aus. H13 8
Badger, Newf., Can. D3 72
Bad Hersfeld, Ger. E9 8
Bad Homburg [vor der Höhe], Ger. E8 8
Bad Honnef, Ger. E7 8
Badin, N.C., U.S. B2 110
Badin Lake, res., N.C., U.S. B2 110
Bad Ischl, Aus. H13 8
Bad Kissingen, Ger. E10 8
Bad Kreuznach, Ger. F7 8
Badlands, hills, S.D., U.S. D3 118
Badlands, reg., U.S. C2 111
Badlands National Park, S.D., U.S. D3 118
Bad Lauterberg, Ger. D10 8
Bad Nauheim, Ger. E8 8
Bad Neustadt an der Saale, Ger. E10 8
Bad Oldesloe, Ger. B10 8
Bad Reichenhall, Ger. H12 8
Bad River Indian Reservation, Wi., U.S. B3 126
Bad Salzungen, Ger. E10 8
Bad Schwartau, Ger. B10 8
Bad Segeberg, Ger. B10 8
Bad Tölz, Ger. H11 8
Badulla, Sri L. I6 37
Badwater Creek, stm., Wy., U.S. C5 127
Bad Wildungen, Ger. D9 8
Bad Wörishofen, Ger. G10 8
Baena, Spain H7 12
Baeza, Spain H8 12
Bafatá, Gui.-B. F3 42
Baffin Bay, b., N.A. B14 61
Baffin Bay, b., Tx., U.S. E4 120
Baffin Island, i., N.W. Ter., Can. C18 66
Bafwasende, Zaire A5 44
Bagaha, India G11 38
Bāgalkot, India D3 37
Bagansiapiapi, Indon. M6 34
Bağarası, Tur. L11 16
Bagdad, Az., U.S. C2 80
Bagdad, Fl., U.S. u14 86
Bagdad see Baghdād, Iraq B3 46
Bagdarin, Russia G16 24
Bagé, Braz. C6 56
Baggs, Wy., U.S. E5 127
Baghdād, Iraq B3 46
Bagheria, Italy K8 14
Baghlān, Afg. B3 38
Baghrān Khowleh, Afg. D1 38
Bagley, Mn., U.S. C3 100
Bagnères-de-Bigorre, Fr. I7 10
Bagnères-de-Luchon, Fr. J7 10
Bagnols-sur-Cèze, Fr. H11 10
Bago, Mya. F4 34
Baguio, Phil. p19 32
Bahamas, ctry., N.A. B9 64
Bahāwalnagar, Pak. F5 38
Bahāwalpur, Pak. F4 38
Bahía, Islas de la, is., Hond. F4 64
Bahía Blanca, Arg. D4 56
Bahía de Caráquez, Ec. H2 58
Bahía Kino, Mex. C4 62
Bahir Dar, Eth. F2 46
Bahraich, India G9 38
Bahrain, ctry., Asia C5 46
Baia-Mare, Rom. B7 16
Bai Bung, Muy, c., Viet. J8 34
Baicheng, China B11 26
Baicheng, China C3 26
Baidoa, Som. H3 46
Baie-Comeau, Que., Can. k13 74
Baie-d'Urfé, Que., Can. q19 74
Baie-Saint-Paul, Que., Can. B7 74
Baie Verte, Newf., Can. D3 72
Baigneux-les-Juifs, Fr. E11 10
Baiju, China B9 28
Bailén, Spain G8 12
Bailey, co., Tx., U.S. B1 120
Bailey Island, Me., U.S. g8 96
Bailey Island, i., S.C., U.S. k11 117
Baileys Crossroads, Va., U.S. g12 123
Bainbridge, Ga., U.S. F2 87
Bainbridge, In., U.S. E4 91
Bainbridge, Oh., U.S. C2 112
Bainbridge Island, i., Wa., U.S. e10 124
Bain-de-Bretagne, Fr. E5 10
Baing, Indon. H7 32
Baird, Tx., U.S. C3 120
Bairdford, Pa., U.S. h14 115
Baird Inlet, b., Ak., U.S. C7 79
Baird Mountains, mts., Ak., U.S. B7 79
Bais, Fr. D6 10
Baise, China C9 34
Baishuijiang, China E8 26
Baiyin, China D7 26
Baiyunebo, China C9 26
Baja, Hung. I18 8
Baja, Punta, c., Mex. C4 62
Baja California, pen., Mex. D3 62
Bajanchongor, Mong. B7 26
Bajkal, Ozero (Lake Baykal), l., Russia G15 24
Bajkal'skoje, Russia F15 24
Bajkit, Russia E13 24
Bajkonyr, Kaz. H11 22
Bajo Baudó, Col. E4 58
Baker, La., U.S. D4 95
Baker, Mt., U.S. D12 103
Baker, Or., U.S. C9 114
Baker, co., Fl., U.S. B4 86
Baker, co., Ga., U.S. E2 87
Baker, co., Or., U.S. C9 114
Baker, stm., N.H., U.S. C3 106
Baker, Mount, mtn., Wa., U.S. A4 124
Baker Air Force Base, mil., Ar., U.S. B6 81
Baker Butte, mtn., Az., U.S. C4 80
Baker Island, i., Ak., U.S. n22 79
Baker Lake, N.W. Ter., Can. D13 66
Baker Lake, l., Me., U.S. B3 96
Baker Lake, res., Wa., U.S. A4 124
Bakersfield, Ca., U.S. E4 82
Bakers Island, i., Ma., U.S. f12 98
Bakerstown, Pa., U.S. h14 115
Bakhtarān, Iran B4 46
Bakhtegān, Daryācheh-ye, l., Iran C5 46
Bakır, stm., Tur. J11 16
Bakoye, stm., Afr. F4 42
Baku, Azer. I7 22
Balabac Island, i., Phil. D6 32
Balabac Strait, strt., Asia D6 32
Ba'labakk (Baalbek), Leb. B5 40
Balachna, Russia E26 18
Bālāghāt, India J9 38
Bālāghāt Range, mts., India C4 37
Balaguer, Spain D12 12
Balakovo, Russia G7 22
Balallan, Scot., U.K. C6 7
Balāngīr, India B7 37
Balašicha, Russia F20 18
Balasore, India J12 38
Balašov, Russia G6 22
Balaton, Mn., U.S. F3 100
Balaton, l., Hung. I17 8
Balbriggan, Ire. H6 7
Balcarres, Sask., Can. G4 75
Balchaš, Ozero, l., Kaz. H9 24
Bald Eagle Lake, l., Mn., U.S. m12 100
Bald Eagle Lake, l., Mn., U.S. C7 100
Baldhill Dam, N.D., U.S. B7 111
Bald Knob, Ar., U.S. B4 81
Bald Knoll, mtn., Wy., U.S. D2 127
Bald Mountain, mtn., Or., U.S. D5 114
Bald Mountain, mtn., Or., U.S. C9 114
Bald Mountain, mtn., Wy., U.S. B5 127
Bald Mountains, mts., N.C., U.S. f10 110
Baldwin, Fl., U.S. B5 86
Baldwin, Ga., U.S. B3 87
Baldwin, La., U.S. E4 95
Baldwin, Mi., U.S. E5 99
Baldwin, Pa., U.S. k14 115
Baldwin, S.C., U.S. B5 117
Baldwin, Wi., U.S. D1 126
Baldwin, co., Al., U.S. E2 78
Baldwin, co., Ga., U.S. C3 87
Baldwin City, Ks., U.S. D8 93
Baldwinsville, N.Y., U.S. B4 109
Baldwinville, Ma., U.S. A3 98
Baldwyn, Ms., U.S. A5 101
Baldy Mountain, mtn., B.C., Can. D7 69
Baldy Mountain, mtn., Man., Can. D1 70
Baldy Mountain, mtn., Mt., U.S. B7 103
Baldy Mountain, mtn., N.M., U.S. A4 108
Baldy Peak, mtn., Az., U.S. D6 80
Baleares, Islas (Balearic Islands), is., Spain F14 12
Balearic Islands see Baleares, Islas, is., Spain E15 12
Baleine, Rivière à la, stm., Que., Can. g13 74
Balej, Russia G17 24
Balfate, Hond. G4 64
Balfour, N.C., U.S. f10 110
Bali, i., Indon. G5 32
Bali, Laut (Bali Sea), Indon. G6 32
Balıkesir, Tur. H13 4
Balikpapan, Indon. F6 32
Balimo, Pap. N. Gui. G11 32
Balingen, Ger. G8 8
Balintang Channel, strt., Phil. B7 32
Baliza, Braz. D2 57
Balkan Mountains see Stara Planina, mts., Eur. G8 16
Balkh, Afg. B2 38
Balkhash, Lake see Balchaš, Ozero, l., Kaz. H9 24
Ball, La., U.S. C3 95
Ballachulish, Scot., U.K. E7 7
Ballālpur, India C5 37
Ballarat, Austl. G8 50
Ballard, co., Ky., U.S. e8 94
Ball Club Lake, l., Mn., U.S. C5 100
Ballenas, Canal de, strt., Mex. C3 62
Ball Ground, Ga., U.S. B2 87
Ballia, India H11 38
Ballina, Ire. G3 7
Ballinger, Tx., U.S. D3 120
Ballinrobe, Ire. H3 7
Ball Mountain Lake, res., Vt., U.S. E3 122
Ballston Spa, N.Y., U.S. B7 109
Ballwin, Mo., U.S. f12 102
Bally, Pa., U.S. F10 115
Ballycastle, N. Ire., U.K. F6 7
Ballymena, N. Ire., U.K. G6 7
Ballyshannon, Ire. G4 7
Balmoral, N.B., Can. B3 71
Balmoral, Scot., U.K. D9 7
Balmville, N.Y., U.S. D6 109
Balovale, Zam. D4 44
Balrāmpur, India G10 38
Balsam Lake, Wi., U.S. C1 126
Balsam Lake, l., Wi., U.S. C1 126
Balsas, Braz. E9 54
Baltasar Brum, Ur. C5 56
Baltic, Ct., U.S. C7 84
Baltic, S.D., U.S. D9 118
Baltic Sea, Eur. H12 6
Baltijsk, Russia G2 18
Baltijskaja Kosa, spit, Eur. A19 8
Baltimore, Ire. J3 7
Baltimore, Md., U.S. B4 97
Baltimore, Oh., U.S. C3 112
Baltimore, co., Md., U.S. B4 97
Baltimore Highlands, Md., U.S. h11 97
Baluchistan, hist. reg., Asia D1 36
Bālurghāt, India H13 38
Balygyčan, Russia E24 24
Balzar, Ec. H3 58
Bamako, Mali F4 42
Bambana, stm., Nic. H6 64
Bambari, Cen. Afr. Rep. G10 42
Bamberg, Ger. F10 8
Bamberg, S.C., U.S. E5 117
Bamberg, co., S.C., U.S. E5 117
Bamenda, Cam. G8 42
Bāmīān, Afg. C2 38
Banalia, Zaire A5 44
Banana, Zaire C2 44
Bananal, Ilha do, i., Braz. F8 54
Banana River, b., Fl., U.S. D6 86
Banās, Ra's, c., Egypt D13 42
Banbridge, N. Ire., U.K. G6 7
Banbury, Eng., U.K. I11 7
Bancroft, Ont., Can. B7 73
Bancroft, Ia., U.S. A3 92
Bānda, India H9 38
Banda, Kepulauan, is., Indon. F8 32
Banda, Laut (Banda Sea), Indon. G8 32
Banda Aceh, Indon. D2 32
Bandama, stm., C. Iv. G4 42
Bandar Beheshtī, Iran C7 46
Bandar-e 'Abbās, Iran C6 46
Bandar-e Būshehr, Iran C5 46
Bandar-e Lengeh, Iran C5 46
Bandar Seri Begawan, Bru. E5 32
Banded Peak, mtn., Co., U.S. D4 83
Bandeira, Pico da, mtn., Braz. F8 57
Bandelier National Monument, N.M., U.S. B3 108
Bandera, co., Tx., U.S. E3 120
Banderas, Bahía de, b., Mex. G7 62
Bandırma, Tur. G13 4
Bandon, Ire. J4 7
Bandon, Or., U.S. D2 114
Bandundu, Zaire B3 44
Bandung, Indon. m13 32
Banes, Cuba D10 64
Banff, Scot., U.K. D10 7
Banff National Park, Alta., Can. D2 68
Bangalore, India F4 37
Bangassou, Cen. Afr. Rep. H10 42
Banggai, Kepulauan, is., Indon. F7 32
Banggi, Pulau, i., Malay. D6 32
Banghāzī, Libya B10 42
Bangil, Indon. m16 33a
Bangka, i., Indon. F4 32
Bangkalan, Indon. m16 33a
Bangkinang, Indon. N6 34
Bangkok see Krung Thep, Thai. H6 34
Bangladesh, ctry., Asia E6 36
Bangor, N. Ire., U.K. G7 7
Bangor, Wales, U.K. H8 7
Bangor, Me., U.S. D4 96
Bangor, Mi., U.S. F4 99
Bangor, Pa., U.S. E11 115
Bangor, Wi., U.S. E3 126
Bangor Township, Mi., U.S. E7 99
Bangs, Tx., U.S. D3 120
Bangs, Mount, mtn., Az., U.S. A2 80
Bangui, Cen. Afr. Rep. H9 42
Bangweulu, Lake, l., Zam. D5 44
Baní, Dom. Rep. E12 64
Banī Mazār, Egypt C12 42
Banister, stm., Va., U.S. D4 123
Banī Suwayf, Egypt C12 42
Bāniyās, Syria B4 40
Banja Luka, Bos. E12 14
Banjarmasin, Indon. F5 32
Banjul, Gam. F2 42
Bankhead Lake, res., Al., U.S. B2 78
Banks, co., Ga., U.S. B3 87
Banks Island, i., B.C., Can. C2 69
Banks Island, i., N.W. Ter., Can. B8 66
Banks Lake, res., Wa., U.S. B6 124
Banks Strait, strt., Austl. H9 50
Bānkura, India I12 38
Bann, stm., N. Ire., U.K. G6 7
Banner, co., Ne., U.S. C2 104
Banner Elk, N.C., U.S. A1 110
Banning, Ca., U.S. F5 82
Bannock, co., Id., U.S. G6 89
Bannock Peak, mtn., Id., U.S. F6 89
Bannock Range, mts., Id., U.S. G6 89
Bannu, Pak. D4 38
Baños de Cerrato, Spain D7 12
Ban Pak Phraek, Thai. J6 34
Ban Phak Phang, Thai. F6 34
Ban Pong, Thai. H5 34
Banská Bystrica, Slov. G19 8
Bānswāra, India I6 38
Bantam, stm., Ct., U.S. B3 84
Bantam Lake, l., Ct., U.S. C3 84
Bantry, Ire. J3 7
Banyak, Kepulauan, is., Indon. M4 34
Banyuwangi, Indon. n17 33a
Baoding, China D10 26
Baofeng, China B2 28
Bao Ha, Viet. C8 34
Baoji, China E8 26
Baoshan, China B5 34
Baotou, China C8 26
Baoying, China B8 28
Ba'qūbah, Iraq B3 46
Baquedano, Chile A3 56
Baraboo, Wi., U.S. E4 126
Baraboo, stm., Wi., U.S. E3 126
Baracoa, Cuba D10 64
Baraga, Mi., U.S. B2 99
Baraga, co., Mi., U.S. B2 99
Barakī Barak, Afg. D3 38
Baram, stm., Malay. E5 32
Bārāmati, India C3 37
Bārāmūla, India C6 38
Bārān, India H7 38
Baranagar, India I13 38
Baranoa, Col. B5 58
Baranof Island, i., Ak., U.S. m22 79
Baranoviči, Bela. H9 18
Barataria, La., U.S. E5 95
Barataria Bay, b., La., U.S. E6 95
Barat Daya, Kepulauan, is., Indon. G8 32
Barbacena, Braz. F7 57
Barbados, ctry., N.A. H18 64
Barbar, Sudan E12 42
Barbas, Cabo, c., W. Sah. D2 42
Barbastro, Spain C12 12
Barbate de Franco, Spain I6 12
Barber, co., Ks., U.S. E5 93
Barbers Point, c., Hi., U.S. B3 88
Barbers Point Naval Air Station, mil., Hi., U.S. g9 88
Barberton, Oh., U.S. A4 112
Barbezieux, Fr. G6 10
Barbosa, Col. E6 58
Barbour, co., Al., U.S. D4 78
Barbour, co., W.V., U.S. B4 125
Barboursville, W.V., U.S. C2 125
Barbourville, Ky., U.S. D6 94
Barbuda, i., Antig. F17 64
Barcaldine, Austl. D9 50
Barcellona Pozzo di Gotto, Italy K10 14
Barcelona, Spain D14 12
Barcelona, Ven. B10 58
Barcelos, Braz. D6 54
Barcelos, Port. D3 12
Barcroft, Lake, res., Va., U.S. g12 123
Barden Reservoir, res., R.I., U.S. C2 116
Bardera, Som. H3 46
Bardīyah, Libya B11 42
Bardstown, Ky., U.S. C4 94
Bardufoss, Nor. B12 6
Bardwell, Ky., U.S. f9 94
Bardwell Lake, res., Tx., U.S. C4 120
Bareilly, India F8 38
Barents Sea, Eur. B8 128
Barfleur, Fr. C5 10
Bargersville, In., U.S. E5 91
Bar Harbor, Me., U.S. D4 96
Bari, Italy H11 14
Barīkowṭ, Afg. C4 38
Barillas, Guat. G2 64
Barinas, Ven. C7 58
Barinitas, Ven. C7 58
Baripāda, India J12 38
Barisāl, Bngl. I14 38
Barisan, Pegunungan, mts., Indon. F3 32
Barito, stm., Indon. F5 32
Barker Heights, N.C., U.S. f10 110
Barkhamsted Reservoir, res., Ct., U.S. B3 84
Barkley, Lake, res., U.S. f10 94
Barkley Sound, strt., B.C., Can. E5 69
Barkly Tableland, plat., Austl. C7 50
Bark Point, c., Wi., U.S. B2 126
Barksdale Air Force Base, mil., La., U.S. B2 95
Bar-le-Duc, Fr. D12 10
Barlee, Lake, l., Austl. E3 50
Barletta, Italy H11 14
Barling, Ar., U.S. B1 81
Barlow, Ky., U.S. e8 94
Barmer, India H4 38
Barmouth, Wales, U.K. I8 7
Barnaul, Russia G10 24
Barnegat Bay, b., N.J., U.S. D4 107
Barnegat Inlet, b., N.J., U.S. D4 107
Barnes, co., N.D., U.S. B7 111
Barnesboro, Pa., U.S. E4 115
Barnes Sound, strt., Fl., U.S. G6 86
Barnesville, Ga., U.S. C2 87
Barnesville, Mn., U.S. D2 100
Barnesville, Oh., U.S. C4 112
Barneville-Carteret, Fr. C5 10
Barnhart, Mo., U.S. C7 102
Barnsdall, Ok., U.S. A5 113
Barnsley, Eng., U.K. H11 7
Barnstable, Ma., U.S. C7 98
Barnstable, co., Ma., U.S. C7 98
Barnstaple, Eng., U.K. J8 7
Barnwell, S.C., U.S. E5 117
Barnwell, co., S.C., U.S. E5 117
Baroda, India I5 38
Barpeta, India G14 38
Barqah (Cyrenaica), reg., Libya B10 42
Barques, Pointe aux, c., Mi., U.S. D8 99
Barquisimeto, Ven. B8 58
Barra, Braz. F10 54
Barra, Ponta da, c., Moz. F7 44
Barrackville, W.V., U.S. B4 125
Barra do Corda, Braz. E9 54
Barra Falsa, Ponta da, c., Moz. F7 44
Barra Mansa, Braz. G6 57

Name | Map Ref | Page

Barrancabermeja, Col. D6 58
Barranca del Cobre, Parque Nacional, Mex. D6 62
Barrancas, Ven. C11 58
Barrancos, Port. G5 12
Barranquilla, Col. B5 58
Barras, Braz. D10 54
Barrax, Spain F9 12
Barre, Vt., U.S. C4 122
Barre, Lake, l., La., U.S. E5 95
Barre Falls Reservoir, res., Ma., U.S. B4 98
Barreiras, Braz. B6 57
Barreiro, Port. G2 12
Barreiros, Braz. E11 54
Barrême, Fr. I13 10
Barren, co., Ky., U.S. D4 94
Barren, stm., Ky., U.S. C3 94
Barren Island, i., Md., U.S. D5 97
Barren Islands, is., Ak., U.S. h15 79
Barren River Lake, res., Ky., U.S. D3 94
Barretos, Braz. F4 57
Barrett, W.V., U.S. D3 125
Barrhead, Alta., Can. B3 68
Barrie, Ont., Can. C5 73
Barrie Island, i., Ont., Can. B2 73
Barrière, B.C., Can. D7 69
Barrington, Il., U.S. A5 90
Barrington, N.J., U.S. D2 107
Barrington, R.I., U.S. D5 116
Barrington, stm., R.I., U.S. C5 116
Barron, Wi., U.S. C2 126
Barron, co., Wi., U.S. C2 126
Barron Lake, Mi., U.S. G4 99
Barrow, Ak., U.S. A8 79
Barrow, co., Ga., U.S. B3 87
Barrow, Point, c., Ak., U.S. A8 79
Barrow Creek, Austl. D6 50
Barrow-in-Furness, Eng., U.K. G9 7
Barrow Island, i., Austl. D3 50
Barrow Strait, strt., N.W. Ter., Can. B14 66
Barry, Il., U.S. D2 90
Barry, co., Mi., U.S. F5 99
Barry, co., Mo., U.S. E4 102
Barrys Bay, Ont., Can. B7 73
Bārsi, India C3 37
Barstow, Ca., U.S. E5 82
Bar-sur-Aube, Fr. D11 10
Barth, Ger. A12 8
Bartholomew, co., In., U.S. F6 91
Bartholomew, Bayou, stm., U.S. D4 81
Bartica, Guy. D13 58
Bartlesville, Ok., U.S. A6 113
Bartlett, N.H., U.S. B4 106
Bartlett, Tn., U.S. B2 119
Bartlett, Tx., U.S. D4 120
Bartlett Reservoir, res., Az., U.S. D4 80
Bartletts Ferry Dam, U.S. C4 78
Barton, Oh., U.S. B5 112
Barton, Vt., U.S. B4 122
Barton, co., Ks., U.S. D5 93
Barton, co., Mo., U.S. D3 102
Barton, stm., Vt., U.S. B4 122
Bartonville, Il., U.S. C4 90
Bartow, Fl., U.S. E5 86
Bartow, co., Ga., U.S. B2 87
Barú, Volcán, vol., Pan. J6 64
Bāruni, India H11 38
Baruun Urt, Mong. B9 26
Barvas, Scot., U.K. C6 7
Basalt, Co., U.S. B3 83
Basankusu, Zaire A3 44
Basatongwula Shan, mtn., China D14 38
Bascuñán, Cabo, c., Chile B2 56
Basehor, Ks., U.S. k16 93
Basel (Bâle), Switz. E14 10
Bashan Lake, l., Ct., U.S. D6 84
Bashaw, Alta., Can. C4 68
Bashi Channel, strt., Asia G11 26
Basilan Island, i., Phil. D7 32
Basildon, Eng., U.K. J13 7
Basile, La., U.S. D3 95
Basin, Wy., U.S. B4 127
Basingstoke, Eng., U.K. J11 7
Basīrhāt, India I13 38
Basīt, Ra's al-, c., Syria B4 40
Baskahegan Lake, l., Me., U.S. C5 96
Baskatong, Réservoir, res., Que., Can. G17 66
Basking Ridge, N.J., U.S. B3 107
Basoko, Zaire A4 44
Basra see Al-Başrah, Iraq B4 46
Bassano, Alta., Can. D4 68
Bassano del Grappa, Italy D6 14
Bassari, Togo G6 42
Bassas da India, rf., Reu. F7 44
Basse-Terre, Guad. F17 64
Basseterre, St. K./N. F16 64
Basse-Terre, i., Guad. F17 64
Bassett, Ne., U.S. B6 104
Bassett, Va., U.S. D3 123
Bassett Peak, mtn., Az., U.S. E5 80
Bass Islands, is., Oh., U.S. A3 112
Bass Lake, In., U.S. B4 91
Bass Strait, strt., Austl. G9 50
Basswood Lake, l., Mn., U.S. B7 100
Basti, India G10 38
Bastogne, Bel. E5 8
Bastrop, La., U.S. B4 95
Bastrop, Tx., U.S. D4 120
Bastrop, co., Tx., U.S. D4 120
Bastuträsk, Swe. D13 6
Bata, Eq. Gui. H7 42
Bataan Peninsula, pen., Phil. q19 33b
Batabanó, Golfo de, b., Cuba C6 64
Batagaj, Russia D20 24
Bataguaçu, Braz. F2 57
Bataiporã, Braz. G2 57
Batāla, India E6 38
Batalha, Port. F3 12
Batamaj, Russia E19 24
Batang, China E6 26
Batangas, Phil. r19 33b
Batan Islands, is., Phil. A7 32
Batanta, Pulau, i., Indon. F9 32
Batatais, Braz. F5 57
Batavia, Il., U.S. B5 90
Batavia, N.Y., U.S. C2 109
Batavia, Oh., U.S. C1 112
Batchelor Bay, b., N.C., U.S. B6 110
Bătdâmbâng, Camb. H7 34
Batepito, Mex. B5 62
Bates, co., Mo., U.S. C3 102
Batesburg, S.C., U.S. D4 117
Batesville, Ar., U.S. B4 81
Batesville, In., U.S. F7 91
Batesville, Ms., U.S. A4 101
Bath, N.B., Can. C2 71
Bath, Ont., Can. C8 73
Bath, Eng., U.K. J10 7
Bath, Me., U.S. E3 96
Bath, N.Y., U.S. C3 109
Bath, Pa., U.S. E11 115
Bath, S.C., U.S. D4 117
Bath, co., Ky., U.S. B6 94
Bath, co., Va., U.S. B3 123
Bathurst, N.B., Can. B4 71
Bathurst, Cape, c., N.W. Ter., Can. B7 66
Bathurst Inlet, N.W. Ter., Can. C11 66
Bathurst Inlet, b., N.W. Ter., Can. C11 66
Bathurst Island, i., Austl. B6 50
Bathurst Island, i., N.W. Ter., Can. A12 66
Batiscan, stm., Que., Can. B5 74
Batna, Alg. A7 42
Baton Rouge, La., U.S. D4 95
Batouri, Cam. H8 42
Batsto, stm., N.J., U.S. D3 107
Batten Kill, stm., U.S. E2 122
Batticaloa, Sri L. I6 37
Battle, stm., Can. F10 66
Battle Creek, Ia., U.S. B2 92
Battle Creek, Mi., U.S. F5 99
Battle Creek, Ne., U.S. C8 104
Battle Ground, In., U.S. C4 91
Battle Ground, Wa., U.S. D3 124
Battle Lake, Mn., U.S. D3 100
Battle Mountain, Nv., U.S. C5 105
Battle Mountain, mtn., Wy., U.S. E5 127
Batu, mtn., Eth. G2 46
Batu, Kepulauan, is., Indon. O5 34
Batumi, Geor. I6 22
Batu Pahat, Malay. N7 34
Baturité, Braz. D11 54
Baubau, Indon. G7 32
Bauchi, Nig. F7 42
Baud, Fr. E3 10
Baudette, Mn., U.S. B4 100
Bauld, Cape, c., Newf., Can. C4 72
Baume-les-Dames, Fr. E13 10
Baunei, Italy I4 14
Bauru, Braz. G4 57
Baús, Braz. E2 57
Bautzen, Ger. D14 8
Bawean, Pulau, i., Indon. G5 32
Baxley, Ga., U.S. E4 87
Baxter, Ia., U.S. C4 92
Baxter, Mn., U.S. D4 100
Baxter, Tn., U.S. C8 119
Baxter, co., Ar., U.S. A3 81
Baxter Springs, Ks., U.S. E9 93
Bay, Ar., U.S. B5 81
Bay, co., Fl., U.S. u16 86
Bay, co., Mi., U.S. E6 99
Bay, Laguna de, l., Phil. q19 33b
Bayamo, Cuba D9 64
Bayan Har Shan, mts., China E6 26
Bayard, Ne., U.S. C2 104
Bayard, N.M., U.S. E1 108
Bayberry, N.Y., U.S. *B4 109
Bayboro, N.C., U.S. B6 110
Bay Bulls, Newf., Can. E5 72
Bay City, Mi., U.S. E7 99
Bay City, Or., U.S. B3 114
Bay City, Tx., U.S. E5 120
Bay de Verde, Newf., Can. D5 72
Bayerische Alpen, mts., Eur. H11 8
Bayeux, Fr. C6 10
Bayfield, Ont., Can. D3 73
Bayfield, Co., U.S. D3 83
Bayfield, Wi., U.S. B3 126
Bayfield, co., Wi., U.S. B2 126
Bayındır, Tur. K11 16
Baykonur see Bajkonyr, Kaz. H11 22
Baylor, co., Tx., U.S. C3 120
Bay Mills Indian Reservation, Mi., U.S. B6 99
Bay Minette, Al., U.S. E2 78
Bayo, Spain B3 12
Bayona, Spain C3 12
Bayonne, Fr. I5 10
Bayonne, N.J., U.S. B4 107
Bayou Bodcau Reservoir, res., La., U.S. B2 95
Bayou D'Arbonne Lake, res., La., U.S. B3 95
Bayou George, Fl., U.S. u16 86
Bayou Goula, La., U.S. D4 95
Bayou La Batre, Al., U.S. E1 78
Bay Point, c., S.C., U.S. G7 117
Bayport, Mn., U.S. E6 100
Bayport, N.Y., U.S. n15 109
Bayramıç, Tur. J10 16
Bayreuth, Ger. F11 8
Bay Ridge, Md., U.S. C5 97
Bay Roberts, Newf., Can. E5 72
Bayrūt (Beirut), Leb. C4 40
Bays, Lake of, l., Ont., Can. B5 73
Bay Saint Louis, Ms., U.S. E4 101
Bay Shore, N.Y., U.S. E7 109
Bayshore Gardens, Fl., U.S. q10 86
Bayside, Wi., U.S. m12 126
Bay Springs, Ms., U.S. D4 101
Bayt Lahm, Isr. Occ. D4 40
Baytown, Tx., U.S. E5 120
Bayview, Al., U.S. f7 78
Bay Village, Oh., U.S. h9 112
Baza, Spain H9 12
Bazaruto, Ilha do, i., Moz. F7 44
Bazas, Fr. H6 10
Be, Nosy, i., Madag. D9 44
Beach, Il., U.S. h9 90
Beach, N.D., U.S. C1 111
Beachburg, Ont., Can. B8 73
Beach City, Oh., U.S. B4 112
Beach Haven Inlet, b., N.J., U.S. D4 107
Beach Pond, res., U.S. C8 84
Beachville, Ont., Can. D4 73
Beachwood, N.J., U.S. D4 107
Beachy Head, c., Eng., U.K. K13 7
Beacon, N.Y., U.S. D7 109
Beacon Falls, Ct., U.S. D3 84
Beaconsfield, Que., Can. q19 74
Beadle, co., S.D., U.S. C7 118
Beagle Gulf, b., Austl. B6 50
Bealanana, Madag. D9 44
Beale, Cape, c., B.C., Can. E5 69
Beale Air Force Base, mil., Ca., U.S. C3 82
Bear, De., U.S. B3 85
Bear, stm., U.S. B3 121
Bear Creek, Al., U.S. A2 78
Bear Creek, stm., U.S. E2 93
Bear Creek, stm., Or., U.S. E4 114
Bear Creek, stm., Wy., U.S. E8 127
Bearden, Ar., U.S. D3 81
Beardstown, Il., U.S. C3 90
Bear Inlet, b., N.C., U.S. C5 110
Bear Lake, co., Id., U.S. G7 89
Bear Lake, l., U.S. A4 121
Bear Lake, l., Wi., U.S. C2 126
Bear Lodge Mountains, mts., Wy., U.S. B8 127
Bear Mountain, mtn., Or., U.S. D4 114
Bearpaw Mountains, mts., Mt., U.S. B7 103
Bear River, N.S., Can. E4 71
Bear River City, Ut., U.S. B3 121
Beartooth Pass, Wy., U.S. B3 127
Beartooth Range, mts., U.S. E7 103
Bear Town, Ms., U.S. D3 101
Beasain, Spain B9 12
Beas de Segura, Spain G9 12
Beata, Isla, i., Dom. Rep. F12 64
Beatrice, Ne., U.S. D9 104
Beatton, stm., B.C., Can. E8 66
Beatty, Nv., U.S. G5 105
Beattyville, Ky., U.S. C6 94
Beaucaire, Fr. I11 10
Beaufort, N.C., U.S. C6 110
Beaufort, S.C., U.S. G6 117
Beaufort, co., N.C., U.S. B5 110
Beaufort, co., S.C., U.S. G6 117
Beaufort Marine Corps Air Station, mil., S.C., U.S. F6 117
Beaufort Sea, N.A. B7 61
Beaufort West, S. Afr. H4 44
Beaugency, Fr. E8 10
Beauharnois, Que., Can. D4 74
Beau Lake, l., Me., U.S. A3 96
Beauly, Scot., U.K. D8 7
Beaumont, Alta., Can. C4 68
Beaumont, Ms., U.S. D5 101
Beaumont, Tx., U.S. D5 120
Beaumont-sur-Sarthe, Fr. D7 10
Beaune, Fr. E11 10
Beauport, Que., Can. n17 74
Beaupré, Que., Can. B7 74
Beaupréau, Fr. E5 10
Beauregard, co., La., U.S. D2 95
Beausejour, Man., Can. D3 70
Beauvais, Fr. C9 10
Beauval, Sask., Can. B2 75
Beauvoir-sur-Niort, Fr. F6 10
Beaver, Ok., U.S. A1 113
Beaver, Pa., U.S. E1 115
Beaver, Ut., U.S. E3 121
Beaver, W.V., U.S. D3 125
Beaver, co., Ok., U.S. e10 113
Beaver, co., Pa., U.S. E1 115
Beaver, co., Ut., U.S. E2 121
Beaver, stm., Can. D7 66
Beaver, stm., Can. B2 75
Beaver, stm., U.S. A2 113
Beaver, stm., N.Y., U.S. B6 109
Beaver, stm., R.I., U.S. E2 116
Beaver, stm., Ut., U.S. E2 121
Beaverbank, N.S., Can. E6 71
Beaver Brook, stm., U.S. E4 106
Beaver City, Ne., U.S. D6 104
Beavercreek, Oh., U.S. C1 112
Beaver Creek, stm., U.S. E4 104
Beaver Creek, stm., U.S. C8 127
Beaver Creek, stm., N.D., U.S. C5 111
Beaver Creek, stm., N.D., U.S. C1 111
Beaver Creek, stm., Ok., U.S. C3 113
Beaver Creek, stm., Tn., U.S. m13 119
Beaver Creek, stm., Wy., U.S. D4 127
Beaverdale, Pa., U.S. F4 115
Beaver Dam, Ky., U.S. C3 94
Beaver Dam, Wi., U.S. E5 126
Beaverdam Branch, stm., De., U.S. F3 85
Beaverdam Lake, res., Wi., U.S. E5 126
Beaver Falls, Pa., U.S. E1 115
Beaverhead, co., Mt., U.S. E3 103
Beaverhead, stm., Mt., U.S. E4 103
Beaverhead Mountains, mts., U.S. D5 89
Beaverhill Lake, l., Alta., Can. C4 68
Beaver Island, i., Mi., U.S. C5 99
Beaver Lake, res., Ar., U.S. A2 81
Beaverlodge, Alta., Can. B1 68
Beaver Meadows, Pa., U.S. E10 115
Beaver Run Reservoir, res., Pa., U.S. F2 115
Beavertail Point, c., R.I., U.S. F4 116
Beaverton, Mi., U.S. E6 99
Beaverton, Or., U.S. B4 114
Beāwar, India G6 38
Bebedouro, Braz. F4 57
Bécancour, Que., Can. C5 74
Bečej, Yugo. D4 16
Becerreá, Spain C4 12
Béchar, Alg. B5 42
Becharof Lake, l., Ak., U.S. D8 79
Beckemeyer, Il., U.S. E4 90
Becker, Mn., U.S. E5 100
Becker, co., Mn., U.S. D3 100
Beckham, co., Ok., U.S. B2 113
Beckley, W.V., U.S. D3 125
Beckum, Ger. D8 8
Becky Peak, mtn., Nv., U.S. D7 105
Bédarieux, Fr. I10 10
Bedford, Que., Can. D5 74
Bedford, Eng., U.K. I12 7
Bedford, In., U.S. G5 91
Bedford, Ia., U.S. D3 92
Bedford, Ky., U.S. B4 94
Bedford, Ma., U.S. B5 98
Bedford, N.H., U.S. E3 106
Bedford, Oh., U.S. A4 112
Bedford, Pa., U.S. F4 115
Bedford, Va., U.S. C3 123
Bedford, co., Pa., U.S. G4 115
Bedford, co., Tn., U.S. B5 119
Bedford, co., Va., U.S. C3 123
Bedford Hills, N.Y., U.S. D7 109
Bee, co., Tx., U.S. E4 120
Beebe, Que., Can. D5 74
Beebe, Ar., U.S. B4 81
Beecher, Il., U.S. B6 90
Beecher, Mi., U.S. *E7 99
Beech Fork, stm., Ky., U.S. C4 94
Beech Grove, In., U.S. E5 91
Beech Island, S.C., U.S. E4 117
Beemer, Ne., U.S. C9 104
Bee Ridge, Fl., U.S. q11 86
Beersheba see Be'er Sheva', Isr. D4 40
Be'er Sheva', Isr. D4 40
Beeton (part of Alliston Beeton Tecumseth and Tottenham), Ont., Can. C5 73
Beeville, Tx., U.S. E4 120
Befale, Zaire A4 44
Befandriana, Madag. E9 44
Beggs, Ok., U.S. B5 113
Begi, Eth. G1 46
Behbehān, Iran B5 46
Behm Canal, strt., Ak., U.S. n24 79
Bei, stm., China G9 26
Bei'an, China B12 26
Beihai, China D10 34
Beijing (Peking), China D10 26
Beijing Shih, China C10 26
Beipiao, China C11 26
Beira, Moz. E6 44
Beirut see Bayrūt, Leb. C4 40
Beja, Port. G4 12
Béja, Tun. M4 14
Bejaïa, Alg. A7 42
Béjar, Spain E6 12
Békéscsaba, Hung. I21 8
Bekily, Madag. F9 44
Bela, India H9 38
Bel Air, Md., U.S. A5 97
Belalcázar, Spain G6 12
Bel Alton, Md., U.S. D4 97
Belampalli, India C5 37
Belarus, ctry., Eur. G3 22
Bela Vista, Braz. A5 56
Belcamp, Md., U.S. B5 97
Belcherāgh, Afg. C1 38
Belcher Islands, is., N.W. Ter., Can. E17 66
Belchertown, Ma., U.S. B3 98
Belchite, Spain D11 12
Belcourt, N.D., U.S. A6 111
Belden, Ms., U.S. A5 101
Belding, Mi., U.S. E5 99
Beled Weyne, Som. H4 46
Belém, Braz. D9 54
Belén, Para. A5 56
Belen, N.M., U.S. C3 108
Belfair, Wa., U.S. B3 124
Belfast, N. Ire., U.K. G7 7
Belfast, Me., U.S. D3 96
Belfield, N.D., U.S. C2 111
Belford, N.J., U.S. C4 107
Belfort, Fr. E13 10
Belfry, Ky., U.S. C7 94
Belgaum, India E3 37
Belgium, Wi., U.S. E6 126
Belgium, ctry., Eur. E8 4
Belgorod, Russia G5 22
Belgrade, Mn., U.S. E3 100
Belgrade, Mt., U.S. E5 103
Belgrade see Beograd, Yugo. E4 16
Belhaven, N.C., U.S. B6 110
Belin, Fr. H6 10
Belington, W.V., U.S. B5 125
Belitung, i., Indon. F4 32
Belize, ctry., N.A. F3 64
Belize City, Belize F3 64
Belknap, co., N.H., U.S. C3 106
Belknap Crater, crat., Or., U.S. C5 114
Bell, co., Ky., U.S. D6 94
Bell, co., Tx., U.S. D4 120
Bellac, Fr. F8 10
Bella Coola, stm., B.C., Can. C4 69
Bellaire, Ks., U.S. g12 93
Bellaire, Mi., U.S. D5 99
Bellaire, Oh., U.S. C5 112
Bellaire, Tx., U.S. r14 120
Bellamy, Al., U.S. C1 78
Bellary, India E4 37
Bellavista, Peru E3 54
Bella Vista, Ar., U.S. A1 81
Bellbrook, Oh., U.S. C1 112
Belle, Mo., U.S. C6 102
Belle, W.V., U.S. C3 125
Belle, stm., La., U.S. k9 95
Belleair, Fl., U.S. p10 86
Belle Bay, b., Newf., Can. E4 72
Belle Chasse, La., U.S. E5 95
Bellefontaine, Oh., U.S. B2 112
Bellefonte, Pa., U.S. E6 115
Belle Fourche, S.D., U.S. C2 118
Belle Fourche, stm., U.S. C3 118
Belle Fourche Reservoir, res., S.D., U.S. C2 118
Bellegarde, Fr. F12 10
Belle Glade, Fl., U.S. F6 86
Belle Isle, Fl., U.S. D5 86
Belle Isle, i., Newf., Can. C4 72
Belle Isle, Strait of, strt., Newf., Can. C3 72
Belle Meade, Tn., U.S. g10 119
Belle Plaine, Ia., U.S. C5 92
Belle Plaine, Ks., U.S. E6 93
Belle Plaine, Mn., U.S. F5 100
Belle River, Ont., Can. E2 73
Belle Rose, La., U.S. D4 95
Belle Vernon, Pa., U.S. F2 115
Belleview, Fl., U.S. C4 86
Belle View, Va., U.S. g12 123
Belleville, Ont., Can. C7 73
Belleville, Il., U.S. E4 90
Belleville, Ks., U.S. C6 93
Belleville, Mi., U.S. p15 99
Belleville, N.J., U.S. B4 107
Belleville, Pa., U.S. E6 115
Belleville, Wi., U.S. F4 126
Belleville Pond, l., R.I., U.S. E4 116
Bellevue, Id., U.S. F4 89
Bellevue, Ia., U.S. B7 92
Bellevue, Ky., U.S. h13 94
Bellevue, Mi., U.S. F5 99
Bellevue, Ne., U.S. C10 104
Bellevue, Oh., U.S. A3 112
Bellevue, Pa., U.S. F1 115
Bellevue, Wa., U.S. e11 124
Belley, Fr. G12 10
Bellflower, Ca., U.S. n12 82
Bellingham, Ma., U.S. B5 98
Bellingham, Wa., U.S. A3 124
Bellingshausen Sea, Ant. B4 47
Bellinzona, Switz. F16 10
Bell Island, i., Newf., Can. C4 72
Bellmawr, N.J., U.S. D2 107
Bello, Col. D5 58
Bellows Falls, Vt., U.S. E4 122
Bell Peninsula, pen., N.W. Ter., Can. D16 66
Bellport, N.Y., U.S. n16 109
Bells, Tn., U.S. B2 119
Bells Creek, stm., W.V., U.S. m13 125
Belluno, Italy C7 14
Bell Ville, Arg. C4 56
Bellville, Oh., U.S. B3 112
Bellville, Tx., U.S. E4 120
Bellwood, Il., U.S. k9 90
Bellwood, Pa., U.S. E5 115
Bellwood, Va., U.S. n18 123
Belmar, N.J., U.S. C4 107
Belmond, Ia., U.S. B4 92
Belmont, Ont., Can. E3 73
Belmont, Ca., U.S. h8 82
Belmont, Ma., U.S. g11 98
Belmont, Ms., U.S. A5 101
Belmont, N.H., U.S. D4 106
Belmont, N.C., U.S. B1 110
Belmont, W.V., U.S. B3 125
Belmont, Wi., U.S. F3 126
Belmont, co., Oh., U.S. C4 112
Belmonte, Braz. C9 57
Belmonte, Port. E4 12
Belmonte, Spain B5 12
Belmonte, Spain F9 12
Belmopan, Belize F3 64
Belmullet, Ire. G2 7
Bel-Nor, Mo., U.S. f13 102
Belo, Madag. E8 44
Beloeil, Que., Can. D4 74
Belogorsk, Russia G19 24
Belo Horizonte, Braz. E7 57
Beloit, Ks., U.S. C5 93
Beloit, Oh., U.S. B5 112
Beloit, Wi., U.S. F4 126
Beloit North, Wi., U.S. *F4 126
Beloje, Ozero, l., Russia A20 18
Beloje more (White Sea), Russia D5 22
Belorado, Spain C8 12
Beloreck, Russia G9 22
Belorussia see Belarus, ctry., Eur. G3 22
Belovo, Russia G11 24
Belpre, Oh., U.S. C4 112
Belt, Mt., U.S. C6 103
Belted Range, mts., Nv., U.S. F5 105
Belton, Mo., U.S. C3 102
Belton, S.C., U.S. B3 117
Belton, Tx., U.S. D4 120
Belton Lake, res., Tx., U.S. D4 120
Beltrami, co., Mn., U.S. B3 100
Beltsville, Md., U.S. B4 97
Belucha, Gora, mtn., Asia H11 24
Belvedere, S.C., U.S. D4 117
Belvedere Marittimo, Italy J10 14
Belvidere, Il., U.S. A5 90
Belvidere, N.J., U.S. B2 107
Belyj, Ostrov, i., Russia C8 24
Belyj Jar, Russia F11 24
Belzoni, Ms., U.S. B3 101
Bement, Il., U.S. D5 90
Bemidji, Mn., U.S. C4 100
Bemidji, Lake, l., Mn., U.S. C4 100
Benabarre, Spain C12 12
Bena-Dibele, Zaire B4 44
Benavente, Port. G3 12
Benavente, Spain C6 12
Benavides, Tx., U.S. F3 120
Benbrook Lake, res., Tx., U.S. n9 120
Bend, Or., U.S. C5 114
Ben Davis Point, c., N.J., U.S. E2 107
Bendeleben, Mount, mtn., Ak., U.S. B7 79
Bendigo, Austl. G8 50
Benedict, Md., U.S. C4 97
Benedito Leite, Braz. E10 54
Benevento, Italy H9 14
Benewah, co., Id., U.S. B2 89
Bengal, Bay of, b., Asia F6 36
Bengbu, China C6 28
Benghazi see Banghāzī, Libya B10 42
Bengkalis, Indon. N7 34
Bengkulu, Indon. F3 32
Benguela, Ang. D2 44
Benham, Ky., U.S. D7 94
Ben Hill, co., Ga., U.S. E3 87
Beni, stm., Bol. F5 54
Béni Abbès, Alg. B5 42
Benicarló, Spain E12 12
Benicia, Ca., U.S. C2 82
Beni-Mellal, Mor. B4 42
Benin, ctry., Afr. G6 42
Benin, Bight of, Afr. G6 42
Benin City, Nig. G7 42
Benisa, Spain G12 12
Benito Juárez, Presa, res., Mex. I12 62
Benjamin Constant, Braz. D4 54
Benjamín Hill, Mex. B4 62

Name	Map Ref	Page
Benkelman, Ne., U.S.	D4	104
Benld, Il., U.S.	D4	90
Bennett, Co., U.S.	B6	83
Bennett, co., S.D., U.S.	D4	118
Bennettsville, S.C., U.S.	B8	117
Bennington, Ne., U.S.	g12	104
Bennington, N.H., U.S.	D3	106
Bennington, Vt., U.S.	F2	122
Bennington, co., Vt., U.S.	E2	122
Benoit, Ms., U.S.	B2	101
Bénoué (Benue), stm., Afr.	G8	42
Bensenville, Il., U.S.	B6	90
Bensheim, Ger.	F8	8
Bensley, Va., U.S.	C5	123
Benson, Az., U.S.	F5	80
Benson, Mn., U.S.	E3	100
Benson, N.C., U.S.	B4	110
Benson, co., N.D., U.S.	A6	111
Bent, co., Co., U.S.	D7	83
Bentley, Alta., Can.	C3	68
Bentleyville, Pa., U.S.	F1	115
Benton, Ar., U.S.	C3	81
Benton, Il., U.S.	E5	90
Benton, Ks., U.S.	E6	93
Benton, Ky., U.S.	f9	94
Benton, La., U.S.	B2	95
Benton, Pa., U.S.	D9	115
Benton, Tn., U.S.	B7	119
Benton, Wi., U.S.	F3	126
Benton, co., Ar., U.S.	A1	81
Benton, co., In., U.S.	C3	91
Benton, co., Ia., U.S.	B5	92
Benton, co., Mn., U.S.	E4	100
Benton, co., Ms., U.S.	A4	101
Benton, co., Mo., U.S.	C4	102
Benton, co., Or., U.S.	C3	114
Benton, co., Tn., U.S.	A3	119
Benton, co., Wa., U.S.	C6	124
Benton City, Wa., U.S.	C6	124
Benton Harbor, Mi., U.S.	F4	99
Benton Heights, Mi., U.S.	F4	99
Bentonville, Ar., U.S.	A1	81
Ben Treang, Viet.	I9	34
Bent's Old Fort National Historic Site, hist., Co., U.S.	C7	83
Benue (Bénoué), stm., Afr.	G7	42
Benwood, W.V., U.S.	f8	125
Benxi, China	C11	26
Benzie, co., Mi., U.S.	D4	99
Beograd (Belgrade), Yugo.	E4	16
Beowawe, Nv., U.S.	C5	105
Beppu, Japan	I4	30
Berau, Teluk, b., Indon.	F9	32
Berbera, Som.	F4	46
Berbérati, Cen. Afr. Rep.	H9	42
Berchtesgaden, Ger.	H13	8
Berck, Fr.	B8	10
Berdigest'ach, Russia	E19	24
Berdsk, Russia	G10	24
Berea, Ky., U.S.	C5	94
Berea, Oh., U.S.	A4	112
Berea, S.C., U.S.	B3	117
Berens, stm., Can.	F13	66
Berens, stm., Can.	C3	70
Beresford, S.D., U.S.	D9	118
Berg, Nor.	B11	6
Berga, Spain	C13	12
Bergama, Tur.	J11	16
Bergamo, Italy	D4	14
Bergen, Nor.	F5	6
Bergen, co., N.J., U.S.	A4	107
Bergen [auf Rügen], Ger.	A13	8
Bergenfield, N.J., U.S.	B4	107
Bergen op Zoom, Neth.	D4	8
Bergerac, Fr.	H7	10
Bergland, Mi., U.S.	m12	99
Bergstrom Air Force Base, mil., Tx., U.S.	D4	120
Berhampore, India	H13	38
Berhampur, India	C8	37
Beringovskij, Russia	E29	24
Bering Sea	D30	128
Bering Strait, strt.	m18	76a
Berja, Spain	I9	12
Berkåk, Nor.	E7	6
Berkeley, Ca., U.S.	D2	82
Berkeley, Mo., U.S.	f13	102
Berkeley, R.I., U.S.	B4	116
Berkeley, co., S.C., U.S.	E8	117
Berkeley, co., W.V., U.S.	B6	125
Berkeley Heights, N.J., U.S.	B4	107
Berkeley Springs, W.V., U.S.	B6	125
Berkley, Mi., U.S.	F7	99
Berkner Island, i., Ant.	B8	47
Berks, co., Pa., U.S.	F9	115
Berkshire, co., Ma., U.S.	B1	98
Berkshire Hills, hills, Ma., U.S.	B1	98
Berlin, Ger.	C13	8
Berlin, Ct., U.S.	C5	84
Berlin, Md., U.S.	D7	97
Berlin, N.H., U.S.	B4	106
Berlin, N.J., U.S.	D3	107
Berlin, Pa., U.S.	G4	115
Berlin, Wi., U.S.	E5	126
Berlin Lake, res., Oh., U.S.	A4	112
Bermeo, Spain	B9	12
Bermuda, dep., N.A.	E14	76
Bern (Berne), Switz.	F14	10
Bernalillo, N.M., U.S.	B3	108
Bernalillo, co., N.M., U.S.	C3	108
Bernardsville, N.J., U.S.	B3	107
Bernasconi, Arg.	D4	56
Bernau bei Berlin, Ger.	C13	8
Bernay, Fr.	C7	10
Bernburg, Ger.	D11	8
Berne, In., U.S.	C8	91
Bernice, La., U.S.	B3	95
Bernie, Mo., U.S.	E8	102
Bernier Island, i., Austl.	D2	50
Bernina, Piz, mtn., Eur.	F16	10
Beroroha, Madag.	F9	44
Berre, Étang de, b., Fr.	I12	10
Berrien, co., Ga., U.S.	E3	87
Berrien, co., Mi., U.S.	F4	99
Berrien Springs, Mi., U.S.	G4	99
Berry, Al., U.S.	B2	78
Berryessa, Lake, res., Ca., U.S.	C2	82
Berry Hill, Tn., U.S.	g10	119
Berry Islands, is., Bah.	B9	64
Berryville, Ar., U.S.	A2	81
Berryville, Va., U.S.	A5	123
Berthierville, Que., Can.	C4	74
Berthoud, Co., U.S.	A5	83
Berthoud Pass, Co., U.S.	B5	83
Bertie, co., N.C., U.S.	A5	110
Bertoua, Cam.	H8	42
Bertrand, Mo., U.S.	E8	102
Bertrand, Ne., U.S.	D6	104
Berwick, Ia., U.S.	e8	92
Berwick, La., U.S.	E4	95
Berwick, Me., U.S.	E2	96
Berwick, Pa., U.S.	D9	115
Berwick-upon-Tweed, Eng., U.K.	F10	7
Berwyn, Alta., Can.	A2	68
Berwyn, Il., U.S.	k9	90
Berwyn, Pa., U.S.	o20	115
Besalampy, Madag.	E8	44
Besançon, Fr.	E13	10
Beskid Mountains, mts., Eur.	F19	8
Bessemer, Al., U.S.	B3	78
Bessemer, Mi., U.S.	n11	99
Bessemer, Pa., U.S.	E1	115
Bessemer City, N.C., U.S.	B1	110
Best'ach, Russia	E19	24
Betanzos, Spain	B3	12
Bétaré Oya, Cam.	G8	42
Betatakin Ruin, hist., Az., U.S.	A5	80
Bethalto, Il., U.S.	E3	90
Bethany, Ct., U.S.	D4	84
Bethany, Il., U.S.	D5	90
Bethany, Mo., U.S.	A3	102
Bethany, Ok., U.S.	B4	113
Bethany, W.V., U.S.	A4	125
Bethany Beach, De., U.S.	F5	85
Bethel, Ak., U.S.	C7	79
Bethel, Ct., U.S.	D2	84
Bethel, Me., U.S.	D2	96
Bethel, N.C., U.S.	B5	110
Bethel, Oh., U.S.	D1	112
Bethel, Vt., U.S.	D3	122
Bethel Park, Pa., U.S.	k14	115
Bethel Springs, Tn., U.S.	B3	119
Bethesda, Md., U.S.	C3	97
Bethesda, Oh., U.S.	B4	112
Bethlehem, S. Afr.	G5	44
Bethlehem, Ct., U.S.	C3	84
Bethlehem, N.H., U.S.	B3	106
Bethlehem, Pa., U.S.	E11	115
Bethlehem see Bayt Laḥm, Jord.	D4	40
Béthune, Fr.	B9	10
Beticos, Sistemas, mts., Spain	H9	12
Betioky, Madag.	F8	44
Betong, Malay.	M6	34
Betroka, Madag.	F9	44
Betsiboka, stm., Madag.	E9	44
Betsie, Point, c., Mi., U.S.	D4	99
Betsy Layne, Ky., U.S.	C7	94
Bette, mtn., Libya	D9	42
Bettendorf, Ia., U.S.	C7	92
Bettiah, India	G11	38
Betūl, India	B4	37
Betzdorf, Ger.	E7	8
Beulah, Co., U.S.	C6	83
Beulah, N.D., U.S.	B4	111
Beulah, Lake, l., Ms., U.S.	B3	101
Beulaville, N.C., U.S.	C5	110
B. Everett Jordan Lake, res., N.C., U.S.	B3	110
Beverley, Austl.	F3	50
Beverley, Eng., U.K.	H12	7
Beverley Head, c., Newf., Can.	D2	72
Beverly, Ma., U.S.	A6	98
Beverly, N.J., U.S.	C3	107
Beverly, Oh., U.S.	C4	112
Beverly, W.V., U.S.	C5	125
Beverly Hills, Ca., U.S.	m12	82
Beverly Shores, In., U.S.	A4	91
Bexar, co., Tx., U.S.	E3	120
Bexley, Oh., U.S.	m11	112
Beypore, India	G3	37
Bežeck, Russia	D19	18
Béziers, Fr.	I10	10
Bhadrakh, India	J12	38
Bhadrāvati, India	F3	37
Bhāgalpur, India	H12	38
Bhakkar, Pak.	E4	38
Bhaktapur, Nepal	G11	38
Bhandāra, India	B5	37
Bharatpur, India	G7	38
Bhatinda, India	E6	38
Bhātpāra, India	I13	38
Bhāvnagar, India	J5	38
Bhilai, India	B6	37
Bhīlwāra, India	H6	38
Bhīma, stm., India	D4	37
Bhīmavaram, India	D6	37
Bhind, India	G8	38
Bhiwandi, India	C2	37
Bhiwāni, India	F7	38
Bhopāl, India	I7	38
Bhubaneswar, India	J11	38
Bhuj, India	I3	38
Bhusāwal, India	B3	37
Bhutan, ctry., Asia	D7	36
Bia, Phou, mtn., Laos	E7	34
Biafra, Bight of, Afr.	H7	42
Biak, i., Indon.	F10	32
Biała Podlaska, Pol.	C23	8
Białystok, Pol.	B23	8
Biarritz, Fr.	I5	10
Biasca, Switz.	F15	10
Bibai, Japan	p19	30a
Bibb, co., Al., U.S.	C2	78
Bibb, co., Ga., U.S.	D3	87
Biberach an der Riss, Ger.	G9	8
Bic, Que., Can.	A9	74
Bic, Île du, i., Que., Can.	A9	74
Biche, Lac la, l., Alta., Can.	B4	68
Bicknell, In., U.S.	G3	91
Bida, Nig.	G7	42
Bīdar, India	D4	37
Biddeford, Me., U.S.	E2	96
Bideford, Eng., U.K.	J8	7
Bidwell, Mount, mtn., Ca., U.S.	B3	82
Biel [Bienne], Switz.	E14	10
Bielefeld, Ger.	C8	8
Bieler Lake, l., N.W. Ter., Can.	B18	66
Bielersee, l., Switz.	E14	10
Biella, Italy	D3	14
Bielsko-Biała, Pol.	F19	8
Bien Hoa, Viet.	I9	34
Bienville, co., La., U.S.	B2	95
Bienville, Lac, l., Que., Can.	g12	74
Big, stm., Mo., U.S.	c7	102
Biga, Tur.	I11	16
Bigadiç, Tur.	J12	16
Big Bald, mtn., Ga., U.S.	B2	87
Big Bald Mountain, mtn., N.B., Can.	B3	71
Big Baldy, mtn., Id., U.S.	E3	89
Big Baldy Mountain, mtn., Mt., U.S.	D6	103
Big Bay De Noc, b., Mi., U.S.	C4	99
Big Bear City, Ca., U.S.	E5	82
Big Belt Mountains, mts., Mt., U.S.	D5	103
Big Bend, Wi., U.S.	n11	126
Big Bend Dam, S.D., U.S.	C6	118
Big Bend National Park, Tx., U.S.	E1	120
Big Birch Lake, l., Mn., U.S.	E4	100
Big Black, stm., Me., U.S.	B3	96
Big Black, stm., Ms., U.S.	C3	101
Big Blue, stm., In., U.S.	E6	91
Big Burro Mountains, mts., N.M., U.S.	E1	108
Big Cabin Creek, stm., Ok., U.S.	A6	113
Big Coal, stm., W.V., U.S.	C3	125
Big Costilla Peak, mtn., N.M., U.S.	A4	108
Big Creek, stm., Tn., U.S.	e8	119
Big Creek Lake, res., Al., U.S.	E1	78
Big Creek Peak, mtn., Id., U.S.	E5	89
Big Cypress Indian Reservation, Fl., U.S.	F5	86
Big Cypress Swamp, sw., Fl., U.S.	F5	86
Big Darby Creek, stm., Oh., U.S.	C2	112
Big Delta, Ak., U.S.	C10	79
Big Duke Dam, N.C., U.S.	B2	110
Big Eau Pleine, stm., Wi., U.S.	D3	126
Big Eau Pleine Reservoir, res., Wi., U.S.	D4	126
Big Escambia Creek, stm., U.S.	D2	78
Big Flats, N.Y., U.S.	C4	109
Bigfork, Mt., U.S.	B2	103
Big Fork, stm., Mn., U.S.	B5	100
Biggs, Ca., U.S.	C3	82
Big Hatchet Peak, mtn., N.M., U.S.	F1	108
Big Hole, stm., Mt., U.S.	E4	103
Big Hole National Battlefield, hist., Mt., U.S.	E3	103
Big Horn, co., Mt., U.S.	E9	103
Big Horn, co., Wy., U.S.	B4	127
Bighorn Canyon National Recreation Area, U.S.	F8	103
Bighorn Lake, res., U.S.	E8	103
Bighorn Mountains, mts., U.S.	B5	127
Big Horn Mountains, mts., Az., U.S.	D2	80
Big Kandiyohi Lake, l., Mn., U.S.	F4	100
Big Lake, Mn., U.S.	E5	100
Big Lake, Tx., U.S.	D2	120
Big Lake, l., Me., U.S.	C5	96
Biglerville, Pa., U.S.	G7	115
Big Lookout Mountain, mtn., Or., U.S.	C9	114
Big Lost, stm., Id., U.S.	F5	89
Big Mossy Point, c., Man., Can.	C2	70
Big Mountain, mtn., Nv., U.S.	B2	105
Big Muddy, stm., Il., U.S.	F4	90
Big Nemaha, stm., Ne., U.S.	D10	104
Big Otter, stm., Va., U.S.	C3	123
Big Pine Lake, l., Mn., U.S.	D3	100
Big Pine Mountain, mtn., Ca., U.S.	E4	82
Big Piney, Wy., U.S.	D2	127
Big Piney, stm., Mo., U.S.	D5	102
Bigpoint, Ms., U.S.	E5	101
Big Rapids, Mi., U.S.	E5	99
Big Rib, stm., Wi., U.S.	C3	126
Big River, Sask., Can.	D2	75
Big Sable Point, c., Mi., U.S.	D4	99
Big Sandy, Mt., U.S.	B6	103
Big Sandy, Tx., U.S.	C5	120
Big Sandy, stm., U.S.	C2	125
Big Sandy, stm., Az., U.S.	C2	80
Big Sandy, stm., Tn., U.S.	B3	119
Big Sandy, stm., Wy., U.S.	D3	127
Big Sandy Creek, stm., W.V., U.S.	C3	125
Big Sandy Lake, l., Mn., U.S.	D5	100
Big Sandy Reservoir, res., Wy., U.S.	D3	127
Big Sheep Mountain, mtn., Mt., U.S.	C11	103
Big Sioux, stm., U.S.	E9	118
Big Smoky Valley, val., Nv., U.S.	E4	105
Big Snowy Mountains, mts., Mt., U.S.	D7	103
Big Southern Butte, mtn., Id., U.S.	F5	89
Big South Fork, stm., Ky., U.S.	k13	94
Big Spring, Tx., U.S.	C2	120
Big Stone, co., Mn., U.S.	E2	100
Big Stone City, S.D., U.S.	B9	118
Big Stone Gap, Va., U.S.	f9	123
Big Stone Lake, l., U.S.	E2	100
Big Sunflower, stm., Ms., U.S.	B3	101
Big Thompson, stm., Co., U.S.	A5	83
Big Timber, Mt., U.S.	E7	103
Big Trout Lake, l., Ont., Can.	n17	73
Big Walnut Creek, stm., Oh., U.S.	m11	112
Big Wood, stm., Id., U.S.	F4	89
Bihać, Bos.	E10	14
Bihār, India	H11	38
Bihār, state, India	H11	38
Biharamulo, Tan.	B6	44
Bihoro, Japan	p22	30a
Bija, stm., Russia	G11	24
Bijāpur, India	C6	37
Bijāpur, India	D3	37
Bijsk, Russia	G11	24
Bīkaner, India	F5	38
Bikin, Russia	H20	24
Bikoro, Zaire	B3	44
Bilāspur, India	I10	38
Bila Tserkva, Ukr.	H4	22
Bilauktaung Range, mts., Asia	G5	34
Bilbao, Spain	B9	12
Bilimora, India	B2	37
Bilk Creek Mountains, mts., Nv., U.S.	B3	105
Billerica, Ma., U.S.	A5	98
Billings, Mo., U.S.	D4	102
Billings, Mt., U.S.	E8	103
Billings, co., N.D., U.S.	B2	111
Billings Heights, Mt., U.S.	E8	103
Bill Williams, stm., Az., U.S.	C1	80
Bill Williams Mountain, mtn., Az., U.S.	B3	80
Bilma, Niger	E8	42
Biloxi, Ms., U.S.	E5	101
Biloxi, stm., Ms., U.S.	E4	101
Biloxi Bay, b., Ms., U.S.	f8	101
Biltmore Forest, N.C., U.S.	f10	110
Bimini Islands, is., Bah.	B8	64
Bīna-Etāwa, India	H8	38
Bindura, Zimb.	E6	44
Binéfar, Spain	D12	12
Binga, Monte, mtn., Afr.	E6	44
Bingamon Creek, stm., W.V., U.S.	k10	125
Bingen, Ger.	F7	8
Bingen, Wa., U.S.	D4	124
Binger, Ok., U.S.	B3	113
Bingham, Me., U.S.	C3	96
Bingham, co., Id., U.S.	F6	89
Binghamton, N.Y., U.S.	C5	109
Binhai (Dongkan), China	A8	28
Binjai, Indon.	M5	34
Bintimani, mtn., S.L.	G3	42
Biograd, Cro.	F10	14
Bioko, i., Eq. Gui.	H7	42
Bīr, India	C3	37
Birao, Cen. Afr. Rep.	F10	42
Birātnagar, Nepal	G12	38
Birch, stm., W.V., U.S.	C4	125
Birch Island, i., Man., Can.	C2	70
Birch Lake, l., Mn., U.S.	C7	100
Birch River, Man., Can.	C1	70
Birch Run, Mi., U.S.	E7	99
Birchwood City, Md., U.S.	*f9	97
Birchy Bay, Newf., Can.	D4	72
Bird Creek, stm., Ok., U.S.	A6	113
Bird Island, Mn., U.S.	F4	100
Bird Island, i., N.C., U.S.	D4	110
Birdsboro, Pa., U.S.	F10	115
Birdum, Austl.	C6	50
Birecik, Tur.	A5	40
Bīrganj, Nepal	G11	38
Birigui, Braz.	F3	57
Biril'ussy, Russia	F12	24
Bīrjand, Iran	K9	22
Birkenfeld, Ger.	F7	8
Birkenhead, Eng., U.K.	H9	7
Bîrlad, Rom.	C11	16
Birmingham, Eng., U.K.	I11	7
Birmingham, Al., U.S.	B3	78
Birmingham, Mi., U.S.	F7	99
Birmitrapur, India	I11	38
Bir Mogreïn, Maur.	C3	42
Birobidžan, Russia	H20	24
Biron, Wi., U.S.	D4	126
Birr, Ire.	H5	7
Bi'r Safājah, Egypt	C12	42
Birtle, Man., Can.	D1	70
Bisbee, Az., U.S.	F6	80
Biscarrosse, Fr.	H5	10
Biscay, Bay of, b., Eur.	G7	4
Biscayne, Key, i., Fl., U.S.	s13	86
Biscayne Bay, b., Fl., U.S.	G6	86
Biscayne National Monument, Fl., U.S.	G6	86
Biscayne Park, Fl., U.S.	s13	86
Bisceglie, Italy	H11	14
Bischofshofen, Aus.	H13	8
Biscoe, N.C., U.S.	B3	110
Bishnupur, India	I12	38
Bishop, Ca., U.S.	D4	82
Bishop, Tx., U.S.	F4	120
Bishop Auckland, Eng., U.K.	G11	7
Bishop's Falls, Newf., Can.	D4	72
Bishopville, S.C., U.S.	C7	117
Biškek (Bishkek), Kyrg.	I12	22
Biskra, Alg.	B7	42
Bismarck, Il., U.S.	C6	90
Bismarck, Mo., U.S.	D7	102
Bismarck, N.D., U.S.	C5	111
Bismarck Archipelago, is., Pap. N. Gui.	m16	50a
Bismarck Range, mts., Pap. N. Gui.	m15	50a
Bison Peak, mtn., Co., U.S.	B5	83
Bissau, Gui.-B.	F2	42
Bistineau, Lake, res., La., U.S.	B2	95
Bistrița, Rom.	B8	16
Bitola, Mac.	H5	16
Bitonto, Italy	H11	14
Bitter Creek, stm., Wy., U.S.	E4	127
Bitterfeld, Ger.	D12	8
Bitterfontein, S. Afr.	H3	44
Bitter Lake, l., S.D., U.S.	B8	118
Bitterroot, stm., Mt., U.S.	D2	103
Bitterroot Range, mts., U.S.	B3	89
Bitti, Italy	I4	14
Biwabik, Mn., U.S.	C6	100
Biwa-ko, l., Japan	G9	30
Bixby, Ok., U.S.	B6	113
Biyang, China	C2	28
Bizen, Japan	H7	30
Bizerte, Tun.	L4	14
Bjelovar, Cro.	D11	14
Black (Lixian) (Da), stm., Asia	D8	34
Black, stm., Az., U.S.	D5	80
Black, stm., Ar., U.S.	B4	81
Black, stm., La., U.S.	C4	95
Black, stm., Mi., U.S.	E8	99
Black, stm., N.Y., U.S.	B4	109
Black, stm., N.C., U.S.	C4	110
Black, stm., S.C., U.S.	D8	117
Black, stm., Vt., U.S.	B4	122
Black, stm., Vt., U.S.	E3	122
Black, stm., Wi., U.S.	D3	126
Blackall, Austl.	D9	50
Black Bear Creek, stm., Ok., U.S.	A4	113
Blackbeard Island, i., Ga., U.S.	E5	87
Blackburn, Eng., U.K.	H10	7
Blackburn, Mount, mtn., Ak., U.S.	C11	79
Black Butte, mtn., Mt., U.S.	F5	103
Black Butte Lake, res., Ca., U.S.	C2	82
Black Canyon, val., Co., U.S.	C3	83
Black Canyon City, Az., U.S.	C3	80
Black Canyon of the Gunnison National Monument, Co., U.S.	C3	83
Black Creek, B.C., Can.	E5	69
Black Creek, Wi., U.S.	D5	126
Black Creek, stm., U.S.	B1	108
Black Creek, stm., S.C., U.S.	B7	117
Black Diamond, Alta., Can.	D3	68
Black Diamond, Wa., U.S.	B4	124
Blackduck, Mn., U.S.	C4	100
Black Eagle, Mt., U.S.	C5	103
Black Earth, Wi., U.S.	E4	126
Blackfalds, Alta., Can.	C4	68
Blackfeet Indian Reservation, Mt., U.S.	B4	103
Blackfoot, Id., U.S.	F6	89
Blackfoot, stm., Mt., U.S.	C3	103
Blackfoot Mountains, mts., Id., U.S.	F7	89
Blackfoot Reservoir, res., Id., U.S.	G7	89
Blackford, co., In., U.S.	D7	91
Black Forest, Co., U.S.	C6	83
Black Forest see Schwarzwald, mts., Ger.	G8	8
Blackhall Mountain, mtn., Wy., U.S.	E6	127
Black Hawk, S.D., U.S.	C2	118
Black Hawk, co., Ia., U.S.	B5	92
Black Hills, mts., U.S.	C2	118
Blackjack Mountain, mtn., Ga., U.S.	h8	87
Black Lake, Que., Can.	C6	74
Black Lake, l., Mi., U.S.	C6	99
Black Lake, l., N.Y., U.S.	f9	109
Black Lick, Pa., U.S.	F3	115
Blacklick Estates, Oh., U.S.	*m11	112
Black Mesa, mtn., Ok., U.S.	e8	113
Black Mingo Creek, stm., S.C., U.S.	D9	117
Blackmore, Mount, mtn., Mt., U.S.	E6	103
Black Mountain, N.C., U.S.	f10	110
Black Mountain, mtn., U.S.	D7	94
Black Mountain, mtn., Az., U.S.	E4	80
Black Mountain, mtn., Co., U.S.	A5	83
Black Mountain, mtn., Id., U.S.	C3	89
Black Mountain, mtn., Mt., U.S.	D4	103
Black Mountain, mtn., Or., U.S.	B7	114
Black Mountain, mtn., Wy., U.S.	B5	127
Black Mountain, mtn., Wy., U.S.	D7	127
Black Mountains, mts., Az., U.S.	B1	80
Black Peak, mtn., Az., U.S.	C1	80
Black Pine Peak, mtn., Id., U.S.	G5	89
Blackpool, Eng., U.K.	H9	7
Black Range, mts., N.M., U.S.	D2	108
Black River Falls, Wi., U.S.	D3	126
Black Rock, Ar., U.S.	A4	81
Black Rock, N.M., U.S.	B1	108
Black Rock Desert, des., Nv., U.S.	B3	105
Black Rock Range, mts., Nv., U.S.	B3	105
Blacksburg, S.C., U.S.	A4	117
Blacksburg, Va., U.S.	C2	123
Black Sea	G14	4
Blacks Fork, stm., U.S.	E3	127
Blacks Harbour, N.B., Can.	D3	71
Blackshear, Ga., U.S.	E4	87
Blackstone, Ma., U.S.	B4	98
Blackstone, Va., U.S.	C5	123
Blackstone, stm., R.I., U.S.	B4	116
Black Thunder Creek, stm., Wy., U.S.	C8	127
Blackville, N.B., Can.	C4	71
Blackville, S.C., U.S.	E5	117
Black Volta (Volta Noire), stm., Afr.	G5	42
Blackwalnut Point, c., Md., U.S.	C5	97
Black Warrior, stm., Al., U.S.	C2	78
Blackwater, stm., Fl., U.S.	u15	86
Blackwater, stm., Md., U.S.	D5	97
Blackwater, stm., N.H., U.S.	D3	106
Blackwater, stm., Va., U.S.	D6	123
Blackwater Reservoir, res., N.H., U.S.	D3	106
Blackwell, Ok., U.S.	A4	113
Blackwood, N.J., U.S.	D2	107
Bladen, co., N.C., U.S.	C4	110
Bladenboro, N.C., U.S.	C4	110
Bladensburg, Md., U.S.	f9	97
Blades, De., U.S.	F3	85
Blagoevgrad, Bul.	G7	16
Blagoveščensk, Russia	G19	24
Blaine, Me., U.S.	B5	96
Blaine, Mn., U.S.	m12	100
Blaine, Tn., U.S.	C10	119
Blaine, Wa., U.S.	A3	124
Blaine, co., Id., U.S.	F4	89
Blaine, co., Mt., U.S.	B7	103
Blaine, co., Ne., U.S.	C6	104
Blaine, co., Ok., U.S.	B3	113
Blaine Lake, Sask., Can.	E2	75
Blair, Ne., U.S.	C9	104
Blair, Ok., U.S.	C2	113
Blair, W.V., U.S.	n12	125
Blair, Wi., U.S.	D2	126
Blair, co., Pa., U.S.	E5	115
Blair Athol, Austl.	D9	50
Blairstown, Ia., U.S.	C5	92
Blairsville, Pa., U.S.	F3	115
Blake Island, i., Wa., U.S.	e11	124
Blakely, Ga., U.S.	E2	87
Blakely, Pa., U.S.	m18	115
Blake Point, c., Mi., U.S.	h10	99
Blanc, Cap, c., Afr.	D2	42
Blanc, Mont (Monte Bianco), mtn., Eur.	G13	10
Blanca Peak, mtn., Co., U.S.	D5	83
Blanchard, La., U.S.	B2	95
Blanchard, Ok., U.S.	B4	113
Blanchard, stm., Oh., U.S.	A1	112
Blanchardville, Wi., U.S.	F4	126
Blanchester, Oh., U.S.	C2	112
Blanco, Tx., U.S.	D3	120

Index

Name	Map Ref	Page
Blanco, co., Tx., U.S.	D3	120
Blanco, Cape, c., Or., U.S.	E2	114
Bland, Mo., U.S.	C6	102
Bland, co., Va., U.S.	C1	123
Blanding, Ut., U.S.	F6	121
Blandinsville, Il., U.S.	C3	90
Blanes, Spain	D14	12
Blangkedjeren, Indon.	M4	34
Blangy-sur-Bresle, Fr.	C8	10
Blanquilla, Isla, i., Ven.	B10	58
Blantyre, Mwi.	E7	44
Blasdell, N.Y., U.S.	C2	109
Blawnox, Pa., U.S.	k14	115
Blaye-et-Sainte-Luce, Fr.	G6	10
Bleckley, co., Ga., U.S.	D3	87
Bled, Slo.	C9	14
Bledsoe, co., Tn., U.S.	D8	119
Blende, Co., U.S.	C6	83
Blenheim, Ont., Can.	E3	73
Blenheim, N.Z.	D4	52
Blennerhassett, W.V., U.S.	B3	125
Bléré, Fr.	E7	10
Blida, Alg.	A6	42
Blind, stm., La., U.S.	h10	95
Blind River, Ont., Can.	A2	73
Blissfield, Mi., U.S.	G7	99
Blitar, Indon.	n16	32
Block Island, R.I., U.S.	h7	116
Block Island, i., R.I., U.S.	h7	116
Block Island Sound, strt., U.S.	G2	116
Bloemfontein, S. Afr.	G5	44
Bloemhof, S. Afr.	G5	44
Blois, Fr.	E8	10
Blood Mountain, mtn., Ga., U.S.	B3	87
Bloodsworth Island, i., Md., U.S.	D5	97
Bloodvein, stm., Can.	D3	70
Bloody Foreland, c., Ire.	F4	7
Bloomer, Wi., U.S.	C2	126
Bloomfield, Ont., Can.	D7	73
Bloomfield, Ct., U.S.	B5	84
Bloomfield, In., U.S.	F4	91
Bloomfield, Ia., U.S.	D5	92
Bloomfield, Ky., U.S.	C4	94
Bloomfield, Mo., U.S.	E8	102
Bloomfield, Ne., U.S.	B8	104
Bloomfield, N.J., U.S.	h8	107
Bloomfield, N.M., U.S.	A2	108
Bloomfield Hills, Mi., U.S.	o15	99
Bloomingdale, Ga., U.S.	D5	87
Bloomingdale, Il., U.S.	k8	90
Bloomingdale, N.J., U.S.	A4	107
Bloomingdale, Tn., U.S.	C11	119
Blooming Prairie, Mn., U.S.	G5	100
Bloomington, Il., U.S.	C4	90
Bloomington, In., U.S.	F4	91
Bloomington, Mn., U.S.	F5	100
Bloomington, Tx., U.S.	E4	120
Bloomington, Wi., U.S.	F3	126
Bloomington, Lake, res., Il., U.S.	C5	90
Bloomsburg, Pa., U.S.	E9	115
Bloomville, Oh., U.S.	A2	112
Blora, Indon.	m15	33a
Blossburg, Pa., U.S.	C7	115
Blossom, Tx., U.S.	C5	120
Blount, co., Al., U.S.	B3	78
Blount, co., Tn., U.S.	D10	119
Blountstown, Fl., U.S.	B1	86
Blountsville, Al., U.S.	A3	78
Blountville, Tn., U.S.	C11	119
Blowing Rock, N.C., U.S.	A1	110
Bludenz, Aus.	H9	8
Blue, stm., Co., U.S.	B4	83
Blue, stm., In., U.S.	H5	91
Blue, stm., Mo., U.S.	k10	102
Blue, stm., Ok., U.S.	C5	113
Blue Ash, Oh., U.S.	o13	112
Blue Buck Point, c., La., U.S.	E2	95
Blue Creek, W.V., U.S.	m13	125
Blue Creek, stm., W.V., U.S.	m13	125
Blue Cypress Lake, l., Fl., U.S.	E6	86
Blue Diamond, Nv., U.S.	G6	105
Blue Earth, Mn., U.S.	G4	100
Blue Earth, co., Mn., U.S.	G4	100
Blue Earth, stm., Mn., U.S.	G4	100
Bluefield, Va., U.S.	C1	123
Bluefield, W.V., U.S.	D3	125
Bluefields, Nic.	H6	64
Blue Grass, Ia., U.S.	C7	92
Blue Hill, Me., U.S.	D4	96
Blue Hill, Ne., U.S.	D7	104
Blue Hill Range, hills, Ma., U.S.	h11	98
Blue Hills, Ct., U.S.	B5	84
Blue Island, Il., U.S.	B6	90
Bluejoint Lake, l., Or., U.S.	E7	114
Blue Lake, Ca., U.S.	B2	82
Blue Mesa Reservoir, res., Co., U.S.	C3	83
Blue Mound, Il., U.S.	D4	90
Blue Mountain, Ms., U.S.	A4	101
Blue Mountain, mtn., Mt., U.S.	C12	103
Blue Mountain, mtn., N.M., U.S.	D2	108
Blue Mountain, mtn., Pa., U.S.	F6	115
Blue Mountain Lake, res., Ar., U.S.	B2	81
Blue Mountain Peak, mtn., Jam.	E9	64
Blue Nile (Al-Bahr al-Azraq), stm., Afr.	F12	42
Blue Point, Me., U.S.	g7	96
Blue Rapids, Ks., U.S.	C7	93
Blue Ridge, Ga., U.S.	B2	87
Blue Ridge, Va., U.S.	C3	123
Blue Ridge, mtn., U.S.	E10	76
Blue Ridge Summit, Pa., U.S.	G7	115
Blue Springs, Mo., U.S.	h11	102
Bluestone, stm., W.V., U.S.	D3	125
Bluestone Lake, res., U.S.	D4	125
Bluewell, W.V., U.S.	D3	125
Bluff City, Tn., U.S.	C11	119
Bluff Creek, stm., Ok., U.S.	A4	113
Bluff Lake, res., Ms., U.S.	B5	101
Bluff Park, Al., U.S.	g7	78
Bluffs, Il., U.S.	D3	90
Bluffton, In., U.S.	C7	91
Bluffton, Oh., U.S.	B2	112
Bluffton, S.C., U.S.	G6	117
Blumenau, Braz.	B7	56
Bly, Or., U.S.	E5	114
Blying Sound, strt., Ak., U.S.	h17	79
Blyth, Ont., Can.	D3	73
Blyth, Eng., U.K.	F11	7
Blythe, Ca., U.S.	F6	82
Blytheville, Ar., U.S.	B6	81
Bø, Nor.	B10	6
Bø, Nor.	G7	6
Bo, S.L.	G3	42
Boaco, Nic.	H5	64
Boalsburg, Pa., U.S.	E6	115
Boa Nova, Braz.	C8	57
Boardman, Oh., U.S.	A5	112
Boardman, Or., U.S.	B7	114
Boa Vista, Braz.	C6	54
Boavita, Col.	D6	58
Boaz, Al., U.S.	A3	78
Bobbili, India	C7	37
Bobbio, Italy	E4	14
Bobcaygeon, Ont., Can.	C6	73
Böblingen, Ger.	G9	8
Bobo Dioulasso, Burkina	F5	42
Bobrujsk, Bela.	H12	18
Bobtown, Pa., U.S.	G2	115
Bobures, Ven.	C7	58
Boby, Pic, mtn., Madag.	F9	44
Boca Chica Key, i., Fl., U.S.	H5	86
Boca Ciega Bay, b., Fl., U.S.	p10	86
Bôca do Acre, Braz.	E5	54
Boca Grande, Fl., U.S.	F4	86
Boca Raton, Fl., U.S.	F6	86
Bocas del Toro, Pan.	J6	64
Bocholt, Ger.	D6	8
Bochum, Ger.	D7	8
Bodajbo, Russia	F16	24
Bodega Head, c., Ca., U.S.	C2	82
Bodele, reg., Chad	E9	42
Boden, Swe.	D13	6
Bodensee, l., Eur.	H9	8
Bodhan, India	C4	37
Bodie Island, i., N.C., U.S.	B7	110
Bodināyakkanūr, India	G4	37
Bodkin Point, c., Md., U.S.	B5	97
Bodø, Nor.	C10	6
Boende, Zaire	B4	44
Boën-sur-Lignon, Fr.	G10	10
Boerne, Tx., U.S.	E3	120
Boeuf, stm., La., U.S.	C4	95
Boeuf, Lake, l., La., U.S.	k10	95
Bogale, Mya.	F3	34
Bogalusa, La., U.S.	D6	95
Bogart, Ga., U.S.	C3	87
Bogata, Tx., U.S.	C5	120
Bogenfels, Nmb.	G3	44
Boger City, N.C., U.S.	B1	110
Bognes, Nor.	B10	6
Bogor, Indon.	m13	32
Bogorodick, Russia	H21	18
Bogorodsk, Russia	E26	18
Bogota, N.J., U.S.	h8	107
Bogotá see Santa Fe de Bogotá, Col.	E5	58
Bogotol, Russia	F11	24
Bogra, Bngl.	H13	38
Bogučany, Russia	F13	24
Bogue Chitto, Ms., U.S.	D3	101
Bogue Chitto, stm., U.S.	D5	95
Bogue Inlet, b., N.C., U.S.	C5	110
Bogue Phalia, stm., Ms., U.S.	B3	101
Bo Hai, b., China	D10	26
Bohain-en-Vermandois, Fr.	C10	10
Bohemia see Čechy, hist. reg., Czech.	F14	8
Bohemian Forest, mts., Eur.	F12	8
Bohol, i., Phil.	D7	32
Boiano, Italy	H9	14
Boigu, i., Austl.	A8	50
Boiling Springs, N.C., U.S.	B1	110
Boiling Springs, Pa., U.S.	F7	115
Bois Blanc Island, i., Mi., U.S.	C6	99
Bois Brule, stm., Wi., U.S.	B2	126
Boischâtel, Que., Can.	C6	74
Bois-des-Filion, Que., Can.	p19	74
Bois de Sioux, stm., Mn., U.S.	E2	100
Boise, Id., U.S.	F2	89
Boise, co., Id., U.S.	F3	89
Boise City, Ok., U.S.	e8	113
Boissevain, Man., Can.	E1	70
Boissevain, Va., U.S.	e10	123
Boistfort Peak, mtn., Wa., U.S.	C2	124
Boizenburg, Ger.	B10	8
Bojador, Cabo, c., W. Sah.	C3	42
Bojeador, Cape, c., Phil.	B7	32
Bojnūrd, Iran	J9	22
Bojonegoro, Indon.	m15	33a
Boké, Gui.	F3	42
Boketu, China	B11	26
Boknafjorden, Nor.	G5	6
Boksitogorsk, Russia	B16	18
Bokungu, Zaire	B4	44
Bolama, Gui.-B.	F2	42
Bolbec, Fr.	C7	10
Bolesławiec, Pol.	D15	8
Boley, Ok., U.S.	B5	113
Bolgatanga, Ghana	F5	42
Boli, China	B13	26
Bolingbrook, Il., U.S.	k8	90
Bolívar, Arg.	D4	56
Bolivar, Mo., U.S.	D4	102
Bolivar, Oh., U.S.	B4	112
Bolivar, Tn., U.S.	B3	119
Bolivar, W.V., U.S.	B7	125
Bolivar, co., Ms., U.S.	B3	101
Bolívar, Cerro, mtn., Ven.	D11	58
Bolivar, Lake, l., Ms., U.S.	B3	101
Bolívar, Pico, mtn., Ven.	C7	58
Bolivia, ctry., S.A.	G5	54
Bollène, Fr.	H11	10
Bollinger, co., Mo., U.S.	D7	102
Bollnäs, Swe.	F11	6
Bollullos par del Condado, Spain	H5	12
Bolobo, Zaire	B3	44
Bologna, Italy	E6	14
Bologoje, Russia	D17	18
Bolotnoje, Russia	F10	24
Bolsena, Italy	G6	14
Bol'šereck, Russia	G25	24
Bol'ševik, Russia	E23	24
Bol'ševik, Ostrov, i., Russia	B14	24
Bol'šoj An'uj, stm., Russia	D26	24
Bol'šoj Begičev, Ostrov, i., Russia	C16	24
Bol'šoj L'achovskij, Ostrov, i., Russia	C22	24
Bolton, Eng., U.K.	H10	7
Bolton, Ms., U.S.	C3	101
Bolton Lakes, l., Ct., U.S.	B6	84
Bolton Landing, N.Y., U.S.	B7	109
Bolzano (Bozen), Italy	C6	14
Boma, Zaire	C2	44
Bombala, Austl.	G9	50
Bombarral, Port.	F2	12
Bombay, India	C2	37
Bombay Hook Island, i., De., U.S.	C4	85
Bom Despacho, Braz.	E6	57
Bom Jesus da Lapa, Braz.	B7	57
Bomoseen, Lake, l., Vt., U.S.	D2	122
Bomu (Mbomou), stm., Afr.	H10	42
Bon, Cap, c., Tun.	A8	42
Bon Accord, Alta., Can.	C4	68
Bon Air, Va., U.S.	C5	123
Bonaire, Ga., U.S.	D3	87
Bonaire, i., Neth. Ant.	H13	64
Bonanza Peak, mtn., Wa., U.S.	A5	124
Bonao, Dom. Rep.	E12	64
Bonaparte, Mount, mtn., Wa., U.S.	A6	124
Bonaparte Archipelago, is., Austl.	B5	50
Bonarbridge, Scot., U.K.	D8	7
Bonasila Dome, mtn., Ak., U.S.	C7	79
Bonaventure, Que., Can.	A4	71
Bonavista, Newf., Can.	D5	72
Bonavista, Cape, c., Newf., Can.	D5	72
Bonavista Bay, b., Newf., Can.	G22	66
Bonavista Bay, b., Newf., Can.	D5	72
Bond, co., Il., U.S.	E4	90
Bondeno, Italy	E6	14
Bondo, Zaire	H10	42
Bondoukou, C. Iv.	G5	42
Bondowoso, Indon.	m16	33a
Bondsville, Ma., U.S.	B3	98
Bonduel, Wi., U.S.	D5	126
Bondurant, Ia., U.S.	C4	92
Bone, Teluk, b., Indon.	F7	32
Bone Lake, l., Wi., U.S.	C1	126
Bongandanga, Zaire	A4	44
Bongor, Chad	F9	42
Bonham, Tx., U.S.	C4	120
Bon Homme, co., S.D., U.S.	D8	118
Bonifati, Capo, c., Italy	J10	14
Bonifay, Fl., U.S.	u16	86
Bonita Springs, Fl., U.S.	F5	86
Bonn, Ger.	E7	8
Bonneauville, Pa., U.S.	G7	115
Bonne Bay, b., Newf., Can.	D3	72
Bonner, co., Id., U.S.	A2	89
Bonners Ferry, Id., U.S.	A2	89
Bonner Springs, Ks., U.S.	C9	93
Bonnet Carre Floodway, La., U.S.	h11	95
Bonne Terre, Mo., U.S.	D7	102
Bonneval, Fr.	D8	10
Bonneville, Fr.	F13	10
Bonneville, co., Id., U.S.	F7	89
Bonneville Dam, U.S.	B4	114
Bonneville Peak, mtn., Id., U.S.	F6	89
Bonneville Salt Flats, pl., Ut., U.S.	C2	121
Bonney Lake, Wa., U.S.	B3	124
Bonnie Doone, N.C., U.S.	B4	110
Bonny Reservoir, res., Co., U.S.	B8	83
Bonnyville, Alta., Can.	B5	68
Bono, Ar., U.S.	B5	81
Bonorva, Italy	I3	14
Bon Secour, Al., U.S.	E2	78
Bonthe, S.L.	G3	42
Booker, Tx., U.S.	A2	120
Booker T. Washington National Monument, Va., U.S.	C3	123
Boomer, W.V., U.S.	C3	125
Boone, Ia., U.S.	B4	92
Boone, N.C., U.S.	A1	110
Boone, co., Ar., U.S.	A2	81
Boone, co., Il., U.S.	A5	90
Boone, co., In., U.S.	D4	91
Boone, co., Ia., U.S.	B3	92
Boone, co., Ky., U.S.	B5	94
Boone, co., Mo., U.S.	B5	102
Boone, co., Ne., U.S.	C7	104
Boone, co., W.V., U.S.	C3	125
Boone, stm., Ia., U.S.	B4	92
Boone Lake, res., Tn., U.S.	C11	119
Booneville, Ar., U.S.	B2	81
Booneville, Ms., U.S.	A5	101
Boonsboro, Md., U.S.	A2	97
Boonton, N.J., U.S.	B4	107
Boonville, In., U.S.	H3	91
Boonville, Mo., U.S.	C5	102
Boonville, N.Y., U.S.	B5	109
Boonville, N.C., U.S.	A2	110
Boothbay Harbor, Me., U.S.	E3	96
Boothia, Gulf of, b., N.W. Ter., Can.	B14	66
Boothia Peninsula, pen., N.W. Ter., Can.	B14	66
Booths Creek, stm., W.V., U.S.	h11	125
Boothville, La., U.S.	E6	95
Booué, Gabon	B2	44
Boquete, Pan.	J6	64
Boquillas del Carmen, Mex.	C8	62
Bor, Russia	E27	18
Bor, Sudan	G12	42
Boraha, Nosy, i., Madag.	E9	44
Borah Peak, mtn., Id., U.S.	E5	89
Borås, Swe.	H9	6
Bordeaux, Fr.	H6	10
Borden, co., Tx., U.S.	C2	120
Borden Peninsula, pen., N.W. Ter., Can.	B16	66
Bordentown, N.J., U.S.	C3	107
Bordertown, Austl.	G8	50
Borgå (Porvoo), Fin.	F15	6
Borgarnes, Ice.	C3	4
Borger, Tx., U.S.	B2	120
Borgne, Lake, b., La., U.S.	D6	95
Borgo, Italy	C6	14
Borgo San Dalmazzo, Italy	E2	14
Borgosesia, Italy	D3	14
Borgo Val di Taro, Italy	E4	14
Borisov, Bela.	G11	18
Borja, Spain	D10	12
Borjas Blancas, Spain	D12	12
Borken, Ger.	D6	8
Borlänge, Swe.	F10	6
Borlu, Tur.	K12	16
Borneo (Kalimantan), i., Asia	E5	32
Bornholm, i., Den.	I10	6
Bornova, Tur.	K11	16
Borogoncy, Russia	E20	24
Boron, Ca., U.S.	E5	82
Boronga Islands, is., Mya.	E2	34
Boroviči, Russia	C16	18
Borrego Springs, Ca., U.S.	F5	82
Bort-les-Orgues, Fr.	G9	10
Borūjerd, Iran	B4	46
Borz'a, Russia	G17	24
Bosa, Italy	I3	14
Bosanska Gradiška, Bos.	D12	14
Bosanska Krupa, Bos.	E11	14
Bosanski Novi, Bos.	D11	14
Bosanski Petrovac, Bos.	E11	14
Bosaso, Som.	F4	46
Boscobel, Wi., U.S.	E3	126
Boshan, China	D10	26
Bosnia and Herzegovina, ctry., Eur.	E12	14
Bosporus see İstanbul Boğazı, strt., Tur.	H13	16
Bosque, co., Tx., U.S.	D4	120
Bossangoa, Cen. Afr. Rep.	G9	42
Bossembélé, Cen. Afr. Rep.	G9	42
Bossier, co., La., U.S.	B2	95
Bossier City, La., U.S.	B2	95
Bosten Hu, l., China	C4	26
Boston, Eng., U.K.	I12	7
Boston, Ga., U.S.	F3	87
Boston, Ma., U.S.	B5	98
Boston Bay, b., Ma., U.S.	B6	98
Boston Mountains, mts., Ar., U.S.	B2	81
Boswell, In., U.S.	C3	91
Boswell, Ok., U.S.	C6	113
Boswell, Pa., U.S.	F3	115
Botād, India	I4	38
Boteti, stm., Bots.	F4	44
Botetourt, co., Va., U.S.	C3	123
Bothell, Wa., U.S.	B3	124
Bothnia, Gulf of, b., Eur.	E12	6
Bothwell, Ont., Can.	E3	73
Botkins, Oh., U.S.	B1	112
Botoşani, Rom.	B10	16
Botswana, ctry., Afr.	F4	44
Bottenhavet (Selkämeri), b., Eur.	F12	6
Bottenviken (Perämeri), b., Eur.	D14	6
Bottineau, N.D., U.S.	A5	111
Bottineau, co., N.D., U.S.	A4	111
Botucatu, Braz.	G4	57
Botwood, Newf., Can.	D4	72
Bouaflé, C. Iv.	G4	42
Bouaké, C. Iv.	G4	42
Bouar, Cen. Afr. Rep.	G9	42
Bou Arada, Tun.	M4	14
Boucherville, Que., Can.	D4	74
Bouctouche, N.B., Can.	C5	71
Boudreaux, Lake, l., La., U.S.	E5	95
Bou Ficha, Tun.	M5	14
Bougainville Reef, rf., Austl.	C9	50
Bougouni, Mali	F4	42
Bouillon, Bel.	F5	8
Boulder, Co., U.S.	A5	83
Boulder, Mt., U.S.	D4	103
Boulder, co., Co., U.S.	A5	83
Boulder City, Nv., U.S.	H7	105
Boulevard Heights, Md., U.S.	f9	97
Boulogne-Billancourt, Fr.	D9	10
Boulogne-sur-Gesse, Fr.	I7	10
Boulogne-sur-Mer, Fr.	B8	10
Bouna, C. Iv.	G5	42
Boundary, co., Id., U.S.	A2	89
Boundary Bay, b., Wa., U.S.	A3	124
Boundary Peak, mtn., Nv., U.S.	F3	105
Bound Brook, N.J., U.S.	B3	107
Bountiful, Ut., U.S.	C4	121
Bourbeuse, stm., Mo., U.S.	C6	102
Bourbon, In., U.S.	B5	91
Bourbon, Mo., U.S.	C6	102
Bourbon, co., Ks., U.S.	E9	93
Bourbon, co., Ky., U.S.	B5	94
Bourbonnais, Il., U.S.	B6	90
Bourbonnais, hist. reg., Fr.	F9	10
Bourbonne-les-Bains, Fr.	E12	10
Bourem, Mali	E5	42
Bourg, La., U.S.	E5	95
Bourganeuf, Fr.	G8	10
Bourg-en-Bresse, Fr.	F12	10
Bourges, Fr.	E9	10
Bourg-Lastic, Fr.	G9	10
Bourgogne, hist. reg., Fr.	E11	10
Bourgoin, Fr.	G12	10
Bourg-Saint-Andéol, Fr.	H11	10
Bourg-Saint-Maurice, Fr.	G13	10
Bourke, Austl.	F9	50
Bournemouth, Eng., U.K.	K11	7
Bou Saâda, Alg.	A6	42
Bouse, Az., U.S.	D2	80
Boussac, Fr.	F9	10
Bousso, Chad	F9	42
Boutte, La., U.S.	k11	95
Bøvågen, Nor.	F5	6
Bovalino Marina, Italy	K11	14
Bovec, Slo.	C8	14
Bøverdal, Nor.	F7	6
Bovey, Mn., U.S.	C5	100
Bovina, Tx., U.S.	B1	120
Bow, N.H., U.S.	D3	106
Bow, stm., Alta., Can.	D4	68
Bowden, Alta., Can.	D4	68
Bowdish Reservoir, res., R.I., U.S.	B1	116
Bowdon, Ga., U.S.	C1	87
Bowen, Austl.	C9	50
Bowie, Az., U.S.	E6	80
Bowie, Md., U.S.	C4	97
Bowie, Tx., U.S.	C4	120
Bowie, co., Tx., U.S.	C5	120
Bow Island, Alta., Can.	E5	68
Bow Lake, l., N.H., U.S.	D4	106
Bowling Green, Fl., U.S.	E5	86
Bowling Green, Ky., U.S.	D3	94
Bowling Green, Mo., U.S.	B6	102
Bowling Green, Oh., U.S.	A2	112
Bowling Green, S.C., U.S.	A5	117
Bowling Green, Va., U.S.	B5	123
Bowman, Ga., U.S.	B3	87
Bowman, N.D., U.S.	C2	111
Bowman, S.C., U.S.	E6	117
Bowman, co., N.D., U.S.	C2	111
Bowman Creek, stm., Pa., U.S.	m16	115
Bowman-Haley Lake, res., N.D., U.S.	C2	111
Bowron, stm., B.C., Can.	C7	69
Bowstring Lake, l., Mn., U.S.	C5	100
Box Butte, co., Ne., U.S.	B2	104
Box Butte Reservoir, res., Ne., U.S.	B2	104
Box Elder, S.D., U.S.	C2	118
Box Elder, co., Ut., U.S.	B2	121
Boxford, Ma., U.S.	A6	98
Boxian, China	B4	28
Boyce, La., U.S.	C3	95
Boyceville, Wi., U.S.	C1	126
Boyd, Tx., U.S.	C4	120
Boyd, co., Ky., U.S.	B7	94
Boyd, co., Ne., U.S.	B7	104
Boyden, Ia., U.S.	A2	92
Boyd Lake, l., Me., U.S.	C4	96
Boyer, stm., Ia., U.S.	C2	92
Boyertown, Pa., U.S.	F10	115
Boykins, Va., U.S.	D5	123
Boyle, Alta., Can.	B4	68
Boyle, Ire.	H4	7
Boyle, Ms., U.S.	B3	101
Boyle, co., Ky., U.S.	C5	94
Boyne City, Mi., U.S.	C6	99
Boynton Beach, Fl., U.S.	F6	86
Boysen Reservoir, res., Wy., U.S.	C4	127
Boys Town, Ne., U.S.	g12	104
Bozburun, Tur.	M12	16
Boz Dağ, mtn., Tur.	L13	16
Bozeman, Mt., U.S.	E5	103
Bozeman Pass, Mt., U.S.	E6	103
Bozoum, Cen. Afr. Rep.	G9	42
Bra, Italy	E2	14
Bracciano, Italy	G7	14
Bracebridge, Ont., Can.	B5	73
Bräcke, Swe.	E10	6
Bracken, co., Ky., U.S.	B5	94
Brackenridge, Pa., U.S.	h15	115
Brackettville, Tx., U.S.	E2	120
Braddock, Pa., U.S.	k14	115
Braddock Heights, Md., U.S.	B2	97
Braddock Point, c., S.C., U.S.	G6	117
Bradenton, Fl., U.S.	E4	86
Bradenville, Pa., U.S.	F3	115
Bradford, Eng., U.K.	H11	7
Bradford, Ar., U.S.	B4	81
Bradford, Oh., U.S.	B1	112
Bradford, Pa., U.S.	C4	115
Bradford, R.I., U.S.	F2	116
Bradford, Tn., U.S.	A3	119
Bradford, Vt., U.S.	D4	122
Bradford, co., Fl., U.S.	C4	86
Bradford, co., Pa., U.S.	C8	115
Bradford [West Gwillimbury], Ont., Can.	C5	73
Bradfordwoods, Pa., U.S.	h13	115
Bradley, Il., U.S.	B6	90
Bradley, Me., U.S.	D4	96
Bradley, W.V., U.S.	D3	125
Bradley, co., Ar., U.S.	D3	81
Bradley, co., Tn., U.S.	D9	119
Bradley Beach, N.J., U.S.	C4	107
Bradner, Oh., U.S.	A2	112
Bradshaw, Md., U.S.	B5	97
Bradshaw Mountains, mts., Az., U.S.	C3	80
Brady, Tx., U.S.	D3	120
Braga, Port.	D3	12
Bragado, Arg.	D4	56
Bragança, Port.	D5	12
Braham, Mn., U.S.	E5	100
Brāhmanbāria, Bngl.	I14	38
Brāhmani, stm., India	J11	38
Brahmaputra (Yarlung), stm., Asia	G15	38
Braich y Pwll, c., Wales, U.K.	I8	7
Braidwood, Il., U.S.	B5	90
Brăila, Rom.	D11	16
Brainerd, Mn., U.S.	D4	100
Braintree, Ma., U.S.	B5	98
Brake, Ger.	B8	8
Brampton, Ont., Can.	D5	73
Bramsche, Ger.	C7	8
Bramwell, W.V., U.S.	D3	125
Branch, co., Mi., U.S.	G5	99
Branch, stm., R.I., U.S.	B3	116
Branch, stm., Wi., U.S.	h10	126
Branch Lake, l., Me., U.S.	D4	96
Branch Village, R.I., U.S.	B3	116
Branchville, S.C., U.S.	E6	117
Branco, stm., Braz.	C6	54
Brandberg, mtn., Nmb.	F2	44
Brandbu, Nor.	F8	6
Brandenburg, Ger.	C12	8
Brandenburg, Ky., U.S.	C3	94
Brandon, Man., Can.	E2	70
Brandon, Fl., U.S.	E4	86
Brandon, Ms., U.S.	C4	101
Brandon, S.C., U.S.	B3	117
Brandon, S.D., U.S.	D9	118
Brandon, Vt., U.S.	D2	122
Brandon, Wi., U.S.	E5	126
Brandvlei, S. Afr.	H4	44
Brandy Peak, mtn., Or., U.S.	E3	114
Brandywine, Md., U.S.	C4	97
Brandywine Creek, stm., U.S.	A3	85
Branford, Ct., U.S.	D4	84
Branford Hills, Ct., U.S.	D4	84
Br'ansk, Russia	H17	18
Branson, Mo., U.S.	E4	102
Brantford, Ont., Can.	D4	73
Brantley, Al., U.S.	D3	78
Brantley, co., Ga., U.S.	E4	87
Brantôme, Fr.	G7	10
Brant Rock, Ma., U.S.	B6	98
Brantville, N.B., Can.	B5	71
Bras d'Or Lake, l., N.S., Can.	D9	71
Brasília, Braz.	C5	57
Braşov, Rom.	D9	16
Brasstown Bald, mtn., Ga., U.S.	B3	87
Brassua Lake, res., Me., U.S.	C3	96
Bratenahl, Oh., U.S.	g9	112

Name	Map Ref	Page
Bratislava, Slov.	G17	8
Bratsk, Russia	F14	24
Bratskoje Vodochranilišče, res., Russia	F14	24
Brattleboro, Vt., U.S.	F3	122
Braunau [am Inn], Aus.	G13	8
Braunschweig, Ger.	C10	8
Brava, Som.	H3	46
Brava, Costa, Spain	D15	12
Bravo del Norte (Rio Grande), stm., N.A.	F6	76
Brawley, Ca., U.S.	F6	82
Brawley Peaks, mts., Nv., U.S.	E3	105
Braxton, co., W.V., U.S.	C4	125
Bray, Ire.	H6	7
Bray, Ok., U.S.	C4	113
Bray Island, i., N.W. Ter., Can.	C17	66
Braymer, Mo., U.S.	B4	102
Brazeau, stm., Alta., Can.	C2	68
Brazil, In., U.S.	E3	91
Brazil, ctry., S.A.	E7	54
Brazoria, Tx., U.S.	r14	120
Brazoria, co., Tx., U.S.	E5	120
Brazos, co., Tx., U.S.	D4	120
Brazos, stm., Tx., U.S.	D4	120
Brazzaville, Congo	B3	44
Brčko, Bos.	E2	16
Brea, Ca., U.S.	n13	82
Breakenridge, Mount, mtn., B.C., Can.	E7	69
Breathitt, co., Ky., U.S.	C6	94
Breaux Bridge, La., U.S.	D4	95
Brebes, Indon.	m14	33a
Breckenridge, Co., U.S.	B4	83
Breckenridge, Mi., U.S.	E6	99
Breckenridge, Mn., U.S.	D2	100
Breckenridge, Tx., U.S.	C3	120
Breckinridge, co., Ky., U.S.	C3	94
Brecksville, Oh., U.S.	A4	112
Brecon Beacons National Park, Wales, U.K.	J9	7
Breda, Neth.	D4	8
Bredstedt, Ger.	A8	8
Breese, Il., U.S.	E4	90
Bréhal, Fr.	D5	10
Brekstad, Nor.	E7	6
Bremen, Ger.	B8	8
Bremen, Ga., U.S.	C1	87
Bremen, In., U.S.	B5	91
Bremen, Oh., U.S.	C3	112
Bremer, co., Ia., U.S.	B5	92
Bremerhaven, Ger.	B8	8
Bremerton, Wa., U.S.	B3	124
Bremond, Tx., U.S.	D4	120
Brenham, Tx., U.S.	D4	120
Brenner Pass, Eur.	B6	14
Breno, Italy	D5	14
Brent, Al., U.S.	C2	78
Brent, Fl., U.S.	u14	86
Brenton Point, c., R.I., U.S.	F5	116
Brentwood, Ca., U.S.	h9	82
Brentwood, Md., U.S.	f9	97
Brentwood, Mo., U.S.	f13	102
Brentwood, N.Y., U.S.	E7	109
Brentwood, Pa., U.S.	k14	115
Brentwood, S.C., U.S.	k11	117
Brentwood, Tn., U.S.	A5	119
Brescia, Italy	D5	14
Breslau see Wrocław, Pol.	D17	8
Bressanone, Italy	C6	14
Bressuire, Fr.	F6	10
Brest, Bela.	I6	18
Brest, Fr.	D2	10
Bretagne, hist. reg., Fr.	D3	10
Breton Islands, is., La., U.S.	E6	95
Breton Sound, strt., La., U.S.	E6	95
Brevard, N.C., U.S.	f10	110
Brevard, co., Fl., U.S.	E6	86
Brevoort Lake, l., Mi., U.S.	B6	99
Brewer, Me., U.S.	D4	96
Brewster, Ma., U.S.	C7	98
Brewster, N.Y., U.S.	D7	109
Brewster, Oh., U.S.	B4	112
Brewster, Wa., U.S.	A6	124
Brewster, co., Tx., U.S.	E1	120
Brewster Islands, is., Ma., U.S.	g12	98
Brewton, Al., U.S.	D2	78
Brežice, Slo.	D10	14
Bria, Cen. Afr. Rep.	G10	42
Brian Boru Peak, mtn., B.C., Can.	B4	69
Briançon, Fr.	H13	10
Brian Head, mtn., Ut., U.S.	F3	121
Briare, Fr.	E9	10
Briceville, Tn., U.S.	C9	119
Brick [Township], N.J., U.S.	C4	107
Bricquebec, Fr.	C5	10
Bridal Veil Falls, wtfl, Ut., U.S.	C4	121
Bridgehampton, N.Y., U.S.	n16	109
Bridgeport, Al., U.S.	A4	78
Bridgeport, Ct., U.S.	E3	84
Bridgeport, Il., U.S.	E6	90
Bridgeport, Mi., U.S.	E7	99
Bridgeport, Ne., U.S.	C2	104
Bridgeport, Oh., U.S.	B5	112
Bridgeport, Pa., U.S.	o20	115
Bridgeport, Tx., U.S.	C4	120
Bridgeport, Wa., U.S.	B6	124
Bridgeport, W.V., U.S.	B4	125
Bridger, Mt., U.S.	E8	103
Bridger Peak, mtn., Wy., U.S.	E5	127
Bridger Range, mts., Mt., U.S.	E6	103
Bridgeton, Mo., U.S.	C7	102
Bridgeton, N.J., U.S.	E2	107
Bridgetown, Barb.	H18	64
Bridgetown, N.S., Can.	E4	71
Bridgeville, De., U.S.	F3	85
Bridgeville, Pa., U.S.	k13	115
Bridgewater, Ma., U.S.	C6	98
Bridgewater, N.J., U.S.	B3	107
Bridgewater, Va., U.S.	B4	123
Bridgman, Mi., U.S.	G4	99
Bridgton, Me., U.S.	D2	96
Bridgwater, Eng., U.K.	J9	7
Bridlington, Eng., U.K.	G12	7
Briec, Fr.	D2	10
Brielle, N.J., U.S.	C4	107
Brienne-le-Château, Fr.	D11	10
Brienz, Switz.	F15	10
Brig, Switz.	F14	10
Brigantine, N.J., U.S.	E4	107
Brigantine Beach, N.J., U.S.	E4	107
Brigden, Ont., Can.	E2	73
Briggs Marsh, sw., R.I., U.S.	F6	116
Brigham City, Ut., U.S.	B3	121
Brighton, Ont., Can.	C7	73
Brighton, Eng., U.K.	K12	7
Brighton, Al., U.S.	B3	78
Brighton, Co., U.S.	B6	83
Brighton, Il., U.S.	D3	90
Brighton, Ia., U.S.	C6	92
Brighton, Mi., U.S.	F7	99
Brighton, N.Y., U.S.	B3	109
Brighton, Tn., U.S.	B2	119
Brighton Indian Reservation, Fl., U.S.	E5	86
Brihuega, Spain	E9	12
Brilliant, Al., U.S.	A2	78
Brilliant, Oh., U.S.	B5	112
Brillion, Wi., U.S.	D5	126
Brilon, Ger.	D8	8
Brimfield, Il., U.S.	C4	90
Brindisi, Italy	I12	14
Brinkley, Ar., U.S.	C4	81
Brinnon, Wa., U.S.	B3	124
Brioude, Fr.	G10	10
Brisbane, Austl.	E10	50
Briscoe, co., Tx., U.S.	B2	120
Bristol, N.B., Can.	C2	71
Bristol, Eng., U.K.	J10	7
Bristol, Ct., U.S.	C4	84
Bristol, In., U.S.	A6	91
Bristol, N.H., U.S.	C3	106
Bristol, R.I., U.S.	D5	116
Bristol, Tn., U.S.	C11	119
Bristol, Vt., U.S.	C2	122
Bristol, Va., U.S.	f9	123
Bristol, co., Ma., U.S.	C5	98
Bristol, co., R.I., U.S.	D5	116
Bristol Bay, b., Ak., U.S.	D7	79
Bristol Channel, strt., U.K.	J8	7
Bristol [Township], Pa., U.S.	F12	115
Bristow, Ok., U.S.	B5	113
British Columbia, prov., Can.	C6	69
British Honduras see Belize, ctry., N.A.	F3	64
British Indian Ocean Territory, dep., Afr.	G17	2
British Mountains, mts., N.A.	C5	66
British Solomon Islands see Solomon Islands, ctry., Oc.	G23	2
Britstown, S. Afr.	H4	44
Britt, Ia., U.S.	A4	92
Brittany see Bretagne, hist. reg., Fr.	D3	10
Britton, S.D., U.S.	B8	118
Brive-la-Gaillarde, Fr.	G8	10
Briviesca, Spain	C8	12
Brno, Czech.	F16	8
Broach, India	B2	37
Broad, stm., S.C., U.S.	C5	117
Broad Brook, Ct., U.S.	B5	84
Broadford, Scot., U.K.	D7	7
Broadkill, stm., De., U.S.	E4	85
Broadkill Beach, De., U.S.	E5	85
Broad Law, mtn., Scot., U.K.	F9	7
Broad Run, stm., Va., U.S.	g11	123
Broadus, Mt., U.S.	E11	103
Broadview Heights, Oh., U.S.	h9	112
Broadwater, co., Mt., U.S.	D5	103
Broadway, N.C., U.S.	B3	110
Broadway, Va., U.S.	B4	123
Brockport, N.Y., U.S.	B3	109
Brockton, Ma., U.S.	B5	98
Brockton Reservoir, res., Ma., U.S.	h11	98
Brockville, Ont., Can.	C9	73
Brockway, Pa., U.S.	D4	115
Brodeur Peninsula, pen., N.W. Ter., Can.	B15	66
Brodhead, Ky., U.S.	C5	94
Brodhead, Wi., U.S.	F4	126
Brodheadsville, Pa., U.S.	E11	115
Broken Arrow, Ok., U.S.	A6	113
Broken Bow, Ne., U.S.	C6	104
Broken Bow, Ok., U.S.	C7	113
Broken Bow Lake, res., Ok., U.S.	C7	113
Broken Hill, Austl.	F8	50
Brokopondo, Sur.	B8	54
Brome, Lac, l., Que., Can.	D5	74
Bromptonville, Que., Can.	D6	74
Bromsgrove, Eng., U.K.	I10	7
Bronlund Peak, mtn., B.C., Can.	E7	66
Brønnøysund, Nor.	D9	6
Bronson, Mi., U.S.	G5	99
Bronte, Italy	L9	14
Bronx, co., N.Y., U.S.	E7	109
Bronxville, N.Y., U.S.	h13	109
Brook, In., U.S.	C3	91
Brooke, co., W.V., U.S.	A4	125
Brookfield, N.S., Can.	D6	71
Brookfield, Ct., U.S.	D2	84
Brookfield, Il., U.S.	k9	90
Brookfield, Mo., U.S.	B4	102
Brookfield, Va., U.S.	*B5	123
Brookfield, Wi., U.S.	m11	126
Brookfield Center, Ct., U.S.	D2	84
Brookhaven, Ms., U.S.	D3	101
Brookhaven, W.V., U.S.	h11	125
Brookings, Or., U.S.	E2	114
Brookings, S.D., U.S.	C9	118
Brookings, co., S.D., U.S.	C9	118
Brookland, Ar., U.S.	B5	81
Brooklandville, Md., U.S.	g10	97
Brooklet, Ga., U.S.	D5	87
Brookline, Ma., U.S.	B5	98
Brooklyn, N.S., Can.	E5	71
Brooklyn, Ct., U.S.	B8	84
Brooklyn, In., U.S.	E5	91
Brooklyn, Ia., U.S.	C5	92
Brooklyn, Mi., U.S.	F6	99
Brooklyn, Ms., U.S.	D4	101
Brooklyn, Oh., U.S.	h9	112
Brooklyn, S.C., U.S.	B6	117
Brooklyn, Wi., U.S.	F4	126
Brooklyn Center, Mn., U.S.	E5	100
Brooklyn Park, Md., U.S.	h11	97
Brooklyn Park, Mn., U.S.	m12	100
Brookneal, Va., U.S.	C4	123
Brook Park, Oh., U.S.	h9	112
Brookport, Il., U.S.	F5	90
Brooks, Alta., Can.	D5	68
Brooks, Ky., U.S.	g11	94
Brooks, co., Ga., U.S.	F3	87
Brooks, co., Tx., U.S.	F3	120
Brooks Air Force Base, mil., Tx., U.S.	k7	120
Brookshire, Tx., U.S.	E5	120
Brookside, Al., U.S.	f7	78
Brookside, De., U.S.	B3	85
Brooks Range, mts., Ak., U.S.	B9	79
Brookston, In., U.S.	C4	91
Brooksville, Fl., U.S.	D4	86
Brooksville, Ky., U.S.	B5	94
Brooksville, Ms., U.S.	B5	101
Brookville, In., U.S.	F8	91
Brookville, Oh., U.S.	C1	112
Brookville, Pa., U.S.	D3	115
Brookville Lake, res., In., U.S.	E7	91
Brookwood, Al., U.S.	B2	78
Brookwood, N.J., U.S.	C4	107
Broomall, Pa., U.S.	p20	115
Broome, Austl.	C4	50
Broome, co., N.Y., U.S.	C5	109
Broomfield, Co., U.S.	B5	83
Broons, Fr.	D4	10
Brossard, Que., Can.	q20	74
Brou, Fr.	D8	10
Broussard, La., U.S.	D4	95
Broward, co., Fl., U.S.	F6	86
Browerville, Mn., U.S.	D4	100
Brown, co., Il., U.S.	D3	90
Brown, co., In., U.S.	F5	91
Brown, co., Ks., U.S.	C8	93
Brown, co., Mn., U.S.	F4	100
Brown, co., Ne., U.S.	B6	104
Brown, co., Oh., U.S.	D2	112
Brown, co., S.D., U.S.	B7	118
Brown, co., Tx., U.S.	D3	120
Brown, co., Wi., U.S.	D6	126
Brown, Point, c., Wa., U.S.	C1	124
Brown City, Mi., U.S.	E8	99
Brown Deer, Wi., U.S.	m12	126
Brownfield, Tx., U.S.	C1	120
Browning, Mt., U.S.	B3	103
Brownlee Dam, U.S.	E2	89
Brownlee Reservoir, res., U.S.	C10	114
Browns, stm., Vt., U.S.	B2	122
Browns Branch, stm., De., U.S.	E3	85
Brownsburg, Que., Can.	D3	74
Brownsburg, In., U.S.	E5	91
Brownsdale, Mn., U.S.	G6	100
Browns Inlet, b., N.C., U.S.	C5	110
Browns Mills, N.J., U.S.	D3	107
Browns Peak, mtn., Az., U.S.	D4	80
Brownstown, In., U.S.	G5	91
Browns Valley, Mn., U.S.	E2	100
Brownsville, Fl., U.S.	s13	86
Brownsville, Ky., U.S.	C3	94
Brownsville, Or., U.S.	C4	114
Brownsville, Pa., U.S.	F2	115
Brownsville, Tn., U.S.	B2	119
Brownsville, Tx., U.S.	G4	120
Brownton, Mn., U.S.	F4	100
Brownville Junction, Me., U.S.	C3	96
Brownwood, Tx., U.S.	D3	120
Brownwood, Lake, res., Tx., U.S.	D3	120
Broxton, Ga., U.S.	E4	87
Bruay-en-Artois, Fr.	B9	10
Bruce, Ms., U.S.	B4	101
Bruce, Wi., U.S.	C2	126
Bruce, Mount, mtn., Austl.	D3	50
Bruce National Park, Ont., Can.	B3	73
Bruce Peninsula, pen., Ont., Can.	B3	73
Bruceton, Tn., U.S.	A3	119
Bruchsal, Ger.	F8	8
Bruck an der Leitha, Aus.	H16	8
Bruck an der Mur, Aus.	H15	8
Bruderheim, Alta., Can.	C4	68
Brugge, Bel.	D3	8
Bruin Point, mtn., Ut., U.S.	D5	121
Brule, co., S.D., U.S.	D6	118
Brule, stm., U.S.	C5	126
Brule Lake, l., Mn., U.S.	k9	100
Brundidge, Al., U.S.	D4	78
Bruneau, stm., U.S.	G3	89
Brunei, ctry., Asia	E5	32
Brunico, Italy	C6	14
Brunkeberg, Nor.	G7	6
Bruno, Sask., Can.	E3	75
Brunsbüttel, Ger.	B9	8
Brunswick, Ga., U.S.	E5	87
Brunswick, Me., U.S.	E3	96
Brunswick, Md., U.S.	B2	97
Brunswick, Mo., U.S.	B4	102
Brunswick, Oh., U.S.	A4	112
Brunswick, co., N.C., U.S.	C4	110
Brunswick, co., Va., U.S.	D5	123
Brunswick Naval Air Station, mil., Me., U.S.	E3	96
Brush, Co., U.S.	A7	83
Brushy Mountains, mts., N.C., U.S.	B1	110
Brus Laguna, Hond.	G5	64
Brusly, La., U.S.	D4	95
Brussels, Ont., Can.	D3	73
Brussels see Bruxelles, Bel.	E4	8
Bruxelles (Brussel), Bel.	E4	8
Bryan, Oh., U.S.	A1	112
Bryan, Tx., U.S.	D4	120
Bryan, co., Ga., U.S.	D5	87
Bryan, co., Ok., U.S.	D5	113
Bryans Road, Md., U.S.	C3	97
Bryant, Ar., U.S.	C3	81
Bryantville, Ma., U.S.	B6	98
Bryce Canyon National Park, Ut., U.S.	F3	121
Bryn Mawr, Wa., U.S.	e11	124
Bryson City, N.C., U.S.	f9	110
Brzeg, Pol.	E17	8
Bsharrī, Leb.	B5	40
Būbiyān, i., Kuw.	C4	46
Bucaramanga, Col.	D6	58
Buccaneer Archipelago, is., Austl.	C4	50
Buchanan, Lib.	G3	42
Buchanan, Ga., U.S.	C1	87
Buchanan, Mi., U.S.	G4	99
Buchanan, Va., U.S.	C3	123
Buchanan, co., Ia., U.S.	B6	92
Buchanan, co., Mo., U.S.	B3	102
Buchanan, co., Va., U.S.	e9	123
Buchan Gulf, b., N.W. Ter., Can.	B18	66
Buchans, Newf., Can.	D3	72
Buchara, Uzb.	J10	22
Bucharest see București, Rom.	E10	16
Buchholz, Ger.	B9	8
Buckatunna, Ms., U.S.	D5	101
Bückeburg, Ger.	C9	8
Buckeye, Az., U.S.	D3	80
Buckeye Lake, Oh., U.S.	C3	112
Buckhannon, W.V., U.S.	C4	125
Buck Hill Falls, Pa., U.S.	D11	115
Buckhorn Lake, res., Ky., U.S.	C6	94
Buckingham, Que., Can.	D2	74
Buckingham, co., Va., U.S.	C4	123
Buckley, Wa., U.S.	B3	124
Bucklin, Ks., U.S.	E4	93
Bucklin, Mo., U.S.	B5	102
Buck Mountain, mtn., Wa., U.S.	A6	124
Buckner, Mo., U.S.	h11	102
Bucks, co., Pa., U.S.	F11	115
Buckskin Mountains, mts., Az., U.S.	C2	80
Bucksport, Me., U.S.	D4	96
Bucksport, S.C., U.S.	D9	117
București (Bucharest), Rom.	E10	16
Bucyrus, Oh., U.S.	B3	112
Buda, Tx., U.S.	D4	120
Budapest, Hung.	H19	8
Budaun, India	F8	38
Budd Lake, l., N.J., U.S.	B3	107
Buddusò, Italy	I4	14
Bude, Eng., U.K.	K8	7
Bude, Ms., U.S.	D3	101
Buea, Cam.	H7	42
Buechel, Ky., U.S.	B4	94
Buena, N.J., U.S.	D3	107
Buena, Wa., U.S.	C5	124
Buena Park, Ca., U.S.	n12	82
Buena Vista, Bol.	G6	54
Buena Vista, Co., U.S.	C4	83
Buena Vista, Fl., U.S.	D4	86
Buena Vista, Ga., U.S.	D2	87
Buena Vista, Va., U.S.	C3	123
Buena Vista, co., Ia., U.S.	B2	92
Buenópolis, Braz.	D6	57
Buenos Aires, Arg.	C5	56
Buffalo, Ia., U.S.	C7	92
Buffalo, Mn., U.S.	E5	100
Buffalo, Mo., U.S.	D4	102
Buffalo, N.Y., U.S.	C2	109
Buffalo, Ok., U.S.	A2	113
Buffalo, S.C., U.S.	B4	117
Buffalo, Tx., U.S.	D5	120
Buffalo, W.V., U.S.	C3	125
Buffalo, Wi., U.S.	D2	126
Buffalo, Wy., U.S.	B6	127
Buffalo, co., Ne., U.S.	D6	104
Buffalo, co., S.D., U.S.	C6	118
Buffalo, co., Wi., U.S.	D2	126
Buffalo, stm., Ar., U.S.	B3	81
Buffalo, stm., Mn., U.S.	D2	100
Buffalo, stm., Tn., U.S.	B4	119
Buffalo, stm., Wi., U.S.	D2	126
Buffalo Bill Reservoir, res., Wy., U.S.	B3	127
Buffalo Center, Ia., U.S.	A4	92
Buffalo Creek, stm., U.S.	f8	125
Buffalo Creek, stm., W.V., U.S.	h10	125
Buffalo Creek, stm., W.V., U.S.	n12	125
Buffalo Grove, Il., U.S.	h9	90
Buffalo Lake, Mn., U.S.	F4	100
Buffalo Lake, l., Alta., Can.	C4	68
Buffalo Lake, l., N.W. Ter., Can.	D9	66
Buffalo Lake, res., Tx., U.S.	B1	120
Buffalo Lake, res., Wi., U.S.	E4	126
Buffumville Lake, res., Ma., U.S.	B4	98
Buford, Ga., U.S.	B2	87
Bug, stm., Eur.	E12	4
Buga, Col.	F4	58
Bugøynes, Nor.	B17	6
Bugsuk Island, i., Phil.	D6	32
Bugul'ma, Russia	G8	22
Buhl, Id., U.S.	G4	89
Buhl, Mn., U.S.	C6	100
Buhler, Ks., U.S.	D6	93
Buies Creek, N.C., U.S.	B4	110
Buj, Russia	C24	18
Bujalance, Spain	H7	12
Bujaraloz, Spain	D11	12
Bujumbura, Bdi.	B5	44
Bukačača, Russia	G17	24
Bukama, Zaire	C5	44
Bukavu, Zaire	B5	44
Bukittinggi, Indon.	F3	32
Bukoba, Tan.	B6	44
Bukovina, hist. reg., Eur.	B9	16
Bula, Indon.	F9	32
Bulan, Ky., U.S.	C6	94
Bulandshahr, India	F7	38
Bulawayo, Zimb.	F5	44
Buldan, Tur.	K12	16
Buldāna, India	B4	37
Bulgan, Mong.	B5	26
Bulgaria, ctry., Eur.	G12	4
Bulkley, stm., B.C., Can.	B4	69
Bull Creek, stm., S.D., U.S.	B2	118
Bulle, Switz.	F14	10
Bullfinch, Austl.	F3	50
Bullfrog Creek, stm., Ut., U.S.	F5	121
Bullhead City, Az., U.S.	B1	80
Bull Island, i., S.C., U.S.	G6	117
Bull Island, i., S.C., U.S.	D9	117
Bull Island, i., S.C., U.S.	F8	117
Bullitt, co., Ky., U.S.	C4	94
Bull Mountain, mtn., Mt., U.S.	D4	103
Bulloch, co., Ga., U.S.	D5	87
Bullock, co., Al., U.S.	C4	78
Bullock Creek, Mi., U.S.	E6	99
Bull Run, stm., Va., U.S.	g11	123
Bullrun Rock, mtn., Or., U.S.	C8	114
Bulls Bay, b., S.C., U.S.	F8	117
Bulls Gap, Tn., U.S.	C10	119
Bull Shoals, Ar., U.S.	A3	81
Bull Shoals Lake, res., U.S.	A3	81
Bully Creek Reservoir, res., Or., U.S.	C9	114
Bulsār, India	B2	37
Bulukumba, Indon.	G7	32
Bumba, Zaire	A4	44
Bumping, stm., Wa., U.S.	C4	124
Buna, Tx., U.S.	D6	120
Bunbury, Austl.	F3	50
Buncombe, co., N.C., U.S.	f10	110
Buncrana, Ire.	F5	7
Bundaberg, Austl.	D10	50
Būndi, India	H6	38
Bundoran, Ire.	G4	7
Bungo-suidō, strt., Japan	I5	30
Bunia, Zaire	A6	44
Bunker Hill, Il., U.S.	D4	90
Bunker Hill, In., U.S.	C5	91
Bunker Hill, W.V., U.S.	B6	125
Bunker Hill, W.V., U.S.	m12	125
Bunker Hill, mtn., Nv., U.S.	D4	105
Bunkerville, Nv., U.S.	G7	105
Bunkie, La., U.S.	D3	95
Bunnell, Fl., U.S.	C5	86
Buñol, Spain	F11	12
Buntok, Indon.	F5	32
Buolkalach, Russia	C17	24
Buon Me Thuot, Viet.	H10	34
Buor-Chaja, Guba, b., Russia	C20	24
Buor-Chaja, Mys, c., Russia	C20	24
Bura, Kenya	B7	44
Burao, Som.	G4	46
Buras, La., U.S.	E6	95
Buraydah, Sau. Ar.	C3	46
Burbank, Ca., U.S.	E4	82
Burbank, Il., U.S.	k9	90
Burbank, Wa., U.S.	C7	124
Burdickville, R.I., U.S.	F2	116
Burdur, Tur.	H14	4
Burdwān, India	I12	38
Bureau, co., Il., U.S.	B4	90
Bureinskij Chrebet, mts., Russia	G20	24
Bureja, stm., Russia	G20	24
Burfjord, Nor.	B13	6
Burgas, Bul.	G11	16
Bur Gavo, Som.	B8	44
Burgaw, N.C., U.S.	C5	110
Burg [bei Magdeburg], Ger.	C11	8
Burgdorf, Switz.	E14	10
Burgeo, Newf., Can.	E3	72
Burgettstown, Pa., U.S.	F1	115
Burghausen, Ger.	G12	8
Burghūth, Sabkhat al-, l., Syria	B7	40
Burgin, China	B4	26
Burgin, Ky., U.S.	C5	94
Burglengenfeld, Ger.	F12	8
Burgos, Spain	C8	12
Burgsteinfurt, Ger.	C7	8
Burgundy see Bourgogne, hist. reg., Fr.	E11	10
Burhaniye, Tur.	J10	16
Burhānpur, India	B4	37
Burica, Punta, c., N.A.	J6	64
Burin, Newf., Can.	E4	72
Burin Peninsula, pen., Newf., Can.	E4	72
Buriram, Thai.	G7	34
Burjasot, Spain	F11	12
Burkburnett, Tx., U.S.	B3	120
Burke, S.D., U.S.	D6	118
Burke, co., Ga., U.S.	C4	87
Burke, co., N.C., U.S.	B1	110
Burke, co., N.D., U.S.	A3	111
Burke Channel, strt., B.C., Can.	C4	69
Burkesville, Ky., U.S.	D4	94
Burketown, Austl.	C7	50
Burkina Faso, ctry., Afr.	F5	42
Burk's Falls, Ont., Can.	B5	73
Burleigh, co., N.D., U.S.	C5	111
Burleson, Tx., U.S.	n9	120
Burleson, co., Tx., U.S.	D4	120
Burley, Id., U.S.	G5	89
Burlingame, Ca., U.S.	h8	82
Burlingame, Ks., U.S.	D8	93
Burlington, Ont., Can.	D5	73
Burlington, Co., U.S.	B8	83
Burlington, Ia., U.S.	D6	92
Burlington, Ks., U.S.	D8	93
Burlington, Ky., U.S.	A5	94
Burlington, Ma., U.S.	f11	98
Burlington, N.J., U.S.	C3	107
Burlington, N.C., U.S.	A3	110
Burlington, N.D., U.S.	A4	111
Burlington, Vt., U.S.	C2	122
Burlington, Wa., U.S.	A3	124
Burlington, Wi., U.S.	F5	126
Burlington, co., N.J., U.S.	D3	107
Burlington Beach, In., U.S.	B3	91
Burlington Junction, Mo., U.S.	A2	102
Burma, ctry., Asia	A2	32
Burnaby, B.C., Can.	E6	69
Burnet, Tx., U.S.	D3	120
Burnet, co., Tx., U.S.	D3	120
Burnett, co., Wi., U.S.	C1	126
Burney, Ca., U.S.	B3	82
Burnham, Pa., U.S.	E6	115
Burnie, Austl.	H9	50
Burns, Or., U.S.	D7	114
Burns, Tn., U.S.	A4	119
Burns, Wy., U.S.	E8	127
Burns Flat, Ok., U.S.	B2	113
Burnside, Ky., U.S.	D5	94
Burns Lake, B.C., Can.	B5	69
Burns Paiute Indian Reservation, Or., U.S.	D7	114
Burnsville, Mn., U.S.	F5	100
Burnsville, Ms., U.S.	A5	101
Burnsville, N.C., U.S.	f10	110
Burnsville Lake, res., W.V., U.S.	C4	125
Burnt Islands, Newf., Can.	E2	72
Burnt Mills, Lake, l., Va., U.S.	k14	123
Burntside Lake, l., Mn., U.S.	C6	100
Burntwood, stm., Man., Can.	B2	70
Burravoe, Scot., U.K.	A11	7
Burr Oak, Mi., U.S.	G5	99
Burr Oak Reservoir, res., Oh., U.S.	C3	112
Burrton, Ks., U.S.	D6	93
Bursa, Tur.	G13	4
Būr Saʿīd (Port Said), Egypt	B12	42

Name	Map Ref	Page
Būr Sūdān (Port Sudan), Sudan	E13	42
Burt, co., Ne., U.S.	C9	104
Burt Lake, l., Mi., U.S.	C6	99
Burton, Mi., U.S.	F7	99
Burton, Oh., U.S.	A4	112
Burton upon Trent, Eng., U.K.	I11	7
Burtts Corner, N.B., Can.	C3	71
Buru, i., Indon.	F8	32
Burundi, ctry., Afr.	B5	44
Burwell, Ne., U.S.	C6	104
Burwick, Scot., U.K.	C10	7
Bury Saint Edmunds, Eng., U.K.	I13	7
Busalla, Italy	E3	14
Buşayrah, Syria	B7	40
Bushnell, Fl., U.S.	D4	86
Bushnell, Il., U.S.	C3	90
Bush River, b., Md., U.S.	B5	97
Buşrá ash-Shām, Syria	C5	40
Busselton, Austl.	F3	50
Busto Arsizio, Italy	D3	14
Busuanga Island, i., Phil.	C7	32
Buta, Zaire	H10	42
Butare, Rw.	B5	44
Butehaqi, China	B11	26
Bute Inlet, b., B.C., Can.	D5	69
Butler, Al., U.S.	C1	78
Butler, Ga., U.S.	D2	87
Butler, In., U.S.	B8	91
Butler, Ky., U.S.	B5	94
Butler, Mo., U.S.	C3	102
Butler, N.J., U.S.	B4	107
Butler, Oh., U.S.	B3	112
Butler, Pa., U.S.	E2	115
Butler, Wi., U.S.	m11	126
Butler, co., Al., U.S.	D3	78
Butler, co., Ia., U.S.	B5	92
Butler, co., Ks., U.S.	E7	93
Butler, co., Ky., U.S.	C3	94
Butler, co., Mo., U.S.	E7	102
Butler, co., Ne., U.S.	C8	104
Butler, co., Oh., U.S.	C1	112
Butler, co., Pa., U.S.	E2	115
Butner, N.C., U.S.	A4	110
Buttahatchee, stm., U.S.	B5	101
Butte, Mt., U.S.	E4	103
Butte, co., Ca., U.S.	C3	82
Butte, co., Id., U.S.	F5	89
Butte, co., S.D., U.S.	C2	118
Butte des Morts, Lake, l., Wi., U.S.	D5	126
Butte Mountains, mts., Nv., U.S.	D6	105
Butternut Lake, l., Wi., U.S.	C5	126
Butterworth, Malay.	L6	34
Butt of Lewis, c., Scot., U.K.	C6	7
Buttonwillow, Ca., U.S.	E4	82
Butts, co., Ga., U.S.	C3	87
Butuan, Phil.	D8	32
Butung, Pulau, i., Indon.	F7	32
Bützow, Ger.	B11	8
Buxtehude, Ger.	B9	8
Buxton, N.C., U.S.	B7	110
Büyükmenderes, stm., Tur.	L11	16
Buzançais, Fr.	F8	10
Buzău, Rom.	D10	16
Búzi, stm., Moz.	F6	44
Buzuluk, Russia	G8	22
Buzzards Bay, Ma., U.S.	C6	98
Buzzards Bay, b., Ma., U.S.	C6	98
Byam Channel, strt., N.W. Ter., Can.	A11	66
Byam Martin Island, i., N.W. Ter., Can.	A12	66
Bydgoszcz, Pol.	B18	8
Byers, Co., U.S.	B6	83
Byesville, Oh., U.S.	C4	112
Byhalia, Ms., U.S.	A4	101
Bylas, Az., U.S.	D5	80
Bylot Island, i., N.W. Ter., Can.	B17	66
Byng, Ok., U.S.	C5	113
Byrdstown, Tn., U.S.	C8	119
Byron, Ga., U.S.	D3	87
Byron, Il., U.S.	A4	90
Byron, Mn., U.S.	F6	100
Byron, Wy., U.S.	B4	127
Byrranga, Gory, mts., Russia	B14	24
Bytantaj, stm., Russia	D20	24
Bytom (Beuthen), Pol.	E18	8
Byxelkrok, Swe.	H11	6

C

Caacupé, Para.	B5	56
Cabaiguán, Cuba	C8	64
Caballo Mountains, mts., N.M., U.S.	E2	108
Caballo Reservoir, res., N.M., U.S.	E2	108
Cabanatuan, Phil.	q19	32
Cabano, Que., Can.	B9	74
Cabarrus, co., N.C., U.S.	B2	110
Cabbage Swamp, sw., Fl., U.S.	m9	86
Cabell, co., W.V., U.S.	C2	125
Cabeza del Buey, Spain	G6	12
Cabimas, Ven.	B7	58
Cabin Creek, W.V., U.S.	m13	125
Cabin Creek, stm., W.V., U.S.	m13	125
Cabinda, Ang.	C2	44
Cabinda, dept., Ang.	C2	44
Cabinet Gorge Reservoir, res., U.S.	B1	103
Cabinet Mountains, mts., Mt., U.S.	B1	103
Cabin John, Md., U.S.	C3	97
Cabo Frio, Braz.	G7	57
Cabonga, Réservoir, res., Que., Can.	k11	74
Cabool, Mo., U.S.	D5	102
Caborca, Mex.	B3	62
Cabot, Ar., U.S.	C3	81
Cabot, Mount, mtn., N.H., U.S.	A4	106
Cabot Head, c., Ont., Can.	B3	73
Cabot Strait, strt., Can.	G21	66
Cabra, Spain	H7	12
Cabri, Sask., Can.	G1	75
Cabrillo National Monument, Ca., U.S.	o15	82
Cabrobó, Braz.	E11	54
Cabruta, Ven.	D9	58
Çaçador, Braz.	B6	56
Čačak, Yugo.	F4	16
Cacapon, stm., W.V., U.S.	B6	125
Cáceres, Braz.	G7	54
Cáceres, Col.	D5	58
Cáceres, Spain	F5	12
Cache, Ok., U.S.	C3	113
Cache, co., Ut., U.S.	B4	121
Cache, stm., Ar., U.S.	C4	81
Cache, stm., Il., U.S.	F4	90
Cache Bay, Ont., Can.	A5	73
Cache Creek, B.C., Can.	D7	69
Cache la Poudre, stm., Co., U.S.	A5	83
Cache Mountain, mtn., Ak., U.S.	B10	79
Cache Peak, mtn., Id., U.S.	G5	89
Cachimbo, Serra do, mts., Braz.	E7	54
Cachoeira, Braz.	B9	57
Cachoeira do Sul, Braz.	C6	56
Cachoeiro de Itapemirim, Braz.	F8	57
Cacólo, Ang.	D3	44
Caconda, Ang.	D3	44
Cactus Flat, pl., Nv., U.S.	F5	105
Cactus Peak, mtn., Nv., U.S.	F5	105
Caddo, Ok., U.S.	C5	113
Caddo, co., La., U.S.	B2	95
Caddo, co., Ok., U.S.	B3	113
Caddo, stm., Ar., U.S.	C2	81
Caddo Creek, stm., Ok., U.S.	C4	113
Caddo Lake, res., U.S.	B2	95
Cader Idris, mtn., Wales, U.K.	I9	7
Cadillac, Fr.	H6	10
Cadillac, Mi., U.S.	D5	99
Cadillac Mountain, mtn., Me., U.S.	D4	96
Cádiz, Spain	I5	12
Cadiz, Ky., U.S.	D2	94
Cadiz, Oh., U.S.	B4	112
Cádiz, Golfo de, b., Eur.	I4	12
Cadott, Wi., U.S.	D2	126
Caen, Fr.	C6	10
Caernarvon, Wales, U.K.	H8	7
Caesar Creek Lake, res., Oh., U.S.	C2	112
Caeté, Braz.	E7	57
Cagayan de Oro, Phil.	D7	32
Cagayan Islands, is., Phil.	D7	32
Čagda, Russia	F20	24
Cagles Mill Lake, res., In., U.S.	F4	91
Cagli, Italy	F7	14
Cagliari, Italy	J4	14
Caguas, P.R.	E14	64
Cahaba, stm., Al., U.S.	C2	78
Caha Mountains, mts., Ire.	J3	7
Cahirciveen, Ire.	J2	7
Cahokia, Il., U.S.	E3	90
Cahore Point, c., Ire.	I6	7
Cahors, Fr.	H8	10
Caiapó, Serra, mts., Braz.	D2	57
Caibarién, Cuba	C8	64
Caicara, Ven.	D9	58
Caicos Islands, is., T./C. Is.	D12	64
Caicos Passage, strt., N.A.	C11	64
Caillou Bay, b., La., U.S.	E5	95
Caillou Lake, l., La., U.S.	E5	95
Cairnbrook, Pa., U.S.	F4	115
Cairngorm Mountains, mts., Scot., U.K.	D9	7
Cairns, Austl.	C9	50
Cairo, Ga., U.S.	F2	87
Cairo, Il., U.S.	F4	90
Cairo, Ne., U.S.	D7	104
Cairo see Al-Qāhirah, Egypt	B12	42
Caiundo, Ang.	E3	44
Cajamarca, Peru	E3	54
Çajàzeiras, Braz.	E11	54
Čakovec, Cro.	C11	14
Calabar, Nig.	H7	42
Calabozo, Ven.	C9	58
Calahorra, Spain	C10	12
Calais, Fr.	B8	10
Calais, Me., U.S.	C5	96
Calais, Pas de (Strait of Dover), strt., Eur.	K14	7
Calamar, Col.	B5	58
Calamian Group, is., Phil.	C6	32
Calamocha, Spain	E10	12
Calamus, stm., Ne., U.S.	B6	104
Calanda, Spain	E11	12
Calapan, Phil.	r19	33b
Călăraşi, Rom.	E11	16
Calatayud, Spain	D10	12
Calaveras, co., Ca., U.S.	C3	82
Calcasieu, co., La., U.S.	D2	95
Calcasieu, stm., La., U.S.	D2	95
Calcasieu Lake, l., La., U.S.	E2	95
Calcasieu Pass, strt., La., U.S.	E2	95
Calçoene, Braz.	C8	54
Calcutta, India	I13	38
Calcutta, Oh., U.S.	B5	112
Calcutta Lake, l., Nv., U.S.	B2	105
Caldas da Rainha, Port.	F2	12
Calderwood, Tn., U.S.	D10	119
Caldron Falls Reservoir, res., Wi., U.S.	C5	126
Caldwell, Id., U.S.	F2	89
Caldwell, Ks., U.S.	E6	93
Caldwell, N.J., U.S.	B4	107
Caldwell, Oh., U.S.	C4	112
Caldwell, Tx., U.S.	D4	120
Caldwell, co., Ky., U.S.	C2	94
Caldwell, co., La., U.S.	B3	95
Caldwell, co., Mo., U.S.	B3	102
Caldwell, co., N.C., U.S.	B1	110
Caldwell, co., Tx., U.S.	E4	120
Caledon, Ont., Can.	D5	73
Caledonia, Mi., U.S.	F5	99
Caledonia, Mn., U.S.	G7	100
Caledonia, Ms., U.S.	B5	101
Caledonia, N.Y., U.S.	C3	109
Caledonia, co., Vt., U.S.	C4	122
Calera, Al., U.S.	B3	78
Calera, Ok., U.S.	D5	113
Calexico, Ca., U.S.	F6	82
Calgary, Alta., Can.	D3	68
Calhoun, Ga., U.S.	B2	87
Calhoun, Ky., U.S.	C2	94
Calhoun, co., Al., U.S.	B4	78
Calhoun, co., Ar., U.S.	D3	81
Calhoun, co., Fl., U.S.	B1	86
Calhoun, co., Ga., U.S.	E2	87
Calhoun, co., Il., U.S.	D3	90
Calhoun, co., Ia., U.S.	B3	92
Calhoun, co., Mi., U.S.	F5	99
Calhoun, co., Ms., U.S.	B4	101
Calhoun, co., S.C., U.S.	D6	117
Calhoun, co., Tx., U.S.	E4	120
Calhoun, co., W.V., U.S.	C3	125
Calhoun City, Ms., U.S.	B4	101
Calhoun Falls, S.C., U.S.	C2	117
Cali, Col.	F4	58
Calico Rock, Ar., U.S.	A3	81
Calicut, India	G3	37
Caliente, Nv., U.S.	F7	105
California, Mo., U.S.	C5	102
California, Pa., U.S.	F2	115
California, state, U.S.	D4	82
California, Golfo de, b., Mex.	D4	62
California Aqueduct, Ca., U.S.	E4	82
Calimere, Point, c., India	G5	37
Calipatria, Ca., U.S.	F6	82
Calispell Peak, mtn., Wa., U.S.	A8	124
Calistoga, Ca., U.S.	C2	82
Calitri, Italy	I10	14
Callac, Fr.	D3	10
Callaghan, Mount, mtn., Nv., U.S.	D5	105
Callahan, co., Tx., U.S.	C3	120
Callao, Peru	F3	54
Callaway, co., Mo., U.S.	C6	102
Calling Lake, l., Alta., Can.	B4	68
Callosa de Ensarriá, Spain	G11	12
Calloway, co., Ky., U.S.	f9	94
Calmar, Alta., Can.	C4	68
Calmar, Ia., U.S.	A6	92
Caloosahatchee, stm., Fl., U.S.	F5	86
Caltagirone, Italy	L9	14
Caltanissetta, Italy	L9	14
Calumet, Que., Can.	D3	74
Calumet, Mi., U.S.	A2	99
Calumet, co., Wi., U.S.	D5	126
Calumet, Lake, l., Il., U.S.	k9	90
Calumet City, Il., U.S.	B6	90
Calunda, Ang.	D4	44
Calvert, Tx., U.S.	D4	120
Calvert, co., Md., U.S.	C4	97
Calvert City, Ky., U.S.	e9	94
Calverton, Md., U.S.	*B4	97
Calverton Park, Mo., U.S.	f13	102
Calvinia, S. Afr.	H3	44
Camacho, Mex.	E8	62
Camacupa, Ang.	D3	44
Camaguán, Ven.	C9	58
Camagüey, Cuba	D9	64
Camaná, Peru	G4	54
Camanche, Ia., U.S.	C7	92
Camano Island, i., Wa., U.S.	A3	124
Camapuã, Braz.	E1	57
Camaquã, Braz.	C6	56
Camas, Spain	H5	12
Camas, Wa., U.S.	D3	124
Camas, co., Id., U.S.	F4	89
Ca Mau, Viet.	J8	34
Cambados, Spain	C3	12
Cambay, India	I5	38
Cambodia (Kampuchea), ctry., Asia	C3	32
Cambrai, Fr.	B10	10
Cambria, Ca., U.S.	E3	82
Cambria, Wi., U.S.	E4	126
Cambria, co., Pa., U.S.	E4	115
Cambrian Mountains, mts., Wales, U.K.	I9	7
Cambridge, Ont., Can.	D4	73
Cambridge, Eng., U.K.	I13	7
Cambridge, Il., U.S.	B3	90
Cambridge, Ia., U.S.	C4	92
Cambridge, Md., U.S.	C5	97
Cambridge, Ma., U.S.	B5	98
Cambridge, Mn., U.S.	E5	100
Cambridge, Ne., U.S.	D5	104
Cambridge, N.Y., U.S.	B7	109
Cambridge, Oh., U.S.	B4	112
Cambridge, Wi., U.S.	F4	126
Cambridge Bay, N.W. Ter., Can.	C11	66
Cambridge City, In., U.S.	E7	91
Cambridge Reservoir, res., Ma., U.S.	g10	98
Cambridge Springs, Pa., U.S.	C1	115
Cambuci, Braz.	F8	57
Camden, Al., U.S.	D2	78
Camden, Ar., U.S.	D3	81
Camden, De., U.S.	D3	85
Camden, In., U.S.	C4	91
Camden, Me., U.S.	D3	96
Camden, N.J., U.S.	D2	107
Camden, N.Y., U.S.	B5	109
Camden, Oh., U.S.	C1	112
Camden, S.C., U.S.	C6	117
Camden, Tn., U.S.	A3	119
Camden, co., Ga., U.S.	F5	87
Camden, co., Mo., U.S.	C5	102
Camden, co., N.J., U.S.	D3	107
Camden, co., N.C., U.S.	A6	110
Camdenton, Mo., U.S.	D5	102
Camelback Mountain, mtn., Az., U.S.	k9	80
Cameron, Az., U.S.	B4	80
Cameron, La., U.S.	E2	95
Cameron, Mo., U.S.	B3	102
Cameron, Tx., U.S.	D4	120
Cameron, W.V., U.S.	B4	125
Cameron, Wi., U.S.	C2	126
Cameron, co., La., U.S.	E2	95
Cameron, co., Pa., U.S.	D5	115
Cameron, co., Tx., U.S.	F4	120
Cameron Highlands, Malay.	L6	34
Cameron Hills, hills, Can.	E9	66
Cameroon, ctry., Afr.	G8	42
Cameroon Mountain, mtn., Cam.	H7	42
Cametá, Braz.	D9	54
Camilla, Ga., U.S.	E2	87
Camino, Ca., U.S.	C3	82
Camiranga, Braz.	D9	54
Camissombo, Ang.	C4	44
Cam Lo, Viet.	F9	34
Cammack Village, Ar., U.S.	C3	81
Camooweal, Austl.	C7	50
Camorta Island, i., India	J2	34
Camp, co., Tx., U.S.	C5	120
Campana, Isla, i., Chile	F1	56
Campanero, Cerro, mtn., Ven.	E10	58
Campbell, Ca., U.S.	k8	82
Campbell, Fl., U.S.	D5	86
Campbell, Mo., U.S.	E7	102
Campbell, Oh., U.S.	A5	112
Campbell, co., Ky., U.S.	B5	94
Campbell, co., S.D., U.S.	B5	118
Campbell, co., Tn., U.S.	C9	119
Campbell, co., Va., U.S.	C3	123
Campbell, co., Wy., U.S.	B7	127
Campbellford, Ont., Can.	C7	73
Campbell Hill, hill, Oh., U.S.	B2	112
Campbell Lake, l., Or., U.S.	E7	114
Campbellsburg, In., U.S.	G5	91
Campbellsburg, Ky., U.S.	B4	94
Campbells Creek, stm., W.V., U.S.	m13	125
Campbellsport, Wi., U.S.	E5	126
Campbellsville, Ky., U.S.	C4	94
Campbellton, N.B., Can.	A3	71
Campbellton, Newf., Can.	D4	72
Campbeltown, Scot., U.K.	F7	7
Campeche, Mex.	H14	62
Campeche, Bahía de, b., Mex.	H13	62
Camperville, Man., Can.	D1	70
Camp Hill, Al., U.S.	C4	78
Camp Hill, Pa., U.S.	F8	115
Camp H. M. Smith Marine Corps Base, mil., Hi., U.S.	g10	88
Camp Howard Ridge, mtn., Id., U.S.	D2	89
Campina Grande, Braz.	E11	54
Campinas, Braz.	G5	57
Camp Lejeune Marine Corps Base, mil., N.C., U.S.	C5	110
Campoalegre, Col.	F5	58
Campo Alegre de Goiás, Braz.	D5	57
Campobasso, Italy	H9	14
Campobello Island, i., N.B., Can.	E3	71
Campo Belo, Braz.	F6	57
Campo de Criptana, Spain	F8	12
Campo de la Cruz, Col.	B5	58
Campo Grande, Braz.	F1	57
Campo Maior, Braz.	D10	54
Campos, Braz.	F8	57
Campos do Jordão, Braz.	G6	57
Camp Pendleton Marine Corps Base, mil., Ca., U.S.	F5	82
Camp Point, Il., U.S.	C2	90
Camp Springs, Md., U.S.	f9	97
Campti, La., U.S.	C2	95
Campton, N.H., U.S.	C3	106
Camp Verde, Az., U.S.	C4	80
Camp Verde Indian Reservation, Az., U.S.	C4	80
Cam Ranh, Viet.	I10	34
Camrose, Alta., Can.	C4	68
Canaan, Ct., U.S.	A2	84
Canaan, N.H., U.S.	C2	106
Canaan, stm., N.B., Can.	C4	71
Canada, ctry., N.A.	D14	66
Canada Bay, b., Newf., Can.	C3	72
Canada Falls Lake, res., Me., U.S.	C2	96
Canadensis, Pa., U.S.	D11	115
Canadian, Tx., U.S.	B2	120
Canadian, co., Ok., U.S.	B3	113
Canadian, stm., U.S.	D6	76
Canajoharie, N.Y., U.S.	C6	109
Çanakkale, Tur.	G13	4
Çanakkale Boğazi (Dardanelles), strt., Tur.	I10	16
Canal Flats, B.C., Can.	D10	69
Canal Fulton, Oh., U.S.	B4	112
Canal Winchester, Oh., U.S.	C3	112
Canandaigua, N.Y., U.S.	C3	109
Canandaigua Lake, l., N.Y., U.S.	C3	109
Cananea, Mex.	B4	62
Cañar, Ec.	I3	58
Canarias, Islas (Canary Islands), is., Spain	p24	136
Canary Islands see Canarias, Islas, is., Spain	p24	136
Cañas, C.R.	I5	64
Canastota, N.Y., U.S.	B5	109
Canaveral, Cape, c., Fl., U.S.	D6	86
Canaveral National Seashore, Fl., U.S.	D6	86
Canavieiras, Braz.	C9	57
Canberra, Austl.	G9	50
Canby, Mn., U.S.	F2	100
Canby, Or., U.S.	B4	114
Cancale, Fr.	D5	10
Cancon, Fr.	H7	10
Cancún, Mex.	G16	62
Candeleda, Spain	E6	12
Candiac, Que., Can.	q19	74
Candle Lake, l., Sask., Can.	D3	75
Candler, co., Ga., U.S.	D4	87
Candlewood, Lake, l., Ct., U.S.	D1	84
Candlewood Isle, Ct., U.S.	D2	84
Candlewood Shores, Ct., U.S.	D2	84
Cando, N.D., U.S.	A6	111
Candor, N.C., U.S.	B3	110
Cane, stm., La., U.S.	C2	95
Cañete, Spain	E10	12
Caney, Ks., U.S.	E8	93
Caney, stm., Ok., U.S.	A5	113
Caney Creek, stm., Tx., U.S.	r14	120
Caney Fork, stm., Tn., U.S.	C8	119
Canfield, Oh., U.S.	A5	112
Canfranc, Spain	C11	12
Cangas de Onís, Spain	B6	12
Cangombe, Ang.	D3	44
Canguçu, Braz.	C6	56
Cangzhou, China	D10	26
Caniapiscau, stm., Que., Can.	g13	74
Caniapiscau, Lac, l., Que., Can.	F19	66
Canicattì, Italy	L8	14
Canistear Reservoir, res., N.J., U.S.	A4	107
Canisteo, N.Y., U.S.	C3	109
Canisteo, stm., N.Y., U.S.	C3	109
Canistota, S.D., U.S.	D8	118
Cañitas, Mex.	F8	62
Çankırı, Tur.	G14	4
Canmore, Alta., Can.	D3	68
Cannanore, India	G3	37
Cannelton, In., U.S.	I4	91
Cannes, Fr.	I14	10
Canning, N.S., Can.	D5	71
Cannon, co., Tn., U.S.	B5	119
Cannon, stm., Mn., U.S.	F5	100
Cannon Air Force Base, mil., N.M., U.S.	C6	108
Cannonball, stm., N.D., U.S.	C5	111
Cannon Beach, Or., U.S.	B3	114
Cannondale, Ct., U.S.	E2	84
Cannon Falls, Mn., U.S.	F6	100
Cannonsburg, Ky., U.S.	B7	94
Cannonsville Reservoir, res., N.Y., U.S.	C5	109
Canon, Ga., U.S.	B3	87
Canon City, Co., U.S.	C5	83
Canonsburg, Pa., U.S.	F1	115
Canosa [di Puglia], Italy	H11	14
Cantábrica, Cordillera, mts., Spain	B7	12
Cantalejo, Spain	D8	12
Cantanhede, Port.	E3	12
Cantaura, Ven.	C10	58
Canterbury, Eng., U.K.	J14	7
Canterbury, De., U.S.	D3	85
Canterbury Bight, N.Z.	F3	52
Can Tho, Viet.	I8	34
Canton, Ct., U.S.	B4	84
Canton, Ga., U.S.	B2	87
Canton, Il., U.S.	C3	90
Canton, Ks., U.S.	D6	93
Canton, Ma., U.S.	B5	98
Canton, Ms., U.S.	C3	101
Canton, Mo., U.S.	A6	102
Canton, N.Y., U.S.	f9	109
Canton, N.C., U.S.	f10	110
Canton, Oh., U.S.	B4	112
Canton, Ok., U.S.	A3	113
Canton, Pa., U.S.	C8	115
Canton, S.D., U.S.	D9	118
Canton, Tx., U.S.	C5	120
Canton see Guangzhou, China	L2	28
Canton Lake, res., Ok., U.S.	A3	113
Cantonment, Fl., U.S.	u14	86
Cantù, Italy	D4	14
Canutillo, Tx., U.S.	o11	120
Canyon, Tx., U.S.	B2	120
Canyon, co., Id., U.S.	F2	89
Canyon City, Or., U.S.	C8	114
Canyon de Chelly National Monument, Az., U.S.	A6	80
Canyon Ferry Lake, res., Mt., U.S.	D5	103
Canyon Lake, Tx., U.S.	E3	120
Canyon Lake, res., Tx., U.S.	E3	120
Canyonlands National Park, Ut., U.S.	E6	121
Canyonville, Or., U.S.	E3	114
Cao Bang, Viet.	C9	34
Capac, Mi., U.S.	F8	99
Cap-à-l'Aigle, Que., Can.	B7	74
Cap-aux-Meules, Que., Can.	B8	71
Cap-de-la-Madeleine, Que., Can.	C5	74
Cape Breton Highlands National Park, N.S., Can.	C9	71
Cape Breton Island, i., N.S., Can.	C9	71
Cape Broyle, Newf., Can.	E5	72
Cape Canaveral, Fl., U.S.	D6	86
Cape Charles, Va., U.S.	C6	123
Cape Coast, Ghana	G5	42
Cape Cod Bay, b., Ma., U.S.	C7	98
Cape Cod Canal, Ma., U.S.	C6	98
Cape Cod National Seashore, Ma., U.S.	C7	98
Cape Coral, Fl., U.S.	F5	86
Cape Dorset, N.W. Ter., Can.	D17	66
Cape Elizabeth, Me., U.S.	E2	96
Cape Fear, stm., N.C., U.S.	C4	110
Cape Girardeau, Mo., U.S.	D8	102
Cape Girardeau, co., Mo., U.S.	D8	102
Cape Hatteras National Seashore, N.C., U.S.	B7	110
Cape Horn Mountain, mtn., Id., U.S.	E3	89
Cape Island, i., S.C., U.S.	E9	117
Cape Lookout National Seashore, N.C., U.S.	C6	110
Cape May, N.J., U.S.	F3	107
Cape May, co., N.J., U.S.	E3	107
Cape May Court House, N.J., U.S.	E3	107
Capers Inlet, b., S.C., U.S.	k12	117
Capers Island, i., S.C., U.S.	G6	117
Capers Island, i., S.C., U.S.	F8	117
Cape Sable Island, i., N.S., Can.	F4	71
Cape Town (Kaapstad), S. Afr.	H3	44
Cape Verde, ctry., Afr.	E11	2
Cape York Peninsula, pen., Austl.	B8	50
Cap-Haïtien, Haiti	E11	64
Capim, stm., Braz.	D9	54
Capitan, N.M., U.S.	D4	108
Capitan Mountains, mts., N.M., U.S.	D4	108
Capitan Peak, mtn., N.M., U.S.	D4	108
Capitol Heights, Ia., U.S.	e8	92
Capitol Heights, Md., U.S.	C4	97
Capitol Peak, mtn., Nv., U.S.	B4	105
Capitol Reef National Park, Ut., U.S.	E4	121
Čapljina, Bos.	F12	14
Cap-Pelé, N.B., Can.	C5	71
Capreol, Ont., Can.	p19	73
Capri, Italy	I9	14
Caprivi Strip, hist. reg., Nmb.	E4	44
Cap-Rouge, Que., Can.	n17	74
Cap-Saint-Ignace, Que., Can.	B7	74
Captain Cook, Hi., U.S.	D6	88
Captieux, Fr.	H6	10
Captiva, Fl., U.S.	F4	86
Captiva Island, i., Fl., U.S.	F4	86
Capua, Italy	H9	14
Capulin Volcano National Monument, N.M., U.S.	A6	108
Caquetá (Japurá), stm., S.A.	D5	54
Čara, Russia	F17	24
Čara, stm., Russia	F17	24
Caracaraí, Braz.	C6	54
Caracas, Ven.	B9	58
Carajás, Serra dos, mts., Braz.	E8	54

Name	Map Ref	Page
Carangola, Braz.	F7	57
Caraquet, N.B., Can.	B5	71
Caratasca, Laguna de, b., Hond.	G6	64
Caratinga, Braz.	E7	57
Carauari, Braz.	D5	54
Caravaca, Spain	G10	12
Caravelas, Braz.	D9	57
Caraway, Ar., U.S.	B5	81
Carballo, Spain	B3	12
Carberry, Man., Can.	E2	70
Carbon, co., Mt., U.S.	E7	103
Carbon, co., Pa., U.S.	E10	115
Carbon, co., Ut., U.S.	D5	121
Carbon, co., Wy., U.S.	E5	127
Carbondale, Co., U.S.	B3	83
Carbondale, Il., U.S.	F4	90
Carbondale, Ks., U.S.	D8	93
Carbondale, Pa., U.S.	C10	115
Carbonear, Newf., Can.	E5	72
Carboneras de Guadazaon, Spain	F10	12
Carbon Hill, Al., U.S.	B2	78
Carbonia, Italy	J3	14
Carcagente, Spain	F11	12
Carcassonne, Fr.	I9	10
Carcross, Yukon, Can.	D6	66
Cárdenas, Cuba	C7	64
Cárdenas, Mex.	F10	62
Cardiff, Wales, U.K.	J9	7
Cardigan, Wales, U.K.	I8	7
Cardigan Bay, b., P.E.I., Can.	C7	71
Cardigan Bay, b., Wales, U.K.	I8	7
Cardinal, Ont., Can.	C9	73
Cardington, Oh., U.S.	B3	112
Cardston, Alta., Can.	E4	68
Cardwell, Mo., U.S.	E7	102
Čardžou, Turk.	J10	22
Carencro, La., U.S.	D3	95
Carentan, Fr.	C5	10
Caretta, W.V., U.S.	D3	125
Carey, Id., U.S.	F5	89
Carey, Oh., U.S.	B2	112
Carey, Lake, l., Austl.	E4	50
Caribbean Sea	G10	64
Cariboo Mountains, mts., B.C., Can.	C7	69
Caribou, Me., U.S.	B5	96
Caribou, co., Id., U.S.	G7	89
Caribou Island, i., N.S., Can.	D7	71
Caribou Lake, l., Me., U.S.	C3	96
Caribou Mountain, mtn., Id., U.S.	F7	89
Caribou Mountains, mts., Alta., Can.	f7	68
Caribou Range, mts., Id., U.S.	F7	89
Carignan, Fr.	C12	10
Cariñena, Spain	D10	12
Carinhanha, Braz.	C7	57
Carini, Italy	K8	14
Caripito, Ven.	B11	58
Carl Blackwell, Lake, res., Ok., U.S.	A4	113
Carleton, Mi., U.S.	F7	99
Carleton, Mount, mtn., N.B., Can.	B3	71
Carleton Place, Ont., Can.	B8	73
Carlin, Nv., U.S.	C5	105
Carlinville, Il., U.S.	D4	90
Carlisle, Eng., U.K.	G10	7
Carlisle, Ar., U.S.	C4	81
Carlisle, In., U.S.	G3	91
Carlisle, Ia., U.S.	C4	92
Carlisle, Ky., U.S.	B5	94
Carlisle, Oh., U.S.	C1	112
Carlisle, Pa., U.S.	F7	115
Carlisle, co., Ky., U.S.	f8	94
Carl Junction, Mo., U.S.	D3	102
Carlow, Ire.	I6	7
Carlsbad, Ca., U.S.	F5	82
Carlsbad, N.M., U.S.	E5	108
Carlsbad Caverns National Park, N.M., U.S.	E5	108
Carlstadt, N.J., U.S.	h8	107
Carlton, Mn., U.S.	D6	100
Carlton, Or., U.S.	B3	114
Carlton, co., Mn., U.S.	D6	100
Carlyle, Il., U.S.	E4	90
Carlyle Lake, res., Il., U.S.	E4	90
Carmacks, Yukon, Can.	D5	66
Carmagnola, Italy	E2	14
Carman, Man., Can.	E2	70
Carmanville, Newf., Can.	D4	72
Carmarthen, Wales, U.K.	J8	7
Carmaux, Fr.	H9	10
Carmel, Ca., U.S.	D3	82
Carmel, In., U.S.	E5	91
Carmel, N.Y., U.S.	D7	109
Carmel Head, c., Wales, U.K.	H8	7
Carmen, Isla, i., Mex.	E4	62
Carmen, Isla del, i., Mex.	H14	62
Carmen de Patagones, Arg.	E4	56
Carmi, Il., U.S.	E5	90
Carmi, Lake, l., Vt., U.S.	B3	122
Carmona, Spain	H6	12
Carnarvon, Austl.	D2	50
Carnarvon, S. Afr.	H4	44
Carnation, Wa., U.S.	B4	124
Carndonagh, Ire.	F5	7
Carnegie, Ok., U.S.	B3	113
Carnegie, Pa., U.S.	F1	115
Carnegie, Lake, l., Austl.	E4	50
Carneys Point, N.J., U.S.	D2	107
Carniche, Alpi, mts., Eur.	C8	14
Car Nicobar Island, i., India	J2	34
Carnsore Point, c., Ire.	I6	7
Caro, Mi., U.S.	E7	99
Carol City, Fl., U.S.	s13	86
Caroleen, N.C., U.S.	B1	110
Carolina, Braz.	E9	54
Carolina, Col.	D5	58
Carolina, R.I., U.S.	F2	116
Carolina, W.V., U.S.	k10	125
Carolina Beach, N.C., U.S.	C5	110
Caroline, co., Md., U.S.	C6	97
Caroline, co., Va., U.S.	C5	123
Caroní, stm., Ven.	D11	58
Carora, Ven.	B7	58
Carpathian Mountains, mts., Eur.	F12	4
Carpații Meridionali, mts., Rom.	D8	16
Carpentaria, Gulf of, b., Austl.	B7	50
Carpenter Dam, Ar., U.S.	g7	81
Carpentersville, Il., U.S.	A5	90
Carpentras, Fr.	H12	10
Carpi, Italy	E5	14
Carpinteria, Ca., U.S.	E4	82
Carquefou, Fr.	E5	10
Carrabelle, Fl., U.S.	C2	86
Carrara, Italy	E5	14
Carrauntoohill, mtn., Ire.	I3	7
Carrboro, N.C., U.S.	B3	110
Carreta, Punta, c., Peru	F3	54
Carrickfergus, N. Ire., U.K.	G7	7
Carrickmacross, Ire.	H6	7
Carrie, Mount, mtn., Wa., U.S.	B2	124
Carriere, Ms., U.S.	E4	101
Carrier Mills, Il., U.S.	F5	90
Carrillo, Mex.	D8	62
Carrington, N.D., U.S.	B6	111
Carrington Island, i., Ut., U.S.	C3	121
Carrión de los Condes, Spain	C7	12
Carrizo Creek, stm., U.S.	A1	120
Carrizo Mountain, mtn., N.M., U.S.	D4	108
Carrizo Mountains, mts., U.S.	A6	80
Carrizo Springs, Tx., U.S.	*E3	120
Carrizozo, N.M., U.S.	D4	108
Carroll, Ia., U.S.	B3	92
Carroll, co., Ar., U.S.	A2	81
Carroll, co., Ga., U.S.	C1	87
Carroll, co., Il., U.S.	A4	90
Carroll, co., In., U.S.	C4	91
Carroll, co., Ia., U.S.	B3	92
Carroll, co., Ky., U.S.	B4	94
Carroll, co., Md., U.S.	A3	97
Carroll, co., Ms., U.S.	B4	101
Carroll, co., Mo., U.S.	B4	102
Carroll, co., N.H., U.S.	C4	106
Carroll, co., Oh., U.S.	B4	112
Carroll, co., Tn., U.S.	B3	119
Carroll, co., Va., U.S.	D2	123
Carrollton, Al., U.S.	B1	78
Carrollton, Ga., U.S.	C1	87
Carrollton, Il., U.S.	D3	90
Carrollton, Ky., U.S.	B4	94
Carrollton, Mi., U.S.	E7	99
Carrollton, Mo., U.S.	B4	102
Carrollton, Oh., U.S.	B4	112
Carrolltown, Pa., U.S.	E4	115
Carrot, stm., Can.	D4	75
Carry Falls Reservoir, res., N.Y., U.S.	f10	109
Čarsk, Kaz.	H10	24
Carson, Ia., U.S.	C2	92
Carson, Wa., U.S.	D4	124
Carson, co., Tx., U.S.	B2	120
Carson, stm., Nv., U.S.	D2	105
Carson City, Mi., U.S.	E6	99
Carson City, Nv., U.S.	D2	105
Carson Lake, l., Nv., U.S.	D3	105
Carson Sink, l., Nv., U.S.	D3	105
Carson Spring, Tn., U.S.	D10	119
Carstairs, Alta., Can.	D3	68
Carswell Air Force Base, mil., Tx., U.S.	n9	120
Cartagena, Col.	B5	58
Cartagena, Spain	H11	12
Cartago, Col.	E5	58
Cartago, C.R.	J6	64
Carter, co., Ky., U.S.	B6	94
Carter, co., Mo., U.S.	E7	102
Carter, co., Mt., U.S.	E12	103
Carter, co., Ok., U.S.	C4	113
Carter, co., Tn., U.S.	C11	119
Carteret, N.J., U.S.	B4	107
Carteret, co., N.C., U.S.	C6	110
Carter Lake, Ia., U.S.	C2	92
Carter Mountain, mtn., Wy., U.S.	B3	127
Carters Lake, res., Ga., U.S.	B2	87
Cartersville, Ga., U.S.	B2	87
Carterville, Il., U.S.	F4	90
Carterville, Mo., U.S.	D3	102
Carthage, Il., U.S.	C2	90
Carthage, In., U.S.	E6	91
Carthage, Ms., U.S.	C4	101
Carthage, Mo., U.S.	D3	102
Carthage, N.Y., U.S.	B5	109
Carthage, N.C., U.S.	B3	110
Carthage, Tn., U.S.	C8	119
Carthage, Tx., U.S.	C5	120
Cartier Island, i., Austl.	B4	50
Cartwright, Newf., Can.	B3	72
Cartwright, Ok., U.S.	D5	113
Caruaru, Braz.	E11	54
Carúpano, Ven.	B11	58
Caruthersville, Mo., U.S.	E8	102
Carver, Ma., U.S.	C6	98
Carver, Mn., U.S.	F5	100
Carver, co., Mn., U.S.	F5	100
Carville, La., U.S.	h9	95
Cary, Il., U.S.	A5	90
Cary, N.C., U.S.	B4	110
Caryville, Tn., U.S.	C9	119
Casablanca (Dar-el-Beida), Mor.	B4	42
Casacalenda, Italy	H9	14
Casa Grande, Az., U.S.	E4	80
Casa Grande National Monument, Az., U.S.	E4	80
Casale Monferrato, Italy	D3	14
Casarano, Italy	I13	14
Casas Adobes, Az., U.S.	E5	80
Casas Ibáñez, Spain	F10	12
Cascade, Co., U.S.	C6	83
Cascade, Id., U.S.	E2	89
Cascade, Ia., U.S.	B6	92
Cascade, Mt., U.S.	C5	103
Cascade, co., Mt., U.S.	C5	103
Cascade Locks, Or., U.S.	B5	114
Cascade Range, mts., N.A.	C2	76
Cascade Reservoir, res., Id., U.S.	E3	89
Cascade Tunnel, Wa., U.S.	B4	124
Cascais, Port.	G2	12
Cascina, Italy	F5	14
Casco Bay, b., Me., U.S.	E3	96
Caserta, Italy	H9	14
Caseville, Mi., U.S.	E7	99
Casey, Il., U.S.	D6	90
Casey, co., Ky., U.S.	C5	94
Casey, Mount, mtn., Id., U.S.	A2	89
Casey Key, i., Fl., U.S.	E4	86
Cashion, Az., U.S.	m8	80
Cashmere, Wa., U.S.	B5	124
Cashton, Wi., U.S.	E3	126
Casigua, Ven.	C6	58
Caspe, Spain	D11	12
Casper, Wy., U.S.	D6	127
Casper Mountain, mtn., Wy., U.S.	D6	127
Caspian, Mi., U.S.	B2	99
Caspian Lake, l., Vt., U.S.	B4	122
Caspian Sea	G17	4
Cass, co., Il., U.S.	D3	90
Cass, co., In., U.S.	C5	91
Cass, co., Ia., U.S.	C3	92
Cass, co., Mi., U.S.	G4	99
Cass, co., Mn., U.S.	D4	100
Cass, co., Mo., U.S.	C3	102
Cass, co., Ne., U.S.	D9	104
Cass, co., N.D., U.S.	C8	111
Cass, co., Tx., U.S.	C5	120
Cass, stm., Mi., U.S.	E7	99
Cassai (Kasai), stm., Afr.	C4	44
Cassano allo Ionio, Italy	J11	14
Cass City, Mi., U.S.	E7	99
Casselberry, Fl., U.S.	D5	86
Casselman, Ont., Can.	B9	73
Casselman, stm., U.S.	k12	97
Casselton, N.D., U.S.	C8	111
Cassia, co., Id., U.S.	G5	89
Cassiar, B.C., Can.	m17	69
Cassinga, Ang.	E3	44
Cassino, Italy	H8	14
Cass Lake, Mn., U.S.	C4	100
Cass Lake, l., Mn., U.S.	C4	100
Cassopolis, Mi., U.S.	G4	99
Cassville, Ga., U.S.	B2	87
Cassville, Mo., U.S.	E4	102
Cassville, Wi., U.S.	F3	126
Castalia, Oh., U.S.	A3	112
Castanea, Pa., U.S.	D7	115
Castanheira de Pêra, Port.	E3	12
Castel del Piano, Italy	G6	14
Castelfranco Veneto, Italy	D6	14
Castellamare del Golfo, Italy	K7	14
Castellammare [di Stabia], Italy	I9	14
Castellane, Fr.	I13	10
Castellón de la Plana, Spain	F11	12
Castelnaudary, Fr.	I8	10
Castelo Branco, Port.	F4	12
Castelsarrasin, Fr.	H8	10
Castelvetrano, Italy	L7	14
Castets, Fr.	I5	10
Castiglione del Lago, Italy	F7	14
Castilla, Peru	E2	54
Castilla la Nueva, hist. reg., Spain	F8	12
Castillo de San Marcos National Monument, Fl., U.S.	n9	86
Castine, Me., U.S.	D4	96
Castle Air Force Base, mil., Ca., U.S.	D3	82
Castlebar, Ire.	H3	7
Castleberry, Al., U.S.	D2	78
Castle Dale, Ut., U.S.	D4	121
Castle Dome Mountains, mts., Az., U.S.	D1	80
Castle Dome Peak, mtn., Az., U.S.	D1	80
Castlegar, B.C., Can.	E9	69
Castle Hayne, N.C., U.S.	C5	110
Castle Hills, De., U.S.	i7	85
Castle Mountain, mtn., Yukon, Can.	D5	66
Castle Mountains, mts., Mt., U.S.	D6	103
Castle Peak, mtn., Co., U.S.	B4	83
Castle Peak, mtn., Id., U.S.	E4	89
Castle Point, Mo., U.S.	f13	102
Castle Rock, Co., U.S.	B6	83
Castle Rock, Wa., U.S.	C3	124
Castle Rock, mtn., Or., U.S.	C8	114
Castle Rock Lake, res., Wi., U.S.	E4	126
Castleton, Vt., U.S.	D2	122
Castletown, I. of Man	G8	7
Castletown Berehaven, Ire.	J3	7
Castlewood, Va., U.S.	f9	123
Castor, Alta., Can.	C5	68
Castor, stm., Mo., U.S.	D7	102
Castres, Fr.	I9	10
Castries, St. Luc.	G17	64
Castro, co., Tx., U.S.	B1	120
Castro Daire, Port.	E4	12
Castro del Río, Spain	H7	12
Castropol, Spain	B4	12
Castro Valley, Ca., U.S.	h8	82
Castrovillari, Italy	J11	14
Castroville, Tx., U.S.	E3	120
Castuera, Spain	G6	12
Caswell, co., N.C., U.S.	A3	110
Catacamas, Hond.	G5	64
Cataguases, Braz.	F7	57
Catahoula, co., La., U.S.	C4	95
Catahoula Lake, l., La., U.S.	C3	95
Catalão, Braz.	E5	57
Catalina, Newf., Can.	D5	72
Catalina, Chile	B3	56
Catamarca, Arg.	B3	56
Catamayo, Ec.	I3	58
Catanduanes Island, i., Phil.	C7	32
Catanduva, Braz.	F4	57
Catania, Italy	L10	14
Catanzaro, Italy	K11	14
Cataouatche, Lake, l., La., U.S.	k11	95
Catarman, Phil.	C7	32
Catasauqua, Pa., U.S.	E11	115
Catastrophe, Cape, c., Austl.	F7	50
Cataumet, Ma., U.S.	C6	98
Catawba, co., N.C., U.S.	B1	110
Catawba, stm., S.C., U.S.	B6	117
Catawba, South Fork, stm., N.C., U.S.	B1	110
Catawissa, Pa., U.S.	E9	115
Catete, Ang.	C2	44
Cathance, Lake, l., Me., U.S.	D5	96
Cathcart, S. Afr.	H5	44
Cathedral City, Ca., U.S.	F5	82
Cathedral of the Pines, N.H., U.S.	E3	106
Catherine, Lake, res., Ar., U.S.	C3	81
Cat Island, i., Bah.	B10	64
Cat Island, i., Ma., U.S.	f12	98
Cat Island, i., Ms., U.S.	E4	101
Cat Island, i., S.C., U.S.	E9	117
Catlettsburg, Ky., U.S.	B7	94
Catlin, Il., U.S.	C6	90
Catnip Mountain, mtn., Nv., U.S.	B2	105
Catoche, Cabo, c., Mex.	G16	62
Cato Island, i., Austl.	D11	50
Catonsville, Md., U.S.	B4	97
Catoosa, Ok., U.S.	A6	113
Catoosa, co., Ga., U.S.	B1	87
Catorce, Mex.	F9	62
Catron, co., N.M., U.S.	D1	108
Catskill, N.Y., U.S.	C7	109
Catskill Mountains, mts., N.Y., U.S.	C6	109
Catt, Mount, mtn., B.C., Can.	B3	69
Cattaraugus, co., N.Y., U.S.	C2	109
Cattaraugus Creek, stm., N.Y., U.S.	C2	109
Cattaraugus Indian Reservation, N.Y., U.S.	C2	109
Cattolica, Italy	F7	14
Catus, Fr.	H8	10
Caubvick, Mount (Mont d'Iberville), mtn., Can.	f9	72
Cauca, stm., Col.	D5	58
Caucasia, Col.	C5	58
Caucasus, mts., Eur.	I6	22
Caucomgomoc Lake, l., Me., U.S.	B3	96
Caudry, Fr.	B10	10
Caulonia, Italy	K11	14
Caúngula, Ang.	C3	44
Čaunskaja Guba, b., Russia	D27	24
Cauquenes, Chile	D2	56
Caura, stm., Ven.	D10	58
Caussade, Fr.	H8	10
Cauvery, stm., India	G5	37
Cavalaire-sur-Mer, Fr.	I13	10
Cavalier, N.D., U.S.	A8	111
Cavalier, co., N.D., U.S.	A7	111
Cavan, Ire.	G5	7
Cave City, Ar., U.S.	B4	81
Cave City, Ky., U.S.	C4	94
Cave Creek, Az., U.S.	D4	80
Cave Junction, Or., U.S.	E3	114
Cave Point, c., Wi., U.S.	D6	126
Cave Run Lake, res., Ky., U.S.	B6	94
Cave Spring, Ga., U.S.	B1	87
Cave Spring, Va., U.S.	C2	123
Cavetown, Md., U.S.	A2	97
Caviana, Ilha, i., Braz.	C8	54
Cavite, Phil.	q19	33b
Cawood, Ky., U.S.	D6	94
Cawston, B.C., Can.	E8	69
Caxambu, Braz.	F6	57
Caxias, Braz.	D10	54
Caxias do Sul, Braz.	B6	56
Caxito, Ang.	C2	44
Cayambe, Ec.	G3	58
Cayambe, vol., Ec.	H4	58
Cayce, S.C., U.S.	D5	117
Cayenne, Fr. Gu.	C8	54
Cayman Brac, i., Cay. Is.	E8	64
Cayman Islands, dep., N.A.	E7	64
Cayuga, In., U.S.	E3	91
Cayuga, co., N.Y., U.S.	C4	109
Cayuga Heights, N.Y., U.S.	C4	109
Cayuga Lake, l., N.Y., U.S.	C4	109
Cazenovia, N.Y., U.S.	C5	109
Cazères, Fr.	I8	10
Cazin, Bos.	E10	14
Cazorla, Spain	H8	12
Čeboksary, Russia	F7	22
Cebollar, Arg.	B3	56
Cebreros, Spain	E7	12
Cebu, Phil.	C7	32
Cebu, i., Phil.	C7	32
Cecerleg, Mong.	B7	26
Čechov, Russia	F20	18
Čechy, hist. reg., Czech.	F14	8
Cecil, co., Md., U.S.	A6	97
Cecil Field Naval Air Station, mil., Fl., U.S.	B5	86
Cecilia, Ky., U.S.	C4	94
Cecina, Italy	F5	14
Cedar, co., Ia., U.S.	C6	92
Cedar, co., Mo., U.S.	D4	102
Cedar, co., Ne., U.S.	B8	104
Cedar, stm., U.S.	C6	92
Cedar, stm., Ne., U.S.	B7	104
Cedar, stm., Wa., U.S.	B4	124
Cedar Bluff, Al., U.S.	A4	78
Cedar Bluff Reservoir, res., Ks., U.S.	D4	93
Cedar Bluff Two, Tn., U.S.	D9	119
Cedar Breaks National Monument, Ut., U.S.	F3	121
Cedarburg, Wi., U.S.	E6	126
Cedar City, Ut., U.S.	F2	121
Cedar Creek, stm., N.J., U.S.	D4	107
Cedar Creek, stm., N.D., U.S.	C3	111
Cedar Creek, stm., Oh., U.S.	e7	112
Cedar Creek Lake, res., Tx., U.S.	C4	120
Cedar Crest, N.M., U.S.	k8	108
Cedaredge, Co., U.S.	C3	83
Cedar Falls, Ia., U.S.	B5	92
Cedar Grove, N.J., U.S.	B4	107
Cedar Grove, W.V., U.S.	C3	125
Cedar Grove, Wi., U.S.	E6	126
Cedar Hill, Mo., U.S.	g12	102
Cedar Hill, Tx., U.S.	n10	120
Cedarhurst, N.Y., U.S.	k13	109
Cedar Island, i., N.C., U.S.	C6	110
Cedar Island, i., S.C., U.S.	E9	117
Cedar Island, i., Va., U.S.	C7	123
Cedar Key, Fl., U.S.	C3	86
Cedar Keys, is., Fl., U.S.	C3	86
Cedar Lake, In., U.S.	B3	91
Cedar Lake, res., Man., Can.	C1	70
Cedar Lake, res., Il., U.S.	F4	90
Cedar Mountain, mtn., Ca., U.S.	B3	82
Cedar Point, c., Md., U.S.	D5	97
Cedar Point, c., Oh., U.S.	A3	112
Cedar Point, c., Oh., U.S.	e7	112
Cedar Rapids, Ia., U.S.	C6	92
Cedar Springs, Mi., U.S.	E5	99
Cedartown, Ga., U.S.	B1	87
Cedar Vale, Ks., U.S.	E7	93
Cedarville, Oh., U.S.	C2	112
Cedros, Isla, i., Mex.	C2	62
Ceduna, Austl.	F6	50
Cefalù, Italy	K9	14
Čegdomyn, Russia	G20	24
Cegléd, Hung.	H19	8
Cehegín, Spain	G10	12
Cela, Ang.	D3	44
Čel'abinsk, Russia	F10	22
Celano, Italy	G8	14
Celanova, Spain	C4	12
Celaya, Mex.	G9	62
Cele, China	B9	38
Celebes Sea, Asia	E7	32
Celebes see Sulawesi, i., Indon.	F7	32
Celina, Oh., U.S.	B1	112
Celina, Tn., U.S.	C8	119
Celina, Tx., U.S.	C4	120
Celinograd, Kaz.	G8	24
Celje, Slo.	C10	14
Celle, Ger.	C10	8
Cement, Ok., U.S.	C3	113
Cementon, Pa., U.S.	E10	115
Centennial Mountains, mts., Id., U.S.	E7	89
Center, Co., U.S.	D4	83
Center, N.D., U.S.	B4	111
Center, Tx., U.S.	D5	120
Centerbrook, Ct., U.S.	D6	84
Centerburg, Oh., U.S.	B3	112
Centereach, N.Y., U.S.	n15	109
Centerfield, Ut., U.S.	D4	121
Center Hill Lake, res., Tn., U.S.	C8	119
Center Moriches, N.Y., U.S.	n16	109
Center Mountain, mtn., Id., U.S.	D3	89
Center Point, Al., U.S.	f7	78
Center Point, Ia., U.S.	B6	92
Centerville, In., U.S.	E8	91
Centerville, Ia., U.S.	D5	92
Centerville, La., U.S.	E4	95
Centerville, Ma., U.S.	C7	98
Centerville, Oh., U.S.	C1	112
Centerville, Pa., U.S.	F2	115
Centerville, S.D., U.S.	D9	118
Centerville, Tn., U.S.	B4	119
Centerville, Ut., U.S.	C4	121
Cento, Italy	E6	14
Central, N.M., U.S.	E1	108
Central, S.C., U.S.	B2	117
Central, Cordillera, mts., Bol.	G6	54
Central, Cordillera, mts., Col.	E5	58
Central, Cordillera, mts., Peru	E3	54
Central, Massif, mts., Fr.	G10	10
Central, Planalto, plat., Braz.	G9	54
Central, Sistema, mts., Spain	E6	12
Central African Republic, ctry., Afr.	G10	42
Central City, Co., U.S.	B5	83
Central City, Il., U.S.	E4	90
Central City, Ia., U.S.	B6	92
Central City, Ky., U.S.	C2	94
Central City, Ne., U.S.	C7	104
Central City, Pa., U.S.	F4	115
Central Falls, R.I., U.S.	B4	116
Central Heights, Az., U.S.	D5	80
Centralia, Il., U.S.	E4	90
Centralia, Mo., U.S.	B5	102
Centralia, Wa., U.S.	C3	124
Central Islip, N.Y., U.S.	n15	109
Central Lake, Mi., U.S.	C5	99
Central Makrān Range, mts., Pak.	D1	36
Central Park, Wa., U.S.	C2	124
Central Point, Or., U.S.	E4	114
Central Square, N.Y., U.S.	B4	109
Central Valley, Ca., U.S.	B2	82
Central Valley, N.Y., U.S.	D6	109
Central Village, Ct., U.S.	C8	84
Centre, Al., U.S.	A4	78
Centre, co., Pa., U.S.	E6	115
Centre Hall, Pa., U.S.	E6	115
Centreville, Al., U.S.	C2	78
Centreville, Il., U.S.	E3	90
Centreville, Md., U.S.	B5	97
Centreville, Mi., U.S.	G5	99
Centreville, Ms., U.S.	D2	101
Centuria, Wi., U.S.	C1	126
Century, Fl., U.S.	u14	86
Cepu, Indon.	m15	33a
Ceram Sea see Seram, Laut, Indon.	F8	32
Cerbat Mountains, mts., Az., U.S.	B1	80
Ceredo, W.V., U.S.	C2	125
Čeremchovo, Russia	G14	24
Čerepovec, Russia	B20	18
Ceres, Ca., U.S.	D3	82
Ceresco, Ne., U.S.	C9	104
Céret, Fr.	J9	10
Cereté, Col.	C5	58
Cerf Island, i., Sey.	C10	44
Cerignola, Italy	H10	14
Cérilly, Fr.	F9	10
Čerkassy, Ukr.	H4	22
Čerkessk, Russia	I6	22
Čern'achovsk, Russia	G4	18
Černigov, Ukr.	G4	22
Černogorsk, Russia	G12	24
Černyševskij, Russia	E16	24
Cerralvo, Isla, i., Mex.	E5	62
Cerritos, Mex.	F9	62
Cerro de Pasco, Peru	F3	54
Cerro Gordo, Il., U.S.	D5	90
Cerro Gordo, co., Ia., U.S.	A4	92
Čerskij, Russia	D26	24
Čerskogo, Chrebet, mts., Russia	E23	24
Cervera del Río Alhama, Spain	C10	12
Cervera de Pisuerga, Spain	C7	12
Cervia, Italy	E7	14
Cesena, Italy	E7	14
Cesenatico, Italy	E7	14
České Budějovice, Czech.	G14	8
Cessnock, Austl.	F10	50
Ceuta, Sp. N. Afr.	A4	42
Ceyhan, Tur.	A4	40
Ceylânpınar, Tur.	A7	40
Ceylon see Sri Lanka, ctry., Asia	H5	36
Chabanais, Fr.	G7	10
Chabarovsk, Russia	H21	24
Chachoengsao, Thai.	H6	34
Chaco, stm., N.M., U.S.	A1	108
Chaco Culture National Historic Park, N.M., U.S.	A2	108

Chac-Chit

Index

Name	Map Ref	Page
Chacon, Cape, c., Ak., U.S.	n24	79
Chad, ctry., Afr.	E9	42
Chad, Lake (Lac Tchad), l., Afr.	F8	42
Chadbourn, N.C., U.S.	C4	110
Chadds Ford, Pa., U.S.	G10	115
Chadileuvú, stm., Arg.	D3	56
Chadron, Ne., U.S.	B3	104
Chadwicks, N.Y., U.S.	B5	109
Chaffee, Mo., U.S.	D8	102
Chaffee, co., Co., U.S.	C4	83
Chaffin, Ma., U.S.	B4	98
Chaghcharān, Afg.	C1	38
Chagny, Fr.	F11	10
Chagos Archipelago, is., B.I.O.T.	G17	2
Chagrin Falls, Oh., U.S.	A4	112
Chāībāsā, India	I11	38
Chaîne Annamitique, mts., Asia	F9	34
Chakachamna Lake, l., Ak., U.S.	g15	79
Chake Chake, Tan.	C7	44
Chalais, Fr.	G7	10
Chalbi Desert, des., Kenya	H2	46
Chalcuapa, El Sal.	H3	64
Chaleur Bay, b., Can.	B4	71
Chalfonte, De., U.S.	h7	85
Chālisgaon, India	B3	37
Chalk River, Ont., Can.	A7	73
Challans, Fr.	F5	10
Challis, Id., U.S.	E4	89
Chalmette, La., U.S.	E6	95
Chalonnes-sur-Loire, Fr.	E6	10
Châlons-sur-Marne, Fr.	D11	10
Chalon-sur-Saône, Fr.	F11	10
Châlus, Fr.	G7	10
Cham, Ger.	F12	8
Chama, N.M., U.S.	A3	108
Chama, Rio, stm., N.M., U.S.	A3	108
Chaman, Pak.	E2	38
Chambal, stm., India	G7	38
Chamberlain, S.D., U.S.	D6	118
Chamberlain Lake, l., Me., U.S.	B3	96
Chamberlin, Mount, mtn., Ak., U.S.	B10	79
Chambers, co., Al., U.S.	C4	78
Chambers, co., Tx., U.S.	E5	120
Chambersburg, Pa., U.S.	G6	115
Chambers Island, i., Wi., U.S.	C6	126
Chambéry, Fr.	G12	10
Chambi, Jebel, mtn., Tun.	A7	42
Chamblee, Ga., U.S.	h8	87
Chambly, Que., Can.	D4	74
Chambon-sur-Voueize, Fr.	F9	10
Chamisal, N.M., U.S.	A4	108
Chamonix-Mont-Blanc, Fr.	G13	10
Champagne, hist. reg., Fr.	D11	10
Champagnole, Fr.	F12	10
Champaign, Il., U.S.	C5	90
Champaign, co., Il., U.S.	C5	90
Champaign, co., Oh., U.S.	B2	112
Champassak, Laos	G8	34
Champion, Oh., U.S.	A5	112
Champlain, Lake, l., N.A.	C12	76
Champlin, Mn., U.S.	m12	100
Chāmrājnagar Rāmasamudram, India	G4	37
Chañaral, Chile	B2	56
Chance, Md., U.S.	D6	97
Chanch, Mong.	A7	26
Chanchelulla Peak, mtn., Ca., U.S.	B2	82
Chandalar, stm., Ak., U.S.	B10	79
Chandausi, India	F8	38
Chandeleur Islands, is., La., U.S.	E7	95
Chandeleur Sound, strt., La., U.S.	E6	95
Chandīgarh, India	E7	38
Chandler, Que., Can.	k14	74
Chandler, Az., U.S.	D4	80
Chandler, In., U.S.	H3	91
Chandler, Ok., U.S.	B5	113
Chandler, Tx., U.S.	C5	120
Chandler Heights, Az., U.S.	m9	80
Chāndpur, Bngl.	I14	38
Chāndpur, India	F8	38
Chandrapur, India	C5	37
Chandyga, Russia	E21	24
Chang (Yangtze), stm., China	E10	26
Changajn Nuruu, mts., Mong.	B6	26
Changchun, China	C12	26
Changde, China	F9	26
Changhua, Tai.	K9	28
Changjiang, China	J5	28
Changli, China	D10	26
Changsha, China	G1	28
Changshu, China	D9	28
Changzhi, China	D9	26
Changzhou (Changchow), China	D8	28
Chanhassen, Mn., U.S.	n11	100
Chanka, Ozero (Xingkathu), l., Asia	I20	24
Channahon, Il., U.S.	B5	90
Channapatna, India	F4	37
Channel Islands, is., Eur.	C4	10
Channel Islands National Park, Ca., U.S.	F4	82
Channel Lake, Il., U.S.	H8	90
Channel-Port-aux-Basques, Newf., Can.	E2	72
Channelview, Tx., U.S.	r14	120
Chantada, Spain	C4	12
Chantajskoje, Ozero, l., Russia	D12	24
Chanthaburi, Thai.	H7	34
Chantilly, Va., U.S.	g12	123
Chantrey Inlet, b., N.W. Ter., Can.	C13	66
Chanute, Ks., U.S.	E8	93
Chanute Air Force Base, mil., Il., U.S.	C5	90
Chaoan, China	L5	28
Chao Phraya, stm., Thai.	G6	34
Chapala, Lago de, l., Mex.	G8	62
Chaparral, Col.	F5	58
Chapčeranga, Russia	H16	24
Chapel Hill, N.C., U.S.	B3	110
Chapel Hill, Tn., U.S.	B5	119
Chaplin, stm., Ky., U.S.	C4	94
Chaplin Lake, l., Sask., Can.	G2	75
Chapman, Ks., U.S.	D6	93
Chapman Pond, l., R.I., U.S.	F1	116
Chapmanville, W.V., U.S.	D2	125
Chappaquiddick Island, i., Ma., U.S.	D7	98
Chappell, Ne., U.S.	C3	104
Chāpra, India	H11	38
Chapultepec, mtn., Mex.	F8	62
Charadai, Arg.	B5	56
Charcas, Mex.	F9	62
Chardon, Oh., U.S.	A4	112
Chardzhou see Čardžou, Turk.	J10	22
Charenton, La., U.S.	E4	95
Chari, stm., Afr.	F9	42
Chārīkār, Afg.	C3	38
Chariton, Ia., U.S.	C4	92
Chariton, co., Mo., U.S.	B4	102
Chariton, stm., U.S.	A5	102
Charity, Guy.	D13	58
Charleroi, Bel.	E4	8
Charleroi, Pa., U.S.	F2	115
Charles, co., Md., U.S.	C3	97
Charles, stm., Ma., U.S.	B5	98
Charles, Cape, c., Va., U.S.	C6	123
Charles A. Goodwin Dam, Ct., U.S.	B3	84
Charlesbourg, Que., Can.	n17	74
Charles City, Ia., U.S.	A5	92
Charles City, co., Va., U.S.	C5	123
Charles Island, i., N.W. Ter., Can.	D18	66
Charles Mill Lake, res., Oh., U.S.	B3	112
Charles Mix, co., S.D., U.S.	D7	118
Charles Mound, hill, Il., U.S.	A3	90
Charleston, Ar., U.S.	B1	81
Charleston, Il., U.S.	D5	90
Charleston, Ms., U.S.	A3	101
Charleston, Mo., U.S.	E8	102
Charleston, Or., U.S.	D2	114
Charleston, S.C., U.S.	F8	117
Charleston, Tn., U.S.	D9	119
Charleston, W.V., U.S.	C3	125
Charleston, co., S.C., U.S.	F8	117
Charleston Air Force Base, mil., S.C., U.S.	k11	117
Charleston Naval Shipyard, mil., S.C., U.S.	k12	117
Charleston Peak, mtn., Nv., U.S.	G6	105
Charlestown, In., U.S.	H6	91
Charlestown, N.H., U.S.	D2	106
Charlestown, R.I., U.S.	F2	116
Charles Town, W.V., U.S.	B7	125
Charleville, Austl.	E9	50
Charleville-Mézières, Fr.	C11	10
Charlevoix, Mi., U.S.	C5	99
Charlevoix, co., Mi., U.S.	C5	99
Charlevoix, Lake, l., Mi., U.S.	C5	99
Charlo, N.B., Can.	B3	71
Charlotte, Mi., U.S.	F6	99
Charlotte, N.C., U.S.	B2	110
Charlotte, Tn., U.S.	A4	119
Charlotte, Tx., U.S.	E3	120
Charlotte, co., Fl., U.S.	F5	86
Charlotte, co., Va., U.S.	C4	123
Charlotte Amalie, V.I.U.S.	E15	64
Charlotte Hall, Md., U.S.	D4	97
Charlotte Harbor, Fl., U.S.	F4	86
Charlotte Harbor, b., Fl., U.S.	F4	86
Charlottenberg, Swe.	G9	6
Charlottesville, Va., U.S.	B4	123
Charlottetown, P.E.I., Can.	C6	71
Charlton, co., Ga., U.S.	F4	87
Charmco, W.V., U.S.	C4	125
Charmes, Fr.	D13	10
Charny, Que., Can.	C6	74
Charolles, Fr.	F11	10
Chārsadda, Pak.	C4	38
Charters Towers, Austl.	D9	50
Chartres, Fr.	D8	10
Char Us Nuur, l., Mong.	B5	26
Chascomús, Arg.	D5	56
Chase, B.C., Can.	D8	69
Chase, Md., U.S.	B5	97
Chase, co., Ks., U.S.	D7	93
Chase, co., Ne., U.S.	D4	104
Chase City, Va., U.S.	D4	123
Chase Field Naval Air Station, mil., Tx., U.S.	E4	120
Chaska, Mn., U.S.	F5	100
Chassahowitzka Bay, b., Fl., U.S.	D4	86
Chassell, Mi., U.S.	B2	99
Chatanbulag, Mong.	C8	26
Chatanga, Russia	C14	24
Chatanga, stm., Russia	C14	24
Chatangskij Zaliv, b., Russia	C15	24
Châteaubriant, Fr.	E5	10
Château-du-Loir, Fr.	E7	10
Châteaudun, Fr.	D8	10
Château-Gontier, Fr.	E6	10
Châteauguay, Que., Can.	D4	74
Château-Landon, Fr.	D9	10
Châteaulin, Fr.	D2	10
Châteaumeillant, Fr.	F9	10
Châteauneuf-sur-Charente, Fr.	G6	10
Châteauneuf-sur-Loire, Fr.	E9	10
Château-Renault, Fr.	E7	10
Château-Richer, Que., Can.	C6	74
Châteauroux, Fr.	F8	10
Château-Thierry, Fr.	C10	10
Châtellerault, Fr.	F7	10
Chatfield, Mn., U.S.	G6	100
Chatgal, Mong.	A7	26
Chatham, N.B., Can.	B4	71
Chatham, Ont., Can.	E2	73
Chatham, Eng., U.K.	J13	7
Chatham, Il., U.S.	D4	90
Chatham, La., U.S.	B3	95
Chatham, Ma., U.S.	C8	98
Chatham, N.J., U.S.	B4	107
Chatham, N.Y., U.S.	C7	109
Chatham, Va., U.S.	D3	123
Chatham, co., Ga., U.S.	E5	87
Chatham, co., N.C., U.S.	B3	110
Chatham Strait, strt., Ak., U.S.	m22	79
Châtillon, Italy	D2	14
Châtillon-Coligny, Fr.	E9	10
Châtillon-sur-Indre, Fr.	F8	10
Châtillon-sur-Seine, Fr.	E11	10
Chatom, Al., U.S.	D1	78
Chatsworth, Ga., U.S.	B2	87
Chatsworth, Il., U.S.	C5	90
Chatsworth Reservoir, res., Ca., U.S.	m11	82
Chattahoochee, Fl., U.S.	B2	86
Chattahoochee, co., Ga., U.S.	D2	87
Chattahoochee, stm., U.S.	E1	87
Chattanooga, Tn., U.S.	D8	119
Chattaroy, W.V., U.S.	D2	125
Chattooga, co., Ga., U.S.	B1	87
Chattooga, stm., U.S.	B1	117
Chatuge Lake, res., U.S.	g9	110
Chatyrka, Russia	E29	24
Chaudière, stm., Que., Can.	C7	74
Chau Doc, Viet.	I8	34
Chauk, Mya.	D3	34
Chaumont, Fr.	D12	10
Chauncey, Oh., U.S.	C3	112
Chauny, Fr.	C10	10
Chautauqua, co., Ks., U.S.	E7	93
Chautauqua, co., N.Y., U.S.	C1	109
Chautauqua Lake, l., N.Y., U.S.	C1	109
Chauvigny, Fr.	F7	10
Chauvin, La., U.S.	E5	95
Chavakkad, India	G4	37
Chaves, Port.	D4	12
Chaves, co., N.M., U.S.	D5	108
Cháviva, Col.	E6	58
Chbukha Dzong, Bhu.	G13	38
Cheaha Mountain, mtn., Al., U.S.	B4	78
Cheat, Shavers Fork, stm., W.V., U.S.	B5	125
Cheatham, co., Tn., U.S.	A4	119
Chebanse, Il., U.S.	C6	90
Cheboygan, Mi., U.S.	C6	99
Cheboygan, co., Mi., U.S.	C6	99
Chech, Erg, des., Afr.	C5	42
Checotah, Ok., U.S.	B6	113
Chedabucto Bay, b., N.S., Can.	D8	71
Cheduba Island, i., Mya.	E2	34
Cheektowaga, N.Y., U.S.	C2	109
Cheeseman Lake, res., Co., U.S.	B5	83
Chehalem Mountains, mts., Or., U.S.	h12	114
Chehalis, Wa., U.S.	C3	124
Chehalis, stm., Wa., U.S.	C2	124
Cheju-do, i., S. Kor.	E12	26
Chelan, Wa., U.S.	B5	124
Chelan, co., Wa., U.S.	B4	124
Chelan, Lake, l., Wa., U.S.	A5	124
Chelan Mountains, mts., Wa., U.S.	A5	124
Chełm, Pol.	D23	8
Chełmno, Pol.	B18	8
Chelmsford, Eng., U.K.	J13	7
Chelmsford, Ma., U.S.	A5	98
Chelsea, Que., Can.	D2	74
Chelsea, Al., U.S.	g7	78
Chelsea, Ma., U.S.	B5	98
Chelsea, Mi., U.S.	F6	99
Chelsea, Ok., U.S.	A6	113
Cheltenham, Eng., U.K.	J10	7
Cheltenham, Md., U.S.	C4	97
Chelva, Spain	F11	12
Chelyabinsk see Čel'abinsk, Russia	F10	22
Chelyan, W.V., U.S.	C3	125
Chemehuevi Indian Reservation, Ca., U.S.	E6	82
Chemnitz, Ger.	E12	8
Chemquasabamticook Lake (Ross Lake), l., Me., U.S.	B3	96
Chemung, co., N.Y., U.S.	C4	109
Chemung, stm., Pa., U.S.	C8	115
Chemung Lake, l., Ont., Can.	C6	73
Chenāb, stm., Asia	E5	38
Chenachane, Alg.	C6	42
Chenango, co., N.Y., U.S.	C5	109
Chenango, stm., N.Y., U.S.	C5	109
Chenango Bridge, N.Y., U.S.	C5	109
Chenes, River Aux, b., La., U.S.	k12	95
Chénéville, Que., Can.	D2	74
Cheney, Ks., U.S.	E6	93
Cheney, Wa., U.S.	B8	124
Cheney Reservoir, res., Ks., U.S.	E6	93
Cheneyville, La., U.S.	C3	95
Chengde, China	C10	26
Chengdu, China	E7	26
Chengutu, Zimb.	E6	44
Chenoa, Il., U.S.	C5	90
Chenoweth, Or., U.S.	B5	114
Chepachet, R.I., U.S.	B2	116
Chepachet, stm., R.I., U.S.	B2	116
Chepo, Pan.	J8	64
Chequamegon Bay, b., Wi., U.S.	B3	126
Cheraw, S.C., U.S.	B8	117
Cherbourg, Fr.	C5	10
Chergui, Chott ech, l., Alg.	B6	42
Cherkasy, Ukr.	H4	22
Chernihiv, Ukr.	G4	22
Chernivtsi, Ukr.	H3	22
Cherokee, Al., U.S.	A2	78
Cherokee, Ia., U.S.	B2	92
Cherokee, Ks., U.S.	E9	93
Cherokee, Ok., U.S.	A3	113
Cherokee, co., Al., U.S.	A4	78
Cherokee, co., Ga., U.S.	B2	87
Cherokee, co., Ia., U.S.	B2	92
Cherokee, co., Ks., U.S.	E9	93
Cherokee, co., N.C., U.S.	f8	110
Cherokee, co., Ok., U.S.	B6	113
Cherokee, co., S.C., U.S.	A4	117
Cherokee, co., Tx., U.S.	D5	120
Cherokee Indian Reservation, N.C., U.S.	f9	110
Cherokee Lake, res., Tn., U.S.	C10	119
Cherokees, Lake O' The, res., Ok., U.S.	A7	113
Cherokee Village, Ar., U.S.	A4	81
Cherry, co., Ne., U.S.	B4	104
Cherry Creek, stm., S.D., U.S.	C3	118
Cherry Hill, N.J., U.S.	D2	107
Cherry Point, c., Va., U.S.	C6	123
Cherry Point Marine Corps Air Station, mil., N.C., U.S.	C6	110
Cherryvale, Ks., U.S.	E8	93
Cherry Valley, Ar., U.S.	B5	81
Cherry Valley, Il., U.S.	A5	90
Cherryville, N.C., U.S.	B1	110
Chesaning, Mi., U.S.	E6	99
Chesapeake, Oh., U.S.	D3	112
Chesapeake, Va., U.S.	D6	123
Chesapeake, W.V., U.S.	C3	125
Chesapeake and Delaware Canal, U.S.	B3	85
Chesapeake Bay, b., U.S.	D11	76
Chesapeake Bay Bridge-Tunnel, Va., U.S.	D7	123
Chesapeake Beach, Md., U.S.	C4	97
Chesapeake City, Md., U.S.	A6	97
Chesdin, Lake, res., Va., U.S.	C5	123
Cheshire, Ct., U.S.	D4	84
Cheshire, co., N.H., U.S.	E2	106
Cheshire Reservoir, res., Ma., U.S.	A1	98
Chesley, Ont., Can.	C3	73
Chesnee, S.C., U.S.	A4	117
Chester, Eng., U.K.	H10	7
Chester, Ca., U.S.	B3	82
Chester, Ct., U.S.	D6	84
Chester, Ga., U.S.	D3	87
Chester, Il., U.S.	F4	90
Chester, Md., U.S.	C5	97
Chester, Mt., U.S.	B6	103
Chester, N.H., U.S.	E4	106
Chester, N.Y., U.S.	D6	109
Chester, Pa., U.S.	G11	115
Chester, S.C., U.S.	B5	117
Chester, Vt., U.S.	E3	122
Chester, Va., U.S.	C5	123
Chester, W.V., U.S.	A4	125
Chester, co., Pa., U.S.	G10	115
Chester, co., S.C., U.S.	B5	117
Chester, co., Tn., U.S.	B3	119
Chester, stm., Md., U.S.	B5	97
Chester Basin, N.S., Can.	E5	71
Chester Depot, Vt., U.S.	E3	122
Chesterfield, In., U.S.	D6	91
Chesterfield, S.C., U.S.	B7	117
Chesterfield, co., S.C., U.S.	B7	117
Chesterfield, co., Va., U.S.	C5	123
Chesterfield, Îles, is., N. Cal.	C11	50
Chesterfield Inlet, N.W. Ter., Can.	D14	66
Chesterfield Inlet, b., N.W. Ter., Can.	D14	66
Chesterton, In., U.S.	A3	91
Chestertown, Md., U.S.	B5	97
Chesterville, Ont., Can.	B9	73
Chesuncook Lake, l., Me., U.S.	C3	96
Cheswick, Pa., U.S.	h14	115
Cheswold, De., U.S.	D3	85
Cheta, stm., Russia	C13	24
Chetac, Lake, l., Wi., U.S.	C2	126
Chetco, stm., Or., U.S.	E2	114
Chetek, Wi., U.S.	C2	126
Chetek, Lake, l., Wi., U.S.	C2	126
Chetopa, Ks., U.S.	E8	93
Chetumal Bay, b., N.A.	H15	62
Chetwynd, B.C., Can.	B7	69
Chevak, Ak., U.S.	C6	79
Cheval Blanc, Pointe du, c., Haiti	E11	64
Cheviot, Oh., U.S.	C1	112
Chevreuil, Point, c., La., U.S.	E4	95
Chevy Chase, Md., U.S.	C3	97
Chewack, stm., Wa., U.S.	A5	124
Chew Bahir (Lake Stefanie), l., Afr.	H2	46
Chewelah, Wa., U.S.	A8	124
Cheyenne, Ok., U.S.	B2	113
Cheyenne, Wy., U.S.	E8	127
Cheyenne, co., Co., U.S.	C8	83
Cheyenne, co., Ks., U.S.	C2	93
Cheyenne, co., Ne., U.S.	C2	104
Cheyenne, stm., U.S.	C4	118
Cheyenne, Dry Fork, stm., Wy., U.S.	C7	127
Cheyenne River Indian Reservation, S.D., U.S.	B4	118
Cheyenne Wells, Co., U.S.	C8	83
Chezhou, China	J1	28
Chhatarpur, India	H8	38
Chhindwāra, India	I8	38
Chi, stm., Thai.	G8	34
Chiai, Tai.	L9	28
Chiali, Tai.	L9	28
Chiang Khan, Thai.	F6	34
Chiang Mai, Thai.	E5	34
Chiang Rai, Thai.	E5	34
Chiari, Italy	D4	14
Chiavari, Italy	E4	14
Chiavenna, Italy	C4	14
Chiba, Japan	G13	30
Chiblow Lake, l., Ont., Can.	A1	73
Chibougamau, Que., Can.	k12	74
Chibuto, Moz.	F6	44
Chicago, Il., U.S.	B6	90
Chicago Heights, Il., U.S.	B6	90
Chicago Sanitary and Ship Canal, Il., U.S.	k8	90
Chicamacomico, stm., Md., U.S.	D6	97
Chicapa, stm., Afr.	C4	44
Chichagof Island, i., Ak., U.S.	m22	79
Chīchāwatni, Pak.	E5	38
Chichén Itzá, Mex.	G15	62
Chichibu, Japan	G12	30
Chickahominy, stm., Va., U.S.	C5	123
Chickamauga, Ga., U.S.	B1	87
Chickamauga and Chattanooga National Military Park, U.S.	k11	119
Chickamauga Dam, Tn., U.S.	h11	119
Chickamauga Lake, res., Tn., U.S.	D8	119
Chickasaw, Al., U.S.	E1	78
Chickasaw, co., Ia., U.S.	A5	92
Chickasaw, co., Ms., U.S.	B5	101
Chickasawhay, stm., Ms., U.S.	D5	101
Chickasaw National Recreation Area, Ok., U.S.	C5	113
Chickasha, Ok., U.S.	B4	113
Chickasha, Lake, res., Ok., U.S.	B3	113
Chickwolnepy Stream, stm., N.H., U.S.	A4	106
Chiclana de la Frontera, Spain	I5	12
Chiclayo, Peru	E3	54
Chico, Ca., U.S.	C3	82
Chicoa, Moz.	E6	44
Chicopee, Ga., U.S.	B3	87
Chicopee, Ma., U.S.	B2	98
Chicora, Pa., U.S.	E2	115
Chicot, Lake, l., Ar., U.S.	D4	81
Chicot Island, i., La., U.S.	E6	95
Chicoutimi, Que., Can.	A6	74
Chicoutimi, stm., Que., Can.	A6	74
Chidambaram, India	G5	37
Chidley, Cape, c., Can.	D20	66
Chiefland, Fl., U.S.	C4	86
Chieri, Italy	D2	14
Chieti, Italy	G9	14
Chifeng, China	C10	26
Chigasaki, Japan	G12	30
Chignecto, Cape, c., N.S., Can.	D5	71
Chignecto Bay, b., Can.	D5	71
Ch'ihu, Tai.	L9	28
Chihuahua, Mex.	C6	62
Chikaskia, stm., U.S.	A4	113
Chik Ballāpur, India	F4	37
Chikmagalūr, India	F3	37
Chilakalūrupet, India	D6	37
Chilapa de Alvarez, Mex.	I10	62
Chilās, Pak.	C6	38
Childersburg, Al., U.S.	B3	78
Childress, Tx., U.S.	B2	120
Childress, co., Tx., U.S.	B2	120
Chile, ctry., S.A.	C2	56
Chilete, Peru	E3	54
Chilhowie, Va., U.S.	f10	123
Chililabombwe (Bancroft), Zam.	D5	44
Chilka Lake, l., India	C8	37
Chilko, stm., B.C., Can.	D6	69
Chilko Lake, l., B.C., Can.	D5	69
Chillán, Chile	D2	56
Chillicothe, Il., U.S.	C4	90
Chillicothe, Mo., U.S.	B4	102
Chillicothe, Oh., U.S.	C3	112
Chilliwack, B.C., Can.	E7	69
Chillum, Md., U.S.	f9	97
Chiloé, Isla de, i., Chile	E2	56
Chilok, Russia	G16	24
Chiloquin, Or., U.S.	E5	114
Chilpancingo [de los Bravos], Mex.	I10	62
Chilton, Wi., U.S.	D5	126
Chilton, co., Al., U.S.	C3	78
Chilung, Tai.	J10	28
Chilwa, Lake, l., Afr.	E7	44
Chimacum, Wa., U.S.	A3	124
Chimayo, N.M., U.S.	A4	108
Chimborazo, vol., Ec.	H3	58
Chimbote, Peru	E3	54
Chimkent see Čimkent, Kaz.	I11	22
Chimki, Russia	F20	18
Chimney Rock, mtn., Ne., U.S.	C2	104
China, ctry., Asia	D7	26
China Grove, N.C., U.S.	B2	110
China Lake, l., Me., U.S.	D3	96
Chinandega, Nic.	H4	64
Chincha Alta, Peru	F3	54
Chincilla de Monte Aragón, Spain	G10	12
Chincoteague, Va., U.S.	C7	123
Chincoteague Bay, b., U.S.	D7	97
Chinde, Moz.	E7	44
Chindwinn, stm., Mya.	C3	34
Chingleput, India	F5	37
Chingola, Zam.	D5	44
Ch'ingshui, Tai.	K9	28
Chin Hills, hills, Mya.	D2	34
Chinhoyi, Zimb.	E6	44
Chiniot, Pak.	E5	38
Chinitna Point, c., Ak., U.S.	h15	79
Chinju, S. Kor.	D12	26
Chinko, stm., Cen. Afr. Rep.	G10	42
Chinkuashih, Tai.	J10	28
Chinle, Az., U.S.	A6	80
Chinmen Tao, i., Tai.	K7	28
Chino, Ca., U.S.	F5	82
Chinon, Fr.	E7	10
Chinook, Mt., U.S.	B7	103
Chinook, Wa., U.S.	C2	124
Chinook, Lake, res., Or., U.S.	C5	114
Chino Valley, Az., U.S.	C3	80
Chinshan, Tai.	J10	28
Chioggia, Italy	D7	14
Chipata, Zam.	D6	44
Chipita Park, Co., U.S.	C6	83
Chipley, Fl., U.S.	u16	86
Chipman, N.B., Can.	C4	71
Chipola, stm., Fl., U.S.	B1	86
Chippewa, co., Mi., U.S.	B6	99
Chippewa, co., Mn., U.S.	E3	100
Chippewa, co., Wi., U.S.	C2	126
Chippewa, stm., Mn., U.S.	E3	100
Chippewa, stm., Wi., U.S.	D2	126
Chippewa, Lake, l., Wi., U.S.	C2	126
Chippewa Falls, Wi., U.S.	D2	126
Chipuxet, stm., R.I., U.S.	F3	116
Chiquimula, Guat.	G3	64
Chiquinquirá, Col.	E6	58
Chīrāla, India	E6	37
Chirfa, Niger	D8	42
Chirgis Nuur, l., Mong.	B5	26
Chiricahua Mountains, mts., Az., U.S.	E6	80
Chiricahua National Monument, Az., U.S.	F6	80
Chiricahua Peak, mtn., Az., U.S.	F6	80
Chiriguaná, Col.	C6	58
Chirikof Island, i., Ak., U.S.	D8	79
Chiriquí, Golfo, b., Pan.	K6	64
Chiriquí, Laguna de, b., Pan.	J7	64
Chirripó, Cerro, mtn., C.R.	J6	64
Chisago, co., Mn., U.S.	E6	100
Chisago City, Mn., U.S.	E6	100
Chisholm, Me., U.S.	D2	96
Chisholm, Mn., U.S.	C6	100
Chishtiān Mandi, Pak.	F5	38
Chişinău, Mol.	H3	22
Chisos Mountains, mts., Tx., U.S.	E1	120
Chitato, Ang.	C4	44
Chitembo, Ang.	D3	44
Chitina, stm., Ak., U.S.	g19	79
Chitipa, Mwi.	C6	44
Chitorgarh, India	H6	38
Chitose, Japan	q19	30a
Chitradurga, India	E4	37
Chitrāl, Pak.	C4	38
Chitré, Pan.	K7	64
Chittagong, Bngl.	I14	38
Chittenango, N.Y., U.S.	B5	109
Chittenden, co., Vt., U.S.	C2	122
Chittenden Reservoir, res., Vt., U.S.	D3	122
Chittoor, India	F5	37

Name Map Ref Page

Chiusi, Italy F6 14
Chivasso, Italy D2 14
Choapan, Mex. I12 62
Chocolate Mountains, mts., U.S. F6 82
Chocontá, Col. E6 58
Choctaw, Ok., U.S. B4 113
Choctaw, co., Al., U.S. C1 78
Choctaw, co., Ms., U.S. B4 101
Choctaw, co., Ok., U.S. C6 113
Choctawhatchee Bay, b., Fl., U.S. u15 86
Choctaw Indian Reservation, Ms., U.S. C4 101
Choele-Choel, Arg. D3 56
Cholet, Fr. E6 10
Cholmsk, Russia H22 24
Choluteca, Hond. H4 64
Choma, Zam. E5 44
Chomutov, Czech. E13 8
Chon Buri, Thai. H6 34
Chone, Ec. H2 58
Ch'ŏngjin, N. Kor. C12 26
Ch'ŏngju, S. Kor. D12 26
Chongmingdao, i., China D10 28
Chongqing, China F8 26
Chŏnju, S. Kor. D12 26
Chonos, Archipiélago de los, is., Chile F2 56
Chonuu, Russia D22 24
Choptank, stm., Md., U.S. C6 97
Chōshi, Japan G13 30
Chos Malal, Arg. D2 56
Choteau, Mt., U.S. C4 103
Chouteau, Ok., U.S. A6 113
Chouteau, co., Mt., U.S. C6 103
Chovd, Mong. B5 26
Chövsgöl Nuur, l., Mong. A7 26
Chowan, co., N.C., U.S. A6 110
Chowan, stm., N.C., U.S. A6 110
Chowchilla, Ca., U.S. D3 82
Chrisman, Il., U.S. D6 90
Christianshåb, Grnld. C22 66
Christchurch, N.Z. E4 52
Christian, co., Il., U.S. D4 90
Christian, co., Ky., U.S. D2 94
Christian, co., Mo., U.S. E4 102
Christian, Cape, c., N.W. Ter., Can. B19 66
Christiana, De., U.S. B3 85
Christiana, Pa., U.S. G9 115
Christiansburg, Va., U.S. C2 123
Christian Sound, strt., Ak., U.S. n22 79
Christiansted, V.I.U.S. F15 64
Christina, stm., Alta., Can. A5 68
Christina, stm., De., U.S. B3 85
Christina, Lake, l., Mn., U.S. D3 100
Christina Peak, mtn., Nv., U.S. D6 105
Christmas, Fl., U.S. D5 86
Christmas Island, dep., Oc. H4 32
Christmas Lake, l., Or., U.S. D6 114
Christopher, Il., U.S. F4 90
Chroma, stm., Russia C22 24
Chrzanów, Pol. E19 8
Chubbuck, Id., U.S. G6 89
Chugach Islands, is., Ak., U.S. h16 79
Chugach Mountains, mts., Ak., U.S. g18 79
Chūgoku-sanchi, mts., Japan H5 30
Chugwater, Wy., U.S. E8 127
Chugwater Creek, stm., Wy., U.S. E8 127
Chukai, Malay. L7 34
Chukchi Sea C30 128
Chula Vista, Ca., U.S. F5 82
Chulucanas, Peru E2 54
Chumphon, Thai. I5 34
Chum Saeng, Thai. G6 34
Chunchi, Ec. I3 58
Ch'unch'ŏn, S. Kor. D12 26
Chunchula, Al., U.S. E1 78
Ch'ungju, S. Kor. D12 26
Chungking see Chongqing, China F8 26
Chungli, Tai. K10 28
Chungyang Shanmo, mts., Tai. L10 28
Chuŏr Phnum Krâvanh, mts., Asia H7 34
Chupadera Mesa, mtn., N.M., U.S. D3 108
Chupaderos, Mex. F8 62
Chuquicamata, Chile A3 56
Chur, Switz. F16 10
Church Hill, Tn., U.S. C11 119
Churchill, Man., Can. f9 70
Churchill, co., Nv., U.S. D3 105
Churchill, stm., Can. E13 66
Churchill, stm., Newf., Can. h9 72
Churchill, Cape, c., Man., Can. f9 70
Churchill, Mount, mtn., B.C., Can. E6 69
Churchill Falls, wtfl, Newf., Can. h8 72
Churchill Lake, l., Sask., Can. m7 75
Churchill Lake, l., Me., U.S. B3 96
Church Point, La., U.S. D3 95
Church Rock, N.M., U.S. B1 108
Churchton, Md., U.S. C4 97
Churchville, N.Y., U.S. B3 109
Churu, India F6 38
Churubusco, In., U.S. B7 91
Churuguara, Ven. B8 58
Chuska Mountains, mts., Az., U.S. A6 80
Chutag, Mong. B7 26
Chuxian, China C7 28
Chuxiong, China B6 34
Chužir, Russia G15 24
Cianjur, Indon. G4 32
Cibecue, Az., U.S. C5 80
Cibinong, Indon. m13 33a
Cibola, co., N.M., U.S. C1 108
Cibolo Creek, stm., Tx., U.S. h7 120
Cicero, Il., U.S. B6 90
Cicero, In., U.S. D5 91
Ciechanów, Pol. C20 8
Ciego de Avila, Cuba D8 64
Ciempozuelos, Spain E8 12
Ciénaga, Col. B5 58
Cienfuegos, Cuba C7 64
Cieszyn, Pol. F18 8
Cieza, Spain G10 12
Cifuentes, Spain E9 12
Cikampek, Indon. m13 33a
Cilacap, Indon. m14 33a
Cilleruelo de Bezana, Spain C8 12
Cimarron, Ks., U.S. E3 93
Cimarron, N.M., U.S. A5 108
Cimarron, co., Ok., U.S. e8 113
Čimkent, Kaz. I11 22
Çınarcık, Tur. I13 16
Cincinnati, Oh., U.S. C1 112
Çine, Tur. L12 16
Ciney, Bel. E5 8
Cinnaminson, N.J., U.S. D3 107
Cipa, stm., Russia F17 24
Cipolletti, Arg. D3 56
Circle, Ak., U.S. B11 79
Circle, Mt., U.S. C11 103
Circle Pines, Mn., U.S. m12 100
Circleville, Oh., U.S. C3 112
Cirebon, Indon. m14 32
Cirencester, Eng., U.K. J11 7
Ciriè, Italy D2 14
Cirò Marina, Italy J12 14
Cisco, Tx., U.S. C3 120
Cispus, stm., Wa., U.S. C4 124
Cissna Park, Il., U.S. C6 90
Cistierna, Spain C6 12
Čita, Russia G16 24
Citra, Fl., U.S. C4 86
Citronelle, Al., U.S. D1 78
Citrus, co., Fl., U.S. D4 86
Città di Castello, Italy F7 14
City of Refuge National Historical Park, Hi., U.S. D5 88
City View, S.C., U.S. B3 117
Ciudad, Mex. F7 62
Ciudad Acuña, Mex. C9 62
Ciudad Altamirano, Mex. H9 62
Ciudad Bolívar, Ven. C11 58
Ciudad Bolivia, Ven. C7 58
Ciudad Camargo, Mex. D7 62
Ciudad Chetumal, Mex. H15 62
Ciudad del Carmen, Mex. H14 62
Ciudad del Maíz, Mex. F10 62
Ciudad de México (Mexico City), Mex. H10 62
Ciudad de Nutrias, Ven. C8 58
Ciudad de Valles, Mex. G10 62
Ciudadela, Spain E15 12
Ciudad Guayana, Ven. C11 58
Ciudad Guzmán, Mex. H8 62
Ciudad Hidalgo, Mex. H9 62
Ciudad Ixtepec, Mex. I12 62
Ciudad Jiménez, Mex. D7 62
Ciudad Juárez, Mex. B6 62
Ciudad Madero, Mex. F11 62
Ciudad Mante, Mex. F10 62
Ciudad Melchor Múzquiz, Mex. D9 62
Ciudad Obregón, Mex. D5 62
Ciudad Ojeda (Lagunillas), Ven. B7 58
Ciudad Piar, Ven. D11 58
Ciudad Real, Spain G8 12
Ciudad Rodrigo, Spain E5 12
Ciudad Victoria, Mex. F10 62
Civita Castellana, Italy G7 14
Civitanova Marche, Italy F8 14
Civitavecchia, Italy G6 14
Civray, Fr. F7 10
C.J. Strike Reservoir, res., Id., U.S. G3 89
Clackamas, Or., U.S. h12 114
Clackamas, co., Or., U.S. B4 114
Clacton-on-Sea, Eng., U.K. J14 7
Claflin, Ks., U.S. D5 93
Claiborne, co., La., U.S. B2 95
Claiborne, co., Ms., U.S. D3 101
Claiborne, co., Tn., U.S. C10 119
Claiborne, Lake, res., La., U.S. B3 95
Clair, N.B., Can. B1 71
Claire, Lake, l., Alta., Can. f8 68
Clair Engle Lake, res., Ca., U.S. B2 82
Clairton, Pa., U.S. F2 115
Clallam, co., Wa., U.S. B1 124
Clallam Bay, Wa., U.S. A1 124
Clamecy, Fr. E10 10
Clam Lake, l., Wi., U.S. C1 126
Clan Alpine Mountains, mts., Nv., U.S. D4 105
Clanton, Al., U.S. C3 78
Clanwilliam, S. Afr. H3 44
Clara City, Mn., U.S. F3 100
Clara Peak, mtn., Az., U.S. C2 80
Clare, Mi., U.S. E6 99
Clare, co., Mi., U.S. E6 99
Claremont, Ca., U.S. m13 82
Claremont, N.H., U.S. D2 106
Claremont, N.C., U.S. B1 110
Claremont, mtn., Ca., U.S. C3 82
Claremore, Ok., U.S. A6 113
Claremorris, Ire. H3 7
Clarence, Ia., U.S. C6 92
Clarence, Mo., U.S. B5 102
Clarence Strait, strt., Ak., U.S. n23 79
Clarendon, Ar., U.S. C4 81
Clarendon, Tx., U.S. B2 120
Clarendon, co., S.C., U.S. D7 117
Clarendon, stm., Vt., U.S. E2 122
Clarendon Hills, Il., U.S. k9 90
Clarenville, Newf., Can. D4 72
Claresholm, Alta., Can. D4 68
Claridge, Pa., U.S. F2 115
Clarinda, Ia., U.S. D2 92
Clarines, Ven. C10 58
Clarion, Ia., U.S. B4 92
Clarion, Pa., U.S. D3 115
Clarion, co., Pa., U.S. D3 115
Clarion, stm., Pa., U.S. D3 115
Clarión, Isla, i., Mex. H2 62
Clarissa, Mn., U.S. D4 100
Clark, N.J., U.S. B4 107
Clark, S.D., U.S. C8 118
Clark, co., Ar., U.S. C2 81
Clark, co., Id., U.S. E6 89
Clark, co., Il., U.S. D6 90
Clark, co., In., U.S. H6 91
Clark, co., Ks., U.S. E4 93
Clark, co., Ky., U.S. C5 94
Clark, co., Mo., U.S. A6 102
Clark, co., Nv., U.S. G6 105
Clark, co., Oh., U.S. C2 112
Clark, co., S.D., U.S. C8 118
Clark, co., Wa., U.S. D3 124
Clark, co., Wi., U.S. D3 126
Clark, Lake, l., Ak., U.S. C9 79
Clark, Point, c., Ont., Can. C3 73
Clarkdale, Az., U.S. C3 80
Clarkdale, Ga., U.S. h7 87
Clarke, co., Al., U.S. D2 78
Clarke, co., Ga., U.S. C3 87
Clarke, co., Ia., U.S. D4 92
Clarke, co., Ms., U.S. C5 101
Clarke, co., Va., U.S. A4 123
Clarkesville, Ga., U.S. B3 87
Clarkfield, Mn., U.S. F3 100
Clark Fork, stm., U.S. C1 103
Clarks, La., U.S. B3 95
Clarks, stm., Ky., U.S. f9 94
Clarksburg, Md., U.S. B3 97
Clarksburg, W.V., U.S. B4 125
Clarksdale, Ms., U.S. A3 101
Clarks Grove, Mn., U.S. G5 100
Clark's Harbour, N.S., Can. F4 71
Clarks Hill, In., U.S. D4 91
Clarkson, Ky., U.S. C3 94
Clarkson, Ne., U.S. C8 104
Clarks Summit, Pa., U.S. m18 115
Clarkston, Ga., U.S. h8 87
Clarkston, Mi., U.S. F7 99
Clarkston, Ut., U.S. B3 121
Clarkston, Wa., U.S. C8 124
Clarksville, Ar., U.S. B2 81
Clarksville, De., U.S. F5 85
Clarksville, In., U.S. H6 91
Clarksville, Ia., U.S. B5 92
Clarksville, Tn., U.S. A4 119
Clarksville, Tx., U.S. C5 120
Clarksville, Va., U.S. D4 123
Clarkton, Mo., U.S. E8 102
Clarkton, N.C., U.S. C4 110
Clatskanie, Or., U.S. A3 114
Clatsop, co., Or., U.S. A3 114
Claude, Tx., U.S. B2 120
Clausthal-Zellerfeld, Ger. D10 8
Clawson, Mi., U.S. o15 99
Claxton, Ga., U.S. D5 87
Clay, Ky., U.S. C2 94
Clay, co., Al., U.S. B4 78
Clay, co., Ar., U.S. A5 81
Clay, co., Fl., U.S. B5 86
Clay, co., Ga., U.S. E2 87
Clay, co., Il., U.S. E5 90
Clay, co., In., U.S. F3 91
Clay, co., Ia., U.S. A2 92
Clay, co., Ks., U.S. C6 93
Clay, co., Ky., U.S. C6 94
Clay, co., Mn., U.S. D2 100
Clay, co., Ms., U.S. B5 101
Clay, co., Mo., U.S. B3 102
Clay, co., Ne., U.S. D7 104
Clay, co., N.C., U.S. f9 110
Clay, co., S.D., U.S. E8 118
Clay, co., Tn., U.S. C8 119
Clay, co., Tx., U.S. C3 120
Clay, co., W.V., U.S. C3 125
Clay Center, Ks., U.S. C6 93
Clay Center, Ne., U.S. D7 104
Clay City, Il., U.S. E5 90
Clay City, In., U.S. F3 91
Clay City, Ky., U.S. C6 94
Clay Creek, stm., S.D., U.S. D8 118
Claymont, De., U.S. A4 85
Clayoquot Sound, strt., B.C., Can. E4 69
Claypool, Az., U.S. D5 80
Claysburg, Pa., U.S. F5 115
Claysville, Pa., U.S. F1 115
Clayton, Al., U.S. D4 78
Clayton, De., U.S. C3 85
Clayton, Ga., U.S. B3 87
Clayton, In., U.S. E4 91
Clayton, La., U.S. C4 95
Clayton, Mo., U.S. f13 102
Clayton, N.J., U.S. D2 107
Clayton, N.M., U.S. A6 108
Clayton, N.Y., U.S. A4 109
Clayton, N.C., U.S. B4 110
Clayton, Ok., U.S. C6 113
Clayton, co., Ga., U.S. C2 87
Clayton, co., Ia., U.S. B6 92
Claytor Lake, res., Va., U.S. C2 123
Clear, stm., R.I., U.S. B2 116
Clear Boggy Creek, stm., Ok., U.S. C5 113
Clear Creek, co., Co., U.S. B5 83
Clear Creek, stm., Tn., U.S. C9 119
Clear Creek, stm., Wy., U.S. B6 127
Cleare, Cape, c., Ak., U.S. D10 79
Clearfield, Ky., U.S. B6 94
Clearfield, Pa., U.S. D5 115
Clearfield, Ut., U.S. B3 121
Clearfield, co., Pa., U.S. D5 115
Clear Fork, stm., W.V., U.S. D3 125
Clear Fork, stm., W.V., U.S. n13 125
Clearlake, Ca., U.S. C2 82
Clear Lake, Ia., U.S. A4 92
Clear Lake, S.D., U.S. C9 118
Clearlake, Wa., U.S. A3 124
Clear Lake, Wi., U.S. C1 126
Clear Lake, l., Ia., U.S. A4 92
Clear Lake, l., Ut., U.S. D3 121
Clear Lake, res., Ca., U.S. C2 82
Clear Lake Reservoir, res., Ca., U.S. B3 82
Clear Lake Shores, Tx., U.S. r15 120
Clear Stream, stm., N.H., U.S. g7 106
Clearwater, B.C., Can. D7 69
Clearwater, Fl., U.S. E4 86
Clearwater, Ks., U.S. E6 93
Clearwater, S.C., U.S. E4 117
Clearwater, co., Id., U.S. C3 89
Clearwater, co., Mn., U.S. C3 100
Clearwater, stm., Can. A5 68
Clearwater, stm., Id., U.S. C2 89
Clearwater, stm., Mn., U.S. C3 100
Clearwater Lake, res., Mo., U.S. D7 102
Clearwater Mountains, mts., Id., U.S. C2 89
Cleburne, Tx., U.S. C4 120
Cleburne, co., Al., U.S. B4 78
Cleburne, co., Ar., U.S. B3 81
Cle Elum, Wa., U.S. B5 124
Cle Elum, stm., Wa., U.S. B4 124
Cle Elum Lake, res., Wa., U.S. B4 124
Clementon, N.J., U.S. D3 107
Clemmons, N.C., U.S. A2 110
Clemson, S.C., U.S. B2 117
Clendenin, W.V., U.S. C3 125
Clendening Lake, res., Oh., U.S. B4 112
Cleona, Pa., U.S. F9 115
Clermont, Que., Can. B7 74
Clermont, Fr. C9 10
Clermont, Fl., U.S. D5 86
Clermont, co., Oh., U.S. C1 112
Clermont-Ferrand, Fr. G10 10
Cles, Italy C6 14
Cleveland, Al., U.S. A3 78
Cleveland, Ga., U.S. B3 87
Cleveland, Mn., U.S. F5 100
Cleveland, Ms., U.S. B3 101
Cleveland, N.C., U.S. B2 110
Cleveland, Oh., U.S. A4 112
Cleveland, Ok., U.S. A5 113
Cleveland, Tn., U.S. D9 119
Cleveland, Tx., U.S. D5 120
Cleveland, Wi., U.S. k10 126
Cleveland, co., Ar., U.S. D3 81
Cleveland, co., N.C., U.S. B1 110
Cleveland, co., Ok., U.S. B4 113
Cleveland, Mount, mtn., Mt., U.S. B3 103
Cleveland Heights, Oh., U.S. A4 112
Cleves, Oh., U.S. o12 112
Clewiston, Fl., U.S. F6 86
Clifden, Ire. H2 7
Cliff Island, i., Me., U.S. g7 96
Clifford, Ont., Can. D4 73
Cliffside, N.C., U.S. B1 110
Cliffside Park, N.J., U.S. h9 107
Clifton, Az., U.S. D6 80
Clifton, Co., U.S. B2 83
Clifton, Il., U.S. C6 90
Clifton, N.J., U.S. B4 107
Clifton, S.C., U.S. B4 117
Clifton, Tn., U.S. B4 119
Clifton, Tx., U.S. D4 120
Clifton Forge, Va., U.S. C3 123
Clifton Knolls, N.Y., U.S. C7 109
Clifton Springs, N.Y., U.S. C3 109
Clinch, co., Ga., U.S. F4 87
Clinch, stm., U.S. D9 119
Clinchco, Va., U.S. e9 123
Clinch Mountain, mtn., U.S. C10 119
Clingmans Dome, mtn., U.S. D10 119
Clinton, B.C., Can. D7 69
Clinton, Ont., Can. D3 73
Clinton, Ar., U.S. B3 81
Clinton, Ct., U.S. D5 84
Clinton, Il., U.S. C5 90
Clinton, In., U.S. E3 91
Clinton, Ia., U.S. C7 92
Clinton, Ky., U.S. f9 94
Clinton, La., U.S. D4 95
Clinton, Me., U.S. D3 96
Clinton, Md., U.S. C4 97
Clinton, Ma., U.S. B4 98
Clinton, Mi., U.S. F7 99
Clinton, Ms., U.S. C3 101
Clinton, Mo., U.S. C4 102
Clinton, N.Y., U.S. B5 109
Clinton, N.C., U.S. C4 110
Clinton, Ok., U.S. B3 113
Clinton, S.C., U.S. C4 117
Clinton, Tn., U.S. C9 119
Clinton, Ut., U.S. B3 121
Clinton, Wa., U.S. B3 124
Clinton, Wi., U.S. F5 126
Clinton, co., Il., U.S. E4 90
Clinton, co., In., U.S. D4 91
Clinton, co., Ia., U.S. C7 92
Clinton, co., Ky., U.S. D4 94
Clinton, co., Mi., U.S. F6 99
Clinton, co., Mo., U.S. B3 102
Clinton, co., N.Y., U.S. f11 109
Clinton, co., Oh., U.S. C2 112
Clinton, co., Pa., U.S. D6 115
Clinton, Lake, res., Il., U.S. C5 90
Clinton-Colden Lake, l., N.W. Ter., Can. D11 66
Clinton Lake, res., Ks., U.S. m15 93
Clinton Reservoir, res., N.J., U.S. A4 107
Clintonville, Wi., U.S. D5 126
Clintwood, Va., U.S. e9 123
Clio, Al., U.S. D4 78
Clio, Mi., U.S. E7 99
Clio, S.C., U.S. B8 117
Clive, Ia., U.S. e8 92
Clogher Head, c., Ire. H6 7
Cloncurry, Austl. D8 50
Clonmel, Ire. I5 7
Cloppenburg, Ger. C8 8
Cloquet, Mn., U.S. D6 100
Cloquet, stm., Mn., U.S. C6 100
Closter, N.J., U.S. B5 107
Clothier, W.V., U.S. n12 125
Cloud, co., Ks., U.S. C6 93
Cloudcroft, N.M., U.S. E4 108
Cloud Peak, mtn., Wy., U.S. B5 127
Clover, S.C., U.S. A5 117
Cloverdale, Al., U.S. A2 78
Cloverdale, Ca., U.S. C2 82
Cloverdale, In., U.S. E4 91
Cloverport, Ky., U.S. C3 94
Clovis, Ca., U.S. D4 82
Clovis, N.M., U.S. C6 108
Cluj-Napoca, Rom. C7 16
Cluny, Fr. F11 10
Cluses, Fr. F13 10
Clusone, Italy D4 14
Clute, Tx., U.S. r14 120
Clutha, stm., N.Z. G2 52
Clyde, N.W. Ter., Can. B19 66
Clyde, Ks., U.S. C6 93
Clyde, N.Y., U.S. B4 109
Clyde, N.C., U.S. f10 110
Clyde, Oh., U.S. A3 112
Clyde, Tx., U.S. C3 120
Clyde, stm., Scot., U.K. F9 7
Clyde, Firth of, est., Scot., U.K. F7 7
Clymer, Pa., U.S. E3 115
Coachella, Ca., U.S. F5 82
Coachella Canal, Ca., U.S. F6 82
Coacoyole, Mex. E6 62
Coahoma, Tx., U.S. C2 120
Coahoma, co., Ms., U.S. A3 101
Coal, co., Ok., U.S. C5 113
Coal, stm., W.V., U.S. C3 125
Coal Branch, N.B., Can. C4 71
Coal City, Il., U.S. B5 90
Coalcomán de Matamoros, Mex. H8 62
Coal Creek, stm., Ok., U.S. B6 113
Coaldale, Alta., Can. E4 68
Coal Fork, W.V., U.S. C3 125
Coal Fork, stm., W.V., U.S. m13 125
Coalgate, Ok., U.S. C5 113
Coal Grove, Oh., U.S. D3 112
Coal Hill, Ar., U.S. B2 81
Coalhurst, Alta., Can. E4 68
Coalinga, Ca., U.S. D3 82
Coalmont, Tn., U.S. D8 119
Coalville, Ut., U.S. C4 121
Coalwood, W.V., U.S. D3 125
Coari, Braz. D6 54
Coasters Harbor Island, i., R.I., U.S. E5 116
Coast Mountains, mts., N.A. E6 66
Coast Ranges, mts., U.S. C2 76
Coatepeque, Guat. G2 64
Coatesville, Pa., U.S. G10 115
Coaticook, Que., Can. D6 74
Coats, N.C., U.S. B4 110
Coats Island, i., N.W. Ter., Can. D16 66
Coats Land, reg., Ant. B10 47
Coatzacoalcos, Mex. H12 62
Cobalt, Ont., Can. p19 73
Cobb, co., Ga., U.S. C2 87
Cobb, stm., Mn., U.S. G5 100
Cobble Mountain Reservoir, res., Ma., U.S. B2 98
Cobbosseecontee Lake, l., Me., U.S. D3 96
Cobden, Ont., Can. B8 73
Cobden, Il., U.S. F4 90
Cobequid Mountains, mts., N.S., Can. D5 71
Cobham, stm., Can. C4 70
Cobija, Bol. F5 54
Cobleskill, N.Y., U.S. C6 109
Cobourg, Ont., Can. D6 73
Cóbuè, Moz. D6 44
Cobun Creek, stm., W.V., U.S. h11 125
Coburg, Ger. E10 8
Coburg, Or., U.S. C3 114
Coburg Island, i., N.W. Ter., Can. A17 66
Cochabamba, Bol. G5 54
Cocheco, stm., N.H., U.S. D5 106
Cochin, India H4 37
Cochise, co., Az., U.S. F5 80
Cochise Head, mtn., Az., U.S. E6 80
Cochiti Indian Reservation, N.M., U.S. h8 108
Cochiti Reservoir, res., N.M., U.S. B3 108
Cochituate, Ma., U.S. g10 98
Cochituate, Lake, l., Ma., U.S. g10 98
Cochran, Ga., U.S. D3 87
Cochran, co., Tx., U.S. C1 120
Cochrane, Alta., Can. D3 68
Cochrane, Ont., Can. o19 73
Cochranton, Pa., U.S. C1 115
Cocke, co., Tn., U.S. D10 119
Cockeysville, Md., U.S. B4 97
Cockrell Hill, Tx., U.S. n10 120
Coco, stm., N.A. G6 64
Coco, Isla del, i., C.R. B1 54
Cocoa, Fl., U.S. D6 86
Cocoa Beach, Fl., U.S. D6 86
Coco Channel, strt., Asia H2 34
Coco Islands, is., Mya. G2 34
Coconino, co., Az., U.S. B3 80
Cocopah Indian Reservation, Az., U.S. E1 80
Côcos, Braz. C6 57
Cocula, Mex. G8 62
Cod, Cape, c., Ma., U.S. C7 98
Codajás, Braz. D6 54
Coden, Al., U.S. E1 78
Codigoro, Italy E7 14
Codington, co., S.D., U.S. C8 118
Codogno, Italy D4 14
Codroipo, Italy D7 14
Cody, Wy., U.S. B3 127
Coeburn, Va., U.S. f9 123
Coen, Austl. B8 50
Coetivy Island, i., Sey. C11 44
Coeur d'Alene, Id., U.S. B2 89
Coeur d'Alene, stm., Id., U.S. B2 89
Coeur d'Alene Indian Reservation, Id., U.S. B2 89
Coeur d'Alene Lake, res., Id., U.S. B2 89
Coeur d'Alene Mountains, mts., Id., U.S. B2 89
Coffee, co., Al., U.S. D3 78
Coffee, co., Ga., U.S. E4 87
Coffee, co., Tn., U.S. B5 119
Coffeeville, Ms., U.S. B4 101
Coffey, co., Ks., U.S. D8 93
Coffeyville, Ks., U.S. E8 93
Coffs Harbour, Austl. F10 50
Coggon, Ia., U.S. B6 92
Cognac, Fr. G6 10
Cohansey, stm., N.J., U.S. E2 107
Cohasset, Ma., U.S. B6 98
Cohasset, Mn., U.S. C5 100
Cohocton, stm., N.Y., U.S. C3 109
Cohoes, N.Y., U.S. C7 109
Cohoon, Lake, res., Va., U.S. k14 123
Cohutta Mountain, mtn., Ga., U.S. B2 87
Coiba, Isla de, i., Pan. K7 64
Coimbatore, India G4 37
Coimbra, Braz. F7 57
Coimbra, Port. E3 12
Coín, Spain I7 12
Čojbalsan, Mong. B9 26
Cokato, Mn., U.S. E4 100
Coke, co., Tx., U.S. D2 120
Cokeville, Wy., U.S. D2 127
Čokurdach, Russia C23 24
Colatina, Braz. E8 57
Colbert, Ok., U.S. D5 113
Colbert, co., Al., U.S. A2 78

Name	Map Ref	Page
Colborne, Ont., Can.	C7	73
Colby, Ks., U.S.	C2	93
Colby, Wi., U.S.	D3	126
Colchester, Eng., U.K.	J13	7
Colchester, Ct., U.S.	C6	84
Colchester, Il., U.S.	C3	90
Colcord, Ok., U.S.	A7	113
Cold, stm., N.H., U.S.	C4	106
Cold, stm., N.H., U.S.	D2	106
Cold Bay, Ak., U.S.	E7	79
Cold Lake, Alta., Can.	B5	68
Cold Spring, Ky., U.S.	A5	94
Cold Spring, Mn., U.S.	E4	100
Coldwater, Ont., Can.	C5	73
Coldwater, Ks., U.S.	E4	93
Coldwater, Mi., U.S.	G5	99
Coldwater, Ms., U.S.	A4	101
Coldwater, Oh., U.S.	B1	112
Coldwater, stm., Ms., U.S.	A3	101
Coldwater Creek, stm., U.S.	e9	113
Cole, co., Mo., U.S.	C5	102
Colebrook, N.H., U.S.	g7	106
Colebrook River Lake, res., Ct., U.S.	A3	84
Cole Camp, Mo., U.S.	C4	102
Coleen, stm., Ak., U.S.	B11	79
Coleman, Mi., U.S.	E6	99
Coleman, Tx., U.S.	D3	120
Coleman, Wi., U.S.	C5	126
Coleman, co., Tx., U.S.	D3	120
Coleraine, N. Ire., U.K.	F6	7
Coleraine, Mn., U.S.	C5	100
Coles, co., Il., U.S.	D5	90
Colesberg, S. Afr.	H5	44
Colfax, Ca., U.S.	C3	82
Colfax, Il., U.S.	C5	90
Colfax, In., U.S.	D4	91
Colfax, Ia., U.S.	C4	92
Colfax, La., U.S.	C3	95
Colfax, Wa., U.S.	C8	124
Colfax, Wi., U.S.	D2	126
Colfax, co., Ne., U.S.	C8	104
Colfax, co., N.M., U.S.	A5	108
Colhué Huapi, Lago, l., Arg.	F3	56
Colima, Mex.	H8	62
Colima, Nevado de, mtn., Mex.	H8	62
Colinas, Braz.	E10	54
Coll, i., Scot., U.K.	E6	7
College, Ak., U.S.	B10	79
Collegedale, Tn., U.S.	h11	119
College Park, Ga., U.S.	C2	87
College Park, Md., U.S.	C4	97
College Place, Wa., U.S.	C7	124
College Station, Ar., U.S.	C3	81
College Station, Tx., U.S.	D4	120
Collegeville, In., U.S.	C3	91
Collegeville, Pa., U.S.	F11	115
Colleton, co., S.C., U.S.	F6	117
Collier, co., Fl., U.S.	F5	86
Collier Bay, b., Austl.	C4	50
Colliers, W.V., U.S.	f8	125
Collierville, Tn., U.S.	B2	119
Collin, co., Tx., U.S.	C4	120
Collingdale, Pa., U.S.	p20	115
Collingswood, N.J., U.S.	D2	107
Collingsworth, co., Tx., U.S.	B2	120
Collingwood, Ont., Can.	C4	73
Collins, Ms., U.S.	D4	101
Collins Park, De., U.S.	B3	85
Collinsville, Al., U.S.	A4	78
Collinsville, Ct., U.S.	B4	84
Collinsville, Il., U.S.	E4	90
Collinsville, Ms., U.S.	C5	101
Collinsville, Ok., U.S.	A6	113
Collinsville, Va., U.S.	D3	123
Collinwood, Tn., U.S.	B4	119
Collooney, Ire.	G4	7
Colmar, Fr.	D14	10
Colmar Manor, Md., U.S.	f9	97
Colmenar, Spain	I7	12
Colmenar de Oreja, Spain	E8	12
Colmenar Viejo, Spain	E8	12
Colo, Ia., U.S.	B4	92
Cologne see Köln, Ger.	E6	8
Coloma, Mi., U.S.	F4	99
Colomb-Béchar see Béchar, Alg.	B5	42
Colombia, ctry., S.A.	C4	54
Colombo, Sri L.	I5	37
Colón, Cuba	C7	64
Colón, Pan.	J8	64
Colon, Mi., U.S.	G5	99
Colon, Archipiélago de (Galapagos Islands), is., Ec.	m15	58a
Colonia Dora, Arg.	B4	56
Colonia Las Heras, Arg.	F3	56
Colonial Beach, Va., U.S.	B6	123
Colonial Heights, Tn., U.S.	C11	119
Colonial Heights, Va., U.S.	C5	123
Colonial National Historical Park, Va., U.S.	C6	123
Colonia Vicente Guerrero, Mex.	B1	62
Colonie, N.Y., U.S.	C7	109
Coloradas, Lomas, hills, Arg.	E3	56
Colorado, co., Tx., U.S.	E4	120
Colorado, state, U.S.	B5	83
Colorado, stm., Arg.	D4	56
Colorado, stm., N.A.	E4	76
Colorado, stm., Tx., U.S.	D3	120
Colorado City, Az., U.S.	A3	80
Colorado City, Co., U.S.	D6	83
Colorado City, Tx., U.S.	C2	120
Colorado City, Lake, res., Tx., U.S.	C2	120
Colorado National Monument, Co., U.S.	B2	83
Colorado River Aqueduct, Ca., U.S.	F6	82
Colorado River Indian Reservation, U.S.	D1	80
Colorado Springs, Co., U.S.	C6	83
Colotlán, Mex.	F8	62
Colquitt, Ga., U.S.	E2	87
Colquitt, co., Ga., U.S.	E3	87
Colstrip, Mt., U.S.	E10	103
Colton, S.D., U.S.	D9	118
Coltons Point, Md., U.S.	D4	97
Columbia, Al., U.S.	D4	78
Columbia, Il., U.S.	E3	90
Columbia, Ky., U.S.	C4	94
Columbia, Md., U.S.	B4	97
Columbia, Ms., U.S.	D4	101
Columbia, Mo., U.S.	C5	102
Columbia, N.C., U.S.	B6	110
Columbia, Pa., U.S.	F9	115
Columbia, S.C., U.S.	C5	117
Columbia, Tn., U.S.	B4	119
Columbia, co., Ar., U.S.	D2	81
Columbia, co., Fl., U.S.	B4	86
Columbia, co., Ga., U.S.	C4	87
Columbia, co., N.Y., U.S.	C7	109
Columbia, co., Or., U.S.	B3	114
Columbia, co., Pa., U.S.	D9	115
Columbia, co., Wa., U.S.	C7	124
Columbia, co., Wi., U.S.	E4	126
Columbia, stm., N.A.	G8	66
Columbia, Mount, mtn., Can.	C2	68
Columbia City, In., U.S.	B7	91
Columbia City, Or., U.S.	B4	114
Columbia Falls, Mt., U.S.	B2	103
Columbia Heights, Mn., U.S.	m12	100
Columbia Lake, res., Ct., U.S.	C6	84
Columbia Mountains, mts., B.C., Can.	C7	69
Columbiana, Al., U.S.	B3	78
Columbiana, Oh., U.S.	B5	112
Columbiana, co., Oh., U.S.	B5	112
Columbiaville, Mi., U.S.	E7	99
Columbus, Ga., U.S.	D2	87
Columbus, In., U.S.	F6	91
Columbus, Ks., U.S.	E9	93
Columbus, Ms., U.S.	B5	101
Columbus, Mt., U.S.	E7	103
Columbus, Ne., U.S.	C8	104
Columbus, N.M., U.S.	F2	108
Columbus, N.C., U.S.	f10	110
Columbus, Oh., U.S.	C2	112
Columbus, Tx., U.S.	E4	120
Columbus, Wi., U.S.	E4	126
Columbus, co., N.C., U.S.	C4	110
Columbus Air Force Base, mil., Ms., U.S.	B5	101
Columbus Grove, Oh., U.S.	B1	112
Columbus Junction, Ia., U.S.	C6	92
Columbus Lake, res., Ms., U.S.	B5	101
Colusa, Ca., U.S.	C2	82
Colusa, co., Ca., U.S.	C2	82
Colver, Pa., U.S.	E4	115
Colville, Wa., U.S.	A8	124
Colville, stm., Ak., U.S.	B9	79
Colville, stm., Wa., U.S.	A8	124
Colville Indian Reservation, Wa., U.S.	A6	124
Colvos Passage, strt., Wa., U.S.	f10	124
Colwich, Ks., U.S.	E6	93
Colwood, B.C., Can.	h12	69
Comacchio, Italy	E7	14
Comal, co., Tx., U.S.	E3	120
Comanche, Ok., U.S.	C4	113
Comanche, Tx., U.S.	D3	120
Comanche, co., Ks., U.S.	E4	93
Comanche, co., Ok., U.S.	C3	113
Comanche, co., Tx., U.S.	D3	120
Comandante Fontana, Arg.	B5	56
Comayagua, Hond.	G4	64
Combahee, stm., S.C., U.S.	F6	117
Combarbalá, Chile	C2	56
Combeaufontaine, Fr.	E12	10
Comber, Ont., Can.	E2	73
Combermere Bay, b., Mya.	E2	34
Combined Locks, Wi., U.S.	h9	126
Combourg, Fr.	D5	10
Combs, Ky., U.S.	C6	94
Comer, Ga., U.S.	B3	87
Comfort, Tx., U.S.	E3	120
Comilla, Bngl.	I14	38
Comitán [de Domínguez], Mex.	I13	62
Comite, stm., La., U.S.	D4	95
Commentry, Fr.	F9	10
Commerce, Ga., U.S.	B3	87
Commerce, Ok., U.S.	A7	113
Commerce, Tx., U.S.	C5	120
Commerce City, Co., U.S.	B6	83
Committee Bay, b., N.W. Ter., Can.	C15	66
Common Fence Point, R.I., U.S.	D6	116
Como, Italy	D4	14
Como, Ms., U.S.	A4	101
Como, Lago di, l., Italy	C4	14
Comodoro Rivadavia, Arg.	F3	56
Comorin, Cape, c., India	H4	37
Comoros, ctry., Afr.	D8	44
Comox, B.C., Can.	E5	69
Compiègne, Fr.	C9	10
Compton, Que., Can.	D6	74
Compton, Ca., U.S.	n12	82
Comstock, Mi., U.S.	F5	99
Çon, stm., Viet.	E8	34
Çona, stm., Russia	E16	24
Conakry, Gui.	G3	42
Conanicut Island, i., R.I., U.S.	E5	116
Conanicut Point, c., R.I., U.S.	E5	116
Concarneau, Fr.	E3	10
Conceição do Araguaia, Braz.	E9	54
Concepción, Arg.	B3	56
Concepción, Bol.	G6	54
Concepción, Chile	D2	56
Concepción, Para.	A5	56
Concepción, Laguna, l., Bol.	G6	54
Concepción, Volcán, vol., Nic.	I5	64
Concepción del Oro, Mex.	E9	62
Concepción del Uruguay, Arg.	C5	56
Conception, Point, c., Ca., U.S.	E3	82
Conception Bay, b., Newf., Can.	E5	72
Conception Bay South, Newf., Can.	E5	72
Conchas Lake, res., N.M., U.S.	B5	108
Conches, Fr.	D7	10
Concho, co., Tx., U.S.	D3	120
Concho, stm., Tx., U.S.	D2	120
Conchos, stm., Mex.	C7	62
Concord, Ca., U.S.	h8	82
Concord, Ma., U.S.	B5	98
Concord, Mi., U.S.	F6	99
Concord, Mo., U.S.	g13	102
Concord, N.H., U.S.	D3	106
Concord, N.C., U.S.	B2	110
Concord, stm., Ma., U.S.	A5	98
Concordia, Arg.	C5	56
Concordia, Mex.	F6	62
Concordia, Ks., U.S.	C6	93
Concordia, Mo., U.S.	C4	102
Concordia, co., La., U.S.	C4	95
Concrete, Wa., U.S.	A4	124
Condé, Fr.	D6	10
Condom, Fr.	I7	10
Condon, Or., U.S.	B6	114
Condoto, Col.	E4	58
Conecuh, co., Al., U.S.	D2	78
Conecuh, stm., U.S.	D3	78
Conegliano, Italy	D7	14
Conejos, co., Co., U.S.	D4	83
Conejos, stm., Co., U.S.	D4	83
Conejos Peak, mtn., Co., U.S.	D4	83
Conemaugh, Pa., U.S.	F4	115
Conemaugh River Lake, res., Pa., U.S.	F3	115
Confolens, Fr.	F7	10
Congamond Lakes, l., U.S.	A4	84
Congaree, stm., S.C., U.S.	D6	117
Congaree Swamp National Monument, S.C., U.S.	D6	117
Congo, ctry., Afr.	B2	44
Congo (Zaire), stm., Afr.	C2	44
Congress, Az., U.S.	C3	80
Conimicut Point, c., R.I., U.S.	D5	116
Conitaca, Mex.	E6	62
Conklin, N.Y., U.S.	C5	109
Conn, Lough, l., Ire.	G3	7
Connaught, hist. reg., Ire.	H3	7
Conneaut, Oh., U.S.	A5	112
Conneaut Creek, stm., Oh., U.S.	A5	112
Conneaut Lake, l., Pa., U.S.	C1	115
Connecticut, state, U.S.	C5	84
Connecticut, stm., U.S.	C12	76
Connell, Wa., U.S.	C7	124
Connellsville, Pa., U.S.	F2	115
Connemara, reg., Ire.	H3	7
Connersville, In., U.S.	E7	91
Conover, N.C., U.S.	B1	110
Conowingo, Md., U.S.	A5	97
Conrad, Ia., U.S.	B5	92
Conrad, Mt., U.S.	B5	103
Conroe, Tx., U.S.	D5	120
Conselheiro Lafaiete, Braz.	F7	57
Conshohocken, Pa., U.S.	F11	115
Con Son, is., Viet.	J9	34
Consort, Alta., Can.	C5	68
Constance, Lake see Bodensee, l., Eur.	H9	8
Constanța, Rom.	E12	16
Constantina, Spain	H6	12
Constantine (Qacentina), Alg.	A7	42
Constantine, Mi., U.S.	G5	99
Constantine, Cape, c., Ak., U.S.	D8	79
Consuegra, Spain	F8	12
Contai, India	J12	38
Contas, Rio de, stm., Braz.	C9	57
Content Keys, is., Fl., U.S.	H5	86
Continental, Oh., U.S.	A1	112
Continental Peak, mtn., Wy., U.S.	D4	127
Continental Reservoir, res., Co., U.S.	D3	83
Contoocook, N.H., U.S.	D3	106
Contoocook, stm., N.H., U.S.	D3	106
Contra Costa, co., Ca., U.S.	D3	82
Contrecoeur, Que., Can.	D4	74
Contres, Fr.	E8	10
Contwoyto Lake, l., N.W. Ter., Can.	C10	66
Convención, Col.	C6	58
Conversano, Italy	I12	14
Converse, In., U.S.	C6	91
Converse, S.C., U.S.	B4	117
Converse, co., Wy., U.S.	C7	127
Convoy, Oh., U.S.	B1	112
Conway, Ar., U.S.	B3	81
Conway, Fl., U.S.	D5	86
Conway, Mo., U.S.	D5	102
Conway, N.H., U.S.	C4	106
Conway, N.C., U.S.	A5	110
Conway, Pa., U.S.	E1	115
Conway, S.C., U.S.	D9	117
Conway, co., Ar., U.S.	B3	81
Conway, Lake, res., Ar., U.S.	B3	81
Conway Lake, l., N.H., U.S.	C4	106
Conway Springs, Ks., U.S.	E6	93
Conyers, Ga., U.S.	C2	87
Cooch Behār, India	G13	38
Cook, Mn., U.S.	C6	100
Cook, co., Ga., U.S.	E3	87
Cook, co., Il., U.S.	B6	90
Cook, co., Mn., U.S.	k9	100
Cook, Cape, c., B.C., Can.	D4	69
Cook, Mount, mtn., N.Z.	E3	52
Cooke, co., Tx., U.S.	C4	120
Cookes Peak, mtn., N.M., U.S.	E2	108
Cookeville, Tn., U.S.	C8	119
Cook Inlet, b., Ak., U.S.	D9	79
Cook Islands, dep., Oc.	H2	2
Cook Point, c., Md., U.S.	C5	97
Cookshire, Que., Can.	D6	74
Cookson, Ok., U.S.	B7	113
Cookstown, N. Ire., U.K.	G6	7
Cook Strait, strt., N.Z.	D5	52
Cooktown, Austl.	C9	50
Cooleemee, N.C., U.S.	B2	110
Coolgardie, Austl.	F4	50
Coolidge, Az., U.S.	E4	80
Coolidge, Ga., U.S.	E3	87
Cooma, Austl.	G9	50
Coonoor, India	G4	37
Coon Rapids, Ia., U.S.	C3	92
Coon Rapids, Mn., U.S.	E5	100
Coon Valley, Wi., U.S.	E2	126
Cooper, Tx., U.S.	C5	120
Cooper, co., Mo., U.S.	C5	102
Cooper, stm., S.C., U.S.	F8	117
Cooper Mountain, mtn., Ak., U.S.	g17	79
Coopersburg, Pa., U.S.	F11	115
Cooperstown, N.Y., U.S.	C6	109
Cooperstown, N.D., U.S.	B7	111
Coopersville, Mi., U.S.	E5	99
Coos, co., N.H., U.S.	A4	106
Coos, co., Or., U.S.	D2	114
Coos, stm., Or., U.S.	D2	114
Coosa, co., Al., U.S.	C3	78
Coosa, stm., U.S.	C3	78
Coosada, Al., U.S.	C3	78
Coosawhatchie, stm., S.C., U.S.	F5	117
Coos Bay, Or., U.S.	D2	114
Copalis Beach, Wa., U.S.	B1	124
Copan, Ok., U.S.	A6	113
Copan Reservoir, res., Ok., U.S.	A6	113
Copenhagen see København, Den.	I9	6
Copiah, co., Ms., U.S.	D3	101
Copiapó, Chile	B2	56
Coplay, Pa., U.S.	E10	115
Copparo, Italy	E6	14
Copper, stm., Ak., U.S.	C11	79
Copperas Cove, Tx., U.S.	D4	120
Copper Butte, mtn., Wa., U.S.	A7	124
Coppermine, N.W. Ter., Can.	C9	66
Coppermine, stm., N.W. Ter., Can.	C10	66
Copper Mountain, mtn., Wy., U.S.	C5	127
Copper Mountains, mts., Az., U.S.	E2	80
Coquille, Or., U.S.	D2	114
Coquimbo, Chile	B2	56
Coral Gables, Fl., U.S.	G6	86
Coral Harbour, N.W. Ter., Can.	D16	66
Coral Sea, Oc.	B10	50
Coralville, Ia., U.S.	C6	92
Coralville Lake, res., Ia., U.S.	C5	92
Corantijn (Corentyne), stm., S.A.	E14	58
Coraopolis, Pa., U.S.	E1	115
Corato, Italy	H11	14
Corbeil-Essonnes, Fr.	D9	10
Corbigny, Fr.	E10	10
Corbin, Ky., U.S.	D5	94
Corcoran, Ca., U.S.	D4	82
Corcoran, Mn., U.S.	m11	100
Corcovado, Golfo, b., Chile	E2	56
Corcovado, Volcán, vol., Chile	E2	56
Corcubión, Spain	C2	12
Cordele, Ga., U.S.	E3	87
Cordell, Ok., U.S.	B3	113
Cordell Hull Lake, res., Tn., U.S.	C8	119
Cordes, Fr.	H8	10
Córdoba, Arg.	C4	56
Córdoba, Mex.	H11	62
Córdoba, Spain	H7	12
Cordova, Al., U.S.	B2	78
Cordova, Ak., U.S.	C10	79
Cordova, N.M., U.S.	A4	108
Cordova, N.C., U.S.	C3	110
Cordova Peak, mtn., Ak., U.S.	C10	79
Corentyne (Corantijn), stm., S.A.	E14	58
Corfu see Kérkira, Grc.	J3	16
Coria, Spain	F5	12
Coria del Río, Spain	H5	12
Corigliano Calabro, Italy	J11	14
Coringa Islets, is., Austl.	C9	50
Corinna, Me., U.S.	D3	96
Corinne, Ut., U.S.	B3	121
Corinne Key, i., Fl., U.S.	G6	86
Corinth, Ms., U.S.	A5	101
Corinth, N.Y., U.S.	B7	109
Corinth see Kórinthos, Grc.	L6	16
Corinto, Braz.	E6	57
Cork, Ire.	J4	7
Corlay, Fr.	D3	10
Corleone, Italy	L8	14
Corleto Perticara, Italy	I11	14
Çorlu, Tur.	H11	16
Cormorant Lake, l., Man., Can.	B1	70
Cornelia, Ga., U.S.	B3	87
Cornélio Procópio, Braz.	G3	57
Cornelius, N.C., U.S.	B2	110
Cornelius, Or., U.S.	g11	114
Cornell, Wi., U.S.	C2	126
Corner Brook, Newf., Can.	D3	72
Cornersville, Tn., U.S.	B5	119
Cornfield Point, c., Ct., U.S.	D6	84
Cornie Bayou, stm., U.S.	D3	81
Corning, Ar., U.S.	A5	81
Corning, Ca., U.S.	C2	82
Corning, Ia., U.S.	D3	92
Corning, N.Y., U.S.	C3	109
Cornish, Me., U.S.	E2	96
Corn Islands, is., Nic.	H6	64
Corno Grande, mtn., Italy	G8	14
Cornville, Az., U.S.	C4	80
Cornwall, Ont., Can.	B10	73
Cornwall, Pa., U.S.	F9	115
Cornwallis Island, i., N.W. Ter., Can.	A14	66
Cornwall on Hudson, N.Y., U.S.	D6	109
Coro, Ven.	B8	58
Corocoro, Bol.	G5	54
Coroico, Bol.	G5	54
Coromandel Coast, India	F6	37
Coromandel Peninsula, pen., N.Z.	B5	52
Corona, Ca., U.S.	F5	82
Coronado, Ca., U.S.	F5	82
Coronado National Memorial, Az., U.S.	F5	80
Coronation, Alta., Can.	C5	68
Coronation Gulf, b., N.W. Ter., Can.	C10	66
Coronation Island, i., Ak., U.S.	n22	79
Coronel Dorrego, Arg.	D4	56
Coronel Fabriciano, Braz.	E7	57
Coronel Pringles, Arg.	D4	56
Coronel Suárez, Arg.	D4	56
Coropuna, Nevado, mtn., Peru	G4	54
Corpus Christi, Tx., U.S.	F4	120
Corpus Christi Naval Air Station, mil., Tx., U.S.	F4	120
Corral de Almaguer, Spain	F8	12
Correctionville, Ia., U.S.	B2	92
Correggio, Italy	E5	14
Corrente, stm., Braz.	B7	57
Corrib, Lough, l., Ire.	H3	7
Corrientes, Arg.	B5	56
Corrientes, Cabo, c., Col.	E4	58
Corrientes, Cabo, c., Cuba	D5	64
Corrientes, Cabo, c., Mex.	G7	62
Corrigan, Tx., U.S.	D5	120
Corriganville, Md., U.S.	k13	97
Corry, Pa., U.S.	C2	115
Corse (Corsica), i., Fr.	m19	11a
Corsica, S.D., U.S.	D7	118
Corsica see Corse, i., Fr.	m19	11a
Corsicana, Tx., U.S.	C4	120
Corson, co., S.D., U.S.	B4	118
Corson Inlet, b., N.J., U.S.	E3	107
Cortemilia, Italy	E3	14
Cortez, Co., U.S.	D2	83
Cortez, Fl., U.S.	q10	86
Cortez Mountains, mts., Nv., U.S.	C5	105
Cortina d'Ampezzo, Italy	C7	14
Cortland, Il., U.S.	B5	90
Cortland, N.Y., U.S.	C4	109
Cortland, Oh., U.S.	A5	112
Cortland, co., N.Y., U.S.	C4	109
Çorum, Tur.	G14	4
Corumbá, Braz.	G7	54
Corumbá, stm., Braz.	E4	57
Corunna, Mi., U.S.	F6	99
Corvallis, Or., U.S.	C3	114
Corydon, In., U.S.	H5	91
Corydon, Ia., U.S.	D4	92
Corydon, Ky., U.S.	C2	94
Coryell, co., Tx., U.S.	D4	120
Cosamaloapan [de Carpio], Mex.	H12	62
Cosenza, Italy	J11	14
Coshocton, Oh., U.S.	B4	112
Coshocton, co., Oh., U.S.	B4	112
Cosmoledo Group, is., Sey.	C9	44
Cosmopolis, Wa., U.S.	C2	124
Cosmos, Mn., U.S.	F4	100
Cosne-sur-Loire, Fr.	E9	10
Cossatot, stm., Ar., U.S.	C1	81
Costa Mesa, Ca., U.S.	n13	82
Costa Rica, Mex.	C4	62
Costa Rica, ctry., N.A.	I5	64
Costilla, co., Co., U.S.	D5	83
Cotabato, Phil.	D7	32
Coteau-Landing, Que., Can.	D3	74
Cotentin, pen., Fr.	C5	10
Cotonou, Benin	G6	42
Cotopaxi, vol., Ec.	H3	58
Cottage Grove, Mn., U.S.	n13	100
Cottage Grove, Or., U.S.	D3	114
Cottage Grove Reservoir, res., Or., U.S.	D3	114
Cottam, Ont., Can.	E2	73
Cottbus, Ger.	D14	8
Cotter, Ar., U.S.	A3	81
Cottiennes, Alpes (Alpi Cozie), mts., Eur.	H13	10
Cottle, co., Tx., U.S.	B2	120
Cottleville, Mo., U.S.	f12	102
Cotton, co., Ok., U.S.	C3	113
Cottondale, Al., U.S.	B2	78
Cotton Plant, Ar., U.S.	B4	81
Cottonport, La., U.S.	C3	95
Cotton Valley, La., U.S.	B2	95
Cottonwood, Al., U.S.	D4	78
Cottonwood, Az., U.S.	C3	80
Cottonwood, Ca., U.S.	B2	82
Cottonwood, Id., U.S.	C2	89
Cottonwood, Mn., U.S.	F3	100
Cottonwood, co., Mn., U.S.	F3	100
Cottonwood, stm., Ks., U.S.	D7	93
Cottonwood, stm., Mn., U.S.	F3	100
Cottonwood Creek, stm., Wy., U.S.	C4	127
Cottonwood Falls, Ks., U.S.	D7	93
Cotuit, Ma., U.S.	C7	98
Cotulla, Tx., U.S.	E3	120
Coudersport, Pa., U.S.	C5	115
Cougar Reservoir, res., Or., U.S.	C4	114
Couhé, Fr.	F7	10
Coulee Creek, stm., Wa., U.S.	g13	124
Coulee Dam, Wa., U.S.	B7	124
Coulee Dam National Recreation Area, Wa., U.S.	A7	124
Coulommiers, Fr.	D10	10
Coulterville, Il., U.S.	E4	90
Counce, Tn., U.S.	B3	119
Council, Id., U.S.	E2	89
Council Bluffs, Ia., U.S.	C2	92
Council Grove, Ks., U.S.	D7	93
Council Grove Lake, res., Ks., U.S.	D7	93
Council Mountain, mtn., Id., U.S.	E2	89
Country Homes, Wa., U.S.	B8	124
Coupeville, Wa., U.S.	A3	124
Courtenay, B.C., Can.	E5	69
Courte Oreilles, Lac, l., Wi., U.S.	C2	126
Courtland, Ont., Can.	E4	73
Courtland, Al., U.S.	A2	78
Courtland, Va., U.S.	D5	123
Coushatta, La., U.S.	B2	95
Coutances, Fr.	C5	10
Coutras, Fr.	G6	10
Cove Creek, stm., Ut., U.S.	E3	121
Covedale, Oh., U.S.	o12	112
Coventry, Eng., U.K.	I11	7
Coventry, Ct., U.S.	B6	84
Coventry, R.I., U.S.	D3	116
Cove Point, c., Md., U.S.	D5	97
Covilhã, Port.	E4	12
Covina, Ca., U.S.	m13	82
Covington, Ga., U.S.	C3	87
Covington, In., U.S.	D3	91
Covington, Ky., U.S.	A5	94
Covington, La., U.S.	D5	95
Covington, Oh., U.S.	B1	112
Covington, Tn., U.S.	B2	119
Covington, Va., U.S.	C3	123
Covington, co., Al., U.S.	D3	78
Covington, co., Ms., U.S.	D4	101
Cowan, Tn., U.S.	B5	119
Cowan, Lake, l., Austl.	F4	50
Cowansville, Que., Can.	D5	74
Cowarts, Al., U.S.	D4	78
Cow Creek, stm., Wa., U.S.	C7	124
Cowee Mountains, mts., N.C., U.S.	f9	110
Cowen, Mount, mtn., Mt., U.S.	E6	103
Coweta, Ok., U.S.	B6	113
Coweta, co., Ga., U.S.	C2	87
Cow Head, Newf., Can.	D3	72
Cowichan Bay, B.C., Can.	g12	69
Cow Lakes, l., Or., U.S.	D9	114
Cowley, Wy., U.S.	B4	127
Cowley, co., Ks., U.S.	E7	93
Cowlington, Ok., U.S.	B7	113
Cowlitz, co., Wa., U.S.	C2	124

Name	Map Ref	Page
Cowlitz, stm., Wa., U.S.	C3	124
Cowpasture, stm., Va., U.S.	B3	123
Cowpen Mountain, mtn., Ga., U.S.	B2	87
Cowpens, S.C., U.S.	A4	117
Coxim, Braz.	E1	57
Coxsackie, N.Y., U.S.	C7	109
Cox's Bāzār, Bngl.	J14	38
Cox's Cove, Newf., Can.	D2	72
Coyhaique, Chile	F2	56
Cozad, Ne., U.S.	D6	104
Cozumel, Isla de, i., Mex.	G16	62
Crab Creek, stm., Wa., U.S.	C6	124
Crab Creek, stm., Wa., U.S.	B7	124
Crab Orchard, Ky., U.S.	C5	94
Crab Orchard, Tn., U.S.	D9	119
Crab Orchard, W.V., U.S.	n13	125
Crab Orchard Lake, res., Il., U.S.	F4	90
Crabtree, Pa., U.S.	F3	115
Crabtree Mills, Que., Can.	D4	74
Cradock, S. Afr.	H5	44
Crafton, Pa., U.S.	k13	115
Craig, Ak., U.S.	D13	79
Craig, Co., U.S.	A3	83
Craig, co., Ok., U.S.	A6	113
Craig, co., Va., U.S.	C2	123
Craig Air Force Base, mil., Al., U.S.	C3	78
Craig Creek, stm., Va., U.S.	C2	123
Craighead, co., Ar., U.S.	B5	81
Craigsville, Va., U.S.	B3	123
Craigsville, W.V., U.S.	C4	125
Crailsheim, Ger.	F10	8
Craiova, Rom.	E7	16
Cramerton, N.C., U.S.	B1	110
Cranberry Lake, l., N.Y., U.S.	A6	109
Cranberry Portage, Man., Can.	B1	70
Cranbrook, B.C., Can.	E10	69
Crandall, Tx., U.S.	n10	120
Crandon, Wi., U.S.	C5	126
Crane, Az., U.S.	*E1	80
Crane, Mo., U.S.	E4	102
Crane, Tx., U.S.	D1	120
Crane, co., Tx., U.S.	D1	120
Crane Creek, stm., Oh., U.S.	e7	112
Crane Creek Reservoir, res., Id., U.S.	E2	89
Crane Lake, l., Il., U.S.	C3	90
Crane Lake, l., Mn., U.S.	B6	100
Crane Mountain, mtn., Or., U.S.	E6	114
Crane Prairie Reservoir, res., Or., U.S.	D5	114
Cranford, N.J., U.S.	B4	107
Cranston, R.I., U.S.	C4	116
Craon, Fr.	E6	10
Craponne, Fr.	G10	10
Crater Lake, l., Or., U.S.	E4	114
Crater Lake National Park, Or., U.S.	E4	114
Craters of the Moon National Monument, Id., U.S.	F5	89
Cratéus, Braz.	E10	54
Crato, Braz.	E11	54
Crauford, Cape, c., N.W. Ter., Can.	B16	66
Craven, co., N.C., U.S.	B5	110
Crawford, Ga., U.S.	C3	87
Crawford, Ms., U.S.	B5	101
Crawford, Ne., U.S.	B2	104
Crawford, co., Ar., U.S.	B1	81
Crawford, co., Ga., U.S.	D3	87
Crawford, co., Il., U.S.	D6	90
Crawford, co., In., U.S.	H4	91
Crawford, co., Ia., U.S.	B2	92
Crawford, co., Ks., U.S.	E9	93
Crawford, co., Mi., U.S.	D6	99
Crawford, co., Mo., U.S.	D6	102
Crawford, co., Oh., U.S.	B3	112
Crawford, co., Pa., U.S.	C1	115
Crawford, co., Wi., U.S.	E3	126
Crawford Lake, l., Me., U.S.	C5	96
Crawford Notch State Park, N.H., U.S.	B4	106
Crawfordsville, Ar., U.S.	B5	81
Crawfordsville, In., U.S.	D4	91
Crawfordville, Fl., U.S.	B2	86
Crazy Mountains, mts., Mt., U.S.	D6	103
Crazy Peak, mtn., Mt., U.S.	D6	103
Crazy Woman Creek, stm., Wy., U.S.	B6	127
Creal Springs, Il., U.S.	F5	90
Cree, stm., Sask., Can.	E11	66
Creedmoor, N.C., U.S.	A4	110
Creek, co., Ok., U.S.	B5	113
Cree Lake, l., Sask., Can.	m7	75
Creemore, Ont., Can.	C4	73
Creighton, Ne., U.S.	B8	104
Creighton, Pa., U.S.	h14	115
Creil, Fr.	C9	10
Crema, Italy	D4	14
Cremona, Italy	D5	14
Crenshaw, Ms., U.S.	A3	101
Crenshaw, co., Al., U.S.	D3	78
Creola, Al., U.S.	E1	78
Cres, Cro.	E9	14
Cresaptown, Md., U.S.	k13	97
Crescent, Ok., U.S.	B4	113
Crescent, Or., U.S.	D5	114
Crescent, Lake, l., Wa., U.S.	A2	124
Crescent City, Ca., U.S.	B1	82
Crescent City, Fl., U.S.	C5	86
Crescent Lake, l., Fl., U.S.	C5	86
Crescent Lake, l., Or., U.S.	D5	114
Crescent Springs, Ky., U.S.	h13	94
Cresco, Ia., U.S.	A5	92
Cresskill, N.J., U.S.	h9	107
Cresson, Pa., U.S.	F4	115
Cressona, Pa., U.S.	E9	115
Crest, Fr.	H12	10
Crested Butte, Co., U.S.	C4	83
Crest Hill, Il., U.S.	k8	90
Crestline, Oh., U.S.	B3	112
Creston, B.C., Can.	E9	69
Creston, Ia., U.S.	C3	92
Creston, Oh., U.S.	B4	112
Crestone Peak, mtn., Co., U.S.	D5	83
Crestview, Fl., U.S.	u15	86
Crestview, Hi., U.S.	g10	88
Crestwood, Ky., U.S.	B4	94
Crestwood Village, N.J., U.S.	D4	107
Creswell, Or., U.S.	D3	114
Crete, Il., U.S.	B6	90
Crete, Ne., U.S.	D9	104
Crete see Kríti, i., Grc.	N8	16
Creve Coeur, Il., U.S.	C4	90
Crevillente, Spain	G11	12
Crewe, Eng., U.K.	H10	7
Crewe, Va., U.S.	C4	123
Criciúma, Braz.	B7	56
Cricket, N.C., U.S.	A1	110
Cridersville, Oh., U.S.	B1	112
Crikvenica, Cro.	D9	14
Crimea see Kryms'kyy pivostriv, pen., Ukr.	H4	22
Crimmitschau, Ger.	E12	8
Crisfield, Md., U.S.	E6	97
Crisp, co., Ga., U.S.	E3	87
Cristalândia, Braz.	F9	54
Cristalina, Braz.	D5	57
Cristianópolis, Braz.	D4	57
Cristóbal Colón, Pico, mtn., Col.	B6	58
Crittenden, Ky., U.S.	B5	94
Crittenden, co., Ar., U.S.	B5	81
Crittenden, co., Ky., U.S.	e9	94
Crivitz, Wi., U.S.	C6	126
Črnomelj, Slo.	D10	14
Croatia, ctry., Eur.	D10	14
Crocker, Mo., U.S.	D5	102
Crockett, Ca., U.S.	g8	82
Crockett, Tx., U.S.	D5	120
Crockett, co., Tn., U.S.	B2	119
Crockett, co., Tx., U.S.	D2	120
Crofton, Ky., U.S.	C2	94
Crofton, Md., U.S.	B4	97
Crofton, Ne., U.S.	B8	104
Croix, Lac la, l., Mn., U.S.	B6	100
Croker, Cape, c., Ont., Can.	C4	73
Croker Island, i., Austl.	B6	50
Cromarty, Scot., U.K.	D8	7
Cromona, Ky., U.S.	C7	94
Cromwell, Ct., U.S.	C5	84
Crook, co., Or., U.S.	C6	114
Crook, co., Wy., U.S.	B8	127
Crooked, stm., Or., U.S.	C6	114
Crooked Creek, stm., U.S.	E3	93
Crooked Creek, stm., Pa., U.S.	C7	115
Crooked Creek Lake, res., Pa., U.S.	E3	115
Crooked Island, i., Bah.	C10	64
Crooked Island Passage, strt., Bah.	C10	64
Crooked Lake, l., Fl., U.S.	E5	86
Crooked Lake, l., Mn., U.S.	B7	100
Crooks, S.D., U.S.	D9	118
Crooks Lake, l., Nv., U.S.	B2	105
Crookston, Mn., U.S.	C2	100
Crooksville, Oh., U.S.	C3	112
Crosby, Mn., U.S.	D5	100
Crosby, N.D., U.S.	A2	111
Crosby, Tx., U.S.	r14	120
Crosby, co., Tx., U.S.	C2	120
Crosby, Mount, mtn., Wy., U.S.	C3	127
Crosbyton, Tx., U.S.	C2	120
Cross, co., Ar., U.S.	B5	81
Cross Bay, b., Man., Can.	C2	70
Cross City, Fl., U.S.	C3	86
Cross Creek, stm., W.V., U.S.	f8	125
Crossett, Ar., U.S.	D4	81
Crossfield, Alta., Can.	D3	68
Cross Island, i., Me., U.S.	D5	96
Cross Lake, Man., Can.	B3	70
Crosslake, Mn., U.S.	D4	100
Cross Lake, l., Me., U.S.	A4	96
Cross Lake, res., La., U.S.	B2	95
Cross Lanes, W.V., U.S.	C3	125
Crossman Peak, mtn., Az., U.S.	C1	80
Cross Plains, Tn., U.S.	A5	119
Cross Plains, Tx., U.S.	C3	120
Cross Plains, Wi., U.S.	E4	126
Cross Sound, strt., Ak., U.S.	k21	79
Crossville, Al., U.S.	A4	78
Crossville, Il., U.S.	E5	90
Crossville, Tn., U.S.	D8	119
Croswell, Mi., U.S.	E8	99
Crothersville, In., U.S.	G6	91
Crotone, Italy	J12	14
Croton-on-Hudson, N.Y., U.S.	D7	109
Crouse, N.C., U.S.	B1	110
Crow, stm., Mn., U.S.	F4	100
Crow Agency, Mt., U.S.	E9	103
Crow Creek, stm., U.S.	A6	83
Crow Creek Indian Reservation, S.D., U.S.	C6	118
Crowder, Ms., U.S.	A3	101
Crowell, Tx., U.S.	C3	120
Crow Indian Reservation, Mt., U.S.	E9	103
Crowley, La., U.S.	D3	95
Crowley, Tx., U.S.	n9	120
Crowley, co., Co., U.S.	C7	83
Crowley, Lake, res., Ca., U.S.	D4	82
Crowleys Ridge, mtn., U.S.	B5	81
Crown Point, In., U.S.	B3	91
Crown Point, La., U.S.	k11	95
Crownpoint, N.M., U.S.	B1	108
Crown Prince Frederick Island, i., N.W. Ter., Can.	B15	66
Crow Peak, mtn., Mt., U.S.	D5	103
Crowsnest Pass, Alta., Can.	E3	68
Crowsnest Pass, Can.	E3	68
Crow Wing, co., Mn., U.S.	D4	100
Crow Wing, stm., Mn., U.S.	D4	100
Croydon, Austl.	C8	50
Crozet, Va., U.S.	B4	123
Crozon, Fr.	D2	10
Cruces, Cuba	C7	64
Crump Lake, l., Or., U.S.	E7	114
Cruz Alta, Braz.	B6	56
Cruz del Eje, Arg.	C4	56
Cruzeiro do Sul, Braz.	E4	54
Crystal, Mn., U.S.	m12	100
Crystal, stm., Co., U.S.	B3	83
Crystal Bay, Nv., U.S.	D1	105
Crystal Bay, b., Fl., U.S.	D4	86
Crystal Beach, Fl., U.S.	D4	86
Crystal City, Man., Can.	E2	70
Crystal City, Mo., U.S.	C7	102
Crystal City, Tx., U.S.	E3	120
Crystal Falls, Mi., U.S.	B2	99
Crystal Lake, Ct., U.S.	B6	84
Crystal Lake, Fl., U.S.	u16	86
Crystal Lake, Il., U.S.	A5	90
Crystal Lake, l., Ct., U.S.	B6	84
Crystal Lake, l., Mi., U.S.	D4	99
Crystal Lake, l., N.H., U.S.	D4	106
Crystal Lake, l., Vt., U.S.	B4	122
Crystal Lawns, Il., U.S.	k8	90
Crystal Pond, res., Ct., U.S.	B7	84
Crystal River, Fl., U.S.	D4	86
Crystal Springs, Ms., U.S.	D3	101
Cuando (Kwando), stm., Afr.	E4	44
Cuangar, Ang.	E3	44
Cuango, Ang.	C3	44
Cuango (Kwango), stm., Afr.	C3	44
Cuanza, stm., Ang.	C3	44
Cuauhtémoc, Mex.	C6	62
Cuautla, Mex.	H10	62
Cuba, Port.	G4	12
Cuba, Il., U.S.	C3	90
Cuba, Mo., U.S.	C6	102
Cuba, N.M., U.S.	A3	108
Cuba, N.Y., U.S.	C2	109
Cuba, ctry., N.A.	D8	64
Cuba City, Wi., U.S.	F3	126
Cubango (Okavango), stm., Afr.	E3	44
Cubero, N.M., U.S.	B2	108
Cucharas, Mex.	F7	62
Cucharas, stm., Co., U.S.	D6	83
Cudahy, Wi., U.S.	F6	126
Cuddalore, India	G5	37
Cuddapah, India	E5	37
Cuddy Mountain, mtn., Id., U.S.	E2	89
Čudskoje Ozero (Peipsi Järv), l., Eur.	C10	18
Cuéllar, Spain	D7	12
Cuenca, Ec.	I3	58
Cuenca, Spain	E9	12
Cuencamé [de Ceniceros], Mex.	E8	62
Cuernavaca, Mex.	H10	62
Cuero, Tx., U.S.	E4	120
Cuers, Fr.	I13	10
Cuervos, Mex.	A2	62
Cuevas del Almanzora, Spain	H10	12
Cuglieri, Italy	I3	14
Cuiabá, Braz.	G7	54
Cuiseaux, Fr.	F12	10
Cuito, stm., Ang.	E3	44
Cuito-Cuanavale, Ang.	E3	44
Cuivre, West Fork, stm., Mo., U.S.	B6	102
Čukotskij, Mys, c., Russia	E31	24
Čukotskij Poluostrov, pen., Russia	D30	24
Culberson, co., Tx., U.S.	o12	120
Culbertson, Mt., U.S.	B12	103
Culbertson, Ne., U.S.	D5	104
Culebra Peak, mtn., Co., U.S.	D5	83
Culiacán, Mex.	E6	62
Cullen, La., U.S.	B2	95
Cullman, Al., U.S.	A3	78
Cullman, co., Al., U.S.	A3	78
Culloden, W.V., U.S.	C2	125
Cullowhee, N.C., U.S.	f9	110
Čul'man, Russia	F18	24
Culpeper, Va., U.S.	B4	123
Culpeper, co., Va., U.S.	B5	123
Culver, In., U.S.	B5	91
Culver City, Ca., U.S.	m12	82
Culvers Lake, l., N.J., U.S.	A3	107
Culym, Russia	F10	24
Cumalı, Tur.	M11	16
Cumaná, Ven.	B10	58
Cumanacoa, Ven.	B11	58
Cumbal, Nevado de, mtn., Col.	G4	58
Cumberland, B.C., Can.	E5	69
Cumberland, Ky., U.S.	D7	94
Cumberland, Md., U.S.	k13	97
Cumberland, Wi., U.S.	C2	126
Cumberland, co., Il., U.S.	D5	90
Cumberland, co., Ky., U.S.	D4	94
Cumberland, co., Me., U.S.	E2	96
Cumberland, co., N.J., U.S.	E2	107
Cumberland, co., N.C., U.S.	C4	110
Cumberland, co., Pa., U.S.	F7	115
Cumberland, co., Tn., U.S.	D8	119
Cumberland, co., Va., U.S.	C4	123
Cumberland, stm., U.S.	D4	94
Cumberland, Lake, res., Ky., U.S.	D5	94
Cumberland Center, Me., U.S.	g7	96
Cumberland Foreside, Me., U.S.	E2	96
Cumberland Gap, U.S.	D6	94
Cumberland Gap National Historical Park, U.S.	D6	94
Cumberland Hill, R.I., U.S.	B4	116
Cumberland Island National Seashore, Ga., U.S.	F5	87
Cumberland Islands, is., Austl.	D9	50
Cumberland Lake, l., Sask., Can.	C4	75
Cumberland Peninsula, pen., N.W. Ter., Can.	C19	66
Cumberland Sound, strt., N.W. Ter., Can.	C19	66
Cumbres Pass, Co., U.S.	D4	83
Čumikan, Russia	G21	24
Cuming, co., Ne., U.S.	C9	104
Cumming, Ga., U.S.	B2	87
Cumnock, Scot., U.K.	F8	7
Čuna, stm., Russia	F13	24
Čun'a, stm., Russia	E13	24
Cunani, Braz.	C8	54
Cunene, stm., Afr.	E2	44
Cuneo, Italy	E2	14
Cunnamulla, Austl.	E9	50
Cunningham, Ky., U.S.	f9	94
Cupar, Sask., Can.	G3	75
Curaçao, i., Neth. Ant.	H13	64
Curecanti National Recreation Area, Co., U.S.	C3	83
Curepipe, Mrts.	F11	44
Curiapo, Ven.	C12	58
Curicó, Chile	C2	56
Curitiba, Braz.	B7	56
Curlew Creek, stm., Wa., U.S.	A7	124
Curlew Lake, l., Wa., U.S.	A7	124
Curralinho, Braz.	D9	54
Currant Mountain, mtn., Nv., U.S.	E6	105
Current, stm., U.S.	A5	81
Currituck, co., N.C., U.S.	A6	110
Curry, co., N.M., U.S.	C6	108
Curry, co., Or., U.S.	E2	114
Curtis, Ne., U.S.	D5	104
Curtisville, Pa., U.S.	E2	115
Curvelo, Braz.	E6	57
Curwensville, Pa., U.S.	E4	115
Curwensville Lake, res., Pa., U.S.	E4	115
Curwood, Mount, mtn., Mi., U.S.	B2	99
Cushing, Ok., U.S.	B5	113
Cushman, Lake, res., Wa., U.S.	B2	124
Cusseta, Ga., U.S.	D2	87
Custer, S.D., U.S.	D2	118
Custer, co., Co., U.S.	C5	83
Custer, co., Id., U.S.	E4	89
Custer, co., Mt., U.S.	D11	103
Custer, co., Ne., U.S.	C6	104
Custer, co., Ok., U.S.	B2	113
Custer, co., S.D., U.S.	D2	118
Custer Battlefield National Monument, Mt., U.S.	E9	103
Cut Bank, Mt., U.S.	B4	103
Cut Bank Creek, stm., N.D., U.S.	A4	111
Cutchogue, N.Y., U.S.	m16	109
Cuthbert, Ga., U.S.	E2	87
Cutler Ridge, Fl., U.S.	s13	86
Cut Off, La., U.S.	E5	95
Cutro, Italy	J11	14
Cuttack, India	J11	38
Cuttyhunk Island, i., Ma., U.S.	D6	98
Cuxhaven, Ger.	B8	8
Cuyahoga, co., Oh., U.S.	A4	112
Cuyahoga, stm., Oh., U.S.	A4	112
Cuyahoga Falls, Oh., U.S.	A4	112
Cuyama, stm., Ca., U.S.	E4	82
Cuyamaca Peak, mtn., Ca., U.S.	F5	82
Cuyo Islands, is., Phil.	C7	32
Cuyuni, stm., S.A.	D13	58
Cuzco, Peru	F4	54
C.W. McConaughy, Lake, res., Ne., U.S.	C4	104
Cyclades see Kikládhes, is., Grc.	L8	16
Cynthiana, In., U.S.	H2	91
Cynthiana, Ky., U.S.	B5	94
Cypress Creek, stm., Tx., U.S.	r14	120
Cypress Hills Provincial Park, Sask., Can.	H1	75
Cypress Lake, l., Fl., U.S.	D5	86
Cypress Quarters, Fl., U.S.	E6	86
Cypress Swamp, sw., U.S.	F4	85
Cyprus, ctry., Asia	B3	40
Cyril, Ok., U.S.	C3	113
Czech Republic, ctry., Eur.	F11	4
Częstochowa, Pol.	E19	8

D

Name	Map Ref	Page
Dabeiba, Col.	D4	58
Dabhoi, India	I5	38
Dabie Shan, mts., China	D4	28
Dabola, Gui.	F3	42
Dacca see Dhaka, Bngl.	I14	38
Dachaidan, China	B16	38
Dachau, Ger.	G11	8
Dacono, Co., U.S.	A6	83
Dacula, Ga., U.S.	C3	87
Dadanawa, Guy.	F13	58
Dade, co., Fl., U.S.	G6	86
Dade, co., Ga., U.S.	B1	87
Dade, co., Mo., U.S.	D4	102
Dade City, Fl., U.S.	D4	86
Dadeville, Al., U.S.	C4	78
Dādra and Nagar Haveli, ter., India	B2	37
Dādu, Pak.	G2	38
Daet, Phil.	q20	33b
Daggett, co., Ut., U.S.	C6	121
Dagsboro, De., U.S.	F5	85
Dagupan, Phil.	p19	33b
Dahan-e Qowmghī, Afg.	C2	38
Da Hinggan Ling, mts., China	C11	26
Dahlak Archipelago, is., Erit.	E3	46
Dahlak Kebir Island, i., Erit.	E3	46
Dahlonega, Ga., U.S.	B3	87
Dahomey see Benin, ctry., Afr.	G6	42
Dahra, Libya	C9	42
Dahy, Nafūd ad-, des., Sau. Ar.	D4	46
Daimiel, Spain	F8	12
Daingerfield, Tx., U.S.	C5	120
Dairen see Dalian, China	D11	26
Dakar, Sen.	F2	42
Dakhla, W. Sah.	D2	42
Dakota, co., Mn., U.S.	F5	100
Dakota, co., Ne., U.S.	B9	104
Dakota City, Ia., U.S.	B3	92
Dakota City, Ne., U.S.	B9	104
Dalandzadgad, Mong.	C7	26
Da Lat, Viet.	I10	34
Dālbandin, Pak.	D1	36
Dalby, Austl.	E10	50
Dale, In., U.S.	H4	91
Dale, co., Al., U.S.	D4	78
Dale City, Va., U.S.	B5	123
Dale Hollow Lake, res., U.S.	C8	119
Daleville, Al., U.S.	D4	78
Daleville, In., U.S.	D6	91
Dalhart, Tx., U.S.	A1	120
Dalhousie, N.B., Can.	A3	71
Dalhousie, Cape, c., N.W. Ter., Can.	B7	66
Dali, China	B6	34
Dalian, China	D11	26
Dall, Mount, mtn., Ak., U.S.	f15	79
Dallam, co., Tx., U.S.	A1	120
Dallas, Ga., U.S.	C2	87
Dallas (part of Melcher), Ia., U.S.	C4	92
Dallas, N.C., U.S.	B1	110
Dallas, Or., U.S.	C3	114
Dallas, Pa., U.S.	D10	115
Dallas, Tx., U.S.	C4	120
Dallas, co., Al., U.S.	C2	78
Dallas, co., Ar., U.S.	D3	81
Dallas, co., Ia., U.S.	C3	92
Dallas, co., Mo., U.S.	D4	102
Dallas, co., Tx., U.S.	C4	120
Dallas Center, Ia., U.S.	C4	92
Dallas City, Il., U.S.	C2	90
Dallas Naval Air Station, mil., Tx., U.S.	n9	120
Dallastown, Pa., U.S.	G8	115
Dall Island, i., Ak., U.S.	n23	79
Dalmacija, hist. reg., Eur.	F11	14
Dalmatia see Dalmacija, hist. reg., Eur.	F11	14
Daloa, C. Iv.	G4	42
Dalqū, Sudan	D12	42
Dalton, Ga., U.S.	B2	87
Dalton, Ma., U.S.	B1	98
Dalton, Oh., U.S.	B4	112
Dalton, Pa., U.S.	C10	115
Daltonganj, India	H11	38
Dalton Gardens, Id., U.S.	B2	89
Dalwallinu, Austl.	F3	50
Daly City, Ca., U.S.	h8	82
Damān, India	B2	37
Damān, ter., India	B2	37
Damar, Pulau, i., Indon.	G8	32
Damariscotta, Me., U.S.	D3	96
Damariscotta Lake, l., Me., U.S.	D3	96
Damascus, Md., U.S.	B3	97
Damascus, Va., U.S.	f10	123
Damascus see Dimashq, Syria	C5	40
Damāvand, Qolleh-ye, mtn., Iran	J8	22
Damba, Ang.	C3	44
Damoh, India	I8	38
Dampar, Tasek, l., Malay.	M7	34
Dampier, Austl.	D3	50
Dampier, Selat, strt., Indon.	F9	32
Dampier Archipelago, is., Austl.	D3	50
Dan, stm., U.S.	D3	123
Dana, In., U.S.	E3	91
Danakil Plain, pl., Erit.	F3	46
Da Nang, Viet.	F10	34
Danbury, Ct., U.S.	D2	84
Danbury, Tx., U.S.	r14	120
Dand, Afg.	E1	38
Dandridge, Tn., U.S.	C10	119
Dane, co., Wi., U.S.	E4	126
Dangla, Eth.	F2	46
Dania, Fl., U.S.	F6	86
Daniels, co., Mt., U.S.	B11	103
Danielson, Ct., U.S.	B8	84
Daniels Pass, Ut., U.S.	C4	121
Danilov, Russia	C23	18
Danlí, Hond.	G4	64
Dannemora, N.Y., U.S.	f11	109
Dansville, N.Y., U.S.	C3	109
Dante, Va., U.S.	f9	123
Danube, stm., Eur.	G13	4
Danube, Mouths of the, mth., Eur.	D13	16
Danvers, Il., U.S.	C4	90
Danvers, Ma., U.S.	A6	98
Danville, Que., Can.	D5	74
Danville, Ar., U.S.	B2	81
Danville, Ca., U.S.	h9	82
Danville, Il., U.S.	C6	90
Danville, In., U.S.	E4	91
Danville, Ia., U.S.	D6	92
Danville, Ky., U.S.	C5	94
Danville, Oh., U.S.	B3	112
Danville, Pa., U.S.	E8	115
Danville, Va., U.S.	D3	123
Danyang, China	C8	28
Danzig, Gulf of, b., Eur.	A19	8
Danzig see Gdańsk, Pol.	A18	8
Daocheng, China	F7	26
Dapango, Togo	F6	42
Daphne, Al., U.S.	E2	78
Dar'ā, Syria	C5	40
Darakht-e Yahyā, Afg.	E3	38
Dārayyā, Syria	C5	40
Darbāsīyah, Syria	A7	40
Darbhanga, India	G11	38
Darby, Mt., U.S.	D2	103
Darby, Pa., U.S.	G11	115
Darchan, Mong.	B8	26
Dardanelle, Ar., U.S.	B2	81
Dardanelle Lake, res., Ar., U.S.	B2	81
Dardanelles see Çanakkale Boğazı, strt., Tur.	I10	16
Dare, co., N.C., U.S.	B7	110
Dar es Salaam, Tan.	C7	44
Dargaville, N.Z.	A4	52
Dari, China	E6	26
Darien, Ct., U.S.	E2	84
Darien, Ga., U.S.	E5	87
Darien, Wi., U.S.	F5	126
Dariganga, Mong.	B9	26
Darjeeling, India	G13	38
Darke, co., Oh., U.S.	B1	112
Darley Woods, De., U.S.	h8	85
Darling, stm., Austl.	F9	50
Darling, Lake, res., N.D., U.S.	A4	111
Darling Range, mts., Austl.	F3	50
Darlington, Eng., U.K.	G11	7
Darlington, In., U.S.	D4	91
Darlington, Md., U.S.	A5	97
Darlington, S.C., U.S.	C8	117
Darlington, Wi., U.S.	F3	126
Darlington, co., S.C., U.S.	C8	117
Darmstadt, Ger.	F8	8
Darnah, Libya	B10	42
Daroca, Spain	D10	12
Darrah, Mount, mtn., Can.	E3	68
Darrington, Wa., U.S.	A4	124
Dartmoor National Park, Eng., U.K.	K9	7
Dartmouth, Eng., U.K.	K9	7
Daru, Pap. N. Gui.	G11	32
Darwin, Austl.	B6	50
Dašinčilen, Mong.	B7	26
Dassel, Mn., U.S.	E4	100
Datia, India	H8	38
Datil Mountains, mts., N.M., U.S.	C2	108
D'at'kovo, Russia	H17	18
Datong, China	C9	26
Datu, Tanjung, c., Asia	M10	34
Dāūd Khel, Pak.	D4	38
Daufuskie Island, i., S.C., U.S.	G6	117
Daugavpils, Lat.	F9	18
Daulatābād (Shirin Tagāo), Afg.	B1	38
Daule, Ec.	G2	58
Dauphin, Man., Can.	D1	70
Dauphin, co., Pa., U.S.	F8	115
Dauphin, stm., Man., Can.	D2	70

Name	Map Ref	Page
Dauphin Island, Al., U.S.	E1	78
Dauphin Island, i., Al., U.S.	E1	78
Dauphin Lake, l., Man., Can.	D2	70
Dāvangere, India	E3	37
Davao, Phil.	D8	32
Davao Gulf, b., Phil.	D8	32
Daveluyville, Que., Can.	C5	74
Davenport, Fl., U.S.	D5	86
Davenport, Ia., U.S.	C7	92
Davenport, Ok., U.S.	B5	113
Davenport, Wa., U.S.	B7	124
David, Pan.	J6	64
David City, Ne., U.S.	C8	104
Davidson, N.C., U.S.	B2	110
Davidson, co., N.C., U.S.	B2	110
Davidson, co., Tn., U.S.	A5	119
Davidsville, Pa., U.S.	F4	115
Davie, Fl., U.S.	F6	86
Davie, co., N.C., U.S.	B2	110
Daviess, co., In., U.S.	G3	91
Daviess, co., Ky., U.S.	C2	94
Daviess, co., Mo., U.S.	B3	102
Davis, Ca., U.S.	C3	82
Davis, Ok., U.S.	C4	113
Davis, W.V., U.S.	B5	125
Davis, co., Ia., U.S.	D5	92
Davis, co., Ut., U.S.	C3	121
Davis, Mount, mtn., Pa., U.S.	G3	115
Davis Creek, stm., W.V., U.S.	m12	125
Davis Dam, U.S.	H7	105
Davis Islands, is., Fl., U.S.	p11	86
Davis Lake, l., Or., U.S.	E5	114
Davis-Monthan Air Force Base, mil., Az., U.S.	E5	80
Davison, Mi., U.S.	E7	99
Davison, co., S.D., U.S.	D7	118
Davis Strait, strt., N.A.	C21	66
Davisville, R.I., U.S.	E4	116
Davos, Switz.	F16	10
Dawa (Daua), stm., Afr.	H3	46
Dawei, Mya.	G5	34
Dawes, co., Ne., U.S.	B2	104
Daws Island, i., S.C., U.S.	G6	117
Dawson, Ga., U.S.	E2	87
Dawson, Mn., U.S.	F2	100
Dawson, co., Ga., U.S.	B2	87
Dawson, co., Mt., U.S.	C11	103
Dawson, co., Ne., U.S.	D6	104
Dawson, co., Tx., U.S.	C1	120
Dawson, Mount, mtn., B.C., Can.	D9	69
Dawson Creek, B.C., Can.	B7	69
Dawson Springs, Ky., U.S.	C2	94
Dax, Fr.	I5	10
Day, co., S.D., U.S.	B8	118
Dayr az-Zawr, Syria	B7	40
Daysland, Alta., Can.	C4	68
Dayton, In., U.S.	D4	91
Dayton, Ia., U.S.	B3	92
Dayton, Ky., U.S.	h14	94
Dayton, Md., U.S.	B4	97
Dayton, Mn., U.S.	m12	100
Dayton, Nv., U.S.	D2	105
Dayton, Oh., U.S.	C1	112
Dayton, Or., U.S.	B3	114
Dayton, Tn., U.S.	D8	119
Dayton, Tx., U.S.	D5	120
Dayton, Va., U.S.	B4	123
Dayton, Wa., U.S.	C8	124
Dayton, Wy., U.S.	B5	127
Daytona Beach, Fl., U.S.	C5	86
Da Yunhe, China	E10	26
Dayville, Ct., U.S.	B8	84
De Aar, S. Afr.	H4	44
Dead, North Branch, stm., Me., U.S.	C2	96
Dead, South Branch, stm., Me., U.S.	C2	96
Dead Creek, stm., Vt., U.S.	C2	122
Dead Diamond, stm., N.H., U.S.	g7	106
Dead Indian Peak, mtn., Wy., U.S.	B3	127
Dead Lake, l., Mn., U.S.	D3	100
Dead Lakes, l., Fl., U.S.	B1	86
Deadman Bay, b., Fl., U.S.	C3	86
Deadman Creek, stm., Wa., U.S.	g14	124
Deadmans Cay, Bah.	C10	64
Dead Sea, l., Asia	D4	40
Deadwood, S.D., U.S.	C2	118
Deadwood Reservoir, res., Id., U.S.	E3	89
Deaf Smith, co., Tx., U.S.	B1	120
Deale, Md., U.S.	C4	97
Deal Island, Md., U.S.	D6	97
Deal Island, i., Md., U.S.	D6	97
Dean, stm., B.C., Can.	C4	69
Dean Channel, strt., B.C., Can.	C4	69
Deán Funes, Arg.	C4	56
Dearborn, Mi., U.S.	F7	99
Dearborn, co., In., U.S.	F7	91
Dearborn Heights, Mi., U.S.	p15	99
Dearg, Beinn, mtn., Scot., U.K.	D8	7
Dease Strait, strt., N.W. Ter., Can.	C11	66
Death Valley, val., Ca., U.S.	D5	82
Death Valley National Monument, U.S.	D5	82
Deauville, Fr.	C7	10
De Baca, co., N.M., U.S.	C5	108
De Bary, Fl., U.S.	D5	86
Debauch Mountain, mtn., Ak., U.S.	C8	79
Dębica, Pol.	E21	8
Debrecen, Hung.	H21	8
Debre Markos, Eth.	F2	46
Debre Tabor, Eth.	F2	46
De Cade, Lake, l., La., U.S.	E5	95
Decatur, Al., U.S.	A3	78
Decatur, Ar., U.S.	A1	81
Decatur, Ga., U.S.	C2	87
Decatur, Il., U.S.	D5	90
Decatur, In., U.S.	C8	91
Decatur, Mi., U.S.	F5	99
Decatur, Ms., U.S.	C4	101
Decatur, Ne., U.S.	B9	104
Decatur, Tn., U.S.	D9	119
Decatur, Tx., U.S.	C4	120
Decatur, co., Ga., U.S.	F2	87
Decatur, co., In., U.S.	F6	91
Decatur, co., Ia., U.S.	D4	92
Decatur, co., Ks., U.S.	C3	93
Decatur, co., Tn., U.S.	B3	119
Decatur, Lake, res., Il., U.S.	D5	90
Decaturville, Tn., U.S.	B3	119
Decazeville, Fr.	H9	10
Deccan, plat., India	E4	37
Deception, Mount, mtn., Wa., U.S.	B2	124
Decherd, Tn., U.S.	B5	119
Děčín, Czech.	E14	8
Decize, Fr.	F10	10
Deckerville, Mi., U.S.	E8	99
Decorah, Ia., U.S.	A6	92
Dedham, Ma., U.S.	B5	98
Dédougou, Burkina	F5	42
Dedovsk, Russia	F20	18
Deep, stm., N.C., U.S.	B3	110
Deep Creek, stm., Ut., U.S.	C2	121
Deep Creek, stm., Ut., U.S.	B3	121
Deep Creek, stm., Ut., U.S.	F3	121
Deep Creek, stm., Wa., U.S.	g13	124
Deep Creek Lake, res., Md., U.S.	K12	97
Deep Creek Mountains, mts., Id., U.S.	G6	89
Deep Fork, stm., Ok., U.S.	B5	113
Deep Inlet, b., Newf., Can.	g10	72
Deep Red Creek, stm., Ok., U.S.	C3	113
Deep River, Ont., Can.	A7	73
Deep River, Ct., U.S.	D6	84
Deer Creek, stm., Oh., U.S.	C2	112
Deer Creek Indian Reservation, Mn., U.S.	C5	100
Deerfield, Il., U.S.	h9	90
Deerfield, Ks., U.S.	E2	93
Deerfield, Ma., U.S.	A2	98
Deerfield, Mi., U.S.	G7	99
Deerfield, Wi., U.S.	E4	126
Deerfield, stm., U.S.	A2	98
Deerfield Beach, Fl., U.S.	F6	86
Deer Island, pen., Ma., U.S.	g12	98
Deer Island, i., Ms., U.S.	f8	101
Deer Isle, i., Me., U.S.	D4	96
Deer Lake, Newf., Can.	D3	72
Deer Lake, l., Newf., Can.	D3	72
Deer Lake, l., Mn., U.S.	C5	100
Deer Lodge, Mt., U.S.	D4	103
Deer Lodge, co., Mt., U.S.	E3	103
Deer Park, N.Y., U.S.	n15	109
Deer Park, Oh., U.S.	o13	112
Deer Park, Wa., U.S.	B8	124
Deer Peak, mtn., Co., U.S.	C5	83
Deer River, Mn., U.S.	C5	100
Deesa, India	H5	38
Defiance, Oh., U.S.	A1	112
Defiance, co., Oh., U.S.	A1	112
Defiance, Mount, mtn., Or., U.S.	B5	114
De Forest, Wi., U.S.	E4	126
De Funiak Springs, Fl., U.S.	u15	86
Degeh-Bur, Eth.	G3	46
Dégelis, Que., Can.	B9	74
Deggendorf, Ger.	G12	8
De Graff, Oh., U.S.	B2	112
De Gray Lake, res., Ar., U.S.	C2	81
Dehiwala-Mount Lavinia, Sri L.	I5	37
Dehra Dūn, India	E8	38
Dehri, India	H11	38
Dehu, India	C2	37
Dehui, China	C12	26
Dej, Rom.	B7	16
Deje, Swe.	G9	6
De Kalb, Il., U.S.	B5	90
De Kalb, Ms., U.S.	C5	101
De Kalb, Tx., U.S.	C5	120
De Kalb, co., Al., U.S.	A4	78
De Kalb, co., Ga., U.S.	C2	87
De Kalb, co., Il., U.S.	B5	90
De Kalb, co., In., U.S.	B7	91
De Kalb, co., Mo., U.S.	B3	102
De Kalb, co., Tn., U.S.	D8	119
Dekese, Zaire	B4	44
Delafield, Wi., U.S.	m11	126
Delanco, N.J., U.S.	C3	107
De Land, Fl., U.S.	C5	86
Delano, Ca., U.S.	E4	82
Delano, Mn., U.S.	E5	100
Delano Peak, mtn., Ut., U.S.	E3	121
Delaronde Lake, l., Sask., Can.	C2	75
Delavan, Il., U.S.	C4	90
Delavan, Wi., U.S.	F5	126
Delaware, Oh., U.S.	B2	112
Delaware, co., In., U.S.	D7	91
Delaware, co., Ia., U.S.	B6	92
Delaware, co., N.Y., U.S.	C5	109
Delaware, co., Oh., U.S.	B2	112
Delaware, co., Ok., U.S.	A7	113
Delaware, co., Pa., U.S.	G11	115
Delaware, state, U.S.	D3	85
Delaware, stm., U.S.	G11	115
Delaware, stm., Ks., U.S.	C8	93
Delaware, East Branch, stm., N.Y., U.S.	C5	109
Delaware Bay, b., U.S.	D11	76
Delaware City, De., U.S.	B3	85
Delaware Lake, res., Oh., U.S.	B3	112
Delaware Water Gap, N.J., U.S.	B2	107
Delaware Water Gap National Recreation Area, U.S.	B2	107
Delbarton, W.V., U.S.	D2	125
Delcambre, La., U.S.	E4	95
Del City, Ok., U.S.	B4	113
Delémont, Switz.	E14	10
De Leon, Tx., U.S.	C3	120
De Leon Springs, Fl., U.S.	C5	86
Delft, Neth.	C4	8
Delfzijl, Neth.	B6	8
Delgado, Cabo, c., Moz.	D8	44
Delhi, India	F7	38
Delhi, La., U.S.	B4	95
Delhi, N.Y., U.S.	C6	109
Delicias, Mex.	C7	62
De Lisle, Ms., U.S.	E4	101
Delitzsch, Ger.	D12	8
Dellenbaugh, Mount, mtn., Az., U.S.	A2	80
Dell Rapids, S.D., U.S.	D9	118
Del Mar, Ca., U.S.	o15	82
Delmar, De., U.S.	G3	85
Delmar, Md., U.S.	D6	97
Delmar, N.Y., U.S.	C7	109
Delmenhorst, Ger.	B8	8
Delnice, Cro.	D9	14
Del Norte, Co., U.S.	D4	83
Del Norte, co., Ca., U.S.	B2	82
De-Longa, Ostrova, is., Russia	B23	24
Deloraine, Man., Can.	E1	70
Del Park Manor, De., U.S.	i7	85
Delphi, In., U.S.	C4	91
Delphos, Oh., U.S.	B1	112
Delran, N.J., U.S.	C3	107
Delray Beach, Fl., U.S.	F6	86
Del Rio, Tx., U.S.	E2	120
Delson, Que., Can.	q19	74
Delta, Co., U.S.	C2	83
Delta, Oh., U.S.	A2	112
Delta, Ut., U.S.	D3	121
Delta, co., Co., U.S.	C3	83
Delta, co., Mi., U.S.	C3	99
Delta, co., Tx., U.S.	C5	120
Delta, reg., Ms., U.S.	B3	101
Delta Junction, Ak., U.S.	C10	79
Delta Peak, mtn., B.C., Can.	A3	69
Delta Reservoir, res., N.Y., U.S.	B5	109
Deltaville, Va., U.S.	C6	123
Deltona, Fl., U.S.	D5	86
Demarest, N.J., U.S.	h9	107
Deming, N.M., U.S.	E2	108
Demirci, Tur.	J12	16
Demirköy, Tur.	H11	16
Demmin, Ger.	B13	8
Demopolis, Al., U.S.	C2	78
Demorest, Ga., U.S.	B3	87
Demotte, In., U.S.	B3	91
Denain, Fr.	B10	10
Denali National Park, Ak., U.S.	C9	79
Denare Beach, Sask., Can.	C4	75
Denham Springs, La., U.S.	D5	95
Den Helder, Neth.	C4	8
Denia, Spain	G12	12
Denison, Ia., U.S.	B2	92
Denison, Tx., U.S.	C4	120
Denison Dam, U.S.	D5	113
Denizli, Tur.	H13	4
Denmark, S.C., U.S.	E5	117
Denmark, Wi., U.S.	D6	126
Denmark, ctry., Eur.	D9	4
Denmark Strait, strt.	C15	128
Dennehotso, Az., U.S.	A6	80
Dennis, Ma., U.S.	C7	98
Dennison, Oh., U.S.	B4	112
Dennis Port, Ma., U.S.	C7	98
Denny Terrace, S.C., U.S.	C5	117
Denpasar, Indon.	G6	32
Dent, co., Mo., U.S.	D6	102
Denton, Md., U.S.	C6	97
Denton, N.C., U.S.	B2	110
Denton, Tx., U.S.	C4	120
Denton, co., Tx., U.S.	C4	120
D'Entrecasteaux Islands, is., Pap. N. Gui.	m17	50a
Dentsville, S.C., U.S.	C6	117
Denver, Co., U.S.	B6	83
Denver, Ia., U.S.	B5	92
Denver, Pa., U.S.	F9	115
Denver, co., Co., U.S.	B6	83
Denver City, Tx., U.S.	C1	120
Denville, N.J., U.S.	B4	107
Deoghar, India	H12	38
Deolāli, India	C2	37
Deoria, India	G10	38
De Pere, Wi., U.S.	D5	126
Depew, N.Y., U.S.	C2	109
Depoe Bay, Or., U.S.	C2	114
Depok, Indon.	m13	33a
Deposit, N.Y., U.S.	C5	109
Depue, Il., U.S.	B4	90
Deqin, China	F6	26
De Queen, Ar., U.S.	C1	81
De Queen Reservoir, res., Ar., U.S.	C1	81
De Quincy, La., U.S.	D2	95
Dera Ghāzi Khān, Pak.	E4	38
Dera Ismāīl Khān, Pak.	E4	38
Derby, Austl.	C4	50
Derby, Eng., U.K.	I11	7
Derby, Ct., U.S.	D3	84
Derby, Ks., U.S.	E6	93
Derby, Vt., U.S.	B4	122
Derby Line, Vt., U.S.	A4	122
Derg, Lough, l., Ire.	I4	7
De Ridder, La., U.S.	D2	95
Derma, Ms., U.S.	B4	101
Dermott, Ar., U.S.	D4	81
Dernieres, Isles, is., La., U.S.	E5	95
Derry, N.H., U.S.	E4	106
Derry, Pa., U.S.	F3	115
Derval, Fr.	E5	10
Derventa, Bos.	E12	14
Derwood, Md., U.S.	B3	97
Desaguadero, stm., Arg.	C3	56
Des Allemands, La., U.S.	E5	95
Des Arc, Ar., U.S.	C4	81
Desbiens, Que., Can.	A6	74
Descartes, Fr.	F7	10
Deschaillons [-sur-Saint-Laurent], Que., Can.	C5	74
Deschambault, Que., Can.	C6	74
Deschambault Lake, l., Sask., Can.	C4	75
Deschutes, co., Or., U.S.	D5	114
Deschutes, stm., Or., U.S.	B6	114
Dese, Eth.	F2	46
Deseado, stm., Arg.	F3	56
Deseret Peak, mtn., Ut., U.S.	C3	121
Deseronto, Ont., Can.	C7	73
Desert Creek Peak, mtn., Nv., U.S.	E2	105
Desert Hot Springs, Ca., U.S.	F5	82
Desert Peak, mtn., Ut., U.S.	B2	121
Desert Valley, val., Nv., U.S.	B3	105
Desha, Ar., U.S.	B4	81
Desha, co., Ar., U.S.	D4	81
Deshler, Ne., U.S.	D8	104
Deshler, Oh., U.S.	A2	112
Des Lacs, stm., N.D., U.S.	A4	111
Desloge, Mo., U.S.	D7	102
De Smet, S.D., U.S.	C8	118
Des Moines, Ia., U.S.	C4	92
Des Moines, Wa., U.S.	B3	124
Des Moines, co., Ia., U.S.	D6	92
Des Moines, stm., U.S.	D5	92
Desolación, Isla, i., Chile	G2	56
De Soto, Il., U.S.	F4	90
De Soto, Ia., U.S.	C3	92
De Soto, Ks., U.S.	D9	93
De Soto, Mo., U.S.	C7	102
De Soto, co., Fl., U.S.	E5	86
De Soto, co., La., U.S.	B2	95
De Soto, co., Ms., U.S.	A3	101
Despard, W.V., U.S.	k10	125
Des Peres, Mo., U.S.	f13	102
Des Plaines, Il., U.S.	A6	90
Des Plaines, stm., U.S.	k8	90
Desroches, Île, i., Sey.	C10	44
Dessau, Ger.	D12	8
Destin, Fl., U.S.	u15	86
Destrehan, La., U.S.	E5	95
Desvres, Fr.	B8	10
Detmold, Ger.	D8	8
Detour, Point, c., Mi., U.S.	C4	99
Detroit, Mi., U.S.	F7	99
Detroit Lake, res., Or., U.S.	C4	114
Detroit Lakes, Mn., U.S.	D3	100
Deuel, co., Ne., U.S.	C3	104
Deuel, co., S.D., U.S.	C9	118
Deutsche Bucht, b., Ger.	A7	8
Deutschlandsberg, Aus.	I15	8
Deux-Montagnes, Que., Can.	p19	74
Deux Montagnes, Lac des, l., Que., Can.	q19	74
Deva, Rom.	D6	16
Devakottai, India	H5	37
De Valls Bluff, Ar., U.S.	C4	81
Deventer, Neth.	C6	8
DeView, Bayou, stm., Ar., U.S.	B4	81
Devil's Island see Diable, Île du, i., Fr. Gu.	B8	54
Devils Lake, N.D., U.S.	A7	111
Devils Lake, l., N.D., U.S.	A6	111
Devils Paw, mtn., Ak., U.S.	k23	79
Devils Postpile National Monument, Ca., U.S.	D4	82
Devils Tower National Monument, Wy., U.S.	B8	127
Devil Track Lake, l., Mn., U.S.	k9	100
Devine, Tx., U.S.	E3	120
DeVola, Oh., U.S.	C4	112
Devon, Alta., Can.	C4	68
Devon Island, i., N.W. Ter., Can.	A15	66
Devonport, Austl.	H9	50
Devonport, N.Z.	B5	52
Devonshire, De., U.S.	h7	85
Dewa-kyūryō, hills, Japan	C13	30
Dewar, Ok., U.S.	B6	113
Dewās, India	I7	38
Dewees Inlet, b., S.C., U.S.	k12	117
Dewees Island, i., S.C., U.S.	F8	117
Dewey, Az., U.S.	C3	80
Dewey, Ok., U.S.	A6	113
Dewey, co., Ok., U.S.	B2	113
Dewey, co., S.D., U.S.	B4	118
Dewey Beach, De., U.S.	F5	85
Dewey Lake, res., Ky., U.S.	C7	94
Deweyville, Tx., U.S.	D6	120
De Witt, Ar., U.S.	C4	81
De Witt, Ia., U.S.	C7	92
De Witt, Mi., U.S.	F6	99
De Witt, N.Y., U.S.	B4	109
De Witt, co., Il., U.S.	C4	90
De Witt, co., Tx., U.S.	E4	120
Dexter, Ia., U.S.	C3	92
Dexter, Me., U.S.	C3	96
Dexter, Mi., U.S.	F7	99
Dexter, Mo., U.S.	E8	102
Dexter, N.M., U.S.	D5	108
Dexter, Lake, l., Fl., U.S.	C5	86
Dezfūl, Iran	B4	46
Dezhou, China	D10	26
Dhaka, Bngl.	I14	38
Dhamār, Yemen	F3	46
Dhamtari, India	B6	37
Dhānbād, India	I12	38
Dhār, India	I6	38
Dharmapuri, India	F5	37
Dharmavaram, India	E4	37
Dhārwār, India	E3	37
Dhawlāgiri, mtn., Nepal	F10	38
Dhodhekánisos (Dodecanese), is., Grc.	M10	16
Dholpur, India	G7	38
Dhorāji, India	J4	38
Dhrol, India	I4	38
Dhubri, India	G13	38
Dhule, India	B3	37
Diable, Île du, i., Fr. Gu.	B8	54
Diablo, Canyon, val., Az., U.S.	C4	80
Diablo, Mount, mtn., Ca., U.S.	h9	82
Diablo Dam, Wa., U.S.	A4	124
Diablo Lake, res., Wa., U.S.	A4	124
Diablo Range, mts., Ca., U.S.	D3	82
Diamante, Arg.	C4	56
Diamantina, Braz.	E7	57
Diamantino, Braz.	F7	54
Diamond Head, crat., Hi., U.S.	B4	88
Diamond Hill, R.I., U.S.	B4	116
Diamond Hill Reservoir, res., R.I., U.S.	A4	116
Diamond Lake, Il., U.S.	h9	90
Diamond Lake, l., Or., U.S.	D4	114
Diamond Mountains, mts., Nv., U.S.	D6	105
Diamond Peak, mtn., Co., U.S.	A2	83
Diamond Peak, mtn., Id., U.S.	E5	89
Diamond Peak, mtn., Or., U.S.	D4	114
Diamond Peak, mtn., Wa., U.S.	C8	124
Diamondville, Wy., U.S.	E2	127
Diaz, Ar., U.S.	B4	81
Dibaya, Zaire	C4	44
D'Iberville, Ms., U.S.	E5	101
Diboll, Tx., U.S.	D5	120
Dibrugarh, India	G16	38
Dickens, co., Tx., U.S.	C2	120
Dickenson, co., Va., U.S.	e9	123
Dickerson, Md., U.S.	B3	97
Dickey, co., N.D., U.S.	C7	111
Dickeyville, Wi., U.S.	F3	126
Dickinson, N.D., U.S.	C3	111
Dickinson, co., Ia., U.S.	A2	92
Dickinson, co., Ks., U.S.	D6	93
Dickinson, co., Mi., U.S.	B3	99
Dickinson Dam, N.D., U.S.	C3	111
Dickson, Ok., U.S.	C5	113
Dickson, Tn., U.S.	A4	119
Dickson, co., Tn., U.S.	A4	119
Dickson City, Pa., U.S.	D10	115
Didsbury, Alta., Can.	D3	68
Die, Fr.	H12	10
Dieburg, Ger.	F8	8
Dieciocho de Marzo, Mex.	E11	62
Diefenbaker, Lake, res., Sask., Can.	F2	75
Diégo-Suarez see Antsiranana, Madag.	D9	44
Dien Bien Phu, Viet.	D7	34
Diepholz, Ger.	C8	8
Dieppe, N.B., Can.	C5	71
Dieppe, Fr.	C8	10
Dierks, Ar., U.S.	C1	81
Dieuze, Fr.	D13	10
Digboi, India	G16	38
Dighton, Ks., U.S.	D3	93
Digne, Fr.	H13	10
Digoin, Fr.	F10	10
Dijon, Fr.	E12	10
Dike, Ia., U.S.	B5	92
Dikson, Russia	C10	24
Dili, Indon.	G8	32
Dillard, Or., U.S.	D3	114
Dill City, Ok., U.S.	B2	113
Dilley, Tx., U.S.	E3	120
Dillingen [an der Donau], Ger.	G10	8
Dillingham, Ak., U.S.	D8	79
Dillon, Mt., U.S.	E4	103
Dillon, S.C., U.S.	C9	117
Dillon, co., S.C., U.S.	C9	117
Dillon Lake, res., Oh., U.S.	B3	112
Dillon Reservoir, res., Co., U.S.	B4	83
Dillonvale, Oh., U.S.	B5	112
Dillsboro, In., U.S.	F7	91
Dillsburg, Pa., U.S.	F7	115
Dilolo, Zaire	D4	44
Dilworth, Mn., U.S.	D2	100
Dimāpur, India	H15	38
Dimashq (Damascus), Syria	C5	40
Dimitrovgrad, Bul.	G9	16
Dimitrovgrad, Russia	G7	22
Dimmit, co., Tx., U.S.	E3	120
Dimmitt, Tx., U.S.	B1	120
Dimona, Isr.	D4	40
Dimondale, Mi., U.S.	F6	99
Dinagat Island, i., Phil.	C8	32
Dinājpur, Bngl.	H13	38
Dinan, Fr.	D4	10
Dinant, Bel.	E4	8
Dinara, mts., Eur.	F11	14
Dinard, Fr.	D4	10
Dinaric Alps see Dinara, mts., Eur.	F11	14
Dindigul, India	G4	37
Dinghai, China	E11	28
Dingle, Ire.	I2	7
Dingmans Ferry, Pa., U.S.	D12	115
Dingolfing, Ger.	G12	8
Dingqing, China	E16	38
Dingri, China	F12	38
Dingshan, China	D8	28
Dingwall, Scot., U.K.	D8	7
Dinh Lap, Viet.	D9	34
Dinner Point, c., Fl., U.S.	D4	86
Dinosaur National Monument, U.S.	C6	121
Dinuba, Ca., U.S.	D4	82
Dinwiddie, co., Va., U.S.	C5	123
Diourbel, Sen.	F2	42
Dipkarpaz, N. Cyp.	B4	40
Dipolog, Phil.	D7	32
Dire Dawa, Eth.	G3	46
Diriamba, Nic.	I4	64
Dirico, Ang.	E4	44
Dirk Hartog Island, i., Austl.	E2	50
Dirty Devil, stm., Ut., U.S.	E5	121
Disappointment, Cape, c., Falk. Is.	G9	56
Disappointment, Cape, c., Wa., U.S.	C1	124
Disappointment, Lake, l., Austl.	D4	50
Disentis, Switz.	F15	10
Dishman, Wa., U.S.	g14	124
Disko, i., Grnld.	C22	66
Disko Bugt, b., Grnld.	C22	66
Dismal, stm., Ne., U.S.	C5	104
Disraëli, Que., Can.	D6	74
District of Columbia, dept., U.S.	f8	97
Diu, India	J4	38
Diu, ter., India	J4	38
Divernon, Il., U.S.	D4	90
Divide, co., N.D., U.S.	A2	111
Divide Peak, mtn., Wy., U.S.	E5	127
Divinópolis, Braz.	F6	57
Divisor, Serra do, plat., S.A.	E4	54
Dix, stm., Ky., U.S.	C5	94
Dixfield, Me., U.S.	D2	96
Dixie, co., Fl., U.S.	C3	86
Dixie Valley, val., Nv., U.S.	D4	105
Dixon, Ca., U.S.	C3	82
Dixon, Il., U.S.	B4	90
Dixon, Mo., U.S.	D5	102
Dixon, N.M., U.S.	A4	108
Dixon, co., Ne., U.S.	B9	104
Dixon Entrance, strt., N.A.	F6	66
Dixonville, Pa., U.S.	E3	115
Diyarbakır, Tur.	H16	4
Dja, stm., Afr.	H8	42
Djakarta see Jakarta, Indon.	m13	32
Djambala, Congo	B2	44
Djanet, Alg.	D7	42
Djebel Abiod, Tun.	M4	14
Djebibina, Tun.	M5	14
Djemmal, Tun.	N5	14
Djerba, Île de, i., Tun.	B8	42
Djerid, Chott, sw., Tun.	B7	42
Djibouti, Dji.	F3	46
Djibouti, ctry., Afr.	F3	46
Dmitrija Lapteva, Proliv, strt., Russia	C22	24
Dmitrov, Russia	E20	18
Dnieper, stm., Eur.	H4	22
Dniester, stm., Eur.	H3	22

Name Map Ref Page

Dniprodzerzhyns'k, Ukr. H4 22
Dnipropetrovs'k, Ukr. H4 22
Dno, Russia D12 18
Do Āb-e Mīkh-e Zarrīn, Afg. C2 38
Doaktown, N.B., Can. C3 71
Doany, Madag. D9 44
Doba, Chad E9 42
Dobbiaco, Italy C7 14
Dobbs Ferry, N.Y., U.S. g13 109
Döbeln, Ger. D13 8
Doberai, Jazirah, pen., Indon. F9 32
Dobo, Indon. G9 32
Doboj, Bos. E2 16
Dobrič, Bul. F11 16
Dobruš, Bela. I14 18
Dobson, N.C., U.S. A2 110
Doce, stm., Braz. E8 57
Docena, Al., U.S. f7 78
Dock Junction, Ga., U.S. *E5 87
Doctors Lake, l., Fl., U.S. m8 86
Doddridge, co., W.V., U.S. B4 125
Dodecanese see Dhodhekánisos, is., Grc. M10 16
Dodge, Ne., U.S. C9 104
Dodge, co., Ga., U.S. D3 87
Dodge, co., Mn., U.S. G6 100
Dodge, co., Ne., U.S. C9 104
Dodge, co., Wi., U.S. E5 126
Dodge Center, Mn., U.S. F6 100
Dodge City, Ks., U.S. E3 93
Dodgeville, Wi., U.S. F3 126
Dodoma, Tan. C7 44
Doerun, Ga., U.S. E3 87
Doe Run, Mo., U.S. D7 102
Doetinchem, Neth. D6 8
Dog, stm., Vt., U.S. C3 122
Dogai Coring, l., China C13 38
Dog Island, i., Fl., U.S. C2 86
Dog Keys Pass, strt., Ms., U.S. g8 101
Dog Lake, l., Man., Can. D2 70
Dogondoutchi, Niger F6 42
Doha see Ad-Dawḥah, Qatar C5 46
Dohad, India I6 38
Doiran, Lake, l., Eur. H6 16
Dokka, Nor. F8 6
Dokkum, Neth. B5 8
Dolak, Pulau, i., Indon. G10 32
Dolbeau, Que., Can. k12 74
Dol-de-Bretagne, Fr. D5 10
Dolgeville, N.Y., U.S. B6 109
Dolianova, Italy J4 14
Dolisie, Congo B2 44
Dollar Bay, Mi., U.S. A2 99
Dolo, Som. H3 46
Dolomite, Al., U.S. B3 78
Dolomites see Dolomiti, mts., Italy C6 14
Dolomiti, mts., Italy C6 14
Dolores, Arg. D5 56
Dolores, Col. F5 58
Dolores, Co., U.S. D2 83
Dolores, co., Co., U.S. D2 83
Dolores, stm., U.S. E7 121
Dolores Hidalgo, Mex. G9 62
Dolphin and Union Strait, strt., N.W. Ter., Can. C9 66
Dolphin Island, i., Ut., U.S. B3 121
Dolton, Il., U.S. k9 90
Dombås, Nor. E7 6
Dome Mountain, mtn., Az., U.S. k9 80
Dome Peak, mtn., Co., U.S. B3 83
Domeyko, Chile B2 56
Domeyko, Cordillera, mts., Chile A3 56
Domfront, Fr. D6 10
Dominica, ctry., N.A. G17 64
Dominica Channel, strt., N.A. G17 64
Dominican Republic, ctry., N.A. E12 64
Dominion, Cape, c., N.W. Ter., Can. C18 66
Domodedovo, Russia F20 18
Domodossola, Italy C3 14
Domžale, Slo. C9 14
Don, stm., Russia H6 22
Dona Ana, N.M., U.S. E3 108
Dona Ana, co., N.M., U.S. E2 108
Donaldsonville, La., U.S. D4 95
Donalsonville, Ga., U.S. E2 87
Donaueschingen, Ger. H8 8
Donauwörth, Ger. G10 8
Don Benito, Spain G6 12
Doncaster, Eng., U.K. H11 7
Dondo, Ang. C2 44
Dondra Head, c., Sri L. J6 37
Donegal Bay, b., Ire. G4 7
Doneraile, S.C., U.S. C8 117
Donetsk, Ukr. H5 22
Donga, stm., Nig. G8 42
Dongara, Austl. E2 50
Dongchuan, China A7 34
Dongfang, China H8 26
Dongfang (Basuo), China E10 34
Dongguan, China L2 28
Donghai Dao, i., China D11 34
Dong Hoi, Viet. F9 34
Dongshan, China L6 28
Dongtai, China C9 28
Dongting Hu, l., China F1 28
Doniphan, Mo., U.S. E7 102
Doniphan, Ne., U.S. D7 104
Doniphan, co., Ks., U.S. C8 93
Donkey Creek, stm., Wy., U.S. B7 127
Donkin, N.S., Can. C10 71
Donley, co., Tx., U.S. B2 120
Donna, Tx., U.S. F3 120
Donnacona, Que., Can. C6 74
Donnellson, Ia., U.S. D6 92
Donner Pass, Ca., U.S. C3 82
Donora, Pa., U.S. F2 115
Donskoj, Russia H21 18
Dooly, co., Ga., U.S. D3 87
Doonerak, Mount, mtn., Ak., U.S. B9 79
Door, co., Wi., U.S. D6 126
Dora, Al., U.S. B2 78
Doraville, Ga., U.S. h8 87
Dorcheat, Bayou, stm., U.S. B2 95
Dorchester, N.B., Can. D5 71
Dorchester, Eng., U.K. K10 7
Dorchester, Ne., U.S. D8 104
Dorchester, co., Md., U.S. D5 97
Dorchester, co., S.C., U.S. E7 117
Dorchester, Cape, c., N.W. Ter., Can. C17 66
Dordogne, stm., Fr. H8 10
Dordrecht, Neth. D4 8
Doré Lake, l., Sask., Can. C2 75
Dorena Lake, res., Or., U.S. D3 114
Dores do Indaiá, Braz. E6 57
Dorgali, Italy I4 14
Dori, Burkina F5 42
Dorion-Vaudreuil, Que., Can. q18 74
Dormont, Pa., U.S. k13 115
Dornbirn, Aus. H9 8
Dorothy Pond, Ma., U.S. B4 98
Dorr, Mi., U.S. F5 99
Dorset, Vt., U.S. E2 122
Dorsey, Md., U.S. B4 97
Dortmund, Ger. D7 8
Dorton, Ky., U.S. C7 94
Dorval, Que., Can. q19 74
Dos Bahías, Cabo, c., Arg. E3 56
Dothan, Al., U.S. D4 78
Douai, Fr. B10 10
Douala, Cam. H7 42
Douarnenez, Fr. D2 10
Double Beach, Ct., U.S. D4 84
Doublespring Pass, Id., U.S. E5 89
Double Springs, Al., U.S. A2 78
Doubletop Peak, mtn., Wy., U.S. C2 127
Doubs, stm., Eur. E12 10
Dougherty, co., Ga., U.S. E2 87
Douglas, I. of Man G8 7
Douglas, Az., U.S. F6 80
Douglas, Ga., U.S. E4 87
Douglas, Mi., U.S. F4 99
Douglas, Wy., U.S. D7 127
Douglas, co., Co., U.S. B6 83
Douglas, co., Ga., U.S. C2 87
Douglas, co., Il., U.S. D5 90
Douglas, co., Ks., U.S. D8 93
Douglas, co., Mn., U.S. E3 100
Douglas, co., Mo., U.S. E5 102
Douglas, co., Ne., U.S. C9 104
Douglas, co., Nv., U.S. E2 105
Douglas, co., Or., U.S. D3 114
Douglas, co., S.D., U.S. D7 118
Douglas, co., Wa., U.S. B6 124
Douglas, co., Wi., U.S. B2 126
Douglas, Mount, mtn., Ak., U.S. D9 79
Douglas Channel, strt., B.C., Can. C3 69
Douglas Lake, l., Mi., U.S. C6 99
Douglas Lake, res., Tn., U.S. D10 119
Douglass, Ks., U.S. E7 93
Douglastown, N.B., Can. B4 71
Douglasville, Ga., U.S. C2 87
Dourada, Serra, plat., Braz. B4 57
Dourados, Braz. G1 57
Douro (Duero), stm., Eur. D4 12
Dousman, Wi., U.S. E5 126
Dove Creek, Co., U.S. D2 83
Dover, Eng., U.K. J14 7
Dover, Ar., U.S. B2 81
Dover, De., U.S. D3 85
Dover, Fl., U.S. D4 86
Dover, Ma., U.S. h10 98
Dover, N.H., U.S. D5 106
Dover, N.J., U.S. B3 107
Dover, Oh., U.S. B4 112
Dover, Pa., U.S. F8 115
Dover, Tn., U.S. A4 119
Dover, Strait of (Pas de Calais), strt., Eur. J14 7
Dover Air Force Base, mil., De., U.S. D4 85
Dover-Foxcroft, Me., U.S. C3 96
Dover Plains, N.Y., U.S. D7 109
Dowagiac, Mi., U.S. G4 99
Dowlat Yār, Afg. C1 38
Downers Grove, Il., U.S. B5 90
Downey, Ca., U.S. n12 82
Downey, Id., U.S. G6 89
Downingtown, Pa., U.S. F10 115
Downpatrick, N. Ire., U.K. G7 7
Downpatrick Head, c., Ire. G3 7
Downs, Ks., U.S. C5 93
Downs Mountain, mtn., Wy., U.S. C3 127
Downton, Mount, mtn., B.C., Can. C5 69
Dows, Ia., U.S. B4 92
Dowshī, Afg. C3 38
Doylestown, Oh., U.S. B4 112
Doylestown, Pa., U.S. F11 115
Doyline, La., U.S. B2 95
Drâa, Oued, val., Afr. C4 42
Dracena, Braz. F3 57
Drachten, Neth. B6 8
Dracut, Ma., U.S. A5 98
Draguignan, Fr. I13 10
Drain, Or., U.S. D3 114
Drake Passage, strt. D6 47
Drake Peak, mtn., Or., U.S. E6 114
Dráma, Grc. H8 16
Drammen, Nor. G8 6
Draper, Ut., U.S. C4 121
Drau (Drava), stm., Eur. C8 14
Drava (Drau), stm., Eur. D13 14
Drayton, Ont., Can. D4 73
Drayton, N.D., U.S. A8 111
Drayton, S.C., U.S. B4 117
Drayton Plains, Mi., U.S. F7 99
Drayton Valley, Alta., Can. C3 68
Dresden, Ont., Can. E2 73
Dresden, Ger. D13 8
Dresden, Oh., U.S. B3 112
Dresden, Tn., U.S. A3 119
Dresslerville, Nv., U.S. E2 105
Dreux, Fr. D8 10
Drew, Ms., U.S. B3 101
Drew, co., Ar., U.S. D4 81
Drews Reservoir, res., Or., U.S. E6 114
Drexel, Mo., U.S. C3 102
Drexel, N.C., U.S. B1 110
Drexel, Oh., U.S. C1 112
Drift, Ky., U.S. C7 94
Driggs, Id., U.S. F7 89
Driskill Mountain, hill, La., U.S. B3 95
Drogheda, Ire. H6 7
Drumheller, Alta., Can. D4 68
Drum Island, i., S.C., U.S. k12 117
Drummond, Lake, l., Va., U.S. D6 123
Drummond Island, i., Mi., U.S. C7 99
Drummondville, Que., Can. D5 74
Drumright, Ok., U.S. B5 113
Družina, Russia D23 24
Drybranch, W.V., U.S. m13 125
Dry Cimarron, stm., U.S. A6 108
Dry Creek Mountain, mtn., Nv., U.S. B5 105
Dryden, Ont., Can. o16 73
Dryden, N.Y., U.S. C4 109
Dry Fork, stm., Mo., U.S. D6 102
Dry Fork, stm., W.V., U.S. D3 125
Dry Fork, stm., W.V., U.S. B5 125
Dry Ridge, Ky., U.S. B5 94
Dry Tortugas, is., Fl., U.S. H5 86
Duarte, Pico, mtn., Dom. Rep. E12 64
Dubach, La., U.S. B3 95
Dubai see Dubayy, U.A.E. C6 46
Dubawnt, stm., N.W. Ter., Can. D12 66
Dubawnt Lake, l., N.W. Ter., Can. D12 66
Du Bay, Lake, res., Wi., U.S. D4 126
Dubayy (Dubai), U.A.E. C6 46
Dubbo, Austl. F9 50
Dublin (Baile Átha Cliath), Ire. H6 7
Dublin, Ga., U.S. D4 87
Dublin, In., U.S. E7 91
Dublin, N.H., U.S. E2 106
Dublin, Oh., U.S. k10 112
Dublin, Pa., U.S. F11 115
Dublin, Tx., U.S. C3 120
Dublin, Va., U.S. C2 123
Dubna, Russia E20 18
Dubois, In., U.S. H4 91
Du Bois, Pa., U.S. D4 115
Dubois, Wy., U.S. C3 127
Dubois, co., In., U.S. H4 91
Duboistown, Pa., U.S. D7 115
Dubrovnik, Cro. G13 14
Dubuque, Ia., U.S. B7 92
Dubuque, co., Ia., U.S. B7 92
Duchesne, Ut., U.S. C5 121
Duchesne, co., Ut., U.S. C5 121
Duchesne, stm., Ut., U.S. C5 121
Duchess, Austl. D7 50
Duck, stm., Tn., U.S. B4 119
Duck Bay, Man., Can. C1 70
Duck Creek, stm., Oh., U.S. C4 112
Duck Creek, stm., Wi., U.S. h9 126
Duck Lake, Sask., Can. E2 75
Duck Lake, l., Me., U.S. C4 96
Duck Mountain Provincial Park, Sask., Can. F5 75
Duck Valley Indian Reservation, U.S. B5 105
Duckwater Indian Reservation, Nv., U.S. E6 105
Duckwater Peak, mtn., Nv., U.S. E6 105
Dudelange, Lux. F6 8
Dudinka, Russia D11 24
Dudley, Ma., U.S. B4 98
Duenweg, Mo., U.S. D3 102
Duero (Douro), stm., Eur. D5 12
Due West, S.C., U.S. C3 117
Duffer Peak, mtn., Nv., U.S. B3 105
Dufour Spitze, mtn., Eur. G14 10
Duga Resa, Cro. D10 14
Dugdemona, stm., La., U.S. B3 95
Dugger, In., U.S. F3 91
Duida, Cerro, mtn., Ven. F10 58
Duifken Point, c., Austl. B8 50
Duisburg, Ger. D6 8
Duke Island, i., Ak., U.S. n24 79
Dukes, co., Ma., U.S. D6 98
Duk Fadiat, Sudan G12 42
Dulce, N.M., U.S. A2 108
Dulgalach, stm., Russia D20 24
Duluth, Ga., U.S. B2 87
Duluth, Mn., U.S. D6 100
Dūmā, Syria C5 40
Dumaguete, Phil. D7 32
Dumaran Island, i., Phil. C6 32
Dumaring, Indon. E6 32
Dumas, Ar., U.S. D4 81
Dumas, Tx., U.S. B2 120
Dumbarton, Scot., U.K. F8 7
Dumfries, Scot., U.K. F9 7
Dumfries, Va., U.S. B5 123
Dumont, Ia., U.S. B5 92
Dumont, N.J., U.S. B5 107
Dumyāṭ, Egypt B12 42
Dunaújváros, Hung. I18 8
Dunbar, Pa., U.S. G2 115
Dunbar, W.V., U.S. C3 125
Duncan, B.C., Can. E6 69
Duncan, Az., U.S. E6 80
Duncan, Ok., U.S. C4 113
Duncan, S.C., U.S. B3 117
Duncan Falls, Oh., U.S. C4 112
Duncan Lake, res., B.C., Can. D9 69
Duncannon, Pa., U.S. F7 115
Duncansville, Pa., U.S. F5 115
Duncanville, Tx., U.S. n10 120
Dundalk, Ont., Can. C4 73
Dundalk, Ire. G6 7
Dundalk, Md., U.S. B4 97
Dundas, Ont., Can. D5 73
Dundas Peninsula, pen., N.W. Ter., Can. B10 66
Dundee, S. Afr. G6 44
Dundee, Scot., U.K. E9 7
Dundee, Fl., U.S. D5 86
Dundee, Il., U.S. A5 90
Dundee, Mi., U.S. G7 99
Dundee, N.Y., U.S. C4 109
Dundee, Or., U.S. h11 114
Dundy, co., Ne., U.S. D4 104
Dunedin, N.Z. F3 52
Dunedin, Fl., U.S. D4 86
Dunellen, N.J., U.S. B4 107
Dunfermline, Scot., U.K. E9 7
Dungarvan, Ire. I5 7
Dungeness, stm., Wa., U.S. A2 124
Dungun, Malay. L7 34
Dunham, Que., Can. D5 74
Dunhua, China C12 26
Dunhuang, China C5 26
Dunkard Creek, stm., U.S. B4 125
Dunkerque, Fr. A9 10
Dunkerton, Ia., U.S. B5 92
Dunkirk, In., U.S. D7 91
Dunkirk, N.Y., U.S. C1 109
Dunkirk, Oh., U.S. B2 112
Dunklin, co., Mo., U.S. E7 102
Dunkwa, Ghana G5 42
Dún Laoghaire, Ire. H6 7
Dunlap, Il., U.S. C4 90
Dunlap, In., U.S. A6 91
Dunlap, Ia., U.S. C2 92
Dunlap, Tn., U.S. D8 119
Dunleith, De., U.S. i7 85
Dunloup Creek, stm., W.V., U.S. n13 125
Dunmore, Pa., U.S. D10 115
Dunmore, Lake, l., Vt., U.S. D2 122
Dunn, N.C., U.S. B4 110
Dunn, co., N.D., U.S. B3 111
Dunn, co., Wi., U.S. D2 126
Dunnellon, Fl., U.S. C4 86
Dunnville, Ont., Can. E5 73
Dunqulah, Sudan E12 42
Duns, Scot., U.K. F10 7
Dunseith, N.D., U.S. A5 111
Dunsmuir, Ca., U.S. B2 82
Duntou, China F8 28
Dunville, Newf., Can. E5 72
Dunwoody, Ga., U.S. h8 87
Duomaer, China E2 26
Du Page, co., Il., U.S. B5 90
Du Page, stm., Il., U.S. k8 90
Duplin, co., N.C., U.S. C5 110
Dupont, Co., U.S. B6 83
Dupont, Pa., U.S. n18 115
Dupont City, W.V., U.S. m12 125
Dupont Manor, De., U.S. B1 41
Dupont Manor, De., U.S. D3 85
Duque de Caxias, Braz. G7 57
Duque de York, Isla, i., Chile G1 56
Duquesne, Pa., U.S. F2 115
Du Quoin, Il., U.S. E4 90
Durand, Il., U.S. A4 90
Durand, Mi., U.S. F6 99
Durand, Wi., U.S. D2 126
Durango, Mex. E7 62
Durango, Spain B9 12
Durango, Co., U.S. D3 83
Durant, Ia., U.S. C7 92
Durant, Ms., U.S. B4 101
Durant, Ok., U.S. D5 113
Durazno, Ur. C5 56
Durban, S. Afr. G6 44
Đurđevac, Cro. C12 14
Düren, Ger. E6 8
Durg, India B6 37
Durgāpur, India I12 38
Durham, Ont., Can. C4 73
Durham, Eng., U.K. G11 7
Durham, Ca., U.S. C3 82
Durham, Ct., U.S. D5 84
Durham, N.H., U.S. D5 106
Durham, N.C., U.S. B4 110
Durham, co., N.C., U.S. A4 110
Durness, Scot., U.K. C8 7
Durrell, Newf., Can. D4 72
Durrës, Alb. H3 16
Dursunbey, Tur. J12 16
D'Urville, Tanjung, c., Indon. F10 32
Duryea, Pa., U.S. D10 115
Dušanbe, Taj. J11 22
Dušekan, Russia E15 24
Dushan, China B9 34
Dushanbe see Dušanbe, Taj. J11 22
Duson, La., U.S. D3 95
Düsseldorf, Ger. D6 8
Dutchess, co., N.Y., U.S. D7 109
Dutch Island, i., R.I., U.S. F4 116
Dutton, Ont., Can. E3 73
Dutton, Mount, mtn., Ut., U.S. E3 121
Duval, co., Fl., U.S. B5 86
Duval, co., Tx., U.S. F3 120
Duxbury, Ma., U.S. B6 98
Duyun, China A9 34
Dwight, Il., U.S. B5 90
Dwight D. Eisenhower Lock, N.Y., U.S. f9 109
Dworshak Reservoir, res., Id., U.S. C3 89
Dyer, In., U.S. A2 91
Dyer, Tn., U.S. A3 119
Dyer, co., Tn., U.S. A2 119
Dyer, Cape, c., N.W. Ter., Can. C20 66
Dyer Island, i., R.I., U.S. E5 116
Dyersburg, Tn., U.S. A2 119
Dyersville, Ia., U.S. B6 92
Dyess Air Force Base, mil., Tx., U.S. C3 120
Dysart, Ia., U.S. B5 92
Džalinda, Russia G18 24
Džambul, Kaz. I12 22
Dzaoudzi, May. D9 44
Džardžan, Russia D18 24
Dzavchan, stm., Mong. B5 26
Dzeržinsk, Russia E26 18
Dzeržinskoje, Kaz. H10 24
Džezkazgan, Kaz. H11 22
Dzhambul see Džambul, Kaz. I12 22
Dzierżoniów (Reichenbach), Pol. E16 8
Džugdžur, Chrebet, mts., Russia F21 24

E

Eads, Co., U.S. C8 83
Eagan, Mn., U.S. n12 100
Eagar, Az., U.S. C6 80
Eagle, Co., U.S. B4 83
Eagle, Id., U.S. F2 89
Eagle, Ne., U.S. h12 104
Eagle, Wi., U.S. F5 126
Eagle, co., Co., U.S. B4 83
Eagle, stm., Newf., Can. B2 72
Eagle Creek Reservoir, res., In., U.S. E5 91
Eagle Grove, Ia., U.S. B4 92
Eagle Key, i., Fl., U.S. G6 86
Eagle Lake, Me., U.S. A4 96
Eagle Lake, Mn., U.S. F5 100
Eagle Lake, Tx., U.S. E4 120
Eagle Lake, l., Ca., U.S. B3 82
Eagle Lake, l., Me., U.S. A4 96
Eagle Lake, l., Me., U.S. B3 96
Eagle Lake, l., Ms., U.S. C3 101
Eagle Lake, l., Wi., U.S. C4 126
Eagle Mountain, mtn., Mn., U.S. k9 100
Eagle Mountain Lake, res., Tx., U.S. m9 120
Eagle Nest Lake, l., N.M., U.S. A4 108
Eagle Pass, Tx., U.S. E2 120
Eagle Peak, mtn., Ca., U.S. B3 82
Eagle Point, Or., U.S. E4 114
Eagle River, Wi., U.S. C4 126
Eagletail Mountains, mts., Az., U.S. D2 80
Eagletail Peak, mtn., Az., U.S. D2 80
Eagletown, Ok., U.S. C7 113
Earle, Ar., U.S. B5 81
Earlham, Ia., U.S. C3 92
Earlimart, Ca., U.S. E4 82
Earlington, Ky., U.S. C2 94
Earlville, Il., U.S. B5 90
Earlville, Ia., U.S. B6 92
Early, Ia., U.S. B2 92
Early, co., Ga., U.S. E2 87
Earth, Tx., U.S. B1 120
Easley, S.C., U.S. B2 117
East, stm., Ct., U.S. D5 84
East, stm., N.Y., U.S. k13 109
East, stm., Wi., U.S. h9 126
East Alton, Il., U.S. E3 90
East Angus, Que., Can. D6 74
East Arlington, Vt., U.S. E2 122
East Aurora, N.Y., U.S. C2 109
East Bangor, Pa., U.S. E11 115
East Bank, W.V., U.S. m13 125
East Barre, Vt., U.S. C4 122
East Baton Rouge, co., La., U.S. D4 95
East Bay, b., Fl., U.S. u16 86
East Bay, b., Tx., U.S. R15 120
East Beckwith Mountain, mtn., Co., U.S. C3 83
East Berlin, Ct., U.S. C5 84
East Berlin, Pa., U.S. G8 115
East Bernard, Tx., U.S. E4 120
East Bernstadt, Ky., U.S. C5 94
East Bethel, Mn., U.S. E5 100
East Billerica, Ma., U.S. f11 98
Eastborough, Ks., U.S. g12 93
Eastbourne, Eng., U.K. K13 7
East Brady, Pa., U.S. E2 115
East Branch Clarion River Lake, res., Pa., U.S. C4 115
East Brewton, Al., U.S. D2 78
East Bridgewater, Ma., U.S. B6 98
East Brimfield Lake, res., Ma., U.S. B3 98
East Brooklyn, Ct., U.S. B8 84
East Broughton, Que., Can. C6 74
East Brunswick, N.J., U.S. C4 107
East Butte, mtn., Mt., U.S. B5 103
East Cache Creek, stm., Ok., U.S. C3 113
East Cape, c., Fl., U.S. G5 86
East Carbon, Ut., U.S. D5 121
East Carroll, co., La., U.S. B4 95
East Chicago, In., U.S. A3 91
East China Sea, Asia E12 26
East Chop, c., Ma., U.S. D6 98
East Cleveland, Oh., U.S. g9 112
East Cote Blanche Bay, b., La., U.S. E4 95
East Dennis, Ma., U.S. C7 98
East Derry, N.H., U.S. E4 106
East Detroit, Mi., U.S. p16 99
East Douglas, Ma., U.S. B4 98
East Dubuque, Il., U.S. A3 90
Eastend, Sask., Can. H1 75
Easter Island see Pascua, Isla de, i., Chile H5 2
Eastern Bay, b., Md., U.S. C5 97
Eastern Channel see Tsushima-kaikyō, strt., Japan I2 30
Eastern Ghāts, mts., India F5 37
Eastern Neck Island, i., Md., U.S. B5 97
Eastern Point, c., Ma., U.S. f13 98
Easterville, Man., Can. C2 70
East Falkland, i., Falk. Is. G5 56
East Falmouth, Ma., U.S. C6 98
East Feliciana, co., La., U.S. D4 95
East Flat Rock, N.C., U.S. f10 110
East Fork, stm., Wy., U.S. D3 127
East Fork Lake, res., Oh., U.S. C1 112
East Gaffney, S.C., U.S. A4 117
East Galesburg, Il., U.S. C3 90
East Granby, Ct., U.S. B5 84
East Grand Forks, Mn., U.S. C2 100
East Grand Rapids, Mi., U.S. F5 99
East Greenville, Pa., U.S. F10 115
East Greenwich, R.I., U.S. D4 116
East Gwillimbury, Ont., Can. C5 73
East Hampstead, N.H., U.S. E4 106
East Hampton, Ct., U.S. C5 84
Easthampton, Ma., U.S. B2 98
East Hanover, N.J., U.S. *B4 107
East Hartford, Ct., U.S. B5 84
East Hartland, Ct., U.S. B4 84
East Haven, Ct., U.S. D4 84
East Helena, Mt., U.S. D5 103
East Jordan, Mi., U.S. C5 99
Eastlake, Oh., U.S. A4 112
East Lake Tohopekaliga, l., Fl., U.S. D5 86
Eastland, Tx., U.S. C3 120
Eastland, co., Tx., U.S. C3 120
East Lansing, Mi., U.S. F6 99
East Las Vegas, Nv., U.S. G6 105
East Liverpool, Oh., U.S. B5 112
East London (Oos-Londen), S. Afr. H5 44
East Longmeadow, Ma., U.S. B2 98
East Los Angeles, Ca., U.S. m12 82
East Lyme, Ct., U.S. D7 84
East Lynn Lake, res., W.V., U.S. C2 125
Eastmain, stm., Que., Can. F17 66
Eastmain-Opinaca, Réservoir, res., Que., Can. h11 74
Eastman, Que., Can. D5 74
Eastman, Ga., U.S. D3 87

Name	Map Ref	Page
East Matunuck, R.I., U.S.	F3	116
East Middlebury, Vt., U.S.	D2	122
East Millinocket, Me., U.S.	C4	96
East Moline, Il., U.S.	B3	90
East Montpelier, Vt., U.S.	C4	122
East Naples, Fl., U.S.	F5	86
East Newnan, Ga., U.S.	C2	87
East Nishnabotna, stm., Ia., U.S.	C2	92
East Norriton, Pa., U.S.	o20	115
East Olympia, Wa., U.S.	C3	124
Easton, Md., U.S.	C5	97
Easton, Pa., U.S.	E11	115
Easton Reservoir, res., Ct., U.S.	E2	84
East Orange, N.J., U.S.	B4	107
East Orleans, Ma., U.S.	C8	98
Eastover, S.C., U.S.	D6	117
East Palatka, Fl., U.S.	C5	86
East Palestine, Oh., U.S.	B5	112
East Pass, strt., Fl., U.S.	C2	86
East Pea Ridge, W.V., U.S.	C2	125
East Peoria, Il., U.S.	C4	90
East Pepperell, Ma., U.S.	A4	98
East Petersburg, Pa., U.S.	F9	115
East Pittsburgh, Pa., U.S.	k14	115
Eastpoint, Fl., U.S.	C2	86
East Point, Ga., U.S.	C2	87
East Point, c., P.E.I., Can.	C8	71
East Point, c., Ma., U.S.	B6	98
East Point, c., N.J., U.S.	E2	107
Eastport, Newf., Can.	D5	72
Eastport, Me., U.S.	D6	96
East Prairie, Mo., U.S.	E8	102
East Providence, R.I., U.S.	C4	116
East Pryor Mountain, mtn., Mt., U.S.	E8	103
East Quogue, N.Y., U.S.	n16	109
East Range, mts., Nv., U.S.	C4	105
East Ridge, Tn., U.S.	h11	119
East River, Ct., U.S.	D5	84
East Rochester, N.Y., U.S.	B3	109
East Rockingham, N.C., U.S.	C3	110
East Rutherford, N.J., U.S.	h8	107
East Saint Louis, Il., U.S.	E3	90
East Selkirk, Man., Can.	D3	70
Eastsound, Wa., U.S.	A3	124
East Spencer, N.C., U.S.	B2	110
East Stroudsburg, Pa., U.S.	D11	115
East Tawas, Mi., U.S.	D7	99
East Troy, Wi., U.S.	F5	126
East Vestal, N.Y., U.S.	C4	109
East View, W.V., U.S.	k10	125
East Walker, stm., U.S.	E2	105
East Walpole, Ma., U.S.	h11	98
East Wareham, Ma., U.S.	C6	98
East Washington, Pa., U.S.	F1	115
East Wenatchee, Wa., U.S.	B5	124
East Windsor, N.J., U.S.	C3	107
East York, Ont., Can.	D5	73
Eaton, Co., U.S.	A6	83
Eaton, In., U.S.	D7	91
Eaton, Oh., U.S.	C1	112
Eaton, co., Mi., U.S.	F6	99
Eaton Rapids, Mi., U.S.	F6	99
Eatonton, Ga., U.S.	C3	87
Eatontown, N.J., U.S.	C4	107
Eatonville, Wa., U.S.	C3	124
Eau Claire, Wi., U.S.	D2	126
Eau Claire, co., Wi., U.S.	D2	126
Eau Claire, stm., Wi., U.S.	D2	126
Eau Claire, Lac à l', l., Que., Can.	g11	74
Eauze, Fr.	I7	10
Ebano, Mex.	F10	62
Ebba Ksour, Tun.	N3	14
Ebbw Vale, Wales, U.K.	J9	7
Ebensburg, Pa., U.S.	F4	115
Eberndorf, Aus.	I14	8
Eberswalde, Ger.	C13	8
Ebetsu, Japan	p19	30a
Ebingen, Ger.	G9	8
Ebinur Hu, l., China	B3	26
Eboli, Italy	I10	14
Ebolowa, Cam.	H8	42
Ebro, stm., Spain	E12	12
Ebro, Delta del, Spain	E12	12
Eccles, W.V., U.S.	n13	125
Echo Bay, Nv., U.S.	G7	105
Echo Lake, l., Me., U.S.	D3	96
Echo Lake, l., Vt., U.S.	B5	122
Echols, co., Ga., U.S.	F4	87
Écija, Spain	H6	12
Eckernförde, Ger.	A9	8
Eckhart Mines, Md., U.S.	k13	97
Eckville, Alta., Can.	C3	68
Eclectic, Al., U.S.	C3	78
Eclipse Sound, strt., N.W. Ter., Can.	B17	66
Écommoy, Fr.	E7	10
Econfina, stm., Fl., U.S.	B3	86
Economy, Pa., U.S.	*h13	115
Écorces, Rivière aux, stm., Que., Can.	A6	74
Ecorse, Mi., U.S.	p15	99
Ecru, Ms., U.S.	A4	101
Ector, co., Tx., U.S.	D1	120
Ecuador, ctry., S.A.	D3	54
Ed, Swe.	G8	6
Edcouch, Tx., U.S.	F4	120
Eddy, co., N.M., U.S.	E5	108
Eddy, co., N.D., U.S.	B7	111
Eddystone, Pa., U.S.	p20	115
Eddyville, Ia., U.S.	C5	92
Eddyville, Ky., U.S.	e9	94
Ede, Neth.	C5	8
Edéa, Cam.	H8	42
Eden, Ga., U.S.	D5	87
Eden, Md., U.S.	D6	97
Eden, N.Y., U.S.	C2	109
Eden, N.C., U.S.	A3	110
Eden, Tx., U.S.	D3	120
Edenderry, Ire.	H5	7
Eden Prairie, Mn., U.S.	n12	100
Edenton, N.C., U.S.	A6	110
Eden Valley, Mn., U.S.	E4	100
Edgar, Ne., U.S.	D8	104
Edgar, Wi., U.S.	D4	126
Edgar, co., Il., U.S.	D6	90
Edgard, La., U.S.	D5	95
Edgartown, Ma., U.S.	D6	98
Edgecombe, co., N.C., U.S.	B5	110
Edgecumbe, Cape, c., Ak., U.S.	m21	79
Edgefield, S.C., U.S.	D4	117
Edgefield, co., S.C., U.S.	D4	117
Edgeley, N.D., U.S.	C7	111
Edgemere, Md., U.S.	B5	97
Edgemont, S.D., U.S.	D2	118
Edgemoor, De., U.S.	A3	85
Edgerton, Ks., U.S.	D8	93
Edgerton, Mn., U.S.	G2	100
Edgerton, Oh., U.S.	A1	112
Edgerton, Wi., U.S.	F4	126
Edgerton, Wy., U.S.	C6	127
Edgewater, Al., U.S.	f7	78
Edgewater, Fl., U.S.	D6	86
Edgewater, Md., U.S.	C4	97
Edgewater, N.J., U.S.	h9	107
Edgewater Park, N.J., U.S.	C3	107
Edgewood, In., U.S.	D6	91
Edgewood, Ia., U.S.	B6	92
Edgewood, Ky., U.S.	h13	94
Edgewood, Md., U.S.	B5	97
Edgewood, N.M., U.S.	B3	108
Edgewood, Oh., U.S.	A5	112
Edgewood, Pa., U.S.	k14	115
Edgewood, Wa., U.S.	f11	124
Edgeworth, Pa., U.S.	h13	115
Edina, Mn., U.S.	F5	100
Edina, Mo., U.S.	A5	102
Edinboro, Pa., U.S.	C1	115
Edinburg, Il., U.S.	D4	90
Edinburg, Tx., U.S.	F3	120
Edinburg, Va., U.S.	B4	123
Edinburgh, Scot., U.K.	F9	7
Edinburgh, In., U.S.	F6	91
Edirne, Tur.	G13	4
Edison, Ga., U.S.	E2	87
Edison, N.J., U.S.	B4	107
Edisto, stm., S.C., U.S.	E6	117
Edisto Island, i., S.C., U.S.	F7	117
Edith, Mount, mtn., Mt., U.S.	D5	103
Edjeleh, Alg.	C7	42
Edmond, Ok., U.S.	B4	113
Edmonds, Wa., U.S.	B3	124
Edmondson Heights, Md., U.S.	*g10	97
Edmonson, co., Ky., U.S.	C3	94
Edmonton, Alta., Can.	C4	68
Edmonton, Ky., U.S.	D4	94
Edmore, Mi., U.S.	E5	99
Edmunds, co., S.D., U.S.	B6	118
Edmundston, N.B., Can.	B1	71
Edna, Tx., U.S.	E4	120
Edon, Oh., U.S.	A1	112
Édouard, Lac, l., Que., Can.	B5	74
Edremit, Tur.	J11	16
Edrengijn Nuruu, mts., Mong.	C6	26
Edsbyn, Swe.	F10	6
Edson, Alta., Can.	C2	68
Edson Butte, mtn., Or., U.S.	E2	114
Eduardo Castex, Arg.	D4	56
Edward, Lake, l., Afr.	B5	44
Edwards, Ms., U.S.	C3	101
Edwards, co., Il., U.S.	E5	90
Edwards, co., Ks., U.S.	E4	93
Edwards, co., Tx., U.S.	E2	120
Edwards Air Force Base, mil., Ca., U.S.	E5	82
Edwardsburg, Mi., U.S.	G4	99
Edwards Butte, mtn., Or., U.S.	B3	114
Edwardsville, Il., U.S.	E4	90
Edwardsville, Ks., U.S.	k16	93
Edwardsville, Pa., U.S.	n17	115
Eel, stm., Ca., U.S.	B2	82
Eel, stm., In., U.S.	F3	91
Eel, stm., In., U.S.	C6	91
Effigy Mounds National Monument, Ia., U.S.	A6	92
Effingham, Il., U.S.	D5	90
Effingham, co., Ga., U.S.	D5	87
Effingham, co., Il., U.S.	D5	90
Efland, N.C., U.S.	A3	110
Egan Range, mts., Nv., U.S.	E7	105
Eganville, Ont., Can.	B7	73
Egede og Rothes Fjord, Grnld.	C25	66
Egedesminde, Grnld.	C22	66
Eger, Hung.	H20	8
Egersund, Nor.	G5	6
Eggenfelden, Ger.	G12	8
Egg Harbor City, N.J., U.S.	D3	107
Egg Island Point, c., N.J., U.S.	E2	107
Égletons, Fr.	G9	10
Eglin Air Force Base, mil., Fl., U.S.	u15	86
Egmont, Mount, mtn., N.Z.	C5	52
Egmont Bay, b., P.E.I., Can.	C5	71
Egmont Channel, strt., Fl., U.S.	p10	86
Egmont Key, i., Fl., U.S.	p10	86
Egvekinot, Russia	D29	24
Egypt, ctry., Afr.	C11	42
Egypt, Lake of, res., Il., U.S.	F5	90
Ehingen, Ger.	G9	8
Ehrenberg, Az., U.S.	D1	80
Éibar, Spain	B9	12
Eichstätt, Ger.	G11	8
Eidsvoll, Nor.	F8	6
Eielson Air Force Base, mil., Ak., U.S.	C10	79
Eifel, mts., Ger.	E6	8
Eighty Mile Beach, Austl.	C4	50
Eil, Som.	G4	46
Eilenburg, Ger.	D12	8
Eindhoven, Neth.	D5	8
Einsiedeln, Switz.	E15	10
Eirunepé, Braz.	E5	54
Eisenach, Ger.	E10	8
Eisenberg, Ger.	E11	8
Eisenerz, Aus.	H14	8
Eisenhower, Mount, mtn., N.H., U.S.	B4	106
Eisenhüttenstadt, Ger.	C14	8
Eisenstadt, Aus.	H16	8
Eisleben, Ger.	D11	8
Ejea de los Caballeros, Spain	C10	12
Ekiatapskij Chrebet, mts., Russia	D29	24
Ekimčan, Russia	G20	24
Ekwan, stm., Ont., Can.	F16	66
El Aaiún, W. Sah.	C3	42
Elaine, Ar., U.S.	C5	81
El Asnam, Alg.	A6	42
Elat, Isr.	E4	40
El Avión, Mex.	E6	62
Elâzığ, Tur.	H15	4
Elba, Al., U.S.	D3	78
Elba, Isola d', i., Italy	G5	14
El Banco, Col.	C6	58
El Barco de Valdeorras, Spain	C5	12
Elbasan, Alb.	H4	16
El Baúl, Ven.	C8	58
Elbe (Labe), stm., Eur.	B9	8
Elberfeld, In., U.S.	H3	91
Elbert, co., Co., U.S.	B6	83
Elbert, co., Ga., U.S.	B4	87
Elbert, Mount, mtn., Co., U.S.	B4	83
Elberta, Ga., U.S.	D3	87
Elberton, Ga., U.S.	B4	87
Elbeuf, Fr.	C8	10
Elbląg (Elbing), Pol.	A19	8
El Bonillo, Spain	G9	12
El Bordo, Col.	F4	58
Elbow, stm., Alta., Can.	D3	68
Elbow Lake, Mn., U.S.	E3	100
El'brus, gora (Mount Elbrus), mtn., Russia	I6	22
El Burgo de Osma, Spain	D8	12
Elburn, Il., U.S.	B5	90
Elburz Mountains see Alborz, Reshteh-ye Kūhhā-ye, mts., Iran	J8	22
El Cajon, Ca., U.S.	F5	82
El Callao, Ven.	D12	58
El Campo, Tx., U.S.	E4	120
El Capitan, mtn., Mt., U.S.	D2	103
El Capitan Reservoir, res., Ca., U.S.	o16	82
El Carmen, Arg.	A3	56
El Carmen de Bolívar, Col.	C5	58
El Centro, Ca., U.S.	F6	82
El Cerrito, Col.	F4	58
El Cerrito, Ca., U.S.	h8	82
Elche, Spain	G11	12
Elche de la Sierra, Spain	G9	12
El Cozón, Mex.	B3	62
El Cuervo Butte, mtn., N.M., U.S.	k9	108
Elda, Spain	G11	12
El Desemboque, Mex.	C3	62
El Diviso, Col.	G3	58
El Djouf, des., Afr.	D4	42
Eldon, Ia., U.S.	D5	92
Eldon, Mo., U.S.	C5	102
Eldora, Ia., U.S.	B4	92
Eldorado, Mex.	E6	62
El Dorado, Ar., U.S.	D3	81
Eldorado, Il., U.S.	F5	90
El Dorado, Ks., U.S.	E7	93
Eldorado, Tx., U.S.	D2	120
El Dorado, co., Ca., U.S.	C3	82
Eldorado Peak, mtn., Wa., U.S.	A4	124
Eldorado Springs, Co., U.S.	B5	83
El Dorado Springs, Mo., U.S.	D3	102
Eldoret, Kenya	A7	44
Eldridge, Ia., U.S.	C7	92
Eleanor, W.V., U.S.	C3	125
Electra, Tx., U.S.	C3	120
Electra Lake, res., Co., U.S.	D3	83
Electric Peak, mtn., Co., U.S.	C5	83
Electric Peak, mtn., Mt., U.S.	E6	103
Elektrostal', Russia	F21	18
El Encanto, Col.	H6	58
Elephant Butte Reservoir, res., N.M., U.S.	D2	108
El Estor, Guat.	G3	64
Eleuthera, i., Bah.	B9	64
Eleven Mile Canyon Reservoir, res., Co., U.S.	C5	83
Eleven Point, stm., U.S.	A4	81
Elevsís, Grc.	K7	16
El Fahs, Tun.	M4	14
El Ferrol del Caudillo, Spain	B3	12
El Galpón, Arg.	B4	56
Elgin, Scot., U.K.	D9	7
Elgin, Il., U.S.	A5	90
Elgin, Ia., U.S.	B6	92
Elgin, Mn., U.S.	F6	100
Elgin, Ne., U.S.	C7	104
Elgin, N.D., U.S.	C4	111
Elgin, Ok., U.S.	C3	113
Elgin, Or., U.S.	B9	114
Elgin, S.C., U.S.	B6	117
Elgin, Tx., U.S.	D4	120
El Goléa, Alg.	B6	42
El Golfo de Santa Clara, Mex.	B2	62
Elgon, Mount, mtn., Afr.	A6	44
El Hank, clf, Afr.	D4	42
El Haouaria, Tun.	L6	14
Elida, Oh., U.S.	B1	112
Élisabethville see Lubumbashi, Zaire	D5	44
Elizabeth, Austl.	F7	50
Elizabeth, Co., U.S.	B6	83
Elizabeth, N.J., U.S.	B4	107
Elizabeth, W.V., U.S.	B3	125
Elizabeth, Cape, c., Wa., U.S.	B1	124
Elizabeth City, N.C., U.S.	A6	110
Elizabeth Islands, is., Ma., U.S.	D6	98
Elizabeth Reef, atoll, Austl.	E11	50
Elizabethton, Tn., U.S.	C11	119
Elizabethtown, Ky., U.S.	C4	94
Elizabethtown, N.C., U.S.	C4	110
Elizabethtown, Pa., U.S.	F8	115
Elizabethville, Pa., U.S.	E8	115
El-Jadida, Mor.	B4	42
El Jebel, Co., U.S.	B3	83
Ełk, Pol.	B22	8
Elk, co., Ks., U.S.	E7	93
Elk, co., Pa., U.S.	D4	115
Elk, stm., U.S.	A2	78
Elk, stm., Co., U.S.	A4	83
Elk, stm., Ks., U.S.	E7	93
Elk, stm., W.V., U.S.	C3	125
Elk, stm., Wi., U.S.	C3	126
Elkader, Ia., U.S.	B6	92
El Kairouan, Tun.	N5	14
Elk City, Id., U.S.	D3	89
Elk City, Ok., U.S.	B2	113
Elk City Lake, res., Ks., U.S.	E7	93
Elk Creek, stm., Ok., U.S.	B2	113
Elk Creek, stm., S.D., U.S.	C3	118
El Kef, Tun.	M3	14
Elkford, B.C., Can.	D10	69
Elk Grove, Ca., U.S.	C3	82
Elk Grove Village, Il., U.S.	h9	90
Elkhart, In., U.S.	A6	91
Elkhart, Ks., U.S.	E2	93
Elkhart, Tx., U.S.	D5	120
Elkhart, co., In., U.S.	A6	91
Elkhart, stm., In., U.S.	B6	91
Elkhart Lake, Wi., U.S.	E5	126
Elkhead Mountains, mts., Co., U.S.	A3	83
Elkhorn, Man., Can.	E1	70
Elk Horn, Ia., U.S.	C2	92
Elkhorn, Ne., U.S.	g12	104
Elkhorn, Wi., U.S.	F5	126
Elkhorn, stm., Ne., U.S.	B7	104
Elkhorn City, Ky., U.S.	C7	94
Elkhorn Peaks, mts., Id., U.S.	F7	89
Elkin, N.C., U.S.	A2	110
Elkins, Ar., U.S.	A1	81
Elkins, W.V., U.S.	C5	125
Elkland, Pa., U.S.	C7	115
Elk Mills, Md., U.S.	A6	97
Elk Mound, Wi., U.S.	D2	126
Elk Mountain, Wy., U.S.	E6	127
Elk Mountain, mtn., N.M., U.S.	D1	108
Elk Mountain, mtn., Wy., U.S.	E6	127
Elk Mountains, mts., U.S.	D1	118
Elk Mountains, mts., Co., U.S.	B3	83
Elko, Nv., U.S.	C6	105
Elko, co., Nv., U.S.	B6	105
Elk Peak, mtn., Mt., U.S.	D6	103
Elk Point, Alta., Can.	C5	68
Elk Point, S.D., U.S.	E9	118
Elk Rapids, Mi., U.S.	D5	99
El Krib, Tun.	M4	14
Elkridge, Md., U.S.	B4	97
Elk River, Mn., U.S.	E5	100
Elkton, Ky., U.S.	D2	94
Elkton, Md., U.S.	A6	97
Elkton, Mi., U.S.	E7	99
Elkton, S.D., U.S.	C9	118
Elkton, Va., U.S.	B4	123
Elkview, W.V., U.S.	m13	125
Elkville, Il., U.S.	F4	90
Ellaville, Ga., U.S.	D2	87
Ellen, Mount, mtn., Ut., U.S.	E5	121
Ellendale, De., U.S.	E4	85
Ellendale, N.D., U.S.	C7	111
Ellensburg, Wa., U.S.	C5	124
Ellenton, Fl., U.S.	E4	86
Ellenville, N.Y., U.S.	D6	109
Ellerbe, N.C., U.S.	B3	110
Ellerslie, Md., U.S.	k13	97
Ellesmere Island, i., N.W. Ter., Can.	A21	128
Ellettsville, In., U.S.	F4	91
Ellice Islands see Tuvalu, ctry., Oc.	G24	2
Ellicott City, Md., U.S.	B4	97
Ellijay, Ga., U.S.	B2	87
Ellington, Ct., U.S.	B6	84
Ellington, Mo., U.S.	D7	102
Ellinwood, Ks., U.S.	D5	93
Elliot Lake, Ont., Can.	A2	73
Elliott, Ms., U.S.	B4	101
Elliott, co., Ky., U.S.	B6	94
Elliott Bay, b., Wa., U.S.	e11	124
Elliott Key, i., Fl., U.S.	G6	86
Ellis, Ks., U.S.	D4	93
Ellis, co., Ks., U.S.	D4	93
Ellis, co., Ok., U.S.	A2	113
Ellis, co., Tx., U.S.	C4	120
Ellis, stm., N.H., U.S.	B4	106
Elliston, Va., U.S.	C2	123
Ellisville, Ms., U.S.	D4	101
Ellisville, Mo., U.S.	f12	102
Ellon, Scot., U.K.	D10	7
Elloree, S.C., U.S.	D6	117
Ellport, Pa., U.S.	E1	115
Ellsworth, Ks., U.S.	D5	93
Ellsworth, Me., U.S.	D4	96
Ellsworth, Pa., U.S.	F1	115
Ellsworth, Wi., U.S.	D1	126
Ellsworth, co., Ks., U.S.	D5	93
Ellsworth Air Force Base, mil., S.D., U.S.	C2	118
Ellwangen, Ger.	G10	8
Ellwood City, Pa., U.S.	E1	115
Elm, stm., N.D., U.S.	B8	111
Elma, Ia., U.S.	A5	92
Elma, Wa., U.S.	C2	124
El Mahdia, Tun.	N6	14
El Manteco, Ven.	D11	58
Elm City, N.C., U.S.	B5	110
Elm Creek, Ne., U.S.	D6	104
El Médano, Mex.	E4	62
Elmendorf Air Force Base, mil., Ak., U.S.	C10	79
Elm Grove, Wi., U.S.	m11	126
Elmhurst, Il., U.S.	B6	90
Elmhurst, Pa., U.S.	D10	115
Elmira, N.Y., U.S.	C4	109
El Mirage, Az., U.S.	k8	80
Elmira Heights, N.Y., U.S.	C4	109
El Mokrine, Tun.	N5	14
Elmont, N.Y., U.S.	k13	109
Elmora, Pa., U.S.	E4	115
Elmore, Mn., U.S.	G4	100
Elmore, Oh., U.S.	A2	112
Elmore, co., Al., U.S.	C3	78
Elmore, co., Id., U.S.	F3	89
El Morro National Monument, N.M., U.S.	B1	108
Elmsdale, N.S., Can.	E6	71
Elmshorn, Ger.	B9	8
Elm Springs, Ar., U.S.	A1	81
Elmvale, Ont., Can.	C5	73
Elmwood, Il., U.S.	C3	90
Elmwood, Wi., U.S.	D1	126
Elmwood Park, Il., U.S.	k9	90
Elmwood Park, N.J., U.S.	h8	107
Elmwood Place, Oh., U.S.	o13	112
Elne, Fr.	J9	10
Elnora, In., U.S.	G3	91
Eloise, Fl., U.S.	E5	86
Elon College, N.C., U.S.	A3	110
Elora, Ont., Can.	D4	73
Elorza, Ven.	D8	58
El Oued, Alg.	B7	42
Eloy, Az., U.S.	E4	80
El Palmar, Ven.	D12	58
El Paso, Il., U.S.	C4	90
El Paso, Tx., U.S.	o11	120
El Paso, co., Co., U.S.	C6	83
El Paso, co., Tx., U.S.	o11	120
El Pilar, Ven.	B11	58
El Pital, Cerro, mtn., N.A.	G3	64
El Portal, Fl., U.S.	s13	86
El Prado, N.M., U.S.	A4	108
El Progreso, Hond.	G4	64
El Puente del Arzobispo, Spain	F6	12
El Puerto de Santa María, Spain	I5	12
El Quelite, Mex.	F6	62
El Reno, Ok., U.S.	B4	113
Elrose, Sask., Can.	F1	75
Elroy, Wi., U.S.	E3	126
Elsa, Yukon, Can.	D5	66
Elsa, Tx., U.S.	F3	120
Elsah, Il., U.S.	E3	90
El Salto, Mex.	F7	62
El Salvador, ctry., N.A.	H3	64
El Sauce, Nic.	H4	64
El Sauzal, Mex.	B1	62
Elsberry, Mo., U.S.	B7	102
Elsie, Mi., U.S.	E6	99
Elsinore, Ut., U.S.	E3	121
Elsmere, De., U.S.	B3	85
Elsmere, Ky., U.S.	B5	94
El Socorro, Ven.	C10	58
El Sombrero, Ven.	C9	58
Elspe, Ger.	D8	8
Elsterwerda, Ger.	D13	8
El Tigre, Col.	F8	58
El Tigre, Ven.	C10	58
El Tocuyo, Ven.	C8	58
Elton, La., U.S.	D3	95
El Toro Marine Corps Air Station, mil., Ca., U.S.	n13	82
El Trapiche, Col.	F4	58
El Triunfo, Mex.	F4	62
El Turbio, Arg.	G2	56
Elūru, India	D6	37
El Vado Reservoir, res., N.M., U.S.	A3	108
Elvas, Port.	G4	12
Elverum, Nor.	F8	6
El Vigía, Ven.	C7	58
Elvins, Mo., U.S.	D7	102
Elwell, Lake, res., Mt., U.S.	B5	103
Elwha, stm., Wa., U.S.	A2	124
Elwood, In., U.S.	D6	91
Elwood, Ks., U.S.	C9	93
Elwood, Ne., U.S.	D6	104
Ely, Eng., U.K.	I13	7
Ely, Mn., U.S.	C7	100
Ely, Nv., U.S.	D7	105
Elyria, Oh., U.S.	A3	112
Elysburg, Pa., U.S.	E8	115
Emanuel, co., Ga., U.S.	D4	87
Embarcación, Arg.	A4	56
Embarras, stm., Il., U.S.	E6	90
Embarrass, stm., Wi., U.S.	D5	126
Embro, Ont., Can.	D4	73
Embrun, Fr.	H13	10
Emden, Ger.	B7	8
Emerald, Austl.	D9	50
Emerson, Man., Can.	E3	70
Emerson, Ga., U.S.	B2	87
Emerson, Ne., U.S.	B9	104
Emerson, N.J., U.S.	h8	107
Emery, co., Ut., U.S.	E5	121
Emet, Tur.	J13	16
Emily, Mn., U.S.	D5	100
Emily, Lake, l., Mn., U.S.	E3	100
Eminence, Ky., U.S.	B4	94
Emmaus, Pa., U.S.	E11	115
Emmen, Neth.	C6	8
Emmendingen, Ger.	G7	8
Emmet, co., Ia., U.S.	A3	92
Emmet, co., Mi., U.S.	C6	99
Emmetsburg, Ia., U.S.	A3	92
Emmett, Id., U.S.	F2	89
Emmigan̄ūru, India	E4	37
Emmitsburg, Md., U.S.	A3	97
Emmonak, Ak., U.S.	C7	79
Emmons, co., N.D., U.S.	C5	111
Emory Peak, mtn., Tx., U.S.	E1	120
Empalme, Mex.	D4	62
Empangeni, S. Afr.	G6	44
Empedrado, Arg.	B5	56
Empire, La., U.S.	E6	95
Empire, Nv., U.S.	C2	105
Empoli, Italy	F5	14
Emporia, Ks., U.S.	D7	93
Emporia, Va., U.S.	D5	123
Emporium, Pa., U.S.	D5	115
Empty Quarter see Ar-Rab' al-Khālī, des., Asia	D5	46
Emsdetten, Ger.	C7	8
Emsworth, Pa., U.S.	h13	115
Encampment, Wy., U.S.	E6	127
Encarnación, Para.	B5	56
Encinitas, Ca., U.S.	F5	82
Encontrados, Ven.	C6	58
Ende, Indon.	G7	32
Enderby, B.C., Can.	D8	69
Enderby Land, reg., Ant.	C18	47
Enderlin, N.D., U.S.	C8	111
Enders Reservoir, res., Ne., U.S.	D4	104
Endicott, N.Y., U.S.	C4	109
Endicott Mountains, mts., Ak., U.S.	B9	79
Endless Lake, l., Me., U.S.	C4	96
Endwell, N.Y., U.S.	C4	109
Enfida, Tun.	M5	14
Enfield (Thompsonville), Ct., U.S.	B5	84
Enfield, N.H., U.S.	C2	106
Enfield, N.C., U.S.	A5	110
Engel's, Russia	G7	22
Enggano, Pulau, i., Indon.	G3	32
England, Ar., U.S.	C4	81
England, ter., U.K.	I11	7
England Air Force Base, mil., La., U.S.	C3	95
Englee, Newf., Can.	C3	72
Engleside, Va., U.S.	g12	123

Name	Map Ref	Page
Englewood, Co., U.S.	B6	83
Englewood, Fl., U.S.	F4	86
Englewood, N.J., U.S.	B5	107
Englewood, Oh., U.S.	C1	112
Englewood, Tn., U.S.	D9	119
Englewood Cliffs, N.J., U.S.	h9	107
English, In., U.S.	H5	91
English Bāzār, India	H13	38
English Channel (La Manche), strt., Eur.	B5	10
Enguera, Spain	G11	12
Enid, Ok., U.S.	A4	113
Enid Lake, res., Ms., U.S.	A4	101
Enigma, Ga., U.S.	E3	87
Enka, N.C., U.S.	f10	110
Enkhuizen, Neth.	C5	8
Enköping, Swe.	G11	6
Enmelen, Russia	D30	24
Enna, Italy	L9	14
Ennadai Lake, l., N.W. Ter., Can.	D12	66
Ennedi, plat., Chad	E10	42
Ennis, Ire.	I4	7
Ennis, Mt., U.S.	E5	103
Ennis, Tx., U.S.	C4	120
Enniskillen, N. Ire., U.K.	G5	7
Enoch, Ut., U.S.	F2	121
Enola, Pa., U.S.	F8	115
Enon, Oh., U.S.	*C2	112
Enoree, S.C., U.S.	B4	117
Enoree, stm., S.C., U.S.	B3	117
Enosburg Falls, Vt., U.S.	B3	122
Enriquillo, Dom. Rep.	F12	64
Enschede, Neth.	C6	8
Ensenada, Mex.	B1	62
Enshi, China	E8	26
Enshū-nada, Japan	H10	30
Ensley, Fl., U.S.	u14	86
Entebbe, Ug.	A6	44
Enterprise, Al., U.S.	D4	78
Enterprise, Ks., U.S.	D6	93
Enterprise, Or., U.S.	B9	114
Enterprise, Ut., U.S.	F2	121
Enterprise, W.V., U.S.	B4	125
Entiat, stm., Wa., U.S.	B5	124
Entiat, Lake, l., Wa., U.S.	B5	124
Entiat Mountains, mts., Wa., U.S.	B5	124
Entraygues, Fr.	H9	10
Entre-Rios, Moz.	D7	44
Enugu, Nig.	G7	42
Enumclaw, Wa., U.S.	B4	124
Envigado, Col.	D5	58
Eola Hills, hills, Or., U.S.	h11	114
Épernay, Fr.	C10	10
Ephraim, Ut., U.S.	D4	121
Ephrata, Pa., U.S.	F9	115
Ephrata, Wa., U.S.	B6	124
Épila, Spain	D10	12
Épinal, Fr.	D13	10
Epping, N.H., U.S.	D4	106
Epworth, Ia., U.S.	B7	92
Equatorial Guinea, ctry., Afr.	H7	42
Eraclea, Italy	D7	14
Erath, La., U.S.	E3	95
Erath, co., Tx., U.S.	C3	120
Erdek, Tur.	I11	16
Erdemli, Tur.	A4	40
Erebus, Mount, mtn., Ant.	B29	47
Erechim, Braz.	B6	56
Erfurt, Ger.	E11	8
Erichsen Lake, l., N.W. Ter., Can.	B16	66
Erick, Ok., U.S.	B2	113
Erickson, Man., Can.	D2	70
Erie, Co., U.S.	A5	83
Erie, Il., U.S.	B3	90
Erie, Ks., U.S.	E8	93
Erie, Mi., U.S.	G7	99
Erie, Pa., U.S.	B1	115
Erie, co., N.Y., U.S.	C2	109
Erie, co., Oh., U.S.	A3	112
Erie, co., Pa., U.S.	C1	115
Erie, Lake, l., N.A.	C10	76
Erie Canal, N.Y., U.S.	B5	109
Erimo-misaki, c., Japan	r21	30a
Erin, Ont., Can.	D4	73
Erin, Tn., U.S.	A4	119
Eritrea, ctry., Afr.	E2	46
Erlangen, Ger.	F11	8
Erlanger, Ky., U.S.	A5	94
Erlian, China	C9	26
Erling, Lake, res., Ar., U.S.	D2	81
Ermelo, S. Afr.	G5	44
Ermenak, Tur.	A3	40
Ernākulam, India	H4	37
Erne, Lower Lough, l., N. Ire., U.K.	G5	7
Ernée, Fr.	D6	10
Erode, India	G4	37
Errigal, mtn., Ire.	F4	7
Ertai, China	B5	26
Erwin, N.C., U.S.	B4	110
Erwin, Tn., U.S.	C11	119
Erzgebirge (Krušné hory), mts., Eur.	E12	8
Erzincan, Tur.	H15	4
Erzurum, Tur.	H16	4
Esashi, Japan	A13	30
Esbjerg, Den.	I7	6
Escalante, Ut., U.S.	F4	121
Escalante, stm., Ut., U.S.	F4	121
Escalón, Mex.	D7	62
Escalon, Ca., U.S.	D3	82
Escambia, co., Al., U.S.	D2	78
Escambia, co., Fl., U.S.	u14	86
Escambia, stm., Fl., U.S.	u14	86
Escanaba, Mi., U.S.	C3	99
Escanaba, stm., Mi., U.S.	B3	99
Escarpada Point, c., Phil.	B7	32
Escatawpa, Ms., U.S.	E5	101
Escatawpa, stm., U.S.	D5	101
Esch-sur-Alzette, Lux.	F5	8
Eschwege, Ger.	D10	8
Escondido, Ca., U.S.	F5	82
Escoumins, Rivière des, stm., Que., Can.	A8	74
Escuinapa [de Hidalgo], Mex.	F7	62
Escuintla, Guat.	G2	64
Escuintla, Mex.	J13	62
Escuminac, Point, c., N.B., Can.	B5	71
Eşfahān, Iran	B5	46
Eshkāshem, Afg.	B4	38
Eskilstuna, Swe.	G11	6
Eskimo Lakes, l., N.W. Ter., Can.	C6	66
Eskimo Point, N.W. Ter., Can.	D14	66
Eskişehir, Tur.	H14	4
Eşme, Tur.	K12	16
Esmeralda, co., Nv., U.S.	F4	105
Esmeraldas, Ec.	G3	58
Esmond, R.I., U.S.	B4	116
Espalion, Fr.	H9	10
Espanola, Ont., Can.	A3	73
Espanola, N.M., U.S.	B3	108
Esparto, Ca., U.S.	C2	82
Espelkamp, Ger.	C8	8
Esperance, Austl.	F4	50
Espinal, Col.	E5	58
Espinhaço, Serra do, mts., Braz.	C7	57
Espinho, Port.	D3	12
Espíritu Santo, Bahía del, b., Mex.	H16	62
Espíritu Santo, Isla del, i., Mex.	E4	62
Espoo (Esbo), Fin.	F15	6
Espy, Pa., U.S.	D9	115
Esquel, Arg.	E2	56
Esquimalt, B.C., Can.	E6	69
Esquina, Arg.	B5	56
Essaouira, Mor.	B4	42
Essen, Ger.	D7	8
Essendon, Mount, mtn., Austl.	D4	50
Essequibo, stm., Guy.	E13	58
Es Sers, Tun.	M4	14
Essex, Ont., Can.	E2	73
Essex, Ct., U.S.	D6	84
Essex, Ia., U.S.	D2	92
Essex, Md., U.S.	B5	97
Essex, Ma., U.S.	A6	98
Essex, Vt., U.S.	B2	122
Essex, co., Ma., U.S.	A5	98
Essex, co., N.J., U.S.	B4	107
Essex, co., N.Y., U.S.	B7	109
Essex, co., Vt., U.S.	B5	122
Essex, co., Va., U.S.	C6	123
Essex Junction, Vt., U.S.	C2	122
Essexville, Mi., U.S.	E7	99
Esslingen, Ger.	G9	8
Es Smala es Souassi, Tun.	N5	14
Est, Cap, c., Madag.	E10	44
Est, Pointe de l', c., Que., Can.	G20	66
Estacada, Or., U.S.	B4	114
Estaca de Bares, Punta de la, c., Spain	B4	12
Estacado, Llano, pl., U.S.	C1	120
Estados, Isla de los, i., Arg.	G4	56
Estancia, N.M., U.S.	C3	108
Estcourt, S. Afr.	G5	44
Este, Italy	D6	14
Estelí, Nic.	H4	64
Estella, Spain	C9	12
Estelline, S.D., U.S.	C9	118
Estepona, Spain	I6	12
Esternay, Fr.	D10	10
Estero Bay, b., Ca., U.S.	E3	82
Estero Bay, b., Fl., U.S.	F5	86
Estero Island, i., Fl., U.S.	F5	86
Estes Park, Co., U.S.	A5	83
Estherville, Ia., U.S.	A3	92
Estherwood, La., U.S.	D3	95
Estill, S.C., U.S.	F5	117
Estill, co., Ky., U.S.	C6	94
Estill Springs, Tn., U.S.	B5	119
Estonia, ctry., Eur.	C9	18
Estremoz, Port.	G4	12
Esztergom, Hung.	H18	8
Etah, Grnld.	B20	128
Etah, India	G8	38
Étampes, Fr.	D9	10
Étang-du-Nord, Que., Can.	B8	71
Étaples, Fr.	B8	10
Etāwah, India	G8	38
Ethel, W.V., U.S.	n12	125
Ethiopia, ctry., Afr.	G2	46
Etna, Pa., U.S.	k14	115
Etna, Monte, vol., Italy	L9	14
Etobicoke, Ont., Can.	D5	73
Etolin Island, i., Ak., U.S.	m23	79
Etolin Strait, strt., Ak., U.S.	C6	79
Etosha Pan, pl., Nmb.	E3	44
Etowah, Tn., U.S.	D9	119
Etowah, co., Al., U.S.	A3	78
Etowah, stm., Ga., U.S.	B2	87
Ettelbruck, Lux.	F6	8
Ettlingen, Ger.	G8	8
Ettrick, Va., U.S.	C5	123
Eu, Fr.	B8	10
Eucla, Austl.	F5	50
Euclid, Oh., U.S.	A4	112
Eudora, Ar., U.S.	D4	81
Eudora, Ks., U.S.	D8	93
Eufaula, Al., U.S.	D4	78
Eufaula, Ok., U.S.	B6	113
Eufaula Lake, res., Ok., U.S.	B6	113
Eugene, Or., U.S.	C3	114
Eugenia, Punta, c., Mex.	D2	62
Eunice, La., U.S.	D3	95
Eunice, N.M., U.S.	E6	108
Euphrates (Al-Furāt), stm., Asia	A2	46
Eupora, Ms., U.S.	B4	101
Eureka, Ca., U.S.	B1	82
Eureka, Il., U.S.	C4	90
Eureka, Ks., U.S.	E7	93
Eureka, Mo., U.S.	f12	102
Eureka, Mt., U.S.	B1	103
Eureka, Nv., U.S.	D6	105
Eureka, S.C., U.S.	B5	117
Eureka, S.D., U.S.	B6	118
Eureka, co., Nv., U.S.	D5	105
Eureka Springs, Ar., U.S.	A2	81
Europa, Île, i., Reu.	F8	44
Europa Point, c., Gib.	I6	12
Europe	E11	4
Euskirchen, Ger.	E6	8
Eustis, Fl., U.S.	D5	86
Eutaw, Al., U.S.	C2	78
Eutin, Ger.	A10	8
Eutsuk Lake, l., B.C., Can.	C4	69
Evangeline, co., La., U.S.	D3	95
Evans, Co., U.S.	A6	83
Evans, Ga., U.S.	C4	87
Evans, W.V., U.S.	C3	125
Evans, co., Ga., U.S.	D5	87
Evans, Lac, l., Que., Can.	F17	66
Evans, Mount, mtn., Co., U.S.	B5	83
Evansburg, Alta., Can.	C3	68
Evans City, Pa., U.S.	E1	115
Evansdale, Ia., U.S.	B5	92
Evans Strait, strt., N.W. Ter., Can.	D16	66
Evanston, Il., U.S.	A6	90
Evanston, Wy., U.S.	E2	127
Evansville, Il., U.S.	E4	90
Evansville, In., U.S.	I2	91
Evansville, Wi., U.S.	F4	126
Evansville, Wy., U.S.	D6	127
Evart, Mi., U.S.	E5	99
Evarts, Ky., U.S.	D6	94
Eveleth, Mn., U.S.	C6	100
Everard, Lake, l., Austl.	F7	50
Everest, Mount, mtn., Asia	G12	38
Everett, Ma., U.S.	g11	98
Everett, Pa., U.S.	F5	115
Everett, Wa., U.S.	B3	124
Everett Lake, res., N.H., U.S.	D3	106
Everglades National Park, Fl., U.S.	G5	86
Evergreen, Al., U.S.	D3	78
Evergreen, Co., U.S.	B5	83
Evergreen Park, Il., U.S.	k9	90
Everly, Ia., U.S.	A2	92
Everson, Wa., U.S.	A3	124
Evesham, Eng., U.K.	I11	7
Evje, Nor.	G6	6
Évora, Port.	G4	12
Évreux, Fr.	C8	10
Évros (Marica) (Meriç), stm., Eur.	H10	16
E.V. Spence Reservoir, res., Tx., U.S.	D2	120
Évvoia, i., Grc.	K7	16
Ewa, Hi., U.S.	B3	88
Ewa Beach, Hi., U.S.	B3	88
Ewa Beach, Hi., U.S.	g9	88
Ewing Township, N.J., U.S.	C3	107
Ewo, Congo	B2	44
Excelsior Mountain, mtn., Ca., U.S.	C4	82
Excelsior Mountains, mts., Nv., U.S.	E3	105
Excelsior Springs, Mo., U.S.	B3	102
Executive Committee Range, mts., Ant.	B36	47
Exeter, Ont., Can.	D3	73
Exeter, Eng., U.K.	K9	7
Exeter, Ca., U.S.	D4	82
Exeter, Ne., U.S.	D8	104
Exeter, N.H., U.S.	E5	106
Exeter, Pa., U.S.	D10	115
Exeter, stm., N.H., U.S.	E5	106
Exeter Sound, strt., N.W. Ter., Can.	C20	66
Exira, Ia., U.S.	C3	92
Exmore, Va., U.S.	C7	123
Exmouth, Eng., U.K.	K9	7
Exmouth Gulf, b., Austl.	D2	50
Experiment, Ga., U.S.	C2	87
Exploits, stm., Newf., Can.	D3	72
Exploits, Bay of, b., Newf., Can.	D4	72
Export, Pa., U.S.	F2	115
Exuma Sound, strt., Bah.	B9	64
Eyasi, Lake, l., Tan.	B6	44
Eylar Mountain, mtn., Ca., U.S.	D3	82
Eymoutiers, Fr.	G8	10
Eyota, Mn., U.S.	G6	100
Eyre (North), Lake, l., Austl.	E7	50
Eyre (South), Lake, l., Austl.	E7	50
Eyre Peninsula, pen., Austl.	F7	50

F

Name	Map Ref	Page
Fabens, Tx., U.S.	o11	120
Fabius, stm., Mo., U.S.	A6	102
Fabriano, Italy	F7	14
Facatativá, Col.	E5	58
Factoryville, Pa., U.S.	C10	115
Fada, Chad	E10	42
Fada Ngourma, Burkina	F6	42
Faddejevskij, Ostrov, i., Russia	B22	24
Faenza, Italy	E6	14
Faeroe Islands, dep., Eur.	C6	4
Fagernes, Nor.	F7	6
Fagersta, Swe.	F10	6
Fairacres, N.M., U.S.	E3	108
Fairbank, Ia., U.S.	B5	92
Fairbanks, Ak., U.S.	C10	79
Fair Bluff, N.C., U.S.	C3	110
Fairborn, Oh., U.S.	C1	112
Fairburn, Ga., U.S.	C2	87
Fairbury, Il., U.S.	C5	90
Fairbury, Ne., U.S.	D8	104
Fairchance, Pa., U.S.	G2	115
Fairchild Air Force Base, mil., Wa., U.S.	g13	124
Fairdale, Ky., U.S.	B4	94
Fairfax, Ca., U.S.	C2	82
Fairfax, De., U.S.	A3	85
Fairfax, Ia., U.S.	C6	92
Fairfax, Mn., U.S.	F4	100
Fairfax, Mo., U.S.	A2	102
Fairfax, Ok., U.S.	A5	113
Fairfax, S.C., U.S.	F5	117
Fairfax, Va., U.S.	B5	123
Fairfax, co., Va., U.S.	B5	123
Fairfield, Al., U.S.	B3	78
Fairfield, Ca., U.S.	C2	82
Fairfield, Ct., U.S.	E2	84
Fairfield, Il., U.S.	E5	90
Fairfield, Ia., U.S.	C6	92
Fairfield, Me., U.S.	D3	96
Fairfield, Mt., U.S.	C5	103
Fairfield, Oh., U.S.	n12	112
Fairfield, Tx., U.S.	D4	120
Fairfield, co., Ct., U.S.	D2	84
Fairfield, co., Oh., U.S.	C3	112
Fairfield, co., S.C., U.S.	C5	117
Fairfield Bay, Ar., U.S.	B3	81
Fairfield Pond, l., Vt., U.S.	B3	122
Fair Grove, Mo., U.S.	D4	102
Fair Grove, N.C., U.S.	B2	110
Fairhaven, Ma., U.S.	C6	98
Fair Haven, Mi., U.S.	F8	99
Fair Haven, N.J., U.S.	C4	107
Fair Haven, Vt., U.S.	D2	122
Fairhope, Al., U.S.	E2	78
Fair Isle, i., Scot., U.K.	B11	7
Fairland, In., U.S.	E6	91
Fairland, Ok., U.S.	A7	113
Fair Lawn, N.J., U.S.	h8	107
Fairlawn, Va., U.S.	C2	123
Fairlea, W.V., U.S.	D4	125
Fairmont, Il., U.S.	C6	90
Fairmont, Mn., U.S.	G4	100
Fairmont, Ne., U.S.	D8	104
Fairmont, N.C., U.S.	C3	110
Fairmont, W.V., U.S.	B4	125
Fairmount, Ga., U.S.	B2	87
Fairmount, In., U.S.	D6	91
Fairmount Heights, Md., U.S.	f9	97
Fair Oaks, Ga., U.S.	h7	87
Fairoaks, Pa., U.S.	h13	115
Fair Plain, Mi., U.S.	F4	99
Fairport, N.Y., U.S.	B3	109
Fairport Harbor, Oh., U.S.	A4	112
Fairvale, N.B., Can.	D4	71
Fairview, Alta., Can.	A1	68
Fairview, Mt., U.S.	C12	103
Fairview, N.J., U.S.	h8	107
Fairview, Ok., U.S.	A3	113
Fairview, Pa., U.S.	B1	115
Fairview, Tn., U.S.	B4	119
Fairview, Ut., U.S.	D4	121
Fairview Heights, Il., U.S.	E3	90
Fairview Park, In., U.S.	E3	91
Fairview Park, Oh., U.S.	g9	112
Fairview Peak, mtn., Nv., U.S.	D3	105
Fairview Peak, mtn., Or., U.S.	D4	114
Fairway, Ks., U.S.	k16	93
Fairweather, Mount, mtn., N.A.	E5	66
Faisalabad, Pak.	E5	38
Faison, N.C., U.S.	B4	110
Faizābād, India	G10	38
Fakenham, Eng., U.K.	I13	7
Fakfak, Indon.	F9	32
Falaise, Fr.	D6	10
Falam, Mya.	C2	34
Falconer, N.Y., U.S.	C1	109
Falcon Heights, Mn., U.S.	n12	100
Falcon Heights, Or., U.S.	E5	114
Falcon Reservoir, res., N.A.	D10	62
Falfurrias, Tx., U.S.	F3	120
Falher, Alta., Can.	B2	68
Falkenberg, Swe.	H9	6
Falkensee, Ger.	C13	8
Falkenstein, Ger.	E12	8
Falkland Islands (Islas Malvinas), dep., S.A.	G5	56
Falköping, Swe.	G9	6
Falkville, Al., U.S.	A3	78
Fall, stm., Ks., U.S.	E7	93
Fall Branch, Tn., U.S.	C11	119
Fallbrook, Ca., U.S.	F5	82
Fall City, Wa., U.S.	B4	124
Fall Creek, Wi., U.S.	D2	126
Falling Creek, stm., Va., U.S.	n17	123
Falling Rock Creek, stm., W.V., U.S.	m13	125
Fall Mountain Lake, Ct., U.S.	C4	84
Fallon, Nv., U.S.	D3	105
Fallon, co., Mt., U.S.	D12	103
Fallon Indian Reservation, Nv., U.S.	D3	105
Fallon Naval Air Station, mil., Nv., U.S.	D3	105
Fall River, Ma., U.S.	C5	98
Fall River, Wi., U.S.	E4	126
Fall River, co., S.D., U.S.	D2	118
Fall River Lake, res., Ks., U.S.	E7	93
Falls, co., Tx., U.S.	D4	120
Falls Church, Va., U.S.	g12	123
Falls City, Ne., U.S.	D10	104
Falls City, Or., U.S.	C3	114
Falls Creek, Pa., U.S.	D4	115
Fallston, Md., U.S.	A5	97
Falmouth, N.S., Can.	E5	71
Falmouth, Eng., U.K.	K7	7
Falmouth, Ky., U.S.	B5	94
Falmouth, Me., U.S.	E2	96
Falmouth, Ma., U.S.	C6	98
Falmouth, Va., U.S.	B5	123
False Cape, c., Fl., U.S.	D6	86
False Cape, c., Va., U.S.	D7	123
False Divi Point, c., India	E6	37
Falset, Spain	D12	12
Falun, Swe.	F10	6
Famagusta see Gazimağusa, N. Cyp.	B3	40
Famatina, Nevado de, mts., Arg.	B3	56
Fancy Farm, Ky., U.S.	f9	94
Fangcheng, China	B1	28
Fannin, co., Ga., U.S.	B2	87
Fannin, co., Tx., U.S.	C4	120
Fanny, Mount, mtn., Or., U.S.	B9	114
Fano, Italy	F8	14
Faradje, Zaire	H11	42
Faradofay, Madag.	G9	44
Farafangana, Madag.	F9	44
Farāh, Afg.	C1	36
Faranah, Gui.	F3	42
Farasān, Jazā'ir, is., Sau. Ar.	E3	46
Farewell, Cape, c., N.Z.	D4	52
Fargo, Ga., U.S.	F4	87
Fargo, N.D., U.S.	C9	111
Faribault, Mn., U.S.	F5	100
Faribault, co., Mn., U.S.	G4	100
Farīdpur, Bngl.	I13	38
Färjestaden, Swe.	H11	6
Farley, Ia., U.S.	B6	92
Farmer City, Il., U.S.	C5	90
Farmers Branch, Tx., U.S.	n10	120
Farmersburg, In., U.S.	F3	91
Farmerville, La., U.S.	B3	95
Farmingdale, Me., U.S.	D3	96
Farmington, Ar., U.S.	A1	81
Farmington, Ct., U.S.	C4	84
Farmington, Il., U.S.	C3	90
Farmington, Ia., U.S.	D6	92
Farmington, Me., U.S.	D2	96
Farmington, Mi., U.S.	p15	99
Farmington, Mn., U.S.	F5	100
Farmington, Mo., U.S.	D7	102
Farmington, N.H., U.S.	D4	106
Farmington, N.M., U.S.	A1	108
Farmington, Ut., U.S.	C4	121
Farmington, stm., Ct., U.S.	B4	84
Farmington Hills, Mi., U.S.	o15	99
Farmland, In., U.S.	D7	91
Farmville, N.C., U.S.	B5	110
Farmville, Va., U.S.	C4	123
Farnham, Que., Can.	D5	74
Faro, Braz.	D7	54
Faro, Port.	H4	12
Faro, Punta del, c., Italy	K10	14
Fårösund, Swe.	H12	6
Farquhar Group, is., Sey.	D10	44
Farrell, Pa., U.S.	D1	115
Farrukhābād, India	G8	38
Fartak, Ra's, c., Yemen	E5	46
Farvel, Kap, c., Grnld.	E24	66
Farwell, Mi., U.S.	E6	99
Farwell, Tx., U.S.	B1	120
Fasano, Italy	I12	14
Fatehpur, India	H9	38
Fatehpur, India	G6	38
Faulk, co., S.D., U.S.	B6	118
Faulkland Heights, De., U.S.	i7	85
Faulkner, co., Ar., U.S.	B3	81
Faulkton, S.D., U.S.	B6	118
Fauquier, co., Va., U.S.	B5	123
Fauske, Nor.	C10	6
Favara, Italy	L8	14
Faverges, Fr.	G13	10
Fawnie Nose, mtn., B.C., Can.	C5	69
Fayette, Al., U.S.	B2	78
Fayette, Ia., U.S.	B6	92
Fayette, Ms., U.S.	D2	101
Fayette, Mo., U.S.	B5	102
Fayette, Oh., U.S.	A1	112
Fayette, co., Al., U.S.	B3	78
Fayette, co., Ga., U.S.	C2	87
Fayette, co., Il., U.S.	D5	90
Fayette, co., In., U.S.	E7	91
Fayette, co., Ia., U.S.	B6	92
Fayette, co., Ky., U.S.	B5	94
Fayette, co., Oh., U.S.	C2	112
Fayette, co., Pa., U.S.	G2	115
Fayette, co., Tn., U.S.	B2	119
Fayette, co., Tx., U.S.	E4	120
Fayette, co., W.V., U.S.	C3	125
Fayetteville, Ar., U.S.	A1	81
Fayetteville, Ga., U.S.	C2	87
Fayetteville, N.C., U.S.	B4	110
Fayetteville, Pa., U.S.	G6	115
Fayetteville, Tn., U.S.	B5	119
Fayetteville, W.V., U.S.	C3	125
Fāzilka, India	E6	38
Fazzān (Fezzan), reg., Libya	C8	42
Fdérik, Maur.	D3	42
Fear, Cape, c., N.C., U.S.	D5	110
Feather, stm., Ca., U.S.	C3	82
Fécamp, Fr.	C7	10
Federalsburg, Md., U.S.	C6	97
Feeding Hills, Ma., U.S.	B2	98
Fehmarn Belt, strt., Eur.	A11	8
Feijó, Braz.	E4	54
Feira de Santana, Braz.	B9	57
Felanitx, Spain	F15	12
Feldbach, Aus.	I15	8
Feldkirch, Aus.	H9	8
Feldkirchen in Kärnten, Aus.	I14	8
Félix Gómez, Mex.	C4	62
Felletin, Fr.	G9	10
Fellsmere, Fl., U.S.	E6	86
Felton, Ca., U.S.	D2	82
Felton, De., U.S.	D3	85
Feltre, Italy	C6	14
Femundsenden, Nor.	F8	6
Fence, stm., Mi., U.S.	B2	99
Fence Lake, l., Wi., U.S.	C4	126
Fenelon Falls, Ont., Can.	C6	73
Fengcheng, China	G4	28
Fengzhen, China	C9	26
Fenimore Pass, strt., Ak., U.S.	E4	79
Fennimore, Wi., U.S.	F3	126
Fennville, Mi., U.S.	F4	99
Fenton, Mi., U.S.	F7	99
Fentress, co., Tn., U.S.	C9	119
Fenwick Island, i., S.C., U.S.	k11	117
Fenyang, China	D9	26
Feodosiya, Ukr.	H5	22
Fer, Point au, c., La., U.S.	E4	95
Ferdinand, In., U.S.	H4	91
Fergana, Uzb.	I12	22
Fergus, Ont., Can.	D4	73
Fergus, co., Mt., U.S.	C7	103
Fergus Falls, Mn., U.S.	D2	100
Ferguson, Ky., U.S.	C5	94
Ferguson, Mo., U.S.	C7	102
Ferme-Neuve, Que., Can.	C2	74
Fermo, Italy	F8	14
Fermont, Que., Can.	h13	74
Fermoy, Ire.	I4	7
Fernandina Beach, Fl., U.S.	B5	86
Fernando de Noronha, Ilha, i., Braz.	D12	54
Fernandópolis, Braz.	F3	57
Fernando Póo see Bioko, i., Eq. Gui.	H7	42
Fernán-Núñez, Spain	H7	12
Fern Creek, Ky., U.S.	g11	94
Ferndale, Ca., U.S.	B1	82
Ferndale, Md., U.S.	B4	97
Ferndale, Mi., U.S.	P15	99
Ferndale, Pa., U.S.	F4	115
Ferndale, Wa., U.S.	A3	124
Fernie, B.C., Can.	E10	69
Fernley, Nv., U.S.	D2	105
Fern Ridge Lake, res., Or., U.S.	C3	114
Fernwood, Id., U.S.	B2	89
Fernwood, Ms., U.S.	D3	101
Ferrara, Italy	E6	14
Ferreira do Alentejo, Port.	G3	12
Ferrelo, Cape, c., Or., U.S.	E2	114
Ferriday, La., U.S.	C4	95
Ferris, Tx., U.S.	C4	120
Ferris Mountains, mts., Wy., U.S.	D5	127
Ferron, Ut., U.S.	D4	121

Name	Map Ref	Page
Ferrum, Va., U.S.	D2	123
Ferry, co., Wa., U.S.	A7	124
Ferry Farms, Va., U.S.	B5	123
Ferryland, Newf., Can.	E5	72
Ferry Point, c., N.J., U.S.	k7	107
Fertile, Mn., U.S.	C2	100
Fès, Mor.	B5	42
Feshi, Zaire	C3	44
Fessenden, N.D., U.S.	B6	111
Festus, Mo., U.S.	C7	102
Fethiye, Tur.	M13	16
Feuilles, Rivière aux, stm., Que., Can.	g12	74
Feurs, Fr.	G11	10
Feyẕābād, Afg.	B4	38
Fez see Fès, Mor.	B5	42
Fianarantsoa, Madag.	F9	44
Ficksburg, S. Afr.	G5	44
Fidalgo Island, i., Wa., U.S.	A3	124
Fidenza, Italy	E5	14
Fieldale, Va., U.S.	D3	123
Fields, Lake, l., Fl., U.S.	B3	86
Fields, Lake, l., La., U.S.	k10	95
Fier, Alb.	I3	16
Fifteenmile Creek, stm., Wy., U.S.	B4	127
Fifteen Mile Falls Reservoir, res., U.S.	C5	122
Figeac, Fr.	H9	10
Figueira da Foz, Port.	E3	12
Figueras, Spain	C14	12
Figuig, Mor.	B5	42
Fiji, ctry., Oc.	H1	2
Filchner Ice Shelf, Ant.	B9	47
Filer, Id., U.S.	G4	89
Fillmore, Ca., U.S.	E4	82
Fillmore, Ut., U.S.	E3	121
Fillmore, co., Mn., U.S.	G6	100
Fillmore, co., Ne., U.S.	D8	104
Finale Ligure, Italy	E3	14
Findlay, Il., U.S.	D5	90
Findlay, Oh., U.S.	A2	112
Finisterre, Cabo de, c., Spain	C2	12
Finland, ctry., Eur.	C13	4
Finland, Gulf of, b., Eur.	G16	6
Finlay, stm., B.C., Can.	E7	66
Finley, Tn., U.S.	A2	119
Finney, co., Ks., U.S.	D3	93
Finn Mountain, mtn., Ak., U.S.	C8	79
Finse, Nor.	F6	6
Finspång, Swe.	G10	6
Finsterwalde, Ger.	D13	8
Fiorenzuola d'Arda, Italy	E4	14
Fircrest, Wa., U.S.	f10	124
Firebaugh, Ca., U.S.	D3	82
Firenze (Florence), Italy	F6	14
Firenzuola, Italy	E6	14
Firestone, Co., U.S.	A6	83
Firminy, Fr.	G11	10
Fīrozābād, India	G8	38
Fīrozpur, India	E6	38
First Connecticut Lake, l., N.H., U.S.	f7	106
Fish, stm., Al., U.S.	E2	78
Fish, stm., Me., U.S.	A4	96
Fish Creek, stm., W.V., U.S.	g8	125
Fisher, Il., U.S.	C5	90
Fisher, co., Tx., U.S.	C2	120
Fisher Bay, b., Man., Can.	D3	70
Fishermans Island, i., Va., U.S.	h15	123
Fishers, In., U.S.	E5	91
Fishers Island, i., N.Y., U.S.	m16	109
Fishers Peak, mtn., Co., U.S.	D6	83
Fisher Strait, strt., N.W. Ter., Can.	D16	66
Fishersville, Va., U.S.	B4	123
Fishing Bay, b., Md., U.S.	D5	97
Fishing Creek, Md., U.S.	D5	97
Fishing Creek, stm., N.C., U.S.	A5	110
Fishing Creek, stm., S.C., U.S.	B5	117
Fishing Creek, stm., W.V., U.S.	B4	125
Fishing Creek Reservoir, res., S.C., U.S.	B6	117
Fishkill, N.Y., U.S.	D7	109
Fish Lake, l., Ut., U.S.	E4	121
Fish River Lake, l., Me., U.S.	B4	96
Fishtrap Lake, res., Ky., U.S.	C7	94
Fiskdale, Ma., U.S.	B3	98
Fitchburg, Ma., U.S.	A4	98
Fitzgerald, Ga., U.S.	E3	87
Fitz Roy, Arg.	F3	56
Fitzroy, stm., Austl.	C4	50
Fitzroy, Monte (Cerro Chaltel), mtn., S.A.	F2	56
Fitzroy Crossing, Austl.	C5	50
Fitzwilliam, N.H., U.S.	E2	106
Fitzwilliam Island, i., Ont., Can.	B3	73
Five Island Lake, l., Ia., U.S.	A3	92
Fivemile Creek, stm., Wy., U.S.	C4	127
Five Points, N.M., U.S.	B3	108
Flagler, co., Fl., U.S.	C5	86
Flagler Beach, Fl., U.S.	C5	86
Flagstaff, Az., U.S.	B4	80
Flagstaff Lake, l., Or., U.S.	E7	114
Flambeau, stm., Wi., U.S.	C3	126
Flamborough Head, c., Eng., U.K.	G12	7
Flaming Gorge Dam, Ut., U.S.	C6	121
Flaming Gorge National Recreation Area, U.S.	E3	127
Flaming Gorge Reservoir, res., U.S.	E3	127
Flanagan, Il., U.S.	C5	90
Flandreau, S.D., U.S.	C9	118
Flandreau Indian Reservation, S.D., U.S.	C9	118
Flat, stm., Mi., U.S.	E5	99
Flat, stm., N.C., U.S.	A4	110
Flat, stm., R.I., U.S.	E2	116
Flat Brook, stm., N.J., U.S.	A3	107
Flathead, co., Mt., U.S.	B2	103
Flathead, South Fork, stm., Mt., U.S.	C3	103
Flathead Indian Reservation, Mt., U.S.	C2	103
Flathead Lake, l., Mt., U.S.	C2	103
Flathead Valley, val., Mt., U.S.	C2	103
Flat Lake, l., La., U.S.	k9	95
Flat Lick, Ky., U.S.	D6	94
Flatonia, Tx., U.S.	E4	120
Flat River, Mo., U.S.	D7	102
Flat River Reservoir, res., R.I., U.S.	D3	116
Flat Rock, Mi., U.S.	F7	99
Flat Rock, N.C., U.S.	f10	110
Flatrock, stm., In., U.S.	F6	91
Flattery, Cape, c., Wa., U.S.	A1	124
Flatwoods, Ky., U.S.	B7	94
Fleetwood, Eng., U.K.	H9	7
Fleetwood, Pa., U.S.	F10	115
Flekkefjord, Nor.	G6	6
Fleming, co., Ky., U.S.	B6	94
Fleming-Neon, Ky., U.S.	C7	94
Flemingsburg, Ky., U.S.	B6	94
Flemington, N.J., U.S.	B3	107
Flemington, Pa., U.S.	D7	115
Flensburg, Ger.	A9	8
Flers, Fr.	D6	10
Fletcher, N.C., U.S.	f10	110
Fletcher, Ok., U.S.	C3	113
Fleurance, Fr.	I7	10
Flinders, stm., Austl.	C8	50
Flinders Island, i., Austl.	G9	50
Flin Flon, Man., Can.	B1	70
Flint, Wales, U.K.	H9	7
Flint, Mi., U.S.	E7	99
Flint, stm., Ga., U.S.	E2	87
Flint City, Al., U.S.	A3	78
Flint Creek Range, mts., Mt., U.S.	D3	103
Flint Run, stm., W.V., U.S.	k9	125
Flippin, Ar., U.S.	A3	81
Flomaton, Al., U.S.	D2	78
Flora, Il., U.S.	E5	90
Flora, In., U.S.	C4	91
Flora, Ms., U.S.	C3	101
Florac, Fr.	H10	10
Florala, Al., U.S.	D3	78
Floral City, Fl., U.S.	D4	86
Florence, Al., U.S.	A2	78
Florence, Az., U.S.	D4	80
Florence, Co., U.S.	C5	83
Florence, Ks., U.S.	D7	93
Florence, Ky., U.S.	A5	94
Florence, Ms., U.S.	C3	101
Florence, N.J., U.S.	C3	107
Florence, Or., U.S.	D2	114
Florence, S.C., U.S.	C8	117
Florence, co., S.C., U.S.	C8	117
Florence, co., Wi., U.S.	C5	126
Florence see Firenze, Italy	F6	14
Florenceville, N.B., Can.	C2	71
Florencia, Col.	G5	58
Flores, i., Indon.	G7	32
Flores, Laut (Flores Sea), Indon.	G6	32
Floresville, Tx., U.S.	E3	120
Florham Park, N.J., U.S.	B4	107
Floriano, Braz.	E10	54
Florianópolis, Braz.	B7	56
Florida, Col.	F4	58
Florida, Cuba	D8	64
Florida, N.Y., U.S.	D6	109
Florida, state, U.S.	E5	86
Florida, Cape, c., Fl., U.S.	G6	86
Florida, Straits of, strt., N.A.	B7	64
Florida Bay, b., Fl., U.S.	H6	86
Floridablanca, Col.	D6	58
Florida City, Fl., U.S.	G6	86
Florida Keys, is., Fl., U.S.	H6	86
Florida Mountains, mts., N.M., U.S.	E2	108
Florida State Indian Reservation, Fl., U.S.	F5	86
Florien, La., U.S.	C2	95
Florissant, Mo., U.S.	f13	102
Florissant Fossil Beds National Monument, Co., U.S.	C5	83
Florø, Nor.	F5	6
Flossmoor, Il., U.S.	k9	90
Flovilla, Ga., U.S.	C3	87
Flower Brook, stm., Vt., U.S.	E2	122
Flowery Branch, Ga., U.S.	B3	87
Flowood, Ms., U.S.	C3	101
Floyd, co., Ga., U.S.	B1	87
Floyd, co., In., U.S.	H6	91
Floyd, co., Ia., U.S.	A5	92
Floyd, co., Ky., U.S.	C7	94
Floyd, co., Tx., U.S.	B2	120
Floyd, co., Va., U.S.	D2	123
Floyd, stm., Ia., U.S.	B1	92
Floydada, Tx., U.S.	C2	120
Floyds Fork, stm., Ky., U.S.	B4	94
Floyds Knobs, In., U.S.	H6	91
Flushing, Mi., U.S.	E7	99
Flushing, Oh., U.S.	B4	112
Flushing see Vlissingen, Neth.	D3	8
Fluvanna, co., Va., U.S.	C4	123
Fly, stm.	m15	50a
Foard, co., Tx., U.S.	B3	120
Foça, Tur.	K10	16
Focşani, Rom.	D11	16
Fogang (Shijiao), China	L2	28
Foggia, Italy	H10	14
Fogland Point, c., R.I., U.S.	E6	116
Fogo, Newf., Can.	D4	72
Fogo, Cape, c., Newf., Can.	D5	72
Fogo Island, i., Newf., Can.	D4	72
Fohnsdorf, Aus.	H14	8
Foix, Fr.	J8	10
Foley, Al., U.S.	E2	78
Foley, Mn., U.S.	E5	100
Foley Island, i., N.W. Ter., Can.	C17	66
Foligno, Italy	G7	14
Folkestone, Eng., U.K.	J14	7
Folkston, Ga., U.S.	F4	87
Follansbee, W.V., U.S.	A4	125
Follonica, Italy	G5	14
Folly Beach, S.C., U.S.	F8	117
Folly Island, i., S.C., U.S.	F8	117
Folsom, Ca., U.S.	C3	82
Fonda, Ia., U.S.	B3	92
Fond du Lac, Wi., U.S.	E5	126
Fond du Lac, co., Wi., U.S.	E5	126
Fond du Lac Indian Reservation, Mn., U.S.	D6	100
Fondi, Italy	H8	14
Fondouk el Aouareb, Tun.	N4	14
Fonni, Italy	I4	14
Fonseca, Col.	B6	58
Fonseca, Golfo de, b., N.A.	H4	64
Fontainebleau, Fr.	D9	10
Fontana, Ca., U.S.	m14	82
Fontana, Wi., U.S.	F5	126
Fontana Lake, res., N.C., U.S.	f9	110
Fontanelle, Ia., U.S.	C3	92
Fonte Boa, Braz.	D5	54
Fontenay-le-Comte, Fr.	F6	10
Fontenelle Reservoir, res., Wy., U.S.	D2	127
Fontur, c., Ice.	B5	4
Foochow see Fuzhou, China	I8	28
Footville, Wi., U.S.	F4	126
Foraker, Mount, mtn., Ak., U.S.	f16	79
Forbach, Fr.	C13	10
Forbach, Ger.	G8	8
Forbes, Mount, mtn., Alta., Can.	D2	68
Forcalquier, Fr.	I12	10
Forchheim, Ger.	F11	8
Ford, co., Il., U.S.	C5	90
Ford, co., Ks., U.S.	E4	93
Ford, stm., Mi., U.S.	C3	99
Ford City, Ca., U.S.	E4	82
Ford City, Pa., U.S.	E2	115
Førde, Nor.	F5	6
Fordoche, La., U.S.	D4	95
Fords Prairie, Wa., U.S.	C2	124
Fordyce, Ar., U.S.	D3	81
Forel, Mont, mtn., Grnld.	C25	66
Foreman, Ar., U.S.	D1	81
Forest, Ont., Can.	D2	73
Forest, Ms., U.S.	C4	101
Forest, Oh., U.S.	B2	112
Forest, co., Pa., U.S.	C3	115
Forest, co., Wi., U.S.	C5	126
Forest, stm., N.D., U.S.	A8	111
Forest Acres, S.C., U.S.	C6	117
Forestburg, Alta., Can.	C4	68
Forest City, Ia., U.S.	A4	92
Forest City, N.C., U.S.	B1	110
Forest City, Pa., U.S.	C11	115
Forestdale, R.I., U.S.	B3	116
Forest Dale, Vt., U.S.	D2	122
Forest Glen, La., U.S.	h12	95
Forest Grove, Or., U.S.	B3	114
Forest Hill, Md., U.S.	A5	97
Forest Hills, Pa., U.S.	k14	115
Forest Knolls, Ca., U.S.	g7	82
Forest Lake, Mn., U.S.	E6	100
Forest Park, Ga., U.S.	h8	87
Forest Park, Il., U.S.	k9	90
Forest Park, La., U.S.	*B3	95
Forest Park, Oh., U.S.	*n12	112
Forfar, Scot., U.K.	E10	7
Forillon, Parc National de, Que., Can.	k14	74
Fork Creek, stm., W.V., U.S.	m12	125
Forked Deer, stm., Tn., U.S.	B2	119
Forkland, Al., U.S.	C2	78
Forks, Wa., U.S.	B1	124
Forlì, Italy	E7	14
Formia, Italy	H8	14
Formiga, Braz.	F6	57
Formosa, Arg.	B5	56
Formosa, Braz.	C5	57
Formosa, Serra, plat., Braz.	F8	54
Formosa see Taiwan, i., Asia	L9	28
Forney, Tx., U.S.	C4	120
Fornovo di Taro, Italy	E5	14
Forrest, Austl.	F5	50
Forrest, Il., U.S.	C5	90
Forrest, co., Ms., U.S.	D4	101
Forrest City, Ar., U.S.	B5	81
Forrester Island, i., Ak., U.S.	n23	79
Forreston, Il., U.S.	A4	90
Forsayth, Austl.	C8	50
Forst, Ger.	D14	8
Forsyth, Ga., U.S.	C3	87
Forsyth, Il., U.S.	D5	90
Forsyth, Mo., U.S.	E4	102
Forsyth, Mt., U.S.	D10	103
Forsyth, co., Ga., U.S.	B2	87
Forsyth, co., N.C., U.S.	A2	110
Fortaleza, Braz.	D11	54
Fort Apache Indian Reservation, Az., U.S.	D5	80
Fort-Archambault see Sarh, Chad	G9	42
Fort Ashby, W.V., U.S.	B6	125
Fort Atkinson, Wi., U.S.	F5	126
Fort Augustus, Scot., U.K.	D8	7
Fort Beaufort, S. Afr.	H5	44
Fort Belknap Indian Reservation, Mt., U.S.	B8	103
Fort Belvoir, mil., Va., U.S.	g12	123
Fort Bend, co., Tx., U.S.	E5	120
Fort Benjamin Harrison, mil., In., U.S.	k10	91
Fort Benning, mil., Ga., U.S.	D2	87
Fort Benton, Mt., U.S.	C6	103
Fort Berthold Indian Reservation, N.D., U.S.	B3	111
Fort Bidwell Indian Reservation, Ca., U.S.	B3	82
Fort Bliss, mil., Tx., U.S.	o11	120
Fort Bragg, Ca., U.S.	C2	82
Fort Bragg, mil., N.C., U.S.	B3	110
Fort Branch, In., U.S.	H2	91
Fort Calhoun, Ne., U.S.	C9	104
Fort Campbell, mil., U.S.	A4	119
Fort Carson, mil., Co., U.S.	C6	83
Fort Chipewyan, Alta., Can.	f8	68
Fort Clatsop National Memorial, hist., Or., U.S.	A3	114
Fort Cobb, Ok., U.S.	B3	113
Fort Cobb Reservoir, res., Ok., U.S.	B3	113
Fort Collins, Co., U.S.	A5	83
Fort Coulonge, Que., Can.	B8	73
Fort Davis, Tx., U.S.	o13	120
Fort Davis National Historic Site, hist., Tx., U.S.	o13	120
Fort Defiance, Az., U.S.	B6	80
Fort-de-France, Mart.	G17	64
Fort Deposit, Al., U.S.	D3	78
Fort Detrick, mil., Md., U.S.	B3	97
Fort Devens, mil., Ma., U.S.	f9	98
Fort Dix, mil., N.J., U.S.	C3	107
Fort Dodge, Ia., U.S.	B3	92
Fort Donelson National Battlefield, Tn., U.S.	A4	119
Fort Edward, N.Y., U.S.	B7	109
Fort Erie, Ont., Can.	E6	73
Fortescue, stm., Austl.	D3	50
Fort Eustis, mil., Va., U.S.	h14	123
Fort Fairfield, Me., U.S.	B5	96
Fort Frances, Ont., Can.	o16	73
Fort Franklin, N.W. Ter., Can.	C8	66
Fort Gaines, Ga., U.S.	E1	87
Fort Gay, W.V., U.S.	C2	125
Fort Gibson, Ok., U.S.	B6	113
Fort Gibson Lake, res., Ok., U.S.	A6	113
Fort Good Hope, N.W. Ter., Can.	C7	66
Fort Gordon, mil., Ga., U.S.	C4	87
Fort Greely, mil., Ak., U.S.	C10	79
Forth, Firth of, est., Scot., U.K.	E10	7
Fort Hall, Id., U.S.	F6	89
Fort Hall Indian Reservation, Id., U.S.	F6	89
Fort Hood, mil., Tx., U.S.	D4	120
Fort Howard, Md., U.S.	B5	97
Fort Huachuca, mil., Az., U.S.	F5	80
Fortín Coronel Eugenio Garay, Para.	H6	54
Fort Jackson, mil., S.C., U.S.	C6	117
Fort Jefferson National Monument, Fl., U.S.	H4	86
Fort Kent, Me., U.S.	A4	96
Fort Knox, mil., Ky., U.S.	B4	94
Fort-Lamy see N'Djamena, Chad	F9	42
Fort Laramie, Wy., U.S.	D8	127
Fort Laramie National Historic Site, hist., Wy., U.S.	D8	127
Fort Lauderdale, Fl., U.S.	F6	86
Fort Lawn, S.C., U.S.	B6	117
Fort Leavenworth, mil., Ks., U.S.	C9	93
Fort Lee, N.J., U.S.	B5	107
Fort Lee, mil., Va., U.S.	C5	123
Fort Leonard Wood, mil., Mo., U.S.	D5	102
Fort Lewis, mil., Wa., U.S.	B3	124
Fort Liard, N.W. Ter., Can.	D8	66
Fort Loramie, Oh., U.S.	B1	112
Fort Loudon, Pa., U.S.	G6	115
Fort Loudoun Lake, res., Tn., U.S.	D9	119
Fort Lupton, Co., U.S.	A6	83
Fort MacArthur, mil., Ca., U.S.	n12	82
Fort Macleod, Alta., Can.	E4	68
Fort Madison, Ia., U.S.	D6	92
Fort Matanzas National Monument, Fl., U.S.	C5	86
Fort McClellan, mil., Al., U.S.	B4	78
Fort McDermitt Indian Reservation, U.S.	B4	105
Fort McDowell Indian Reservation, Az., U.S.	D4	80
Fort McHenry National Monument And Historic Shrine, Md., U.S.	g11	97
Fort McMurray, Alta., Can.	A5	68
Fort Meade, Fl., U.S.	E5	86
Fort Meade, mil., Md., U.S.	B4	97
Fort Meadow Reservoir, res., Ma., U.S.	g9	98
Fort Mill, S.C., U.S.	A6	117
Fort Mitchell, Al., U.S.	C4	78
Fort Mitchell, Ky., U.S.	h13	94
Fort Mojave Indian Reservation, U.S.	C1	80
Fort Monmouth, mil., N.J., U.S.	C4	107
Fort Monroe, mil., Va., U.S.	h15	123
Fort Morgan, Co., U.S.	A7	83
Fort Myer, mil., Va., U.S.	g12	123
Fort Myers, Fl., U.S.	F5	86
Fort Myers Beach, Fl., U.S.	F5	86
Fort Nelson, B.C., Can.	m18	69
Fort Norman, N.W. Ter., Can.	D7	66
Fort Oglethorpe, Ga., U.S.	B1	87
Fort Ord, mil., Ca., U.S.	D3	82
Fort Payne, Al., U.S.	A4	78
Fort Peck Indian Reservation, Mt., U.S.	B11	103
Fort Peck Lake, res., Mt., U.S.	C9	103
Fort Pierce, Fl., U.S.	E6	86
Fort Pierce Inlet, b., Fl., U.S.	E6	86
Fort Pierre, S.D., U.S.	C5	118
Fort Plain, N.Y., U.S.	C6	109
Fort Polk, mil., La., U.S.	C2	95
Fort Portal, Ug.	A6	44
Fort Providence, N.W. Ter., Can.	D9	66
Fort Randall Dam, S.D., U.S.	D7	118
Fort Recovery, Oh., U.S.	B1	112
Fort Reliance, N.W. Ter., Can.	D11	66
Fort Resolution, N.W. Ter., Can.	D10	66
Fortress Mountain, mtn., Wy., U.S.	B3	127
Fort Richardson, mil., Ak., U.S.	C10	79
Fort Riley, mil., Ks., U.S.	C7	93
Fort Ritchie, mil., Md., U.S.	A3	97
Fort Rucker, mil., Al., U.S.	D4	78
Fort Saint James, B.C., Can.	B5	69
Fort Saint John, B.C., Can.	A7	69
Fort Sam Houston, mil., Tx., U.S.	k7	120
Fort Sandeman, Pak.	E3	38
Fort Saskatchewan, Alta., Can.	C4	68
Fort Scott, Ks., U.S.	E9	93
Fort Shafter, mil., Hi., U.S.	g10	88
Fort Shawnee, Oh., U.S.	B1	112
Fort Sheridan, mil., Il., U.S.	h9	90
Fort Sill, mil., Ok., U.S.	C3	113
Fort Simpson, N.W. Ter., Can.	D8	66
Fort Smith, N.W. Ter., Can.	D10	66
Fort Smith, Ar., U.S.	B1	81
Fort Stewart, mil., Ga., U.S.	D5	87
Fort Stockton, Tx., U.S.	D1	120
Fort Sumner, N.M., U.S.	C5	108
Fort Sumter National Monument, S.C., U.S.	k12	117
Fort Supply Lake, res., Ok., U.S.	A2	113
Fort Thomas, Ky., U.S.	h14	94
Fort Totten, N.D., U.S.	B7	111
Fort Totten Indian Reservation, N.D., U.S.	B7	111
Fortuna, Ca., U.S.	B1	82
Fortune, Newf., Can.	E4	72
Fortune Bay, b., Newf., Can.	E4	72
Fort Union National Monument, N.M., U.S.	B5	108
Fort Valley, Ga., U.S.	D3	87
Fort Vermilion, Alta., Can.	f7	68
Fortville, In., U.S.	E6	91
Fort Wainwright, mil., Ak., U.S.	C10	79
Fort Walton Beach, Fl., U.S.	u15	86
Fort Washington Forest, Md., U.S.	C4	97
Fort Wayne, In., U.S.	B7	91
Fort William, Scot., U.K.	E7	7
Fort Wingate, N.M., U.S.	B1	108
Fort Worth, Tx., U.S.	C4	120
Fort Wright, Ky., U.S.	h13	94
Forty Fort, Pa., U.S.	D10	115
Fort Yukon, Ak., U.S.	B10	79
Fort Yuma Indian Reservation, Ca., U.S.	F6	82
Foshan, China	L2	28
Fossano, Italy	E2	14
Fossil Butte National Monument, Wy., U.S.	E2	127
Fossil Lake, l., Or., U.S.	D6	114
Fossombrone, Italy	F7	14
Foss Reservoir, res., Ok., U.S.	B2	113
Fosston, Mn., U.S.	C3	100
Foster, Or., U.S.	C4	114
Foster, co., N.D., U.S.	B6	111
Foster Village, Hi., U.S.	g10	88
Fostoria, Oh., U.S.	A2	112
Fougamou, Gabon	B2	44
Fougères, Fr.	D5	10
Fouke, Ar., U.S.	D2	81
Foula, i., Scot., U.K.	A10	7
Foumban, Cam.	G8	42
Fountain, Co., U.S.	C6	83
Fountain, co., In., U.S.	D3	91
Fountain City, In., U.S.	E8	91
Fountain City, Wi., U.S.	D2	126
Fountain Hill, Pa., U.S.	E11	115
Fountain Inn, S.C., U.S.	B3	117
Fountain Peak, mtn., Ca., U.S.	E6	82
Fountain Place, La., U.S.	*D4	95
Fourche LaFave, stm., Ar., U.S.	C2	81
Fourche Maline, stm., Ok., U.S.	C6	113
Fourmies, Fr.	B11	10
Four Mountains, Islands of, is., Ak., U.S.	E6	79
Four Oaks, N.C., U.S.	B4	110
Fowler, Ca., U.S.	D4	82
Fowler, Co., U.S.	C6	83
Fowler, In., U.S.	C3	91
Fowler, Mi., U.S.	E6	99
Fowlerville, Mi., U.S.	F6	99
Fox, stm., Man., Can.	B4	70
Fox, stm., U.S.	B5	90
Fox, stm., U.S.	A6	102
Fox, stm., Mi., U.S.	B4	99
Fox, stm., Wi., U.S.	D5	126
Foxboro, Ont., Can.	C7	73
Foxboro, Ma., U.S.	B5	98
Fox Creek, Alta., Can.	B2	68
Foxe Basin, b., N.W. Ter., Can.	C17	66
Foxe Channel, strt., N.W. Ter., Can.	D16	66
Foxe Peninsula, pen., N.W. Ter., Can.	D17	66
Fox Island, i., R.I., U.S.	E4	116
Fox Island, i., Wa., U.S.	f10	124
Fox Islands, is., Ak., U.S.	E6	79
Fox Lake, Il., U.S.	A5	90
Fox Lake, Wi., U.S.	E5	126
Fox Lake, l., Il., U.S.	h8	90
Fox Mountain, mtn., Nv., U.S.	B2	105
Fox Point, Wi., U.S.	E6	126
Fox River Grove, Il., U.S.	h8	90
Foxworth, Ms., U.S.	D4	101
Foz do Cunene, Ang.	E2	44
Foz do Iguaçu, Braz.	B6	56
Frackville, Pa., U.S.	E9	115
Fraga, Spain	D12	12
Framingham, Ma., U.S.	B5	98
Franca, Braz.	F5	57
Francavilla Fontana, Italy	I12	14
France, ctry., Eur.	F8	4
Francesville, In., U.S.	C4	91
Franceville, Gabon	B2	44
Francis, Lake, l., N.H., U.S.	f7	106
Francis Case, Lake, res., S.D., U.S.	D6	118
Francistown, Bots.	F5	44
Francofonte, Italy	L9	14
Franconia, N.H., U.S.	B3	106
Franconia Notch, N.H., U.S.	B3	106
Francs Peak, mtn., Wy., U.S.	C3	127
Frankenberg, Ger.	E13	8
Frankenberg-Eder, Ger.	D8	8
Frankenmuth, Mi., U.S.	E7	99
Frankford, Ont., Can.	C7	73
Frankford, De., U.S.	F5	85
Frankfort, Il., U.S.	m9	90
Frankfort, In., U.S.	D4	91
Frankfort, Ks., U.S.	C7	93
Frankfort, Ky., U.S.	B5	94
Frankfort, Mi., U.S.	D4	99
Frankfort, N.Y., U.S.	B5	109
Frankfort, Oh., U.S.	C2	112
Frankfurt am Main, Ger.	E8	8
Frankfurt an der Oder, Ger.	C14	8
Franklin, Ga., U.S.	C1	87
Franklin, In., U.S.	F5	91
Franklin, Ky., U.S.	D3	94
Franklin, La., U.S.	E4	95
Franklin, Ma., U.S.	B5	98
Franklin, Ne., U.S.	D7	104
Franklin, N.H., U.S.	D3	106
Franklin, N.J., U.S.	A3	107
Franklin, N.C., U.S.	f9	110
Franklin, Oh., U.S.	C1	112
Franklin, Pa., U.S.	D2	115
Franklin, Tn., U.S.	B5	119
Franklin, Tx., U.S.	D4	120
Franklin, Va., U.S.	D6	123
Franklin, W.V., U.S.	C5	125
Franklin, Wi., U.S.	n11	126
Franklin, co., Al., U.S.	A2	78
Franklin, co., Ar., U.S.	B2	81
Franklin, co., Fl., U.S.	C2	86
Franklin, co., Ga., U.S.	B3	87
Franklin, co., Id., U.S.	G7	89
Franklin, co., Il., U.S.	E4	90
Franklin, co., In., U.S.	F7	91
Franklin, co., Ia., U.S.	B4	92

Name — Map Ref — Page
Franklin, co., Ks., U.S. D8 93
Franklin, co., Ky., U.S. B5 94
Franklin, co., La., U.S. B4 95
Franklin, co., Me., U.S. C2 96
Franklin, co., Ma., U.S. A2 98
Franklin, co., Ms., U.S. D3 101
Franklin, co., Mo., U.S. C6 102
Franklin, co., Ne., U.S. D7 104
Franklin, co., N.Y., U.S. f10 109
Franklin, co., N.C., U.S. A4 110
Franklin, co., Oh., U.S. B2 112
Franklin, co., Pa., U.S. G6 115
Franklin, co., Tn., U.S. B5 119
Franklin, co., Tx., U.S. C5 120
Franklin, co., Vt., U.S. B2 122
Franklin, co., Va., U.S. D3 123
Franklin, co., Wa., U.S. C6 124
Franklin, Point, c., Ak., U.S. A8 79
Franklin Bay, b., N.W. Ter., Can. C7 66
Franklin D. Roosevelt Lake, res., Wa., U.S. B7 124
Franklin Falls Reservoir, res., N.H., U.S. C3 106
Franklin Grove, Il., U.S. B4 90
Franklin Lake, l., N.W. Ter., Can. C13 66
Franklin Lake, l., Nv., U.S. C6 105
Franklin Mountains, mts., N.W. Ter., Can. D8 66
Franklin Park, Il., U.S. k9 90
Franklin Park, Pa., U.S. *h13 115
Franklin Strait, strt., N.W. Ter., Can. B13 66
Franklinton, La., U.S. D5 95
Franklinton, N.C., U.S. A4 110
Franklinville, N.Y., U.S. C2 109
Frankston, Tx., U.S. C5 120
Frankton, In., U.S. D6 91
Frascati, Italy H7 14
Fraser, stm., B.C., Can. E7 69
Fraser, stm., Newf., Can. g9 72
Fraser, Mount, mtn., Can. C8 69
Fraserburgh, Scot., U.K. D10 7
Fraser Lake, B.C., Can. B5 69
Fraser Plateau, plat., B.C., Can. D6 69
Frauenfeld, Switz. E15 10
Frazee, Mn., U.S. D3 100
Frazeysburg, Oh., U.S. B3 112
Frazier Park, Ca., U.S. E4 82
Fr'azino, Russia F21 18
Frederic, Wi., U.S. C1 126
Frederica, De., U.S. D4 85
Fredericia, Den. I7 6
Frederick, Co., U.S. A6 83
Frederick, Md., U.S. B3 97
Frederick, Ok., U.S. C2 113
Frederick, co., Md., U.S. B3 97
Frederick, co., Va., U.S. A4 123
Fredericksburg, Ia., U.S. B5 92
Fredericksburg, Tx., U.S. D3 120
Fredericksburg, Va., U.S. B5 123
Frederick Sound, strt., Ak., U.S. m23 79
Fredericktown, Mo., U.S. D7 102
Fredericktown, Oh., U.S. B3 112
Fredericktown, Pa., U.S. F1 115
Fredericton, N.B., Can. D3 71
Fredericton Junction, N.B., Can. D3 71
Frederikshåb, Grnld. D23 66
Frederikshavn, Den. H8 6
Fredonia, Az., U.S. A3 80
Fredonia, Ks., U.S. E8 93
Fredonia, N.Y., U.S. C1 109
Fredonia, Wi., U.S. E6 126
Fredrikstad, Nor. G8 6
Freeborn, co., Mn., U.S. G5 100
Freeburg, Il., U.S. E4 90
Freedom, Pa., U.S. E1 115
Freedom, Wy., U.S. D2 127
Freehold, N.J., U.S. C4 107
Freeland, Mi., U.S. E6 99
Freeland, Pa., U.S. D10 115
Freelandville, In., U.S. G3 91
Freel Peak, mtn., Ca., U.S. C4 82
Freels, Cape, c., Newf., Can. D5 72
Freels, Cape, c., Newf., Can. E5 72
Freeman, S.D., U.S. D8 118
Freeman, Lake, l., In., U.S. C4 91
Freemansburg, Pa., U.S. E11 115
Freemason Island, i., La., U.S. E7 95
Freeport, Bah. A8 64
Freeport, Il., U.S. A4 90
Freeport, Me., U.S. E2 96
Freeport, N.Y., U.S. n15 109
Freeport, Pa., U.S. E2 115
Freeport, Tx., U.S. E5 120
Freer, Tx., U.S. F3 120
Freestone, co., Tx., U.S. D4 120
Freetown, S.L. G3 42
Freetown, In., U.S. G5 91
Freezeout Mountains, mts., Wy., U.S. D6 127
Fregenal de la Sierra, Spain G5 12
Freiberg, Ger. E13 8
Freiburg [im Breisgau], Ger. H7 8
Freising, Ger. G11 8
Freistadt, Aus. G14 8
Freital, Ger. D13 8
Fréjus, Fr. I13 10
Fremont, Ca., U.S. D2 82
Fremont, In., U.S. A8 91
Fremont, Ia., U.S. C5 92
Fremont, Mi., U.S. E5 99
Fremont, Ne., U.S. C9 104
Fremont, N.C., U.S. B5 110
Fremont, Oh., U.S. A2 112
Fremont, co., Co., U.S. C5 83
Fremont, co., Id., U.S. E7 89
Fremont, co., Ia., U.S. D2 92
Fremont, co., Wy., U.S. C4 127
Fremont, stm., Ut., U.S. E4 121
Fremont Island, i., Ut., U.S. B3 121
Fremont Lake, l., Wy., U.S. D3 127
Fremont Peak, mtn., Wy., U.S. C3 127
French Broad, stm., U.S. D10 119
Frenchburg, Ky., U.S. C6 94
French Creek, stm., Pa., U.S. C2 115
French Frigate Shoals, rf., Hi., U.S. m14 88
French Guiana, dep., S.A. C8 54
French Lick, In., U.S. G4 91
Frenchman Bay, b., Me., U.S. D4 96
Frenchman Creek, stm., U.S. D4 104
Frenchman Hills, hills, Wa., U.S. C6 124
Frenchman Lake, l., Nv., U.S. G6 105
French Polynesia, dep., Oc. G3 2
French Settlement, La., U.S. D5 95
Freshfield, Mount, mtn., Can. D2 68
Fresnillo, Mex. F8 62
Fresno, Ca., U.S. D4 82
Fresno, co., Ca., U.S. D4 82
Fresno Reservoir, res., Mt., U.S. B6 103
Freudenstadt, Ger. G8 8
Frewsburg, N.Y., U.S. C1 109
Fria, Cape, c., Nmb. E2 44
Friars Point, Ms., U.S. A3 101
Frías, Arg. B3 56
Fribourg (Freiburg), Switz. F14 10
Friday Harbor, Wa., U.S. A2 124
Fridley, Mn., U.S. m12 100
Friedberg, Aus. H16 8
Friedrichshafen, Ger. H9 8
Friend, Ne., U.S. D8 104
Friendsville, Tn., U.S. D9 119
Fries, Va., U.S. D2 123
Friesland, hist. reg., Neth. B5 8
Frio, co., Tx., U.S. E3 120
Frio, stm., Tx., U.S. E3 120
Frio, Cabo, c., Braz. G7 57
Friona, Tx., U.S. B1 120
Fripps Island, i., S.C., U.S. G7 117
Frisco, Co., U.S. B4 83
Frisco City, Al., U.S. D2 78
Frisco Peak, mtn., Ut., U.S. E2 121
Frissell, Mount, mtn., U.S. A2 84
Fritch, Tx., U.S. B2 120
Fritzlar, Ger. D9 8
Friza, Proliv, strt., Russia H23 24
Frobisher Bay, b., N.W. Ter., Can. D19 66
Frobisher Lake, l., Sask., Can. m7 75
Frohnleiten, Aus. H15 8
Frontenac, Ks., U.S. E9 93
Frontier, co., Ne., U.S. D5 104
Front Range, mts., Co., U.S. A5 83
Front Royal, Va., U.S. B4 123
Frosinone, Italy H8 14
Frostburg, Md., U.S. k13 97
Frostproof, Fl., U.S. E5 86
Fruita, Co., U.S. B2 83
Fruit Heights, Ut., U.S. B4 121
Fruitland, Id., U.S. F2 89
Fruitland, Md., U.S. D6 97
Fruitland, N.M., U.S. A1 108
Fruitland Park, Fl., U.S. D5 86
Fruitport, Mi., U.S. E4 99
Fruitvale, B.C., Can. E9 69
Fruitvale, Co., U.S. B2 83
Fruitvale, Wa., U.S. C5 124
Fruitville, Fl., U.S. E4 86
Frunze see Biškek, Kyrg. I12 22
Frutigen, Switz. F14 10
Fryeburg, Me., U.S. D2 96
Fuchū, Japan H6 30
Fuencaliente, Spain G7 12
Fuente de Cantos, Spain G5 12
Fuente-obejuna, Spain G6 12
Fuerteventura, i., Spain p27 13b
Fuji, Japan G11 30
Fuji, Mount see Fuji-san, vol., Japan G11 30
Fujian, prov., China F10 26
Fujin, China B13 26
Fujinomiya, Japan G11 30
Fuji-san (Fujiyama), vol., Japan G11 30
Fujisawa, Japan G12 30
Fujiyama see Fuji-san, vol., Japan G11 30
Fuji-yoshida, Japan G11 30
Fukagawa, Japan p20 30a
Fukaya, Japan F12 30
Fukuchiyama, Japan G8 30
Fukue, Japan J1 30
Fukui, Japan F9 30
Fukuoka, Japan I3 30
Fukushima, Japan E13 30
Fukushima, Japan r18 30a
Fukuyama, Japan H6 30
Fūlādī, Kūh-e, mtn., Afg. C2 38
Fulda, Ger. E9 8
Fulda, Mn., U.S. G3 100
Fullerton, Ca., U.S. n13 82
Fullerton, Ne., U.S. C8 104
Fulton, Il., U.S. B3 90
Fulton, Ky., U.S. f9 94
Fulton, Md., U.S. B4 97
Fulton, Ms., U.S. A5 101
Fulton, Mo., U.S. C6 102
Fulton, N.Y., U.S. B4 109
Fulton, co., Ar., U.S. A4 81
Fulton, co., Ga., U.S. C2 87
Fulton, co., Il., U.S. C3 90
Fulton, co., In., U.S. B5 91
Fulton, co., Ky., U.S. f8 94
Fulton, co., N.Y., U.S. B6 109
Fulton, co., Oh., U.S. A1 112
Fulton, co., Pa., U.S. G5 115
Fultondale, Al., U.S. f7 78
Funabashi, Japan G13 30
Funchal, Port. n21 13a
Fundación, Col. B5 58
Fundy, Bay of, b., Can. D4 71
Fundy National Park, N.B., Can. D4 71
Funkstown, Md., U.S. A2 97
Fuquay-Varina, N.C., U.S. B4 110
Furano, Japan p20 30a
Furmanov, Russia D24 18
Furnace Brook, stm., Vt., U.S. D3 122
Furnas, co., Ne., U.S. D6 104
Furnas, Represa de, res., Braz. F5 57
Furneaux Group, is., Austl. H9 50
Furqlus, Syria B5 40
Fürstenfeld, Aus. H16 8
Fürstenfeldbruck, Ger. G11 8
Fürstenwalde, Ger. C14 8
Fürth, Ger. F10 8
Furth im Wald, Ger. F12 8
Furudal, Swe. F10 6
Fushun, China C11 26
Füssen, Ger. H10 8
Fuxian, China D11 26
Fuxian, China D8 26
Fuxinshi, China C11 26
Fuyang, China C4 28
Fuzhou, China G5 28
Fuzhou (Foochow), China I8 28
Fyffe, Al., U.S. A4 78

G

Gabbs, Nv., U.S. E4 105
Gabès, Tun. B8 42
Gabès, Golfe de, b., Tun. B8 42
Gabon, ctry., Afr. B2 44
Gaborone, Bots. F5 44
Gabriel Strait, strt., N.W. Ter., Can. D19 66
Gabriola, B.C., Can. f12 69
Gabrovo, Bul. G9 16
Gadag, India E3 37
Gäddede, Swe. D10 6
Gadsden, Al., U.S. A3 78
Gadsden, co., Fl., U.S. B2 86
Gaeta, Italy H8 14
Gaffney, S.C., U.S. A4 117
Gafsa, Tun. B7 42
Gage, co., Ne., U.S. D9 104
Gagetown, N.B., Can. D3 71
Gagliano del Capo, Italy J13 14
Gagnoa, C. Iv. G4 42
Gahanna, Oh., U.S. k11 112
Gaillac, Fr. I8 10
Gaillard, Lake, l., Ct., U.S. D5 84
Gaines, co., Tx., U.S. C1 120
Gainesboro, Tn., U.S. C8 119
Gaines Creek, stm., Ok., U.S. C6 113
Gainesville, Fl., U.S. C4 86
Gainesville, Ga., U.S. B3 87
Gainesville, Mo., U.S. E5 102
Gainesville, Tx., U.S. C4 120
Gainesville, Va., U.S. g11 123
Gairdner, Lake, l., Austl. F7 50
Gaithersburg, Md., U.S. B3 97
Galán, Cerro, mtn., Arg. B3 56
Galapagos Islands see Colón, Archipiélago de, is., Ec. m15 58a
Galashiels, Scot., U.K. F10 7
Galați, Rom. D12 16
Galatia, Il., U.S. F5 90
Galatina, Italy I13 14
Galax, Va., U.S. D2 123
Galena, Ak., U.S. C8 79
Galena, Il., U.S. A3 90
Galena, Ks., U.S. E9 93
Galeota Point, c., Trin. I17 64
Galera, Punta, c., Chile D2 56
Galera, Punta, c., Ec. G2 58
Galesburg, Il., U.S. C3 90
Galesburg, Mi., U.S. F5 99
Gales Ferry, Ct., U.S. D7 84
Galesville, Md., U.S. C4 97
Galesville, Wi., U.S. D2 126
Galeton, Pa., U.S. C6 115
Galič, Russia C25 18
Galicia, hist. reg., Eur. F21 8
Galicia, hist. reg., Spain B3 12
Galilee, Sea of see Kinneret, Yam, l., Isr. C4 40
Galion, Oh., U.S. B3 112
Galisteo Creek, stm., N.M., U.S. k8 108
Galiuro Mountains, mts., Az., U.S. E5 80
Galka'yo, Som. G4 46
Gallant, Al., U.S. B3 78
Gallarate, Italy D3 14
Gallatin, Mo., U.S. B4 102
Gallatin, Tn., U.S. A5 119
Gallatin, co., Il., U.S. F5 90
Gallatin, co., Ky., U.S. B5 94
Gallatin, co., Mt., U.S. E5 103
Gallatin, stm., Mt., U.S. E5 103
Gallatin Range, mts., Mt., U.S. E5 103
Gallaway, Tn., U.S. B2 119
Galle, Sri L. I6 37
Gallia, co., Oh., U.S. D3 112
Galliano, La., U.S. E5 95
Gallinas, Punta, c., Col. A7 58
Gallinas Mountains, mts., N.M., U.S. C2 108
Gallipoli, Italy I12 14
Gallipoli see Gelibolu, Tur. I10 16
Gallipolis, Oh., U.S. D3 112
Gallitzin, Pa., U.S. F4 115
Gällivare, Swe. C13 6
Gallo Mountains, mts., N.M., U.S. C1 108
Galloo Island, i., N.Y., U.S. B4 109
Galloway, Mull of, c., Scot., U.K. G8 7
Gallup, N.M., U.S. B1 108
Galt, Ca., U.S. C3 82
Galtür, Aus. I10 8
Galty Mountains, mts., Ire. I4 7
Galva, Il., U.S. B3 90
Galva, Ks., U.S. D6 93
Galveston, In., U.S. C5 91
Galveston, Tx., U.S. E5 120
Galveston, co., Tx., U.S. E5 120
Galveston Bay, b., Tx., U.S. E5 120
Galveston Island, i., Tx., U.S. E5 120
Gálvez, Arg. C4 56
Galway, Ire. H3 7
Gambela, Eth. G1 46
Gambell, Ak., U.S. C5 79
Gambia, ctry., Afr. F2 42
Gambia (Gambie), stm., Afr. F2 42
Gambier, Oh., U.S. B3 112
Gambo, Newf., Can. D4 72
Gambrills, Md., U.S. B4 97
Gamleby, Swe. H11 6
Ganado, Az., U.S. B6 80
Ganado, Tx., U.S. E4 120
Gananoque, Ont., Can. C8 73
Ganda, Ang. D2 44
Gandak, stm., Asia G11 38
Gander, Newf., Can. D4 72
Gander, stm., Newf., Can. D4 72
Ganderkesee, Ger. B8 8
Gander Lake, l., Newf., Can. D4 72
Gandesa, Spain D12 12
Gāndhinagar, India I5 38
Gāndhi Sāgar, res., India H6 38
Gandia, Spain G11 12
Gangāpur, India G7 38
Gangāwati, India E4 37
Gangdisê Shan, mts., China E10 38
Ganges, B.C., Can. g12 69
Ganges (Ganga) (Padma), stm., Asia I13 38
Ganges, Mouths of the, mth., Asia J13 38
Gang Mills, N.Y., U.S. C3 109
Gangtok, India G13 38
Gangu, China E8 26
Gannat, Fr. F10 10
Gannett Peak, mtn., Wy., U.S. C3 127
Gansu, prov., China D7 26
Gantt, S.C., U.S. B3 117
Gantt Lake, res., Al., U.S. D3 78
Ganzhou, China J3 28
Ganzi, China E7 26
Gao, Mali E5 42
Gaokeng, China H2 28
Gaoyou, China C8 28
Gaozhou, China D11 34
Gap, Fr. H13 10
Gap, Pa., U.S. G9 115
Gar, China E9 38
Garanhuns, Braz. E11 54
Garber, Ok., U.S. A4 113
Garberville, Ca., U.S. B2 82
Garça, Braz. G4 57
Garda, Lago di, l., Italy D5 14
Gardelegen, Ger. C11 8
Garden, co., Ne., U.S. C3 104
Gardena, Ca., U.S. n12 82
Garden City, Ga., U.S. D5 87
Garden City, Id., U.S. F2 89
Garden City, Ks., U.S. E3 93
Garden City, Mi., U.S. p15 99
Garden City, Mo., U.S. C3 102
Gardendale, Al., U.S. B3 78
Garden Grove, Ca., U.S. n13 82
Garden Island, i., Mi., U.S. C5 99
Garden Plain, Ks., U.S. E6 93
Garden Reach, India I13 38
Gardēz, Afg. D3 38
Gardiner, Me., U.S. D3 96
Gardiner, Mt., U.S. E6 103
Gardiner, Or., U.S. D2 114
Gardiners Island, i., N.Y., U.S. m16 109
Gardner, Il., U.S. B5 90
Gardner, Ks., U.S. D9 93
Gardner, Ma., U.S. A4 98
Gardner Canal, strt., B.C., Can. C3 69
Gardner Lake, l., Ct., U.S. C6 84
Gardner Lake, l., Me., U.S. D5 96
Gardner Pinnacles, Hi., U.S. k14 88
Gardnerville, Nv., U.S. E2 105
Gardone Val Trompia, Italy D5 14
Garfield, N.J., U.S. h8 107
Garfield, co., Co., U.S. B2 83
Garfield, co., Mt., U.S. C9 103
Garfield, co., Ne., U.S. C6 104
Garfield, co., Ok., U.S. A4 113
Garfield, co., Ut., U.S. F4 121
Garfield, co., Wa., U.S. C8 124
Garfield Heights, Oh., U.S. h9 112
Garfield Mountain, mtn., Mt., U.S. F4 103
Garfield Peak, mtn., Wy., U.S. D5 127
Garibaldi, Or., U.S. B3 114
Garibaldi, Mount, mtn., B.C., Can. E6 69
Garies, S. Afr. H3 44
Garissa, Kenya B7 44
Garland, N.C., U.S. C4 110
Garland, Tx., U.S. n10 120
Garland, Ut., U.S. B3 121
Garland, co., Ar., U.S. C2 81
Garlin, Fr. I6 10
Garm Āb, Afg. D1 38
Garmisch-Partenkirchen, Ger. H11 8
Garnavillo, Ia., U.S. B6 92
Garner, Ia., U.S. A4 92
Garner, N.C., U.S. B4 110
Garnet Range, mts., Mt., U.S. D3 103
Garnett, Ks., U.S. D8 93
Garnish, Newf., Can. E4 72
Garonne, stm., Eur. H6 10
Garoua, Cam. G8 42
Garrard, co., Ky., U.S. C5 94
Garretson, S.D., U.S. D9 118
Garrett, In., U.S. B7 91
Garrett, co., Md., U.S. k12 97
Garrett Park, Md., U.S. B3 97
Garrettsville, Oh., U.S. A4 112
Garrison, Ky., U.S. B6 94
Garrison, Md., U.S. B4 97
Garrison, N.D., U.S. B4 111
Garrison Dam, N.D., U.S. B4 111
Garrovillas, Spain F5 12
Garry Lake, l., N.W. Ter., Can. C12 66
Garsen, Kenya B8 44
Garut, Indon. m13 33a
Garvin, co., Ok., U.S. C4 113
Gary, In., U.S. A3 91
Gary, W.V., U.S. D3 125
Garysburg, N.C., U.S. A5 110
Garyville, La., U.S. D5 95
Garza, co., Tx., U.S. C2 120
Garza-Little Elm Reservoir, res., Tx., U.S. C4 120
Garzón, Col. F5 58
Gas City, In., U.S. D6 91
Gasconade, co., Mo., U.S. C6 102
Gasconade, stm., Mo., U.S. C6 102
Gascoyne, stm., Austl. E3 50
Gasparilla Island, i., Fl., U.S. F4 86
Gaspé, Que., Can. k14 74
Gaspésie, Péninsule de la, pen., Que., Can. k13 74
Gassaway, W.V., U.S. C4 125
Gassville, Ar., U.S. A3 81
Gaston, In., U.S. D7 91
Gaston, N.C., U.S. A5 110
Gaston, S.C., U.S. D5 117
Gaston, co., N.C., U.S. B1 110
Gaston, Lake, res., U.S. A5 110
Gaston Dam, N.C., U.S. A5 110
Gastonia, N.C., U.S. B1 110
Gátas, Akrotírion, c., Cyp. B3 40
Gatčina, Russia B13 18
Gate City, Va., U.S. f9 123
Gates, N.Y., U.S. *B3 109
Gates, Tn., U.S. B2 119
Gates, co., N.C., U.S. A6 110
Gateshead, Eng., U.K. G11 7
Gateshead Island, i., N.W. Ter., Can. B12 66
Gates of the Arctic National Park, Ak., U.S. B9 79
Gatesville, Tx., U.S. D4 120
Gatineau, Que., Can. D2 74
Gatineau, stm., Que., Can. D2 74
Gatineau, Parc de la, Que., Can. D2 74
Gatlinburg, Tn., U.S. D10 119
Gaucín, Spain I6 12
Gauhāti, India G14 38
Gauley, stm., W.V., U.S. C3 125
Gauley Bridge, W.V., U.S. C3 125
Gautier, Ms., U.S. f8 101
Gauting, Ger. G11 8
Gavá, Spain D14 12
Gavins Point Dam, U.S. B8 104
Gävle, Swe. F11 6
Gavrilov-Jam, Russia D22 18
Gawler Ranges, mts., Austl. F7 50
Gaya, India H11 38
Gay Head, c., Ma., U.S. D6 98
Gaylord, Mi., U.S. C6 99
Gaylord, Mn., U.S. F4 100
Gayndah, Austl. E10 50
Gaza see Ghazzah, Isr. Occ. D4 40
Gaziantep, Tur. H15 4
Gazimağusa, N. Cyp. B3 40
Gazimağusa Körfezi, b., N. Cyp. B4 40
Gbarnga, Lib. G4 42
Gdańsk (Danzig), Pol. A18 8
Gdynia, Pol. A18 8
Gearhart, Or., U.S. A3 114
Gearhart Mountain, mtn., Or., U.S. E6 114
Geary, N.B., Can. D3 71
Geary, Ok., U.S. B3 113
Geary, co., Ks., U.S. D7 93
Geauga, co., Oh., U.S. A4 112
Gebze, Tur. I13 16
Gediz, stm., Tur. K11 16
Geel, Bel. D4 8
Geelong, Austl. G8 50
Ge'ermu, China B16 38
Geesthacht, Ger. B10 8
Geilo, Nor. F7 6
Geislingen, Ger. G9 8
Geistown, Pa., U.S. F4 115
Geist Reservoir, res., In., U.S. E6 91
Gejiu (Kokiu), China C7 34
Gela, Italy L9 14
Gelibolu, Tur. I10 16
Gelibolu Yarımadası (Gallipoli Peninsula), pen., Tur. I10 16
Gelsenkirchen, Ger. D7 8
Gem, co., Id., U.S. E2 89
Gembloux, Bel. E4 8
Gemena, Zaire H9 42
Gemlik, Tur. I13 16
Gemona del Friuli, Italy C8 14
Genale (Juba), stm., Afr. G3 46
General Alvear, Arg. C3 56
General Bravo, Mex. E10 62
General Carneiro, Braz. C2 57
General Levalle, Arg. C4 56
General Pico, Arg. D4 56
General Pinedo, Arg. B4 56
General Roca, Arg. D3 56
General Villegas, Arg. D4 56
Genesee, Id., U.S. C2 89
Genesee, Mi., U.S. E7 99
Genesee, co., Mi., U.S. E7 99
Genesee, co., N.Y., U.S. B2 109
Genesee, stm., N.Y., U.S. C2 109
Geneseo, Il., U.S. B3 90
Geneseo, N.Y., U.S. C3 109
Geneva, Al., U.S. D4 78
Geneva, Il., U.S. B5 90
Geneva, In., U.S. C8 91
Geneva, Ne., U.S. D8 104
Geneva, N.Y., U.S. C4 109
Geneva, Oh., U.S. A5 112
Geneva, co., Al., U.S. D4 78
Geneva, Lake, l., Eur. F13 10
Geneva, Lake, l., Wi., U.S. F5 126
Geneva see Genève, Switz. F13 10
Geneva-on-the-Lake, Oh., U.S. A5 112
Genève, Switz. F13 10
Genk, Bel. E5 8
Genkai-nada, Japan I3 30
Genoa, Il., U.S. A5 90
Genoa, Ne., U.S. C8 104
Genoa, Nv., U.S. D2 105
Genoa, Oh., U.S. A2 112
Genoa City, Wi., U.S. F5 126
Genoa see Genova, Italy E3 14
Genola, Ut., U.S. D4 121
Genova (Genoa), Italy E3 14
Genova, Golfo di, b., Italy E3 14
Gent (Gand), Bel. D3 8
Genteng, Indon. n17 33a
Genthin, Ger. C12 8
Gentry, Ar., U.S. A1 81
Gentry, co., Mo., U.S. A3 102
Geographe Bay, b., Austl. F3 50
George, S. Afr. H4 44
George, Ia., U.S. A2 92
George, co., Ms., U.S. E5 101
George, stm., Que., Can. g13 74
George, Cape, c., N.S., Can. D8 71
George, Lake, l., Ug. B6 44
George, Lake, l., Fl., U.S. C5 86
George, Lake, l., N.Y., U.S. B7 109
George Air Force Base, mil., Ca., U.S. E5 82
George B. Stevenson Reservoir, res., Pa., U.S. D6 115
George Peak, mtn., Ut., U.S. B2 121
Georgetown, P.E.I., Can. C7 71
Georgetown, Cay. Is. E7 64

Name | Map Ref | Page

Georgetown, Gam. F3 42
Georgetown, Guy. D13 58
George Town (Pinang), Malay. L6 34
Georgetown, Ca., U.S. C3 82
Georgetown, Co., U.S. B5 83
Georgetown, Ct., U.S. D2 84
Georgetown, De., U.S. F4 85
Georgetown, Ga., U.S. E1 87
Georgetown, Il., U.S. D6 90
Georgetown, In., U.S. H6 91
Georgetown, Ky., U.S. B5 94
Georgetown, Ma., U.S. A6 98
Georgetown, Oh., U.S. D2 112
Georgetown, S.C., U.S. E9 117
Georgetown, Tx., U.S. D4 120
Georgetown, co., S.C., U.S. E9 117
George Washington Birthplace National Monument, Va., U.S. B6 123
George Washington Carver National Monument, Mo., U.S. E3 102
George West, Tx., U.S. E3 120
Georgia, ctry., Asia I6 22
Georgia, state, U.S. D3 87
Georgia, Strait of, strt., N.A. B2 76
Georgiana, Al., U.S. D3 78
Georgian Bay, b., Ont., Can. B3 73
Georgina, stm., Austl. D7 50
Gera, Ger. E12 8
Gerald, Mo., U.S. C6 102
Geraldine, Al., U.S. A4 78
Geral do Paranã, Serra, hills, Braz. C5 57
Geraldton, Austl. E2 50
Geraldton, Ont., Can. o18 73
Gérardmer, Fr. D13 10
Gerber Reservoir, res., Or., U.S. E5 114
Gerdine, Mount, mtn., Ak., U.S. C9 79
Gereshk, Afg. E1 38
Gérgal, Spain H9 12
Gering, Ne., U.S. C2 104
Gerlach, Nv., U.S. C2 105
Germantown, Il., U.S. E4 90
Germantown, Md., U.S. B3 97
Germantown, Oh., U.S. C1 112
Germantown, Tn., U.S. B2 119
Germantown, Wi., U.S. E5 126
Germany, ctry., Eur. E10 4
Germiston, S. Afr. G5 44
Gerona, Spain D14 12
Geronimo, Ok., U.S. C3 113
Gervais, Or., U.S. B4 114
Geseke, Ger. D8 8
Getafe, Spain E8 12
Gettysburg, Pa., U.S. G7 115
Gettysburg, S.D., U.S. C6 118
Ghāghra, stm., Asia G10 38
Ghana, ctry., Afr. G5 42
Ghanzi, Bots. F4 44
Gharbīyah, Aṣ-Ṣaḥrā' al- (Western Desert), des., Egypt C11 42
Ghardaïa, Alg. B6 42
Gharyān, Libya B8 42
Ghāt, Libya D8 42
Għawdex, i., Malta M9 14
Ghazāl, Baḥr al-, stm., Sudan G12 42
Ghāziābād, India F7 38
Ghāzīpur, India H10 38
Ghaznī, Afg. D3 38
Ghazzah (Gaza), Isr. Occ. D4 40
Ghedi, Italy D5 14
Gheen, Mn., U.S. C6 100
Ghent see Gent, Bel. D3 8
Ghīn, Tall, mtn., Syria C5 40
Ghudāmis, Libya B7 42
Giants Neck, Ct., U.S. D7 84
Gibbon, Mn., U.S. F4 100
Gibbon, Ne., U.S. D7 104
Gibbons, Alta., Can. C4 68
Gibbstown, N.J., U.S. D2 107
Gibeon, Nmb. G3 44
Gibraltar, Gib. I6 12
Gibraltar, dep., Eur. H6 4
Gibraltar, Strait of (Estrecho de Gibraltar), strt. J6 12
Gibraltar Point, c., Eng., U.K. H13 7
Gibsland, La., U.S. B2 95
Gibson, Ga., U.S. C4 87
Gibson, co., In., U.S. H2 91
Gibson, co., Tn., U.S. A3 119
Gibsonburg, Oh., U.S. A2 112
Gibson City, Il., U.S. C5 90
Gibson Desert, des., Austl. D4 50
Gibsonia, Pa., U.S. h14 115
Gibson Island, i., Md., U.S. B5 97
Gibsons, B.C., Can. E6 69
Gibsonton, Fl., U.S. p11 86
Gibsonville, N.C., U.S. A3 110
Giddings, Tx., U.S. D4 120
Gideon, Mo., U.S. E8 102
Gien, Fr. E9 10
Giessen, Ger. E8 8
Gifford, Fl., U.S. E6 86
Gifford, Il., U.S. C5 90
Gifu, Japan G9 30
Gig Harbor, Wa., U.S. B3 124
Gihon, stm., Vt., U.S. B3 122
Gijón, Spain B6 12
Gila, co., Az., U.S. D5 80
Gila, stm., U.S. E4 76
Gila Bend, Az., U.S. E3 80
Gila Bend Indian Reservation, Az., U.S. D3 80
Gila Bend Mountains, mts., Az., U.S. D2 80
Gila Cliff Dwellings National Monument, N.M., U.S. D1 108
Gila Mountains, mts., Az., U.S. D6 80
Gila Peak, mtn., Az., U.S. D6 80
Gila River Indian Reservation, Az., U.S. D4 80
Gilbert, Az., U.S. D4 80
Gilbert, Ia., U.S. B4 92
Gilbert, La., U.S. B4 95
Gilbert, Mn., U.S. C6 100
Gilbert Islands see Kiribati, ctry., Oc. G24 2
Gilbert Peak, mtn., Wa., U.S. C4 124
Gilbert Plains, Man., Can. D1 70
Gilbertsville, Ky., U.S. f9 94
Gilbertsville, Pa., U.S. F10 115
Gilbertville, Ia., U.S. B5 92
Gilbués, Braz. E9 54
Gilchrist, Or., U.S. D5 114
Gilchrist, co., Fl., U.S. C4 86
Gilcrest, Co., U.S. A6 83
Giles, co., Tn., U.S. B4 119
Giles, co., Va., U.S. C2 123
Gilford Island, i., B.C., Can. D4 69
Gilgit, Pak. C6 38
Gillam, Man., Can. A4 70
Gillespie, Il., U.S. D4 90
Gillespie, co., Tx., U.S. D3 120
Gillespie Dam, Az., U.S. D3 80
Gillett, Ar., U.S. C4 81
Gillett, Wi., U.S. D5 126
Gillette, Wy., U.S. B7 127
Gilliam, co., Or., U.S. B6 114
Gilman, Il., U.S. C5 90
Gilman, Vt., U.S. C5 122
Gilmanton, N.H., U.S. D4 106
Gilmer, Tx., U.S. C5 120
Gilmer, co., Ga., U.S. B2 87
Gilmer, co., W.V., U.S. C4 125
Gilo, stm., Eth. G1 46
Gilpin, co., Co., U.S. B5 83
Gilroy, Ca., U.S. D3 82
Gil'uj, stm., Russia G19 24
Giluwe, Mount, mtn., Pap. N. Gui. m15 50a
Gimli, Man., Can. D3 70
Ginosa, Italy I11 14
Ginowan, Japan y27 31b
Gioia del Colle, Italy I11 14
Gioia Tauro, Italy K10 14
Girard, Il., U.S. D4 90
Girard, Ks., U.S. E9 93
Girard, Oh., U.S. A5 112
Girard, Pa., U.S. B1 115
Girardot, Col. E5 58
Girardville, Pa., U.S. E9 115
Giridih, India H12 38
Girifalco, Italy K11 14
Girne, N. Cyp. B3 40
Girwa, stm., Asia F9 38
Gisborne, N.Z. C7 52
Gisenyi, Rw. B5 44
Gisors, Fr. C8 10
Giugliano [in Campania], Italy I9 14
Giulianova, Italy G8 14
Giurgiu, Rom. F9 16
Givet, Fr. B11 10
Givors, Fr. G11 10
Giyon, Eth. G2 46
Giza see Al-Jīzah, Egypt B12 42
Gižiga, Russia E26 24
Gižiginskaja Guba, b., Russia E25 24
Gjandža, Azer. I7 22
Gjirokastër, Alb. I4 16
Gjoa Haven, N.W. Ter., Can. C13 66
Glacier, co., Mt., U.S. B3 103
Glacier Bay, b., Ak., U.S. k21 79
Glacier Bay National Park, Ak., U.S. D12 79
Glacier National Park, B.C., Can. D9 69
Glacier National Park, Mt., U.S. B2 103
Glacier Peak, mtn., Wa., U.S. A4 124
Gladbrook, Ia., U.S. B5 92
Glade Creek, stm., Wa., U.S. C6 124
Glade Creek, stm., W.V., U.S. n13 125
Glade Creek, stm., W.V., U.S. n14 125
Glades, co., Fl., U.S. F5 86
Glade Spring, Va., U.S. f10 123
Gladewater, Tx., U.S. C5 120
Gladstone, Austl. D10 50
Gladstone, Man., Can. D2 70
Gladstone, Mi., U.S. C4 99
Gladstone, Mo., U.S. h10 102
Gladstone, Or., U.S. B4 114
Gladwin, Mi., U.S. E6 99
Gladwin, co., Mi., U.S. D6 99
Glåma, stm., Nor. F8 6
Glarner Alpen, mts., Switz. F15 10
Glarus, Switz. E16 10
Glascock, co., Ga., U.S. C4 87
Glasford, Il., U.S. C4 90
Glasgow, Scot., U.K. F8 7
Glasgow, Ky., U.S. C4 94
Glasgow, Mo., U.S. B5 102
Glasgow, Mt., U.S. B10 103
Glasgow, Va., U.S. C3 123
Glasgow, W.V., U.S. m13 125
Glassboro, N.J., U.S. D2 107
Glasscock, co., Tx., U.S. D2 120
Glassport, Pa., U.S. F2 115
Glastonbury, Ct., U.S. C5 84
Glauchau, Ger. E12 8
Glazier Lake, l., Me., U.S. A3 96
Glazov, Russia F8 22
Gleason, Tn., U.S. A3 119
Gleisdorf, Aus. H15 8
Glen Allan, Ms., U.S. B2 101
Glen Allen, Va., U.S. C5 123
Glenboro, Man., Can. E2 70
Glenbrook, Nv., U.S. D2 105
Glen Burnie, Md., U.S. B4 97
Glen Canyon Dam, Az., U.S. A4 80
Glen Canyon National Recreation Area, U.S. F5 121
Glencoe, Ont., Can. E3 73
Glencoe, Al., U.S. B4 78
Glencoe, Il., U.S. A6 90
Glencoe, Mn., U.S. F4 100
Glen Cove, N.Y., U.S. h13 109
Glendale, Az., U.S. D3 80
Glendale, Ca., U.S. m12 82
Glendale, Ms., U.S. D4 101
Glendale, Oh., U.S. C1 112
Glendale, Or., U.S. E3 114
Glendale, R.I., U.S. B2 116
Glendale, S.C., U.S. B4 117
Glen Dale, W.V., U.S. B4 125
Glendale, Wi., U.S. m12 126
Glendale Heights, W.V., U.S. g8 125
Glendive, Mt., U.S. C12 103
Glendo, Wy., U.S. D7 127
Glendora, Ca., U.S. m13 82
Glendo Reservoir, res., Wy., U.S. D8 127
Glenelg, Md., U.S. B4 97
Glen Ellis Falls, wtfl, N.H., U.S. B4 106
Glen Ellyn, Il., U.S. k8 90
Glenham, N.Y., U.S. D7 109
Glen Innes, Austl. E10 50
Glen Jean, W.V., U.S. D3 125
Glen Lake, l., Mi., U.S. D5 99
Glen Lyon, Pa., U.S. D9 115
Glenmora, La., U.S. D3 95
Glenn, co., Ca., U.S. C2 82
Glennallen, Ak., U.S. f19 79
Glenns Ferry, Id., U.S. G3 89
Glennville, Ga., U.S. E5 87
Glenolden, Pa., U.S. p20 115
Glenpool, Ok., U.S. B5 113
Glen Raven, N.C., U.S. A3 110
Glen Ridge, N.J., U.S. h8 107
Glen Rock, N.J., U.S. h8 107
Glen Rock, Pa., U.S. G8 115
Glenrock, Wy., U.S. D7 127
Glen Rose, Tx., U.S. C4 120
Glens Falls, N.Y., U.S. B7 109
Glen Ullin, N.D., U.S. C4 111
Glenview, Il., U.S. h9 90
Glenview Naval Air Station, mil., Il., U.S. h9 90
Glenville, Mn., U.S. G5 100
Glenville, W.V., U.S. C4 125
Glenwood, Newf., Can. D4 72
Glenwood, Ar., U.S. C2 81
Glenwood, Ga., U.S. D4 87
Glenwood, Ia., U.S. C2 92
Glenwood, Mn., U.S. E3 100
Glenwood, Va., U.S. D3 123
Glenwood City, Wi., U.S. C1 126
Glenwood Springs, Co., U.S. B3 83
Glidden, Ia., U.S. B3 92
Glide, Or., U.S. D3 114
Glina, Cro. D11 14
Glittertinden, mtn., Nor. F7 6
Gliwice (Gleiwitz), Pol. E18 8
Globe, Az., U.S. D5 80
Gloggnitz, Aus. H15 8
Gloster, Ms., U.S. D2 101
Gloucester, Ont., Can. h12 73
Gloucester, Eng., U.K. J10 7
Gloucester, Ma., U.S. A6 98
Gloucester, Va., U.S. C6 123
Gloucester, co., N.J., U.S. D2 107
Gloucester, co., Va., U.S. C6 123
Gloucester City, N.J., U.S. D2 107
Gloucester Point, Va., U.S. C6 123
Glouster, Oh., U.S. C3 112
Glover Island, i., Newf., Can. D3 72
Gloversville, N.Y., U.S. B6 109
Glovertown, Newf., Can. D4 72
Gloverville, S.C., U.S. E4 117
Gluck, S.C., U.S. C2 117
Glücksburg, Ger. A9 8
Glückstadt, Ger. B9 8
Glyndon, Md., U.S. B4 97
Glyndon, Mn., U.S. D2 100
Glynn, co., Ga., U.S. E5 87
Gmünd, Aus. G14 8
Gmunden, Aus. H13 8
Gnadenhutten, Oh., U.S. B4 112
Gnarp, Swe. E11 6
Gniezno, Pol. C17 8
Gnjilane, Yugo. G5 16
Gō, stm., Japan H5 30
Goa, ter., India E2 37
Goat Island, i., R.I., U.S. F5 116
Goat Mountain, mtn., Mt., U.S. C3 103
Goat Rock Dam, U.S. C4 78
Goba, Eth. G3 46
Gobabis, Nmb. F3 44
Gobi, des., Asia C7 26
Gobles, Mi., U.S. F5 99
Godāvari, stm., India D6 37
Goddard, Ks., U.S. E6 93
Goderich, Ont., Can. D3 73
Godfrey, Il., U.S. E3 90
Godhavn, Grnld. C22 66
Godhra, India I5 38
Godoy Cruz, Arg. C3 56
Gods, stm., Man., Can. A5 70
Gods Lake, l., Man., Can. B4 70
Godthåb, Grnld. D22 66
Godwin Austen see K2, mtn., Asia C7 38
Goéland, Lac au, l., Que., Can. G17 66
Goélands, Lac aux, l., Que., Can. E20 66
Goff Creek, stm., Ok., U.S. e9 113
Goffstown, N.H., U.S. D3 106
Gogebic, co., Mi., U.S. n12 99
Gogebic, Lake, l., Mi., U.S. m12 99
Goiana, Braz. G9 54
Goiânia, Braz. D4 57
Goiás, Braz. C3 57
Gojra, Pak. E5 38
Gokāk, India D3 37
Gökçeada, i., Tur. I9 16
Gol'čicha, Russia C10 24
Golconda, Il., U.S. F5 90
Golconda, Nv., U.S. C4 105
Gold Bar, Wa., U.S. B4 124
Gold Beach, Or., U.S. E2 114
Golden, B.C., Can. D9 69
Golden, Co., U.S. B5 83
Golden City, Mo., U.S. D3 102
Goldendale, Wa., U.S. D5 124
Golden Gate Bridge, Ca., U.S. h7 82
Golden Gate National Recreation Area, Ca., U.S. h7 82
Golden Hinde, mtn., B.C., Can. E5 69
Golden Meadow, La., U.S. E5 95
Golden Spike National Historic Site, hist., Ut., U.S. B3 121
Golden Valley, Mn., U.S. n12 100
Golden Valley, co., Mt., U.S. D7 103
Golden Valley, co., N.D., U.S. B2 111
Goldfield, Ia., U.S. B4 92
Goldfield, Nv., U.S. F4 105
Gold Hill, Or., U.S. E3 114
Goldsboro, N.C., U.S. B5 110
Goldsby, Ok., U.S. B4 113
Goldthwaite, Tx., U.S. D3 120
Goleta, Ca., U.S. E4 82
Golf Manor, Oh., U.S. o13 112
Goliad, Tx., U.S. E4 120
Goliad, co., Tx., U.S. E4 120
Golspie, Scot., U.K. D9 7
Gomati, stm., India G9 38
Gombe, stm., Tan. B6 44
Gomel', Bela. I14 18
Gomera, i., Spain C2 42
Gómez Palacio, Mex. E8 62
Gonābād, Iran K9 22
Gonaïves, Haiti E11 64
Gonam, Russia F20 24
Gonam, stm., Russia F28 24
Gonâve, Golfe de la, b., Haiti E11 64
Gonâve, Île de la, i., Haiti E11 64
Gonda, India G9 38
Gondal, India J4 38
Gonder, Eth. F2 46
Gondia, India B6 37
Gondomar, Port. D3 12
Gondrecourt-le-Château, Fr. D12 10
Gönen, Tur. I11 16
Gōnoura, Japan I2 30
Gonzales, Ca., U.S. D3 82
Gonzales, La., U.S. D5 95
Gonzales, Tx., U.S. E4 120
Gonzales, co., Tx., U.S. E4 120
Gonzalez, Fl., U.S. u14 86
Goochland, co., Va., U.S. C5 123
Goode, Mount, mtn., Ak., U.S. g18 79
Goodfellow Air Force Base, mil., Tx., U.S. D2 120
Good Hope, Cape of, c., S. Afr. H3 44
Good Hope Mountain, mtn., B.C., Can. D5 69
Goodhue, co., Mn., U.S. F6 100
Gooding, Id., U.S. G4 89
Gooding, co., Id., U.S. F4 89
Goodland, In., U.S. C3 91
Goodland, Ks., U.S. C2 93
Goodlettsville, Tn., U.S. g10 119
Goodman, Ms., U.S. C4 101
Goodman, Mo., U.S. E3 102
Good Pine, La., U.S. C3 95
Goodsprings, Nv., U.S. H6 105
Goodview, Mn., U.S. F7 100
Goodwater, Al., U.S. B3 78
Goodwell, Ok., U.S. e9 113
Goodyear, Az., U.S. D3 80
Goole, Eng., U.K. H12 7
Goondiwindi, Austl. E10 50
Goose, stm., N.D., U.S. B8 111
Goose Bay, b., Newf., Can. B1 72
Gooseberry Creek, stm., Wy., U.S. B4 127
Goose Creek, S.C., U.S. F7 117
Goose Creek, stm., U.S. G5 89
Goose Creek, stm., Va., U.S. C3 123
Goose Creek Reservoir, res., S.C., U.S. k11 117
Goose Lake, l., U.S. B3 82
Goose Pond, l., N.H., U.S. C2 106
Göppingen, Ger. G9 8
Gorakhpur, India G10 38
Gorda, Punta, c., Cuba C6 64
Gordil, Cen. Afr. Rep. G10 42
Gordo, Al., U.S. B2 78
Gordon, Ga., U.S. D3 87
Gordon, Ne., U.S. B3 104
Gordon, co., Ga., U.S. B2 87
Gordonsville, Tn., U.S. C8 119
Gordonsville, Va., U.S. B4 123
Gore, Eth. G2 46
Gore, N.Z. G2 52
Gore, Ok., U.S. B6 113
Gore Bay, Ont., Can. B2 73
Gore Point, c., Ak., U.S. h16 79
Gore Range, mts., Co., U.S. B4 83
Goreville, Il., U.S. F5 90
Gorey, Ire. I6 7
Gorgān, Iran J8 22
Gorge High Dam, Wa., U.S. A4 124
Gorham, Me., U.S. E2 96
Gorham, N.H., U.S. B4 106
Gorinchem, Neth. D4 8
Gorizia, Italy D8 14
Gorki, Bela. G13 18
Gorki see Nižnij Novgorod, Russia E27 18
Gorkovskoje Vodochranilišče, res., Russia D26 18
Görlitz, Ger. B13 8
Gorman, Tx., U.S. C3 120
Gornja Radgona, Slo. C10 14
Gorno-Altajsk, Russia G11 24
Gorodec, Russia E26 18
Gorontalo, Indon. E7 32
Gort, Ire. H4 7
Gorzów Wielkopolski (Landsberg an der Warthe), Pol. C15 8
Goshen, In., U.S. A6 91
Goshen, N.Y., U.S. D6 109
Goshen, Oh., U.S. C1 112
Goshen, co., Wy., U.S. D8 127
Goshute Indian Reservation, U.S. D7 105
Goshute Lake, l., Nv., U.S. C7 105
Goshute Mountains, mts., Nv., U.S. C7 105
Goslar, Ger. D10 8
Gosper, co., Ne., U.S. D6 104
Gosport, In., U.S. F4 91
Göteborg (Gothenburg), Swe. H8 6
Gotemba, Japan G11 30
Gotha, Ger. E10 8
Gothenburg, Ne., U.S. D5 104
Gothenburg see Göteborg, Swe. H8 6
Gotland, i., Swe. H12 6
Gotō-rettō, is., Japan J1 30
Göttingen, Ger. D9 8
Gouda, Neth. C4 8
Gouin, Réservoir, res., Que., Can. k12 74
Goulburn, Austl. F9 50
Goulburn Islands, is., Austl. B6 50
Gould, Ar., U.S. D4 81
Goulding, Fl., U.S. u14 86
Gould Island, i., R.I., U.S. E5 116
Goulds, Fl., U.S. s13 86
Gourdon, Fr. H8 10
Gouré, Niger F8 42
Gourin, Fr. D3 10
Gournay-en-Bray, Fr. C8 10
Gouverneur, N.Y., U.S. f9 109
Gove, co., Ks., U.S. D3 93
Governador Valadares, Braz. E8 57
Governors Harbour, Bah. B9 64
Govind Balabh Pant Sāgar, res., India H10 38
Govind Sāgar, res., India E7 38
Gowanda, N.Y., U.S. C2 109
Gower, Mo., U.S. B3 102
Gowmal (Gumal), stm., Asia D3 38
Gowmal Kalay, Afg. D3 38
Gowrie, Ia., U.S. B3 92
Goya, Arg. B5 56
Gozo see Għawdex, i., Malta M9 14
Graaff-Reinet, S. Afr. H4 44
Grabill, In., U.S. B8 91
Grace, Id., U.S. G7 89
Graceville, Fl., U.S. u16 86
Graceville, Mn., U.S. E2 100
Gracewood, Ga., U.S. C4 87
Gracias a Dios, Cabo, c., N.A. G6 64
Gradaús, Braz. E8 54
Gradaús, Serra dos, plat., Braz. E8 54
Grado, Italy D8 14
Grady, co., Ga., U.S. F2 87
Grady, co., Ok., U.S. C4 113
Graettinger, Ia., U.S. A3 92
Grafton, Austl. E10 50
Grafton, Il., U.S. E3 90
Grafton, Ma., U.S. B4 98
Grafton, N.D., U.S. A8 111
Grafton, Oh., U.S. A3 112
Grafton, Va., U.S. h15 123
Grafton, W.V., U.S. B4 125
Grafton, Wi., U.S. E6 126
Grafton, co., N.H., U.S. C3 106
Grafton, Cape, c., Austl. C9 50
Graham, N.C., U.S. A3 110
Graham, Tx., U.S. C3 120
Graham, co., Az., U.S. E5 80
Graham, co., Ks., U.S. C4 93
Graham, co., N.C., U.S. f9 110
Graham, Lake, res., Tx., U.S. C3 120
Graham, Mount, mtn., Az., U.S. E6 80
Graham Island, i., B.C., Can. C1 69
Graham Lake, l., Me., U.S. D4 96
Graham Moore, Cape, c., N.W. Ter., Can. B17 66
Grahamstown, S. Afr. H5 44
Grahn, Ky., U.S. B6 94
Grainger, co., Tn., U.S. C10 119
Grain Valley, Mo., U.S. B3 102
Grajaú, Braz. E9 54
Gramat, Fr. H8 10
Grambling, La., U.S. B3 95
Gramercy, La., U.S. h10 95
Grammichele, Italy L9 14
Grampian Mountains, mts., Scot., U.K. E8 7
Granada, Col. F6 58
Granada, Nic. I5 64
Granada, Spain H8 12
Granard, Ire. H5 7
Granbury, Tx., U.S. C4 120
Granby, Que., Can. D5 74
Granby, Co., U.S. A5 83
Granby, Ct., U.S. B4 84
Granby, Mo., U.S. E3 102
Granby, Lake, res., Co., U.S. A5 83
Gran Canaria, i., Spain p25 13a
Gran Chaco, pl., S.A. A4 56
Grand, co., Co., U.S. A4 83
Grand, co., Ut., U.S. E6 121
Grand, stm., Ont., Can. D4 73
Grand, stm., Mi., U.S. E5 99
Grand, stm., Mo., U.S. A3 102
Grand, stm., Oh., U.S. A4 112
Grand, stm., S.D., U.S. B4 118
Grandas, Spain B5 12
Grand Bahama, i., Bah. A8 64
Grand Bank, Newf., Can. E4 72
Grand-Bassam, C. Iv. G5 42
Grand Bay, N.B., Can. D3 71
Grand Bay, Al., U.S. E1 78
Grand Bend, Ont., Can. D3 73
Grand Blanc, Mi., U.S. F7 99
Grand Caillou, La., U.S. E5 95
Grand Canal, Ire. H5 7
Grand Canal see Da Yunhe, China E10 26
Grand Canyon, Az., U.S. A3 80
Grand Canyon, val., Az., U.S. A3 80
Grand Canyon National Park, Az., U.S. B3 80
Grand Cayman, i., Cay. Is. E7 64
Grand Centre, Alta., Can. B5 68
Grand Coteau, La., U.S. D3 95
Grand Coulee, Wa., U.S. B6 124
Grand Coulee Dam, Wa., U.S. B6 124
Grande, stm., Bol. G6 54
Grande, stm., Braz. E3 57
Grande, Bahía, b., Arg. G3 56
Grande, Boca, mth., Ven. C12 58
Grande, Ilha, i., Braz. G6 57
Grande, Ilha, i., Braz. G1 57
Grande, Rio (Bravo del Norte), stm., N.A. F7 76
Grande-Anse, N.B., Can. B4 71
Grande Cache, Alta., Can. C1 68
Grande Comore, i., Com. D8 44
Grande de Matagalpa, stm., Nic. H5 64
Grande de Santiago, Río, stm., Mex. G7 62
Grande do Gurupá, Ilha, i., Braz. D8 54
Grand-Entrée, Que., Can. B8 71
Grande Prairie, Alta., Can. B1 68
Grand Erg de Bilma, des., Niger E8 42
Grand Erg Occidental, des., Alg. B6 42
Grand Erg Oriental, des., Alg. B7 42
Grande rivière de la Baleine, stm., Que., Can. g11 74
Grande Ronde, stm., U.S. C8 124
Grandes, Salinas, pl., Arg. B4 56
Grandes-Bergeronnes, Que., Can. A8 74
Grande-Terre, i., Guad. F17 64
Grand Falls (Grand-Sault), N.B., Can. B2 71
Grand Falls, wtfl, Me., U.S. C5 96

Name	Map Ref	Page
Grand Falls [-Windsor], Newf., Can.	D4	72
Grandfather Mountain, mtn., N.C., U.S.	A1	110
Grandfield, Ok., U.S.	C3	113
Grand Forks, B.C., Can.	E8	69
Grand Forks, N.D., U.S.	B8	111
Grand Forks, co., N.D., U.S.	B8	111
Grand Forks Air Force Base, mil., N.D., U.S.	B8	111
Grand-Fougeray, Fr.	E5	10
Grand Harbour, N.B., Can.	E3	71
Grand Haven, Mi., U.S.	E4	99
Grand Island, Ne., U.S.	D7	104
Grand Island, i., La., U.S.	D6	95
Grand Island, i., Mi., U.S.	B4	99
Grand Isle, La., U.S.	E6	95
Grand Isle, co., Vt., U.S.	B2	122
Grand Isle, i., La., U.S.	E6	95
Grand Junction, Co., U.S.	B2	83
Grand Junction, Ia., U.S.	B3	92
Grand Lake, l., N.B., Can.	D3	71
Grand Lake, l., Newf., Can.	D3	72
Grand Lake, l., La., U.S.	E6	95
Grand Lake, l., La., U.S.	E3	95
Grand Lake, l., Mi., U.S.	C7	99
Grand Lake, l., Oh., U.S.	B1	112
Grand Lake Matagamon, l., Me., U.S.	B4	96
Grand Lake Seboeis, l., Me., U.S.	B4	96
Grand Ledge, Mi., U.S.	F6	99
Grand Manan Island, i., N.B., Can.	E3	71
Grand Marais, Mn., U.S.	k9	100
Grand Meadow, Mn., U.S.	G6	100
Grand-Mère, Que., Can.	C5	74
Grand Mound, Ia., U.S.	C7	92
Grand Portage Indian Reservation, Mn., U.S.	k10	100
Grand Portage National Monument, Mn., U.S.	h10	100
Grand Prairie, Tx., U.S.	n10	120
Grand Rapids, Mi., U.S.	F5	99
Grand Rapids, Mn., U.S.	C5	100
Grand Rapids, Oh., U.S.	f6	112
Grand Rivière de la Baleine, stm., Que., Can.	E17	66
Grand-Saint-Bernard, Tunnel du, Eur.	G14	10
Grand Saline, Tx., U.S.	C5	120
Grand Terre Islands, is., La., U.S.	E6	95
Grand Teton, mtn., Wy., U.S.	C2	127
Grand Teton National Park, Wy., U.S.	C2	127
Grand Tower, Il., U.S.	F4	90
Grand Traverse, co., Mi., U.S.	D5	99
Grand Traverse Bay, b., Mi., U.S.	C5	99
Grand Turk, T./C. Is.	D12	64
Grand Valley, Ont., Can.	D4	73
Grandview, Man., Can.	D1	70
Grandview, In., U.S.	I4	91
Grandview, Mo., U.S.	C3	102
Grandview, Wa., U.S.	C6	124
Grandview Heights, Oh., U.S.	m10	112
Grandville, Mi., U.S.	F5	99
Grandy, N.C., U.S.	A7	110
Granger, In., U.S.	A5	91
Granger, Ia., U.S.	C4	92
Granger, Tx., U.S.	D4	120
Granger, Wa., U.S.	C5	124
Grangeville, Id., U.S.	D2	89
Granisle, B.C., Can.	B4	69
Granite, Ok., U.S.	C2	113
Granite, co., Mt., U.S.	D3	103
Granite City, Il., U.S.	E3	90
Granite Falls, Mn., U.S.	F3	100
Granite Falls, N.C., U.S.	B1	110
Granite Falls, Wa., U.S.	A4	124
Granite Lake, res., Newf., Can.	D3	72
Granite Mountain, mtn., Ak., U.S.	B7	79
Granite Mountains, mts., Az., U.S.	E2	80
Granite Mountains, mts., Wy., U.S.	D5	127
Granite Pass, Wy., U.S.	B5	127
Granite Peak, mtn., Mt., U.S.	E7	103
Granite Peak, mtn., Nv., U.S.	C2	105
Granite Peak, mtn., Nv., U.S.	B4	105
Granite Peak, mtn., Ut., U.S.	C2	121
Granite Peak, mtn., Ut., U.S.	E3	121
Granite Peak, mtn., Wy., U.S.	D4	127
Granite Quarry, N.C., U.S.	B2	110
Granite Range, mts., Nv., U.S.	C2	105
Graniteville, S.C., U.S.	D4	117
Graniteville, Vt., U.S.	C4	122
Granollers, Spain	D14	12
Grant, Al., U.S.	A3	78
Grant, Mi., U.S.	E5	99
Grant, Ne., U.S.	D4	104
Grant, co., Ar., U.S.	C3	81
Grant, co., In., U.S.	D6	91
Grant, co., Ks., U.S.	E2	93
Grant, co., Ky., U.S.	B5	94
Grant, co., La., U.S.	C3	95
Grant, co., Mn., U.S.	E2	100
Grant, co., Ne., U.S.	C4	104
Grant, co., N.M., U.S.	E1	108
Grant, co., N.D., U.S.	C4	111
Grant, co., Ok., U.S.	A4	113
Grant, co., Or., U.S.	C7	114
Grant, co., S.D., U.S.	B8	118
Grant, co., Wa., U.S.	B6	124
Grant, co., W.V., U.S.	B5	125
Grant, co., Wi., U.S.	F3	126
Grant, Mount, mtn., Nv., U.S.	E3	105
Grant City, Mo., U.S.	A3	102
Grantham, Eng., U.K.	I12	7
Grant Park, Il., U.S.	B6	90
Grant Range, mts., Nv., U.S.	E6	105
Grants, N.M., U.S.	B2	108
Grantsburg, Wi., U.S.	C1	126
Grants Pass, Or., U.S.	E3	114
Grantsville, Ut., U.S.	C3	121
Grantsville, W.V., U.S.	C3	125
Grant Town, W.V., U.S.	B4	125
Grantville, Ga., U.S.	C2	87
Granville, Fr.	D5	10
Granville, Il., U.S.	B4	90
Granville, N.Y., U.S.	B7	109
Granville, Oh., U.S.	B3	112
Granville, W.V., U.S.	h11	125
Granville, co., N.C., U.S.	A4	110
Granville Lake, l., Man., Can.	A1	70
Granvin, Nor.	F6	6
Grapeland, Tx., U.S.	D5	120
Grapeview, Wa., U.S.	B3	124
Grapevine, Tx., U.S.	C4	120
Grapevine Lake, res., Tx., U.S.	n9	120
Grapevine Peak, mtn., Nv., U.S.	G4	105
Gras, Lac de, l., N.W. Ter., Can.	D10	66
Grasonville, Md., U.S.	C5	97
Grass, stm., Man., Can.	B2	70
Grass, stm., N.Y., U.S.	f9	109
Grasse, Fr.	I13	10
Grass Lake, Il., U.S.	h8	90
Grass Lake, Mi., U.S.	F6	99
Grass Lake, l., Il., U.S.	h8	90
Grass Valley, Ca., U.S.	C3	82
Grassy Brook, stm., Vt., U.S.	E3	122
Grassy Lake, l., La., U.S.	k9	95
Grates Point, c., Newf., Can.	D5	72
Gratiot, co., Mi., U.S.	E6	99
Gratis, Oh., U.S.	C1	112
Grave Creek, stm., W.V., U.S.	g8	125
Gravelly Branch, stm., De., U.S.	F4	85
Gravelly Range, mts., Mt., U.S.	E4	103
Gravenhurst, Ont., Can.	C5	73
Grave Peak, mtn., Id., U.S.	C4	89
Graves, co., Ky., U.S.	f9	94
Gravette, Ar., U.S.	A1	81
Gravina in Puglia, Italy	I11	14
Gray, Fr.	E12	10
Gray, Ga., U.S.	C3	87
Gray, Ky., U.S.	D5	94
Gray, La., U.S.	k10	95
Gray, Me., U.S.	g7	96
Gray, co., Ks., U.S.	E3	93
Gray, co., Tx., U.S.	B2	120
Grayback Mountain, mtn., Or., U.S.	E3	114
Gray Court, S.C., U.S.	B3	117
Grayland, Wa., U.S.	C1	124
Grayling, Mi., U.S.	D6	99
Graylyn Crest, De., U.S.	A3	85
Grays Harbor, co., Wa., U.S.	B2	124
Grays Harbor, b., Wa., U.S.	C1	124
Grayslake, Il., U.S.	A5	90
Grays Lake, sw., Id., U.S.	F7	89
Grayson, Ky., U.S.	B7	94
Grayson, co., Ky., U.S.	C3	94
Grayson, co., Tx., U.S.	C4	120
Grayson, co., Va., U.S.	D1	123
Grayson Lake, res., Ky., U.S.	B7	94
Grays Peak, mtn., Co., U.S.	B5	83
Gray Summit, Mo., U.S.	g12	102
Graysville, Al., U.S.	f7	78
Graysville, Tn., U.S.	D8	119
Grayville, Il., U.S.	E5	90
Graz, Aus.	H15	8
Gr'azi, Russia	I22	18
Great Abaco, i., Bah.	A9	64
Great Artesian Basin, Austl.	D8	50
Great Australian Bight, Austl.	F5	50
Great Averill Pond, l., Vt., U.S.	B5	122
Great Barrier Reef, rf., Austl.	C9	50
Great Barrington, Ma., U.S.	B1	98
Great Basin National Park, Nv., U.S.	E7	105
Great Bay, b., N.H., U.S.	D5	106
Great Bay, b., N.J., U.S.	D4	107
Great Bear Lake, l., N.W. Ter., Can.	C9	66
Great Bend, Ks., U.S.	D5	93
Great Captain Island, i., Ct., U.S.	F1	84
Great Channel, strt., Asia	K3	34
Great Dismal Swamp, sw., U.S.	D6	123
Great Divide Basin, Wy., U.S.	E4	127
Great Dividing Range, mts., Austl.	D9	50
Great East Lake, l., U.S.	C5	106
Great Egg Harbor, stm., N.J., U.S.	D3	107
Greater Antilles, is., N.A.	D10	64
Greater Sunda Islands, is., Asia	F4	32
Great Exuma, i., Bah.	C10	64
Great Falls, Mt., U.S.	C5	103
Great Falls, S.C., U.S.	B6	117
Great Falls, wtfl, Md., U.S.	B3	97
Great Falls Dam, Tn., U.S.	D6	119
Great Guana Cay, i., Bah.	B9	64
Great Himalaya Range, mts., Asia	F10	38
Greathouse Peak, mtn., Mt., U.S.	D7	103
Great Inagua, i., Bah.	D11	64
Great Indian Desert (Thar Desert), des., Asia	G4	38
Great Island, spit, Ma., U.S.	C7	98
Great Island, i., N.C., U.S.	B6	110
Great Karroo, plat., S. Afr.	H4	44
Great Lakes Naval Training Center, mil., Il., U.S.	h9	90
Great Miami, stm., U.S.	C1	112
Great Misery Island, i., Ma., U.S.	f12	98
Great Moose Lake, l., Me., U.S.	D3	96
Great Neck, N.Y., U.S.	h13	109
Great Nicobar, i., India	K2	34
Great Pee Dee, stm., U.S.	D9	117
Great Plain of the Koukdjuak, pl., N.W. Ter., Can.	C18	66
Great Plains, pl., N.A.	E10	61
Great Point, c., Ma., U.S.	D7	98
Great Ruaha, stm., Tan.	C7	44
Great Sacandaga Lake, l., N.Y., U.S.	C6	109
Great Salt Lake, l., Ut., U.S.	B3	121
Great Salt Lake Desert, des., Ut., U.S.	C2	121
Great Salt Plains Lake, res., Ok., U.S.	A3	113
Great Salt Pond, b., R.I., U.S.	h7	116
Great Sand Dunes National Monument, Co., U.S.	D5	83
Great Sandy Desert, des., Austl.	D4	50
Great Slave Lake, l., N.W. Ter., Can.	D10	66
Great Smoky Mountains, mts., U.S.	B8	119
Great Smoky Mountains National Park, U.S.	B8	119
Great Swamp, sw., R.I., U.S.	F3	116
Great Victoria Desert, des., Austl.	E5	50
Great Village, N.S., Can.	D6	71
Great Wass Island, i., Me., U.S.	D5	96
Great Yarmouth, Eng., U.K.	I14	7
Greece, N.Y., U.S.	B3	109
Greece, ctry., Eur.	H12	4
Greeley, Co., U.S.	A6	83
Greeley, Pa., U.S.	D12	115
Greeley, co., Ks., U.S.	D2	93
Greeley, co., Ne., U.S.	C7	104
Green, Or., U.S.	D3	114
Green, co., Ky., U.S.	C4	94
Green, co., Wi., U.S.	F4	126
Green, stm., U.S.	D5	76
Green, stm., U.S.	A1	83
Green, stm., U.S.	F3	122
Green, stm., Il., U.S.	B4	90
Green, stm., Ky., U.S.	C2	94
Green, stm., Wa., U.S.	B3	124
Green Acres, De., U.S.	h8	85
Greenacres, Wa., U.S.	B8	124
Greenacres City, Fl., U.S.	F6	86
Greenback, Tn., U.S.	D9	119
Green Bay, Wi., U.S.	D6	126
Green Bay, b., U.S.	D3	99
Greenbelt, Md., U.S.	C4	97
Greenbriar, Va., U.S.	g12	123
Greenbrier, Ar., U.S.	B3	81
Green Brier, Tn., U.S.	A5	119
Greenbrier, co., W.V., U.S.	D4	125
Greenbrier, stm., W.V., U.S.	D4	125
Greenbush, Mn., U.S.	B2	100
Greencastle, In., U.S.	E4	91
Greencastle, Pa., U.S.	G6	115
Green City, Mo., U.S.	A5	102
Green Cove Springs, Fl., U.S.	C5	86
Greendale, In., U.S.	F8	91
Greendale, Wi., U.S.	F6	126
Greene, Ia., U.S.	B5	92
Greene, N.Y., U.S.	C5	109
Greene, co., Al., U.S.	C1	78
Greene, co., Ar., U.S.	A5	81
Greene, co., Ga., U.S.	C3	87
Greene, co., Il., U.S.	D3	90
Greene, co., In., U.S.	F4	91
Greene, co., Ia., U.S.	B3	92
Greene, co., Ms., U.S.	D5	101
Greene, co., Mo., U.S.	D4	102
Greene, co., N.Y., U.S.	C6	109
Greene, co., N.C., U.S.	B5	110
Greene, co., Oh., U.S.	C2	112
Greene, co., Pa., U.S.	G1	115
Greene, co., Tn., U.S.	C11	119
Greene, co., Va., U.S.	B4	123
Greeneville, Tn., U.S.	C11	119
Green Fall, stm., U.S.	F1	116
Greenfield, Ca., U.S.	D3	82
Greenfield, Il., U.S.	D3	90
Greenfield, In., U.S.	E6	91
Greenfield, Ia., U.S.	C3	92
Greenfield, Ma., U.S.	A2	98
Greenfield, Mo., U.S.	D4	102
Greenfield, N.H., U.S.	E3	106
Greenfield, Oh., U.S.	C2	112
Greenfield, Tn., U.S.	A3	119
Greenfield, Wi., U.S.	n12	126
Greenfield Plaza, Ia., U.S.	e8	92
Green Forest, Ar., U.S.	A2	81
Green Harbor, Ma., U.S.	B6	98
Green Hill Pond, l., R.I., U.S.	G3	116
Greenhills, Oh., U.S.	n12	112
Green Lake, Wi., U.S.	E5	126
Green Lake, co., Wi., U.S.	E4	126
Green Lake, l., Me., U.S.	D4	96
Green Lake, l., Wi., U.S.	E5	126
Greenland, Ar., U.S.	B1	81
Greenland, N.H., U.S.	D5	106
Greenland, dep., N.A.	B16	61
Greenland Sea	B13	128
Greenlee, co., Az., U.S.	D6	80
Green Lookout Mountain, mtn., Wa., U.S.	D3	124
Green Mountain, mtn., Wy., U.S.	D5	127
Green Mountain Reservoir, res., Co., U.S.	B4	83
Green Mountains, mts., Vt., U.S.	F2	122
Greenock, Scot., U.K.	F8	7
Greenock, Pa., U.S.	F2	115
Green Peter Lake, res., Or., U.S.	C4	114
Green Pond, Al., U.S.	B2	78
Green Pond, l., N.J., U.S.	A4	107
Greenport, N.Y., U.S.	m16	109
Green River, Ut., U.S.	E5	121
Green River, Wy., U.S.	E3	127
Green River Lake, res., Ky., U.S.	C4	94
Green River Lock and Dam, U.S.	I2	91
Green River Reservoir, res., Vt., U.S.	B3	122
Green Rock, Il., U.S.	B3	90
Greensboro, Al., U.S.	C2	78
Greensboro, Ga., U.S.	C3	87
Greensboro, Md., U.S.	C6	97
Greensboro, N.C., U.S.	A3	110
Greensburg, In., U.S.	F7	91
Greensburg, Ks., U.S.	E4	93
Greensburg, Ky., U.S.	C4	94
Greensburg, Pa., U.S.	F2	115
Greens Peak, mtn., Az., U.S.	C6	80
Green Springs, Oh., U.S.	A2	112
Greensville, co., Va., U.S.	D5	123
Green Swamp, sw., N.C., U.S.	C4	110
Greentown, In., U.S.	D6	91
Greenup, Il., U.S.	D5	90
Greenup, Ky., U.S.	B7	94
Greenup, co., Ky., U.S.	B7	94
Green Valley, Az., U.S.	F5	80
Greenview, Il., U.S.	C4	90
Greenville, Lib.	G4	42
Greenville, Al., U.S.	D3	78
Greenville, Ca., U.S.	B3	82
Greenville, De., U.S.	A3	85
Greenville, Ga., U.S.	C2	87
Greenville, Il., U.S.	E4	90
Greenville, Ky., U.S.	C2	94
Greenville, Me., U.S.	C3	96
Greenville, Mi., U.S.	E5	99
Greenville, Ms., U.S.	B2	101
Greenville, N.H., U.S.	E3	106
Greenville, N.C., U.S.	B5	110
Greenville, Oh., U.S.	B1	112
Greenville, Pa., U.S.	D1	115
Greenville, R.I., U.S.	C3	116
Greenville, S.C., U.S.	B3	117
Greenville, Tx., U.S.	C4	120
Greenville, co., S.C., U.S.	B3	117
Greenville Creek, stm., Oh., U.S.	B1	112
Greenville Junction, Me., U.S.	C3	96
Greenwich, Ct., U.S.	E1	84
Greenwich, N.Y., U.S.	B7	109
Greenwich, Oh., U.S.	A3	112
Greenwich Bay, b., R.I., U.S.	D4	116
Greenwich Point, c., Ct., U.S.	E1	84
Greenwood, B.C., Can.	E8	69
Greenwood, Ar., U.S.	B1	81
Greenwood, De., U.S.	E3	85
Greenwood, In., U.S.	E5	91
Greenwood, La., U.S.	B2	95
Greenwood, Ms., U.S.	B3	101
Greenwood, Mo., U.S.	k11	102
Greenwood, Pa., U.S.	E5	115
Greenwood, S.C., U.S.	C3	117
Greenwood, Wi., U.S.	D3	126
Greenwood, co., Ks., U.S.	E7	93
Greenwood, co., S.C., U.S.	C3	117
Greenwood, Lake, res., In., U.S.	G4	91
Greenwood, Lake, res., S.C., U.S.	C4	117
Greenwood Lake, N.Y., U.S.	D6	109
Greenwood Lake, l., U.S.	A4	107
Greenwood Lake, l., Mn., U.S.	C7	100
Greer, S.C., U.S.	B3	117
Greer, co., Ok., U.S.	C2	113
Greers Ferry Lake, res., Ar., U.S.	B3	81
Greeson, Lake, res., Ar., U.S.	C2	81
Gregg, co., Tx., U.S.	C5	120
Gregory, S.D., U.S.	D6	118
Gregory, co., S.D., U.S.	D6	118
Greifswald, Ger.	A13	8
Greilickville, Mi., U.S.	D5	99
Greiz, Ger.	E12	8
Grenada, Ms., U.S.	B4	101
Grenada, co., Ms., U.S.	B4	101
Grenada, ctry., N.A.	H17	64
Grenada Lake, res., Ms., U.S.	B4	101
Grenadine Islands, is., N.A.	H17	64
Grenchen, Switz.	E14	10
Grenoble, Fr.	G12	10
Grenville, Que., Can.	D3	74
Grenville, Cape, c., Austl.	B8	50
Grenville, Point, c., Wa., U.S.	B1	124
Gresham, Or., U.S.	B4	114
Gresik, Indon.	m16	33a
Gretna, Man., Can.	E3	70
Gretna, Fl., U.S.	B2	86
Gretna, La., U.S.	E5	95
Gretna, Ne., U.S.	C9	104
Gretna, Va., U.S.	D3	123
Greven, Ger.	C7	8
Grevená, Grc.	I5	16
Grevesmühlen, Ger.	B11	8
Grey, stm., Newf., Can.	E3	72
Greybull, Wy., U.S.	B4	127
Greybull, stm., Wy., U.S.	B4	127
Greylock, Mount, mtn., Ma., U.S.	A1	98
Greymouth, N.Z.	E3	52
Greys, stm., Wy., U.S.	C2	127
Gridley, Ca., U.S.	C3	82
Gridley, Il., U.S.	C5	90
Griffin, Ga., U.S.	C2	87
Griffiss Air Force Base, mil., N.Y., U.S.	B5	109
Griffith, Austl.	F9	50
Griffith, In., U.S.	A3	91
Grifton, N.C., U.S.	B5	110
Griggs, co., N.D., U.S.	B7	111
Griggsville, Il., U.S.	D3	90
Grik, Malay.	L6	34
Grimes, Ia., U.S.	C4	92
Grimes, co., Tx., U.S.	D4	120
Grimmen, Ger.	A13	8
Grimsby, Ont., Can.	D5	73
Grimsby, Eng., U.K.	H12	7
Grimselpass, Switz.	F15	10
Grimshaw, Alta., Can.	A2	68
Grimsley, Tn., U.S.	C9	119
Grimstad, Nor.	G7	6
Grindall Creek, Va., U.S.	n18	123
Grinnell, Ia., U.S.	C5	92
Grinnell Peninsula, pen., N.W. Ter., Can.	A14	66
Gris-Nez, Cap, c., Fr.	B8	10
Grissom Air Force Base, mil., In., U.S.	C5	91
Griswold, Ia., U.S.	C2	92
Grizzly Mountain, mtn., Id., U.S.	B2	89
Grizzly Mountain, mtn., Or., U.S.	C6	114
Grizzly Mountain, mtn., Wa., U.S.	A7	124
Groais Island, i., Newf., Can.	C4	72
Grodno, Bela.	H6	18
Groesbeck, Tx., U.S.	D4	120
Grombalia, Tun.	M5	14
Gronau, Ger.	C6	8
Grong, Nor.	D9	6
Groningen, Neth.	B6	8
Groom Lake, l., Nv., U.S.	F6	105
Groom Range, mts., Nv., U.S.	F6	105
Groote Eylandt, i., Austl.	B7	50
Grootfontein, Nmb.	E3	44
Gros Morne National Park, Newf., Can.	D3	72
Grosse Isle Naval Air Station, mil., Mi., U.S.	p15	99
Grossenhain, Ger.	D13	8
Grosse Pointe, Mi., U.S.	*p16	99
Grosse Pointe Park, Mi., U.S.	p16	99
Grosse Pointe Woods, Mi., U.S.	p16	99
Grosseto, Italy	G6	14
Grossglockner, mtn., Aus.	H12	8
Grossmont, Ca., U.S.	o16	82
Gros Ventre, stm., Wy., U.S.	C2	127
Gros Ventre Range, mts., Wy., U.S.	C2	127
Groswater Bay, b., Newf., Can.	F21	66
Groton, Ct., U.S.	D7	84
Groton, N.Y., U.S.	C4	109
Groton, S.D., U.S.	B7	118
Groton Long Point, Ct., U.S.	D7	84
Grottaglie, Italy	I12	14
Grottaminarda, Italy	H10	14
Grottoes, Va., U.S.	B4	123
Grouse Creek, stm., Ut., U.S.	B2	121
Grouse Creek Mountain, mtn., Id., U.S.	E5	89
Grove, Ok., U.S.	A7	113
Grove City, Fl., U.S.	F4	86
Grove City, Oh., U.S.	C2	112
Grove City, Pa., U.S.	D1	115
Grove Hill, Al., U.S.	D2	78
Groveland, Fl., U.S.	D5	86
Groveland, Ma., U.S.	A5	98
Grove Point, c., Md., U.S.	B5	97
Groveport, Oh., U.S.	C3	112
Grover City, Ca., U.S.	E3	82
Groves, Tx., U.S.	E6	120
Groveton, N.H., U.S.	A3	106
Groveton, Tx., U.S.	D5	120
Groveton, Va., U.S.	g12	123
Groveton Gardens, Va., U.S.	*B5	123
Grovetown, Ga., U.S.	C4	87
Groveville, N.J., U.S.	C3	107
Growler Peak, mtn., Az., U.S.	E2	80
Groznyj, Russia	I7	22
Grudziądz, Pol.	B18	8
Gruetli-Laager, Tn., U.S.	D8	119
Grulla, Tx., U.S.	F3	120
Grundy, Va., U.S.	e9	123
Grundy, co., Il., U.S.	B5	90
Grundy, co., Ia., U.S.	B5	92
Grundy, co., Mo., U.S.	A4	102
Grundy, co., Tn., U.S.	D8	119
Grundy Center, Ia., U.S.	B5	92
Grunthal, Man., Can.	E3	70
Gruver, Tx., U.S.	A2	120
Guacanayabo, Golfo de, b., Cuba	D9	64
Guachochic, Mex.	D6	62
Guadalajara, Mex.	G8	62
Guadalajara, Spain	E8	12
Guadalcanal, i., Sol.Is.	A11	50
Guadalquivir, stm., Spain	H6	12
Guadalupe, Mex.	E9	62
Guadalupe, Az., U.S.	m9	80
Guadalupe, Ca., U.S.	E3	82
Guadalupe, co., N.M., U.S.	C5	108
Guadalupe, co., Tx., U.S.	E4	120
Guadalupe Garzarón, Mex.	E9	62
Guadalupe Mountains, mts., U.S.	E5	108
Guadalupe Mountains National Park, Tx., U.S.	o12	120
Guadalupe Peak, mtn., Tx., U.S.	o12	120
Guadeloupe, dep., N.A.	F17	64
Guadeloupe Passage, strt., N.A.	F17	64
Guadiana, stm., Eur.	H4	12
Guadix, Spain	H8	12
Guafo, Isla, i., Chile	E2	56
Guajará Mirim, Braz.	F5	54
Gualeguaychú, Arg.	C5	56
Gualicho, Salina, pl., Arg.	E3	56
Guam, dep., Oc.	F22	2
Guaminí, Arg.	D4	56
Guamo, Col.	E5	58
Guampí, Sierra de, mts., Ven.	B5	54
Guanaja, Isla de, i., Hond.	F5	64
Guanajuato, Mex.	G9	62
Guanambi, Braz.	C7	57
Guanare, Ven.	C8	58
Guanarito, Ven.	C8	58
Guanay, Cerro, mtn., Ven.	E9	58
Guane, Cuba	C5	64
Guang'an, China	E8	26
Guangdong, prov., China	G9	26
Guanghua, China	E9	26
Guangxi Zhuang Zizhiqu, prov., China	G8	26
Guangyuan, China	E8	26
Guangzhou (Canton), China	L2	28
Guano Lake, l., Or., U.S.	E7	114
Guantánamo, Cuba	D10	64
Guanxian, China	E7	26
Guápiles, C.R.	I6	64
Guaporé (Iténez), stm., S.A.	F6	54
Guaqui, Bol.	G5	54
Guarabira, Braz.	E11	54
Guaranda, Ec.	H3	58
Guarapuava, Braz.	B6	56
Guaratinguetá, Braz.	G6	57
Guarda, Port.	E4	12
Guardo, Spain	C7	12
Guárico, Embalse del, res., Ven.	C9	58
Guarulhos, Braz.	G5	57
Guarus, Braz.	F8	57
Guasave, Mex.	E5	62
Guasdualito, Ven.	D7	58
Guatemala, Guat.	G2	64
Guatemala, ctry., N.A.	G2	64
Guaviare, stm., Col.	F8	58
Guaxupé, Braz.	F5	57
Guayama, P.R.	F14	64
Guayaquil, Ec.	I3	58
Guayaquil, Golfo de, b., S.A.	I2	58
Guaymallén, Arg.	C3	56
Guaymas, Mex.	D4	62
Gubbio, Italy	F7	14
Guben, Ger.	D14	8
Guchengzi, China	D7	26
Gūdalūr, India	G4	37
Gudiyāttam, India	F5	37
Gūdūr, India	E5	37
Guebwiller, Fr.	E14	10
Guelma, Alg.	A7	42
Guelph, Ont., Can.	D4	73
Guérande, Fr.	E4	10
Guéret, Fr.	F8	10
Guernsey, Wy., U.S.	D8	127
Guernsey, co., Oh., U.S.	B4	112
Guernsey, dep., Eur.	C4	10
Gueydan, La., U.S.	D3	95
Guga, Russia	G21	24
Guibes, Nmb.	G3	44
Güicán, Col.	D6	58
Guichen, Fr.	E5	10
Guiding, China	A9	34
Guijuelo, Spain	E6	12
Guilford, Ct., U.S.	D5	84
Guilford, Me., U.S.	C3	96
Guilford, co., N.C., U.S.	A3	110
Guilin (Kweilin), China	B11	34
Guillaumes, Fr.	H13	10
Guimarães, Port.	D3	12

Index

Name — Map Ref — Page

Guin, Al., U.S. B2 78
Guinea, ctry., Afr. F3 42
Guinea, Gulf of, b., Afr. H6 42
Guinea-Bissau, ctry., Afr. F2 42
Güines, Cuba C6 64
Guingamp, Fr. D3 10
Güira de Melena, Cuba C6 64
Guiratinga, Braz. G8 54
Güiria, Ven. B11 58
Guixian, China C10 34
Guiyang (Kweiyang), China A9 34
Guizhou, prov., China F8 26
Gujarat, state, India I4 38
Gūjar Khān, Pak. D5 38
Gujrānwāla, Pak. D6 38
Gujrāt, Pak. D6 38
Gulbarga, India D4 37
Guledagudda, India D3 37
Gulf, co., Fl., U.S. C1 86
Gulf Gate Estates, Fl., U.S. E4 86
Gulf Islands National Seashore, U.S. E5 101
Gulfport, Fl., U.S. E4 86
Gulfport, Ms., U.S. E4 101
Gulf Shores, Al., U.S. E2 78
Gull Island, i., N.C., U.S. B7 110
Gullivan Bay, b., Fl., U.S. G5 86
Gull Lake, l., Alta., Can. C4 68
Gull Lake, l., Mn., U.S. D4 100
Güllük, Tur. L11 16
Gülpinar, Tur. J10 16
Gulu, Ug. H12 42
Gumal (Gowmal), stm., Asia D3 38
Gumboro, De., U.S. G4 85
Gummersbach, Ger. D7 8
Guna, India H7 38
Gunisao, stm., Man., Can. C3 70
Gunnarn, Swe. D11 6
Gunnison, Co., U.S. C4 83
Gunnison, Ms., U.S. B3 101
Gunnison, Ut., U.S. D4 121
Gunnison, co., Co., U.S. C3 83
Gunnison, stm., Co., U.S. C2 83
Gunnison, Mount, mtn., Co., U.S. C3 83
Gunpowder Neck, c., Md., U.S. B5 97
Gunpowder River, b., Md., U.S. B5 97
Guntakal, India E4 37
Gunter Air Force Base, mil., Al., U.S. C3 78
Guntersville, Al., U.S. A3 78
Guntersville Lake, res., Al., U.S. A3 78
Guntown, Ms., U.S. A5 101
Guntūr, India D6 37
Gunungsitoli, Indon. N4 34
Günzburg, Ger. G10 8
Gunzenhausen, Ger. F10 8
Gurdāspur, India D6 38
Gurdon, Ar., U.S. D2 81
Guri, Embalse, res., Ven. D11 58
Gurley, Al., U.S. A3 78
Gurnee, Il., U.S. h9 90
Gurnet Point, c., Ma., U.S. B6 98
Gurupi, Braz. F9 54
Gurupi, stm., Braz. D9 54
Gusau, Nig. F7 42
Gus'-Chrustal'nyj, Russia F23 18
Gusev, Russia G5 18
Gushi, China C4 28
Gushikawa, Japan y27 31b
Gusinoozersk, Russia G15 24
Guspini, Italy J3 14
Gustav Holm, Kap, c., Grnld. C26 66
Gustine, Ca., U.S. D3 82
Güstrow, Ger. B12 8
Gütersloh, Ger. D8 8
Guthrie, Ky., U.S. D2 94
Guthrie, Ok., U.S. B4 113
Guthrie, W.V., U.S. m12 125
Guthrie, co., Ia., U.S. C3 92
Guthrie Center, Ia., U.S. C3 92
Guttenberg, Ia., U.S. B6 92
Guttenberg, N.J., U.S. h8 107
Guyana, ctry., S.A. B7 54
Guyandotte, stm., W.V., U.S. C2 125
Guymon, Ok., U.S. e9 113
Guysborough, N.S., Can. D8 71
Guyton, Ga., U.S. D5 87
Güzelyurt Körfezi, b., N. Cyp. B3 40
Gwādar, Pak. D1 36
Gwai, Zimb. E5 44
Gwalior, India G8 38
Gwanda, Zimb. F5 44
Gweru, Zimb. E5 44
Gwinhurst, De., U.S. h8 85
Gwinn, Mi., U.S. B3 99
Gwinner, N.D., U.S. C8 111
Gwinnett, co., Ga., U.S. C2 87
Gwydyr Bay, b., Ak., U.S. A10 79
Gwynns Falls, stm., Md., U.S. g10 97
Gympie, Austl. E10 50
Gyöngyös, Hung. H19 8
Győr, Hung. H17 8
Gypsum, Co., U.S. B4 83

H

Haakon, co., S.D., U.S. C4 118
Haapajärvi, Fin. E15 6
Haapamäki, Fin. E15 6
Haar, Ger. G11 8
Haarlem, Neth. C4 8
Haast, N.Z. E2 52
Habersham, co., Ga., U.S. B3 87
Habiganj, Bngl. H14 38
Hachijō-jima, i., Japan E14 26
Hachinohe, Japan B14 30
Hachiōji, Japan G12 30
Hackberry, La., U.S. E2 95
Hackensack, N.J., U.S. B4 107
Hackensack, stm., N.J., U.S. h8 107
Hackettstown, N.J., U.S. B3 107
Hackleburg, Al., U.S. A2 78
Hadd, Ra's al-, c., Oman D6 46
Haddam, Ct., U.S. D5 84
Haddock, Ga., U.S. C3 87
Haddonfield, N.J., U.S. D2 107
Haddon Heights, N.J., U.S. D2 107
Hadejia, stm., Nig. F8 42
Hadera, Isr. C4 40
Haderslev, Den. I7 6
Hadīyah, Sau. Ar. C2 46
Hadjeb el Aïoun, Tun. N4 14
Hadley Bay, b., N.W. Ter., Can. B11 66
Hadley Lake, l., Me., U.S. D5 96
Hadlock, Wa., U.S. A3 124
Ha Dong, Viet. D8 34
Hadramawt, reg., Yemen E4 46
Haeju, N. Kor. D12 26
Hāfizābād, Pak. D5 38
Hafun, Ras, c., Som. F5 46
Hagan, Ga., U.S. D5 87
Hagemeister Island, i., Ak., U.S. D7 79
Hagen, Ger. D7 8
Hagerman, Id., U.S. G4 89
Hagerman, N.M., U.S. D5 108
Hagerstown, In., U.S. E7 91
Hagerstown, Md., U.S. A2 97
Hagfors, Swe. F9 6
Haggin, Mount, mtn., Mt., U.S. D3 103
Hagi, Japan H4 30
Ha Giang, Viet. C8 34
Hague, Sask., Can. E2 75
Hague, Cap de la, c., Fr. C5 10
Haguenau, Fr. D14 10
Hagues Peak, mtn., Co., U.S. A5 83
Ha90 Ha90, Baie des, b., Que., Can. C2 72
Hahira, Ga., U.S. F3 87
Hahnville, La., U.S. E5 95
Haian, China C9 28
Haicheng, China C11 26
Hai Duong, Viet. D9 34
Haifa see Hefa, Isr. C4 40
Haikou, China D11 34
Haiku, Hi., U.S. C5 88
Hā'il, Sau. Ar. C3 46
Hailaer, China B10 26
Hailey, Id., U.S. F4 89
Haileybury, Ont., Can. p20 73
Haileyville, Ok., U.S. C6 113
Haimen, China G10 28
Haimen, China L5 28
Hainan, China H8 26
Hainan Dao, i., China E10 34
Haines, Ak., U.S. D12 79
Haines City, Fl., U.S. D5 86
Haines Junction, Yukon, Can. D5 66
Hainfeld, Aus. G15 8
Haining, China E9 28
Hai Phong, Viet. D9 34
Haiti (Haïti), ctry., N.A. E11 64
Haizhou, China A8 28
Hakodate, Japan r18 30a
Hāla, Pak. H3 38
Halab (Aleppo), Syria A5 40
Halā'ib, Sudan D13 42
Halawa, Cape, c., Hi., U.S. B5 88
Halawa Heights, Hi., U.S. g10 88
Halbā, Leb. B5 40
Halberstadt, Ger. D11 8
Halden, Nor. G8 6
Haldensleben, Ger. C11 8
Haldimand, Ont., Can. E5 73
Haldwāni, India F8 38
Hale, co., Al., U.S. C2 78
Hale, co., Tx., U.S. B2 120
Haleakala Crater, crat., Hi., U.S. C5 88
Haleakala National Park, Hi., U.S. C6 88
Hale Center, Tx., U.S. B2 120
Haleiwa, Hi., U.S. B3 88
Hales Corners, Wi., U.S. n11 126
Halethorpe, Md., U.S. B4 97
Haleyville, Al., U.S. A2 78
Half Moon Bay, Ca., U.S. k8 82
Halfway, Md., U.S. A2 97
Haliburton, Ont., Can. B6 73
Halibut Point, c., Ma., U.S. A6 98
Halifax, N.S., Can. E6 71
Halifax, Va., U.S. D4 123
Halifax, co., N.C., U.S. A5 110
Halifax, co., Va., U.S. D4 123
Halifax Bay, b., Austl. C9 50
Haliimaile, Hi., U.S. C5 88
Halkirk, Scot., U.K. C9 7
Hall, co., Ga., U.S. B3 87
Hall, co., Ne., U.S. D7 104
Hall, co., Tx., U.S. B2 120
Hallam Peak, mtn., B.C., Can. C8 69
Hallandale, Fl., U.S. G6 86
Halla-san, mtn., S. Kor. E12 26
Halle, Ger. D11 8
Hällefors, Swe. G10 6
Hallein, Aus. H13 8
Hallettsville, Tx., U.S. E4 120
Hallie, Wi., U.S. D2 126
Hall Island, i., Ak., U.S. C5 79
Hall Meadow Brook Reservoir, res., Ct., U.S. B3 84
Hall Mountain, mtn., Wa., U.S. A8 124
Hällnäs, Swe. D12 6
Hallock, Mn., U.S. B2 100
Hallowell, Me., U.S. D3 96
Hall Peninsula, pen., N.W. Ter., Can. D19 66
Halls, Tn., U.S. B2 119
Hallsberg, Swe. G10 6
Halls Creek, Austl. C5 50
Halls Creek, stm., Ut., U.S. F5 121
Halls Crossroads, Tn., U.S. m14 119
Halls Stream, stm., N.H., U.S. f7 106
Hallstavik, Swe. F12 6
Hallstead, Pa., U.S. C10 115
Hallsville, Mo., U.S. B5 102
Hallsville, Tx., U.S. C5 120
Halmahera, i., Indon. E8 32
Halmahera, Laut, Indon. F8 32
Halmstad, Swe. H9 6
Halsey, Or., U.S. C3 114
Hälsingborg see Helsingborg, Swe. H9 6
Halstad, Mn., U.S. C2 100
Halstead, Ks., U.S. E6 93
Haltern, Ger. D7 8
Haltiatunturi, mtn., Eur. B13 6
Halton Hills, Ont., Can. D5 73
Hamada, Japan H5 30
Hamadān, Iran B4 46
Hamāh, Syria B5 40
Hamamatsu, Japan H10 30
Hamar, Nor. F8 6
Hamblen, co., Tn., U.S. C10 119
Hamburg, Ger. B9 8
Hamburg, Ar., U.S. D4 81
Hamburg, Ia., U.S. D2 92
Hamburg, N.Y., U.S. C2 109
Hamburg, Pa., U.S. E10 115
Hamden, Ct., U.S. D4 84
Hamden, Oh., U.S. C3 112
Hämeenlinna, Fin. F15 6
Hamel, Mn., U.S. m11 100
Hameln, Ger. C9 8
Hamersley Range, mts., Austl. D3 50
Hamhŭng, N. Kor. D12 26
Hami, China C5 26
Hamilton, Ber. E14 76
Hamilton, Ont., Can. D5 73
Hamilton, N.Z. B5 52
Hamilton, Scot., U.K. F8 7
Hamilton, Al., U.S. A2 78
Hamilton, Il., U.S. C2 90
Hamilton, In., U.S. A8 91
Hamilton, Mi., U.S. F4 99
Hamilton, Ms., U.S. B5 101
Hamilton, Mo., U.S. B3 102
Hamilton, Mt., U.S. D2 103
Hamilton, N.Y., U.S. C5 109
Hamilton, Oh., U.S. C1 112
Hamilton, Tx., U.S. D3 120
Hamilton, Va., U.S. A5 123
Hamilton, co., Fl., U.S. B3 86
Hamilton, co., Il., U.S. E5 90
Hamilton, co., In., U.S. D5 91
Hamilton, co., Ia., U.S. B4 92
Hamilton, co., Ks., U.S. E2 93
Hamilton, co., Ne., U.S. D7 104
Hamilton, co., N.Y., U.S. B6 109
Hamilton, co., Oh., U.S. C1 112
Hamilton, co., Tn., U.S. D8 119
Hamilton, co., Tx., U.S. D3 120
Hamilton, Lake, res., Ar., U.S. C2 81
Hamilton, Mount, mtn., Ak., U.S. C8 79
Hamilton, Mount, mtn., Ca., U.S. k9 82
Hamilton, Mount, mtn., Nv., U.S. D6 105
Hamilton Inlet, b., Newf., Can. A2 72
Hamilton Reservoir, res., Ma., U.S. B3 98
Hamilton Sound, strt., Newf., Can. D4 72
Hamilton Square, N.J., U.S. C3 107
Hamiota, Man., Can. D1 70
Hamlet, In., U.S. B4 91
Hamlet, N.C., U.S. C3 110
Hamlet, Mount, mtn., Ak., U.S. B6 79
Hamlin, Pa., U.S. D11 115
Hamlin, Tx., U.S. C2 120
Hamlin, W.V., U.S. C2 125
Hamlin, co., S.D., U.S. C8 118
Hamlin Lake, l., Mi., U.S. D4 99
Hamm, Ger. D7 8
Hammamet, Tun. M5 14
Hammam Lif, Tun. M5 14
Hammerdal, Swe. E10 6
Hammon, Ok., U.S. B2 113
Hammonasset, stm., Ct., U.S. D5 84
Hammonasset Point, c., Ct., U.S. E5 84
Hammond, In., U.S. A2 91
Hammond, La., U.S. D5 95
Hammond, Wi., U.S. D1 126
Hammond Bay, b., Mi., U.S. C6 99
Hammonton, N.J., U.S. D3 107
Hampden, Newf., Can. D3 72
Hampden, Me., U.S. D4 96
Hampden, co., Ma., U.S. B2 98
Hampden Highlands, Me., U.S. D4 96
Hampshire, Il., U.S. A5 90
Hampshire, co., Ma., U.S. B2 98
Hampshire, co., W.V., U.S. B6 125
Hampstead, Md., U.S. A4 97
Hampstead, N.C., U.S. C5 110
Hampton, N.B., Can. D4 71
Hampton, Ar., U.S. D3 81
Hampton, Ga., U.S. C2 87
Hampton, Ia., U.S. B4 92
Hampton, N.H., U.S. E5 106
Hampton, S.C., U.S. F5 117
Hampton, Tn., U.S. C11 119
Hampton, Va., U.S. C6 123
Hampton, co., S.C., U.S. F5 117
Hampton Bays, N.Y., U.S. n16 109
Hampton Beach, N.H., U.S. E5 106
Hampton Butte, mtn., Or., U.S. D6 114
Hampton Roads, Va., U.S. k15 123
Hampton Roads Bridge-Tunnel, Va., U.S. k15 123
Hams Fork, stm., Wy., U.S. E2 127
Hamtramck, Mi., U.S. p15 99
Hana, Hi., U.S. C6 88
Hanahan, S.C., U.S. F7 117
Hanalei Bay, b., Hi., U.S. A2 88
Hanamaki, Japan C14 30
Hanamaulu, Hi., U.S. B2 88
Hanapepe, Hi., U.S. B2 88
Hanau, Ger. E8 8
Hanceville, Al., U.S. A3 78
Hancock, Md., U.S. A1 97
Hancock, Mi., U.S. A2 99
Hancock, Mn., U.S. E3 100
Hancock, co., Ga., U.S. C3 87
Hancock, co., Il., U.S. C2 90
Hancock, co., In., U.S. E6 91
Hancock, co., Ia., U.S. A4 92
Hancock, co., Ky., U.S. C3 94
Hancock, co., Me., U.S. D4 96
Hancock, co., Ms., U.S. E4 101
Hancock, co., Oh., U.S. A2 112
Hancock, co., Tn., U.S. C10 119
Hancock, co., W.V., U.S. A4 125
Hand, co., S.D., U.S. C6 118
Handa, Japan H9 30
Handan, China D9 26
Hando, Som. F5 46
HaNegev, reg., Isr. D4 40
Hanford, Ca., U.S. D4 82
Hangchow see Hangzhou, China E9 28
Hangman Creek, stm., Wa., U.S. B8 124
Hangö (Hanko), Fin. G14 6
Hangzhou (Hangchow), China E9 28
Hangzhou Wan, b., China E9 28
Ḥanīsh, Jazā'ir, is., Yemen F3 46
Hanjiang, China J8 28
Hankinson, N.D., U.S. C9 111
Hanna, Alta., Can. D5 68
Hanna, Wy., U.S. E6 127
Hanna City, Il., U.S. C4 90
Hannahville Indian Reservation, Mi., U.S. C3 99
Hannibal, Mo., U.S. B6 102
Hannover, Ger. C9 8
Ha Noi, Viet. D8 34
Hanover, Ont., Can. C3 73
Hanover, Il., U.S. A3 90
Hanover, In., U.S. G7 91
Hanover, Ks., U.S. C7 93
Hanover, Ma., U.S. B6 98
Hanover, Mn., U.S. m11 100
Hanover, N.H., U.S. C2 106
Hanover, Pa., U.S. G8 115
Hanover, co., Va., U.S. C5 123
Hanover Park, Il., U.S. k8 90
Hansen, Id., U.S. G4 89
Hansford, co., Tx., U.S. A2 120
Hanson, Ma., U.S. B6 98
Hanson, co., S.D., U.S. D8 118
Hantsport, N.S., Can. D5 71
Hanzhong, China E8 26
Haparanda, Swe. D15 6
Hapeville, Ga., U.S. C2 87
Happy Valley, N.M., U.S. E5 108
Happy Valley-Goose Bay, Newf., Can. B1 72
Harahan, La., U.S. k11 95
Haralson, co., Ga., U.S. C1 87
Harare, Zimb. E6 44
Harash, Bi'r al-, well, Libya C10 42
Harbeson, De., U.S. F4 85
Harbin, China B12 26
Harbor, Or., U.S. E2 114
Harbor Beach, Mi., U.S. E8 99
Harborcreek, Pa., U.S. B2 115
Harbor Springs, Mi., U.S. C6 99
Harbour Breton, Newf., Can. E4 72
Harbour Grace, Newf., Can. E5 72
Harcuvar Mountains, mts., Az., U.S. D2 80
Harda, India I7 38
Hardangerfjorden, Nor. F5 6
Hardee, co., Fl., U.S. E5 86
Hardeeville, S.C., U.S. G5 117
Hardeman, co., Tn., U.S. B2 119
Hardeman, co., Tx., U.S. B3 120
Hardin, Il., U.S. D3 90
Hardin, Mt., U.S. E9 103
Hardin, co., Il., U.S. F5 90
Hardin, co., Ia., U.S. B4 92
Hardin, co., Ky., U.S. C4 94
Hardin, co., Oh., U.S. B2 112
Hardin, co., Tn., U.S. B3 119
Hardin, co., Tx., U.S. D5 120
Harding, co., N.M., U.S. B5 108
Harding, co., S.D., U.S. B2 118
Harding, Lake, res., U.S. C4 78
Hardinsburg, Ky., U.S. C3 94
Hardisty, Alta., Can. C5 68
Hardwār, India F8 38
Hardwick, Ga., U.S. C3 87
Hardwick, Vt., U.S. B4 122
Hardwood Ridge, mtn., Pa., U.S. D11 115
Hardy, co., W.V., U.S. B6 125
Hardy Lake, res., In., U.S. G6 91
Hare Bay, Newf., Can. D4 72
Hare Bay, b., Newf., Can. C4 72
Harer, Eth. G3 46
Harford, co., Md., U.S. A5 97
Hargeysa, Som. G3 46
Harihar, India E3 37
Harīrūd (Tedžen), stm., Asia J10 22
Harkers Island, N.C., U.S. C6 110
Harlan, In., U.S. B8 91
Harlan, Ia., U.S. C2 92
Harlan, Ky., U.S. D6 94
Harlan, co., Ky., U.S. D6 94
Harlan, co., Ne., U.S. D6 104
Harlan County Lake, res., Ne., U.S. E6 104
Harlem, Fl., U.S. F6 86
Harlem, Ga., U.S. C4 87
Harlem, Mt., U.S. B8 103
Harleyville, S.C., U.S. E7 117
Harlingen, Neth. B5 8
Harlingen, Tx., U.S. F4 120
Harlow, Eng., U.K. J13 7
Harlowton, Mt., U.S. D7 103
Harmon, co., Ok., U.S. C2 113
Harmon Creek, stm., W.V., U.S. f8 125
Harmony, In., U.S. E3 91
Harmony, Mn., U.S. G6 100
Harmony, Pa., U.S. E1 115
Harmony, R.I., U.S. B3 116
Harnett, co., N.C., U.S. B4 110
Harney, co., Or., U.S. D7 114
Harney, Lake, l., Fl., U.S. D5 86
Harney Lake, l., Or., U.S. D7 114
Harney Peak, mtn., S.D., U.S. D2 118
Härnösand, Swe. E11 6
Haro, Spain C9 12
Haro Strait, strt., Wa., U.S. A2 124
Harper, Lib. H4 42
Harper, Ks., U.S. E5 93
Harper, co., Ks., U.S. E5 93
Harper, co., Ok., U.S. A2 113
Harper, Mount, mtn., Ak., U.S. C11 79
Harpers Ferry, W.V., U.S. B7 125
Harpers Ferry National Historical Park, W.V., U.S. B7 125
Harpersville, Al., U.S. B3 78
Harpeth, stm., Tn., U.S. A5 119
Harquahala Mountain, mtn., Az., U.S. D2 80
Harquahala Mountains, mts., Az., U.S. D2 80
Harrah, Ok., U.S. B4 113
Harricana, stm., Can. F17 66
Harriman, Tn., U.S. D9 119
Harriman Reservoir, res., Vt., U.S. F3 122
Harrington, De., U.S. E3 85
Harrington Park, N.J., U.S. h9 107
Harris, Mn., U.S. E6 100
Harris, R.I., U.S. D3 116
Harris, co., Ga., U.S. D2 87
Harris, co., Tx., U.S. E5 120
Harris, Lake, l., Fl., U.S. D5 86
Harrisburg, Ar., U.S. B5 81
Harrisburg, Il., U.S. F5 90
Harrisburg, Or., U.S. C3 114
Harrisburg, Pa., U.S. F8 115
Harrisburg, S.D., U.S. D9 118
Harrison, Ar., U.S. A2 81
Harrison, Mi., U.S. D6 99
Harrison, N.J., U.S. k8 107
Harrison, N.Y., U.S. h13 109
Harrison, Oh., U.S. C1 112
Harrison, Tn., U.S. h11 119
Harrison, co., In., U.S. H5 91
Harrison, co., Ia., U.S. C2 92
Harrison, co., Ky., U.S. B5 94
Harrison, co., Ms., U.S. E4 101
Harrison, co., Mo., U.S. A3 102
Harrison, co., Oh., U.S. B4 112
Harrison, co., Tx., U.S. C5 120
Harrison, co., W.V., U.S. B4 125
Harrison, Cape, c., Newf., Can. g10 72
Harrison Bay, b., Ak., U.S. A9 79
Harrisonburg, Va., U.S. B4 123
Harrison Hot Springs, B.C., Can. f14 69
Harrison Lake, l., B.C., Can. E7 69
Harrisonville, Mo., U.S. C3 102
Harriston, Ont., Can. D4 73
Harristown, Il., U.S. D4 90
Harrisville, R.I., U.S. B2 116
Harrisville, Ut., U.S. B4 121
Harrisville, W.V., U.S. B3 125
Harrodsburg, Ky., U.S. C5 94
Harrogate, Eng., U.K. G11 7
Harrow, Ont., Can. E2 73
Harry S. Truman Reservoir, res., Mo., U.S. C4 102
Harry Strunk Lake, res., Ne., U.S. D5 104
Harstad, Nor. B11 6
Hart, Mi., U.S. E4 99
Hart, Tx., U.S. B1 120
Hart, co., Ga., U.S. B4 87
Hart, co., Ky., U.S. C4 94
Hart, Lake, l., Fl., U.S. D5 86
Hartford, Al., U.S. D4 78
Hartford, Ar., U.S. B1 81
Hartford, Ct., U.S. B5 84
Hartford, Il., U.S. E3 90
Hartford, Ia., U.S. C4 92
Hartford, Ky., U.S. C3 94
Hartford, Mi., U.S. F4 99
Hartford, S.D., U.S. D9 118
Hartford, Vt., U.S. D4 122
Hartford, Wi., U.S. E5 126
Hartford, co., Ct., U.S. B4 84
Hartford City, In., U.S. D7 91
Hartington, Ne., U.S. B8 104
Hart Lake, l., Or., U.S. E7 114
Hartland, N.B., Can. C2 71
Hartland, Me., U.S. D3 96
Hartland, Wi., U.S. E5 126
Hartland Point, c., Eng., U.K. J8 7
Hartlepool, Eng., U.K. G11 7
Hartley, Ia., U.S. A2 92
Hartley, co., Tx., U.S. B1 120
Hartney, Man., Can. E1 70
Hartselle, Al., U.S. A3 78
Hartshorne, Ok., U.S. C6 113
Hartsville, S.C., U.S. C7 117
Hartsville, Tn., U.S. A5 119
Hartville, Oh., U.S. B4 112
Hartwell, Ga., U.S. B4 87
Hartwell Lake, res., U.S. B1 117
Hārūnābād, Pak. F5 38
Hārūt, stm., Afg. C1 36
Harvard, Il., U.S. A5 90
Harvard, Ne., U.S. D7 104
Harvard, Mount, mtn., Co., U.S. C4 83
Harvey, Il., U.S. B6 90
Harvey, La., U.S. E5 95
Harvey, Mi., U.S. B3 99
Harvey, N.D., U.S. B6 111
Harvey, co., Ks., U.S. D6 93
Harvey Lake, res., Pa., U.S. m16 115
Harveys Creek, stm., Pa., U.S. n16 115
Harwich, Eng., U.K. J14 7
Harwich Port, Ma., U.S. C7 98
Harwinton, Ct., U.S. B3 84
Haryana, state, India F7 38
Harz, mts., Ger. D10 8
Hasbrouck Heights, N.J., U.S. h8 107
Haskell, Ar., U.S. C3 81
Haskell, Ok., U.S. B6 113
Haskell, Tx., U.S. C3 120
Haskell, co., Ks., U.S. E3 93
Haskell, co., Ok., U.S. B6 113
Haskell, co., Tx., U.S. C3 120
Haskovo, Bul. H9 16
Hassan, India F4 37
Hassayampa, stm., Az., U.S. D3 80
Hasselt, Bel. E5 8
Hassfurt, Ger. E10 8
Hässleholm, Swe. H9 6
Hastings, Ont., Can. C7 73
Hastings, N.Z. C6 52
Hastings, Eng., U.K. K13 7
Hastings, Mi., U.S. F5 99
Hastings, Mn., U.S. F6 100
Hastings, Ne., U.S. D7 104
Hastings, Pa., U.S. E4 115
Hastings-on-Hudson, N.Y., U.S. h13 109
Hatch, N.M., U.S. E2 108
Hatchet Lake, N.S., Can. E6 71
Hatchie, stm., Tn., U.S. B2 119
Hatchineha, Lake, l., Fl., U.S. D5 86
Hat Creek, stm., S.D., U.S. E2 118
Hatfield, In., U.S. I3 91
Hatfield, Pa., U.S. F11 115
Hāthras, India G8 38
Ha Tinh, Viet. E8 34
Hat Mountain, mtn., Az., U.S. E3 80
Hatteras, N.C., U.S. B7 110

Name	Map Ref	Page
Hatteras, Cape, c., N.C., U.S.	B7	110
Hatteras Inlet, b., N.C., U.S.	B7	110
Hattiesburg, Ms., U.S.	D4	101
Hatton, N.D., U.S.	B8	111
Hat Yai, Thai.	K6	34
Haubstadt, In., U.S.	H2	91
Haugesund, Nor.	G5	6
Haughton, La., U.S.	B2	95
Haukivuori, Fin.	E16	6
Hauser, Or., U.S.	D2	114
Haut, Isle au, i., Me., U.S.	D4	96
Haut Atlas, mts., Mor.	B4	42
Hauula, Hi., U.S.	B4	88
Havana, Fl., U.S.	B2	86
Havana, Il., U.S.	C3	90
Havana see La Habana, Cuba	C6	64
Havant, Eng., U.K.	K12	7
Havasu, Lake, res., U.S.	C1	80
Havasupai Indian Reservation, Az., U.S.	A3	80
Havelberg, Ger.	C12	8
Havelock, Ont., Can.	C7	73
Havelock, N.C., U.S.	C6	110
Haven, Ks., U.S.	E6	93
Haverford [Township], Pa., U.S.	o20	115
Haverhill, Ma., U.S.	A5	98
Hāveri, India	E3	37
Haverstraw, N.Y., U.S.	D7	109
Haviland, Ks., U.S.	E4	93
Havířov, Czech.	F18	8
Havre, Mt., U.S.	B7	103
Havre de Grace, Md., U.S.	A5	97
Havre North, Mt., U.S.	B7	103
Haw, stm., N.C., U.S.	B3	110
Hawaii, co., Hi., U.S.	D6	88
Hawaii, state, U.S.	C5	88
Hawaii, i., Hi., U.S.	D6	88
Hawaiian Islands, is., Hi., U.S.	m14	88
Hawaii Volcanoes National Park, Hi., U.S.	D6	88
Hawarden, Ia., U.S.	A1	92
Hawesville, Ky., U.S.	C3	94
Hawi, Hi., U.S.	C6	88
Hawick, Scot., U.K.	F10	7
Hawke Bay, b., N.Z.	C6	52
Hawkesbury, Ont., Can.	B10	73
Hawkesbury Island, i., B.C., Can.	C3	69
Hawkins, co., Tn., U.S.	C11	119
Hawkinsville, Ga., U.S.	D3	87
Hawley, Mn., U.S.	D2	100
Hawley, Pa., U.S.	D11	115
Haworth, N.J., U.S.	h9	107
Haw River, N.C., U.S.	A3	110
Hawthorne, Ca., U.S.	n12	82
Hawthorne, Fl., U.S.	C4	86
Hawthorne, Nv., U.S.	E3	105
Hawthorne, N.J., U.S.	B4	107
Hawthorne, N.Y., U.S.	g13	109
Haxtun, Co., U.S.	A8	83
Hay, Austl.	F8	50
Hay, stm., Austl.	D7	50
Hay, stm., Can.	E9	66
Hay, Cape, c., N.W. Ter., Can.	B10	66
Hayange, Fr.	C13	10
Hayden, Az., U.S.	E5	80
Hayden, Co., U.S.	A3	83
Hayden Lake, l., Id., U.S.	B2	89
Hayes, La., U.S.	D3	95
Hayes, co., Ne., U.S.	D4	104
Hayes, stm., Man., Can.	B5	70
Hayes, Mount, mtn., Ak., U.S.	C10	79
Hayfield, Mn., U.S.	G6	100
Hayford Peak, mtn., Nv., U.S.	G6	105
Haymock Lake, l., Me., U.S.	B3	96
Haynesville, La., U.S.	B2	95
Hayneville, Al., U.S.	C3	78
Hayrabolu, Tur.	H11	16
Hay River, N.W. Ter., Can.	D9	66
Hays, Ks., U.S.	D4	93
Hays, N.C., U.S.	A1	110
Hays, co., Tx., U.S.	D3	120
Hays Canyon Peak, mtn., Nv., U.S.	B2	105
Hay Springs, Ne., U.S.	B3	104
Haystack Mountain, mtn., Nv., U.S.	B6	105
Haysville, Ks., U.S.	g12	93
Hayti, Mo., U.S.	E8	102
Hayti Heights, Mo., U.S.	E8	102
Hayward, Ca., U.S.	h8	82
Hayward, Wi., U.S.	B2	126
Haywood, co., N.C., U.S.	f9	110
Haywood, co., Tn., U.S.	B2	119
Hazard, Ky., U.S.	C6	94
Hazardville, Ct., U.S.	B5	84
Hazāribāgh, India	I11	38
Hazel Crest, Il., U.S.	k9	90
Hazel Dell, Wa., U.S.	D3	124
Hazel Green, Al., U.S.	A3	78
Hazel Green, Wi., U.S.	F3	126
Hazel Park, Mi., U.S.	p15	99
Hazelton Pyramid, mtn., Wy., U.S.	B5	127
Hazelwood, N.C., U.S.	f10	110
Hazen, Ar., U.S.	C4	81
Hazen, N.D., U.S.	B4	111
Hazen Bay, b., Ak., U.S.	C6	79
Hazlehurst, Ga., U.S.	E4	87
Hazlehurst, Ms., U.S.	D3	101
Hazlet, N.J., U.S.	C4	107
Hazleton, Ia., U.S.	B6	92
Hazleton, Pa., U.S.	E10	115
Head Harbor Island, i., Me., U.S.	D5	96
Headland, Al., U.S.	D4	78
Headley, Mount, mtn., Mt., U.S.	C1	103
Healdsburg, Ca., U.S.	C2	82
Healdton, Ok., U.S.	C4	113
Healy, Ak., U.S.	C10	79
Heard, co., Ga., U.S.	C1	87
Hearne, Tx., U.S.	D4	120
Hearst, Ont., Can.	o19	73
Heart, stm., N.D., U.S.	C3	111
Heart Butte Dam, N.D., U.S.	C4	111
Heart Lake, l., Wy., U.S.	B2	127
Heart's Content, Newf., Can.	E5	72
Heath, Oh., U.S.	B3	112
Heath Springs, S.C., U.S.	B6	117
Heavener, Ok., U.S.	C7	113
Hebbronville, Tx., U.S.	F3	120
Hebei, prov., China	D10	26
Heber, Az., U.S.	C5	80
Heber City, Ut., U.S.	C4	121
Heber Springs, Ar., U.S.	B3	81
Hébertville, Que., Can.	A6	74
Hebgen Lake, res., Mt., U.S.	F5	103
Hebrides, is., Scot., U.K.	D6	4
Hebron, N.S., Can.	F3	71
Hebron, Il., U.S.	A5	90
Hebron, In., U.S.	B3	91
Hebron, Ky., U.S.	h13	94
Hebron, Md., U.S.	D6	97
Hebron, Ne., U.S.	D8	104
Hebron, N.D., U.S.	C3	111
Hebron, Oh., U.S.	C3	112
Hebron see Al-Khalīl, Jord.	D4	40
Hecate Strait, strt., B.C., Can.	C2	69
Heceta Island, i., Ak., U.S.	n23	79
Hechi, China	B9	34
Hechingen, Ger.	G8	8
Hechuan, China	E8	26
Hecla Island, i., Man., Can.	D3	70
Hector, Mn., U.S.	F4	100
Hedemora, Swe.	F10	6
He Devil, mtn., Id., U.S.	D2	89
Hedrick, Ia., U.S.	C5	92
Heerenveen, Neth.	C5	8
Heerlen, Neth.	E5	8
Ḥefa (Haifa), Isr.	C4	40
Hefei, China	D6	28
Heflin, Al., U.S.	B4	78
Hefner, Lake, res., Ok., U.S.	B4	113
Hegang, China	B13	26
Hegins, Pa., U.S.	E9	115
Heide, Ger.	A9	8
Heidelberg, Ger.	F8	8
Heidelberg, Ms., U.S.	D5	101
Heidenheim, Ger.	F10	8
Heidenreichstein, Aus.	G15	8
Heidrick, Ky., U.S.	D6	94
Heihe (Naquka), China	E14	38
Heilbron, S. Afr.	G5	44
Heilbronn, Ger.	F9	8
Heiligenstadt, Ger.	D10	8
Heilongjiang, prov., China	B12	26
Heilongjiang (Amur), stm., Asia	G19	24
Heinola, Fin.	F16	6
Hejaz see Al-Ḥijāz, reg., Sau. Ar.	C2	46
Hekla, vol., Ice.	C4	4
Hekou, China	C7	34
Helena, Al., U.S.	B3	78
Helena, Ar., U.S.	C5	81
Helena, Ga., U.S.	D4	87
Helena, Mt., U.S.	D4	103
Helena, Ok., U.S.	A3	113
Helensburgh, Scot., U.K.	E8	7
Helgoland, i., Ger.	A7	8
Helgoländer Bucht, b., Ger.	A8	8
Hellam, Pa., U.S.	G8	115
Hellertown, Pa., U.S.	E11	115
Hellesylt, Nor.	E6	6
Hellín, Spain	G10	12
Hells Canyon, val., U.S.	B10	114
Hells Canyon National Recreation Area, U.S.	B10	114
Hell-Ville, Madag.	D9	44
Helmand, stm., Asia	C2	36
Helmond, Neth.	D5	8
Helmsdale, Scot., U.K.	C9	7
Helmstedt, Ger.	C10	8
Helotes, Tx., U.S.	h7	120
Helper, Ut., U.S.	D5	121
Helsingborg, Swe.	H9	6
Helsingfors see Helsinki, Fin.	F15	6
Helsingør (Elsinore), Den.	H9	6
Helsinki (Helsingfors), Fin.	F15	6
Hematite, Mo., U.S.	C7	102
Hemet, Ca., U.S.	F5	82
Hemingford, Ne., U.S.	B2	104
Hemingway, S.C., U.S.	D9	117
Hemlock, Mi., U.S.	E6	99
Hemlock Reservoir, res., Ct., U.S.	E2	84
Hemmingford, Que., Can.	D4	74
Hemphill, Tx., U.S.	D6	120
Hemphill, co., Tx., U.S.	B2	120
Hempstead, N.Y., U.S.	n15	109
Hempstead, Tx., U.S.	D4	120
Hempstead, co., Ar., U.S.	D2	81
Hemse, Swe.	H12	6
Henagar, Al., U.S.	A4	78
Henan, prov., China	E9	26
Henderson, Ky., U.S.	C2	94
Henderson, La., U.S.	D4	95
Henderson, Mn., U.S.	F5	100
Henderson, Ne., U.S.	D8	104
Henderson, Nv., U.S.	G7	105
Henderson, N.C., U.S.	A4	110
Henderson, Tn., U.S.	B3	119
Henderson, Tx., U.S.	C5	120
Henderson, co., Il., U.S.	C3	90
Henderson, co., Ky., U.S.	C2	94
Henderson, co., N.C., U.S.	f10	110
Henderson, co., Tn., U.S.	B3	119
Henderson, co., Tx., U.S.	C5	120
Henderson's Point, Ms., U.S.	g7	101
Hendersonville, N.C., U.S.	f10	110
Hendersonville, Tn., U.S.	A5	119
Hendricks, Mn., U.S.	F2	100
Hendricks, co., In., U.S.	E4	91
Hendry, co., Fl., U.S.	F5	86
Hengelo, Neth.	C6	8
Hengshan, China	H1	28
Hengyang, China	F9	26
Henlawson, W.V., U.S.	n12	125
Henlopen, Cape, c., De., U.S.	E5	85
Hennef, Ger.	E7	8
Hennepin, co., Mn., U.S.	E5	100
Hennessey, Ok., U.S.	A4	113
Henniker, N.H., U.S.	D3	106
Henning, Mn., U.S.	D3	100
Henning, Tn., U.S.	B2	119
Henrico, co., Va., U.S.	C5	123
Henrietta, N.C., U.S.	B1	110
Henrietta, Tx., U.S.	C3	120
Henrietta Maria, Cape, c., Ont., Can.	n19	73
Henry, Il., U.S.	B4	90
Henry, co., Al., U.S.	D4	78
Henry, co., Ga., U.S.	C2	87
Henry, co., Il., U.S.	B3	90
Henry, co., In., U.S.	E7	91
Henry, co., Ia., U.S.	C6	92
Henry, co., Ky., U.S.	B4	94
Henry, co., Mo., U.S.	C4	102
Henry, co., Oh., U.S.	A1	112
Henry, co., Tn., U.S.	A3	119
Henry, co., Va., U.S.	D3	123
Henry, Mount, mtn., Mt., U.S.	B1	103
Henryetta, Ok., U.S.	B6	113
Henry Kater, Cape, c., N.W. Ter., Can.	C19	66
Henrys Fork, stm., U.S.	E2	127
Henryville, Que., Can.	D4	74
Henryville, In., U.S.	G6	91
Hensall, Ont., Can.	D3	73
Henzada, Mya.	F3	34
Hephzibah, Ga., U.S.	C4	87
Heppner, Or., U.S.	B7	114
Hepu (Lianzhou), China	D10	34
Herāt, Afg.	C1	36
Herbes, Isle aux, i., Al., U.S.	E1	78
Herbignac, Fr.	E4	10
Herculaneum, Mo., U.S.	C7	102
Hereford, Eng., U.K.	I10	7
Hereford, Md., U.S.	A4	97
Hereford, Tx., U.S.	B1	120
Hereford Inlet, b., N.J., U.S.	E3	107
Herford, Ger.	C8	8
Herington, Ks., U.S.	D7	93
Herkimer, N.Y., U.S.	B6	109
Herkimer, co., N.Y., U.S.	B5	109
Hermann, Mo., U.S.	C6	102
Hermano Peak, mtn., Co., U.S.	D2	83
Hermantown, Mn., U.S.	D6	100
Hermanus, S. Afr.	H3	44
Herminie, Pa., U.S.	F2	115
Hermiston, Or., U.S.	B7	114
Hermitage, Newf., Can.	E4	72
Hermitage, Ar., U.S.	D3	81
Hermitage Bay, b., Newf., Can.	E3	72
Hermosillo, Mex.	C4	62
Hernando, Fl., U.S.	D4	86
Hernando, Ms., U.S.	A4	101
Hernando, co., Fl., U.S.	D4	86
Herndon, Va., U.S.	B5	123
Herning, Den.	H7	6
Heron Lake, Mn., U.S.	G3	100
Herrera del Duque, Spain	F6	12
Herrera de Pisuerga, Spain	C7	12
Herrin, Il., U.S.	F4	90
Herring Bay, b., Md., U.S.	C4	97
Herring Cove, N.S., Can.	E6	71
Herrington Lake, res., Ky., U.S.	C5	94
Herscher, Il., U.S.	B5	90
Hershey, Pa., U.S.	F8	115
Hertford, N.C., U.S.	A6	110
Hertford, co., N.C., U.S.	A5	110
Hervás, Spain	E6	12
Hesdin, Fr.	B9	10
Hesperia, Ca., U.S.	E5	82
Hesperia, Mi., U.S.	E4	99
Hesperus Mountain, mtn., Co., U.S.	D2	83
Hesston, Ks., U.S.	D6	93
Hetian, China	B8	38
Hettinger, N.D., U.S.	D3	111
Hettinger, co., N.D., U.S.	C3	111
Heyburn, Id., U.S.	G5	89
Heyworth, Il., U.S.	C5	90
Hialeah, Fl., U.S.	G6	86
Hiawatha, Ia., U.S.	B6	92
Hiawatha, Ks., U.S.	C8	93
Hibbing, Mn., U.S.	C6	100
Hickam Air Force Base, mil., Hi., U.S.	g10	88
Hickman, Ky., U.S.	f8	94
Hickman, Ne., U.S.	D9	104
Hickman, co., Ky., U.S.	f8	94
Hickman, co., Tn., U.S.	B4	119
Hickory, N.C., U.S.	B1	110
Hickory, co., Mo., U.S.	D4	102
Hicksville, N.Y., U.S.	E7	109
Hicksville, Oh., U.S.	A1	112
Hico, Tx., U.S.	D3	120
Hico, W.V., U.S.	C3	125
Hidaka-sammyaku, mts., Japan	q20	30a
Hidalgo, Mex.	E10	62
Hidalgo, Tx., U.S.	F3	120
Hidalgo, co., N.M., U.S.	F1	108
Hidalgo, co., Tx., U.S.	F3	120
Hidalgo del Parral, Mex.	D7	62
Hiddenite, N.C., U.S.	B1	110
Hieroglyphic Mountains, mts., Az., U.S.	k8	80
Hierro, i., Spain	C2	42
Higashiōsaka, Japan	H8	30
Higbee, Mo., U.S.	B5	102
Higganum, Ct., U.S.	D5	84
Higgins Lake, l., Mi., U.S.	D6	99
Higgins Millpond, res., Md., U.S.	C6	97
Higginsville, Mo., U.S.	B4	102
High Bridge, N.J., U.S.	B3	107
High Falls Reservoir, res., Wi., U.S.	C5	126
High Island, i., Mi., U.S.	C5	99
Highland, Il., U.S.	E4	90
Highland, In., U.S.	A3	91
Highland, Ks., U.S.	C8	93
Highland, Mi., U.S.	o14	99
Highland, N.Y., U.S.	D7	109
Highland, Wi., U.S.	E3	126
Highland, co., Oh., U.S.	C2	112
Highland, co., Va., U.S.	B3	123
Highland Lake, l., Me., U.S.	g7	96
Highland Lakes, N.J., U.S.	A4	107
Highland Park, Il., U.S.	A6	90
Highland Park, Mi., U.S.	p15	99
Highland Park, Tx., U.S.	n10	120
Highland Peak, mtn., Ca., U.S.	C4	82
Highland Point, c., Fl., U.S.	G5	86
Highlands, N.J., U.S.	C5	107
Highlands, N.C., U.S.	f9	110
Highlands, Tx., U.S.	r14	120
Highlands, co., Fl., U.S.	E5	86
Highland Springs, Va., U.S.	C5	123
High Level, Alta., Can.	F7	68
Highmore, S.D., U.S.	C6	118
High Point, N.C., U.S.	B2	110
High Prairie, Alta., Can.	B2	68
High Ridge, Mo., U.S.	g12	102
High River, Alta., Can.	D4	68
Highrock Lake, l., Man., Can.	B1	70
High Rock Lake, res., N.C., U.S.	B2	110
High Spire, Pa., U.S.	F8	115
High Springs, Fl., U.S.	C4	86
Hightstown, N.J., U.S.	C3	107
Highwood, Il., U.S.	A6	90
Highwood Baldy, mtn., Mt., U.S.	C6	103
Highwood Mountains, mts., Mt., U.S.	C6	103
Higuerote, Ven.	B9	58
Higüey, Dom. Rep.	E13	64
Híjar, Spain	D11	12
Hikari, Japan	I4	30
Hikone, Japan	G9	30
Hiko Range, mts., Nv., U.S.	F6	105
Hilbert, Wi., U.S.	D5	126
Hildale, Ut., U.S.	F3	121
Hilden, N.S., Can.	D6	71
Hildesheim, Ger.	C9	8
Hill, co., Mt., U.S.	B6	103
Hill, co., Tx., U.S.	D4	120
Hill City, Ks., U.S.	C4	93
Hill City, S.D., U.S.	D2	118
Hillcrest, Il., U.S.	B4	90
Hillcrest Heights, Md., U.S.	C4	97
Hilliard, Fl., U.S.	B5	86
Hilliard, Oh., U.S.	k10	112
Hill Island Lake, l., N.W. Ter., Can.	D11	66
Hill Lake, l., Ar., U.S.	h10	81
Hills, Ia., U.S.	C6	92
Hills, Mn., U.S.	G2	100
Hillsboro, Il., U.S.	D4	90
Hillsboro, Ks., U.S.	D6	93
Hillsboro, Mo., U.S.	C7	102
Hillsboro, N.H., U.S.	D3	106
Hillsboro, N.D., U.S.	B8	111
Hillsboro, Oh., U.S.	C2	112
Hillsboro, Or., U.S.	B4	114
Hillsboro, Tx., U.S.	C4	120
Hillsboro, Wi., U.S.	E3	126
Hillsboro Canal, Fl., U.S.	F6	86
Hillsborough, N.B., Can.	D5	71
Hillsborough, N.C., U.S.	A3	110
Hillsborough, co., Fl., U.S.	E4	86
Hillsborough, co., N.H., U.S.	E3	106
Hillsborough Bay, b., P.E.I., Can.	C6	71
Hillsburgh, Ont., Can.	D4	73
Hills Creek Lake, res., Or., U.S.	D4	114
Hillsdale, Mi., U.S.	G6	99
Hillsdale, N.J., U.S.	g8	107
Hillsdale, co., Mi., U.S.	G6	99
Hillside, N.J., U.S.	k8	107
Hillsville, Pa., U.S.	D1	115
Hillsville, Va., U.S.	D2	123
Hilo, Hi., U.S.	D6	88
Hilo Bay, b., Hi., U.S.	D6	88
Hilton, N.Y., U.S.	B3	109
Hilton Head Island, S.C., U.S.	G6	117
Hilton Head Island, i., S.C., U.S.	G6	117
Hilversum, Neth.	C5	8
Himachal Pradesh, ter., India	E7	38
Himalayas, mts., Asia	F10	38
Himeji, Japan	H7	30
Himi, Japan	F9	30
Ḥimṣ (Homs), Syria	B5	40
Hinchinbrook Island, i., Austl.	C9	50
Hinchinbrook Island, i., Ak., U.S.	g18	79
Hinckley, Il., U.S.	B5	90
Hinckley, Mn., U.S.	D6	100
Hinckley, Ut., U.S.	D3	121
Hinckley Reservoir, res., N.Y., U.S.	B5	109
Hindaun, India	G7	38
Hindman, Ky., U.S.	C7	94
Hinds, co., Ms., U.S.	C3	101
Hindu Kush, mts., Asia	B4	38
Hindupur, India	F4	37
Hines, Or., U.S.	D7	114
Hinesville, Ga., U.S.	E5	87
Hinganghāt, India	B5	37
Hingham, Ma., U.S.	B6	98
Hingham Bay, b., Ma., U.S.	g12	98
Hingoli, India	C4	37
Hinojosa del Duque, Spain	G6	12
Hinsdale, Il., U.S.	k9	90
Hinsdale, N.H., U.S.	E2	106
Hinsdale, co., Co., U.S.	D3	83
Hinton, Alta., Can.	C2	68
Hinton, Ia., U.S.	B1	92
Hinton, Ok., U.S.	B3	113
Hinton, W.V., U.S.	D4	125
Hirado, Japan	I2	30
Hīrākud, res., India	J10	38
Hiram, Ga., U.S.	C2	87
Hiram, Oh., U.S.	A4	112
Hirara, Japan	G12	26
Hiratsuka, Japan	G12	30
Hirosaki, Japan	B13	30
Hiroshima, Japan	H5	30
Hirson, Fr.	C11	10
Hisār, India	F6	38
Hispaniola, i., N.A.	E12	64
Hita, Japan	I3	30
Hitachi, Japan	F13	30
Hitchcock, Tx., U.S.	r14	120
Hitchcock, co., Ne., U.S.	D4	104
Hitchcock Lake, Ct., U.S.	C4	84
Hitoyoshi, Japan	J3	30
Hitra, i., Nor.	E7	6
Hiwassee, stm., Tn., U.S.	D9	119
Hiwassee Lake, res., N.C., U.S.	f8	110
Hjørring, Den.	H7	6
Ho, Ghana	G6	42
Hoa Binh, Viet.	D8	34
Hoagland, In., U.S.	C8	91
Hoback, stm., Wy., U.S.	C2	127
Hobart, Austl.	H9	50
Hobart, In., U.S.	A3	91
Hobart, Ok., U.S.	B2	113
Hobbs, N.M., U.S.	E6	108
Hobe Sound, Fl., U.S.	E6	86
Hobo, Col.	F5	58
Hoboken, N.J., U.S.	k8	107
Höchstadt an der Aisch, Ger.	F10	8
Hockessin, De., U.S.	A3	85
Hocking, co., Oh., U.S.	C3	112
Hocking, stm., Oh., U.S.	C3	112
Hockley, co., Tx., U.S.	C1	120
Hodgeman, co., Ks., U.S.	D4	93
Hodgenville, Ky., U.S.	C4	94
Hodges Village Reservoir, res., Ma., U.S.	B4	98
Hódmezővásárhely, Hung.	I20	8
Hodna, Chott el, l., Alg.	J16	12
Hodonín, Czech.	G17	8
Hof, Ger.	E11	8
Hoffman Estates, Il., U.S.	h8	90
Hofgeismar, Ger.	D9	8
Hofheim in Unterfranken, Ger.	E10	8
Hofors, Swe.	F11	6
Hōfu, Japan	H4	30
Hogansville, Ga., U.S.	C2	87
Hogback Mountain, mtn., Mt., U.S.	F4	103
Hog Island, i., Fl., U.S.	C3	86
Hog Island, i., Mi., U.S.	C5	99
Hog Island, i., N.C., U.S.	B6	110
Hog Island, i., R.I., U.S.	D5	116
Hog Island, i., Va., U.S.	C7	123
Hoh, stm., Wa., U.S.	B1	124
Hohenau an der March, Aus.	G16	8
Hohenwald, Tn., U.S.	B4	119
Hohe Tauern, mts., Aus.	H12	8
Hoh Head, c., Wa., U.S.	B1	124
Hohhot, China	C9	26
Hohoe, Ghana	G5	42
Hōhoku, Japan	H3	30
Ho-Ho-Kus, N.J., U.S.	h8	107
Hoh Xil Shan, mts., China	C13	38
Hoi An, Viet.	G10	34
Hoisington, Ks., U.S.	D5	93
Hokah, Mn., U.S.	G7	100
Hoke, co., N.C., U.S.	B3	110
Hokes Bluff, Al., U.S.	B4	78
Hokitika, N.Z.	E3	52
Hokkaidō, i., Japan	p20	30a
Holbrook, Az., U.S.	C5	80
Holbrook, Ma., U.S.	B5	98
Holcomb, Ks., U.S.	E3	93
Holden, Ma., U.S.	B4	98
Holden, Mo., U.S.	C4	102
Holden, W.V., U.S.	D2	125
Holdenville, Ok., U.S.	B5	113
Holdrege, Ne., U.S.	D6	104
Hole in the Mountain Peak, mtn., Nv., U.S.	C6	105
Holgate, Oh., U.S.	A1	112
Holguín, Cuba	D9	64
Höljes, Swe.	F9	6
Hollabrunn, Aus.	G16	8
Holladay, Ut., U.S.	C4	121
Holland, In., U.S.	H3	91
Holland, Mi., U.S.	F4	99
Holland, Oh., U.S.	A2	112
Holland, Tx., U.S.	D4	120
Hollandale, Ms., U.S.	B3	101
Holland Island, i., Md., U.S.	D5	97
Holland see Netherlands, ctry., Eur.	E9	4
Holland Point, c., Md., U.S.	C4	97
Holland Straits, strt., Md., U.S.	D5	97
Holley, N.Y., U.S.	B2	109
Holliday, Tx., U.S.	C3	120
Hollidaysburg, Pa., U.S.	F5	115
Hollins, Va., U.S.	C3	123
Hollis, Ok., U.S.	C2	113
Hollister, Ca., U.S.	D3	82
Hollister, Mo., U.S.	E4	102
Holliston, Ma., U.S.	B5	98
Holloman Air Force Base, mil., N.M., U.S.	E3	108
Hollow Rock, Tn., U.S.	A3	119
Hollowtop Mountain, mtn., Mt., U.S.	E4	103
Holly, Co., U.S.	C8	83
Holly, Mi., U.S.	F7	99
Holly Grove, Ar., U.S.	C4	81
Holly Hill, Fl., U.S.	C5	86
Holly Hill, S.C., U.S.	E7	117
Holly Pond, Al., U.S.	A3	78
Holly Ridge, N.C., U.S.	C5	110
Holly Shelter Swamp, sw., N.C., U.S.	C5	110
Holly Springs, Ga., U.S.	B2	87
Holly Springs, Ms., U.S.	A4	101
Holly Springs, N.C., U.S.	B4	110
Hollywood, Al., U.S.	A4	78
Hollywood, Fl., U.S.	F6	86
Hollywood, Md., U.S.	D4	97
Hollywood, S.C., U.S.	k11	117
Hollywood Indian Reservation, Fl., U.S.	r3	86
Holman Island, N.W. Ter., Can.	B9	66
Holmen, Wi., U.S.	E2	126
Holmes, co., Fl., U.S.	u16	86
Holmes, co., Ms., U.S.	B3	101
Holmes, co., Oh., U.S.	B4	112
Holmes, Mount, mtn., Wy., U.S.	B2	127
Holmes Reefs, rf., Austl.	C9	50
Holstebro, Den.	H7	6
Holstein, Ia., U.S.	B2	92
Holsteinsborg, Grnld.	C22	66
Holston, stm., Tn., U.S.	C11	119
Holston, Middle Fork, stm., Va., U.S.	f10	123
Holston High Knob, mtn., Tn., U.S.	C11	119
Holsworthy, Eng., U.K.	K8	7
Holt, Al., U.S.	B2	78
Holt, Mi., U.S.	F6	99
Holt, co., Mo., U.S.	A2	102
Holt, co., Ne., U.S.	B7	104
Holt Lake, res., Al., U.S.	B2	78
Holton, Ks., U.S.	C8	93
Holtville, Ca., U.S.	F6	82
Holualoa, Hi., U.S.	D6	88
Holy Cross, Mountain of the, mtn., Co., U.S.	B4	83
Holyhead, Wales, U.K.	H8	7
Holyoke, Co., U.S.	A8	83
Holyoke, Ma., U.S.	B2	98
Holyoke Range, hills, Ma., U.S.	B2	98

Name — Map Ref — Page

Holzminden, Ger. D9 8
Hombori Tondo, mtn., Mali E5 42
Homburg, Ger. F7 8
Home Bay, b., N.W. Ter., Can. C19 66
Homecroft, In., U.S. m10 91
Homedale, Id., U.S. F2 89
Home Hill, Austl. C9 50
Homeland, Ga., U.S. F4 87
Home Place, In., U.S. E5 91
Homer, Ak., U.S. D9 79
Homer, Ga., U.S. B3 87
Homer, Il., U.S. C6 90
Homer, La., U.S. B2 95
Homer, Mi., U.S. F6 99
Homer, N.Y., U.S. C4 109
Homer City, Pa., U.S. E3 115
Homerville, Ga., U.S. E4 87
Homer Youngs Peak, mtn., Mt., U.S. E3 103
Homestead, Fl., U.S. G6 86
Homestead, Pa., U.S. k14 115
Homestead Air Force Base, mil., Fl., U.S. G6 86
Homestead National Monument of America, Ne., U.S. D9 104
Homewood, Al., U.S. g7 78
Homewood, Il., U.S. B6 90
Homewood, Oh., U.S. C1 112
Hominy, Ok., U.S. A5 113
Hominy Creek, stm., Ok., U.S. A5 113
Homme Dam, N.D., U.S. A8 111
Homochitto, stm., Ms., U.S. D2 101
Homosassa, Fl., U.S. D4 86
Homs see Ḩimṣ, Syria B5 40
Honaker, Va., U.S. e10 123
Honaunau, Hi., U.S. D6 88
Honda, Col. E5 58
Hondo, Japan J3 30
Hondo, Tx., U.S. E3 120
Hondo, stm., N.A. H15 62
Hondo, Rio, stm., N.M., U.S. D4 108
Honduras, ctry., N.A. G4 64
Honduras, Gulf of, b., N.A. F4 64
Honea Path, S.C., U.S. C3 117
Hønefoss, Nor. F8 6
Honeoye Falls, N.Y., U.S. C3 109
Honesdale, Pa., U.S. C11 115
Honey Brook, Pa., U.S. F10 115
Honey Grove, Tx., U.S. C5 120
Honey Lake, l., Ca., U.S. B3 82
Honeypot Glen, Ct., U.S. C4 84
Honeyville, Ut., U.S. B3 121
Hon Gai, Viet. D9 34
Honga River, b., Md., U.S. D5 97
Hongdong, China D9 26
Honghu, China F2 28
Hong Kong, dep., Asia M3 28
Hongliuyuan, China C6 26
Honguedo, Détroit d', strt., Que., Can. G20 66
Hongze Hu, l., China B7 28
Honiara, Sol.Is. A11 50
Honjō, Japan F12 30
Honningsvåg, Nor. A15 6
Honokaa, Hi., U.S. C6 88
Honolulu, Hi., U.S. B4 88
Honolulu, co., Hi., U.S. B3 88
Honolulu International Airport, Hi., U.S. g10 88
Honomu, Hi., U.S. D6 88
Honouliuli, Hi., U.S. g9 88
Honshū, i., Japan F10 30
Honuapo Bay, b., Hi., U.S. D6 88
Hood, co., Tx., U.S. C4 120
Hood, Mount, mtn., Or., U.S. B5 114
Hood Canal, b., Wa., U.S. B2 124
Hoodoo Peak, mtn., Wa., U.S. A5 124
Hood River, Or., U.S. B5 114
Hood River, co., Or., U.S. B5 114
Hoodsport, Wa., U.S. B2 124
Hoogeveen, Neth. C6 8
Hooker, Ok., U.S. e9 113
Hooker, co., Ne., U.S. C4 104
Hook Head, c., Ire. I6 7
Hooksett, N.H., U.S. D4 106
Hoonah, Ak., U.S. D12 79
Hoopa Valley Indian Reservation, Ca., U.S. B2 82
Hooper, Ne., U.S. C9 104
Hooper Bay, Ak., U.S. C6 79
Hooper Islands, is., Md., U.S. D5 97
Hooper Strait, strt., Md., U.S. D5 97
Hoopes Reservoir, res., De., U.S. A3 85
Hoopeston, Il., U.S. C6 90
Hoorn, Neth. C5 8
Hoosac Range, mts., U.S. A1 98
Hoosic, stm., U.S. C7 109
Hoosick Falls, N.Y., U.S. C7 109
Hoover Dam, U.S. G7 105
Hoover Reservoir, res., Oh., U.S. B3 112
Hooverson Heights, W.V., U.S. f8 125
Hopatcong, N.J., U.S. B3 107
Hopatcong, Lake, l., N.J., U.S. A3 107
Hope, B.C., Can. E7 69
Hope, Ar., U.S. D2 81
Hope, In., U.S. F6 91
Hope, R.I., U.S. D3 116
Hope, Ben, mtn., Scot., U.K. C8 7
Hope, Point, c., Ak., U.S. B6 79
Hopedale, Il., U.S. C4 90
Hopedale, Ma., U.S. B4 98
Hope Island, i., R.I., U.S. E5 116
Hope Mills, N.C., U.S. C4 110
Hopes Advance, Cap, c., Que., Can. f13 74
Hopetown, S. Afr. G4 44
Hope Valley, R.I., U.S. E2 116
Hopewell, Va., U.S. C5 123
Hopewell Junction, N.Y., U.S. D7 109
Hopi Indian Reservation, Az., U.S. A5 80
Hopkins, Mn., U.S. n12 100
Hopkins, S.C., U.S. D6 117
Hopkins, co., Ky., U.S. C2 94
Hopkins, co., Tx., U.S. C5 120
Hopkinsville, Ky., U.S. D2 94
Hopkinton, Ia., U.S. B6 92
Hopkinton, Ma., U.S. B4 98
Hopkinton, R.I., U.S. F1 116
Hopkinton Lake, res., N.H., U.S. D3 106
Hopwood, Pa., U.S. G2 115
Hoquiam, Wa., U.S. C2 124
Horace, N.D., U.S. C9 111
Horace Mountain, mtn., Ak., U.S. B10 79
Horatio, Ar., U.S. D1 81
Horgen, Switz. E15 10
Horicon, Wi., U.S. E5 126
Horine, Mo., U.S. C7 102
Horlivka, Ukr. H5 22
Hormuz, Strait of, strt., Asia C6 46
Horn, Aus. G15 8
Horn, Cape see Hornos, Cabo de, c., Chile H3 56
Hornell, N.Y., U.S. C3 109
Hornersville, Mo., U.S. E7 102
Horn Island, i., Ms., U.S. E5 101
Horn Island Pass, strt., Ms., U.S. g8 101
Horn Lake, Ms., U.S. A3 101
Hornos, Cabo de (Cape Horn), c., Chile H3 56
Horn Plateau, plat., N.W. Ter., Can. D9 66
Horqin Youyi Qianqi, China B11 26
Horry, co., S.C., U.S. D10 117
Horse, stm., Ct., U.S. C6 84
Horse Cave, Ky., U.S. C4 94
Horse Creek, stm., U.S. E8 127
Horse Creek Reservoir, res., Co., U.S. C7 83
Horsehead Lake, l., N.D., U.S. B6 111
Horseheads, N.Y., U.S. C4 109
Horse Heaven Hills, hills, Wa., U.S. C6 124
Horsens, Den. I7 6
Horse Peak, mtn., N.M., U.S. D1 108
Horseshoe Bend, Id., U.S. F2 89
Horseshoe Bend National Military Park, Al., U.S. C4 78
Horseshoe Cove, b., Fl., U.S. C3 86
Horseshoe Point, c., Fl., U.S. C3 86
Horseshoe Reservoir, res., Az., U.S. C4 80
Horsham, Austl. G8 50
Horten, Nor. G8 6
Horton, Ks., U.S. C8 93
Hortonia, Lake, l., Vt., U.S. D2 122
Hortonville, Wi., U.S. D5 126
Hoschton, Ga., U.S. B3 87
Hoshangābād, India I7 38
Hoshiārpur, India E6 38
Hospers, Ia., U.S. A2 92
Hospet, India E4 37
Hospitalet, Spain D14 12
Hosta Butte, mtn., N.M., U.S. B1 108
Hoste, Isla, i., Chile H3 56
Hotchkiss, Co., U.S. C3 83
Hot Creek Range, mts., Nv., U.S. E5 105
Hot Creek Valley, val., Nv., U.S. E5 105
Hoting, Swe. D11 6
Hot Spring, co., Ar., U.S. C2 81
Hot Springs, S.D., U.S. D2 118
Hot Springs, co., Wy., U.S. C4 127
Hot Springs National Park, Ar., U.S. C2 81
Hot Springs National Park, Ar., U.S. C2 81
Hot Springs Peak, mtn., Ca., U.S. B3 82
Hot Springs Peak, mtn., Nv., U.S. B4 105
Hottah Lake, l., N.W. Ter., Can. C9 66
Houghton, Mi., U.S. A2 99
Houghton, N.Y., U.S. C2 109
Houghton, co., Mi., U.S. B2 99
Houghton Lake, Mi., U.S. D6 99
Houghton Lake, l., Mi., U.S. D6 99
Houghton Lake Heights, Mi., U.S. D6 99
Houlton, Me., U.S. B5 96
Houma, China D9 26
Houma, La., U.S. E5 95
Housatonic, stm., U.S. D3 84
House Springs, Mo., U.S. g12 102
Houston, De., U.S. E3 85
Houston, Mn., U.S. G7 100
Houston, Ms., U.S. B4 101
Houston, Mo., U.S. D6 102
Houston, Pa., U.S. F1 115
Houston, Tx., U.S. E5 120
Houston, co., Al., U.S. D4 78
Houston, co., Ga., U.S. D3 87
Houston, co., Mn., U.S. G7 100
Houston, co., Tn., U.S. A4 119
Houston, co., Tx., U.S. D5 120
Houston, stm., La., U.S. D2 95
Houston, Lake, res., Tx., U.S. r14 120
Houston Intercontinental Airport, Tx., U.S. r14 120
Houtman Rocks, Austl. E2 50
Houtzdale, Pa., U.S. E5 115
Hovenweep National Monument, Ut., U.S. F6 121
Hovmantorp, Swe. H10 6
Howard, Ks., U.S. E7 93
Howard, S.D., U.S. C8 118
Howard, Wi., U.S. D5 126
Howard, co., Ar., U.S. C2 81
Howard, co., In., U.S. C5 91
Howard, co., Ia., U.S. A5 92
Howard, co., Md., U.S. B4 97
Howard, co., Mo., U.S. B5 102
Howard, co., Ne., U.S. C7 104
Howard, co., Tx., U.S. C2 120
Howard City, Mi., U.S. E5 99
Howard Hanson Reservoir, res., Wa., U.S. B4 124
Howard Lake, Mn., U.S. E4 100
Howard Prairie Lake, res., Or., U.S. E4 114
Howards Grove-Millersville, Wi., U.S. E6 126
Howell, Mi., U.S. F7 99
Howell, co., Mo., U.S. E6 102
Howells, Ne., U.S. C8 104
Howe Sound, strt., B.C., Can. E6 69
Howick, Que., Can. D4 74
Howland, Me., U.S. C4 96
Howrah, India I13 38
Hoxie, Ar., U.S. A5 81
Hoxie, Ks., U.S. C3 93
Höxter, Ger. D9 8
Hoy, i., Scot., U.K. C9 7
Høyanger, Nor. F6 6
Hoyerswerda, Ger. D14 8
Hoyos, Spain E5 12
Hoyt Lakes, Mn., U.S. C6 100
Hradec Králové, Czech. E15 8
Hsilo, Tai. L9 28
Hsinchu, Tai. K9 28
Hsüehchia, Tai. L9 28
Huacho, Peru F3 54
Huachuca City, Az., U.S. F5 80
Hua Hin, Thai. H5 34
Huahua, stm., Nic. G6 64
Huaian, China B8 28
Huainan, China C6 28
Huaiyang, China B3 28
Huaiyin, China B8 28
Huaiyuan, China C6 28
Hualalai, vol., Hi., U.S. D6 88
Hualapai Indian Reservation, Az., U.S. B2 80
Hualapai Mountains, mts., Az., U.S. C2 80
Hualapai Peak, mtn., Az., U.S. B2 80
Hualien, Tai. L10 28
Huallaga, stm., Peru E3 54
Huallanca, Peru E3 54
Huamachuco, Peru E3 54
Huambo, Ang. D3 44
Huancayo, Peru F3 54
Huang (Yellow), stm., China D10 26
Huangchuan, China C4 28
Huangling, China D8 26
Huangshi, China E4 28
Huangyan, China G10 28
Huánuco, Peru E3 54
Huaraz, Peru E3 54
Huascarán, Nevado, mtn., Peru E3 54
Huasco, Chile B2 56
Huatabampo, Mex. D5 62
Huauchinango, Mex. G10 62
Hubbard, Ia., U.S. B4 92
Hubbard, Oh., U.S. A5 112
Hubbard, Or., U.S. B4 114
Hubbard, Tx., U.S. D4 120
Hubbard, co., Mn., U.S. C4 100
Hubbard Creek Lake, res., Tx., U.S. C3 120
Hubbard Lake, l., Mi., U.S. D7 99
Hubbardton, stm., Vt., U.S. D2 122
Hubbell, Mi., U.S. A2 99
Hubei, prov., China E9 26
Hubli, India E3 37
Huckleberry Mountain, mtn., Or., U.S. D4 114
Huddersfield, Eng., U.K. H11 7
Huddinge, Swe. G11 6
Hudiksvall, Swe. F11 6
Hudson, Que., Can. D3 74
Hudson, Co., U.S. A6 83
Hudson, Fl., U.S. D4 86
Hudson, Il., U.S. C5 90
Hudson, Ia., U.S. B5 92
Hudson, Ma., U.S. B4 98
Hudson, Mi., U.S. G6 99
Hudson, N.H., U.S. E4 106
Hudson, N.Y., U.S. C7 109
Hudson, N.C., U.S. B1 110
Hudson, Oh., U.S. A4 112
Hudson, Wi., U.S. D1 126
Hudson, Wy., U.S. D4 127
Hudson, co., N.J., U.S. B4 107
Hudson, stm., U.S. E7 109
Hudson, Lake, res., Ok., U.S. A6 113
Hudson Bay, b., Can. D15 66
Hudson Falls, N.Y., U.S. B7 109
Hudson Hope, B.C., Can. A6 69
Hudson Lake, In., U.S. A4 91
Hudson Strait, strt., Can. D18 66
Hudsonville, Mi., U.S. F5 99
Hudspeth, co., Tx., U.S. o12 120
Hue, Viet. F9 34
Huehuetenango, Guat. G2 64
Huelma, Spain H8 12
Huelva, Spain H5 12
Huércal-Overa, Spain H10 12
Huerfano, co., Co., U.S. D5 83
Huerfano, stm., Co., U.S. D6 83
Huerfano Mountain, mtn., N.M., U.S. A2 108
Huesca, Spain C11 12
Hueytown, Al., U.S. g6 78
Huffakers, Nv., U.S. D2 105
Hugh Butler Lake, res., Ne., U.S. D5 104
Hughenden, Austl. D8 50
Hughes, Ar., U.S. C5 81
Hughes, co., Ok., U.S. B5 113
Hughes, co., S.D., U.S. C5 118
Hughes, North Fork, stm., W.V., U.S. B3 125
Hughes, South Fork, stm., W.V., U.S. B3 125
Hughesville, Md., U.S. C4 97
Hughesville, Pa., U.S. D8 115
Hugo, Co., U.S. B7 83
Hugo, Mn., U.S. m13 100
Hugo, Ok., U.S. C6 113
Hugo Lake, res., Ok., U.S. C6 113
Hugoton, Ks., U.S. E2 93
Huidong, China A7 34
Huila, Nevado del, mtn., Col. F4 58
Huili, China A7 34
Huinan, China C12 26
Huittinen (Lauttakylä), Fin. F14 6
Huitzuco [de los Figueroa], Mex. H10 62
Huixtla, Mex. J13 62
Huiyang (Huizhou), China L3 28
Hulah Lake, res., Ok., U.S. A5 113
Hulan, China B12 26
Hulett, Wy., U.S. B8 127
Hull, Que., Can. D2 74
Hull, Ia., U.S. A1 92
Hull, Ma., U.S. B6 98
Hultsfred, Swe. H10 6
Hulun Nur, l., China B10 26
Humaitá, Braz. E6 54
Humansville, Mo., U.S. D4 102
Humber, stm., Eng., U.K. H12 7
Humble, Tx., U.S. E5 120
Humboldt, Az., U.S. C3 80
Humboldt, Ia., U.S. B3 92
Humboldt, Ks., U.S. E8 93
Humboldt, Ne., U.S. D10 104
Humboldt, Tn., U.S. B3 119
Humboldt, co., Ca., U.S. B2 82
Humboldt, co., Ia., U.S. B3 92
Humboldt, co., Nv., U.S. B3 105
Humboldt, stm., Nv., U.S. C3 105
Humboldt Range, mts., Nv., U.S. C3 105
Hummels Wharf, Pa., U.S. E8 115
Humphrey, Ar., U.S. C4 81
Humphrey, Ne., U.S. C8 104
Humphreys, co., Ms., U.S. B3 101
Humphreys, co., Tn., U.S. A4 119
Humphreys, Mount, mtn., Ca., U.S. D4 82
Humphreys Peak, mtn., Az., U.S. B4 80
Hunan, prov., China F9 26
Hundred Acre Pond, l., R.I., U.S. E3 116
Hunedoara, Rom. D6 16
Hünfeld, Ger. E9 8
Hungary, ctry., Eur. F11 4
Hungf'ou Hsü, i., Tai. M10 28
Hŭngnam, N. Kor. D12 26
Hungry Horse, Mt., U.S. B2 103
Hungry Horse Reservoir, res., Mt., U.S. B3 103
Hunsrück, mts., Ger. F6 8
Hunt, co., Tx., U.S. C4 120
Hunt, stm., R.I., U.S. D4 116
Hunterdon, co., N.J., U.S. B3 107
Hunter Island, i., Austl. H8 50
Hunter Island, i., B.C., Can. D3 69
Huntertown, In., U.S. B7 91
Huntingburg, In., U.S. H4 91
Huntingdon, Que., Can. D3 74
Huntingdon, Pa., U.S. F6 115
Huntingdon, Tn., U.S. A3 119
Huntingdon, co., Pa., U.S. F5 115
Hunting Island, i., S.C., U.S. G7 117
Huntington, Ar., U.S. B1 81
Huntington, In., U.S. C7 91
Huntington, N.Y., U.S. E7 109
Huntington, Tx., U.S. D5 120
Huntington, Ut., U.S. D5 121
Huntington, W.V., U.S. C2 125
Huntington, co., In., U.S. C6 91
Huntington Beach, Ca., U.S. F4 82
Huntington Lake, res., In., U.S. C7 91
Huntington Woods, Mi., U.S. p15 99
Huntingtown, Md., U.S. C4 97
Huntland, Tn., U.S. B5 119
Huntley, Il., U.S. A5 90
Hunt Mountain, mtn., Wy., U.S. B5 127
Huntsville, Ont., Can. B5 73
Huntsville, Al., U.S. A3 78
Huntsville, Ar., U.S. A2 81
Huntsville, Mo., U.S. B5 102
Huntsville, Tn., U.S. C9 119
Huntsville, Tx., U.S. D5 120
Huon Gulf, b., Pap. N. Gui. m16 50a
Hurao, China B13 26
Hurd, Cape, c., Ont., Can. B3 73
Hurley, Ms., U.S. E5 101
Hurley, N.M., U.S. E1 108
Hurley, N.Y., U.S. D6 109
Hurley, Wi., U.S. B3 126
Hurlock, Md., U.S. C6 97
Huron, Oh., U.S. A3 112
Huron, S.D., U.S. C7 118
Huron, co., Mi., U.S. E7 99
Huron, co., Oh., U.S. A3 112
Huron, stm., Mi., U.S. p14 99
Huron, Lake, l., N.A. C10 76
Huron Mountains, hills, Mi., U.S. B3 99
Hurricane, Ut., U.S. F2 121
Hurricane, W.V., U.S. C2 125
Hurst, Il., U.S. F4 90
Hurt, Va., U.S. C3 123
Hurtsboro, Al., U.S. C4 78
Húsavík, Ice. B4 4
Huskvarna, Swe. H10 6
Hustisford, Wi., U.S. E5 126
Husum, Ger. A9 8
Hutchins, Tx., U.S. n10 120
Hutchinson, Ks., U.S. D6 93
Hutchinson, Mn., U.S. F4 100
Hutchinson, co., S.D., U.S. D8 118
Hutchinson, co., Tx., U.S. B2 120
Hutchinson Island, i., Fl., U.S. E6 86
Hutchinson Island, i., S.C., U.S. k11 117
Hutch Mountain, mtn., Az., U.S. C4 80
Hüttental, Ger. E8 8
Huttig, Ar., U.S. D3 81
Huwei, Tai. L9 28
Huxley, Ia., U.S. C4 92
Huy, Bel. E5 8
Huzhou, China E9 28
Hvannadalshnúkur, mtn., Ice. C4 4
Hvar, Cro. F11 14
Hwange, Zimb. E5 44
Hwang Ho see Huang, stm., China D10 26
Hyannis, Ma., U.S. C7 98
Hyannis Port, Ma., U.S. C7 98
Hyattsville, Md., U.S. C4 97
Hybla Valley, Va., U.S. g12 123
Hyco, stm., Va., U.S. D3 123
Hyco Lake, res., N.C., U.S. A3 110
Hydaburg, Ak., U.S. D13 79
Hyde, Pa., U.S. D5 115
Hyde, co., N.C., U.S. B6 110
Hyde, co., S.D., U.S. C6 118
Hyde Park, Guy. D13 58
Hyde Park, N.Y., U.S. D7 109
Hyde Park, Ut., U.S. B4 121
Hyder, Ak., U.S. D13 79
Hyderābād, India D5 37
Hyderābād, Pak. H3 38
Hydeville, Vt., U.S. D2 122
Hydro, Ok., U.S. B3 113
Hyères, Fr. I13 10
Hyesan, N. Kor. C12 26
Hymera, In., U.S. F3 91
Hyndman, Pa., U.S. G4 115
Hyndman Peak, mtn., Id., U.S. F4 89
Hyrum, Ut., U.S. B4 121
Hythe, Alta., Can. B1 68
Hyūga, Japan J4 30
Hyūga-nada, Japan J4 30
Hyvinkää, Fin. F15 6

I

Iamonia, Lake, l., Fl., U.S. B2 86
Iaşi, Rom. B11 16
Iatt, Lake, res., La., U.S. C3 95
Ibadan, Nig. G6 42
Ibagué, Col. E5 58
Ibapah Peak, mtn., Ut., U.S. D2 121
Ibarra, Ec. G3 58
Ibb, Yemen F3 46
Iberia, Mo., U.S. C5 102
Iberia, co., La., U.S. E4 95
Iberville, Que., Can. D4 74
Iberville, co., La., U.S. D4 95
Iberville, Mont d' (Mount Caubvick), mtn., Can. g14 74
Ibiá, Braz. E5 57
Ibicaraí, Braz. C9 57
Ibiza, Spain G13 12
Ibiza, i., Spain G13 12
Ibo, Moz. D8 44
Ica, Peru F3 54
Içá (Putumayo), stm., S.A. I8 58
Içana, Braz. C5 54
Içana, stm., S.A. C5 54
Ice Harbor Dam, Wa., U.S. C7 124
Içel, Tur. H14 4
Iceland, ctry., Eur. B4 4
Ichalkaranji, India D3 37
Ich Bogd Uul, mts., Mong. C7 26
Ichinomiya, Japan G9 30
Ichinoseki, Japan D14 30
Icicle Creek, stm., Wa., U.S. B5 124
Icó, Braz. E11 54
Icy Cape, c., Ak., U.S. A7 79
Icy Strait, strt., Ak., U.S. k22 79
Ida, Mi., U.S. G7 99
Ida, co., Ia., U.S. B2 92
Ida, Lake, l., Mn., U.S. D3 100
Idabel, Ok., U.S. D7 113
Ida Grove, Ia., U.S. B2 92
Idaho, co., Id., U.S. D3 89
Idaho, state, U.S. E3 89
Idaho Falls, Id., U.S. F6 89
Idaho Springs, Co., U.S. B5 83
Idalou, Tx., U.S. C2 120
Idamay, W.V., U.S. k10 125
Idanha-a-Nova, Port. F4 12
Idappādi, India G4 37
Idar-Oberstein, Ger. F7 8
Idaville, In., U.S. C4 91
Ider, Al., U.S. A4 78
Idfū, Egypt D12 42
Idlib, Syria B5 40
Ídolo, Isla del, i., Mex. G11 62
Ieper, Bel. E2 8
Ierápetra, Grc. N9 16
Iesi, Italy F8 14
Ife, Nig. G6 42
Iferouâne, Niger E7 42
Iforas, Adrar des, mts., Afr. D6 42
Iglesias, Italy J3 14
Igloolik, N.W. Ter., Can. C16 66
Ignacio, Co., U.S. D3 83
Iguaçu, Saltos do (Iguassu Falls), wtfl, S.A. B6 56
Iguala, Mex. H10 62
Igualada, Spain D13 12
Iguape, Braz. A7 56
Iguatu, Braz. E11 54
Iguéla, Gabon B1 44
Iguidi, Erg, dunes, Afr. C4 42
Ihosy, Madag. F9 44
Iida, Japan G10 30
Iisalmi, Fin. E16 6
Iizuka, Japan I3 30
IJmuiden, Neth. C4 8
IJsselmeer (Zuiderzee), Neth. C5 8
Ika, Russia F15 24
Ikela, Zaire B4 44
Ikerre, Nig. G7 42
Ila, Nig. G6 42
Ilagan, Phil. B7 32
Ilan, Tai. K10 28
Ilbenge, Russia E18 24
Île-à-la-Crosse, Lac, l., Sask., Can. B2 75
Ilebo, Zaire B4 44
Île-de-France, hist. reg., Fr. C9 10
Île-Perrot, Que., Can. q19 74
Ilhéus, Braz. C9 57
Ili, stm., Asia I13 22
Iliamna Lake, l., Ak., U.S. D8 79
Iliamna Volcano, vol., Ak., U.S. C9 79
Ilion, N.Y., U.S. B5 109
Ilio Point, c., Hi., U.S. B4 88
Ilirska Bistrica, Slo. D9 14
Il'jinskij, Russia H22 24
Ilkal, India E4 37
Illampu, Nevado, mtn., Bol. G5 54
Illapel, Chile C2 56
Illescas, Mex. F8 62
Illiers, Fr. D8 10
Illimani, Nevado, mtn., Bol. G5 54
Illinois, state, U.S. C4 90
Illinois, stm., U.S. A7 113
Illinois, stm., Il., U.S. B5 90
Illinois, stm., Or., U.S. E3 114
Illinois Peak, mtn., Id., U.S. B3 89
Illiopolis, Il., U.S. D4 90
Illizi, Alg. C7 42
Illmo, Mo., U.S. D8 102
Il'men', Ozero, l., Russia C14 18
Ilo, Peru G4 54
Iloilo, Phil. C7 32
Ilomantsi, Fin. E18 6
Ilorin, Nig. G6 42
Il'pyrskij, Russia F26 24
Ilwaco, Wa., U.S. C1 124
Imabari, Japan H6 30
Iman, Russia H20 24

Name	Map Ref	Page
Imari, Japan	I2	30
Imatra, Fin.	F17	6
Imboden, Ar., U.S.	A4	81
Imlay, Nv., U.S.	C3	105
Imlay City, Mi., U.S.	E7	99
Immenstadt, Ger.	H10	8
Immokalee, Fl., U.S.	F5	86
Imnaha, stm., Or., U.S.	B10	114
Imola, Italy	E6	14
Imperatriz, Braz.	E9	54
Imperia, Italy	F3	14
Imperial, Ca., U.S.	F6	82
Imperial, Mo., U.S.	C7	102
Imperial, Ne., U.S.	D4	104
Imperial, Pa., U.S.	k13	115
Imperial, co., Ca., U.S.	F6	82
Imperial Beach, Ca., U.S.	o15	82
Imperial Dam, U.S.	E1	80
Imperial Reservoir, res., U.S.	E1	80
Imperial Valley, val., Ca., U.S.	F6	82
Impfondo, Congo	A3	44
Imphāl, India	H15	38
Imst, Aus.	H10	8
Imuris, Mex.	B4	62
Ina, Japan	G10	30
Inari, Fin.	B16	6
Inca, Spain	F14	12
İncekum Burnu, c., Tur.	A3	40
Inch'ŏn, S. Kor.	D12	26
Incline Village, Nv., U.S.	D2	105
Independence, Ia., U.S.	B6	92
Independence, Ks., U.S.	E8	93
Independence, Ky., U.S.	B5	94
Independence, La., U.S.	D5	95
Independence, Mo., U.S.	B3	102
Independence, Or., U.S.	C3	114
Independence, Va., U.S.	D1	123
Independence, Wi., U.S.	D2	126
Independence, co., Ar., U.S.	B4	81
Independence, stm., N.Y., U.S.	B5	109
Independence Mountains, mts., Nv., U.S.	C5	105
Independence National Historical Park, Pa., U.S.	p21	115
Independence Rock, mtn., Wy., U.S.	D5	127
India, ctry., Asia	E4	36
Indian, stm., Ont., Can.	B7	73
Indian, stm., De., U.S.	F4	85
Indian, stm., Mi., U.S.	B4	99
Indian, stm., N.Y., U.S.	A5	109
Indiana, Pa., U.S.	E3	115
Indiana, co., Pa., U.S.	E3	115
Indiana, state, U.S.	E5	91
Indiana Dunes National Lakeshore, In., U.S.	A3	91
Indianapolis, In., U.S.	E5	91
Indian Bay, b., Fl., U.S.	D4	86
Indian Cedar Swamp, sw., R.I., U.S.	F2	116
Indian Creek, stm., Oh., U.S.	C1	112
Indian Creek, stm., S.D., U.S.	B2	118
Indian Creek, stm., Tn., U.S.	B3	119
Indian Creek, stm., W.V., U.S.	k9	125
Indian Creek, stm., W.V., U.S.	D4	125
Indian Head, Md., U.S.	C3	97
Indian Island, i., N.C., U.S.	B6	110
Indian Lake, l., Mi., U.S.	C4	99
Indian Lake, l., N.Y., U.S.	B6	109
Indian Lake, l., Oh., U.S.	B2	112
Indian Lake, l., R.I., U.S.	F4	116
Indian Neck, Ct., U.S.	D4	84
Indian Ocean	G17	2
Indianola, Ia., U.S.	C4	92
Indianola, Ms., U.S.	B3	101
Indianola, Ne., U.S.	D5	104
Indian Peak, mtn., Ut., U.S.	E2	121
Indian Peak, mtn., Wy., U.S.	B3	127
Indian Prairie Canal, Fl., U.S.	E5	86
Indian River, co., Fl., U.S.	E6	86
Indian River, b., Fl., U.S.	D6	86
Indian River Bay, b., De., U.S.	F5	85
Indian Rock, mtn., Wa., U.S.	D5	124
Indian Rocks Beach, Fl., U.S.	p10	86
Indian Springs, Nv., U.S.	G6	105
Indian Stream, stm., N.H., U.S.	f7	106
Indiantown, Fl., U.S.	E6	86
Indian Trail, N.C., U.S.	B2	110
Indigirka, stm., Russia	C23	24
Indio, Ca., U.S.	F5	82
Indispensable Reefs, rf., Sol.Is.	B12	50
Indonesia, ctry., Asia	F6	32
Indore, India	I6	38
Indoukâl-n-Taghès, mtn., Niger	E7	42
Indramayu, Indon.	m14	33a
Indrāvati, stm., India	C6	37
Indus, stm., Asia	H2	38
İnegöl, Tur.	I13	16
Infiernillo, Presa del, res., Mex.	H9	62
I-n-Gall, Niger	E7	42
Ingalls, In., U.S.	E6	91
Ingalls Park, Il., U.S.	B5	90
Ingersoll, Ont., Can.	D4	73
Ingham, Austl.	C9	50
Ingham, co., Mi., U.S.	F6	99
Ingleside, Tx., U.S.	F4	120
Inglewood, Ca., U.S.	n12	82
Ingolstadt, Ger.	G11	8
Ingraham, Lake, l., Fl., U.S.	G5	86
Ingram, Pa., U.S.	k13	115
In Guezzam, Alg.	E7	42
Inhambane, Moz.	F7	44
Inhambupe, Braz.	F11	54
Inhaminga, Moz.	E6	44
Inharrime, Moz.	F7	44
Inírida, stm., Col.	F8	58
Inkerman, N.B., Can.	B5	71
Inkom, Id., U.S.	G6	89
Inkster, Mi., U.S.	p15	99
Inland Sea see Seto-naikai, Japan	H6	30
Inle Lake, l., Mya.	D4	34
Inman, Ks., U.S.	D6	93
Inman, S.C., U.S.	A3	117
Inn (En), stm., Eur.	G13	8
Innamincka, Austl.	E8	50
Inner Hebrides, is., Scot., U.K.	E6	7
Innisfail, Alta., Can.	C4	68
Innsbruck, Aus.	H11	8
Inola, Ok., U.S.	A6	113
Inongo, Zaire	B3	44
Inowrocław, Pol.	C18	8
In Salah, Alg.	C6	42
Inscription House Ruin, hist., Az., U.S.	A5	80
Insein, Mya.	F4	34
Institute, W.V., U.S.	m12	125
Interlachen, Fl., U.S.	C5	86
Interlaken, Switz.	F14	10
International Falls, Mn., U.S.	B5	100
Inthanon, Doi, mtn., Thai.	E5	34
Intiyaco, Arg.	B4	56
Intracoastal Waterway, U.S.	E4	95
Inukjuak, Que., Can.	g11	74
Inveraray, Scot., U.K.	E7	7
Invercargill, N.Z.	G2	52
Inverell, Austl.	E10	50
Inver Grove Heights, Mn., U.S.	n12	100
Invermere, B.C., Can.	D9	69
Inverness, Scot., U.K.	D8	7
Inverness, Ca., U.S.	C2	82
Inverness, Fl., U.S.	D4	86
Inverness, Ms., U.S.	B3	101
Inverurie, Scot., U.K.	D10	7
Investigator Group, is., Austl.	F6	50
Investigator Strait, strt., Austl.	G7	50
Invisible Mountain, mtn., Id., U.S.	F5	89
Inwood, Ia., U.S.	A1	92
Inwood, N.Y., U.S.	k13	109
Inwood, W.V., U.S.	B6	125
Inyangani, mtn., Zimb.	E6	44
Inyan Kara Creek, stm., Wy., U.S.	B8	127
Inyan Kara Mountain, mtn., Wy., U.S.	B8	127
Inyo, co., Ca., U.S.	D5	82
Inyo, Mount, mtn., Ca., U.S.	D5	82
Inyo Mountains, mts., Ca., U.S.	D4	82
Ioánnina, Grc.	J4	16
Iola, Ks., U.S.	E8	93
Iola, Wi., U.S.	D4	126
Iona, Id., U.S.	F7	89
Ione, Ca., U.S.	C3	82
Ionia, Mi., U.S.	F5	99
Ionia, co., Mi., U.S.	F5	99
Ionian Islands see Iónioi Nísoi, is., Grc.	K4	16
Ionian Sea, Eur.	H11	4
Iónioi Nísoi, is., Grc.	K4	16
Iosco, co., Mi., U.S.	D7	99
Iota, La., U.S.	D3	95
Iowa, La., U.S.	D2	95
Iowa, co., Ia., U.S.	C5	92
Iowa, co., Wi., U.S.	E3	126
Iowa, state, U.S.	C4	92
Iowa, stm., Ia., U.S.	C6	92
Iowa, West Branch, stm., Ia., U.S.	B4	92
Iowa City, Ia., U.S.	C6	92
Iowa Falls, Ia., U.S.	B4	92
Iowa Indian Reservation, U.S.	C8	93
Iowa Lake, l., U.S.	A3	92
Iowa Park, Tx., U.S.	C3	120
Ipameri, Braz.	D4	57
Iphigenia Bay, b., Ak., U.S.	n22	79
Ipiales, Col.	G4	58
Ipiaú, Braz.	C9	57
Ipoh, Malay.	L6	34
Ipswich, Austl.	E10	50
Ipswich, Eng., U.K.	I14	7
Ipswich, Ma., U.S.	A6	98
Ipswich, S.D., U.S.	B6	118
Ipswich, stm., Ma., U.S.	A5	98
Ipu, Braz.	D10	54
Iqaluit, N.W. Ter., Can.	D19	66
Iquique, Chile	H4	54
Iquitos, Peru	D4	54
Iraan, Tx., U.S.	D2	120
Iráklion, Grc.	N9	16
Iran, ctry., Asia	B5	46
Iran Mountains, mts., Asia	E5	32
Īrānshahr, Iran	C7	46
Irapa, Ven.	B11	58
Irapuato, Mex.	G9	62
Iraq, ctry., Asia	B3	46
Irazú, Volcán, vol., C.R.	J6	64
Irbid, Jord.	C4	40
Irbīl, Iraq	A3	46
Iredell, co., N.C., U.S.	B2	110
Ireland, ctry., Eur.	E6	4
Iriga, Phil.	r20	32
Iringa, Tan.	C7	44
Irion, co., Tx., U.S.	D2	120
Iriri, stm., Braz.	D8	54
Irish, Mount, mtn., Nv., U.S.	F6	105
Irish Sea, Eur.	H8	7
Irkutsk, Russia	G14	24
Irmo, S.C., U.S.	C5	117
Iron, co., Mi., U.S.	B2	99
Iron, co., Mo., U.S.	D7	102
Iron, co., Ut., U.S.	F2	121
Iron, co., Wi., U.S.	B3	126
Irondale, Al., U.S.	f7	78
Irondequoit, N.Y., U.S.	B3	109
Iron Gate, val., Eur.	E6	16
Iron Gate Reservoir, res., Eur.	E5	16
Iron Gate Reservoir, res., Ca., U.S.	B2	82
Iron Mountain, Mi., U.S.	C2	99
Iron Mountain, mtn., Az., U.S.	D4	80
Iron Mountains, mts., U.S.	D1	123
Iron Ridge, Wi., U.S.	E5	126
Iron River, Mi., U.S.	B2	99
Iron River, Wi., U.S.	B2	126
Ironton, Mo., U.S.	D7	102
Ironton, Oh., U.S.	D3	112
Ironwood, Mi., U.S.	n11	99
Iroquois, Ont., Can.	C9	73
Iroquois, co., Il., U.S.	C6	90
Iroquois, stm., U.S.	C6	90
Iroquois, Lake, l., Vt., U.S.	B2	122
Iroquois Falls, Ont., Can.	o19	73
Irrawaddy see Ayeyarwady, stm., Mya.	G3	34
Irricana, Alta., Can.	D4	68
Irrigon, Or., U.S.	B7	114
Irtyš (Ertix), stm., Asia	F11	22
Irumu, Zaire	A5	44
Irún, Spain	B10	12
Irurzun, Spain	C10	12
Irú Tepuy, mtn., Ven.	E12	58
Irvine, Scot., U.K.	F8	7
Irvine, Ca., U.S.	n13	82
Irvine, Ky., U.S.	C6	94
Irving, Tx., U.S.	n10	120
Irvington, Al., U.S.	E1	78
Irvington, Il., U.S.	E4	90
Irvington, Ky., U.S.	C3	94
Irvington, N.J., U.S.	k8	107
Irvington, N.Y., U.S.	g13	109
Irwin, Pa., U.S.	F2	115
Irwin, co., Ga., U.S.	E3	87
Irwinton, Ga., U.S.	D3	87
Isabel, Mount, mtn., Wy., U.S.	D2	127
Isabella, co., Mi., U.S.	E6	99
Isabella, Cordillera, mts., Nic.	G5	64
Isabella Indian Reservation, Mi., U.S.	E6	99
Isabella Lake, l., Mn., U.S.	C7	100
Ísafjördur, Ice.	B3	4
Isahaya, Japan	J3	30
Isanti, Mn., U.S.	E5	100
Isanti, co., Mn., U.S.	E5	100
Isar, stm., Eur.	G11	8
Ischia, Italy	I8	14
Ise, Japan	H9	30
Isernia, Italy	H9	14
Isesaki, Japan	F12	30
Ise-wan, b., Japan	H9	30
Isherton, Guy.	F13	58
Ishikari-wan, b., Japan	p18	30a
Ishinomaki, Japan	D14	30
Ishpeming, Mi., U.S.	B3	99
Isinglass, stm., N.H., U.S.	D4	106
Isiolo, Kenya	A7	44
Isiro, Zaire	H11	42
İskele, N. Cyp.	B3	40
İskenderun, Tur.	H15	4
İskenderun Körfezi, b., Tur.	A4	40
Iskitim, Russia	G10	24
İslâhiye, Tur.	A5	40
Islāmābād, Pak.	D5	38
Islamorada, Fl., U.S.	H6	86
Isla Mujeres, Mex.	G16	62
Island, co., Wa., U.S.	A3	124
Island Beach, N.J., U.S.	D4	107
Island City, Or., U.S.	B8	114
Island Falls, Me., U.S.	B4	96
Island Lake, l., Man., Can.	C4	70
Island Park, R.I., U.S.	E6	116
Island Park Reservoir, res., Id., U.S.	E7	89
Island Pond, Vt., U.S.	B5	122
Island Pond, l., N.H., U.S.	E4	106
Islands, Bay of, b., Newf., Can.	D2	72
Isla Vista, Ca., U.S.	E4	82
Islay, i., Scot., U.K.	F6	7
Isle-aux-Morts, Newf., Can.	E2	72
Isle of Man, dep., Eur.	E7	4
Isle of Palms, S.C., U.S.	k12	117
Isle of Wight, co., Va., U.S.	D6	123
Isle of Wight Bay, b., Md., U.S.	D7	97
Isle Royale National Park, Mi., U.S.	h9	99
Islesboro Island, i., Me., U.S.	D4	96
Isleta, N.M., U.S.	C3	108
Isleta Indian Reservation, N.M., U.S.	C3	108
Islington, Ma., U.S.	h11	98
Isola, Ms., U.S.	B3	101
Isola della Scala, Italy	D5	14
Ispica, Italy	M9	14
Israel (Yisra'el), ctry., Asia	D4	40
Israel, stm., N.H., U.S.	B3	106
Issano, Guy.	E13	58
Issaquah, Wa., U.S.	B3	124
Issaquena, co., Ms., U.S.	C2	101
Issoire, Fr.	G10	10
Issoudun, Fr.	F8	10
Is-sur-Tille, Fr.	E12	10
Issyk-Kul', Kyrg.	I13	22
İstanbul, Tur.	G13	4
İstanbul Boğazı (Bosporus), strt., Tur.	H13	16
Isto, Mount, mtn., Ak., U.S.	B11	79
Istokpoga, Lake, l., Fl., U.S.	E5	86
Itabaiana, Braz.	F11	54
Itaberaí, Braz.	G9	54
Itabira, Braz.	E7	57
Itabuna, Braz.	C9	57
Itacoatiara, Braz.	D7	54
Itagüí, Col.	D5	58
Itaituba, Braz.	D7	54
Itajaí, Braz.	B7	56
Itajubá, Braz.	G6	57
Italy, Tx., U.S.	C4	120
Italy, ctry., Eur.	G10	4
Itaperuna, Braz.	F8	57
Itapetinga, Braz.	C8	57
Itapetininga, Braz.	G4	57
Itapeva, Braz.	G4	57
Itapicuru, stm., Braz.	D10	54
Itapira, Braz.	G5	57
Itaquari, Braz.	F8	57
Itararé, Braz.	H4	57
Itārsi, India	I7	38
Itasca, Il., U.S.	k8	90
Itasca, Tx., U.S.	C4	120
Itasca, co., Mn., U.S.	C5	100
Itasca, Lake, l., Mn., U.S.	C3	100
Itawamba, co., Ms., U.S.	A5	101
Ithaca, Mi., U.S.	E6	99
Ithaca, N.Y., U.S.	C4	109
Itō, Japan	H12	30
Itta Bena, Ms., U.S.	B3	101
Ittiri, Italy	I3	14
Ituberá, Braz.	B9	57
Ituiutaba, Braz.	E4	57
Itumbiara, Braz.	E4	57
Ituni, Guy.	E13	58
Ituri, stm., Zaire	A5	44
Iturup, Ostrov (Etorofu-tō), i., Russia	I23	24
Ituverava, Braz.	F5	57
Ituxi, stm., Braz.	E5	54
Itzehoe, Ger.	B9	8
Iuka, Ms., U.S.	A5	101
Iva, S.C., U.S.	C2	117
Ivalo, Fin.	B16	6
Ivanhoe, Mn., U.S.	F2	100
Ivanić Grad, Cro.	D11	14
Ivano-Frankivs'k, Ukr.	H2	22
Ivanovo, Russia	D23	18
Ivigtut, Grnld.	D23	66
Ivinheima, stm., Braz.	G2	57
Ivins, Ut., U.S.	F2	121
Ivory Coast, ctry., Afr.	G4	42
Ivoryton, Ct., U.S.	D6	84
Ivrea, Italy	D2	14
Iwaki (Taira), Japan	E13	30
Iwakuni, Japan	H5	30
Iwanai, Japan	q18	30a
Iwanuma, Japan	D13	30
Iwo, Nig.	G6	42
Ixtacihuatl, vol., Mex.	H10	62
Iyo-nada, Japan	I5	30
Izabal, Lago de, l., Guat.	G3	64
Izard, co., Ar., U.S.	A4	81
Izegem, Bel.	E3	8
Iževsk, Russia	F8	22
İzmir, Tur.	H13	4
İzmit, Tur.	G13	4
Iznalloz, Spain	H8	12
İznik Gölü, l., Tur.	I13	16
Izozog, Bañados de, sw., Bol.	G6	54
Izúcar de Matamoros, Mex.	H10	62
Izuhara, Japan	H2	30
Izumo, Japan	G5	30
Izu-shotō, is., Japan	H12	30
Izvestij CIK, Ostrova, is., Russia	B10	24

J

Name	Map Ref	Page
Jabalpur, India	I8	38
Jabbūl, Sabkhat al-, l., Syria	A5	40
Jablah, Syria	B4	40
Jablonec nad Nisou, Czech.	E15	8
Jaboatão, Braz.	E11	54
Jabrīn, well, Sau. Ar.	D4	46
Jaca, Spain	C11	12
Jacarèzinho, Braz.	G4	57
Jáchal, Arg.	C3	56
Jacinto City, Tx., U.S.	r14	120
Jack, co., Tx., U.S.	C3	120
Jackfish Lake, l., Sask., Can.	D1	75
Jackman, Me., U.S.	C2	96
Jackman Station, Me., U.S.	C2	96
Jack Mountain, mtn., Mt., U.S.	D4	103
Jack Mountain, mtn., Wa., U.S.	A5	124
Jackpot, Nv., U.S.	B7	105
Jacksboro, Tn., U.S.	C9	119
Jacksboro, Tx., U.S.	C3	120
Jacks Mountain, mtn., Pa., U.S.	E6	115
Jackson, Al., U.S.	D2	78
Jackson, Ca., U.S.	C3	82
Jackson, Ga., U.S.	C3	87
Jackson, Ky., U.S.	C6	94
Jackson, La., U.S.	D4	95
Jackson, Mi., U.S.	F6	99
Jackson, Mn., U.S.	G4	100
Jackson, Ms., U.S.	C3	101
Jackson, Mo., U.S.	D8	102
Jackson, Oh., U.S.	C3	112
Jackson, S.C., U.S.	E4	117
Jackson, Tn., U.S.	B3	119
Jackson, Wi., U.S.	E5	126
Jackson, Wy., U.S.	C2	127
Jackson, co., Al., U.S.	A3	78
Jackson, co., Ar., U.S.	B4	81
Jackson, co., Co., U.S.	A4	83
Jackson, co., Fl., U.S.	B1	86
Jackson, co., Ga., U.S.	B3	87
Jackson, co., Il., U.S.	F4	90
Jackson, co., In., U.S.	G5	91
Jackson, co., Ia., U.S.	B7	92
Jackson, co., Ks., U.S.	C8	93
Jackson, co., Ky., U.S.	C5	94
Jackson, co., La., U.S.	B3	95
Jackson, co., Mi., U.S.	F6	99
Jackson, co., Mn., U.S.	G3	100
Jackson, co., Ms., U.S.	E5	101
Jackson, co., Mo., U.S.	B3	102
Jackson, co., N.C., U.S.	f9	110
Jackson, co., Oh., U.S.	C3	112
Jackson, co., Ok., U.S.	C2	113
Jackson, co., Or., U.S.	E4	114
Jackson, co., S.D., U.S.	D4	118
Jackson, co., Tn., U.S.	C8	119
Jackson, co., Tx., U.S.	E4	120
Jackson, co., W.V., U.S.	C3	125
Jackson, co., Wi., U.S.	D3	126
Jackson, stm., Va., U.S.	C3	123
Jackson, Lake, l., Fl., U.S.	E5	86
Jackson, Lake, l., Fl., U.S.	B2	86
Jackson, Mount, mtn., N.H., U.S.	B4	106
Jackson Center, Oh., U.S.	B1	112
Jackson Lake, res., Wy., U.S.	C2	127
Jackson Mountains, mts., Nv., U.S.	B3	105
Jackson's Arm, Newf., Can.	D3	72
Jacksons Gap, Al., U.S.	C4	78
Jacksonville, Al., U.S.	B4	78
Jacksonville, Ar., U.S.	C3	81
Jacksonville, Fl., U.S.	B5	86
Jacksonville, Il., U.S.	D3	90
Jacksonville, N.C., U.S.	C5	110
Jacksonville, Or., U.S.	E4	114
Jacksonville, Tx., U.S.	D5	120
Jacksonville Beach, Fl., U.S.	B5	86
Jacksonville Naval Air Station, mil., Fl., U.S.	B5	86
Jacks Peak, mtn., Ut., U.S.	E3	121
Jacmel, Haiti	E11	64
Jacobābād, Pak.	F3	38
Jacques-Cartier, stm., Que., Can.	B6	74
Jacques-Cartier, Détroit de, strt., Que., Can.	h8	72
Jacquet River, N.B., Can.	B4	71
Jadraque, Spain	E9	12
Jaén, Peru	E3	54
Jaén, Spain	H8	12
Jaffna, Sri L.	H6	37
Jaffrey, N.H., U.S.	E2	106
Jafr, Qā' al-, depr., Jord.	D5	40
Jagādhri, India	E7	38
Jagdalpur, India	C7	37
Jagersfontein, S. Afr.	G5	44
Jagodnoje, Russia	E23	24
Jagtiāl, India	C5	37
Jaguarão, Braz.	C6	56
Jahrom, Iran	C5	46
Jaidak, Afg.	E2	38
Jaipur, India	G6	38
Jajce, Bos.	E12	14
Jakarta, Indon.	m13	32
Jakobshavn, Grnld.	C22	66
Jakobstad (Pietarsaari), Fin.	E14	6
Jakutsk, Russia	E19	24
Jal, N.M., U.S.	E6	108
Jalālābād, Afg.	C4	38
Jalapa, Guat.	G3	64
Jalapa Enríquez, Mex.	H11	62
Jālgaon, India	B3	37
Jālna, India	C3	37
Jalostotitlán, Mex.	G8	62
Jalpaiguri, India	G13	38
Jaltepec, stm., Mex.	I12	62
Jamaica, ctry., N.A.	E9	64
Jamaica Bay, b., N.Y., U.S.	k13	109
Jamaica Channel, strt., N.A.	E10	64
Jamālpur, Bngl.	H13	38
Jamālpur, India	H12	38
Jamame, Som.	A8	44
Jambi, Indon.	F3	32
Jambol, Bul.	G10	16
James, stm., U.S.	C7	76
James, stm., Mo., U.S.	E4	102
James, stm., Va., U.S.	C5	123
James, Lake, l., In., U.S.	A7	91
James, Lake, res., N.C., U.S.	B1	110
James Bay, b., Can.	F16	66
James Branch, stm., De., U.S.	F3	85
Jamesburg, N.J., U.S.	C4	107
James City, N.C., U.S.	B5	110
James City, co., Va., U.S.	C6	123
James Island, S.C., U.S.	k12	117
James Island, i., Md., U.S.	C5	97
James Island, i., S.C., U.S.	F8	117
James River Bridge, Va., U.S.	k15	123
Jamestown, In., U.S.	E4	91
Jamestown, Ky., U.S.	D4	94
Jamestown, N.Y., U.S.	C1	109
Jamestown, N.C., U.S.	B3	110
Jamestown, N.D., U.S.	C7	111
Jamestown, Oh., U.S.	C2	112
Jamestown, R.I., U.S.	F5	116
Jamestown, Tn., U.S.	C9	119
James Town, Wy., U.S.	E3	127
Jamestown Dam, N.D., U.S.	C7	111
Jamestown Reservoir, res., N.D., U.S.	C7	111
Jamiltepec, Mex.	I11	62
Jamkhandi, India	D3	37
Jammu, India	D6	38
Jammu and Kashmir, dep., Asia	C6	38
Jāmnagar, India	I4	38
Jāmpur, Pak.	F4	38
Jämsä, Fin.	F15	6
Jamshedpur, India	I12	38
Jamsk, Russia	F24	24
Jamūi, India	H12	38
Jamuna, stm., Bngl.	H13	38
Jana, stm., Russia	C21	24
Janaucu, Ilha, i., Braz.	C8	54
Janesville, Ca., U.S.	B3	82
Janesville, Ia., U.S.	B5	92
Janesville, Mn., U.S.	F5	100
Janesville, Wi., U.S.	F4	126
Jangipur, India	H13	38
Janīn, Jord.	C4	40
Janskij, Russia	D20	24
Janskij Zaliv, b., Russia	C21	24
Januária, Braz.	C6	57
Jaora, India	I6	38
Japan, ctry., Asia	D14	26
Japan, Sea of, Asia	D13	26
Japurá (Caquetá), stm., S.A.	D5	54
Jaqué, Pan.	K8	64
Jarābulus, Syria	A6	40
Jaraiz de la Vera, Spain	E6	12
Jarash, Jord.	C4	40
Jarcevo, Russia	F15	18
Jardines de la Reina, is., Cuba	D8	64
Jari, stm., Braz.	D8	54
Jaridih, India	I12	38
Jaroslavl', Russia	D22	18
Jarosław, Pol.	E22	8
Jarrettsville, Md., U.S.	A5	97
Järvenpää, Fin.	F15	6
Järvsö, Swe.	F11	6
Jask, Iran	C6	46
Jasmine Estates, Fl., U.S.	D4	86
Jasnyj, Russia	G19	24
Jasonville, In., U.S.	F3	91
Jasper, Al., U.S.	B2	78
Jasper, Fl., U.S.	B4	86
Jasper, Ga., U.S.	B2	87
Jasper, In., U.S.	H4	91
Jasper, Mo., U.S.	D3	102
Jasper, Tn., U.S.	D8	119
Jasper, Tx., U.S.	D6	120
Jasper, co., Ga., U.S.	C3	87
Jasper, co., Il., U.S.	D5	90
Jasper, co., In., U.S.	B3	91
Jasper, co., Ia., U.S.	C4	92
Jasper, co., Ms., U.S.	C4	101
Jasper, co., Mo., U.S.	D3	102
Jasper, co., S.C., U.S.	G5	117
Jasper, co., Tx., U.S.	D5	120
Jasper National Park, Alta., Can.	C1	68
Jataí, Braz.	D3	57
Játiva, Spain	G11	12
Jatni, India	J11	38
Jaú, Braz.	G4	57
Jauaperi, stm., Braz.	C6	54
Jauja, Peru	F3	54
Jaunpur, India	H10	38
Java see Jawa, i., Indon.	G4	32
Javari (Yavarí), stm., S.A.	D4	54

Name	Map Ref	Page
Java Sea see Jawa, Laut, Indon.	G4	32
Jävre, Swe.	D13	6
Jawa, i., Indon.	G4	32
Jawa, Laut (Java Sea), Indon.	G4	32
Jaworzno, Pol.	E19	8
Jay, Ok., U.S.	A7	113
Jay, co., In., U.S.	D7	91
Jaya, Puncak, mtn., Indon.	F10	32
Jayapura, Indon.	F11	32
Jayb, Wādī al-, val., Asia	D4	40
J. B. Thomas, Lake, res., Tx., U.S.	C2	120
Jean, Nv., U.S.	H6	105
Jeanerette, La., U.S.	E4	95
Jean Lafitte National Historical Park, La., U.S.	k12	95
Jeannette, Pa., U.S.	F2	115
Jebba, Nig.	G6	42
Jeddore Lake, res., Newf., Can.	D3	72
Jeff Davis, co., Ga., U.S.	E4	87
Jeff Davis, co., Tx., U.S.	o12	120
Jefferson, Ga., U.S.	B3	87
Jefferson, Ia., U.S.	B3	92
Jefferson, La., U.S.	k11	95
Jefferson, N.C., U.S.	A1	110
Jefferson, Oh., U.S.	A5	112
Jefferson, Or., U.S.	C3	114
Jefferson, S.C., U.S.	B7	117
Jefferson, Tx., U.S.	C5	120
Jefferson, Wi., U.S.	E5	126
Jefferson, co., Al., U.S.	B3	78
Jefferson, co., Ar., U.S.	C3	81
Jefferson, co., Co., U.S.	B5	83
Jefferson, co., Fl., U.S.	B3	86
Jefferson, co., Ga., U.S.	C4	87
Jefferson, co., Id., U.S.	F6	89
Jefferson, co., Il., U.S.	E5	90
Jefferson, co., In., U.S.	G6	91
Jefferson, co., Ia., U.S.	C5	92
Jefferson, co., Ks., U.S.	C8	93
Jefferson, co., Ky., U.S.	B4	94
Jefferson, co., La., U.S.	E5	95
Jefferson, co., Ms., U.S.	D2	101
Jefferson, co., Mo., U.S.	C7	102
Jefferson, co., Mt., U.S.	D4	103
Jefferson, co., Ne., U.S.	D8	104
Jefferson, co., N.Y., U.S.	A5	109
Jefferson, co., Oh., U.S.	B5	112
Jefferson, co., Ok., U.S.	C4	113
Jefferson, co., Or., U.S.	C5	114
Jefferson, co., Pa., U.S.	D3	115
Jefferson, co., Tn., U.S.	C10	119
Jefferson, co., Tx., U.S.	E5	120
Jefferson, co., Wa., U.S.	B1	124
Jefferson, co., W.V., U.S.	B7	125
Jefferson, co., Wi., U.S.	E5	126
Jefferson, stm., Mt., U.S.	E5	103
Jefferson, Mount, mtn., Id., U.S.	E7	89
Jefferson, Mount, mtn., Nv., U.S.	E5	105
Jefferson, Mount, mtn., Or., U.S.	C5	114
Jefferson City, Mo., U.S.	C5	102
Jefferson City, Tn., U.S.	C10	119
Jefferson Davis, co., La., U.S.	D3	95
Jefferson Davis, co., Ms., U.S.	D4	101
Jefferson Farms, De., U.S.	i7	85
Jefferson Proving Ground, mil., In., U.S.	G7	91
Jeffersontown, Ky., U.S.	B4	94
Jeffersonville, Ga., U.S.	D3	87
Jeffersonville, In., U.S.	H6	91
Jeffersonville, Ky., U.S.	C6	94
Jeffersonville, Oh., U.S.	C2	112
Jeffrey, W.V., U.S.	D3	125
Jeffrey City, Wy., U.S.	D5	127
Jeffries Creek, stm., S.C., U.S.	C8	117
Jefremov, Russia	H21	18
Jegorjevsk, Russia	F22	18
Jehossee Island, i., S.C., U.S.	k11	117
Jejsk, Russia	H5	22
Jekaterinburg, Russia	F10	22
Jekyll Island, i., Ga., U.S.	E5	87
Jelec, Russia	I21	18
Jelenia Góra (Hirschberg), Pol.	E15	8
Jelgava, Lat.	E6	18
Jellico, Tn., U.S.	C9	119
Jelm Mountain, mtn., Wy., U.S.	E7	127
Jeloguj, stm., Russia	E11	24
Jember, Indon.	n16	32
Jemez, stm., N.M., U.S.	k7	108
Jemez Canyon Dam, N.M., U.S.	k7	108
Jemez Indian Reservation, N.M., U.S.	h7	108
Jemez Pueblo, N.M., U.S.	B3	108
Jemison, Al., U.S.	C3	78
Jena, Ger.	E11	8
Jena, La., U.S.	C3	95
Jenašimskij Polkan, Gora, mtn., Russia	F12	24
Jendouba (Souk el Arba), Tun.	M3	14
Jenisej, stm., Russia	D11	24
Jenisejsk, Russia	F12	24
Jenisejskij Zaliv, b., Russia	C10	24
Jenkins, Ky., U.S.	C7	94
Jenkins, co., Ga., U.S.	D5	87
Jenkintown, Pa., U.S.	o21	115
Jenks, Ok., U.S.	A6	113
Jennings, La., U.S.	D3	95
Jennings, Mo., U.S.	f13	102
Jennings, co., In., U.S.	G6	91
Jensen Beach, Fl., U.S.	E6	86
Jepara, Indon.	m15	33a
Jequié, Braz.	B8	57
Jequitinhonha, stm., Braz.	D9	57
Jerada, Mor.	B5	42
Jerauld, co., S.D., U.S.	C7	118
Jérémie, Haiti	E10	64
Jeremoabo, Braz.	F11	54
Jerevan, Arm.	I6	22
Jerez de García Salinas, Mex.	F8	62
Jerez de la Frontera, Spain	I5	12
Jerez de los Caballeros, Spain	G5	12
Jericho, Vt., U.S.	B3	122
Jericho see Arīḥā, Jord.	D4	40
Jerimoth Hill, hill, R.I., U.S.	C1	116
Jermyn, Pa., U.S.	C10	115
Jerofej Pavlovič, Russia	G18	24
Jerome, Id., U.S.	G4	89
Jerome, Pa., U.S.	F4	115
Jerome, co., Id., U.S.	G4	89
Jeropol, Russia	D27	24
Jersey, co., Il., U.S.	D3	90
Jersey, dep., Eur.	C4	10
Jersey City, N.J., U.S.	B4	107
Jersey Mountain, mtn., Id., U.S.	E3	89
Jersey Shore, Pa., U.S.	D7	115
Jerseyville, Il., U.S.	D3	90
Jerusalem see Yerushalayim, Isr.	D4	40
Jervis Inlet, b., B.C., Can.	D6	69
Jesenice, Slo.	C9	14
Jessamine, co., Ky., U.S.	C5	94
Jessore, Bngl.	I13	38
Jessup, Md., U.S.	B4	97
Jessup, Pa., U.S.	m18	115
Jesup, Ga., U.S.	E5	87
Jesup, Ia., U.S.	B5	92
Jesup, Lake, l., Fl., U.S.	D5	86
Jésus, Île, i., Que., Can.	p19	74
Jesús Carranza, Mex.	I12	62
Jetmore, Ks., U.S.	D4	93
Jeumont, Fr.	B11	10
Jever, Ger.	B7	8
Jewel Cave National Monument, S.D., U.S.	D2	118
Jewell, Ia., U.S.	B4	92
Jewell, co., Ks., U.S.	C5	93
Jewett City, Ct., U.S.	C8	84
Jeypore, India	C7	37
Jhang Maghiāna, Pak.	E5	38
Jhānsi, India	H8	38
Jharia, India	I12	38
Jhelum, Pak.	D5	38
Jhelum, stm., Asia	E5	38
Jiading, China	D10	28
Jiaganj, India	H13	38
Jiamusi, China	B13	26
Jian, China	H3	28
Jianchuan, China	A5	34
Jiangmen, China	M2	28
Jiangsu, prov., China	E10	26
Jiangxi, prov., China	F10	26
Jiangyin, China	D9	28
Jiangzi, China	F13	38
Jianou, China	H7	28
Jianshui, China	C7	34
Jiaoxian, China	D10	26
Jiaozuo, China	D9	26
Jiashan, China	C6	28
Jiawang, China	A6	28
Jiaxian, China	A2	28
Jiaxing, China	E9	28
Jiazi, China	M5	28
Jicarilla Apache Indian Reservation, N.M., U.S.	A2	108
Jiddah, Sau. Ar.	D2	46
Jieshou, China	B4	28
Jieyang, China	L5	28
Jihlava, Czech.	F15	8
Jijiga, Eth.	G3	46
Jijona, Spain	G11	12
Jilemutu, China	A11	26
Jilin, China	C12	26
Jilin, prov., China	C12	26
Jill, Kediet ej, mtn., Maur.	D3	42
Jima, Eth.	G2	46
Jimena de la Frontera, Spain	I6	12
Jim Hogg, co., Tx., U.S.	F3	120
Jim Lake, res., N.D., U.S.	B7	111
Jim Thorpe, Pa., U.S.	E10	115
Jim Wells, co., Tx., U.S.	F3	120
Jinan (Tsinan), China	D10	26
Jīnd, India	F7	38
Jingdezhen (Kingtechen), China	F6	28
Jingjiang, China	C9	28
Jingxi, China	C9	34
Jinhua, China	F8	28
Jining, China	C9	26
Jining, China	D10	26
Jinja, Ug.	A6	44
Jinning (Jiukunyang), China	B7	34
Jinotega, Nic.	H4	64
Jinshi, China	F9	26
Jinxian, China	D11	26
Jinzhou, China	C11	26
Jiparaná, stm., Braz.	E6	54
Jipijapa, Ec.	H2	58
Jirjā, Egypt	C12	42
Jisr ash-Shughūr, Syria	B5	40
Jiujiang, China	F4	28
Jiuling Shan, mts., China	G3	28
Jiumangya, China	B14	38
Jiuquan, China	D6	26
Jixi, China	B13	26
Joaçaba, Braz.	B6	56
Joanna, S.C., U.S.	C4	117
João Pessoa, Braz.	E12	54
Joaquín V. González, Arg.	B4	56
Job Peak, mtn., Nv., U.S.	D3	105
Jobson (Vera), Arg.	B4	56
Jocassee, Lake, res., U.S.	B1	117
Jódar, Spain	H8	12
Jo Daviess, co., Il., U.S.	A3	90
Jodhpur, India	G5	38
Joe Batt's Arm [-Barr'd Islands-Shoal Bay], Newf., Can.	D4	72
Joensuu, Fin.	E17	6
Joes Brook, stm., Vt., U.S.	C4	122
Joes Creek, stm., W.V., U.S.	m12	125
Joffre, Mount, mtn., Can.	D3	68
Jogjakarta see Yogyakarta, Indon.	G5	32
Johannesburg, S. Afr.	G5	44
Johar, Som.	H4	46
John, Cape, c., N.S., Can.	D6	71
John Day, Or., U.S.	C8	114
John Day, stm., Or., U.S.	B6	114
John Day Dam, U.S.	D5	124
John Day Fossil Beds National Monument, Or., U.S.	C6	114
John F. Kennedy Space Center, sci., Fl., U.S.	D6	86
John H. Kerr Dam, Va., U.S.	D4	123
John H. Kerr Reservoir, res., U.S.	D4	123
John Martin Reservoir, res., Co., U.S.	C7	83
John Muir National Historical Site, hist., Ca., U.S.	h8	82
John o' Groats, Scot., U.K.	C9	7
John Redmond Reservoir, res., Ks., U.S.	D8	93
John Sevier, Tn., U.S.	m14	119
Johns Island, i., S.C., U.S.	F7	117
Johnson, Ks., U.S.	E2	93
Johnson, Vt., U.S.	B3	122
Johnson, co., Ar., U.S.	B2	81
Johnson, co., Ga., U.S.	D4	87
Johnson, co., Il., U.S.	F5	90
Johnson, co., In., U.S.	F5	91
Johnson, co., Ia., U.S.	C6	92
Johnson, co., Ks., U.S.	D9	93
Johnson, co., Ky., U.S.	C7	94
Johnson, co., Mo., U.S.	C4	102
Johnson, co., Ne., U.S.	D9	104
Johnson, co., Tn., U.S.	C12	119
Johnson, co., Tx., U.S.	C4	120
Johnson, co., Wy., U.S.	B6	127
Johnsonburg, Pa., U.S.	D4	115
Johnson City, N.Y., U.S.	C5	109
Johnson City, Tn., U.S.	C11	119
Johnson City, Tx., U.S.	D3	120
Johnson Creek, Wi., U.S.	E5	126
Johnsonville, S.C., U.S.	D9	117
Johns Pass, strt., Fl., U.S.	p10	86
Johnston, Ia., U.S.	e8	92
Johnston, R.I., U.S.	C4	116
Johnston, S.C., U.S.	D4	117
Johnston, co., N.C., U.S.	B4	110
Johnston, co., Ok., U.S.	C5	113
Johnston City, Il., U.S.	F5	90
Johnston Key, i., Fl., U.S.	H5	86
Johnstown, Co., U.S.	A6	83
Johnstown, N.Y., U.S.	B6	109
Johnstown, Oh., U.S.	B3	112
Johnstown, Pa., U.S.	F4	115
John W. Flannagan Reservoir, res., Va., U.S.	e9	123
Johor Baharu, Malay.	N7	34
Joigny, Fr.	E10	10
Joiner, Ar., U.S.	B5	81
Joinvile, Braz.	B7	56
Joinville, Fr.	D12	10
Jokkmokk, Swe.	C12	6
Joliet, Il., U.S.	B5	90
Joliette, Que., Can.	C4	74
Jolo Island, i., Phil.	D7	32
Jombang, Indon.	m16	33a
Jones, Ok., U.S.	B4	113
Jones, co., Ga., U.S.	C3	87
Jones, co., Ia., U.S.	B6	92
Jones, co., Ms., U.S.	D4	101
Jones, co., N.C., U.S.	B5	110
Jones, co., S.D., U.S.	D5	118
Jones, co., Tx., U.S.	C3	120
Jonesboro, Ar., U.S.	B5	81
Jonesboro, Ga., U.S.	C2	87
Jonesboro, Il., U.S.	F4	90
Jonesboro, In., U.S.	D6	91
Jonesboro, La., U.S.	B3	95
Jonesborough, Tn., U.S.	C11	119
Jonesburg, Mo., U.S.	C6	102
Jones Creek, Tx., U.S.	s14	120
Jones Mill, Ar., U.S.	C3	81
Jonesport, Me., U.S.	D5	96
Jones Sound, strt., N.W. Ter., Can.	A15	66
Jonestown, Ms., U.S.	A3	101
Jonesville, La., U.S.	C4	95
Jonesville, Mi., U.S.	G6	99
Jonesville, N.C., U.S.	A2	110
Jonesville, S.C., U.S.	B4	117
Jonesville, Va., U.S.	f8	123
Jongkha, China	F11	38
Jönköping, Swe.	H10	6
Jonquière, Que., Can.	A6	74
Jonzac, Fr.	G6	10
Joplin, Mo., U.S.	D3	102
Joppatowne, Md., U.S.	B5	97
Jordan, Mn., U.S.	F5	100
Jordan, ctry., Asia	D5	40
Jordan, stm., Asia	C4	40
Jordan, stm., Ut., U.S.	C4	121
Jordan Creek, stm., U.S.	E9	114
Jordan Lake, res., Al., U.S.	C3	78
Jorhāt, India	G16	38
Jörn, Swe.	D13	6
Jornado del Muerto, des., N.M., U.S.	D3	108
Jos, Nig.	G7	42
José Battle y Ordóñez, Ur.	C5	56
Joseph, Or., U.S.	B9	114
Joseph, Lac, l., Newf., Can.	h8	72
Joseph Bonaparte Gulf, b., Austl.	B5	50
Joseph City, Az., U.S.	C5	80
Josephine, co., Or., U.S.	E3	114
Joshua, Tx., U.S.	n9	120
Joshua Tree, Ca., U.S.	E5	82
Joshua Tree National Monument, Ca., U.S.	F6	82
Joškar-Ola, Russia	F7	22
Jourdanton, Tx., U.S.	E3	120
Joutsijärvi, Fin.	C16	6
Jovellanos, Cuba	C7	64
J. Percy Priest Lake, res., Tn., U.S.	A5	119
Juab, co., Ut., U.S.	D2	121
Juan Aldama, Mex.	E8	62
Juan de Fuca, Strait of, strt., N.A.	G8	66
Juan de Nova, Île, i., Reu.	E8	44
Juárez, Arg.	D5	56
Juàzeiro, Braz.	E10	54
Juàzeiro do Norte, Braz.	E11	54
Jūbā, Sudan	H12	42
Juba (Genale), stm., Afr.	H3	46
Juchitán [de Zaragoza], Mex.	I12	62
Judenburg, Aus.	H14	8
Judith, stm., Mt., U.S.	C7	103
Judith, Point, c., R.I., U.S.	G4	85
Judith Basin, co., Mt., U.S.	C6	103
Judith Island, i., N.C., U.S.	B6	110
Judith Mountains, mts., Mt., U.S.	C7	103
Judith Peak, mtn., Mt., U.S.	C7	103
Judoma, stm., Russia	F21	24
Judsonia, Ar., U.S.	B4	81
Juigalpa, Nic.	H5	64
Juiz de Fora, Braz.	F7	57
Jukagirskoje Ploskogorje, plat., Russia	D24	24
Jukte, Russia	E15	24
Julesburg, Co., U.S.	A8	83
Juliaca, Peru	G4	54
Julian, Ca., U.S.	F5	82
Julian, W.V., U.S.	C3	125
Julian Alps, mts., Eur.	C8	14
Juliana Top, mtn., Sur.	C7	54
Julianehåb, Grnld.	D23	66
Jülich, Ger.	E6	8
Jullundur, India	E6	38
Jumbo Peak, mtn., Nv., U.S.	G7	105
Jumentos Cays, is., Bah.	C10	64
Jumet, Bel.	E4	8
Jumilla, Spain	G10	12
Jump, stm., Wi., U.S.	C3	126
Junāgadh, India	J4	38
Junction, Tx., U.S.	D3	120
Junction City, Ar., U.S.	D3	81
Junction City, Ks., U.S.	C7	93
Junction City, Ky., U.S.	C5	94
Junction City, La., U.S.	A3	95
Junction City, Or., U.S.	C3	114
Jundiaí, Braz.	G5	57
Juneau, Ak., U.S.	D13	79
Juneau, Wi., U.S.	E5	126
Juneau, co., Wi., U.S.	E3	126
June in Winter, Lake, l., Fl., U.S.	E5	86
Jungfrau, mtn., Switz.	F14	10
Junggar Pendi, China	B4	26
Juniata, Ne., U.S.	D7	104
Juniata, co., Pa., U.S.	F7	115
Juniata, stm., Pa., U.S.	F7	115
Junín, Arg.	C4	56
Junín, Lago de, l., Peru	F3	54
Junín de los Andes, Arg.	D2	56
Junior Lake, l., Me., U.S.	C4	96
Juniper Mountains, mts., Az., U.S.	B2	80
Junipero Serra Peak, mtn., Ca., U.S.	D3	82
Junsele, Swe.	E11	6
Jupiter, Fl., U.S.	F6	86
Jupiter Inlet, b., Fl., U.S.	F6	86
Jupiter Island, i., Fl., U.S.	E6	86
Jura, mts., Eur.	F13	10
Jura, i., Scot., U.K.	F7	7
Jurga, Russia	F10	24
Jūrmala, Lat.	E6	18
Juruá, stm., S.A.	D5	54
Juruena, stm., Braz.	E7	54
Justin, Tx., U.S.	C4	120
Justo Daract, Arg.	C3	56
Jutaí, stm., Braz.	D5	54
Jüterbog, Ger.	D13	8
Jutiapa, Guat.	G3	64
Juticalpa, Hond.	G4	64
Jutland see Jylland, pen., Den.	H7	6
Juventud, Isla de la (Isle of Pines), i., Cuba	D6	64
Juwara, Oman	E6	46
Juža, Russia	E25	18
Južno-Sachalinsk, Russia	H22	24
Južnyj, Mys, c., Russia	F25	24
Jwayyā, Leb.	C4	40
Jylland, pen., Den.	H7	6
Jyväskylä, Fin.	E15	6

K

Name	Map Ref	Page
K2 (Qogir Feng), mtn., Asia	C7	38
Kaaawa, Hi., U.S.	f10	88
Kaala, mtn., Hi., U.S.	f9	88
Kaala Djerda, Tun.	N3	14
Kaalualu Bay, b., Hi., U.S.	E6	88
Kaaumakua, Puu, mtn., Hi., U.S.	f10	88
Kabale, Ug.	B5	44
Kabalo, Zaire	C5	44
Kabambare, Zaire	B5	44
Kåbdalis, Swe.	C12	6
Kabetogama Lake, l., Mn., U.S.	B5	100
Kabīr Kūh, mts., Iran	B4	46
Kābol, Afg.	C3	38
Kabompo, stm., Zam.	D4	44
Kabongo, Zaire	C5	44
Kābul, stm., Asia	C4	38
Kabwe (Broken Hill), Zam.	D5	44
Kachess Lake, res., Wa., U.S.	B4	124
K'achta, Russia	G15	24
Kačug, Russia	G15	24
Kadan Kyun, i., Mya.	H5	34
Kadiri, India	E5	37
Kadoka, S.D., U.S.	D4	118
Kaduna, Nig.	F7	42
Kāduqlī, Sudan	F11	42
Kadykčan, Russia	E23	24
Kaédi, Maur.	E3	42
Kaena Point, c., Hi., U.S.	B3	88
Kaesŏng, N. Kor.	D12	26
Kafia Kingi, Sudan	G10	42
Kafue, stm., Zam.	D5	44
Kaga, Japan	F9	30
Kagamigahara, Japan	G9	30
Kagaznagar, India	C5	37
Kagoshima, Japan	K3	30
Kahaluu, Hi., U.S.	D6	88
Kahaluu, Hi., U.S.	g10	88
Kahana Bay, b., Hi., U.S.	f10	88
Kahemba, Zaire	C3	44
Kahoka, Mo., U.S.	A6	102
Kahoolawe, i., Hi., U.S.	C5	88
Kahramanmaraş, Tur.	H15	4
Kahuku, Hi., U.S.	B4	88
Kahuku Point, c., Hi., U.S.	B4	88
Kahului, Hi., U.S.	C5	88
Kahului Bay, b., Hi., U.S.	C5	88
Kai, Kepulauan, is., Indon.	G9	32
Kaibab Indian Reservation, Az., U.S.	A3	80
Kaieteur Fall, wtfl, Guy.	E13	58
Kaifeng, China	E9	26
Kaikoura, N.Z.	E4	52
Kaili, China	A10	34
Kailua, Hi., U.S.	B4	88
Kailua Bay, b., Hi., U.S.	g11	88
Kailua Kona, Hi., U.S.	D6	88
Kaimana, Indon.	F9	32
Kaimanawa Mountains, mts., N.Z.	C5	52
Kainan, Japan	H8	30
Kaiserslautern, Ger.	F7	8
Kaitangata, N.Z.	G2	52
Kaiwi Channel, strt., Hi., U.S.	B4	88
Kajaani, Fin.	D16	6
Kajakī, Band-e, res., Afg.	D1	38
Kajan, stm., Indon.	E6	32
Kajang, Malay.	M6	34
Kakamas, S. Afr.	G4	44
Kaka Point, c., Hi., U.S.	C5	88
Kake, Ak., U.S.	D13	79
Kakegawa, Japan	H11	30
Kakie, Bots.	F4	44
Kākināda, India	D7	37
Kakogawa, Japan	H7	30
Kaladan, stm., Asia	D2	34
Ka Lae, c., Hi., U.S.	E6	88
Kalahari Desert, des., Afr.	F4	44
Kālahasti, India	F5	37
Kalaheo, Hi., U.S.	B2	88
Kalajoki, Fin.	D14	6
Kalakan, Russia	F17	24
Kalām, Pak.	C5	38
Kalama, Wa., U.S.	C3	124
Kalámai, Grc.	L6	16
Kalamazoo, Mi., U.S.	F5	99
Kalamazoo, co., Mi., U.S.	F5	99
Kalamazoo, stm., Mi., U.S.	F5	99
Kalasin, Thai.	F7	34
Kalāt, Pak.	F2	38
Kalaupapa Peninsula, pen., Hi., U.S.	B5	88
Kalawao, co., Hi., U.S.	B5	88
Kalb, Ra's al-, c., Yemen	F4	46
Kale, Tur.	L12	16
Kaleden, B.C., Can.	E8	69
Kalemie (Albertville), Zaire	C5	44
Kalena, Puu, mtn., Hi., U.S.	g9	88
Kalgin Island, i., Ak., U.S.	g16	79
Kalgoorlie, Austl.	F4	50
Kalima, Zaire	B5	44
Kálimnos, Grc.	M10	16
Kaliningrad (Königsberg), Russia	G3	18
Kalinkoviči, Bela.	I12	18
Kalispel Indian Reservation, Wa., U.S.	A8	124
Kalispell, Mt., U.S.	B2	103
Kalisz, Pol.	D18	8
Kalkaska, Mi., U.S.	D5	99
Kalkaska, co., Mi., U.S.	D5	99
Kalmar, Swe.	H11	6
Kalohi Channel, strt., Hi., U.S.	C4	88
Kālol, India	I5	38
Kaloli Point, c., Hi., U.S.	D7	88
Kalona, Ia., U.S.	C6	92
Kalone Peak, mtn., B.C., Can.	C4	69
Kaluga, Russia	G19	18
Kalutara, Sri L.	I5	37
Kamaishi, Japan	C14	30
Kamakou, mtn., Hi., U.S.	B5	88
Kamakura, Japan	G12	30
Kamālia, Pak.	E5	38
Kamarān, i., Yemen	E3	46
Kamas, Ut., U.S.	C4	121
Kamba, China	F13	38
Kambam, India	H4	37
Kambar, Pak.	G2	38
Kamčatka, stm., Russia	F25	24
Kamčatka, Poluostrov, pen., Russia	F25	24
Kamčatskij Zaliv, b., Russia	F26	24
Kamen', Gora, mtn., Russia	D12	24
Kamen'-na-Obi, Russia	G10	24
Kamenz, Ger.	D14	8
Kamiah, Id., U.S.	C2	89
Kamiak Butte, mtn., Wa., U.S.	C8	124
Kamienna Góra, Pol.	E16	8
Kamilukuak Lake, l., N.W. Ter., Can.	D12	66
Kamina, Zaire	C5	44
Kaminak Lake, l., N.W. Ter., Can.	D13	66
Kaminuriak Lake, l., N.W. Ter., Can.	D13	66
Kamitsushima, Japan	H2	30
Kamloops, B.C., Can.	D7	69
Kamo, Japan	E12	30
Kāmoke, Pak.	E6	38
Kampala, Ug.	A6	44
Kampar, Malay.	L6	34
Kampen, Neth.	C5	8
Kampeska, Lake, l., S.D., U.S.	C8	118
Kâmpóng Cham, Camb.	H8	34
Kâmpóng Chhnăng, Camb.	H8	34
Kâmpóng Saôm, Camb.	I7	34
Kâmpóng Saôm, Chhâk, b., Camb.	I7	34
Kâmpóng Thum, Camb.	H8	34
Kâmpôt, Camb.	I8	34
Kāmthi, India	B5	37
Kamuela (Waimea), Hi., U.S.	C6	88
Kamui-misaki, c., Japan	p18	30a
Kan, stm., Asia	H9	34
Kanab, Ut., U.S.	F3	121
Kanab Creek, stm., U.S.	A3	80
Kanabec, co., Mn., U.S.	E5	100
Kanaga Island, i., Ak., U.S.	E4	79
Kanairiktok, stm., Newf., Can.	g9	72
Kananga (Luluabourg), Zaire	C4	44
Kanapou Bay, b., Hi., U.S.	C5	88
Kanata, Ont., Can.	B9	73
Kanawha, Ia., U.S.	B4	92
Kanawha, co., W.V., U.S.	C3	125
Kanawha, stm., W.V., U.S.	C3	125
Kanazawa, Japan	F9	30
Kanchanaburi, Thai.	G5	34

Name	Map Ref	Page
Kānchenjunga, mtn., Asia	G13	38
Kānchipuram, India	F5	37
Kandhkot, Pak.	F3	38
Kāndi, India	I13	38
Kandiyohi, co., Mn., U.S.	E3	100
Kandy, Sri L.	I6	37
Kane, Pa., U.S.	C4	115
Kane, co., Il., U.S.	B5	90
Kane, co., Ut., U.S.	F3	121
Kaneohe, Hi., U.S.	B4	88
Kaneohe Bay, b., Hi., U.S.	g10	88
Kaneohe Bay Marine Corps Air Station, mil., Hi., U.S.	g10	88
Kangar, Malay.	K6	34
Kangaroo Island, i., Austl.	G7	50
Kangean, Kepulauan, is., Indon.	G6	32
Kangnŭng, S. Kor.	D12	26
Kango, Gabon	A2	44
Kangto, mtn., Asia	G15	38
Kaniama, Zaire	C4	44
Kankakee, Il., U.S.	B6	90
Kankakee, co., Il., U.S.	B6	90
Kankakee, stm., U.S.	B5	90
Kankan, Gui.	F4	42
Kanmaw Kyun, i., Mya.	I5	34
Kannapolis, N.C., U.S.	B2	110
Kannauj, India	G8	38
Kannonkoski, Fin.	E15	6
Kannus, Fin.	E14	6
Kano, Nig.	F7	42
Kanonji, Japan	H6	30
Kanopolis, Ks., U.S.	D5	93
Kanopolis Lake, res., Ks., U.S.	D5	93
Kanoya, Japan	K3	30
Kānpur, India	G9	38
Kansas, Il., U.S.	D6	90
Kansas, state, U.S.	D5	93
Kansas, stm., Ks., U.S.	C7	93
Kansas City, Ks., U.S.	C9	93
Kansas City, Mo., U.S.	B3	102
Kansk, Russia	F13	24
Kantō-sammyaku, mts., Japan	F11	30
Kanuma, Japan	F12	30
Kanye, Bots.	F5	44
Kaohsiung, Tai.	M9	28
Kaohsiunghsien, Tai.	M9	28
Kaokoveld, plat., Nmb.	E2	44
Kaolack, Sen.	F2	42
Kapaa, Hi., U.S.	A2	88
Kapaau, Hi., U.S.	C6	88
Kapadvanj, India	I5	38
Kapanga, Zaire	C4	44
Kapapa Island, i., Hi., U.S.	g10	88
Kapfenberg, Aus.	H15	8
Kaplan, La., U.S.	D3	95
Kaposvár, Hung.	I17	8
Kaptai, Bngl.	I15	38
Kapuas, stm., Indon.	F4	32
Kapūrthala, India	E6	38
Kapuskasing, Ont., Can.	o19	73
Karabük, Tur.	G14	4
Karacabey, Tur.	I12	16
Karacaköy, Tur.	H12	16
Karāchi, Pak.	H2	38
Karād, India	D3	37
Karaganda, Kaz.	H8	24
Karaginskij, Ostrov, i., Russia	F26	24
Karaginskij Zaliv, b., Russia	F26	24
Karagoš, Gora, mtn., Russia	G11	24
Kāraikkudi, India	G5	37
Karakelong, Pulau, i., Indon.	E8	32
Karakoram Range, mts., Asia	C7	38
Karakumskij kanal, Turk.	J10	22
Karaman, Tur.	H14	4
Karaman, Tur.	L13	16
Karamay, China	B3	26
Karamürsel, Tur.	I13	16
Kāranja, India	B4	37
Karasburg, Nmb.	G3	44
Karasjok, Nor.	B15	6
Karatsu, Japan	I2	30
Karaul, Russia	C10	24
Karauli, India	G7	38
Karawang, Indon.	m13	33a
Karawanken, mts., Eur.	C9	14
Karbalā', Iraq	B3	46
Kårböle, Swe.	F10	6
Karcag, Hung.	H20	8
Kardeljevo, Cro.	F12	14
Kardhítsa, Grc.	J5	16
Kărdžali, Bul.	H9	16
Kargasok, Russia	F10	24
Karhula, Fin.	F16	6
Kariba, Zimb.	E5	44
Kariba, Lake, res., Afr.	E5	44
Karibib, Nmb.	F3	44
Karigasniemi, Fin.	B15	6
Karimata, Kepulauan, is., Indon.	F4	32
Karimata, Selat (Karimata Strait), strt., Indon.	F4	32
Karīmganj, India	H15	38
Karīmnagar, India	C5	37
Karin, Som.	F4	46
Karis (Karjaa), Fin.	F14	6
Kariya, Japan	H9	30
Karkabet, Erit.	E2	46
Karlovac, Cro.	D10	14
Karlovo, Bul.	G8	16
Karlovy Vary, Czech.	E12	8
Karlshamn, Swe.	H10	6
Karlskoga, Swe.	G10	6
Karlskrona, Swe.	H10	6
Karlsruhe, Ger.	F8	8
Karlstad, Swe.	G9	6
Karlstad, Mn., U.S.	B2	100
Karnāl, India	F7	38
Karnaphuli Reservoir, res., Bngl.	I15	38
Karnataka, state, India	E3	37
Karnes, co., Tx., U.S.	E4	120
Karnes City, Tx., U.S.	E4	120
Karns, Tn., U.S.	n13	119
Karonga, Mwi.	C6	44
Kárpathos, i., Grc.	N11	16
Karpenísion, Grc.	K5	16
Kars, Tur.	G16	4
Kärsämäki, Fin.	E15	6
Karši, Uzb.	J11	22
Kartal, Tur.	I13	16
Karufa, Indon.	F9	32
Karungi, Swe.	C14	6
Karūr, India	G5	37
Karviná, Czech.	F18	8
Kārwār, India	E3	37
Kasai (Cassai), stm., Afr.	B3	44
Kasaji, Zaire	D4	44
Kasama, Zam.	D6	44
Kasanga, Tan.	C6	44
Kasaoka, Japan	H6	30
Kāsaragod, India	F3	37
Kasba Lake, l., N.W. Ter., Can.	D12	66
Kaseda, Japan	K3	30
Kasempa, Zam.	D5	44
Kasenga, Zaire	D5	44
Kasese, Zaire	B5	44
Kāsganj, India	G8	38
Kāshān, Iran	B5	46
Kashi, China	D2	26
Kashima-nada, Japan	F13	30
Kashīpur, India	F8	38
Kashiwa, Japan	G12	30
Kashiwazaki, Japan	E11	30
Kashmir see Jammu and Kashmir, dep., Asia	C6	38
Kasimov, Russia	G24	18
Kašin, Russia	D20	18
Kašira, Russia	G21	18
Kaskaskia, stm., Il., U.S.	D5	90
Kaskö (Kaskinen), Fin.	E13	6
Kaslo, B.C., Can.	E9	69
Kasongo, Zaire	B5	44
Kasota, Mn., U.S.	F5	100
Kasr, Ra's, c., Sudan	E13	42
Kassalā, Sudan	E13	42
Kassel, Ger.	D9	8
Kasson, Mn., U.S.	F6	100
Kastoría, Grc.	I5	16
Kasugai, Japan	G9	30
Kasūr, Pak.	E6	38
Katahdin, Mount, mtn., Me., U.S.	C4	96
Katanga Plateau, plat., Zaire	D5	44
Katchall Island, i., India	K2	34
Kateríni, Grc.	I6	16
Kates Needle, mtn., Ak., U.S.	m24	79
Katherine, Austl.	B6	50
Kāthiāwār, pen., India	I4	38
Kathleen, Fl., U.S.	D4	86
Kathmāndau, Nepal	G11	38
Katihār, India	H12	38
Katiola, C. Iv.	G4	42
Katmai, Mount, mtn., Ak., U.S.	D9	79
Katmai National Park, Ak., U.S.	D9	79
Katmandu see Kāthmāndau, Nepal	G11	38
Katowice, Pol.	E19	8
Kātrīnā, Jabal, mtn., Egypt	C12	42
Katrineholm, Swe.	G11	6
Katsina, Nig.	F7	42
Katsuta, Japan	F13	30
Kattegat, strt., Eur.	H8	6
Katy, Tx., U.S.	r14	120
Kauai, co., Hi., U.S.	B1	88
Kauai, i., Hi., U.S.	A2	88
Kauai Channel, strt., Hi., U.S.	B3	88
Kau Desert, des., Hi., U.S.	D6	88
Kaufbeuren, Ger.	H10	8
Kaufman, Tx., U.S.	C4	120
Kaufman, co., Tx., U.S.	C4	120
Kauiki Head, c., Hi., U.S.	C6	88
Kaukauna, Wi., U.S.	D5	126
Kaukauveld, mts., Afr.	F3	44
Kaula Island, i., Hi., U.S.	m15	88
Kaulakahi Channel, strt., Hi., U.S.	A2	88
Kaumakani, Hi., U.S.	B2	88
Kaunakakai, Hi., U.S.	B4	88
Kauna Point, c., Hi., U.S.	D6	88
Kaunas, Lith.	G6	18
Kaura Namoda, Nig.	F7	42
Kaustinen, Fin.	E14	6
Kavača, Russia	E27	24
Kavacık, Tur.	J12	16
Kavalerovo, Russia	I21	24
Kavála, Grc.	I8	16
Kavaratti, India	G2	37
Kavieng, Pap. N. Gui.	k17	50a
Kawagoe, Japan	G12	30
Kawaguchi, Japan	G12	30
Kawaihoa Point, c., Hi., U.S.	B1	88
Kawaikini, mtn., Hi., U.S.	A2	88
Kawambwa, Zam.	C5	44
Kawanoe, Japan	H6	30
Kawasaki, Japan	G12	30
Kawich Peak, mtn., Nv., U.S.	F5	105
Kawich Range, mts., Nv., U.S.	F5	105
Kaw Lake, res., Ok., U.S.	A5	113
Kawm Umbū, Egypt	D12	42
Kay, co., Ok., U.S.	A4	113
Kayankulam, India	H4	37
Kaycee, Wy., U.S.	C6	127
Kayenta, Az., U.S.	A5	80
Kayes, Mali	F3	42
Kayseri, Tur.	H15	4
Kaysville, Ut., U.S.	B4	121
Kažačinskoje, Russia	F12	24
Kazačje, Russia	C21	24
Kazakhstan, ctry., Asia	H11	22
Kazan', Russia	F7	22
Kazanlâk, Bul.	G9	16
Kāzerūn, Iran	C5	46
Keaau, Hi., U.S.	D6	88
Keahiakahoe, Puu, mtn., Hi., U.S.	g10	88
Keahole Point, c., Hi., U.S.	D5	88
Kealaikahiki Channel, strt., Hi., U.S.	C5	88
Kealaikahiki Point, c., Hi., U.S.	C5	88
Kealakekua, Hi., U.S.	D6	88
Kealia, Hi., U.S.	A2	88
Keams Canyon, Az., U.S.	B5	80
Keanapapa Point, c., Hi., U.S.	C4	88
Keansburg, N.J., U.S.	C4	107
Kearney, Mo., U.S.	B3	102
Kearney, Ne., U.S.	D6	104
Kearney, co., Ne., U.S.	D7	104
Kearns, Ut., U.S.	C4	121
Kearny, Az., U.S.	D5	80
Kearny, N.J., U.S.	h8	107
Kearny, co., Ks., U.S.	D2	93
Kebri Dehar, Eth.	G3	46
Kechika, stm., B.C., Can.	E7	66
Kecskemét, Hung.	I19	8
Kedges Straits, strt., Md., U.S.	D5	97
Kedgwick, N.B., Can.	B2	71
Kediri, Indon.	m16	32
Kedon, Russia	E25	24
Kédougou, Sen.	F3	42
Kędzierzyn, Pol.	E18	8
Keego Harbor, Mi., U.S.	o15	99
Keele Peak, mtn., Yukon, Can.	D6	66
Keelung see Chilung, Tai.	J10	28
Keene, N.H., U.S.	E2	106
Keene, Tx., U.S.	n9	120
Keeper Hill, hill, Ire.	I4	7
Keeseville, N.Y., U.S.	f11	109
Keesler Air Force Base, mil., Ms., U.S.	E5	101
Keetmanshoop, Nmb.	G3	44
Keet Seel Ruin, hist., Az., U.S.	A5	80
Keewatin, Ont., Can.	E4	70
Keewatin, Mn., U.S.	C5	100
Kefallinía, i., Grc.	K4	16
Keffi, Nig.	G7	42
Keflavík, Ice.	C3	4
Ke Ga, Mui, c., Viet.	H10	34
Kegonsa, Lake, l., Wi., U.S.	F4	126
Keiser, Ar., U.S.	B5	81
Keith, Scot., U.K.	D10	7
Keith, co., Ne., U.S.	C4	104
Keizer, Or., U.S.	C3	114
Kejimkujik National Park, N.S., Can.	E4	71
Kekaha, Hi., U.S.	B2	88
Kelafo, Eth.	G3	46
Kelang, Malay.	M6	34
Kelheim, Ger.	G11	8
Kelibia, Tun.	M6	14
Keller, Tx., U.S.	n9	120
Kellett, Cape, c., N.W. Ter., Can.	B7	66
Kelleys Island, i., Oh., U.S.	A3	112
Kellogg, Id., U.S.	B2	89
Kellogg, Ia., U.S.	C5	92
Kelloselkä, Fin.	C17	6
Kelly Air Force Base, mil., Tx., U.S.	k7	120
Kelly Island, i., De., U.S.	D4	85
Kellyville, Ok., U.S.	B5	113
Kélo, Chad	G9	42
Kelottijärvi, Fin.	B14	6
Kelowna, B.C., Can.	E8	69
Kelso, Wa., U.S.	C3	124
Keluang, Malay.	M7	34
Kemerovo, Russia	F11	24
Kemi, Fin.	D15	6
Kemijärvi, Fin.	C16	6
Kemijoki, stm., Fin.	C15	6
Kemmerer, Wy., U.S.	E2	127
Kemp, Tx., U.S.	C4	120
Kemp, Lake, res., Tx., U.S.	C3	120
Kemper, co., Ms., U.S.	C5	101
Kemps Bay, Bah.	B9	64
Kempt, Lac, l., Que., Can.	G18	66
Kempten [Allgäu], Ger.	H10	8
Kemptville, Ont., Can.	B9	73
Kemul, Kong, mtn., Indon.	E6	32
Kenai, Ak., U.S.	C9	79
Kenai Fjords National Park, Ak., U.S.	D10	79
Kenai Mountains, mts., Ak., U.S.	h16	79
Kenai Peninsula, pen., Ak., U.S.	h16	79
Kenansville, N.C., U.S.	C5	110
Kenbridge, Va., U.S.	D4	123
Kendall, Fl., U.S.	s13	86
Kendall, co., Il., U.S.	B5	90
Kendall, co., Tx., U.S.	E3	120
Kendall, Cape, c., N.W. Ter., Can.	D15	66
Kendall Park, N.J., U.S.	C3	107
Kendallville, In., U.S.	B7	91
Kendari, Indon.	F7	32
Kenedy, Tx., U.S.	E4	120
Kenedy, co., Tx., U.S.	F4	120
Kenema, S.L.	G3	42
Kenesaw, Ne., U.S.	D7	104
Kēng Tung, Mya.	D5	34
Kenhardt, S. Afr.	G4	44
Kenilworth, Il., U.S.	h9	90
Kenitra, Mor.	B4	42
Kenly, N.C., U.S.	B4	110
Kenmare, N.D., U.S.	A3	111
Kenmore, N.Y., U.S.	C2	109
Kennaday Peak, mtn., Wy., U.S.	E6	127
Kennebago Lake, l., Me., U.S.	C2	96
Kennebec, co., Me., U.S.	D3	96
Kennebec, stm., Me., U.S.	D3	96
Kennebunk, Me., U.S.	E2	96
Kennebunkport, Me., U.S.	E2	96
Kennedy Entrance, strt., Ak., U.S.	D9	79
Kennedy Peak, mtn., Mya.	C2	34
Kenner, La., U.S.	E5	95
Kennesaw, Ga., U.S.	B2	87
Kennesaw Mountain, mtn., Ga., U.S.	C2	87
Kennett, Mo., U.S.	E7	102
Kennett Square, Pa., U.S.	G10	115
Kennewick, Wa., U.S.	C6	124
Kenn Reefs, rf., Austl.	D11	50
Kennydale, Wa., U.S.	e11	124
Keno, Or., U.S.	E5	114
Kénogami, Lac, l., Que., Can.	A6	74
Kenora, Ont., Can.	o16	73
Kenosha, Wi., U.S.	F6	126
Kenosha, co., Wi., U.S.	F5	126
Kenova, W.V., U.S.	C2	125
Kensett, Ar., U.S.	B4	81
Kensico Reservoir, res., N.Y., U.S.	g13	109
Kensington, P.E.I., Can.	C6	71
Kensington, Ct., U.S.	C4	84
Kensington, Md., U.S.	B3	97
Kent, Oh., U.S.	A4	112
Kent, Wa., U.S.	B3	124
Kent, co., De., U.S.	D3	85
Kent, co., Md., U.S.	B5	97
Kent, co., Mi., U.S.	E5	99
Kent, co., R.I., U.S.	D2	116
Kent, co., Tx., U.S.	C2	120
Kent City, Mi., U.S.	E5	99
Kent Island, i., De., U.S.	D4	85
Kent Island, i., Md., U.S.	C5	97
Kentland, In., U.S.	C3	91
Kenton, De., U.S.	D3	85
Kenton, Oh., U.S.	B2	112
Kenton, Tn., U.S.	A2	119
Kenton, co., Ky., U.S.	B5	94
Kent Peninsula, pen., N.W. Ter., Can.	C11	66
Kent Point, c., Md., U.S.	C5	97
Kentucky, state, U.S.	C4	94
Kentucky, stm., Ky., U.S.	B5	94
Kentwood, La., U.S.	D5	95
Kentwood, Mi., U.S.	F5	99
Kenvil, N.J., U.S.	B3	107
Kenvir, Ky., U.S.	D6	94
Kenya, ctry., Afr.	B7	44
Kenya, Mount see Kirinyaga, mtn., Kenya	B7	44
Kenyon, Mn., U.S.	F6	100
Kenyon, R.I., U.S.	F2	116
Keokea, Hi., U.S.	C5	88
Keokuk, Ia., U.S.	D6	92
Keokuk, co., Ia., U.S.	C5	92
Keokuk Lock and Dam, U.S.	D6	92
Keosauqua, Ia., U.S.	D6	92
Keota, Ia., U.S.	C6	92
Keota, Ok., U.S.	B7	113
Keowee, Lake, res., S.C., U.S.	B2	117
Kepi, Indon.	G10	32
Kerala, state, India	G4	37
Kerch, Ukr.	H5	22
Keremeos, B.C., Can.	E8	69
Keren, Erit.	E2	46
Kerens, Tx., U.S.	C4	120
Kerguélen, Îles, is., F.S.A.T.	J17	2
Kerhonkson, N.Y., U.S.	D6	109
Kericho, Kenya	B7	44
Kerinci, Gunung, mtn., Indon.	F3	32
Kerkhoven, Mn., U.S.	E3	100
Kérkira (Corfu), Grc.	J3	16
Kérkira, i., Grc.	J3	16
Kermān, Iran	B6	46
Kerme Körfezi, b., Tur.	M11	16
Kermit, Tx., U.S.	D1	120
Kermode, Mount, mtn., B.C., Can.	C2	69
Kern, co., Ca., U.S.	E4	82
Kern, stm., Ca., U.S.	E4	82
Kernersville, N.C., U.S.	A2	110
Kernville, Ca., U.S.	E4	82
Kerr, co., Tx., U.S.	D3	120
Kerr, Lake, l., Fl., U.S.	C5	86
Kerrville, Tx., U.S.	D3	120
Kerry Head, c., Ire.	I3	7
Kersey, Co., U.S.	A6	83
Kershaw, S.C., U.S.	B6	117
Kershaw, co., S.C., U.S.	C6	117
Kerulen (Cherlen), stm., Asia	B9	26
Kesagami Lake, l., Ont., Can.	F16	66
Keşan, Tur.	I10	16
Kesennuma, Japan	D14	30
Keshena, Wi., U.S.	D5	126
Ket', stm., Russia	F11	24
Keta, Ozero, l., Russia	D11	24
Ketchikan, Ak., U.S.	D13	79
Ketchum, Id., U.S.	F4	89
Kettering, Eng., U.K.	I12	7
Kettering, Oh., U.S.	C1	112
Kettle, stm., Mn., U.S.	D6	100
Kettle Creek, stm., Pa., U.S.	D6	115
Kettle Creek Lake, res., Pa., U.S.	D6	115
Kettle Falls, Wa., U.S.	A7	124
Keuka Lake, l., N.Y., U.S.	C3	109
Kew, T./C. Is.	D11	64
Kewanee, Il., U.S.	B4	90
Kewaskum, Wi., U.S.	E5	126
Kewaunee, Wi., U.S.	D6	126
Kewaunee, co., Wi., U.S.	D6	126
Keweenaw, co., Mi., U.S.	A2	99
Keweenaw Bay, b., Mi., U.S.	B2	99
Keweenaw Peninsula, pen., Mi., U.S.	A3	99
Keweenaw Point, c., Mi., U.S.	A3	99
Keya Paha, co., Ne., U.S.	B6	104
Keya Paha, stm., U.S.	A5	104
Keyhole Reservoir, res., Wy., U.S.	B8	127
Key Largo, Fl., U.S.	G6	86
Keyport, N.J., U.S.	C4	107
Keyser, W.V., U.S.	B6	125
Keystone, W.V., U.S.	D3	125
Keystone Heights, Fl., U.S.	C4	86
Keystone Lake, res., Ok., U.S.	A5	113
Keystone Peak, mtn., Az., U.S.	F4	80
Keysville, Va., U.S.	C4	123
Key West, Fl., U.S.	H5	86
Key West Naval Air Station, mil., Fl., U.S.	H5	86
Kezar Falls, Me., U.S.	E2	96
Kezar Lake, l., Me., U.S.	D2	96
Kežma, Russia	F14	24
Khadki (Kirkee), India	C2	37
Khairpur, Pak.	G3	38
Khalkís, Grc.	K7	16
Khambhāliya, India	I3	38
Khambhāt, Gulf of, b., India	B2	37
Khāmgaon, India	B4	37
Khammam, India	D6	37
Khānābād, Afg.	B3	38
Khānaqīn, Iraq	B4	46
Khandwa, India	B4	37
Khānewāl, Pak.	E4	38
Khaniá, Grc.	N8	16
Khanna, India	E7	38
Khānpur, Pak.	F4	38
Khān Yūnus, Isr. Occ.	D4	40
Kharagpur, India	I12	38
Khargon, India	J6	38
Kharkiv, Ukr.	G5	22
Khartoum see Al-Kharṭūm, Sudan	E12	42
Kherson, Ukr.	H4	22
Khíos, Grc.	K10	16
Kholm, Afg.	B2	38
Khong, Laos	G8	34
Khong Sédone, Laos	G8	34
Khon Kaen, Thai.	F7	34
Khóra Sfakíon, Grc.	N8	16
Khorramābād, Iran	B4	46
Khorramshahr, Iran	B4	46
Khouribga, Mor.	B4	42
Khowst, Afg.	D3	38
Khulna, Bngl.	I13	38
Khunjerab Pass, Asia	B6	38
Khurja, India	F7	38
Khūryān Mūryān (Kuria Muria Isla, is., Oman	E6	46
Khushāb, Pak.	D5	38
Khvājeh Moḥammad, Kūh-e, mts., Afg.	B4	38
Khvoy, Iran	J6	22
Khyber Pass, Asia	C4	38
Kiamichi, stm., Ok., U.S.	C6	113
Kiamika, stm., Que., Can.	C2	74
Kiana, Ak., U.S.	B7	79
Kiawah Island, i., S.C., U.S.	F7	117
Kibangou, Congo	B2	44
Kibombo, Zaire	B5	44
Kibre Mengist, Eth.	G2	46
Kičevo, Mac.	H4	16
Kichčik, Russia	G25	24
Kickamuit, stm., R.I., U.S.	D5	116
Kickapoo, stm., Wi., U.S.	E3	126
Kickapoo, Lake, res., Tx., U.S.	C3	120
Kickapoo Indian Reservation, Ks., U.S.	C8	93
Kicking Horse Pass, Can.	D2	68
Kidal, Mali	E6	42
Kidder, co., N.D., U.S.	C6	111
Kidira, Sen.	F3	42
Kiefer, Ok., U.S.	B5	113
Kiel, Ger.	A10	8
Kiel, Wi., U.S.	E5	126
Kielce, Pol.	E20	8
Kieler Bucht, b., Ger.	A10	8
Kiester, Mn., U.S.	G5	100
Kiev see Kyyiv, Ukr.	G4	22
Kiffa, Maur.	E3	42
Kigali, Rw.	B6	44
Kigoma, Tan.	B5	44
Kihei, Hi., U.S.	C5	88
Kihniö, Fin.	E14	6
Kiholo Bay, b., Hi., U.S.	D5	88
Kii-suidō, strt., Japan	I7	30
Kikinda, Yugo.	D4	16
Kikládhes, is., Grc.	L8	16
Kikwit, Zaire	C3	44
Kilauea, Hi., U.S.	A2	88
Kilauea Crater, crat., Hi., U.S.	D6	88
Kilauea Point, c., Hi., U.S.	A2	88
Kilgore, Tx., U.S.	C5	120
Kilimanjaro, mtn., Tan.	B7	44
Kilis, Tur.	A5	40
Kilkee, Ire.	I3	7
Kilkenny, Ire.	I5	7
Kilkís, Grc.	H6	16
Killala, Ire.	G3	7
Killaloe Station, Ont., Can.	B7	73
Killam, Alta., Can.	C5	68
Killarney, Man., Can.	E2	70
Killarney, Ire.	I3	7
Killarney Provincial Park, Ont., Can.	A3	73
Killdeer, N.D., U.S.	B3	111
Killeen, Tx., U.S.	D4	120
Killen, Al., U.S.	A2	78
Killian, La., U.S.	h10	95
Killik, stm., Ak., U.S.	B9	79
Killona, La., U.S.	h11	95
Killorglin, Ire.	I3	7
Kilmarnock, Scot., U.K.	F8	7
Kilmarnock, Va., U.S.	C6	123
Kilmichael, Ms., U.S.	B4	101
Kiln, Ms., U.S.	E4	101
Kilombero, stm., Tan.	C7	44
Kilosa, Tan.	C7	44
Kilpisjärvi, Fin.	B13	6
Kilwa, Zaire	C5	44
Kilwa Kivinje, Tan.	C7	44
Kimball, Mn., U.S.	E4	100
Kimball, Ne., U.S.	C2	104
Kimball, S.D., U.S.	D7	118
Kimball, co., Ne., U.S.	C2	104
Kimball, Mount, mtn., Ak., U.S.	C11	79
Kimberley, B.C., Can.	E9	69
Kimberley, S. Afr.	G4	44
Kimberley Plateau, plat., Austl.	C5	50
Kimberlin Heights, Tn., U.S.	n14	119
Kimberly, Al., U.S.	B3	78
Kimberly, Id., U.S.	G4	89
Kimberly, W.V., U.S.	m13	125
Kimberly, Wi., U.S.	h9	126
Kimble, co., Tx., U.S.	D3	120
Kimch'aek, N. Kor.	C12	26
Kimovsk, Russia	H21	18
Kimry, Russia	E20	18
Kinabalu, Gunong, mtn., Malay.	D6	32
Kinbasket Lake, res., B.C., Can.	D8	69
Kincaid, Il., U.S.	D4	90
Kincaid, W.V., U.S.	m13	125
Kincaid, Lake, res., Il., U.S.	D4	90
Kincardine, Ont., Can.	C3	73
Kincheloe Air Force Base, mil., Mi., U.S.	B6	99
Kinder, La., U.S.	D3	95
Kindia, Gui.	F3	42
Kindu, Zaire	B5	44
Kinešma, Russia	D25	18
King, N.C., U.S.	A2	110
King, Wi., U.S.	D4	126
King, co., Tx., U.S.	C2	120
King, co., Wa., U.S.	B3	124
King and Queen, co., Va., U.S.	C6	123
Kingaroy, Austl.	E10	50
King City, Ca., U.S.	D3	82
King City, Mo., U.S.	A3	102

Name	Map Ref	Page
King Cove, Ak., U.S.	E7	79
Kingfield, Me., U.S.	D2	96
Kingfisher, Ok., U.S.	B4	113
Kingfisher, co., Ok., U.S.	B3	113
King George, co., Va., U.S.	B5	123
King Island, i., Austl.	G8	50
King Island, i., B.C., Can.	C4	69
King Lear Peak, mtn., Nv., U.S.	B3	105
King Leopold Ranges, mts., Austl.	C5	50
Kingman, Az., U.S.	B1	80
Kingman, Ks., U.S.	E5	93
Kingman, co., Ks., U.S.	E5	93
King Mountain, mtn., Or., U.S.	E3	114
King Mountain, mtn., Or., U.S.	D8	114
King Peak, mtn., Ca., U.S.	B1	82
Kings, Ms., U.S.	C3	101
Kings, co., Ca., U.S.	D4	82
Kings, co., N.Y., U.S.	E7	109
Kings, stm., Ar., U.S.	A2	81
Kings, stm., Ca., U.S.	D4	82
Kings, stm., Nv., U.S.	B3	105
King Salmon, Ak., U.S.	D8	79
Kingsburg, Ca., U.S.	D4	82
Kingsbury, co., S.D., U.S.	C8	118
Kings Canyon National Park, Ca., U.S.	D4	82
Kingsey-Falls, Que., Can.	D5	74
Kingsford, Mi., U.S.	C2	99
Kingsland, Ga., U.S.	F5	87
Kingsland, Tx., U.S.	D3	120
Kingsley, Ia., U.S.	B2	92
Kingsley, Mi., U.S.	D5	99
King's Lynn, Eng., U.K.	I13	7
Kings Mountain, N.C., U.S.	B1	110
King Sound, strt., Austl.	C4	50
Kings Park West, Va., U.S.	*B5	123
Kings Peak, mtn., Ut., U.S.	C5	121
King's Point, Newf., Can.	D3	72
Kingsport, Tn., U.S.	C11	119
Kingston, Ont., Can.	C8	73
Kingston, Jam.	E9	64
Kingston, Ga., U.S.	B2	87
Kingston, Id., U.S.	B2	89
Kingston, Ma., U.S.	C6	98
Kingston, N.H., U.S.	E4	106
Kingston, N.Y., U.S.	D6	109
Kingston, Oh., U.S.	C3	112
Kingston, Ok., U.S.	D5	113
Kingston, Pa., U.S.	D10	115
Kingston, R.I., U.S.	F3	116
Kingston, Tn., U.S.	D9	119
Kingston Springs, Tn., U.S.	A4	119
Kingston upon Hull, Eng., U.K.	H12	7
Kingstown, St. Vin.	H17	64
Kingstown, Md., U.S.	B5	97
Kingstree, S.C., U.S.	D8	117
Kingsville, Ont., Can.	E2	73
Kingsville, Md., U.S.	B5	97
Kingsville (North Kingsville), Oh., U.S.	A5	112
Kingsville, Tx., U.S.	F4	120
Kingsville Naval Air Station, mil., Tx., U.S.	F4	120
King William, co., Va., U.S.	C5	123
King William Island, i., N.W. Ter., Can.	C13	66
King William's Town, S. Afr.	H5	44
Kingwood, W.V., U.S.	B5	125
Kinistino, Sask., Can.	E3	75
Kinkaid Lake, res., Il., U.S.	F4	90
Kinloch, Mo., U.S.	f13	102
Kinmundy, Il., U.S.	E5	90
Kinna, Swe.	H9	6
Kinnairds Head, c., Scot., U.K.	D10	7
Kinnelon, N.J., U.S.	B4	107
Kinneret, Yam, l., Isr.	C4	40
Kinney, co., Tx., U.S.	E2	120
Kinross, Scot., U.K.	E9	7
Kinsale, Ire.	J4	7
Kinsarvik, Nor.	F6	6
Kinsey, Al., U.S.	D4	78
Kinshasa (Léopoldville), Zaire	B3	44
Kinsley, Ks., U.S.	E4	93
Kinston, N.C., U.S.	B5	110
Kintyre, pen., Scot., U.K.	F7	7
Kintyre, Mull of, c., Scot., U.K.	F7	7
Kinyeti, mtn., Sudan	H12	42
Kiowa, Ks., U.S.	E5	93
Kiowa, Ok., U.S.	C6	113
Kiowa, co., Co., U.S.	C8	83
Kiowa, co., Ks., U.S.	E4	93
Kiowa, co., Ok., U.S.	C2	113
Kiowa Creek, stm., Ok., U.S.	A1	113
Kipembawe, Tan.	C6	44
Kipili, Tan.	C6	44
Kipnuk, Ak., U.S.	C7	79
Kipushi, Zaire	D5	44
Kirbyville, Tx., U.S.	D6	120
Kirchdorf an der Krems, Aus.	H14	8
Kirenga, stm., Russia	F15	24
Kirensk, Russia	F15	24
Kirghizia see Kyrgyzstan, state, Asia	I12	22
Kiribati, ctry., Oc.	G24	2
Kırıkhan, Tur.	A5	40
Kırıkkale, Tur.	H14	4
Kirin see Jilin, China	C12	26
Kirinyaga (Mount Kenya), mtn., Kenya	B7	44
Kırkağaç, Tur.	J11	16
Kirkcaldy, Scot., U.K.	E9	7
Kirkcudbright, Scot., U.K.	G8	7
Kirkenes, Nor.	B18	6
Kirkland, Il., U.S.	A5	90
Kirkland, Wa., U.S.	B3	124
Kirkland Lake, Ont., Can.	o19	73
Kırklareli, Tur.	H11	16
Kirklin, In., U.S.	D5	91
Kirksville, Mo., U.S.	A5	102
Kirkūk, Iraq	A3	46
Kirkwall, Scot., U.K.	C10	7
Kirkwood, De., U.S.	B3	85
Kirkwood, Il., U.S.	C3	90
Kirkwood, Mo., U.S.	f13	102
Kirov, Russia	G17	18
Kirov, Russia	F7	22
Kirovohrad, Ukr.	H4	22
Kirovskij, Russia	G25	24
Kırşehir, Tur.	H14	4
Kīrthar Range, mts., Pak.	G2	38
Kirtland, N.M., U.S.	A1	108
Kirtland Air Force Base, mil., N.M., U.S.	k7	108
Kiruna, Swe.	C13	6
Kirwin Reservoir, res., Ks., U.S.	C4	93
Kiryū, Japan	F12	30
Kisa, Swe.	H10	6
Kisangani (Stanleyville), Zaire	A5	44
Kisarazu, Japan	G12	30
K.I. Sawyer Air Force Base, mil., Mi., U.S.	B3	99
Kisel'ovsk, Russia	G11	24
Kishanganj, India	G12	38
Kishangarh, India	G6	38
Kishinev see Chişinău, Mol.	H3	22
Kishiwada, Japan	H8	30
Kishorganj, Bngl.	H14	38
Kishwaukee, stm., Il., U.S.	A5	90
Kiska Island, i., Ak., U.S.	E3	79
Kiskunfélegyháza, Hung.	I19	8
Kiskunhalas, Hung.	I19	8
Kislovodsk, Russia	I6	22
Kismayu, Som.	B8	44
Kissidougou, Gui.	G3	42
Kissimmee, Fl., U.S.	D5	86
Kissimmee, stm., Fl., U.S.	E5	86
Kissimmee, Lake, l., Fl., U.S.	E5	86
Kississing Lake, l., Man., Can.	B1	70
Kistanje, Cro.	F10	14
Kistler, W.V., U.S.	D3	125
Kisumu, Kenya	B6	44
Kitaibaraki, Japan	F13	30
Kitakami, stm., Japan	C14	30
Kitakami-sanchi, mts., Japan	C14	30
Kitakyūshū, Japan	I3	30
Kitale, Kenya	A6	44
Kitami, Japan	p21	30a
Kitami-sanchi, mts., Japan	o20	30a
Kit Carson, co., Co., U.S.	B8	83
Kitchener, Ont., Can.	D4	73
Kíthira, i., Grc.	M6	16
Kitimat, B.C., Can.	B3	69
Kitsap, co., Wa., U.S.	B3	124
Kitscoty, Alta., Can.	C5	68
Kittanning, Pa., U.S.	E2	115
Kittatinny Mountain, mtn., U.S.	B2	107
Kittery, Me., U.S.	E2	96
Kittery Point, Me., U.S.	E2	96
Kittilä, Fin.	C15	6
Kittitas, Wa., U.S.	C5	124
Kittitas, co., Wa., U.S.	B4	124
Kitts, Ky., U.S.	D6	94
Kittson, co., Mn., U.S.	B2	100
Kitty Hawk, N.C., U.S.	A7	110
Kitty Hawk Bay, b., N.C., U.S.	A7	110
Kitwe, Zam.	D5	44
Kitzbühel, Aus.	H12	8
Kitzingen, Ger.	F10	8
Kivu, Lac, l., Afr.	B5	44
Kızıl, stm., Tur.	G14	4
Kjustendil, Bul.	G6	16
Kladno, Czech.	E14	8
Klagenfurt, Aus.	I14	8
Klaipėda (Memel), Lith.	F4	18
Klamath, co., Or., U.S.	E5	114
Klamath, stm., U.S.	B2	82
Klamath Falls, Or., U.S.	E5	114
Klamath Mountains, mts., U.S.	E2	114
Klangenan, Indon.	m14	33a
Klarälven, stm., Eur.	F9	6
Klawock, Ak., U.S.	D13	79
Kleberg, co., Tx., U.S.	F4	120
Klerksdorp, S. Afr.	G5	44
Kleve, Ger.	D6	8
Klickitat, Wa., U.S.	D4	124
Klickitat, co., Wa., U.S.	D4	124
Klickitat, stm., Wa., U.S.	C4	124
Klimovsk, Russia	F20	18
Klin, Russia	E19	18
Klincy, Russia	I15	18
Kłodzko, Pol.	E16	8
Klondike, hist. reg., Yukon, Can.	D5	66
Klondike Gold Rush National Historical Park, Ak., U.S.	k22	79
Klosterneuburg, Aus.	G16	8
Kluane Lake, l., Yukon, Can.	D5	66
Klutina Lake, l., Ak., U.S.	g19	79
Knapp Creek, stm., W.V., U.S.	C5	125
Knee Lake, l., Man., Can.	B4	70
Kneža, Bul.	F8	16
Knife, stm., N.D., U.S.	B3	111
Knightdale, N.C., U.S.	B4	110
Knight Inlet, b., B.C., Can.	D5	69
Knight Island, i., Ak., U.S.	g18	79
Knightstown, In., U.S.	E6	91
Knightsville, In., U.S.	E3	91
Knightville Reservoir, res., Ma., U.S.	B2	98
Knin, Cro.	E11	14
Knittelfeld, Aus.	H14	8
Knob Noster, Mo., U.S.	C4	102
Knokke, Bel.	D3	8
Knollwood, W.V., U.S.	m12	125
Knott, co., Ky., U.S.	C6	94
Knox, In., U.S.	B4	91
Knox, Pa., U.S.	D2	115
Knox, co., Il., U.S.	B3	90
Knox, co., In., U.S.	G3	91
Knox, co., Ky., U.S.	D6	94
Knox, co., Me., U.S.	D4	96
Knox, co., Mo., U.S.	A5	102
Knox, co., Ne., U.S.	B8	104
Knox, co., Oh., U.S.	B3	112
Knox, co., Tn., U.S.	C10	119
Knox, co., Tx., U.S.	C3	120
Knox, Cape, c., B.C., Can.	B1	69
Knox City, Tx., U.S.	C3	120
Knoxville, Il., U.S.	C3	90
Knoxville, Ia., U.S.	C4	92
Knoxville, Tn., U.S.	D10	119
Knysna, S. Afr.	H4	44
Kōbe, Japan	H8	30
København (Copenhagen), Den.	I9	6
Koblenz, Ger.	E7	8
Kobrin, Bela.	I7	18
Kobuk, stm., Ak., U.S.	B8	79
Kobuk Valley National Park, Ak., U.S.	B8	79
Kočani, Mac.	H6	16
Kočevje, Slo.	D9	14
Kōchi, Japan	I6	30
Koch Peak, mtn., Mt., U.S.	E5	103
Kodiak, Ak., U.S.	D9	79
Kodiak Island, i., Ak., U.S.	D9	79
Koes, Nmb.	G3	44
Kofa Mountains, mts., Az., U.S.	D2	80
Köflach, Aus.	H15	8
Kōfu, Japan	G11	30
Koga, Japan	F12	30
Kogaluc, Baie, b., Que., Can.	E17	66
Kogaluk, stm., Newf., Can.	g9	72
Køge Bugt, b., Grnld.	D24	66
Kohala Mountains, mts., Hi., U.S.	C6	88
Kohāt, Pak.	D4	38
Kohīma, India	H16	38
Kohler, Wi., U.S.	E6	126
Kohtla-Järve, Est.	B10	18
Kokand, Uzb.	I12	22
Kokanee Glacier Provincial Park, B.C., Can.	E9	69
Kokemäki, Fin.	F14	6
Kokkola (Gamlakarleby), Fin.	E14	6
Koko Head, c., Hi., U.S.	B4	88
Kokolik, stm., Ak., U.S.	B7	79
Kokomo, In., U.S.	D5	91
Kokonau, Indon.	F10	32
Kokopo, Pap. N. Gui.	k17	50a
Kokosing, stm., Oh., U.S.	B3	112
Koksoak, stm., Que., Can.	E19	66
Kokstad, S. Afr.	H5	44
Kolaka, Indon.	F7	32
Kola Peninsula see Kol'skij poluostrov, pen., Russia	D5	22
Kolār, India	F5	37
Kolār Gold Fields, India	F5	37
Kol'čugino, Russia	E22	18
Kolda, Sen.	F3	42
Kolding, Den.	I7	6
Kolhāpur, India	D3	37
Kolín, Czech.	E15	8
Kollegāl, India	F4	37
Köln (Cologne), Ger.	E6	8
Koloa, Hi., U.S.	B2	88
Kołobrzeg, Pol.	A15	8
Kolomna, Russia	F21	18
Kolpaševo, Russia	F10	24
Kolpino, Russia	B13	18
Kol'skij poluostrov (Kola Peninsula), pen., Russia	D5	22
Kolwezi, Zaire	D5	44
Kolyma, stm., Russia	D25	24
Kolymskaja Nizmennost', pl., Russia	D24	24
Komárno, Slov.	H18	8
Komatsu, Japan	F9	30
Komló, Hung.	I18	8
Kommunizma, pik, mtn., Taj.	J12	22
Komoé, stm., Afr.	G5	42
Komotiní, Grc.	H9	16
Komsomolec, Ostrov, i., Russia	A12	24
Komsomol'sk-na-Amure, Russia	G21	24
Komsomol'skoj Pravdy, Ostrova, is., Russia	B15	24
Konahuanui, Puu, mtn., Hi., U.S.	g10	88
Konakovo, Russia	E19	18
Konawa, Ok., U.S.	C5	113
Konch, India	H8	38
Kondrovo, Russia	G18	18
Kông, Kaôh, i., Camb.	I7	34
Kongolo, Zaire	C5	44
Kongsberg, Nor.	G7	6
Kongsvinger, Nor.	F8	6
Kongsvoll, Nor.	E7	6
Kongur Shan, mtn., China	A6	38
Königs Wusterhausen, Ger.	C13	8
Konin, Pol.	C18	8
Konjic, Bos.	F12	14
Konomoc, Lake, res., Ct., U.S.	D7	84
Konqi, stm., China	C4	26
Konstanz, Ger.	H9	8
Kontagora, Nig.	F7	42
Kontiomäki, Fin.	D17	6
Kon Tum, Viet.	G10	34
Konya, Tur.	H14	4
Konza, Kenya	B7	44
Koochiching, co., Mn., U.S.	B4	100
Koolau Range, mts., Hi., U.S.	f10	88
Koontz Lake, In., U.S.	B5	91
Kooskia, Id., U.S.	C3	89
Kootenai, co., Id., U.S.	B2	89
Kootenay Lake, l., B.C., Can.	E9	69
Kootenay National Park, B.C., Can.	D9	69
Kopargaon, India	C3	37
Koper, Slo.	D8	14
Kopetdag, chrebet, mts., Asia	J9	22
Köping, Swe.	G10	6
Koppal, India	E4	37
Koppang, Nor.	F8	6
Koppel, Pa., U.S.	E1	115
Koprivnica, Cro.	C11	14
Kor'akskoje Nagorje, mts., Russia	E27	24
Korba, India	I10	38
Korbach, Ger.	D8	8
Korçë, Alb.	I4	16
Korčula, Cro.	G12	14
Korea, North, ctry., Asia	C12	26
Korea, South, ctry., Asia	D12	26
Korea Bay, b., Asia	D11	26
Korea Strait, strt., Asia	E12	26
Korf, Russia	E27	24
Korhogo, C. Iv.	G4	42
Korinthiakós Kólpos, b., Grc.	K6	16
Kórinthos (Corinth), Grc.	L6	16
Kōriyama, Japan	E13	30
Korliki, Russia	E10	24
Korogwe, Tan.	C7	44
Koronis, Lake, l., Mn., U.S.	E4	100
Koro Toro, Chad	E9	42
Korovin Volcano, vol., Ak., U.S.	E5	79
Korsakov, Russia	H22	24
Korsnäs, Fin.	E13	6
Korso, Fin.	F15	6
Kortrijk (Courtrai), Bel.	E3	8
Koruçam Burnu, c., N. Cyp.	B3	40
Koš-Agač, Russia	G11	24
Kosciusko, Ms., U.S.	B4	101
Kosciusko, co., In., U.S.	B6	91
Kosciusko, Mount, mtn., Austl.	G9	50
Koshkonong, Lake, l., Wi., U.S.	F5	126
Košice, Slov.	G21	8
Kosovska Mitrovica, Yugo.	G4	16
Kossuth, co., Ia., U.S.	A3	92
Kostroma, Russia	D23	18
Koszalin (Köslin), Pol.	A16	8
Kota, India	H6	38
Kota Baharu, Malay.	K7	34
Kotabumi, Indon.	F3	32
Kot Addu, Pak.	E4	38
Kota Kinabalu (Jesselton), Malay.	D6	32
Kotel'nyj, Ostrov, i., Russia	B21	24
Köthen, Ger.	D11	8
Kotka, Fin.	F16	6
Kot Kapūra, India	E6	38
Kotlas, Russia	E7	22
Kotlik, Ak., U.S.	C7	79
Kotor Varoš, Bos.	E12	14
Kotovsk, Russia	I24	18
Kotri, Pak.	H3	38
Kötschach [-Mauthen], Aus.	I12	8
Kottagūdem, India	D6	37
Kottayam, India	H4	37
Kotte, Sri L.	I5	37
Kotto, stm., Cen. Afr. Rep.	G10	42
Kotuj, stm., Russia	C14	24
Kotzebue, Ak., U.S.	B7	79
Kotzebue Sound, strt., Ak., U.S.	B7	79
Kouchibouguac National Park, N.B., Can.	C5	71
Koudougou, Burkina	F5	42
Koula-Moutou, Gabon	B2	44
Koumra, Chad	G9	42
Kountze, Tx., U.S.	D5	120
Koussi, Emi, mtn., Chad	E9	42
Koutiala, Mali	F4	42
Kouts, In., U.S.	B3	91
Kouvola, Fin.	F16	6
Kovrov, Russia	E24	18
Kowkcheh, stm., Afg.	B4	38
Kowloon (Jiulong), H.K.	M3	28
Kowt-e 'Ashrow, Afg.	C3	38
Koyukuk, stm., Ak., U.S.	B8	79
Koza, Japan	y27	31b
Kozáni, Grc.	I5	16
Kra, Isthmus of, Asia	I5	34
Krâchéh, Camb.	H9	34
Kragerø, Nor.	G7	6
Kragujevac, Yugo.	E4	16
Kraków, Pol.	E19	8
Kraljevica, Cro.	D9	14
Kraljevo, Yugo.	F4	16
Kramfors, Swe.	E11	6
Krångede, Swe.	E11	6
Kranj, Slo.	C9	14
Krasneno, Russia	E28	24
Krasnodar, Russia	H5	22
Krasnogorsk, Russia	F20	18
Krasnojarsk, Russia	F12	24
Krasnoje, Ozero, l., Russia	E28	24
Krasnosel'kup, Russia	D10	24
Krasnozavodsk, Russia	E21	18
Krebs, Ok., U.S.	C6	113
Kremenchuk, Ukr.	H4	22
Kremmling, Co., U.S.	A4	83
Krems an der Donau, Aus.	G15	8
Kresta, Zaliv, b., Russia	D30	24
Kribi, Cam.	H7	42
Kričov, Bela.	H14	18
Krishna, stm., India	D5	37
Krishnanagar, India	I13	38
Kristiansand, Nor.	G7	6
Kristianstad, Swe.	H10	6
Kristiansund, Nor.	E6	6
Kristinehamn, Swe.	G10	6
Kríti, i., Grc.	N8	16
Kritikón Pélagos, Grc.	N8	16
Krivoy Rog see Kryvyy Rih, Ukr.	H4	22
Krnov, Czech.	E17	8
Kroken, Nor.	D10	6
Kroměříž, Czech.	F17	8
Kronach, Ger.	E11	8
Krŏng Khémôreáh Phumint, Camb.	I7	34
Kronockij Zaliv, b., Russia	G26	24
Kronoki, Russia	G26	24
Kronštadt, Russia	B12	18
Kroonstad, S. Afr.	G5	44
Kropotkin, Russia	F17	24
Krosno, Pol.	F21	8
Krotz Springs, La., U.S.	D4	95
Krško, Slo.	D10	14
Kr'ukovo, Russia	D25	24
Krung Thep (Bangkok), Thai.	H6	34
Kruševac, Yugo.	F5	16
Krušné hory (Erzgebirge), mts., Eur.	E12	8
Kruzenšterna, Proliv, strt., Russia	H24	24
Kruzof Island, i., Ak., U.S.	m21	79
Kryms'kyy pivostriv (Crimea), pen., Ukr.	H4	22
Kryvyy Rih, Ukr.	H4	22
Ksenjevka, Russia	G17	24
Ksour Essaf, Tun.	N5	14
Kuala Kangsar, Malay.	L6	34
Kualakapuas, Indon.	F5	32
Kuala Krai, Malay.	L7	34
Kuala Kubu Baharu, Malay.	M6	34
Kuala Lumpur, Malay.	M6	34
Kuala Nerang, Malay.	K6	34
Kuala Pilah, Malay.	M7	34
Kuala Terengganu, Malay.	L7	34
Kuantan, Malay.	M7	34
Kubokawa, Japan	I6	30
Kuche, China	C3	26
Kuching, Malay.	E5	32
Kudat, Malay.	D6	32
Kudus, Indon.	m15	32
Kuee Ruins, hist., Hi., U.S.	D6	88
Kufstein, Aus.	H12	8
Kuhmo, Fin.	D17	6
Kuito, Ang.	D3	44
Kuiu Island, i., Ak., U.S.	m23	79
Kuivaniemi, Fin.	D15	6
Kukawa, Nig.	F8	42
Kula, Tur.	K12	16
Kula, Hi., U.S.	C5	88
Kul'ab, Taj.	B3	38
Kula Kangri, mtn., Bhu.	F14	38
Kulebaki, Russia	F25	18
Kulen Vakuf, Bos.	E11	14
Kulim, Malay.	L6	34
Kulmbach, Ger.	E11	8
Kulpmont, Pa., U.S.	E9	115
Kulunqi, China	C11	26
Kumagaya, Japan	F12	30
Kumajri, Arm.	I6	22
Kumamoto, Japan	J3	30
Kumano, Japan	I9	30
Kumano-nada, Japan	I9	30
Kumanovo, Mac.	G5	16
Kumasi, Ghana	G5	42
Kumbakonam, India	G5	37
Kume-shima, i., Japan	y26	31b
Kumo, Nig.	F8	42
Kumon Range, mts., Mya.	B4	34
Kumukahi, Cape, c., Hi., U.S.	D7	88
Kuna, Id., U.S.	F2	89
Kunašir, Ostrov (Kunashiri-tō), i., Russia	I23	24
Kundiān, Pak.	D4	38
Kundla, India	J4	38
Kunes, Nor.	A16	6
Kunghit Island, i., B.C., Can.	C2	69
Kuningan, Indon.	m14	33a
Kunlun Shan, mts., China	B12	38
Kunming, China	B7	34
Kunsan, S. Kor.	D12	26
Kunshan, China	D9	28
Kuopio, Fin.	E16	6
Kupang, Indon.	H7	32
Kupreanof Island, i., Ak., U.S.	m23	79
Kupres, Bos.	E12	14
Kura, stm., Asia	I7	22
Kurashiki, Japan	H6	30
Kurayoshi, Japan	G6	30
Kure, Japan	H5	30
Kure Island, i., Hi., U.S.	k12	88
Kurejka, stm., Russia	D11	24
Kurenalus, Fin.	D16	6
Kurgan-T'ube, Taj.	B3	38
Kurikka, Fin.	E14	6
Kuril'sk, Russia	H23	24
Kuril'skije Ostrova (Kuril Islands), is., Russia	H23	24
Kurmuk, Sudan	F12	42
Kurnool, India	E5	37
Kurow, N.Z.	F3	52
Kursk, Russia	G5	22
Kurtistown, Hi., U.S.	D6	88
Kuruman, S. Afr.	G4	44
Kurume, Japan	I3	30
Kurumkan, Russia	G16	24
Kurunegala, Sri L.	I6	37
Kuşadası Körfezi, b., Tur.	L11	16
Kuş Gölü, l., Tur.	I11	16
Kushima, Japan	K4	30
Kushiro, Japan	q22	30a
Kushtia, Bngl.	I13	38
Kushui, China	C5	26
Kuskokwim, stm., Ak., U.S.	C8	79
Kuskokwim Bay, b., Ak., U.S.	D7	79
Kuskokwim Mountains, mts., Ak., U.S.	C8	79
Kūstī, Sudan	F12	42
K'us'ur, Russia	C19	24
Kut, Ko, i., Thai.	I7	34
Kutaisi, Geor.	I6	22
Kūt al-Imāra, Iraq	B4	46
Kutch, Gulf of, b., India	I3	38
Kutina, Cro.	D11	14
Kutno, Pol.	C19	8
Kutu, Zaire	B3	44
Kutztown, Pa., U.S.	E10	115
Kuujjuaq, Que., Can.	g13	74
Kuusamo, Fin.	D17	6
Kuusankoski, Fin.	F16	6
Kuvango, Ang.	D3	44
Kuwait, ctry., Asia	C4	46
Kuwait see Al-Kuwayt, Kuw.	C4	46
Kuwana, Japan	G9	30
Kuybyshev see Samara, Russia	G8	22
Kuzneck, Russia	G7	22
Kvikkjokk, Swe.	C11	6
Kwando (Cuando), stm., Afr.	E4	44
Kwangchow see Guangzhou, China	L2	28
Kwangju, S. Kor.	D12	26
Kwango (Cuango), stm., Afr.	B3	44
Kwekwe, Zimb.	E5	44
Kwethluk, Ak., U.S.	C7	79
Kwidzyn, Pol.	B18	8
Kwigillingok, Ak., U.S.	D7	79
Kwilu (Cuilo), stm., Afr.	B3	44
Kyaiklat, Mya.	F3	34
Kyaikto, Mya.	F4	34
Kyle, Tx., U.S.	E4	120
Kyle of Lochalsh, Scot., U.K.	D7	7
Kyoga, Lake, l., Ug.	A6	44
Kyōto, Japan	G8	30
Kyrgyzstan, ctry., Asia	I12	22
Kyuquot Sound, strt., B.C., Can.	E4	69
Kyūshū, i., Japan	I3	30
Kyūshū-sanchi, mts., Japan	J4	30
Kyyiv, Ukr.	G4	22
Kyyjärvi, Fin.	E15	6
Kyzyl, Russia	G12	24

Name — Map Ref — Page

Kzyl-Orda, Kaz. I11 22

L

Laa an der Thaya, Aus. G16 8
La Almunia de Doña Godina, Spain D10 12
La Asunción, Ven. B11 58
Laau Point, c., Hi., U.S. B4 88
L'Abacou, Pointe, c., Haiti E11 64
Labadieville, La., U.S. E5 95
La Bañeza, Spain C6 12
La Barca, Mex. G8 62
La Barge, Wy., U.S. D2 127
La Barge Creek, stm., Wy., U.S. D2 127
La Baule, Fr. E4 10
Labé, Gui. F3 42
Labe (Elbe), stm., Eur. E14 8
La Belle, Fl., U.S. F5 86
La Belle, Mo., U.S. A6 102
Labette, co., Ks., U.S. E8 93
Labin, Cro. D9 14
La Bisbal, Spain D15 12
Labouheyre, Fr. H6 10
Labrador, reg., Newf., Can. g9 72
Labrador City, Newf., Can. h8 72
Labrador Sea, N.A. E22 66
Lábrea, Braz. E6 54
Labutta, Mya. F3 34
La Canada Flintridge, Ca., U.S. m12 82
Lacanau, Fr. H5 10
La Cañiza, Spain C3 12
La Canourgue, Fr. H10 10
La Carolina, Spain G8 12
Lacaune, Fr. I9 10
Lac-Bouchette, Que., Can. A5 74
Lac-Brome, Que., Can. D5 74
Laccadive Sea, Asia H3 37
Lac-Carré, Que., Can. C3 74
Lac Courte Oreilles Indian Reservation, Wi., U.S. C2 126
Lac du Bonnet, Man., Can. D3 70
Lac du Flambeau, Wi., U.S. B4 126
Lac du Flambeau Indian Reservation, Wi., U.S. C3 126
La Ceiba, Hond. G4 64
La Ceiba, Ven. C7 58
La Center, Ky., U.S. e9 94
Lac-Etchemin, Que., Can. C7 74
Lacey, Wa., U.S. B3 124
La Charité [-sur-Loire], Fr. E10 10
La Châtre, Fr. F8 10
La Chaux-de-Fonds, Switz. E13 10
Lachine, Que., Can. D4 74
La Chorrera, Col. H6 58
La Chorrera, Pan. J8 64
Lachute, Que., Can. D3 74
La Ciotat, Fr. I12 10
Lackawanna, N.Y., U.S. C2 109
Lackawanna, co., Pa., U.S. D10 115
Lackland Air Force Base, mil., Tx., U.S. k7 120
Lac La Biche, Alta., Can. B5 68
Lac la Hache, B.C., Can. D7 69
Laclede, co., Mo., U.S. D5 102
Lac-Mégantic, Que., Can. D7 74
Lacolle, Que., Can. D4 74
Lacombe, Alta., Can. C4 68
Lacombe, La., U.S. D6 95
Lacon, Il., U.S. B4 90
Laconia, N.H., U.S. C4 106
La Conner, Wa., U.S. A3 124
Lacoochee, Fl., U.S. D4 86
La Coruña, Spain B3 12
Lac qui Parle, co., Mn., U.S. F2 100
Lac qui Parle, stm., Mn., U.S. F2 100
La Creek Lake, l., S.D., U.S. D4 118
La Crescent, Mn., U.S. G7 100
La Crete, Alta., Can. f7 68
La Crosse, In., U.S. B4 91
La Crosse, Ks., U.S. D4 93
La Crosse, Wi., U.S. E2 126
La Crosse, co., Wi., U.S. E2 126
La Crosse, stm., Wi., U.S. E3 126
La Cruz, Nic. H5 64
La Cygne, Ks., U.S. D9 93
Ladd, Il., U.S. B4 90
Ladies Island, i., S.C., U.S. G6 117
Lādīz, Iran C7 46
Lādnun, India G6 38
Ladoga, In., U.S. E4 91
Ladoga, Lake see Ladožskoje Ozero, l., Russia F18 6
La Dorada, Col. E5 58
Ladožskoje Ozero (Lake Ladoga), l., Russia F18 6
Ladson, S.C., U.S. F7 117
Lady Lake, Fl., U.S. D5 86
Lady Laurier, Mount, mtn., B.C., Can. A6 69
Ladysmith, B.C., Can. E6 69
Ladysmith, S. Afr. G5 44
Ladysmith, Wi., U.S. C2 126
Lae, Pap. N. Gui. m16 50a
La Encantada, Cerro de, mtn., Mex. B2 62
La Esmeralda, Ven. F10 58
La Esperanza, Hond. G3 64
La Estrada, Spain C3 12
La Farge, Wi., U.S. E3 126
Lafayette, Al., U.S. C4 78
Lafayette, Co., U.S. B5 83
Lafayette, Ga., U.S. B1 87
Lafayette, In., U.S. D4 91
Lafayette, La., U.S. D3 95
Lafayette, N.C., U.S. B3 110
Lafayette, Or., U.S. B3 114
La Fayette, R.I., U.S. E4 116
Lafayette, Tn., U.S. A5 119
Lafayette, co., Ar., U.S. D2 81
Lafayette, co., Fl., U.S. C3 86
Lafayette, co., La., U.S. D3 95
Lafayette, co., Ms., U.S. A4 101
Lafayette, co., Mo., U.S. B4 102
Lafayette, co., Wi., U.S. F3 126
Lafayette, Mount, mtn., N.H., U.S. B3 106
La Feria, Tx., U.S. F4 120
La Ferté-Bernard, Fr. D7 10
La Ferté-Macé, Fr. D6 10
La Ferté-Saint-Aubin, Fr. E8 10
Lafia, Nig. G7 42
Lafitte, La., U.S. k11 95
La Flèche, Fr. E6 10
La Follette, Tn., U.S. C9 119
La Fontaine, In., U.S. C6 91
La Fortuna, C.R. I5 64
Lafourche, La., U.S. E5 95
Lafourche, co., La., U.S. E5 95
La France, S.C., U.S. B2 117
La Fregeneda, Spain E5 12
La Fría, Ven. C6 58
La Fuente de San Esteban, Spain E5 12
Lågen, stm., Nor. F8 6
Laghouat, Alg. B6 42
Lago, Mount, mtn., Wa., U.S. A5 124
Lagonegro, Italy I10 14
Lagos, Nig. G6 42
Lagos de Moreno, Mex. G9 62
La Goulette, Tun. M5 14
La Grand'Combe, Fr. H11 10
La Grande, Or., U.S. B8 114
La Grande, stm., Que., Can. h11 74
La Grande Deux, Réservoir, res., Que., Can. h11 74
La Grange, Austl. C4 50
La Grange, Ga., U.S. C1 87
La Grange, Il., U.S. B6 90
Lagrange, In., U.S. A7 91
La Grange, Ky., U.S. B4 94
La Grange, Mo., U.S. A6 102
La Grange, N.C., U.S. B5 110
Lagrange, Oh., U.S. A3 112
La Grange, Tx., U.S. E4 120
Lagrange, co., In., U.S. A7 91
La Grange Park, Il., U.S. k9 90
La Gran Sabana, pl., Ven. E12 58
La Grita, Ven. C7 58
La Guadeloupe (Saint-Evariste), Que., Can. D7 74
La Guaira, Ven. B9 58
La Guajira, Península de, pen., S.A. A7 58
Laguardia, Spain C9 12
La Guardia, Spain D3 12
La Guerche-de-Bretagne, Fr. E5 10
La Guerche-sur-l'aubois, Fr. F9 10
Laguiole, Fr. H9 10
Laguna, N.M., U.S. B2 108
Laguna Beach, Ca., U.S. F5 82
Laguna Dam, U.S. E1 80
Laguna Indian Reservation, N.M., U.S. C2 108
Lagunillas, Bol. G6 54
La Habana (Havana), Cuba C6 64
La Habra, Ca., U.S. n13 82
Lahaina, Hi., U.S. C5 88
La Harpe, Il., U.S. C3 90
La Harpe, Ks., U.S. E8 93
Lahat, Indon. F3 32
La Have, stm., N.S., Can. E5 71
La Haye-du-Puits, Fr. C5 10
Laḥij, Yemen F3 46
Laholm, Swe. H9 6
Lahoma, Ok., U.S. A3 113
Lahontan Reservoir, res., Nv., U.S. D2 105
Lahore, Pak. E6 38
Lahr, Ger. G7 8
Lahti, Fin. F15 6
Laie, Hi., U.S. B4 88
L'Aigle, Fr. D7 10
Laignes, Fr. E11 10
Laihia, Fin. E14 6
Laingsburg, S. Afr. H4 44
Laingsburg, Mi., U.S. F6 99
Lairg, Scot., U.K. C8 7
Laissac, Fr. H9 10
Laiyang, China D11 26
La Jara, Co., U.S. D5 83
Lajes, Braz. E11 54
La Jolla, Point, c., Ca., U.S. o15 82
La Joya, Mex. A2 62
La Junta, Mex. C6 62
La Junta, Co., U.S. D7 83
Lake, co., Ca., U.S. C2 82
Lake, co., Co., U.S. B4 83
Lake, co., Fl., U.S. D5 86
Lake, co., Il., U.S. A6 90
Lake, co., In., U.S. B3 91
Lake, co., Mi., U.S. E5 99
Lake, co., Mn., U.S. C7 100
Lake, co., Mt., U.S. C2 103
Lake, co., Oh., U.S. A4 112
Lake, co., Or., U.S. E6 114
Lake, co., S.D., U.S. C8 118
Lake, co., Tn., U.S. A2 119
Lake Alfred, Fl., U.S. D5 86
Lake Andes, S.D., U.S. D7 118
Lake Ariel, Pa., U.S. D11 115
Lake Arrowhead, Ca., U.S. E5 82
Lake Arthur, La., U.S. D3 95
Lake Barcroft, Va., U.S. *B5 123
Lake Benton, Mn., U.S. F2 100
Lake Bluff, Il., U.S. A6 90
Lake Butler, Fl., U.S. B4 86
Lake Charles, La., U.S. D2 95
Lake Chelan National Recreation Area, Wa., U.S. A5 124
Lake City, Ar., U.S. B5 81
Lake City, Fl., U.S. B4 86
Lake City, Ia., U.S. B3 92
Lake City, Mi., U.S. D5 99
Lake City, Mn., U.S. F6 100
Lake City, Pa., U.S. B1 115
Lake City, S.C., U.S. D8 117
Lake City, Tn., U.S. C9 119
Lake Clark National Park, Ak., U.S. C9 79
Lake Cowichan, B.C., Can. g11 69
Lake Creek, stm., Wa., U.S. B7 124
Lake Crystal, Mn., U.S. F4 100
Lake Delta, N.Y., U.S. B5 109
Lake Delton, Wi., U.S. E4 126
Lake District National Park, Eng., U.K. G9 7
Lake Elsinore, Ca., U.S. F5 82
Lake Erie Beach, N.Y., U.S. C1 109
Lakefield, Ont., Can. C6 73
Lakefield, Mn., U.S. G3 100
Lake Forest, Il., U.S. A6 90
Lake Fork, stm., Ut., U.S. C5 121
Lake Geneva, Wi., U.S. F5 126
Lake Hamilton, Ar., U.S. g7 81
Lake Harbour, N.W. Ter., Can. D19 66
Lake Havasu City, Az., U.S. C1 80
Lake Helen, Fl., U.S. D5 86
Lakehurst, N.J., U.S. C4 107
Lakehurst Naval Air Station, mil., N.J., U.S. C4 107
Lake in the Hills, Il., U.S. h8 90
Lake Jackson, Tx., U.S. r14 120
Lake Katrine, N.Y., U.S. D7 109
Lakeland, Fl., U.S. D5 86
Lakeland, Ga., U.S. E3 87
Lake Linden, Mi., U.S. A2 99
Lake Louise, Alta., Can. D2 68
Lake Magdalene, Fl., U.S. o11 86
Lake Mary, Fl., U.S. D5 86
Lake Mead National Recreation Area, U.S. H7 105
Lake Meredith National Recreation Area, Tx., U.S. B2 120
Lake Mills, Ia., U.S. A4 92
Lake Mills, Wi., U.S. E5 126
Lakemore, Oh., U.S. A4 112
Lake Mountain, mtn., Wy., U.S. E6 127
Lake Nebagamon, Wi., U.S. B2 126
Lake Odessa, Mi., U.S. F5 99
Lake of the Woods, co., Mn., U.S. B4 100
Lake Orion, Mi., U.S. F7 99
Lake Oswego, Or., U.S. B4 114
Lake Ozark, Mo., U.S. C5 102
Lake Park, Fl., U.S. F6 86
Lake Park, Ia., U.S. A2 92
Lake Park, Mn., U.S. D2 100
Lake Placid, Fl., U.S. E5 86
Lake Placid, N.Y., U.S. A7 109
Lake Pontchartrain Causeway, La., U.S. h11 95
Lakeport, Ca., U.S. C2 82
Lake Preston, S.D., U.S. C8 118
Lake Providence, La., U.S. B4 95
Lake Range, mts., Nv., U.S. C2 105
Lake Ridge, Va., U.S. *B5 123
Lake Shore, Md., U.S. B5 97
Lakeshore, Ms., U.S. E4 101
Lakeside, Az., U.S. C6 80
Lakeside, Ca., U.S. F5 82
Lakeside, Ct., U.S. D3 84
Lakeside, Mt., U.S. B2 103
Lakeside, Oh., U.S. A3 112
Lakeside, Or., U.S. D2 114
Lakeside Park, Ky., U.S. h13 94
Lake Station, In., U.S. A3 91
Lake Station, Ok., U.S. A5 113
Lake Stevens, Wa., U.S. A3 124
Lake Superior Provincial Park, Ont., Can. p18 73
Lake Swamp, stm., S.C., U.S. D8 117
Lake Tansi Village, Tn., U.S. D8 119
Lake Valley, val., Nv., U.S. E7 105
Lake View, Ia., U.S. B2 92
Lakeview, Mi., U.S. E5 99
Lakeview, Oh., U.S. B2 112
Lakeview, Or., U.S. E6 114
Lake View, S.C., U.S. C9 117
Lake Villa, Il., U.S. h8 90
Lake Village, Ar., U.S. D4 81
Lake Village, In., U.S. B3 91
Lakeville, Ct., U.S. B2 84
Lakeville, In., U.S. A5 91
Lakeville, Ma., U.S. C6 98
Lakeville, Mn., U.S. F5 100
Lake Waccamaw, N.C., U.S. C4 110
Lake Wales, Fl., U.S. E5 86
Lakewood, Ca., U.S. n12 82
Lakewood, Co., U.S. B5 83
Lakewood, Il., U.S. D5 90
Lakewood, Ia., U.S. f8 92
Lakewood, N.J., U.S. C4 107
Lakewood, N.Y., U.S. C1 109
Lakewood, Oh., U.S. A4 112
Lakewood Center, Wa., U.S. B3 124
Lake Worth, Fl., U.S. F6 86
Lake Worth Inlet, b., Fl., U.S. F7 86
Lake Zurich, Il., U.S. h8 90
Lakhīmpur, India G9 38
Lakin, Ks., U.S. E2 93
Lakota, N.D., U.S. A7 111
Lakselv, Nor. A15 6
Lakshadweep, state, India H3 37
Lakshadweep, is., India H2 37
Lalbenque, Fr. H8 10
La Libertad, Guat. F2 64
La Libertad, Mex. C3 62
Lalinde, Fr. H7 10
La Línea, Spain I6 12
Lalitpur, India H8 38
Lalitpur, Nepal G11 38
La Loupe, Fr. D8 10
La Luz, N.M., U.S. E4 108
Lama, Ozero, l., Russia D12 24
La Maddalena, Italy H4 14
La Madrid, Arg. B3 56
La Malbaie, Que., Can. B7 74
La Mancha, Mex. E8 62
La Mancha, reg., Spain G8 12
Lamar, Ar., U.S. B2 81
Lamar, Co., U.S. C8 83
Lamar, Mo., U.S. D3 102
Lamar, Pa., U.S. D7 115
Lamar, S.C., U.S. C7 117
Lamar, co., Al., U.S. B1 78
Lamar, co., Ga., U.S. C2 87
Lamar, co., Ms., U.S. D4 101
Lamar, co., Tx., U.S. C5 120
Lamar, stm., Wy., U.S. B2 127
Lamarche, Fr. D12 10
La Mauricie, Parc National de, Que., Can. C5 74
Lamb, co., Tx., U.S. B1 120
Lamballe, Fr. D4 10
Lambaréné, Gabon B2 44
Lambert, Ms., U.S. A3 101
Lambert Glacier, Ant. B19 47
Lamberton, Mn., U.S. F3 100
Lambert's Bay, S. Afr. H3 44
Lambertville, Mi., U.S. G7 99
Lambertville, N.J., U.S. C3 107
Lambton, Cape, c., N.W. Ter., Can. B8 66
Lame Deer, Mt., U.S. E10 103
Lamego, Port. D4 12
Lamèque, N.B., Can. B5 71
Lamèque, Île, i., N.B., Can. B5 71
La Mesa, Ca., U.S. F5 82
La Mesa, N.M., U.S. E3 108
Lamesa, Tx., U.S. C2 120
Lamía, Grc. K6 16
Lamoille, Nv., U.S. C6 105
Lamoille, co., Vt., U.S. B3 122
Lamoille, stm., Vt., U.S. B3 122
La Moine, stm., Il., U.S. C3 90
Lamoni, Ia., U.S. D4 92
Lamont, Alta., Can. C4 68
Lamont, Ca., U.S. E4 82
La Monte, Mo., U.S. C4 102
La Motte, Isle, i., Vt., U.S. B2 122
Lamotte-Beuvron, Fr. E9 10
La Moure, N.D., U.S. C7 111
La Moure, co., N.D., U.S. C7 111
Lampang, Thai. E5 34
Lampasas, Tx., U.S. D3 120
Lampasas, co., Tx., U.S. D3 120
Lampedusa, Isola di, i., Italy N7 14
Lampertheim, Ger. F8 8
Lampman, Sask., Can. H4 75
Lamprey, stm., N.H., U.S. D4 106
Lamu, Kenya B8 44
La Mure, Fr. H12 10
Lanai, i., Hi., U.S. C4 88
Lanai City, Hi., U.S. C5 88
Lanaihale, mtn., Hi., U.S. C5 88
Lanark, Ont., Can. C8 73
Lanark, Il., U.S. A4 90
Lanark, W.V., U.S. D3 125
Lanbi Kyun, i., Mya. I5 34
Lancaster, Ont., Can. B10 73
Lancaster, Eng., U.K. G10 7
Lancaster, Ca., U.S. E4 82
Lancaster, Ky., U.S. C5 94
Lancaster, Mo., U.S. A5 102
Lancaster, N.H., U.S. B3 106
Lancaster, N.Y., U.S. C2 109
Lancaster, Oh., U.S. C3 112
Lancaster, Pa., U.S. F9 115
Lancaster, S.C., U.S. B6 117
Lancaster, Tx., U.S. n10 120
Lancaster, Wi., U.S. F3 126
Lancaster, co., Ne., U.S. D9 104
Lancaster, co., Pa., U.S. G9 115
Lancaster, co., S.C., U.S. B6 117
Lancaster, co., Va., U.S. C6 123
Lancaster Sound, strt., N.W. Ter., Can. B16 66
Lance Creek, stm., Wy., U.S. C8 127
Lanciano, Italy G9 14
Landau, Ger. F8 8
Landau an der Isar, Ger. G12 8
Land Between the Lakes, U.S. f9 94
Lander, Wy., U.S. D4 127
Lander, co., Nv., U.S. C4 105
Landerneau, Fr. D2 10
Landess, In., U.S. C6 91
Landete, Spain F10 12
Landis, N.C., U.S. B2 110
Lando, S.C., U.S. B5 117
Landquart, Switz. F16 10
Landrum, S.C., U.S. A3 117
Land's End, c., Eng., U.K. K7 7
Lands End, c., R.I., U.S. F5 116
Landshut, Ger. G12 8
Landskrona, Swe. I9 6
Lane, co., Ks., U.S. D3 93
Lane, co., Or., U.S. C4 114
Lanesboro, Mn., U.S. G7 100
Lanett, Al., U.S. C4 78
Langar, Afg. B5 38
Långban, Swe. G10 6
Langdon, N.D., U.S. A7 111
Langeac, Fr. G10 10
Langeais, Fr. E7 10
Langeloth, Pa., U.S. F1 115
Langenhagen, Ger. C9 8
Langenthal, Switz. E14 10
Langholm, Scot., U.K. F9 7
Langhorne, Pa., U.S. F12 115
Langlade, co., Wi., U.S. C4 126
Langley, B.C., Can. f13 69
Langley, S.C., U.S. E4 117
Langley, Wa., U.S. A3 124
Langley Air Force Base, mil., Va., U.S. h15 123
Langley Park, Md., U.S. f9 97
Langnau, Switz. F14 10
Langogne, Fr. H10 10
Langon, Fr. H6 10
Langres, Fr. E1 10
Langsa, Indon. E2 32
Lang Son, Viet. D9 34
Langston, Ok., U.S. B4 113
Languedoc, hist. reg., Fr. I9 10
L'Anguille, stm., Ar., U.S. B5 81
Langzhong, China E8 26
Lanham, Md., U.S. C4 97
Lanier, co., Ga., U.S. E3 87
Lannemezan, Fr. I7 10
Lannilis, Fr. D2 10
Lannion, Fr. D3 10
Lannon, Wi., U.S. m11 126
L'Annonciation, Que., Can. C3 74
Lansdale, Pa., U.S. F11 115
Lansdowne, Md., U.S. B4 97
L'Anse, Mi., U.S. B2 99
L'Anse-au-Loup, Newf., Can. C3 72
L'Anse Indian Reservation, Mi., U.S. B2 99
Lansford, Pa., U.S. E10 115
Lansing, Il., U.S. B6 90
Lansing, Ia., U.S. A6 92
Lansing, Ks., U.S. C9 93
Lansing, Mi., U.S. F6 99
Lantana, Fl., U.S. F6 86
Lantau Island, i., H.K. M2 28
Lanusei, Italy J4 14
Lanxi, China F8 28
Lanzarote, i., Spain p27 13b
Lanzhou, China D7 26
Laoag, Phil. B7 32
Lao Cai, Viet. C7 34
Laon, Fr. C10 10
La Oroya, Peru F3 54
Laos, ctry., Asia B3 32
Lapalisse, Fr. F10 10
La Palma, Col. E5 58
La Palma, Pan. J8 64
La Palma, i., Spain p23 13b
La Paragua, Ven. D11 58
La Paz, Arg. C5 56
La Paz, Arg. C3 56
La Paz, Bol. G5 54
La Paz, Mex. E4 62
La Paz, co., Az., U.S. D2 80
La Paz, Bahía de, b., Mex. E4 62
Lapeer, Mi., U.S. E7 99
Lapeer, co., Mi., U.S. E7 99
Lapel, In., U.S. D6 91
La Perouse Strait, strt., Asia B15 26
La Piedad [Cavadas], Mex. G8 62
La Pine, Or., U.S. D5 114
Lapinlahti, Fin. E16 6
La Place, La., U.S. h11 95
Lapland, reg., Eur. C14 6
La Plata, Arg. C5 56
La Plata, Md., U.S. C4 97
La Plata, Mo., U.S. A5 102
La Plata, co., Co., U.S. D3 83
La Plata Mountains, mts., Co., U.S. D3 83
La Plata Peak, mtn., Co., U.S. B4 83
La Platte, stm., Vt., U.S. C2 122
La Pocatière, Que., Can. B7 74
Laporte, Co., U.S. A5 83
La Porte, In., U.S. A4 91
La Porte, Tx., U.S. r14 120
La Porte, co., In., U.S. A4 91
La Porte City, Ia., U.S. B5 92
Lappeenranta, Fin. F17 6
La Prairie, Que., Can. D4 74
La Pryor, Tx., U.S. E3 120
Laptevych, More (Laptev Sea), Russia B19 24
Lapua, Fin. E14 6
La Puebla, Spain F15 12
La Puebla de Montalbán, Spain F7 12
La Push, Wa., U.S. B1 124
Lapwai, Id., U.S. C2 89
La Quiaca, Arg. A3 56
L'Aquila, Italy G8 14
Lār, Iran C5 46
Larache, Mor. A4 42
Laramie, Wy., U.S. E7 127
Laramie, co., Wy., U.S. E8 127
Laramie, stm., U.S. E7 127
Laramie Mountains, mts., Wy., U.S. D7 127
Laramie Peak, mtn., Wy., U.S. D7 127
Larantuka, Indon. G7 32
L'Arbresle, Fr. G11 10
Lärbro, Swe. H12 6
Larche, Col de, Eur. H13 10
Larchmont, N.Y., U.S. h13 109
Larchwood, Ia., U.S. A1 92
Laredo, Tx., U.S. F3 120
La Réole, Fr. H6 10
Largeau, Chad E9 42
L'argentière-la-Bessée, Fr. H13 10
Lar Gerd, Afg. C2 38
Largo, Fl., U.S. E4 86
Largo, Cañon, val., N.M., U.S. A2 108
Largo, Key, i., Fl., U.S. G6 86
Largs, Scot., U.K. F8 7
Larimer, co., Co., U.S. A5 83
Larimore, N.D., U.S. B8 111
La Rioja, Arg. B3 56
Lárisa, Grc. J6 16
Larjak, Russia E10 24
Lārkāna, Pak. G3 38
Lark Harbour, Newf., Can. D2 72
Larkspur, Ca., U.S. h7 82
Larksville, Pa., U.S. n17 115
Lárnax (Larnaca), Cyp. B3 40
Larne, N. Ire., U.K. G7 7
Larned, Ks., U.S. D4 93
La Robla, Spain C6 12
La Roca de la Sierra, Spain F5 12
La Rochefoucauld, Fr. G7 10
La Rochelle, Fr. F5 10
La Roche-sur-Yon, Fr. F5 10
La Roda, Spain F9 12
La Romana, Dom. Rep. E13 64
Laroquebrou, Fr. H9 10
Larose, La., U.S. E5 95
La Rubia, Arg. C4 56
Larue, co., Ky., U.S. C4 94
Laruns, Fr. J6 10
Larvik, Nor. G7 6
LaSalle, Que., Can. q19 74
La Salle, Co., U.S. A6 83
La Salle, Il., U.S. B4 90
La Salle, co., Il., U.S. B4 90
La Salle, co., La., U.S. C3 95
La Salle, co., Tx., U.S. E3 120
Las Animas, Co., U.S. C7 83
Las Animas, co., Co., U.S. D6 83
Las Anod, Som. G4 46

Name — Map Ref — Page

La Sarre, Que., Can. k11 74
Las Casitas, Cerro, mtn., Mex. F5 62
Las Choapas, Mex. I12 62
La Scie, Newf., Can. D4 72
Las Colimas, Mex. E10 62
Las Cruces, N.M., U.S. E3 108
Las Delicias, Mex. J14 62
La Selle, Pic, mtn., Haiti E11 64
La Serena, Chile B2 56
Las Escobas, Mex. B2 62
La Seyne, Fr. I12 10
Las Flores, Arg. D5 56
Lashio, Mya. C4 34
Laško, Slo. C10 14
Las Lomitas, Arg. A4 56
Las Minas, Cerro, mtn., Hond. G3 64
La Solana, Spain G8 12
Las Palmas de Gran Canaria, Spain p25 13b
La Spezia, Italy E4 14
Las Piedras, Ur. C5 56
Las Plumas, Arg. E3 56
Lassen, co., Ca., U.S. B3 82
Lassen Peak, vol., Ca., U.S. B3 82
Lassen Volcanic National Park, Ca., U.S. B3 82
L'Assomption, Que., Can. D4 74
Las Termas, Arg. B4 56
Last Mountain Lake, l., Sask., Can. F3 75
Las Tórtolas, Cerro, mtn., S.A. B3 56
Las Varas, Mex. C5 62
Las Vegas, Nv., U.S. G6 105
Las Vegas, N.M., U.S. B4 108
Latacunga, Ec. H3 58
Latah, co., Id., U.S. C2 89
Latakia see Al-Lādhiqīyah, Syria B4 40
La Teste-de-Buch, Fr. H5 10
Lathrop, Mo., U.S. B3 102
Lathrop Wells, Nv., U.S. G5 105
Latimer, co., Ok., U.S. C6 113
Latina, Italy H7 14
Laton, Ca., U.S. D4 82
La Tortuga, Isla, i., Ven. B10 58
Latour Peak, mtn., Id., U.S. B2 89
Latrobe, Pa., U.S. F3 115
Latta, S.C., U.S. C9 117
La Tuque, Que., Can. B5 74
Lātūr, India C4 37
Latvia, ctry., Eur. E7 18
Lauchhammer, Ger. D13 8
Lauderdale, Ms., U.S. C5 101
Lauderdale, co., Al., U.S. A2 78
Lauderdale, co., Ms., U.S. C5 101
Lauderdale, co., Tn., U.S. B2 119
Lauderdale Lakes, Fl., U.S. r13 86
Lauenburg, Ger. B10 8
Laughlin, Nv., U.S. H7 105
Laughlin Air Force Base, mil., Tx., U.S. E2 120
Laughlin Peak, mtn., N.M., U.S. A5 108
Laughlintown, Pa., U.S. F3 115
Launceston, Austl. H9 50
Launceston, Eng., U.K. K8 7
Launching Point, c., P.E.I., Can. C7 71
La Union, El Sal. H4 64
La Unión, Spain H11 12
La Unión, Ven. C9 58
La Urbana, Ven. D9 58
Laurel, De., U.S. F3 85
Laurel, Fl., U.S. E4 86
Laurel, Md., U.S. B4 97
Laurel, Ms., U.S. D4 101
Laurel, Mt., U.S. E8 103
Laurel, Ne., U.S. B8 104
Laurel, Va., U.S. C5 123
Laurel, co., Ky., U.S. C5 94
Laurel, stm., Ky., U.S. D5 94
Laurel Bay, S.C., U.S. G6 117
Laurel Creek, stm., W.V., U.S. n14 125
Laurel Creek, stm., W.V., U.S. m12 125
Laureldale, Pa., U.S. F10 115
Laurel Fork, stm., W.V., U.S. C5 125
Laurel Hill, N.C., U.S. C3 110
Laurel River Lake, res., Ky., U.S. D5 94
Laurence G. Hanscom Air Force Base, mil., Ma., U.S. g10 98
Laurence Harbor, N.J., U.S. C4 107
Laurens, Ia., U.S. B3 92
Laurens, S.C., U.S. C3 117
Laurens, co., Ga., U.S. D4 87
Laurens, co., S.C., U.S. C4 117
Laurentides, Que., Can. D4 74
Laurentides, Parc Provincial des, Que., Can. B6 74
Laurier, Que., Can. C6 74
Laurière, Fr. F8 10
Laurierville, Que., Can. C6 74
Laurinburg, N.C., U.S. C3 110
Laurium, Mi., U.S. A2 99
Lausanne, Switz. F13 10
Laut, Pulau, i., Indon. F6 32
Laut, Pulau, i., Indon. L9 34
Lautaro, Chile D2 56
Lauterbach, Ger. E9 8
Laut Kecil, Kepulauan, is., Indon. F6 32
Lauzon (part of Lévis-Lauzon), Que., Can. C6 74
Lava Beds National Monument, Ca., U.S. B3 82
Lavaca, Ar., U.S. B1 81
Lavaca, co., Tx., U.S. E4 120
Lavagh More, mtn., Ire. G4 7
Laval, Que., Can. D4 74
Laval, Fr. D6 10
La Vale, Md., U.S. k13 97
Lavaltrie, Que., Can. D4 74
Lavapié, Punta, c., Chile D2 56
Laveen, Az., U.S. m8 80
La Vega, Dom. Rep. E12 64
La Vela, Cabo de, c., Col. A6 58
Lavello, Italy H10 14
L'Avenir, Que., Can. D5 74
La Vergne, Tn., U.S. A5 119
La Verkin, Ut., U.S. F2 121
La Verne, Ca., U.S. m13 82
Laverne, Ok., U.S. A2 113
La Veta, Co., U.S. D5 83
Lavia, Fin. F14 6
La Vista, Ga., U.S. *h8 87
La Vista, Ne., U.S. g12 104
Lavonia, Ga., U.S. B3 87
Lavon Lake, res., Tx., U.S. m10 120
La Voulte-sur-Rhône, Fr. H11 10
Lavras, Braz. F6 57
Lawai, Hi., U.S. B2 88
Lawang, Indon. m16 33a
Lawers, Ben, mtn., Scot., U.K. E8 7
Lawn, Newf., Can. E4 72
Lawrence, In., U.S. E5 91
Lawrence, Ks., U.S. D8 93
Lawrence, Ma., U.S. A5 98
Lawrence, Mi., U.S. F4 99
Lawrence, N.Y., U.S. k13 109
Lawrence, co., Al., U.S. A2 78
Lawrence, co., Ar., U.S. A4 81
Lawrence, co., Il., U.S. E6 90
Lawrence, co., In., U.S. G4 91
Lawrence, co., Ky., U.S. B7 94
Lawrence, co., Ms., U.S. D3 101
Lawrence, co., Mo., U.S. D4 102
Lawrence, co., Oh., U.S. D3 112
Lawrence, co., Pa., U.S. E1 115
Lawrence, co., Tn., U.S. B4 119
Lawrenceburg, In., U.S. F8 91
Lawrenceburg, Ky., U.S. B5 94
Lawrenceburg, Tn., U.S. B4 119
Lawrence Park, Pa., U.S. B1 115
Lawrenceville, Ga., U.S. C3 87
Lawrenceville, Il., U.S. E6 90
Lawrenceville, Va., U.S. D5 123
Lawson, Mo., U.S. B3 102
Lawsonia, Md., U.S. E6 97
Lawtell, La., U.S. D3 95
Lawton, Mi., U.S. F5 99
Lawton, Ok., U.S. C3 113
Lawz, Jabal al-, mtn., Sau. Ar. C2 46
Lay Lake, res., Al., U.S. B3 78
Laysan Island, i., Hi., U.S. k13 88
Layton, Ut., U.S. B4 121
La Zarca, Mex. E7 62
Lazarev, Russia G22 24
Lazi, China F12 38
Lea, co., N.M., U.S. D6 108
Leachville, Ar., U.S. B5 81
Lead, S.D., U.S. C2 118
Leadbetter Point, c., Wa., U.S. C1 124
Leadville, Co., U.S. B4 83
Leadwood, Mo., U.S. D7 102
Leaf, stm., Ms., U.S. D5 101
Leaf Rapids, Man., Can. A1 70
Leake, co., Ms., U.S. C4 101
Leakesville, Ms., U.S. D5 101
Lealman, Fl., U.S. p10 86
Leamington, Ont., Can. E2 73
Leary, Ga., U.S. E2 87
Leatherman Peak, mtn., Id., U.S. E5 89
Leavenworth, Ks., U.S. C9 93
Leavenworth, Wa., U.S. B5 124
Leavenworth, co., Ks., U.S. C8 93
Leavittsburg, Oh., U.S. A5 112
Leawood, Ks., U.S. D9 93
Lebanon, De., U.S. D4 85
Lebanon, Il., U.S. E4 90
Lebanon, In., U.S. D5 91
Lebanon, Ky., U.S. C4 94
Lebanon, Mo., U.S. D5 102
Lebanon, N.H., U.S. C2 106
Lebanon, Oh., U.S. C1 112
Lebanon, Or., U.S. C4 114
Lebanon, Pa., U.S. F9 115
Lebanon, Tn., U.S. A5 119
Lebanon, Va., U.S. f9 123
Lebanon, co., Pa., U.S. F8 115
Lebanon, ctry., Asia C4 40
Lebanon Junction, Ky., U.S. C4 94
Le Blanc, Fr. F8 10
Lebo, Ks., U.S. D8 93
Lębork, Pol. A17 8
Lebrija, Spain I5 12
Lecce, Italy I13 14
Lecco, Italy D4 14
Le Center, Mn., U.S. F5 100
Le Cheylard, Fr. H11 10
Le Claire, Ia., U.S. C7 92
Lecompte, La., U.S. C3 95
Lecompton, Ks., U.S. C8 93
Le Creusot, Fr. F11 10
Le Dorat, Fr. F8 10
Leduc, Alta., Can. C4 68
Lee, Ma., U.S. B1 98
Lee, co., Al., U.S. C4 78
Lee, co., Ar., U.S. C5 81
Lee, co., Fl., U.S. F5 86
Lee, co., Ga., U.S. E2 87
Lee, co., Il., U.S. B4 90
Lee, co., Ia., U.S. D6 92
Lee, co., Ky., U.S. C6 94
Lee, co., Ms., U.S. A5 101
Lee, co., N.C., U.S. B3 110
Lee, co., S.C., U.S. C7 117
Lee, co., Tx., U.S. D4 120
Lee, co., Va., U.S. f8 123
Lee, Lake, l., Ms., U.S. B3 101
Leechburg, Pa., U.S. E2 115
Leech Lake, l., Mn., U.S. C4 100
Leech Lake Indian Reservation, Mn., U.S. C4 100
Lee Creek, stm., U.S. B1 81
Leeds, Eng., U.K. H11 7
Leeds, Al., U.S. B3 78
Leelanau, co., Mi., U.S. D5 99
Leelanau, Lake, l., Mi., U.S. C5 99
Lee Park, Pa., U.S. n17 115
Leer, Ger. B7 8
Leesburg, Fl., U.S. D5 86
Leesburg, Ga., U.S. E2 87
Leesburg, Oh., U.S. C2 112
Leesburg, Va., U.S. A5 123
Lees Summit, Mo., U.S. C3 102
Leesville, La., U.S. C2 95
Leesville, S.C., U.S. D4 117
Leesville Lake, res., Va., U.S. C3 123
Leeton, Mo., U.S. C4 102
Leetonia, Oh., U.S. B5 112
Leetsdale, Pa., U.S. h13 115
Leeuwarden, Neth. B5 8
Leeuwin, Cape, c., Austl. F3 50
Leeward Islands, is., N.A. F17 64
Leflore, co., Ms., U.S. B3 101
Le Flore, co., Ok., U.S. C7 113
Legal, Alta., Can. C4 68
Legazpi, Phil. r20 33b
Leghorn see Livorno, Italy F5 14
Legnago, Italy D6 14
Legnano, Italy D3 14
Legnica (Liegnitz), Pol. D16 8
Le Grand, Ca., U.S. D3 82
Le Grand, Ia., U.S. B5 92
Le Havre, Fr. C7 10
Lehi, Ut., U.S. C4 121
Lehigh, co., Pa., U.S. E10 115
Lehigh, stm., Pa., U.S. E10 115
Lehigh Acres, Fl., U.S. F5 86
Lehighton, Pa., U.S. E10 115
Lehua Island, i., Hi., U.S. A1 88
Lehututu, Bots. F4 44
Leiah, Pak. E4 38
Leibnitz, Aus. I15 8
Leicester, Eng., U.K. I11 7
Leicester, Ma., U.S. B4 98
Leichhardt, stm., Austl. C7 50
Leiden, Neth. C4 8
Leighton, Al., U.S. A2 78
Leikanger, Nor. F6 6
Leinster, hist. reg., Ire. H5 7
Leinster, Mount, mtn., Ire. I6 7
Leipsic, De., U.S. D3 85
Leipsic, Oh., U.S. A2 112
Leipsic, stm., De., U.S. C3 85
Leipzig, Ger. D12 8
Leiria, Port. F3 12
Leisler, Mount, mtn., Austl. D5 50
Leisure City, Fl., U.S. s13 86
Leitchfield, Ky., U.S. C3 94
Leitrim, Ire. G4 7
Leiyang, China I1 28
Leizhou Bandao, pen., China D11 34
Leland, Il., U.S. B5 90
Leland, Ms., U.S. B3 101
Leleiwi Point, c., Hi., U.S. D7 88
Leleque, Arg. E2 56
Le Lion-d'Angers, Fr. E6 10
Leli Shan, mtn., China D9 38
Le Locle, Switz. E13 10
Le Lude, Fr. E7 10
Le Maire, Estrecho de, strt., Arg. G4 56
Le Mans, Fr. D7 10
Le Mars, Ia., U.S. B1 92
Leme, Braz. G5 57
Lemesós (Limassol), Cyp. B3 40
Lemgo, Ger. C8 8
Lemhi, co., Id., U.S. E4 89
Lemhi, stm., Id., U.S. E5 89
Lemhi Pass, Id., U.S. E5 89
Lemhi Range, mts., Id., U.S. E5 89
Lemmon, S.D., U.S. B3 118
Lemmon, Mount, mtn., Az., U.S. E5 80
Lemmon Valley, Nv., U.S. D2 105
Lemon, Lake, l., In., U.S. F5 91
Lemon Fair, stm., Vt., U.S. C2 122
Lemon Grove, Ca., U.S. o15 82
Lemon Island, i., S.C., U.S. G6 117
Lemont, Il., U.S. B5 90
Lemont, Pa., U.S. E6 115
Lemonweir, stm., Wi., U.S. D3 126
Lemoore, Ca., U.S. D4 82
Lemoore Naval Air Station, mil., Ca., U.S. D4 82
Lempa, stm., N.A. H3 64
Lem Peak, mtn., Id., U.S. E5 89
Lena, Il., U.S. A4 90
Lena, stm., Russia C19 24
Lenawee, co., Mi., U.S. G6 99
Lencloître, Fr. F7 10
Lenexa, Ks., U.S. D9 93
Lenghu, China D5 26
Leninabad, Taj. I11 22
Leningrad see Sankt-Peterburg, Russia B13 18
Leninogorsk, Kaz. G10 24
Leninsk-Kuzneckij, Russia G11 24
Leninskoje, Russia H20 24
Lennox, S.D., U.S. D9 118
Lennoxville, Que., Can. D6 74
Lenoir, N.C., U.S. B1 110
Lenoir, co., N.C., U.S. B5 110
Lenoir City, Tn., U.S. D9 119
Lenore Lake, l., Sask., Can. E3 75
Lenore Lake, l., Wa., U.S. B6 124
Lenox, Ga., U.S. E3 87
Lenox, Ia., U.S. D3 92
Lenox, Ma., U.S. B1 98
Lens, Fr. B9 10
Lensk, Russia E16 24
Lentini, Italy L10 14
Leo, In., U.S. B7 91
Leoben, Aus. H15 8
Leominster, Eng., U.K. I10 7
Leominster, Ma., U.S. A4 98
León, Nic. H4 64
León, Spain C6 12
Leon, Ia., U.S. D4 92
Leon, Ks., U.S. E7 93
Leon, co., Fl., U.S. B2 86
Leon, co., Tx., U.S. D4 120
Leonard, Tx., U.S. C4 120
Leonardo, N.J., U.S. C4 107
Leonardtown, Md., U.S. D4 97
Leonberg, Ger. G9 8
León [de los Aldamas], Mex. G9 62
Leonia, N.J., U.S. h9 107
Leonora, Austl. E4 50
Leonville, La., U.S. D4 95
Léopold II, Lac see Mai-Ndombe, Lac, l., Zaire B3 44
Leopoldina, Braz. F7 57
Léopoldville see Kinshasa, Zaire B3 44
Leoti, Ks., U.S. D2 93
Le Palais, Fr. E3 10
Lepanto, Ar., U.S. B5 81
Lepe, Spain H4 12
Leping, China G6 28
L'Épiphanie, Que., Can. D4 74
Lepontine, Alpi, mts., Eur. F15 10
Le Puy, Fr. G10 10
Lercara Friddi, Italy L8 14
Lerici, Italy E4 14
Lérida, Col. G7 58
Lérida, Spain D12 12
Lerma, Spain C8 12
Le Roy, Il., U.S. C5 90
Le Roy, Mn., U.S. G6 100
Le Roy, N.Y., U.S. C3 109
Lerwick, Scot., U.K. A11 7
Léry, Que., Can. q19 74
Lery, Lake, l., La., U.S. k12 95
Les Andelys, Fr. C8 10
Lesbos see Lésvos, i., Grc. J10 16
Les Cayes, Haiti E11 64
Les Échelles, Fr. G12 10
Les Herbiers, Fr. F5 10
Leskovac, Yugo. G5 16
Leslie, Mi., U.S. F6 99
Leslie, S.C., U.S. B6 117
Leslie, co., Ky., U.S. C6 94
Lesotho, ctry., Afr. G5 44
Lesozavodsk, Russia H20 24
Les Sables-d'Olonne, Fr. F5 10
Lesser Antilles, is. G17 64
Lesser Slave Lake, l., Alta., Can. B3 68
Lesser Sunda Islands, is., Indon. G6 32
Lester Prairie, Mn., U.S. F4 100
Le Sueur, Mn., U.S. F5 100
Le Sueur, co., Mn., U.S. F5 100
Lésvos (Lesbos), i., Grc. J10 16
Leszno, Pol. D16 8
Letcher, co., Ky., U.S. C7 94
Lethbridge, Alta., Can. E4 68
Lethbridge, Newf., Can. D5 72
Lethem, Guy. F13 58
Le Thillot, Fr. E13 10
Leti, Kepulauan, is., Indon. G8 32
Leticia, Col. J8 58
Le Tréport, Fr. B8 10
Letsôk-Aw Kyun, i., Mya. I5 34
Letterkenny, Ire. G5 7
Leutkirch, Ger. H10 8
Leuven, Bel. E4 8
Levádhia, Grc. K6 16
Levante, Riviera di, Italy E4 14
Levelland, Tx., U.S. C1 120
Leveque, Cape, c., Austl. C4 50
Leverkusen, Ger. D6 8
Le Vigan, Fr. I10 10
Levisa Fork, stm., U.S. C7 94
Lévis [-Lauzon], Que., Can. C6 74
Levittown, N.Y., U.S. E7 109
Levittown, Pa., U.S. F12 115
Levy, co., Fl., U.S. C4 86
Levy Lake, l., Fl., U.S. C4 86
Lewes, Eng., U.K. K13 7
Lewes, De., U.S. E5 85
Lewes and Rehoboth Canal, De., U.S. F5 85
Lewis, co., Id., U.S. C2 89
Lewis, co., Ky., U.S. B6 94
Lewis, co., Mo., U.S. A6 102
Lewis, co., N.Y., U.S. B5 109
Lewis, co., Tn., U.S. B4 119
Lewis, co., Wa., U.S. C3 124
Lewis, co., W.V., U.S. C4 125
Lewis, stm., Wa., U.S. C4 124
Lewis, stm., Wy., U.S. B2 127
Lewis, Isle of, i., Scot., U.K. C6 7
Lewis, Mount, mtn., Nv., U.S. C5 105
Lewis and Clark, co., Mt., U.S. C4 103
Lewis and Clark Cavern, Mt., U.S. D5 103
Lewis and Clark Lake, res., U.S. E8 118
Lewisburg, Ky., U.S. D3 94
Lewisburg, Oh., U.S. C1 112
Lewisburg, Pa., U.S. E8 115
Lewisburg, Tn., U.S. B5 119
Lewisburg, W.V., U.S. D4 125
Lewis Creek, stm., Vt., U.S. C2 122
Lewis Lake, l., Wy., U.S. B2 127
Lewisport, Ky., U.S. C3 94
Lewisporte, Newf., Can. D4 72
Lewis Smith Lake, res., Al., U.S. B2 78
Lewiston, Id., U.S. C1 89
Lewiston, Me., U.S. D2 96
Lewiston, Mn., U.S. G7 100
Lewiston, N.Y., U.S. B1 109
Lewiston, Ut., U.S. B4 121
Lewiston Peak, mtn., Ut., U.S. C3 121
Lewiston Woodville, N.C., U.S. A5 110
Lewistown, Il., U.S. C3 90
Lewistown, Mt., U.S. C7 103
Lewistown, Pa., U.S. E6 115
Lewisville, Ar., U.S. D2 81
Lewisville, Tx., U.S. C4 120
Lewisville Lake, res., Tx., U.S. C4 120
Lexington, Al., U.S. A2 78
Lexington, Il., U.S. C5 90
Lexington, Ky., U.S. B5 94
Lexington, Ma., U.S. B5 98
Lexington, Mi., U.S. E8 99
Lexington, Ms., U.S. B3 101
Lexington, Mo., U.S. B4 102
Lexington, Ne., U.S. D6 104
Lexington, N.C., U.S. B2 110
Lexington, Oh., U.S. B3 112
Lexington, Ok., U.S. B4 113
Lexington, S.C., U.S. D5 117
Lexington, Tn., U.S. B3 119
Lexington, Va., U.S. C3 123
Lexington, co., S.C., U.S. D5 117
Lexington Park, Md., U.S. D5 97
Leyte, i., Phil. C7 32
Leyte Gulf, b., Phil. C8 32
Lhasa, China F14 38
Lhokseumawe, Indon. D2 32
Lianhua Shan, mts., China L4 28
Lianxian, China G9 26
Lianyungang, China E10 26
Liao, stm., China C11 26
Liaocheng, China D10 26
Liaodong Wan, b., China C11 26
Liaoning, prov., China C11 26
Liaotung, Gulf of see Liaodong Wan, b., China C11 26
Liaoyang, China C11 26
Liaoyuan, China C12 26
Liard, stm., Can. E8 66
Libby, Mt., U.S. B1 103
Libenge, Zaire H9 42
Liberal, Ks., U.S. E3 93
Liberal, Mo., U.S. D3 102
Liberec, Czech. E15 8
Liberia, C.R. I5 64
Liberia, ctry., Afr. G4 42
Libertad, Ven. C8 58
Liberty, In., U.S. E8 91
Liberty, Ky., U.S. C5 94
Liberty, Ms., U.S. D3 101
Liberty, Mo., U.S. B3 102
Liberty, N.Y., U.S. D6 109
Liberty, N.C., U.S. B3 110
Liberty, S.C., U.S. B2 117
Liberty, Tx., U.S. D5 120
Liberty, co., Fl., U.S. B2 86
Liberty, co., Ga., U.S. E5 87
Liberty, co., Mt., U.S. B5 103
Liberty, co., Tx., U.S. D5 120
Liberty Center, Oh., U.S. A1 112
Liberty Lake, Wa., U.S. g14 124
Liberty Lake, res., Md., U.S. B4 97
Libertyville, Il., U.S. A6 90
Lībīyah, Aṣ-Ṣaḥrā' al- (Libyan Desert), des., Afr. D11 42
Libourne, Fr. H6 10
Libreville, Gabon A1 44
Libuse, La., U.S. C3 95
Libya, ctry., Afr. C9 42
Libyan Desert see Lībīyah, Aṣ-Ṣaḥrā' al-, des., Afr. D11 42
Licata, Italy L8 14
Lichinga, Moz. D7 44
Lichtenfels, Ger. E11 8
Lick Creek, stm., Tn., U.S. C11 119
Licking, Mo., U.S. D6 102
Licking, co., Oh., U.S. B3 112
Licking, stm., Ky., U.S. B6 94
Lida, Bela. H8 18
Lida, Lake, l., Mn., U.S. D3 100
Lidgerwood, N.D., U.S. C8 111
Lidköping, Swe. G9 6
Lido di Ostia, Italy H7 14
Liechtenstein, ctry., Eur. F9 4
Liège, Bel. E5 8
Lieksa, Fin. E18 6
Lienz, Aus. I12 8
Liepāja, Lat. E4 18
Lier, Bel. D4 8
Liestal, Switz. E14 10
Liévin, Fr. B9 10
Lièvre, Rivière du, stm., Que., Can. D2 74
Liezen, Aus. H14 8
Lifford, Ire. G5 7
Ligao, Phil. r20 33b
Lighthouse Inlet, b., S.C., U.S. k12 117
Lighthouse Point, c., Fl., U.S. C2 86
Lighthouse Point, c., La., U.S. E3 95
Lighthouse Point, c., Mi., U.S. C5 99
Lightning Creek, stm., Wy., U.S. C8 127
Ligny-en-Barrois, Fr. D12 10
Ligonier, In., U.S. B6 91
Ligonier, Pa., U.S. F3 115
Ligurian Sea, Eur. F3 14
Lihou Reefs, rf., Austl. C10 50
Lihue, Hi., U.S. B2 88
Lijiang, China F7 26
Likasi (Jadotville), Zaire D5 44
Likino-Dulevo, Russia F22 18
Liknes, Nor. G6 6
Likouala, stm., Congo B3 44
Lilbourn, Mo., U.S. E8 102
Lilburn, Ga., U.S. h8 87
Liling, China H2 28
Lille, Fr. B10 10
Lillehammer, Nor. F8 6
Lillestrøm, Nor. G8 6
Lillian, Al., U.S. E2 78
Lillington, N.C., U.S. B4 110
Lillinonah, Lake, l., Ct., U.S. C2 84
Lillo, Spain F8 12
Lillooet, B.C., Can. D7 69
Lillooet, stm., B.C., Can. D6 69
Lilly, Pa., U.S. F4 115
Lilly Fork, stm., W.V., U.S. m13 125
Lilly Grove, W.V., U.S. D3 125
Lilongwe, Mwi. D6 44
Lily, Ky., U.S. C5 94
Lima, Peru F3 54
Lima, N.Y., U.S. C3 109
Lima, Oh., U.S. B1 112
Lima Reservoir, res., Mt., U.S. F4 103
Limassol see Lemesós, Cyp. B3 40
Limbdi, India I4 38
Limburg an der Lahn, Ger. E8 8
Limeira, Braz. G5 57
Limerick, Ire. I4 7
Limestone, Me., U.S. B5 96
Limestone, co., Al., U.S. A2 78
Limestone, co., Tx., U.S. D4 120
Limestone Point, pen., Man., Can. C2 70
Liminka, Fin. D15 6
Limmen Bight, Austl. B7 50
Límnos, i., Grc. J9 16
Limoges, Ont., Can. B9 73
Limoges, Fr. G8 10
Limón, C.R. I6 64
Limón, Hond. G5 64
Limon, Co., U.S. B7 83
Limousins, Plateau du, plat., Fr. G8 10

Name — Map Ref — Page

Limoux, Fr. **I9** 10
Limpopo, stm., Afr. **F6** 44
Linares, Chile **D2** 56
Linares, Col. **G4** 58
Linares, Mex. **E10** 62
Linares, Spain **G8** 12
Lincoln, Arg. **C4** 56
Lincoln, Ont., Can. **D5** 73
Lincoln, Eng., U.K. **H12** 7
Lincoln, Al., U.S. **B3** 78
Lincoln, Ar., U.S. **B1** 81
Lincoln, Ca., U.S. **C3** 82
Lincoln, De., U.S. **E4** 85
Lincoln, Id., U.S. **F6** 89
Lincoln, Il., U.S. **C4** 90
Lincoln, Ks., U.S. **C5** 93
Lincoln, Me., U.S. **C4** 96
Lincoln, Ma., U.S. **g10** 98
Lincoln, Mo., U.S. **C4** 102
Lincoln, Ne., U.S. **D9** 104
Lincoln, N.H., U.S. **B3** 106
Lincoln, co., Ar., U.S. **D4** 81
Lincoln, co., Co., U.S. **C7** 83
Lincoln, co., Ga., U.S. **C4** 87
Lincoln, co., Id., U.S. **G4** 89
Lincoln, co., Ks., U.S. **C5** 93
Lincoln, co., Ky., U.S. **C5** 94
Lincoln, co., La., U.S. **B3** 95
Lincoln, co., Me., U.S. **D3** 96
Lincoln, co., Mn., U.S. **F2** 100
Lincoln, co., Ms., U.S. **D3** 101
Lincoln, co., Mo., U.S. **B7** 102
Lincoln, co., Mt., U.S. **B1** 103
Lincoln, co., Ne., U.S. **D5** 104
Lincoln, co., Nv., U.S. **F6** 105
Lincoln, co., N.M., U.S. **D4** 108
Lincoln, co., N.C., U.S. **B1** 110
Lincoln, co., Ok., U.S. **B5** 113
Lincoln, co., Or., U.S. **C3** 114
Lincoln, co., S.D., U.S. **D9** 118
Lincoln, co., Tn., U.S. **B5** 119
Lincoln, co., Wa., U.S. **B7** 124
Lincoln, co., W.V., U.S. **C2** 125
Lincoln, co., Wi., U.S. **C4** 126
Lincoln, co., Wy., U.S. **D2** 127
Lincoln, Mount, mtn., Co., U.S. **B4** 83
Lincoln Acres, Ca., U.S. **o15** 82
Lincoln City, Or., U.S. **C3** 114
Lincoln Heights, Oh., U.S. **o13** 112
Lincoln Park, Co., U.S. **C5** 83
Lincoln Park, Ga., U.S. **D2** 87
Lincoln Park, Mi., U.S. **p15** 99
Lincoln Park, N.J., U.S. **B4** 107
Lincolnshire, Il., U.S. **h9** 90
Lincoln Tomb State Memorial, hist., Il., U.S. **D4** 90
Lincolnton, Ga., U.S. **C4** 87
Lincolnton, N.C., U.S. **B1** 110
Lincolnville, S.C., U.S. **h11** 117
Lincolnwood, Il., U.S. **h9** 90
Lincroft, N.J., U.S. **C4** 107
Lindale, Ga., U.S. **B1** 87
Lindale, Tx., U.S. **C5** 120
Lindau, Ger. **H9** 8
Linden, Al., U.S. **C2** 78
Linden, In., U.S. **D4** 91
Linden, Mi., U.S. **F7** 99
Linden, N.J., U.S. **k8** 107
Linden, Tn., U.S. **B4** 119
Linden, Tx., U.S. **C5** 120
Lindenhurst, Il., U.S. **h8** 90
Lindenhurst, N.Y., U.S. **n15** 109
Lindenwold, N.J., U.S. **D3** 107
Lindesnes, c., Nor. **G6** 6
Lindi, Tan. **C7** 44
Lindon, Ut., U.S. **C4** 121
Lindsay, Ont., Can. **C6** 73
Lindsay, Ca., U.S. **D4** 82
Lindsay, Ok., U.S. **C4** 113
Lindsborg, Ks., U.S. **D6** 93
Lindstrom, Mn., U.S. **E6** 100
Linesville, Pa., U.S. **C1** 115
Lineville, Al., U.S. **B4** 78
Lingao, China **D10** 34
Lingayen, Phil. **B7** 32
Lingen, Ger. **C7** 8
Lingga, Kepulauan, is., Indon. **F3** 32
Lingle, Wy., U.S. **D8** 127
Linglestown, Pa., U.S. **F8** 115
Lingling, China **A11** 34
Linh, Ngoc, mtn., Viet. **G9** 34
Linhai, China **G10** 28
Linière, Que., Can. **C7** 74
Linjiang, China **C12** 26
Linköping, Swe. **G10** 6
Linkou, China **B13** 26
Linn, Mo., U.S. **C6** 102
Linn, co., Ia., U.S. **B6** 92
Linn, co., Ks., U.S. **D9** 93
Linn, co., Mo., U.S. **B4** 102
Linn, co., Or., U.S. **C4** 114
Lino Lakes, Mn., U.S. **m12** 100
Linqing, China **D10** 26
Linru, China **A1** 28
Lins, Braz. **F4** 57
Lintao, China **D7** 26
Linthicum Heights, Md., U.S. **B4** 97
Linton, In., U.S. **F3** 91
Linton, N.D., U.S. **C5** 111
Linwood, N.J., U.S. **E3** 107
Linxi, China **C10** 26
Linxia, China **D7** 26
Linyi, China **D10** 26
Linz, Aus. **G14** 8
Lion, Golfe du, b., Fr. **I11** 10
Lipa, Phil. **r19** 33b
Lipeck, Russia **I22** 18
Lippstadt, Ger. **D8** 8
Lipscomb, Al., U.S. **B3** 78
Lipscomb, co., Tx., U.S. **A2** 120
Lira, Ug. **H12** 42
Liria, Spain **F11** 12
Lisala, Zaire **A4** 44
Lisboa (Lisbon), Port. **G2** 12
Lisbon, Ia., U.S. **C6** 92
Lisbon, Me., U.S. **D2** 96
Lisbon, Md., U.S. **B3** 97
Lisbon, N.H., U.S. **B3** 106
Lisbon, N.D., U.S. **C8** 111
Lisbon, Oh., U.S. **B5** 112
Lisbon Center, Me., U.S. **f7** 96
Lisbon Falls, Me., U.S. **E2** 96
Lisbon see Lisboa, Port. **G2** 12
Lisburne, Cape, c., Ak., U.S. **B6** 79
Lishui, China **G8** 28
Lisianski Island, i., Hi., U.S. **k13** 88
Lisieux, Fr. **C7** 10
Lisle, Il., U.S. **k8** 90
L'Isle Jourdain, Fr. **F7** 10
L'Isle-Jourdain, Fr. **I8** 10
L'Islet-sur-Mer, Que., Can. **B7** 74
L'Isle-Verte, Que., Can. **A8** 74
Lismore, Austl. **E10** 50
Listowel, Ont., Can. **D4** 73
Listowel, Ire. **I3** 7
Lit, Swe. **E10** 6
Litang, China **G8** 26
Litchfield, Ct., U.S. **C3** 84
Litchfield, Il., U.S. **D4** 90
Litchfield, Mi., U.S. **F6** 99
Litchfield, Mn., U.S. **E4** 100
Litchfield, co., Ct., U.S. **B2** 84
Litchfield Park, Az., U.S. **m8** 80
Lithia Springs, Ga., U.S. **h7** 87
Lithonia, Ga., U.S. **C2** 87
Lithuania, ctry., Eur. **F6** 18
Litija, Slo. **C9** 14
Lititz, Pa., U.S. **F9** 115
Litovko, Russia **H21** 24
Little, stm., U.S. **B5** 81
Little, stm., U.S. **D7** 113
Little, stm., Ct., U.S. **C7** 84
Little, stm., Ky., U.S. **D2** 94
Little, stm., La., U.S. **C3** 95
Little, stm., N.C., U.S. **B3** 110
Little, stm., Ok., U.S. **B5** 113
Little, stm., S.C., U.S. **C2** 117
Little, stm., Tn., U.S. **n14** 119
Little, stm., Vt., U.S. **C3** 122
Little, stm., Va., U.S. **D2** 123
Little Abaco Island, i., Bah. **A9** 64
Little Acres, Az., U.S. **D5** 80
Little Andaman, i., India **I2** 34
Little Arkansas, stm., Ks., U.S. **D6** 93
Little Belt Mountains, mts., Mt., U.S. **D6** 103
Little Bighorn, stm., U.S. **E9** 103
Little Black, stm., Me., U.S. **A3** 96
Little Blue, stm., U.S. **C6** 93
Little Blue, stm., In., U.S. **H5** 91
Little Bow, stm., Alta., Can. **D4** 68
Little Cacapon, stm., W.V., U.S. **B6** 125
Little Catalina, Newf., Can. **D5** 72
Little Cayman, i., Cay. Is. **E7** 64
Little Cedar, stm., Ia., U.S. **A5** 92
Little Churchill, stm., Man., Can. **A4** 70
Little Chute, Wi., U.S. **D5** 126
Little Coal, stm., W.V., U.S. **C3** 125
Little Colorado, stm., Az., U.S. **B4** 80
Little Compton, R.I., U.S. **E6** 116
Little Creek, De., U.S. **D4** 85
Little Creek Naval Amphibious Base, mil., Va., U.S. **k15** 123
Little Creek Peak, mtn., Ut., U.S. **F3** 121
Little Current, Ont., Can. **B3** 73
Little Diomede Island, i., Ak., U.S. **B6** 79
Little Egg Harbor, b., N.J., U.S. **D4** 107
Little Egg Inlet, b., N.J., U.S. **E4** 107
Little Falls, Mn., U.S. **E4** 100
Little Falls, N.J., U.S. **B4** 107
Little Falls, N.Y., U.S. **B6** 109
Little Ferry, N.J., U.S. **h8** 107
Littlefield, Tx., U.S. **C1** 120
Little Fishing Creek, stm., W.V., U.S. **h9** 125
Littlefork, Mn., U.S. **B5** 100
Little Fork, stm., Mn., U.S. **B5** 100
Little Goose Creek, stm., Wy., U.S. **B6** 127
Little Gunpowder Falls, stm., Md., U.S. **A4** 97
Little Humboldt, stm., Nv., U.S. **B4** 105
Little Inagua, i., Bah. **D11** 64
Little Kanawha, stm., W.V., U.S. **C4** 125
Little Lake, Mi., U.S. **B3** 99
Little Lake, l., La., U.S. **E5** 95
Little Lynches, stm., S.C., U.S. **C7** 117
Little Manatee, stm., Fl., U.S. **p11** 86
Little Mecatina, stm., Can. **h9** 72
Little Miami, stm., Oh., U.S. **C1** 112
Little Minch, strt., Scot., U.K. **D6** 7
Little Missouri, stm., U.S. **B6** 76
Little Missouri, stm., Ar., U.S. **D2** 81
Little Muddy, stm., Il., U.S. **E4** 90
Little Muddy, stm., N.D., U.S. **A2** 111
Little Nicobar, i., India **K2** 34
Little Osage, stm., U.S. **E9** 93
Little Otter Creek, stm., Vt., U.S. **C2** 122
Little Owyhee, stm., U.S. **B5** 105
Little Pee Dee, stm., S.C., U.S. **C9** 117
Little Powder, stm., U.S. **F11** 103
Little Red, stm., Ar., U.S. **B4** 81
Little River, co., Ar., U.S. **D1** 81
Little River Inlet, b., S.C., U.S. **D10** 117
Little Rock, Ar., U.S. **C3** 81
Little Rock, stm., U.S. **A1** 92
Little Rock Air Force Base, mil., Ar., U.S. **C3** 81
Little Sable Point, c., Mi., U.S. **E4** 99
Little Salt Lake, l., Ut., U.S. **F3** 121
Little Sandy, stm., Ky., U.S. **B6** 94
Little Sandy Creek, stm., Wy., U.S. **D3** 127
Little Sebago Lake, l., Me., U.S. **g7** 96
Little Silver, N.J., U.S. **C4** 107
Little Sioux, stm., U.S. **B2** 92
Little Sioux, West Fork, stm., Ia., U.S. **B2** 92
Little Smoky, stm., Alta., Can. **B2** 68
Little Snake, stm., U.S. **A2** 83
Little Spokane, stm., Wa., U.S. **B8** 124
Littlestown, Pa., U.S. **G7** 115
Little Tallapoosa, stm., U.S. **B4** 78
Little Tenmile Creek, stm., W.V., U.S. **k10** 125
Little Tennessee, stm., U.S. **D9** 119
Littleton, Co., U.S. **B6** 83
Littleton, Me., U.S. **B5** 96
Littleton, Ma., U.S. **f10** 98
Littleton, N.H., U.S. **B3** 106
Littleton, N.C., U.S. **A5** 110
Littleville, Al., U.S. **A2** 78
Little Wabash, stm., Il., U.S. **E5** 90
Little Walnut, stm., Ks., U.S. **g13** 93
Little White, stm., S.D., U.S. **D5** 118
Little Wolf, stm., Wi., U.S. **D4** 126
Little Wood, stm., Id., U.S. **F4** 89
Liuan, China **D5** 28
Liuhe, China **C7** 28
Liuzhou, China **B10** 34
Live Oak, Ca., U.S. **C3** 82
Live Oak, Fl., U.S. **B4** 86
Live Oak, co., Tx., U.S. **E3** 120
Livermore, Ca., U.S. **h9** 82
Livermore, Ky., U.S. **C2** 94
Livermore, Mount, mtn., Tx., U.S. **o12** 120
Livermore Falls, Me., U.S. **D2** 96
Liverpool, Eng., U.K. **H10** 7
Liverpool, Cape, c., N.W. Ter., Can. **B17** 66
Livingston, Al., U.S. **C1** 78
Livingston, Ca., U.S. **D3** 82
Livingston, Il., U.S. **E4** 90
Livingston, La., U.S. **D5** 95
Livingston, Mt., U.S. **E6** 103
Livingston, N.J., U.S. **B4** 107
Livingston, Tn., U.S. **C8** 119
Livingston, Tx., U.S. **D5** 120
Livingston, co., Il., U.S. **C5** 90
Livingston, co., Ky., U.S. **e9** 94
Livingston, co., La., U.S. **D5** 95
Livingston, co., Mi., U.S. **F7** 99
Livingston, co., Mo., U.S. **B4** 102
Livingston, co., N.Y., U.S. **C3** 109
Livingston, Lake, res., Tx., U.S. **D5** 120
Livingstone, Zam. **E5** 44
Livingstonia, Mwi. **D6** 44
Livno, Bos. **F12** 14
Livny, Russia **I20** 18
Livonia, La., U.S. **D4** 95
Livonia, Mi., U.S. **F7** 99
Livorno (Leghorn), Italy **F5** 14
Liyang, China **D8** 28
Lizard Head Pass, Co., U.S. **D3** 83
Lizard Head Peak, mtn., Wy., U.S. **D3** 127
Lizard Point, c., Eng., U.K. **L7** 7
Lizella, Ga., U.S. **D3** 87
Ljubljana, Slo. **C9** 14
Ljungby, Swe. **H9** 6
Ljusdal, Swe. **F11** 6
Llandudno, Wales, U.K. **H9** 7
Llanelli, Wales, U.K. **J8** 7
Llanes, Spain **B7** 12
Llanidloes, Wales, U.K. **I9** 7
Llano, Tx., U.S. **D3** 120
Llano, co., Tx., U.S. **D3** 120
Llano, stm., Tx., U.S. **D3** 120
Llanos, pl., S.A. **E7** 58
Llanwrtyd Wells, Wales, U.K. **I9** 7
Llera, Mex. **F10** 62
Llerena, Spain **G5** 12
Lloyd, Ky., U.S. **B7** 94
Lloydminster, Alta., Can. **C5** 68
Lloyds, stm., Newf., Can. **D3** 72
Lluchmayor, Spain **F14** 12
Llullaillaco, Volcán, vol., S.A. **A3** 56
Lo, stm., Viet. **C8** 34
Loami, Il., U.S. **D4** 90
Loange, stm., Afr. **C3** 44
Löbau, Ger. **D14** 8
Lobaye, stm., Cen. Afr. Rep. **G9** 42
Lobelville, Tn., U.S. **B4** 119
Lobito, Ang. **D2** 44
Lobos de Afuera, Islas, is., Peru **E2** 54
Lobos de Tierra, Isla, i., Peru **E2** 54
Lobster Lake, l., Me., U.S. **C3** 96
Locarno, Switz. **F15** 10
Lochaline, Scot., U.K. **E7** 7
Lochboisdale, Scot., U.K. **D5** 7
Loches, Fr. **E7** 10
Lochgilphead, Scot., U.K. **E7** 7
Loch Lomond, Va., U.S. ***B5** 123
Loch Raven Reservoir, res., Md., U.S. **B4** 97
Lochsa, stm., Id., U.S. **C3** 89
Lockeport, N.S., Can. **F4** 71
Lockesburg, Ar., U.S. **D1** 81
Lockhart, Tx., U.S. **E4** 120
Lock Haven, Pa., U.S. **D7** 115
Lockland, Oh., U.S. **o13** 112
Lockney, Tx., U.S. **B2** 120
Lockport, Il., U.S. **B5** 90
Lockport, La., U.S. **E5** 95
Lockport, N.Y., U.S. **B2** 109
Lockwood, Mo., U.S. **D4** 102
Lockwood, Mt., U.S. **E8** 103
Loc Ninh, Viet. **I9** 34
Locust, N.C., U.S. **B2** 110
Locust Fork, stm., Al., U.S. **B3** 78
Locust Grove, Ga., U.S. **C2** 87
Locust Grove, Ok., U.S. **A6** 113
Lod, Isr. **D4** 40
Lodejnoje Polje, Russia **A16** 18
Lodève, Fr. **I10** 10
Lodgepole Creek, stm., U.S. **C3** 104
Lodi, Italy **D4** 14
Lodi, Ca., U.S. **C3** 82
Lodi, N.J., U.S. **h8** 107
Lodi, Oh., U.S. **A3** 112
Lodi, Wi., U.S. **E4** 126
Lodja, Zaire **B4** 44
Lodore, Canyon of, val., Co., U.S. **A2** 83
Lodwar, Kenya **H2** 46
Łódź, Pol. **D19** 8
Loffa, stm., Afr. **G3** 42
Logan, Ia., U.S. **C2** 92
Logan, Ks., U.S. **C4** 93
Logan, N.M., U.S. **B6** 108
Logan, Oh., U.S. **C3** 112
Logan, Ut., U.S. **B4** 121
Logan, W.V., U.S. **D3** 125
Logan, co., Ar., U.S. **B2** 81
Logan, co., Co., U.S. **A7** 83
Logan, co., Il., U.S. **C4** 90
Logan, co., Ks., U.S. **D2** 93
Logan, co., Ky., U.S. **D3** 94
Logan, co., Ne., U.S. **C5** 104
Logan, co., N.D., U.S. **C6** 111
Logan, co., Oh., U.S. **B2** 112
Logan, co., Ok., U.S. **B4** 113
Logan, co., W.V., U.S. **D3** 125
Logan, Mount, mtn., Yukon, Can. **D4** 66
Logan, Mount, mtn., Wa., U.S. **A5** 124
Logandale, Nv., U.S. **G7** 105
Logan Lake, B.C., Can. **D7** 69
Logan Martin Lake, res., Al., U.S. **B3** 78
Logan Pass, Mt., U.S. **B2** 103
Logansport, In., U.S. **C5** 91
Logansport, La., U.S. **C2** 95
Loganville, Ga., U.S. **C3** 87
Loganville, Pa., U.S. **G8** 115
Loggieville, N.B., Can. **B4** 71
Log Lane Village, Co., U.S. **A7** 83
Logone, stm., Afr. **F9** 42
Logroño, Spain **C9** 12
Logrosán, Spain **F6** 12
Lohr, Ger. **E9** 8
Loi-Kaw, Mya. **E4** 34
Loimaa, Fin. **F14** 6
Loire, stm., Fr. **E5** 10
Loja, Ec. **J3** 58
Loja, Spain **H7** 12
Lokolama, Zaire **B3** 44
Lol, stm., Sudan **G11** 42
Lola, Mount, mtn., Ca., U.S. **C3** 82
Lolo, Mt., U.S. **D2** 103
Lolo Pass, U.S. **C4** 89
Lomami, stm., Zaire **B4** 44
Lombard, Il., U.S. **k8** 90
Lomblen, Pulau, i., Indon. **G7** 32
Lombok, i., Indon. **G6** 32
Lomé, Togo **G6** 42
Lomela, Zaire **B4** 44
Lomela, stm., Zaire **B4** 44
Lomira, Wi., U.S. **E5** 126
Lomond, Loch, l., Scot., U.K. **E8** 7
Lomonosov, Russia **B12** 18
Lompoc, Ca., U.S. **E3** 82
Łomża, Pol. **B22** 8
Lonaconing, Md., U.S. **k13** 97
Lonāvale, India **C2** 37
Loncoche, Chile **D2** 56
London, Ont., Can. **E3** 73
London, Eng., U.K. **J12** 7
London, Ar., U.S. **B2** 81
London, Ky., U.S. **C5** 94
London, Oh., U.S. **C2** 112
Londonderry, N. Ire., U.K. **G5** 7
Londonderry, N.H., U.S. **E4** 106
Londonderry, Cape, c., Austl. **B5** 50
Londonderry, Isla, i., Chile **H2** 56
Londontown, Md., U.S. **C4** 97
Londrina, Braz. **G3** 57
Lone Grove, Ok., U.S. **C4** 113
Lone Mountain, mtn., Nv., U.S. **E4** 105
Lone Pine, Ca., U.S. **D4** 82
Lone Tree, Ia., U.S. **C6** 92
Long, co., Ga., U.S. **E5** 87
Longa, Proliv, strt., Russia **C29** 24
Longarone, Italy **C7** 14
Long Bar Harbor, Md., U.S. **B5** 97
Long Beach, Ca., U.S. **F4** 82
Long Beach, In., U.S. **A4** 91
Long Beach, Md., U.S. **D5** 97
Long Beach, Ms., U.S. **g7** 101
Long Beach, N.Y., U.S. **E7** 109
Long Beach, Wa., U.S. **C1** 124
Long Beach Naval Shipyard, mil., Ca., U.S. **n12** 82
Longboat Key, Fl., U.S. **q10** 86
Longboat Key, i., Fl., U.S. **E4** 86
Longboat Pass, strt., Fl., U.S. **q10** 86
Long Branch, N.J., U.S. **C5** 107
Longbranch, Wa., U.S. **B3** 124
Long Creek Mountain, mtn., Wy., U.S. **D5** 127
Longeau, Fr. **E12** 10
Long Grove, Ia., U.S. **C7** 92
Long Harbour [-Mount Arlington Heights], Newf., Can. **E5** 72
Long Island, i., Bah. **C10** 64
Long Island, i., N.S., Can. **E3** 71
Long Island, i., Me., U.S. **g7** 96
Long Island, i., Ma., U.S. **g12** 98
Long Island, i., N.Y., U.S. **E7** 109
Long Island Sound, strt., U.S. **E7** 109
Longjiang, China **B11** 26
Long Key, i., Fl., U.S. **H6** 86
Long Lake, Il., U.S. **h8** 90
Long Lake, l., Me., U.S. **A4** 96
Long Lake, l., Me., U.S. **D2** 96
Long Lake, l., Mi., U.S. **D5** 99
Long Lake, l., Mi., U.S. **C7** 99
Long Lake, l., Mn., U.S. **D4** 100
Long Lake, l., N.Y., U.S. **B6** 109
Long Lake, l., N.D., U.S. **C6** 111
Long Lake, l., Wa., U.S. **f10** 124
Long Lake, l., Wi., U.S. **C2** 126
Longli, China **A9** 34
Longmeadow, Ma., U.S. **B2** 98
Longmont, Co., U.S. **A5** 83
Long Point, c., Man., Can. **C2** 70
Long Point, pen., Ont., Can. **E4** 73
Long Pond, res., Fl., U.S. **C4** 86
Long Prairie, Mn., U.S. **E4** 100
Long Range Mountains, mts., Newf., Can. **D3** 72
Longreach, Austl. **D8** 50
Longsheng, China **B11** 34
Longs Peak, mtn., Co., U.S. **A5** 83
Longué, Fr. **E6** 10
Longueuil, Que., Can. **D4** 74
Longuyon, Fr. **C12** 10
Long View, N.C., U.S. **B1** 110
Longview, Tx., U.S. **C5** 120
Longview, Wa., U.S. **C3** 124
Longwy, Fr. **C12** 10
Long Xuyen, Viet. **I8** 34
Lonigo, Italy **D6** 14
Löningen, Ger. **C7** 8
Lonoke, Ar., U.S. **C4** 81
Lonoke, co., Ar., U.S. **C4** 81
Lønsdal, Nor. **C10** 6
Lonsdale, Mn., U.S. **F5** 100
Lonsdale, R.I., U.S. **B4** 116
Lons-le-Saunier, Fr. **F12** 10
Loogootee, In., U.S. **G4** 91
Lookout, Ky., U.S. **C7** 94
Lookout, Cape, c., N.C., U.S. **C6** 110
Lookout, Point, c., Mi., U.S. **d7** 99
Lookout Mountain, Tn., U.S. **h11** 119
Lookout Mountain, mtn., U.S. **D8** 119
Lookout Mountain, mtn., Or., U.S. **C6** 114
Lookout Pass, U.S. **B3** 89
Lookout Point Lake, res., Or., U.S. **D4** 114
Loon Lake, Wa., U.S. **A8** 124
Loon Lake, l., Me., U.S. **B3** 96
Loop Creek, stm., W.V., U.S. **m13** 125
Loop Head, c., Ire. **I3** 7
Loosahatchie, stm., Tn., U.S. **B2** 119
Lopatina, Gora, mtn., Russia **G22** 24
Lopatka, Mys, c., Russia **G25** 24
Lop Buri, Thai. **G6** 34
Lopez, Cap, c., Gabon **B1** 44
López Collada, Mex. **B3** 62
Lopez Island, i., Wa., U.S. **A3** 124
Lop Nur, l., China **C5** 26
Lora del Río, Spain **H6** 12
Lorain, Oh., U.S. **A3** 112
Lorain, co., Oh., U.S. **A3** 112
Loramie, Lake, res., Oh., U.S. **B1** 112
Lorca, Spain **H10** 12
Lord Howe Island, i., Austl. **F11** 50
Lordsburg, N.M., U.S. **E1** 108
Loreauville, La., U.S. **D4** 95
Lorena, Braz. **G6** 57
Lorenzo, Tx., U.S. **C2** 120
Loreto, Braz. **E9** 54
Loreto, Col. **I7** 58
Loreto, Mex. **F9** 62
Lorette, Man., Can. **E3** 70
Loretteville, Que., Can. **C6** 74
Loretto, Ky., U.S. **C4** 94
Loretto, Pa., U.S. **F4** 115
Loretto, Tn., U.S. **B4** 119
Lorica, Col. **C5** 58
Lorient, Fr. **E3** 10
L'Orignal, Ont., Can. **B10** 73
Loring Air Force Base, mil., Me., U.S. **B5** 96
Loriol [-du-Comtat], Fr. **H11** 10
Loris, S.C., U.S. **C10** 117
Lorne, N.B., Can. **B3** 71
Lörrach, Ger. **H7** 8
Lorraine, hist. reg., Fr. **D13** 10
Los Alamos, N.M., U.S. **B3** 108
Los Alamos, co., N.M., U.S. **B3** 108
Los Aldamas, Mex. **D10** 62
Los Altos, Ca., U.S. **k8** 82
Los Ángeles, Chile **D2** 56
Los Angeles, Ca., U.S. **E4** 82
Los Angeles, co., Ca., U.S. **E4** 82
Los Angeles Aqueduct, Ca., U.S. **E4** 82
Los Banos, Ca., U.S. **D3** 82
Los Blancos, Arg. **A4** 56
Los Fresnos, Tx., U.S. **F4** 120
Los Gatos, Ca., U.S. **D2** 82
Los Lagos, Chile **D2** 56
Los Lunas, N.M., U.S. **C3** 108
Los Mochis, Mex. **E5** 62
Los Palacios y Villafranca, Spain **H6** 12
Los Pinos, stm., Co., U.S. **D3** 83
Los Ranchos de Albuquerque, N.M., U.S. **B3** 108
Los Roques, Islas, is., Ven. **B9** 58
Lost, stm., In., U.S. **G4** 91
Lost, stm., Wa., U.S. **A5** 124
Lost, stm., W.V., U.S. **B6** 125
Lost Creek, stm., Wy., U.S. **D4** 127
Los Teques, Ven. **B9** 58
Los Testigos, Islas, is., Ven. **B11** 58
Lost Peak, mtn., Ut., U.S. **F2** 121
Lost Ranger Peak, mtn., Co., U.S. **A4** 83
Lost River Glacial Caverns, N.H., U.S. **B3** 106
Lost River Range, mts., Id., U.S. **E5** 89
Lost Trail Pass, U.S. **D5** 89
Los Vilos, Chile **C2** 56
Los Yébenes, Spain **F8** 12
Lota, Chile **D2** 56
Lotawana, Lake, res., Mo., U.S. **k11** 102
Lotbinière, Que., Can. **C6** 74
Louang Namtha, Laos **D6** 34
Louangphrabang, Laos **E7** 34
Loudéac, Fr. **D4** 10
Loudon, Tn., U.S. **D9** 119
Loudon, co., Tn., U.S. **D9** 119
Loudonville, Oh., U.S. **B3** 112
Loudoun, co., Va., U.S. **A5** 123
Loudun, Fr. **E7** 10
Louga, Sen. **E2** 42
Loughrea, Ire. **H4** 7
Louhans, Fr. **F12** 10
Louisa, Ky., U.S. **B7** 94
Louisa, Va., U.S. **B4** 123
Louisa, co., Ia., U.S. **C6** 92
Louisa, co., Va., U.S. **C5** 123
Louisa, Lake, l., Fl., U.S. **D5** 86
Louisbourg, N.S., Can. **D10** 71
Louisburg, Ks., U.S. **D9** 93
Louisburg, N.C., U.S. **A4** 110
Louisdale, N.S., Can. **D8** 71
Louise, Lake, l., Ak., U.S. **f18** 79
Louise Island, i., B.C., Can. **C2** 69
Louiseville, Que., Can. **C5** 74

Name — Map Ref — Page

Louisiade Archipelago, is., Pap. N. Gui. B10 50
Louisiana, Mo., U.S. B6 102
Louisiana, state, U.S. C3 95
Louisiana Point, c., La., U.S. E2 95
Louis Trichardt, S. Afr. F5 44
Louisville, Al., U.S. D4 78
Louisville, Co., U.S. B5 83
Louisville, Ga., U.S. C4 87
Louisville, Il., U.S. E5 90
Louisville, Ky., U.S. B4 94
Louisville, Ms., U.S. B4 101
Louisville, Ne., U.S. D9 104
Louisville, Oh., U.S. B4 112
Louis-XIV, Pointe, c., Que., Can. h11 74
Loulé, Port. H3 12
Loup, co., Ne., U.S. C6 104
Loup, stm., Ne., U.S. C8 104
Loup City, Ne., U.S. C7 104
Lourdes, Newf., Can. D2 72
Lourdes, Fr. I6 10
Lourenço Marques see Maputo, Moz. G6 44
Louth, Eng., U.K. H12 7
Louviers, Fr. C8 10
Louviers, Co., U.S. B6 83
Love, co., Ok., U.S. D4 113
Loveč, Bul. F8 16
Loveland, Co., U.S. A5 83
Loveland, Oh., U.S. n13 112
Loveland Park, Oh., U.S. C1 112
Loveland Pass, Co., U.S. B5 83
Lovell, Wy., U.S. B4 127
Lovelock, Nv., U.S. C3 105
Lovely, Ky., U.S. C7 94
Lovenia, Mount, mtn., Ut., U.S. C5 121
Love Point, c., Md., U.S. B5 97
Lovere, Italy D5 14
Loves Park, Il., U.S. A4 90
Lovettsville, Va., U.S. A5 123
Loving, N.M., U.S. E5 108
Loving, co., Tx., U.S. D1 120
Lovington, Il., U.S. D5 90
Lovington, Ia., U.S. e8 92
Lovington, N.M., U.S. E6 108
Lövstabruk, Swe. F11 6
Low, Cape, c., N.W. Ter., Can. D15 66
Lowden, Ia., U.S. C7 92
Lowell, Ar., U.S. A1 81
Lowell, In., U.S. B3 91
Lowell, Ma., U.S. A5 98
Lowell, Mi., U.S. F5 99
Lowell, N.C., U.S. B1 110
Lowell, Or., U.S. D4 114
Lowell, Lake, res., Id., U.S. F2 89
Lowellville, Oh., U.S. A5 112
Lower Arrow Lake, res., B.C., Can. E8 69
Lower Brule Indian Reservation, S.D., U.S. C6 118
Lower California see Baja California, pen., Mex. D3 62
Lower Hutt, N.Z. D5 52
Lower Klamath Lake, l., Ca., U.S. B3 82
Lower Matecumbe Key, i., Fl., U.S. H6 86
Lower Monumental Lake, res., Wa., U.S. C7 124
Lower New York Bay, b., N.J., U.S. B4 107
Lower Otay Lake, res., Ca., U.S. o16 82
Lower Paia, Hi., U.S. C5 88
Lower Red Lake, l., Mn., U.S. C3 100
Lower Rice Lake, l., Mn., U.S. C3 100
Lower Salmon Dam, Id., U.S. G4 89
Lower West Pubnico, N.S., Can. F4 71
Lowestoft, Eng., U.K. I14 7
Lowndes, co., Al., U.S. C3 78
Lowndes, co., Ga., U.S. F3 87
Lowndes, co., Ms., U.S. B5 101
Lowry Air Force Base, mil., Co., U.S. B6 83
Lowry City, Mo., U.S. C4 102
Lowville, N.Y., U.S. B5 109
Loxley, Al., U.S. E2 78
Loyal, Wi., U.S. D3 126
Loyall, Ky., U.S. D6 94
Loyalsock Creek, stm., Pa., U.S. D8 115
Loznica, Yugo. E3 16
Lozoyuela, Spain E8 12
Lua, stm., Zaire H9 42
Lualaba, stm., Zaire B5 44
Lua Makika, crat., Hi., U.S. C5 88
Luanda, Ang. C2 44
Luang Praban Range, mts., Asia E6 34
Luanguinga, stm., Afr. D4 44
Luangwa, stm., Afr. D6 44
Luanshya, Zam. D5 44
Luarca, Spain B5 12
Luau, Ang. D4 44
Lubang Island, i., Phil. C7 32
Lubango, Ang. D2 44
Lübben, Ger. D13 8
Lübbenau, Ger. D13 8
Lubbock, Tx., U.S. C2 120
Lubbock, co., Tx., U.S. C2 120
Lubec, Me., U.S. D6 96
Lübeck, Ger. B10 8
Lübecker Bucht, b., Ger. A11 8
L'ubercy, Russia F20 18
Lubilash, stm., Zaire C4 44
Lubin, Pol. D16 8
Lublin, Pol. D22 8
Lubudi, Zaire C4 44
Lubuksikaping, Indon. N6 34
Lubumbashi (Elisabethville), Zaire D5 44
Lubutu, Zaire B5 44
Lucama, N.C., U.S. B4 110
Lucan, Ont., Can. D3 73
Lucania, Mount, mtn., Yukon, Can. D4 66
Lucas, co., Ia., U.S. C4 92
Lucas, co., Oh., U.S. A2 112
Lucasville, Oh., U.S. D3 112
Lucca, Italy F5 14
Luce, co., Mi., U.S. B5 99
Luce Bay, b., Scot., U.K. G8 7
Lucedale, Ms., U.S. E5 101
Lucena, Phil. r19 33b
Lucena, Spain H7 12
Lucena del Cid, Spain E11 12
Luc-en-Diois, Fr. H12 10
Lucera, Italy H10 14
Lucerne, Ca., U.S. C2 82
Lucerne see Luzern, Switz. E15 10
Lucernemines, Pa., U.S. E3 115
Lucerne Valley, Ca., U.S. E5 82
Luceville, Que., Can. A9 74
Luchiang, Tai. K9 28
Lüchow, Ger. C11 8
Lucira, Ang. D2 44
Luck, Wi., U.S. C1 126
Luckeesarai, India H12 38
Luckenwalde, Ger. C13 8
Lucknow, Ont., Can. D3 73
Lucknow, India G9 38
Lucky Peak Lake, res., Id., U.S. F3 89
Luçon, Fr. F5 10
Lüderitz, Nmb. G3 44
Ludhiāna, India E6 38
Ludington, Mi., U.S. E4 99
L'udinovo, Russia H17 18
Ludlow, Ky., U.S. h13 94
Ludlow, Ma., U.S. B3 98
Ludlow, Vt., U.S. E3 122
Ludowici, Ga., U.S. E5 87
Ludvika, Swe. F10 6
Ludwigsburg, Ger. G9 8
Ludwigsfelde, Ger. C13 8
Ludwigshafen, Ger. F8 8
Luena, stm., Ang. D4 44
Luene, Ang. D3 44
Lufeng, China M4 28
Lufkin, Tx., U.S. D5 120
Luga, Russia C12 18
Lugano, Switz. F15 10
Lugenda, stm., Moz. D7 44
Lugh Ganane, Som. H3 46
Lugnaquillia Mountain, mtn., Ire. I6 7
Lugo, Italy E6 14
Lugo, Spain B4 12
Lugoff, S.C., U.S. C6 117
Lugoj, Rom. D5 16
Luhans'k, Ukr. H5 22
Luhit, stm., Asia G16 38
Luilaka, stm., Zaire B4 44
Luino, Italy C3 14
Lukachukai, Az., U.S. A6 80
Luke Air Force Base, mil., Az., U.S. D3 80
Lukulu, Zam. D4 44
Lula, Ga., U.S. B3 87
Luleå, Swe. D14 6
Lüleburgaz, Tur. H11 16
Luling, La., U.S. k11 95
Luling, Tx., U.S. E4 120
Lulonga, stm., Zaire A3 44
Lumajang, Indon. n16 33a
Lumber, stm., U.S. C9 117
Lumber City, Ga., U.S. E4 87
Lumberport, W.V., U.S. B4 125
Lumberton, Ms., U.S. D4 101
Lumberton, N.C., U.S. C3 110
Lumbrales, Spain E5 12
Lumby, B.C., Can. D8 69
Lumding, India H15 38
Lummi Indian Reservation, Wa., U.S. A3 124
Lumpkin, Ga., U.S. D2 87
Lumpkin, co., Ga., U.S. B2 87
Lumsden, Newf., Can. D5 72
Luna, co., N.M., U.S. E2 108
Luna Pier, Mi., U.S. G7 99
Lund, Swe. I9 6
Lund, Nv., U.S. E6 105
Lundar, Man., Can. D2 70
Lundazi, Zam. D6 44
Lüneburg, Ger. B10 8
Lüneburger Heide, reg., Ger. B10 8
Lunel, Fr. I11 10
Lunenburg, Ma., U.S. A4 98
Lunenburg, co., Va., U.S. D4 123
Lunéville, Fr. D13 10
Lunga, stm., Zam. D5 44
Luohe, China B3 28
Luolong, China E17 38
Luopu, China B9 38
Luoyang, China E9 26
Lūrah, stm., Afg. D2 38
Luray, Va., U.S. B4 123
Lure, Fr. E13 10
Lure, Lake, res., N.C., U.S. f10 110
Lurgan, N. Ire., U.K. G6 7
Lúrio, stm., Moz. D7 44
Lusaka, Zam. E5 44
Lusambo, Zaire B4 44
Lusby, Md., U.S. D5 97
Luseland, Sask., Can. E1 75
Lushan, China B1 28
Lushnje, Alb. I3 16
Lushoto, Tan. B7 44
Lüshun (Port Arthur), China D11 26
Lusk, Wy., U.S. D8 127
Lussac-les-Châteaux, Fr. F7 10
Lūt, Dasht-e, des., Iran B6 46
Lutcher, La., U.S. D5 95
Luther, Ok., U.S. B4 113
Luthersville, Ga., U.S. C2 87
Lutherville-Timonium, Md., U.S. B4 97
Luton, Eng., U.K. J12 7
Luts'k, Ukr. G3 22
Luttrell, Tn., U.S. C10 119
Lutz, Fl., U.S. D4 86
Luverne, Al., U.S. D3 78
Luverne, Mn., U.S. G2 100
Luwegu, stm., Tan. C7 44
Luxapallila Creek, stm., U.S. B5 101
Luxembourg, Lux. F6 8
Luxembourg, ctry., Eur. F9 4
Luxemburg, Wi., U.S. D6 126
Luxomni, Ga., U.S. h8 87
Luxora, Ar., U.S. B6 81
Luzern, Switz. E15 10
Luzerne, Pa., U.S. n17 115
Luzerne, co., Pa., U.S. D9 115
Luzhou, China F8 26
Luzon, i., Phil. B7 32
Luzon Strait, strt., Asia G11 26
Luzy, Fr. F10 10
L'viv, Ukr. H2 22
Lycksele, Swe. D12 6
Lycoming, co., Pa., U.S. D7 115
Lycoming Creek, stm., Pa., U.S. D7 115
Lydenburg, S. Afr. G6 44
Lyell, Mount, mtn., Can. D2 68
Lyford, Tx., U.S. F4 120
Lykens, Pa., U.S. E8 115
Lyle, Wa., U.S. D4 124
Lyman, S.C., U.S. B3 117
Lyman, Wy., U.S. E2 127
Lyman, co., S.D., U.S. D6 118
Lyman Lake, res., Az., U.S. C6 80
Lynch, Ky., U.S. D7 94
Lynchburg, Oh., U.S. C2 112
Lynchburg, Tn., U.S. B5 119
Lynchburg, Va., U.S. C3 123
Lynches, stm., S.C., U.S. D8 117
Lynden, Wa., U.S. A3 124
Lynde Point, c., Ct., U.S. D6 84
Lyndhurst, N.J., U.S. h8 107
Lyndhurst, Oh., U.S. g9 112
Lyndon, Ks., U.S. D8 93
Lyndon, Ky., U.S. g11 94
Lyndon B. Johnson National Historical Site, hist., Tx., U.S. D3 120
Lyndon B. Johnson Space Center, sci., Tx., U.S. r14 120
Lyndonville, Vt., U.S. B4 122
Lyndora, Pa., U.S. E2 115
Lynher Reef, rf., Austl. C4 50
Lynn, Al., U.S. A2 78
Lynn, In., U.S. D8 91
Lynn, Ma., U.S. B6 98
Lynn, co., Tx., U.S. C2 120
Lynn, Lake, res., W.V., U.S. B5 125
Lynn Canal, b., Ak., U.S. k22 79
Lynne Acres, Md., U.S. *B4 97
Lynnfield, Ma., U.S. f11 98
Lynn Garden, Tn., U.S. C11 119
Lynn Garden, Tn., U.S. A9 119
Lynn Haven, Fl., U.S. u16 86
Lynnhaven Roads, b., Va., U.S. k15 123
Lynnville, In., U.S. H3 91
Lynnwood, Wa., U.S. B3 124
Lynton, Eng., U.K. J9 7
Lynwood, Ca., U.S. n12 82
Lyon, Fr. G11 10
Lyon, co., Ia., U.S. A1 92
Lyon, co., Ks., U.S. D7 93
Lyon, co., Ky., U.S. C1 94
Lyon, co., Mn., U.S. F3 100
Lyon, co., Nv., U.S. D2 105
Lyons, Co., U.S. A5 83
Lyons, Ga., U.S. D4 87
Lyons, Il., U.S. k9 90
Lyons, In., U.S. G3 91
Lyons, Ks., U.S. D5 93
Lyons, Mi., U.S. F6 99
Lyons, Ne., U.S. C9 104
Lyons, N.Y., U.S. B3 109
Lyons, Or., U.S. C4 114
Lyster Station, Que., Can. C6 74
Lysychans'k, Ukr. H5 22
Lytle, Tx., U.S. E3 120

M

Ma, stm., Asia D8 34
Maalaea Bay, b., Hi., U.S. C5 88
Ma'ān, Jord. D4 40
Maanshan, China D7 28
Ma'arrat an-Nu'mān, Syria B5 40
Maas (Meuse), stm., Eur. D5 8
Maastricht, Neth. E5 8
Mabank, Tx., U.S. C4 120
Mabaruma, Guy. C13 58
Mabel, Mn., U.S. G7 100
Maben, Ms., U.S. B4 101
Mableton, Ga., U.S. h7 87
Mabscott, W.V., U.S. D3 125
Mabton, Wa., U.S. C5 124
Mača, Russia F17 24
Macaé, Braz. G8 57
Macão, Port. F3 12
Macao see Macau, dep., Asia M2 28
Macapá, Braz. C8 54
Macará, Ec. J3 58
Macarani, Braz. C8 57
Macas, Ec. I3 58
Macau, Braz. E11 54
Macau (Aomen), Macao M2 28
Macau (Aomen), dep., Asia M2 28
MacClenny, Fl., U.S. B4 86
MacDill Air Force Base, mil., Fl., U.S. E4 86
Macdonnell Ranges, mts., Austl. D6 50
MacDowell Reservoir, res., N.H., U.S. E2 106
Macduff, Scot., U.K. D10 7
Macdui, Ben, mtn., Scot., U.K. D9 7
Macedo de Cavaleiros, Port. D5 12
Macedonia, Oh., U.S. A4 112
Macedonia, hist. reg., Eur. H6 16
Macedonia, ctry., Eur. H5 16
Maceió, Braz. E11 54
Macerata, Italy F8 14
Maces Bay, b., N.B., Can. D3 71
MacGregor, Man., Can. E2 70
Machačkala, Russia I7 22
Machagai, Arg. B4 56
Machala, Ec. I3 58
Machecoul, Fr. E5 10
Machias, Me., U.S. D5 96
Machias, stm., Me., U.S. B4 96
Machias, stm., Me., U.S. D5 96
Machias Bay, b., Me., U.S. D5 96
Machias Lakes, l., Me., U.S. C5 96
Machilīpatnam (Bandar), India D6 37
Machiques, Ven. B6 58
Macho, Arroyo del, val., N.M., U.S. C4 108
Machupicchu, Peru F4 54
Macina, reg., Mali F4 42
Mackay, Austl. D9 50
Mackay, Lake, l., Austl. D5 50
MacKenzie, B.C., Can. B6 69
Mackenzie, stm., N.W. Ter., Can. C6 66
Mackenzie Bay, b., Can. C5 66
Mackenzie Mountains, mts., Can. D7 66
Mackinac, co., Mi., U.S. B5 99
Mackinac, Straits of, strt., Mi., U.S. C6 99
Mackinac Bridge, Mi., U.S. C6 99
Mackinac Island, i., Mi., U.S. C6 99
Mackinaw, Il., U.S. C4 90
Mackinaw, stm., Il., U.S. C4 90
Mackinaw City, Mi., U.S. C6 99
Maclear, S. Afr. H5 44
Macmillan, stm., Yukon, Can. D6 66
Macomb, Il., U.S. C3 90
Macomb, co., Mi., U.S. F8 99
Macomer, Italy I3 14
Mâcon, Fr. F11 10
Macon, Ga., U.S. D3 87
Macon, Il., U.S. D5 90
Macon, Ms., U.S. B5 101
Macon, Mo., U.S. B5 102
Macon, co., Al., U.S. C4 78
Macon, co., Ga., U.S. D2 87
Macon, co., Il., U.S. D4 90
Macon, co., Mo., U.S. B5 102
Macon, co., N.C., U.S. f9 110
Macon, co., Tn., U.S. A5 119
Macon, Bayou, stm., U.S. B4 95
Macoupin, co., Il., U.S. D4 90
MacTier, Ont., Can. B5 73
Macungie, Pa., U.S. E10 115
Mad, stm., Ca., U.S. B2 82
Mad, stm., Ct., U.S. B3 84
Mad, stm., N.H., U.S. C3 106
Mad, stm., Oh., U.S. C2 112
Mad, stm., Vt., U.S. C3 122
Ma'dabā, Jord. D4 40
Madagascar, ctry., Afr. E9 44
Madame, Isle, i., N.S., Can. D9 71
Madanapalle, India F5 37
Madang, Pap. N. Gui. m16 50a
Mādārīpur, Bngl. I14 38
Madawaska, Me., U.S. A4 96
Madawaska, stm., Can. B9 74
Madawaska, stm., Ont., Can. B7 73
Madawaska Lake, l., Me., U.S. A4 96
Maddaloni, Italy H9 14
Madeira, Oh., U.S. o13 112
Madeira, i., Port. B2 42
Madeira, stm., S.A. E6 54
Madeira, Arquipélago da (Madeira Islands), is., Port. m20 13a
Mädelegabel, mtn., Eur. E17 10
Madeleine, Îles de la, is., Que., Can. B8 71
Madelia, Mn., U.S. F4 100
Madeline Island, i., Wi., U.S. B3 126
Madera, Ca., U.S. D3 82
Madera, co., Ca., U.S. D4 82
Madhubani, India G12 38
Madhya Pradesh, state, India I8 38
Madill, Ok., U.S. C5 113
Madīnat ash-Sha'b, Yemen F3 46
Madingou, Congo B2 44
Madison, Al., U.S. A3 78
Madison, Ar., U.S. B5 81
Madison, Ct., U.S. D5 84
Madison, Fl., U.S. B3 86
Madison, Ga., U.S. C3 87
Madison, Il., U.S. E3 90
Madison, In., U.S. G7 91
Madison, Ks., U.S. D7 93
Madison, Me., U.S. D3 96
Madison, Mn., U.S. E2 100
Madison, Ms., U.S. C3 101
Madison, Ne., U.S. C8 104
Madison, N.J., U.S. B4 107
Madison, N.C., U.S. A3 110
Madison, Oh., U.S. A4 112
Madison, S.D., U.S. D8 118
Madison, W.V., U.S. C3 125
Madison, Wi., U.S. E4 126
Madison, co., Al., U.S. A3 78
Madison, co., Ar., U.S. B2 81
Madison, co., Fl., U.S. B3 86
Madison, co., Ga., U.S. B3 87
Madison, co., Id., U.S. F7 89
Madison, co., Il., U.S. E4 90
Madison, co., In., U.S. D6 91
Madison, co., Ia., U.S. C3 92
Madison, co., Ky., U.S. C5 94
Madison, co., La., U.S. B4 95
Madison, co., Ms., U.S. C4 101
Madison, co., Mo., U.S. D7 102
Madison, co., Mt., U.S. E5 103
Madison, co., Ne., U.S. C8 104
Madison, co., N.Y., U.S. C5 109
Madison, co., N.C., U.S. f10 110
Madison, co., Oh., U.S. C2 112
Madison, co., Tn., U.S. B3 119
Madison, co., Tx., U.S. D5 120
Madison, co., Va., U.S. B4 123
Madison, stm., Mt., U.S. E5 103
Madison Heights, Mi., U.S. o15 99
Madison Heights, Va., U.S. C3 123
Madison Lake, Mn., U.S. F5 100
Madison Range, mts., Mt., U.S. E5 103
Madisonville, Ky., U.S. C2 94
Madisonville, La., U.S. D5 95
Madisonville, Tn., U.S. D9 119
Madisonville, Tx., U.S. D5 120
Madiun, Indon. m15 32
Madoc, Ont., Can. C7 73
Mado Gashi, Kenya B7 44
Madras, India F6 37
Madras, Or., U.S. C5 114
Madre, Laguna, b., Mex. E11 62
Madre, Laguna, b., Tx., U.S. F4 120
Madre, Sierra, mts., N.A. J14 62
Madre, Sierra, mts., Phil. B7 32
Madre de Dios, stm., S.A. F5 54
Madre de Dios, Isla, i., Chile G1 56
Madre del Sur, Sierra, mts., Mex. I10 62
Madre Occidental, Sierra, mts., Mex. E6 62
Madre Oriental, Sierra, mts., Mex. F9 62
Madrid, Spain E8 12
Madrid, Ia., U.S. C4 92
Madridejos, Spain F8 12
Maduo, China E6 26
Madura, i., Indon. G5 32
Madurai, India H5 37
Maebashi, Japan F12 30
Mae Hong Son, Thai. E4 34
Maeser, Ut., U.S. C6 121
Mae Sot, Thai. F5 34
Maestra, Sierra, mts., Cuba D9 64
Maevatanana, Madag. E9 44
Mafia Island, i., Tan. C7 44
Mafikeng, S. Afr. G5 44
Mafra, Braz. B7 56
Magadan, Russia F24 24
Magadi, Kenya B7 44
Magallanes, Estrecho de (Strait of Magellan), strt., S.A. G2 56
Magangué, Col. C5 58
Magazine, Ar., U.S. B2 81
Magazine Mountain, mtn., Ar., U.S. B2 81
Magdagači, Russia G19 24
Magdalena, Bol. F6 54
Magdalena, Mex. B4 62
Magdalena, N.M., U.S. C2 108
Magdalena, stm., Col. B5 58
Magdalena, Bahía, b., Mex. E3 62
Magdalena, Isla, i., Chile E2 56
Magdalena Mountains, mts., N.M., U.S. D2 108
Magdeburg, Ger. C11 8
Magee, Ms., U.S. D4 101
Magelang, Indon. m15 33a
Magellan, Strait of see Magallanes, Estrecho de, strt., S.A. G2 56
Magenta, Italy D3 14
Maggie Creek, stm., Nv., U.S. C5 105
Maggiore, Lago, l., Eur. C3 14
Magic Reservoir, res., Id., U.S. F4 89
Magione, Italy F7 14
Magna, Ut., U.S. C3 121
Magnetawan, stm., Ont., Can. B4 73
Magnitogorsk, Russia G9 22
Magnolia, Ar., U.S. D2 81
Magnolia, Ky., U.S. C4 94
Magnolia, Ms., U.S. D3 101
Magnolia, N.C., U.S. C4 110
Magnolia, Oh., U.S. B4 112
Magoffin, co., Ky., U.S. C6 94
Magog, Que., Can. D5 74
Magothy River, b., Md., U.S. B4 97
Magpie, Lac, l., Que., Can. F20 66
Magrath, Alta., Can. E4 68
Magruder Mountain, mtn., Nv., U.S. F4 105
Maguarinho, Cabo, c., Braz. D9 54
Magway, Mya. D3 34
Mahābād, Iran J7 22
Mahābhārat Range, mts., Nepal F10 38
Mahaicony Village, Guy. D14 58
Mahajamba, Baie de la, b., Madag. E9 44
Mahajanga, Madag. E9 44
Mahakam, stm., Indon. E6 32
Mahānadi, stm., India J11 38
Mahanoro, Madag. E9 44
Mahanoy City, Pa., U.S. E9 115
Mahārāshtra, state, India C3 37
Maha Sarakham, Thai. F7 34
Mahaska, co., Ia., U.S. C5 92
Mahaṭṭat al-Qaṭrānah, Jord. D5 40
Mahaṭṭat Ḥaraḍ, Sau. Ar. D4 46
Mahbūbnagar, India D4 37
Mahé Island, i., Sey. B11 44
Mahenge, Tan. C7 44
Mahi, stm., India I5 38
Mahmūd-e 'Erāqī, Afg. C3 38
Mahnomen, Mn., U.S. C3 100
Mahnomen, co., Mn., U.S. C3 100
Mahoba, India H8 38
Mahogany Mountain, mtn., Or., U.S. D9 114
Mahomet, Il., U.S. C5 90
Mahón, Spain F16 12
Mahone Bay, N.S., Can. E5 71
Mahoning, co., Oh., U.S. B5 112
Mahoning, stm., U.S. A5 112
Mahopac, N.Y., U.S. D7 109
Mahuva, India J4 38
Mahwah, N.J., U.S. A4 107
Maiden, N.C., U.S. B1 110
Maidstone, Eng., U.K. J13 7
Maidstone Lake, l., Vt., U.S. B5 122
Maiduguri, Nig. F8 42
Maili, Hi., U.S. g9 88
Maili Point, c., Hi., U.S. g9 88
Maillezais, Fr. F6 10
Main, stm., Ger. F9 8
Mainburg, Ger. G11 8
Main Channel, strt., Ont., Can. B3 73
Mai-Ndombe, Lac, l., Zaire B3 44
Maine, state, U.S. C3 96
Mainland, i., Scot., U.K. B9 7
Mainland, i., Scot., U.K. A11 7
Main Pass, strt., La., U.S. E6 95
Mainz, Ger. E8 8
Maipo, Volcán, vol., S.A. C3 56
Maipú, Arg. D5 56
Maiquetía, Ven. B9 58
Maisonnette, N.B., Can. B4 71
Maitland, Austl. F10 50

Name — Map Ref — Page

Maitland, Ont., Can. C9 73
Maize, Ks., U.S. g12 93
Maizuru, Japan G8 30
Maja, stm., Russia F20 24
Majene, Indon. F6 32
Majī, Eth. G2 46
Majkop, Russia I6 22
Majno-Pyl'gino, Russia E29 24
Major, co., Ok., U.S. A3 113
Majorca see Mallorca, i., Spain F15 12
Makaha, Hi., U.S. g9 88
Makaha Point, c., Hi., U.S. A2 88
Makah Indian Reservation, Wa., U.S. A1 124
Makahuena Point, c., Hi., U.S. B2 88
Makakilo City, Hi., U.S. g9 88
Makale, Indon. F6 32
Makapuu Head, c., Hi., U.S. B4 88
Makarska, Cro. F12 14
Makasar, Selat (Makassar Strait), strt., Indon. F6 32
Makasar see Ujungpandang, Indon. G6 32
Makawao, Hi., U.S. C5 88
Makaweli, Hi., U.S. B2 88
Makeni, S.L. G3 42
Makgadikgadi Pans, pl., Bots. F5 44
Makhachkala see Machačkala, Russia I7 22
Makindu, Kenya B7 44
M'akit, Russia E24 24
Makkah (Mecca), Sau. Ar. D2 46
Maklakovo, Russia F12 24
Makó, Hung. I20 8
Makokou, Gabon A2 44
Makthar, Tun. N4 14
Makumbi, Zaire C4 44
Makurazaki, Japan K3 30
Makurdi, Nig. G7 42
Makushin Volcano, vol., Ak., U.S. E6 79
Malabar, Fl., U.S. D6 86
Malabar Coast, India G4 37
Malabo, Eq. Gui. H7 42
Malacca, Strait of, strt., Asia M6 34
Malad City, Id., U.S. G6 89
Málaga, Col. D6 58
Málaga, Spain I7 12
Malagón, Spain F8 12
Malaimbandy, Madag. F9 44
Malaja Kuril'skaja Gr'ada (Habomai-shotō), is., Russia p24 30a
Malakāl, Sudan G12 42
Malakoff, Tx., U.S. C4 120
Malang, Indon. m16 32
Malanje, Ang. C3 44
Malanville, Benin F6 42
Mälaren, l., Swe. G11 6
Malargüe, Arg. D3 56
Malartic, Que., Can. k11 74
Malaspina Glacier, Ak., U.S. D11 79
Malatya, Tur. H15 4
Malawi, ctry., Afr. D6 44
Malaya, reg., Malay. M7 34
Malay Peninsula, pen., Asia K6 34
Malaysia, ctry., Asia E3 32
Malbaie, stm., Que., Can. B7 74
Malbork, Pol. A19 8
Malcolm, Austl. E4 50
Malden, Ma., U.S. B5 98
Malden, Mo., U.S. E8 102
Malden, W.V., U.S. m12 125
Maldives, ctry., Asia I2 37
Maldonado, Ur. C6 56
Mālegaon, India B3 37
Malek Dīn, Afg. D3 38
Malha Wells, Sudan E11 42
Malheur, co., Or., U.S. D9 114
Malheur, stm., Or., U.S. D9 114
Malheur Lake, l., Or., U.S. D8 114
Mali, ctry., Afr. E5 42
Malibu, Ca., U.S. m11 82
Malik, Wādī al-, val., Sudan E11 42
Malin, Or., U.S. E5 114
Malindi, Kenya B8 44
Malino, Bukit, mtn., Indon. E7 32
Malka, Russia G25 24
Malkāpur, India B4 37
Malkara, Tur. I10 16
Mallaig, Scot., U.K. D7 7
Mallawī, Egypt C12 42
Malletts Bay, b., Vt., U.S. B2 122
Mallnitz, Aus. I13 8
Mallorca, i., Spain F14 12
Mallow, Ire. I4 7
Malmberget, Swe. C13 6
Malmédy, Bel. E6 8
Malmesbury, S. Afr. H3 44
Malmö, Swe. I9 6
Malmstrom Air Force Base, mil., Mt., U.S. C5 103
Malolos, Phil. q19 33b
Malone, N.Y., U.S. f10 109
Maloney Reservoir, res., Ne., U.S. C5 104
Måløy, Nor. F5 6
Malpaso, Presa de, res., Mex. I13 62
Malpelo, Isla de, i., Col. C2 54
Malpeque Bay, b., P.E.I., Can. C6 71
Malta, Il., U.S. B5 90
Malta, Mt., U.S. B9 103
Malta, ctry., Eur. H10 4
Malta Channel, strt., Eur. M9 14
Maltahöhe, Nmb. F3 44
Maluku (Moluccas), is., Indon. F8 32
Maluku, Laut (Molucca Sea), Indon. F7 32
Malung, Swe. F9 6
Malvern, Ar., U.S. C3 81
Malvern, Ia., U.S. D2 92
Malvern, Oh., U.S. B4 112
Malvern, Pa., U.S. o19 115
Malverne, N.Y., U.S. k13 109
Malyj An'uj, stm., Russia D26 24
Malyj Tajmyr, Ostrov, i., Russia B15 24
Mama, Russia F16 24
Mamala Bay, b., Hi., U.S. g10 88
Mamaroneck, N.Y., U.S. h13 109
Mamberamo, stm., Indon. F10 32
Mamers, Fr. D7 10
Mamfe, Cam. G7 42
Mammoth, Az., U.S. E5 80
Mammoth Cave National Park, Ky., U.S. C4 94
Mammoth Lakes, Ca., U.S. D4 82
Mammoth Spring, Ar., U.S. A4 81
Mamoré, stm., S.A. F5 54
Mamou, Gui. F3 42
Mamou, La., U.S. D3 95
Man, C. Iv. G4 42
Man, W.V., U.S. D3 125
Manacapuru, Braz. D6 54
Manacor, Spain F15 12
Manado, Indon. E7 32
Managua, Nic. H4 64
Managua, Lago de, l., Nic. H4 64
Manakara, Madag. F9 44
Manama see Al-Manāmah, Bahr. C5 46
Manana Island, i., Hi., U.S. g11 88
Mananara, Madag. E9 44
Mananjary, Madag. F9 44
Manantico Creek, stm., N.J., U.S. E3 107
Mana Point, c., Hi., U.S. A2 88
Manas, China C4 26
Manasquan, N.J., U.S. C4 107
Manasquan, stm., N.J., U.S. C4 107
Manassa, Co., U.S. D5 83
Manassas, Va., U.S. B5 123
Manassas National Battlefield Park, Va., U.S. g11 123
Manassas Park, Va., U.S. B5 123
Manatee, co., Fl., U.S. E4 86
Manatee, stm., Fl., U.S. E4 86
Manaus, Braz. D6 54
Manawa, Wi., U.S. D5 126
Manbij, Syria A5 40
Mancelona, Mi., U.S. D5 99
Mancha Real, Spain H8 12
Manchester, Eng., U.K. H10 7
Manchester, Ct., U.S. B5 84
Manchester, Ga., U.S. D2 87
Manchester, Ia., U.S. B6 92
Manchester, Ky., U.S. C6 94
Manchester, Me., U.S. D3 96
Manchester, Md., U.S. A4 97
Manchester, Ma., U.S. A6 98
Manchester, Mi., U.S. F6 99
Manchester, Mo., U.S. f12 102
Manchester, N.H., U.S. E4 106
Manchester, N.Y., U.S. C3 109
Manchester, Oh., U.S. D2 112
Manchester, Pa., U.S. F8 115
Manchester, Tn., U.S. B5 119
Manchester, Vt., U.S. E2 122
Manchester Center, Vt., U.S. E2 122
Manchuria, reg., China B12 26
Manciano, Italy G6 14
Mancos, Co., U.S. D2 83
Mancos, stm., U.S. D2 83
Mand, stm., Iran C5 46
Manda, Tan. D6 44
Mandal, Nor. G6 6
Mandalay, Mya. C4 34
Mandalgov', Mong. B8 26
Mandan, N.D., U.S. C5 111
Mandas, Italy J4 14
Mandasor, India H6 38
Mandeb, Bāb el-, strt. F3 46
Mandeville, Ar., U.S. D2 81
Mandeville, La., U.S. D5 95
Mandi Bahāuddīn, Pak. D5 38
Mandimba, Moz. D7 44
Mandla, India I9 38
Manduria, Italy I12 14
Māndvi, India I3 38
Mandya, India F4 37
Manerbio, Italy D5 14
Manfredonia, Italy H10 14
Mangabeiras, Chapada das, hills, Braz. F9 54
Mangalore, India F3 37
Mangkalihat, Tanjung, c., Indon. E6 32
Manglares, Cabo, c., Col. G3 58
Mangoche, Mwi. D7 44
Mangoky, stm., Madag. F8 44
Mangole, Pulau, i., Indon. F8 32
Māngrol, India J4 38
Mangrove Cay, i., Bah. B9 64
Mangualde, Port. E4 12
Mangum, Ok., U.S. C2 113
Mangya, China D5 26
Manhattan, Ks., U.S. C7 93
Manhattan, Mt., U.S. E5 103
Manhattan Beach, Ca., U.S. n12 82
Manhattan Island, i., N.Y., U.S. h13 109
Manheim, Pa., U.S. F9 115
Manhuaçu, Braz. F7 57
Manicoré, Braz. E6 54
Manicouagan, stm., Que., Can. F19 66
Manicouagan, Réservoir, res., Que., Can. h13 74
Manila, Phil. q19 32
Manila, Ar., U.S. B5 81
Manila Bay, b., Phil. C7 32
Manilla, Ia., U.S. C2 92
Manipur, ter., India H15 38
Manisa, Tur. K11 16
Manistee, Mi., U.S. D4 99
Manistee, co., Mi., U.S. D4 99
Manistee, stm., Mi., U.S. D5 99
Manistique, Mi., U.S. C4 99
Manistique, stm., Mi., U.S. B4 99
Manistique Lake, l., Mi., U.S. B5 99
Manito, Il., U.S. C4 90
Manitoba, prov., Can. C3 70
Manitoba, Lake, l., Man., Can. D2 70
Manitou, Man., Can. E2 70
Manitou, Lake, l., Ont., Can. B3 73
Manitou Island, i., Mi., U.S. A3 99
Manitou Lake, l., Sask., Can. E1 75
Manitoulin Island, i., Ont., Can. B2 73
Manitou Springs, Co., U.S. C6 83
Manitowoc, Wi., U.S. D6 126
Manitowoc, co., Wi., U.S. D6 126
Manitowoc, stm., Wi., U.S. h10 126
Maniwaki, Que., Can. C2 74
Manizales, Col. E5 58
Manjacaze, Moz. F6 44
Mānjra, stm., India C4 37
Mankato, Ks., U.S. C5 93
Mankato, Mn., U.S. F5 100
Mankoya, Zam. D4 44
Manlius, N.Y., U.S. C5 109
Manlléu, Spain C14 12
Manly, Ia., U.S. A4 92
Manmād, India B3 37
Mannar, Gulf of, b., Asia H5 37
Mannārgudi, India G5 37
Mannar Island, i., Sri L. H5 37
Mannford, Ok., U.S. A5 113
Mannheim, Ger. F8 8
Manning, Alta., Can. A2 68
Manning, Ia., U.S. C2 92
Manning, S.C., U.S. D7 117
Mannington, W.V., U.S. B4 125
Manns Creek, stm., W.V., U.S. n14 125
Mannville, Alta., Can. C5 68
Manokin, stm., Md., U.S. D6 97
Manokotak, Ak., U.S. D8 79
Manokwari, Indon. F9 32
Manomet, Ma., U.S. C6 98
Manomet Point, c., Ma., U.S. C6 98
Manono, Zaire C5 44
Manor, Tx., U.S. D4 120
Manosque, Fr. I12 10
Manouane, Lac, l., Que., Can. h12 74
Manresa, Spain D13 12
Mānsa, India F6 38
Mansa, Zam. D5 44
Manseau, Que., Can. C5 74
Mansel Island, i., N.W. Ter., Can. D17 66
Mansfield, Eng., U.K. H11 7
Mansfield, Ar., U.S. B1 81
Mansfield, Il., U.S. C5 90
Mansfield, La., U.S. B2 95
Mansfield, Ma., U.S. B5 98
Mansfield, Mo., U.S. D5 102
Mansfield, Oh., U.S. B3 112
Mansfield, Pa., U.S. C7 115
Mansfield, Tx., U.S. n9 120
Mansfield, Mount, mtn., Vt., U.S. B3 122
Mansfield Center, Ct., U.S. B7 84
Mansfield Hollow Lake, res., Ct., U.S. B7 84
Manson, Ia., U.S. B3 92
Manson, Wa., U.S. B5 124
Mansonville, Que., Can. D5 74
Mansura, La., U.S. C3 95
Manta, Ec. H2 58
Mantachie, Ms., U.S. A5 101
Manteca, Ca., U.S. D3 82
Manteno, Il., U.S. B6 90
Manteo, N.C., U.S. B7 110
Mantes-la-Jolie, Fr. D8 10
Manti, Ut., U.S. D4 121
Mantiqueira, Serra da, mts., Braz. F6 57
Manton, Mi., U.S. D5 99
Mantorville, Mn., U.S. F6 100
Mantova, Italy D5 14
Mantua, Oh., U.S. A4 112
Mantua, Ut., U.S. B4 121
Manturovo, Russia C27 18
Manukau Harbour, b., N.Z. B5 52
Manumuskin, stm., N.J., U.S. E3 107
Manus Island, i., Pap. N. Gui. k16 50a
Manvel, Tx., U.S. r14 120
Manville, N.J., U.S. B3 107
Manville, R.I., U.S. B4 116
Many, La., U.S. C2 95
Many Farms, Az., U.S. A6 80
Manzanares, Spain F8 12
Manzanillo, Cuba D9 64
Manzanillo, Mex. H7 62
Manzano Mountains, mts., N.M., U.S. C3 108
Manzano Peak, mtn., N.M., U.S. C3 108
Manzhouli, China B10 26
Mao, Chad F9 42
Maoke, Pegunungan, mts., Indon. F10 32
Mapastepec, Mex. J13 62
Mapi, Indon. G10 32
Mapia, Kepulauan, is., Indon. E9 32
Mapimí, Mex. E8 62
Mapimí, Bolsón de, des., Mex. D8 62
Mapire, Ven. D10 58
Maple, stm., U.S. A7 118
Maple, stm., Ia., U.S. B2 92
Maple, stm., N.D., U.S. C8 111
Maple Bluff, Wi., U.S. E4 126
Maple Grove, Mn., U.S. m12 100
Maple Heights, Oh., U.S. h9 112
Maple Lake, Mn., U.S. E5 100
Maple Plain, Mn., U.S. m11 100
Maple Shade, N.J., U.S. D2 107
Maplesville, Al., U.S. C3 78
Mapleton, Ia., U.S. B2 92
Mapleton, Mn., U.S. G5 100
Mapleton, N.D., U.S. C8 111
Mapleton, Or., U.S. C3 114
Mapleton, Ut., U.S. C4 121
Maple Valley, Wa., U.S. f11 124
Mapleville, R.I., U.S. B2 116
Maplewood, Mn., U.S. n12 100
Maplewood, Mo., U.S. f13 102
Maplewood, N.J., U.S. B4 107
Mapuera, stm., Braz. D7 54
Maputo (Lourenço Marques), Moz. G6 44
Maqueda, Spain E7 12
Maquela do Zombo, Ang. C3 44
Maquinchao, Arg. E3 56
Maquoketa, Ia., U.S. B7 92
Maquoketa, stm., Ia., U.S. B6 92
Maquoketa, North Fork, stm., Ia., U.S. B7 92
Mar, Serra do, clf, Braz. A7 56
Marabá, Braz. E9 54
Maracá, Ilha de, i., Braz. C8 54
Maracaibo, Ven. B7 58
Maracaibo, Lago de, l., Ven. C7 58
Maracay, Ven. B9 58
Marādah, Libya C9 42
Maradi, Niger F7 42
Marāgheh, Iran J7 22
Maragogipe, Braz. B9 57
Marahuaca, Cerro, mtn., Ven. F10 58
Marais des Cygnes, stm., U.S. D8 93
Marajó, Baía de, b., Braz. D9 54
Marajó, Ilha de, i., Braz. D9 54
Maralal, Kenya A7 44
Marambaia, Ilha da, i., Braz. G7 57
Marana, Az., U.S. E4 80
Marang, Malay. L7 34
Marañón, stm., Peru D3 54
Marans, Fr. F5 10
Marapanim, Braz. D9 54
Marathon, Fl., U.S. H5 86
Marathon, Wi., U.S. D4 126
Marathon, co., Wi., U.S. D4 126
Marawī, Sudan E1 46
Marble, Mn., U.S. C5 100
Marble, N.C., U.S. f9 110
Marble Bar, Austl. D3 50
Marble Canyon, val., Az., U.S. A4 80
Marble Falls, Tx., U.S. D3 120
Marblehead, Ma., U.S. B6 98
Marble Hill, Mo., U.S. D8 102
Marbleton, Wy., U.S. D2 127
Marburg an der Lahn, Ger. E8 8
Marbury, Md., U.S. C3 97
Marcaria, Italy D5 14
Marceline, Mo., U.S. B5 102
Marcellus, Mi., U.S. F5 99
March (Morava), stm., Eur. G16 8
Marcha, Russia E18 24
March Air Force Base, mil., Ca., U.S. F5 82
Marche-en-Famenne, Bel. E5 8
Marchena, Spain H6 12
Mar Chiquita, Laguna, l., Arg. C4 56
Marco, Fl., U.S. G5 86
Marcus, Ia., U.S. B2 92
Marcus Baker, Mount, mtn., Ak., U.S. g18 79
Marcus Hook, Pa., U.S. G11 115
Marcy, Mount, mtn., N.Y., U.S. A7 109
Mardān, Pak. C5 38
Mar del Plata, Arg. D5 56
Mardin, Tur. H16 4
Mareeba, Austl. C9 50
Mareg, Som. H4 46
Marengo, Il., U.S. A5 90
Marengo, In., U.S. H5 91
Marengo, Ia., U.S. C5 92
Marengo, co., Al., U.S. C2 78
Marennes, Fr. G5 10
Marfa, Tx., U.S. o12 120
Margaret, Al., U.S. B3 78
Margarita, Isla de, i., Ven. B10 58
Margate, Fl., U.S. F6 86
Margate City, N.J., U.S. E3 107
Margherita Peak, mtn., Afr. A5 44
Marghī, Afg. C2 38
Margrethe, Lake, l., Mi., U.S. D6 99
María Cleofas, Isla, i., Mex. G6 62
María Madre, Isla, i., Mex. G6 62
María Magdalena, Isla, i., Mex. G6 62
Marian, Lake, l., Fl., U.S. E5 86
Marianao, Cuba C6 64
Marianna, Ar., U.S. C5 81
Marianna, Fl., U.S. B1 86
Marias, stm., Mt., U.S. B4 103
Marías, Islas, is., Mex. G6 62
Marias Pass, Mt., U.S. B3 103
Mariato, Punta, c., Pan. K7 64
Mariazell, Aus. H15 8
Maribor, Slo. C10 14
Marica (Évros) (Meriç), stm., Eur. G9 16
Maricopa, Az., U.S. E3 80
Maricopa, Ca., U.S. E4 82
Maricopa, co., Az., U.S. D3 80
Maricopa Mountains, mts., Az., U.S. m7 80
Marie-Galante, i., Guad. G17 64
Mariehamn, Fin. F12 6
Mariemont, Oh., U.S. o13 112
Mariental, Nmb. F3 44
Marienville, Pa., U.S. D3 115
Maries, co., Mo., U.S. C6 102
Mariestad, Swe. G9 6
Marietta, Ga., U.S. C2 87
Marietta, Oh., U.S. C4 112
Marietta, Ok., U.S. D4 113
Marietta, S.C., U.S. A2 117
Marieville, Que., Can. D4 74
Marília, Braz. G4 57
Marimba, Ang. C3 44
Marín, Spain C3 12
Marin, co., Ca., U.S. C2 82
Marinduque Island, i., Phil. C7 32
Marine, Il., U.S. E4 90
Marine City, Mi., U.S. F8 99
Marine On St. Croix, Mn., U.S. E6 100
Marinette, Wi., U.S. C6 126
Marinette, co., Wi., U.S. C5 126
Maringá, Braz. G3 57
Maringouin, La., U.S. D4 95
Marinha Grande, Port. F3 12
Marion, Al., U.S. C2 78
Marion, Ar., U.S. B5 81
Marion, Il., U.S. F5 90
Marion, In., U.S. C6 91
Marion, Ia., U.S. B6 92
Marion, Ks., U.S. D6 93
Marion, Ky., U.S. e9 94
Marion, La., U.S. B3 95
Marion, Mi., U.S. D5 99
Marion, Ms., U.S. C5 101
Marion, N.C., U.S. B1 110
Marion, Oh., U.S. B2 112
Marion, Pa., U.S. G6 115
Marion, S.C., U.S. C9 117
Marion, S.D., U.S. D8 118
Marion, Va., U.S. f10 123
Marion, Wi., U.S. D5 126
Marion, co., Al., U.S. A2 78
Marion, co., Ar., U.S. A3 81
Marion, co., Fl., U.S. C4 86
Marion, co., Ga., U.S. D2 87
Marion, co., Il., U.S. E4 90
Marion, co., In., U.S. E5 91
Marion, co., Ia., U.S. C4 92
Marion, co., Ks., U.S. D6 93
Marion, co., Ky., U.S. C4 94
Marion, co., Ms., U.S. D4 101
Marion, co., Mo., U.S. B6 102
Marion, co., Oh., U.S. B2 112
Marion, co., Or., U.S. C4 114
Marion, co., S.C., U.S. C9 117
Marion, co., Tn., U.S. D8 119
Marion, co., Tx., U.S. C5 120
Marion, co., W.V., U.S. B4 125
Marion, Lake, res., S.C., U.S. E7 117
Marion Station, Md., U.S. D6 97
Marionville, Mo., U.S. D4 102
Maripa, Ven. D10 58
Mariposa, co., Ca., U.S. D3 82
Mariscal Estigarribia, Para. A4 56
Marissa, Il., U.S. E4 90
Maritime Alps, mts., Eur. H14 10
Mariupol' (Ždanov), Ukr. H5 22
Marka, Som. H3 46
Markaryd, Swe. H9 6
Markdale, Ont., Can. C4 73
Marked Tree, Ar., U.S. B5 81
Markesan, Wi., U.S. E5 126
Markham, Ont., Can. D5 73
Markham, Il., U.S. k9 90
Markham, Tx., U.S. E4 120
Markham, Mount, mtn., Ant. A29 47
Markland Lock and Dam, U.S. B5 94
Markle, In., U.S. C7 91
Markovo, Russia E28 24
Marks, Ms., U.S. A3 101
Marksville, La., U.S. C3 95
Marktredwitz, Ger. E12 8
Mark Twain Lake, res., Mo., U.S. B6 102
Marlboro, N.Y., U.S. D6 109
Marlboro, Va., U.S. n17 123
Marlboro, co., S.C., U.S. B8 117
Marlborough, Ct., U.S. C6 84
Marlborough, Ma., U.S. B4 98
Marlborough, N.H., U.S. E2 106
Marle, Fr. C10 10
Marlette, Mi., U.S. E7 99
Marley, Md., U.S. B4 97
Marlin, Tx., U.S. D4 120
Marlinton, W.V., U.S. C4 125
Marlow, Ok., U.S. C4 113
Marlowe, W.V., U.S. B7 125
Marlton, N.J., U.S. D3 107
Marmaduke, Ar., U.S. A5 81
Marmande, Fr. H7 10
Marmara Adası, i., Tur. I11 16
Marmara Denizi (Sea of Marmara), Tur. I12 16
Marmaris, Tur. M12 16
Marmet, W.V., U.S. C3 125
Marmora, Ont., Can. C7 73
Marne, stm., Fr. C10 10
Maroa, Il., U.S. C5 90
Maroa, Ven. F9 58
Maroantsetra, Madag. E9 44
Maromokotro, mtn., Madag. D9 44
Marondera, Zimb. E6 44
Maros (Mureș), stm., Eur. C4 16
Maroua, Cam. F8 42
Marovoay, Madag. E9 44
Marquesas Keys, is., Fl., U.S. H4 86
Marquette, Mi., U.S. B3 99
Marquette, co., Mi., U.S. B3 99
Marquette, co., Wi., U.S. E4 126
Marquette Heights, Il., U.S. C4 90
Marquise, Fr. B8 10
Marrah, Jabal, mtn., Sudan F10 42
Marrakech, Mor. B4 42
Marrero, La., U.S. E5 95
Mars, Pa., U.S. E1 115
Marsabit, Kenya H2 46
Marsala, Italy L7 14
Marsā Maṭrūḥ, Egypt B11 42
Marseille, Fr. J12 10
Marseille-en-Beauvaisis, Fr. C8 10
Marseilles, Il., U.S. B5 90
Marshall, Sask., Can. D1 75
Marshall, Ar., U.S. B3 81
Marshall, Il., U.S. D6 90
Marshall, Mi., U.S. F6 99
Marshall, Mn., U.S. F3 100
Marshall, Mo., U.S. B4 102
Marshall, N.C., U.S. f10 110
Marshall, Tx., U.S. C5 120
Marshall, Va., U.S. B5 123
Marshall, Wi., U.S. E4 126
Marshall, co., Al., U.S. A3 78
Marshall, co., Il., U.S. B4 90
Marshall, co., In., U.S. B5 91
Marshall, co., Ia., U.S. C4 92
Marshall, co., Ks., U.S. C7 93
Marshall, co., Ky., U.S. f9 94
Marshall, co., Mn., U.S. B2 100
Marshall, co., Ms., U.S. A4 101
Marshall, co., Ok., U.S. C5 113
Marshall, co., S.D., U.S. B8 118
Marshall, co., Tn., U.S. B5 119
Marshall, co., W.V., U.S. B4 125
Marshalltown, De., U.S. B3 85
Marshalltown, Ia., U.S. B5 92
Marshallville, Ga., U.S. D3 87
Marshes Siding, Ky., U.S. D5 94
Marshfield, Ma., U.S. B6 98
Marshfield, Mo., U.S. D5 102
Marshfield, Wi., U.S. D3 126
Marshfield Hills, Ma., U.S. B6 98
Marsh Fork, stm., W.V., U.S. n13 125
Marsh Harbour, Bah. A9 64
Mars Hill, Me., U.S. B5 96
Mars Hill, N.C., U.S. f10 110
Marsh Island, i., La., U.S. E4 95

Name	Map Ref	Page
Marsh Lake, res., Mn., U.S.	E2	100
Marsh Peak, mtn., Ut., U.S.	C6	121
Marshville, N.C., U.S.	C2	110
Marsing, Id., U.S.	F2	89
Märsta, Swe.	G11	6
Marston, Mo., U.S.	E8	102
Mart, Tx., U.S.	D4	120
Martaban, Gulf of, b., Mya.	F4	34
Marthasville, Mo., U.S.	C6	102
Martha's Vineyard, i., Ma., U.S.	D6	98
Martigny, Switz.	F14	10
Martigues, Fr.	I12	10
Martin, Slov.	F18	8
Martin, Ky., U.S.	C7	94
Martin, S.D., U.S.	D4	118
Martin, Tn., U.S.	A3	119
Martin, co., Fl., U.S.	E6	86
Martin, co., In., U.S.	G4	91
Martin, co., Ky., U.S.	C7	94
Martin, co., Mn., U.S.	G4	100
Martin, co., N.C., U.S.	B5	110
Martin, co., Tx., U.S.	C2	120
Martina Franca, Italy	I12	14
Martinez, Ca., U.S.	C2	82
Martinez, Ga., U.S.	C4	87
Martínez de la Torre, Mex.	G11	62
Martinique, dep., N.A.	G17	64
Martin Lake, res., Al., U.S.	C4	78
Martin Point, c., Ak., U.S.	A11	79
Martinsberg, Aus.	G15	8
Martinsburg, Pa., U.S.	F5	115
Martinsburg, W.V., U.S.	B7	125
Martins Ferry, Oh., U.S.	B5	112
Martinsville, Il., U.S.	D6	90
Martinsville, In., U.S.	F5	91
Martinsville, Va., U.S.	D3	123
Martos, Spain	H8	12
Martre, Lac la, l., N.W. Ter., Can.	D9	66
Martti, Fin.	C17	6
Marugame, Japan	H6	30
Ma'rūt, Afg.	E2	38
Marvejols, Fr.	H10	10
Marvell, Ar., U.S.	C5	81
Marvine, Mount, mtn., Ut., U.S.	E4	121
Mary, Turk.	J10	22
Mary, Lake, l., Mn., U.S.	E3	100
Mary, Lake, l., Ms., U.S.	D2	101
Maryborough, Austl.	E10	50
Maryland, state, U.S.	B4	97
Maryland City, Md., U.S.	B4	97
Maryland Heights, Mo., U.S.	f13	102
Maryland Point, c., Md., U.S.	D3	97
Maryport, Eng., U.K.	G9	7
Marys, stm., Nv., U.S.	B6	105
Marys Peak, mtn., Or., U.S.	C3	114
Marystown, Newf., Can.	E4	72
Marysville, Ca., U.S.	C3	82
Marysville, Ks., U.S.	C7	93
Marysville, Mi., U.S.	F8	99
Marysville, Oh., U.S.	B2	112
Marysville, Pa., U.S.	F8	115
Marysville, Wa., U.S.	A3	124
Maryville, Mo., U.S.	A3	102
Maryville, Tn., U.S.	D10	119
Marzūq, Libya	C8	42
Marzūq, Idehan, reg., Libya	C8	42
Masai Steppe, plat., Tan.	B7	44
Masaka, Ug.	B6	44
Masan, S. Kor.	D12	26
Masasi, Tan.	D7	44
Masaya, Nic.	I4	64
Masbate Island, i., Phil.	C7	32
Mascarene Islands, is., Afr.	F11	44
Mascoma, stm., N.H., U.S.	C2	106
Mascoma Lake, l., N.H., U.S.	C2	106
Mascot, Tn., U.S.	C10	119
Mascota, Mex.	G7	62
Mascouche, Que., Can.	D4	74
Mascoutah, Il., U.S.	E4	90
Maseru, Leso.	G5	44
Mashābih, i., Sau. Ar.	C2	46
Mashapaug Pond, l., Ct., U.S.	A7	84
Masherbrum, mtn., Pak.	C7	38
Mashhad, Iran	J9	22
Masi Manimba, Zaire	B3	44
Masindi, Ug.	H12	42
Masjed Soleymān, Iran	B4	46
Mask, Lough, l., Ire.	H3	7
Maskanah, Syria	A6	40
Maskinongé, Que., Can.	C4	74
Mason, Mi., U.S.	F6	99
Mason, Nv., U.S.	E2	105
Mason, Oh., U.S.	C1	112
Mason, Tx., U.S.	D3	120
Mason, W.V., U.S.	B2	125
Mason, co., Il., U.S.	C4	90
Mason, co., Ky., U.S.	B6	94
Mason, co., Mi., U.S.	D4	99
Mason, co., Tx., U.S.	D3	120
Mason, co., Wa., U.S.	B2	124
Mason, co., W.V., U.S.	C3	125
Mason City, Il., U.S.	C4	90
Mason City, Ia., U.S.	A4	92
Masontown, Pa., U.S.	G2	115
Masontown, W.V., U.S.	B5	125
Masqaṭ (Muscat), Oman	D6	46
Massa, Italy	E5	14
Massabesic Lake, l., N.H., U.S.	E4	106
Massac, co., Il., U.S.	F5	90
Massachusetts, state, U.S.	B4	98
Massachusetts Bay, b., Ma., U.S.	B6	98
Massacre Lake, l., Nv., U.S.	B2	105
Massafra, Italy	I12	14
Massa Marittima, Italy	F5	14
Massangena, Moz.	F6	44
Massapoag Lake, l., Ma., U.S.	h11	98
Massarosa, Italy	F5	14
Massasecum, Lake, l., N.H., U.S.	D3	106
Massena, N.Y., U.S.	f10	109
Massenya, Chad	F9	42
Masset, B.C., Can.	C1	69
Massey, Ont., Can.	A2	73
Massif Central see Central, Massif, mts., Fr.	G10	10
Massillon, Oh., U.S.	B4	112
Massive, Mount, mtn., Co., U.S.	B4	83
Masterton, N.Z.	D5	52
Mastic Beach, N.Y., U.S.	n16	109
Mastung, Pak.	F2	38
Masuda, Japan	H4	30
Masury, Oh., U.S.	A5	112
Matadi, Zaire	C2	44
Matagalpa, Nic.	H5	64
Matagorda, co., Tx., U.S.	E5	120
Matagorda Bay, b., Tx., U.S.	E4	120
Matagorda Island, i., Tx., U.S.	E4	120
Matagorda Peninsula, pen., Tx., U.S.	E5	120
Matale, Sri L.	I6	37
Matamoras, Pa., U.S.	D12	115
Matamoros, Mex.	E11	62
Matamoros de la Laguna, Mex.	E8	62
Matandu, stm., Tan.	C7	44
Matane, Que., Can.	k13	74
Matanuska, stm., Ak., U.S.	g18	79
Matanzas, Cuba	C7	64
Matanzas Inlet, b., Fl., U.S.	C5	86
Matara, Sri L.	J6	37
Mataró, Spain	D14	12
Matatiele, S. Afr.	H5	44
Matawan, N.J., U.S.	C4	107
Matehuala, Mex.	F9	62
Mateira, Braz.	E3	57
Matelica, Italy	F7	14
Matera, Italy	I11	14
Mateur, Tun.	L4	14
Matewan, W.V., U.S.	D2	125
Mather, Pa., U.S.	G1	115
Mather Air Force Base, mil., Ca., U.S.	C3	82
Mather Peaks, mts., Wy., U.S.	B5	127
Mathews, La., U.S.	E5	95
Mathews, Va., U.S.	C6	123
Mathews, co., Va., U.S.	C6	123
Mathews, Lake, l., Ca., U.S.	n14	82
Mathis, Tx., U.S.	E4	120
Mathiston, Ms., U.S.	B4	101
Mathura, India	G7	38
Matías Romero, Mex.	I12	62
Matinicus Island, i., Me., U.S.	E3	96
Mātli, Pak.	H3	38
Mato, Cerro, mtn., Ven.	D10	58
Matoaca, Va., U.S.	n18	123
Mato Grosso, Braz.	F7	54
Mato Grosso, Planalto do, plat., Braz.	G7	54
Matosinhos, Port.	D3	12
Matou, Tai.	L9	28
Maṭraḥ, Oman	D6	46
Matsqui, B.C., Can.	f13	69
Matsudo, Japan	G12	30
Matsue, Japan	G6	30
Matsumae, Japan	r18	30a
Matsumoto, Japan	F10	30
Matsusaka, Japan	H9	30
Matsu Tao, i., Tai.	I8	28
Matsuyama, Japan	I5	30
Mattagami, stm., Ont., Can.	F16	66
Mattamiscontis Lake, l., Me., U.S.	C4	96
Mattamuskeet, Lake, l., N.C., U.S.	B6	110
Mattāncheri, India	H4	37
Mattapoisett, Ma., U.S.	C6	98
Mattaponi, stm., Va., U.S.	C5	123
Mattawa, Ont., Can.	A6	73
Mattawamkeag, Me., U.S.	C4	96
Mattawamkeag, stm., Me., U.S.	C4	96
Mattawamkeag Lake, l., Me., U.S.	C4	96
Matterhorn, mtn., Eur.	G14	10
Matterhorn, mtn., Nv., U.S.	B6	105
Matteson, Il., U.S.	k9	90
Matthews, Mo., U.S.	E8	102
Matthews, N.C., U.S.	B2	110
Matthews Ridge, Guy.	D12	58
Matthew Town, Bah.	D11	64
Mattighofen, Aus.	G13	8
Mattituck, N.Y., U.S.	n16	109
Mattoon, Il., U.S.	D5	90
Mattoon, Lake, res., Il., U.S.	D5	90
Mattydale, N.Y., U.S.	B4	109
Matunuck, R.I., U.S.	G3	116
Maturín, Ven.	C11	58
Maúa, Moz.	D7	44
Maubeuge, Fr.	B10	10
Maud, Ok., U.S.	B5	113
Maugansville, Md., U.S.	A2	97
Maui, co., Hi., U.S.	B5	88
Maui, i., Hi., U.S.	C6	88
Mauldin, S.C., U.S.	B3	117
Mauléon-Licharre, Fr.	I6	10
Maulvi Bāzār, Bngl.	H14	38
Maumee, Oh., U.S.	A2	112
Maumee, stm., U.S.	A2	112
Maumee Bay, b., U.S.	G7	99
Maumelle, Lake, res., Ar., U.S.	C3	81
Maun, Bots.	E4	44
Mauna Kea, vol., Hi., U.S.	D6	88
Maunaloa, Hi., U.S.	B4	88
Mauna Loa, vol., Hi., U.S.	D6	88
Maunalua Bay, b., Hi., U.S.	g10	88
Maunath Bhanjan, India	H10	38
Maunawili, Hi., U.S.	g10	88
Mau Rānīpur, India	H8	38
Maurepas, Lake, l., La., U.S.	D5	95
Mauriac, Fr.	G9	10
Maurice, Ia., U.S.	B1	92
Maurice, stm., N.J., U.S.	E2	107
Mauritania, ctry., Afr.	D3	42
Mauritius, ctry., Afr.	F11	44
Maurs, Fr.	H9	10
Maury, co., Tn., U.S.	B4	119
Maury City, Tn., U.S.	B2	119
Maury Island, i., Wa., U.S.	f11	124
Mauston, Wi., U.S.	E3	126
Mauterndorf, Aus.	H13	8
Mauthausen, Aus.	G14	8
Maverick, co., Tx., U.S.	E2	120
Maw-Daung Pass, Asia	I5	34
Mawlaik, Mya.	C3	34
Mawlamyine (Moulmein), Mya.	F4	34
Maw Taung, mtn., Asia	I5	34
Maxinkuckee, Lake, l., In., U.S.	B5	91
Max Meadows, Va., U.S.	D2	123
Maxton, N.C., U.S.	C3	110
Maxville, Ont., Can.	B10	73
Maxwell, Ia., U.S.	C4	92
Maxwell Acres, W.V., U.S.	g8	125
Maxwell Air Force Base, mil., Al., U.S.	C3	78
Mayaguana, i., Bah.	C11	64
Mayaguana Passage, strt., Bah.	C11	64
Mayagüez, P.R.	E14	64
Maya Mountains, mts., N.A.	F3	64
Maybole, Scot., U.K.	F8	7
Mayen, Ger.	E7	8
Mayenne, Fr.	D6	10
Mayer, Az., U.S.	C3	80
Mayerthorpe, Alta., Can.	C3	68
Mayes, co., Ok., U.S.	A6	113
Mayesville, S.C., U.S.	D7	117
Mayfield, Ky., U.S.	f9	94
Mayfield, Pa., U.S.	C10	115
Mayfield Heights, Oh., U.S.	A4	112
Mayfield Lake, res., Wa., U.S.	C3	124
Mayflower, Ar., U.S.	C3	81
Mayking, Ky., U.S.	C7	94
Maykop see Majkop, Russia	I6	22
Maymyo, Mya.	C4	34
Maynard, Ma., U.S.	B5	98
Maynardville, Tn., U.S.	C10	119
Mayne, B.C., Can.	g12	69
Mayo, Yukon, Can.	D5	66
Mayo, Md., U.S.	C4	97
Mayo, S.C., U.S.	A4	117
Mayodan, N.C., U.S.	A3	110
Mayotte, ter., Afr.	D9	44
Mayotte, i., May.	D9	44
May Park, Or., U.S.	B8	114
Mayport Naval Station, mil., Fl., U.S.	B5	86
Maysville, Ga., U.S.	B3	87
Maysville, Ky., U.S.	B6	94
Maysville, Mo., U.S.	B3	102
Maysville, N.C., U.S.	C5	110
Maysville, Ok., U.S.	C4	113
Mayumba, Gabon	B2	44
Māyūram, India	G5	37
Mayville, Mi., U.S.	E7	99
Mayville, N.Y., U.S.	C1	109
Mayville, N.D., U.S.	B8	111
Mayville, Wi., U.S.	E5	126
Maywood, Il., U.S.	k9	90
Maywood, N.J., U.S.	h8	107
Maywood Park, Or., U.S.	*B4	114
Mazabuka, Zam.	E5	44
Mazamet, Fr.	I9	10
Mazara del Vallo, Italy	L7	14
Mazār-e Sharīf, Afg.	B2	38
Mazaruni, stm., Guy.	E13	58
Mazatenango, Guat.	G2	64
Mazatlán, Mex.	F6	62
Mazatzal Mountains, mts., Az., U.S.	C4	80
Mazatzal Peak, mtn., Az., U.S.	C4	80
Mazeppa, Mn., U.S.	F6	100
Mazoe, stm., Afr.	E6	44
Mazomanie, Wi., U.S.	E4	126
Mazon, Il., U.S.	B5	90
Mbabane, Swaz.	G6	44
Mbaïki, Cen. Afr. Rep.	H9	42
Mbala, Zam.	C6	44
Mbale, Ug.	A6	44
Mbandaka (Coquilhatville), Zaire	A3	44
Mbanza-Ngungu, Zaire	C2	44
M'banz Congo, Ang.	C2	44
Mbeya, Tan.	C6	44
Mbomou (Bomu), stm., Afr.	H10	42
Mbout, Maur.	E3	42
Mbuji-Mayi (Bakwanga), Zaire	C4	44
McAdam, N.B., Can.	D2	71
McAdoo, Pa., U.S.	E9	115
McAfee Peak, mtn., Nv., U.S.	B6	105
McAlester, Ok., U.S.	C6	113
McAlester, Lake, res., Ok., U.S.	B6	113
McAllen, Tx., U.S.	F3	120
McAlmont, Ar., U.S.	h10	81
McAlpine, Md., U.S.	B4	97
McAlpine Lock and Dam, U.S.	H6	91
McArthur, Oh., U.S.	C3	112
McBee, S.C., U.S.	C7	117
McCall, Id., U.S.	E2	89
McCalla, Al., U.S.	g6	78
McCamey, Tx., U.S.	D1	120
McCammon, Id., U.S.	G6	89
McCandless, Pa., U.S.	h13	115
McCartney Mountain, mtn., Mt., U.S.	E4	103
McCaysville, Ga., U.S.	B2	87
McChord Air Force Base, mil., Wa., U.S.	f11	124
McClain, co., Ok., U.S.	C4	113
McCleary, Wa., U.S.	B2	124
McClellan Air Force Base, mil., Ca., U.S.	C3	82
McClintock, Mount, mtn., Ant.	A28	47
McCloud, Ca., U.S.	B2	82
McClure, Pa., U.S.	E7	115
McColl, S.C., U.S.	B8	117
McComas, W.V., U.S.	D3	125
McComb, Ms., U.S.	D3	101
McComb, Oh., U.S.	A2	112
McCone, co., Mt., U.S.	C11	103
McConnell Air Force Base, mil., Ks., U.S.	g12	93
McConnellsburg, Pa., U.S.	G6	115
McConnelsville, Oh., U.S.	C4	112
McCook, Ne., U.S.	D5	104
McCook, co., S.D., U.S.	D8	118
McCordsville, In., U.S.	E6	91
McCormick, S.C., U.S.	D3	117
McCormick, co., S.C., U.S.	D3	117
McCracken, co., Ky., U.S.	e9	94
McCreary, Man., Can.	D2	70
McCreary, co., Ky., U.S.	D5	94
McCrory, Ar., U.S.	B4	81
McCulloch, co., Tx., U.S.	D3	120
McCullough Mountain, mtn., Nv., U.S.	H6	105
McCurtain, co., Ok., U.S.	C7	113
McDermitt, Nv., U.S.	B4	105
McDonald, co., Mo., U.S.	E3	102
McDonough, Ga., U.S.	C2	87
McDonough, co., Il., U.S.	C3	90
McDougall, Mount, mtn., Wy., U.S.	D2	127
McDowell, Ky., U.S.	C7	94
McDowell, co., N.C., U.S.	f10	110
McDowell, co., W.V., U.S.	D3	125
McDowell Mountains, mts., Az., U.S.	k9	80
McDowell Peak, mtn., Az., U.S.	k9	80
McDuffie, co., Ga., U.S.	C4	87
McElroy Creek, stm., W.V., U.S.	k9	125
Mcensk, Russia	H19	18
McEwen, Tn., U.S.	A4	119
McFarland, Ca., U.S.	E4	82
McFarland, Wi., U.S.	E4	126
McGehee, Ar., U.S.	D4	81
McGill, Nv., U.S.	D7	105
McGrath, Ak., U.S.	C8	79
McGregor, Ia., U.S.	A6	92
McGregor, Tx., U.S.	D4	120
McGregor, stm., B.C., Can.	B7	69
McGregor Lake, l., Alta., Can.	D4	68
McGuire, Mount, mtn., Id., U.S.	D4	89
McGuire Air Force Base, mil., N.J., U.S.	C3	107
McHenry, Il., U.S.	A5	90
McHenry, Md., U.S.	k12	97
McHenry, co., Il., U.S.	A5	90
McHenry, co., N.D., U.S.	A5	111
McIntosh, Mn., U.S.	C3	100
McIntosh, co., Ga., U.S.	E5	87
McIntosh, co., N.D., U.S.	C6	111
McIntosh, co., Ok., U.S.	B6	113
McKean, co., Pa., U.S.	C4	115
McKee, Ky., U.S.	C6	94
McKeesport, Pa., U.S.	F2	115
McKees Rocks, Pa., U.S.	F1	115
McKenzie, Tn., U.S.	A3	119
McKenzie, co., N.D., U.S.	B2	111
McKenzie, stm., Or., U.S.	C4	114
McKinley, co., N.M., U.S.	B1	108
McKinley, Mount, mtn., Ak., U.S.	C9	79
McKinleyville, Ca., U.S.	B1	82
McKinney, Tx., U.S.	C4	120
McKinney, Lake, l., Ks., U.S.	E2	93
McKittrick Summit, mtn., Ca., U.S.	E4	82
McLaughlin, S.D., U.S.	B5	118
McLean, Il., U.S.	C4	90
McLean, Va., U.S.	g12	123
McLean, co., Il., U.S.	C4	90
McLean, co., Ky., U.S.	C2	94
McLean, co., N.D., U.S.	B4	111
McLeansboro, Il., U.S.	E5	90
McLennan, Alta., Can.	B2	68
McLennan, co., Tx., U.S.	D4	120
McLeod, co., Mn., U.S.	F4	100
McLeod, Lake, l., Austl.	D2	50
M'Clintock Channel, strt., N.W. Ter., Can.	B12	66
McLoud, Ok., U.S.	B4	113
McLoughlin, Mount, mtn., Or., U.S.	D4	114
McLouth, Ks., U.S.	C8	93
McMechen, W.V., U.S.	B4	125
McMillan, Lake, res., N.M., U.S.	E5	108
McMinn, co., Tn., U.S.	D9	119
McMinnville, Or., U.S.	B3	114
McMinnville, Tn., U.S.	D8	119
McMullen, co., Tx., U.S.	E3	120
McNairy, co., Tn., U.S.	B3	119
McNary, Az., U.S.	C6	80
McNary Dam, U.S.	B7	114
McNeil, Ar., U.S.	D2	81
McNeil, Mount, mtn., B.C., Can.	B2	69
McNeil Island, i., Wa., U.S.	f10	124
McNeill, Ms., U.S.	E4	101
McPherson, Ks., U.S.	D6	93
McPherson, co., Ks., U.S.	D6	93
McPherson, co., Ne., U.S.	C4	104
McPherson, co., S.D., U.S.	B6	118
McQueeney, Tx., U.S.	h7	120
McRae, Ar., U.S.	B4	81
McRae, Ga., U.S.	D4	87
McRoberts, Ky., U.S.	C7	94
McSherrystown, Pa., U.S.	G7	115
Mead, Wa., U.S.	B8	124
Mead, Lake, res., U.S.	A1	80
Meade, Ks., U.S.	E3	93
Meade, co., Ks., U.S.	E3	93
Meade, co., Ky., U.S.	C3	94
Meade, co., S.D., U.S.	C3	118
Meade, stm., Ak., U.S.	B8	79
Meaden Peak, mtn., Co., U.S.	A3	83
Meade Peak, mtn., Id., U.S.	G7	89
Meadow, stm., W.V., U.S.	C4	125
Meadow Creek, stm., W.V., U.S.	n14	125
Meadow Lands, Pa., U.S.	F1	115
Meadow Valley Wash, val., Nv., U.S.	F7	105
Meadowview, Va., U.S.	f10	123
Meadville, Pa., U.S.	C1	115
Meaford, Ont., Can.	C4	73
Meagher, co., Mt., U.S.	D6	103
Mealhada, Port.	E3	12
Meander Creek Reservoir, res., Oh., U.S.	A5	112
Meath, hist. reg., Ire.	H5	7
Meaux, Fr.	D9	10
Mebane, N.C., U.S.	A3	110
Mecca, Ca., U.S.	F5	82
Mecca see Makkah, Sau. Ar.	D2	46
Mechanic Falls, Me., U.S.	D2	96
Mechanicsburg, Oh., U.S.	B2	112
Mechanicsburg, Pa., U.S.	F7	115
Mechanicsville, Ia., U.S.	C6	92
Mechanicsville, Md., U.S.	D4	97
Mechanicsville, Va., U.S.	C5	123
Mechanicville, N.Y., U.S.	C7	109
Mechant, Lake, l., La., U.S.	E4	95
Mechelen, Bel.	D4	8
Mecklenburg, co., N.C., U.S.	B2	110
Mecklenburg, co., Va., U.S.	D4	123
Mecklenburg, hist. reg., Ger.	B12	8
Mecklenburger Bucht, b., Ger.	A11	8
Mecosta, co., Mi., U.S.	E5	99
Medan, Indon.	E2	32
Medanosa, Punta, c., Arg.	F3	56
Medaryville, In., U.S.	B4	91
Meddybumps Lake, l., Me., U.S.	C5	96
Medeiros Neto, Braz.	D8	57
Medellín, Col.	D5	58
Médenine, Tun.	B8	42
Medfield, Ma., U.S.	h10	98
Medford, Ma., U.S.	B5	98
Medford, Mn., U.S.	F5	100
Medford, Ok., U.S.	A4	113
Medford, Or., U.S.	E4	114
Medford, Wi., U.S.	C3	126
Medford Lakes, N.J., U.S.	D3	107
Medgidia, Rom.	E12	16
Media, Pa., U.S.	G11	115
Mediapolis, Ia., U.S.	C6	92
Mediaș, Rom.	C8	16
Medical Lake, Wa., U.S.	B8	124
Medicine Bow, Wy., U.S.	E6	127
Medicine Bow, stm., Wy., U.S.	E6	127
Medicine Bow Mountains, mts., U.S.	E6	127
Medicine Bow Peak, mtn., Wy., U.S.	E6	127
Medicine Hat, Alta., Can.	D5	68
Medicine Lodge, Ks., U.S.	E5	93
Medicine Lodge, stm., U.S.	E4	93
Medina, N.Y., U.S.	B2	109
Medina, Oh., U.S.	A4	112
Medina, Tn., U.S.	B3	119
Medina, Wa., U.S.	e11	124
Medina, co., Oh., U.S.	A4	112
Medina, co., Tx., U.S.	E3	120
Medina, stm., Tx., U.S.	k7	120
Medina see Al-Madīnah, Sau. Ar.	D2	46
Medinaceli, Spain	D9	12
Medina del Campo, Spain	D7	12
Medina de Ríoseco, Spain	D6	12
Mediterranean Sea	D14	2
Medjez el Bab, Tun.	M4	14
Médoc, reg., Fr.	G5	10
Medora, In., U.S.	G5	91
Médouneu, Gabon	A2	44
Medway, Me., U.S.	C4	96
Medway, Ma., U.S.	B5	98
Medway, stm., N.S., Can.	E5	71
Meekatharra, Austl.	E3	50
Meeker, Co., U.S.	A3	83
Meeker, Ok., U.S.	B5	113
Meeker, co., Mn., U.S.	E4	100
Meelpaeg Lake, res., Newf., Can.	D3	72
Meerut, India	F7	38
Meeteetse, Wy., U.S.	B4	127
Mega, Eth.	H2	46
Mégantic, Lac, l., Que., Can.	D7	74
Mégantic, Mont, mtn., Que., Can.	D6	74
Mégara, Grc.	K7	16
Meggett, S.C., U.S.	F7	117
Meghalaya, state, India	H14	38
Meherrin, stm., U.S.	A4	110
Mehlville, Mo., U.S.	f13	102
Mehsāna, India	I5	38
Mehtar Lām, Afg.	C4	38
Mehun-sur-Yèvre, Fr.	E9	10
Meigs, Ga., U.S.	E2	87
Meigs, co., Oh., U.S.	C3	112
Meigs, co., Tn., U.S.	D9	119
Meiktila, Mya.	D3	34
Meiningen, Ger.	E10	8
Meissen, Ger.	D13	8
Meixian, China	K5	28
Mekambo, Gabon	A2	44
Mekele, Eth.	F2	46
Meknès, Mor.	B4	42
Mekong, stm., Asia	H8	34
Melaka, Malay.	M7	34
Melanesia, is., Oc.	G23	2
Melbourne, Austl.	G8	50
Melbourne, Ar., U.S.	A4	81
Melbourne, Fl., U.S.	D6	86
Melbourne, Ia., U.S.	C4	92
Melbourne, Ky., U.S.	h14	94
Melbourne Beach, Fl., U.S.	D6	86
Melcher, Ia., U.S.	C4	92
Meldorf, Ger.	A9	8
Mélèzes, Rivière aux, stm., Que., Can.	g12	74
Melfi, Chad	F9	42
Melfi, Italy	I10	14
Melgaço, Port.	C3	12
Melhus, Nor.	E8	6
Melilla, Sp. N. Afr.	A5	42
Melita, Man., Can.	E1	70
Melito di Porto Salvo, Italy	L10	14
Melitopol', Ukr.	H5	22
Melk, Aus.	G15	8
Mellansel, Swe.	E12	6
Melle, Fr.	F6	10
Mellen, Wi., U.S.	B3	126
Mellerud, Swe.	G9	6
Mellette, co., S.D., U.S.	D5	118
Mellish Reef, atoll, Austl.	C11	50
Melo, Ur.	C6	56
Melocheville, Que., Can.	q19	74
Melrhir, Chott, l., Alg.	B7	42
Melrose, Fl., U.S.	C4	86
Melrose, Ma., U.S.	B5	98
Melrose, Mn., U.S.	E4	100
Melrose, N.M., U.S.	C6	108
Meltaus, Fin.	C15	6
Melton Hill Lake, res., Tn., U.S.	D9	119
Melton Mowbray, Eng., U.K.	I12	7
Melun, Fr.	D9	10
Melvern Lake, res., Ks., U.S.	D8	93
Melville, La., U.S.	D4	95
Melville, Lake, l., Newf., Can.	B2	72
Melville Hills, hills, N.W. Ter., Can.	C8	66
Melville Island, i., Austl.	B6	50
Melville Island, i., N.W. Ter., Can.	A10	66

Name — Map Ref — Page

Melville Peninsula, pen., N.W. Ter., Can. C16 66
Melvin, Ky., U.S. C7 94
Memmingen, Ger. H10 8
Memphis, Fl., U.S. p10 86
Memphis, Mi., U.S. F8 99
Memphis, Mo., U.S. A5 102
Memphis, Tn., U.S. B1 119
Memphis, Tx., U.S. B2 120
Memphis Naval Air Station, mil., Tn., U.S. B2 119
Mena, Ar., U.S. C1 81
Menahga, Mn., U.S. D3 100
Ménaka, Mali E6 42
Menan, Id., U.S. F7 89
Menands, N.Y., U.S. C7 109
Menard, Tx., U.S. D3 120
Menard, co., Il., U.S. C4 90
Menard, co., Tx., U.S. D3 120
Menasha, Wi., U.S. D5 126
Mendawai, stm., Indon. F5 32
Mende, Fr. H10 10
Mendenhall, Ms., U.S. D4 101
Méndez, Ec. I3 58
Mendham, N.J., U.S. B3 107
Mendi, Eth. G2 46
Mendip Hills, hills, Eng., U.K. J10 7
Mendocino, co., Ca., U.S. C2 82
Mendon, Il., U.S. C2 90
Mendon, Mi., U.S. F5 99
Mendon, Ut., U.S. B4 121
Mendota, Ca., U.S. D3 82
Mendota, Il., U.S. B4 90
Mendota, Lake, l., Wi., U.S. E4 126
Mendoza, Arg. C3 56
Mene de Mauroa, Ven. B7 58
Mene Grande, Ven. C7 58
Menemen, Tur. K11 16
Menfi, Italy L7 14
Mengzhi, China C7 34
Mengzi, China B5 34
Menifee, co., Ky., U.S. C6 94
Menlo Park, Ca., U.S. k8 82
Menno, S.D., U.S. D8 118
Menominee, Mi., U.S. C3 99
Menominee, co., Mi., U.S. C3 99
Menominee, co., Wi., U.S. C5 126
Menominee, stm., U.S. C6 126
Menominee Indian Reservation, Wi., U.S. C5 126
Menomonee, stm., Wi., U.S. m11 126
Menomonee Falls, Wi., U.S. E5 126
Menomonie, Wi., U.S. D2 126
Menongue, Ang. D3 44
Menorca, i., Spain F16 12
Mentawai, Kepulauan, is., Indon. F2 32
Menton, Fr. I14 10
Mentone, In., U.S. B5 91
Mentor, Oh., U.S. A4 112
Mentor-on-the-Lake, Oh., U.S. A4 112
Menzel Bourguiba, Tun. L4 14
Meoqui, Mex. C7 62
Meppel, Neth. C6 8
Meppen, Ger. C7 8
Mequon, Wi., U.S. E6 126
Mer, Fr. E8 10
Meramec, stm., Mo., U.S. C7 102
Merano (Meran), Italy C6 14
Merasheen Island, i., Newf., Can. E4 72
Merauke, Indon. G11 32
Meraux, La., U.S. k12 95
Mercaderes, Col. G4 58
Merced, Ca., U.S. D3 82
Merced, co., Ca., U.S. D3 82
Merced, stm., Ca., U.S. D3 82
Mercedes, Arg. B5 56
Mercedes, Arg. C3 56
Mercedes, Tx., U.S. F4 120
Mercedes, Ur. C5 56
Mercer, Pa., U.S. D1 115
Mercer, Wi., U.S. B3 126
Mercer, co., Il., U.S. B3 90
Mercer, co., Ky., U.S. C5 94
Mercer, co., Mo., U.S. A4 102
Mercer, co., N.J., U.S. C3 107
Mercer, co., N.D., U.S. B4 111
Mercer, co., Oh., U.S. B1 112
Mercer, co., Pa., U.S. D1 115
Mercer, co., W.V., U.S. D3 125
Mercer Island, Wa., U.S. B3 124
Mercer Island, i., Wa., U.S. e11 124
Mercersburg, Pa., U.S. G6 115
Mercerville, N.J., U.S. C3 107
Mercier, Que., Can. D4 74
Meredith, N.H., U.S. C3 106
Meredith, Lake, l., Co., U.S. C7 83
Meredith, Lake, res., Tx., U.S. B2 120
Meredosia, Il., U.S. D3 90
Meredosia Lake, l., Il., U.S. D3 90
Mergui (Myeik), Mya. H5 34
Mergui Archipelago, is., Mya. H4 34
Meriç (Marica) (évros), stm., Eur. H10 16
Mérida, Mex. G15 62
Mérida, Spain G5 12
Mérida, Ven. C7 58
Meriden, Ct., U.S. C4 84
Meriden, Ks., U.S. C8 93
Meridian, Id., U.S. F2 89
Meridian, Ms., U.S. C5 101
Meridian, Pa., U.S. E2 115
Meridian, Tx., U.S. D4 120
Meridian Hills, In., U.S. k10 91
Meridian Naval Air Station, mil., Ms., U.S. C5 101
Meridianville, Al., U.S. A3 78
Mérignac, Fr. H6 10
Merikarvia, Fin. F13 6
Meriwether, co., Ga., U.S. C2 87
Merkel, Tx., U.S. C2 120
Merlin, Ont., Can. E2 73
Mermentau, La., U.S. D3 95
Mermentau, stm., La., U.S. E3 95
Meron, Hare, mtn., Isr. C4 40
Merriam, Ks., U.S. k16 93
Merrick, co., Ne., U.S. C7 104
Merrickville, Ont., Can. C9 73
Merrill, Ia., U.S. B1 92
Merrill, Mi., U.S. E6 99
Merrill, Or., U.S. E5 114
Merrill, Wi., U.S. C4 126
Merrillville, In., U.S. B3 91
Merrimac, Ma., U.S. A5 98
Merrimack, N.H., U.S. E4 106
Merrimack, co., N.H., U.S. D3 106
Merrimack, stm., U.S. A5 98
Merritt, B.C., Can. D7 69
Merritt Island, Fl., U.S. D6 86
Merritt Reservoir, res., Ne., U.S. B5 104
Merrymeeting Lake, l., N.H., U.S. D4 106
Merryville, La., U.S. D2 95
Merseburg, Ger. D11 8
Merthyr Tydfil, Wales, U.K. J9 7
Mértola, Port. H4 12
Merton, Wi., U.S. m11 126
Méru, Fr. C9 10
Merwin Lake, res., Wa., U.S. C3 124
Merzig, Ger. F6 8
Mesa, Az., U.S. D4 80
Mesa, co., Co., U.S. C2 83
Mesabi Range, hills, Mn., U.S. C6 100
Mesagne, Italy I12 14
Mesa Mountain, mtn., Co., U.S. D4 83
Mesa Verde National Park, Co., U.S. D2 83
Mescalero, N.M., U.S. D4 108
Mescalero Indian Reservation, N.M., U.S. D4 108
Mesilla, N.M., U.S. E3 108
Mesolóngion, Grc. K5 16
Mesopotamia, reg., Asia B3 46
Mesquite, Nv., U.S. G7 105
Mesquite, N.M., U.S. E3 108
Mesquite, Tx., U.S. n10 120
Messalo, stm., Moz. D7 44
Messalonskee Lake, l., Me., U.S. D3 96
Messina, Italy K10 14
Messina, S. Afr. F5 44
Messina, Stretto di, strt., Italy K10 14
Mesta (Néstos), stm., Eur. H7 16
Mestre, Italy D7 14
Meta, stm., S.A. D9 58
Métabetchouan, Que., Can. A6 74
Métabetchouane, stm., Que., Can. A5 74
Metairie, La., U.S. k11 95
Metamora, Il., U.S. C4 90
Metán, Arg. B3 56
Metcalfe, Ont., Can. B9 73
Metcalfe, Ms., U.S. B2 101
Metcalfe, co., Ky., U.S. C4 94
Metedeconk, North Branch, stm., N.J., U.S. C4 107
Metedeconk, South Branch, stm., N.J., U.S. C3 107
Meteghan, N.S., Can. E3 71
Meteghan River, N.S., Can. E3 71
Meteor Crater, crat., Az., U.S. C4 80
Methow, stm., Wa., U.S. A5 124
Methuen, Ma., U.S. A5 98
Metković, Cro. F12 14
Metlakatla, Ak., U.S. D13 79
Metlatonoc, Mex. I10 62
Metlika, Slo. D10 14
Metonga, Lake, l., Wi., U.S. C5 126
Metro, Indon. k12 33a
Metropolis, Il., U.S. F5 90
Mettawee, stm., U.S. E2 122
Metter, Ga., U.S. D4 87
Mettūr, India G4 37
Metuchen, N.J., U.S. B4 107
Metz, Fr. C13 10
Metzger, Or., U.S. h12 114
Meuse (Maas), stm., Eur. E5 8
Mexia, Tx., U.S. D4 120
Mexia, Lake, res., Tx., U.S. D4 120
Mexiana, Ilha, i., Braz. D9 54
Mexicali, Mex. A2 62
Mexico, In., U.S. C5 91
Mexico, Me., U.S. D2 96
Mexico, Mo., U.S. B6 102
Mexico (México), ctry., N.A. F8 62
Mexico, Gulf of, b., N.A. F9 76
Mexico City see Ciudad de México, Mex. H10 62
Meximieux, Fr. G12 10
Meycauayan, Phil. q19 33b
Meyersdale, Pa., U.S. G3 115
Meymaneh, Afg. C1 38
Meyrueis, Fr. H10 10
Meždurečensk, Russia G11 24
Mèze, Fr. I10 10
Mezőtúr, Hung. H20 8
Mezquital, Mex. F7 62
Mezzolombardo, Italy C6 14
Mhow, India I6 38
Miami, Az., U.S. D5 80
Miami, Fl., U.S. G6 86
Miami, Ok., U.S. A7 113
Miami, co., In., U.S. C5 91
Miami, co., Ks., U.S. D9 93
Miami, co., Oh., U.S. B1 112
Miami Beach, Fl., U.S. G6 86
Miami Canal, Fl., U.S. F6 86
Miami International Airport, Fl., U.S. G6 86
Miamisburg, Oh., U.S. C1 112
Miami Shores, Fl., U.S. G6 86
Miami Springs, Fl., U.S. G6 86
Miandrivazo, Madag. E9 44
Mīāneh, Iran J7 22
Mianus Reservoir, res., U.S. E1 84
Miānwāli, Pak. D4 38
Mica Mountain, mtn., Az., U.S. E5 80
Micco, Fl., U.S. E6 86
Miccosukee, Lake, res., Fl., U.S. B2 86
Michelson, Mount, mtn., Ak., U.S. B11 79
Michie, Tn., U.S. B3 119
Michigamme, Lake, l., Mi., U.S. B2 99
Michigamme Reservoir, res., Mi., U.S. B2 99
Michigan, state, U.S. E6 99
Michigan, stm., Co., U.S. A4 83
Michigan, Lake, l., U.S. C9 76
Michigan Center, Mi., U.S. F6 99
Michigan City, In., U.S. A4 91
Michigan Island, i., Wi., U.S. B3 126
Michikamau Lake, l., Newf., Can. F20 66
Michipicoten Island, i., Ont., Can. G15 66
Micronesia, is., Oc. F23 2
Mičurinsk, Russia I23 18
Middelburg, Neth. D3 8
Middelburg, S. Afr. H4 44
Middelharnis, Neth. D4 8
Middle, stm., Ia., U.S. C3 92
Middle, stm., Mn., U.S. B2 100
Middle Andaman, i., India H2 34
Middleboro (Middleborough Center), Ma., U.S. C6 98
Middlebourne, W.V., U.S. B4 125
Middleburg, Fl., U.S. B5 86
Middleburg, Pa., U.S. E7 115
Middleburg Heights, Oh., U.S. h9 112
Middlebury, Ct., U.S. C3 84
Middlebury, In., U.S. A6 91
Middlebury, Vt., U.S. C2 122
Middlefield, Ct., U.S. C5 84
Middlefield, Oh., U.S. A4 112
Middle Island Creek, stm., W.V., U.S. B3 125
Middle Nodaway, stm., Ia., U.S. C3 92
Middle Park, val., Co., U.S. A4 83
Middle Patuxent, stm., Md., U.S. B4 97
Middleport, N.Y., U.S. B2 109
Middleport, Oh., U.S. C3 112
Middle Raccoon, stm., Ia., U.S. C3 92
Middle River, Md., U.S. B5 97
Middlesboro, Ky., U.S. D6 94
Middlesex, N.J., U.S. B4 107
Middlesex, N.C., U.S. B4 110
Middlesex, co., Ct., U.S. D5 84
Middlesex, co., Ma., U.S. A5 98
Middlesex, co., N.J., U.S. C4 107
Middlesex, co., Va., U.S. C6 123
Middlesex Fells Reservation, Ma., U.S. g11 98
Middleton, N.S., Can. E4 71
Middleton, Id., U.S. F2 89
Middleton, Ma., U.S. A5 98
Middleton, Wi., U.S. E4 126
Middleton Reef, atoll, Austl. E11 50
Middletown, Ca., U.S. C2 82
Middletown, Ct., U.S. C5 84
Middletown, De., U.S. C3 85
Middletown, In., U.S. D6 91
Middletown, Ky., U.S. g11 94
Middletown, Md., U.S. B2 97
Middletown, N.J., U.S. C4 107
Middletown, N.Y., U.S. D6 109
Middletown, Oh., U.S. C1 112
Middletown, Pa., U.S. F8 115
Middletown, R.I., U.S. E5 116
Middletown, Va., U.S. A4 123
Middleville, Mi., U.S. F5 99
Midfield, Al., U.S. g7 78
Midland, Ont., Can. C5 73
Midland, Mi., U.S. E6 99
Midland, N.C., U.S. B2 110
Midland, Pa., U.S. E1 115
Midland, Tx., U.S. D1 120
Midland, co., Mi., U.S. E6 99
Midland, co., Tx., U.S. D1 120
Midland City, Al., U.S. D4 78
Midland Park, Ks., U.S. g12 93
Midland Park, N.J., U.S. B4 107
Midland Park, S.C., U.S. k11 117
Midleton, Ire. J4 7
Midlothian, Il., U.S. k9 90
Midlothian, Tx., U.S. C4 120
Midnapore, India I12 38
Midongy Sud, Madag. F9 44
Midvale, Ut., U.S. C4 121
Midville, Ga., U.S. D4 87
Midway, B.C., Can. E8 69
Midway, De., U.S. F5 85
Midway, Ky., U.S. B5 94
Midway, Pa., U.S. G7 115
Midway, Ut., U.S. C4 121
Midway Islands, dep., Oc. E1 2
Midwest, Wy., U.S. C6 127
Midwest City, Ok., U.S. B4 113
Mielec, Pol. E21 8
Mieres, Spain B6 12
Miesbach, Ger. H11 8
Mifflin, co., Pa., U.S. E6 115
Mifflinburg, Pa., U.S. E7 115
Mifflinville, Pa., U.S. D9 115
Miguel Alemán, Presa, res., Mex. H11 62
Miguel Auza, Mex. E8 62
Mihajlovgrad, Bul. F7 16
Mihara, Japan H6 30
Mikasa, Japan p19 30a
Mikkeli, Fin. F16 6
Mikumi, Tan. C7 44
Milaca, Mn., U.S. E5 100
Milagro, Arg. C3 56
Milagro, Ec. I3 58
Milam, co., Tx., U.S. D4 120
Milan, Ga., U.S. D3 87
Milan, Il., U.S. B3 90
Milan, In., U.S. F7 91
Milan, Mi., U.S. F7 99
Milan, Mo., U.S. A4 102
Milan, N.M., U.S. B2 108
Milan, Oh., U.S. A3 112
Milan, Tn., U.S. B3 119
Milan see Milano, Italy D4 14
Milano (Milan), Italy D4 14
Milâs, Tur. L11 16
Milazzo, Italy K10 14
Milbank, S.D., U.S. B9 118
Mildmay, Ont., Can. C3 73
Mildura, Austl. F8 50
Milesburg, Pa., U.S. E6 115
Miles City, Mt., U.S. D11 103
Milestone, Sask., Can. G3 75
Milford, Ct., U.S. E3 84
Milford, De., U.S. E4 85
Milford, Il., U.S. C6 90
Milford, In., U.S. B6 91
Milford, Ia., U.S. A2 92
Milford, Me., U.S. D4 96
Milford, Ma., U.S. B4 98
Milford, Mi., U.S. F7 99
Milford, Ne., U.S. D8 104
Milford, N.H., U.S. E3 106
Milford, Oh., U.S. C1 112
Milford, Pa., U.S. D12 115
Milford, Ut., U.S. E2 121
Milford Haven, Wales, U.K. J7 7
Milford Lake, res., Ks., U.S. C6 93
Milford Station, N.S., Can. D6 71
Mililani Town, Hi., U.S. g9 88
Mil'kovo, Russia G25 24
Milk River, Alta., Can. E4 68
Mill, stm., Ma., U.S. h9 98
Millard, co., Ut., U.S. D2 121
Millau, Fr. H10 10
Millbrae, Ca., U.S. h8 82
Millbrook, Ont., Can. C6 73
Millbrook, Al., U.S. C3 78
Mill Brook, stm., Vt., U.S. B5 122
Millburn, N.J., U.S. B4 107
Millbury, Ma., U.S. B4 98
Millbury, Oh., U.S. e7 112
Mill City, Or., U.S. C4 114
Millcreek, Ut., U.S. C4 121
Mill Creek, W.V., U.S. C5 125
Mill Creek, stm., N.J., U.S. D4 107
Mill Creek, stm., Oh., U.S. B2 112
Mill Creek, stm., Tn., U.S. g10 119
Mill Creek, stm., W.V., U.S. m13 125
Mill Creek, stm., W.V., U.S. C3 125
Millcreek Township, Pa., U.S. B1 115
Milledgeville, Ga., U.S. C3 87
Milledgeville, Il., U.S. B4 90
Mille Îles, Rivière des, stm., Que., Can. p19 74
Mille Lacs, co., Mn., U.S. E5 100
Mille Lacs, Lac des, l., Ont., Can. G14 66
Mille Lacs Indian Reservation, Mn., U.S. D5 100
Mille Lacs Lake, l., Mn., U.S. D5 100
Millen, Ga., U.S. D5 87
Miller, S.D., U.S. C7 118
Miller, co., Ar., U.S. D2 81
Miller, co., Ga., U.S. E2 87
Miller, co., Mo., U.S. C5 102
Miller, Mount, mtn., Ak., U.S. C11 79
Miller Peak, mtn., Az., U.S. F5 80
Miller Run, stm., Vt., U.S. B4 122
Millers, stm., Ma., U.S. A3 98
Millersburg, In., U.S. A6 91
Millersburg, Ky., U.S. B5 94
Millersburg, Oh., U.S. B4 112
Millersburg, Pa., U.S. E8 115
Millersport, Oh., U.S. C3 112
Millersville, Pa., U.S. F9 115
Millet, Alta., Can. C4 68
Mill Hall, Pa., U.S. D7 115
Milliken, Co., U.S. A6 83
Millington, Mi., U.S. E7 99
Millington, Tn., U.S. B2 119
Millinocket, Me., U.S. C4 96
Millinocket Lake, l., Me., U.S. C4 96
Millinocket Lake, l., Me., U.S. B4 96
Millis, Ma., U.S. B5 98
Millport, Al., U.S. B1 78
Millry, Al., U.S. D1 78
Mills, Wy., U.S. D6 127
Mills, co., Ia., U.S. C2 92
Mills, co., Tx., U.S. D3 120
Millsboro, De., U.S. F4 85
Millsboro, Pa., U.S. G1 115
Millstadt, Il., U.S. E3 90
Millstone, stm., N.J., U.S. C4 107
Milltown, In., U.S. H5 91
Milltown, N.J., U.S. C4 107
Milltown, Wi., U.S. C1 126
Milltown [-Head of Bay d'Espoir], Newf., Can. E4 72
Milltown Malbay, Ire. I3 7
Millvale, Pa., U.S. k14 115
Mill Valley, Ca., U.S. D2 82
Millville, Ma., U.S. B4 98
Millville, N.J., U.S. E2 107
Millville, Pa., U.S. D9 115
Millville, Ut., U.S. B4 121
Millville Lake, N.H., U.S. E4 106
Millwood, Wa., U.S. g14 124
Millwood Lake, res., Ar., U.S. D1 81
Milner Dam, Id., U.S. G5 89
Milnor, N.D., U.S. C8 111
Milo, Ia., U.S. C4 92
Milo, Me., U.S. C4 96
Milparinka, Austl. E8 50
Milroy, In., U.S. F7 91
Milroy, Pa., U.S. E6 115
Milstead, Ga., U.S. C3 87
Milton, Ont., Can. D5 73
Milton, De., U.S. E4 85
Milton, Fl., U.S. u14 86
Milton, In., U.S. E7 91
Milton, Ma., U.S. B5 98
Milton, N.H., U.S. D5 106
Milton, Pa., U.S. D8 115
Milton, Vt., U.S. B2 122
Milton, Wa., U.S. f11 124
Milton, W.V., U.S. C2 125
Milton, Wi., U.S. F5 126
Milton, Lake, l., Oh., U.S. A4 112
Miltona, Lake, l., Mn., U.S. D3 100
Milton-Freewater, Or., U.S. B8 114
Milton Reservoir, res., Co., U.S. A6 83
Milverton, Ont., Can. D4 73
Milwaukee, Wi., U.S. E6 126
Milwaukee, co., Wi., U.S. E6 126
Milwaukee, stm., Wi., U.S. m12 126
Milwaukie, Or., U.S. B4 114
Mimizan, Fr. H5 10
Mims, Fl., U.S. D6 86
Min, stm., China I7 28
Mina, Nv., U.S. E3 105
Minahasa, pen., Indon. E7 32
Minamata, Japan J3 30
Minas, Ur. C5 56
Minas, Sierra de las, mts., Guat. G3 64
Minas Basin, b., N.S., Can. D5 71
Minas Channel, strt., N.S., Can. D5 71
Minas de Barroterán, Mex. D9 62
Minas Novas, Braz. D7 57
Minatare, Ne., U.S. C2 104
Minatitlán, Mex. I12 62
Minco, Ok., U.S. B4 113
Mindanao, i., Phil. D7 32
Mindanao, stm., Phil. D7 32
Mindanao Sea, Phil. D7 32
Mindelheim, Ger. G10 8
Minden, Ger. C8 8
Minden, La., U.S. B2 95
Minden, Ne., U.S. D7 104
Minden, Nv., U.S. E2 105
Minden, W.V., U.S. D3 125
Mindoro, i., Phil. C7 32
Mindoro Strait, strt., Phil. C7 32
Mine Hill, N.J., U.S. B3 107
Mineiros, Braz. D2 57
Mineola, N.Y., U.S. E7 109
Mineola, Tx., U.S. C5 120
Miner, Mo., U.S. E8 102
Miner, co., S.D., U.S. D8 118
Mineral, co., Co., U.S. D4 83
Mineral, co., Mt., U.S. C1 103
Mineral, co., Nv., U.S. E3 105
Mineral, co., W.V., U.S. B6 125
Mineral Point, Wi., U.S. F3 126
Mineral Springs, Ar., U.S. D2 81
Mineral Wells, Tx., U.S. C3 120
Minersville, Pa., U.S. E9 115
Minersville, Ut., U.S. E3 121
Minerva, Oh., U.S. B4 112
Minervino Murge, Italy H11 14
Minetto, N.Y., U.S. B4 109
Mingo, co., W.V., U.S. D2 125
Mingo Junction, Oh., U.S. B5 112
Minho (Miño), stm., Eur. D3 12
Minidoka, co., Id., U.S. G5 89
Minidoka Dam, Id., U.S. G5 89
Minier, Il., U.S. C4 90
Minisink Island, i., N.J., U.S. A3 107
Minitonas, Man., Can. C1 70
Minna, Nig. G7 42
Minneapolis, Ks., U.S. C6 93
Minneapolis, Mn., U.S. F5 100
Minnedosa, Man., Can. D2 70
Minnedosa, stm., Man., Can. D1 70
Minnehaha, co., S.D., U.S. D9 118
Minneola, Ks., U.S. E3 93
Minneota, Mn., U.S. F3 100
Minnesota, state, U.S. E4 100
Minnesota, stm., Mn., U.S. F2 100
Minnesota Lake, Mn., U.S. G5 100
Minnetonka, Mn., U.S. n12 100
Minnetonka, Lake, l., Mn., U.S. n11 100
Minnewaska, Lake, l., Mn., U.S. E3 100
Miño (Minho), stm., Eur. D3 12
Minocqua, Wi., U.S. C4 126
Minonk, Il., U.S. C4 90
Minooka, Il., U.S. B5 90
Minot, N.D., U.S. A4 111
Minot Air Force Base, mil., N.D., U.S. A4 111
Minquadale, De., U.S. i7 85
Minsk, Bela. H10 18
Mińsk Mazowiecki, Pol. C21 8
Minster, Oh., U.S. B1 112
Mint Hill, N.C., U.S. B2 110
Minto, N.B., Can. C3 71
Minto Inlet, b., N.W. Ter., Can. B9 66
Minturn, Co., U.S. B4 83
Minturno, Italy H8 14
Minusinsk, Russia G12 24
Minute Man National Historical Park, Ma., U.S. g10 98
Minxian, China E7 26
Mio, Mi., U.S. D6 99
Mira, Italy D7 14
Mirabel, Que., Can. D3 74
Miraflores, Col. E6 58
Miraflores, Col. G6 58
Miraj, India D3 37
Miramar, Fl., U.S. s13 86
Miramar Naval Air Station, mil., Ca., U.S. F5 82
Miramas, Fr. I11 10
Mirambeau, Fr. G6 10
Miramichi Bay, b., N.B., Can. B5 71
Miranda de Ebro, Spain C9 12
Miranda do Douro, Port. D5 12
Mirande, Fr. I7 10
Mirandela, Port. D4 12
Mirandola, Italy E6 14
Mirbāṭ, Oman E5 46
Mirebeau-sur-Bèze, Fr. E12 10
Miri, Malay. E5 32
Mirnyj, Russia E16 24
Mīrpur Khās, Pak. H3 38
Mirror Lake, l., N.H., U.S. C4 106
Mirzāpur, India H10 38
Misawa, Japan B14 30
Miscouche, P.E.I., Can. C6 71
Miscou Island, i., N.B., Can. B5 71
Miscou Point, c., N.B., Can. A5 71
Misenheimer, N.C., U.S. B2 110
Mishawaka, In., U.S. A5 91
Misheguk Mountain, mtn., Ak., U.S. B7 79
Mishicot, Wi., U.S. D6 126
Mishmi Hills, hills, Asia F16 38
Misima Island, i., Pap. N. Gui. B10 50
Miskitos, Cayos, is., Nic. G6 64
Miskolc, Hung. G20 8
Misool, Pulau, i., Indon. F9 32
Mispillion, stm., De., U.S. E4 85
Misrātah, Libya B9 42
Missaukee, co., Mi., U.S. D5 99
Missaukee, Lake, l., Mi., U.S. D5 99
Mission, Ks., U.S. m16 93
Mission, S.D., U.S. D5 118

Name — Map Ref — Page

Mission, Tx., U.S. F3 120
Mission Range, mts., Mt., U.S. C3 103
Mission Viejo, Ca., U.S. n13 82
Missisquoi, stm., Vt., U.S. B3 122
Missisquoi Bay, b., Vt., U.S. A2 122
Mississauga, Ont., Can. D5 73
Mississinewa, stm., U.S. D7 91
Mississinewa Lake, res., In., U.S. C6 91
Mississippi, co., Ar., U.S. B5 81
Mississippi, co., Mo., U.S. E8 102
Mississippi, state, U.S. C4 101
Mississippi, stm., U.S. E8 76
Mississippi Delta, La., U.S. E6 95
Mississippi Sound, strt., U.S. E5 101
Mississippi State, Ms., U.S. B5 101
Missoula, Mt., U.S. D2 103
Missoula, co., Mt., U.S. D2 103
Missouri, state, U.S. C5 102
Missouri, stm., U.S. C7 76
Missouri City, Tx., U.S. r14 120
Missouri Valley, Ia., U.S. C2 92
Mistassini, Que., Can. h12 74
Mistassini, Lac, l., Que., Can. h12 74
Misti, Volcán, vol., Peru G4 54
Mistretta, Italy L9 14
Mita, Punta de, c., Mex. G7 62
Mitchell, Austl. E9 50
Mitchell, Ont., Can. D3 73
Mitchell, Il., U.S. E3 90
Mitchell, In., U.S. G5 91
Mitchell, Ne., U.S. C2 104
Mitchell, S.D., U.S. D7 118
Mitchell, co., Ga., U.S. E2 87
Mitchell, co., Ia., U.S. A5 92
Mitchell, co., Ks., U.S. C5 93
Mitchell, co., N.C., U.S. e10 110
Mitchell, co., Tx., U.S. C2 120
Mitchell, stm., Austl. C8 50
Mitchell, Lake, l., Mi., U.S. D5 99
Mitchell, Lake, res., Al., U.S. C3 78
Mitchell, Mount, mtn., N.C., U.S. f10 110
Mitchell Island, i., La., U.S. E6 95
Mitchellville, Ia., U.S. C4 92
Mitilíni, Grc. J10 16
Mitkof Island, i., Ak., U.S. m23 79
Mito, Japan F13 30
Mitsiwa, Erit. E2 46
Mitsuke, Japan E11 30
Mittenwald, Ger. H11 8
Mittweida, Ger. E12 8
Mitú, Col. G7 58
Mitumba, Monts, mts., Zaire C5 44
Mitwaba, Zaire C5 44
Mitzic, Gabon A2 44
Miura, Japan G12 30
Mixian, China A2 28
Miyako, Japan C14 30
Miyako-jima, i., Japan G12 26
Miyakonojō, Japan K4 30
Miyazaki, Japan K4 30
Miyoshi, Japan H5 30
Miyun, China C10 26
Mizdah, Libya B8 42
Mizen Head, c., Ire. J3 7
Mizoram, ter., India I15 38
Mizpe Ramon, Isr. D4 40
Mizque, Bol. G5 54
Mjölby, Swe. G10 6
Mjøsa, l., Nor. F8 6
Mkalama, Tan. B6 44
Mladá Boleslav, Czech. E14 8
Mława, Pol. B20 8
Mo, Nor. C10 6
Moab, Ut., U.S. E6 121
Moanda, Gabon B2 44
Moapa River Indian Reservation, Nv., U.S. G7 105
Moate, Ire. H5 7
Mobara, Japan G13 30
Mobaye, Cen. Afr. Rep. H10 42
Moberly, Mo., U.S. B5 102
Mobile, Al., U.S. E1 78
Mobile, co., Al., U.S. E1 78
Mobile, stm., Al., U.S. E1 78
Mobile Bay, b., Al., U.S. E1 83
Mobridge, S.D., U.S. B5 118
Moçambique, Moz. E8 44
Mocanaqua, Pa., U.S. D9 115
Mocha, Isla, i., Chile D2 56
Mochudi, Bots. F5 44
Mocksville, N.C., U.S. B2 110
Moclips, Wa., U.S. B1 124
Môco, Serra do, mtn., Ang. D3 44
Mocoa, Col. G4 58
Mococa, Braz. F5 57
Moctezuma, Mex. C5 62
Mocuba, Moz. E7 44
Modane, Fr. G13 10
Model Reservoir, res., Co., U.S. D6 83
Modena, Italy E5 14
Modesto, Ca., U.S. D3 82
Modica, Italy M9 14
Mödling, Aus. G16 8
Modoc, co., Ca., U.S. B3 82
Modowi, Indon. F9 32
Moengo, Sur. B8 54
Moenkopi, Az., U.S. A4 80
Moffat, Scot., U.K. F9 7
Moffat, co., Co., U.S. A2 83
Moffat Tunnel, Co., U.S. B5 83
Moffett Field Naval Air Station, mil., Ca., U.S. k8 82
Moga, India E6 38
Mogadisho see Muqdisho, Som. H4 46
Mogadore, Oh., U.S. A4 112
Mogadouro, Port. D5 12
Mogaung, Mya. B4 34
Mogi das Cruzes, Braz. G5 57
Mogil'ov, Bela. H13 18
Mogi-Mirim, Braz. G5 57
Mogincual, Moz. E8 44
Mogoča, Russia G17 24
Mogočin, Russia F10 24
Mogok, Mya. C4 34
Mogollon Mountains, mts., N.M., U.S. D1 108
Mogollon Rim, clf, Az., U.S. C5 80
Mogotón, Pico, mtn., N.A. H4 64
Mohall, N.D., U.S. A4 111
Mohave, co., Az., U.S. B1 80
Mohave, Lake, res., U.S. H7 105
Mohave Mountains, mts., Az., U.S. C1 80
Mohave Valley, Az., U.S. C1 80
Mohawk, N.Y., U.S. C5 109
Mohawk, stm., N.H., U.S. g7 106
Mohawk, stm., N.Y., U.S. C6 109
Mohawk Lake, l., N.J., U.S. A3 107
Mohawk Mountains, mts., Az., U.S. E2 80
Moheli, i., Com. D8 44
Mohican, stm., Oh., U.S. B3 112
Mohinora, Cerro, mtn., Mex. D6 62
Mohnton, Pa., U.S. F10 115
Moi, Nor. G6 6
Moisie, Que., Can. h8 72
Moisie, stm., Que., Can. F19 66
Moissac, Fr. H8 10
Mojave, Ca., U.S. E4 82
Mojave, stm., Ca., U.S. E5 82
Mojave Desert, des., Ca., U.S. E5 82
Mojjero, stm., Russia D14 24
Mojo, Eth. G2 46
Mokapu Peninsula, pen., Hi., U.S. g10 88
Mokapu Point, c., Hi., U.S. g11 88
Mokelumne, stm., Ca., U.S. C3 82
Mokena, Il., U.S. k9 90
Mokp'o, S. Kor. E12 26
Moku Manu, i., Hi., U.S. g11 88
Mol, Bel. D5 8
Molalla, Or., U.S. B4 114
Moldau see Vltava, stm., Czech. F14 8
Moldavia see Moldova, ctry., Eur. H3 22
Molde, Nor. E6 6
Moldova, ctry., Eur. H3 22
Molepolole, Bots. F5 44
Molfetta, Italy H11 14
Molina de Aragón, Spain E10 12
Molina de Segura, Spain G10 12
Moline, Il., U.S. B3 90
Moline, Mi., U.S. F5 99
Molino, Fl., U.S. u14 86
Molins de Rey, Spain D14 12
Mollendo, Peru G4 54
Mölln, Ger. B10 8
Mölndal, Swe. H9 6
Molodečno, Bela. G9 18
Molokai, i., Hi., U.S. B5 88
Molokini, i., Hi., U.S. C5 88
Molson Lake, l., Man., Can. B3 70
Molucca Sea see Maluku, Laut, Indon. F7 32
Moluccas see Maluku, is., Indon. F8 32
Moma, Moz. E7 44
Moma, stm., Russia D22 24
Mombasa, Kenya B7 44
Mombetsu, Japan o21 30a
Momence, Il., U.S. B6 90
Momotombo, Volcán, vol., Nic. H4 64
Mon, stm., Mya. D3 34
Mona, Canal de la, strt., N.A. E14 64
Mona, Isla, i., P.R. E14 64
Monaca, Pa., U.S. E1 115
Monaco, ctry., Eur. G9 4
Monadhliath Mountains, mts., Scot., U.K. D8 7
Monadnock, Mount, mtn., N.H., U.S. E2 106
Monadnock Mountain, mtn., Vt., U.S. B5 122
Monahans, Tx., U.S. D1 120
Monarch Mills, S.C., U.S. B4 117
Monarch Pass, Co., U.S. C4 83
Monashee Mountains, mts., B.C., Can. D8 69
Monastir, Tun. N5 14
Moncalieri, Italy D2 14
Monção, Braz. D9 54
Mönchengladbach, Ger. D6 8
Monchique, Port. H3 12
Moncks Corner, S.C., U.S. E7 117
Monclova, Mex. D9 62
Moncton, N.B., Can. C5 71
Mondoñedo, Spain B4 12
Mondovi, Italy E2 14
Mondovi, Wi., U.S. D2 126
Mondragone, Italy H8 14
Monee, Il., U.S. B6 90
Monessen, Pa., U.S. F2 115
Monett, Mo., U.S. E4 102
Monette, Ar., U.S. B5 81
Monfalcone, Italy D8 14
Monforte de Lemos, Spain C4 12
Monfort Heights, Oh., U.S. *o12 112
Mong Cai, Viet. D9 34
Mōng Hsat, Mya. D5 34
Monghyr, India H12 38
Mongo, Chad F9 42
Mongol Altajn Nuruu, mts., Asia B5 26
Mongolia, ctry., Asia B7 26
Mongu, Zam. E4 44
Monhegan Island, i., Me., U.S. E3 96
Monida Pass, U.S. E6 89
Moniteau, co., Mo., U.S. C5 102
Monitor Range, mts., Nv., U.S. E5 105
Monitor Valley, val., Nv., U.S. D5 105
Monmouth, Il., U.S. C3 90
Monmouth, Or., U.S. C3 114
Monmouth, co., N.J., U.S. C4 107
Monmouth Beach, N.J., U.S. C5 107
Monmouth Mountain, mtn., B.C., Can. D6 69
Mono, co., Ca., U.S. D4 82
Monocacy, stm., Md., U.S. B3 97
Mono Lake, l., Ca., U.S. D4 82
Monomonac, Lake, l., U.S. E3 106
Monomoy Island, i., Ma., U.S. C7 98
Monomoy Point, c., Ma., U.S. C7 98
Monon, In., U.S. C4 91
Monona, Ia., U.S. A6 92
Monona, Wi., U.S. E4 126
Monona, co., Ia., U.S. B1 92
Monona, Lake, l., Wi., U.S. E4 126
Monongah, W.V., U.S. B4 125
Monongahela, Pa., U.S. F2 115
Monongahela, stm., U.S. G2 115
Monongalia, co., W.V., U.S. B4 125
Monopoli, Italy I12 14
Monóvar, Spain G11 12
Monreal del Campo, Spain E10 12
Monroe, Ga., U.S. C3 87
Monroe, In., U.S. C8 91
Monroe, Ia., U.S. C4 92
Monroe, La., U.S. B3 95
Monroe, Mi., U.S. G7 99
Monroe, N.Y., U.S. D6 109
Monroe, N.C., U.S. C2 110
Monroe, Oh., U.S. C1 112
Monroe, Ut., U.S. E3 121
Monroe, Wa., U.S. B4 124
Monroe, Wi., U.S. F4 126
Monroe, co., Al., U.S. D2 78
Monroe, co., Ar., U.S. C4 81
Monroe, co., Fl., U.S. G5 86
Monroe, co., Ga., U.S. D3 87
Monroe, co., Il., U.S. E3 90
Monroe, co., In., U.S. F4 91
Monroe, co., Ia., U.S. D5 92
Monroe, co., Ky., U.S. D4 94
Monroe, co., Mi., U.S. G7 99
Monroe, co., Ms., U.S. B5 101
Monroe, co., Mo., U.S. B5 102
Monroe, co., N.Y., U.S. B3 109
Monroe, co., Oh., U.S. C4 112
Monroe, co., Pa., U.S. D11 115
Monroe, co., Tn., U.S. D9 119
Monroe, co., W.V., U.S. D4 125
Monroe, co., Wi., U.S. E3 126
Monroe Center, Ct., U.S. D3 84
Monroe City, Mo., U.S. B6 102
Monroe Lake, res., In., U.S. F5 91
Monroe Park, De., U.S. h7 85
Monroeville, Al., U.S. D2 78
Monroeville, In., U.S. C8 91
Monroeville, Oh., U.S. A3 112
Monroeville, Pa., U.S. k14 115
Monrovia, Lib. G3 42
Monrovia, Ca., U.S. m13 82
Monrovia, In., U.S. E5 91
Mons, Bel. E3 8
Monson, Ma., U.S. B3 98
Montague, P.E.I., Can. C7 71
Montague, Ca., U.S. B2 82
Montague, Mi., U.S. E4 99
Montague, co., Tx., U.S. C4 120
Montague, Isla, i., Mex. B2 62
Montague Island, i., Ak., U.S. D10 79
Montague Peak, mtn., Ak., U.S. g18 79
Montague Strait, strt., Ak., U.S. h18 79
Montaigu, Fr. F5 10
Montalbán, Spain E11 12
Montalcino, Italy F6 14
Montalegre, Port. D4 12
Mont Alto, Pa., U.S. G6 115
Montana, state, U.S. D7 103
Montánchez, Spain F5 12
Montargis, Fr. D9 10
Montauban, Fr. H8 10
Montauk, N.Y., U.S. m17 109
Montbard, Fr. E11 10
Montbéliard, Fr. E13 10
Mont Belvieu, Tx., U.S. E5 120
Montblanch, Spain D13 12
Montbrison, Fr. G11 10
Montcalm, co., Mi., U.S. E5 99
Montchanin, De., U.S. h7 85
Montclair, Ca., U.S. m13 82
Montclair, N.J., U.S. B4 107
Mont Clare, Pa., U.S. o19 115
Mont-de-Marsan, Fr. I6 10
Montdidier, Fr. C9 10
Monteagle, Tn., U.S. D8 119
Monteagudo, Bol. G6 54
Monte Azul, Braz. C7 57
Montebello, Que., Can. D3 74
Montebello, Ca., U.S. m12 82
Monte Caseros, Arg. C5 56
Montecatini Terme, Italy F5 14
Monte Comán, Arg. C3 56
Montecristi, Dom. Rep. E12 64
Montecristi, Ec. H2 58
Montefiascone, Italy G7 14
Montego Bay, Jam. E9 64
Montegut, La., U.S. E5 95
Montélimar, Fr. H11 10
Montello, Nv., U.S. B7 105
Montello, Wi., U.S. E4 126
Montemorelos, Mex. E10 62
Montemor-o-Novo, Port. G3 12
Montendre, Fr. G6 10
Montenero di Bisaccia, Italy H9 14
Montepuez, Moz. D8 44
Montepulciano, Italy F6 14
Monte Quemado, Arg. B4 56
Montereau-faut-Yonne, Fr. D9 10
Monterey, Ca., U.S. D3 82
Monterey, Tn., U.S. C8 119
Monterey, co., Ca., U.S. D3 82
Monterey Bay, b., Ca., U.S. D2 82
Monterey Park, Ca., U.S. m12 82
Montería, Col. C5 58
Monterotondo, Italy G7 14
Monterrey, Mex. E9 62
Montesano, Wa., U.S. C2 124
Monte Sant'Angelo, Italy H10 14
Montes Claros, Braz. D7 57
Montevallo, Al., U.S. B3 78
Montevarchi, Italy F6 14
Montevideo, Mn., U.S. F3 100
Montevideo, Ur. C5 56
Monte Vista, Co., U.S. D4 83
Montezuma, Ga., U.S. D2 87
Montezuma, In., U.S. E3 91
Montezuma, Ia., U.S. C5 92
Montezuma, Ks., U.S. E3 93
Montezuma, co., Co., U.S. D2 83
Montezuma Castle National Monument, Az., U.S. C4 80
Montezuma Peak, mtn., Az., U.S. D3 80
Montgomery, Al., U.S. C3 78
Montgomery, Il., U.S. B5 90
Montgomery, La., U.S. C3 95
Montgomery, Mn., U.S. F5 100
Montgomery, N.Y., U.S. D6 109
Montgomery, Oh., U.S. o13 112
Montgomery, Pa., U.S. D8 115
Montgomery, W.V., U.S. C3 125
Montgomery, co., Al., U.S. C3 78
Montgomery, co., Ar., U.S. C2 81
Montgomery, co., Ga., U.S. D4 87
Montgomery, co., Il., U.S. D4 90
Montgomery, co., In., U.S. D4 91
Montgomery, co., Ia., U.S. C2 92
Montgomery, co., Ks., U.S. E8 93
Montgomery, co., Ky., U.S. B6 94
Montgomery, co., Md., U.S. B3 97
Montgomery, co., Ms., U.S. B4 101
Montgomery, co., Mo., U.S. C6 102
Montgomery, co., N.Y., U.S. C6 109
Montgomery, co., N.C., U.S. B3 110
Montgomery, co., Oh., U.S. C1 112
Montgomery, co., Pa., U.S. F11 115
Montgomery, co., Tn., U.S. A4 119
Montgomery, co., Tx., U.S. D5 120
Montgomery, co., Va., U.S. C2 123
Montgomery City, Mo., U.S. C6 102
Monthey, Switz. F13 10
Monticello, Ar., U.S. D4 81
Monticello, Fl., U.S. B3 86
Monticello, Ga., U.S. C3 87
Monticello, Il., U.S. C5 90
Monticello, In., U.S. C4 91
Monticello, Ia., U.S. B6 92
Monticello, Ky., U.S. D5 94
Monticello, Mn., U.S. E5 100
Monticello, Ms., U.S. D3 101
Monticello, N.Y., U.S. D6 109
Monticello, Ut., U.S. F6 121
Monticello, Wi., U.S. F4 126
Montichiari, Italy D5 14
Montignac, Fr. G8 10
Montijo, Port. G3 12
Montijo, Spain G5 12
Montilla, Spain H7 12
Montivilliers, Fr. C7 10
Mont-Joli, Que., Can. A9 74
Mont-Laurier, Que., Can. C2 74
Mont-Louis, Fr. J9 10
Montluçon, Fr. F9 10
Montmagny, Que., Can. C7 74
Montmorenci, S.C., U.S. D4 117
Montmorency, co., Mi., U.S. C6 99
Montmorillon, Fr. F7 10
Montmort, Fr. D10 10
Montoro, Spain G7 12
Montour, co., Pa., U.S. D8 115
Montour Falls, N.Y., U.S. C4 109
Montoursville, Pa., U.S. D8 115
Montpelier, Id., U.S. G7 89
Montpelier, In., U.S. C7 91
Montpelier, Oh., U.S. A1 112
Montpelier, Vt., U.S. C3 122
Montpellier, Fr. I10 10
Montréal, Que., Can. D4 74
Montreal, Wi., U.S. B3 126
Montréal, Île de, i., Que., Can. q19 74
Montreal Lake, l., Sask., Can. C3 75
Montréal-Nord, Que., Can. p19 74
Montreat, N.C., U.S. f10 110
Montreuil-Bellay, Fr. E6 10
Montreux, Switz. F13 10
Mont-Rolland, Que., Can. D3 74
Montrose, B.C., Can. E9 69
Montrose, Scot., U.K. E10 7
Montrose, Al., U.S. E2 78
Montrose, Co., U.S. C3 83
Montrose, Ia., U.S. D6 92
Montrose, Mi., U.S. E7 99
Montrose, Pa., U.S. C10 115
Montrose, Va., U.S. m18 123
Montrose, co., Co., U.S. C2 83
Mont-Royal, Que., Can. p19 74
Montserrat, dep., N.A. F16 64
Mont-Tremblant, Parc Provincial du, Que., Can. C3 74
Montvale, N.J., U.S. A4 107
Montville, Ct., U.S. D7 84
Monument, Co., U.S. B6 83
Monument Beach, Ma., U.S. C6 98
Monument Peak, mtn., Co., U.S. B3 83
Monument Peak, mtn., Id., U.S. G4 89
Monument Valley, val., Az., U.S. A5 80
Monywa, Mya. C3 34
Monza, Italy D4 14
Monzón, Spain D12 12
Moodus, Ct., U.S. D6 84
Moodus Reservoir, res., Ct., U.S. C6 84
Moody, Tx., U.S. D4 120
Moody, co., S.D., U.S. C9 118
Moon Lake, l., Ms., U.S. A3 101
Moora, Austl. F3 50
Moorcroft, Wy., U.S. B8 127
Moore, Ok., U.S. B4 113
Moore, co., N.C., U.S. B3 110
Moore, co., Tn., U.S. B5 119
Moore, co., Tx., U.S. B2 120
Moore Dam, U.S. B3 106
Moorefield, W.V., U.S. B6 125
Moore Haven, Fl., U.S. F5 86
Mooreland, Ok., U.S. A2 113
Moore Reservoir, res., U.S. B3 106
Moores Creek National Military Park, N.C., U.S. C4 110
Moores Hill, In., U.S. F7 91
Moorestown, N.J., U.S. D3 107
Mooresville, In., U.S. E5 91
Mooresville, N.C., U.S. B2 110
Moorhead, Mn., U.S. D2 100
Moorhead, Ms., U.S. B3 101
Mooringsport, La., U.S. B2 95
Moose, stm., N.H., U.S. B4 106
Moose, stm., N.Y., U.S. B5 109
Moose, stm., Vt., U.S. B5 122
Moosehead Lake, l., Me., U.S. C3 96
Moose Jaw, stm., Sask., Can. G3 75
Moose Lake, Man., Can. C1 70
Moose Lake, Mn., U.S. D6 100
Moose Lake, l., Wi., U.S. B2 126
Mooseleuk Stream, stm., Me., U.S. B4 96
Mooselookmeguntic Lake, l., Me., U.S. D2 96
Moose Mountain Creek, stm., Sask., Can. H4 75
Moose Mountain Provincial Park, Sask., Can. H4 75
Moosic, Pa., U.S. m18 115
Moosup, Ct., U.S. C8 84
Moosup, stm., U.S. C1 116
Mopang Lake, l., Me., U.S. D5 96
Mopti, Mali F5 42
Moquegua, Peru G4 54
Mora, Port. G3 12
Mora, Spain F8 12
Mora, Swe. F10 6
Mora, Mn., U.S. E5 100
Mora, N.M., U.S. B4 108
Mora, co., N.M., U.S. A5 108
Mora, stm., N.M., U.S. B5 108
Morādābād, India F8 38
Morada Nova de Minas, Braz. E6 57
Morafenobe, Madag. E8 44
Moraleda, Canal, strt., Chile E2 56
Morant Cays, is., Jam. F9 64
Mor'arovskij Zaton, Russia F10 24
Moratuwa, Sri L. I5 37
Morava, hist. reg., Czech. F17 8
Morava (March), stm., Eur. G16 8
Moravia, Ia., U.S. D5 92
Moravia see Morava, hist. reg., Czech. F17 8
Morawhanna, Guy. C13 58
Moray Firth, est., Scot., U.K. D9 7
Morden, Man., Can. E2 70
More, Ben, mtn., Scot., U.K. E8 7
More Assynt, Ben, mtn., Scot., U.K. C8 7
Moreau, stm., S.D., U.S. B3 118
Moreauville, La., U.S. C4 95
Morecambe, Eng., U.K. G10 7
Moree, Austl. E9 50
Morehead, Ky., U.S. B6 94
Morehead City, N.C., U.S. C6 110
Morehouse, Mo., U.S. E8 102
Morehouse, co., La., U.S. B4 95
Morelia, Mex. H9 62
Morella, Spain E11 12
Morena, India G8 38
Morenci, Az., U.S. D6 80
Morenci, Mi., U.S. G6 99
Moresby Island, i., B.C., Can. C2 69
Moreuil, Fr. C9 10
Morey, Lake, l., Vt., U.S. D4 122
Morey Peak, mtn., Nv., U.S. E5 105
Morgan, Mn., U.S. F4 100
Morgan, Ut., U.S. B4 121
Morgan, co., Al., U.S. A3 78
Morgan, co., Co., U.S. A7 83
Morgan, co., Ga., U.S. C3 87
Morgan, co., Il., U.S. D3 90
Morgan, co., In., U.S. F5 91
Morgan, co., Ky., U.S. C6 94
Morgan, co., Mo., U.S. C5 102
Morgan, co., Oh., U.S. C4 112
Morgan, co., Tn., U.S. C9 119
Morgan, co., Ut., U.S. B4 121
Morgan, co., W.V., U.S. B6 125
Morgan City, La., U.S. E4 95
Morganfield, Ky., U.S. C2 94
Morgan Hill, Ca., U.S. D3 82
Morgan Island, i., S.C., U.S. G6 117
Morgan Point, c., Ct., U.S. E4 84
Morganton, N.C., U.S. B1 110
Morgantown, In., U.S. F5 91
Morgantown, Ky., U.S. C3 94
Morgantown, Ms., U.S. D2 101
Morgantown, Tn., U.S. D8 119
Morgantown, W.V., U.S. B5 125
Morganza, La., U.S. D4 95
Mori, Japan q18 30a
Moriah, Mount, mtn., Nv., U.S. D7 105
Moriarty, N.M., U.S. C3 108
Morinville, Alta., Can. C4 68
Morioka, Japan C14 30
Morkoka, stm., Russia D16 24
Morlaix, Fr. D3 10
Morley, Mo., U.S. D8 102
Mormon Peak, mtn., Nv., U.S. G7 105
Morning Sun, Ia., U.S. C6 92
Mornington Island, i., Austl. C7 50
Morobe, Pap. N. Gui. m16 50a
Morocco, In., U.S. C3 91
Morocco, ctry., Afr. B4 42
Morogoro, Tan. C7 44
Moro Gulf, b., Phil. D7 32
Morombe, Madag. F8 44
Morón, Cuba C8 64
Morondava, Madag. F8 44
Morón de la Frontera, Spain H6 12
Moroni, Com. D8 44
Moroni, Ut., U.S. D4 121
Morošečnoje, Russia F25 24
Morotai, i., Indon. E8 32
Morrill, Ne., U.S. C2 104
Morrill, co., Ne., U.S. C2 104
Morrilton, Ar., U.S. B3 81
Morrinhos, Braz. D4 57
Morris, Man., Can. E3 70
Morris, Al., U.S. B3 78
Morris, Il., U.S. B5 90
Morris, Mn., U.S. E3 100
Morris, Ok., U.S. B6 113
Morris, co., Ks., U.S. D7 93
Morris, co., N.J., U.S. B3 107
Morris, co., Tx., U.S. C5 120
Morrisburg, Ont., Can. C9 73
Morris Island, i., S.C., U.S. F8 117

Name | Map Ref | Page

Morrison, Il., U.S. B4 90
Morrison, Ok., U.S. A4 113
Morrison, co., Mn., U.S. D4 100
Morrison City, Tn., U.S. C11 119
Morrisonville, Il., U.S. D4 90
Morrisonville, N.Y., U.S. f11 109
Morris Plains, N.J., U.S. B4 107
Morristown, In., U.S. E6 91
Morristown, Mn., U.S. F5 100
Morristown, N.J., U.S. B4 107
Morristown, Tn., U.S. C10 119
Morristown National Historical Park, N.J., U.S. B3 107
Morrisville, N.Y., U.S. C5 109
Morrisville, Pa., U.S. F12 115
Morrisville, Vt., U.S. B3 122
Morro, Ec. I2 58
Morro, Punta, c., Chile B2 56
Morro Bay, Ca., U.S. E3 82
Morro do Chapéu, Braz. F10 54
Morrow, Ga., U.S. C2 87
Morrow, Oh., U.S. C1 112
Morrow, co., Oh., U.S. B3 112
Morrow, co., Or., U.S. B7 114
Moršansk, Russia H24 18
Morse, La., U.S. D3 95
Morse Reservoir, res., In., U.S. D5 91
Morses Creek, stm., N.J., U.S. k8 107
Mortagne, Fr. D7 10
Mortagne-sur-Sèvre, Fr. E6 10
Mortara, Italy D3 14
Mortes, Rio das, stm., Braz. G8 54
Morton, Il., U.S. C4 90
Morton, Ms., U.S. C4 101
Morton, Tx., U.S. C1 120
Morton, Wa., U.S. C3 124
Morton, co., Ks., U.S. E2 93
Morton, co., N.D., U.S. C4 111
Morton Grove, Il., U.S. h9 90
Morton Pass, Wy., U.S. E7 127
Mortons Gap, Ky., U.S. C2 94
Morven, mtn., Scot., U.K. C9 7
Morvi, India I4 38
Morwell, Austl. G9 50
Mosbach, Ger. F9 8
Moscos Islands, is., Mya. G4 34
Moscow, Id., U.S. C2 89
Moscow, Pa., U.S. m18 115
Moscow Mills, Mo., U.S. C7 102
Moscow see Moskva, Russia F20 18
Mosel (Moselle), stm., Eur. F6 8
Moselle, Ms., U.S. D4 101
Moselle (Mosel), stm., Eur. F6 8
Moses Coulee, val., Wa., U.S. B6 124
Moses Lake, Wa., U.S. B6 124
Moses Lake, l., Wa., U.S. B6 124
Mosheim, Tn., U.S. C11 119
Moshi, Tan. B7 44
Mosinee, Wi., U.S. D4 126
Mosjøen, Nor. D9 6
Moskva (Moscow), Russia F20 18
Mosquera, Col. F3 58
Mosquito Creek Lake, res., Oh., U.S. A5 112
Mosquito Lagoon, b., Fl., U.S. D6 86
Mosquitos, Golfo de los, b., Pan. J7 64
Moss, Nor. G8 6
Mossaka, Congo B3 44
Moss Bluff, La., U.S. D2 95
Mosselbaai, S. Afr. H4 44
Mossendjo, Congo B2 44
Mossoró, Braz. E11 54
Moss Point, Ms., U.S. E5 101
Most, Czech. E13 8
Mostaganem, Alg. A6 42
Mostar, Bos. F12 14
Mostardas, Braz. C6 56
Møsting, Kap, c., Grnld. D24 66
Moswansicut Pond, l., R.I., U.S. C3 116
Mota del Marqués, Spain D6 12
Motala, Swe. G10 6
Motherwell, Scot., U.K. F8 7
Motīhāri, India G11 38
Motilla del Palancar, Spain F10 12
Motley, co., Tx., U.S. B2 120
Motril, Spain I8 12
Mott, N.D., U.S. C3 111
Motueka, N.Z. D4 52
Motul de Felipe Carrillo Puerto, Mex. G15 62
Motygino, Russia F12 24
Mouchoir Passage, strt., N.A. D12 64
Moudjéria, Maur. E3 42
Mouila, Gabon B2 44
Moulamein Creek, stm., Austl. G8 50
Moulins, Fr. F10 10
Moulmeingyun, Mya. F3 34
Moulouya, Oued, stm., Mor. B5 42
Moulton, Al., U.S. A2 78
Moulton, Ia., U.S. D5 92
Moultrie, Ga., U.S. E3 87
Moultrie, co., Il., U.S. D5 90
Moultrie, Lake, res., S.C., U.S. E7 117
Mound, Mn., U.S. n11 100
Mound Bayou, Ms., U.S. B3 101
Mound City, Il., U.S. F4 90
Mound City, Ks., U.S. D9 93
Mound City, Mo., U.S. A2 102
Mound City Group National Monument, Oh., U.S. C2 112
Moundou, Chad G9 42
Moundridge, Ks., U.S. D6 93
Mounds, Il., U.S. F4 90
Mounds, Ok., U.S. B5 113
Mounds View, Mn., U.S. m12 100
Moundsville, W.V., U.S. B4 125
Moundville, Al., U.S. C2 78
Mountainair, N.M., U.S. C3 108
Mountainaire, Az., U.S. B4 80
Mountain Brook, Al., U.S. g7 78
Mountain City, Ga., U.S. B3 87
Mountain City, Nv., U.S. B6 105
Mountain City, Tn., U.S. C12 119
Mountain Fork, stm., U.S. C7 113
Mountain Grove, Mo., U.S. D5 102
Mountain Home, Ar., U.S. A3 81
Mountain Home, Id., U.S. F3 89
Mountain Home Air Force Base, mil., Id., U.S. F3 89
Mountain Iron, Mn., U.S. C6 100
Mountain Lake, Mn., U.S. G4 100
Mountain Lake Park, Md., U.S. m12 97
Mountain Nile (Bahr al-Jabal), stm., Sudan G12 42
Mountain Pine, Ar., U.S. C2 81
Mountainside, N.J., U.S. B4 107
Mountain View, Ar., U.S. B3 81
Mountain View, Ca., U.S. k8 82
Mountain View, Mo., U.S. D6 102
Mountain View, N.M., U.S. C3 108
Mountain View, Ok., U.S. B3 113
Mountain View, Wy., U.S. E2 127
Mountain Village, Ak., U.S. C7 79
Mount Airy, Md., U.S. B3 97
Mount Airy, N.C., U.S. A2 110
Mount Albert, Ont., Can. C5 73
Mount Angel, Or., U.S. B4 114
Mount Arlington, N.J., U.S. B3 107
Mount Ayr, Ia., U.S. D3 92
Mount Carmel, Il., U.S. E6 90
Mount Carmel, Oh., U.S. o13 112
Mount Carmel, Pa., U.S. E9 115
Mount Carmel [-Mitchell's Brook-Saint Catherine's], Newf., Can. E5 72
Mount Carroll, Il., U.S. A4 90
Mount Clare, W.V., U.S. B4 125
Mount Clemens, Mi., U.S. F8 99
Mount Desert Island, i., Me., U.S. D4 96
Mount Dora, Fl., U.S. D5 86
Mount Forest, Ont., Can. D4 73
Mount Gambier, Austl. G8 50
Mount Gay, W.V., U.S. D2 125
Mount Gilead, N.C., U.S. B3 110
Mount Gilead, Oh., U.S. B3 112
Mount Healthy, Oh., U.S. o12 112
Mount Holly, N.J., U.S. D3 107
Mount Holly, N.C., U.S. B1 110
Mount Holly Springs, Pa., U.S. F7 115
Mount Hope, Austl. F7 50
Mount Hope, Ks., U.S. E6 93
Mount Hope, W.V., U.S. D3 125
Mount Hope, stm., Ct., U.S. B7 84
Mount Hope Bay, b., U.S. D6 116
Mount Horeb, Wi., U.S. E4 126
Mount Ida, Ar., U.S. C2 81
Mount Isa, Austl. D7 50
Mount Jackson, Va., U.S. B4 123
Mount Jewett, Pa., U.S. C4 115
Mount Joy, Pa., U.S. F9 115
Mount Juliet, Tn., U.S. A5 119
Mount Kisco, N.Y., U.S. D7 109
Mount Lebanon, Pa., U.S. F1 115
Mount Magnet, Austl. E3 50
Mount Morris, Il., U.S. A4 90
Mount Morris, Mi., U.S. E7 99
Mount Morris, N.Y., U.S. C3 109
Mount Olive, Al., U.S. B3 78
Mount Olive, Il., U.S. D4 90
Mount Olive, Ms., U.S. D4 101
Mount Olive, N.C., U.S. B4 110
Mount Olive, Tn., U.S. n14 119
Mount Orab, Oh., U.S. C2 112
Mount Pearl, Newf., Can. E5 72
Mount Penn, Pa., U.S. F10 115
Mount Pleasant, Ia., U.S. D6 92
Mount Pleasant, Mi., U.S. E6 99
Mount Pleasant, N.C., U.S. B2 110
Mount Pleasant, Pa., U.S. F2 115
Mount Pleasant, S.C., U.S. F8 117
Mount Pleasant, Tn., U.S. B4 119
Mount Pleasant, Tx., U.S. C5 120
Mount Pleasant, Ut., U.S. D4 121
Mount Pocono, Pa., U.S. D11 115
Mount Prospect, Il., U.S. A6 90
Mount Pulaski, Il., U.S. C4 90
Mountrail, co., N.D., U.S. A3 111
Mount Rainier, Md., U.S. f9 97
Mount Rainier National Park, Wa., U.S. C4 124
Mount Revelstoke National Park, B.C., Can. D8 69
Mount Rogers National Recreation Area, Va., U.S. D1 123
Mount Rushmore National Memorial, hist., S.D., U.S. D2 118
Mount Savage, Md., U.S. k13 97
Mount Shasta, Ca., U.S. B2 82
Mount Sterling, Il., U.S. D3 90
Mount Sterling, Ky., U.S. B6 94
Mount Sterling, Oh., U.S. C2 112
Mount Uniacke, N.S., Can. E6 71
Mount Union, Pa., U.S. F6 115
Mount Vernon, Al., U.S. D1 78
Mount Vernon, Ga., U.S. D4 87
Mount Vernon, Il., U.S. E5 90
Mount Vernon, In., U.S. I2 91
Mount Vernon, Ia., U.S. C6 92
Mount Vernon, Ky., U.S. C5 94
Mount Vernon, Mo., U.S. D4 102
Mount Vernon, N.Y., U.S. h13 109
Mount Vernon, Oh., U.S. B3 112
Mount Vernon, Tx., U.S. C5 120
Mount Vernon, Wa., U.S. A3 124
Mount View, R.I., U.S. D4 116
Mount Washington, Ky., U.S. B4 94
Mount Wolf, Pa., U.S. F8 115
Mount Zion, Il., U.S. D5 90
Moura, Braz. D6 54
Moura, Port. G4 12
Mourne Mountains, mts., N. Ire., U.K. G6 7
Moussoro, Chad F9 42
Moutong, Indon. E7 32
Moville, Ia., U.S. B1 92
Moweaqua, Il., U.S. D4 90
Mower, co., Mn., U.S. G6 100
Moxee City, Wa., U.S. C5 124
Moxos, Llanos de, pl., Bol. G6 54
Moyahua, Mex. G8 62
Moyale, Kenya H2 46
Moyen Atlas, mts., Mor. B5 42
Moyeuvre-Grande, Fr. C13 10
Moyock, N.C., U.S. A6 110
Moyu, China B8 38
Možajsk, Russia F19 18
Mozambique, ctry., Afr. E6 44
Mozambique Channel, strt., Afr. E8 44
Mozyr', Bela. G3 22
Mpanda, Tan. C6 44
Mpika, Zam. D6 44
Mrkonjić Grad, Bos. E12 14
Msaken, Tun. N5 14
Mtwara, Tan. D8 44
Muang Khammouan, Laos F8 34
Muang Pakxan, Laos E7 34
Muar, Malay. M7 34
Muaratewe, Indon. F5 32
Muāri, Rās, c., Pak. H2 38
Mücheln, Ger. D11 8
Muchinga Mountains, mts., Zam. D6 44
Muckleshoot Indian Reservation, Wa., U.S. f11 124
Mud, stm., Ky., U.S. C3 94
Mud, stm., Mn., U.S. B3 100
Mud, stm., W.V., U.S. C2 125
Mudanjiang, China C12 26
Mud Creek, stm., Ok., U.S. C4 113
Muddy Boggy Creek, stm., Ok., U.S. C6 113
Muddy Creek, stm., Ut., U.S. E4 121
Muddy Creek, stm., Wy., U.S. E2 127
Muddy Creek, stm., Wy., U.S. E5 127
Muddy Creek, stm., Wy., U.S. D6 127
Muddy Creek, stm., Wy., U.S. C4 127
Muddy Mountains, mts., Nv., U.S. G7 105
Muddy Peak, mtn., Nv., U.S. G7 105
Mud Lake, l., Me., U.S. A4 96
Mud Lake, l., Nv., U.S. F4 105
Mudon, Mya. F4 34
Muenster, Tx., U.S. C4 120
Mufulira, Zam. D5 44
Mu Gia, Deo (Mu Gia Pass), Asia F8 34
Muğla, Tur. H13 4
Mühldorf, Ger. G12 8
Muhlenberg, co., Ky., U.S. C2 94
Mühlhausen, Ger. D10 8
Mühlviertel, reg., Aus. G14 8
Muhola, Fin. E15 6
Muirkirk, Md., U.S. B4 97
Muiron Islands, is., Austl. D2 50
Muir Woods National Monument, Ca., U.S. h7 82
Mukden see Shenyang, China C11 26
Mukilteo, Wa., U.S. B3 124
Mukwonago, Wi., U.S. F5 126
Mula, Spain G10 12
Mulanje, Mwi. E7 44
Mulberry, Ar., U.S. B1 81
Mulberry, Fl., U.S. E4 86
Mulberry, In., U.S. D4 91
Mulberry, N.C., U.S. A1 110
Mulberry, stm., Ar., U.S. B1 81
Mulberry Fork, stm., Al., U.S. B3 78
Muldraugh, Ky., U.S. C4 94
Muldrow, Ok., U.S. B7 113
Muleshoe, Tx., U.S. B1 120
Mulgrave, N.S., Can. D8 71
Mulhacén, mtn., Spain H8 12
Mulhouse, Fr. E14 10
Mull, Island of, i., Scot., U.K. E6 7
Mullan, Id., U.S. B3 89
Mullan Pass, Mt., U.S. D4 103
Mullens, W.V., U.S. D3 125
Muller, Pegunungan, mts., Indon. E5 32
Mullet Key, i., Fl., U.S. p10 86
Mullett Lake, l., Mi., U.S. C6 99
Mullewa, Austl. E3 50
Mullica, stm., N.J., U.S. D3 107
Mullins, S.C., U.S. C9 117
Multān, Pak. E4 38
Multnomah, co., Or., U.S. B4 114
Mulvane, Ks., U.S. E6 93
Mumbwa, Zam. D5 44
Mummy Range, mts., Co., U.S. A5 83
Muna, Pulau, i., Indon. F7 32
Muncar, Indon. n17 33a
München (Munich), Ger. G11 8
Muncie, In., U.S. D7 91
Muncy, Pa., U.S. D8 115
Munday, Tx., U.S. C3 120
Mundelein, Il., U.S. A5 90
Münden, Ger. D9 8
Munford, Al., U.S. B4 78
Munford, Tn., U.S. B2 119
Munfordville, Ky., U.S. C4 94
Mungbere, Zaire H11 42
Munhall, Pa., U.S. k14 115
Munhango, Ang. D3 44
Munich see München, Ger. G11 8
Munising, Mi., U.S. B4 99
Munster, Ger. C10 8
Münster, Ger. D7 8
Munster, In., U.S. A2 91
Munster, hist. reg., Ire. I4 7
Munsungan Lake, l., Me., U.S. B3 96
Munuscong Lake, l., Mi., U.S. B6 99
Muong Sing, Laos D6 34
Muqayshiṭ, i., U.A.E. D5 46
Muqdisho, Som. H4 46
Mur (Mura), stm., Eur. I15 8
Mura (Mur), stm., Eur. I16 8
Murat, Fr. G9 10
Murat, stm., Tur. H16 4
Murau, Aus. H14 8
Muravera, Italy J4 14
Murča, Port. D4 12
Murchison, stm., Austl. E3 50
Murcia, Spain H10 12
Murderkill, stm., De., U.S. D4 85
Murdo, S.D., U.S. D5 118
Mureș (Maros), stm., Eur. C5 16
Muret, Fr. I8 10
Murfreesboro, Ar., U.S. C2 81
Murfreesboro, N.C., U.S. A5 110
Murfreesboro, Tn., U.S. B5 119
Mūrīān, Hāmūn-e, l., Iran C6 46
Murmansk, Russia D4 22
Murom, Russia F25 18
Muroran, Japan q18 30a
Muros, Spain C2 12
Muroto, Japan I7 30
Muroto-zaki, c., Japan I7 30
Murphy, Mo., U.S. g13 102
Murphy, N.C., U.S. f8 110
Murphy Island, i., S.C., U.S. E9 117
Murphysboro, Il., U.S. F4 90
Murray, Ia., U.S. C4 92
Murray, Ky., U.S. f9 94
Murray, Ut., U.S. C4 121
Murray, co., Ga., U.S. B2 87
Murray, co., Mn., U.S. F3 100
Murray, co., Ok., U.S. C4 113
Murray, stm., Austl. F7 50
Murray, Lake, res., Ok., U.S. C4 113
Murray, Lake, res., S.C., U.S. C5 117
Murray Head, c., P.E.I., Can. C7 71
Murraysburg, S. Afr. H4 44
Murrayville, Ga., U.S. B3 87
Murrells Inlet, S.C., U.S. D9 117
Murrells Inlet, b., S.C., U.S. D10 117
Murten, Switz. F14 10
Murukta, Russia D14 24
Murwāra, India I9 38
Murwillumbah, Austl. E10 50
Mürzzuschlag, Aus. H15 8
Muş, Tur. H16 4
Musay'īd, Qatar D5 46
Muscat and Oman see Oman, ctry., Asia D6 46
Muscatatuck, stm., In., U.S. G5 91
Muscatine, Ia., U.S. C6 92
Muscatine, co., Ia., U.S. C6 92
Muscat see Masqaṭ, Oman D6 46
Mus-Chaja, Gora, mtn., Russia E22 24
Muscle Shoals, Al., U.S. A2 78
Musclow, Mount, mtn., B.C., Can. C4 69
Muscoda, Wi., U.S. E3 126
Muscogee, co., Ga., U.S. D2 87
Musconetcong, stm., N.J., U.S. B4 107
Muscooten Bay, l., Il., U.S. C3 90
Muse, Pa., U.S. F1 115
Musgrave, Austl. B8 50
Musgrave Harbour, Newf., Can. D5 72
Musgrave Ranges, mts., Austl. E6 50
Musgravetown, Newf., Can. D5 72
Mushin, Nig. G6 42
Muskeg Bay, b., Mn., U.S. B3 100
Muskeget Island, i., Ma., U.S. D7 98
Muskego, Wi., U.S. F5 126
Muskego Lake, l., Wi., U.S. n11 126
Muskegon, Mi., U.S. E4 99
Muskegon, co., Mi., U.S. E4 99
Muskegon, stm., Mi., U.S. E4 99
Muskegon Heights, Mi., U.S. E4 99
Muskegon Lake, l., Mi., U.S. E4 99
Muskingum, co., Oh., U.S. B4 112
Muskingum, stm., Oh., U.S. C4 112
Muskogee, Ok., U.S. B6 113
Muskogee, co., Ok., U.S. B6 113
Musoma, Tan. B6 44
Musquacook Lakes, l., Me., U.S. B3 96
Musquodoboit Harbour, N.S., Can. E6 71
Musselshell, co., Mt., U.S. D8 103
Musselshell, stm., Mt., U.S. D9 103
Mussidan, Fr. G7 10
Mussuma, Ang. D4 44
Mustafakemalpaşa, Tur. I12 16
Mustang, Ok., U.S. B4 113
Mustinka, stm., Mn., U.S. E2 100
Mut, Tur. A3 40
Mutare, Zimb. E6 44
Mutoraj, Russia E14 24
Mutsu, Japan A14 30
Mutsu-wan, b., Japan A13 30
Mutton Mountains, mts., Or., U.S. C5 114
Muzaffarābād, Pak. C5 38
Muzaffarnagar, India F7 38
Muzaffarpur, India G11 38
Muzon, Cape, c., Ak., U.S. n23 79
Muztag, mtn., China B9 38
Muztag, mtn., China B12 38
Mvuma, Zimb. E6 44
Mwanza, Tan. B6 44
Mweelrea, mtn., Ire. H3 7
Mweka, Zaire B4 44
Mwenezi, Zimb. F6 44
Mweru, Lake, l., Afr. C5 44
Mwinilunga, Zam. D4 44
Myakka, stm., Fl., U.S. E4 86
Myanaung, Mya. E3 34
Myaungmya, Mya. F3 34
Myerstown, Pa., U.S. F9 115
Myingyan, Mya. D3 34
Myitkyinā, Mya. B4 34
Mykolayiv, Ukr. H4 22
Myllymäki, Fin. E15 6
Mymensingh, Bngl. H14 38
Mynämäki, Fin. F13 6
Myrskylä (Mörskom), Fin. F15 6
Myrtle Beach, S.C., U.S. D10 117
Myrtle Beach Air Force Base, mil., S.C., U.S. D10 117
Myrtle Grove, Fl., U.S. u14 86
Myrtle Point, Or., U.S. D2 114
Mysen, Nor. G8 6
Mysore, India F4 37
Mys Šmidta, Russia D30 24
Mystic, Ct., U.S. D8 84
Mystic Lakes, l., Ma., U.S. g11 98
My Tho, Viet. I9 34
Mytišči, Russia F20 18
Mzimba, Mwi. D6 44
Mzuzu, Mwi. D6 44

N

Naalehu, Hi., U.S. D6 88
Naas, Ire. H6 7
Nabadwīp, India I13 38
Naberežnyje Čelny, Russia F8 22
Nabeul, Tun. M5 14
Nabī Shu'ayb, Jabal an-, mtn., Yemen E3 46
Nabnasset, Ma., U.S. A5 98
Nābulus, Isr. Occ. C4 40
Nacala-Velha, Moz. D8 44
Naches, stm., Wa., U.S. C5 124
Nachingwea, Tan. D7 44
Nachodka, Russia I20 24
Nacimiento, Lake, res., Ca., U.S. E3 82
Naco, Mex. B5 62
Naco, Az., U.S. F6 80
Nacogdoches, Tx., U.S. D5 120
Nacogdoches, co., Tx., U.S. D5 120
Nadiād, India I5 38
Nadym, stm., Russia E8 24
Næstved, Den. I8 6
Naga, Phil. r20 32
Nagahama, Japan G9 30
Nagaland, state, India H16 38
Nagano, Japan F11 30
Nagaoka, Japan E11 30
Nāgappattinam, India G5 37
Nagasaki, Japan J2 30
Nāgaur, India G5 38
Nāgda, India I6 38
Nāgercoil, India H4 37
Nago, Japan y27 31b
Nagornyj, Russia F18 24
Nagoya, Japan G9 30
Nāgpur, India B5 37
Nags Head, N.C., U.S. B7 110
Nagykanizsa, Hung. I16 8
Nagykőrös, Hung. H19 8
Naha, Japan y27 31b
Nahant, Ma., U.S. g12 98
Nahariya, Isr. C4 40
Nahmakanta Lake, l., Me., U.S. C3 96
Nahunta, Ga., U.S. E5 87
Naidong, China F14 38
Nain, Newf., Can. g9 72
Nā'īn, Iran B5 46
Nairn, Scot., U.K. D9 7
Nairobi, Kenya B7 44
Najafābād, Iran B5 46
Nájera, Spain C9 12
Najin, N. Kor. C13 26
Nakaminato, Japan F13 30
Nakatsu, Japan I4 30
Nakatsugawa, Japan G10 30
Nakhon Pathom, Thai. H6 34
Nakhon Phanom, Thai. F8 34
Nakhon Ratchasima, Thai. G7 34
Nakhon Sawan, Thai. G6 34
Nakhon Si Thammarat, Thai. J5 34
Nakina, Ont., Can. o18 73
Naknek, Ak., U.S. D8 79
Naknek Lake, l., Ak., U.S. D8 79
Nakskov, Den. I8 6
Nakuru, Kenya B7 44
Nakusp, B.C., Can. D9 69
Nalchik see Nal'čik, Russia I6 22
Nal'čik, Russia I6 22
Nalgonda, India D5 37
Nālūt, Libya B8 42
Namak, Daryācheh-ye, l., Iran K8 22
Namangan, Uzb. I12 22
Namanock Island, i., N.J., U.S. A3 107
Namapa, Moz. D7 44
Namatanai, Pap. N. Gui. k17 50a
Nambour, Austl. E10 50
Namcha Barwa see Namjagbarwa Feng, mtn., China F16 38
Nam Co, l., China E14 38
Nam Dinh, Viet. D9 34
Namekagon, stm., Wi., U.S. B2 126
Namekagon Lake, l., Wi., U.S. B2 126
Namhkam, Mya. C4 34
Namib Desert, des., Nmb. F2 44
Namibe, Ang. E2 44
Namibia, ctry., Afr. F3 44
Namjagbarwa Feng, mtn., China F16 38
Namlea, Indon. F8 32
Nampa, Id., U.S. F2 89
Namp'o, N. Kor. D12 26
Nampula, Moz. E7 44
Namsos, Nor. D8 6
Namur, Bel. E4 8
Nanaimo, B.C., Can. E5 69
Nanakuli, Hi., U.S. B3 88
Nanao, Japan E9 30
Nance, co., Ne., U.S. C7 104
Nanchang, China G4 28
Nanchong, China E8 26
Nancy, Fr. D13 10
Nanda Devi, mtn., India E8 38
Nānded, India C4 37
Nandurbār, India B3 37
Nandyāl, India E5 37
Nānga Parbat, mtn., Pak. C6 38
Nangqian (Xiangda), China D17 38
Nanjing (Nanking), China C7 28
Nanking see Nanjing, China C7 28
Nankoku, Japan I6 30
Nankou, China C10 26
Nan Ling, mts., China F9 26
Nanning, China C10 34
Nanping, China I7 28
Nansei-shotō (Ryukyu Islands), is., Japan F12 26
Nansemond, stm., Va., U.S. k14 123
Nantes, Fr. E5 10
Nanticoke, Ont., Can. E4 73
Nanticoke, Pa., U.S. D10 115
Nanticoke, stm., U.S. D6 97
Nanton, Alta., Can. D4 68
Nantong, China C9 28
Nant'ou, Tai. L9 28
Nantua, Fr. F12 10
Nantucket, Ma., U.S. D7 98
Nantucket, co., Ma., U.S. D7 98
Nantucket Island, i., Ma., U.S. D7 98
Nantucket Sound, strt., Ma., U.S. C7 98
Nantuxent Point, c., N.J., U.S. E2 107
Nanty Glo, Pa., U.S. F4 115

Name	Map Ref	Page
Nanuet, N.Y., U.S.	g12	109
Nanuque, Braz.	D8	57
Nanxiang, China	D10	28
Nanxiong, China	J3	28
Nanyang, China	B1	28
Naoetsu, Japan	E11	30
Naoma, W.V., U.S.	n13	125
Naomi Peak, mtn., Ut., U.S.	B4	121
Náousa, Grc.	I6	16
Napa, Ca., U.S.	C2	82
Napa, co., Ca., U.S.	C2	82
Napanee, Ont., Can.	C8	73
Napatree Point, c., R.I., U.S.	G1	116
Napavine, Wa., U.S.	C3	124
Naperville, Il., U.S.	B5	90
Napier, N.Z.	C6	52
Napierville, Que., Can.	D4	74
Naples, Fl., U.S.	F5	86
Naples, Tx., U.S.	C5	120
Naples, Ut., U.S.	C6	121
Naples see Napoli, Italy	I9	14
Napo, stm., S.A.	I6	58
Napoleon, N.D., U.S.	C6	111
Napoleon, Oh., U.S.	A1	112
Napoleonville, La., U.S.	E4	95
Napoli (Naples), Italy	I9	14
Nappanee, In., U.S.	B5	91
Nara, Japan	H8	30
Nara, Mali	E4	42
Naracoorte, Austl.	G8	50
Naramata, B.C., Can.	E8	69
Naranja, Fl., U.S.	G6	86
Narasapur, India	D6	37
Narasaraopet, India	D6	37
Narathiwat, Thai.	K6	34
Nārāyanganj, Bngl.	I14	38
Narberth, Pa., U.S.	p20	115
Narbonne, Fr.	I9	10
Nardò, Italy	I13	14
Narew, stm., Eur.	C21	8
Nārīn Ghar, Afg.	B3	38
Narita, Japan	G13	30
Narmada, stm., India	J5	38
Nārnaul, India	F7	38
Narni, Italy	G7	14
Naro-Fominsk, Russia	F19	18
Narragansett, R.I., U.S.	F4	116
Narragansett Bay, b., R.I., U.S.	E5	116
Narraguagus, stm., Me., U.S.	D5	96
Narrows, Va., U.S.	C2	123
Narsimhapur, India	I8	38
Narssag, Grnld.	D23	66
Naruto, Japan	H7	30
Narva, Est.	B11	18
Narvik, Nor.	B11	6
Naselle, Wa., U.S.	C2	124
Nash, Tx., U.S.	C5	120
Nash, co., N.C., U.S.	A4	110
Nashawena Island, i., Ma., U.S.	D6	98
Nash Stream, stm., N.H., U.S.	A4	106
Nashua, Ia., U.S.	B5	92
Nashua, N.H., U.S.	E4	106
Nashua, stm., U.S.	E3	106
Nashville, Ar., U.S.	D2	81
Nashville, Ga., U.S.	E3	87
Nashville, Il., U.S.	E4	90
Nashville, In., U.S.	F5	91
Nashville, Mi., U.S.	F5	99
Nashville, N.C., U.S.	B5	110
Nashville, Tn., U.S.	A5	119
Nashwauk, Mn., U.S.	C5	100
Nāsik, India	C2	37
Nāsir, Sudan	G12	42
Naskaupi, stm., Newf., Can.	g9	72
Nassau, Bah.	B9	64
Nassau, co., Fl., U.S.	B5	86
Nassau, co., N.Y., U.S.	E7	109
Nassau, stm., Fl., U.S.	k8	86
Nassau Sound, b., Fl., U.S.	B5	86
Nasser, Lake, res., Afr.	D12	42
Nässjö, Swe.	H10	6
Nasukoin Mountain, mtn., Mt., U.S.	B2	103
Natal, Braz.	E11	54
Natalbany, La., U.S.	D5	95
Natalia, Tx., U.S.	E3	120
Natashquan, stm., Can.	h9	72
Natchaug, stm., Ct., U.S.	B7	84
Natchez, Ms., U.S.	D2	101
Natchitoches, La., U.S.	C2	95
Natchitoches, co., La., U.S.	C2	95
Nāthdwāra, India	H5	38
Natick, Ma., U.S.	B5	98
National City, Ca., U.S.	F5	82
Natron, Lake, l., Afr.	B7	44
Natrona, co., Wy., U.S.	D5	127
Natrona Heights, Pa., U.S.	E2	115
Nattaung, mtn., Mya.	E4	34
Natuna Besar, i., Indon.	M10	34
Natuna Besar, Kepulauan, is., Indon.	M10	34
Natuna Selatan, Kepulauan, is., Indon.	M10	34
Natural Bridge, Ut., U.S.	F3	121
Natural Bridge, Va., U.S.	C3	123
Natural Bridges National Monument, Ut., U.S.	F6	121
Naturaliste, Cape, c., Austl.	F3	50
Nauen, Ger.	C12	8
Naugatuck, Ct., U.S.	D3	84
Naugatuck, stm., Ct., U.S.	D3	84
Naumburg, Ger.	D11	8
Naushon Island, i., Ma., U.S.	D6	98
Nautilus Park, Ct., U.S.	D7	84
Nauvoo, Il., U.S.	C2	90
Nava del Rey, Spain	D6	12
Navahermosa, Spain	F7	12
Navajo, co., Az., U.S.	B5	80
Navajo Dam, N.M., U.S.	A2	108
Navajo Indian Reservation, U.S.	A4	80
Navajo Mountain, mtn., Ut., U.S.	F5	121
Navajo National Monument, Az., U.S.	A5	80
Navajo Reservoir, res., U.S.	A2	108
Navalcarnero, Spain	E7	12
Navalmoral de la Mata, Spain	F6	12
Navalvillar de Pela, Spain	F6	12
Navan, Ont., Can.	B9	73
Navan, Ire.	H6	7
Navarin, Mys, c., Russia	E29	24
Navarino, Isla, i., Chile	H3	56
Navarre, Oh., U.S.	B4	112
Navarro, co., Tx., U.S.	D4	120
Navasota, Tx., U.S.	D4	120
Navassa Island, i., N.A.	E10	64
Navoi, Uzb.	I11	22
Navojoa, Mex.	D5	62
Navolato, Mex.	E6	62
Navsāri, India	B2	37
Nawābganj, Bngl.	H13	38
Nawābganj, India	G9	38
Nawābshāh, Pak.	G3	38
Nāwah, Afg.	D2	38
Nawalgarh, India	G6	38
Nawiliwili Bay, b., Hi., U.S.	B2	88
Náxos, i., Grc.	L9	16
Nayak, Afg.	C2	38
Naylor, Mo., U.S.	E7	102
Nayoro, Japan	o20	30a
Nazaré, Braz.	B9	57
Nazaré, Port.	F2	12
Nazareth, Pa., U.S.	E11	115
Nazca, Peru	F4	54
Naze, Japan	w29	31b
Nazilli, Tur.	L12	16
Nazko, stm., B.C., Can.	C6	69
Ndélé, Cen. Afr. Rep.	G10	42
N'Djamena (Fort-Lamy), Chad	F9	42
Ndola, Zam.	D5	44
Neagh, Lough, l., N. Ire., U.K.	G6	7
Neah Bay, Wa., U.S.	A1	124
Néa Páfos (Paphos), Cyp.	B3	40
Neápolis, Grc.	M7	16
Near Islands, is., Ak., U.S.	E2	79
Nebo, Mount, mtn., Ut., U.S.	D4	121
Nebraska, state, U.S.	C6	104
Nebraska City, Ne., U.S.	D10	104
Nechako, stm., B.C., Can.	C5	69
Neches, stm., Tx., U.S.	D5	120
Nechí, Col.	C5	58
Neckar, stm., Ger.	F9	8
Necker Island, i., Hi., U.S.	m15	88
Necochea, Arg.	D5	56
Nederland, Co., U.S.	B5	83
Nederland, Tx., U.S.	E6	120
Nedrow, N.Y., U.S.	C4	109
Needham, Ma., U.S.	g11	98
Needle Mountain, mtn., Wy., U.S.	B3	127
Needles, Ca., U.S.	E6	82
Needville, Tx., U.S.	r14	120
Neenah, Wi., U.S.	D5	126
Neepawa, Man., Can.	D2	70
Neffs, Oh., U.S.	B5	112
Neffsville, Pa., U.S.	F9	115
Negage, Ang.	C3	44
Negaunee, Mi., U.S.	B3	99
Negele, Eth.	G2	46
Negev Desert see Hanegev, reg., Isr.	D4	40
Negley, Oh., U.S.	B5	112
Negombo, Sri L.	I5	37
Negra, Punta, c., Peru	E2	54
Negro, stm., Arg.	E4	56
Negro, stm., S.A.	H12	58
Negros, i., Phil.	C7	32
Neguac, N.B., Can.	B4	71
Nehalem, stm., Or., U.S.	A3	114
Nehbandān, Iran	B7	46
Neheim-Hüsten, Ger.	D7	8
Neiba, Bahía de, b., Dom. Rep.	E12	64
Neijiang, China	F8	26
Neill Point, c., Wa., U.S.	f11	124
Neillsville, Wi., U.S.	D3	126
Nei Monggol Zizhiqu (Inner Mongolia), prov., China	C10	26
Neisse (Nysa Łużycka), stm., Eur.	D14	8
Neiva, Col.	F5	58
Neja, Russia	C26	18
Nekemte, Eth.	G2	46
Nekoosa, Wi., U.S.	D4	126
Nelidovo, Russia	E15	18
Neligh, Ne., U.S.	B7	104
Nel'kan, Russia	F21	24
Nellikuppam, India	G5	37
Nellis Air Force Base, mil., Nv., U.S.	G6	105
Nellore, India	E5	37
Nelson, B.C., Can.	E9	69
Nelson, N.Z.	D4	52
Nelson, Ne., U.S.	D7	104
Nelson, co., Ky., U.S.	C4	94
Nelson, co., N.D., U.S.	B7	111
Nelson, co., Va., U.S.	C4	123
Nelson, stm., Man., Can.	A4	70
Nelsonville, Oh., U.S.	C3	112
Néma, Maur.	E4	42
Nemacolin, Pa., U.S.	G2	115
Nemadji, stm., U.S.	B1	126
Nemaha, co., Ks., U.S.	C7	93
Nemaha, co., Ne., U.S.	D10	104
Nemours, Fr.	D9	10
Nemuro, Japan	p23	30a
Nemuro Strait, strt., Asia	o23	30a
Nenagh, Ire.	I4	7
Nenana, Ak., U.S.	C10	79
Neodesha, Ks., U.S.	E8	93
Neoga, Il., U.S.	D5	90
Neola, Ia., U.S.	C2	92
Neola, Ut., U.S.	C5	121
Neopit, Wi., U.S.	D5	126
Neosho, Mo., U.S.	E3	102
Neosho, co., Ks., U.S.	E8	93
Neosho, stm., Ok., U.S.	A6	113
Nepal (Nepāl), ctry., Asia	D5	36
Nepālganj, Nepal	F9	38
Nepaug Reservoir, res., Ct., U.S.	B3	84
Nepean, Ont., Can.	h12	73
Nepewassi Lake, l., Ont., Can.	A4	73
Nephi, Ut., U.S.	D4	121
Nepisiguit, stm., N.B., Can.	B3	71
Nepisiguit Bay, b., N.B., Can.	B4	71
Neponset, stm., Ma., U.S.	h11	98
Neptune, N.J., U.S.	C4	107
Neptune Beach, Fl., U.S.	B5	86
Neptune City, N.J., U.S.	C4	107
Nérac, Fr.	H7	10
Nerastro, Sarīr, des., Libya	D10	42
Nerčinskij Zavod, Russia	G17	24
Nerechta, Russia	D23	18
Neriquinha, Ang.	E4	44
Nerva, Spain	H5	12
Nesbyen, Nor.	F7	6
Nescopeck, Pa., U.S.	D9	115
Neshanic, stm., N.J., U.S.	C3	107
Neshoba, co., Ms., U.S.	C4	101
Neskaupstaður, Ice.	B5	4
Nesna, Nor.	C9	6
Nesowadnehunk, l., Me., U.S.	B3	96
Nesquehoning, Pa., U.S.	E10	115
Ness, co., Ks., U.S.	D4	93
Ness, Loch, l., Scot., U.K.	D8	7
Ness City, Ks., U.S.	D4	93
Néstos (Mesta), stm., Eur.	H8	16
Netanya, Isr.	C4	40
Netcong, N.J., U.S.	B3	107
Netherlands, ctry., Eur.	E9	4
Netherlands Antilles (Nederlandse Antillen), dep., N.A.	H13	64
Netrakona, Bngl.	H14	38
Nettie, W.V., U.S.	C4	125
Nettilling Lake, l., N.W. Ter., Can.	C18	66
Nett Lake, l., Mn., U.S.	B5	100
Nett Lake Indian Reservation, Mn., U.S.	B6	100
Nettleton, Ms., U.S.	A5	101
Nettuno, Italy	H7	14
Neubrandenburg, Ger.	B13	8
Neuburg an der Donau, Ger.	G11	8
Neuchâtel, Switz.	F13	10
Neuchâtel, Lac de, l., Switz.	F13	10
Neufchâteau, Bel.	F5	8
Neufchâteau, Fr.	D12	10
Neufchâtel-en-Bray, Fr.	C8	10
Neuillé-Pont-Pierre, Fr.	E7	10
Neumarkt in der Oberpfalz, Ger.	F11	8
Neumünster, Ger.	A9	8
Neunkirchen, Aus.	H16	8
Neunkirchen/Saar, Ger.	F7	8
Neuquén, Arg.	D3	56
Neuruppin, Ger.	C12	8
Neuse, stm., N.C., U.S.	B6	110
Neusiedler See, l., Eur.	H16	8
Neuss, Ger.	D6	8
Neustadt [an der Aisch—], Ger.	F10	8
Neustadt an der Weinstrasse, Ger.	F8	8
Neustadt in Holstein, Ger.	A10	8
Neustrelitz, Ger.	B13	8
Neu-Ulm, Ger.	G10	8
Neuville, Que., Can.	C6	74
Neuville-de-Poitou, Fr.	F7	10
Neuwied, Ger.	E7	8
Nevada, Ia., U.S.	B4	92
Nevada, Mo., U.S.	D3	102
Nevada, co., Ar., U.S.	D2	81
Nevada, co., Ca., U.S.	C3	82
Nevada, state, U.S.	D5	105
Nevada, Sierra, mts., Spain	H8	12
Nevada, Sierra, mts., Ca., U.S.	D4	82
Nevada City, Ca., U.S.	C3	82
Nevado, Cerro, mtn., Arg.	D3	56
Nevado, Cerro, mtn., Col.	F5	58
Never, Russia	G18	24
Nevers, Fr.	E10	10
Neversink, stm., N.Y., U.S.	D6	109
Nevis, i., St. K./N.	F16	64
Nevis, Ben, mtn., Scot., U.K.	E7	7
New, stm., U.S.	C3	125
New, stm., Az., U.S.	k8	80
New, stm., N.C., U.S.	C5	110
New Albany, In., U.S.	H6	91
New Albany, Ms., U.S.	A4	101
New Albany, Oh., U.S.	k11	112
New Amsterdam, Guy.	D14	58
Newark, Ar., U.S.	B4	81
Newark, Ca., U.S.	h8	82
Newark, De., U.S.	B3	85
Newark, Il., U.S.	B5	90
Newark, N.J., U.S.	B4	107
Newark, N.Y., U.S.	B3	109
Newark, Oh., U.S.	B3	112
Newark Bay, b., N.J., U.S.	k8	107
Newark Lake, l., Nv., U.S.	D6	105
New Athens, Il., U.S.	E4	90
New Augusta, Ms., U.S.	D4	101
Newaygo, Mi., U.S.	E5	99
Newaygo, co., Mi., U.S.	E5	99
New Baden, Il., U.S.	E4	90
New Baltimore, Mi., U.S.	F8	99
New Bedford, Ma., U.S.	C6	98
New Bedford, Pa., U.S.	D1	115
Newberg, Or., U.S.	B4	114
New Berlin, Il., U.S.	D4	90
New Berlin, Wi., U.S.	n11	126
New Bern, N.C., U.S.	B5	110
Newbern, Tn., U.S.	A2	119
Newberry, Fl., U.S.	C4	86
Newberry, Mi., U.S.	B5	99
Newberry, S.C., U.S.	C4	117
Newberry, co., S.C., U.S.	C4	117
New Bethlehem, Pa., U.S.	D3	115
New Bloomfield, Pa., U.S.	F7	115
New Boston, Mi., U.S.	p15	99
New Boston, Oh., U.S.	D3	112
New Boston, Tx., U.S.	C5	120
New Braunfels, Tx., U.S.	E3	120
New Bremen, Oh., U.S.	B1	112
New Brighton, Mn., U.S.	m12	100
New Brighton, Pa., U.S.	E1	115
New Britain, Ct., U.S.	C4	84
New Britain, i., Pap. N. Gui.	m16	50a
New Brockton, Al., U.S.	D4	78
New Brunswick, N.J., U.S.	C4	107
New Brunswick, prov., Can.	C3	71
New Buffalo, Mi., U.S.	G4	99
Newburg, Wi., U.S.	E5	126
Newburgh, Ont., Can.	C8	73
Newburgh, In., U.S.	I3	91
Newburgh, N.Y., U.S.	D6	109
Newburgh Heights, Oh., U.S.	h9	112
Newburyport, Ma., U.S.	A6	98
New Caledonia, dep., Oc.	H24	2
New Canaan, Ct., U.S.	E2	84
New Carlisle, In., U.S.	A4	91
New Carlisle, Oh., U.S.	C1	112
Newcastle, Austl.	F10	50
Newcastle, N.B., Can.	C4	71
Newcastle, Ont., Can.	D6	73
Newcastle, S. Afr.	G5	44
Newcastle, N. Ire., U.K.	G7	7
New Castle, Al., U.S.	B3	78
New Castle, Co., U.S.	B3	83
New Castle, De., U.S.	B3	85
New Castle, In., U.S.	E7	91
New Castle, Ky., U.S.	B4	94
Newcastle, Ok., U.S.	B4	113
New Castle, Pa., U.S.	D1	115
Newcastle, Wy., U.S.	C8	127
New Castle, co., De., U.S.	B3	85
Newcastle upon Tyne, Eng., U.K.	G11	7
Newcastle Waters, Austl.	C6	50
New City, N.Y., U.S.	D6	109
Newcomerstown, Oh., U.S.	B4	112
New Concord, Oh., U.S.	C4	112
New Cumberland, Pa., U.S.	F8	115
New Cumberland, W.V., U.S.	A4	125
Newdegate, Austl.	F3	50
New Delhi, India	F7	38
Newell, Ia., U.S.	B2	92
Newell, S.D., U.S.	C2	118
Newell, W.V., U.S.	A4	125
New Ellenton, S.C., U.S.	E4	117
Newellton, La., U.S.	B4	95
New England, N.D., U.S.	C3	111
Newenham, Cape, c., Ak., U.S.	D7	79
New Fairfield, Ct., U.S.	D2	84
Newfane, N.Y., U.S.	B2	109
Newfields, N.H., U.S.	D5	106
New Florence, Mo., U.S.	C6	102
Newfound Gap, U.S.	f9	110
Newfound Lake, l., N.H., U.S.	C3	106
Newfoundland, prov., Can.	D4	72
Newfoundland, i., Newf., Can.	D3	72
New Franklin, Mo., U.S.	B5	102
New Freedom, Pa., U.S.	G8	115
New Georgia, i., Sol.Is.	A11	50
New Germany, N.S., Can.	E5	71
New Glarus, Wi., U.S.	F4	126
New Guinea, i.	m14	50a
Newhall, Ia., U.S.	C6	92
New Hampshire, state, U.S.	C3	106
New Hampton, Ia., U.S.	A5	92
New Hanover, co., N.C., U.S.	C5	110
New Hanover, i., Pap. N. Gui.	k17	50a
New Harbour, Newf., Can.	E5	72
New Harmony, In., U.S.	H2	91
New Hartford, Ct., U.S.	B4	84
New Hartford, Ia., U.S.	B5	92
New Haven, Ct., U.S.	D4	84
New Haven, In., U.S.	B7	91
New Haven, Ky., U.S.	C4	94
New Haven, Mi., U.S.	F8	99
New Haven, Mo., U.S.	C6	102
New Haven, W.V., U.S.	C3	125
New Haven, co., Ct., U.S.	D4	84
New Haven, stm., Vt., U.S.	C2	122
New Haven Harbor, b., Ct., U.S.	E4	84
New Hazelton, B.C., Can.	B4	69
New Hebrides see Vanuatu, ctry., Oc.	H24	2
New Holland, Ga., U.S.	B3	87
New Holland, Pa., U.S.	F9	115
New Holstein, Wi., U.S.	E5	126
New Hope, Al., U.S.	A3	78
New Hope, Ky., U.S.	C4	94
New Hope, Mn., U.S.	m12	100
New Hope, Pa., U.S.	F12	115
New Hudson, Mi., U.S.	o14	99
New Iberia, La., U.S.	D4	95
Newington, Ct., U.S.	C5	84
New Inlet, b., N.C., U.S.	D5	110
New Ireland, i., Pap. N. Gui.	k17	50a
New Jersey, state, U.S.	C4	107
New Johnsonville, Tn., U.S.	A4	119
New Kensington, Pa., U.S.	E2	115
New Kent, co., Va., U.S.	C5	123
Newkirk, Ok., U.S.	A4	113
New Laguna, N.M., U.S.	B2	108
New Lenox, Il., U.S.	B6	90
New Lexington, Oh., U.S.	C3	112
New Lisbon, Wi., U.S.	E3	126
New Liskeard, Ont., Can.	p20	73
Newllano, La., U.S.	C2	95
New London, Ct., U.S.	D7	84
New London, Ia., U.S.	D6	92
New London, Mn., U.S.	E4	100
New London, Mo., U.S.	B6	102
New London, N.H., U.S.	D3	106
New London, Oh., U.S.	A3	112
New London, Wi., U.S.	D5	126
New London, co., Ct., U.S.	C7	84
New London Submarine Base, mil., Ct., U.S.	D7	84
New Madison, Oh., U.S.	C1	112
New Madrid, Mo., U.S.	E8	102
New Madrid, co., Mo., U.S.	E8	102
Newman, Ca., U.S.	D3	82
Newman, Il., U.S.	D6	90
New Manchester, W.V., U.S.	e8	125
Newman Grove, Ne., U.S.	C8	104
Newman Lake, l., Wa., U.S.	B8	124
Newmanstown, Pa., U.S.	F9	115
Newmarket, Ont., Can.	C5	73
New Market, Al., U.S.	A3	78
New Market, In., U.S.	E4	91
Newmarket, N.H., U.S.	D5	106
New Market, Tn., U.S.	C10	119
New Market, Va., U.S.	B4	123
New Martinsville, W.V., U.S.	B4	125
New Matamoras, Oh., U.S.	C4	112
New Mexico, state, U.S.	C3	108
New Miami, Oh., U.S.	C1	112
New Milford, Ct., U.S.	C2	84
New Milford, N.J., U.S.	h8	107
New Milford, Pa., U.S.	C10	115
Newnan, Ga., U.S.	C2	87
Newnans Lake, l., Fl., U.S.	C4	86
New Norfolk, Austl.	H9	50
New Orleans, La., U.S.	E5	95
New Orleans Naval Air Station, mil., La., U.S.	k11	95
New Oxford, Pa., U.S.	G7	115
New Palestine, In., U.S.	E6	91
New Paltz, N.Y., U.S.	D6	109
New Paris, In., U.S.	B6	91
New Paris, Oh., U.S.	C1	112
New Philadelphia, Oh., U.S.	B4	112
New Philadelphia, Pa., U.S.	E9	115
New Plymouth, N.Z.	C5	52
New Plymouth, Id., U.S.	F2	89
New Point Comfort, c., Va., U.S.	C6	123
Newport, Eng., U.K.	K11	7
Newport, Wales, U.K.	J9	7
Newport, Ar., U.S.	B4	81
Newport, De., U.S.	B3	85
Newport, In., U.S.	E3	91
Newport, Ky., U.S.	A5	94
Newport, Me., U.S.	D3	96
Newport, Mi., U.S.	G7	99
Newport, Mn., U.S.	n13	100
Newport, N.H., U.S.	D2	106
Newport, N.C., U.S.	C6	110
Newport, Oh., U.S.	C4	112
Newport, Or., U.S.	C2	114
Newport, Pa., U.S.	F7	115
Newport, R.I., U.S.	F5	116
Newport, Tn., U.S.	D10	119
Newport, Vt., U.S.	B4	122
Newport, Wa., U.S.	A8	124
Newport, co., R.I., U.S.	E5	116
Newport Beach, Ca., U.S.	n13	82
Newport News, Va., U.S.	D6	123
New Port Richey, Fl., U.S.	D4	86
New Prague, Mn., U.S.	F5	100
New Preston, Ct., U.S.	C2	84
New Providence, N.J., U.S.	B4	107
New Providence, i., Bah.	B9	64
Newquay, Eng., U.K.	K7	7
New Richland, Mn., U.S.	G5	100
New Richmond, Que., Can.	A4	71
New Richmond, Oh., U.S.	D1	112
New Richmond, Wi., U.S.	C1	126
New River Inlet, b., N.C., U.S.	C5	110
New Roads, La., U.S.	D4	95
New Rochelle, N.Y., U.S.	E7	109
New Rockford, N.D., U.S.	B6	111
New Ross, Ire.	I6	7
Newry, N. Ire., U.K.	G6	7
New Salem, N.D., U.S.	C4	111
New Sarpy, La., U.S.	k11	95
New Sharon, Ia., U.S.	C5	92
New Site, Al., U.S.	B4	78
New Smyrna Beach, Fl., U.S.	C6	86
New South Wales, state, Austl.	F9	50
New Straitsville, Oh., U.S.	C3	112
New Tazewell, Tn., U.S.	C10	119
Newton, Al., U.S.	D4	78
Newton, Ga., U.S.	E2	87
Newton, Il., U.S.	E5	90
Newton, Ia., U.S.	C4	92
Newton, Ks., U.S.	D6	93
Newton, Ma., U.S.	B5	98
Newton, Ms., U.S.	C4	101
Newton, N.J., U.S.	A3	107
Newton, N.C., U.S.	B1	110
Newton, Tx., U.S.	D6	120
Newton, Ut., U.S.	B4	121
Newton, co., Ar., U.S.	B2	81
Newton, co., Ga., U.S.	C3	87
Newton, co., In., U.S.	B3	91
Newton, co., Ms., U.S.	C4	101
Newton, co., Mo., U.S.	E3	102
Newton, co., Tx., U.S.	D6	120
Newton Falls, Oh., U.S.	A5	112
Newton Lake, res., Il., U.S.	E5	90
Newton Stewart, Scot., U.K.	G8	7
Newtown, Ct., U.S.	D2	84
New Town, N.D., U.S.	B3	111
Newtown, Oh., U.S.	C1	112
Newtownabbey, N. Ire., U.K.	G7	7
Newtownards, N. Ire., U.K.	G7	7
Newtown Square, Pa., U.S.	p20	115
New Ulm, Mn., U.S.	F4	100
New Vienna, Oh., U.S.	C2	112
Newville, Pa., U.S.	F7	115
New Washington, In., U.S.	G6	91
New Washington, Oh., U.S.	B3	112
New Waterford, Oh., U.S.	B5	112
New Westminster, B.C., Can.	E6	69
New Whiteland, In., U.S.	E5	91
New Wilmington, Pa., U.S.	D1	115
New Windsor, Il., U.S.	B3	90
New Windsor, Md., U.S.	A3	97
New Windsor, N.Y., U.S.	D6	109
New World Island, i., Newf., Can.	D4	72
New York, N.Y., U.S.	E7	109
New York, co., N.Y., U.S.	k13	109
New York, state, U.S.	C6	109
New York Mills, Mn., U.S.	D3	100
New Zealand, ctry., Oc.	D4	52
Nez Perce, co., Id., U.S.	C2	89
Nez Perce Indian Reservation, Id., U.S.	C2	89
Ngami, Lake, l., Bots.	F4	44
Nganglong Kangri, mts., China	D10	38
Nganjuk, Indon.	m15	33a
Ngaoundéré, Cam.	G8	42
Nguigmi, Niger	F8	42
Nguru, Nig.	F8	42
Nha Trang, Viet.	H10	34
Niafounké, Mali	E5	42
Niagara, Wi., U.S.	C6	126
Niagara, co., N.Y., U.S.	B2	109
Niagara Falls, Ont., Can.	D5	73
Niagara Falls, N.Y., U.S.	B1	109
Niagara-on-the-Lake, Ont., Can.	D5	73

Name — Map Ref — Page

Niamey, Niger **F6** 42
Niangara, Zaire **H11** 42
Niangua, stm., Mo., U.S. **D5** 102
Niantic, Ct., U.S. **D7** 84
Nias, Pulau, i., Indon. **N4** 34
Nibley, Ut., U.S. **B4** 121
Nicaragua, ctry., N.A. **H5** 64
Nicaragua, Lago de, l., Nic. **I5** 64
Nicastro (Lamezia Terme), Italy **K11** 14
Nicatous Lake, l., Me., U.S. **C4** 96
Nice, Fr. **I14** 10
Niceville, Fl., U.S. **u15** 86
Nichinan, Japan **K4** 30
Nicholas, co., Ky., U.S. **B6** 94
Nicholas, co., W.V., U.S. **C4** 125
Nicholas Channel, strt., N.A. **C7** 64
Nicholasville, Ky., U.S. **C5** 94
Nicholls, Ga., U.S. **E4** 87
Nichols Hills, Ok., U.S. **B4** 113
Nicholson, Ms., U.S. **E4** 101
Nickajack Lake, res., Tn., U.S. **D8** 119
Nickel Centre, Ont., Can. **p19** 73
Nickerson, Ks., U.S. **D5** 93
Nicobar Islands, is., India **J2** 34
Nicolet, Que., Can. **C5** 74
Nicolet, stm., Que., Can. **C5** 74
Nicolet, Lake, l., Mi., U.S. **B6** 99
Nicollet, Mn., U.S. **F4** 100
Nicollet, co., Mn., U.S. **F4** 100
Nicolls Town, Bah. **B8** 64
Nicoma Park, Ok., U.S. **B4** 113
Nicosia, Cyp. **B3** 40
Nicosia, N. Cyp. **B3** 40
Nicosia, Italy **L9** 14
Nicoya, Golfo de, b., C.R. **J5** 64
Nicoya, Península de, pen., C.R. **I5** 64
Niebüll, Ger. **A8** 8
Nienburg, Ger. **C9** 8
Nieuw Nickerie, Sur. **B7** 54
Nieves, Mex. **E8** 62
Nigadoo, N.B., Can. **B4** 71
Niger, ctry., Afr. **E7** 42
Niger, stm., Afr. **G7** 42
Nigeria, ctry., Afr. **F7** 42
Nigríta, Grc. **I7** 16
Nihoa, i., Hi., U.S. **m15** 88
Niigata, Japan **E12** 30
Niihama, Japan **I6** 30
Niihau, i., Hi., U.S. **B1** 88
Niinisalo, Fin. **F14** 6
Niitsu, Japan **E12** 30
Níjar, Spain **I9** 12
Nijmegen, Neth. **D5** 8
Nikishka, Ak., U.S. **g16** 79
Nikkō, Japan **F12** 30
Nikolajevsk-na-Amure, Russia **G22** 24
Nikšić, Yugo. **G2** 16
Niland, Ca., U.S. **F6** 82
Nile (Nahr an-Nīl), stm., Afr. **C12** 42
Niles, Il., U.S. **h9** 90
Niles, Mi., U.S. **G4** 99
Niles, Oh., U.S. **A5** 112
Nileshwar, India **F3** 37
Nīmach, India **H6** 38
Nimba, Mont, mtn., Afr. **G4** 42
Nîmes, Fr. **I11** 10
Nimrod Lake, res., Ar., U.S. **C2** 81
Nine Degree Channel, strt., India **H2** 37
Nine Mile Creek, stm., Ut., U.S. **D5** 121
Ninemile Point, c., Mi., U.S. **C6** 99
Ninety Six, S.C., U.S. **C3** 117
Ningbo, China **F10** 28
Ningming, China **C9** 34
Ningxia Huizu Zizhiqu, prov., China **D8** 26
Ninh Binh, Viet. **D8** 34
Ninigret Pond, l., R.I., U.S. **G2** 116
Ninilchik, Ak., U.S. **C9** 79
Ninnescah, stm., Ks., U.S. **E6** 93
Niobrara, co., Wy., U.S. **C8** 127
Niobrara, stm., U.S. **B7** 104
Niono, Mali **F4** 42
Nioro du Sahel, Mali **E4** 42
Niort, Fr. **F6** 10
Niota, Tn., U.S. **D9** 119
Nipāni, India **D3** 37
Nipigon, Lake, l., Ont., Can. **o17** 73
Nipissing, Lake, l., Ont., Can. **A5** 73
Nipomo, Ca., U.S. **E3** 82
Nipple Mountain, mtn., Co., U.S. **D2** 83
Nirmal, India **C5** 37
Niš, Yugo. **F5** 16
Nisa, Port. **F4** 12
Nishinoomote, Japan **u30** 31b
Nishiwaki, Japan **H7** 30
Niskayuna, N.Y., U.S. **C7** 109
Nisqually, stm., Wa., U.S. **C3** 124
Nisswa, Mn., U.S. **D4** 100
Niterói, Braz. **G7** 57
Nitra, Slov. **G18** 8
Nitro, W.V., U.S. **C3** 125
Niue, dep., Oc. **H1** 2
Nivelles, Bel. **E4** 8
Niverville, Man., Can. **E3** 70
Niwot, Co., U.S. **A5** 83
Nixa, Mo., U.S. **D4** 102
Nixon, Nv., U.S. **D2** 105
Nixon, Tx., U.S. **E4** 120
Nizāmābād, India **C5** 37
Nizip, Tur. **A5** 40
Nižn'aja Pojma, Russia **F13** 24
Nižn'aja Tunguska, stm., Russia **E12** 24
Nižneangarsk, Russia **F15** 24
Nižneilimsk, Russia **F14** 24
Nižneudinsk, Russia **G13** 24
Nižnij Novgorod (Gorki), Russia **E27** 18
Nizza Monferrato, Italy **E3** 14
Njombe, Tan. **C6** 44
Nkhota Kota, Mwi. **D6** 44
Nkongsamba, Cam. **H7** 42
Noākhāli, Bngl. **I14** 38
Noank, Ct., U.S. **D8** 84
Noatak, Ak., U.S. **B7** 79
Noatak, stm., Ak., U.S. **B7** 79
Nobel, Ont., Can. **B4** 73
Nobeoka, Japan **J4** 30
Noble, Ok., U.S. **B4** 113
Noble, co., In., U.S. **B7** 91
Noble, co., Oh., U.S. **C4** 112
Noble, co., Ok., U.S. **A4** 113
Nobles, co., Mn., U.S. **G3** 100
Noblesville, In., U.S. **D6** 91
Noboribetsu, Japan **q19** 30a
Nocatee, Fl., U.S. **E5** 86
Nocera [Inferiore], Italy **I9** 14
Nochixtlán, Mex. **I11** 62
Nocona, Tx., U.S. **C4** 120
Nodaway, co., Mo., U.S. **A3** 102
Nodaway, stm., U.S. **A2** 102
Noel, Mo., U.S. **E3** 102
Nogales, Mex. **B4** 62
Nogales, Az., U.S. **F5** 80
Nōgata, Japan **I3** 30
Nogent-le-Rotrou, Fr. **D7** 10
Noginsk, Russia **F21** 18
Nogoyá, Arg. **C5** 56
Noirmoutier, Fr. **E4** 10
Nojima-zaki, c., Japan **H12** 30
Nokia, Fin. **F14** 6
Nokomis, Fl., U.S. **E4** 86
Nokomis, Il., U.S. **D4** 90
Nokomis, Lake, res., Wi., U.S. **C4** 126
Nolan, co., Tx., U.S. **C2** 120
Nolichucky, stm., Tn., U.S. **C10** 119
Nolin, stm., Ky., U.S. **C3** 94
Nolin Lake, res., Ky., U.S. **C3** 94
Nomans Land, i., Ma., U.S. **D6** 98
Nombre de Dios, Mex. **F7** 62
Nome, Ak., U.S. **C6** 79
Nominingue, Que., Can. **C2** 74
Nonacho Lake, l., N.W. Ter., Can. **D11** 66
Nonesuch, stm., Me., U.S. **g7** 96
Nong'an, China **C12** 26
Nong Khai, Thai. **F7** 34
Nonquit Pond, l., R.I., U.S. **E6** 116
Nontron, Fr. **G7** 10
Nooksack, North Fork, stm., Wa., U.S. **A4** 124
Nooksack, South Fork, stm., Wa., U.S. **A3** 124
Noordoost Polder, reg., Neth. **C5** 8
Noorvik, Ak., U.S. **B7** 79
Nootka Island, i., B.C., Can. **G7** 66
Nootka Sound, strt., B.C., Can. **E4** 69
No Point, Point, c., Md., U.S. **D5** 97
Noquebay, Lake, l., Wi., U.S. **C6** 126
Noranda (part of Rouyn [-Noranda]), Que., Can. **k11** 74
Nora Springs, Ia., U.S. **A5** 92
Norborne, Mo., U.S. **B4** 102
Norco, La., U.S. **E5** 95
Norcross, Ga., U.S. **C2** 87
Norden, Ger. **B7** 8
Nordenham, Ger. **B8** 8
Nordenšel'da, Archipelag, is., Russia **B13** 24
Norderney, i., Ger. **B7** 8
Nordfjordeid, Nor. **F5** 6
Nordfold, Nor. **C10** 6
Nordhausen, Ger. **D10** 8
Nordhorn, Ger. **C7** 8
Nordkapp, c., Nor. **A15** 6
Nordkjosbotn, Nor. **B12** 6
Nördlingen, Ger. **G10** 8
Nordmaling, Swe. **E12** 6
Nordreisa, Nor. **B13** 6
Nordre Strømfjord, Grnld. **C22** 66
Nordvik, Russia **C16** 24
Norfolk, Ct., U.S. **B3** 84
Norfolk, Ne., U.S. **B8** 104
Norfolk, N.Y., U.S. **f9** 109
Norfolk, Va., U.S. **D6** 123
Norfolk, co., Ma., U.S. **B5** 98
Norfolk Naval Base, mil., Va., U.S. **k15** 123
Norfolk Naval Shipyard, mil., Va., U.S. **k15** 123
Norfork Dam, Ar., U.S. **A3** 81
Norfork Lake, res., U.S. **A3** 81
Noril'sk, Russia **D11** 24
Norland, Fl., U.S. **s13** 86
Norlina, N.C., U.S. **A4** 110
Normal, Il., U.S. **C5** 90
Norman, Ok., U.S. **B4** 113
Norman, co., Mn., U.S. **C2** 100
Norman, Lake, res., N.C., U.S. **B2** 110
Normandie, hist. reg., Fr. **D6** 10
Normandy, Mo., U.S. **f13** 102
Normandy see Normandie, hist. reg., Fr. **D6** 10
Norman Park, Ga., U.S. **E3** 87
Normanton, Austl. **C8** 50
Norman Wells, N.W. Ter., Can. **C7** 66
Norphlet, Ar., U.S. **D3** 81
Ñorquincó, Arg. **E2** 56
Norridge, Il., U.S. **k9** 90
Norridgewock, Me., U.S. **D3** 96
Norris, S.C., U.S. **B2** 117
Norris, Tn., U.S. **C9** 119
Norris Arm, Newf., Can. **D4** 72
Norris City, Il., U.S. **F5** 90
Norris Dam, Tn., U.S. **C9** 119
Norris Lake, res., Tn., U.S. **C10** 119
Norris Point, Newf., Can. **D3** 72
Norristown, Pa., U.S. **F11** 115
Norrköping, Swe. **G11** 6
Norrtälje, Swe. **G12** 6
Norseman, Austl. **F4** 50
Norsk, Russia **G19** 24
Norte, Serra do, plat., Braz. **F7** 54
North, S.C., U.S. **D5** 117
North, stm., Al., U.S. **B2** 78
North, stm., Ia., U.S. **f8** 92
North, stm., Ma., U.S. **h12** 98
North, stm., W.V., U.S. **B6** 125
North, Cape, c., N.S., Can. **B9** 71
North Adams, Ma., U.S. **A1** 98
North Albany, Or., U.S. **k11** 114
Northam, Austl. **F3** 50
North America **E10** 61
North Amherst, Ma., U.S. **B2** 98
Northampton, Eng., U.K. **I12** 7
Northampton, Ma., U.S. **B2** 98
Northampton, Pa., U.S. **E11** 115
Northampton, co., N.C., U.S. **A5** 110
Northampton, co., Pa., U.S. **E11** 115
Northampton, co., Va., U.S. **C7** 123
North Andaman, i., India **H2** 34
North Andover, Ma., U.S. **A5** 98
North Andrews Gardens, Fl., U.S. ***r13** 86
North Anna, stm., Va., U.S. **B5** 123
North Anson, Me., U.S. **D3** 96
North Apollo, Pa., U.S. **E2** 115
North Arapaho Peak, mtn., Co., U.S. **A5** 83
North Arlington, N.J., U.S. **h8** 107
North Atlanta, Ga., U.S. **h8** 87
North Attleboro, Ma., U.S. **C5** 98
North Augusta, S.C., U.S. **D4** 117
North Aurora, Il., U.S. **k8** 90
North Baltimore, Oh., U.S. **A2** 112
North Bay, Ont., Can. **A5** 73
North Beach, Md., U.S. **C4** 97
North Belmont, N.C., U.S. **B1** 110
North Bend, Ne., U.S. **C9** 104
North Bend, Or., U.S. **D2** 114
North Bend, Wa., U.S. **B4** 124
North Bennington, Vt., U.S. **F2** 122
North Bergen, N.J., U.S. **h8** 107
North Berwick, Me., U.S. **E2** 96
North Billerica, Ma., U.S. **A5** 98
Northborough, Ma., U.S. **B4** 98
North Branch, Mi., U.S. **E7** 99
North Branch, Mn., U.S. **E6** 100
North Branch, N.H., U.S. **D3** 106
North Branch, N.J., U.S. **B3** 107
North Branford, Ct., U.S. **D4** 84
Northbridge, Ma., U.S. **B4** 98
Northbrook, Il., U.S. **h9** 90
North Brookfield, Ma., U.S. **B3** 98
North Brunswick, N.J., U.S. **C4** 107
North Caldwell, N.J., U.S. **B4** 107
North Canadian, stm., Ok., U.S. **A5** 113
North Canton, Ga., U.S. **B2** 87
North Canton, Oh., U.S. **B4** 112
North Cape, c., P.E.I., Can. **B6** 71
North Cape May, N.J., U.S. **F3** 107
North Cape see Nordkapp, c., Nor. **A15** 6
North Caribou Lake, l., Ont., Can. **F14** 66
North Carolina, state, U.S. **B3** 110
North Cascades National Park, Wa., U.S. **A4** 124
North Channel, strt., Ont., Can. **A2** 73
North Channel, strt., U.K. **F7** 7
North Charleston, S.C., U.S. **F8** 117
North Chicago, Il., U.S. **A6** 90
North Clarendon, Vt., U.S. **D3** 122
North College Hill, Oh., U.S. **o12** 112
North Conway, N.H., U.S. **B4** 106
North Corbin, Ky., U.S. **D5** 94
North Crossett, Ar., U.S. **D4** 81
North Cyprus, ctry., Asia **B3** 40
North Dakota, state, U.S. **B5** 111
North Dartmouth, Ma., U.S. **C6** 98
North Druid Hills, Ga., U.S. ***h8** 87
North Eagle Butte, S.D., U.S. **B4** 118
North East, Md., U.S. **A6** 97
North East, Pa., U.S. **B2** 115
Northeast, stm., Md., U.S. **A6** 97
Northeast Cape, c., Ak., U.S. **C6** 79
Northeast Cape Fear, stm., N.C., U.S. **C5** 110
Northeast Harbor, Me., U.S. **D4** 96
Northeast Henrietta, N.Y., U.S. ***B3** 109
North Easton, Ma., U.S. **B5** 98
Northeast Pond, l., N.H., U.S. **D5** 106
Northeast Providence Channel, strt., Bah. **B9** 64
North Edisto, stm., S.C., U.S. **k11** 117
Northeim, Ger. **D9** 8
North English, Ia., U.S. **C5** 92
North English, stm., Ia., U.S. **C5** 92
North Enid, Ok., U.S. **A4** 113
Northern Cheyenne Indian Reservation, Mt., U.S. **E10** 103
Northern Indian Lake, l., Man., Can. **A3** 70
Northern Ireland, ter., U.K. **G6** 7
Northern Territory, ter., Austl. **C6** 50
North Falmouth, Ma., U.S. **C6** 98
Northfield, Mn., U.S. **F5** 100
Northfield, N.H., U.S. **D3** 106
Northfield, N.J., U.S. **E3** 107
Northfield, Oh., U.S. **h9** 112
Northfield, Vt., U.S. **C3** 122
Northfield Falls, Vt., U.S. **C3** 122
North Flinders Ranges, mts., Austl. **F7** 50
North Fond du Lac, Wi., U.S. **E5** 126
Northford, Ct., U.S. **D4** 84
North Fork Reservoir, res., Or., U.S. **B4** 114
North Fort Myers, Fl., U.S. **F5** 86
North Fox Island, i., Mi., U.S. **C5** 99
North Frisian Islands, is., Eur. **A8** 8
Northglenn, Co., U.S. **B6** 83
North Gower, Ont., Can. **B9** 73
North Grafton, Ma., U.S. **B4** 98
North Grosvenordale, Ct., U.S. **B8** 84
North Gulfport, Ms., U.S. **E4** 101
North Haledon, N.J., U.S. **B4** 107
North Hampton, N.H., U.S. **E5** 106
North Hartland Reservoir, res., Vt., U.S. **D4** 122
North Hatley, Que., Can. **D6** 74
North Haven, Ct., U.S. **D4** 84
North Head, N.B., Can. **E3** 71
North Hero Island, i., Vt., U.S. **B2** 122
North Horn Lake, l., Tn., U.S. **e8** 119
North Industry, Oh., U.S. **B4** 112
North Inlet, b., S.C., U.S. **E9** 117
North Island, i., N.Z. **C5** 52
North Island, i., S.C., U.S. **E9** 117
North Island Naval Air Station, mil., Ca., U.S. **o15** 82
North Islands, is., La., U.S. **E7** 95
North Judson, In., U.S. **B4** 91
North Kansas City, Mo., U.S. **h10** 102
North Kingstown, R.I., U.S. **E4** 116
North Kingsville, Oh., U.S. **A5** 112
North La Junta, Co., U.S. **C7** 83
Northlake, Il., U.S. **k9** 90
North Laramie, stm., Wy., U.S. **D7** 127
North Las Vegas, Nv., U.S. **G6** 105
North La Veta Pass, Co., U.S. **D5** 83
North Lewisburg, Oh., U.S. **B2** 112
North Liberty, In., U.S. **A5** 91
North Liberty, Ia., U.S. **C6** 92
North Lima, Oh., U.S. **B5** 112
North Little Rock, Ar., U.S. **C3** 81
North Logan, Ut., U.S. **B4** 121
North Loon Mountain, mtn., Id., U.S. **D3** 89
North Magnetic Pole **B22** 128
North Mamm Peak, mtn., Co., U.S. **B3** 83
North Manchester, In., U.S. **C6** 91
North Manitou Island, i., Mi., U.S. **C4** 99
North Mankato, Mn., U.S. **F4** 100
North Merrydale, La., U.S. ***D4** 95
North Miami, Fl., U.S. **G6** 86
North Miami Beach, Fl., U.S. **s13** 86
North Middletown, Ky., U.S. **B5** 94
North Moose Lake, l., Man., Can. **B1** 70
North Mountain, mtn., Pa., U.S. **D9** 115
North Muskegon, Mi., U.S. **E4** 99
North Myrtle Beach, S.C., U.S. **D10** 117
North Naples, Fl., U.S. **F5** 86
North New River Canal, Fl., U.S. **F6** 86
North Ogden, Ut., U.S. **B4** 121
North Olmsted, Oh., U.S. **h9** 112
North Palisade, mtn., Ca., U.S. **D4** 82
North Park, Il., U.S. **A4** 90
North Park, val., Co., U.S. **A4** 83
North Pass, strt., La., U.S. **E7** 95
North Pembroke, Ma., U.S. **B6** 98
North Plainfield, N.J., U.S. **B4** 107
North Plains, Or., U.S. **B4** 114
North Plains, pl., N.M., U.S. **C1** 108
North Platte, Ne., U.S. **C5** 104
North Platte, stm., U.S. **C6** 76
North Point, c., Md., U.S. **B5** 97
North Point, c., Mi., U.S. **C7** 99
North Pole **A12** 128
Northport, Al., U.S. **B2** 78
North Prairie, Wi., U.S. **F5** 126
North Providence, R.I., U.S. **C4** 116
North Raccoon, stm., Ia., U.S. **C3** 92
North Reading, Ma., U.S. **f11** 98
North Richland Hills, Tx., U.S. **n9** 120
Northridge, Oh., U.S. **C2** 112
North Ridgeville, Oh., U.S. **A3** 112
North Royalton, Oh., U.S. **h9** 112
North Rustico, P.E.I., Can. **C6** 71
North Salem, N.H., U.S. **E4** 106
North Salt Lake, Ut., U.S. **C4** 121
North Santee, stm., S.C., U.S. **E9** 117
North Saskatchewan, stm., Can. **F10** 66
North Schell Peak, mtn., Nv., U.S. **D7** 105
North Scituate, Ma., U.S. **h12** 98
North Sea, Eur. **D8** 4
North Shoshone Peak, mtn., Nv., U.S. **D4** 105
North Sioux City, S.D., U.S. **E9** 118
North Skunk, stm., Ia., U.S. **C5** 92
North Springfield, Vt., U.S. **E3** 122
North Springfield Reservoir, res., Vt., U.S. **E4** 122
North Star, De., U.S. **A3** 85
North St. Paul, Mn., U.S. **m13** 100
North Stratford, N.H., U.S. **A3** 106
North Sudbury, Ma., U.S. **g10** 98
North Swanzey, N.H., U.S. **E2** 106
North Syracuse, N.Y., U.S. **B4** 109
North Tarrytown, N.Y., U.S. **D7** 109
North Terre Haute, In., U.S. **E3** 91
North Thompson, stm., B.C., Can. **D8** 69
North Tonawanda, N.Y., U.S. **B2** 109
North Troy, Vt., U.S. **B4** 122
North Tunica, Ms., U.S. **A3** 101
North Twin Lake, l., Wi., U.S. **B4** 126
Northumberland, Pa., U.S. **E8** 115
Northumberland, co., Pa., U.S. **D8** 115
Northumberland, co., Va., U.S. **C6** 123
Northumberland National Park, Eng., U.K. **F10** 7
Northumberland Strait, strt., Can. **C6** 71
North Umpqua, stm., Or., U.S. **D3** 114
North Uxbridge, Ma., U.S. **B4** 98
Northvale, N.J., U.S. **g9** 107
North Vancouver, B.C., Can. **E6** 69
North Vassalboro, Me., U.S. **D3** 96
North Vernon, In., U.S. **F6** 91
Northville, Mi., U.S. **p15** 99
North Wales, Pa., U.S. **F11** 115
North Walpole, N.H., U.S. **D2** 106
North Warren, Pa., U.S. **C3** 115
North Webster, In., U.S. **B6** 91
North West Cape, c., Austl. **D2** 50
Northwest Miramichi, stm., N.B., Can. **B3** 71
Northwest Providence Channel, strt., Bah. **A8** 64
Northwest Territories, prov., Can. **C13** 66
North Wildwood, N.J., U.S. **E3** 107
North Wilkesboro, N.C., U.S. **A1** 110
North Windham, Ct., U.S. **C7** 84
North Windham, Me., U.S. **E2** 96
Northwood, Ia., U.S. **A4** 92
Northwood, N.D., U.S. **B8** 111
North Woodstock, N.H., U.S. **B3** 106
North York, Ont., Can. **D5** 73
North York, Pa., U.S. **G8** 115
North York Moors National Park, Eng., U.K. **G12** 7
Norton, N.B., Can. **D4** 71
Norton, Ks., U.S. **C4** 93
Norton, Ma., U.S. **C5** 98
Norton, Oh., U.S. **A4** 112
Norton, Va., U.S. **f9** 123
Norton, co., Ks., U.S. **C4** 93
Norton Air Force Base, mil., Ca., U.S. **E5** 82
Norton Bay, b., Ak., U.S. **C7** 79
Norton Pond, l., Vt., U.S. **B5** 122
Norton Reservoir, res., Ks., U.S. **C3** 93
Norton Shores, Mi., U.S. **E4** 99
Norton Sound, strt., Ak., U.S. **C6** 79
Nortonville, Ks., U.S. **C8** 93
Nortonville, Ky., U.S. **C2** 94
Norwalk, Ca., U.S. **n12** 82
Norwalk, Ct., U.S. **E2** 84
Norwalk, Ia., U.S. **C4** 92
Norwalk, Oh., U.S. **A3** 112
Norwalk, stm., Ct., U.S. **E2** 84
Norwalk Islands, is., Ct., U.S. **E2** 84
Norway, Me., U.S. **D2** 96
Norway, Mi., U.S. **C3** 99
Norway, ctry., Eur. **C9** 4
Norway Bay, b., N.W. Ter., Can. **B12** 66
Norway House, Man., Can. **C3** 70
Norway Lake, l., Mn., U.S. **E3** 100
Norwegian Sea, Eur. **C12** 128
Norwich, Eng., U.K. **I14** 7
Norwich, Ct., U.S. **C7** 84
Norwich, N.Y., U.S. **C5** 109
Norwich, Vt., U.S. **D4** 122
Norwood, Ont., Can. **C7** 73
Norwood, Ma., U.S. **B5** 98
Norwood, Mn., U.S. **F5** 100
Norwood, N.J., U.S. **h9** 107
Norwood, N.Y., U.S. **f10** 109
Norwood, N.C., U.S. **B2** 110
Norwood, Oh., U.S. **o13** 112
Norwood, Pa., U.S. **p20** 115
Norwoodville, Ia., U.S. **e8** 92
Noshiro, Japan **B13** 30
Notasulga, Al., U.S. **C4** 78
Notch Peak, mtn., Ut., U.S. **D2** 121
Noto, Italy **M10** 14
Notodden, Nor. **G7** 6
Notre Dame, Monts, mts., Que., Can. **k13** 74
Notre Dame Bay, b., Newf., Can. **D4** 72
Notre Dame de Lourdes, Man., Can. **E2** 70
Notre-Dame-du-Lac, Que., Can. **B9** 74
Nottawasaga Bay, b., Ont., Can. **C4** 73
Nottaway, stm., Que., Can. **h11** 74
Nottingham, Eng., U.K. **I11** 7
Nottingham Island, i., N.W. Ter., Can. **D17** 66
Nottoway, co., Va., U.S. **C4** 123
Nottoway, stm., Va., U.S. **D5** 123
Nouadhibou, Maur. **D2** 42
Nouakchott, Maur. **E2** 42
Nouamrhar, Maur. **E2** 42
Noupoort, S. Afr. **H4** 44
Nouveau-Québec, Cratère du, crat., Que., Can. **D18** 66
Nova América, Braz. **C4** 57
Nova Cruz, Braz. **E11** 54
Nova Freixo, Moz. **D7** 44
Nova Friburgo, Braz. **G7** 57
Nova Gaia, Ang. **D3** 44
Nova Gradiška, Cro. **D12** 14
Nova Iguaçu, Braz. **G7** 57
Novaja Sibir', Ostrov, i., Russia **B23** 24
Novaja Zeml'a, is., Russia **C5** 24
Nova Lima, Braz. **E7** 57
Nova Lisboa see Huambo, Ang. **D3** 44
Nova Mambone, Moz. **F7** 44
Novara, Italy **D3** 14
Nova Scotia, prov., Can. **D6** 71
Nova Sofala, Moz. **F6** 44
Novato, Ca., U.S. **C2** 82
Novelda, Spain **G11** 12
Nové Zámky, Slov. **H18** 8
Novgorod, Russia **C14** 18
Novi, Mi., U.S. **p15** 99
Novi Ligure, Italy **E3** 14
Novi Pazar, Bul. **F11** 16
Novi Pazar, Yugo. **F4** 16
Novi Sad, Yugo. **D3** 16
Novoaltajsk, Russia **G10** 24
Novo Aripuanã, Braz. **E6** 54
Novogrudok, Bela. **H8** 18
Novokuzneck, Russia **G11** 24
Novo Mesto, Slo. **D10** 14
Novo Redondo, Ang. **D2** 44
Novorossijsk, Russia **I5** 22
Novorybnoje, Russia **C15** 24
Novosibirsk, Russia **D4** 128
Novosibirskije Ostrova, is., Russia **B22** 24
Novosibirskoje Vodochranilišče, res., Russia **G10** 24
Novotroick, Russia **G9** 22
Novozybkov, Russia **I14** 18
Novska, Cro. **D11** 14
Nowa Sól (Neusalz), Pol. **D15** 8
Nowata, Ok., U.S. **A6** 113
Nowata, co., Ok., U.S. **A6** 113
Nowgong, India **G15** 38
Nowood, stm., Wy., U.S. **B5** 127
Nowshāk, mtn., Asia **B4** 38
Nowshera, Pak. **C4** 38
Nowy Sącz, Pol. **F20** 8
Nowy Targ, Pol. **F20** 8
Noxon Reservoir, res., Mt., U.S. **C1** 103
Noxontown Lake, res., De., U.S. **C3** 85
Noxubee, co., Ms., U.S. **B5** 101
Noxubee, stm., U.S. **B5** 101
Noyes Island, i., Ak., U.S. **n22** 79
Noyon, Fr. **C9** 10
Nozay, Fr. **E5** 10
Nsanje, Mwi. **E7** 44
Nsawam, Ghana **G5** 42
Nubanusit Lake, l., N.H., U.S. **E2** 106
Nubian Desert, des., Sudan **D12** 42
Nuckolls, co., Ne., U.S. **D7** 104
Nucla, Co., U.S. **C2** 83
Nueces, co., Tx., U.S. **F4** 120
Nueces, stm., Tx., U.S. **E3** 120
Nueltin Lake, l., Can. **E13** 66
Nueva Casas Grandes, Mex. **B6** 62
Nueva Rosita, Mex. **D9** 62
Nueva San Salvador, El Sal. **H3** 64

Name — Map Ref — Page

Nueve de Julio, Arg. D4 56
Nuevitas, Cuba D9 64
Nuevo, Golfo, b., Arg. E4 56
Nuevo Laredo, Mex. D10 62
Nuevo Rocafuerte, Ec. H5 58
Nuits-Saint-Georges, Fr. E11 10
Nukus, Uzb. I9 22
Nulato, Ak., U.S. C8 79
Nulhegan, stm., Vt., U.S. B5 122
Nullagine, Austl. D4 50
Nullarbor Plain, pl., Austl. F5 50
Numata, Japan F12 30
Numazu, Japan G11 30
Numfoor, Pulau, i., Indon. F9 32
Nun, stm., China A12 26
Nunivak Island, i., Ak., U.S. D6 79
Nunjiang, China B12 26
Nuoro, Italy I4 14
N'urba, Russia E17 24
Nuremberg, Pa., U.S. E9 115
Nuremberg see Nürnberg, Ger. F11 8
Nürnberg, Ger. F11 8
Nurri, Italy J4 14
Nutley, N.J., U.S. B4 107
Nutter Fort, W.V., U.S. k10 125
Nutting Lake, Ma., U.S. f10 98
Nuuanu Pali, Hi., U.S. g10 88
Nyack, N.Y., U.S. D7 109
Nyainqêntanglha Shan, mts., China E13 38
Nyala, Sudan F10 42
Nyanda, Zimb. F6 44
Nyasa, Lake, l., Afr. D6 44
Nyaunglebin, Mya. F4 34
Nybro, Swe. H10 6
Nye, co., Nv., U.S. E5 105
Nyenyam, China F11 38
Nyeri, Kenya B7 44
Nyíregyháza, Hung. H21 8
Nykøbing, Den. I8 6
Nyköping, Swe. G11 6
Nylstroom, S. Afr. F5 44
Nynäshamn, Swe. G11 6
Nyngan, Austl. F9 50
Nyon, Switz. F13 10
Nyons, Fr. H12 10
Nysa, Pol. E17 8
Nysa Łużycka (Neisse) (Nisa), stm., Eur. D14 8
Nyssa, Or., U.S. D9 114
Nzérékoré, Gui. G4 42
N'zeto, Ang. C2 44

O

Oahe, Lake, res., U.S. B6 76
Oahe Dam, S.D., U.S. C5 118
Oahu, i., Hi., U.S. B4 88
Oak Bay, B.C., Can. h12 69
Oak Bluffs, Ma., U.S. D6 98
Oak Creek, Co., U.S. A4 83
Oak Creek, Wi., U.S. n12 126
Oakdale, Ca., U.S. D3 82
Oakdale, Ga., U.S. h8 87
Oakdale, La., U.S. D3 95
Oakdale, Pa., U.S. k13 115
Oakes, N.D., U.S. C7 111
Oakfield, N.Y., U.S. B2 109
Oakfield, Wi., U.S. E5 126
Oak Forest, Il., U.S. k9 90
Oak Grove, Ky., U.S. D2 94
Oak Grove, La., U.S. B4 95
Oak Grove, Or., U.S. B4 114
Oak Harbor, Oh., U.S. A2 112
Oak Harbor, Wa., U.S. A3 124
Oak Hill, Mi., U.S. D4 99
Oak Hill, Oh., U.S. D3 112
Oak Hill, W.V., U.S. D3 125
Oak Hill, mtn., Ma., U.S. f9 98
Oakhurst, Ok., U.S. A5 113
Oak Island, i., Wi., U.S. B3 126
Oak Lake, l., Man., Can. E1 70
Oakland, Ca., U.S. D2 82
Oakland, Il., U.S. D5 90
Oakland, Ia., U.S. C2 92
Oakland, Me., U.S. D3 96
Oakland, Md., U.S. m12 97
Oakland, Ne., U.S. C9 104
Oakland, N.J., U.S. A4 107
Oakland, Ok., U.S. C5 113
Oakland, Or., U.S. D3 114
Oakland, R.I., U.S. B2 116
Oakland, co., Mi., U.S. F7 99
Oakland City, In., U.S. H3 91
Oakland Park, Fl., U.S. r13 86
Oak Lawn, Il., U.S. B6 90
Oaklawn, Ks., U.S. g12 93
Oakley, Id., U.S. G5 89
Oakley, Ks., U.S. C3 93
Oakman, Al., U.S. B2 78
Oakmont, Pa., U.S. E2 115
Oak Mountain, mtn., Ga., U.S. D2 87
Oak Orchard, De., U.S. F5 85
Oak Park, Il., U.S. B6 90
Oak Park, Mi., U.S. p15 99
Oak Ridge, N.C., U.S. A3 110
Oakridge, Or., U.S. D4 114
Oak Ridge, Tn., U.S. C9 119
Oak Ridge Reservoir, res., N.J., U.S. A3 107
Oakton, Va., U.S. g12 123
Oaktown, In., U.S. G3 91
Oak Valley, N.J., U.S. D2 107
Oakville, Ont., Can. D5 73
Oakville, Ct., U.S. C3 84
Oakville, Mo., U.S. g13 102
Oakwood, Ga., U.S. B3 87
Oakwood, Il., U.S. C6 90
Oakwood, Oh., U.S. C1 112
Oamaru, N.Z. F3 52
Oaxaca [de Juárez], Mex. I11 62
Ob', stm., Russia D7 24
Oban, Scot., U.K. E7 7
Obbia, Som. G4 46
Obed, stm., Tn., U.S. C9 119
Oberlin, Ks., U.S. C3 93
Oberlin, La., U.S. D3 95
Oberlin, Oh., U.S. A3 112
Oberwart, Aus. H16 8
Obetz, Oh., U.S. C3 112
Obi, Kepulauan, is., Indon. F8 32
Obi, Pulau, i., Indon. F8 32
Óbidos, Braz. D7 54
Obihiro, Japan q21 30a
Obion, Tn., U.S. A2 119
Obion, co., Tn., U.S. A2 119
Obion, stm., Tn., U.S. A2 119
Oblong, Il., U.S. D6 90
Oblučje, Russia H20 24
Obninsk, Russia F19 18
Obock, Dji. F3 46
O'Brien, co., Ia., U.S. A2 92
Obrovac, Cro. E10 14
Observation Peak, mtn., Ca., U.S. B3 82
Observatoire, Caye de l', i., N. Cal. D11 50
Obuasi, Ghana G5 42
Ocala, Fl., U.S. C4 86
Ocaña, Col. C6 58
Ocaña, Spain F8 12
Occidental, Cordillera, mts., Col. E4 58
Occidental, Cordillera, mts., Peru F4 54
Ocean, co., N.J., U.S. D4 107
Oceana, W.V., U.S. D3 125
Oceana, co., Mi., U.S. E4 99
Oceana Naval Air Station, mil., Va., U.S. k15 123
Ocean Bluff, Ma., U.S. B6 98
Ocean City, Fl., U.S. u15 86
Ocean City, Md., U.S. D7 97
Ocean City, N.J., U.S. E3 107
Ocean Grove, Ma., U.S. C5 98
Ocean Park, Wa., U.S. C1 124
Oceanport, N.J., U.S. C4 107
Oceanside, Ca., U.S. F5 82
Ocean Springs, Ms., U.S. E5 101
Ocean [Township], N.J., U.S. C4 107
Ocean View, De., U.S. F5 85
Ocha, Russia G22 24
Ocheda Lake, l., Mn., U.S. G3 100
Ocheyedan, stm., Ia., U.S. A2 92
Ochiltree, co., Tx., U.S. A2 120
Ochlockonee, stm., Fl., U.S. B2 86
Ochoco Lake, res., Or., U.S. C6 114
Ocho Rios, Jam. E9 64
Ochota, stm., Russia F22 24
Ochotsk, Russia F22 24
Ochsenfurt, Ger. F10 8
Ocilla, Ga., U.S. E3 87
Ockelbo, Swe. F11 6
Ocmulgee, stm., Ga., U.S. D3 87
Ocoee, Fl., U.S. D5 86
Ocoee, Lake, res., Tn., U.S. D9 119
Oconee, co., Ga., U.S. C3 87
Oconee, co., S.C., U.S. B1 117
Oconee, stm., Ga., U.S. C3 87
Oconee, Lake, res., Ga., U.S. C3 87
Oconomowoc, Wi., U.S. E5 126
Oconto, Wi., U.S. D6 126
Oconto, co., Wi., U.S. D5 126
Oconto, stm., Wi., U.S. D5 126
Oconto Falls, Wi., U.S. D5 126
Ocotal, Nic. H4 64
Ocotlán, Mex. G8 62
Ocracoke Inlet, b., N.C., U.S. B6 110
Ocracoke Island, i., N.C., U.S. B7 110
Octoraro Creek, stm., U.S. A5 97
Ocumare del Tuy, Ven. B9 58
Ocussi, Indon. G7 32
Oda, Ghana G5 42
Oda, Jabal, mtn., Sudan D13 42
Ōdate, Japan B13 30
Odawara, Japan G12 30
Odda, Nor. F6 6
Odebolt, Ia., U.S. B2 92
Odell, Il., U.S. B5 90
Odell, Or., U.S. B5 114
Odell Lake, l., Or., U.S. E5 114
Odem, Tx., U.S. F4 120
Odemira, Port. H3 12
Ödemiş, Tur. K11 16
Odense, Den. I8 6
Odenton, Md., U.S. B4 97
Odenville, Al., U.S. B3 78
Oder (Odra), stm., Eur. C14 8
Oderberg, Ger. C14 8
Odesa, Ukr. H4 22
Odessa, Ont., Can. C8 73
Odessa, De., U.S. C3 85
Odessa, Mo., U.S. C4 102
Odessa, Tx., U.S. D1 120
Odessa, Wa., U.S. B7 124
Odienné, C. Iv. G4 42
Odin, Il., U.S. E4 90
Odincovo, Russia F20 18
Odon, In., U.S. G4 91
O'Donnell, Tx., U.S. C2 120
Odra (Oder), stm., Eur. C14 8
Oelsnitz, Ger. E12 8
Oelwein, Ia., U.S. B6 92
O'Fallon, Il., U.S. E4 90
O'Fallon, Mo., U.S. f12 102
Offenbach, Ger. E8 8
Offenburg, Ger. G7 8
Offutt Air Force Base, mil., Ne., U.S. g3 104
Ōfunato, Japan C14 30
Ōgaki, Japan G9 30
Ogallala, Ne., U.S. C4 104
Ogbomosho, Nig. G6 42
Ogden, Ia., U.S. B3 92
Ogden, Ks., U.S. C7 93
Ogden, Ut., U.S. B4 121
Ogden, Mount, mtn., N.A. k23 79
Ogdensburg, N.J., U.S. A3 107
Ogdensburg, N.Y., U.S. f9 109
Ogeechee, stm., Ga., U.S. D5 87
Ogemaw, co., Mi., U.S. D6 99
Ogilvie Mountains, mts., Yukon, Can. D5 66
Ogle, co., Il., U.S. A4 90
Oglesby, Il., U.S. B4 90
Oglethorpe, Ga., U.S. D2 87
Oglethorpe, co., Ga., U.S. C3 87
Oglethorpe, Mount, mtn., Ga., U.S. B2 87
Ogooué, stm., Afr. B2 44
Ogulin, Cro. D10 14
Ogunquit, Me., U.S. E2 96
Oğuzeli, Tur. A5 40
Ohanet, Alg. C7 42
Ōhata, Japan A14 30
Ohatchee, Al., U.S. B3 78
O'Higgins, Lago (Lago San Martín), l., S.A. F2 56
Ohio, co., In., U.S. G7 91
Ohio, co., Ky., U.S. C3 94
Ohio, co., W.V., U.S. A4 125
Ohio, state, U.S. B3 112
Ohio, stm., U.S. D9 76
Ohio Brush Creek, stm., Oh., U.S. D2 112
Ohio City, Oh., U.S. B1 112
Ohio Peak, mtn., Co., U.S. C3 83
Ohioville, Pa., U.S. E1 115
Ohoopee, stm., Ga., U.S. D4 87
Ohrid, Lake, l., Eur. H4 16
Öhringen, Ger. F9 8
Oiapoque, Braz. C8 54
Oil City, La., U.S. B2 95
Oil City, Pa., U.S. D2 115
Oil Creek, stm., Pa., U.S. C2 115
Oildale, Ca., U.S. E4 82
Oil Springs, Ont., Can. E2 73
Oilton, Ok., U.S. A5 113
Ōita, Japan I4 30
Ojai, Ca., U.S. E4 82
Ojinaga, Mex. C7 62
Ojm'akon, Russia E22 24
Ojos de Liebre, Laguna, b., Mex. D2 62
Ojos del Salado, Cerro, mtn., S.A. B3 56
Oka, stm., Russia F25 18
Oka, stm., Russia G14 24
Okaba, Indon. G10 32
Okahandja, Nmb. F3 44
Okaloosa, co., Fl., U.S. u15 86
Okamanpeedan Lake, l., U.S. A3 92
Okanagan Falls, B.C., Can. E8 69
Okanagan Lake, l., B.C., Can. D8 69
Okanagan Landing, B.C., Can. D8 69
Okanogan, Wa., U.S. A6 124
Okanogan, co., Wa., U.S. A5 124
Okāra, Pak. E5 38
Okarche, Ok., U.S. B4 113
Okatibee Reservoir, res., Ms., U.S. C5 101
Okauchee Lake, Wi., U.S. *E5 126
Okavango (Cubango), stm., Afr. E3 44
Okavango Swamp, sw., Bots. E4 44
Ōkawa, Japan I3 30
Okawville, Il., U.S. E4 90
Okaya, Japan F11 30
Okayama, Japan H6 30
Okazaki, Japan H10 30
Okeechobee, Fl., U.S. E6 86
Okeechobee, co., Fl., U.S. E6 86
Okeechobee, Lake, l., Fl., U.S. F6 86
Okeene, Ok., U.S. A3 113
Okefenokee Swamp, sw., U.S. F4 87
Okemah, Ok., U.S. B5 113
Okfuskee, co., Ok., U.S. B5 113
Okhotsk, Sea of (Ochotskoje More), Asia G23 24
Oki-guntō, is., Japan F6 30
Okinawa-jima, i., Japan y27 31b
Okinoerabu-shima, i., Japan x28 31b
Okino-Tori-shima, i., Japan G14 26
Oklahoma, co., Ok., U.S. B4 113
Oklahoma, state, U.S. B4 113
Oklahoma City, Ok., U.S. B4 113
Oklawaha, Fl., U.S. C5 86
Oklawaha, stm., Fl., U.S. C5 86
Oklawaha, Lake, res., Fl., U.S. C5 86
Okmulgee, Ok., U.S. B6 113
Okmulgee, co., Ok., U.S. B5 113
Okoboji, Ia., U.S. A2 92
Okobojo Creek, stm., S.D., U.S. C5 118
Okolona, Ky., U.S. g11 94
Okolona, Ms., U.S. B5 101
Okotoks, Alta., Can. D4 68
Okt'abr'skoj Revol'ucii, Ostrov, i., Russia B13 24
Oktibbeha, co., Ms., U.S. B5 101
Ola, Ar., U.S. B2 81
Olancha Peak, mtn., Ca., U.S. D4 82
Olanchito, Hond. G4 64
Öland, i., Swe. H11 6
Olanta, S.C., U.S. D8 117
Olathe, Co., U.S. C3 83
Olathe, Ks., U.S. D9 93
Olavarría, Arg. D4 56
Olbia, Italy I4 14
Ol'chon, Ostrov, i., Russia G15 24
Olcott, N.Y., U.S. B2 109
Old Bahama Channel, strt., N.A. C8 64
Old Bridge, N.J., U.S. C4 107
Oldenburg, Ger. B8 8
Oldenburg, In., U.S. F7 91
Oldenburg [in Holstein], Ger. A10 8
Old Faithful Geyser, Wy., U.S. B2 127
Old Forge, Pa., U.S. D10 115
Old Fort, N.C., U.S. f10 110
Oldham, co., Ky., U.S. B4 94
Oldham, co., Tx., U.S. B1 120
Old Harbor, Ak., U.S. D9 79
Old Head of Kinsale, c., Ire. J4 7
Old Hickory Lake, res., Tn., U.S. A5 119
Oldman, stm., Alta., Can. E4 68
Old Man of the Mountain, N.H., U.S. B3 106
Oldmans Creek, stm., N.J., U.S. D2 107
Old Orchard Beach, Me., U.S. E2 96
Old Perlican, Newf., Can. D5 72
Old Point Comfort, c., Va., U.S. h15 123
Old Rhodes Key, i., Fl., U.S. G6 86
Old River Lake, l., Ar., U.S. k10 81
Olds, Alta., Can. D3 68
Old Saybrook, Ct., U.S. D6 84
Oldsmar, Fl., U.S. o10 86
Old Tampa Bay, b., Fl., U.S. p10 86
Old Tappan, N.J., U.S. g9 107
Old Topsail Inlet, b., N.C., U.S. C5 110
Old Town, Me., U.S. D4 96
Old Wives Lake, l., Sask., Can. G2 75
Olean, N.Y., U.S. C2 109
O'Leary, P.E.I., Can. C5 71
Ølen, Nor. G5 6
Olenij, Ostrov, i., Russia C9 24
Olen'ok, Russia D16 24
Olen'ok, stm., Russia C18 24
Olen'okskij Zaliv, b., Russia C18 24
Olentangy, stm., Oh., U.S. B3 112
Oleśnica, Pol. D17 8
Ol'ga, Russia I21 24
Olga, Mount, mtn., Austl. E6 50
Olhão, Port. H3 12
Ólimbos, mtn., Cyp. B3 40
Ólimbos, Óros, mtn., Grc. I6 16
Olímpia, Braz. F4 57
Olin, Ia., U.S. B6 92
Olinda, Braz. E12 54
Olite, Spain C10 12
Oliva, Arg. C4 56
Oliva, Spain G11 12
Oliva de la Frontera, Spain G5 12
Olive Branch, Ms., U.S. A4 101
Olive Hill, Ky., U.S. B6 94
Olivehurst, Ca., U.S. C3 82
Oliveira, Braz. F6 57
Olivenza, Spain G4 12
Oliver, B.C., Can. E8 69
Oliver, Pa., U.S. G2 115
Oliver, co., N.D., U.S. B4 111
Oliver Dam, U.S. C5 78
Oliver Springs, Tn., U.S. C9 119
Olivet, Mi., U.S. F6 99
Olivia, Mn., U.S. F4 100
Olla, La., U.S. C3 95
Ollagüe, Chile A3 56
Olmedo, Spain D7 12
Olmito, Tx., U.S. F4 120
Olmos, Peru E3 54
Olmos Park, Tx., U.S. k7 120
Olmsted, co., Mn., U.S. G6 100
Olmsted Falls, Oh., U.S. h9 112
Olney, Il., U.S. E5 90
Olney, Md., U.S. B3 97
Olney, Tx., U.S. C3 120
Oloj, stm., Russia D26 24
Ol'okma, stm., Russia F18 24
Ol'okminsk, Russia E18 24
Olomouc, Czech. F17 8
Olongapo, Phil. q19 33b
Oloron-Sainte-Marie, Fr. I6 10
Olot, Spain C14 12
Olov'annaja, Russia G17 24
Olsztyn (Allenstein), Pol. B20 8
Olten, Switz. E14 10
Olton, Tx., U.S. B1 120
Oluan Pi, c., Tai. N9 28
Olustee, Ok., U.S. C2 113
Ol'utorskij, Mys, c., Russia F28 24
Olympia, Wa., U.S. B3 124
Olympic Mountains, mts., Wa., U.S. B2 124
Olympic National Park, Wa., U.S. B2 124
Olympus, Mount, mtn., Wa., U.S. B2 124
Olympus, Mount see Ólimbos, Óros, mtn., Grc. I6 16
Olyphant, Pa., U.S. D10 115
Omae-zaki, c., Japan H11 30
Omagh, N. Ire., U.K. G5 7
Omaha, Ne., U.S. C10 104
Omaha Indian Reservation, Ne., U.S. B9 104
Omak, Wa., U.S. A6 124
Omak Lake, l., Wa., U.S. A6 124
Oman, ctry., Asia D6 46
Oman, Gulf of, b., Asia D6 46
Omar, W.V., U.S. D3 125
Ōma-zaki, c., Japan A13 30
Omčak, Russia E23 24
Omega, Ga., U.S. E3 87
Omegna, Italy D3 14
Omemee, Ont., Can. C6 73
Omerville, Que., Can. D5 74
Ometepe, Isla de, i., Nic. I5 64
Ometepec, Mex. I10 62
Omineca, stm., B.C., Can. B5 69
Omineca Mountains, mts., B.C., Can. A4 69
Ōmiya, Japan G12 30
Ommaney, Cape, c., Ak., U.S. D12 79
Ommanney Bay, b., N.W. Ter., Can. B12 66
Ommen, Neth. C6 8
Omo, stm., Eth. G2 46
Omolon, stm., Russia D25 24
Ompompanoosuc, stm., Vt., U.S. D4 122
Omro, Wi., U.S. D5 126
Omsk, Russia F8 24
Omsukčan, Russia E25 24
Ōmura, Japan J2 30
Ōmuta, Japan I3 30
Onaga, Ks., U.S. C7 93
Onalaska, Wa., U.S. C3 124
Onalaska, Wi., U.S. E2 126
Onamia, Mn., U.S. D5 100
Onancock, Va., U.S. C7 123
Onarga, Il., U.S. C6 90
Onawa, Ia., U.S. B1 92
Onawa, Lake, l., Me., U.S. C3 96
Onaway, Mi., U.S. C6 99
Onda, Spain F11 12
Ondangua, Nmb. E3 44
Ondjiva, Ang. E3 44
Öndörchaan, Mong. B9 26
Oneco, Fl., U.S. E4 86
Onega, Lake see Onežskoje ozero, l., Russia E5 22
One Hundred Fifty Mile House, B.C., Can. C7 69
One Hundred Mile House, B.C., Can. D7 69
Oneida, Ky., U.S. C6 94
Oneida, N.Y., U.S. B5 109
Oneida, Oh., U.S. C1 112
Oneida, Tn., U.S. C9 119
Oneida, co., Id., U.S. G6 89
Oneida, co., N.Y., U.S. B5 109
Oneida, co., Wi., U.S. C4 126
Oneida Lake, l., N.Y., U.S. B5 109
O'Neill, Ne., U.S. B7 104
Onekotan, Ostrov, i., Russia H24 24
Oneonta, Al., U.S. B3 78
Oneonta, N.Y., U.S. C5 109
Onești, Rom. C10 16
Onežskoje ozero, l., Russia E5 22
Ongole, India E6 37
Onida, S.D., U.S. C5 118
Onitsha, Nig. G7 42
Onoda, Japan I4 30
Onomichi, Japan H6 30
Onondaga, co., N.Y., U.S. C4 109
Onondaga Indian Reservation, N.Y., U.S. C4 109
Onota Lake, l., Ma., U.S. B1 98
Onoway, Alta., Can. C3 68
Onset, Ma., U.S. C6 98
Onslow, Austl. D3 50
Onslow, co., N.C., U.S. C5 110
Onslow Bay, b., N.C., U.S. C5 110
Onsted, Mi., U.S. F6 99
Ontario, Ca., U.S. E5 82
Ontario, Oh., U.S. B3 112
Ontario, Or., U.S. C10 114
Ontario, co., N.Y., U.S. C3 109
Ontario, prov., Can. C6 73
Ontario, Lake, l., N.A. C11 76
Onteniente, Spain G11 12
Ontonagon, Mi., U.S. m12 99
Ontonagon, co., Mi., U.S. m12 99
Ontonagon Indian Reservation, Mi., U.S. B1 99
Onverwacht, Sur. B7 54
Oodnadatta, Austl. E7 50
Ooldea, Austl. F6 50
Oolitic, In., U.S. G4 91
Oologah, Ok., U.S. A6 113
Oologah Lake, res., Ok., U.S. A6 113
Ooltewah, Tn., U.S. D8 119
Oostburg, Wi., U.S. E6 126
Oostende (Ostende), Bel. D2 8
Oosterhout, Neth. D4 8
Ootacamund, India G4 37
Ootsa Lake, l., B.C., Can. C4 69
Opala, Zaire B4 44
Opa-Locka, Fl., U.S. s13 86
Opatija, Cro. D9 14
Opava, Czech. F17 8
Opelika, Al., U.S. C4 78
Opelousas, La., U.S. D3 95
Opequon Creek, stm., W.V., U.S. B6 125
Opiscotéo, Lac, l., Que., Can. F19 66
Opole (Oppeln), Pol. E17 8
Opotiki, N.Z. C6 52
Opp, Al., U.S. D3 78
Oppdal, Nor. E7 6
Oppelo, Ar., U.S. B3 81
Opportunity, Wa., U.S. B8 124
Optima Reservoir, res., Ok., U.S. e9 113
Oquawka, Il., U.S. C3 90
Ora, Italy C6 14
Oracle, Az., U.S. E5 80
Oradea, Rom. B5 16
Oradell, N.J., U.S. h8 107
Oradell Reservoir, res., N.J., U.S. h9 107
Orai, India H8 38
Oraibi, Az., U.S. B5 80
Oran (Wahran), Alg. A5 42
Oran, Mo., U.S. D8 102
Orange, Austl. F9 50
Orange, Fr. H11 10
Orange, Ca., U.S. n13 82
Orange, Ct., U.S. D3 84
Orange, Ma., U.S. A3 98
Orange, N.J., U.S. B4 107
Orange, Tx., U.S. D6 120
Orange, Va., U.S. B4 123
Orange, co., Ca., U.S. F5 82
Orange, co., Fl., U.S. D5 86
Orange, co., In., U.S. G4 91
Orange, co., N.Y., U.S. D6 109
Orange, co., N.C., U.S. A3 110
Orange, co., Tx., U.S. D6 120
Orange, co., Vt., U.S. D3 122
Orange, co., Va., U.S. B4 123
Orange (Oranje), stm., Afr. G3 44
Orange, Cabo, c., Braz. C8 54
Orange Beach, Al., U.S. E2 78
Orangeburg, S.C., U.S. E6 117
Orangeburg, co., S.C., U.S. E6 117
Orange City, Fl., U.S. D5 86
Orange City, Ia., U.S. B1 92
Orange Grove, Ms., U.S. E5 101
Orange Grove, Tx., U.S. F4 120
Orange Lake, l., Fl., U.S. C4 86
Orange Park, Fl., U.S. B5 86
Orangeville, Ont., Can. D4 73
Orangeville, Ut., U.S. D4 121
Orange Walk, Belize E3 64
Orani, Phil. q19 33b
Oranienburg, Ger. C13 8
Oranjestad, Aruba H12 64
Orbetello, Italy G6 14
Orbost, Austl. G9 50
Örbyhus, Swe. F11 6
Orcas Island, i., Wa., U.S. A3 124
Orcera, Spain G9 12
Orchard City, Co., U.S. C3 83
Orchard Homes, Mt., U.S. D2 103
Orchard Park, N.Y., U.S. C2 109
Orchards, Wa., U.S. D3 124
Orchard Valley, Wy., U.S. E8 127
Orchila, Isla, i., Ven. B9 58
Orchon, stm., Mong. B7 26

Name	Map Ref	Page
Orcutt, Ca., U.S.	E3	82
Ord, Ne., U.S.	C7	104
Ord, Mount, mtn., Austl.	C5	50
Ordenes, Spain	B3	12
Ordway, Co., U.S.	C7	83
Ordzhonikidze see Vladikavkaz, Russia	I6	22
Oreana, Il., U.S.	D5	90
Örebro, Swe.	G10	6
Orechovo-Zujevo, Russia	F21	18
Oregon, Il., U.S.	A4	90
Oregon, Mo., U.S.	B2	102
Oregon, Oh., U.S.	A2	112
Oregon, Wi., U.S.	F4	126
Oregon, co., Mo., U.S.	E6	102
Oregon, state, U.S.	C6	114
Oregon Caves National Monument, Or., U.S.	E2	114
Oregon City, Or., U.S.	B4	114
Oregon Inlet, b., N.C., U.S.	B7	110
Orel, Russia	I19	18
Orem, Ut., U.S.	C4	121
Orenburg, Russia	G9	22
Orense, Spain	C4	12
Orestiás, Grc.	H10	16
Orfordville, Wi., U.S.	F4	126
Organ Mountains, mts., N.M., U.S.	E3	108
Organ Pipe Cactus National Monument, Az., U.S.	E3	80
Orgūn, Afg.	D3	38
Oriental, N.C., U.S.	B6	110
Oriental, Cordillera, mts., Col.	E6	58
Oriental, Cordillera, mts., Peru	F4	54
Orihuela, Spain	G11	12
Orillia, Ont., Can.	C5	73
Orinoco, stm., S.A.	C11	58
Orinoco, Delta del, Ven.	C12	58
Orion, Il., U.S.	B3	90
Oripää, Fin.	F14	6
Orissa, state, India	J11	38
Oristano, Italy	I3	14
Orivesi, Fin.	F15	6
Orizaba, Mex.	H11	62
Orizaba, Pico de (Volcán Citlaltépetl), vol., Mex.	H11	62
Orkney Islands, is., Scot., U.K.	B9	7
Orland, Ca., U.S.	C2	82
Orlando, Fl., U.S.	D5	86
Orland Park, Il., U.S.	k9	90
Orléans, Fr.	E8	10
Orleans, Ma., U.S.	C7	98
Orleans, Vt., U.S.	B4	122
Orleans, co., La., U.S.	E6	95
Orleans, co., N.Y., U.S.	B2	109
Orleans, co., Vt., U.S.	B4	122
Orléans, Île d', i., Que., Can.	C6	74
Orman Dam, S.D., U.S.	C2	118
Ormond Beach, Fl., U.S.	C5	86
Ormož, Slo.	C11	14
Ormstown, Que., Can.	D3	74
Ornans, Fr.	E13	10
Örnsköldsvik, Swe.	E12	6
Orocué, Col.	E7	58
Orofino, Id., U.S.	C2	89
Oromocto, N.B., Can.	D3	71
Oromocto Lake, l., N.B., Can.	D2	71
Orono, Me., U.S.	D4	96
Oronoco, Mn., U.S.	F6	100
Oroville, Ca., U.S.	C3	82
Oroville, Wa., U.S.	A6	124
Oroville, Lake, res., Ca., U.S.	C3	82
Orrick, Mo., U.S.	B3	102
Orrville, Oh., U.S.	B4	112
Orsk, Russia	G9	22
Orta Nova, Italy	H10	14
Ortegal, Cabo, c., Spain	B4	12
Orting, Wa., U.S.	B3	124
Ortiz, Ven.	C9	58
Ortona, Italy	G9	14
Ortonville, Mi., U.S.	F7	99
Ortonville, Mn., U.S.	E2	100
Orūmīyeh (Reẓā'īyeh), Iran	J7	22
Orūmīyeh, Daryācheh-ye, l., Iran	J7	22
Oruro, Bol.	G5	54
Orūzgān (Qala-I-Hazār Qadam), Afg.	D2	38
Orvieto, Italy	G7	14
Orwell, Oh., U.S.	A5	112
Orwigsburg, Pa., U.S.	E9	115
Oš, Kyrg.	I12	22
Osa, Península de, pen., C.R.	J6	64
Osage, Ia., U.S.	A5	92
Osage, Wy., U.S.	C8	127
Osage, co., Ks., U.S.	D8	93
Osage, co., Mo., U.S.	C6	102
Osage, co., Ok., U.S.	A5	113
Osage, stm., Mo., U.S.	C3	102
Osage Beach, Mo., U.S.	C5	102
Osage City, Ks., U.S.	D8	93
Ōsaka, Japan	H8	30
Ōsaka-wan, b., Japan	H8	30
Osakis, Mn., U.S.	E3	100
Osakis, Lake, l., Mn., U.S.	E3	100
Osawatomie, Ks., U.S.	D9	93
Osborne, Ks., U.S.	C5	93
Osborne, co., Ks., U.S.	C5	93
Osburn, Id., U.S.	B3	89
Osceola, Ar., U.S.	B6	81
Osceola, In., U.S.	A5	91
Osceola, Ia., U.S.	C4	92
Osceola, Mo., U.S.	C4	102
Osceola, Ne., U.S.	C8	104
Osceola, Wi., U.S.	C1	126
Osceola, co., Fl., U.S.	E5	86
Osceola, co., Ia., U.S.	A2	92
Osceola, co., Mi., U.S.	E5	99
Osceola Mills, Pa., U.S.	E5	115
Oschersleben, Ger.	C11	8
Oscoda, Mi., U.S.	D7	99
Oscoda, co., Mi., U.S.	D6	99
Oscura Mountains, mts., N.M., U.S.	D3	108
Osen, Nor.	D8	6
Osgood, In., U.S.	F7	91
Oshawa, Ont., Can.	D6	73
Oshima-hantō, pen., Japan	q18	30a
Oshkosh, Ne., U.S.	C3	104
Oshkosh, Wi., U.S.	D5	126
Oshogbo, Nig.	G6	42
Osh see Oš, Kyrg.	I12	22
Oshwe, Zaire	B3	44
Osijek, Cro.	D2	16
Osimo, Italy	F8	14
Osinniki, Russia	G11	24
Osipoviči, Bela.	H11	18
Oskaloosa, Ia., U.S.	C5	92
Oskaloosa, Ks., U.S.	C8	93
Oskarshamn, Swe.	H11	6
Oslo, Nor.	G8	6
Osmānābād, India	C4	37
Osmaniye, Tur.	A5	40
Osmond, Ne., U.S.	B8	104
Osnabrück, Ger.	C8	8
Osorno, Chile	E2	56
Osorno, Spain	C7	12
Osoyoos, B.C., Can.	E8	69
Osoyoos Lake, l., Wa., U.S.	A6	124
Ospino, Ven.	C8	58
Osprey, Fl., U.S.	E4	86
Osprey Reef, rf., Austl.	B9	50
Ossa, Mount, mtn., Austl.	H9	50
Ossabaw Island, i., Ga., U.S.	E5	87
Osseo, Mn., U.S.	m12	100
Osseo, Wi., U.S.	D2	126
Ossian, In., U.S.	C7	91
Ossian, Ia., U.S.	A6	92
Ossining, N.Y., U.S.	D7	109
Ossipee, stm., U.S.	C5	106
Ossipee Lake, l., N.H., U.S.	C4	106
Ostaškov, Russia	D16	18
Osterholz-Scharmbeck, Ger.	B8	8
Osterode, Ger.	D10	8
Östersund, Swe.	E10	6
Osterville, Ma., U.S.	C7	98
Ostrava, Czech.	F18	8
Ostrołęka, Pol.	B21	8
Ostrov, Russia	D11	18
Ostrowiec Świętokrzyski, Pol.	E21	8
Ostrów Wielkopolski, Pol.	D17	8
Ostuni, Italy	I12	14
Ōsumi-kaikyō, strt., Japan	L3	30
Ōsumi-shotō, is., Japan	u30	31b
Osuna, Spain	H6	12
Osvaldo Cruz, Braz.	F3	57
Oswegatchie, stm., N.Y., U.S.	f9	109
Oswego, Il., U.S.	B5	90
Oswego, Ks., U.S.	E8	93
Oswego, N.Y., U.S.	B4	109
Oswego, co., N.Y., U.S.	B4	109
Oswego, stm., N.J., U.S.	D4	107
Oswego, stm., N.Y., U.S.	B4	109
Oswestry, Eng., U.K.	I9	7
Oświęcim, Pol.	E19	8
Ōta, Japan	F12	30
Otaki, N.Z.	D5	52
Otaru, Japan	p18	30a
Otavi, Nmb.	E3	44
Oteen, N.C., U.S.	f10	110
Otero, co., Co., U.S.	D7	83
Otero, co., N.M., U.S.	E3	108
Othello, Wa., U.S.	C6	124
Oti, stm., Afr.	G6	42
Otish, Monts, mts., Que., Can.	F18	66
Otis Orchards, Wa., U.S.	g14	124
Otis Reservoir, res., Ma., U.S.	B1	98
Otisville, Mi., U.S.	E7	99
Otjiwarongo, Nmb.	F3	44
Otočac, Cro.	E10	14
Otoe, co., Ne., U.S.	D9	104
Otranto, Italy	I13	14
Otranto, Strait of, mth., Eur.	I2	16
Otsego, Mi., U.S.	F5	99
Otsego, co., Mi., U.S.	C6	99
Otsego, co., N.Y., U.S.	C5	109
Otsego Lake, l., N.Y., U.S.	C6	109
Ōtsu, Japan	G8	30
Otta, Nor.	F7	6
Ottauquechee, stm., Vt., U.S.	D4	122
Ottawa, Ont., Can.	B9	73
Ottawa, Il., U.S.	B5	90
Ottawa, Ks., U.S.	D8	93
Ottawa, Oh., U.S.	A1	112
Ottawa, co., Ks., U.S.	C6	93
Ottawa, co., Mi., U.S.	F4	99
Ottawa, co., Oh., U.S.	A2	112
Ottawa, co., Ok., U.S.	A7	113
Ottawa, stm., Can.	G17	66
Ottawa, stm., Oh., U.S.	e6	112
Ottawa Hills, Oh., U.S.	e6	112
Ottawa Islands, is., N.W. Ter., Can.	E16	66
Ottenby, Swe.	H11	6
Otterbein, In., U.S.	D3	91
Otter Brook, stm., N.H., U.S.	E2	106
Otter Brook Lake, res., N.H., U.S.	E2	106
Otter Creek, stm., Ut., U.S.	E4	121
Otter Creek, stm., Vt., U.S.	C2	122
Otter Creek Reservoir, res., Ut., U.S.	E4	121
Otter Islands, is., S.C., U.S.	m11	117
Otter Tail, co., Mn., U.S.	D3	100
Otter Tail, stm., Mn., U.S.	D2	100
Otter Tail Lake, l., Mn., U.S.	D3	100
Otterville, Ont., Can.	E4	73
Ottumwa, Ia., U.S.	C5	92
Otwock, Pol.	C21	8
Ötztaler Alpen, mts., Eur.	C5	14
Ouachita, co., Ar., U.S.	D3	81
Ouachita, co., La., U.S.	B3	95
Ouachita, Lake, res., Ar., U.S.	C2	81
Ouachita Mountains, mts., U.S.	E8	76
Ouadda, Cen. Afr. Rep.	G10	42
Ouagadougou, Burkina	F5	42
Ouahigouya, Burkina	F5	42
Oualâta, Maur.	E4	42
Ouallene, Alg.	D6	42
Ouanda Djallé, Cen. Afr. Rep.	G10	42
Ouarane, reg., Maur.	D3	42
Ouargla, Alg.	B7	42
Ouarzazate, Mor.	B4	42
Oubangui, stm., Afr.	A3	44
Oudtshoorn, S. Afr.	H4	44
Oued Meliz, Tun.	M3	14
Oued Zarga, Tun.	M4	14
Ouémé, stm., Benin	G6	42
Ouesso, Congo	A3	44
Ouezzane, Mor.	B4	42
Oujda, Mor.	B5	42
Oulu, Fin.	D15	6
Oulujärvi, l., Fin.	D16	6
Oum Chalouba, Chad	E10	42
Ounianga Kébir, Chad	E10	42
Ouray, Co., U.S.	C3	83
Ouray, co., Co., U.S.	C3	83
Ouray, Mount, mtn., Co., U.S.	C4	83
Ourinhos, Braz.	G4	57
Ourique, Port.	H3	12
Ouro Prêto, Braz.	F7	57
Ōu-sammyaku, mts., Japan	D13	30
Outagamie, co., Wi., U.S.	D5	126
Outardes Quatre, Réservoir, res., Que., Can.	h13	74
Outer Hebrides, is., Scot., U.K.	D5	7
Outer Island, i., Wi., U.S.	A3	126
Outer Santa Barbara Passage, strt., Ca., U.S.	F4	82
Outpost Mountain, mtn., Ak., U.S.	B9	79
Outremont, Que., Can.	p19	74
Ovalle, Chile	C2	56
Ovamboland, hist. reg., Nmb.	E3	44
Ovana, Cerro, mtn., Ven.	E9	58
Ovar, Port.	E3	12
Overbrook, Ks., U.S.	D8	93
Overgaard, Az., U.S.	C5	80
Overland, Mo., U.S.	f13	102
Overland Park, Ks., U.S.	m16	93
Overlea, Md., U.S.	B4	97
Overton, Nv., U.S.	G7	105
Overton, Tx., U.S.	C5	120
Overton, co., Tn., U.S.	C8	119
Övertorneå, Swe.	C14	6
Ovett, Ms., U.S.	D4	101
Ovid, Mi., U.S.	E6	99
Oviedo, Spain	B6	12
Owando, Congo	B3	44
Owasco Lake, l., N.Y., U.S.	C4	109
Owase, Japan	H9	30
Owasso, Ok., U.S.	A6	113
Owatonna, Mn., U.S.	F5	100
Owego, N.Y., U.S.	C4	109
Owen, Wi., U.S.	D3	126
Owen, co., In., U.S.	F4	91
Owen, co., Ky., U.S.	B5	94
Owen, Lake, l., Wi., U.S.	B2	126
Owen, Mount, mtn., Co., U.S.	C3	83
Owens, stm., Ca., U.S.	D4	82
Owensboro, Ky., U.S.	C2	94
Owens Cross Roads, Al., U.S.	A3	78
Owens Lake, l., Ca., U.S.	D5	82
Owen Sound, Ont., Can.	C4	73
Owen Sound, b., Ont., Can.	C4	73
Owen Stanley Range, mts., Pap. N. Gui.	m16	50a
Owensville, In., U.S.	H2	91
Owensville, Mo., U.S.	C6	102
Owensville, Oh., U.S.	C1	112
Owenton, Ky., U.S.	B5	94
Owings Mills, Md., U.S.	B4	97
Owingsville, Ky., U.S.	B6	94
Owl Creek, stm., Wy., U.S.	C4	127
Owl Creek Mountains, mts., Wy., U.S.	C4	127
Owo, Nig.	G7	42
Owosso, Mi., U.S.	E6	99
Owsley, co., Ky., U.S.	C6	94
Owyhee, Nv., U.S.	B5	105
Owyhee, co., Id., U.S.	G2	89
Owyhee, stm., U.S.	E9	114
Owyhee, Lake, res., Or., U.S.	D9	114
Owyhee Dam, Or., U.S.	D9	114
Owyhee Mountains, mts., U.S.	G2	89
Oxbow Dam, U.S.	E2	89
Oxelösund, Swe.	G11	6
Oxford, N.S., Can.	D6	71
Oxford, N.Z.	E4	52
Oxford, Eng., U.K.	J11	7
Oxford, Al., U.S.	B4	78
Oxford, Ct., U.S.	D3	84
Oxford, Ga., U.S.	C3	87
Oxford, In., U.S.	C3	91
Oxford, Ia., U.S.	C6	92
Oxford, Ks., U.S.	E6	93
Oxford, Me., U.S.	D2	96
Oxford, Md., U.S.	C5	97
Oxford, Ma., U.S.	B4	98
Oxford, Mi., U.S.	F7	99
Oxford, Ms., U.S.	A4	101
Oxford, Ne., U.S.	D6	104
Oxford, N.Y., U.S.	C5	109
Oxford, N.C., U.S.	A4	110
Oxford, Oh., U.S.	C1	112
Oxford, Pa., U.S.	G10	115
Oxford, co., Me., U.S.	D2	96
Oxford Lake, l., Man., Can.	B4	70
Oxford Peak, mtn., Id., U.S.	G6	89
Oxnard, Ca., U.S.	E4	82
Oxon Hill, Md., U.S.	f9	97
Oxus see Amu Darya, stm., Asia	I10	22
Oyama, B.C., Can.	D8	69
Oyama, Japan	F12	30
Oyem, Gabon	A2	44
Oyen, Alta., Can.	D5	68
Oyonnax, Fr.	F12	10
Oyster Bay, N.Y., U.S.	E7	109
Oyster Keys, is., Fl., U.S.	G6	86
Ozamiz, Phil.	D7	32
Ozark, Al., U.S.	D4	78
Ozark, Ar., U.S.	B2	81
Ozark, Mo., U.S.	D4	102
Ozark, co., Mo., U.S.	E5	102
Ozark Plateau, plat., U.S.	D8	76
Ozark Reservoir, res., Ar., U.S.	B1	81
Ozarks, Lake of the, res., Mo., U.S.	C5	102
Ozaukee, co., Wi., U.S.	E6	126
Ózd, Hung.	G20	8
Ozernovskij, Russia	G25	24
Ozette Lake, l., Wa., U.S.	A1	124
Ozieri, Italy	I3	14
Ožogino, Ozero, l., Russia	D23	24
Ozona, Fl., U.S.	o10	86
Ozona, Tx., U.S.	D2	120
Ōzu, Japan	I5	30
P		
Paarl, S. Afr.	H3	44
Paauilo, Hi., U.S.	C6	88
Pabianice, Pol.	D19	8
Pābna, Bngl.	H13	38
Pacasmayo, Peru	E3	54
Pace, Fl., U.S.	u14	86
Pachaug Pond, l., Ct., U.S.	C8	84
Pachino, Italy	M10	14
Pachuca [de Soto], Mex.	G10	62
Pacific, Mo., U.S.	C7	102
Pacific, Wa., U.S.	f11	124
Pacific, co., Wa., U.S.	C2	124
Pacifica, Ca., U.S.	h8	82
Pacific Beach, Wa., U.S.	B1	124
Pacific City, Or., U.S.	B3	114
Pacific Creek, stm., Wy., U.S.	D3	127
Pacific Grove, Ca., U.S.	D3	82
Pacific Ocean	F2	2
Pacific Palisades, Hi., U.S.	g10	88
Pacific Ranges, mts., B.C., Can.	D4	69
Pacific Rim National Park, B.C., Can.	E5	69
Pack Monadnock Mountain, mtn., N.H., U.S.	E3	106
Packwood, Wa., U.S.	C4	124
Pacolet, S.C., U.S.	B4	117
Pacolet, stm., S.C., U.S.	A4	117
Pacolet Mills, S.C., U.S.	B4	117
Pactola Reservoir, res., S.D., U.S.	C2	118
Padang, Indon.	F3	32
Padangpanjang, Indon.	O6	34
Padangsidempuan, Indon.	N5	34
Paddock Lake, Wi., U.S.	n11	126
Paden City, W.V., U.S.	B4	125
Paderborn, Ger.	D8	8
Padova, Italy	D6	14
Padre Island, i., Tx., U.S.	F4	120
Padre Island National Seashore, Tx., U.S.	F4	120
Padrón, Spain	C3	12
Padstow, Eng., U.K.	K8	7
Padua see Padova, Italy	D6	14
Paducah, Ky., U.S.	e9	94
Paducah, Tx., U.S.	B2	120
Paektu-san, mtn., Asia	C12	26
Pafúri, Moz.	F6	44
Pag, Cro.	E10	14
Pagai Selatan, Pulau, i., Indon.	F3	32
Pagai Utara, Pulau, i., Indon.	F3	32
Page, Az., U.S.	A4	80
Page, W.V., U.S.	C3	125
Page, co., Ia., U.S.	D2	92
Page, co., Va., U.S.	B4	123
Pageland, S.C., U.S.	B7	117
Pagoda Peak, mtn., Co., U.S.	A3	83
Pagoda Point, c., Mya.	G3	34
Pagosa Springs, Co., U.S.	D3	83
Paguate, N.M., U.S.	B2	108
Pahala, Hi., U.S.	D6	88
Pahang, stm., Malay.	M7	34
Pahoa, Hi., U.S.	D7	88
Pahokee, Fl., U.S.	F6	86
Pahrump, Nv., U.S.	G6	105
Pahute Mesa, mtn., Nv., U.S.	F5	105
Paia, Hi., U.S.	C5	88
Päijänne, l., Fin.	F15	6
Pailolo Channel, strt., Hi., U.S.	B5	88
Paimpol, Fr.	D3	10
Paincourtville, La., U.S.	k9	95
Painesville, Oh., U.S.	A4	112
Paint, stm., Mi., U.S.	B2	99
Paint Creek, stm., Oh., U.S.	C2	112
Paint Creek, stm., W.V., U.S.	m13	125
Paint Creek, North Fork, stm., Oh., U.S.	C2	112
Paint Creek Lake, res., Oh., U.S.	C2	112
Painted Desert, des., Az., U.S.	B4	80
Painted Post, N.Y., U.S.	C3	109
Painted Rock Reservoir, res., Az., U.S.	D3	80
Paintsville, Ky., U.S.	C7	94
Paisley, Ont., Can.	C3	73
Paisley, Scot., U.K.	F8	7
Paita, Peru	E2	54
Pajala, Swe.	C14	6
Paján, Ec.	H2	58
Pakanbaru, Indon.	E3	32
Pakaraima Mountains, mts., S.A.	E12	58
Pakistan (Pākistān), ctry., Asia	D2	36
Pakistan, East see Bangladesh, ctry., Asia	E6	36
Pakokku, Mya.	D3	34
Pakowki Lake, l., Alta., Can.	E5	68
P'akupur, stm., Russia	E9	24
Pakxé, Laos	G8	34
Pala, Chad	G8	42
Palacios, Tx., U.S.	E4	120
Palamós, Spain	D15	12
Palana, Russia	F25	24
Pālanpur, India	H5	38
Palaoa Point, c., Hi., U.S.	C4	88
Palapye, Bots.	F5	44
Palatine, Il., U.S.	A5	90
Palatka, Russia	E24	24
Palatka, Fl., U.S.	C5	86
Palawan, i., Phil.	D6	32
Pālayankottai, India	H4	37
Palembang, Indon.	F3	32
Palencia, Spain	C7	12
Palermo, Italy	K8	14
Palestine, Ar., U.S.	C5	81
Palestine, Il., U.S.	D6	90
Palestine, Tx., U.S.	D5	120
Palestine, ctry., Asia	C4	40
Palestine, Lake, res., Tx., U.S.	C5	120
Paletwa, Mya.	D2	34
Pālghāt, India	G4	37
Pāli, India	H5	38
Palikea, mtn., Hi., U.S.	g9	88
Palisade, Co., U.S.	B2	83
Palisades Park, N.J., U.S.	h8	107
Palisades Reservoir, res., U.S.	F7	89
Pālitāna, India	J4	38
Palk Strait, strt., Asia	H5	37
Pallastunturi, mtn., Fin.	B14	6
Palma, Moz.	D8	44
Palma del Río, Spain	H6	12
Palma [de Mallorca], Spain	F14	12
Palma di Montechiaro, Italy	L8	14
Palmanova, Italy	D8	14
Palmarito, Ven.	D7	58
Palmas, Cape, c., Lib.	H4	42
Palma Soriano, Cuba	D9	64
Palm Bay, Fl., U.S.	D6	86
Palm Beach, Fl., U.S.	F6	86
Palm Beach, co., Fl., U.S.	F6	86
Palm Beach Gardens, Fl., U.S.	*F6	86
Palmdale, Ca., U.S.	E4	82
Palmelo, Braz.	D4	57
Palmer, Ak., U.S.	C10	79
Palmer, Ma., U.S.	B3	98
Palmer, Mi., U.S.	B3	99
Palmer, Ms., U.S.	D4	101
Palmer, Ne., U.S.	C7	104
Palmer, Tn., U.S.	D8	119
Palmer, Tx., U.S.	n10	120
Palmer Lake, Co., U.S.	B6	83
Palmerston, Ont., Can.	D4	73
Palmerston, Cape, c., Austl.	D9	50
Palmerston North, N.Z.	D5	52
Palmerton, Pa., U.S.	E10	115
Palmetto, Fl., U.S.	E4	86
Palmetto, Ga., U.S.	C2	87
Palm Harbor, Fl., U.S.	o10	86
Palmi, Italy	K10	14
Palmira, Col.	F4	58
Palmira, Ec.	I3	58
Palms, Isle of, i., S.C., U.S.	F8	117
Palm Springs, Ca., U.S.	F5	82
Palm Springs, Fl., U.S.	*F6	86
Palmyra, In., U.S.	H5	91
Palmyra, Mo., U.S.	B6	102
Palmyra, N.J., U.S.	C2	107
Palmyra, N.Y., U.S.	B3	109
Palmyra, Pa., U.S.	F8	115
Palmyra, Wi., U.S.	F5	126
Palni, India	G4	37
Palo Alto, Ca., U.S.	D2	82
Palo Alto, co., Ia., U.S.	A3	92
Paloich, Sudan	F12	42
Palomar Mountain, mtn., Ca., U.S.	F5	82
Palomas Mountains, mts., Az., U.S.	D2	80
Palo Pinto, co., Tx., U.S.	C3	120
Palos Park, Il., U.S.	k9	90
Palos Verdes Estates, Ca., U.S.	n12	82
Palourde, Lake, l., La., U.S.	k9	95
Palouse, Wa., U.S.	C8	124
Palouse, stm., Wa., U.S.	C7	124
Palu, Indon.	F6	32
Palwal, India	F7	38
Pamekasan, Indon.	m16	33a
Pamiers, Fr.	I8	10
Pamir, mts., Asia	B3	36
Pamlico, co., N.C., U.S.	B6	110
Pamlico, stm., N.C., U.S.	B6	110
Pamlico Sound, strt., N.C., U.S.	B6	110
Pampa, Tx., U.S.	B2	120
Pampas, reg., Arg.	C4	56
Pamplico, S.C., U.S.	D8	117
Pamplona, Col.	D6	58
Pamplona, Spain	C10	12
Pamunkey, stm., Va., U.S.	C5	123
Pana, Il., U.S.	D4	90
Panaca, Nv., U.S.	F7	105
Panache, Lake, l., Ont., Can.	A3	73
Panaji (Panjim), India	E2	37
Panamá, Pan.	J8	64
Panama, Ok., U.S.	B7	113
Panama, ctry., N.A.	J7	64
Panama, Gulf of, b., Pan.	J8	64
Panama, Isthmus of, Pan.	J8	64
Panama Canal, Pan.	J8	64
Panama City, Fl., U.S.	u16	86
Panama City Beach, Fl., U.S.	u16	86
Panamint Range, mts., Ca., U.S.	D5	82
Panay, i., Phil.	C7	32
Pancake Range, mts., Nv., U.S.	E6	105
Pandharpur, India	D3	37
Pandora, Oh., U.S.	B2	112
P'andž (Panj), stm., Asia	A4	38
Panevėžys, Lith.	F7	18
Pangala, Congo	B2	44
Pangburn, Ar., U.S.	B4	81
Pangkalanbuun, Indon.	F5	32
Pangkalpinang, Indon.	F4	32
Pangnirtung, N.W. Ter., Can.	C19	66
Panguitch, Ut., U.S.	F3	121
Pangutaran Group, is., Phil.	D7	32
Panhandle, Tx., U.S.	B2	120
Paniau, mtn., Hi., U.S.	B1	88
Pānīpat, India	F7	38
Panj (P'andž), stm., Asia	B4	38
Panjāb, Afg.	C2	38
Panjgūr, Pak.	D1	36
Panola, co., Ms., U.S.	A3	101
Panola, co., Tx., U.S.	C5	120
Panora, Ia., U.S.	C3	92
Pantelleria, Italy	M6	14
Panvel, India	C2	37
Panxian, China	B8	34
Panyam, Nig.	G7	42
Panyu, China	M2	28
Paola, Italy	J11	14
Paola, Ks., U.S.	D9	93
Paoli, In., U.S.	G5	91
Paoli, Pa., U.S.	o20	115
Paonia, Co., U.S.	C3	83
Pápa, Hung.	H17	8

Name	Map Ref	Page
Papago Indian Reservation, Az., U.S.	E3	80
Papaikou, Hi., U.S.	D6	88
Papantla [de Olarte], Mex.	G11	62
Papawai Point, c., Hi., U.S.	C5	88
Papenburg, Ger.	B7	8
Papillion, Ne., U.S.	C9	104
Papineauville, Que., Can.	D2	74
Papua, Gulf of, b., Pap. N. Gui.	m15	50a
Papua New Guinea, ctry., Oc.	m15	50a
Pará, stm., Braz.	D9	54
Paracatu, Braz.	D5	57
Paracatu, stm., Braz.	D6	57
Paracel Islands, is., Asia	B5	32
Parachute, Co., U.S.	B2	83
Paradis, La., U.S.	k11	95
Paradise, Ca., U.S.	C3	82
Paradise, Nv., U.S.	G6	105
Paradise, stm., Newf., Can.	B3	72
Paradise Hills, N.M., U.S.	B3	108
Paradise Valley, Az., U.S.	k9	80
Paradise Valley, Nv., U.S.	B4	105
Paragould, Ar., U.S.	A5	81
Paraguaçu Paulista, Braz.	G3	57
Paraguaipoa, Ven.	B7	58
Paraguaná, Península de, pen., Ven.	B7	58
Paraguarí, Para.	B5	56
Paraguay, ctry., S.A.	A5	56
Paraguay, stm., S.A.	B5	56
Paraíba do Sul, stm., Braz.	F7	57
Parakou, Benin	G6	42
Paramagudi, India	H5	37
Paramaribo, Sur.	B7	54
Paramirim, Braz.	B7	57
Paramount, Md., U.S.	A2	97
Paramus, N.J., U.S.	h8	107
Paramušir, Ostrov, i., Russia	G25	24
Paraná, Arg.	C4	56
Paranã, Braz.	B5	57
Paranã, stm., Braz.	B5	57
Paraná, stm., S.A.	C5	56
Paranaguá, Braz.	B7	56
Paranaíba, Braz.	E3	57
Paranaíba, stm., Braz.	E3	57
Paranapanema, stm., Braz.	G3	57
Paranavaí, Braz.	G2	57
Parangaba, Braz.	D11	54
Paratinga, Braz.	B7	57
Paraúna, Braz.	D3	57
Paray-le-Monial, Fr.	F11	10
Pārbati, stm., India	H7	38
Parbhani, India	C4	37
Parchim, Ger.	B11	8
Parchment, Mi., U.S.	F5	99
Pardeeville, Wi., U.S.	E4	126
Pardo, stm., Braz.	F5	57
Pardubice, Czech.	E15	8
Parece Vela see Okino-Tori-shima, i., Japan	G14	26
Parecis, Serra dos, mts., Braz.	F7	54
Paredes de Nava, Spain	C7	12
Paren', Russia	E26	24
Parepare, Indon.	F6	32
Pargas (Parainen), Fin.	F14	6
Paria, stm., U.S.	A4	80
Paria, Gulf of, b.	I16	64
Pariaguán, Ven.	C10	58
Pariaman, Indon.	O6	34
Parícutin, vol., Mex.	H8	62
Parikkala, Fin.	F17	6
Parima, Sierra, mts., S.A.	F10	58
Pariñas, Punta, c., Peru	D2	54
Parintins, Braz.	D7	54
Paris, Ont., Can.	D4	73
Paris, Fr.	D9	10
Paris, Ar., U.S.	B2	81
Paris, Il., U.S.	D6	90
Paris, Ky., U.S.	B5	94
Paris, Mo., U.S.	B5	102
Paris, Tn., U.S.	A3	119
Paris, Tx., U.S.	C5	120
Paris Peak, mtn., Id., U.S.	G7	89
Parit Buntar, Malay.	L6	34
Park, co., Co., U.S.	B5	83
Park, co., Mt., U.S.	E6	103
Park, co., Wy., U.S.	B3	127
Park, stm., N.D., U.S.	A8	111
Parkano, Fin.	E14	6
Park City, Ks., U.S.	g12	93
Park City, Ut., U.S.	C4	121
Parkdale, P.E.I., Can.	C6	71
Parke, co., In., U.S.	E3	91
Parker, Az., U.S.	C1	80
Parker, Co., U.S.	B6	83
Parker, Fl., U.S.	u16	86
Parker, S.D., U.S.	D8	118
Parker, co., Tx., U.S.	C4	120
Parker, Cape, c., N.W. Ter., Can.	A17	66
Parker City, In., U.S.	D7	91
Parker Dam, U.S.	C1	80
Parkersburg, Ia., U.S.	B5	92
Parkersburg, W.V., U.S.	B3	125
Parkers Prairie, Mn., U.S.	D3	100
Parkesburg, Pa., U.S.	G10	115
Park Falls, Wi., U.S.	C3	126
Park Forest, Il., U.S.	B6	90
Park Hall, Md., U.S.	D5	97
Parkhill, Ont., Can.	D3	73
Park Hills, Ky., U.S.	h13	94
Parkin, Ar., U.S.	B5	81
Parkland, Wa., U.S.	f11	124
Park Layne, Oh., U.S.	C1	112
Park Range, mts., Co., U.S.	A4	83
Park Rapids, Mn., U.S.	D3	100
Park Ridge, Il., U.S.	B6	90
Park Ridge, N.J., U.S.	g8	107
Park River, N.D., U.S.	A8	111
Parkrose, Or., U.S.	B4	114
Parksley, Va., U.S.	C7	123
Parkston, S.D., U.S.	D8	118
Parksville, B.C., Can.	E5	69
Parkville, Md., U.S.	B4	97
Parkville, Mo., U.S.	B3	102
Parkwater, Wa., U.S.	g14	124
Parkwood, N.C., U.S.	B4	110
Parlākimidi, India	C8	37
Parle, Lac qui, l., Mn., U.S.	E3	100
Parlier, Ca., U.S.	D4	82
Parma, Italy	E5	14
Parma, Id., U.S.	F2	89
Parma, Mi., U.S.	F6	99
Parma, Mo., U.S.	E8	102
Parma, Oh., U.S.	A4	112
Parmachenee Lake, l., Me., U.S.	C2	96
Parma Heights, Oh., U.S.	h9	112
Parmer, co., Tx., U.S.	B1	120
Parnaíba, Braz.	D10	54
Parnaíba, stm., Braz.	D10	54
Pärnu, Est.	C7	18
Paro, Bhu.	G13	38
Parowan, Ut., U.S.	F3	121
Par Pond, res., S.C., U.S.	D5	117
Parral, Chile	D2	56
Parramore Island, i., Va., U.S.	C7	123
Parras de la Fuente, Mex.	E8	62
Parrish, Al., U.S.	B2	78
Parrsboro, N.S., Can.	D5	71
Parry, Cape, c., N.W. Ter., Can.	B8	66
Parry, Mount, mtn., B.C., Can.	C3	69
Parry Bay, b., N.W. Ter., Can.	C16	66
Parry Sound, Ont., Can.	B4	73
Parshall, N.D., U.S.	B3	111
Parsons, Ks., U.S.	E8	93
Parsons, Tn., U.S.	B3	119
Parsons, W.V., U.S.	B5	125
Parsonsburg, Md., U.S.	D7	97
Parthenay, Fr.	F6	10
Partinico, Italy	K8	14
Partridge Point, c., Newf., Can.	C3	72
Paru, stm., Braz.	D8	54
Pārvatīpuram, India	C7	37
Parys, S. Afr.	G5	44
Pasadena, Newf., Can.	D3	72
Pasadena, Ca., U.S.	E4	82
Pasadena, Md., U.S.	B4	97
Pasadena, Tx., U.S.	r14	120
Pascagoula, Ms., U.S.	E5	101
Pascagoula, stm., Ms., U.S.	E5	101
Pascagoula Bay, b., Ms., U.S.	f8	101
Pasco, Wa., U.S.	C6	124
Pasco, co., Fl., U.S.	D4	86
Pascoag, R.I., U.S.	B2	116
Pascoag Reservoir, res., R.I., U.S.	B2	116
Pascua, Isla de (Easter Island), i., Chile	H5	2
Pasewalk, Ger.	B13	8
Pasig, Phil.	q19	33b
P'asina, stm., Russia	C11	24
P'asino, Ozero, l., Russia	D11	24
P'asinskij Zaliv, b., Russia	C10	24
Pasirpengarajan, Indon.	N6	34
Pasir Puteh, Malay.	L7	34
Pasni, Pak.	D1	36
Paso de Indios, Arg.	E3	56
Paso de los Libres, Arg.	B5	56
Paso Robles, Ca., U.S.	E3	82
Pasque Island, i., Ma., U.S.	D6	98
Pasquotank, co., N.C., U.S.	A6	110
Passagem, Braz.	B7	57
Passaic, N.J., U.S.	B4	107
Passaic, co., N.J., U.S.	A4	107
Passaic, stm., N.J., U.S.	h8	107
Passamaquoddy Bay, b., Me., U.S.	C6	96
Passau, Ger.	G13	8
Pass Christian, Ms., U.S.	E4	101
Passo Fundo, Braz.	B6	56
Passos, Braz.	F5	57
Passumpsic, stm., Vt., U.S.	C4	122
Pasto, Col.	G4	58
Pastora Peak, mtn., Az., U.S.	A6	80
Pastrana, Spain	E9	12
Pasuruan, Indon.	m16	33a
Patagonia, Az., U.S.	F5	80
Patagonia, reg., Arg.	E3	56
Pātan, India	I5	38
Patapsco, stm., Md., U.S.	B4	97
Pataskala, Oh., U.S.	C3	112
Patchet Brook Reservoir, res., R.I., U.S.	E6	116
Patchogue, N.Y., U.S.	n15	109
Pate Island, i., Kenya	B8	44
Paternò, Italy	L9	14
Paterson, N.J., U.S.	B4	107
Pathānkot, India	D6	38
Pathein, Mya.	F3	34
Pathfinder Reservoir, res., Wy., U.S.	D6	127
Pati, Indon.	m15	33a
Patiāla, India	E7	38
Patience Island, i., R.I., U.S.	D5	116
P'atigorsk, Russia	I6	22
Pātkai Range, mts., Asia	G16	38
Patman, Lake, res., Tx., U.S.	C5	120
Patna, India	H11	38
Patoka, In., U.S.	H2	91
Patoka, stm., In., U.S.	H2	91
Patoka Lake, res., In., U.S.	H4	91
Patos, Braz.	E11	54
Patos, Lagoa dos, b., Braz.	C6	56
Patos de Minas, Braz.	E5	57
Patquía, Arg.	C3	56
Pátrai, Grc.	K5	16
Patricio Lynch, Isla, i., Chile	F1	56
Patrick, co., Va., U.S.	D2	123
Patrick Air Force Base, mil., Fl., U.S.	D6	86
Patrocínio, Braz.	E5	57
Pattani, Thai.	K6	34
Patten, Me., U.S.	C4	96
Patterson, Ga., U.S.	E4	87
Patterson, La., U.S.	E4	95
Patterson Creek, stm., W.V., U.S.	B5	125
Pattoki, Pak.	E5	38
Patton, Pa., U.S.	E4	115
Patuākhāli, Bngl.	I14	38
Patuca, stm., Hond.	G5	64
Patuxent, stm., Md., U.S.	D4	97
Patuxent Naval Air Test Center, mil., Md., U.S.	D5	97
Pátzcuaro, Mex.	H9	62
Pau, Fr.	I6	10
Paul, Id., U.S.	G5	89
Paulding, Oh., U.S.	A1	112
Paulding, co., Ga., U.S.	C2	87
Paulding, co., Oh., U.S.	A1	112
Paulina, La., U.S.	h10	95
Paulina Mountains, mts., Or., U.S.	D5	114
Paulina Peak, mtn., Or., U.S.	E5	114
Paulins Kill, stm., N.J., U.S.	A3	107
Paulistana, Braz.	E10	54
Paulistas, Braz.	E7	57
Paullina, Ia., U.S.	B2	92
Paulo Afonso, Braz.	E11	54
Paulsboro, N.J., U.S.	D2	107
Paul Stream, stm., Vt., U.S.	B5	122
Pauls Valley, Ok., U.S.	C4	113
Paungde, Mya.	E3	34
Pavia, Italy	D4	14
Pavilion Key, i., Fl., U.S.	G5	86
Pavlodar, Kaz.	G9	24
Pavlof Volcano, vol., Ak., U.S.	D7	79
Pavlovo, Russia	F26	18
Pavlovsk, Russia	G7	24
Pavlovskij Posad, Russia	F21	18
Pavo, Ga., U.S.	F3	87
Pavón, Col.	F6	58
Pavullo nel Frignano, Italy	E5	14
Pawcatuck, Ct., U.S.	D8	84
Pawcatuck, stm., R.I., U.S.	G1	116
Paw Creek, N.C., U.S.	B2	110
Pawhuska, Ok., U.S.	A5	113
Pawling, N.Y., U.S.	D7	109
Pawnee, Il., U.S.	D4	90
Pawnee, Ok., U.S.	A5	113
Pawnee, co., Ks., U.S.	D4	93
Pawnee, co., Ne., U.S.	D9	104
Pawnee, co., Ok., U.S.	A5	113
Pawnee, stm., Ks., U.S.	D3	93
Pawnee City, Ne., U.S.	D9	104
Pawpaw, Il., U.S.	B5	90
Paw Paw, Mi., U.S.	F5	99
Paw Paw, stm., Mi., U.S.	F4	99
Pawpaw Creek, stm., W.V., U.S.	h10	125
Pawtuckaway Pond, l., N.H., U.S.	D4	106
Pawtucket, R.I., U.S.	C4	116
Pawtuxet, stm., R.I., U.S.	C4	116
Paxton, Il., U.S.	C5	90
Paxton, Ma., U.S.	B4	98
Payakumbuh, Indon.	O6	34
Payette, Id., U.S.	E2	89
Payette, co., Id., U.S.	E2	89
Payette, North Fork, stm., Id., U.S.	E2	89
Payette, South Fork, stm., Id., U.S.	E3	89
Payette Lake, res., Id., U.S.	E3	89
Payne, Oh., U.S.	A1	112
Payne, co., Ok., U.S.	A4	113
Paynesville, Mn., U.S.	E4	100
Paysandú, Ur.	C5	56
Payson, Az., U.S.	C4	80
Payson, Il., U.S.	D2	90
Payson, Ut., U.S.	C4	121
Pazardžik, Bul.	G8	16
Pazarköy, Tur.	J11	16
Paz de Río, Col.	E6	58
Pazin, Cro.	D8	14
Pea, stm., Al., U.S.	D3	78
Peabody, Ks., U.S.	D6	93
Peabody, Ma., U.S.	A6	98
Peabody, stm., N.H., U.S.	B4	106
Peace, stm., Can.	E9	66
Peace, stm., Fl., U.S.	E5	86
Peace Dale, R.I., U.S.	F3	116
Peace River, Alta., Can.	A2	68
Peach, co., Ga., U.S.	D3	87
Peacham Pond, res., Vt., U.S.	C4	122
Peach Point, c., Ma., U.S.	f12	98
Peach Springs, Az., U.S.	B2	80
Peak District National Park, Eng., U.K.	H11	7
Peaks Island, i., Me., U.S.	g7	96
Peale, Mount, mtn., Ut., U.S.	E6	121
Pea Patch Island, i., De., U.S.	B3	85
Pea Ridge, Ar., U.S.	A1	81
Pea Ridge National Military Park, Ar., U.S.	A1	81
Pearisburg, Va., U.S.	C2	123
Pearl, Ms., U.S.	C3	101
Pearl, stm., U.S.	D3	101
Pearland, Tx., U.S.	r14	120
Pearl and Hermes Reef, rf., Hi., U.S.	k12	88
Pearl City, Hi., U.S.	B4	88
Pearl Harbor, b., Hi., U.S.	B3	88
Pearl Harbor Naval Station, mil., Hi., U.S.	g10	88
Pearlington, Ms., U.S.	E4	101
Pearl River, La., U.S.	D6	95
Pearl River, N.Y., U.S.	g12	109
Pearl River, co., Ms., U.S.	E4	101
Pearsall, Tx., U.S.	E3	120
Pearsoll Peak, mtn., Or., U.S.	E3	114
Pearson, Ga., U.S.	E4	87
Peary Land, reg., Grnld.	A16	128
Pease, stm., Tx., U.S.	B3	120
Pease Air Force Base, mil., N.H., U.S.	D5	106
Pebane, Moz.	E7	44
Peć, Yugo.	G4	16
Pecatonica, Il., U.S.	A4	90
Pecatonica, stm., U.S.	A4	90
Pecatonica, East Branch, stm., Wi., U.S.	F4	126
Peckerwood Lake, res., Ar., U.S.	C4	81
Pečora, stm., Russia	D5	24
Pecos, N.M., U.S.	B4	108
Pecos, Tx., U.S.	D1	120
Pecos, co., Tx., U.S.	D1	120
Pecos, stm., U.S.	E6	76
Pecos National Monument, N.M., U.S.	B4	108
Pécs, Hung.	I18	8
Peculiar, Mo., U.S.	C3	102
Peddocks Island, i., Ma., U.S.	g12	98
Pedernales, Ven.	C11	58
Pedregal, Ven.	B7	58
Pedro, Point, c., Sri L.	H6	37
Pedro de Valdivia, Chile	A3	56
Pedro Juan Caballero, Para.	G1	57
Peebles, Oh., U.S.	D2	112
Peekskill, N.Y., U.S.	D7	109
Peel, I. of Man	G8	7
Peel, stm., Can.	C5	66
Peel Point, c., N.W. Ter., Can.	B10	66
Peel Sound, strt., N.W. Ter., Can.	B13	66
Pegram, Tn., U.S.	A4	119
Pehuajó, Arg.	D4	56
Peikang, Tai.	L9	28
Peine, Ger.	C10	8
Pekalongan, Indon.	m14	32
Pekin, Il., U.S.	C4	90
Pekin, In., U.S.	G5	91
Peking see Beijing, China	D10	26
Pelagie, Isole, is., Italy	N7	14
Pelahatchie, Ms., U.S.	C4	101
Pelée, Montagne, mtn., Mart.	G17	64
Pelee Island, i., Ont., Can.	F2	73
Peleng, Pulau, i., Indon.	F7	32
Pelham, Ont., Can.	D5	73
Pelham, Al., U.S.	B3	78
Pelham, Ga., U.S.	E2	87
Pelham, N.H., U.S.	E4	106
Pelham Manor, N.Y., U.S.	h13	109
Pelican Bay, b., Man., Can.	C1	70
Pelican Lake, l., Man., Can.	C1	70
Pelican Lake, l., Mn., U.S.	D4	100
Pelican Lake, l., Mn., U.S.	D3	100
Pelican Lake, l., Mn., U.S.	B6	100
Pelican Lake, l., Mn., U.S.	E5	100
Pelican Lake, l., Wi., U.S.	C4	126
Pelican Mountain, mtn., Alta., Can.	B4	68
Pelican Rapids, Mn., U.S.	D2	100
Pella, Ia., U.S.	C5	92
Pell City, Al., U.S.	B3	78
Pell Lake, Wi., U.S.	n11	126
Pello, Fin.	C14	6
Pelly Mountains, mts., Yukon, Can.	D6	66
Pelopónnisos, reg., Grc.	L5	16
Pelotas, Braz.	C6	56
Pelton, Lake, l., La., U.S.	E5	95
Pemadumcook Lake, l., Me., U.S.	C3	96
Pemalang, Indon.	m14	33a
Pematangsiantar, Indon.	E2	32
Pemba, Moz.	D8	44
Pemba Island, i., Tan.	C7	44
Pemberton, Austl.	F3	50
Pemberville, Oh., U.S.	A2	112
Pembina, N.D., U.S.	A8	111
Pembina, co., N.D., U.S.	A8	111
Pembina, stm., Alta., Can.	C3	68
Pembroke, Ont., Can.	B7	73
Pembroke, Wales, U.K.	J8	7
Pembroke, Ga., U.S.	D5	87
Pembroke, Ky., U.S.	D2	94
Pembroke, Ma., U.S.	B6	98
Pembroke, N.C., U.S.	C3	110
Pembroke, Va., U.S.	C2	123
Pembroke Pines, Fl., U.S.	r13	86
Pemigewasset, stm., N.H., U.S.	C3	106
Pemiscot, co., Mo., U.S.	E8	102
Peñafiel, Spain	D7	12
Penápolis, Braz.	F3	57
Peñaranda de Bracamonte, Spain	E6	12
Pen Argyl, Pa., U.S.	E11	115
Peñarroya-Pueblonuevo, Spain	G6	12
Penas, Golfo de, b., Chile	F1	56
Penasco, N.M., U.S.	A4	108
Peñasco, Rio, stm., N.M., U.S.	E4	108
Penbrook, Pa., U.S.	F8	115
Pender, Ne., U.S.	B9	104
Pender, co., N.C., U.S.	C4	110
Pendleton, In., U.S.	E6	91
Pendleton, Or., U.S.	B8	114
Pendleton, S.C., U.S.	B2	117
Pendleton, co., Ky., U.S.	B5	94
Pendleton, co., W.V., U.S.	C5	125
Pendley Hills, Ga., U.S.	*h8	87
Pend Oreille, co., Wa., U.S.	A8	124
Pend Oreille, Lake, l., Id., U.S.	A2	89
Pend Oreille, Mount, mtn., Id., U.S.	A2	89
Penetanguishene, Ont., Can.	C5	73
P'enghu Liehtao, is., Tai.	L8	28
Penglai, China	D11	26
Penhold, Alta., Can.	C4	68
Peniche, Port.	F2	12
Penjamo, Mex.	G9	62
Pennant Point, c., N.S., Can.	E6	71
Pennask Mountain, mtn., B.C., Can.	E7	69
Penne, Italy	G8	14
Pennell, Mount, mtn., Ut., U.S.	F5	121
Penner, stm., India	E5	37
Penn Hills, Pa., U.S.	k14	115
Pennines, mts., Eng., U.K.	G10	7
Pennines, Alpes, mts., Eur.	F14	10
Pennington, co., Mn., U.S.	B2	100
Pennington, co., S.D., U.S.	D2	118
Pennington Gap, Va., U.S.	f8	123
Pennsauken, N.J., U.S.	D2	107
Pennsboro, W.V., U.S.	B4	125
Pennsburg, Pa., U.S.	F11	115
Penns Grove, N.J., U.S.	D2	107
Pennsville, N.J., U.S.	D1	107
Pennsylvania, state, U.S.	E7	115
Pennville, In., U.S.	D7	91
Penn Yan, N.Y., U.S.	C3	109
Penobscot, co., Me., U.S.	C4	96
Penobscot, stm., Me., U.S.	C4	96
Penobscot Bay, b., Me., U.S.	D3	96
Penobscot Lake, l., Me., U.S.	C2	96
Penonomé, Pan.	J7	64
Penrith, Eng., U.K.	G10	7
Pensacola, Fl., U.S.	u14	86
Pensacola Bay, b., Fl., U.S.	u14	86
Pensacola Dam, Ok., U.S.	A6	113
Pensacola Naval Air Station, mil., Fl., U.S.	u14	86
Pentagon Mountain, mtn., Mt., U.S.	C3	103
Penticton, B.C., Can.	E8	69
Pentland Firth, strt., Scot., U.K.	C9	7
Pentwater, Mi., U.S.	E4	99
Penyu, Kepulauan, is., Indon.	G8	32
Penza, Russia	G7	22
Penzance, Eng., U.K.	K7	7
Penžina, stm., Russia	E27	24
Penžinskaja Guba, b., Russia	E26	24
Penžinskij Chrebet, mts., Russia	E27	24
Peonan Point, c., Man., Can.	D2	70
Peoria, Az., U.S.	D3	80
Peoria, Il., U.S.	C4	90
Peoria, co., Il., U.S.	C4	90
Peoria Heights, Il., U.S.	C4	90
Peotone, Il., U.S.	B6	90
Pepacton Reservoir, res., N.Y., U.S.	C6	109
Pepeekeo, Hi., U.S.	D6	88
Pepin, Wi., U.S.	D1	126
Pepin, co., Wi., U.S.	D2	126
Pepin, Lake, l., U.S.	D1	126
Pepperell, Ma., U.S.	A4	98
Pequannock, N.J., U.S.	B4	107
Pequest, stm., N.J., U.S.	B2	107
Pequop Mountains, mts., Nv., U.S.	C7	105
Pequot Lakes, Mn., U.S.	D4	100
Perabumulih, Indon.	F3	32
Percy, Il., U.S.	E4	90
Perdido, Al., U.S.	D2	78
Perdido, stm., U.S.	E2	78
Perdido Bay, b., Al., U.S.	E2	78
Pereira, Col.	E5	58
Pere Marquette, stm., Mi., U.S.	E4	99
Pereslavl'-Zalesskij, Russia	E21	18
Pergamino, Arg.	C4	56
Pergine Valsugana, Italy	C6	14
Perham, Mn., U.S.	D3	100
Péribonca, stm., Que., Can.	G18	66
Peridot, Az., U.S.	D5	80
Périgueux, Fr.	G7	10
Perijá, Sierra de, mts., S.A.	B6	58
Perkasie, Pa., U.S.	F11	115
Perkins, Ok., U.S.	B4	113
Perkins, co., Ne., U.S.	D4	104
Perkins, co., S.D., U.S.	B3	118
Perkinston, Ms., U.S.	E4	101
Perlas, Archipiélago de las, is., Pan.	J8	64
Perlas, Laguna de, b., Nic.	H6	64
Perleberg, Ger.	B11	8
Perm', Russia	F9	22
Pernik, Bul.	G7	16
Péronne, Fr.	C9	10
Perpignan, Fr.	J9	10
Perquimans, co., N.C., U.S.	A6	110
Perrine, Fl., U.S.	G6	86
Perris, Ca., U.S.	F5	82
Perro, Laguna del, l., N.M., U.S.	C4	108
Perros-Guirec, Fr.	D3	10
Perrot, Île, i., Que., Can.	q19	74
Perry, Fl., U.S.	B3	86
Perry, Ga., U.S.	D3	87
Perry, Ia., U.S.	C3	92
Perry, Ks., U.S.	C8	93
Perry, Mi., U.S.	F6	99
Perry, Mo., U.S.	B6	102
Perry, N.Y., U.S.	C2	109
Perry, Oh., U.S.	A4	112
Perry, Ok., U.S.	A4	113
Perry, Ut., U.S.	B3	121
Perry, co., Al., U.S.	C2	78
Perry, co., Ar., U.S.	C3	81
Perry, co., Il., U.S.	E4	90
Perry, co., In., U.S.	H4	91
Perry, co., Ky., U.S.	C6	94
Perry, co., Ms., U.S.	D4	101
Perry, co., Mo., U.S.	D8	102
Perry, co., Oh., U.S.	C3	112
Perry, co., Pa., U.S.	F7	115
Perry, co., Tn., U.S.	B4	119
Perry Hall, Md., U.S.	B5	97
Perry Lake, res., Ks., U.S.	C8	93
Perryman, Md., U.S.	B5	97
Perrysburg, Oh., U.S.	A2	112
Perry Stream, stm., N.H., U.S.	f7	106
Perry's Victory and International Peace Memorial, hist., Oh., U.S.	A2	112
Perryton, Tx., U.S.	A2	120
Perryville, Ar., U.S.	B3	81
Perryville, Ky., U.S.	C5	94
Perryville, Md., U.S.	A5	97
Perryville, Mo., U.S.	D8	102
Pershing, co., Nv., U.S.	C3	105
Persia see Iran, ctry., Asia	B5	46
Persian Gulf, b., Asia	C5	46
Person, co., N.C., U.S.	A3	110
Perth, Austl.	F3	50
Perth, Ont., Can.	C8	73
Perth, Scot., U.K.	E9	7
Perth Amboy, N.J., U.S.	B4	107
Perth-Andover, N.B., Can.	D10	71
Pertuis, Fr.	I12	10
Peru, Il., U.S.	B4	90
Peru, In., U.S.	C5	91
Peru, Ne., U.S.	D10	104
Peru, N.Y., U.S.	f11	109
Peru (Perú), ctry., S.A.	E3	54
Perugia, Italy	F7	14
Perušić, Cro.	E10	14
Pesaro, Italy	F7	14
Pescadores see P'enghu Liehtao, is., Tai.	L8	28
Pescara, Italy	G9	14
Pescia, Italy	F5	14
Peshastin, Wa., U.S.	B5	124
Peshāwar, Pak.	C4	38
Peshtigo, Wi., U.S.	C6	126
Peshtigo, stm., Wi., U.S.	C5	126
Pesqueira, Braz.	E11	54
Pessac, Fr.	H6	10
Petaḥ Tiqwa, Isr.	C4	40

Name	Map Ref	Page
Petal, Ms., U.S.	D4	101
Petaluma, Ca., U.S.	C2	82
Petatlán, Mex.	I9	62
Petawawa, Ont., Can.	B7	73
Petawawa, stm., Ont., Can.	A6	73
Petenwell Lake, res., Wi., U.S.	D4	126
Peterborough, Austl.	F7	50
Peterborough, Ont., Can.	C6	73
Peterborough, Eng., U.K.	I12	7
Peterborough, N.H., U.S.	E3	106
Peterhead, Scot., U.K.	D11	7
Peter Pond Lake, l., Sask., Can.	m7	75
Petersburg, Ak., U.S.	D13	79
Petersburg, Il., U.S.	C4	90
Petersburg, In., U.S.	H3	91
Petersburg, Mi., U.S.	G7	99
Petersburg, Oh., U.S.	B5	112
Petersburg, Tx., U.S.	C2	120
Petersburg, Va., U.S.	C5	123
Petersburg, W.V., U.S.	B5	125
Peters Creek, stm., W.V., U.S.	m14	125
Peterson, Al., U.S.	B2	78
Peterson Field, mil., Co., U.S.	C6	83
Petersville, Al., U.S.	A2	78
Petit Bois Island, i., Ms., U.S.	E5	101
Petitcodiac, N.B., Can.	D4	71
Petitcodiac, stm., N.B., Can.	C5	71
Petite Amite, stm., La., U.S.	h10	95
Petit Jean, stm., Ar., U.S.	B2	81
Petit Lac Des Allemands, l., La., U.S.	k11	95
Petit Lake, l., La., U.S.	k12	95
Petitot, stm., Can.	E8	66
Petit-Rocher, N.B., Can.	B4	71
Petitsikapau Lake, l., Newf., Can.	g8	72
Petlād, India	I5	38
Petone, N.Z.	D5	52
Petoskey, Mi., U.S.	C6	99
Petrified Forest National Park, Az., U.S.	B6	80
Petrila, Rom.	D7	16
Petrinja, Cro.	D11	14
Petroleum, co., Mt., U.S.	C8	103
Petrolia, Ont., Can.	E2	73
Petrolina, Braz.	E10	54
Petropavlovsk-Kamčatskij, Russia	G25	24
Petrópolis, Braz.	G7	57
Petros, Tn., U.S.	C9	119
Petroşani, Rom.	D7	16
Petrovsk-Zabajkal'skij, Russia	G15	24
Petrozavodsk, Russia	E4	22
Pettaquamscutt Lake Shores, R.I., U.S.	F4	116
Pettingell Peak, mtn., Co., U.S.	B5	83
Pettis, co., Mo., U.S.	C4	102
Pevek, Russia	D28	24
Pevely, Mo., U.S.	g13	102
Pewaukee, Wi., U.S.	E5	126
Pewaukee Lake, l., Wi., U.S.	m11	126
Pewee Valley, Ky., U.S.	B4	94
Pézenas, Fr.	I10	10
Pforzheim, Ger.	G8	8
Pfungstadt, Ger.	F8	8
Pha-an, Mya.	F4	34
Phagwāra, India	E6	38
Phalsbourg, Fr.	D14	10
Phaltan, India	D3	37
Phangan, Ko, i., Thai.	J6	34
Phangnga, Thai.	J5	34
Phanom Dongrak, Thiu Khao, mts., Asia	G7	34
Phan Rang, Viet.	I10	34
Phan Si Pan, mtn., Viet.	C7	34
Phan Thiet, Viet.	I10	34
Pharr, Tx., U.S.	F3	120
Phatthalung, Thai.	K6	34
Phayao, Thai.	E5	34
Phelps, Ky., U.S.	C7	94
Phelps, N.Y., U.S.	C3	109
Phelps, Wi., U.S.	B4	126
Phelps, co., Mo., U.S.	D6	102
Phelps, co., Ne., U.S.	D6	104
Phelps Lake, l., N.C., U.S.	B6	110
Phenix City, Al., U.S.	C4	78
Phetchaburi, Thai.	H5	34
Philadelphia, Ms., U.S.	C4	101
Philadelphia, Pa., U.S.	G11	115
Philadelphia, co., Pa., U.S.	G12	115
Philadelphia Naval Shipyard, mil., Pa., U.S.	P21	115
Phil Campbell, Al., U.S.	A2	78
Philip, S.D., U.S.	C4	118
Philippeville, Bel.	E4	8
Philippi, W.V., U.S.	B4	125
Philippines, ctry., Asia	C7	32
Philippine Sea	E21	2
Philipsburg, Mt., U.S.	D3	103
Philipsburg, Pa., U.S.	E5	115
Philleo Lake, l., Wa., U.S.	h14	124
Phillips, Me., U.S.	D2	96
Phillips, Tx., U.S.	B2	120
Phillips, Wi., U.S.	C3	126
Phillips, co., Ar., U.S.	C5	81
Phillips, co., Co., U.S.	A8	83
Phillips, co., Ks., U.S.	C4	93
Phillips, co., Mt., U.S.	B8	103
Phillips Brook, stm., N.H., U.S.	A4	106
Phillipsburg, Ks., U.S.	C4	93
Phillipsburg, N.J., U.S.	B2	107
Philmont, N.Y., U.S.	C7	109
Philo, Il., U.S.	C5	90
Philomath, Or., U.S.	C3	114
Philpots Island, i., N.W. Ter., Can.	B17	66
Philpott Reservoir, res., Va., U.S.	D2	123
Phitsanulok, Thai.	F6	34
Phnom Penh see Phnum Pénh, Camb.	I8	34
Phnum Pénh (Phnom Penh), Camb.	I8	34
Phoenix, Az., U.S.	D3	80
Phoenix, Il., U.S.	k9	90
Phoenix, N.Y., U.S.	B4	109
Phoenix, Or., U.S.	E4	114
Phoenixville, Pa., U.S.	F10	115
Phôngsali, Laos	D7	34
Phrae, Thai.	E6	34
Phra Nakhon Si Ayutthaya, Thai.	G6	34
Phuket, Thai.	K5	34
Phuket, Ko, i., Thai.	K5	34
Phu Ly, Viet.	D8	34
Phumĭ Béng, Camb.	H8	34
Phumĭ Kâmpóng Trâbêk, Camb.	H8	34
Phu Quoc, Dao, i., Viet.	I7	34
Phu Tho, Viet.	D8	34
Piacenza, Italy	D4	14
Piatra-Neamţ, Rom.	C10	16
Piatt, co., Il., U.S.	D5	90
Piazza Armerina, Italy	L9	14
Pibor Post, Sudan	G12	42
Picacho, Az., U.S.	E4	80
Picardie, hist. reg., Fr.	C9	10
Picayune, Ms., U.S.	E4	101
Piccadilly, Newf., Can.	D2	72
Pichanal, Arg.	A4	56
Picher, Ok., U.S.	A7	113
Pickaway, co., Oh., U.S.	C2	112
Pickens, Ms., U.S.	C4	101
Pickens, S.C., U.S.	B2	117
Pickens, co., Al., U.S.	B1	78
Pickens, co., Ga., U.S.	B2	87
Pickens, co., S.C., U.S.	B2	117
Pickerel Lake, l., Wi., U.S.	C5	126
Pickering, Ont., Can.	D5	73
Pickerington, Oh., U.S.	C3	112
Pickett, co., Tn., U.S.	C8	119
Pickwick Lake, res., U.S.	A6	101
Pickworth Point, c., Ma., U.S.	f12	98
Pico Rivera, Ca., U.S.	n12	82
Picos, Braz.	E10	54
Picquigny, Fr.	C9	10
Picton, Ont., Can.	D7	73
Pictou Island, i., N.S., Can.	D7	71
Picture Butte, Alta., Can.	E4	68
Pictured Rocks National Lakeshore, Mi., U.S.	B4	99
Pidálion, Akrotírion, c., Cyp.	B4	40
Pidurutalagala, mtn., Sri L.	I6	37
Piedmont, Al., U.S.	B4	78
Piedmont, Ca., U.S.	h8	82
Piedmont, Mo., U.S.	D7	102
Piedmont, Ok., U.S.	B4	113
Piedmont, S.C., U.S.	B3	117
Piedmont, W.V., U.S.	B5	125
Piedmont Lake, res., Oh., U.S.	B4	112
Piedra, stm., Co., U.S.	D3	83
Piedrabuena, Spain	F7	12
Piedrahita, Spain	E6	12
Piedras Blancas, Point, c., Ca., U.S.	E3	82
Piedras Negras, Guat.	F2	64
Piedras Negras, Mex.	C9	62
Pieksämäki, Fin.	E16	6
Pierce, Co., U.S.	A6	83
Pierce, Id., U.S.	C3	89
Pierce, Ne., U.S.	B8	104
Pierce, co., Ga., U.S.	E4	87
Pierce, co., Ne., U.S.	B8	104
Pierce, co., N.D., U.S.	A5	111
Pierce, co., Wa., U.S.	C3	124
Pierce, co., Wi., U.S.	D1	126
Pierce, Lake, l., Fl., U.S.	E5	86
Pierce City, Mo., U.S.	E3	102
Pierceton, In., U.S.	B6	91
Pierre, S.D., U.S.	C5	118
Pierre-Buffière, Fr.	G8	10
Pierrefonds, Que., Can.	q19	74
Pierre Part, La., U.S.	k9	95
Pierreville, Que., Can.	C5	74
Pierson, Fl., U.S.	C5	86
Pierz, Mn., U.S.	E4	100
Pietermaritzburg, S. Afr.	G6	44
Pietersburg, S. Afr.	F5	44
Pietrasanta, Italy	F5	14
Piet Retief, S. Afr.	G6	44
Pigeon, Mi., U.S.	E7	99
Pigeon, stm., U.S.	f9	110
Pigeon, stm., In., U.S.	A6	91
Pigeon, stm., Mn., U.S.	h10	100
Pigeon, stm., Wi., U.S.	k10	126
Pigeon Cove, Ma., U.S.	A6	98
Pigeon Forge, Tn., U.S.	D10	119
Pigeon Point, c., Mn., U.S.	h10	100
Pigg, stm., Va., U.S.	D3	123
Piggott, Ar., U.S.	A5	81
Pihlajavesi, l., Fin.	F17	6
Pihtipudas, Fin.	E15	6
Pijijiapan, Mex.	J13	62
Pikal'ovo, Russia	B17	18
Pike, co., Al., U.S.	D4	78
Pike, co., Ar., U.S.	C2	81
Pike, co., Ga., U.S.	C2	87
Pike, co., Il., U.S.	D2	90
Pike, co., In., U.S.	H3	91
Pike, co., Ky., U.S.	C7	94
Pike, co., Ms., U.S.	D3	101
Pike, co., Mo., U.S.	B6	102
Pike, co., Oh., U.S.	C2	112
Pike, co., Pa., U.S.	D11	115
Pike, stm., Wi., U.S.	C6	126
Pike Island Dam, U.S.	f8	125
Pike Lake, Mn., U.S.	D6	100
Pikes Peak, mtn., Co., U.S.	C5	83
Pikesville, Md., U.S.	B4	97
Piketberg, S. Afr.	H3	44
Piketon, Oh., U.S.	C2	112
Pikeville, Ky., U.S.	C7	94
Pikeville, Tn., U.S.	D8	119
Piła (Schneidemühl), Pol.	B16	8
Pilar do Sul, Braz.	G5	57
Pilcomayo, stm., S.A.	A4	56
Pīlībhīt, India	F8	38
Pillar Point, c., Ca., U.S.	k7	82
Pilot Grove, Mo., U.S.	C5	102
Pilot Knob, Mo., U.S.	D7	102
Pilot Knob, mtn., Id., U.S.	D3	89
Pilot Mound, Man., Can.	E2	70
Pilot Mountain, N.C., U.S.	A2	110
Pilot Peak, mtn., Nv., U.S.	B7	105
Pilot Peak, mtn., Nv., U.S.	E4	105
Pilot Peak, mtn., Wy., U.S.	B3	127
Pilot Point, Tx., U.S.	C4	120
Pilot Range, mts., Nv., U.S.	B7	105
Pilot Rock, Or., U.S.	B8	114
Pilot Station, Ak., U.S.	C7	79
Pima, Az., U.S.	E6	80
Pima, co., Az., U.S.	E3	80
Pimentel, Peru	E3	54
Pimmit Hills, Va., U.S.	g12	123
Pina, Spain	D11	12
Pinal, co., Az., U.S.	E4	80
Pinaleno Mountains, mts., Az., U.S.	E5	80
Pinal Mountains, mts., Az., U.S.	D5	80
Pinang see George Town, Malay.	L6	34
Pinar del Río, Cuba	C6	64
Pinardville, N.H., U.S.	E3	106
Pincher Creek, Alta., Can.	E4	68
Pinckard, Al., U.S.	D4	78
Pinckney, Mi., U.S.	F7	99
Pinckney Island, i., S.C., U.S.	G6	117
Pinckneyville, Il., U.S.	E4	90
Pinconning, Mi., U.S.	E7	99
Píndhos Óros, mts., Grc.	J5	16
Pindi Gheb, Pak.	D5	38
Pindus Mountains see Píndhos Óros, mts., Grc.	J5	16
Pine, Az., U.S.	C4	80
Pine, co., Mn., U.S.	D6	100
Pine, stm., Mi., U.S.	D7	99
Pine, stm., Mi., U.S.	D5	99
Pine, stm., N.H., U.S.	C4	106
Pine, stm., Wi., U.S.	C5	126
Pine, stm., Wi., U.S.	C4	126
Pine Barrens, reg., N.J., U.S.	D3	107
Pine Bluff, Ar., U.S.	C3	81
Pinebluff, N.C., U.S.	B3	110
Pine Bluffs, Wy., U.S.	E8	127
Pine Bridge, Ct., U.S.	D3	84
Pine Castle, Fl., U.S.	D5	86
Pine City, Mn., U.S.	E6	100
Pine Creek, stm., Nv., U.S.	C5	105
Pine Creek, stm., Pa., U.S.	C6	115
Pine Creek, stm., Wa., U.S.	B8	124
Pine Creek Lake, res., Ok., U.S.	C6	113
Pinedale, Wy., U.S.	D3	127
Pine Falls, Man., Can.	D3	70
Pine Forest Range, mts., Nv., U.S.	B3	105
Pine Grove, Pa., U.S.	E9	115
Pine Grove Mills, Pa., U.S.	E6	115
Pine Hill, N.J., U.S.	D3	107
Pine Hills, Fl., U.S.	D5	86
Pinehouse Lake, Sask., Can.	B2	75
Pinehouse Lake, l., Sask., Can.	B2	75
Pinehurst, Ma., U.S.	f11	98
Pinehurst, N.C., U.S.	B3	110
Pine Island, Mn., U.S.	F6	100
Pine Island, i., Fl., U.S.	F4	86
Pine Island Sound, strt., Fl., U.S.	F4	86
Pine Key, i., Fl., U.S.	p10	86
Pine Knot, Ky., U.S.	D5	94
Pine Lake, Ga., U.S.	h8	87
Pine Lake, l., In., U.S.	A4	91
Pine Lake, l., Wi., U.S.	C5	126
Pine Lawn, Mo., U.S.	f13	102
Pine Level, N.C., U.S.	B4	110
Pinellas, co., Fl., U.S.	D4	86
Pinellas, Point, c., Fl., U.S.	p10	86
Pinellas Park, Fl., U.S.	E4	86
Pine Mountain, Ga., U.S.	D2	87
Pine Mountain, mtn., Or., U.S.	D6	114
Pine Mountain, mtn., Wy., U.S.	E3	127
Pine Point, N.W. Ter., Can.	D10	66
Pine Point, Me., U.S.	E2	96
Pine Prairie, La., U.S.	D3	95
Pine Ridge, S.D., U.S.	D3	118
Pine Ridge Indian Reservation, S.D., U.S.	D3	118
Pine River, Mn., U.S.	D4	100
Pinerolo, Italy	E2	14
Pines, Lake O' the, res., Tx., U.S.	C5	120
Pinesdale, Mt., U.S.	D2	103
Pinetops, N.C., U.S.	B5	110
Pine Valley, val., Ut., U.S.	E2	121
Pineville, Ky., U.S.	D6	94
Pineville, La., U.S.	C3	95
Pineville, N.C., U.S.	B2	110
Pineville, W.V., U.S.	D3	125
Pinewood, S.C., U.S.	D7	117
Piney Creek, stm., W.V., U.S.	n13	125
Piney Fork, stm., W.V., U.S.	h9	125
Piney Point, Md., U.S.	D4	97
Piney View, W.V., U.S.	n13	125
Ping, stm., Thai.	F5	34
Pingdingshan, China	E9	26
Pinghu, China	E10	28
Pingliang, China	D8	26
Pingtan Dao, i., China	J8	28
P'ingtung, Tai.	M9	28
Pingxiang, China	H2	28
Pingyao, China	D9	26
Pinhel, Port.	E4	12
Pinnacles National Monument, Ca., U.S.	D3	82
Pinneberg, Ger.	B9	8
Pinole, Ca., U.S.	h8	82
Pinopolis Dam, S.C., U.S.	E8	117
Pinos, Mount, mtn., Ca., U.S.	E4	82
Pins, Pointe aux, c., Ont., Can.	E3	73
Pinsk, Bela.	I9	18
Pinson, Al., U.S.	f7	78
Pinta, Sierra, mts., Az., U.S.	E2	80
Pintwater Range, mts., Nv., U.S.	G6	105
Pioche, Nv., U.S.	F7	105
Piombino, Italy	G5	14
Pioneer, Oh., U.S.	A1	112
Pioneer Mountains, mts., Id., U.S.	F5	89
Pioneer Mountains, mts., Mt., U.S.	E3	103
Pionér, Ostrov, i., Russia	B12	24
Piotrków Trybunalski, Pol.	D19	8
Pipe Spring National Monument, Az., U.S.	A3	80
Pipestem Creek, stm., N.D., U.S.	B6	111
Pipestone, Mn., U.S.	G2	100
Pipestone, co., Mn., U.S.	F2	100
Pipestone, stm., Ont., Can.	F14	66
Pipestone National Monument, Mn., U.S.	G2	100
Pipestone Pass, Mt., U.S.	E4	103
Pipmuacan, Réservoir, res., Que., Can.	k12	74
Piqua, Oh., U.S.	B1	112
Piracicaba, Braz.	G5	57
Piraeus see Piraiévs, Grc.	L7	16
Piraí do Sul, Braz.	A7	56
Piraiévs (Piraeus), Grc.	L7	16
Piraju, Braz.	G4	57
Piran, Slo.	D8	14
Pirané, Arg.	B5	56
Pirapora, Braz.	D6	57
Pires do Rio, Braz.	D4	57
Pírgos, Grc.	L5	16
Pirmasens, Ger.	F7	8
Pirna, Ger.	E13	8
Pirtleville, Az., U.S.	F6	80
Piru, Indon.	F8	32
Pisa, Italy	F5	14
Pisagua, Chile	G4	54
Piscataqua, stm., N.H., U.S.	D5	106
Piscataquis, co., Me., U.S.	C3	96
Piscataquis, stm., Me., U.S.	C3	96
Piscataquog, stm., N.H., U.S.	D3	106
Piscataway, N.J., U.S.	B4	107
Pisco, Peru	F3	54
Piseco Lake, l., N.Y., U.S.	B6	109
Písek, Czech.	F14	8
Pisgah, Al., U.S.	A4	78
Pisgah, Oh., U.S.	n13	112
Pisgah, Mount, mtn., Wy., U.S.	B8	127
Pisgah Forest, N.C., U.S.	f10	110
Pishan, China	B8	38
Pismo Beach, Ca., U.S.	E3	82
Pisticci, Italy	I11	14
Pistoia, Italy	F5	14
Pistolet Bay, b., Newf., Can.	C4	72
Pit, stm., Ca., U.S.	B3	82
Pitalito, Col.	G4	58
Pitcairn, Pa., U.S.	k14	115
Pitcairn, dep., Oc.	H4	2
Piteå, Swe.	D13	6
Piteşti, Rom.	E8	16
Pithāpuram, India	D7	37
Pithiviers, Fr.	D9	10
Pitiquito, Mex.	B3	62
Pitkin, co., Co., U.S.	B4	83
Pitlochry, Scot., U.K.	E9	7
Pitman, N.J., U.S.	D2	107
Pitt, co., N.C., U.S.	B5	110
Pitt Island, i., B.C., Can.	C3	69
Pittsboro, In., U.S.	E5	91
Pittsboro, N.C., U.S.	B3	110
Pittsburg, Ca., U.S.	g9	82
Pittsburg, Ks., U.S.	E9	93
Pittsburg, Ky., U.S.	C5	94
Pittsburg, Tx., U.S.	C5	120
Pittsburg, co., Ok., U.S.	C6	113
Pittsburgh, Pa., U.S.	F1	115
Pittsfield, Il., U.S.	D3	90
Pittsfield, Me., U.S.	D3	96
Pittsfield, Ma., U.S.	B1	98
Pittsfield, N.H., U.S.	D4	106
Pittsford, Vt., U.S.	D2	122
Pittston, Pa., U.S.	D10	115
Pittsville, Md., U.S.	D7	97
Pittsville, Wi., U.S.	D3	126
Pittsylvania, co., Va., U.S.	D3	123
Piu, Cerro, mtn., Nic.	H5	64
Piura, Peru	E2	54
Piute, co., Ut., U.S.	E3	121
Piute Peak, mtn., Ca., U.S.	E4	82
Piute Reservoir, res., Ut., U.S.	E3	121
Pivdennyy Buh, stm., Ukr.	H3	22
Pixley, Ca., U.S.	E4	82
Pizzo, Italy	K11	14
Placentia, Newf., Can.	E5	72
Placentia Bay, b., Newf., Can.	E4	72
Placer, co., Ca., U.S.	C3	82
PLacer Mountain, mtn., N.M., U.S.	k8	108
Placerville, Ca., U.S.	C3	82
Placetas, Cuba	C8	64
Placid, Lake, l., Fl., U.S.	E5	86
Placid, Lake, l., N.Y., U.S.	f11	109
Placitas, N.M., U.S.	B3	108
Plain City, Oh., U.S.	B2	112
Plain City, Ut., U.S.	B3	121
Plain Dealing, La., U.S.	B2	95
Plainfield, Ct., U.S.	C8	84
Plainfield, Il., U.S.	B5	90
Plainfield, In., U.S.	E5	91
Plainfield, N.J., U.S.	B4	107
Plainfield, Vt., U.S.	C4	122
Plainfield, Wi., U.S.	D4	126
Plainfield Heights, Mi., U.S.	*E5	99
Plains, Ga., U.S.	D2	87
Plains, Ks., U.S.	E3	93
Plains, Mt., U.S.	C2	103
Plains, Pa., U.S.	n17	115
Plains, Tx., U.S.	C1	120
Plainview, Ar., U.S.	C2	81
Plainview, Mn., U.S.	F6	100
Plainview, Ne., U.S.	B8	104
Plainview, Tx., U.S.	B2	120
Plainville, Ct., U.S.	C4	84
Plainville, Ks., U.S.	C4	93
Plainville, Ma., U.S.	B5	98
Plainwell, Mi., U.S.	F5	99
Plaistow, N.H., U.S.	E4	106
Plankinton, S.D., U.S.	D7	118
Plano, Il., U.S.	B5	90
Plano, Tx., U.S.	C4	120
Plantagenet, Ont., Can.	B9	73
Plantation, Fl., U.S.	r13	86
Plant City, Fl., U.S.	D4	86
Plantersville, Al., U.S.	C3	78
Plantersville, Ms., U.S.	A5	101
Plantsite, Az., U.S.	D6	80
Plantsville, Ct., U.S.	C4	84
Plaquemine, La., U.S.	D4	95
Plaquemines, co., La., U.S.	E6	95
Plasencia, Spain	E5	12
Plaški, Cro.	D10	14
Plaster Rock, N.B., Can.	C2	71
Plata, Río de la, est., S.A.	D5	56
Platte, S.D., U.S.	D7	118
Platte, co., Mo., U.S.	B3	102
Platte, co., Ne., U.S.	C8	104
Platte, co., Wy., U.S.	D7	127
Platte, stm., U.S.	B3	102
Platte, stm., Mn., U.S.	E4	100
Platte, stm., Ne., U.S.	D6	104
Platte City, Mo., U.S.	B3	102
Platte Island, i., Sey.	C11	44
Platteville, Co., U.S.	A6	83
Platteville, Wi., U.S.	F3	126
Plattling, Ger.	G12	8
Plattsburg, Mo., U.S.	B3	102
Plattsburgh, N.Y., U.S.	f11	109
Plattsburgh Air Force Base, mil., N.Y., U.S.	f11	109
Plattsmouth, Ne., U.S.	D10	104
Plau, Ger.	B12	8
Plauen, Ger.	E12	8
Playas Lake, l., N.M., U.S.	F2	108
Play Cu, Viet.	H9	34
Playgreen Lake, l., Man., Can.	B2	70
Pleasant, stm., Me., U.S.	C3	96
Pleasant, Lake, res., Az., U.S.	D3	80
Pleasant Gap, Pa., U.S.	E6	115
Pleasant Garden, N.C., U.S.	B3	110
Pleasant Grove, Al., U.S.	g7	78
Pleasant Grove, Ut., U.S.	C4	121
Pleasant Hill, Ca., U.S.	h8	82
Pleasant Hill, Il., U.S.	D3	90
Pleasant Hill, Ia., U.S.	e8	92
Pleasant Hill, La., U.S.	C2	95
Pleasant Hill, Mo., U.S.	C3	102
Pleasant Hill, Oh., U.S.	B1	112
Pleasant Lake, In., U.S.	A7	91
Pleasant Lake, l., Me., U.S.	C5	96
Pleasant Lake, l., N.H., U.S.	D4	106
Pleasanton, Ca., U.S.	h9	82
Pleasanton, Ks., U.S.	D9	93
Pleasanton, Tx., U.S.	E3	120
Pleasant Prairie, Wi., U.S.	n12	126
Pleasants, co., W.V., U.S.	B3	125
Pleasant Valley, Ia., U.S.	g11	92
Pleasant Valley, Mo., U.S.	h11	102
Pleasant View, Ut., U.S.	B3	121
Pleasantville, Ia., U.S.	C4	92
Pleasantville, N.J., U.S.	E3	107
Pleasantville, N.Y., U.S.	D7	109
Pleasantville, Oh., U.S.	C3	112
Pleasure Beach, Ct., U.S.	D7	84
Pleasure Ridge Park, Ky., U.S.	g11	94
Pleasureville, Ky., U.S.	B4	94
Pleiku see Play Cu, Viet.	H9	34
Pléneuf, Fr.	D4	10
Plenty, Bay of, b., N.Z.	B6	52
Plentywood, Mt., U.S.	B12	103
Plessisville, Que., Can.	C6	74
Pleternica, Cro.	D12	14
Plétipi, Lac, l., Que., Can.	F18	66
Pleven, Bul.	F8	16
Pljevlja, Yugo.	F3	16
Płock, Pol.	C19	8
Ploërmel, Fr.	E4	10
Ploieşti, Rom.	E10	16
Plomosa Mountains, mts., Az., U.S.	D1	80
Plonge, Lac la, l., Sask., Can.	B2	75
Plouguenast, Fr.	D4	10
Plovdiv, Bul.	G8	16
Plover, Wi., U.S.	D4	126
Plover, stm., Wi., U.S.	D4	126
Plum, Pa., U.S.	k14	115
Plumas, co., Ca., U.S.	B3	82
Plum Coulee, Man., Can.	E3	70
Plumerville, Ar., U.S.	B3	81
Plum Island, i., Ma., U.S.	A6	98
Plummer, Id., U.S.	B2	89
Plumsteadville, Pa., U.S.	F11	115
Plumtree, Zimb.	F5	44
Plymouth, Monts.	F16	64
Plymouth, Eng., U.K.	K8	7
Plymouth, Ct., U.S.	C3	84
Plymouth, Fl., U.S.	D5	86
Plymouth, In., U.S.	B5	91
Plymouth, Ma., U.S.	C6	98
Plymouth, Mi., U.S.	p15	99
Plymouth, Mn., U.S.	m12	100
Plymouth, N.H., U.S.	C3	106
Plymouth, N.C., U.S.	B6	110
Plymouth, Oh., U.S.	A3	112
Plymouth, Pa., U.S.	D10	115
Plymouth, Wi., U.S.	E6	126
Plymouth, co., Ia., U.S.	B1	92
Plymouth, co., Ma., U.S.	C6	98
Plymouth Bay, b., Ma., U.S.	C6	98
Plzeň, Czech.	F13	8
Po, stm., Italy	E7	14
Po, stm., Va., U.S.	B5	123
Pobeda, Gora, mtn., Russia	D23	24
Pocahontas, Ar., U.S.	A5	81
Pocahontas, Il., U.S.	E4	90
Pocahontas, Ia., U.S.	B3	92
Pocahontas, co., Ia., U.S.	B3	92
Pocahontas, co., W.V., U.S.	C4	125
Pocasset, Ma., U.S.	C6	98
Pocatalico, W.V., U.S.	C3	125
Pocatalico, stm., W.V., U.S.	C3	125
Pocatello, Id., U.S.	G6	89
Počep, Russia	I16	18
Pochutla, Mex.	J11	62
Poções, Braz.	C8	57
Pocola, Ok., U.S.	B7	113
Pocomoke, stm., Md., U.S.	D7	97
Pocomoke City, Md., U.S.	D6	97
Pocomoke Sound, strt., Md., U.S.	E6	97
Pocono Mountains, hills, Pa., U.S.	E11	115
Pocono Pines, Pa., U.S.	D11	115
Poços de Caldas, Braz.	F5	57
Pocotopaug Lake, res., Ct., U.S.	C6	84
Podensac, Fr.	H6	10
Podgorica, Yugo.	G3	16
Podkamennaja Tunguska, Russia	E12	24

Name Map Ref Page

Podkamennaja Tunguska, stm., Russia E13 24
Podol'sk, Russia F20 18
Podor, Sen. E3 42
Podravska Slatina, Cro. D12 14
Pofadder, S. Afr. G3 44
Poge, Cape, c., Ma., U.S. D7 98
Poggibonsi, Italy F6 14
P'ohang, S. Kor. D12 26
Pohénégamook, Que., Can. B8 74
Pohue Bay, b., Hi., U.S. E6 88
Poinsett, co., Ar., U.S. B5 81
Poinsett, Lake, l., Fl., U.S. D6 86
Poinsett, Lake, l., S.D., U.S. C8 118
Point Clear, Al., U.S. E2 78
Pointe a la Hache, La., U.S. E6 95
Pointe-à-Pitre, Guad. F17 64
Pointe-au-Pic, Que., Can. B7 74
Pointe-Calumet, Que., Can. p19 74
Pointe-Claire, Que., Can. D4 74
Pointe Coupee, co., La., U.S. D4 95
Pointe-des-Cascades, Que., Can. q19 74
Point Edward, Ont., Can. D2 73
Pointe-Noire, Congo B2 44
Pointe-Verte, N.B., Can. B4 71
Point Fortin, Trin. I17 64
Point Hope, Ak., U.S. B6 79
Point Imperial, mtn., Az., U.S. A4 80
Point Judith Pond, l., R.I., U.S. F4 116
Point Lake, l., N.W. Ter., Can. C10 66
Point Leamington, Newf., Can. D4 72
Point Marion, Pa., U.S. G2 115
Point Mugu Naval Air Station, mil., Ca., U.S. E4 82
Point of Rocks, Md., U.S. B2 97
Point Pelee National Park, Ont., Can. F2 73
Point Pleasant, N.J., U.S. C4 107
Point Pleasant, W.V., U.S. C2 125
Point Pleasant Beach, N.J., U.S. C4 107
Point Reyes National Seashore, Ca., U.S. C2 82
Point Roberts, Wa., U.S. A2 124
Poipu, Hi., U.S. B2 88
Poison Creek, stm., Wy., U.S. C5 127
Poisson Blanc, Lac du, res., Que., Can. C2 74
Poitiers, Fr. F7 10
Poitou, reg., Fr. F6 10
Poix, Fr. C8 10
Pokegama Lake, l., Mn., U.S. C5 100
Pokegama Lake, l., Wi., U.S. C2 126
Polacca, Az., U.S. B5 80
Poland, ctry., Eur. E11 4
Polar Bear Provincial Park, Ont., Can. n18 73
Polecat Creek, stm., Ok., U.S. B5 113
Pol-e Khomrī, Afg. C3 38
Polesje, reg., Eur. I10 18
Pólis, Cyp. B3 40
Polistena, Italy K11 14
Polk, Pa., U.S. D2 115
Polk, co., Ar., U.S. C1 81
Polk, co., Fl., U.S. E5 86
Polk, co., Ga., U.S. C1 87
Polk, co., Ia., U.S. C4 92
Polk, co., Mn., U.S. C2 100
Polk, co., Mo., U.S. D4 102
Polk, co., Ne., U.S. C8 104
Polk, co., N.C., U.S. f10 110
Polk, co., Or., U.S. C3 114
Polk, co., Tn., U.S. D9 119
Polk, co., Tx., U.S. D5 120
Polk, co., Wi., U.S. C1 126
Polk City, Fl., U.S. D5 86
Polk City, Ia., U.S. C4 92
Pol'kino, Russia C13 24
Pollāchi, India G4 37
Polo, Il., U.S. B4 90
Polock, Bela. F11 18
Polson, Mt., U.S. C2 103
Poltava, Ukr. H4 22
Polynesia, is., Oc. G2 2
Pomabamba, Peru E3 54
Pomaro, Mex. H8 62
Pombal, Port. F3 12
Pomerania, hist. reg., Pol. A16 8
Pomeranian Bay, b., Eur. A14 8
Pomeroy, Ia., U.S. B3 92
Pomeroy, Oh., U.S. C3 112
Pomeroy, Wa., U.S. C8 124
Pomme de Terre, stm., Mn., U.S. E3 100
Pomme de Terre, stm., Mo., U.S. D4 102
Pomme de Terre Lake, res., Mo., U.S. D4 102
Pomona, Ca., U.S. E5 82
Pomona, Ks., U.S. D8 93
Pomona Lake, res., Ks., U.S. D7 93
Pompano Beach, Fl., U.S. F6 86
Pompton Lakes, N.J., U.S. A4 107
Ponaganset, stm., R.I., U.S. C2 116
Ponaganset Reservoir, res., R.I., U.S. B2 116
Ponca, Ne., U.S. B9 104
Ponca City, Ok., U.S. A4 113
Ponca Creek, stm., U.S. A6 104
Ponca Indian Reservation, Ne., U.S. B7 104
Ponce, P.R. E14 64
Ponce de Leon Bay, b., Fl., U.S. G5 86
Ponce de Leon Inlet, b., Fl., U.S. C6 86
Poncha Pass, Co., U.S. C4 83
Ponchatoula, La., U.S. D5 95
Pond, stm., Ky., U.S. C2 94
Pond Creek, Ok., U.S. A3 113
Pondera, co., Mt., U.S. B4 103
Pond Fork, stm., W.V., U.S. D3 125
Pondicherry, India G5 37
Pondicherry, ter., India G5 37
Pond Inlet, N.W. Ter., Can. B17 66
Pone Island, i., Md., U.S. D5 97
Ponferrada, Spain C5 12
Ponoka, Alta., Can. C4 68
Ponorogo, Indon. m15 33a
Pons, Fr. G6 10
Ponta Grossa, Braz. B6 56
Pont-à-Mousson, Fr. D13 10
Ponta Porã, Braz. G1 57
Pontarlier, Fr. F13 10
Pontassieve, Italy F6 14
Pont-Audemer, Fr. C7 10
Pontchartrain, Lake, l., La., U.S. D5 95
Pontchâteau, Fr. E4 10
Pont de Suert, Spain C12 12
Ponte Branca, Braz. D2 57
Ponte da Barca, Port. D3 12
Pontedera, Italy F5 14
Ponte de Sor, Port. F3 12
Ponteix, Sask., Can. H2 75
Ponte Nova, Braz. F7 57
Pontevedra, Spain C3 12
Ponte Vedra Beach, Fl., U.S. B5 86
Pontgibaud, Fr. F9 10
Pontiac, Il., U.S. C5 90
Pontiac, Mi., U.S. F7 99
Pontianak, Indon. F4 32
Pontivy, Fr. D4 10
Pont-l'Abbé, Fr. E2 10
Pontoise, Fr. C9 10
Pontoosuc Lake, l., Ma., U.S. B1 98
Pontorson, Fr. D5 10
Pontotoc, Ms., U.S. A4 101
Pontotoc, co., Ms., U.S. A4 101
Pontotoc, co., Ok., U.S. C5 113
Pont-Rouge, Que., Can. C6 74
Pontypool, Ont., Can. C6 73
Pontypool, Wales, U.K. J9 7
Poole, Eng., U.K. K11 7
Pooler, Ga., U.S. D5 87
Pooles Island, i., Md., U.S. B5 97
Poolesville, Md., U.S. B3 97
Poopó, Lago de, l., Bol. G5 54
Popayán, Col. F4 58
Pope, co., Ar., U.S. B2 81
Pope, co., Il., U.S. F5 90
Pope, co., Mn., U.S. E3 100
Pope Air Force Base, mil., N.C., U.S. B3 110
Poplar, Mt., U.S. B11 103
Poplar, stm., Can. C3 70
Poplar, stm., Mn., U.S. C2 100
Poplar Bluff, Mo., U.S. E7 102
Poplar Island, i., Md., U.S. C5 97
Poplarville, Ms., U.S. E4 101
Popocatépetl, Volcán, vol., Mex. H10 62
Popokabaka, Zaire C3 44
Popomanasiu, Mount, mtn., Sol.Is. A11 50
Popondetta, Pap. N. Gui. m16 50a
Popple, stm., Wi., U.S. C5 126
Poquonock, Ct., U.S. B5 84
Poquonock Bridge, Ct., U.S. D7 84
Poquoson, Va., U.S. C6 123
Porangatu, Braz. F9 54
Porbandar, India J3 38
Porcher Island, i., B.C., Can. C2 69
Porcupine Mountains, mts., Mi., U.S. m12 99
Pordenone, Italy D7 14
Poreč, Cro. D8 14
Pori, Fin. F13 6
Porkkala, Fin. G15 6
Porlamar, Ven. B11 58
Poronajsk, Russia H22 24
Porsgrunn, Nor. G7 6
Portadown, N. Ire., U.K. G6 7
Portage, In., U.S. A3 91
Portage, Mi., U.S. F5 99
Portage, Pa., U.S. F4 115
Portage, Wi., U.S. E4 126
Portage, co., Oh., U.S. A4 112
Portage, co., Wi., U.S. D4 126
Portage, stm., Oh., U.S. B2 112
Portage Bay, b., Man., Can. D2 70
Portage Head, c., Wa., U.S. A1 124
Portage Lake, l., Me., U.S. B4 96
Portage Lakes, Oh., U.S. B4 112
Portage la Prairie, Man., Can. E2 70
Portageville, Mo., U.S. E8 102
Port Alberni, B.C., Can. E5 69
Portalegre, Port. F4 12
Portales, N.M., U.S. C6 108
Port Alice, B.C., Can. D4 69
Port Allegany, Pa., U.S. C5 115
Port Allen, La., U.S. D4 95
Port Angeles, Wa., U.S. A2 124
Port Antonio, Jam. E9 64
Port Aransas, Tx., U.S. F4 120
Port Arthur, Tx., U.S. E6 120
Port Arthur see Lüshun, China D11 26
Port Augusta, Austl. F7 50
Port au Port Bay, b., Newf., Can. D2 72
Port au Port [West-Aguathuna-Felix Cove], Newf., Can. D2 72
Port-au-Prince, Haiti E11 64
Port au Prince Peninsula, pen., Newf., Can. D2 72
Port Austin, Mi., U.S. D7 99
Port Barre, La., U.S. D4 95
Port-Bergé, Madag. E9 44
Port Blair, India I2 34
Port Blandford, Newf., Can. D4 72
Port Bolivar, Tx., U.S. E5 120
Port Burwell, Ont., Can. E4 73
Port Byron, Il., U.S. B3 90
Port Carbon, Pa., U.S. E9 115
Port Carling, Ont., Can. B5 73
Port-Cartier-Ouest, Que., Can. k13 74
Port Chalmers, N.Z. F3 52
Port Charlotte, Fl., U.S. F4 86
Port Chester, N.Y., U.S. E7 109
Port Clinton, Oh., U.S. A3 112
Port Colborne, Ont., Can. E5 73
Port Coquitlam, B.C., Can. E6 69
Port Deposit, Md., U.S. A5 97
Port Dickinson, N.Y., U.S. C5 109
Port Dickson, Malay. M6 34
Port Edward, B.C., Can. B2 69
Port Edwards, Wi., U.S. D4 126
Portel, Braz. D8 54
Portel, Port. G4 12
Port Elgin, Ont., Can. C3 73
Port Elizabeth, S. Afr. H5 44
Port Ellen, Scot., U.K. F6 7
Porter, In., U.S. A3 91
Porter, Tx., U.S. D5 120
Porter, co., In., U.S. B3 91
Porter Creek, stm., W.V., U.S. m13 125
Porterdale, Ga., U.S. C3 87
Porterville, Ca., U.S. D4 82
Port Ewen, N.Y., U.S. D7 109
Port Gamble Indian Reservation, Wa., U.S. B3 124
Port-Gentil, Gabon B1 44
Port Gibson, Ms., U.S. D3 101
Port Harcourt, Nig. H7 42
Port Hedland, Austl. D3 50
Port Hood, N.S., Can. C8 71
Port Hope, Ont., Can. D6 73
Port Hope Simpson, Newf., Can. B3 72
Port Hueneme, Ca., U.S. E4 82
Port Huron, Mi., U.S. F8 99
Portimão, Port. H3 12
Port Isabel, Tx., U.S. F4 120
Port Jefferson, N.Y., U.S. n15 109
Port Jervis, N.Y., U.S. D6 109
Portland, Austl. G8 50
Portland, Ct., U.S. C5 84
Portland, In., U.S. D8 91
Portland, Me., U.S. E2 96
Portland, Mi., U.S. F6 99
Portland, N.D., U.S. B8 111
Portland, Or., U.S. B4 114
Portland, Tn., U.S. A5 119
Portland, Tx., U.S. F4 120
Portland, Bill of, c., Eng., U.K. K10 7
Portland Inlet, b., B.C., Can. B2 69
Portland Point, c., Jam. F9 64
Port Lavaca, Tx., U.S. E4 120
Port Lincoln, Austl. F7 50
Port Loko, S.L. G3 42
Port Louis, Mrts. F11 44
Port Ludlow, Wa., U.S. B3 124
Port-Lyautey see Kenitra, Mor. B4 42
Port Macquarie, Austl. F10 50
Port Madison Indian Reservation, Wa., U.S. B3 124
Port McNeil, B.C., Can. D4 69
Port McNicoll, Ont., Can. C5 73
Port Monmouth, N.J., U.S. C4 107
Port Moresby, Pap. N. Gui. m16 50a
Port Morien, N.S., Can. C10 71
Port Neches, Tx., U.S. E6 120
Portneuf, Que., Can. C6 74
Port Nolloth, S. Afr. G3 44
Porto, Port. D3 12
Porto Alegre, Braz. C6 56
Porto Amboim, Ang. D2 44
Portobelo, Pan. J8 64
Porto de Moz, Braz. D8 54
Porto Esperança, Braz. G7 54
Porto Esperidião, Braz. G7 54
Pôrto Feliz, Braz. G5 57
Portoferraio, Italy G5 14
Pôrto Ferreira, Braz. F5 57
Port of Spain, Trin. I17 64
Portogruaro, Italy D7 14
Portola, Ca., U.S. C3 82
Porto Murtinho, Braz. H7 54
Porto Nacional, Braz. F9 54
Porto-Novo, Benin G6 42
Port Orange, Fl., U.S. C6 86
Port Orchard, Wa., U.S. B3 124
Port Orford, Or., U.S. E2 114
Porto San Giorgio, Italy F8 14
Porto Santo Stefano, Italy G6 14
Pôrto São José, Braz. G2 57
Pôrto Seguro, Braz. D9 57
Porto Torres, Italy I3 14
Porto União, Braz. B6 56
Porto Velho, Braz. E6 54
Portoviejo, Ec. H2 58
Port Penn, De., U.S. B3 85
Port Pirie, Austl. F7 50
Port Richey, Fl., U.S. D4 86
Port Rowan, Ont., Can. E4 73
Port Royal, S.C., U.S. G6 117
Port Royal Island, i., S.C., U.S. G6 117
Port Royal Sound, strt., S.C., U.S. G6 117
Port Said see Būr Sa'īd, Egypt B12 42
Port-Sainte-Marie, Fr. H7 10
Port Saint Joe, Fl., U.S. C1 86
Port Saint Johns, S. Afr. H5 44
Port Saint Lucie, Fl., U.S. E6 86
Port Salerno, Fl., U.S. E6 86
Port Saunders, Newf., Can. C3 72
Port Shepstone, S. Afr. H6 44
Portsmouth, Eng., U.K. K11 7
Portsmouth, N.H., U.S. D5 106
Portsmouth, Oh., U.S. D3 112
Portsmouth, R.I., U.S. E6 116
Portsmouth, Va., U.S. D6 123
Portsmouth Naval Shipyard, mil., Me., U.S. D5 106
Port Stanley, Ont., Can. E3 73
Port Sulphur, La., U.S. E6 95
Port Talbot, Wales, U.K. J9 7
Port Townsend, Wa., U.S. A3 124
Portugal, ctry., Eur. H6 4
Portugalete, Spain B8 12
Portuguese Guinea see Guinea-Bissau, ctry., Afr. F2 42
Portumna, Ire. H4 7
Port Union, Newf., Can. D5 72
Port-Vendres, Fr. J10 10
Port Washington, N.Y., U.S. h13 109
Port Washington, Wi., U.S. E6 126
Port Wentworth, Ga., U.S. D5 87
Porum, Ok., U.S. B6 113
Porz, Ger. E7 8
Porzuna, Spain F7 12
Posadas, Arg. B5 56
Poschiavo, Switz. F17 10
Posen, Il., U.S. k9 90
Posey, co., In., U.S. H2 91
Poseyville, In., U.S. H2 91
Poso, Indon. F7 32
Posse, Braz. C5 57
Pössneck, Ger. E11 8
Post, Tx., U.S. C2 120
Post Falls, Id., U.S. B2 89
Post Maurice Cortier (Bidon Cinq), Alg. D6 42
Postojna, Slo. D9 14
P'ostraja Dresva, Russia E25 24
Postville, Ia., U.S. A6 92
Potawatomi Indian Reservation, Ks., U.S. C8 93
Potchefstroom, S. Afr. G5 44
Poté, Braz. D8 57
Poteau, Ok., U.S. B7 113
Poteau, stm., U.S. B7 113
Poteet, Tx., U.S. E3 120
Potenza, Italy I10 14
Potes, Spain B7 12
Potgietersrus, S. Afr. F5 44
Poth, Tx., U.S. E3 120
Potholes Reservoir, res., Wa., U.S. B6 124
Potiraguá, Braz. C9 57
Potiskum, Nig. F8 42
Potlatch, Id., U.S. C2 89
Potomac, Md., U.S. B3 97
Potomac, stm., U.S. D4 97
Potomac Heights, Md., U.S. C3 97
Potomac Park, Md., U.S. k13 97
Potosí, Bol. G5 54
Potosi, Mo., U.S. D7 102
Potosí, Cerro, mtn., Mex. E9 62
Potsdam, Ger. C13 8
Potsdam, N.Y., U.S. f10 109
Pottawatomie, co., Ks., U.S. C7 93
Pottawatomie, co., Ok., U.S. B4 113
Pottawattamie, co., Ia., U.S. C2 92
Potter, co., Pa., U.S. C6 115
Potter, co., S.D., U.S. B6 118
Potter, co., Tx., U.S. B2 120
Potter Valley, Ca., U.S. C2 82
Potts Creek, stm., U.S. C2 123
Pottstown, Pa., U.S. F10 115
Pottsville, Ar., U.S. B2 81
Pottsville, Pa., U.S. E9 115
P'otzu, Tai. L9 28
Pouce Coupe, B.C., Can. B7 69
Pouch Cove, Newf., Can. E5 72
Poughkeepsie, N.Y., U.S. D7 109
Poulan, Ga., U.S. E3 87
Poulsbo, Wa., U.S. B3 124
Poultney, Vt., U.S. D2 122
Poultney, stm., Vt., U.S. D2 122
Pound, Va., U.S. e9 123
Pound Gap, U.S. C7 94
Pouso Alegre, Braz. G6 57
Poŭthĭsăt, Camb. H7 34
Pouzauges, Fr. F6 10
Póvoa de Varzim, Port. D3 12
Povungnituk, Que., Can. f11 74
Powassan, Ont., Can. A5 73
Poway, Ca., U.S. F5 82
Powder, stm., U.S. B5 76
Powder, stm., Or., U.S. C9 114
Powder, Middle Fork, stm., Wy., U.S. C6 127
Powder, North Fork, stm., Wy., U.S. C6 127
Powder, South Fork, stm., Wy., U.S. C6 127
Powder River, co., Mt., U.S. E11 103
Powder River Pass, Wy., U.S. B5 127
Powder Springs, Ga., U.S. h8 87
Powell, Oh., U.S. B2 112
Powell, Tn., U.S. m13 119
Powell, Wy., U.S. B4 127
Powell, co., Ky., U.S. C6 94
Powell, co., Mt., U.S. D4 103
Powell, stm., U.S. C10 119
Powell, Lake, res., U.S. F5 121
Powell, Mount, mtn., Co., U.S. B4 83
Powell, Mount, mtn., N.M., U.S. B1 108
Powell Butte, Or., U.S. C5 114
Powell Park, reg., Co., U.S. A2 83
Powell River, B.C., Can. E5 69
Powellton, W.V., U.S. C3 125
Power, co., Id., U.S. G5 89
Powers, Or., U.S. E2 114
Powerview, Man., Can. D3 70
Poweshiek, co., Ia., U.S. C5 92
Powhatan, Va., U.S. C5 123
Powhatan, co., Va., U.S. C5 123
Powhatan Point, Oh., U.S. C5 112
Poxoreu, Braz. C1 57
Poyang, China G5 28
Poyang Hu, l., China F5 28
Poygan, Lake, l., Wi., U.S. D5 126
Poynette, Wi., U.S. E4 126
Poza Rica de Hidalgo, Mex. G11 62
Poznań, Pol. C16 8
Pozo Alcón, Spain H9 12
Pozoblanco, Spain G7 12
Pozo Redondo Mountains, mts., Az., U.S. E3 80
Pozuelo de Alarcón, Spain E8 12
Pozzuoli, Italy I9 14
Prachin Buri, Thai. G6 34
Prachuap Khiri Khan, Thai. I5 34
Prague, Ok., U.S. B5 113
Prague see Praha, Czech. E14 8
Praha (Prague), Czech. E14 8
Prainha, Braz. E6 54
Prairie, co., Ar., U.S. C4 81
Prairie, co., Mt., U.S. D11 103
Prairie, stm., Mn., U.S. C5 100
Prairie, stm., Wi., U.S. C4 126
Prairie City, Ia., U.S. C4 92
Prairie City, Or., U.S. C8 114
Prairie Creek Reservoir, res., In., U.S. D7 91
Prairie Dog Creek, stm., U.S. C3 93
Prairie du Chien, Wi., U.S. E2 126
Prairie du Sac, Wi., U.S. E4 126
Prairie Grove, Ar., U.S. B1 81
Prairies, Rivière des, stm., Que., Can. p19 74
Prairie View, Tx., U.S. D5 120
Prairie Village, Ks., U.S. m16 93
Praslin Island, i., Sey. B11 44
Pratas Islands see Tungsha Tao, is., Tai. G10 26
Prat de Llobregat, Spain D14 12
Prater Mountain, mtn., Wy., U.S. C2 127
Prato, Italy F6 14
Pratt, Ks., U.S. E5 93
Pratt, co., Ks., U.S. E5 93
Prattville, Al., U.S. C3 78
Pravia, Spain B5 12
Preble, co., Oh., U.S. C1 112
Predazzo, Italy C6 14
Predlitz [-Turrach], Aus. H13 8
Pré-en-Pail, Fr. D6 10
Preetz, Ger. A10 8
Premont, Tx., U.S. F3 120
Prentiss, Ms., U.S. D4 101
Prentiss, co., Ms., U.S. A5 101
Prenzlau, Ger. B13 8
Preparis Island, i., Mya. G2 34
Preparis North Channel, strt., Mya. G2 34
Preparis South Channel, strt., Mya. G2 34
Přerov, Czech. F17 8
Prescott, Ont., Can. C9 73
Prescott, Az., U.S. C3 80
Prescott, Ar., U.S. D2 81
Prescott, Wi., U.S. D1 126
Presho, S.D., U.S. D5 118
Presidencia Roca, Arg. B5 56
Presidente Epitácio, Braz. F2 57
Presidente Prudente, Braz. G3 57
Presidential Range, mts., N.H., U.S. B4 106
Presidio, Tx., U.S. p12 120
Presidio, co., Tx., U.S. o12 120
Presidio of San Francisco, mil., Ca., U.S. h8 82
Prešov, Slov. F21 8
Prespa, Lake, l., Eur. I4 16
Presque Isle, Me., U.S. B5 96
Presque Isle, co., Mi., U.S. C6 99
Preston, Eng., U.K. H10 7
Preston, Id., U.S. G7 89
Preston, Ia., U.S. B7 92
Preston, Mn., U.S. G6 100
Preston, co., W.V., U.S. B5 125
Preston Peak, mtn., Ca., U.S. B2 82
Prestonsburg, Ky., U.S. C7 94
Presumpscot, stm., Me., U.S. g7 96
Pretoria, S. Afr. G5 44
Prettyboy Reservoir, res., Md., U.S. A4 97
Pretty Prairie, Ks., U.S. E5 93
Préveza, Grc. K4 16
Prewitt Reservoir, res., Co., U.S. A7 83
Prey Vêng, Camb. I8 34
Pribilof Islands, is., Ak., U.S. D5 79
Příbram, Czech. F14 8
Price, Ut., U.S. D5 121
Price, co., Wi., U.S. C3 126
Price, stm., Ut., U.S. D5 121
Price Inlet, b., S.C., U.S. k12 117
Prichard, Al., U.S. E1 78
Priego, Spain E9 12
Priego de Córdoba, Spain H7 12
Prien, Ger. H12 8
Prieska, S. Afr. G4 44
Priest Lake, l., Id., U.S. A2 89
Priest Rapids Dam, Wa., U.S. C6 124
Priest Rapids Lake, res., Wa., U.S. C6 124
Priest River, Id., U.S. A2 89
Prievidza, Slov. G18 8
Prijedor, Bos. E11 14
Prilep, Mac. H5 16
Prim, Point, c., P.E.I., Can. C6 71
Primghar, Ia., U.S. A2 92
Primrose, R.I., U.S. B3 116
Primrose Lake, l., Can. F11 66
Prince, Lake, res., Va., U.S. k14 123
Prince Albert National Park, Sask., Can. C2 75
Prince Albert Sound, strt., N.W. Ter., Can. B9 66
Prince Charles Island, i., N.W. Ter., Can. C17 66
Prince-de-Galles, Cap du, c., Que., Can. D18 66
Prince Edward, co., Va., U.S. C4 123
Prince Edward Island, prov., Can. C6 71
Prince Edward Island National Park, P.E.I., Can. C6 71
Prince Frederick, Md., U.S. C4 97
Prince George, B.C., Can. C6 69
Prince George, co., Va., U.S. C5 123
Prince Georges, co., Md., U.S. C4 97
Prince of Wales, Cape, c., Ak., U.S. B6 79
Prince of Wales Island, i., Austl. B8 50
Prince of Wales Island, i., N.W. Ter., Can. B13 66
Prince of Wales Island, i., Ak., U.S. n23 79
Prince of Wales Strait, strt., N.W. Ter., Can. B9 66
Prince Regent Inlet, b., N.W. Ter., Can. B14 66
Prince Rupert, B.C., Can. B2 69
Princes Lakes, In., U.S. F5 91
Princess Anne, Md., U.S. D6 97
Princess Royal Channel, strt., B.C., Can. C3 69
Princess Royal Island, i., B.C., Can. C3 69
Princeton, B.C., Can. E7 69
Princeton, Fl., U.S. G6 86
Princeton, Il., U.S. B4 90
Princeton, In., U.S. H2 91
Princeton, Ia., U.S. C7 92
Princeton, Ky., U.S. C2 94

Name — Map Ref — Page

Princeton, Me., U.S. C5 96
Princeton, Mn., U.S. E5 100
Princeton, Mo., U.S. A4 102
Princeton, N.J., U.S. C3 107
Princeton, N.C., U.S. B4 110
Princeton, W.V., U.S. D3 125
Princeton, Wi., U.S. E4 126
Princeton, Mount, mtn., Co., U.S. C4 83
Princeville, Que., Can. C6 74
Princeville, Il., U.S. C4 90
Princeville, N.C., U.S. B5 110
Prince William, co., Va., U.S. B5 123
Prince William Sound, strt., Ak., U.S. g18 79
Príncipe, i., S. Tom./P. A1 44
Principe Channel, strt., B.C., Can. C3 69
Príncipe da Beira, Braz. F6 54
Prineville, Or., U.S. C6 114
Prineville Reservoir, res., Or., U.S. C6 114
Pringsewu, Indon. k12 33a
Prinzapolca, Nic. H6 64
Prior Lake, Mn., U.S. F5 100
Priština, Yugo. G5 16
Pritchards Island, i., S.C., U.S. G6 117
Pritzwalk, Ger. B12 8
Privas, Fr. H11 10
Privolžsk, Russia D24 18
Probolinggo, Indon. m16 33a
Proctor, Mn., U.S. D6 100
Proctor, Vt., U.S. D2 122
Proctor Lake, res., Tx., U.S. C3 120
Proctorsville, Vt., U.S. E3 122
Proddatūr, India E5 37
Professor Dr. Ir. W.J. van Blommestein Meer, res., Sur. C7 54
Progreso, Mex. G15 62
Prokopjevsk, Russia G11 24
Prokuplje, Yugo. F5 16
Promontory Mountains, mts., Ut., U.S. B3 121
Prophetstown, Il., U.S. B4 90
Propriá, Braz. F11 54
Prospect, Ct., U.S. C4 84
Prospect, Ky., U.S. g11 94
Prospect, Oh., U.S. B2 112
Prospect, Or., U.S. E4 114
Prospect, Pa., U.S. E1 115
Prospect Hill, mtn., Or., U.S. k11 114
Prospect Park, N.J., U.S. B4 107
Prospect Park, Pa., U.S. p20 115
Prosperity, S.C., U.S. C4 117
Prosperity, W.V., U.S. n13 125
Prosser, Wa., U.S. C6 124
Prostějov, Czech. F17 8
Protection, Ks., U.S. E4 93
Protville, Tun. M5 14
Provence, hist. reg., Fr. I13 10
Providence, Ky., U.S. C2 94
Providence, R.I., U.S. C4 116
Providence, Ut., U.S. B4 121
Providence, co., R.I., U.S. C2 116
Providence, stm., R.I., U.S. C5 116
Providence Island, i., Sey. C10 44
Providence Point, c., R.I., U.S. D5 116
Providencia, Isla de, i., Col. H7 64
Providenija, Russia E31 24
Province Lake, l., N.H., U.S. C5 106
Provincetown, Ma., U.S. B7 98
Provins, Fr. D10 10
Provo, Ut., U.S. C4 121
Provo, stm., Ut., U.S. C4 121
Provost, Alta., Can. C5 68
Prowers, co., Co., U.S. D8 83
Prozor, Bos. F12 14
Prudence Island, i., R.I., U.S. E5 116
Prudenville, Mi., U.S. D6 99
Prudhoe Bay, Ak., U.S. A10 79
Prudhoe Bay, b., Ak., U.S. A10 79
Prüm, Ger. E6 8
Pruszków, Pol. C20 8
Prut, stm., Eur. D12 16
Pryor, Mt., U.S. E8 103
Pryor, Ok., U.S. A6 113
Pryor Mountains, mts., Mt., U.S. E8 103
Przemyśl, Pol. F22 8
Pskov, Russia D11 18
Ptolemaís, Grc. I5 16
Ptuj, Slo. C10 14
Pucallpa, Peru E4 54
Pucheng, China H7 28
Puckaway Lake, l., Wi., U.S. E4 126
Pudukkottai, India G5 37
Puebla de Sanabria, Spain C5 12
Puebla de Trives, Spain C4 12
Puebla [de Zaragoza], Mex. H10 62
Pueblo, Co., U.S. C6 83
Pueblo, co., Co., U.S. C6 83
Pueblo Hundido, Chile B2 56
Pueblo Mountain, mtn., Or., U.S. E8 114
Pueblo Mountains, mts., Or., U.S. E8 114
Pueblo Reservoir, res., Co., U.S. C6 83
Puentedeume, Spain B3 12
Puente-Genil, Spain H7 12
Pueo Point, c., Hi., U.S. B1 88
Puerco, stm., U.S. C6 80
Puerco, Rio, stm., N.M., U.S. B2 108
Puerto Aisén, Chile F2 56
Puerto Alfonso, Col. I7 58
Puerto Ángel, Mex. J11 62
Puerto Armuelles, Pan. J6 64
Puerto Asís, Col. G4 58
Puerto Ayacucho, Ven. E9 58
Puerto Barrios, Guat. G3 64
Puerto Berrío, Col. D5 58
Puerto Boyacá, Col. E5 58
Puerto Cabello, Ven. B8 58
Puerto Cabezas, Nic. G6 64
Puerto Carreño, Col. D9 58
Puerto Casado, Para. A5 56
Puerto Chicama, Peru E3 54
Puerto Cortés, C.R. J6 64
Puerto Cortés, Hond. G4 64
Puerto Cumarebo, Ven. B8 58
Puerto de Pollensa, Spain F15 12
Puerto de San José, Guat. H2 64
Puerto Deseado, Arg. F3 56
Puerto Escondido, Mex. J11 62
Puerto Francisco de Orellana, Ec. H4 58
Puerto Inírida, Col. F9 58
Puerto Juárez, Mex. G16 62
Puerto la Cruz, Ven. B10 58
Puerto Leguízamo, Col. H5 58
Puerto Limón, Col. F6 58
Puertollano, Spain G7 12
Puerto Lobos, Arg. E3 56
Puerto Madryn, Arg. E3 56
Puerto Maldonado, Peru F5 54
Puerto Montt, Chile E2 56
Puerto Morelos, Mex. G16 62
Puerto Nariño, Col. E9 58
Puerto Natales, Chile G2 56
Puerto Padre, Cuba D9 64
Puerto Peñasco, Mex. B3 62
Puerto Plata, Dom. Rep. E12 64
Puerto Princesa, Phil. D6 32
Puerto Real, Spain I5 12
Puerto Rico, dep., N.A. E14 64
Puerto Rondón, Col. D7 58
Puerto Suárez, Bol. G7 54
Puerto Tejada, Col. F4 58
Puerto Vallarta, Mex. G7 62
Puerto Wilches, Col. D6 58
Puget Sound, strt., Wa., U.S. B3 124
Puget Sound Naval Shipyard, mil., Wa., U.S. e10 124
Pugwash, N.S., Can. D6 71
Puhi, Hi., U.S. B2 88
Puigcerdá, Spain C13 12
Pukalani, Hi., U.S. C5 88
Pukaskwa National Park, Ont., Can. o18 73
Pukch'ŏng, N. Kor. C12 26
Pukë, Alb. G3 16
Pukeashun Mountain, mtn., B.C., Can. D8 69
Pukekohe, N.Z. B5 52
Pukou, China C7 28
Pula, Cro. E8 14
Pulacayo, Bol. H5 54
Pulaski, N.Y., U.S. B4 109
Pulaski, Tn., U.S. B4 119
Pulaski, Va., U.S. C2 123
Pulaski, Wi., U.S. D5 126
Pulaski, co., Ar., U.S. C3 81
Pulaski, co., Ga., U.S. D3 87
Pulaski, co., Il., U.S. F4 90
Pulaski, co., In., U.S. B4 91
Pulaski, co., Ky., U.S. C5 94
Pulaski, co., Mo., U.S. D5 102
Pulaski, co., Va., U.S. C2 123
Puli, Tai. L9 28
Puliyangudi, India H4 37
Pulkkila, Fin. D15 6
Pullman, Wa., U.S. C8 124
Pulog, Mount, mtn., Phil. B7 32
Pumphrey, Md., U.S. h11 97
Puná, Isla, i., Ec. I2 58
Punakha, Bhu. G13 38
Pūnch, India D6 38
Pune (Poona), India C2 37
Pungo Lake, l., N.C., U.S. B6 110
Punjab, state, India E6 38
Puno, Peru G4 54
Punta, Cerro de, mtn., P.R. E14 64
Punta Alta, Arg. D4 56
Punta Arenas, Chile G2 56
Punta Delgada, Arg. E4 56
Punta de Mata, Ven. C11 58
Punta Gorda, Belize F3 64
Punta Gorda, Nic. I6 64
Punta Gorda, Fl., U.S. F4 86
Puntarenas, C.R. J5 64
Punto Fijo, Ven. B7 58
Punxsutawney, Pa., U.S. E4 115
Puolanka, Fin. D16 6
Purcell, Ok., U.S. B4 113
Purcellville, Va., U.S. A5 123
Purdy, Mo., U.S. E4 102
Purgatoire, stm., Co., U.S. D7 83
Purgatoire Peak, mtn., Co., U.S. D5 83
Puri, India K11 38
Purli, India C4 37
Purnea, India H12 38
Purūlia, India I12 38
Purus (Purús), stm., S.A. D6 54
Purvis, Ms., U.S. D4 101
Purwakarta, Indon. m13 33a
Purwokerto, Indon. m14 32
Purworejo, Indon. m15 33a
Pusan, S. Kor. D12 26
Pushaw Lake, l., Me., U.S. D4 96
Pushmataha, co., Ok., U.S. C6 113
Puškin, Russia B13 18
Puškino, Russia E20 18
Putao, Mya. F6 26
Putian, China J8 28
Puting, Tanjung, c., Indon. F5 32
Putnam, Ct., U.S. B8 84
Putnam, co., Fl., U.S. C5 86
Putnam, co., Ga., U.S. C3 87
Putnam, co., Il., U.S. B4 90
Putnam, co., In., U.S. E4 91
Putnam, co., Mo., U.S. A4 102
Putnam, co., N.Y., U.S. D7 109
Putnam, co., Oh., U.S. B1 112
Putnam, co., Tn., U.S. C8 119
Putnam, co., W.V., U.S. C3 125
Putney, Ga., U.S. E2 87
Putney, Vt., U.S. F3 122
Putorana, Plato, plat., Russia D12 24
Puttalam, Sri L. H5 37
Puttgarden, Ger. A11 8
Putumayo (Içá), stm., S.A. I7 58
Putuo, China F11 28
Puukohola Heiau National Historic Site, hist., Hi., U.S. D6 88
Puxico, Mo., U.S. E7 102
Puyallup, Wa., U.S. B3 124
Puyallup, stm., Wa., U.S. C3 124
Puy de Dôme, mtn., Fr. G9 10
Puy de Sancy, mtn., Fr. G9 10
Puylaurens, Fr. I9 10
Puyo, Ec. H4 58
Pweto, Zaire C5 44
Pwllheli, Wales, U.K. I8 7
Pyapon, Mya. F3 34
Pyatigorsk see P'atigorsk, Russia I6 22
Pyè (Prome), Mya. E3 34
Pyhäjoki, Fin. D15 6
Pyhäselkä, Fin. E17 6
Pyinmana, Mya. E4 34
Pyles Fork, stm., W.V., U.S. h10 125
Pymatuning Reservoir, res., U.S. C1 115
P'yŏngyang, N. Kor. D12 26
Pyramid Lake, l., Nv., U.S. C2 105
Pyramid Lake Indian Reservation, Nv., U.S. D2 105
Pyramid Mountains, mts., N.M., U.S. E1 108
Pyramid Peak, mtn., N.M., U.S. E1 108
Pyramid Peak, mtn., Wy., U.S. C2 127
Pyrenees, mts., Eur. C12 12
Pyskowice, Pol. E18 8
Pyu, Mya. E4 34

Q

Qaidam Pendi, China B16 38
Qalāt, Afg. D2 38
Qal'at Bīshah, Sau. Ar. E3 46
Qal'eh-ye Kānsī, Afg. C2 36
Qal'eh-ye Sarkārī, Afg. C2 38
Qallābāt, Sudan F13 42
Qamar, Ghubbat al-, b., Yemen E5 46
Qamdo, China E6 26
Qandahār, Afg. E1 38
Qandala, Som. F4 46
Qarqan, stm., China B11 38
Qarqīn, Afg. B2 38
Qaṣr al-Burayqah, Libya B9 42
Qaṣr al-Farāfirah, Egypt C11 42
Qaṭanā, Syria C5 40
Qatar, ctry., Asia C5 46
Qazvīn, Iran J8 22
Qeshm, i., Iran C6 46
Qeyṣār, Afg. C1 38
Qeẓi'ot, Isr. D4 40
Qiemo, China A11 38
Qijiang, China F8 26
Qinā, Egypt C12 42
Qingdao (Tsingtao), China D11 26
Qinghai, prov., China D6 26
Qinghai Hu, l., China D7 26
Qingjiang, China G4 28
Qinglong, China B8 34
Qingyang, China D8 26
Qingyuan, China G8 26
Qingyuan, China L2 28
Qinhuangdao, China D10 26
Qin Ling, mts., China E8 26
Qinzhou, China D10 34
Qiongzhou Haixia, strt., China D11 34
Qiqihar, China B11 26
Qiryat Shemona, Isr. C4 40
Qitai, China C4 26
Qīzān, Sau. Ar. E3 46
Qom, Iran B5 46
Qomsheh, Iran B5 46
Qondūz, Afg. B3 38
Qondūz, stm., Afg. C3 38
Quabbin Reservoir, res., Ma., U.S. B3 98
Quaddick Reservoir, res., Ct., U.S. B8 84
Quail Oaks, Va., U.S. n18 123
Quaker Hill, Ct., U.S. D7 84
Quakertown, Pa., U.S. F11 115
Qualicum Beach, B.C., Can. E5 69
Quanah, Tx., U.S. B3 120
Quang Ngai, Viet. G10 34
Quannapowitt, Lake, l., Ma., U.S. f11 98
Quantico, Va., U.S. B5 123
Quantico Marine Corps Air Station, mil., Va., U.S. B5 123
Quanzhou, China K7 28
Quapaw, Ok., U.S. A7 113
Qu'Appelle, Sask., Can. G4 75
Qu'Appelle, stm., Can. G4 75
Quarryville, Pa., U.S. G9 115
Quartu Sant'Elena, Italy J4 14
Quartz Lake, l., N.W. Ter., Can. B16 66
Quartz Mountain, mtn., Or., U.S. D4 114
Quartzsite, Az., U.S. D1 80
Quassapaug, Lake, l., Ct., U.S. C3 84
Quatsino Sound, strt., B.C., Can. D3 69
Quay, co., N.M., U.S. C6 108
Qūchān, Iran J9 22
Québec, Que., Can. C6 74
Quebec, prov., Can. C5 74
Quechee, Vt., U.S. D4 122
Quedlinburg, Ger. D11 8
Queen, stm., R.I., U.S. E3 116
Queen Annes, co., Md., U.S. B5 97
Queen Bess, Mount, mtn., B.C., Can. D5 69
Queen Charlotte, B.C., Can. C1 69
Queen Charlotte Islands, is., B.C., Can. C1 69
Queen Charlotte Mountains, mts., B.C., Can. C1 69
Queen Charlotte Sound, strt., B.C., Can. n17 69
Queen Charlotte Strait, strt., B.C., Can. D4 69
Queen City, Mo., U.S. A5 102
Queen City, Tx., U.S. C5 120
Queen Creek, Az., U.S. m9 80
Queen Maud Gulf, b., N.W. Ter., Can. C12 66
Queen Maud Land, reg., Ant. B14 47
Queens, co., N.Y., U.S. E7 109
Queens Channel, strt., N.W. Ter., Can. A13 66
Queensland, state, Austl. D8 50
Queenstown, N.Z. F2 52
Queenstown, S. Afr. H5 44
Quelimane, Moz. E7 44
Quemoy see Chinmen Tao, i., Tai. K7 28
Querétaro, Mex. G9 62
Querobabi, Mex. B4 62
Quesnel, B.C., Can. C6 69
Quesnel, stm., B.C., Can. C6 69
Quesnel Lake, l., B.C., Can. C7 69
Questa, N.M., U.S. A4 108
Questembert, Fr. E4 10
Quetico Provincial Park, Ont., Can. o17 73
Quetta, Pak. E2 38
Quevedo, Ec. H3 58
Quevedo, stm., Ec. H3 58
Quezaltenango, Guat. G2 64
Quezon City, Phil. q19 32
Qufu, China D10 26
Quibdó, Col. E4 58
Quiberon, Fr. E3 10
Quicksand Pond, l., R.I., U.S. E6 116
Quidnessett, R.I., U.S. E4 116
Quidnick, R.I., U.S. D3 116
Quidnick Reservoir, res., R.I., U.S. D2 116
Quilá, Mex. E6 62
Quilcene, Wa., U.S. B3 124
Quileute Indian Reservation, Wa., U.S. B1 124
Quillan, Fr. J9 10
Quilon, India H4 37
Quilpie, Austl. E8 50
Quimilí, Arg. B4 56
Quimper, Fr. D2 10
Quimperlé, Fr. E3 10
Quinault, stm., Wa., U.S. B1 124
Quinault, Lake, l., Wa., U.S. B2 124
Quinault Indian Reservation, Wa., U.S. B1 124
Quincemil, Peru F4 54
Quincy, Ca., U.S. C3 82
Quincy, Fl., U.S. B2 86
Quincy, Il., U.S. D2 90
Quincy, Ma., U.S. B5 98
Quincy, Mi., U.S. G6 99
Quincy, Wa., U.S. B6 124
Quincy Bay, b., Ma., U.S. g12 98
Quinebaug, Ct., U.S. A8 84
Quinebaug, stm., Ct., U.S. C8 84
Quinhagak, Ak., U.S. D7 79
Qui Nhon, Viet. H10 34
Quinlan, Tx., U.S. C4 120
Quinn, stm., Nv., U.S. B3 105
Quinn Canyon Range, mts., Nv., U.S. F6 105
Quinnesec, Mi., U.S. C3 99
Quinnipiac, stm., Ct., U.S. D4 84
Quintanar de la Orden, Spain F8 12
Quinter, Ks., U.S. C3 93
Quinton, Ok., U.S. B6 113
Quiroga, Spain C4 12
Quitman, Ar., U.S. B3 81
Quitman, Ga., U.S. F3 87
Quitman, Ms., U.S. C5 101
Quitman, Tx., U.S. C5 120
Quitman, co., Ga., U.S. E1 87
Quitman, co., Ms., U.S. A3 101
Quito, Ec. H3 58
Quixadá, Braz. D11 54
Qujing, China B7 34
Qumalai (Sewugou), China C16 38
Quoich, stm., N.W. Ter., Can. D14 66
Quonnipaug Lake, l., Ct., U.S. D5 84
Quonochontaug, R.I., U.S. G2 116
Quonochontaug Pond, l., R.I., U.S. G2 116
Quonset Point, c., R.I., U.S. E4 116
Qutdligssat, Grnld. B22 66
Quthing, Leso. H5 44
Quxian, China G7 28

R

Raalte, Neth. C6 8
Rab, Cro. E9 14
Raba, Indon. G6 32
Rába (Raab), stm., Eur. H17 8
Rábade, Spain B4 12
Rabat (Victoria), Malta M9 14
Rabat, Mor. B4 42
Rabaul, Pap. N. Gui. k17 50a
Rabbit Creek, stm., S.D., U.S. B3 118
Rabbit Ears Pass, Co., U.S. A4 83
Rābigh, Sau. Ar. D2 46
Rabun, co., Ga., U.S. B3 87
Rabun Bald, mtn., Ga., U.S. B3 87
Raccoon Creek, stm., Oh., U.S. D3 112
Raccourci Island, i., La., U.S. D4 95
Race, Cape, c., Newf., Can. E5 72
Raceland, Ky., U.S. B7 94
Raceland, La., U.S. E5 95
Race Point, c., Ma., U.S. B7 98
Rach Gia, Viet. I8 34
Racibórz (Ratibor), Pol. E18 8
Racine, W.V., U.S. C3 125
Racine, Wi., U.S. F6 126
Racine, co., Wi., U.S. F5 126
Racine Dam, U.S. C3 125
Radcliff, Ky., U.S. C4 94
Radeberg, Ger. D13 8
Radebeul, Ger. D13 8
Radeče, Slo. C10 14
Radford, Va., U.S. C2 123
Radolfzell, Ger. H8 8
Radom, Pol. D21 8
Radomsko, Pol. D19 8
Rae, N.W. Ter., Can. D9 66
Rāe Bareli, India G9 38
Raeford, N.C., U.S. C3 110
Rae Isthmus, N.W. Ter., Can. C15 66
Rae Strait, strt., N.W. Ter., Can. C13 66
Raetihi, N.Z. C5 52
Rafaela, Arg. C4 56
Rafaḥ, Isr. Occ. D4 40
Rafḥā', Sau. Ar. C3 46
Rafsanjān, Iran K9 22
Rafsanjān, Iran B6 46
Raft, stm., Id., U.S. G5 89
Raft River Mountains, mts., Ut., U.S. B2 121
Raga, Sudan G11 42
Ragged Island, i., Me., U.S. E4 96
Ragged Lake, l., Me., U.S. C3 96
Ragged Top Mountain, mtn., Wy., U.S. E7 127
Ragland, Al., U.S. B3 78
Ragusa, Italy M9 14
Ragusa see Dubrovnik, Cro. G13 14
Rahīmyār Khān, Pak. F4 38
Rahway, N.J., U.S. B4 107
Rahway, stm., N.J., U.S. k7 107
Rāichūr, India D4 37
Raigarh, India B7 37
Railroad Valley, val., Nv., U.S. E6 105
Rainbow Bridge National Monument, Ut., U.S. F5 121
Rainbow Falls, wtfl, Tn., U.S. D10 119
Rainbow Flowage, res., Wi., U.S. C4 126
Rainbow Lake, l., Me., U.S. C3 96
Rainelle, W.V., U.S. D4 125
Rainier, Or., U.S. A4 114
Rainier, Wa., U.S. C3 124
Rainier, Mount, mtn., Wa., U.S. C4 124
Rains, co., Tx., U.S. C5 120
Rainsville, Al., U.S. A4 78
Rainy Lake, l., N.A. G14 66
Rainy Lake, l., Mn., U.S. B5 100
Rainy River, Ont., Can. o16 73
Raipur, India B6 37
Rājahmundry, India D6 37
Raja-Jooseppi, Fin. B17 6
Rājapālaiyam, India H4 37
Rājasthān, prov., India G5 38
Rājasthān Canal, India F5 38
Rajčichinsk, Russia H19 24
Rājkot, India I4 38
Rāj-Nāndgaon, India B6 37
Rājpīpla, India J5 38
Rājshāhi, Bngl. H13 38
Rakaposhi, mtn., Pak. B6 38
Rakata, Pulau, i., Indon. m12 33a
Råkvåg, Nor. E8 6
Raleigh, Ms., U.S. C4 101
Raleigh, N.C., U.S. B4 110
Raleigh, W.V., U.S. n13 125
Raleigh, co., W.V., U.S. D3 125
Raleigh Bay, b., N.C., U.S. C6 110
Ralls, Tx., U.S. C2 120
Ralls, co., Mo., U.S. B6 102
Ralston, Ne., U.S. g12 104
Ralston Valley, val., Nv., U.S. E4 105
Rama, Nic. H5 64
Ramah, N.M., U.S. B1 108
Ramah Indian Reservation, N.M., U.S. C1 108
Rām Allāh, Jord. D4 40
Ramapo, stm., N.J., U.S. A4 107
Ramblewood, N.J., U.S. D3 107
Rambouillet, Fr. D8 10
Ramea, Newf., Can. E3 72
Ramenskoje, Russia F21 18
Rāmeswaram, India H5 37
Rāmgarh, Bngl. I14 38
Ramla, Isr. D4 40
Ramlo, mtn., Erit. F3 46
Ramona, Ca., U.S. F5 82
Rampart Range, mts., Co., U.S. B5 83
Rāmpur, India F8 38
Ramree Island, i., Mya. E2 34
Ramsay, Mi., U.S. n12 99
Ramseur, N.C., U.S. B3 110
Ramsey, I. of Man G8 7
Ramsey, Il., U.S. D4 90
Ramsey, Mn., U.S. *E5 100
Ramsey, N.J., U.S. A4 107
Ramsey, co., Mn., U.S. E5 100
Ramsey, co., N.D., U.S. A7 111
Ramsgate, Eng., U.K. J14 7
Ramshorn Peak, mtn., Mt., U.S. E5 103
Ramshorn Peak, mtn., Wy., U.S. C3 127
Rāmu, Bngl. J15 38
Ramu, stm., Pap. N. Gui. m16 50a
Rancagua, Chile C2 56
Rancharia, Braz. G3 57
Rancheria Rock, mtn., Or., U.S. C6 114
Ranchester, Wy., U.S. B5 127
Rānchī, India I11 38
Rancho Palos Verdes, Ca., U.S. *n12 82
Ranchos de Taos, N.M., U.S. A4 108
Rancocas Creek, stm., N.J., U.S. C3 107
Rand, W.V., U.S. C3 125
Randall, co., Tx., U.S. B2 120
Randallstown, Md., U.S. B4 97
Randazzo, Italy L9 14
Randers, Den. H8 6
Randle, Wa., U.S. C4 124
Randleman, N.C., U.S. B3 110
Randolph, Me., U.S. D3 96
Randolph, Ma., U.S. B5 98
Randolph, Ne., U.S. B8 104
Randolph, Vt., U.S. D3 122
Randolph, Wi., U.S. E5 126
Randolph, co., Al., U.S. B4 78
Randolph, co., Ar., U.S. A4 81
Randolph, co., Ga., U.S. E2 87
Randolph, co., Il., U.S. E4 90
Randolph, co., In., U.S. D7 91
Randolph, co., Mo., U.S. B5 102
Randolph, co., N.C., U.S. B3 110
Randolph, co., W.V., U.S. C5 125
Randolph Air Force Base, mil., Tx., U.S. h7 120
Randolph Hills, Md., U.S. B3 97
Random Island, i., Newf., Can. D5 72
Random Lake, Wi., U.S. E6 126
Rangeley, Me., U.S. D2 96
Rangeley Lake, l., Me., U.S. D2 96
Rangely, Co., U.S. A2 83
Ranger, Tx., U.S. C3 120
Ranger Lake, l., N.M., U.S. D6 108
Rangoon see Yangon, Mya. B2 32
Rangpur, Bngl. H13 38

Name	Map Ref	Page
Rankin, Pa., U.S.	k14	115
Rankin, co., Ms., U.S.	C4	101
Rankin Inlet, N.W. Ter., Can.	D14	66
Rann of Kutch, pl., Asia	H3	38
Ransom, co., N.D., U.S.	C8	111
Ranson, W.V., U.S.	B7	125
Rantauprapat, Indon.	E2	32
Rantekombola, Bulu, mtn., Indon.	F7	32
Rantoul, Il., U.S.	C5	90
Raoping, China	L6	28
Raoul, Ga., U.S.	B3	87
Rapallo, Italy	E4	14
Rapid, stm., Mn., U.S.	B4	100
Rapid City, S.D., U.S.	C2	118
Rapides, co., La., U.S.	C3	95
Rapid River, Mi., U.S.	C4	99
Rapids City, Il., U.S.	B3	90
Rappahannock, co., Va., U.S.	B4	123
Rappahannock, stm., Va., U.S.	B5	123
Raquette, stm., N.Y., U.S.	f10	109
Raquette Lake, l., N.Y., U.S.	B6	109
Raritan, N.J., U.S.	B3	107
Raritan, stm., N.J., U.S.	C4	107
Raritan Bay, b., N.J., U.S.	C4	107
Ra's al-'Ayn, Syria	A7	40
Ra's an-Naqb, Jord.	D4	40
Ras Dashen, mtn., Eth.	F2	46
Ras Djebel, Tun.	L5	14
Rasht, Iran	J7	22
Rāsipuram, India	G5	37
Rasskazovo, Russia	I24	18
Rastatt, Ger.	G8	8
Ratangarh, India	F6	38
Rätansbyn, Swe.	E10	6
Rathbun Lake, res., Ia., U.S.	D5	92
Rathdrum, Id., U.S.	B2	89
Rathenow, Ger.	C12	8
Rathkeale, Ire.	I4	7
Rathlin Island, i., N. Ire., U.K.	F6	7
Rat Islands, is., Ak., U.S.	E3	79
Ratlām, India	I6	38
Ratnāgiri, India	D2	37
Ratnapura, Sri L.	I6	37
Raton, N.M., U.S.	A5	108
Raton Pass, N.M., U.S.	A5	108
Rattlesnake Creek, stm., Oh., U.S.	C2	112
Rattlesnake Creek, stm., Wa., U.S.	C6	124
Rättvik, Swe.	F10	6
Ratz, Mount, mtn., B.C., Can.	E6	66
Ratzeburg, Ger.	B10	8
Raub, Malay.	M6	34
Rauch, Arg.	D5	56
Rauma, Fin.	F13	6
Raurkela, India	I11	38
Ravalli, co., Mt., U.S.	D2	103
Raven, Va., U.S.	e10	123
Ravena, N.Y., U.S.	C7	109
Ravenel, S.C., U.S.	k11	117
Ravenna, Italy	E7	14
Ravenna, Ky., U.S.	C6	94
Ravenna, Mi., U.S.	E5	99
Ravenna, Ne., U.S.	C7	104
Ravenna, Oh., U.S.	A4	112
Raven Park, reg., Co., U.S.	A2	83
Ravensburg, Ger.	H9	8
Ravenshoe, Austl.	C9	50
Ravensthorpe, Austl.	F3	50
Ravenswood, W.V., U.S.	C3	125
Rāwalpindi, Pak.	D5	38
Rawdon, Que., Can.	C4	74
Rawhide Creek, stm., Wy., U.S.	D8	127
Rawlings, Md., U.S.	k13	97
Rawlinna, Austl.	F5	50
Rawlins, Wy., U.S.	E5	127
Rawlins, co., Ks., U.S.	C2	93
Rawson, Arg.	E3	56
Ray, N.D., U.S.	A2	111
Ray, co., Mo., U.S.	B3	102
Ray, Cape, c., Newf., Can.	E2	72
Raya, Bukit, mtn., Indon.	F5	32
Rāyadrug, India	E4	37
Ray City, Ga., U.S.	E3	87
Raymond, Alta., Can.	E4	68
Raymond, Il., U.S.	D4	90
Raymond, Mn., U.S.	E3	100
Raymond, Ms., U.S.	C3	101
Raymond, N.H., U.S.	D4	106
Raymond, Wa., U.S.	C2	124
Raymondville, Tx., U.S.	F4	120
Raymore, Sask., Can.	F3	75
Raymore, Mo., U.S.	C3	102
Rayne, La., U.S.	D3	95
Raynham, Ma., U.S.	C5	98
Raynham Center, Ma., U.S.	C5	98
Raytown, Mo., U.S.	h11	102
Rayville, La., U.S.	B4	95
R'azan', Russia	G22	18
Razgrad, Bul.	F10	16
R'ažsk, Russia	H23	18
Reader, W.V., U.S.	B4	125
Reading, Eng., U.K.	J12	7
Reading, Ma., U.S.	A5	98
Reading, Mi., U.S.	G6	99
Reading, Oh., U.S.	C1	112
Reading, Pa., U.S.	F10	115
Readlyn, Ia., U.S.	B5	92
Reagan, co., Tx., U.S.	D2	120
Real, co., Tx., U.S.	E3	120
Realicó, Arg.	D4	56
Réalmont, Fr.	I9	10
Reamstown, Pa., U.S.	F9	115
Recanati, Italy	F8	14
Recherche, Archipelago of the, is., Austl.	F4	50
Rečica, Bela.	I13	18
Recife, Braz.	E12	54
Recklinghausen, Ger.	D7	8
Recreo, Arg.	B3	56
Rector, Ar., U.S.	A5	81
Red (Hong) (Yuan), stm., Asia	C8	34
Red, stm., N.A.	B7	76
Red, stm., U.S.	E8	76
Red, stm., Ky., U.S.	C6	94
Red, stm., Tn., U.S.	A4	119
Red Bank, N.J., U.S.	C4	107
Red Bank, Tn., U.S.	D8	119
Red Bay, Al., U.S.	A1	78
Redberry Lake, l., Sask., Can.	E2	75
Redbird, Oh., U.S.	A4	112
Red Bird, stm., Ky., U.S.	C6	94
Red Bluff, Ca., U.S.	B2	82
Red Bluff Lake, res., U.S.	o12	120
Red Boiling Springs, Tn., U.S.	C8	119
Red Bud, Il., U.S.	E4	90
Red Butte, mtn., Ut., U.S.	B2	121
Red Cedar, stm., Wi., U.S.	C2	126
Red Cedar Lake, l., Wi., U.S.	C2	126
Redcliff, Alta., Can.	D5	68
Redcliffe, Mount, mtn., Austl.	E4	50
Red Cliff Indian Reservation, Wi., U.S.	B2	126
Red Cloud, Ne., U.S.	D7	104
Redcloud Peak, mtn., Co., U.S.	D3	83
Red Deer, Alta., Can.	C4	68
Red Deer, stm., Can.	D4	68
Red Deer, stm., Can.	E4	75
Redding, Ca., U.S.	B2	82
Redding, Ct., U.S.	D2	84
Redeye, stm., Mn., U.S.	D3	100
Redfield, Ar., U.S.	C3	81
Redfield, Ia., U.S.	C3	92
Redfield, S.D., U.S.	C7	118
Redford, Mi., U.S.	F7	99
Redgranite, Wi., U.S.	D4	126
Red Hook, N.Y., U.S.	C7	109
Red Indian Lake, l., Newf., Can.	D3	72
Red Jacket, W.V., U.S.	D2	125
Redkey, In., U.S.	D7	91
Redlake, Mn., U.S.	C3	100
Red Lake, co., Mn., U.S.	C2	100
Red Lake, l., Az., U.S.	B1	80
Red Lake, stm., Mn., U.S.	C2	100
Red Lake Falls, Mn., U.S.	C2	100
Red Lake Indian Reservation, Mn., U.S.	B3	100
Redlands, Ca., U.S.	E5	82
Red Lion, Pa., U.S.	G8	115
Red Lodge, Mt., U.S.	E7	103
Red Mill Pond, l., De., U.S.	E5	85
Redmond, Or., U.S.	C5	114
Redmond, Ut., U.S.	E4	121
Redmond, Wa., U.S.	e11	124
Red Mountain, mtn., Ca., U.S.	B2	82
Red Mountain, mtn., Mt., U.S.	C4	103
Red Mountain Pass, Co., U.S.	D3	83
Red Oak, Ga., U.S.	h7	87
Red Oak, Ia., U.S.	D2	92
Red Oak, Ok., U.S.	C6	113
Red Oak, Tx., U.S.	n10	120
Red Oaks, La., U.S.	h9	95
Redon, Fr.	E4	10
Redondela, Spain	C3	12
Redondo, Port.	G4	12
Redondo, Wa., U.S.	f11	124
Redondo Beach, Ca., U.S.	n12	82
Redoubt Volcano, vol., Ak., U.S.	g15	79
Red Peak, mtn., Co., U.S.	B4	83
Red River, co., La., U.S.	B2	95
Red River, co., Tx., U.S.	C5	120
Red Rock, stm., Mt., U.S.	F4	103
Red Rock, Lake, res., Ia., U.S.	C4	92
Red Sea	D2	46
Red Springs, N.C., U.S.	C3	110
Red Table Mountain, mts., Co., U.S.	B4	83
Redwater, Alta., Can.	C4	68
Redwater, stm., Mt., U.S.	C11	103
Red Willow, co., Ne., U.S.	D5	104
Redwillow, stm., Can.	B7	69
Red Wing, Mn., U.S.	F6	100
Redwood, co., Mn., U.S.	F3	100
Redwood, stm., Mn., U.S.	F3	100
Redwood City, Ca., U.S.	D2	82
Redwood Falls, Mn., U.S.	F3	100
Redwood National Park, Ca., U.S.	B2	82
Redwood Valley, Ca., U.S.	C2	82
Ree, Lough, l., Ire.	H4	7
Reed City, Mi., U.S.	E5	99
Reedley, Ca., U.S.	D4	82
Reedsburg, Wi., U.S.	E3	126
Reeds Peak, mtn., N.M., U.S.	D2	108
Reedsport, Or., U.S.	D2	114
Reedsville, Pa., U.S.	E6	115
Reedsville, Wi., U.S.	D6	126
Reedy, stm., S.C., U.S.	C3	117
Reedy Lake, l., Fl., U.S.	E5	86
Reelfoot Lake, l., Tn., U.S.	A2	119
Reese, Mi., U.S.	E7	99
Reese, stm., Nv., U.S.	C4	105
Reese Air Force Base, mil., Tx., U.S.	C1	120
Reeves, co., Tx., U.S.	o13	120
Reform, Al., U.S.	B1	78
Refugio, Tx., U.S.	E4	120
Refugio, co., Tx., U.S.	E4	120
Regen, Ger.	G13	8
Regencia, Braz.	E9	57
Regensburg, Ger.	F12	8
Reggane, Alg.	C6	42
Reggio di Calabria, Italy	K10	14
Reggio nell'Emilia, Italy	E5	14
Regina, Sask., Can.	G3	75
Regina Beach, Sask., Can.	G3	75
Rehoboth, Nmb.	E3	44
Rehoboth Bay, b., De., U.S.	F5	85
Rehoboth Beach, De., U.S.	F5	85
Reḥovot, Isr.	D4	40
Reichenbach, Ger.	E12	8
Reid, Mount, mtn., Ak., U.S.	n24	79
Reidland, Ky., U.S.	e9	94
Reidsville, Ga., U.S.	D4	87
Reidsville, N.C., U.S.	A3	110
Reims, Fr.	C11	10
Reina Adelaida, Archipiélago, is., Chile	G2	56
Reinbeck, Ia., U.S.	B5	92
Reindeer Island, i., Man., Can.	C3	70
Reindeer Lake, l., Can.	m8	75
Reinosa, Spain	B7	12
Reisterstown, Md., U.S.	B4	97
Reliance, Wy., U.S.	E3	127
Remada, Tun.	B8	42
Remanso, Braz.	E10	54
Rembang, Indon.	m15	33a
Remington, In., U.S.	C3	91
Remiremont, Fr.	D13	10
Remmel Dam, Ar., U.S.	g8	81
Remscheid, Ger.	D7	8
Remsen, Ia., U.S.	B2	92
Rend Lake, res., Il., U.S.	E5	90
Rendova, i., Sol.Is.	A11	50
Rendsburg, Ger.	A9	8
Renforth, N.B., Can.	D4	71
Renfrew, Ont., Can.	B8	73
Rengat, Indon.	O7	34
Rennell Island, i., Sol.Is.	B12	50
Rennes, Fr.	D5	10
Reno, Nv., U.S.	D2	105
Reno, co., Ks., U.S.	E5	93
Reno, Lake, l., Mn., U.S.	E3	100
Reno Hill, mtn., Wy., U.S.	D6	127
Renovo, Pa., U.S.	D6	115
Rensselaer, In., U.S.	C3	91
Rensselaer, N.Y., U.S.	C7	109
Rensselaer, co., N.Y., U.S.	C7	109
Renton, Wa., U.S.	B3	124
Renville, Mn., U.S.	F3	100
Renville, co., Mn., U.S.	F4	100
Renville, co., N.D., U.S.	A4	111
Reo, Indon.	G7	32
Repentigny, Que., Can.	D4	74
Republic, Mi., U.S.	B3	99
Republic, Mo., U.S.	D4	102
Republic, Pa., U.S.	G2	115
Republic, Wa., U.S.	A7	124
Republic, co., Ks., U.S.	C6	93
Republican, stm., U.S.	C6	93
Repulse Bay, N.W. Ter., Can.	C15	66
Repvåg, Nor.	A15	6
Réquista, Fr.	H9	10
Reschenpass, Eur.	C5	14
Reserve, La., U.S.	h10	95
Resistencia, Arg.	B5	56
Reşiţa, Rom.	D5	16
Resolute, N.W. Ter., Can.	B14	66
Resolution Island, i., N.W. Ter., Can.	D20	66
Reston, Man., Can.	E1	70
Reston, Va., U.S.	B5	123
Resülhınzır, c., Tur.	A4	40
Retalhuleu, Guat.	G2	64
Rethel, Fr.	C11	10
Réthimnon, Grc.	N8	16
Reunion (Réunion), dep., Afr.	F11	44
Reus, Spain	D13	12
Reutlingen, Ger.	G9	8
Revelo, Ky., U.S.	D5	94
Revelstoke, B.C., Can.	D8	69
Revelstoke, Lake, res., B.C., Can.	D8	69
Revere, Ma., U.S.	g11	98
Revillagigedo, Islas de, is., Mex.	H4	62
Revillagigedo Island, i., Ak., U.S.	n24	79
Revin, Fr.	C11	10
Rewa, India	H9	38
Rewāri, India	F7	38
Rex, Ga., U.S.	h8	87
Rexburg, Id., U.S.	F7	89
Rexton, N.B., Can.	C5	71
Rey, Iran	J8	22
Rey, Isla del, i., Pan.	J8	64
Reyes, Bol.	F5	54
Reyes, Point, c., Ca., U.S.	C2	82
Reyhanlı, Tur.	A5	40
Reykjavík, Ice.	C3	4
Reynolds, Ga., U.S.	D2	87
Reynolds, co., Mo., U.S.	D6	102
Reynoldsburg, Oh., U.S.	C3	112
Reynoldsville, Pa., U.S.	D4	115
Reynosa, Mex.	D10	62
Rēzekne, Lat.	E10	18
Rhaetian Alps, mts., Eur.	F16	10
Rhea, co., Tn., U.S.	D9	119
Rheine, Ger.	C7	8
Rheydt, Ger.	D6	8
Rhine (Rhein) (Rhin), stm., Eur.	D6	8
Rhinebeck, N.Y., U.S.	D7	109
Rhinelander, Wi., U.S.	C4	126
Rho, Italy	D4	14
Rhode Island, state, U.S.	D3	116
Rhode Island, i., R.I., U.S.	E5	116
Rhode Island Sound, strt., U.S.	F5	116
Rhodesia see Zimbabwe, ctry., Afr.	E5	44
Rhodes Peak, mtn., Id., U.S.	C4	89
Rhodes see Ródhos, Grc.	M12	16
Rhodope Mountains, mts., Eur.	H8	16
Rhondda, Wales, U.K.	J9	7
Rhône, stm., Eur.	H11	10
Rialto, Ca., U.S.	m14	82
Riau, Kepulauan, is., Indon.	N8	34
Riaza, Spain	D8	12
Ribadeo, Spain	B4	12
Ribadesella, Spain	B6	12
Ribeirão Prêto, Braz.	F5	57
Ribera, Italy	L8	14
Riberalta, Bol.	F5	54
Rib Lake, Wi., U.S.	C3	126
Ribnitz-Damgarten, Ger.	A12	8
Riccione, Italy	F7	14
Rice, Mn., U.S.	E4	100
Rice, co., Ks., U.S.	D5	93
Rice, co., Mn., U.S.	F5	100
Riceboro, Ga., U.S.	E5	87
Rice Lake, Wi., U.S.	C2	126
Rice Lake, l., Ont., Can.	C6	73
Rice Lake, l., Mn., U.S.	D5	100
Riceville, Ia., U.S.	A5	92
Rich, co., Ut., U.S.	B4	121
Rich, Cape, c., Ont., Can.	C4	73
Richards-Gebaur Air Force Base, mil., Mo., U.S.	C3	102
Richards Island, i., N.W. Ter., Can.	C6	66
Richardson, Tx., U.S.	n10	120
Richardson, co., Ne., U.S.	D10	104
Richardson Lakes, l., Me., U.S.	D2	96
Richardson Mountains, mts., Can.	C5	66
Richardton, N.D., U.S.	C3	111
Rich Creek, Va., U.S.	C2	123
Riche, Pointe, c., Newf., Can.	C3	72
Richfield, Mn., U.S.	F5	100
Richfield, Ut., U.S.	E3	121
Richford, Vt., U.S.	B3	122
Rich Hill, Mo., U.S.	C3	102
Richibucto, N.B., Can.	C5	71
Richland, Ga., U.S.	D2	87
Richland, Mo., U.S.	D5	102
Richland, Wa., U.S.	C6	124
Richland, co., Il., U.S.	E5	90
Richland, co., La., U.S.	B4	95
Richland, co., Mt., U.S.	C12	103
Richland, co., N.D., U.S.	C8	111
Richland, co., Oh., U.S.	B3	112
Richland, co., S.C., U.S.	D6	117
Richland, co., Wi., U.S.	E3	126
Richland Balsam, mtn., N.C., U.S.	f10	110
Richland Center, Wi., U.S.	E3	126
Richland Creek, stm., Tn., U.S.	B5	119
Richlands, N.C., U.S.	C5	110
Richlands, Va., U.S.	e10	123
Richlandtown, Pa., U.S.	F11	115
Richmond, Austl.	D8	50
Richmond, B.C., Can.	E6	69
Richmond, Que., Can.	D5	74
Richmond, Ca., U.S.	D2	82
Richmond, Il., U.S.	A5	90
Richmond, In., U.S.	E8	91
Richmond, Ky., U.S.	C5	94
Richmond, Me., U.S.	D3	96
Richmond, Mi., U.S.	F8	99
Richmond, Mn., U.S.	E4	100
Richmond, Mo., U.S.	B4	102
Richmond, Tx., U.S.	E5	120
Richmond, Ut., U.S.	B4	121
Richmond, Vt., U.S.	C3	122
Richmond, Va., U.S.	C5	123
Richmond, co., Ga., U.S.	C4	87
Richmond, co., N.Y., U.S.	E6	109
Richmond, co., N.C., U.S.	B3	110
Richmond, co., Va., U.S.	C6	123
Richmond Beach, Wa., U.S.	B3	124
Richmond Heights, Fl., U.S.	s13	86
Richmond Heights, Mo., U.S.	f13	102
Richmond Highlands, Wa., U.S.	B3	124
Richmond Hill, Ont., Can.	D5	73
Richmond Hill, Ga., U.S.	E5	87
Richmond National Battlefield Park, Va., U.S.	n18	123
Rich Square, N.C., U.S.	A5	110
Richthofen, Mount, mtn., Co., U.S.	A5	83
Richton, Ms., U.S.	D5	101
Richwood, Oh., U.S.	B2	112
Richwood, W.V., U.S.	C4	125
Rickenbacker Air Force Base, mil., Oh., U.S.	m11	112
Rickman, Tn., U.S.	C8	119
Riddle, Or., U.S.	E3	114
Riddle Mountain, mtn., Or., U.S.	D8	114
Rideau, stm., Ont., Can.	B9	73
Ridgecrest, Ca., U.S.	E5	82
Ridge Farm, Il., U.S.	D6	90
Ridgefield, Ct., U.S.	D2	84
Ridgefield, N.J., U.S.	h8	107
Ridgefield, Wa., U.S.	D3	124
Ridgefield Park, N.J., U.S.	B4	107
Ridgeland, Ms., U.S.	C3	101
Ridgeland, S.C., U.S.	G6	117
Ridgeley, W.V., U.S.	B6	125
Ridgely, Md., U.S.	C6	97
Ridgely, Tn., U.S.	A2	119
Ridge Spring, S.C., U.S.	D4	117
Ridgetop, Tn., U.S.	A5	119
Ridgetown, Ont., Can.	E3	73
Ridgeview, W.V., U.S.	C3	125
Ridgeville, In., U.S.	D7	91
Ridgeville, S.C., U.S.	E7	117
Ridgeway, Va., U.S.	D3	123
Ridgewood, N.J., U.S.	B4	107
Ridgway, Il., U.S.	F5	90
Ridgway, Pa., U.S.	D4	115
Riding Mountain National Park, Man., Can.	D1	70
Ridley Park, Pa., U.S.	p20	115
Ried im Innkreis, Aus.	G13	8
Riesa, Ger.	D13	8
Riesi, Italy	L9	14
Rieti, Italy	G7	14
Rif, mts., Mor.	A5	42
Riffe Lake, res., Wa., U.S.	C3	124
Rifle, Co., U.S.	B3	83
Rifle, stm., Mi., U.S.	D6	99
Rift Valley, val., Afr.	B5	44
Rīga, Lat.	E7	18
Riga, Gulf of, b., Eur.	D6	18
Rigaud, Que., Can.	D3	74
Rigby, Id., U.S.	F7	89
Rīgestān, reg., Afg.	C1	36
Riihimäki, Fin.	F15	6
Rijeka, Cro.	D9	14
Riley, Ks., U.S.	C7	93
Riley, co., Ks., U.S.	C7	93
Riley, Mount, mtn., N.M., U.S.	F2	108
Rimbey, Alta., Can.	C3	68
Rimersburg, Pa., U.S.	D3	115
Rimini, Italy	E7	14
Rimouski, Que., Can.	A9	74
Rimouski, stm., Que., Can.	A9	74
Rimouski-Est, Que., Can.	A9	74
Rimrock Lake, res., Wa., U.S.	C4	124
Rincon, Ga., U.S.	D5	87
Rincon Mountains, mts., Az., U.S.	E5	80
Rindal, Nor.	E7	6
Ringebu, Nor.	F8	6
Ringgold, Ga., U.S.	B1	87
Ringgold, La., U.S.	B2	95
Ringgold, co., Ia., U.S.	D3	92
Ringling, Ok., U.S.	C4	113
Ringwood, N.J., U.S.	A4	107
Rio, Fl., U.S.	E6	86
Rio, Wi., U.S.	E4	126
Rio Arriba, co., N.M., U.S.	A2	108
Riobamba, Ec.	H3	58
Río Benito, Eq. Gui.	H7	42
Rio Blanco, co., Co., U.S.	B2	83
Rio Branco, Braz.	E5	54
Rio Claro, Braz.	G5	57
Río Colorado, Arg.	D4	56
Río Cuarto, Arg.	C4	56
Rio de Janeiro, Braz.	G7	57
Rio Dell, Ca., U.S.	B1	82
Rio do Sul, Braz.	B7	56
Río Gallegos, Arg.	G3	56
Río Grande, Arg.	G3	56
Rio Grande, Braz.	C6	56
Río Grande, Mex.	F8	62
Río Grande, Nic.	H6	64
Rio Grande, Oh., U.S.	D3	112
Rio Grande, co., Co., U.S.	D4	83
Rio Grande City, Tx., U.S.	F3	120
Rio Grande Reservoir, res., Co., U.S.	D3	83
Ríohacha, Col.	B6	58
Rio Hondo, Tx., U.S.	F4	120
Rioja, Peru	E3	54
Riom, Fr.	G10	10
Río Mayo, Arg.	F2	56
Río Negro, Embalse del, res., Ur.	C5	56
Rio Negro, Pantanal do, sw., Braz.	G7	54
Rionero in Vulture, Italy	I10	14
Rio Pardo, Braz.	B6	56
Rio Pardo de Minas, Braz.	G10	54
Rio Rancho, N.M., U.S.	B3	108
Río Sucio, Col.	E5	58
Rio Verde, Braz.	D3	57
Ríoverde, Mex.	G10	62
Rio Vista, Ca., U.S.	C3	82
Rioz, Fr.	E13	10
Ripley, Ms., U.S.	A5	101
Ripley, Oh., U.S.	D2	112
Ripley, Tn., U.S.	B2	119
Ripley, W.V., U.S.	C3	125
Ripley, co., In., U.S.	F7	91
Ripley, co., Mo., U.S.	E7	102
Ripoll, Spain	C14	12
Ripon, Eng., U.K.	G11	7
Ripon, Wi., U.S.	E5	126
Rippowam, stm., Ct., U.S.	E1	84
Ririe Lake, res., Id., U.S.	F7	89
Rishon leẒiyyon, Isr.	D4	40
Rising Sun, De., U.S.	D3	85
Rising Sun, In., U.S.	G8	91
Rising Sun, Md., U.S.	A5	97
Rison, Ar., U.S.	D3	81
Ritchie, co., W.V., U.S.	B3	125
Ritter, Mount, mtn., Ca., U.S.	D4	82
Rittman, Oh., U.S.	B4	112
Ritzville, Wa., U.S.	B7	124
Riva, Italy	D5	14
Rivanna, stm., Va., U.S.	C4	123
Rivas, Nic.	I5	64
Rivera, Ur.	C5	56
Riverbank, Ca., U.S.	D3	82
River Bourgeois, N.S., Can.	D9	71
Riverdale, Ca., U.S.	D4	82
Riverdale, Il., U.S.	k9	90
Riverdale, Md., U.S.	C4	97
River Edge, N.J., U.S.	h8	107
River Falls, Al., U.S.	D3	78
River Falls, Wi., U.S.	D1	126
River Forest, Il., U.S.	k9	90
River Grove, Il., U.S.	k9	90
Riverhead, N.Y., U.S.	n16	109
River Hebert, N.S., Can.	D5	71
River Heights, Ut., U.S.	B4	121
River Hills, Wi., U.S.	m12	126
River Pines, Ma., U.S.	f10	98
River Ridge, La., U.S.	k11	95
River Road, Or., U.S.	C3	114
River Rouge, Mi., U.S.	p15	99
Rivers, Man., Can.	D1	70
Riverside, Al., U.S.	B3	78
Riverside, Ca., U.S.	F5	82
Riverside, Il., U.S.	k9	90
Riverside, Ia., U.S.	C6	92
Riverside, N.J., U.S.	C3	107
Riverside, Pa., U.S.	E8	115
Riverside, co., Ca., U.S.	F5	82
Riverside Reservoir, res., Co., U.S.	A6	83
Riverton, Man., Can.	D3	70
Riverton, Il., U.S.	D4	90
Riverton, Ks., U.S.	E9	93
Riverton, N.J., U.S.	C3	107
Riverton, Ut., U.S.	C4	121
Riverton, Vt., U.S.	C3	122
Riverton, Wy., U.S.	C4	127
Riverton Heights, Wa., U.S.	f11	124
River Vale, N.J., U.S.	h8	107
Riverview, Fl., U.S.	p11	86
Riverview, Mi., U.S.	p15	99
Rivesaltes, Fr.	J9	10
Rivesville, W.V., U.S.	B4	125
Riviera Beach, Fl., U.S.	F6	86
Riviera Beach, Md., U.S.	B4	97
Rivière-du-Loup, Que., Can.	B8	74
Rivière-Verte, N.B., Can.	B1	71
Rivne, Ukr.	G3	22
Rivoli, Italy	D2	14
Riyadh see Ar-Riyāḍ, Sau. Ar.	D4	46
Rize, Tur.	G16	4
Roa, Spain	D8	12
Roachdale, In., U.S.	E4	91
Roane, co., Tn., U.S.	D9	119
Roane, co., W.V., U.S.	C3	125
Roan Mountain, Tn., U.S.	C11	119
Roanne, Fr.	F11	10
Roanoke, Al., U.S.	B4	78
Roanoke, Il., U.S.	C4	90
Roanoke, In., U.S.	C7	91
Roanoke, La., U.S.	D3	95
Roanoke, Tx., U.S.	m9	120
Roanoke, Va., U.S.	C3	123
Roanoke, co., Va., U.S.	C2	123

Name — Map Ref — Page
Roanoke, stm., U.S. A5 110
Roanoke Island, i., N.C., U.S. B7 110
Roanoke Rapids, N.C., U.S. A5 110
Roanoke Rapids Lake, res., U.S. A5 110
Roaring Fork, stm., Co., U.S. C4 83
Roaring Spring, Pa., U.S. F5 115
Roatán, Isla de, i., Hond. F4 64
Robbins, Il., U.S. k9 90
Robbins, N.C., U.S. B3 110
Robbinsdale, Mn., U.S. m12 100
Robbinsville, N.C., U.S. f9 110
Röbel, Ger. B12 8
Robersonville, N.C., U.S. B5 110
Roberta, Ga., U.S. D2 87
Robert Lee, Tx., U.S. D2 120
Roberts, Wi., U.S. C1 126
Roberts, co., S.D., U.S. B8 118
Roberts, co., Tx., U.S. B2 120
Roberts, Point, c., Wa., U.S. A2 124
Robert's Arm, Newf., Can. D4 72
Roberts Creek Mountain, mtn., Nv., U.S. D5 105
Robertsdale, Al., U.S. E2 78
Robertsfors, Swe. D13 6
Robert S. Kerr Reservoir, res., Ok., U.S. B6 113
Roberts Mountain, mtn., Ak., U.S. C6 79
Roberts Mountain, mtn., Wy., U.S. D3 127
Robertson, co., Ky., U.S. B5 94
Robertson, co., Tn., U.S. A5 119
Robertson, co., Tx., U.S. D4 120
Robertsonville, Que., Can. C6 74
Roberts Peak, mtn., B.C., Can. F8 66
Robertsport, Lib. G3 42
Robertville, N.B., Can. B4 71
Roberval, Que., Can. A5 74
Robeson, co., N.C., U.S. C3 110
Robins, Ia., U.S. B6 92
Robinson, Il., U.S. D6 90
Robinson Fork, stm., W.V., U.S. m14 125
Robinson Fork, stm., W.V., U.S. k9 125
Roblin, Man., Can. D1 70
Roboré, Bol. G7 54
Robson, Mount, mtn., B.C., Can. C8 69
Robstown, Tx., U.S. F4 120
Roca Partida, Isla, i., Mex. H3 62
Roca Partida, Punta, c., Mex. H12 62
Rocas, Atol das, atoll, Braz. D12 54
Roccastrada, Italy F6 14
Rocha, Ur. C6 56
Rochefort, Fr. G6 10
Rochelle, Ga., U.S. E3 87
Rochelle, Il., U.S. B4 90
Rochelle Park, N.J., U.S. h8 107
Rochester, Il., U.S. D4 90
Rochester, In., U.S. B5 91
Rochester, Mi., U.S. F7 99
Rochester, Mn., U.S. F6 100
Rochester, N.H., U.S. D5 106
Rochester, N.Y., U.S. B3 109
Rochester, Pa., U.S. E1 115
Rochester, Vt., U.S. D3 122
Rochester, Wa., U.S. C2 124
Rochester, Wi., U.S. n11 126
Rock, co., Mn., U.S. G2 100
Rock, co., Ne., U.S. B6 104
Rock, co., Wi., U.S. F4 126
Rock, stm., U.S. B3 90
Rock, stm., U.S. A1 92
Rockall, i., Scot., U.K. D5 4
Rockaway, N.J., U.S. B3 107
Rockaway, Or., U.S. B3 114
Rockbridge, co., Va., U.S. C3 123
Rockcastle, co., Ky., U.S. C5 94
Rockcastle, stm., Ky., U.S. C5 94
Rockcliffe Park, Ont., Can. h12 73
Rock Creek, Mn., U.S. E6 100
Rock Creek, stm., U.S. B3 97
Rock Creek, stm., U.S. h14 124
Rock Creek, stm., Nv., U.S. C5 105
Rock Creek, stm., Or., U.S. B6 114
Rock Creek, stm., Wa., U.S. D5 124
Rock Creek, stm., Wa., U.S. B8 124
Rock Creek, stm., Wy., U.S. E6 127
Rock Creek Butte, mtn., Or., U.S. C8 114
Rockdale, Il., U.S. B5 90
Rockdale, Md., U.S. B4 97
Rockdale, Tx., U.S. D4 120
Rockdale, co., Ga., U.S. C3 87
Rockfall, Ct., U.S. C5 84
Rock Falls, Il., U.S. B4 90
Rockford, Il., U.S. A4 90
Rockford, Ia., U.S. A5 92
Rockford, Mi., U.S. E5 99
Rockford, Mn., U.S. E5 100
Rockford, Oh., U.S. B1 112
Rockford, Tn., U.S. D10 119
Rock Hall, Md., U.S. B5 97
Rockhampton, Austl. D10 50
Rock Hill, S.C., U.S. B5 117
Rockingham, N.C., U.S. C3 110
Rockingham, co., N.H., U.S. D4 106
Rockingham, co., N.C., U.S. A3 110
Rockingham, co., Va., U.S. B4 123
Rock Island, Que., Can. D5 74
Rock Island, Il., U.S. B3 90
Rock Island, co., Il., U.S. B3 90
Rock Island, i., Fl., U.S. C3 86
Rock Island, i., Wi., U.S. C7 126
Rock Lake, l., Wa., U.S. B8 124
Rockland, Ont., Can. B9 73
Rockland, Me., U.S. D3 96
Rockland, Ma., U.S. B6 98
Rockland, co., N.Y., U.S. D6 109
Rockledge, Fl., U.S. D6 86
Rockledge, Pa., U.S. o20 115
Rocklin, Ca., U.S. C3 82
Rockmart, Ga., U.S. B1 87
Rock Mountain, mtn., Co., U.S. D3 83
Rockport, In., U.S. I3 91
Rockport, Me., U.S. D3 96
Rockport, Ma., U.S. A6 98
Rock Port, Mo., U.S. A2 102
Rockport, Tx., U.S. F4 120
Rock Rapids, Ia., U.S. A1 92
Rock River, Wy., U.S. E7 127
Rock Sound, Bah. B9 64
Rocksprings, Tx., U.S. D2 120
Rock Springs, Wy., U.S. E3 127
Rockstone, Guy. E13 58
Rockton, Il., U.S. A4 90
Rock Valley, Ia., U.S. A1 92
Rockville, In., U.S. E3 91
Rockville, Md., U.S. B3 97
Rockville Centre, N.Y., U.S. n15 109
Rockwall, Tx., U.S. C4 120
Rockwall, co., Tx., U.S. C4 120
Rockwell, Ia., U.S. B4 92
Rockwell, N.C., U.S. B2 110
Rockwell City, Ia., U.S. B3 92
Rockwell Park, N.C., U.S. B2 110
Rockwood, Mi., U.S. F7 99
Rockwood, Pa., U.S. G3 115
Rockwood, Tn., U.S. D9 119
Rocky, stm., N.C., U.S. B2 110
Rocky, stm., S.C., U.S. C2 117
Rocky, East Branch, stm., Oh., U.S. h9 112
Rocky, West Branch, stm., Oh., U.S. h9 112
Rocky Boys Indian Reservation, Mt., U.S. B7 103
Rocky Ford, Co., U.S. C7 83
Rocky Fork Lake, l., Oh., U.S. C2 112
Rocky Harbour, Newf., Can. D3 72
Rocky Hill, Ct., U.S. C5 84
Rocky Lake, l., Me., U.S. D5 96
Rocky Mount, N.C., U.S. B5 110
Rocky Mount, Va., U.S. D3 123
Rocky Mountain, mtn., Mt., U.S. C4 103
Rocky Mountain House, Alta., Can. C3 68
Rocky Mountain National Park, Co., U.S. A5 83
Rocky Mountains, mts., N.A. E9 61
Rocky Ripple, In., U.S. k10 91
Rocky River, Oh., U.S. A4 112
Rocky Top, mtn., Or., U.S. C4 114
Roddickton, Newf., Can. C3 72
Roderfield, W.V., U.S. D3 125
Rodez, Fr. H9 10
Ródhos (Rhodes), Grc. M12 16
Ródhos, i., Grc. M11 16
Rodney, Ont., Can. E3 73
Rodney, Cape, c., Ak., U.S. C6 79
Rodney Village, De., U.S. D3 85
Rodniki, Russia D24 18
Roebourne, Austl. D3 50
Roebuck, S.C., U.S. B4 117
Roeland Park, Ks., U.S. k16 93
Roeselare, Bel. E3 8
Roes Welcome Sound, strt., N.W. Ter., Can. D15 66
Roff, Ok., U.S. C5 113
Rogagua, Lago, l., Bol. F5 54
Roger Mills, co., Ok., U.S. B2 113
Rogers, Ar., U.S. A1 81
Rogers, Mn., U.S. E5 100
Rogers, Tx., U.S. D4 120
Rogers, co., Ok., U.S. A6 113
Rogers, Mount, mtn., Va., U.S. f10 123
Rogers City, Mi., U.S. C7 99
Rogers Lake, res., Ct., U.S. D6 84
Rogers Pass, Mt., U.S. C4 103
Rogersville, N.B., Can. C4 71
Rogersville, Al., U.S. A2 78
Rogersville, Mo., U.S. D4 102
Rogersville, Tn., U.S. C10 119
Roggiano Gravina, Italy J11 14
Rogue, stm., Or., U.S. E2 114
Rogue River, Or., U.S. E3 114
Rohtak, India F7 38
Roi Et, Thai. F7 34
Rojo, Cabo, c., Mex. G11 62
Roland, Ia., U.S. B4 92
Roland, Ok., U.S. B7 113
Roland, Lake, res., Md., U.S. g11 97
Rolândia, Braz. G3 57
Røldal, Nor. G6 6
Rolette, N.D., U.S. A6 111
Rolette, co., N.D., U.S. A6 111
Rolfe, Ia., U.S. B3 92
Rolla, Mo., U.S. D6 102
Rolla, N.D., U.S. A6 111
Rollingbay, Wa., U.S. e10 124
Rolling Fork, Ms., U.S. C3 101
Rolling Fork, stm., Ar., U.S. C1 81
Rolling Fork, stm., Ky., U.S. C4 94
Rolling Meadows, Il., U.S. h8 90
Rollingstone, Mn., U.S. F7 100
Rollinsford, N.H., U.S. D5 106
Roma (Rome), Italy H7 14
Roma, Tx., U.S. F3 120
Romain, Cape, c., S.C., U.S. F9 117
Roman, Rom. C10 16
Romania, ctry., Eur. F13 4
Roman Nose Mountain, mtn., Or., U.S. D3 114
Romano, Cape, c., Fl., U.S. G5 86
Romano, Cayo, i., Cuba C8 64
Romans [-sur-Isère], Fr. G12 10
Romanzof, Cape, c., Ak., U.S. C6 79
Romanzof Mountains, mts., Ak., U.S. B11 79
Rome, Ga., U.S. B1 87
Rome, Il., U.S. C4 90
Rome, N.Y., U.S. B5 109
Rome City, In., U.S. B7 91
Romeo, Mi., U.S. F7 99
Romeoville, Il., U.S. k8 90
Rome see Roma, Italy H7 14
Romilly-sur-Seine, Fr. D10 10
Romney, W.V., U.S. B6 125
Romorantin-Lanthenay, Fr. E8 10
Romulus, Mi., U.S. p15 99
Ron, Mui, c., Viet. E9 34
Ronan, Mt., U.S. C2 103
Roncador, Serra do, plat., Braz. F8 54
Roncesvalles, Spain B10 12
Ronceverte, W.V., U.S. D4 125
Ronda, Spain I6 12
Rondônia, Braz. F6 54
Rondonópolis, Braz. D1 57
Ronge, Lac la, l., Sask., Can. B3 75
Rønne, Den. I10 6
Ronneby, Swe. H10 6
Ronne Ice Shelf, Ant. B6 47
Ronse, Bel. E3 8
Roodhouse, Il., U.S. D3 90
Rooks, co., Ks., U.S. C4 93
Roorkee, India F7 38
Roosendaal, Neth. D4 8
Roosevelt, Ut., U.S. C5 121
Roosevelt, co., Mt., U.S. B11 103
Roosevelt, co., N.M., U.S. C6 108
Roosevelt, stm., Braz. E6 54
Roosevelt Park, Mi., U.S. E4 99
Root, stm., Mn., U.S. G7 100
Root, stm., Wi., U.S. n12 126
Roper, N.C., U.S. B6 110
Roquefort, Fr. H6 10
Roraima, Mount, mtn., S.A. E12 58
Røros, Nor. E8 6
Rorschach, Switz. E16 10
Rørvik, Nor. D8 6
Rošal', Russia F22 18
Rosamond, Ca., U.S. E4 82
Rosamorada, Mex. F7 62
Rosario, Arg. C4 56
Rosário, Braz. D10 54
Rosario, Mex. F7 62
Rosario, Mex. B2 62
Rosario, Ven. B6 58
Rosário Oeste, Braz. F7 54
Rosarno, Italy K10 14
Rosas, Golfo de, b., Spain C15 12
Roscoe, Il., U.S. A5 90
Roscoe, Tx., U.S. C2 120
Roscommon, Ire. H4 7
Roscommon, Mi., U.S. D6 99
Roscommon, co., Mi., U.S. D6 99
Roscrea, Ire. I5 7
Rose, Mount, mtn., Nv., U.S. D2 105
Roseau, Dom. G17 64
Roseau, Mn., U.S. B3 100
Roseau, co., Mn., U.S. B3 100
Roseau, South Fork, stm., Mn., U.S. B3 100
Rose-Blanche [-Harbour le Cou], Newf., Can. E2 72
Roseboro, N.C., U.S. C4 110
Rosebud, S.D., U.S. D5 118
Rosebud, Tx., U.S. D4 120
Rosebud, co., Mt., U.S. D10 103
Rosebud Indian Reservation, S.D., U.S. D5 118
Roseburg, Or., U.S. D3 114
Rosedale, In., U.S. E3 91
Rosedale, Md., U.S. g11 97
Rosedale, Ms., U.S. B2 101
Rose Hill, Ks., U.S. E6 93
Rose Hill, N.C., U.S. C4 110
Rose Hill, Va., U.S. f8 123
Roseland, Fl., U.S. E6 86
Roseland, In., U.S. A5 91
Roseland, La., U.S. D5 95
Roseland, Oh., U.S. B3 112
Roselle, Il., U.S. k8 90
Roselle, N.J., U.S. k7 107
Roselle Park, N.J., U.S. k7 107
Rosemère, Que., Can. p19 74
Rosemount, Mn., U.S. F5 100
Rosenberg, Tx., U.S. E5 120
Rosendale, Wi., U.S. E5 126
Rosenheim, Ger. H12 8
Rose Peak, mtn., Az., U.S. D6 80
Rosepine, La., U.S. D2 95
Rose Point, c., B.C., Can. B2 69
Roseto, Pa., U.S. E11 115
Roseville, Ca., U.S. C3 82
Roseville, Il., U.S. C3 90
Roseville, Mi., U.S. o16 99
Roseville, Mn., U.S. m12 100
Roseville, Oh., U.S. C3 112
Rosewood Heights, Il., U.S. E3 90
Rosiclare, Il., U.S. F5 90
Rosignano Marittimo, Italy F5 14
Roskilde, Den. I9 6
Roslags-Näsby, Swe. G12 6
Roslavl', Russia H15 18
Roslyn, Wa., U.S. B4 124
Roslyn Heights, N.Y., U.S. h13 109
Ross, Oh., U.S. C1 112
Ross, co., Oh., U.S. C2 112
Rossano, Italy J11 14
Rossan Point, c., Ire. G4 7
Ross Barnett Reservoir, res., Ms., U.S. C3 101
Rossburn, Man., Can. D1 70
Ross Dam, Wa., U.S. A4 124
Rossel Island, i., Pap. N. Gui. B10 50
Rossford, Oh., U.S. A2 112
Ross Ice Shelf, Ant. A31 47
Rossignol, Lake, l., N.S., Can. E4 71
Ross Island, i., Man., Can. B3 70
Ross Lake National Recreation Area, Wa., U.S. A5 124
Rossland, B.C., Can. E9 69
Rosslare, Ire. I6 7
Rosso, Maur. E2 42
Ross River, Yukon, Can. D6 66
Ross Sea, Ant. B31 47
Rossville, Ga., U.S. B1 87
Rossville, Il., U.S. C6 90
Rossville, In., U.S. D4 91
Rossville, Ks., U.S. C8 93
Rostock, Ger. A12 8
Rostov, Russia D22 18
Rostov-na-Donu, Russia H5 22
Roswell, Ga., U.S. B2 87
Roswell, N.M., U.S. D5 108
Rotan, Tx., U.S. C2 120
Rotenburg, Ger. B9 8
Rothaargebirge, mts., Ger. D8 8
Rothenburg ob der Tauber, Ger. F10 8
Rothesay, N.B., Can. D4 71
Rothschild, Wi., U.S. D4 126
Rothsville, Pa., U.S. F9 115
Roti, Pulau, i., Indon. H7 32
Rotondella, Italy I11 14
Rotorua, N.Z. C6 52
Rotterdam, Neth. D4 8
Rotterdam, N.Y., U.S. C6 109
Rottweil, Ger. G8 8
Roubaix, Fr. B10 10
Rouen, Fr. C8 10
Rouge, stm., Que., Can. D3 74
Rough, stm., Ky., U.S. C3 94
Rough River Lake, res., Ky., U.S. C3 94
Roulette, Pa., U.S. C5 115
Round Island, i., Ms., U.S. g8 101
Round Lake, Il., U.S. h8 90
Round Lake Beach, Il., U.S. h8 90
Round Mountain, Nv., U.S. E4 105
Round Rock, Tx., U.S. D4 120
Roundup, Mt., U.S. D8 103
Round Valley Indian Reservation, Ca., U.S. C2 82
Round Valley Reservoir, res., N.J., U.S. B3 107
Rouses Point, N.Y., U.S. f11 109
Roussillon, hist. reg., Fr. J9 10
Routt, co., Co., U.S. A3 83
Rouyn [-Noranda], Que., Can. k11 74
Rouzerville, Pa., U.S. G6 115
Rovaniemi, Fin. C15 6
Rovato, Italy D4 14
Rovereto, Italy D6 14
Rovigo, Italy D6 14
Rovinj, Cro. D8 14
Rowan, co., Ky., U.S. B6 94
Rowan, co., N.C., U.S. B2 110
Rowland, N.C., U.S. C3 110
Rowlesburg, W.V., U.S. B5 125
Rowley Island, i., N.W. Ter., Can. C17 66
Rowley Shoals, rf., Austl. C3 50
Roxboro, N.C., U.S. A4 110
Roxton Falls, Que., Can. D5 74
Roxton Pond, Que., Can. D5 74
Roy, Ut., U.S. B3 121
Royal, stm., Me., U.S. g7 96
Royal Canal, Ire. H5 7
Royal Center, In., U.S. C4 91
Royale, Isle, i., Mi., U.S. h9 99
Royal Gorge, val., Co., U.S. C5 83
Royal Oak, Mi., U.S. F7 99
Royal Pines, N.C., U.S. f10 110
Royalton, Il., U.S. F4 90
Royalton, Mn., U.S. E4 100
Royan, Fr. G5 10
Royersford, Pa., U.S. F10 115
Royerton, In., U.S. D7 91
Royse City, Tx., U.S. C4 120
Royston, B.C., Can. E5 69
Royston, Ga., U.S. B3 87
Rubbestadneset, Nor. G5 6
Rubcovsk, Russia G10 24
Rubidoux, Ca., U.S. n14 82
Rubio, Ven. D6 58
Ruby Dome, mtn., Nv., U.S. C6 105
Ruby Lake, l., Nv., U.S. C6 105
Ruby Mountains, mts., Nv., U.S. C6 105
Ruby Range, mts., Co., U.S. C3 83
Ruby Range, mts., Mt., U.S. E4 103
Rudolf, Lake, l., Afr. H2 46
Rudolstadt, Ger. E11 8
Rudyard, Mi., U.S. B6 99
Rue, Fr. B8 10
Rufā'ah, Sudan F12 42
Ruffec, Fr. F7 10
Rufino, Arg. C4 56
Rufus Woods Lake, res., Wa., U.S. A6 124
Rugao, China C9 28
Rugby, Eng., U.K. I11 7
Rugby, N.D., U.S. A6 111
Ruian, China H9 28
Ruidoso, N.M., U.S. D4 108
Ruidoso Downs, N.M., U.S. D4 108
Ruijin, China F10 26
Ruijin, China J4 28
Rukwa, Lake, l., Tan. C6 44
Ruleville, Ms., U.S. B3 101
Rum, stm., Mn., U.S. D5 100
Ruma, Yugo. D3 16
Rumbek, Sudan G11 42
Rum Cay, i., Bah. C10 64
Rum Creek, stm., W.V., U.S. n12 125
Rumford, Me., U.S. D2 96
Rumia, Pol. A18 8
Rum Jungle, Austl. B6 50
Rumoi, Japan p19 30a
Rumson, N.J., U.S. C4 107
Rumstick Point, c., R.I., U.S. D5 116
Ru'nan, China B3 28
Runanga, N.Z. E3 52
Runge, Tx., U.S. E4 120
Rungwa, Tan. C6 44
Runnels, co., Tx., U.S. D3 120
Runnemede, N.J., U.S. D2 107
Ruoqiang, China D4 26
Rupert, Id., U.S. G5 89
Rupert, W.V., U.S. D4 125
Rupert, Rivière de, stm., Que., Can. h11 74
Rural Hall, N.C., U.S. A2 110
Rural Retreat, Va., U.S. D1 123
Rusagonis, N.B., Can. D3 71
Ruse, Bul. F9 16
Rush, co., In., U.S. E6 91
Rush, co., Ks., U.S. D4 93
Rush, stm., Mn., U.S. F4 100
Rush, stm., Wi., U.S. D1 126
Rush City, Mn., U.S. E6 100
Rush Creek, stm., Oh., U.S. B2 112
Rush Creek, stm., Ok., U.S. C4 113
Rushford, Mn., U.S. G7 100
Rush Lake, l., Mn., U.S. E5 100
Rush Lake, l., Mn., U.S. D3 100
Rush Lake, l., Wi., U.S. E5 126
Rushmere, Va., U.S. h14 123
Rush Springs, Ok., U.S. C4 113
Rushville, Il., U.S. C3 90
Rushville, In., U.S. E7 91
Rushville, Ne., U.S. B3 104
Rusk, Tx., U.S. D5 120
Rusk, co., Tx., U.S. C5 120
Rusk, co., Wi., U.S. C2 126
Ruskin, Fl., U.S. E4 86
Russas, Braz. D11 54
Russell, Man., Can. D1 70
Russell, Ont., Can. B9 73
Russell, Ks., U.S. D5 93
Russell, Ky., U.S. B7 94
Russell, Pa., U.S. C3 115
Russell, co., Al., U.S. C4 78
Russell, co., Ks., U.S. D5 93
Russell, co., Ky., U.S. D4 94
Russell, co., Va., U.S. f9 123
Russell, Mount, mtn., Ak., U.S. f16 79
Russell Cave National Monument, Al., U.S. A4 78
Russell Fork, stm., U.S. C7 94
Russell Island, i., N.W. Ter., Can. B13 66
Russell Springs, Ky., U.S. C4 94
Russellville, Al., U.S. A2 78
Russellville, Ar., U.S. B2 81
Russellville, Ky., U.S. D3 94
Russellville, Mo., U.S. C5 102
Russellville, Tn., U.S. C10 119
Rüsselsheim, Ger. E8 8
Russia, ctry., Eur. E15 22
Russian, stm., Ca., U.S. C2 82
Russiaville, In., U.S. D5 91
Rustavi, Geor. I7 22
Rustburg, Va., U.S. C3 123
Rustenburg, S. Afr. G5 44
Ruston, La., U.S. B3 95
Ruston, Wa., U.S. B3 124
Ruth, Nv., U.S. D6 105
Rutherford, N.J., U.S. B4 107
Rutherford, Tn., U.S. A3 119
Rutherford, co., N.C., U.S. B1 110
Rutherford, co., Tn., U.S. B5 119
Rutherfordton, N.C., U.S. B1 110
Ruthven, Ia., U.S. A3 92
Rutland, Ma., U.S. B4 98
Rutland, Vt., U.S. D3 122
Rutland, co., Vt., U.S. D2 122
Rutledge, Ga., U.S. C3 87
Rutledge, Tn., U.S. C10 119
Ruukki, Fin. D15 6
Ruvuma (Rovuma), stm., Afr. D7 44
Ružomberok, Slov. F19 8
Rwanda, ctry., Afr. B5 44
Ryan, Ok., U.S. C4 113
Ryan Peak, mtn., Id., U.S. F4 89
Rybinsk, Russia C21 18
Rybinskoje Vodochranilišče, res., Russia C21 18
Rybnik, Pol. E18 8
Rycroft, Alta., Can. B1 68
Ryde, Eng., U.K. K11 7
Rye, N.H., U.S. D5 106
Rye, N.Y., U.S. h13 109
Rye Beach, N.H., U.S. E5 106
Rye Patch Dam, Nv., U.S. C3 105
Rye Patch Reservoir, res., Nv., U.S. C3 105
Ryfoss, Nor. F7 6
Ryōtsu, Japan D11 30
Rysy, mtn., Eur. F20 8
Ryukyu Islands see Nansei-shotō, is., Japan F12 26
Rzeszów, Pol. E21 8
Ržev, Russia E17 18

S

Saalfeld, Ger. E11 8
Saarbrücken, Ger. F6 8
Saaremaa, i., Est. C5 18
Saarijärvi, Fin. E15 6
Saarlouis, Ger. F6 8
Sab, Tônlé, l., Camb. H7 34
Saba, i., Neth. Ant. F16 64
Sabadell, Spain D14 12
Sabae, Japan G9 30
Sabana, Archipiélago de, is., Cuba C8 64
Sabanagrande, Hond. H4 64
Sabanalarga, Col. B5 58
Sabang, Indon. E6 32
Sabanilla, Mex. E9 62
Sabará, Braz. E7 57
Sabattus, Me., U.S. D2 96
Sabetha, Ks., U.S. C8 93
Sabhah, Libya C8 42
Sabi (Save), stm., Afr. F6 44
Sabillasville, Md., U.S. A3 97
Sabina, Oh., U.S. C2 112
Sabinal, Tx., U.S. E3 120
Sabiñánigo, Spain C11 12
Sabinas, Mex. D9 62
Sabinas Hidalgo, Mex. D9 62
Sabine, co., La., U.S. C2 95
Sabine, co., Tx., U.S. D6 120
Sabine, stm., U.S. D6 120
Sabine Lake, l., U.S. E2 95
Sabine Pass, strt., U.S. E2 95
Sable, Cape, c., N.S., Can. H19 66
Sable, Cape, c., Fl., U.S. G5 86
Sable, Îles de, i., N. Cal. C11 50
Sable Island, i., N.S., Can. F10 71
Sabula, Ia., U.S. B7 92
Sabzevār, Iran J9 22
Sac, co., Ia., U.S. B2 92
Sac, stm., Mo., U.S. D4 102
Sacajawea, Lake, res., Wa., U.S. C7 124
Sacajawea Peak, mtn., Or., U.S. B9 114
Sacandaga Lake, l., N.Y., U.S. B6 109
Sac and Fox Indian Reservation, Ia., U.S. C5 92
Sacaton, Az., U.S. D4 80
Sac City, Ia., U.S. B2 92
Sacedón, Spain E9 12

Name | Map Ref | Page

Sachalin, Ostrov (Sakhalin), i., Russia G22 24
Sachalinskij Zaliv, b., Russia G22 24
Sachigo, stm., Ont., Can. F14 66
Sachse, Tx., U.S. n10 120
Sachs Harbour, N.W. Ter., Can. B8 66
Šachty, Russia H6 22
Sachuest Point, c., R.I., U.S. F6 116
Sackville, N.B., Can. D5 71
Saco, Me., U.S. E2 96
Saco, stm., U.S. E2 96
Saco, East Branch, stm., N.H., U.S. B4 106
Sacramento, Ca., U.S. C3 82
Sacramento, co., Ca., U.S. C3 82
Sacramento, stm., Ca., U.S. C3 82
Sacramento, stm., N.M., U.S. E4 108
Sacramento Mountains, mts., N.M., U.S. E4 108
Sacramento Valley, val., Ca., U.S. C2 82
Sacré-Coeur-Saguenay, Que., Can. A8 74
Sacred Heart, Mn., U.S. F3 100
Sádaba, Spain C10 12
Şa'dah, Yemen E3 46
Saddle, stm., N.J., U.S. h8 107
Saddleback Mountain, mtn., Az., U.S. k8 80
Saddle Brook, N.J., U.S. h8 107
Saddlebunch Keys, is., Fl., U.S. H5 86
Saddle Mountain, mtn., Or., U.S. B3 114
Saddle Mountains, mts., Wa., U.S. C5 124
Saddle River, N.J., U.S. A4 107
Sa Dec, Viet. I8 34
Sādiqābad, Pak. F4 38
Sado, i., Japan D11 30
Sado-kaikyō, strt., Japan E11 30
Saegertown, Pa., U.S. C1 115
Safety Harbor, Fl., U.S. E4 86
Säffle, Swe. G9 6
Safford, Az., U.S. E6 80
Safi, Mor. B4 42
Safīd, stm., Afg. B1 38
Safīd Kūh, Selseleh-ye, mts., Afg. C1 36
Safonovo, Russia F16 18
Saga, Japan I3 30
Sagadahoc, co., Me., U.S. E3 96
Sagaing, Mya. D3 34
Sagamihara, Japan G12 30
Sagami-nada, b., Japan G12 30
Sagamore Hills, Oh., U.S. h9 112
Saganaga Lake, l., Mn., U.S. B7 100
Sāgar, India E3 37
Sāgar, India I8 38
Sag Harbor, N.Y., U.S. m16 109
Saginaw, Mi., U.S. E7 99
Saginaw, Tx., U.S. n9 120
Saginaw, co., Mi., U.S. E6 99
Saginaw Bay, b., Mi., U.S. E7 99
Saglek Bay, b., Newf., Can. f9 72
Sagres, Port. H3 12
Saguache, co., Co., U.S. C4 83
Sagua de Tánamo, Cuba D10 64
Sagua la Grande, Cuba C7 64
Saguaro Lake, res., Az., U.S. k10 80
Saguaro National Monument, Az., U.S. E5 80
Saguaro National Monument (Tucson Mountain Section), Az., U.S. E4 80
Saguenay, stm., Que., Can. A7 74
Sagunto, Spain F11 12
Sahagún, Col. C5 58
Sahagún, Spain C6 12
Sahara, des., Afr. D6 42
Sahāranpur, India F7 38
Sāhīwāl (Montgomery), Pak. E5 38
Sahuaripa, Mex. C5 62
Sahuarita, Az., U.S. F5 80
Sahuayo, Mex. G8 62
Saibai, i., Austl. A8 50
Saïda, Alg. B6 42
Saidpur, Bngl. H13 38
Saidu, Pak. C5 38
Saigō, Japan F6 30
Saigon see Thanh Pho Ho Chi Minh, Viet. I9 34
Saijō, Japan I6 30
Saimaa, l., Fin. F16 6
Saint Abb's Head, c., Scot., U.K. F10 7
Saint Adolphe, Man., Can. E3 70
Saint-Affrique, Fr. I9 10
Sainte-Agathe, Que., Can. C6 74
Sainte-Agathe-des-Monts, Que., Can. C3 74
Saint-Aimé (Massueville), Que., Can. D5 74
Saint-Alban, Que., Can. C5 74
Saint Alban's, Newf., Can. E4 72
Saint Albans, Eng., U.K. J12 7
Saint Albans, Vt., U.S. B2 122
Saint Albans, W.V., U.S. C3 125
Saint Albans Bay, b., Vt., U.S. B2 122
Saint Albert, Alta., Can. C4 68
Saint-Amand-Mont-Rond, Fr. F9 10
Saint-Ambroise, Que., Can. A6 74
Saint-Ambroix, Fr. H11 10
Saint-André, Cap, c., Madag. E8 44
Saint-André-Avellin, Que., Can. D2 74
Saint-André-Est, Que., Can. D3 74
Saint-André-les-Alpes, Fr. I13 10
Saint Andrew Bay, b., Fl., U.S. u16 86
Saint Andrews, N.B., Can. D2 71
Saint Andrews, Scot., U.K. E10 7
Saint Andrews, S.C., U.S. F7 117
Saint Andrews, S.C., U.S. C5 117
Saint Anne, Il., U.S. B6 90
Sainte-Anne-de-Beaupré, Que., Can. B7 74
Sainte-Anne [-de-Bellevue], Que., Can. q19 74
Sainte Anne-de-Madawaska, N.B., Can. B1 71
Sainte Anne-des-Chênes, Man., Can. E3 70
Saint-Anselme, Que., Can. C7 74
Saint Ansgar, Ia., U.S. A5 92
Saint Anthony, Newf., Can. C4 72
Saint Anthony, Id., U.S. F7 89
Saint Antoine, N.B., Can. C5 71
Saint-Apollinaire, Que., Can. C6 74
Saint Arthur, N.B., Can. B3 71
Saint-Astier, Fr. G7 10
Saint-Aubert, Que., Can. B7 74
Saint Augustin, stm., Can. C2 72
Saint Augustine, Fl., U.S. C5 86
Saint Austell, Eng., U.K. K8 7
Saint-Avold, Fr. C13 10
Saint-Barthélemy, i., Guad. F16 64
Saint Basile, N.B., Can. B1 71
Saint-Basile [-Sud], Que., Can. C6 74
Saint-Benoît-du-Sault, Fr. F8 10
Saint-Bernard, Que., Can. C6 74
Saint Bernard, Al., U.S. A3 78
Saint Bernard, La., U.S. E6 95
Saint Bernard, Oh., U.S. o13 112
Saint Bernard, co., La., U.S. E6 95
Saint Bernice, In., U.S. E2 91
Saint Bride, Mount, mtn., Alta., Can. D3 68
Saint Bride's, Newf., Can. E4 72
Saint-Brieuc, Fr. D4 10
Saint-Bruno, Que., Can. A6 74
Saint-Calais, Fr. E7 10
Saint-Casimir, Que., Can. C5 74
Saint Catharines, Ont., Can. D5 73
Saint Catherine, Lake, l., Vt., U.S. E2 122
Saint Catherines Island, i., Ga., U.S. E5 87
Saint-Célestin (Annaville), Que., Can. C5 74
Saint-Céré, Fr. H8 10
Saint-Césaire, Que., Can. D4 74
Saint-Chamond, Fr. G11 10
Saint-Charles, Que., Can. C7 74
Saint Charles, Il., U.S. B5 90
Saint Charles, Mi., U.S. E6 99
Saint Charles, Mn., U.S. G6 100
Saint Charles, Mo., U.S. C7 102
Saint Charles, co., La., U.S. E5 95
Saint Charles, co., Mo., U.S. C7 102
Saint-Chély-d'Apcher, Fr. H10 10
Saint Christopher (Saint Kitts), i., St. K./N. F16 64
Saint Christopher-Nevis see Saint Kitts and Nevis, ctry., N.A. F16 64
Saint-Chrysostome, Que., Can. D4 74
Saint Clair, Mi., U.S. F8 99
Saint Clair, Mn., U.S. F5 100
Saint Clair, Mo., U.S. C6 102
Saint Clair, Pa., U.S. E9 115
Saint Clair, co., Al., U.S. B3 78
Saint Clair, co., Il., U.S. E3 90
Saint Clair, co., Mi., U.S. F8 99
Saint Clair, co., Mo., U.S. C4 102
Saint Clair Shores, Mi., U.S. p16 99
Saint Clairsville, Oh., U.S. B5 112
Saint Claude, Man., Can. E2 70
Saint-Claude, Fr. F12 10
Saint Cloud, Fl., U.S. D5 86
Saint Cloud, Mn., U.S. E4 100
Saint-Coeur-de-Marie, Que., Can. A6 74
Saint-Constant, Que., Can. q19 74
Sainte-Croix, Que., Can. C6 74
Saint Croix, co., Wi., U.S. C1 126
Saint Croix, i., V.I.U.S. F15 64
Saint Croix, stm., U.S. C1 126
Saint Croix, Lake, l., U.S. D1 126
Saint Croix Falls, Wi., U.S. C1 126
Saint Croix Stream, stm., Me., U.S. B4 96
Saint-Damase, Que., Can. D4 74
Saint David, Az., U.S. F5 80
Saint-David-de-l'Auberivière, Que., Can. n17 74
Saint David's, Wales, U.K. J7 7
Saint-Denis, Que., Can. D4 74
Saint-Denis, Fr. D9 10
Saint-Denis, Reu. F11 44
Saint-Dié, Fr. D13 10
Saint-Dizier, Fr. D11 10
Saint-Dominique, Que., Can. D5 74
Saint Edward, Ne., U.S. C8 104
Saint Eleanor's, P.E.I., Can. C6 71
Saint Elias, Cape, c., Ak., U.S. D11 79
Saint Elmo, Al., U.S. E1 78
Saint Elmo, Il., U.S. D5 90
Saint-Éphrem [-de-Tring], Que., Can. C7 74
Saint Étienne, Fr. G11 10
Saint-Eustache, Que., Can. D4 74
Saint-Félicien, Que., Can. A5 74
Saint-Félix-de-Valois, Que., Can. C4 74
Saint-Ferdinand (Bernierville), Que., Can. C6 74
Saint-Ferréol [-les-Neiges], Que., Can. B7 74
Saint-Flavien, Que., Can. C6 74
Saint-Florentin, Fr. D10 10
Saint-Florent-sur-Cher, Fr. F9 10
Saint-Flour, Fr. G10 10
Sainte-Foy, Que., Can. n17 74
Sainte-Foy-la-Grande, Fr. H7 10
Saint Francis, Ks., U.S. C2 93
Saint Francis, Mn., U.S. E5 100
Saint Francis, S.D., U.S. D5 118
Saint Francis, Wi., U.S. n12 126
Saint Francis, co., Ar., U.S. B5 81
Saint Francis, stm., U.S. A5 81
Saint Francis, Cape, c., Newf., Can. E5 72
Saint Francisville, Il., U.S. E6 90
Saint Francisville, La., U.S. D4 95
Saint Francois, co., Mo., U.S. D7 102
Saint-François, stm., Que., Can. D5 74
Saint-François, Lac, l., Que., Can. D6 74
Saint Francois Mountains, hills, Mo., U.S. D7 102
Saint Froid Lake, l., Me., U.S. B4 96
Saint-Fulgence, Que., Can. A7 74
Saint-Gabriel, Que., Can. C4 74
Saint-Gaudens, Fr. I7 10
Saint-Gédéon, Que., Can. D7 74
Sainte Genevieve, Mo., U.S. D7 102
Sainte Genevieve, co., Mo., U.S. D7 102
Saint George, Austl. E9 50
Saint George, N.B., Can. D3 71
Saint George, Ont., Can. D4 73
Saint George, S.C., U.S. E6 117
Saint George, Ut., U.S. F2 121
Saint George, Cape, c., Newf., Can. D2 72
Saint George, Cape, c., Fl., U.S. C1 86
Saint George Island, i., Ak., U.S. D6 79
Saint George Island, i., Fl., U.S. C2 86
Saint George's, Newf., Can. D2 72
Saint-Georges, Que., Can. C5 74
Saint-Georges, Fr. Gu. C8 54
Saint George's, Gren. H17 64
Saint Georges, De., U.S. B3 85
Saint George's Bay, b., Newf., Can. D2 72
Saint Georges Bay, b., N.S., Can. D8 71
Saint George's Channel, strt., Eur. J6 7
Saint-Georges-Ouest (part of Ville-Saint-Georges), Que., Can. C7 74
Saint-Germain, Fr. D9 10
Saint-Gervais, Que., Can. C7 74
Saint-Gilles, Que., Can. C6 74
Saint-Gilles-Croix-de-Vie, Fr. F5 10
Saint-Girons, Fr. J8 10
Saint-Grégoire (Larochelle), Que., Can. C5 74
Saint-Guénolé, Fr. E2 10
Saint-Guillaume-d'Upton, Que., Can. D5 74
Saint Helen, Lake, l., Mi., U.S. D6 99
Saint Helena, Ca., U.S. C2 82
Saint Helena, co., La., U.S. D5 95
Saint Helena Bay, b., S. Afr. H3 44
Saint Helena Island, i., S.C., U.S. G6 117
Saint Helena Sound, strt., S.C., U.S. G7 117
Saint Helens, Or., U.S. B4 114
Saint Helens, Mount, vol., Wa., U.S. C3 124
Saint Helier, Jersey C4 10
Saint Henry, Oh., U.S. B1 112
Saint-Hippolyte, Fr. E13 10
Saint-Honoré, Que., Can. D7 74
Saint-Hubert, Que., Can. q20 74
Saint-Hubert-de-Témiscouata, Que., Can. B8 74
Saint-Hyacinthe, Que., Can. D5 74
Saint Ignace, Mi., U.S. C6 99
Saint Ignace Island, i., Ont., Can. G15 66
Saint Ignatius, Mt., U.S. C2 103
Saint Isidore de Prescott, Ont., Can. B10 73
Saint Jacobs, Ont., Can. D4 73
Saint Jacques, N.B., Can. B1 71
Saint-Jacques, Que., Can. D4 74
Saint James, Mn., U.S. G4 100
Saint James, Mo., U.S. D6 102
Saint James, co., La., U.S. D5 95
Saint James, Cape, c., B.C., Can. D2 69
Saint James City, Fl., U.S. F4 86
Saint-Jean, stm., Que., Can. A7 74
Saint-Jean, Lac, l., Que., Can. A5 74
Saint Jean Baptiste, Man., Can. E3 70
Saint-Jean-Chrysostome, Que., Can. o17 74
Saint-Jean-d'Angély, Fr. G6 10
Saint-Jean-de-Luz, Fr. I5 10
Saint-Jean-de-Maurienne, Fr. G13 10
Saint-Jean-de-Monts, Fr. F4 10
Saint-Jean-Pied-de-Port, Fr. I5 10
Saint-Jean-sur-Richelieu, Que., Can. D4 74
Saint-Jérôme, Que., Can. D3 74
Saint Jo, Tx., U.S. C4 120
Saint-Joachim, Que., Can. B7 74
Saint Joe, stm., Id., U.S. B3 89
Saint John, N.B., Can. D3 71
Saint John, In., U.S. B3 91
Saint John, Ks., U.S. E5 93
Saint John, i., V.I.U.S. E15 64
Saint John, stm., N.A. G19 66
Saint John, Cape, c., Newf., Can. D4 72
Saint John Bay, b., Newf., Can. C3 72
Saint Johns, Antig. F17 64
Saint John's, Newf., Can. E5 72
Saint Johns, Az., U.S. C6 80
Saint Johns, Mi., U.S. F6 99
Saint Johns, co., Fl., U.S. C5 86
Saint Johns, stm., Fl., U.S. B5 86
Saint Johnsbury, Vt., U.S. C4 122
Saint Johnsville, N.Y., U.S. B6 109
Saint John the Baptist, co., La., U.S. D5 95
Saint Jones, stm., De., U.S. D4 85
Saint Joseph, N.B., Can. D5 71
Saint Joseph, Il., U.S. C5 90
Saint Joseph, La., U.S. C4 95
Saint Joseph, Mi., U.S. F4 99
Saint Joseph, Mn., U.S. E4 100
Saint Joseph, Mo., U.S. B3 102
Saint Joseph, Tn., U.S. B4 119
Saint Joseph, co., In., U.S. A5 91
Saint Joseph, co., Mi., U.S. G5 99
Saint Joseph, stm., U.S. F5 99
Saint-Joseph, Lac, l., Que., Can. n16 74
Saint Joseph, Lake, l., Ont., Can. o17 73
Saint Joseph Bay, b., Fl., U.S. C1 86
Saint-Joseph-de-Beauce, Que., Can. C7 74
Saint Joseph Point, c., Fl., U.S. v16 86
Saint Joseph Sound, strt., Fl., U.S. o10 86
Saint-Jovite, Que., Can. C3 74
Saint-Julien-en-Born, Fr. H5 10
Saint-Junien, Fr. G7 10
Saint-Just-en-Chaussée, Fr. C9 10
Saint Kilda, i., Scot., U.K. D4 7
Saint Kitts-Nevis, ctry., N.A. F16 64
Saint-Lambert, Que., Can. p19 74
Saint Landry, co., La., U.S. D3 95
Saint-Laurent, Que., Can. p19 74
Saint Lawrence, Newf., Can. E4 72
Saint Lawrence, co., N.Y., U.S. A5 109
Saint Lawrence, stm., N.A. G19 66
Saint Lawrence, Cape, c., N.S., Can. B9 71
Saint Lawrence, Gulf of, b., Can. G20 66
Saint Lawrence Island, i., Ak., U.S. C5 79
Saint Lawrence Islands National Park, Ont., Can. C9 73
Saint Léonard, N.B., Can. B2 71
Saint-Léonard [-d'Aston], Que., Can. C5 74
Saint-Liboire, Que., Can. D5 74
Saint-Lô, Fr. C5 10
Saint-Louis, Sen. E2 42
Saint Louis, Mi., U.S. E6 99
Saint Louis, Mo., U.S. C7 102
Saint Louis, co., Mn., U.S. C6 100
Saint Louis, co., Mo., U.S. C7 102
Saint Louis, stm., U.S. D6 100
Saint-Louis, Lac, l., Que., Can. q19 74
Saint Louis Bay, b., Ms., U.S. f7 101
Saint-Louis-de-Gonzague, Que., Can. D3 74
Saint Louis-de-Kent, N.B., Can. C5 71
Saint-Louis-du-Ha! Ha!, Que., Can. B8 74
Saint Louis Park, Mn., U.S. n12 100
Saint-Luc, Que., Can. D4 74
Saint Lucia, ctry., N.A. H17 64
Saint Lucia Channel, strt., N.A. G17 64
Saint Lucie, co., Fl., U.S. E6 86
Saint Lucie Canal, Fl., U.S. F6 86
Saint Lucie Inlet, b., Fl., U.S. E6 86
Sainte-Madeleine, Que., Can. D4 74
Saint Malo, Man., Can. E3 70
Saint-Malo, Fr. D4 10
Saint-Malo, Golfe de, b., Fr. D4 10
Saint-Marc, Haiti E11 64
Saint-Marc [-des-Carrières], Que., Can. C5 74
Saint-Marcellin, Fr. G12 10
Saint Margaret Bay, b., Newf., Can. C3 72
Sainte-Marguerite, stm., Que., Can. A7 74
Sainte-Marie, Que., Can. C6 74
Sainte-Marie, Cap, c., Madag. G9 44
Saint Maries, Id., U.S. B2 89
Sainte-Marthe, Que., Can. D3 74
Saint Martin, co., La., U.S. D4 95
Saint-Martin (Sint Maarten), i., N.A. E16 64
Saint Martin, Lake, l., Man., Can. D2 70
Saint Martin Island, i., Mi., U.S. C4 99
Saint Martinville, La., U.S. D4 95
Saint Mary, co., La., U.S. E4 95
Saint Mary-of-the-Woods, In., U.S. E3 91
Saint Mary Peak, mtn., Austl. F7 50
Saint Marys, Austl. H9 50
Saint Mary's, Newf., Can. E5 72
Saint Mary's, Ont., Can. D3 73
Saint Marys, Ak., U.S. C7 79
Saint Marys, Ga., U.S. F5 87
Saint Marys, In., U.S. A5 91
Saint Marys, Ks., U.S. C7 93
Saint Marys, Oh., U.S. B1 112
Saint Marys, Pa., U.S. D4 115
Saint Marys, W.V., U.S. B3 125
Saint Marys, co., Md., U.S. D4 97
Saint Marys, stm., N.S., Can. D8 71
Saint Marys, stm., U.S. F5 87
Saint Marys, stm., U.S. C8 91
Saint Marys, stm., Md., U.S. D5 97
Saint Mary's, Cape, c., Newf., Can. E4 72
Saint Mary's Bay, b., Newf., Can. E5 72
Saint Marys Bay, b., N.S., Can. E3 71
Saint Marys City, Md., U.S. D5 97
Saint-Mathieu, Pointe de, c., Fr. D2 10
Saint Matthew Island, i., Ak., U.S. C5 79
Saint Matthews, Ky., U.S. B4 94
Saint Matthews, S.C., U.S. D6 117
Sainte-Maure-du-Touraine, Fr. E7 10
Saint-Maurice, stm., Que., Can. C5 74
Sainte-Maxime, Fr. I13 10
Saint-Méen-le-Grand, Fr. D4 10
Sainte-Menehould, Fr. C11 10
Sainte-Mère-Église, Fr. C5 10
Saint Michael, Mn., U.S. E5 100
Saint Michaels, Md., U.S. C5 97
Saint-Michel [-de-Bellechasse], Que., Can. C7 74
Saint-Mihiel, Fr. D12 10
Saint-Moritz see Sankt Moritz, Switz. F16 10
Saint-Nazaire, Fr. E4 10
Saint-Nicolas, Que., Can. o17 74
Saint-Odilon, Que., Can. C7 74
Saint-Omer, Fr. B9 10
Saint-Ours, Que., Can. D4 74
Saint-Pacôme, Que., Can. B8 74
Saint-Pamphile, Que., Can. C8 74
Saint Paris, Oh., U.S. B2 112
Saint-Pascal, Que., Can. B8 74
Saint Paul, Alta., Can. B5 68
Saint Paul, Ak., U.S. D5 79
Saint Paul, In., U.S. F6 91
Saint Paul, Ks., U.S. E8 93
Saint Paul, Mn., U.S. F5 100
Saint Paul, Mo., U.S. f12 102
Saint Paul, Ne., U.S. C7 104
Saint Paul, Va., U.S. f9 123
Saint Paul Island, i., Ak., U.S. D5 79
Saint Paul Park, Mn., U.S. n12 100
Saint Pauls, N.C., U.S. C4 110
Sainte-Perpétue-de-L'Islet, Que., Can. B8 74
Saint Peter, Mn., U.S. F5 100
Saint Peter Port, Guernsey C4 10
Saint Peters, N.S., Can. D9 71
Saint Peters, Mo., U.S. C7 102
Saint Petersburg, Fl., U.S. E4 86
Saint Petersburg Beach, Fl., U.S. p10 86
Saint Petersburg see Sankt-Peterburg, Russia B13 18
Saint Phillips Island, i., S.C., U.S. G6 117
Saint-Pie, Que., Can. D5 74
Saint-Pierre, Reu. F11 44
Saint-Pierre, St. P./M. E3 72
Saint-Pierre, Lac, l., Que., Can. C5 74
Saint Pierre and Miquelon, dep., N.A. G21 66
Saint Pierre Island, i., Sey. C10 44
Saint Pierre-Jolys, Man., Can. E3 70
Saint-Pierre-le-Moûtier, Fr. F10 10
Saint-Pol-de-Léon, Fr. D3 10
Saint-Pons, Fr. I9 10
Saint-Pourçain-sur-Sioule, Fr. F10 10
Saint-Prime, Que., Can. A5 74
Saint Quentin, N.B., Can. B2 71
Saint-Quentin, Fr. C10 10
Saint-Raphaël, Que., Can. C7 74
Saint-Raphaël, Fr. I13 10
Saint-Raymond, Que., Can. C6 74
Saint-Rédempteur, Que., Can. o17 74
Saint Regis, Mt., U.S. C1 103
Saint Regis, West Branch, stm., N.Y., U.S. f10 109
Saint-Rémi, Que., Can. D4 74
Saint-Romuald, Que., Can. C6 74
Saint Rose, La., U.S. k11 95
Sainte Rose du Lac, Man., Can. D2 70
Saintes, Fr. G6 10
Saint Sauveur, N.B., Can. B4 71
Saint-Sauveur-des-Monts, Que., Can. D3 74
Saint-Sébastien, Cap, c., Madag. D9 44
Saint-Siméon, Que., Can. B8 74
Saint Simons Island, Ga., U.S. E5 87
Saint Simons Island, i., Ga., U.S. E5 87
Saint Stephen, N.B., Can. D2 71
Saint Stephen, S.C., U.S. E8 117
Saint Tammany, co., La., U.S. D5 95
Sainte-Thècle, Que., Can. C5 74
Sainte-Thérèse, Que., Can. D4 74
Saint Thomas, Ont., Can. E3 73
Saint Thomas, i., V.I.U.S. E15 64
Saint Timothée, Que., Can. q18 74
Saint-Tite, Que., Can. C5 74
Saint-Tropez, Fr. I13 10
Saint-Valéry-en-Caux, Fr. C7 10
Saint-Varent, Fr. F6 10
Sainte-Véronique, Que., Can. C3 74
Saint-Victor, Que., Can. C7 74
Saint-Vincent, Cap, c., Madag. F8 44
Saint Vincent, Gulf, b., Austl. F7 50
Saint Vincent and the Grenadines, ctry., N.A. H17 64
Saint Vincent Island, i., Fl., U.S. C1 86
Saint Vincent Passage, strt., N.A. H17 64
Saint Vincent's [-Saint Stephens-Peter's River], Newf., Can. E5 72
Saint-Vith, Bel. E6 8
Saint Walburg, Sask., Can. D1 75
Saint-Zacharie, Que., Can. C7 74
Sairecábur, Cerro, mtn., S.A. A3 56
Saito, Japan J4 30
Saitula, China B8 38
Sajama, Nevado, mtn., Bol. G5 54
Sajia, China F13 38
Sajnšand, Mong. C9 26
Sakai, Japan H8 30
Sakaide, Japan H6 30
Sakai-minato, Japan G6 30
Sakakawea, Lake, res., N.D., U.S. B3 111
Sakami, Lac, l., Que., Can. F17 66
Sakata, Japan D12 30
Sakhalin see Sachalin, Ostrov, i., Russia G22 24
Sākhar, Afg. D1 38
Sakishima-shotō, is., Japan G11 26
Sakon Nakhon, Thai. F8 34
Sakonnet, stm., R.I., U.S. E6 116
Sakonnet Point, c., R.I., U.S. F6 116
Saku, Japan F11 30
Sakurai, Japan H8 30
Sal, Point, c., Ca., U.S. E3 82
Sala, Swe. G11 6
Salaberry-de-Valleyfield, Que., Can. D3 74
Sala Consilina, Italy I10 14
Salado, stm., Arg. C4 56
Salado, Rio, stm., N.M., U.S. C2 108
Şalālah, Oman E5 46
Salamanca, Mex. G9 62
Salamanca, Spain E6 12
Salamanca, N.Y., U.S. C2 109
Salamina, Col. E5 58
Salamonie, stm., In., U.S. C6 91
Salamonie Lake, res., In., U.S. C6 91
Salatiga, Indon. m15 33a
Salavat, Russia G9 22
Salawati, i., Indon. F9 32
Saldanha, S. Afr. H3 44
Sale, Austl. G9 50
Sale Creek, Tn., U.S. D8 119
Salem, India G5 37
Salem, Ar., U.S. A4 81
Salem, Il., U.S. E5 90
Salem, In., U.S. G5 91
Salem, Ky., U.S. e9 94
Salem, Ma., U.S. A6 98
Salem, Mo., U.S. D6 102
Salem, N.H., U.S. E4 106
Salem, N.J., U.S. D2 107
Salem, Oh., U.S. B5 112
Salem, Or., U.S. C4 114
Salem, S.D., U.S. D8 118
Salem, Ut., U.S. C4 121
Salem, Va., U.S. C2 123
Salem, W.V., U.S. B4 125
Salem, Wi., U.S. n11 126
Salem, co., N.J., U.S. D2 107
Salem, stm., N.J., U.S. D2 107

Name	Map Ref	Page
Salem, Lake, l., Vt., U.S.	**B4**	122
Salemi, Italy	**L7**	14
Sälen, Swe.	**F9**	6
Salerno, Italy	**I9**	14
Salford, Eng., U.K.	**H10**	7
Salgótarján, Hung.	**G19**	8
Sali, Cro.	**F10**	14
Salida, Co., U.S.	**C5**	83
Salies-de-Béarn, Fr.	**I6**	10
Salihli, Tur.	**K12**	16
Salina, Ks., U.S.	**D6**	93
Salina, Ok., U.S.	**A6**	113
Salina, Ut., U.S.	**E4**	121
Salina Cruz, Mex.	**I12**	62
Salinas, Braz.	**D7**	57
Salinas, Ca., U.S.	**D3**	82
Salinas, stm., Ca., U.S.	**D3**	82
Salinas de Hidalgo, Mex.	**F9**	62
Salinas Peak, mtn., N.M., U.S.	**D3**	108
Salinas Pueblo Missions National Monument, N.M., U.S.	**C3**	108
Saline, Mi., U.S.	**F7**	99
Saline, co., Ar., U.S.	**C3**	81
Saline, co., Il., U.S.	**F5**	90
Saline, co., Ks., U.S.	**D6**	93
Saline, co., Mo., U.S.	**B4**	102
Saline, co., Ne., U.S.	**D8**	104
Saline, stm., Ar., U.S.	**C1**	81
Saline, stm., Ar., U.S.	**D4**	81
Saline, stm., Ks., U.S.	**C3**	93
Saline, North Fork, stm., Il., U.S.	**F5**	90
Saline Lake, res., La., U.S.	**C3**	95
Salineville, Oh., U.S.	**B5**	112
Salisbury, N.B., Can.	**C4**	71
Salisbury, Eng., U.K.	**J11**	7
Salisbury, Ct., U.S.	**B2**	84
Salisbury, Md., U.S.	**D6**	97
Salisbury, Ma., U.S.	**A6**	98
Salisbury, Mo., U.S.	**B5**	102
Salisbury, N.C., U.S.	**B2**	110
Salisbury see Harare, Zimb.	**E6**	44
Salisbury Island, i., N.W. Ter., Can.	**D17**	66
Salisbury Plain, pl., Eng., U.K.	**J11**	7
Salish Mountains, mts., Mt., U.S.	**B2**	103
Salkehatchie, stm., S.C., U.S.	**E5**	117
Şalkhad, Syria	**C5**	40
Salles-Curan, Fr.	**H9**	10
Sallisaw, Ok., U.S.	**B7**	113
Salluit, Que., Can.	**f11**	74
Salmo, B.C., Can.	**E9**	69
Salmon, Id., U.S.	**D5**	89
Salmon, stm., N.B., Can.	**C4**	71
Salmon, stm., Id., U.S.	**D3**	89
Salmon Creek, Wa., U.S.	**D3**	124
Salmon Creek Reservoir, res., Id., U.S.	**G4**	89
Salmon Falls, stm., U.S.	**D5**	106
Salmon Falls Creek, stm., U.S.	**G4**	89
Salmon Mountains, mts., Ca., U.S.	**B2**	82
Salmon Point, c., Ont., Can.	**D7**	73
Salmon River Mountains, mts., Id., U.S.	**E3**	89
Salmon River Reservoir, res., N.Y., U.S.	**B5**	109
Salo, Fin.	**F14**	6
Salome, Az., U.S.	**D2**	80
Salon-De-Provence, Fr.	**I12**	10
Salonika see Thessaloníki, Grc.	**I6**	16
Salsomaggiore Terme, Italy	**E4**	14
Salt, stm., Az., U.S.	**D4**	80
Salt, stm., Ky., U.S.	**C4**	94
Salt, stm., Mo., U.S.	**B6**	102
Salta, Arg.	**A3**	56
Salt Creek, stm., N.M., U.S.	**D5**	108
Salt Creek, stm., Oh., U.S.	**C3**	112
Salt Creek, stm., Wy., U.S.	**C6**	127
Salter Path, N.C., U.S.	**C6**	110
Salt Fork Lake, res., Oh., U.S.	**B4**	112
Saltillo, Mex.	**E9**	62
Saltillo, Ms., U.S.	**A5**	101
Salt Lake, co., Ut., U.S.	**C3**	121
Salt Lake, l., Hi., U.S.	**g10**	88
Salt Lake, l., N.M., U.S.	**E6**	108
Salt Lake City, Ut., U.S.	**C4**	121
Salto, Ur.	**C5**	56
Salton Sea, l., Ca., U.S.	**F5**	82
Saltonstall, Lake, l., Ct., U.S.	**D4**	84
Salt Point, c., Ca., U.S.	**C2**	82
Salt River Indian Reservation, Az., U.S.	**k9**	80
Salt River Range, mts., Wy., U.S.	**D2**	127
Saltsburg, Pa., U.S.	**F3**	115
Salt Springs, Fl., U.S.	**C5**	86
Saltville, Va., U.S.	**f10**	123
Salt Wells Creek, stm., Wy., U.S.	**E4**	127
Saluda, S.C., U.S.	**C4**	117
Saluda, co., S.C., U.S.	**C4**	117
Saluda, stm., S.C., U.S.	**C4**	117
Saluda Dam, S.C., U.S.	**C5**	117
Sālūr, India	**C7**	37
Saluzzo, Italy	**E2**	14
Salvador, Braz.	**B9**	57
Salvador, Lake, l., La., U.S.	**E5**	95
Salvatierra, Mex.	**G9**	62
Salween (Nu) (Thanlwin), stm., Asia	**D5**	34
Salyersville, Ky., U.S.	**C6**	94
Salzburg, Aus.	**H13**	8
Salzgitter, Ger.	**C10**	8
Salzwedel, Ger.	**C11**	8
Sama [de Langreo], Spain	**B6**	12
Samaná, Bahía de, b., Dom. Rep.	**E13**	64
Samana Cay, i., Bah.	**C11**	64
Samandağı, Tur.	**A4**	40
Samar, i., Phil.	**C8**	32
Samara, Russia	**G8**	22
Samarai, Pap. N. Gui.	**n17**	50a
Samariapo, Ven.	**E9**	58
Samarinda, Indon.	**F6**	32
Samarkand, Uzb.	**J11**	22
Sāmarrā', Iraq	**B3**	46
Samāstipur, India	**H11**	38
Sambalpur, India	**J10**	38
Sambas, Indon.	**E4**	32
Sambava, Madag.	**D10**	44
Sambhal, India	**F8**	38
Sāmbhar, India	**G6**	38
Samborondón, Ec.	**H3**	58
Sammamish Lake, l., Wa., U.S.	**e11**	124
Samneua, Laos	**D8**	34
Samobor, Cro.	**D10**	14
Sámos, i., Grc.	**L10**	16
Samoset, Fl., U.S.	**q10**	86
Sampit, Indon.	**F5**	32
Sampit, stm., S.C., U.S.	**E9**	117
Sampson, co., N.C., U.S.	**B4**	110
Sam Rayburn Reservoir, res., Tx., U.S.	**D5**	120
Samson, Al., U.S.	**D3**	78
Samsun, Tur.	**G15**	4
Samuels, Id., U.S.	**A2**	89
Samui, Ko, i., Thai.	**J6**	34
Samut Prakan, Thai.	**H6**	34
Samut Sakhon, Thai.	**H6**	34
San, Mali	**F5**	42
San, stm., Eur.	**E22**	8
Şan'ā', Yemen	**E3**	46
Sanaga, stm., Cam.	**H7**	42
San Agustín, Col.	**G4**	58
San Agustin, Cape, c., Phil.	**D8**	32
San Agustin, Plains of, pl., N.M., U.S.	**C2**	108
Sanak Islands, is., Ak., U.S.	**E7**	79
Sanana, Pulau, i., Indon.	**F8**	32
Sanandaj, Iran	**A4**	46
San Andreas, Ca., U.S.	**C3**	82
San Andrés, Isla de, i., Col.	**H7**	64
San Andres Mountains, mts., N.M., U.S.	**E3**	108
San Andres Peak, mtn., N.M., U.S.	**E3**	108
San Andrés Tuxtla, Mex.	**H12**	62
San Angelo, Tx., U.S.	**D2**	120
San Anselmo, Ca., U.S.	**h7**	82
San Antonio, Tx., U.S.	**E3**	120
San Antonio, Cabo, c., Arg.	**D5**	56
San Antonio, Cabo, c., Cuba	**D5**	64
San Antonio Abad, Spain	**G13**	12
San Antonio Bay, b., Tx., U.S.	**E4**	120
San Antonio de Bravo, Mex.	**B7**	62
San Antonio de los Cobres, Arg.	**A3**	56
San Antonio del Táchira, Ven.	**D6**	58
San Antonio Mountain, mtn., N.M., U.S.	**A3**	108
San Antonio Oeste, Arg.	**E4**	56
San Augustine, Tx., U.S.	**D5**	120
San Augustine, co., Tx., U.S.	**D5**	120
San Benedetto del Tronto, Italy	**G8**	14
San Benedicto, Isla, i., Mex.	**H4**	62
San Benito, Guat.	**F3**	64
San Benito, Tx., U.S.	**F4**	120
San Benito, co., Ca., U.S.	**D3**	82
San Benito Mountain, mtn., Ca., U.S.	**D3**	82
San Bernardino, Ca., U.S.	**E5**	82
San Bernardino, co., Ca., U.S.	**E5**	82
San Bernardo, Chile	**C2**	56
San Blas, Mex.	**G7**	62
San Blas, Mex.	**D5**	62
San Blas, Cape, c., Fl., U.S.	**v16**	86
San Borja, Bol.	**F5**	54
Sanborn, Ia., U.S.	**A2**	92
Sanborn, co., S.D., U.S.	**D7**	118
Sanbornville, N.H., U.S.	**C4**	106
San Bruno, Ca., U.S.	**D2**	82
San Carlos, Nic.	**I5**	64
San Carlos, Az., U.S.	**D5**	80
San Carlos, Ca., U.S.	**k8**	82
San Carlos, Ven.	**C8**	58
San Carlos de Bariloche, Arg.	**E2**	56
San Carlos de Guaroa, Col.	**F6**	58
San Carlos de la Rápita, Spain	**E12**	12
San Carlos del Zulia, Ven.	**C7**	58
San Carlos de Río Negro, Ven.	**G9**	58
San Carlos Indian Reservation, Az., U.S.	**D5**	80
San Carlos Lake, res., Az., U.S.	**D5**	80
San Cataldo, Italy	**L9**	14
Sancerre, Fr.	**E9**	10
Sánchez, Mex.	**D10**	62
San Clemente, Ca., U.S.	**F5**	82
San Clemente Island, i., Ca., U.S.	**F4**	82
Sancoins, Fr.	**F9**	10
San Cristóbal, Arg.	**C4**	56
San Cristóbal, Ven.	**D6**	58
San Cristóbal, Volcán, vol., Nic.	**H4**	64
San Cristóbal las Casas, Mex.	**I13**	62
Sancti-Spíritus, Cuba	**D8**	64
Sand, Nor.	**G6**	6
Sandakan, Malay.	**D6**	32
Sanday, i., Scot., U.K.	**B10**	7
Sand Creek, stm., Wy., U.S.	**C7**	127
Sanders, Az., U.S.	**B6**	80
Sanders, co., Mt., U.S.	**C1**	103
Sanderson, Tx., U.S.	**D1**	120
Sandersville, Ga., U.S.	**D4**	87
Sandersville, Ms., U.S.	**D4**	101
Sand Hill, Ma., U.S.	**h13**	98
Sand Hill, stm., Mn., U.S.	**C2**	100
Sandia, Peru	**F5**	54
Sandia Crest, mtn., N.M., U.S.	**k8**	108
Sandia Indian Reservation, N.M., U.S.	**k7**	108
Sandia Mountains, mts., N.M., U.S.	**k8**	108
San Diego, Ca., U.S.	**F5**	82
San Diego, Tx., U.S.	**F3**	120
San Diego, co., Ca., U.S.	**F5**	82
San Diego, stm., Ca., U.S.	**o15**	82
San Diego Naval Station, mil., Ca., U.S.	**o15**	82
San Diego Naval Training Center, mil., Ca., U.S.	**o15**	82
Sand Island, i., Hi., U.S.	**g10**	88
Sand Island, i., Wi., U.S.	**B3**	126
Sand Key, i., Fl., U.S.	**E4**	86
Sandlick Creek, stm., W.V., U.S.	**n13**	125
Sandnes, Nor.	**G5**	6
Sandoa, Zaire	**C4**	44
San Donà di Piave, Italy	**D7**	14
Sandoval, Il., U.S.	**E4**	90
Sandoval, co., N.M., U.S.	**B2**	108
Sandoway, Mya.	**E3**	34
Sand Point, Ak., U.S.	**D7**	79
Sandpoint, Id., U.S.	**A2**	89
Sands Key, i., Fl., U.S.	**s3**	86
Sand Springs, Ok., U.S.	**A5**	113
Sandston, Va., U.S.	**m18**	123
Sandstone, Austl.	**E3**	50
Sandstone, Mn., U.S.	**D6**	100
Sandusky, Mi., U.S.	**E8**	99
Sandusky, Oh., U.S.	**A3**	112
Sandusky, co., Oh., U.S.	**A2**	112
Sandusky, stm., Oh., U.S.	**B2**	112
Sandviken, Swe.	**F11**	6
Sandwich, Il., U.S.	**B5**	90
Sandwich, Ma., U.S.	**C7**	98
Sandwich Bay, b., Newf., Can.	**B3**	72
Sandy, Or., U.S.	**B4**	114
Sandy, Ut., U.S.	**C4**	121
Sandy, stm., Me., U.S.	**D2**	96
Sandy Creek, stm., Oh., U.S.	**B4**	112
Sandy Creek, stm., Ok., U.S.	**C2**	113
Sandy Hook, Ct., U.S.	**D2**	84
Sandy Hook, spit, N.J., U.S.	**C5**	107
Sandy Island, i., S.C., U.S.	**D9**	117
Sandy Lake, l., Newf., Can.	**D3**	72
Sandy Lake, l., Ont., Can.	**n16**	73
Sandy Neck, pen., Ma., U.S.	**C7**	98
Sandy Point, c., R.I., U.S.	**h7**	116
Sandy Springs, Ga., U.S.	**h8**	87
Sandy Springs, S.C., U.S.	**B2**	117
Sandyville, Md., U.S.	**A4**	97
San Felipe, Ven.	**B8**	58
San Felipe Indian Reservation, N.M., U.S.	**k8**	108
San Felipe Pueblo, N.M., U.S.	**B3**	108
San Feliu de Guixols, Spain	**D15**	12
San Fernando, Chile	**C2**	56
San Fernando, Mex.	**E10**	62
San Fernando, Phil.	**B7**	32
San Fernando, Phil.	**q19**	32
San Fernando, Spain	**I5**	12
San Fernando, Trin.	**I17**	64
San Fernando, Ca., U.S.	**m12**	82
San Fernando de Apure, Ven.	**D9**	58
San Fernando de Atabapo, Ven.	**E9**	58
Sanford, Co., U.S.	**D5**	83
Sanford, Fl., U.S.	**D5**	86
Sanford, Me., U.S.	**E2**	96
Sanford, Mi., U.S.	**E6**	99
Sanford, N.C., U.S.	**B3**	110
Sanford, Mount, mtn., Ak., U.S.	**C11**	79
San Francisco, Arg.	**C4**	56
San Francisco, Ca., U.S.	**D2**	82
San Francisco, co., Ca., U.S.	**D2**	82
San Francisco, stm., U.S.	**D6**	80
San Francisco Bay, b., Ca., U.S.	**h8**	82
San Francisco de Borja, Mex.	**D6**	62
San Francisco del Oro, Mex.	**D7**	62
San Francisco del Rincón, Mex.	**G9**	62
San Francisco de Macorís, Dom. Rep.	**E12**	64
San Fratello, Italy	**K9**	14
San Gabriel, Ec.	**G4**	58
San Gabriel, Ca., U.S.	***m12**	82
San Gabriel Mountains, mts., Ca., U.S.	**m12**	82
Sangamner, India	**C3**	37
Sangamon, co., Il., U.S.	**D4**	90
Sangamon, stm., Il., U.S.	**C3**	90
San Gavino Monreale, Italy	**J3**	14
Sangay, Volcán, vol., Ec.	**H3**	58
Sang-e Māsheh, Afg.	**D2**	38
Sanger, Ca., U.S.	**D4**	82
Sanger, Tx., U.S.	**C4**	120
Sangerhausen, Ger.	**D11**	8
Sangha, stm., Afr.	**B3**	44
Sanghar, Pak.	**G3**	38
Sangihe, Kepulauan, is., Indon.	**E8**	32
Sangihe, Pulau, i., Indon.	**E8**	32
San Gil, Col.	**D6**	58
San Giovanni in Fiore, Italy	**J11**	14
San Giovanni in Persiceto, Italy	**E6**	14
San Giovanni Valdarno, Italy	**F6**	14
Sāngli, India	**D3**	37
Sangolquí, Ec.	**H3**	58
San Gorgonio Mountain, mtn., Ca., U.S.	**E5**	82
San Gregorio, Ur.	**C5**	56
Sangrūr, India	**E6**	38
Sangüesa, Spain	**C10**	12
Sanibel, Fl., U.S.	**F4**	86
Sanibel Island, i., Fl., U.S.	**F4**	86
San Ignacio, Arg.	**B5**	56
San Ignacio, Hond.	**G4**	64
Sanilac, co., Mi., U.S.	**E8**	99
San Isidro, Arg.	**C5**	56
San Isidro, C.R.	**J6**	64
San Jacinto, Col.	**C5**	58
San Jacinto, Ca., U.S.	**F5**	82
San Jacinto, co., Tx., U.S.	**D5**	120
San Jacinto, stm., Tx., U.S.	**r14**	120
Sanjō, Japan	**E11**	30
San Joaquin, co., Ca., U.S.	**D3**	82
San Joaquin, stm., Ca., U.S.	**D3**	82
San Joaquin Valley, val., Ca., U.S.	**D3**	82
San Jorge, Golfo, b., Arg.	**F3**	56
San Jorge, Golfo de, b., Spain	**E12**	12
San José, C.R.	**J5**	64
San Jose, Ca., U.S.	**D3**	82
San José, Isla, i., Mex.	**E4**	62
San José de Chiquitos, Bol.	**G6**	54
San José de Guanipa, Ven.	**C10**	58
San José del Cabo, Mex.	**F5**	62
San José del Guaviare, Col.	**F6**	58
San José de Mayo, Ur.	**C5**	56
San José de Ocuné, Col.	**E7**	58
San José de Raíces, Mex.	**E9**	62
San Jose Island, i., Tx., U.S.	**E4**	120
San Juan, Arg.	**C3**	56
San Juan, Mex.	**D8**	62
San Juan, P.R.	**E14**	64
San Juan, Tx., U.S.	**F3**	120
San Juan, co., Co., U.S.	**D3**	83
San Juan, co., N.M., U.S.	**A1**	108
San Juan, co., Ut., U.S.	**F5**	121
San Juan, co., Wa., U.S.	**A2**	124
San Juan, stm., N.A.	**I6**	64
San Juan Capistrano, Ca., U.S.	**F5**	82
San Juan de Colón, Ven.	**C6**	58
San Juan [de la Maguana], Dom. Rep.	**E12**	64
San Juan del Norte, Nic.	**I6**	64
San Juan de los Cayos, Ven.	**B8**	58
San Juan de los Morros, Ven.	**C9**	58
San Juan del Río, Mex.	**G9**	62
San Juan del Sur, Nic.	**I5**	64
San Juan Island, i., Wa., U.S.	**A2**	124
San Juan Mountains, mts., Co., U.S.	**D3**	83
San Julián, Arg.	**F3**	56
San Justo, Arg.	**C4**	56
Sankt Gallen, Aus.	**H14**	8
Sankt Gallen, Switz.	**E16**	10
Sankt Johann im Pongau, Aus.	**H13**	8
Sankt Moritz, Switz.	**F16**	10
Sankt Peter, Ger.	**A8**	8
Sankt-Peterburg (Saint Petersburg), Russia	**B13**	18
Sankt Pölten, Aus.	**G15**	8
Sankt Veit an der Glan, Aus.	**I14**	8
Sankt Wendel, Ger.	**F7**	8
Sankuru, stm., Zaire	**B4**	44
San Lázaro, Cabo, c., Mex.	**E3**	62
San Leandro, Ca., U.S.	**h8**	82
Şanlıurfa, Tur.	**H15**	4
San Lope, Col.	**D7**	58
San Lorenzo, Arg.	**C4**	56
San Lorenzo, Ec.	**G3**	58
San Lorenzo, Isla, i., Peru	**F3**	54
San Lorenzo de El Escorial, Spain	**E7**	12
San Lorenzo de la Parrilla, Spain	**F9**	12
Sanlúcar de Barrameda, Spain	**I5**	12
San Lucas, Ec.	**I3**	58
San Lucas, Cabo, c., Mex.	**F5**	62
San Luis, Arg.	**C3**	56
San Luis, Cuba	**D10**	64
San Luis, Guat.	**F3**	64
San Luis, Az., U.S.	**E1**	80
San Luis, Co., U.S.	**D5**	83
San Luis, Ven.	**B8**	58
San Luis, Lago de, l., Bol.	**F6**	54
San Luis, Point, c., Ca., U.S.	**E3**	82
San Luis de la Paz, Mex.	**G9**	62
San Luis Obispo, Ca., U.S.	**E3**	82
San Luis Obispo, co., Ca., U.S.	**E3**	82
San Luis Pass, strt., Tx., U.S.	**r14**	120
San Luis Peak, mtn., Co., U.S.	**D4**	83
San Luis Potosí, Mex.	**F9**	62
San Luis Río Colorado, Mex.	**A2**	62
San Luis Valley, val., Co., U.S.	**D4**	83
San Manuel, Az., U.S.	**E5**	80
San Marcos, Col.	**C5**	58
San Marcos, Mex.	**D8**	62
San Marcos, Mex.	**I10**	62
San Marcos, Tx., U.S.	**E4**	120
San Marcos, stm., Tx., U.S.	**h8**	120
San Marino, Ca., U.S.	**m12**	82
San Marino, ctry., Eur.	**G10**	4
San Martín de Valdeiglesias, Spain	**E7**	12
San Mateo, Spain	**E12**	12
San Mateo, Ca., U.S.	**D2**	82
San Mateo, co., Ca., U.S.	**D2**	82
San Mateo Mountains, mts., N.M., U.S.	**B2**	108
San Mateo Mountains, mts., N.M., U.S.	**D2**	108
San Matías, Golfo, b., Arg.	**E4**	56
San Miguel, El Sal.	**H3**	64
San Miguel, co., Co., U.S.	**D2**	83
San Miguel, co., N.M., U.S.	**B5**	108
San Miguel, stm., Bol.	**F6**	54
San Miguel, stm., Co., U.S.	**C2**	83
San Miguel de Allende, Mex.	**G9**	62
San Miguel del Monte, Arg.	**D5**	56
San Miguel de Tucumán, Arg.	**B3**	56
San Miguel el Alto, Mex.	**G8**	62
San Miguel Island, i., Ca., U.S.	**E3**	82
San Miguel Mountains, mts., Co., U.S.	**D2**	83
Sannār, Sudan	**F12**	42
Sannicandro Garganico, Italy	**H10**	14
San Nicolas, Phil.	**o19**	33b
San Nicolás de los Arroyos, Arg.	**C4**	56
San Nicolas Island, i., Ca., U.S.	**F4**	82
Sannikova, Proliv, strt., Russia	**C21**	24
Sanniquellie, Lib.	**G4**	42
Sano, Japan	**F12**	30
Sanok, Pol.	**F22**	8
San Onofre, Col.	**C5**	58
San Pablo, Col.	**G4**	58
San Pablo, Phil.	**q19**	32
San Pablo Balleza, Mex.	**D6**	62
San Pablo Bay, b., Ca., U.S.	**g8**	82
San Patricio, co., Tx., U.S.	**E4**	120
San Pedro, stm., Az., U.S.	**E5**	80
San Pedro, Punta, c., Chile	**B2**	56
San Pedro, Volcán, vol., Chile	**A3**	56
San Pedro Bay, b., Ca., U.S.	**n12**	82
San Pedro Carchá, Guat.	**G2**	64
San Pedro de las Colonias, Mex.	**E8**	62
San Pedro de Macorís, Dom. Rep.	**E13**	64
San Pedro Mártir, Sierra, mts., Mex.	**B2**	62
San Pedro Peaks, mts., N.M., U.S.	**A3**	108
San Pedro Sula, Hond.	**G4**	64
Sanpete, co., Ut., U.S.	**D4**	121
Sanpoil, stm., Wa., U.S.	**A7**	124
San Quintín, Cabo, c., Mex.	**B1**	62
San Rafael, Arg.	**C3**	56
San Rafael, Mex.	**E9**	62
San Rafael, Ca., U.S.	**D2**	82
San Rafael, N.M., U.S.	**B2**	108
San Rafael, stm., Ut., U.S.	**D5**	121
San Rafael Knob, mtn., Ut., U.S.	**E5**	121
San Rafael Mountains, mts., Ca., U.S.	**E4**	82
San Ramón, Nic.	**G5**	64
San Ramon, Ca., U.S.	**h9**	82
San Remo, Italy	**F2**	14
San Saba, Tx., U.S.	**D3**	120
San Saba, co., Tx., U.S.	**D3**	120
San Salvador, El Sal.	**H3**	64
San Salvador (Watling Island), i., Bah.	**B10**	64
San Salvador de Jujuy, Arg.	**A3**	56
Sansanné-Mango, Togo	**F6**	42
San Sebastián, Spain	**B10**	12
Sansepolcro, Italy	**F7**	14
San Severo, Italy	**H10**	14
San Simon, stm., Az., U.S.	**E6**	80
Sanski Most, Bos.	**E11**	14
Santa Ana, Bol.	**G5**	54
Santa Ana, Bol.	**F5**	54
Santa Ana, El Sal.	**H3**	64
Santa Ana, Mex.	**E9**	62
Santa Ana, Mex.	**B4**	62
Santa Ana, Ca., U.S.	**F5**	82
Santa Ana, stm., Ca., U.S.	**n13**	82
Santa Ana Indian Reservation, N.M., U.S.	**h7**	108
Santa Ana Mountains, mts., Ca., U.S.	**n13**	82
Santa Anna, Tx., U.S.	**D3**	120
Santa Bárbara, Mex.	**D7**	62
Santa Barbara, Ca., U.S.	**E4**	82
Santa Barbara, co., Ca., U.S.	**E3**	82
Santa Barbara Channel, strt., Ca., U.S.	**E3**	82
Santa Barbara Island, i., Ca., U.S.	**F4**	82
Santa Catalina, Gulf of, b., Ca., U.S.	**F5**	82
Santa Catalina Island, i., Ca., U.S.	**F4**	82
Santa Catalina Mountains, mts., Az., U.S.	**E5**	80
Santa Catarina, Ilha de, i., Braz.	**B7**	56
Santa Clara, Cuba	**C8**	64
Santa Clara, Ca., U.S.	**D2**	82
Santa Clara, Ut., U.S.	**F2**	121
Santa Clara, co., Ca., U.S.	**D3**	82
Santa Clara, stm., Ca., U.S.	**E4**	82
Santa Claus, In., U.S.	**H4**	91
Santa Coloma de Farnés, Spain	**D14**	12
Santa Comba Dão, Port.	**E3**	12
Santa Cruz, Arg.	**F3**	56
Santa Cruz, Bol.	**G6**	54
Santa Cruz, C.R.	**I5**	64
Santa Cruz, Phil.	**q19**	33b
Santa Cruz, Ca., U.S.	**D2**	82
Santa Cruz, N.M., U.S.	**B3**	108
Santa Cruz, co., Az., U.S.	**F5**	80
Santa Cruz, co., Ca., U.S.	**D2**	82
Santa Cruz, stm., Az., U.S.	**E4**	80
Santa Cruz del Quiché, Guat.	**G2**	64
Santa Cruz de Tenerife, Spain	**p24**	13b
Santa Cruz do Rio Pardo, Braz.	**G4**	57
Santa Cruz Island, i., Ca., U.S.	**F4**	82
Santa Elena, Ec.	**I2**	58
Santa Elena, Punta, c., Ec.	**I2**	58
Santa Eugenia, Spain	**C2**	12
Santa Eulalia, Spain	**E10**	12
Santa Eulalia del Río, Spain	**G13**	12
Santa Fe, Arg.	**C4**	56
Santa Fé, Braz.	**C3**	57
Santa Fé, Cuba	**D6**	64
Santa Fe, Spain	**H8**	12
Santa Fe, N.M., U.S.	**B4**	108
Santa Fe, Tx., U.S.	**r14**	120
Santa Fe, co., N.M., U.S.	**B3**	108
Santa Fe, stm., N.M., U.S.	**h8**	108
Santa Fe Baldy, mtn., N.M., U.S.	**B4**	108
Santa Fe de Bogotá, Col.	**E5**	58
Santa Inés, Isla, i., Chile	**G2**	56
Santa Isabel, Ec.	**I3**	58
Santa Isabel, i., Sol.Is.	**A11**	50
Santa Isabel see Malabo, Eq. Gui.	**H7**	42
Santa Lucia Range, mts., Ca., U.S.	**E3**	82
Santa Magdalena, Isla, i., Mex.	**E3**	62
Santa Margarita, Ca., U.S.	**E3**	82
Santa Margarita, Isla de, i., Mex.	**E4**	62
Santa Maria, Braz.	**B6**	56
Santa Maria, Ca., U.S.	**E3**	82
Santa Maria, stm., Az., U.S.	**C2**	80
Santa Maria, Cabo de, c., Ang.	**D2**	44
Santa Maria do Suaçuí, Braz.	**E7**	57
Santa Maria Mountains, mts., Az., U.S.	**C3**	80
Santa Marta, Col.	**B5**	58
Santa Monica, Ca., U.S.	**m12**	82
Santana do Livramento, Braz.	**C5**	56
Santander, Col.	**F4**	58
Santander, Spain	**B8**	12
Sant' Antioco, Italy	**J3**	14
Santa Paula, Ca., U.S.	**E4**	82
Santaquin, Ut., U.S.	**D4**	121
Sant'Arcangelo, Italy	**I11**	14
Santarém, Braz.	**D8**	54
Santarém, Port.	**F3**	12
Santa Rita, Col.	**G6**	58
Santa Rita, Hond.	**G4**	64
Santa Rosa, Arg.	**D4**	56
Santa Rosa, Arg.	**C3**	56
Santa Rosa, Ec.	**I3**	58
Santa Rosa, Ca., U.S.	**C2**	82
Santa Rosa, N.M., U.S.	**C5**	108
Santa Rosa, co., Fl., U.S.	**u14**	86
Santa Rosa de Cabal, Col.	**E5**	58
Santa Rosa [de Copán], Hond.	**G3**	64
Santa Rosa Island, i., Ca., U.S.	**F3**	82
Santa Rosa Island, i., Fl., U.S.	**u14**	86
Santa Rosa Range, mts., Nv., U.S.	**B4**	105
Šantarskije Ostrova, is., Russia	**F21**	24
Santa Teresa Gallura, Italy	**H4**	14
Santa Vitória do Palmar, Braz.	**C6**	56
Santa Ynez, Ca., U.S.	**E3**	82
Santee, Ca., U.S.	**o16**	82
Santee, stm., S.C., U.S.	**E8**	117
Santee Dam, S.C., U.S.	**E7**	117

Name — Map Ref — Page

Santee Indian Reservation, Ne., U.S. B8 104
Santhià, Italy D3 14
Santiago, Chile C2 56
Santiago, Dom. Rep. E12 64
Santiago, Pan. J7 64
Santiago de Compostela, Spain C3 12
Santiago de Cuba, Cuba D10 64
Santiago del Estero, Arg. B4 56
Santiago do Cacém, Port. G3 12
Santiago Ixcuintla, Mex. G7 62
Santiago Papasquiaro, Mex. E7 62
Santiago Peak, mtn., Ca., U.S. n13 82
Santiago Reservoir, res., Ca., U.S. n13 82
Santiaguillo, Laguna de, l., Mex. E7 62
Santiam Pass, Or., U.S. C4 114
Sāntipur, India I13 38
Santisteban del Puerto, Spain G8 12
Santo Amaro, Braz. B9 57
Santo Anastácio, Braz. F3 57
Santo André, Braz. G5 57
Santo Ângelo, Braz. B6 56
Santo Antônio de Jesus, Braz. B9 57
Santo Antônio do Içá, Braz. D5 54
Santo Domingo, Dom. Rep. E13 64
Santo Domingo, Nic. H5 64
Santo Domingo de la Calzada, Spain C9 12
Santo Domingo de los Colorados, Ec. H3 58
Santo Domingo Indian Reservation, N.M., U.S. h8 108
Santo Domingo Pueblo, N.M., U.S. B3 108
Santoña, Spain B8 12
Santos, Braz. G5 57
Santos Dumont, Braz. F7 57
Santo Tomás, Mex. B1 62
Santo Tomé, Arg. B5 56
San Valentín, Monte, mtn., Chile F2 56
San Vicente, El Sal. H3 64
San Vicente, Mex. B1 62
San Vicente de Baracaldo, Spain B9 12
San Vicente de la Barquera, Spain B7 12
San Vicente del Caguán, Col. F5 58
San Vicente Reservoir, res., Ca., U.S. o16 82
San Xavier Indian Reservation, Az., U.S. E4 80
Sanzao Dao, i., China M2 28
Sanza Pombo, Ang. C3 44
São Bento, Braz. D10 54
São Borja, Braz. B5 56
São Caetano do Sul, Braz. G5 57
São Carlos, Braz. G5 57
São Domingos, Braz. B5 57
São Francisco, stm., Braz. E11 54
São Francisco do Sul, Braz. B7 56
São Gabriel, Braz. E8 57
São João da Boa Vista, Braz. F5 57
São João da Madeira, Port. E3 12
São João del Rei, Braz. F6 57
São Joaquim da Barra, Braz. F5 57
São José do Rio Prêto, Braz. F4 57
São José dos Campos, Braz. G6 57
São Leopoldo, Braz. B6 56
São Lourenço, Braz. G6 57
São Lourenço, Pantanal de, sw., Braz. G7 54
São Luís, Braz. D10 54
São Manuel, Braz. G4 57
São Mateus, Braz. E9 57
Saona, Isla, i., Dom. Rep. E13 64
Saône, stm., Fr. F11 10
São Paulo, Braz. G5 57
São Pedro do Ivaí, Braz. G3 57
São Pedro do Sul, Port. E3 12
São Romão, Braz. D6 57
São Roque, Cabo de, c., Braz. E11 54
São Sebastião, Ponta, c., Moz. F7 44
São Sebastião do Paraíso, Braz. F5 57
São Tomé, S. Tom./P. A1 44
São Tomé, i., S. Tom./P. A1 44
São Tomé, Cabo de, c., Braz. F8 57
Sao Tome and Principe, ctry., Afr. A1 44
São Vicente, Braz. G5 57
São Vicente, Cabo de, c., Port. H2 12
Sapé, Braz. E11 54
Sapele, Nig. G7 42
Sapelo Island, i., Ga., U.S. E5 87
Sapitwa, mtn., Mwi. E7 44
Sappa Creek, stm., U.S. E5 104
Sapphire Mountains, mts., Mt., U.S. D3 103
Sappington, Mo., U.S. f13 102
Sapporo, Japan p19 30a
Sapri, Italy I10 14
Sapulpa, Ok., U.S. B5 113
Sara Buri, Thai. G6 34
Sarajevo, Bos. F2 16
Saraland, Al., U.S. E1 78
Saranac, Mi., U.S. F5 99
Saranac, stm., N.Y., U.S. F11 109
Saranac Lake, N.Y., U.S. f10 109
Saranac Lakes, l., N.Y., U.S. f10 109
Sarangani Islands, is., Phil. D8 32
Saransk, Russia G7 22
Sarapul, Russia F8 22
Sarasota, Fl., U.S. E4 86
Sarasota, co., Fl., U.S. E4 86
Sarasota Bay, b., Fl., U.S. E4 86
Saratoga, Ca., U.S. k8 82
Saratoga, Tx., U.S. D5 120
Saratoga, Wy., U.S. E6 127
Saratoga, co., N.Y., U.S. B7 109
Saratoga Lake, l., N.Y., U.S. C7 109
Saratoga National Historical Park, N.Y., U.S. B7 109
Saratoga Springs, N.Y., U.S. B7 109
Saratov, Russia G7 22
Saravane, Laos G9 34
Sarcoxie, Mo., U.S. D3 102
Sardalas, Libya C8 42
Sardārshahr, India F6 38
Sardegna, i., Italy I3 14
Sardinia see Sardegna, i., Italy I3 14
Sardis, Ga., U.S. D5 87
Sardis, Ms., U.S. A4 101
Sardis Lake, res., Ms., U.S. A4 101
Sar-e Pol, Afg. B1 38
Sarepta, La., U.S. B2 95
Sarera, Teluk, b., Indon. F10 32
Sargent, Ga., U.S. C2 87
Sargent, Ne., U.S. C6 104
Sargent, co., N.D., U.S. C8 111
Sargodha, Pak. D5 38
Sarh, Chad G9 42
Sariñena, Spain D11 12
Şarköy, Tur. I11 16
Sarlat-la-Canéda, Fr. H8 10
Sarmi, Indon. F10 32
Sarmiento, Arg. F3 56
Särna, Swe. F9 6
Sarnia, Ont., Can. E2 73
Sarpy, co., Ne., U.S. C9 104
Sarralbe, Fr. C14 10
Sarrebourg, Fr. D14 10
Sarreguemines, Fr. C14 10
Sarria, Spain C4 12
Sartang, stm., Russia D20 24
Sartell, Mn., U.S. E4 100
Sarthe, stm., Fr. E6 10
Sarufutsu, Japan n20 30a
Sarzeau, Fr. E4 10
Sasarām, India H11 38
Sasebo, Japan I2 30
Saskatchewan, prov., Can. E3 75
Saskatchewan, stm., Can. F12 66
Saskylach, Russia C16 24
Sasovo, Russia G24 18
Sassafras, stm., Md., U.S. B5 97
Sassafras Mountain, mtn., U.S. A2 117
Sassandra, C. Iv. H4 42
Sassandra, stm., C. Iv. G4 42
Sassari, Italy I3 14
Sassnitz, Ger. A13 8
Sassuolo, Italy E5 14
Sastown, Lib. H4 42
Satah Mountain, mtn., B.C., Can. C5 69
Sata-misaki, c., Japan L3 30
Satanta, Ks., U.S. E3 93
Sātāra, India D2 37
Satilla, stm., Ga., U.S. E5 87
Satkānia, Bngl. I15 38
Satna, India H9 38
Sātpura Range, mts., India B4 37
Satsuma, Al., U.S. E1 78
Satsunan-shotō, is., Japan v29 31b
Şatu Mare, Rom. B6 16
Šatura, Russia F22 18
Satus Creek, stm., Wa., U.S. C5 124
Sauceda Mountains, mts., Az., U.S. E3 80
Sauda, Nor. G6 6
Saudi Arabia, ctry., Asia D4 46
Saufley Field Naval Air Station, mil., Fl., U.S. u14 86
Saugatuck, Mi., U.S. F4 99
Saugatuck, stm., Ct., U.S. D2 84
Saugatucket, stm., R.I., U.S. F4 116
Saugatuck Reservoir, res., Ct., U.S. D2 84
Saugerties, N.Y., U.S. C7 109
Saugus, Ma., U.S. B5 98
Saugus, stm., Ma., U.S. g11 98
Sauk, co., Wi., U.S. E4 126
Sauk, stm., Mn., U.S. E4 100
Sauk, stm., Wa., U.S. A4 124
Sauk Centre, Mn., U.S. E4 100
Sauk City, Wi., U.S. E4 126
Sauk Rapids, Mn., U.S. E4 100
Saukville, Wi., U.S. E6 126
Saulgau, Ger. G9 8
Saulnierville, N.S., Can. E3 71
Sault-au-Mouton, Que., Can. A8 74
Sault Sainte Marie, Ont., Can. p18 73
Sault Sainte Marie, Mi., U.S. B6 99
Saumarez Reef, rf., Austl. D10 50
Saumur, Fr. E6 10
Saunders, co., Ne., U.S. C9 104
Saunderstown, R.I., U.S. E4 116
Saurimo, Ang. C4 44
Sausalito, Ca., U.S. D2 82
Sava, Italy I12 14
Sava, stm., Eur. E3 16
Savage, Md., U.S. B4 97
Savage, stm., Md., U.S. k12 97
Savage River Reservoir, res., Md., U.S. k12 97
Savanna, Il., U.S. A3 90
Savanna, Ok., U.S. C6 113
Savannah, Ga., U.S. D5 87
Savannah, Mo., U.S. B3 102
Savannah, Tn., U.S. B3 119
Savannah, stm., U.S. F5 117
Savannah River Plant, sci., S.C., U.S. E4 117
Savannakhet, Laos F8 34
Savanna Lake, l., Md., U.S. D6 97
Savanna-la-Mar, Jam. E8 64
Savaştepe, Tur. J11 16
Save (Sabi), stm., Afr. F6 44
Savenay, Fr. E5 10
Saverdun, Fr. I8 10
Saverne, Fr. D14 10
Savigliano, Italy E2 14
Saville Dam, Ct., U.S. B4 84
Savona, Italy E3 14
Savonlinna, Fin. F17 6
Savonranta, Fin. E17 6
Savoonga, Ak., U.S. C5 79
Savoy, Il., U.S. C5 90
Savu Sea see Sawu, Laut, Indon. G7 32
Sawai Mādhopur, India G7 38
Sawākin, Sudan E13 42
Sawang, Indon. N7 34
Sawatch Range, mts., Co., U.S. B4 83
Sawdā', Qurnat as-, mtn., Leb. B5 40
Sawel Mountain, mtn., N. Ire., U.K. G5 7
Sawhāj, Egypt C12 42
Sawknah, Libya C9 42
Sawnee Mountain, mtn., Ga., U.S. B2 87
Sawtooth Mountains, mts., Id., U.S. F4 89
Sawtooth National Recreation Area, Id., U.S. E3 89
Sawu, Laut (Savu Sea), Indon. G7 32
Sawu, Pulau, i., Indon. H7 32
Şawwān, Arḑ aş-, pl., Jord. D5 40
Sawyer, co., Wi., U.S. C2 126
Sawyerville, Que., Can. D6 74
Saxmundham, Eng., U.K. I14 7
Saxonburg, Pa., U.S. E2 115
Saxtons, stm., Vt., U.S. E3 122
Saxtons River, Vt., U.S. E3 122
Sayaboury, Laos E6 34
Sayan Mountains (Sajany), mts., Asia G12 24
Sayaxché, Guat. F2 64
Saybrook, Il., U.S. C5 90
Saybrook Manor, Ct., U.S. D6 84
Şaydā (Sidon), Leb. C4 40
Saydel, Ia., U.S. e8 92
Sayhūt, Yemen E5 46
Saylesville, R.I., U.S. B4 116
Saylorsburg, Pa., U.S. E11 115
Saylorville, Ia., U.S. e8 92
Saylorville Lake, res., Ia., U.S. C4 92
Sayre, Al., U.S. B3 78
Sayre, Ok., U.S. B2 113
Sayre, Pa., U.S. C8 115
Sayreville, N.J., U.S. C4 107
Sayula, Mex. H8 62
Say'ūn, Yemen E4 46
Sayville, N.Y., U.S. n15 109
Scafell Pikes, mtn., Eng., U.K. G9 7
Scalp Level, Pa., U.S. F4 115
Scanlon, Mn., U.S. D6 100
Scapegoat Mountain, mtn., Mt., U.S. C3 103
Ščapino, Russia F25 24
Scappoose, Or., U.S. B4 114
Scarborough, Ont., Can. m15 73
Scarborough, Trin. I17 64
Scarborough, Me., U.S. E2 96
Scarbro, W.V., U.S. n13 125
Scarsdale, N.Y., U.S. h13 109
Ščelkovo, Russia F21 18
Ščerbakovo, Russia D26 24
Schaefferstown, Pa., U.S. F9 115
Schaffhausen, Switz. E15 10
Schaller, Ia., U.S. B2 92
Schaumburg, Il., U.S. h8 90
Schell Creek Range, mts., Nv., U.S. D7 105
Schenectady, N.Y., U.S. C7 109
Schenectady, co., N.Y., U.S. C6 109
Schererville, In., U.S. B3 91
Schertz, Tx., U.S. h7 120
Schiller Park, Il., U.S. k9 90
Schio, Italy D6 14
Schladming, Aus. H13 8
Schleicher, co., Tx., U.S. D2 120
Schleiden, Ger. E6 8
Schleswig, Ger. A9 8
Schleswig, Ia., U.S. B2 92
Schley, co., Ga., U.S. D2 87
Schneverdingen, Ger. B9 8
Schofield, Wi., U.S. D4 126
Schofield Barracks, mil., Hi., U.S. g9 88
Schoharie, co., N.Y., U.S. C6 109
Schoharie Creek, stm., N.Y., U.S. C6 109
Schönebeck, Ger. B13 8
Schongau, Ger. H10 8
Schoodic Lake, l., Me., U.S. C4 96
Schoolcraft, Mi., U.S. F5 99
Schoolcraft, co., Mi., U.S. B4 99
Schramberg, Ger. G8 8
Schrobenhausen, Ger. G11 8
Schroon Lake, l., N.Y., U.S. B7 109
Schulenburg, Tx., U.S. E4 120
Schulter, Ok., U.S. B6 113
Schurz, Nv., U.S. E3 105
Schuyler, Ne., U.S. C8 104
Schuyler, co., Il., U.S. C3 90
Schuyler, co., Mo., U.S. A5 102
Schuyler, co., N.Y., U.S. C4 109
Schuylkill, co., Pa., U.S. E9 115
Schuylkill, stm., Pa., U.S. F10 115
Schuylkill Haven, Pa., U.S. E9 115
Schwabach, Ger. F11 8
Schwaben, hist. reg., Ger. G10 8
Schwäbische Alb, mts., Ger. G9 8
Schwäbisch Gmünd, Ger. G9 8
Schwäbisch Hall, Ger. F9 8
Schwandorf in Bayern, Ger. F12 8
Schwaner, Pegunungan, mts., Indon. F5 32
Schwarzwald, mts., Ger. G8 8
Schwaz, Aus. H11 8
Schwechat, Aus. G16 8
Schwedt, Ger. B14 8
Schweinfurt, Ger. E10 8
Schwerin, Ger. B11 8
Schwyz, Switz. E15 10
Sciacca, Italy L8 14
Scicli, Italy M9 14
Science Hill, Ky., U.S. C5 94
Scilly, Isles of, is., Eng., U.K. L6 7
Scio, Or., U.S. C4 114
Scioto, co., Oh., U.S. D3 112
Scioto, stm., Oh., U.S. B2 112
Scituate, Ma., U.S. B6 98
Scituate Reservoir, res., R.I., U.S. C3 116
Scobey, Mt., U.S. B11 103
Scofield Reservoir, res., Ut., U.S. D4 121
Ščokino, Russia G20 18
Scotch Plains, N.J., U.S. B4 107
Scotia, Ca., U.S. B1 82
Scotia, N.Y., U.S. C7 109
Scotland, Ont., Can. D4 73
Scotland, S.D., U.S. D8 118
Scotland, co., Mo., U.S. A5 102
Scotland, co., N.C., U.S. C3 110
Scotland, ter., U.K. D8 7
Scotland Neck, N.C., U.S. A5 110
Scotlandville, La., U.S. D4 95
Scotrun, Pa., U.S. D11 115
Scotstown, Que., Can. D6 74
Scott, La., U.S. D3 95
Scott, co., Ar., U.S. C1 81
Scott, co., Il., U.S. D3 90
Scott, co., In., U.S. G6 91
Scott, co., Ia., U.S. C7 92
Scott, co., Ks., U.S. D3 93
Scott, co., Ky., U.S. B5 94
Scott, co., Mn., U.S. F5 100
Scott, co., Ms., U.S. C4 101
Scott, co., Mo., U.S. D8 102
Scott, co., Tn., U.S. C9 119
Scott, co., Va., U.S. f9 123
Scott, Cape, c., B.C., Can. D3 69
Scott, Mount, mtn., Or., U.S. E4 114
Scott Air Force Base, mil., Il., U.S. E4 90
Scott City, Ks., U.S. D3 93
Scott City, Mo., U.S. D8 102
Scottdale, Ga., U.S. h8 87
Scottdale, Pa., U.S. F2 115
Scott Islands, is., B.C., Can. F7 66
Scott Mountain, mtn., Id., U.S. E3 89
Scott Peak, mtn., Id., U.S. E6 89
Scott Reef, rf., Austl. B4 50
Scott Reservoir, res., N.C., U.S. A1 110
Scottsbluff, Ne., U.S. C2 104
Scotts Bluff, co., Ne., U.S. C2 104
Scotts Bluff National Monument, Ne., U.S. C2 104
Scottsboro, Al., U.S. A3 78
Scottsburg, In., U.S. G6 91
Scottsdale, Austl. H9 50
Scottsdale, Az., U.S. D4 80
Scottsville, Ky., U.S. D3 94
Scottsville, N.Y., U.S. B3 109
Scottville, Mi., U.S. E4 99
Scourie, Scot., U.K. C7 7
Scraggly Lake, l., Me., U.S. B4 96
Scranton, Ks., U.S. D8 93
Scranton, Pa., U.S. D10 115
Scranton, S.C., U.S. D8 117
Screven, Ga., U.S. E4 87
Screven, co., Ga., U.S. D5 87
Scribner, Ne., U.S. C9 104
Scugog, Lake, l., Ont., Can. C6 73
Scurry, co., Tx., U.S. C2 120
Scutari, Lake, l., Eur. G3 16
Seaboard, N.C., U.S. A5 110
Seabreeze, De., U.S. F5 85
Seabrook, N.H., U.S. E5 106
Seabrook, Tx., U.S. r14 120
Seabrook Island, i., S.C., U.S. F7 117
Seadrift, Tx., U.S. E4 120
Seaford, De., U.S. F3 85
Seaford, Va., U.S. h15 123
Seaforth, Ont., Can. D3 73
Seagoville, Tx., U.S. n10 120
Seagraves, Tx., U.S. C1 120
Seaham, Eng., U.K. G11 7
Sea Isle City, N.J., U.S. E3 107
Seal, stm., Man., Can. E13 66
Seal Cove, Newf., Can. D3 72
Seal Point, c., P.E.I., Can. C5 71
Seal Rock, Or., U.S. C2 114
Sealy, Tx., U.S. E4 120
Seaman, Oh., U.S. D2 112
Seaman Range, mts., Nv., U.S. F6 105
Searchlight, Nv., U.S. H7 105
Searcy, Ar., U.S. B4 81
Searcy, co., Ar., U.S. B3 81
Searles Lake, l., Ca., U.S. E5 82
Searsport, Me., U.S. D4 96
Seaside, Or., U.S. B3 114
Seat Pleasant, Md., U.S. C4 97
Seattle, Wa., U.S. B3 124
Seattle-Tacoma International Airport, Wa., U.S. f11 124
Seaview, Wa., U.S. C1 124
Sebago Lake, Me., U.S. E2 96
Šebalino, Russia G11 24
Sebastian, Fl., U.S. E6 86
Sebastian, co., Ar., U.S. B1 81
Sebastian, Cape, c., Or., U.S. E2 114
Sebastian Inlet, b., Fl., U.S. E6 86
Sebastián Vizcaíno, Bahía, b., Mex. C2 62
Sebasticook Lake, l., Me., U.S. D3 96
Sebec Lake, l., Me., U.S. C3 96
Sebeka, Mn., U.S. D3 100
Sebewaing, Mi., U.S. E7 99
Seboeis, stm., Me., U.S. B4 96
Seboeis Lake, l., Me., U.S. C4 96
Seboomook Lake, l., Me., U.S. C3 96
Sebree, Ky., U.S. C2 94
Sebring, Fl., U.S. E5 86
Sebring, Oh., U.S. B4 112
Secaucus, N.J., U.S. h8 107
Sechelt, B.C., Can. E6 69
Second Lake, l., N.H., U.S. f7 106
Second Mesa, Az., U.S. B5 80
Secret Lake, l., R.I., U.S. E4 116
Section, Al., U.S. A4 78
Security, Co., U.S. C6 83
Sedalia, Mo., U.S. C4 102
Sedan, Fr. C11 10
Sedan, Ks., U.S. E7 93
Sedano, Spain C8 12
Sedgewick, Alta., Can. C5 68
Sedgewick, Mount, mtn., N.M., U.S. B1 108
Sedgwick, Ks., U.S. E6 93
Sedgwick, co., Co., U.S. A8 83
Sedgwick, co., Ks., U.S. E6 93
Sedley, Va., U.S. D6 123
Sedona, Az., U.S. C4 80
Sedro Woolley, Wa., U.S. A3 124
Seeheim, Nmb. G3 44
Seekonk, Ma., U.S. C5 98
Seekonk, stm., R.I., U.S. C4 116
Seeley, Ca., U.S. F6 82
Seeley Lake, Mt., U.S. C3 103
Seelyville, In., U.S. F3 91
Sées, Fr. D7 10
Segamat, Malay. M7 34
Ségou, Mali F4 42
Segovia, Col. D5 58
Segovia, Spain E7 12
Segré, Fr. E6 10
Seguam Island, i., Ak., U.S. E5 79
Seguam Pass, strt., Ak., U.S. E5 79
Séguédine, Niger D8 42
Seguin, Tx., U.S. E4 120
Sehore, India I7 38
Seia, Port. E4 12
Seiling, Ok., U.S. A3 113
Seinäjoki, Fin. E14 6
Seine, stm., Fr. C7 10
Seki, Tur. M13 16
Sekiu, Wa., U.S. A1 124
Sekondi-Takoradi, Ghana H5 42
Šelagskij, Mys, c., Russia C28 24
Selah, Wa., U.S. C5 124
Selaru, Pulau, i., Indon. G9 32
Selatan, Tanjung, c., Indon. F5 32
Selawik, Ak., U.S. B7 79
Selawik Lake, l., Ak., U.S. B7 79
Selayar, Pulau, i., Indon. G7 32
Selb, Ger. E12 8
Selby, S.D., U.S. B5 118
Selbyville, De., U.S. G5 85
Selçuk, Tur. L11 16
Seldovia, Ak., U.S. D9 79
Selemdža, stm., Russia G20 24
Selenn'ach, stm., Russia D21 24
Sélestat, Fr. D14 10
Sélibaby, Maur. E3 42
Šelichova, Zaliv, b., Russia E25 24
Seligman, Az., U.S. B3 80
Selinsgrove, Pa., U.S. E8 115
Selkirk, Man., Can. D3 70
Selkirk, Scot., U.K. F10 7
Selkirk Mountains, mts., N.A. F9 66
Sellersburg, In., U.S. H6 91
Sellersville, Pa., U.S. F11 115
Selles-sur-Cher, Fr. E8 10
Sells, Az., U.S. F4 80
Selma, Al., U.S. C2 78
Selma, Ca., U.S. D4 82
Selma, In., U.S. D7 91
Selma, N.C., U.S. B4 110
Selmer, Tn., U.S. B3 119
Selva, Arg. B4 56
Selvas, for., Braz. E6 54
Selway, stm., Id., U.S. C3 89
Selwyn Mountains, mts., Can. D6 66
Semara, W. Sah. C3 42
Semarang, Indon. m15 32
Semeru, Gunung, vol., Indon. n16 33a
Seminoe Mountains, mts., Wy., U.S. D6 127
Seminoe Reservoir, res., Wy., U.S. D6 127
Seminole, Ok., U.S. B5 113
Seminole, Tx., U.S. C1 120
Seminole, co., Fl., U.S. D5 86
Seminole, co., Ga., U.S. F2 87
Seminole, co., Ok., U.S. B5 113
Seminole, Lake, res., U.S. F2 87
Semipalatinsk, Kaz. G10 24
Semisopochnoi Island, i., Ak., U.S. E3 79
Semmes, Al., U.S. E1 78
Semonaicha, Kaz. G10 24
Semur-en-Auxois, Fr. E11 10
Sên, stm., Camb. H8 34
Sena, Moz. E6 44
Senachwine Lake, l., Il., U.S. B4 90
Senador Pompeu, Braz. E11 54
Sena Madureira, Braz. E5 54
Senanga, Zam. E4 44
Senath, Mo., U.S. E7 102
Senatobia, Ms., U.S. A4 101
Sendai, Japan K3 30
Sendai, Japan D13 30
Seneca, Il., U.S. B5 90
Seneca, Ks., U.S. C7 93
Seneca, Mo., U.S. E3 102
Seneca, Pa., U.S. D2 115
Seneca, S.C., U.S. B2 117
Seneca, co., N.Y., U.S. C4 109
Seneca, co., Oh., U.S. A2 112
Seneca Falls, N.Y., U.S. C4 109
Seneca Lake, l., N.Y., U.S. C4 109
Senecaville Lake, res., Oh., U.S. C4 112
Senegal (Sénégal), ctry., Afr. F3 42
Sénégal, stm., Afr. E3 42
Senekal, S. Afr. G5 44
Senftenberg, Ger. D13 8
Senigallia, Italy F8 14
Senise, Italy I11 14
Senmonorom, Camb. H9 34
Senneterre, Que., Can. k11 74
Sennori, Italy I3 14
Senoia, Ga., U.S. C2 87
Sens, Fr. D10 10
Senta, Yugo. D4 16
Sentinel, Ok., U.S. B2 113
Seo de Urgel, Spain C13 12
Seoni, India I8 38
Seoul see Sŏul, S. Kor. D12 26
Sept-Îles (Seven Islands), Que., Can. h13 74
Sepulga, stm., Al., U.S. D3 78
Sepúlveda, Spain D8 12
Sequatchie, co., Tn., U.S. D8 119
Sequatchie, stm., Tn., U.S. D8 119
Sequim, Wa., U.S. A2 124
Sequoia National Park, Ca., U.S. D4 82
Sequoyah, co., Ok., U.S. B7 113
Seraing, Bel. E5 8
Seram, i., Indon. F8 32
Seram, Laut (Ceram Sea), Indon. F8 32
Serang, Indon. m13 33a
Seremban, Malay. M6 34
Serengeti Plain, pl., Tan. B6 44
Serenje, Zam. D6 44
Sergeant Bluff, Ia., U.S. B1 92

Name — Map Ref — Page
Sergeja Kirova, Ostrova, is., Russia B11 24
Sergijev Podad, Russia E21 18
Serowe, Bots. F5 44
Serpa, Port. H4 12
Serpuchov, Russia G20 18
Sérrai, Grc. H7 16
Serra San Bruno, Italy K11 14
Serra Talhada, Braz. E11 54
Serres, Fr. H12 10
Serrezuela, Arg. C3 56
Serri, Italy J4 14
Serrinha, Braz. F11 54
Sertã, Port. F3 12
Sesfontein, Nmb. E2 44
Sesheke, Zam. E4 44
Sessa Aurunca, Italy H8 14
Sesser, Il., U.S. E4 90
Sestri Levante, Italy E4 14
Sète, Fr. I10 10
Sete Lagoas, Braz. E6 57
Seth, W.V., U.S. C3 125
Sétif, Alg. A7 42
Seto, Japan G10 30
Seto-naikai, Japan H6 30
Setúbal, Port. G3 12
Seul, Lac, l., Ont., Can. o16 73
Seul Choix Point, c., Mi., U.S. C5 99
Sevan, ozero, l., Arm. I7 22
Sevastopol', Ukr. I4 22
Seven Devils Lake, res., Ar., U.S. D4 81
Seven Devils Mountains, mts., Id., U.S. D2 89
Seven Hills, Oh., U.S. h9 112
Seven Mile Beach, N.J., U.S. E3 107
Sévérac-le-Château, Fr. H10 10
Severn, Md., U.S. B4 97
Severn, stm., Ont., Can. n17 73
Severn, stm., Eng., U.K. J10 7
Severnaja Dvina, stm., Russia E6 22
Severnaja Zemľa, is., Russia B13 24
Severna Park, Md., U.S. B4 97
Severn River, b., Md., U.S. B4 97
Severodvinsk, Russia E5 22
Severo-Kuril'sk, Russia G25 24
Severo-Sibirskaja Nizmennost', pl., Russia C13 24
Severo-Zadonsk, Russia G21 18
Sevettijärvi, Fin. B17 6
Sevier, co., Ar., U.S. D1 81
Sevier, co., Tn., U.S. D10 119
Sevier, co., Ut., U.S. E4 121
Sevier, stm., Ut., U.S. D3 121
Sevier Bridge Reservoir, res., Ut., U.S. D4 121
Sevier Lake, l., Ut., U.S. E2 121
Sevierville, Tn., U.S. D10 119
Sevilla, Col. E5 58
Sevilla, Spain H6 12
Seville, Oh., U.S. A4 112
Seville see Sevilla, Spain H6 12
Sewanee, Tn., U.S. D8 119
Seward, Ak., U.S. C10 79
Seward, Ne., U.S. D8 104
Seward, co., Ks., U.S. E3 93
Seward, co., Ne., U.S. D8 104
Seward Peninsula, pen., Ak., U.S. B7 79
Sewickley, Pa., U.S. E1 115
Sexsmith, Alta., Can. B1 68
Seychelles, ctry., Afr. B11 44
Seyðisfjörður, Ice. B5 4
Seymour, Ct., U.S. D3 84
Seymour, In., U.S. G6 91
Seymour, Ia., U.S. D4 92
Seymour, Mo., U.S. D5 102
Seymour, Tx., U.S. C3 120
Seymour, Wi., U.S. D5 126
Seymour Inlet, b., B.C., Can. D4 69
Seymour Johnson Air Force Base, mil., N.C., U.S. B5 110
Seymour Lake, l., Vt., U.S. B4 122
Seymourville, La., U.S. h9 95
Seyne, Fr. H13 10
Seyssel, Fr. G12 10
Sézanne, Fr. D10 10
Sezze, Italy H8 14
Sfax, Tun. B8 42
's-Gravenhage (The Hague), Neth. C4 8
Shabbona, Il., U.S. B5 90
Shache, China A7 38
Shackelford, co., Tx., U.S. C3 120
Shackleton Ice Shelf, Ant. C22 47
Shaddādī, Syria A7 40
Shadehill Dam, S.D., U.S. B3 118
Shadehill Reservoir, res., S.D., U.S. B3 118
Shadow Mountain National Recreation Area, Co., U.S. A4 83
Shady Cove, Or., U.S. E4 114
Shady Side, Md., U.S. C4 97
Shadyside, Oh., U.S. C5 112
Shady Spring, W.V., U.S. D3 125
Shafer, Lake, l., In., U.S. C4 91
Shafer Butte, mtn., Id., U.S. F2 89
Shafter, Ca., U.S. E4 82
Shaftsbury, Vt., U.S. E2 122
Shāhdādkot, Pak. G2 38
Shahdol, India I9 38
Shāhjahānpur, India G8 38
Shāh Jūy, Afg. D2 38
Shahrak, Afg. C1 38
Shājāpur, India I7 38
Shakawe, Bots. E4 44
Shaker Heights, Oh., U.S. A4 112
Shakhty see Šachty, Russia H6 22
Shaki, Nig. G6 42
Shakopee, Mn., U.S. F5 100
Shaler Mountains, mts., N.W. Ter., Can. B10 66
Shallotte, N.C., U.S. D4 110
Shallotte Inlet, b., N.C., U.S. D4 110
Shallowater, Tx., U.S. C2 120
Shām, Bādiyat ash-, des., Asia C6 40
Shām, Jabal ash-, mtn., Oman D6 46
Shamokin, Pa., U.S. E8 115
Shamokin Dam, Pa., U.S. E8 115
Shamrock, Tx., U.S. B2 120
Shandī, Sudan E12 42
Shandong, prov., China D10 26
Shandong Bandao, pen., China D11 26
Shanghai, China D10 28
Shanghai Shih, China E11 28
Shangqiu, China A4 28
Shangrao, China G6 28
Shangshui, China B3 28
Shangzhi, China B12 26
Shannock, R.I., U.S. F2 116
Shannon, Ga., U.S. B1 87
Shannon, Il., U.S. A4 90
Shannon, Ms., U.S. A5 101
Shannon, co., Mo., U.S. D6 102
Shannon, co., S.D., U.S. D3 118
Shannon, stm., Ire. I3 7
Shannon, Lake, l., Wa., U.S. A4 124
Shannontown, S.C., U.S. D7 117
Shantou (Swatow), China L5 28
Shantung Peninsula see Shandong Bandao, pen., China D11 26
Shănxī, prov., China D8 26
Shănxī, prov., China D9 26
Shanyin, China D9 26
Shaoguan, China K2 28
Shaowu, China H6 28
Shaoxing, China E9 28
Shaoyang, China F9 26
Shark Bay, b., Austl. E2 50
Sharkey, co., Ms., U.S. C3 101
Shark Point, c., Fl., U.S. H5 86
Sharktooth Mountain, mtn., B.C., Can. E7 66
Sharon, Ct., U.S. B2 84
Sharon, Ma., U.S. B5 98
Sharon, Pa., U.S. D1 115
Sharon, Tn., U.S. A3 119
Sharon, Wi., U.S. F5 126
Sharon Hill, Pa., U.S. p20 115
Sharon Park, Oh., U.S. n12 112
Sharon Springs, Ks., U.S. D2 93
Sharonville, Oh., U.S. n13 112
Sharp, co., Ar., U.S. A4 81
Sharpe, Lake, res., S.D., U.S. C6 118
Sharpes, Fl., U.S. D6 86
Sharpley, De., U.S. h7 85
Sharpsburg, Md., U.S. B2 97
Sharpsburg, N.C., U.S. B5 110
Sharpsburg, Pa., U.S. k14 115
Sharpsville, In., U.S. D5 91
Sharpsville, Pa., U.S. D1 115
Sharptown, Md., U.S. C6 97
Sharqīyah, Aṣ-Ṣaḥrā' ash- (Arabian Desert), des., Egypt C12 42
Shashi, China E9 26
Shashi, stm., Afr. F5 44
Shasta, co., Ca., U.S. B3 82
Shasta, Mount, vol., Ca., U.S. B2 82
Shasta Lake, res., Ca., U.S. B2 82
Shattuck, Ok., U.S. A2 113
Shaw, Ms., U.S. B3 101
Shaw Air Force Base, mil., S.C., U.S. D7 117
Shawano, Wi., U.S. D5 126
Shawano, co., Wi., U.S. D5 126
Shawano Lake, l., Wi., U.S. D5 126
Shawinigan, Que., Can. C5 74
Shawinigan-Sud, Que., Can. C5 74
Shawnee, Ks., U.S. k16 93
Shawnee, Ok., U.S. B5 113
Shawnee, co., Ks., U.S. D8 93
Shawneetown, Il., U.S. F5 90
Shawsheen, stm., Ma., U.S. f11 98
Shaybārā, i., Sau. Ar. C2 46
Shaykh, Jabal ash-, mtn., Asia C4 40
Shebele (Shebelle), stm., Afr. G3 46
Sheberghān, Afg. B1 38
Sheboygan, Wi., U.S. E6 126
Sheboygan, co., Wi., U.S. E6 126
Sheboygan, stm., Wi., U.S. k10 126
Sheboygan Falls, Wi., U.S. E6 126
Shediac, N.B., Can. C5 71
Sheenjek, stm., Ak., U.S. B11 79
Sheep Mountain, mtn., Az., U.S. E1 80
Sheep Mountain, mtn., Wy., U.S. B5 127
Sheep Mountain, mtn., Wy., U.S. C2 127
Sheep Peak, mtn., Nv., U.S. G6 105
Sheep Range, mts., Nv., U.S. G6 105
Sheet Harbour, N.S., Can. E7 71
Sheffield, Eng., U.K. H11 7
Sheffield, Al., U.S. A2 78
Sheffield, Il., U.S. B4 90
Sheffield, Ia., U.S. B4 92
Sheffield, Pa., U.S. C3 115
Sheffield Lake, Oh., U.S. A3 112
Sheila, N.B., Can. B5 71
Shēkhābād, Afg. C3 38
Shekhūpura, Pak. E5 38
Shelagyote Peak, mtn., B.C., Can. B4 69
Shelbiana, Ky., U.S. C7 94
Shelbina, Mo., U.S. B5 102
Shelburn, In., U.S. F3 91
Shelburne, Ont., Can. C4 73
Shelburne Falls, Ma., U.S. A2 98
Shelburne Pond, l., Vt., U.S. C2 122
Shelby, Al., U.S. B3 78
Shelby, In., U.S. B3 91
Shelby, Ia., U.S. C2 92
Shelby, Mi., U.S. E4 99
Shelby, Ms., U.S. B3 101
Shelby, Mt., U.S. B5 103
Shelby, Ne., U.S. C8 104
Shelby, N.C., U.S. B1 110
Shelby, Oh., U.S. B3 112
Shelby, co., Al., U.S. B3 78
Shelby, co., Il., U.S. D5 90
Shelby, co., In., U.S. E6 91
Shelby, co., Ia., U.S. C2 92
Shelby, co., Ky., U.S. B4 94
Shelby, co., Mo., U.S. B5 102
Shelby, co., Oh., U.S. B1 112
Shelby, co., Tn., U.S. B2 119
Shelby, co., Tx., U.S. D5 120
Shelbyville, Il., U.S. D5 90
Shelbyville, In., U.S. F6 91
Shelbyville, Ky., U.S. B4 94
Shelbyville, Tn., U.S. B5 119
Shelbyville, Lake, res., Il., U.S. D5 90
Sheldon, Il., U.S. C6 90
Sheldon, Ia., U.S. A2 92
Sheldon, Tx., U.S. r14 120
Shelikof Strait, strt., Ak., U.S. D9 79
Shell Creek, stm., U.S. A2 83
Shell Creek, stm., Wy., U.S. B5 127
Shelley, Id., U.S. F6 89
Shell Lake, Wi., U.S. C2 126
Shell Lake, l., Mn., U.S. D3 100
Shell Lake, l., Wi., U.S. C2 126
Shellman, Ga., U.S. E2 87
Shell Rock, Ia., U.S. B5 92
Shell Rock, stm., Ia., U.S. B5 92
Shellsburg, Ia., U.S. B6 92
Shelly Mountain, mtn., Id., U.S. F5 89
Shelter Island, N.Y., U.S. m16 109
Shelton, Ct., U.S. D3 84
Shelton, Ne., U.S. D7 104
Shelton, Wa., U.S. B2 124
Shemya Air Force Base, mil., Ak., U.S. E2 79
Shenandoah, Ia., U.S. D2 92
Shenandoah, Pa., U.S. E9 115
Shenandoah, Va., U.S. B4 123
Shenandoah, co., Va., U.S. B4 123
Shenandoah, stm., U.S. A5 123
Shenandoah, North Fork, stm., Va., U.S. B4 123
Shenandoah, South Fork, stm., Va., U.S. B4 123
Shenandoah Mountain, mtn., U.S. B3 123
Shenandoah National Park, Va., U.S. B4 123
Shenango River Lake, res., U.S. D1 115
Shengfang, China D10 26
Shengze, China E9 28
Shenipsit Lake, l., Ct., U.S. B6 84
Shenyang (Mukden), China C11 26
Shenzha, China E13 38
Shepaug, stm., Ct., U.S. C2 84
Shepaug Dam, Ct., U.S. D2 84
Shepaug Reservoir, res., Ct., U.S. C2 84
Shepherd, Mi., U.S. E6 99
Shepherd, Tx., U.S. D5 120
Shepherdstown, W.V., U.S. B7 125
Shepherdsville, Ky., U.S. C4 94
Sheppard Air Force Base, mil., Tx., U.S. C3 120
Shepparton, Austl. G9 50
Sherborn, Ma., U.S. h10 98
Sherbro Island, i., S.L. G3 42
Sherbrooke, Que., Can. D6 74
Sherburn, Mn., U.S. G4 100
Sherburne, co., Mn., U.S. E5 100
Sheridan, Ar., U.S. C3 81
Sheridan, Il., U.S. B5 90
Sheridan, In., U.S. D5 91
Sheridan, Mi., U.S. E5 99
Sheridan, Mt., U.S. E4 103
Sheridan, Or., U.S. B3 114
Sheridan, Wy., U.S. B6 127
Sheridan, co., Ks., U.S. C3 93
Sheridan, co., Mt., U.S. B12 103
Sheridan, co., Ne., U.S. B3 104
Sheridan, co., N.D., U.S. B5 111
Sheridan, co., Wy., U.S. B5 127
Sheridan, Mount, mtn., Wy., U.S. B2 127
Sheringham Cromer, Eng., U.K. I14 7
Sherman, Tx., U.S. C4 120
Sherman, co., Ks., U.S. C2 93
Sherman, co., Ne., U.S. C6 104
Sherman, co., Or., U.S. B6 114
Sherman, co., Tx., U.S. A2 120
Sherman Reservoir, res., Ne., U.S. C7 104
Sherrelwood, Co., U.S. *B6 83
Sherrill, N.Y., U.S. B5 109
's-Hertogenbosch, Neth. D5 8
Sherwood, P.E.I., Can. C6 71
Sherwood, Ar., U.S. C3 81
Sherwood, Or., U.S. h12 114
Sherwood, Wi., U.S. h9 126
Sherwood Manor, Ct., U.S. A5 84
Sherwood Park, De., U.S. i7 85
Shetek, Lake, l., Mn., U.S. G3 100
Shetland Islands, is., Scot., U.K. A11 7
Shetucket, stm., Ct., U.S. C7 84
Sheyenne, stm., N.D., U.S. C8 111
Sheyenne Lake, res., N.D., U.S. B5 111
Shiawassee, co., Mi., U.S. F6 99
Shibata, Japan E12 30
Shibetsu, Japan p23 30a
Shibukawa, Japan F11 30
Shickshinny, Pa., U.S. D9 115
Shijiazhuang, China D9 26
Shijushan, China D8 26
Shikārpur, Pak. G3 38
Shikohābād, India G8 38
Shikoku, i., Japan I6 30
Shikoku-sanchi, mts., Japan I6 30
Shikotsu-ko, l., Japan q19 30a
Shillington, Pa., U.S. F10 115
Shillong, India H14 38
Shiloh National Military Park, Tn., U.S. B3 119
Shilong, China L2 28
Shimabara, Japan J3 30
Shimada, Japan H11 30
Shimbiris, mtn., Som. F4 46
Shimizu, Japan G11 30
Shimminato, Japan F10 30
Shimodate, Japan F12 30
Shimoga, India F3 37
Shimonoseki, Japan I3 30
Shinano, stm., Japan E11 30
Shīndand, Afg. C1 36
Shiner, Tx., U.S. E4 120
Shinglehouse, Pa., U.S. C5 115
Shingū, Japan I8 30
Shinjō, Japan D13 30
Shinnston, W.V., U.S. B4 125
Shinshār, Syria B5 40
Shinyanga, Tan. B6 44
Shiocton, Wi., U.S. D5 126
Shiogama, Japan D14 30
Shiojiri, Japan F10 30
Shiping, China C7 34
Ship Island, i., Ms., U.S. E5 101
Ship Island Pass, strt., Ms., U.S. g7 101
Shippegan, N.B., Can. B5 71
Shippensburg, Pa., U.S. F6 115
Shiprock, N.M., U.S. A1 108
Ship Rock, mtn., N.M., U.S. A1 108
Shirakawa, Japan E13 30
Shīrāz, Iran C5 46
Shire, stm., Afr. E6 44
Shiretoko-misaki, c., Japan o23 30a
Shirley, In., U.S. E6 91
Shirley, Ma., U.S. A4 98
Shirley Mountains, mts., Wy., U.S. D6 127
Shirpur, India B3 37
Shishaldin Volcano, vol., Ak., U.S. E7 79
Shishmaref, Ak., U.S. B6 79
Shively, Ky., U.S. B4 94
Shivpuri, India H7 38
Shizuoka, Japan H11 30
Shkodër, Alb. G3 16
Shoal Creek, stm., U.S. B4 119
Shoal Harbour, Newf., Can. D4 72
Shoal Lake, Man., Can. D1 70
Shoals, In., U.S. G4 91
Shoals, Isles of, is., Me., U.S. E2 96
Shoalwater, Cape, c., Wa., U.S. C1 124
Shōdo-shima, i., Japan H7 30
Shoemakersville, Pa., U.S. F10 115
Sholāpur, India D3 37
Shongopovi, Az., U.S. B5 80
Shonto, Az., U.S. A5 80
Shoreham, Mi., U.S. F4 99
Shores Acres, R.I., U.S. E4 116
Shoreview, Mn., U.S. m12 100
Shorewood, Il., U.S. k8 90
Shorewood, Mn., U.S. n11 100
Shorewood, Wi., U.S. E6 126
Short Beach, Ct., U.S. D4 84
Shoshone, Id., U.S. G4 89
Shoshone, co., Id., U.S. B2 89
Shoshone, stm., Wy., U.S. B4 127
Shoshone Falls, wtfl, Id., U.S. G4 89
Shoshone Lake, l., Wy., U.S. B2 127
Shoshone Mountains, mts., Nv., U.S. E4 105
Shoshone Peak, mtn., Nv., U.S. G5 105
Shoshone Range, mts., Nv., U.S. C5 105
Shoshong, Bots. F5 44
Shoshoni, Wy., U.S. C4 127
Shoup, Id., U.S. D4 89
Shouxian, China C5 28
Show Low, Az., U.S. C5 80
Shreve, Oh., U.S. B3 112
Shreveport, La., U.S. B2 95
Shrewsbury, Eng., U.K. I10 7
Shrewsbury, Ma., U.S. B4 98
Shrewsbury, N.J., U.S. C4 107
Shrewsbury, Pa., U.S. G8 115
Shuajingsi, China E7 26
Shuangcheng, China B12 26
Shuangyashan, China B13 26
Shubenacadie, N.S., Can. D6 71
Shuksan, Mount, mtn., Wa., U.S. A4 124
Shullsburg, Wi., U.S. F3 126
Shumagin Islands, is., Ak., U.S. E7 79
Shunde, China M2 28
Shungnak, Ak., U.S. B8 79
Shuqrā', Yemen F4 46
Shūshtar, Iran B4 46
Shuswap Lake, l., B.C., Can. D8 69
Shwebo, Mya. C3 34
Siaksriinderapura, Indon. N7 34
Siālkot, Pak. D6 38
Siam, Gulf of see Thailand, Gulf of, b., Asia J6 34
Sian see Xi'an, China E8 26
Siargao Island, i., Phil. D8 32
Šiaškotan, Ostrov, i., Russia H24 24
Šiauliai, Lith. F6 18
Šibenik, Cro. F10 14
Siberia see Sibir', reg., Russia D16 24
Siberut, Pulau, i., Indon. F2 32
Sibi, Pak. F2 38
Sibir' (Siberia), reg., Russia D16 24
Sibir'akova, Ostrov, i., Russia C9 24
Sibiti, Congo B2 44
Sibiu, Rom. D8 16
Sibley, Ia., U.S. A2 92
Sibley, La., U.S. B2 95
Sibley, co., Mn., U.S. F4 100
Sibolga, Indon. E2 32
Sibsāgar, India G16 38
Sibu, Malay. E5 32
Sibutu Island, i., Phil. E6 32
Sibuyan Island, i., Phil. C7 32
Sibuyan Sea, Phil. C7 32
Sicamous, B.C., Can. D8 69
Sichote-Alin', mts., Russia H21 24
Sichuan, prov., China E7 26
Sicié, Cap, c., Fr. I12 10
Sicilia, i., Italy L9 14
Sicily, Strait of, strt. L7 14
Sicily see Sicilia, i., Italy L9 14
Sico, stm., Hond. G5 64
Sicuani, Peru F4 54
Siddipet, India C5 37
Siderno, Italy K11 14
Sidhpur, India I5 38
Sidi bel Abbès, Alg. A5 42
Sidi Ifni, Mor. C3 42
Sidmouth, Eng., U.K. K9 7
Sidney, B.C., Can. E6 69
Sidney, Il., U.S. C5 90
Sidney, Ia., U.S. D2 92
Sidney, Mt., U.S. C12 103
Sidney, Ne., U.S. C3 104
Sidney, N.Y., U.S. C5 109
Sidney, Oh., U.S. B1 112
Sidney Lanier, Lake, res., Ga., U.S. B2 87
Sidon see Ṣaydā, Leb. C4 40
Sidra, Gulf of see Surt, Khalīj, b., Libya B9 42
Siedlce, Pol. C22 8
Siegburg, Ger. E7 8
Siegen, Ger. E8 8
Siĕmréab, Camb. H7 34
Siena, Italy F6 14
Sierra, co., Ca., U.S. C3 82
Sierra, co., N.M., U.S. D2 108
Sierra Blanca Peak, mtn., N.M., U.S. D4 108
Sierra Colorada, Arg. E3 56
Sierra Estrella, mts., Az., U.S. m8 80
Sierra Leone, ctry., Afr. G3 42
Sierra Madre, Ca., U.S. m12 82
Sierra Vista, Az., U.S. F5 80
Sierre, Switz. F14 10
Siesta Key, i., Fl., U.S. E4 86
Sighetul Marmaţiei, Rom. B7 16
Sighişoara, Rom. C8 16
Siglufjörður, Ice. B4 4
Signal Mountain, Tn., U.S. D8 119
Signal Peak, mtn., Az., U.S. D1 80
Signal Peak, mtn., Ut., U.S. F2 121
Signy-l'Abbaye, Fr. C11 10
Sigourney, Ia., U.S. C5 92
Sigüenza, Spain D9 12
Sigües, Spain C10 12
Siguiri, Gui. F4 42
Siilinjärvi, Fin. E16 6
Si-Kacha, Thai. H6 34
Sīkar, India G6 38
Sikasso, Mali F4 42
Sikeston, Mo., U.S. E8 102
Sikiá, Grc. I7 16
Síkinos, Grc. M9 16
Sikkim, state, India G13 38
Šikotan, Ostrov (Shikotan-tō), i., Russia I23 24
Sikt'ach, Russia D19 24
Silandro, Italy C5 14
Silao, Mex. G9 62
Silay, Phil. C7 32
Silba, Cro. E9 14
Silchar, India H15 38
Siler City, N.C., U.S. B3 110
Silesia, hist. reg., Pol. E16 8
Siletz, Or., U.S. C3 114
Silifke, Tur. A3 40
Silīguri, India G13 38
Siling Co, l., China E13 38
Silistra, Bul. E11 16
Šilka, Russia G18 24
Šilka, stm., Russia G17 24
Silkeborg, Den. H7 6
Sillamäe, Est. B10 18
Sillé-le-Guillaume, Fr. D6 10
Sillery, Que., Can. n17 74
Sillon de Talbert, pen., Fr. D3 10
Siloam Springs, Ar., U.S. A1 81
Silsbee, Tx., U.S. D5 120
Silt, Co., U.S. B3 83
Silvânia, Braz. G9 54
Silvassa, India B2 37
Silver Bay, Mn., U.S. C7 100
Silver Bow, co., Mt., U.S. E4 103
Silver City, Nv., U.S. D2 105
Silver City, N.M., U.S. E1 108
Silver Creek, Ne., U.S. C8 104
Silver Creek, N.Y., U.S. C1 109
Silver Creek, stm., Or., U.S. D7 114
Silverdale, Wa., U.S. B3 124
Silver Grove, Ky., U.S. h14 94
Silver Hill, Md., U.S. f9 97
Silver Lake, Ks., U.S. C8 93
Silver Lake, Ma., U.S. f11 98
Silver Lake, Mn., U.S. F4 100
Silver Lake, Wi., U.S. F5 126
Silver Lake, l., De., U.S. D3 85
Silver Lake, l., Ia., U.S. A3 92
Silver Lake, l., Me., U.S. C3 96
Silver Lake, l., N.H., U.S. E2 106
Silver Lake, l., N.H., U.S. C4 106
Silver Lake, l., Or., U.S. D7 114
Silver Lake, l., Wa., U.S. g13 124
Silverpeak, Nv., U.S. F4 105
Silver Peak Range, mts., Nv., U.S. F4 105
Silver Spring, Md., U.S. C3 97
Silver Springs, Nv., U.S. D2 105
Silver Star Mountain, mtn., Wa., U.S. A5 124
Silverthrone Mountain, mtn., B.C., Can. D4 69
Silvertip Mountain, mtn., Mt., U.S. C3 103
Silverton, Co., U.S. D3 83
Silverton, Id., U.S. B3 89
Silverton, N.J., U.S. C4 107
Silverton, Oh., U.S. o13 112
Silverton, Or., U.S. C4 114
Silvi, Italy G9 14
Silvies, stm., Or., U.S. D7 114
Silview, De., U.S. B3 85
Silvis, Il., U.S. B3 90
Simanggang, Malay. E5 32
Simanovsk, Russia G19 24
Simav, Tur. J12 16
Simcoe, Ont., Can. E4 73
Simcoe, Lake, l., Ont., Can. C5 73
Simeulue, Pulau, i., Indon. M3 34
Simferopol', Ukr. I4 22
Simi Valley, Ca., U.S. E4 82
Simla, India E7 38
Simmesport, La., U.S. D4 95
Simms Stream, stm., N.H., U.S. g7 106
Simojovel [de Allende], Mex. I13 62
Simonette, stm., Alta., Can. B1 68
Simplon Pass, Switz. F15 10
Simpson, Pa., U.S. C11 115
Simpson, co., Ky., U.S. D3 94
Simpson, co., Ms., U.S. D4 101
Simpson Creek, stm., W.V., U.S. k10 125
Simpson Desert, des., Austl. D7 50

Name — Map Ref — Page

Simpson Peninsula, pen., N.W. Ter., Can. C15 66
Simpsonville, Ky., U.S. B4 94
Simpsonville, S.C., U.S. B3 117
Simsboro, La., U.S. B3 95
Simsbury, Ct., U.S. B4 84
Simušir, Ostrov, i., Russia H24 24
Sīnā', Shibh Jazīrat (Sinai Peninsula), pen., Egypt C12 42
Sinabang, Indon. M4 34
Sinai Peninsula see Sīnā', Shibh Jazīrat, pen., Egypt C12 42
Sin'aja, stm., Russia E18 24
Sinaloa, state, Mex. E5 62
Sīnāwan, Libya B8 42
Sincé, Col. C5 58
Sincé, Col. J10 64
Sincelejo, Col. C5 58
Sinclair, Wy., U.S. E5 127
Sindri, India I12 38
Sines, Port. H3 12
Sinfães, Port. D3 12
Singānallūr, India G4 37
Singapore, Sing. N7 34
Singapore, ctry., Asia E3 32
Singapore Strait, strt., Asia N7 34
Singen [Hohentwiel], Ger. H8 8
Singida, Tan. B6 44
Singkang, Indon. F7 32
Singkawang, Indon. E4 32
Siniscola, Italy I4 14
Sinj, Cro. F11 14
Sinjah, Sudan F12 42
Sinkāt, Sudan E13 42
Sinnamary, Fr. Gu. B8 54
Sinnemahoning Creek, stm., Pa., U.S. D5 115
Sinop, Tur. G15 4
Sinskoje, Russia E19 24
Sintang, Indon. E5 32
Sint Eustatius, i., Neth. Ant. F16 64
Sint Marten (Saint-Martin), i., N.A. E16 64
Sint-Niklaas, Bel. D4 8
Sinton, Tx., U.S. E4 120
Sintra, Port. G2 12
Sinŭiju, N. Kor. C11 26
Sion, Switz. F14 10
Sioux, co., Ia., U.S. A1 92
Sioux, co., Ne., U.S. B2 104
Sioux, co., N.D., U.S. C4 111
Sioux Center, Ia., U.S. A1 92
Sioux City, Ia., U.S. B1 92
Sioux Falls, S.D., U.S. D9 118
Sioux Lookout, Ont., Can. o17 73
Sioux Rapids, Ia., U.S. B2 92
Siping, China C11 26
Sipiwesk Lake, l., Man., Can. B3 70
Sipsey, stm., Al., U.S. B2 78
Sipsey Fork, stm., Al., U.S. A2 78
Siracusa, Italy L10 14
Sirājganj, Bngl. H13 38
Sir Douglas, Mount, mtn., Can. D3 68
Sir Edward Pellew Group, is., Austl. C7 50
Siren, Wi., U.S. C1 126
Siret, stm., Eur. C11 16
Sirevåg, Nor. G5 6
Sir James MacBrien, Mount, mtn., N.W. Ter., Can. D7 66
Sirohi, India H5 38
Sirsa, India F6 38
Sir Sandford, Mount, mtn., B.C., Can. D9 69
Sirsi, India E3 37
Sir Wilfrid Laurier, Mount, mtn., B.C., Can. C8 69
Sisak, Cro. D11 14
Siskiyou, co., Ca., U.S. B2 82
Siskiyou Mountains, mts., U.S. F3 114
Siskiyou Pass, Or., U.S. E4 114
Sisseton, S.D., U.S. B8 118
Sisseton Indian Reservation, U.S. B8 118
Sissiboo, stm., N.S., Can. E4 71
Sisson Branch Reservoir, res., N.B., Can. B2 71
Sissonville, W.V., U.S. C3 125
Sisteron, Fr. H12 10
Sisters, Or., U.S. C5 114
Sistersville, W.V., U.S. B4 125
Sītāpur, India G9 38
Sitka, Ak., U.S. D12 79
Sitka National Historical Park, Ak., U.S. m22 79
Sitka Sound, strt., Ak., U.S. m22 79
Sittard, Neth. D5 8
Sittoung, stm., Mya. E4 34
Sittwe (Akyab), Mya. D2 34
Situbondo, Indon. m16 33a
Sivas, Tur. H15 4
Sīwah, Egypt C11 42
Siwān, India G11 38
Sjælland, i., Den. I8 6
Skagen, Den. H8 6
Skagerrak, strt., Eur. H7 6
Skagit, co., Wa., U.S. A4 124
Skagway, Ak., U.S. D12 79
Skaidi, Nor. A15 6
Skamania, co., Wa., U.S. D3 124
Skaneateles, N.Y., U.S. C4 109
Skaneateles Lake, l., N.Y., U.S. C4 109
Skārdu, Pak. C6 38
Skarżysko-Kamienna, Pol. D20 8
Skeena Mountains, mts., B.C., Can. E7 66
Skegness, Eng., U.K. H13 7
Skeleton Lake, l., Ont., Can. B5 73
Skellefteå, Swe. D13 6
Skelleftehamn, Swe. D13 6
Skiatook, Ok., U.S. A5 113
Skiatook Reservoir, res., Ok., U.S. A5 113
Skibotn, Nor. B13 6
Skiddaw, mtn., Eng., U.K. G9 7
Skien, Nor. G7 6
Skierniewice, Pol. D20 8
Skihist Mountain, mtn., B.C., Can. D7 69
Skikda, Alg. A7 42
Skillet Fork, stm., Il., U.S. E5 90
Skillingaryd, Swe. H10 6
Šklad, Russia C18 24
Škofja Loka, Slo. C9 14
Skokie, Il., U.S. A6 90
Skokomish Indian Reservation, Wa., U.S. B2 124
Skopje, Mac. H5 16
Skövde, Swe. G9 6
Skovorodino, Russia G18 24
Skowhegan, Me., U.S. D3 96
Skull Valley, val., Ut., U.S. C3 121
Skull Valley Indian Reservation, Ut., U.S. C3 121
Skuna, stm., Ms., U.S. B4 101
Skunk, stm., Ia., U.S. D6 92
Skwentna, stm., Ak., U.S. g15 79
Skye, Island of, i., Scot., U.K. D6 7
Skykomish, stm., Wa., U.S. B4 124
Skyland, Nv., U.S. D2 105
Skyland, N.C., U.S. f10 110
Skyline, Al., U.S. A3 78
Slagnäs, Swe. D12 6
Slamet, Gunung, vol., Indon. m14 33a
Slancy, Russia B11 18
Slano, Cro. G12 14
Slater, Ia., U.S. C4 92
Slater, Mo., U.S. B4 102
Slater, S.C., U.S. A3 117
Slatersville, R.I., U.S. A3 116
Slatersville Reservoir, res., R.I., U.S. B3 116
Slatington, Pa., U.S. E10 115
Slaton, Tx., U.S. C2 120
Slaughter, La., U.S. D4 95
Slave, stm., Can. D10 66
Slave Lake, Alta., Can. B3 68
Slavonia see Slavonija, reg., Cro. D12 14
Slavonija, reg., Cro. D12 14
Slavonska Požega, Cro. D12 14
Slavonski Brod, Cro. D2 16
Slayton, Mn., U.S. G3 100
Sleeping Bear Dunes National Lakeshore, Mi., U.S. D4 99
Sleeping Bear Point, c., Mi., U.S. D4 99
Sleepy Eye, Mn., U.S. F4 100
Slickville, Pa., U.S. F2 115
Slidell, La., U.S. D6 95
Sliderock Mountain, mtn., Mt., U.S. D3 103
Sligo, Ire. G4 7
Slinger, Wi., U.S. E5 126
Slippery Rock, Pa., U.S. D1 115
Sliven, Bul. G10 16
Sloan, Ia., U.S. B1 92
Sloan, N.Y., U.S. C2 109
Slocomb, Al., U.S. D4 78
Slonim, Bela. H8 18
Slope, co., N.D., U.S. C2 111
Slovakia, ctry., Eur. G19 8
Slovenia, ctry., Eur. C9 14
Slovenjgradec, Slo. C10 14
Slovenska Bistrica, Slo. C10 14
Sluck, Bela. H10 18
Sl'ud'anka, Russia G14 24
Słupsk (Stolp), Pol. A17 8
Smackover, Ar., U.S. D3 81
Small Point, c., Me., U.S. g8 96
Smallwood Reservoir, res., Newf., Can. g8 72
Smederevo, Yugo. E4 16
Smethport, Pa., U.S. C5 115
Smidovič, Russia H20 24
Šmidta, Ostrov, i., Russia A12 24
Smith, co., Ks., U.S. C5 93
Smith, co., Ms., U.S. C4 101
Smith, co., Tn., U.S. A5 119
Smith, co., Tx., U.S. C5 120
Smith, stm., U.S. D3 123
Smith, stm., Mt., U.S. D5 103
Smith and Sayles Reservoir, res., R.I., U.S. B2 116
Smith Bay, b., Ak., U.S. A9 79
Smith Canyon, val., Co., U.S. D7 83
Smith Center, Ks., U.S. C5 93
Smithers, B.C., Can. B4 69
Smithers, W.V., U.S. C3 125
Smithfield, N.C., U.S. B4 110
Smithfield, Pa., U.S. G2 115
Smithfield, Ut., U.S. B4 121
Smithfield, Va., U.S. D6 123
Smith Island, i., U.S. D5 97
Smith Island, i., Va., U.S. C7 123
Smith Mountain Lake, res., Va., U.S. C3 123
Smith Peak, mtn., Id., U.S. A2 89
Smith Point, c., Ma., U.S. D7 98
Smith Point, c., Va., U.S. C6 123
Smiths, Al., U.S. C4 78
Smithsburg, Md., U.S. A2 97
Smiths Falls, Ont., Can. C8 73
Smiths Grove, Ky., U.S. C3 94
Smithton, Austl. H9 50
Smithton, Il., U.S. E4 90
Smithtown, N.Y., U.S. n15 109
Smithville, Ga., U.S. E2 87
Smithville, Ms., U.S. A5 101
Smithville, Mo., U.S. B3 102
Smithville, Oh., U.S. B4 112
Smithville, Tn., U.S. D8 119
Smithville, Tx., U.S. D4 120
Smithville Lake, res., Mo., U.S. B3 102
Smoke Creek Desert, des., Nv., U.S. C2 105
Smokey, Cape, c., N.S., Can. C9 71
Smokey Dome, mtn., Id., U.S. F4 89
Smoky, stm., Alta., Can. B1 68
Smoky Hill, stm., U.S. D5 93
Smoky Lake, Alta., Can. B4 68
Smoky Mountains, mts., Id., U.S. F4 89
Smolensk, Russia G15 18
Smooth Rock Falls, Ont., Can. o19 73
Smoothstone Lake, l., Sask., Can. C2 75
Smyrna, De., U.S. C3 85
Smyrna, Ga., U.S. C2 87
Smyrna, Tn., U.S. B5 119
Smyrna, stm., De., U.S. C3 85
Smyth, co., Va., U.S. f10 123
Smythe, Mount, mtn., B.C., Can. E8 66
Snake, stm., U.S. D5 100
Snake, stm., Mn., U.S. B1 100
Snake, stm., Ne., U.S. B4 104
Snake Range, mts., Nv., U.S. E7 105
Snake River Plain, pl., Id., U.S. F2 89
Snake River Range, mts., U.S. C2 127
Sneads, Fl., U.S. B2 86
Sneedville, Tn., U.S. C10 119
Sneek, Neth. B5 8
Snipe Keys, is., Fl., U.S. H5 86
Snohomish, Wa., U.S. B3 124
Snohomish, co., Wa., U.S. A4 124
Snoqualmie, Wa., U.S. B4 124
Snoqualmie, stm., Wa., U.S. B4 124
Snoqualmie Pass, Wa., U.S. B4 124
Snowbank Lake, l., Mn., U.S. B7 100
Snowdon, mtn., Wales, U.K. H8 7
Snowdonia National Park, Wales, U.K. I9 7
Snowdrift, N.W. Ter., Can. D10 66
Snowflake, Az., U.S. C5 80
Snow Hill, Md., U.S. D7 97
Snow Hill, N.C., U.S. B5 110
Snowking Mountain, mtn., Wa., U.S. A4 124
Snow Lake, Man., Can. B1 70
Snowmass Mountain, mtn., Co., U.S. B3 83
Snow Peak, mtn., Wa., U.S. A7 124
Snowshoe Lake, l., Me., U.S. B4 96
Snowshoe Peak, mtn., Mt., U.S. B1 103
Snow Water Lake, l., Nv., U.S. C7 105
Snowyside Peak, mtn., Id., U.S. F4 89
Snyder, Ok., U.S. C3 113
Snyder, Tx., U.S. C2 120
Snyder, co., Pa., U.S. E7 115
Soacha, Col. E5 58
Soalala, Madag. E9 44
Soap Lake, Wa., U.S. B6 124
Sobat, stm., Sudan G12 42
Sobinka, Russia F23 18
Sobral, Braz. D10 54
Socastee, S.C., U.S. D9 117
Sochi see Soči, Russia I5 22
Soči, Russia I5 22
Social Circle, Ga., U.S. C3 87
Society Hill, S.C., U.S. B8 117
Socorro, Col. D6 58
Socorro, N.M., U.S. C3 108
Socorro, co., N.M., U.S. D2 108
Socorro, Isla, i., Mex. H4 62
Socotra see Suquṭrā, i., Yemen F5 46
Soc Trang, Viet. J8 34
Socuéllamos, Spain F9 12
Sodankylä, Fin. C16 6
Soda Springs, Id., U.S. G7 89
Soddy-Daisy, Tn., U.S. D8 119
Söderhamn, Swe. F11 6
Södertälje, Swe. G11 6
Sodo, Eth. G2 46
Sodus, N.Y., U.S. B3 109
Soest, Ger. D8 8
Sofia, stm., Madag. E9 44
Sofia see Sofija, Bul. G7 16
Sofija (Sofia), Bul. G7 16
Sogamoso, Col. E6 58
Sognafjorden, Nor. F5 6
Søgne, Nor. G6 6
Soignies, Bel. E4 8
Sointula, B.C., Can. D4 69
Soissons, Fr. C10 10
Sokal'skogo, Proliv, strt., Russia B14 24
Söke, Tur. L11 16
Sokodé, Togo G6 42
Sokol, Russia B23 18
Sokol, Russia C19 24
Sokoto, Nig. F7 42
Sol, Costa del, Spain I7 12
Solana, Fl., U.S. F5 86
Solano, Phil. p19 33b
Solano, co., Ca., U.S. C3 82
Solbad Hall in Tirol, Aus. H11 8
Soldier, stm., Ia., U.S. C2 92
Soldier Key, i., Fl., U.S. s3 86
Soldotna, Ak., U.S. g16 79
Soledad, Col. B5 58
Soledad, Ca., U.S. D3 82
Soledad, Ven. C11 58
Soleduck, stm., Wa., U.S. B1 124
Solingen, Ger. D7 8
Sollefteå, Swe. E11 6
Sollentuna, Swe. G11 6
Sóller, Spain F14 12
Solnečnogorsk, Russia E19 18
Sologoncy, Russia D16 24
Solok, Indon. O6 34
Solomon, Ks., U.S. D6 93
Solomon, stm., Ks., U.S. C6 93
Solomon Islands, ctry., Oc. G23 2
Solomons, Md., U.S. D5 97
Solomon Sea, Oc. A10 50
Solon, Ia., U.S. C6 92
Solon, Oh., U.S. A4 112
Solothurn, Switz. E14 10
Solsona, Spain D13 12
Soltau, Ger. C9 8
Solvay, N.Y., U.S. B4 109
Solwezi, Zam. D5 44
Soma, Tur. J11 16
Somalia, ctry., Afr. G4 46
Sombor, Yugo. D3 16
Sombrerete, Mex. F8 62
Somerdale, N.J., U.S. D2 107
Somers, Ct., U.S. B6 84
Somers, Mt., U.S. B2 103
Somerset, Man., Can. E2 70
Somerset, Ky., U.S. C5 94
Somerset, Ma., U.S. C5 98
Somerset, N.J., U.S. B3 107
Somerset, Oh., U.S. C3 112
Somerset, Pa., U.S. F3 115
Somerset, Tx., U.S. k7 120
Somerset, Wi., U.S. C1 126
Somerset, co., Me., U.S. C2 96
Somerset, co., Md., U.S. D6 97
Somerset, co., N.J., U.S. B3 107
Somerset, co., Pa., U.S. G3 115
Somerset Island, i., N.W. Ter., Can. B14 66
Somerset Reservoir, res., Vt., U.S. E3 122
Somers Point, N.J., U.S. E3 107
Somersville, Ct., U.S. B6 84
Somersworth, N.H., U.S. D5 106
Somerton, Az., U.S. E1 80
Somervell, co., Tx., U.S. C4 120
Somerville, Ma., U.S. B5 98
Somerville, N.J., U.S. B3 107
Somerville, Tn., U.S. B2 119
Somerville, Tx., U.S. D4 120
Somerville Lake, res., Tx., U.S. D4 120
Someș (Szamos), stm., Eur. B6 16
Sömmerda, Ger. D11 8
Somonauk, Il., U.S. B5 90
Somoto, Nic. H4 64
Son, stm., India H10 38
Sønderborg, Den. I7 6
Sondershausen, Ger. D10 8
Søndre Strømfjord, Grnld. C22 66
Sondrio, Italy C4 14
Song Cau, Viet. H10 34
Songea, Tan. D7 44
Songhua, stm., China B12 26
Songjiang, China D10 28
Songkhla, Thai. K6 34
Songnim, N. Kor. D12 26
Sonīpat, India F7 38
Son La, Viet. D7 34
Sonmiāni Bay, b., Pak. H2 38
Sonneberg, Ger. E11 8
Sonoita, Mex. B3 62
Sonoma, Ca., U.S. C2 82
Sonoma, co., Ca., U.S. C2 82
Sonoma Peak, mtn., Nv., U.S. C4 105
Sonoma Range, mts., Nv., U.S. C4 105
Sonora, Ca., U.S. D3 82
Sonora, Tx., U.S. D2 120
Sonora, stm., Mex. C4 62
Sonseca, Spain F8 12
Sonsón, Col. E5 58
Sonsonate, El Sal. H3 64
Sonsorol Islands, is., Palau D9 32
Son Tay, Viet. D8 34
Sonthofen, Ger. H10 8
Soochow see Suzhou, China D9 28
Soperton, Ga., U.S. D4 87
Sophia, W.V., U.S. D3 125
Sopot, Pol. A18 8
Sopron, Hung. H16 8
Sopur, India C6 38
Sora, Italy H8 14
Sore, Fr. H6 10
Sorel, Que., Can. C4 74
Sorgono, Italy I4 14
Sorgues, Fr. H11 10
Soria, Spain D9 12
Sorocaba, Braz. G5 57
Sorong, Indon. F9 32
Soroti, Ug. H12 42
Sorrento, Italy I9 14
Sorrento, La., U.S. D5 95
Sorsele, Swe. D11 6
Sorsogon, Phil. C7 32
Sort, Spain C13 12
Sorūbī, Afg. C3 38
Sos del Rey Católico, Spain C10 12
Sosnovo-Oz'orskoje, Russia G16 24
Sosnowiec, Pol. E19 8
Šoštanj, Slo. C10 14
Sotkamo, Fin. D17 6
Soto la Marina, Mex. F10 62
Sotteville, Fr. C8 10
Soucook, stm., N.H., U.S. D4 106
Soudan, Mn., U.S. C6 100
Souderton, Pa., U.S. F11 115
Souhegan, stm., N.H., U.S. E3 106
Souillac, Fr. H8 10
Soŭl (Seoul), S. Kor. D12 26
Soulac-sur-Mer, Fr. G5 10
Souris, Man., Can. E1 70
Souris, P.E.I., Can. C7 71
Sousa, Braz. E11 54
Sousse, Tun. N5 14
South, stm., Ia., U.S. C4 92
South, stm., N.C., U.S. C4 110
South Acton, Ma., U.S. g10 98
South Africa, ctry., Afr. G5 44
South Amboy, N.J., U.S. C4 107
South America E4 53
South Amherst, Ma., U.S. B2 98
South Amherst, Oh., U.S. A3 112
Southampton, Ont., Can. C3 73
Southampton, Eng., U.K. K11 7
Southampton, N.Y., U.S. n16 109
Southampton, co., Va., U.S. D5 123
Southampton Island, i., N.W. Ter., Can. D16 66
South Andaman, i., India I2 34
South Anna, stm., Va., U.S. C5 123
South Aulatsivik Island, i., Newf., Can. E20 66
South Australia, state, Austl. F7 50
Southaven, Ms., U.S. A3 101
South Bald Mountain, mtn., Co., U.S. A5 83
South Baldy, mtn., N.M., U.S. D2 108
South Barre, Vt., U.S. C3 122
South Bay, Fl., U.S. F6 86
South Beloit, Il., U.S. A4 90
South Bend, In., U.S. A5 91
South Bend, Wa., U.S. C2 124
South Berwick, Me., U.S. E2 96
South Bloomfield, Oh., U.S. C3 112
South Boston, Va., U.S. D4 123
South Bound Brook, N.J., U.S. B3 107
South Branch Lake, l., Me., U.S. C4 96
Southbridge, Ma., U.S. B3 98
South Bristol, Me., U.S. E3 96
South Britain, Ct., U.S. D3 84
South Broadway, Wa., U.S. C5 124
South Bruny, i., Austl. H9 50
South Burlington, Vt., U.S. C2 122
Southbury, Ct., U.S. D3 84
South Carolina, state, U.S. D6 117
South Charleston, Oh., U.S. C2 112
South Charleston, W.V., U.S. C3 125
South Chicago Heights, Il., U.S. m9 90
South China Sea, Asia C5 32
South Coffeyville, Ok., U.S. A6 113
South Congaree, S.C., U.S. D5 117
South Connellsville, Pa., U.S. G2 115
South Dakota, state, U.S. C5 118
South Dartmouth, Ma., U.S. C6 98
South Daytona, Fl., U.S. C5 86
South Deerfield, Ma., U.S. B2 98
South Dennis, Ma., U.S. C7 98
South Duxbury, Ma., U.S. B6 98
South East Cape, c., Austl. H9 50
Southeast Cape, c., Ak., U.S. C6 79
South Easton, Ma., U.S. B5 98
Southeast Pass, strt., La., U.S. E7 95
Southeast Point, c., R.I., U.S. h7 116
South Elgin, Il., U.S. B5 90
Southend-on-Sea, Eng., U.K. J13 7
Southern Alps, mts., N.Z. E3 52
Southern Cross, Austl. F3 50
Southern Indian Lake, l., Man., Can. f8 70
Southern Pines, N.C., U.S. B3 110
Southern Ute Indian Reservation, Co., U.S. D2 83
South Euclid, Oh., U.S. g9 112
Southey, Sask., Can. G3 75
South Fabius, stm., Mo., U.S. A5 102
South Fallsburg, N.Y., U.S. D6 109
Southfield, Mi., U.S. o15 99
South Fork, Pa., U.S. F4 115
South Fox Island, i., Mi., U.S. C5 99
South Fulton, Tn., U.S. A3 119
South Gastonia, N.C., U.S. B1 110
South Gate, Ca., U.S. n12 82
Southgate, Ky., U.S. h14 94
Southgate, Mi., U.S. p15 99
South Georgia, i., Falk. Is. G9 56
South Glastonbury, Ct., U.S. C5 84
South Glens Falls, N.Y., U.S. B7 109
South Grafton, Ma., U.S. B4 98
South Grand, stm., Mo., U.S. C3 102
South Hadley, Ma., U.S. B2 98
South Hadley Falls, Ma., U.S. B2 98
South Hamilton, Ma., U.S. A6 98
South Haven, In., U.S. A3 91
South Haven, Mi., U.S. F4 99
South Henik Lake, l., N.W. Ter., Can. D13 66
South Hero Island, i., Vt., U.S. B2 122
South Hill, Va., U.S. D4 123
South Hingham, Ma., U.S. h12 98
South Holland, Il., U.S. k9 90
South Holston Lake, res., U.S. A9 119
South Hooksett, N.H., U.S. D4 106
South Hopkinton, R.I., U.S. F1 116
South Houston, Tx., U.S. r14 120
South Hutchinson, Ks., U.S. f11 93
South Indian Lake, Man., Can. A2 70
Southington, Ct., U.S. C4 84
South International Falls, Mn., U.S. B5 100
South Island, i., N.Z. E3 52
South Island, i., S.C., U.S. E9 117
South Jacksonville, Il., U.S. D3 90
South Jordan, Ut., U.S. C3 121
South Kenosha, Wi., U.S. F6 126
South Lake Tahoe, Ca., U.S. C4 82
South Lancaster, Ma., U.S. B4 98
South Laurel, Md., U.S. *B4 97
South Lebanon, Oh., U.S. C1 112
South Lyon, Mi., U.S. F7 99
South Magnetic Pole C26 47
South Manitou Island, i., Mi., U.S. C4 99
South Marsh Island, i., Md., U.S. D5 97
South Miami, Fl., U.S. G6 86
South Miami Heights, Fl., U.S. s13 86
South Mills, N.C., U.S. A6 110
South Milwaukee, Wi., U.S. F6 126
Southmont, N.C., U.S. B2 110
South Moose Lake, l., Man., Can. C1 70
South Mountain, mtn., Id., U.S. G2 89
South Mountain, mtn., N.M., U.S. k8 108
South Mountains, mts., Az., U.S. m8 80
South Mountains, mts., N.C., U.S. B1 110
South Nahanni, stm., N.W. Ter., Can. D7 66
South New River Canal, Fl., U.S. r3 86
South Ogden, Ut., U.S. B4 121
Southold, N.Y., U.S. m16 109
South Orange, N.J., U.S. B4 107
South Orkney Islands, is., B.A.T. C8 47
South Paris, Me., U.S. D2 96
South Park, val., Co., U.S. B5 83
South Pass, Wy., U.S. D4 127
South Pass, strt., La., U.S. F6 95
South Patrick Shores, Fl., U.S. D6 86
South Pekin, Il., U.S. C4 90
South Pittsburg, Tn., U.S. D8 119
South Plainfield, N.J., U.S. B4 107
South Platte, stm., U.S. C6 76
South Point, c., Mi., U.S. D7 99
South Pole, Ant. A12 47
Southport, Eng., U.K. H9 7
Southport, Fl., U.S. u16 86
Southport, In., U.S. E5 91
Southport, N.Y., U.S. C4 109
Southport, N.C., U.S. D4 110
South Portland, Me., U.S. E2 96
South Portsmouth, Ky., U.S. B6 94
South Range, Mi., U.S. A2 99
South River, Ont., Can. B5 73
South River, N.J., U.S. C4 107
South River, b., Md., U.S. C4 97
South Ronaldsay, i., Scot., U.K. C10 7

Name / Map Ref / Page

South Royalton, Vt., U.S. D3 122
South Saint Paul, Mn., U.S. n12 100
South Sandwich Islands, is., Falk. Is. D10 47
South San Francisco, Ca., U.S. h8 82
South Saskatchewan, stm., Can. F11 66
South Shetland Islands, is., B.A.T. C7 47
South Shields, Eng., U.K. F11 7
Southside, Al., U.S. B3 78
Southside Place, Tx., U.S. r14 120
South Sioux City, Ne., U.S. B9 104
South Skunk, stm., Ia., U.S. C4 92
South Stony Brook, N.Y., U.S. *n15 109
South Streator, Il., U.S. B5 90
South Toms River, N.J., U.S. D4 107
South Torrington, Wy., U.S. D8 127
South Tucson, Az., U.S. E5 80
South Valley Stream, N.Y., U.S. *n15 109
South Venice, Fl., U.S. E4 86
South Ventana Cone, vol., Ca., U.S. D3 82
South Waverly, Pa., U.S. C8 115
South Wellfleet, Ma., U.S. C8 98
South Wellington, B.C., Can. f12 69
South West Africa see Namibia, ctry., Afr. F3 44
South Westbury, N.Y., U.S. *n15 109
South West Cape, c., Austl. H9 50
Southwest Channel, strt., Fl., U.S. E4 86
South West City, Mo., U.S. E3 102
Southwest Harbor, Me., U.S. D4 96
Southwest Head, c., N.B., Can. E3 71
Southwest Miramichi, stm., N.B., Can. C3 71
Southwest Pass, strt., La., U.S. E3 95
Southwest Pass, strt., La., U.S. F6 95
Southwest Point, c., R.I., U.S. h7 116
South Weymouth Naval Air Station, mil., Ma., U.S. h12 98
South Whitley, In., U.S. B6 91
South Williamson, Ky., U.S. C7 94
South Williamsport, Pa., U.S. D7 115
South Windham, Ct., U.S. C7 84
South Windham, Me., U.S. E2 96
South Windsor, Ct., U.S. B5 84
Southwood, Co., U.S. *B6 83
Southwood Acres, Ct., U.S. A5 84
South Woodstock, Ct., U.S. B8 84
South Yarmouth, Ma., U.S. C7 98
South Zanesville, Oh., U.S. C3 112
Sovetsk (Tilsit), Russia F4 18
Sovetskaja Gavan', Russia H22 24
Spa, Bel. E5 8
Spain, ctry., Eur. G7 4
Spalding, co., Ga., U.S. C2 87
Spanaway, Wa., U.S. B3 124
Spangler, Pa., U.S. E4 115
Spaniard's Bay, Newf., Can. E5 72
Spanish Fork, Ut., U.S. C4 121
Spanish Fort, Al., U.S. E2 78
Spanish Lake, Mo., U.S. f13 102
Spanish North Africa, dep., Afr. A4 42
Spanish Peak, mtn., Or., U.S. C7 114
Spanish Sahara see Western Sahara, dep., Afr. D3 42
Spanish Town, Jam. E9 64
Sparks, Ga., U.S. E3 87
Sparks, Nv., U.S. D2 105
Sparta, Ga., U.S. C4 87
Sparta, Il., U.S. E4 90
Sparta, Mi., U.S. E5 99
Sparta, Mo., U.S. D4 102
Sparta (Lake Mohawk), N.J., U.S. A3 107
Sparta, N.C., U.S. A1 110
Sparta, Tn., U.S. D8 119
Sparta, Wi., U.S. E3 126
Spartanburg, S.C., U.S. B4 117
Spartanburg, co., S.C., U.S. B3 117
Sparta see Spárti, Grc. L6 16
Spartel, Cap, c., Mor. J6 12
Spárti (Sparta), Grc. L6 16
Spartivento, Capo, c., Italy K3 14
Sparwood, B.C., Can. E10 69
Spassk-Dal'nij, Russia I20 24
Spavinaw Creek, stm., Ok., U.S. A7 113
Spear, Cape, c., Newf., Can. E5 72
Spearfish, S.D., U.S. C2 118
Spearman, Tx., U.S. A2 120
Spearville, Ks., U.S. E4 93
Speed, In., U.S. H6 91
Speedway, In., U.S. E5 91
Spence Bay, N.W. Ter., Can. C14 66
Spencer, In., U.S. F4 91
Spencer, Ia., U.S. A2 92
Spencer, Ma., U.S. B4 98
Spencer, N.C., U.S. B2 110
Spencer, Tn., U.S. D8 119
Spencer, W.V., U.S. C3 125
Spencer, Wi., U.S. D3 126
Spencer, co., In., U.S. H4 91
Spencer, co., Ky., U.S. B4 94
Spencer, Cape, c., Ak., U.S. k21 79
Spencer Gulf, b., Austl. F7 50
Spencer Lake, l., Me., U.S. C2 96
Spencerport, N.Y., U.S. B3 109
Spencerville, Md., U.S. B4 97
Spencerville, Oh., U.S. B1 112
Sperry, Ok., U.S. A6 113
Spesutie Island, i., Md., U.S. B5 97
Spey, stm., Scot., U.K. D9 7
Speyer, Ger. F8 8
Spiceland, In., U.S. E7 91
Spicer, Mn., U.S. E4 100
Spider Lake, l., Wi., U.S. B2 126
Spindale, N.C., U.S. B1 110
Spink, co., S.D., U.S. C7 118
Spirit Lake, Id., U.S. B2 89
Spirit Lake, Ia., U.S. A2 92
Spirit Lake, l., Ia., U.S. A2 92
Spirit Lake, l., Wa., U.S. C3 124
Spirit River, Alta., Can. B1 68
Spirit River Flowage, res., Wi., U.S. C4 126
Spiro, Ok., U.S. B7 113
Spittal an der Drau, Aus. I13 8
Spitz, Aus. G15 8
Split, Cro. F11 14
Split, Cape, c., N.S., Can. D5 71
Split Lake, l., Man., Can. A4 70
Split Rock Creek, stm., U.S. G2 100
Splügen, Switz. F16 10
Spofford Lake, l., N.H., U.S. E2 106
Spokane, Wa., U.S. B8 124
Spokane, co., Wa., U.S. B8 124
Spokane, stm., U.S. B8 124
Spokane, Mount, mtn., Wa., U.S. B8 124
Spokane Indian Reservation, Wa., U.S. B8 124
Spoleto, Italy G7 14
Spoon, stm., Il., U.S. C3 90
Spooner, Wi., U.S. C2 126
Spooner Lake, l., Wi., U.S. C2 126
Spornoje, Russia E24 24
Spotswood, N.J., U.S. C4 107
Spotsylvania, co., Va., U.S. B5 123
Sprague, W.V., U.S. n13 125
Sprague, stm., Or., U.S. E5 114
Sprague Lake, l., Wa., U.S. B7 124
Spratly Island, i., Asia D5 32
Spremberg, Ger. D14 8
Spring, stm., Ar., U.S. A4 81
Spring Arbor, Mi., U.S. F6 99
Spring Bay, b., Ut., U.S. B3 121
Springbok, S. Afr. G3 44
Springboro, Oh., U.S. C1 112
Spring Brook, stm., Pa., U.S. n18 115
Spring City, Pa., U.S. F10 115
Spring City, Tn., U.S. D9 119
Spring City, Ut., U.S. D4 121
Spring Creek, stm., U.S. D4 104
Spring Creek, stm., Nv., U.S. C4 105
Spring Creek, stm., N.D., U.S. B3 111
Springdale, Newf., Can. D3 72
Springdale, Ar., U.S. A1 81
Springdale, Oh., U.S. n13 112
Springdale, Pa., U.S. E2 115
Springdale, S.C., U.S. D5 117
Springer, N.M., U.S. A5 108
Springerville, Az., U.S. C6 80
Springfield, Co., U.S. D8 83
Springfield, Fl., U.S. u16 86
Springfield, Ga., U.S. D5 87
Springfield, Il., U.S. D4 90
Springfield, Ky., U.S. C4 94
Springfield, Ma., U.S. B2 98
Springfield, Mn., U.S. F4 100
Springfield, Mo., U.S. D4 102
Springfield, Ne., U.S. C9 104
Springfield, N.J., U.S. B4 107
Springfield, Oh., U.S. C2 112
Springfield, Or., U.S. C4 114
Springfield, Pa., U.S. p20 115
Springfield, S.D., U.S. E8 118
Springfield, Tn., U.S. A5 119
Springfield, Vt., U.S. E4 122
Springfield, Va., U.S. g12 123
Springfield, Lake, res., Il., U.S. D4 90
Springfontein, S. Afr. H5 44
Spring Garden, Guy. D13 58
Spring Glen, Ut., U.S. D5 121
Spring Green, Wi., U.S. E3 126
Spring Grove, Il., U.S. h8 90
Spring Grove, Mn., U.S. G7 100
Spring Grove, Pa., U.S. G8 115
Spring Hill, Fl., U.S. D4 86
Spring Hill, Ks., U.S. D9 93
Springhill, La., U.S. A2 95
Spring Hill, Tn., U.S. B5 119
Spring Hope, N.C., U.S. B4 110
Spring Island, i., S.C., U.S. G6 117
Spring Lake, Mi., U.S. E4 99
Spring Lake, N.J., U.S. C4 107
Spring Lake, N.C., U.S. B4 110
Spring Lake, l., Me., U.S. C2 96
Spring Lake, res., U.S. B3 90
Spring Lake Heights, N.J., U.S. C4 107
Spring Mountains, mts., Nv., U.S. G6 105
Springport, Mi., U.S. F6 99
Springs, S. Afr. G5 44
Springside, Sask., Can. F4 75
Springvale, Me., U.S. E2 96
Spring Valley, Ca., U.S. o16 82
Spring Valley, Il., U.S. B4 90
Spring Valley, Mn., U.S. G6 100
Spring Valley, N.Y., U.S. g12 109
Spring Valley, Wi., U.S. D1 126
Springville, Al., U.S. B3 78
Springville, Ia., U.S. B6 92
Springville, N.Y., U.S. C2 109
Springville, Ut., U.S. C4 121
Spruce Fork, stm., W.V., U.S. m12 125
Spruce Grove, Alta., Can. C4 68
Spruce Knob, mtn., W.V., U.S. C6 125
Spruce Knob-Seneca Rocks National Recreation Area, W.V., U.S. C5 125
Spruce Mountain, mtn., Az., U.S. C3 80
Spruce Mountain, mtn., Nv., U.S. C7 105
Spruce Pine, N.C., U.S. f10 110
Spruce Run Reservoir, res., N.J., U.S. B3 107
Spur, Tx., U.S. C2 120
Spurr, Mount, mtn., Ak., U.S. g15 79
Squam Lake, l., N.H., U.S. C4 106
Squapan Lake, l., Me., U.S. B4 96
Square Lake, l., Me., U.S. A4 96
Squatec, Que., Can. B9 74
Squaw Cap Mountain, mtn., N.B., Can. B3 71
Squaw Hill, mtn., Wy., U.S. E7 127
Squaw Peak, mtn., Mt., U.S. C2 103
Squibnocket Point, c., Ma., U.S. D6 98
Squinzano, Italy I13 14
Squire, W.V., U.S. D3 125
Sragen, Indon. m15 33a
Sredinnyj Chrebet, mts., Russia F26 24
Srednekolymsk, Russia D24 24
Srednerusskaja Vozvyšennost', plat., Russia H20 18
Srednesibirskoje Ploskogorje, plat., Russia D14 24
Sremska Mitrovica, Yugo. E3 16
Sri Gangānagar, India F5 38
Srīkākulam, India C7 37
Sri Lanka, ctry., Asia H5 36
Srīnagar, India C6 38
Srīrampur, India C3 37
Stack Reservoir, res., R.I., U.S. C3 116
Stade, Ger. B9 8
Stadthagen, Ger. C9 8
Stafford, Eng., U.K. I10 7
Stafford, Ks., U.S. E5 93
Stafford, Va., U.S. B5 123
Stafford, co., Ks., U.S. D5 93
Stafford, co., Va., U.S. B5 123
Stafford Pond, l., R.I., U.S. D6 116
Stafford Springs, Ct., U.S. B6 84
Staked Plain see Estacado, Llano, pl., U.S. E6 76
Stalheim, Nor. F6 6
Stalingrad see Volgograd, Russia H6 22
Stalowa Wola, Pol. E22 8
Stambaugh, Mi., U.S. B2 99
Stamford, Ct., U.S. E1 84
Stamford, Tx., U.S. C3 120
Stamford, Vt., U.S. F2 122
Stamford, Lake, res., Tx., U.S. C3 120
Stamping Ground, Ky., U.S. B5 94
Stamps, Ar., U.S. D2 81
Stanaford, W.V., U.S. D3 125
Stanberry, Mo., U.S. A3 102
Standerton, S. Afr. G5 44
Standing Rock Indian Reservation, U.S. B4 118
Standish, Mi., U.S. E7 99
Stanfield, Az., U.S. E3 80
Stanfield, Or., U.S. B7 114
Stanford, Ky., U.S. C5 94
Stanhope, N.J., U.S. B3 107
Stanislaus, co., Ca., U.S. D3 82
Stanke Dimitrov, Bul. G7 16
Stanley, Falk. Is. G5 56
Stanley, N.C., U.S. B1 110
Stanley, N.D., U.S. A3 111
Stanley, Va., U.S. B4 123
Stanley, Wi., U.S. D3 126
Stanley, co., S.D., U.S. C5 118
Stanley Falls, wtfl, Zaire A5 44
Stanleytown, Va., U.S. D3 123
Stanleyville, N.C., U.S. A2 110
Stanleyville see Kisangani, Zaire A5 44
Stanly, co., N.C., U.S. B2 110
Stann Creek, Belize F3 64
Stanovoj Chrebet, mts., Russia F19 24
Stanovoje Nagorje (Stanovoy Mountains), mts., Russia F16 24
Stanstead, Que., Can. D5 74
Stanton, Ia., U.S. D2 92
Stanton, Ky., U.S. C6 94
Stanton, Mi., U.S. E5 99
Stanton, Ne., U.S. C8 104
Stanton, Tx., U.S. C2 120
Stanton, co., Ks., U.S. E2 93
Stanton, co., Ne., U.S. C8 104
Stantonsburg, N.C., U.S. B5 110
Stanwood, Ia., U.S. C6 92
Stanwood, Wa., U.S. A3 124
Staples, Mn., U.S. D4 100
Stapleton, Al., U.S. E2 78
Star, Id., U.S. F2 89
Star, N.C., U.S. B3 110
Starachowice, Pol. D21 8
Staraja Russa, Russia C14 18
Stara Planina (Balkan Mountains), mts., Eur. G8 16
Stara Zagora, Bul. G9 16
Starbuck, Mn., U.S. E3 100
Star City, Ar., U.S. D4 81
Star City, W.V., U.S. B5 125
Stargard Szczeciński (Stargard in Pommern), Pol. B15 8
Stargo, Az., U.S. D6 80
Stark, co., Il., U.S. B4 90
Stark, co., N.D., U.S. C3 111
Stark, co., Oh., U.S. B4 112
Starke, Fl., U.S. C4 86
Starke, co., In., U.S. B4 91
Starks, La., U.S. D2 95
Starkville, Ms., U.S. B5 101
Star Lake, l., Mn., U.S. D3 100
Starnberg, Ger. G11 8
Starogard Gdański, Pol. B18 8
Star Peak, mtn., Nv., U.S. C3 105
Starr, co., Tx., U.S. F3 120
Startex, S.C., U.S. B3 117
Start Point, c., Eng., U.K. K9 7
Startup, Wa., U.S. B4 124
State Center, Ia., U.S. B4 92
State College, Pa., U.S. E6 115
Stateline, Nv., U.S. E2 105
State Line, Pa., U.S. G6 115
Staten Island, i., N.Y., U.S. k12 109
Statenville, Ga., U.S. F4 87
Statesboro, Ga., U.S. D5 87
Statesville, N.C., U.S. B2 110
Statham, Ga., U.S. C3 87
Statue of Liberty National Monument, N.J., U.S. k8 107
Staunton, Il., U.S. D4 90
Staunton, Va., U.S. B3 123
Stavanger, Nor. G5 6
Stavropol', Russia H6 22
Stayner, Ont., Can. C4 73
Stayton, Or., U.S. C4 114
Steamboat, Nv., U.S. D2 105
Steamboat Mountain, mtn., Mt., U.S. C4 103
Steamboat Mountain, mtn., Wy., U.S. E4 127
Steamboat Springs, Co., U.S. A4 83
Stearns, Ky., U.S. D5 94
Stearns, co., Mn., U.S. E4 100
Stearns Brook, stm., N.H., U.S. A4 106
Stebbins, Ak., U.S. C7 79
Steele, Al., U.S. B3 78
Steele, Mo., U.S. E8 102
Steele, N.D., U.S. C6 111
Steele, co., Mn., U.S. F5 100
Steele, co., N.D., U.S. B8 111
Steele, Mount, mtn., Wy., U.S. E6 127
Steeleville, Il., U.S. E4 90
Steelton, Pa., U.S. F8 115
Steelville, Mo., U.S. D6 102
Steenkool, Indon. F9 32
Steens Mountain, mts., Or., U.S. E8 114
Stefansson Island, i., N.W. Ter., Can. B11 66
Steger, Il., U.S. B6 90
Steilacoom, Wa., U.S. f10 124
Steinbach, Man., Can. E3 70
Steinhatchee, stm., Fl., U.S. C3 86
Steinkjer, Nor. D8 6
Stellenbosch, S. Afr. H3 44
Stenay, Fr. C12 10
Stendal, Ger. C11 8
Stephen, Mn., U.S. B2 100
Stephens, Ar., U.S. D2 81
Stephens, co., Ga., U.S. B3 87
Stephens, co., Ok., U.S. C4 113
Stephens, co., Tx., U.S. C3 120
Stephens City, Va., U.S. A4 123
Stephens Lake, res., Man., Can. A4 70
Stephenson, Mi., U.S. C3 99
Stephenson, co., Il., U.S. A4 90
Stephens Passage, strt., Ak., U.S. m23 79
Stephenville, Newf., Can. D2 72
Stephenville, Tx., U.S. C3 120
Stephenville Crossing, Newf., Can. D2 72
Sterling, Ak., U.S. g16 79
Sterling, Co., U.S. A7 83
Sterling, Il., U.S. B4 90
Sterling, Ks., U.S. D5 93
Sterling, Ok., U.S. C3 113
Sterling, Va., U.S. A5 123
Sterling, co., Tx., U.S. D2 120
Sterling City, Tx., U.S. D2 120
Sterling Heights, Mi., U.S. o15 99
Sterling Reservoir, res., Co., U.S. A7 83
Sterlington, La., U.S. B3 95
Sterlitamak, Russia G9 22
Stettin see Szczecin, Pol. B14 8
Stettler, Alta., Can. C4 68
Steuben, co., In., U.S. A7 91
Steuben, co., N.Y., U.S. C3 109
Steubenville, Oh., U.S. B5 112
Stevenage, Eng., U.K. J12 7
Stevens, co., Ks., U.S. E2 93
Stevens, co., Mn., U.S. E3 100
Stevens, co., Wa., U.S. A7 124
Stevens Creek Dam, U.S. C4 87
Stevenson, Al., U.S. A4 78
Stevenson, Ct., U.S. D3 84
Stevenson, Wa., U.S. D4 124
Stevenson Lake, l., Man., Can. C4 70
Stevens Pass, Wa., U.S. B4 124
Stevens Peak, mtn., Id., U.S. B3 89
Stevens Point, Wi., U.S. D4 126
Stevensville, Md., U.S. C5 97
Stevensville, Mi., U.S. F4 99
Stevensville, Mt., U.S. D2 103
Stewart, co., Ga., U.S. D2 87
Stewart, co., Tn., U.S. A4 119
Stewart Island, i., N.Z. G1 52
Stewart Mountain, mtn., Az., U.S. k9 80
Stewartstown, Pa., U.S. G8 115
Stewartsville, Mo., U.S. B3 102
Stewartville, Mn., U.S. G6 100
Stewiacke, N.S., Can. D6 71
Steyr, Aus. G14 8
Stigler, Ok., U.S. B6 113
Stigliano, Italy I11 14
Stikine, stm., B.C., Can. E7 66
Stikine, stm., Ak., U.S. D13 79
Stikine Ranges, mts., B.C., Can. E6 66
Still, stm., Ct., U.S. B3 84
Stillaguamish, North Fork, stm., Wa., U.S. A4 124
Stillaguamish, South Fork, stm., Wa., U.S. A4 124
Stillhouse Hollow Lake, res., Tx., U.S. D4 120
Stillman Valley, Il., U.S. A4 90
Stillmore, Ga., U.S. D4 87
Stillwater, Mn., U.S. E6 100
Stillwater, Ok., U.S. A4 113
Stillwater, co., Mt., U.S. E7 103
Stillwater Range, mts., Nv., U.S. D3 105
Stillwater Reservoir, res., N.Y., U.S. B5 109
Stillwater Reservoir, res., R.I., U.S. B3 116
Stilwell, Ok., U.S. B7 113
Stimson, Mount, mtn., Mt., U.S. B3 103
Stine Mountain, mtn., Mt., U.S. E3 103
Stinking Lake, l., N.M., U.S. A3 108
Stinnett, Tx., U.S. B2 120
Štip, Mac. H6 16
Stirling, Alta., Can. E4 68
Stirling, Ont., Can. C7 73
Stirling, Scot., U.K. E9 7
Stjørdalshalsen, Nor. E8 6
Stockbridge, Ga., U.S. C2 87
Stockbridge, Mi., U.S. F6 99
Stockbridge-Munsee Indian Reservation, Wi., U.S. D5 126
Stockdale, Tx., U.S. E4 120
Stockerau, Aus. G16 8
Stockholm, Swe. G12 6
Stockton, Ca., U.S. D3 82
Stockton, Il., U.S. A3 90
Stockton, Ks., U.S. C4 93
Stockton, Md., U.S. D7 97
Stockton, Mo., U.S. D4 102
Stockton Island, i., Wi., U.S. B3 126
Stockton Lake, res., Mo., U.S. D4 102
Stoddard, Wi., U.S. E2 126
Stoddard, co., Mo., U.S. E8 102
Stoke-on-Trent, Eng., U.K. H10 7
Stokes, co., N.C., U.S. A2 110
Stokesdale, N.C., U.S. A3 110
Stolbovoj, Ostrov, i., Russia C21 24
Stollings, W.V., U.S. n12 125
Ston, Cro. G12 14
Stone, co., Ar., U.S. B3 81
Stone, co., Ms., U.S. E4 101
Stone, co., Mo., U.S. E4 102
Stoneboro, Pa., U.S. D1 115
Stone Corral Lake, l., Or., U.S. E7 114
Stoneham, Ma., U.S. g11 98
Stonehaven, Scot., U.K. E10 7
Stone Mountain, Ga., U.S. C2 87
Stone Mountain, mtn., Ga., U.S. C2 87
Stones River National Battlefield, hist., Tn., U.S. B4 119
Stoneville, N.C., U.S. A3 110
Stonewall, Man., Can. D3 70
Stonewall, La., U.S. B2 95
Stonewall, Ms., U.S. C5 101
Stonewall, co., Tx., U.S. C2 120
Stonewood, W.V., U.S. k10 125
Stoney Creek, Ont., Can. D5 73
Stonington, Ct., U.S. D8 84
Stonington, Il., U.S. D4 90
Stonington, Me., U.S. D4 96
Stono, stm., S.C., U.S. k11 117
Stono Inlet, b., S.C., U.S. F8 117
Stony Brook, N.Y., U.S. n15 109
Stony Brook, stm., N.J., U.S. C3 107
Stony Creek, stm., Va., U.S. C5 123
Stony Island, i., N.Y., U.S. B4 109
Stony Plain, Alta., Can. C3 68
Stony Point, N.C., U.S. B1 110
Storby, Fin. F12 6
Støren, Nor. E8 6
Storey, co., Nv., U.S. D2 105
Storfors, Swe. G10 6
Storkerson Peninsula, pen., N.W. Ter., Can. B11 66
Storlien, Swe. E9 6
Storm Lake, Ia., U.S. B2 92
Storm Lake, l., Ia., U.S. B2 92
Storm Mountain, mtn., Ak., U.S. h16 79
Stornoway, Scot., U.K. C6 7
Storrs, Ct., U.S. B7 84
Storuman, Swe. D11 6
Storvreta, Swe. G11 6
Story, Wy., U.S. B6 127
Story, co., Ia., U.S. B4 92
Story City, Ia., U.S. B4 92
Stoughton, Sask., Can. H4 75
Stoughton, Ma., U.S. B5 98
Stoughton, Wi., U.S. F4 126
Stover, Mo., U.S. C5 102
Stow, Oh., U.S. A4 112
Stow Creek, stm., N.J., U.S. E2 107
Stowe, Pa., U.S. F10 115
Stowe, Vt., U.S. C3 122
Stoyoma Mountain, mtn., B.C., Can. E7 69
Strabane, Pa., U.S. F1 115
Strafford, Mo., U.S. D4 102
Strafford, co., N.H., U.S. D4 106
Straffordville, Ont., Can. E4 73
Strahan, Austl. H9 50
Strakonice, Czech. F13 8
Stralsund, Ger. A13 8
Stranraer, Scot., U.K. G7 7
Strasbourg, Fr. D14 10
Strasburg, Co., U.S. B6 83
Strasburg, Oh., U.S. B4 112
Strasburg, Pa., U.S. G9 115
Strasburg, Va., U.S. B4 123
Stratford, Ont., Can. D3 73
Stratford, Ct., U.S. E3 84
Stratford, Ia., U.S. B4 92
Stratford, N.J., U.S. D2 107
Stratford, Ok., U.S. C5 113
Stratford, Tx., U.S. A1 120
Stratford, Wi., U.S. D3 126
Stratford Point, c., Ct., U.S. E3 84
Stratford-upon-Avon, Eng., U.K. I11 7
Stratham, N.H., U.S. D5 106
Strathmore, Alta., Can. D4 68
Strathmore, Ca., U.S. D4 82
Strathroy, Ont., Can. E3 73
Stratton, Co., U.S. B8 83
Straubing, Ger. G12 8
Strausberg, Ger. C13 8
Strawberry, stm., Ar., U.S. A4 81
Strawberry, stm., Ut., U.S. C5 121
Strawberry Mountain, mtn., Or., U.S. C8 114
Strawberry Point, Ia., U.S. B6 92
Strawberry Point, c., Ma., U.S. B6 98
Strawberry Range, mts., Or., U.S. C8 114
Strawberry Reservoir, res., Ut., U.S. C4 121
Streator, Il., U.S. B5 90
Stretensk, Russia G17 24
Strickland, stm., Pap. N. Gui. m15 50a
Strimón (Struma), stm., Eur. I7 16
Stromness, Scot., U.K. C9 7
Stromsburg, Ne., U.S. C8 104
Strömstad, Swe. G8 6
Strömsund, Swe. E10 6
Strong, Ar., U.S. D3 81
Strong, Me., U.S. D2 96
Strong, stm., Ms., U.S. C4 101
Strong City, Ks., U.S. D7 93
Stronghurst, Il., U.S. C3 90
Strongsville, Oh., U.S. A4 112
Stronsay, i., Scot., U.K. B10 7
Stroud, Ok., U.S. B5 113
Stroudsburg, Pa., U.S. E11 115
Stroudwater, stm., Me., U.S. g7 96
Strum, Wi., U.S. D2 126
Struma (Strimón), stm., Eur. H7 16
Strumble Head, c., Wales, U.K. I7 7
Strumica, Mac. H6 16
Strunino, Russia E21 18
Struthers, Oh., U.S. A5 112
Stryker, Oh., U.S. A1 112
Stuart, Fl., U.S. E6 86
Stuart, Ia., U.S. C3 92
Stuart, Ne., U.S. B6 104
Stuart, Va., U.S. D2 123

Name — Map Ref — Page

Stuart, Mount, mtn., Wa., U.S. B5 124
Stuart Lake, l., B.C., Can. B5 69
Stuarts Draft, Va., U.S. B3 123
Stull, stm., Can. B5 70
Stump Lake, l., N.D., U.S. B7 111
Stump Pond, res., R.I., U.S. D2 116
Stung Treng, Camb. H8 34
Stupino, Russia G21 18
Sturbridge, Ma., U.S. B3 98
Sturgeon, Mo., U.S. B5 102
Sturgeon, stm., Mi., U.S. B4 99
Sturgeon Bay, Wi., U.S. D6 126
Sturgeon Bay, b., Man., Can. C3 70
Sturgeon Falls, Ont., Can. A5 73
Sturgeon Lake, l., Ont., Can. C6 73
Sturgis, Sask., Can. F4 75
Sturgis, Ky., U.S. e10 94
Sturgis, Mi., U.S. G5 99
Sturgis, S.D., U.S. C2 118
Sturtevant, Wi., U.S. F6 126
Stutsman, co., N.D., U.S. B6 111
Stuttgart, Ger. G9 8
Stuttgart, Ar., U.S. C4 81
Suaita, Col. D6 58
Subang, Indon. m13 33a
Subansiri, stm., Asia G16 38
Subiaco, Italy H8 14
Sublette, Ks., U.S. E3 93
Sublette, co., Wy., U.S. D2 127
Sublett Range, mts., Id., U.S. G6 89
Sublimity, Or., U.S. C4 114
Subotica, Yugo. C3 16
Sučan, Russia I20 24
Sucarnoochee, stm., Al., U.S. C1 78
Succasunna, N.J., U.S. B3 107
Suceava, Rom. B10 16
Süchbaatar, Mong. A8 26
Suchumi, Geor. I6 22
Sucre, Bol. G5 54
Sucuaro, Col. E8 58
Sudan, ctry., Afr. F12 42
Sudan, reg., Afr. F7 42
Sudbury, Ont., Can. A4 73
Sudbury, Ma., U.S. B5 98
Sudbury, stm., Ma., U.S. B5 98
Sudbury Center, Ma., U.S. g10 98
Sudbury Reservoir, res., Ma., U.S. g10 98
Sudeten see Sudety, mts., Eur. E15 8
Sudety, mts., Eur. E15 8
Sue, stm., Sudan G11 42
Sueca, Spain F11 12
Suez see As-Suways, Egypt C12 42
Suez Canal see Suways, Qanāt as-, Egypt D3 40
Suffern, N.Y., U.S. D6 109
Suffield, Ct., U.S. B5 84
Suffolk, Va., U.S. D6 123
Suffolk, co., Ma., U.S. B5 98
Suffolk, co., N.Y., U.S. n15 109
Sugar, stm., U.S. F4 126
Sugar, stm., N.H., U.S. D2 106
Sugar City, Id., U.S. F7 89
Sugar Creek, Mo., U.S. h11 102
Sugarcreek, Pa., U.S. D2 115
Sugar Creek, stm., Oh., U.S. C2 112
Sugar Creek, stm., Pa., U.S. C8 115
Sugar Grove, Va., U.S. D1 123
Sugar Hill, Ga., U.S. B2 87
Sugar Island, i., Mi., U.S. B6 99
Sugar Land, Tx., U.S. E5 120
Sugarland Run, Va., U.S. *A5 123
Sugar Loaf, Va., U.S. C3 123
Sugarloaf Mountain, mtn., Mt., U.S. C4 103
Sugar Notch, Pa., U.S. n17 115
Suggi Lake, l., Sask., Can. C4 75
Sugoj, stm., Russia E25 24
Şuḩār, Oman D6 46
Suhl, Ger. E10 8
Suiattle, stm., Wa., U.S. A4 124
Suide, China D9 26
Suihua, China B12 26
Suining, China E8 26
Suiping, China B2 28
Suitland, Md., U.S. C4 97
Suizhong, China C11 26
Suja, Russia E24 18
Sukabumi, Indon. m13 32
Sukagawa, Japan E13 30
Sukhumi see Suchumi, Geor. I6 22
Sukkertoppen, Grnld. C22 66
Sukkur, Pak. G3 38
Sukumo, Japan J5 30
Sula, Kepulauan, is., Indon. F8 32
Sulaimān Range, mts., Pak. F3 38
Sulawesi (Celebes), i., Indon. F7 32
Sullana, Peru D2 54
Sulligent, Al., U.S. B1 78
Sullivan, Il., U.S. D5 90
Sullivan, In., U.S. F3 91
Sullivan, Mo., U.S. C6 102
Sullivan, co., In., U.S. F3 91
Sullivan, co., Mo., U.S. A4 102
Sullivan, co., N.H., U.S. D2 106
Sullivan, co., N.Y., U.S. D6 109
Sullivan, co., Pa., U.S. D9 115
Sullivan, co., Tn., U.S. C11 119
Sullivan Lake, l., Alta., Can. D5 68
Sullivans Island, S.C., U.S. k12 117
Sully, Fr. E9 10
Sully, Ia., U.S. C5 92
Sully, co., S.D., U.S. C5 118
Sulmona, Italy G8 14
Sulphur, La., U.S. D2 95
Sulphur, Ok., U.S. C5 113
Sulphur, stm., U.S. D2 81
Sulphur Spring Range, mts., Nv., U.S. C5 105
Sulphur Springs, Tx., U.S. C5 120
Sultan, Wa., U.S. B4 124
Sultānpur, India G10 38
Sulu Archipelago, is., Phil. D7 32
Sulu Sea, Asia D6 32
Sulzbach-Rosenberg, Ger. F11 8
Sumas, Wa., U.S. A3 124
Sumatera (Sumatra), i., Indon. F3 32
Sumatra see Sumatera, i., Indon. F3 32
Sumba, i., Indon. G7 32
Sumbawa, i., Indon. G6 32
Sumbawanga, Tan. C6 44
Sumedang, Indon. m13 33a
Šumen, Bul. F10 16
Sumenep, Indon. m16 33a
Sumgait, Azer. I7 22
Sumiton, Al., U.S. B2 78
Summerfield, N.C., U.S. A3 110
Summerford, Newf., Can. D4 72
Summer Island, i., Mi., U.S. C4 99
Summer Lake, l., Or., U.S. E6 114
Summerland, B.C., Can. E8 69
Summers, co., W.V., U.S. D4 125
Summerside, P.E.I., Can. C6 71
Summersville, W.V., U.S. C4 125
Summersville Lake, res., W.V., U.S. C4 125
Summerton, S.C., U.S. D7 117
Summertown, Tn., U.S. B4 119
Summerville, Ga., U.S. B1 87
Summerville, S.C., U.S. E7 117
Summit, Il., U.S. k9 90
Summit, Ms., U.S. D3 101
Summit, N.J., U.S. B4 107
Summit, Tn., U.S. h11 119
Summit, co., Co., U.S. B4 83
Summit, co., Oh., U.S. A4 112
Summit, co., Ut., U.S. C5 121
Summit Hill, Pa., U.S. E10 115
Summit Lake, l., Ia., U.S. C3 92
Summit Lake Indian Reservation, Nv., U.S. B2 105
Summit Mountain, mtn., Nv., U.S. D5 105
Summit Peak, mtn., Co., U.S. D4 83
Summitville, In., U.S. D6 91
Sumner, Il., U.S. E6 90
Sumner, Ia., U.S. B5 92
Sumner, Wa., U.S. B3 124
Sumner, co., Ks., U.S. E6 93
Sumner, co., Tn., U.S. A5 119
Sumner, Lake, res., N.M., U.S. C5 108
Sumner Dam, N.M., U.S. C5 108
Sumner Strait, strt., Ak., U.S. m23 79
Sumoto, Japan H7 30
Šumperk, Czech. F16 8
Sumrall, Ms., U.S. D4 101
Šumšu, Ostrov, i., Russia G25 24
Sumter, S.C., U.S. D7 117
Sumter, co., Al., U.S. C1 78
Sumter, co., Fl., U.S. D4 86
Sumter, co., Ga., U.S. D2 87
Sumter, co., S.C., U.S. D7 117
Sumy, Ukr. G4 22
Sun, stm., Mt., U.S. C4 103
Sunagawa, Japan p19 30a
Sunapee, N.H., U.S. D2 106
Sunapee Lake, l., N.H., U.S. D2 106
Sunbright, Tn., U.S. C9 119
Sunbury, Oh., U.S. B3 112
Sunbury, Pa., U.S. E8 115
Sunchales, Arg. C4 56
Sun City, Az., U.S. k8 80
Suncook, N.H., U.S. D4 106
Suncook, stm., N.H., U.S. D4 106
Suncook Lakes, l., N.H., U.S. D4 106
Sunda, Selat, strt., Indon. G4 32
Sundance, Wy., U.S. B8 127
Sundance Mountain, mtn., Wy., U.S. B8 127
Sundarbans, reg., Asia J13 38
Sunderland, Ont., Can. C5 73
Sunderland, Eng., U.K. G11 7
Sundown, Tx., U.S. C1 120
Sundre, Alta., Can. D3 68
Sundridge, Ont., Can. B5 73
Sundsvall, Swe. E11 6
Sunflower, Ms., U.S. B3 101
Sunflower, co., Ms., U.S. B3 101
Sunflower, Mount, mtn., Ks., U.S. C2 93
Sungaidareh, Indon. O6 34
Sungei Patani, Malay. L6 34
Suniteyouqi, China C9 26
Sunland Park, N.M., U.S. F3 108
Sunlight Creek, stm., Wy., U.S. B3 127
Sunman, In., U.S. F7 91
Sunndalsøra, Nor. E7 6
Sunnyside, Newf., Can. E5 72
Sunnyside, Wa., U.S. C5 124
Sunnyvale, Ca., U.S. k8 82
Sun Prairie, Wi., U.S. E4 126
Sunray, Tx., U.S. A2 120
Sunrise Manor, Nv., U.S. *G6 105
Sunset, La., U.S. D3 95
Sunset, Ut., U.S. B4 121
Sunset Beach, Hi., U.S. f9 88
Sunset Crater National Monument, Az., U.S. B4 80
Sunset Lake, l., Vt., U.S. D2 122
Suntar, Russia E17 24
Suntar-Chajata, Chrebet, mts., Russia E22 24
Suntaug Lake, l., Ma., U.S. f11 98
Sun Valley, Id., U.S. F4 89
Sun Valley, Nv., U.S. D2 105
Sunyani, Ghana G5 42
Suō-nada, Japan I4 30
Suonenjoki, Fin. E16 6
Suordach, Russia D20 24
Superior, Az., U.S. D4 80
Superior, Mt., U.S. C2 103
Superior, Ne., U.S. D7 104
Superior, Wi., U.S. B1 126
Superior, Wy., U.S. E4 127
Superior, Lake, l., N.A. B9 76
Superstition Mountains, mts., Az., U.S. m10 80
Supetar, Cro. F11 14
Suphan Buri, Thai. G6 34
Suqian, China B7 28
Suquamish, Wa., U.S. B3 124
Suquṭrā (Socotra), i., Yemen F5 46
Şūr (Tyre), Leb. C4 40
Şūr, Oman D6 46
Sur, Point, c., Ca., U.S. D3 82
Surabaya, Indon. m16 32
Surakarta, Indon. m15 32
Şūrān, Syria B5 40
Surat, India B2 37
Surat Thani (Ban Don), Thai. J5 34
Surendranagar, India I4 38
Surfside, Fl., U.S. s13 86
Surfside Beach, S.C., U.S. D10 117
Surgoinsville, Tn., U.S. C11 119
Sūri, India I12 38
Surigao, Phil. D8 32
Surin, Thai. G7 34
Suriname, ctry., S.A. C7 54
Sūrmaq, Iran B5 46
Surprise, Az., U.S. k8 80
Surrey, N.D., U.S. A4 111
Surry, co., N.C., U.S. A2 110
Surry, co., Va., U.S. C6 123
Surry Mountain Lake, res., N.H., U.S. D2 106
Surt, Libya B9 42
Surt, Khalīj, b., Libya B9 42
Sürüç, Tur. A6 40
Suruga-wan, b., Japan H11 30
Susa, Italy D2 14
Susanville, Ca., U.S. B3 82
Susitna, stm., Ak., U.S. C10 79
Susquehanna, Pa., U.S. C10 115
Susquehanna, co., Pa., U.S. C10 115
Susquehanna, stm., U.S. A5 97
Susquehanna, West Branch, stm., Pa., U.S. D5 115
Sussex, N.B., Can. D4 71
Sussex, N.J., U.S. A3 107
Sussex, Wi., U.S. m11 126
Sussex, co., De., U.S. F4 85
Sussex, co., N.J., U.S. A3 107
Sussex, co., Va., U.S. D5 123
Susurluk, Tur. J12 16
Sutherland, S. Afr. H4 44
Sutherland, Ia., U.S. B2 92
Sutherland, Ne., U.S. C4 104
Sutherlin, Or., U.S. D3 114
Sutlej (Satluj) (Langqên), stm., Asia F4 38
Sutter, co., Ca., U.S. C3 82
Sutter Creek, Ca., U.S. C3 82
Sutton, Que., Can. D5 74
Sutton, Ne., U.S. D8 104
Sutton, W.V., U.S. C4 125
Sutton, co., Tx., U.S. D2 120
Sutton Lake, res., W.V., U.S. C4 125
Sutwik Island, i., Ak., U.S. D8 79
Suur Munamägi, hill, Est. D10 18
Suwa, Japan F11 30
Suwałki, Pol. A22 8
Suwanee, Ga., U.S. B2 87
Suwannee, co., Fl., U.S. B3 86
Suwannee, stm., U.S. C4 86
Suwannee Sound, strt., Fl., U.S. C3 86
Suways, Qanāt as- (Suez Canal), Egypt D3 40
Suwŏn, S. Kor. D12 26
Suxian, China B5 28
Suzaka, Japan F11 30
Suzhou (Soochow), China D9 28
Suzuka, Japan H9 30
Suzu-misaki, c., Japan E10 30
Suzzara, Italy D5 14
Svappavaara, Swe. C13 6
Svartenhuk, pen., Grnld. B22 66
Sv'atoj Nos, Mys, c., Russia C22 24
Sveg, Swe. E10 6
Svenljunga, Swe. H9 6
Svensen, Or., U.S. A3 114
Sverdlovsk see Jekaterinburg, Russia F10 22
Svetlaja, Russia H21 24
Svetlyj, Russia F17 24
Svištov, Bul. F9 16
Svobodnyj, Russia G19 24
Svolvær, Nor. B10 6
Swain, co., N.C., U.S. f9 110
Swainsboro, Ga., U.S. D4 87
Swakopmund, Nmb. F2 44
Swampscott, Ma., U.S. B6 98
Swan, stm., Can. C1 70
Swan Creek, stm., Oh., U.S. e6 112
Swan Falls, wtfl, Id., U.S. F2 89
Swan Hill, Austl. G8 50
Swan Hills, Alta., Can. B3 68
Swan Islands, is., Hond. F6 64
Swan Lake, l., Man., Can. C1 70
Swan Lake, l., Me., U.S. D4 96
Swan Lake, l., Ne., U.S. C3 104
Swannanoa, N.C., U.S. f10 110
Swan Peak, mtn., Mt., U.S. C3 103
Swan Range, mts., Mt., U.S. C3 103
Swan River, Man., Can. C1 70
Swansboro, N.C., U.S. C5 110
Swansea, Wales, U.K. J9 7
Swansea, Il., U.S. E4 90
Swanson Lake, res., Ne., U.S. D4 104
Swanton, Oh., U.S. A2 112
Swanton, Vt., U.S. B2 122
Swanzey Center, N.H., U.S. E2 106
Swarthmore, Pa., U.S. p20 115
Swartswood Lake, l., N.J., U.S. A3 107
Swartz Creek, Mi., U.S. F7 99
Swayzee, In., U.S. C6 91
Swaziland, ctry., Afr. G6 44
Swea City, Ia., U.S. A3 92
Sweden, ctry., Eur. C10 4
Sweeny, Tx., U.S. r14 120
Sweet Grass, co., Mt., U.S. E7 103
Sweet Home, Or., U.S. C4 114
Sweetser, In., U.S. C6 91
Sweet Springs, Mo., U.S. C4 102
Sweetwater, Tn., U.S. D9 119
Sweetwater, Tx., U.S. C2 120
Sweetwater, co., Wy., U.S. E3 127
Sweetwater, stm., Wy., U.S. D4 127
Sweetwater Creek, Fl., U.S. p10 86
Sweetwater Creek, stm., Ok., U.S. B1 113
Swellendam, S. Afr. H4 44
Swepsonville, N.C., U.S. A3 110
Świdnica (Schweidnitz), Pol. E16 8
Swift, co., Mn., U.S. E3 100
Swift, stm., N.H., U.S. B4 106
Swift Creek, stm., N.C., U.S. B5 110
Swift Creek, stm., Va., U.S. n17 123
Swift Creek Reservoir, res., Wa., U.S. C3 124
Swift Diamond, stm., N.H., U.S. g7 106
Swifton, Ar., U.S. B4 81
Swinburne, Cape, c., N.W. Ter., Can. B13 66
Swindon, Eng., U.K. J11 7
Swinford, Ire. H4 7
Swinomish Indian Reservation, Wa., U.S. A3 124
Świnoujście (Swinemünde), Pol. B14 8
Swisher, Ia., U.S. C6 92
Swisher, co., Tx., U.S. B2 120
Swissvale, Pa., U.S. k14 115
Switzer, W.V., U.S. D3 125
Switzerland, Fl., U.S. m8 86
Switzerland, co., In., U.S. G7 91
Switzerland, ctry., Eur. F9 4
Swoyerville, Pa., U.S. D10 115
Syalach, Russia D18 24
Sycamore, Al., U.S. B3 78
Sycamore, Il., U.S. B5 90
Sycamore, Oh., U.S. B2 112
Sycamore Creek, stm., W.V., U.S. m13 125
Sydenham, Ont., Can. C8 73
Sydney, Austl. F10 50
Syke, Ger. C8 8
Sykesville, Md., U.S. B4 97
Sykesville, Pa., U.S. D4 115
Sykkylven, Nor. E6 6
Syktyvkar, Russia E8 22
Sylacauga, Al., U.S. B3 78
Sylhet, Bngl. H14 38
Sylva, N.C., U.S. f9 110
Sylvania, Al., U.S. A4 78
Sylvania, Ga., U.S. D5 87
Sylvania, Oh., U.S. A2 112
Sylvan Lake, Alta., Can. C3 68
Sylvan Lake, Mi., U.S. o15 99
Sylvan Lake, l., In., U.S. B7 91
Sylvan Pass, Wy., U.S. B2 127
Sylvester, Ga., U.S. E3 87
Sym, Russia E11 24
Symmes Creek, stm., Oh., U.S. D3 112
Symsonia, Ky., U.S. f9 94
Syracuse, In., U.S. B6 91
Syracuse, Ks., U.S. E2 93
Syracuse, Ne., U.S. D9 104
Syracuse, N.Y., U.S. B4 109
Syracuse, Ut., U.S. B3 121
Syrdarja (Syr Darya), stm., Asia I11 22
Syria, ctry., Asia B5 40
Syriam, Mya. F4 34
Syrian Desert see Shām, Bādiyat ash-, des., Asia C6 40
Sysladobsis Lake, l., Me., U.S. C4 96
Syzran', Russia G7 22
Szamos (Someș), stm., Eur. B6 16
Szczecin (Stettin), Pol. B14 8
Szczecinek (Neustettin), Pol. B16 8
Szeged, Hung. I20 8
Székesfehérvár, Hung. H18 8
Szentes, Hung. I20 8
Szolnok, Hung. H20 8
Szombathely, Hung. H16 8

T

Taal, Lake, l., Phil. r19 33b
Tabaco, Phil. r20 33b
Tabarka, Tun. M3 14
Tabatinga, Serra da, hills, Braz. F10 54
Tabbys Peak, mtn., Ut., U.S. C3 121
Tabelbala, Alg. C5 42
Taber, Alta., Can. E4 68
Tabernes de Valldigna, Spain F11 12
Tablas Island, i., Phil. C7 32
Table Head, c., Newf., Can. B4 72
Table Mountain, mtn., Az., U.S. E5 80
Table Rock Lake, res., U.S. E4 102
Table Top, mtn., Az., U.S. E3 80
Tabor, Russia C24 24
Tabor, Ia., U.S. D2 92
Tabora, Tan. C6 44
Tabor City, N.C., U.S. C4 110
Tabou, C. Iv. H4 42
Tabrīz, Iran J7 22
Tabūk, Sau. Ar. C2 46
Tacámbaro de Codallos, Mex. H9 62
Tachikawa, Japan G12 30
Tacna, Peru G4 54
Tacoma, Wa., U.S. B3 124
Taconic Range, mts., U.S. A1 98
Tacuarembó, Ur. C5 56
Tacubaya, Mex. C7 62
Tadjeroune, Tun. N3 14
Tadoule Lake, l., Man., Can. E13 66
Tadoussac, Que., Can. A8 74
Tādpatri, India E5 37
Taegu, S. Kor. D12 26
Taejŏn, S. Kor. D12 26
Tafalla, Spain C10 12
Taft, Ca., U.S. E4 82
Taft, Tx., U.S. F4 120
Tagajō, Japan D13 30
Taganrog, Russia H5 22
Taglio di Po, Italy D7 14
Taguatinga, Braz. B5 57
Taguke, China D11 38
Tagula Island, i., Pap. N. Gui. B10 50
Tagus (Tejo) (Tajo), stm., Eur. F3 12
Tahan, Gunong, mtn., Malay. L7 34
Tahat, mtn., Alg. D7 42
Tahlequah, Ok., U.S. B7 113
Tahoe, Lake, l., U.S. E1 105
Tahoe City, Ca., U.S. C3 82
Tahoka, Tx., U.S. C2 120
Taholah, Wa., U.S. B1 124
Tahoua, Niger F7 42
Tahquamenon, stm., Mi., U.S. B5 99
Tahsis, B.C., Can. E4 69
Tahtsa Peak, mtn., B.C., Can. C4 69
T'aichung, Tai. K9 28
T'aichunghsien, Tai. K9 28
Taihape, N.Z. C5 52
Tai Hu, l., China D9 28
Tailai, China B11 26
Tain, Scot., U.K. D8 7
T'ainan, Tai. L9 28
T'aipei, Tai. J10 28
T'aipeihsien, Tai. J10 28
Taiping, Malay. L6 34
Taishun, China H8 28
Taitao, Península de, pen., Chile F2 56
T'aitung, Tai. M10 28
Taivalkoski, Fin. D17 6
Taiwan (T'aiwan), ctry., Asia G11 26
Taiwan Strait, strt., Asia K8 28
Taixian, China C9 28
Taixing, China C9 28
Taiyuan, China D9 26
Taizhou, China C8 28
Ta'izz, Yemen F3 46
Tajikistan, ctry., Asia J12 22
Tajitos, Mex. B3 62
Tajmyr, Ozero, l., Russia C14 24
Tajmyr, Poluostrov, pen., Russia B14 24
Tajšet, Russia F13 24
Tajumulco, Volcán, vol., Guat. G2 64
Tak, Thai. F5 34
Takada, Japan E11 30
Takalar, Indon. G6 32
Takamatsu, Japan H7 30
Takaoka, Japan F10 30
Takapuna, N.Z. B5 52
Takasaki, Japan F12 30
Takatsuki, Japan H8 30
Takawa, Japan I3 30
Takayama, Japan F10 30
Takefu, Japan G9 30
Takêv, Camb. I8 34
Takijuq Lake, l., N.W. Ter., Can. C10 66
Takikawa, Japan p19 30a
Takla Lake, l., B.C., Can. B5 69
Taklimakan Shamo, des., China D3 26
Takoma Park, Md., U.S. f8 97
Taku Glacier, Ak., U.S. k22 79
Tala, Mex. G8 62
Talagang, Pak. D5 38
Talaimannar, Sri L. H5 37
Talara, Peru D2 54
Talarrubias, Spain F6 12
Talasea, Pap. N. Gui. m17 50a
Talaud, Kepulauan, is., Indon. E8 32
Talavera de la Reina, Spain F7 12
Talawdī, Sudan F12 42
Talbot, co., Ga., U.S. D2 87
Talbot, co., Md., U.S. C5 97
Talbot Island, i., Fl., U.S. B5 86
Talbot Lake, l., Man., Can. B2 70
Talbotton, Ga., U.S. D2 87
Talca, Chile D2 56
Talcahuano, Chile D2 56
Talent, Or., U.S. E4 114
Taliabu, Pulau, i., Indon. F7 32
Taliaferro, co., Ga., U.S. C4 87
Talihina, Ok., U.S. C6 113
Talkeetna, Ak., U.S. C10 79
Talkeetna Mountains, mts., Ak., U.S. f17 79
Talladega, Al., U.S. B3 78
Talladega, co., Al., U.S. B3 78
Tallahassee, Fl., U.S. B2 86
Tallahatchie, co., Ms., U.S. B3 101
Tallahatchie, stm., Ms., U.S. B3 101
Tallapoosa, Ga., U.S. C1 87
Tallapoosa, co., Al., U.S. C4 78
Tallapoosa, stm., Al., U.S. C3 78
Tallassee, Al., U.S. C4 78
Talleyville, De., U.S. A3 85
Tallinn, Est. B7 18
Tall Kalakh, Syria B5 40
Tallmadge, Oh., U.S. A4 112
Tall Tamir, Syria A7 40
Tallulah, La., U.S. B4 95
Tal'menka, Russia G10 24
Talo, mtn., Eth. F2 46
Tāloqān, Afg. B3 38
Talquin, Lake, res., Fl., U.S. B2 86
Talu, Indon. N5 34
Taluk, Indon. O6 34
Tama, Ia., U.S. C5 92
Tama, co., Ia., U.S. B5 92
Tamale, Ghana G5 42
Tamalpais, Mount, mtn., Ca., U.S. h7 82
Tamana, Japan J3 30
Tamanrasset, Alg. D7 42
Tamaqua, Pa., U.S. E10 115
Tamaroa, Il., U.S. E4 90
Tamazula de Gordiano, Mex. H8 62
Tamazunchale, Mex. G10 62
Tambacounda, Sen. F3 42
Tambohorano, Madag. E8 44
Tambov, Russia I24 18
Tambura, Sudan G11 42
Tamchaket, Maur. E3 42
Tamel Aike, Arg. F2 56
Tamiahua, Laguna de, b., Mex. G11 62
Tamiami Canal, Fl., U.S. G6 86
Tamil Nadu, state, India G5 37
Tam Ky, Viet. G10 34
Tampa, Fl., U.S. E4 86
Tampa Bay, b., Fl., U.S. E4 86
Tampere, Fin. F14 6
Tampico, Mex. F11 62
Tampico, Il., U.S. B4 90
Tamrida, Yemen F5 46
Tamsagbulag, Mong. B10 26
Tamworth, Austl. F10 50
Tana, Nor. A17 6
Tana, stm., Eur. A16 6
Tana, stm., Kenya B7 44

Name	Map Ref	Page
Tana, Lake, l., Eth.	F2	46
Tanabe, Japan	I8	30
Tanaga Island, i., Ak., U.S.	E4	79
Tanahjampea, Pulau, i., Indon.	G7	32
Tanami Desert, des., Austl.	C5	50
Tanana, Ak., U.S.	B9	79
Tanana, stm., Ak., U.S.	C10	79
Tananarive see Antananarivo, Madag.	E9	44
Tānda, India	G10	38
Tandil, Arg.	D5	56
Tando Ādam, Pak.	H3	38
Tando Muhammad Khān, Pak.	H3	38
Tanega-shima, i., Japan	u30	31b
Taney, co., Mo., U.S.	E4	102
Taneycomo, Lake, res., Mo., U.S.	E4	102
Taneytown, Md., U.S.	A3	97
Tanezrouft, des., Afr.	D5	42
Tanga, Tan.	C7	44
Tangail, Bngl.	H13	38
Tanganyika, Lake, l., Afr.	C5	44
Tanger (Tangier), Mor.	A4	42
Tangerang, Indon.	m13	33a
Tangermünde, Ger.	C11	8
Tanggula Shan, mts., China	D13	38
Tangier, Va., U.S.	C7	123
Tangier Island, i., Va., U.S.	C6	123
Tangier Sound, strt., Md., U.S.	D6	97
Tangier see Tanger, Mor.	A4	42
Tangipahoa, co., La., U.S.	D5	95
Tangipahoa, stm., La., U.S.	D5	95
Tangra Yumco, l., China	E12	38
Tangshan, China	D10	26
Tanimbar, Kepulauan, is., Indon.	G9	32
Tanjungbalai, Indon.	M5	34
Tanjungkarang-Telukbetung, Indon.	k12	32
Tanjungpinang, Indon.	N8	34
Tanjungselor, Indon.	E6	32
Tānk, Pak.	D4	38
Tännäs, Swe.	E9	6
Tanner, Al., U.S.	A3	78
Tânout, Niger	F7	42
Tanshui, Tai.	J10	28
Ṭanṭā, Egypt	B12	42
Tanuku, India	D6	37
Tanzania, ctry., Afr.	C6	44
Taos, Mo., U.S.	C5	102
Taos, N.M., U.S.	A4	108
Taos, co., N.M., U.S.	A4	108
Taos Pueblo, N.M., U.S.	A4	108
Taoudenni, Mali	D5	42
Tapachula, Mex.	J13	62
Tapah, Malay.	L6	34
Tapajós, stm., Braz.	E7	54
Taphan Hin, Thai.	F6	34
Tāpi, stm., India	B2	37
Tappahannock, Va., U.S.	C6	123
Tappan, N.Y., U.S.	g13	109
Tappan, Lake, res., N.J., U.S.	g9	107
Tappan Lake, res., Oh., U.S.	B4	112
Taqātu' Hayyā, Sudan	E13	42
Taquaritinga, Braz.	F4	57
Tar, stm., N.C., U.S.	B5	110
Tara, Ont., Can.	C3	73
Ṭarābulus (Tripoli), Leb.	B4	40
Ṭarābulus (Tripoli), Libya	B8	42
Ṭarābulus (Tripolitania), reg., Libya	B8	42
Tarakan, Indon.	E6	32
Tarancón, Spain	E8	12
Taranto, Italy	I12	14
Taranto, Golfo di, b., Italy	I12	14
Tarapacá, Col.	I8	58
Tarare, Fr.	G11	10
Tarascon, Fr.	J8	10
Tarata, Bol.	G5	54
Tarazona, Spain	D10	12
Tarazona de la Mancha, Spain	F10	12
Tarbert, Scot., U.K.	F7	7
Tarbert, Scot., U.K.	D6	7
Tarbes, Fr.	I7	10
Tarboro, N.C., U.S.	B5	110
Tarcento, Italy	C8	14
Taree, Austl.	F10	50
Tareja, Russia	C12	24
Tarentum, Pa., U.S.	E2	115
Tarfaya, Mor.	C3	42
Targhee Pass, U.S.	E7	89
Tarifa, Punta de, c., Spain	I6	12
Tariffville, Ct., U.S.	B4	84
Tarija, Bol.	H6	54
Tarim, stm., China	C3	26
Tarīn Kowt, Afg.	D1	38
Tarkio, Mo., U.S.	A2	102
Tarkwa, Ghana	G5	42
Tarlac, Phil.	q19	32
Tarn, stm., Fr.	I8	10
Tärnaby, Swe.	D10	6
Tarnak, stm., Afg.	D2	38
Tarnów, Pol.	E20	8
Tarnowskie Góry, Pol.	E18	8
Tarpey, Ca., U.S.	D4	82
Tarpon, Lake, l., Fl., U.S.	o10	86
Tarpon Springs, Fl., U.S.	D4	86
Tarquinia, Italy	G6	14
Tarragona, Spain	D13	12
Tarrant, Al., U.S.	B3	78
Tarrant, co., Tx., U.S.	C4	120
Tarrasa, Spain	D14	12
Tarryall Mountains, mts., Co., U.S.	B5	83
Tarrytown, N.Y., U.S.	D7	109
Tarsus, Tur.	A4	40
Tartagal, Arg.	A4	56
Tartas, Fr.	I6	10
Tartu, Est.	C9	18
Ṭarṭūs, Syria	B4	40
Tarutung, Indon.	M5	34
Tašauz, Turk.	I9	22
Tasejeva, stm., Russia	F12	24
Tasejevo, Russia	F12	24
Taseko Mountain, mtn., B.C., Can.	D6	69
Tashi Gang Dzong, Bhu.	G14	38
Tashkent see Taškent, Uzb.	I11	22
Tasikmalaya, Indon.	m14	32
Taškent, Uzb.	I11	22
Tasmania, state, Austl.	H9	50
Tasman Sea, Oc.	G11	50
Tasso, Tn., U.S.	D9	119
Taštagol, Russia	G11	24
Tatabánya, Hung.	H18	8
Tatarskij Proliv, strt., Russia	H22	24
Tate, Ga., U.S.	B2	87
Tate, co., Ms., U.S.	A4	101
Tateville, Ky., U.S.	D5	94
Tateyama, Japan	H12	30
Tathlina Lake, l., N.W. Ter., Can.	D9	66
Tatnam, Cape, c., Man., Can.	f9	70
Tatta, Pak.	H2	38
Tattnall, co., Ga., U.S.	D4	87
Tatum, N.M., U.S.	D6	108
Tatvan, Tur.	H16	4
Tau, Nor.	G5	6
Taubaté, Braz.	G6	57
Tauberbischofsheim, Ger.	F9	8
Taujskaja Guba, b., Russia	F24	24
Taumarunui, N.Z.	C5	52
Taum Sauk Mountain, mtn., Mo., U.S.	D6	102
Taungdwingyi, Mya.	D3	34
Taunggyi, Mya.	D4	34
Taungup Pass, Mya.	E3	34
Taunton, Eng., U.K.	J9	7
Taunton, Ma., U.S.	C5	98
Taunton, stm., Ma., U.S.	C5	98
Taupo, Lake, l., N.Z.	C5	52
Tauranga, N.Z.	B6	52
Taureau, Réservoir, res., Que., Can.	C4	74
Taurus Mountains see Toros Dağları, mts., Tur.	H14	4
Tauste, Spain	D10	12
Tavares, Fl., U.S.	D5	86
Tavernier, Fl., U.S.	G6	86
Tavira, Port.	H4	12
Tavoy Point, c., Mya.	H5	34
Tavşanlı, Tur.	J13	16
Tawakoni, Lake, res., Tx., U.S.	C4	120
Tawas City, Mi., U.S.	D7	99
Tawas Lake, l., Mi., U.S.	D7	99
Tawau, Malay.	E6	32
Tawitawi Island, i., Phil.	D6	32
Tawkar, Sudan	E13	42
Taxco de Alarcón, Mex.	H10	62
Tay, Loch, l., Scot., U.K.	E8	7
Taylor, B.C., Can.	A7	69
Taylor, Az., U.S.	C5	80
Taylor, Ar., U.S.	D2	81
Taylor, Mi., U.S.	p15	99
Taylor, Pa., U.S.	D10	115
Taylor, Tx., U.S.	D4	120
Taylor, co., Fl., U.S.	B3	86
Taylor, co., Ga., U.S.	D2	87
Taylor, co., Ia., U.S.	D3	92
Taylor, co., Ky., U.S.	C4	94
Taylor, co., Tx., U.S.	C3	120
Taylor, co., W.V., U.S.	B4	125
Taylor, co., Wi., U.S.	C3	126
Taylor, stm., Co., U.S.	C4	83
Taylor, Mount, mtn., N.M., U.S.	B2	108
Taylor Mill, Ky., U.S.	k14	94
Taylor Mountain, mtn., Id., U.S.	E4	89
Taylor Park Reservoir, res., Co., U.S.	C4	83
Taylors, S.C., U.S.	B3	117
Taylors Falls, Mn., U.S.	E6	100
Taylors Island, i., Md., U.S.	D5	97
Taylorsville, In., U.S.	F6	91
Taylorsville, Ky., U.S.	B4	94
Taylorsville, Ms., U.S.	D4	101
Taylorsville, N.C., U.S.	B1	110
Taylorville, Il., U.S.	D4	90
Taymā', Sau. Ar.	C2	46
Tay Ninh, Viet.	I9	34
Tayoltita, Mex.	E7	62
Taytay, Phil.	C6	32
Taz, stm., Russia	D10	24
Taza, Mor.	B5	42
Tazewell, Tn., U.S.	C10	119
Tazewell, Va., U.S.	e10	123
Tazewell, co., Il., U.S.	C4	90
Tazewell, co., Va., U.S.	e10	123
Tazin Lake, l., Sask., Can.	E11	66
Tbessa, Alg.	A7	42
Tbilisi, Geor.	I6	22
Tbong, Camb.	H8	34
Tchefuncta, stm., La., U.S.	D5	95
Tchibanga, Gabon	B2	44
Tchien, Lib.	G4	42
Tchula, Ms., U.S.	B3	101
Tczew, Pol.	A18	8
Tea, S.D., U.S.	D9	118
Teacapán, Mex.	F7	62
Teague, Tx., U.S.	D4	120
Teakean Butte, mtn., Id., U.S.	C2	89
Te Anau, Lake, l., N.Z.	F1	52
Teaneck, N.J., U.S.	h8	107
Teano, Italy	H9	14
Teaticket, Ma., U.S.	C6	98
Tebingtinggi, Indon.	M5	34
Téboursouk, Tun.	M4	14
Tecate, Mex.	A1	62
Tecolotlan, Mex.	G7	62
Tecomán, Mex.	H8	62
Tecpan de Galeana, Mex.	I9	62
Tecuala, Mex.	F7	62
Tecuci, Rom.	D11	16
Tecumseh, Ont., Can.	E2	73
Tecumseh, Ks., U.S.	k14	93
Tecumseh, Mi., U.S.	G7	99
Tecumseh, Ne., U.S.	D9	104
Tecumseh, Ok., U.S.	B5	113
Tedžen (Harīrūd), stm., Asia	J10	22
Teeswater, Ont., Can.	C3	73
Tefé, Braz.	D6	54
Tegal, Indon.	m14	32
Tegucigalpa, Hond.	G4	64
Tehachapi, Ca., U.S.	E4	82
Tehachapi Mountains, mts., Ca., U.S.	E4	82
Tehama, co., Ca., U.S.	B2	82
Tehrān, Iran	J8	22
Tehuacán, Mex.	H11	62
Tehuantepec, Mex.	I12	62
Tehuantepec, Golfo de, b., Mex.	J12	62
Tehuantepec, Istmo de, Mex.	I12	62
Teide, Pico de, mtn., Spain	p24	13b
Tejamén, Mex.	E7	62
Tejkovo, Russia	E23	18
Tejupan, Punta, c., Mex.	H8	62
Tekamah, Ne., U.S.	C9	104
Tekirdağ, Tur.	I11	16
Tekoa, Wa., U.S.	B8	124
Tekonsha, Mi., U.S.	F5	99
Tela, Hond.	G4	64
Telavåg, Nor.	F5	6
Tel Aviv-Yafo, Isr.	C4	40
Teleckoje, Ozero, l., Russia	G11	24
Telén, Arg.	D3	56
Telescope Peak, mtn., Ca., U.S.	D5	82
Teles Pires, stm., Braz.	E7	54
Telfair, co., Ga., U.S.	E4	87
Telford, Pa., U.S.	F11	115
Telfs, Aus.	H11	8
Teli, Russia	G12	24
Telkwa, B.C., Can.	B4	69
Tell City, In., U.S.	I4	91
Teller, co., Co., U.S.	C5	83
Tellicherry, India	G3	37
Tellico Plains, Tn., U.S.	D9	119
Telluride, Co., U.S.	D3	83
Telok Anson, Malay.	L6	34
Telos Lake, l., Me., U.S.	B3	96
Temagami, Lake, l., Ont., Can.	G16	66
Tembeling, stm., Malay.	L7	34
Tembenči, stm., Russia	D13	24
Temecula, Ca., U.S.	F5	82
Temerloh, Malay.	M7	34
Teminabuan, Indon.	F9	32
Témiscouata, Lac, l., Que., Can.	B9	74
Te-Moak Indian Reservation, Nv., U.S.	C6	105
Temósachic, Mex.	C6	62
Tempe, Az., U.S.	D4	80
Temperance, Mi., U.S.	G7	99
Temperance, stm., Mn., U.S.	C6	100
Tempio Pausania, Italy	I4	14
Temple, Ga., U.S.	C1	87
Temple, Ok., U.S.	C3	113
Temple, Pa., U.S.	F10	115
Temple, Tx., U.S.	D4	120
Temple Terrace, Fl., U.S.	o11	86
Templin, Ger.	B13	8
Temuco, Chile	D2	56
Tena, Ec.	H4	58
Tenafly, N.J., U.S.	B5	107
Tenaha, Tx., U.S.	D5	120
Tenāli, India	D6	37
Tendaho, Eth.	F3	46
Tende, Col de, Eur.	H14	10
Ten Degree Channel, strt., India	J2	34
Ténéré, des., Niger	E8	42
Tenerife, i., Spain	p24	13b
Tengchong, China	B5	34
Tenino, Wa., U.S.	C3	124
Tenkāsi, India	H4	37
Tenkiller Ferry Lake, res., Ok., U.S.	B6	113
Tenkodogo, Burkina	F5	42
Tenmile, stm., U.S.	B5	116
Tenmile Creek, stm., W.V., U.S.	k10	125
Tenmile Lake, l., Mn., U.S.	D4	100
Tennant Creek, Austl.	C6	50
Tennessee, state, U.S.	B5	119
Tennessee, stm., U.S.	D9	76
Tennessee Pass, Co., U.S.	B4	83
Tennessee Ridge, Tn., U.S.	A4	119
Tennille, Ga., U.S.	D4	87
Tenom, Malay.	D6	32
Tenryū, stm., Japan	G10	30
Tensas, co., La., U.S.	B4	95
Tensas, stm., La., U.S.	B4	95
Tensaw, stm., Al., U.S.	E2	78
Ten Sleep, Wy., U.S.	B5	127
Tenterfield, Austl.	E10	50
Ten Thousand Islands, is., Fl., U.S.	G5	86
Teocaltiche, Mex.	G8	62
Teófilo Otoni, Braz.	D8	57
Tepa, Indon.	G8	32
Tepatitlán [de Morelos], Mex.	G8	62
Tepic, Mex.	G7	62
Teplice, Czech.	E13	8
Teramo, Italy	G8	14
Teresina, Braz.	E10	54
Teresópolis, Braz.	G7	57
Termez, Uzb.	B2	38
Termini Imerese, Italy	L8	14
Términos, Laguna de, b., Mex.	H14	62
Termoli, Italy	G9	14
Ternej, Russia	H21	24
Terni, Italy	G7	14
Ternopil', Ukr.	H3	22
Terpenija, Mys, c., Russia	H22	24
Terpenija, Zaliv, b., Russia	H22	24
Terra Alta, W.V., U.S.	B5	125
Terrace, B.C., Can.	B3	69
Terracina, Italy	H8	14
Terralba, Italy	J3	14
Terra Nova National Park, Newf., Can.	D4	72
Terrebonne, Que., Can.	D4	74
Terrebonne, Or., U.S.	C5	114
Terrebonne, co., La., U.S.	E5	95
Terrebonne Bay, b., La., U.S.	E5	95
Terre Haute, In., U.S.	F3	91
Terre Hill, Pa., U.S.	F9	115
Terrell, Tx., U.S.	C4	120
Terrell, co., Ga., U.S.	E2	87
Terrell, co., Tx., U.S.	D1	120
Terrell Hills, Tx., U.S.	k7	120
Terrenceville, Newf., Can.	E4	72
Terry, Ms., U.S.	C3	101
Terry, Mt., U.S.	D11	103
Terry, co., Tx., U.S.	C1	120
Terrytown, Ne., U.S.	C2	104
Terryville, Ct., U.S.	C3	84
Teruel, Spain	E10	12
Tervola, Fin.	C15	6
Teseney, Erit.	E2	46
Teshekpuk Lake, l., Ak., U.S.	A9	79
Teshio, Japan	o19	30a
Teslin, Yukon, Can.	D6	66
Teslin, stm., Can.	D6	66
Tesouro, Braz.	D2	57
Tessalit, Mali	D6	42
Tesuque, N.M., U.S.	B4	108
Tete, Moz.	E6	44
Teterow, Ger.	B12	8
Teton, co., Id., U.S.	F7	89
Teton, co., Mt., U.S.	C4	103
Teton, co., Wy., U.S.	C2	127
Teton, stm., Mt., U.S.	C5	103
Teton Pass, Wy., U.S.	C2	127
Teton Range, mts., Wy., U.S.	C2	127
Teton Village, Wy., U.S.	C2	127
Tétouan, Mor.	A4	42
Tetovo, Mac.	G4	16
Tet'uche, Russia	I21	24
Teulada, Italy	K3	14
Teulon, Man., Can.	D3	70
Teutopolis, Il., U.S.	D5	90
Teuva, Fin.	E13	6
Tevere (Tiber), stm., Italy	G7	14
Teverya, Isr.	C4	40
Tewksbury, Ma., U.S.	A5	98
Texada Island, i., B.C., Can.	E5	69
Texarkana, Ar., U.S.	D1	81
Texarkana, Tx., U.S.	C5	120
Texas, co., Mo., U.S.	D5	102
Texas, co., Ok., U.S.	e9	113
Texas, state, U.S.	D3	120
Texas City, Tx., U.S.	E5	120
Texhoma, Ok., U.S.	e9	113
Texico, N.M., U.S.	C6	108
Texoma, Lake, res., U.S.	D5	113
Teyvareh, Afg.	D1	38
Teziutlán, Mex.	H11	62
Tezpur, India	G15	38
Thabazimbi, S. Afr.	F5	44
Thai Binh, Viet.	D9	34
Thailand, ctry., Asia	B3	32
Thailand, Gulf of, b., Asia	J6	34
Thai Nguyen, Viet.	D8	34
Thal, Pak.	D4	38
Thames, stm., Ont., Can.	E3	73
Thames, stm., Eng., U.K.	J14	7
Thames, stm., Ct., U.S.	D7	84
Thamesville, Ont., Can.	E3	73
Thāna, India	C2	37
Thanh Hoa, Viet.	E8	34
Thanh Pho Ho Chi Minh (Saigon), Viet.	I9	34
Thanjāvūr, India	G5	37
Thar Desert (Great Indian Desert), des., Asia	G3	38
Thargomindah, Austl.	E8	50
Thatcher, Az., U.S.	E6	80
Thaton, Mya.	F4	34
Thayer, Mo., U.S.	E6	102
Thayer, co., Ne., U.S.	D8	104
Thayetmyo, Mya.	E3	34
Thayne, Wy., U.S.	D1	127
Thealka, Ky., U.S.	C7	94
The Barrens, plat., Tn., U.S.	B5	119
The Bight, Bah.	B10	64
The Cheviot, mtn., Eng., U.K.	F10	7
The Colony, Tx., U.S.	*C4	120
The Dalles, Or., U.S.	B5	114
The Dells, val., Wi., U.S.	E4	126
Thedford, Ont., Can.	D3	73
The English Company's Islands, is., Austl.	B7	50
The Everglades, sw., Fl., U.S.	G6	86
The Fens, sw., Eng., U.K.	I12	7
The Flat Tops, mts., Co., U.S.	B3	83
The Flume, wtfl, N.H., U.S.	B3	106
The Graves, is., Ma., U.S.	g12	98
The Hague see 's-Gravenhage, Neth.	C4	8
The Heads, c., Or., U.S.	E2	114
Thelon, stm., N.W. Ter., Can.	D12	66
The Narrows, strt., Wa., U.S.	f10	124
Theodore, Austl.	D10	50
Theodore, Al., U.S.	E1	78
Theodore Roosevelt Lake, res., Az., U.S.	D4	80
Theodore Roosevelt National Park (South Unit), N.D., U.S.	C2	111
Theodore Roosevelt National Park (North Unit), N.D., U.S.	B2	111
The Pas, Man., Can.	C1	70
The Plains, Oh., U.S.	C3	112
Theresa, Wi., U.S.	E5	126
Thermopolis, Wy., U.S.	C4	127
The Rockies, mts., Wa., U.S.	C3	124
Thessalon, Ont., Can.	p19	73
Thessaloníki (Salonika), Grc.	I6	16
Thetford Mines, Que., Can.	C6	74
The Thimbles, is., Ct., U.S.	E5	84
The Village, Ok., U.S.	B4	113
The Warburton, stm., Austl.	E7	50
The Wash, b., Eng., U.K.	I13	7
The Weald, reg., Eng., U.K.	J13	7
Thibodaux, La., U.S.	E5	95
Thief, stm., Mn., U.S.	B2	100
Thief Lake, l., Mn., U.S.	B3	100
Thief River Falls, Mn., U.S.	B2	100
Thielsen, Mount, mtn., Or., U.S.	D4	114
Thiene, Italy	D6	14
Thiensville, Wi., U.S.	E6	126
Thiers, Fr.	G10	10
Thiès, Sen.	F2	42
Thika, Kenya	B7	44
Thimphu, Bhu.	G13	38
Thingangyun, Mya.	F4	34
Thionville, Fr.	C13	10
Thíra, i., Grc.	M9	16
Third Lake, l., N.H., U.S.	f7	106
Thirsk, Eng., U.K.	G11	7
Thisted, Den.	H7	6
Thívai (Thebes), Grc.	K7	16
Thiviers, Fr.	G7	10
Thomas, Ok., U.S.	B3	113
Thomas, co., Ga., U.S.	F3	87
Thomas, co., Ks., U.S.	C2	93
Thomas, co., Ne., U.S.	C5	104
Thomasboro, Il., U.S.	C5	90
Thomaston, Ct., U.S.	C3	84
Thomaston, Ga., U.S.	D2	87
Thomaston, Me., U.S.	D3	96
Thomaston Reservoir, res., Ct., U.S.	C3	84
Thomastown, Ire.	I5	7
Thomasville, Al., U.S.	D2	78
Thomasville, Ga., U.S.	F3	87
Thomasville, N.C., U.S.	B2	110
Thompson, Man., Can.	B3	70
Thompson, Ct., U.S.	B8	84
Thompson, N.D., U.S.	B8	111
Thompson, stm., U.S.	A4	102
Thompson Falls, Mt., U.S.	C1	103
Thompson Island, i., Ma., U.S.	g11	98
Thompson Lake, l., U.S.	D2	96
Thompson Peak, mtn., Ca., U.S.	B2	82
Thompson Peak, mtn., N.M., U.S.	h9	108
Thompson Reservoir, res., Or., U.S.	E5	114
Thomsen, stm., N.W. Ter., Can.	B9	66
Thomson, Ga., U.S.	C4	87
Thon Buri, Thai.	H6	34
Thongwa, Mya.	F4	34
Thonon-les-Bains, Fr.	F13	10
Thonotosassa, Fl., U.S.	D4	86
Thonze, Mya.	F3	34
Thorburn, N.S., Can.	D7	71
Thoreau, N.M., U.S.	B1	108
Thornbury, Ont., Can.	C4	73
Thorndale, Tx., U.S.	D4	120
Thornton, Ont., Can.	C5	73
Thorntown, In., U.S.	D4	91
Thorold, Ont., Can.	D5	73
Thorp, Wi., U.S.	D3	126
Thorsby, Al., U.S.	C3	78
Thouars, Fr.	F6	10
Thousand Islands, is., N.Y., U.S.	A4	109
Thousand Lake Mountain, mtn., Ut., U.S.	E4	121
Thousand Springs Creek, stm., U.S.	B7	105
Thrace, hist. reg., Eur.	G13	4
Thrakikón Pélagos, Grc.	I8	16
Three Fingered Jack, mtn., Or., U.S.	C5	114
Three Forks, Mt., U.S.	E5	103
Three Hills, Alta., Can.	D4	68
Three Lakes, Wi., U.S.	C4	126
Three Mile Plains, N.S., Can.	E5	71
Three Oaks, Mi., U.S.	G4	99
Three Pagodas Pass, Asia	G5	34
Three Points, Cape, c., Ghana	H5	42
Three Rivers, Ma., U.S.	B3	98
Three Rivers, Mi., U.S.	G5	99
Three Rivers, Tx., U.S.	E3	120
Three Sisters, mtn., Or., U.S.	C5	114
Three Springs, Austl.	E3	50
Throckmorton, co., Tx., U.S.	C3	120
Throop, Pa., U.S.	m18	115
Throssell Range, mts., Austl.	D4	50
Thu Dao Mot, Viet.	I9	34
Thule, Grnld.	B19	128
Thun, Switz.	F14	10
Thunder Bay, Ont., Can.	o17	73
Thunder Bay, b., Mi., U.S.	D7	99
Thunder Bay, stm., Mi., U.S.	D6	99
Thunderbird, Lake, res., Ok., U.S.	B4	113
Thunderbolt, Ga., U.S.	D5	87
Thunder Butte Creek, stm., S.D., U.S.	B3	118
Thunersee, l., Switz.	F14	10
Thüringen, hist. reg., Ger.	D11	8
Thurles, Ire.	I5	7
Thurmont, Md., U.S.	A3	97
Thurso, Que., Can.	D2	74
Thurso, Scot., U.K.	C9	7
Thurston, co., Ne., U.S.	B9	104
Thurston, co., Wa., U.S.	C2	124
Tiancang, China	C7	26
Tiandong, China	C9	34
Tianjin (Tientsin), China	D10	26
Tianjun, China	D6	26
Tianmen, China	E2	28
Tianshui, China	E8	26
Tiaret, Alg.	A6	42
Tibagi, Braz.	A6	56
Tibasti, Sarīr, des., Libya	D9	42
Tiber see Tevere, stm., Italy	G7	14
Tibesti, mts., Chad	D9	42
Tibet, hist. reg., China	E12	38
Tiburón, Isla, i., Mex.	C3	62
Tice, Fl., U.S.	F5	86
Tīchīt, Maur.	E4	42
Tichvin, Russia	B16	18
Tickfaw, stm., La., U.S.	C5	95
Ticonderoga, N.Y., U.S.	B7	109
Ticul, Mex.	G15	62
Tide Head, N.B., Can.	B3	71
Tidjikdja, Maur.	E3	42
Tieling, China	C11	26
Tienen, Bel.	E4	8
Tien Shan, mts., Asia	C2	26
Tientsin see Tianjin, China	D10	26
Tierra Amarilla, N.M., U.S.	A3	108
Tierra Blanca, Mex.	H11	62
Tierra del Fuego, Isla Grande de, i., S.A.	G3	56
Tierralta, Col.	C4	58
Tietê, stm., Braz.	F3	57
Tieton, Wa., U.S.	C5	124
Tieton, stm., Wa., U.S.	C4	124
Tieton Dam, Wa., U.S.	C4	124
Tiffany Mountain, mtn., Wa., U.S.	A6	124
Tiffin, Oh., U.S.	A2	112
Tiffin, stm., Oh., U.S.	A1	112
Tift, co., Ga., U.S.	E3	87
Tifton, Ga., U.S.	E3	87

Name — Map Ref — Page

Tigard, Or., U.S. h12 114
Tigerton, Wi., U.S. D4 126
Tigil', Russia F25 24
Tignall, Ga., U.S. C4 87
Tignish, P.E.I., Can. C5 71
Tigre, stm., Peru D3 54
Tigris (Dijlah), stm., Asia A3 46
Tiguentourine, Alg. C7 42
Tijesno, Cro. F10 14
Tijuana, Mex. A1 62
Tikamgarh, India H8 38
Tikrīt, Iraq B3 46
Tilburg, Neth. D5 8
Tilbury, Ont., Can. E2 73
Tilden, Il., U.S. E4 90
Tilden, Ne., U.S. B8 104
Tilghman, Md., U.S. C5 97
Tilghman Island, i., Md., U.S. C5 97
Tilhar, India G8 38
Tillabéry, Niger F6 42
Tillamook, Or., U.S. B3 114
Tillamook, co., Or., U.S. B3 114
Tillanchong Island, i., India J2 34
Tillery, Lake, res., N.C., U.S. B2 110
Tillman, co., Ok., U.S. C2 113
Tillmans Corner, Al., U.S. E1 78
Tillsonburg, Ont., Can. E4 73
Tilton, Il., U.S. C6 90
Tilton, N.H., U.S. D3 106
Tiltonsville, Oh., U.S. B5 112
Timaru, N.Z. F3 52
Timbalier Island, i., La., U.S. E5 95
Timberlake, Va., U.S. C3 123
Timberville, Va., U.S. B4 123
Timbuktu see Tombouctou, Mali E5 42
Timimoun, Alg. C6 42
Timiris, Cap, c., Maur. E2 42
Timişoara, Rom. D5 16
Timmins, Ont., Can. o19 73
Timmonsville, S.C., U.S. C8 117
Timms Hill, hill, Wi., U.S. C3 126
Timor, i., Indon. G8 32
Timor Sea B5 50
Timotes, Ven. C7 58
Timpanogos Cave National Monument, Ut., U.S. C4 121
Timpton, stm., Russia F19 24
Tims Ford Lake, res., Tn., U.S. B5 119
Tinaquillo, Ven. C8 58
Tindivanam, India F5 37
Tindouf, Alg. C4 42
Tingmerkpuk Mountain, mtn., Ak., U.S. B7 79
Tingo María, Peru E3 54
Tingvoll, Nor. E7 6
Tinharé, Ilha de, i., Braz. F11 54
Tinker Air Force Base, mil., Ok., U.S. B4 113
Tinley Park, Il., U.S. k9 90
Tinniswood, Mount, mtn., B.C., Can. D6 69
Tinogasta, Arg. B3 56
Tinsukia, India G16 38
Tinton Falls, N.J., U.S. C4 107
Tioga, La., U.S. C3 95
Tioga, N.D., U.S. A3 111
Tioga, co., N.Y., U.S. C4 109
Tioga, co., Pa., U.S. C7 115
Tioga, stm., Pa., U.S. B7 115
Tiogue Lake, res., R.I., U.S. D3 116
Tioman, Pulau, i., Malay. M8 34
Tionesta Creek, stm., Pa., U.S. C3 115
Tionesta Lake, res., Pa., U.S. D3 115
Tioughnioga, stm., N.Y., U.S. C4 109
Tippah, co., Ms., U.S. A5 101
Tippah, stm., Ms., U.S. A4 101
Tipp City, Oh., U.S. C1 112
Tippecanoe, co., In., U.S. D4 91
Tippecanoe, stm., In., U.S. C4 91
Tipperary, Ire. I4 7
Tipton, Ca., U.S. D4 82
Tipton, In., U.S. D5 91
Tipton, Ia., U.S. C6 92
Tipton, Mo., U.S. C5 102
Tipton, Ok., U.S. C2 113
Tipton, co., In., U.S. D5 91
Tipton, co., Tn., U.S. B2 119
Tipton, Mount, mtn., Az., U.S. B1 80
Tiptonville, Tn., U.S. A2 119
Tiquisate, Guat. G2 64
Tiracambu, Serra do, plat., Braz. D9 54
Tīrān, Madīq, strt. F4 40
Tiran, Strait of see Tīrān, Madīq, strt. F4 40
Tiranë, Alb. H3 16
Tirano, Italy C5 14
Tiraspol, Mol. H3 22
Tirat Karmel, Isr. C4 40
Tire, Tur. K11 16
Tiree, i., Scot., U.K. E6 7
Tîrgovişte, Rom. E9 16
Tîrgu-Jiu, Rom. D7 16
Tîrgu Mureş, Rom. C8 16
Tîrgu-Ocna, Rom. C10 16
Tírnavos, Grc. J6 16
Tirschenreuth, Ger. F12 8
Tiruchchirāppalli, India G5 37
Tirunelveli, India H4 37
Tirupati, India F5 37
Tiruppattūr, India F5 37
Tiruppur, India G4 37
Tiruvannāmalai, India F5 37
Tishomingo, Ok., U.S. C5 113
Tishomingo, co., Ms., U.S. A5 101
Tiskilwa, Il., U.S. B4 90
Tisza (Tisa), stm., Eur. C4 16
Tit-Ary, Russia C19 24
Titicaca, Lago, l., S.A. G5 54
Titonka, Ia., U.S. A3 92
Titov Veles, Mac. H5 16
Titule, Zaire H11 42
Titus, co., Tx., U.S. C5 120
Titusville, Fl., U.S. D6 86
Titusville, Pa., U.S. C2 115
Tiverton, Ont., Can. C3 73
Tiverton, Eng., U.K. K9 7
Tiverton, R.I., U.S. D6 116
Tivoli, Italy H7 14
Tizimín, Mex. G15 62
Tizi-Ouzou, Alg. A6 42
Tlahualilo de Zaragoza, Mex. D8 62
Tlaltenango de Sánchez Román, Mex. G8 62
Tlaxiaco, Mex. I11 62
Tlemcen, Alg. B5 42
Tlētē Ouāte Gharbī, Jabal, mtn., Syria B6 40
Toamasina, Madag. E9 44
Toano, Va., U.S. C6 123
Toano Range, mts., Nv., U.S. C7 105
Toast, N.C., U.S. A2 110
Toba, Japan H9 30
Toba, Danau, l., Indon. M5 34
Tobacco Root Mountains, mts., Mt., U.S. E5 103
Tobago, i., Trin. I17 64
Toba Inlet, b., B.C., Can. D5 69
Toba Kākar Range, mts., Pak. E2 38
Tobarra, Spain G10 12
Tobermory, Scot., U.K. E6 7
Tobin, Mount, mtn., Nv., U.S. C4 105
Tobin Lake, l., Sask., Can. D4 75
Tobin Range, mts., Nv., U.S. C4 105
Tobique, stm., N.B., Can. B2 71
Tobruk see Ţubruq, Libya B10 42
Tobyhanna, Pa., U.S. D11 115
Tocantínia, Braz. E9 54
Tocantinópolis, Braz. E9 54
Tocantins, stm., Braz. D9 54
Toccoa, Ga., U.S. B3 87
Toccoa, stm., Ga., U.S. B2 87
Toccoa Falls, Ga., U.S. B3 87
Tochigi, Japan F12 30
Töcksfors, Swe. G8 6
Toco, Chile A3 56
Tocopilla, Chile A2 56
Todd, co., Ky., U.S. D2 94
Todd, co., Mn., U.S. D4 100
Todd, co., S.D., U.S. D5 118
Todi, Italy G7 14
Todos Santos, Mex. F4 62
Todtnau, Ger. H7 8
Tofield, Alta., Can. C4 68
Tofino, B.C., Can. E5 69
Togiak, Ak., U.S. D7 79
Togian, Kepulauan, is., Indon. F7 32
Togo, ctry., Afr. G6 42
Togwotee Pass, Wy., U.S. C2 127
Tohakum Peak, mtn., Nv., U.S. C2 105
Tohatchi, N.M., U.S. B1 108
Tohopekaliga, Lake, l., Fl., U.S. D5 86
Toiyabe Range, mts., Nv., U.S. D4 105
Tok, Ak., U.S. C11 79
Tōkamachi, Japan E11 30
Tokara-kaikyō, strt., Japan u30 31b
Tokara-rettō, is., Japan v29 31b
Tokat, Tur. G15 4
Tokelau Islands, dep., Oc. G1 2
Toki, Japan G10 30
Tokuno-shima, i., Japan x28 31b
Tokushima, Japan H7 30
Tokuyama, Japan H4 30
Tōkyō, Japan G12 30
Tokzār, Afg. C2 38
Toleak Point, c., Wa., U.S. B1 124
Toledo, Spain F7 12
Toledo, Il., U.S. D5 90
Toledo, Ia., U.S. B5 92
Toledo, Oh., U.S. A2 112
Toledo, Or., U.S. C3 114
Toledo Bend Reservoir, res., U.S. C2 95
Tolentino, Italy F8 14
Toler, Ky., U.S. C7 94
Toliara, Madag. F8 44
Toljatti, Russia G7 22
Tol'ka, Russia E10 24
Tolland, Ct., U.S. B6 84
Tolland, co., Ct., U.S. B6 84
Tollesboro, Ky., U.S. B6 94
Tolleson, Az., U.S. m8 80
Tolmezzo, Italy C8 14
Tolmin, Slo. C8 14
Tolo, Teluk, b., Indon. F7 32
Tolono, Il., U.S. D5 90
Tolosa, Spain B9 12
Tolstoj, Mys, c., Russia F25 24
Tolt Reservoir, res., Wa., U.S. B4 124
Toluca, Il., U.S. C4 90
Toluca, Nevado de, vol., Mex. H10 62
Toluca [de Lerdo], Mex. H10 62
Tom', stm., Russia F11 24
Tomah, Wi., U.S. E3 126
Tomahawk, Wi., U.S. C4 126
Tomahawk Lake, l., Wi., U.S. C4 126
Tomakomai, Japan q19 30a
Tomar, Port. F3 12
Tomaszów Mazowiecki, Pol. D20 8
Tomatlán, Mex. H7 62
Tombador, Serra do, plat., Braz. F7 54
Tomball, Tx., U.S. D5 120
Tombigbee, stm., U.S. D1 78
Tombouctou (Timbuktu), Mali E5 42
Tombstone, Az., U.S. F5 80
Tombua, Ang. E2 44
Tomelloso, Spain F9 12
Tom Green, co., Tx., U.S. D2 120
Tomini, Teluk, b., Indon. F7 32
Tommot, Russia F19 24
Tom Nevers Head, c., Ma., U.S. D8 98
Tomo, stm., Col. E8 58
Tompkins, co., N.Y., U.S. C4 109
Tompkinsville, Ky., U.S. D4 94
Tomptokan, Russia F20 24
Tomra, Nor. E6 6
Toms, stm., N.J., U.S. C4 107
Tomsk, Russia F10 24
Toms River, N.J., U.S. D4 107
Tonalá, Mex. I13 62
Tonasket, Wa., U.S. A6 124
Tonawanda Indian Reservation, N.Y., U.S. B2 109
Tondabayashi, Japan H8 30
Tone, stm., Japan F12 30
Tonga, ctry., Oc. H1 2
Tonganoxie, Ks., U.S. C8 93
Tongbai, China C2 28
Tongchuan, China D8 26
Tongeren, Bel. E5 8
Tongguan, China E9 26
Tonghai, China B7 34
Tonghua, China C12 26
Tongliao, China C11 26
Tongling, China E6 28
Tongsa Dzong, Bhu. G14 38
Tongtianheyan, China D15 38
Tongue, Scot., U.K. C8 7
Tongue, stm., Mt., U.S. E10 103
Tongue, stm., Tx., U.S. p13 120
Tongzi, China F8 26
Tonk, India G6 38
Tonkawa, Ok., U.S. A4 113
Tonkin, Gulf of, b., Asia E9 34
Tonle Sap see Sab, Tônlé, l., Camb. H7 34
Tonneins, Fr. H7 10
Tonnerre, Fr. E10 10
Tonopah, Nv., U.S. E4 105
Tønsberg, Nor. G8 6
Tonstad, Nor. G6 6
Tonto National Monument, Az., U.S. D4 80
Tonto Natural Bridge, Az., U.S. C4 80
Tooele, Ut., U.S. C3 121
Tooele, co., Ut., U.S. C2 121
Toole, co., Mt., U.S. B5 103
Toombs, co., Ga., U.S. D4 87
Toomsboro, Ga., U.S. D3 87
Toowoomba, Austl. E10 50
Topeka, In., U.S. A6 91
Topeka, Ks., U.S. C8 93
Topia, Mex. E6 62
Topock, Az., U.S. C1 80
Toppenish, Wa., U.S. C5 124
Topsfield, Ma., U.S. A6 98
Topsham, Me., U.S. E3 96
Topton, Pa., U.S. F10 115
Toquima Range, mts., Nv., U.S. E5 105
Torbay, Newf., Can. E5 72
Torbert, Mount, mtn., Ak., U.S. g15 79
Torch Lake, l., Mi., U.S. D5 99
Tordesillas, Spain D6 12
Töre, Swe. D14 6
Torgau, Ger. D12 8
Torhout, Bel. D3 8
Torino (Turin), Italy D2 14
Torit, Sudan H12 42
Torkestān, Band-e, mts., Afg. C2 38
Torneälven, stm., Eur. B12 4
Torngat Mountains, mts., Can. f8 72
Toro, Spain D6 12
Toronto, Ont., Can. D5 73
Toronto, Oh., U.S. B5 112
Toronto Lake, res., Ks., U.S. E7 93
Toro Peak, mtn., Ca., U.S. F5 82
Tororo, Ug. A6 44
Toros Dağları, mts., Tur. H14 4
Torquay (Torbay), Eng., U.K. K9 7
Torquemada, Spain C7 12
Torrance, Ca., U.S. n12 82
Torrance, co., N.M., U.S. C3 108
Torrão, Port. G3 12
Torre Annunziata, Italy I9 14
Torre Baja, Spain E10 12
Torreblanca, Spain E12 12
Torrecilla en Cameros, Spain C9 12
Torre de Moncorvo, Port. D4 12
Torredonjimeno, Spain H8 12
Torrelaguna, Spain E8 12
Torrelavega, Spain B7 12
Torremaggiore, Italy H10 14
Torremolinos, Spain I7 12
Torrens, Lake, l., Austl. F7 50
Torrente, Spain F11 12
Torreón, Mex. E8 62
Torres Novas, Port. F3 12
Torres Strait, strt., Oc. B8 50
Torres Vedras, Port. F2 12
Torrevieja, Spain H11 12
Torridon, Scot., U.K. D7 7
Torriglia, Italy E4 14
Torrijos, Spain F7 12
Torrington, Ct., U.S. B3 84
Torrington, Wy., U.S. D8 127
Torrox, Spain I8 12
Torsby, Swe. F9 6
Tórshavn, Faer. Is. C6 4
Tortola, i., Br. Vir. Is. E15 64
Tortoli, Italy J4 14
Tortona, Italy E3 14
Tortosa, Spain E12 12
Tortue, Île de la, i., Haiti D11 64
Toruń, Pol. B18 8
Toržok, Russia D17 18
Tosa-shimizu, Japan J5 30
Tosa-wan, b., Japan I6 30
Tostado, Arg. B4 56
Totagatic, stm., Wi., U.S. B2 126
Totana, Spain H10 12
Toteng, Bots. F4 44
Tôtes, Fr. C8 10
Tot'ma, Russia B25 18
Totowa, N.J., U.S. B4 107
Totson Mountain, mtn., Ak., U.S. C8 79
Tottenham (part of Alliston Beeton Tecumseth and Tottenham), Ont., Can. C5 73
Tottori, Japan G7 30
Toubkal, Jbel, mtn., Mor. B4 42
Touchet, stm., Wa., U.S. C7 124
Touggourt, Alg. B7 42
Touisset, Ma., U.S. C5 98
Toul, Fr. D12 10
Toulon, Fr. I12 10
Toulon, Il., U.S. B4 90
Toulouse, Fr. I8 10
Tounan, Tai. L9 28
Toungoo, Mya. E4 34
Tourcoing, Fr. B10 10
Tournai, Bel. E3 8
Tournon, Fr. G11 10
Tournus, Fr. F11 10
Tours, Fr. E7 10
Touside, Pic, mtn., Chad D9 42
Toussaint Creek, stm., Oh., U.S. f7 112
Toutle, North Fork, stm., Wa., U.S. C3 124
Tovar, Ven. C7 58
Towanda, Il., U.S. C5 90
Towanda, Ks., U.S. E7 93
Towanda, Pa., U.S. C9 115
Towanda Creek, stm., Pa., U.S. C8 115
Tower City, Pa., U.S. E8 115
Town Creek, Al., U.S. A2 78
Towner, N.D., U.S. A5 111
Towner, co., N.D., U.S. A6 111
Towns, co., Ga., U.S. B3 87
Townsend, De., U.S. C3 85
Townsend, Mt., U.S. D5 103
Townshend Reservoir, res., Vt., U.S. E3 122
Townsville, Austl. C9 50
Towson, Md., U.S. B4 97
Toyama, Japan F10 30
Toyohashi, Japan H10 30
Toyokawa, Japan H10 30
Toyonaka, Japan H8 30
Toyooka, Japan G7 30
Toyota, Japan G10 30
Tozeur, Tun. B7 42
Trabzon, Tur. G15 4
Tracadie, N.B., Can. B5 71
Tracy, N.B., Can. D3 71
Tracy, Que., Can. C4 74
Tracy, Ca., U.S. D3 82
Tracy, Mn., U.S. F3 100
Tracy City, Tn., U.S. D8 119
Tracyton, Wa., U.S. e10 124
Tradewater, stm., Ky., U.S. C2 94
Traer, Ia., U.S. B5 92
Trafford, Pa., U.S. k14 115
Trafford, Lake, l., Fl., U.S. F5 86
Trail, B.C., Can. E9 69
Trail Creek, In., U.S. A4 91
Traill, co., N.D., U.S. B8 111
Trail Ridge, mtn., U.S. F4 87
Tralee, Ire. I3 7
Tranås, Swe. G10 6
Trancas, Arg. B3 56
Trang, Thai. K5 34
Trangan, Pulau, i., Indon. G9 32
Trani, Italy H11 14
Transylvania, co., N.C., U.S. f10 110
Transylvania, hist. reg., Rom. C7 16
Transylvanian Alps see Carpaţii Meridionali, mts., Rom. D8 16
Trapani, Italy K7 14
Trappe, Md., U.S. C5 97
Trapper Peak, mtn., Mt., U.S. E2 103
Traun, Aus. G14 8
Traunstein, Ger. H12 8
Travelers Rest, S.C., U.S. B3 117
Traverse, co., Mn., U.S. E2 100
Traverse, Lake, l., U.S. B9 118
Traverse City, Mi., U.S. D5 99
Tra Vinh, Viet. J9 34
Travis, co., Tx., U.S. D4 120
Travis Air Force Base, mil., Ca., U.S. C2 82
Travnik, Bos. E12 14
Tray Mountain, mtn., Ga., U.S. B3 87
Treasure, co., Mt., U.S. D9 103
Treasure Island Naval Station, mil., Ca., U.S. h8 82
Trecate, Italy D3 14
Trego, co., Ks., U.S. D4 93
Tregosse Islets, is., Austl. C10 50
Tréguier, Fr. D3 10
Treherne, Man., Can. E2 70
Treinta y Tres, Ur. C6 56
Trélazé, Fr. E6 10
Trelew, Arg. E3 56
Trelleborg, Swe. I9 6
Tremblant, Mont, mtn., Que., Can. C3 74
Tremont, Il., U.S. C4 90
Tremont, Pa., U.S. E9 115
Tremonton, Ut., U.S. B3 121
Tremp, Spain C12 12
Trempealeau, Wi., U.S. D2 126
Trempealeau, co., Wi., U.S. D2 126
Trempealeau, stm., Wi., U.S. D2 126
Trenche, stm., Que., Can. B5 74
Trenčín, Slov. G18 8
Trenque Lauquen, Arg. D4 56
Trent, stm., N.C., U.S. B5 110
Trente et un Milles, Lac des, l., Que., Can. C2 74
Trento, Italy C6 14
Trenton, Ont., Can. C7 73
Trenton, Fl., U.S. C4 86
Trenton, Ga., U.S. B1 87
Trenton, Il., U.S. E4 90
Trenton, Mi., U.S. F7 99
Trenton, Mo., U.S. A4 102
Trenton, Ne., U.S. D4 104
Trenton, N.J., U.S. C3 107
Trenton, Oh., U.S. C1 112
Trenton, Tn., U.S. B3 119
Trepassey, Newf., Can. E5 72
Trepassey Bay, b., Newf., Can. E5 72
Tres Arroyos, Arg. D4 56
Tresckow, Pa., U.S. E10 115
Três Corações, Braz. F6 57
Tres Esquinas, Col. G5 58
Três Lagoas, Braz. F3 57
Três Marias, Représa, res., Braz. E6 57
Tres Picos, Cerro, mtn., Arg. D4 56
Três Pontas, Braz. F6 57
Tres Puntas, Cabo, c., Arg. F3 56
Três Rios, Braz. G7 57
Treutlen, co., Ga., U.S. D4 87
Treviglio, Italy D4 14
Treviso, Italy D7 14
Trevor, Wi., U.S. n11 126
Trevorton, Pa., U.S. E8 115
Treynor, Ia., U.S. C2 92
Trezevant, Tn., U.S. A3 119
Triadelphia, W.V., U.S. A4 125
Triadelphia Reservoir, res., Md., U.S. B3 97
Triangle, Va., U.S. B5 123
Tribune, Ks., U.S. D2 93
Trichūr, India G4 37
Tri City, Or., U.S. E3 114
Trident Peak, mtn., Nv., U.S. B3 105
Trieben, Aus. H14 8
Trier, Ger. F6 8
Trieste, Italy D8 14
Trigg, co., Ky., U.S. D2 94
Triglav, mtn., Slo. C8 14
Trigo Mountains, mts., Az., U.S. D1 80
Trikala, Grc. J5 16
Trikora, Puncak, mtn., Indon. F10 32
Tri Lakes, In., U.S. B7 91
Trim, Ire. H6 7
Trimble, Tn., U.S. A2 119
Trimble, co., Ky., U.S. B4 94
Trimont, Mn., U.S. G4 100
Trincheras, Mex. B4 62
Trincomalee, Sri L. H6 37
Třinec, Czech. F18 8
Tring Jonction, Que., Can. C6 74
Trinidad, Bol. F6 54
Trinidad, Col. E7 58
Trinidad, Cuba D8 64
Trinidad, Co., U.S. D6 83
Trinidad, Tx., U.S. C4 120
Trinidad, i., Trin. I17 64
Trinidad and Tobago, ctry., N.A. I17 64
Trinidad Head, c., Ca., U.S. B1 82
Trinity, Al., U.S. A2 78
Trinity, Tx., U.S. D5 120
Trinity, co., Ca., U.S. B2 82
Trinity, co., Tx., U.S. D5 120
Trinity, stm., Ca., U.S. B2 82
Trinity, stm., Tx., U.S. D5 120
Trinity Bay, b., Newf., Can. D5 72
Trinity Islands, is., Ak., U.S. D9 79
Trinity Mountain, mtn., Id., U.S. F3 89
Trinity Mountains, mts., Ca., U.S. B2 82
Trinity Peak, mtn., Nv., U.S. C3 105
Trinity Range, mts., Nv., U.S. C3 105
Trion, Ga., U.S. B1 87
Tripoli, Ia., U.S. B5 92
Trípolis, Grc. L6 16
Tripoli see Ţarābulus, Leb. B4 40
Tripoli see Ţarābulus, Libya B8 42
Tripp, S.D., U.S. D8 118
Tripp, co., S.D., U.S. D6 118
Triumph, La., U.S. E6 95
Trivandrum, India H4 37
Trnava, Slov. G17 8
Troarn, Fr. C6 10
Trobriand Islands, is., Pap. N. Gui. A10 50
Trochu, Alta., Can. D4 68
Trogir, Cro. F11 14
Trois-Pistoles, Que., Can. A8 74
Trois-Rivières, Que., Can. C5 74
Trois-Rivières-Ouest, Que., Can. C5 74
Trojan, Bul. G8 16
Trollhättan, Swe. G9 6
Trombetas, stm., Braz. C7 54
Tromelin, i., Afr. E10 44
Tromsø, Nor. B12 6
Trona, Ca., U.S. E5 82
Tronador, Monte, mtn., S.A. E2 56
Trondheim, Nor. E8 6
Trondheimsfjorden, Nor. E8 6
Tropea, Italy K10 14
Trophy Mountain, mtn., B.C., Can. D8 69
Trotwood, Oh., U.S. C1 112
Troup, co., Ga., U.S. C1 87
Trousdale, co., Tn., U.S. A5 119
Trout, stm., Fl., U.S. m8 86
Trout, stm., Vt., U.S. B3 122
Trout Creek, Ont., Can. B5 73
Trout Creek Pass, Co., U.S. C5 83
Trout Lake, Wa., U.S. D4 124
Trout Lake, l., N.W. Ter., Can. D8 66
Trout Lake, l., Ont., Can. o16 73
Trout Lake, l., Mn., U.S. B6 100
Trout Lake, l., Wi., U.S. B4 126
Troutman, N.C., U.S. B2 110
Trout Peak, mtn., Wy., U.S. B3 127
Trout River, Newf., Can. D2 72
Trouville [-sur-Mer], Fr. C7 10
Troy, Al., U.S. D4 78
Troy, Id., U.S. C2 89
Troy, Il., U.S. E4 90
Troy, Ks., U.S. C8 93
Troy, Mi., U.S. o15 99
Troy, Mo., U.S. C7 102
Troy, Mt., U.S. B1 103
Troy, N.H., U.S. E2 106
Troy, N.Y., U.S. C7 109
Troy, N.C., U.S. B3 110
Troy, Oh., U.S. B1 112
Troy, Pa., U.S. C8 115
Troy, Tn., U.S. A2 119
Troyes, Fr. D11 10
Troy Peak, mtn., Nv., U.S. E6 105
Truchas Peak, mtn., N.M., U.S. B4 108
Trucial States see United Arab Emirates, ctry., Asia D5 46
Truckee, Ca., U.S. C3 82
Truckee, stm., U.S. D2 105
Trujillo, Hond. G4 64
Trujillo, Peru E3 54
Trujillo, Spain F6 12
Trujillo, Ven. C7 58
Truman, Mn., U.S. G4 100
Trumann, Ar., U.S. B5 81
Trumansburg, N.Y., U.S. C4 109
Trumbull, Ct., U.S. E3 84
Trumbull, co., Oh., U.S. A5 112
Trumbull, Mount, mtn., Az., U.S. A2 80
Truro, Eng., U.K. K7 7
Trussville, Al., U.S. B3 78

Name | Map Ref | Page
Trustom Pond, l., R.I., U.S. G3 116
Truth or Consequences (Hot Springs), N.M., U.S. D2 108
Trutnov, Czech. E15 8
Tryon, N.C., U.S. f10 110
Tržič, Slo. C9 14
Tsala Apopka Lake, l., Fl., U.S. D4 86
Tsaratanana, Madag. E9 44
Tsaratanana, Massif du, mts., Madag. D9 44
Tschida, Lake, res., N.D., U.S. C4 111
Tshabong, Bots. G4 44
Tshangalele, Lac, l., Zaire D5 44
Tshikapa, Zaire C4 44
Tshofa, Zaire C5 44
Tshuapa, stm., Zaire B4 44
Tsoying, Tai. M9 28
Tsu, Japan H9 30
Tsubame, Japan E11 30
Tsuchiura, Japan F13 30
Tsugaru-kaikyō, strt., Japan A13 30
Tsukumi, Japan I4 30
Tsukushi-sanchi, mts., Japan I3 30
Tsumeb, Nmb. E3 44
Tsuruga, Japan G9 30
Tsuruoka, Japan D12 30
Tsushima, is., Japan H2 30
Tsushima-kaikyō, strt., Japan I2 30
Tsuyama, Japan G7 30
Tual, Indon. G9 32
Tualatin, stm., Or., U.S. h11 114
Tuba City, Az., U.S. A4 80
Tuban, Indon. m16 33a
Tubarão, Braz. B7 56
Ţubruq, Libya B10 42
Tucannon, stm., Wa., U.S. C8 124
Tucano, Braz. F11 54
Tuckahoe, N.Y., U.S. h13 109
Tuckahoe, stm., N.J., U.S. E3 107
Tucker, Ga., U.S. h8 87
Tucker, co., W.V., U.S. B5 125
Tucker Island, i., N.J., U.S. E4 107
Tuckerman, Ar., U.S. B4 81
Tuckernuck Island, i., Ma., U.S. D7 98
Tuckerton, N.J., U.S. D4 107
Tucson, Az., U.S. E5 80
Tucumcari, N.M., U.S. B6 108
Tucumcari Mountain, mtn., N.M., U.S. B6 108
Tucupita, Ven. C11 58
Tucuruí, Braz. D9 54
Tudela, Spain C10 12
Tudmur (Palmyra), Syria B6 40
Tugaloo Lake, res., U.S. B1 117
Tug Fork, stm., U.S. C2 125
Tuguegarao, Phil. p19 32
Tugur, Russia G21 24
Tukangbesi, Kepulauan, is., Indon. G7 32
Tuktoyaktuk, N.W. Ter., Can. C6 66
Tukwila, Wa., U.S. f11 124
Tula, Mex. F10 62
Tula, Russia G20 18
Tulalip Indian Reservation, Wa., U.S. A3 124
Tulancingo, Mex. G10 62
Tulare, Ca., U.S. D4 82
Tulare, co., Ca., U.S. D4 82
Tulare Lake, l., Ca., U.S. D4 82
Tularosa, N.M., U.S. D3 108
Tularosa Mountains, mts., N.M., U.S. D1 108
Tularosa Valley, val., N.M., U.S. E3 108
Tulcán, Ec. G4 58
Tulcea, Rom. D12 16
Tule Lake, sw., Ca., U.S. B3 82
Tule River Indian Reservation, Ca., U.S. E4 82
Tule Valley, val., Ut., U.S. D2 121
Tulia, Tx., U.S. B2 120
Ţūlkarm, Jord. C4 40
Tullahoma, Tn., U.S. B5 119
Tullamore, Ire. H5 7
Tulle, Fr. G8 10
Tullins, Fr. G12 10
Tulsa, Ok., U.S. A6 113
Tulsa, co., Ok., U.S. B6 113
Tuluá, Col. E4 58
Tulum, Mex. G16 62
Tulun, Russia G14 24
Tulungagung, Indon. n15 33a
Tuma, stm., Nic. H5 64
Tumacacori National Monument, Az., U.S. F4 80
Tumaco, Col. G3 58
Tuman-gang, stm., Asia C12 26
Tumany, Russia E25 24
Tumatumari, Guy. E13 58
Tumba, Lac, l., Zaire B3 44
Tumbes, Peru D2 54
Tumble Mountain, mtn., Mt., U.S. E7 103
Tumbler Ridge, B.C., Can. B7 69
Tumen, China C12 26
Tumiritinga, Braz. E8 57
Tumkūr, India F4 37
Tummo, Libya D8 42
Tumsar, India B5 37
Tumuc-Humac Mountains, mts., S.A. C8 54
Tumwater, Wa., U.S. B3 124
Tunbridge Wells, Eng., U.K. J13 7
Tunduru, Tan. D7 44
Tundža, stm., Eur. G10 16
T'ung, stm., Russia D17 24
Tungabhadra, stm., India E4 37
Tungabhadra Reservoir, res., India E4 37
Tungchiang, Tai. M9 28
Tungsha Tao (Pratas Islands), is., Tai. G10 26
Tungshih, Tai. K9 28
Tunica, Ms., U.S. A3 101
Tunica, co., Ms., U.S. A3 101
Tunis, Tun. M5 14
Tunisia, ctry., Afr. B7 42
Tunja, Col. E6 58
Tunkhannock, Pa., U.S. C10 115
Tunk Lake, l., Me., U.S. D4 96
Tunnel Hill, Ga., U.S. B1 87
Tunp Range, mts., Wy., U.S. D2 127
Tununak, Ak., U.S. C6 79
Tunxi, China F7 28
Tuobuja, Russia E18 24
Tuolumne, Ca., U.S. D3 82
Tuolumne, co., Ca., U.S. C4 82
Tuolumne, stm., Ca., U.S. D3 82
Tupã, Braz. F3 57
Tupaciguara, Braz. E4 57
Tupanciretã, Braz. B6 56
Tupelo, Ms., U.S. A5 101
Tupiza, Bol. H5 54
Tupper Lake, N.Y., U.S. A6 109
Tupper Lake, l., N.Y., U.S. A6 109
Túquerres, Col. G4 58
Tura, India H14 38
Tura, Russia E14 24
Turan, Russia G12 24
Turbat, Pak. D1 36
Turbeville, S.C., U.S. D7 117
Turbo, Col. C4 58
Turda, Rom. C7 16
Turgutlu, Tur. K11 16
Turimiquire, Cerro, mtn., Ven. B11 58
Turin see Torino, Italy D2 14
Turkey, ctry., Asia H14 4
Turkey, stm., Ia., U.S. B6 92
Turkey Creek, stm., Ok., U.S. A3 113
Turkey Point, c., Md., U.S. B5 97
Turkmenistan, ctry., Asia I9 22
Turks and Caicos Islands, dep., N.A. D12 64
Turks Islands, is., T./C. Is. D12 64
Turku (Åbo), Fin. F14 6
Turley, Ok., U.S. A6 113
Turlock, Ca., U.S. D3 82
Turnbull, Mount, mtn., Az., U.S. D5 80
Turneffe Islands, is., Belize F4 64
Turner, Or., U.S. C4 114
Turner, co., Ga., U.S. E3 87
Turner, co., S.D., U.S. D8 118
Turners Falls, Ma., U.S. A2 98
Turner Valley, Alta., Can. D3 68
Turnhout, Bel. D4 8
Turnor Lake, l., Sask., Can. m7 75
Turnu-Măgurele, Rom. F8 16
Turpan, China C4 26
Turquino, Pico, mtn., Cuba E9 64
Turrell, Ar., U.S. B5 81
Turret Peak, mtn., Az., U.S. C4 80
Turtle Creek, Pa., U.S. k14 115
Turtle Flambeau Flowage, res., Wi., U.S. B3 126
Turtle Lake, N.D., U.S. B5 111
Turtle Lake, Wi., U.S. C1 126
Turtle Lake, l., Sask., Can. D1 75
Turtle Mountain Indian Reservation, N.D., U.S. A6 111
Turu, stm., Russia D14 24
Turuchan, stm., Russia D11 24
Turuchansk, Russia D11 24
Tuscaloosa, Al., U.S. B2 78
Tuscaloosa, co., Al., U.S. B2 78
Tuscarawas, co., Oh., U.S. B4 112
Tuscarawas, stm., Oh., U.S. B4 112
Tuscarora Indian Reservation, N.Y., U.S. B2 109
Tuscarora Mountain, mtn., Pa., U.S. F6 115
Tuscarora Mountains, mts., Nv., U.S. B5 105
Tuscola, Il., U.S. D5 90
Tuscola, co., Mi., U.S. E7 99
Tuscumbia, Al., U.S. A2 78
Tuskegee, Al., U.S. C4 78
Tusket, stm., N.S., Can. E4 71
Tustumena Lake, l., Ak., U.S. g16 79
Tuticorin, India H5 37
Tutóia, Braz. D10 54
Tuttle, Ok., U.S. B4 113
Tuttle Creek Lake, res., Ks., U.S. C7 93
Tututalak Mountain, mtn., Ak., U.S. B7 79
Tutwiler, Ms., U.S. A3 101
Tuvalu, ctry., Oc. G24 2
Ţuwayq, Jabal, mts., Sau. Ar. D4 46
Tuxedo, N.C., U.S. f10 110
Tuxedo Park, De., U.S. i7 85
Tuxpan, Mex. G7 62
Tuxpan de Rodríguez Cano, Mex. G11 62
Tuxtla Gutiérrez, Mex. I13 62
Túy, Spain C3 12
Tuy Hoa, Viet. H10 34
Tuz Gölü, l., Tur. H14 4
Tuzigoot National Monument, Az., U.S. C4 80
Tuzla, Bos. E2 16
Tveitsund, Nor. G7 6
Tver', Russia E18 18
Tweed, Ont., Can. C7 73
Tweedsmuir Provincial Park, B.C., Can. C4 69
Tweedy Mountain, mtn., Mt., U.S. E4 103
Twelvepole Creek, stm., W.V., U.S. C2 125
Twentymile Creek, stm., W.V., U.S. C3 125
Twentynine Palms, Ca., U.S. E5 82
Twentynine Palms Marine Corps Base, mil., Ca., U.S. E5 82
Twiggs, co., Ga., U.S. D3 87
Twillingate, Newf., Can. D4 72
Twin Buttes, mtn., Or., U.S. C4 114
Twin Buttes Reservoir, res., Tx., U.S. D2 120
Twin City, Ga., U.S. D4 87
Twin Creek, stm., Oh., U.S. C1 112
Twin Falls, Id., U.S. G4 89
Twin Falls, co., Id., U.S. G4 89
Twin Knolls, Az., U.S. m9 80
Twin Lakes, Ga., U.S. F3 87
Twin Lakes, Wi., U.S. F5 126
Twin Lakes, l., Ct., U.S. A2 84
Twin Lakes, l., Ia., U.S. B3 92
Twin Lakes, l., Me., U.S. C4 96
Twin Mountains, mtn., Wy., U.S. E7 127
Twin Peaks, mts., Id., U.S. E4 89
Twin Rivers, N.J., U.S. C4 107
Twinsburg, Oh., U.S. A4 112
Twin Valley, Mn., U.S. C2 100
Twisp, Wa., U.S. A5 124
Two Harbors, Mn., U.S. C7 100
Two Hills, Alta., Can. C5 68
Two Mile Beach, N.J., U.S. F3 107
Two Rivers, Wi., U.S. D6 126
Two Rivers, North Branch, stm., Mn., U.S. B2 100
Two Rivers, South Branch, stm., Mn., U.S. B2 100
Tybee Island, Ga., U.S. D6 87
Tychy, Pol. E18 8
Tygart Lake, res., W.V., U.S. B5 125
Tygart River, Falls of the, wtfl, W.V., U.S. k10 125
Tygart Valley, stm., W.V., U.S. B4 125
Tyger, stm., S.C., U.S. B4 117
Tyler, Mn., U.S. F2 100
Tyler, Tx., U.S. C5 120
Tyler, co., Tx., U.S. D5 120
Tyler, co., W.V., U.S. B4 125
Tyler, Lake, res., Tx., U.S. C5 120
Tyler Branch, stm., Vt., U.S. B3 122
Tyler Heights, W.V., U.S. C3 125
Tylertown, Ms., U.S. D3 101
Tymochtee Creek, stm., Oh., U.S. B2 112
Tyndall, S.D., U.S. E8 118
Tyndall Air Force Base, mil., Fl., U.S. u16 86
Tyonek, Ak., U.S. C9 79
Tyre see Şūr, Leb. C4 40
Tyrma, Russia G20 24
Tyrone, N.M., U.S. E1 108
Tyrone, Ok., U.S. e9 113
Tyrone, Pa., U.S. E5 115
Tyronza, Ar., U.S. B5 81
Tyrrell, co., N.C., U.S. B6 110
Tyrrhenian Sea (Mare Tirreno), Eur. I6 14
Tysse, Nor. F5 6
Tzaneen, S. Afr. F6 44

U

Uatumã, stm., Braz. D7 54
Uaupés, Braz. D5 54
Ubá, Braz. F7 57
Ubangi (Oubangui), stm., Afr. H9 42
Ube, Japan I4 30
Úbeda, Spain G8 12
Uberaba, Braz. E5 57
Uberlândia, Braz. E4 57
Ubly, Mi., U.S. E8 99
Ubon Ratchathani, Thai. G8 34
Ubundi, Zaire B5 44
Učami, Russia E13 24
Ucayali, stm., Peru E4 54
Uchiura-wan, b., Japan q18 30a
Ucluelet, B.C., Can. E5 69
Ucon, Id., U.S. F7 89
Uda, stm., Russia G13 24
Uda, stm., Russia G20 24
Udaipur, India H5 38
Udall, Ks., U.S. E6 93
Uddevalla, Swe. G8 6
Udgīr, India C4 37
Udine, Italy C8 14
Udipi, India F3 37
Udon Thani, Thai. F7 34
Udskaja Guba, b., Russia G21 24
Udža, Russia C17 24
Ueckermünde, Ger. B14 8
Ueda, Japan F11 30
Uele, stm., Zaire H10 42
Uelen, Russia D31 24
Uelzen, Ger. C10 8
Ueno, Japan H9 30
Uere, stm., Zaire H11 42
Ufa, Russia G9 22
Uganda, ctry., Afr. A6 44
Ugashik Lakes, l., Ak., U.S. D8 79
Ugine, Fr. G13 10
Uglegorsk, Russia H22 24
Uglič, Russia D21 18
Uhrichsville, Oh., U.S. B4 112
Uíge, Ang. C3 44
Uinta, co., Wy., U.S. E2 127
Uinta, stm., Ut., U.S. C5 121
Uintah, co., Ut., U.S. D6 121
Uintah and Ouray Indian Reservation, Ut., U.S. C5 121
Uinta Mountains, mts., Ut., U.S. C5 121
Uitenhage, S. Afr. H5 44
Uivak, Cape, c., Newf., Can. f9 72
Ujandina, stm., Russia D22 24
Uji, Japan H8 30
Ujiji, Tan. B5 44
Ujjain, India I6 38
Ujungpandang, Indon. G6 32
Uka, Russia F26 24
Ukiah, Ca., U.S. C2 82
Ukraine, ctry., Eur. H4 22
Ulaanbaatar (Ulan Bator), Mong. B8 26
Ulaangom, Mong. B5 26
Ulak Island, i., Ak., U.S. E4 79
Ulan Bator see Ulaanbaatar, Mong. B8 26
Ulan-Ude, Russia G15 24
Ulhāsnagar, India C2 37
Uliastaj, Mong. B6 26
Ulindi, stm., Zaire B5 44
Ulja, Russia F22 24
Uljanovsk, Russia G7 22
Ullapool, Scot., U.K. D7 7
Ullŭng-do, i., S. Kor. D13 26
Ulm, Ger. G10 8
Ulsan, S. Kor. D12 26
Ulster, co., N.Y., U.S. D6 109
Ulster, hist. reg., Eur. G5 7
Ulu, Russia E19 24
Ulubat Gölü, l., Tur. I12 16
Ulungur Hu, l., China B4 26
Ulysses, Ks., U.S. E2 93
Umag, Cro. D8 14
Uman', Ukr. H4 22
Umanak, Grnld. B22 66
Umanak Fjord, Grnld. B22 66
Umatilla, Fl., U.S. D5 86
Umatilla, Or., U.S. B7 114
Umatilla, co., Or., U.S. B8 114
Umatilla, stm., Or., U.S. B7 114
Umatilla Indian Reservation, Or., U.S. B8 114
Umbagog Lake, l., U.S. A4 106
Umcolcus Lake, l., Me., U.S. B4 96
Umeå, Swe. E13 6
Umm Durmān (Omdurman), Sudan E12 42
Umnak Island, i., Ak., U.S. E6 79
Umnäs, Swe. D11 6
Umpqua, stm., Or., U.S. D3 114
Umsaskis Lake, l., Me., U.S. B3 96
Umtata, S. Afr. H5 44
Umzinto, S. Afr. H6 44
Unadilla, Ga., U.S. D3 87
Unadilla, stm., N.Y., U.S. C5 109
Unalakleet, Ak., U.S. C7 79
Unalaska Island, i., Ak., U.S. E6 79
'Unayzah, Sau. Ar. C3 46
Uncasville, Ct., U.S. D7 84
Uncompahgre, stm., Co., U.S. C3 83
Uncompahgre Mountains, mts., Co., U.S. C3 83
Uncompahgre Peak, mtn., Co., U.S. C3 83
Underwood, Al., U.S. B3 78
Underwood, N.D., U.S. B4 111
Ungava, Péninsule d', pen., Que., Can. g12 74
Ungava Bay, b., Can. E19 66
União dos Palmares, Braz. E11 54
Unicoi, Tn., U.S. C11 119
Unicoi, co., Tn., U.S. C11 119
Unicoi Mountains, mts., U.S. D9 119
Unimak Island, i., Ak., U.S. D7 79
Unimak Pass, strt., Ak., U.S. E6 79
Union, Ky., U.S. k13 94
Union, Ms., U.S. C4 101
Union, Mo., U.S. C6 102
Union, Or., U.S. B9 114
Union, S.C., U.S. B4 117
Union, Wa., U.S. B2 124
Union, co., Ar., U.S. D3 81
Union, co., Fl., U.S. B4 86
Union, co., Ga., U.S. B2 87
Union, co., Il., U.S. F4 90
Union, co., In., U.S. E8 91
Union, co., Ia., U.S. C3 92
Union, co., Ky., U.S. C2 94
Union, co., La., U.S. B3 95
Union, co., Ms., U.S. A4 101
Union, co., N.J., U.S. B4 107
Union, co., N.M., U.S. A6 108
Union, co., N.C., U.S. B2 110
Union, co., Oh., U.S. B2 112
Union, co., Or., U.S. B8 114
Union, co., Pa., U.S. E7 115
Union, co., S.C., U.S. B4 117
Union, co., S.D., U.S. E9 118
Union, co., Tn., U.S. C10 119
Union, West Branch, stm., Me., U.S. D4 96
Union Beach, N.J., U.S. C4 107
Union Bridge, Md., U.S. A3 97
Union City, Ca., U.S. h8 82
Union City, Ga., U.S. C2 87
Union City, In., U.S. D8 91
Union City, Mi., U.S. F5 99
Union City, N.J., U.S. h8 107
Union City, Oh., U.S. B1 112
Union City, Ok., U.S. B4 113
Union City, Pa., U.S. C2 115
Union City, Tn., U.S. A2 119
Union Flat Creek, stm., Wa., U.S. C8 124
Union Gap, Wa., U.S. C5 124
Union Grove, Wi., U.S. F5 126
Union Lake, l., N.J., U.S. E2 107
Union Pier, Mi., U.S. G4 99
Union Point, Ga., U.S. C3 87
Union Springs, Al., U.S. C4 78
Uniontown, Al., U.S. C2 78
Uniontown, Ky., U.S. C2 94
Uniontown, Oh., U.S. B4 112
Uniontown, Pa., U.S. G2 115
Union Village, R.I., U.S. B3 116
Union Village Reservoir, res., Vt., U.S. D4 122
Unionville, Ct., U.S. B4 84
Unionville, Mo., U.S. A4 102
United Arab Emirates, ctry., Asia D5 46
United Kingdom, ctry., Eur. E7 4
United Nations Headquarters, N.Y., U.S. h12 109
United States, ctry., N.A. D7 76
United States Air Force Academy, mil., Co., U.S. B6 83
United States Military Academy, mil., N.Y., U.S. C6 109
United States Naval Academy, mil., Md., U.S. C4 97
Unity Reservoir, res., Or., U.S. C8 114
University City, Mo., U.S. C7 102
University Heights, Ia., U.S. C6 92
University Heights, Oh., U.S. h9 112
University Park, Ia., U.S. C5 92
University Park, N.M., U.S. E3 108
University Park, Tx., U.S. n10 120
University Place, Wa., U.S. f10 124
Unnão, India G9 38
Uozu, Japan F10 30
Upata, Ven. C11 58
Upemba, Lac, l., Zaire C5 44
Upernavik, Grnld. B21 66
Upington, S. Afr. G4 44
Upland, Ca., U.S. E5 82
Upland, In., U.S. D7 91
Upleta, India J4 38
Upolu Point, c., Hi., U.S. C6 88
Upper Ammonoosuc, stm., N.H., U.S. A4 106
Upper Arlington, Oh., U.S. B2 112
Upper Arrow Lake, l., B.C., Can. F9 66
Upper Arrow Lake, res., B.C., Can. D9 69
Upperco, Md., U.S. A4 97
Upper Darby, Pa., U.S. G11 115
Upper Greenwood Lake, N.J., U.S. A4 107
Upper Humber, stm., Newf., Can. D3 72
Upper Iowa, stm., Ia., U.S. A5 92
Upper Island Cove, Newf., Can. E5 72
Upper Kapuas Mountains, mts., Asia E5 32
Upper Klamath Lake, l., Or., U.S. E4 114
Upper Marlboro, Md., U.S. C4 97
Upper New York Bay, b., U.S. k8 107
Upper Red Lake, l., Mn., U.S. B4 100
Upper Saddle River, N.J., U.S. A4 107
Upper Sandusky, Oh., U.S. B2 112
Upper Sheila [Haut Sheila], N.B., Can. B5 71
Upper Volta see Burkina Faso, ctry., Afr. F5 42
Uppsala, Swe. G11 6
Upright, Cape, c., Ak., U.S. C5 79
Upshur, co., Tx., U.S. C5 120
Upshur, co., W.V., U.S. C4 125
Upson, co., Ga., U.S. D2 87
Upton, Que., Can. D5 74
Upton, Ky., U.S. C4 94
Upton, Ma., U.S. B4 98
Upton, Wy., U.S. B8 127
Upton, co., Tx., U.S. D2 120
Uquía, Cerro, mtn., Ven. E11 58
Urabá, Golfo de, b., Col. C4 58
Ural, stm., Asia H8 22
Ural Mountains see Ural'skije gory, mts., Russia F9 22
Ural'sk, Kaz. G8 22
Ural'skije gory (Ural Mountains), mts., Russia F9 22
Urania, La., U.S. C3 95
Urbana, Il., U.S. C5 90
Urbana, Oh., U.S. B2 112
Urbancrest, Oh., U.S. m10 112
Urbandale, Ia., U.S. C4 92
Urbino, Italy F7 14
Urgenč, Uzb. I10 22
Uribe, Col. F5 58
Uribia, Col. B6 58
Urla, Tur. K10 16
Uruaçu, Braz. C4 57
Uruapan [del Progreso], Mex. H8 62
Urubamba, stm., Peru F4 54
Urucuia, stm., Braz. D6 57
Uruguaiana, Braz. B5 56
Uruguay, ctry., S.A. C5 56
Uruguay (Uruguai), stm., S.A. C5 56
Ürümqi, China C4 26
Ur'ung-Chaja, Russia C16 24
Urun-Islāmpur, India D3 37
Urup, Ostrov, i., Russia H23 24
Usa, Japan I4 30
Uşak, Tur. K13 16
Usedom, i., Eur. B14 8
Ushibuka, Japan J3 30
Ushuaia, Arg. G3 56
Usolje-Sibirskoje, Russia G14 24
Usquepaug, R.I., U.S. F3 116
Ussel, Fr. G9 10
Ussuri (Wusuli), stm., Asia B14 26
Ussurijsk, Russia I20 24
Ust'-Barguzin, Russia G15 24
Ust'-Belaja, Russia D28 24
Ust'Čaun, Russia D28 24
Ústí nad Labem, Czech. E14 8
Ust'-Kamčatsk, Russia F26 24
Ust'-Kamenogorsk, Kaz. H10 24
Ust'-Kut, Russia F15 24
Ust'-Maja, Russia E20 24
Ust'-Nera, Russia E22 24
Usu, China C3 26
Usuki, Japan I4 30
Usulután, El Sal. H3 64
Usumacinta, stm., N.A. I14 62
Utah, co., Ut., U.S. C4 121
Utah, state, U.S. D4 121
Utah Lake, l., Ut., U.S. C4 121
Utashinai, Japan p20 30a
Ute Creek, stm., N.M., U.S. A6 108
Ute Mountain Indian Reservation, U.S. D2 83
Ute Reservoir, res., N.M., U.S. B6 108
Utete, Tan. C7 44
Uthai Thani, Thai. G6 34
Utiariti, Braz. F7 54
Utica, Il., U.S. B5 90
Utica, Mi., U.S. F7 99
Utica, Ms., U.S. C3 101
Utica, Ne., U.S. D8 104
Utica, N.Y., U.S. B5 109
Utica, Oh., U.S. B3 112
Utiel, Spain F10 12
Utikuma Lake, l., Alta., Can. B3 68
Utrecht, Neth. C5 8
Utrera, Spain H6 12
Utsunomiya, Japan F12 30
Uttar Pradesh, state, India G8 38
Uusikaupunki (Nystad), Fin. F13 6
Uvá, stm., Col. F8 58
Uvalde, Tx., U.S. E3 120
Uvalde, co., Tx., U.S. E3 120
Uvdal, Nor. F7 6
Uvinza, Tan. C6 44
Uvs Nuur, l., Asia A5 26
Uwajima, Japan I5 30
'Uwaynāt, Jabal al-, mtn., Afr. D10 42
Uwharrie, stm., N.C., U.S. B3 110
Uxbridge, Ma., U.S. B4 98
Uyuni, Bol. H5 54
Uyuni, Salar de, pl., Bol. H5 54

Index

Name — Map Ref — Page

Uzbekistan, state, Asia I10 22
Uzerche, Fr. G8 10
Uzès, Fr. H11 10
Užice, Yugo. F3 16
Uzlovaja, Russia H21 18
Uzunköprü, Tur. H10 16
Užur, Russia F11 24

V

Vaala, Fin. D16 6
Vaasa (Vasa), Fin. E13 6
Vác, Hung. H19 8
Vaca Key, i., Fl., U.S. H5 86
Vacaville, Ca., U.S. C3 82
Vaccarès, Étang de, b., Fr. I11 10
Vach, stm., Russia E9 24
Vacherie, La., U.S. h10 95
Vadsø, Nor. A17 6
Vaduz, Liech. H9 8
Váh, stm., Slov. G18 8
Vaiden, Ms., U.S. B4 101
Vail, Co., U.S. B4 83
Vākhān, stm., Afg. B5 38
Vākhān, reg., Afg. B5 38
Vålådalen, Swe. E9 6
Val-Bélair, Que., Can. n17 74
Valcheta, Arg. E3 56
Valcourt, Que., Can. D5 74
Valdagno, Italy D6 14
Val-David, Que., Can. C3 74
Valdecañas, Embalse de, res., Spain F6 12
Valdemarsvik, Swe. G11 6
Valdepeñas, Spain G8 12
Valderrobres, Spain E12 12
Valders, Wi., U.S. D6 126
Valdés, Península, pen., Arg. E4 56
Valdese, N.C., U.S. B1 110
Valdez, Ak., U.S. C10 79
Val-d'Isère, Fr. G13 10
Valdivia, Chile D2 56
Valdivia, Col. D5 58
Val-d'Or, Que., Can. k11 74
Valdosta, Ga., U.S. F3 87
Vale, Or., U.S. D9 114
Valemount, B.C., Can. C8 69
Valença, Braz. B9 57
Valença, Port. C3 12
Valençay, Fr. E8 10
Valence, Fr. H11 10
Valencia, Spain F11 12
Valencia, Az., U.S. m7 80
Valencia, Ven. C8 58
Valencia, co., N.M., U.S. C3 108
Valencia, Golfo de, b., Spain F12 12
Valencia de Alcántara, Spain F4 12
Valencia de Don Juan, Spain C6 12
Valencia Heights, S.C., U.S. D6 117
Valenciennes, Fr. B10 10
Valentine, Ne., U.S. B5 104
Valenza, Italy D3 14
Valera, Ven. C7 58
Valga, Est. D9 18
Valhalla, N.Y., U.S. D7 109
Valhermoso Springs, Al., U.S. A3 78
Valjevo, Yugo. E3 16
Valkeakoski, Fin. F15 6
Valkenswaard, Neth. D5 8
Valladolid, Mex. G15 62
Valladolid, Spain D7 12
Vall de Uxó, Spain F11 12
Vallecito Reservoir, res., Co., U.S. D3 83
Valle de Guanape, Ven. C10 58
Valle de la Pascua, Ven. C9 58
Valle de Santiago, Mex. G9 62
Valle de Zaragoza, Mex. D7 62
Valledupar, Col. B6 58
Vallée-Jonction, Que., Can. C7 74
Valle Hermoso, Mex. E11 62
Vallejo, Ca., U.S. C2 82
Vallelunga Pratameno, Italy L8 14
Vallenar, Chile B2 56
Valletta, Malta N9 14
Valley, Ne., U.S. C9 104
Valley, co., Id., U.S. E3 89
Valley, co., Mt., U.S. B10 103
Valley, co., Ne., U.S. C6 104
Valley, stm., Man., Can. D1 70
Valley Center, Ks., U.S. E6 93
Valley City, N.D., U.S. C8 111
Valley Cottage, N.Y., U.S. g13 109
Valley East, Ont., Can. p19 73
Valley Falls, Ks., U.S. C8 93
Valley Falls, R.I., U.S. B4 116
Valley Forge, Pa., U.S. o20 115
Valley Mills, Tx., U.S. D4 120
Valley Park, Mo., U.S. f12 102
Valley Springs, S.D., U.S. D9 118
Valley Station, Ky., U.S. g11 94
Valley Stream, N.Y., U.S. n15 109
Valleyview, Alta., Can. B2 68
Valley View, Pa., U.S. E8 115
Valliant, Ok., U.S. D6 113
Vallo della Lucania, Italy I10 14
Valls, Spain D13 12
Vallscreek, W.V., U.S. D3 125
Valmeyer, Il., U.S. E3 90
Valognes, Fr. C5 10
Valparai, India G4 37
Valparaíso, Chile C2 56
Valparaíso, Mex. F8 62
Valparaiso, Fl., U.S. u15 86
Valparaiso, In., U.S. B3 91
Valréas, Fr. H11 10
Vals, Tanjung, c., Indon. G10 32
Valtimo, Fin. E17 6
Val Verda, Ut., U.S. C4 121
Valverde, Dom. Rep. E12 64
Val Verde, co., Tx., U.S. E2 120
Valverde del Camino, Spain H5 12
Van, Tur. H16 4
Van, Tx., U.S. C5 120
Van, W.V., U.S. n12 125
Van Alstyne, Tx., U.S. C4 120
Vanavara, Russia E14 24
Van Buren, Ar., U.S. B1 81
Van Buren, In., U.S. C6 91
Van Buren, Me., U.S. A5 96
Van Buren, Mo., U.S. E6 102
Van Buren, co., Ar., U.S. B3 81
Van Buren, co., Ia., U.S. D6 92
Van Buren, co., Mi., U.S. F4 99
Van Buren, co., Tn., U.S. D8 119
Vance, co., N.C., U.S. A4 110
Vance Air Force Base, mil., Ok., U.S. A3 113
Vanceboro, N.C., U.S. B5 110
Vanceburg, Ky., U.S. B6 94
Vancleave, Ms., U.S. E5 101
Vancouver, B.C., Can. E6 69
Vancouver, Wa., U.S. D3 124
Vancouver, Cape, c., Austl. G3 50
Vancouver Island, i., B.C., Can. E4 69
Vancouver Island Ranges, mts., B.C., Can. D4 69
Vandalia, Il., U.S. E4 90
Vandalia, Mo., U.S. B6 102
Vandenberg Air Force Base, mil., Ca., U.S. E3 82
Vander, N.C., U.S. B4 110
Vanderbilt Peak, mtn., N.M., U.S. E1 108
Vanderburgh, co., In., U.S. H2 91
Vandergrift, Pa., U.S. E2 115
Vanderhoof, B.C., Can. C5 69
Van Diemen Gulf, b., Austl. B6 50
Vänern, l., Swe. G9 6
Vänersborg, Swe. G9 6
Vangaindrano, Madag. F9 44
Van Gölü, l., Tur. H16 4
Vangunu, i., Sol.Is. A11 50
Van Horn, Tx., U.S. o12 120
Van Horne, Ia., U.S. B5 92
Vanier, Ont., Can. h12 73
Vāniyambādi, India F5 37
Vankarem, Russia D30 24
Vankleek Hill, Ont., Can. B10 73
Van Kull, Kill, stm., N.J., U.S. k8 107
Van Lear, Ky., U.S. C7 94
Van Meter, Ia., U.S. C4 92
Vännäs, Swe. E12 6
Vannes, Fr. E4 10
Van Rees, Pegunungan, mts., Indon. F10 32
Vanrhynsdorp, S. Afr. H3 44
Vansant, Va., U.S. e9 123
Vansbro, Swe. F10 6
Vansittart Island, i., N.W. Ter., Can. C16 66
Vanuatu, ctry., Oc. H24 2
Van Vleck, Tx., U.S. r14 120
Van Wert, Oh., U.S. B1 112
Van Wert, co., Oh., U.S. B1 112
Van Zandt, co., Tx., U.S. C5 120
Varades, Fr. E5 10
Vārānasi (Benares), India H10 38
Varaždin, Cro. C11 14
Varazze, Italy E3 14
Varberg, Swe. H9 6
Vardaman, Ms., U.S. B4 101
Vardar (Axiós), stm., Eur. H6 16
Vardø, Nor. A18 6
Varennes, Que., Can. D4 74
Varennes-sur-Allier, Fr. F10 10
Varese, Italy D3 14
Varginha, Braz. F6 57
Varina, Va., U.S. C5 123
Varkaus, Fin. E16 6
Varkhān, stm., Afg. D1 38
Varna, Bul. F11 16
Värnamo, Swe. H10 6
Varnville, S.C., U.S. F5 117
Varzy, Fr. E10 10
Vasai (Bassein), India C2 37
Vashon, Point, c., Wa., U.S. e11 124
Vashon Island, i., Wa., U.S. f11 124
Vass, N.C., U.S. B3 110
Vassar, Mi., U.S. E7 99
Västerås, Swe. G11 6
Västervik, Swe. H11 6
Vasto, Italy G9 14
Vas'ugan, stm., Russia F9 24
Vatican City (Città del Vaticano), ctry., Eur. H7 14
Vatnajökull, Ice. C4 4
Vättern, l., Swe. G10 6
Vaucouleurs, Fr. D12 10
Vaudreuil, Que., Can. D3 74
Vaughan, Ont., Can. D5 73
Vaughn, Mt., U.S. C5 103
Vaughn, N.M., U.S. C4 108
Vaupés (Uaupés), stm., S.A. G7 58
Vauxhall, Alta., Can. D4 68
Växjö, Swe. H10 6
Vazante, Braz. D5 57
V'azemskij, Russia H20 24
V'az'ma, Russia F17 18
V'azniki, Russia E25 18
Veazie, Me., U.S. D4 96
Vechta, Ger. C8 8
Veedersburg, In., U.S. D3 91
Veendam, Neth. B6 8
Vegreville, Alta., Can. C4 68
Vejer de la Frontera, Spain I6 12
Vejle, Den. I7 6
Vela Luka, Cro. G11 14
Velda Rose Estates, Az., U.S. *D4 80
Velenje, Slo. C10 14
Vélez-Málaga, Spain I7 12
Vélez Rubio, Spain H9 12
Velhas, Rio das, stm., Braz. D6 57
Velike Lašče, Slo. D9 14
Velikije Luki, Russia E13 18
Veliko Tărnovo, Bul. F9 16
Vella Lavella, i., Sol.Is. A11 50
Velletri, Italy H7 14
Vellore, India F5 37
Velma, Ok., U.S. C4 113
Velva, N.D., U.S. A5 111
Venado Tuerto, Arg. C4 56
Venango, co., Pa., U.S. D2 115
Venda Nova, Braz. E7 57
Vendeuvre-sur-Barse, Fr. D11 10
Vendôme, Fr. E8 10
Veneta, Or., U.S. C3 114
Venezia (Venice), Italy D7 14
Venezuela, ctry., S.A. B5 54
Venezuela, Golfo de, b., S.A. B7 58
Veniaminof, Mount, mtn., Ak., U.S. D8 79
Venice, Fl., U.S. E4 86
Venice, Il., U.S. E3 90
Venice, Gulf of, b., Eur. D7 14
Venice see Venezia, Italy D7 14
Vénissieux, Fr. G11 10
Venlo, Neth. D6 8
Venosa, Italy I10 14
Ventanas, Ec. H3 58
Ventnor City, N.J., U.S. E4 107
Ventspils, Lat. D4 18
Ventuari, stm., Ven. E9 58
Ventura (San Buenaventura), Ca., U.S. E4 82
Ventura, co., Ca., U.S. E4 82
Venustiano Carranza, Mex. I13 62
Vera, Spain H10 12
Veracruz [Llave], Mex. H11 62
Verāval, India J4 38
Verbania, Italy D3 14
Vercelli, Italy D3 14
Verchères, Que., Can. D4 74
Verchn'aja Amga, Russia F19 24
Verchneimbatskoje, Russia E11 24
Verchojansk, Russia D20 24
Verchojanskij Chrebet, mts., Russia D19 24
Verda, Ky., U.S. D6 94
Verde, stm., Az., U.S. C4 80
Verden, Ger. C9 8
Verdi, Nv., U.S. D2 105
Verdigre, Ne., U.S. B7 104
Verdigris, Ok., U.S. A6 113
Verdigris, stm., U.S. A6 113
Verdi Peak, mtn., Nv., U.S. C6 105
Verdun, Que., Can. q19 74
Verdun, Fr. C12 10
Vereeniging, S. Afr. G5 44
Vergara, Spain B9 12
Vergennes, Vt., U.S. C2 122
Veríssimo, Braz. E4 57
Vermilion, Alta., Can. C5 68
Vermilion, Oh., U.S. A3 112
Vermilion, co., Il., U.S. C6 90
Vermilion, co., La., U.S. E3 95
Vermilion, stm., Alta., Can. C5 68
Vermilion, stm., Il., U.S. C5 90
Vermilion, stm., La., U.S. E3 95
Vermilion, stm., Mn., U.S. B6 100
Vermilion, stm., Oh., U.S. A3 112
Vermilion Bay, b., La., U.S. E3 95
Vermilion Lake, l., Mn., U.S. C6 100
Vermilion Pass, Can. D2 68
Vermillion, S.D., U.S. E9 118
Vermillion, co., In., U.S. E2 91
Vermillion, East Fork, stm., S.D., U.S. D8 118
Vermillion, stm., Que., Can. B4 74
Vermont, Il., U.S. C3 90
Vermont, state, U.S. D3 122
Vermontville, Mi., U.S. F5 99
Vernal, Ut., U.S. C6 121
Verneuil-sur-Avre, Fr. D7 10
Vernon, B.C., Can. D8 69
Vernon, Fr. C8 10
Vernon, Al., U.S. B1 78
Vernon, Tx., U.S. B3 120
Vernon, co., La., U.S. C2 95
Vernon, co., Mo., U.S. D3 102
Vernon, co., Wi., U.S. E3 126
Vernon Hills, Il., U.S. h9 90
Vernonia, Or., U.S. B3 114
Vero Beach, Fl., U.S. E6 86
Véroia, Grc. I6 16
Verona, Ont., Can. C8 73
Verona, Italy D6 14
Verona, Ms., U.S. A5 101
Verona, N.J., U.S. B4 107
Verona, Pa., U.S. k14 115
Verona, Wi., U.S. E4 126
Verret, Lake, l., La., U.S. E4 95
Versailles, Fr. D9 10
Versailles, In., U.S. F7 91
Versailles, Ky., U.S. B5 94
Versailles, Mo., U.S. C5 102
Versailles, Oh., U.S. B1 112
Vert, Cap, c., Sen. F2 42
Vertientes, Cuba D8 64
Vertou, Fr. E5 10
Verviers, Bel. E5 8
Vesoul, Fr. E13 10
Vestal, N.Y., U.S. C4 109
Vestavia Hills, Al., U.S. g7 78
Vestmannaeyjar, Ice. C3 4
Vesuvio, vol., Italy I9 14
Vesuvius see Vesuvio, vol., Italy I9 14
Veszprém, Hung. H17 8
Vetlanda, Swe. H10 6
Vevay, In., U.S. G7 91
Vevey, Switz. F13 10
Veynes, Fr. H12 10
Viadana, Italy E5 14
Vian, Ok., U.S. B7 113
Viana del Bollo, Spain C4 12
Viana do Alentejo, Port. G3 12
Viana do Castelo, Port. D3 12
Viangchan, Laos F7 34
Viareggio, Italy F5 14
Viborg, Den. H7 6
Viborg, S.D., U.S. D8 118
Vibo Valentia, Italy K11 14
Viburnum, Mo., U.S. D6 102
Vic-en-Bigorre, Fr. I7 10
Vicente, Point, c., Ca., U.S. n12 82
Vicenza, Italy D6 14
Vich, Spain D14 12
Vichada, stm., Col. E8 58
Vichy, Fr. F10 10
Vici, Ok., U.S. A2 113
Vicksburg, Mi., U.S. F5 99
Vicksburg, Ms., U.S. C3 101
Vicksburg National Military Park, Ms., U.S. C3 101
Viçosa, Braz. F7 57
Victor, Ia., U.S. C5 92
Victor, N.Y., U.S. C3 109
Victoria, B.C., Can. E6 69
Victoria, Newf., Can. E5 72
Victoria (Xianggang), H.K. M3 28
Victoria, Sey. B11 44
Victoria, Ks., U.S. D4 93
Victoria, Tx., U.S. E4 120
Victoria, Va., U.S. *C4 123
Victoria, state, Austl. G9 50
Victoria, co., Tx., U.S. E4 120
Victoria, Lake, l., Afr. B6 44
Victoria, Mount, mtn., Mya. D2 34
Victoria de las Tunas, Cuba D9 64
Victoria Falls, wtfl, Afr. E5 44
Victoria Harbour, Ont., Can. C5 73
Victoria Island, i., N.W. Ter., Can. B10 66
Victoria Lake, res., Newf., Can. D3 72
Victoria Land, reg., Ant. B28 47
Victoria Nile, stm., Ug. H12 42
Victoria Peak, mtn., Belize F3 64
Victoria Strait, strt., N.W. Ter., Can. C12 66
Victoriaville, Que., Can. C6 74
Victoria West, S. Afr. H4 44
Victorville, Ca., U.S. E5 82
Vičuga, Russia D24 18
Vidalia, Ga., U.S. D4 87
Vidalia, La., U.S. C4 95
Vidisha, India I7 38
Vidor, Tx., U.S. D5 120
Viechtach, Ger. F12 8
Viedma, Arg. E4 56
Viedma, Lago, l., Arg. F2 56
Viella, Spain C12 12
Vienna, Ga., U.S. D3 87
Vienna, Il., U.S. F5 90
Vienna, Mo., U.S. C6 102
Vienna, Va., U.S. B5 123
Vienna, W.V., U.S. B3 125
Vienna see Wien, Aus. G16 8
Vienne, Fr. G11 10
Vientiane see Viangchan, Laos F7 34
Vieques, Isla de, i., P.R. E15 64
Vieremä, Fin. E16 6
Vierwaldstätter See, l., Switz. F15 10
Vierzon, Fr. E9 10
Vieste, Italy H11 14
Vietnam, ctry., Asia B4 32
Vieux Desert, Lac, l., Wi., U.S. B4 126
Vigan, Phil. p19 33b
Vigevano, Italy D3 14
Vignola, Italy E5 14
Vigo, Spain C3 12
Vigo, co., In., U.S. F3 91
Vihti, Fin. F15 6
Vijayawāda, India D6 37
Vijosë (Aóös), stm., Eur. I3 16
Vikajärvi, Fin. C16 6
Viking, Alta., Can. C5 68
Vila Coutinho, Moz. D6 44
Vila do Conde, Port. D3 12
Vila Fontes, Moz. E7 44
Vilafranca del Panadés, Spain D13 12
Vila Franca de Xira, Port. G3 12
Vilanculos, Moz. F7 44
Vila Nova de Famalicão, Port. D3 12
Vila Nova de Foz Côa, Port. D4 12
Vila Nova de Gaia, Port. D3 12
Vila Pery, Moz. E6 44
Vila Real, Port. D4 12
Vilas, co., Wi., U.S. B4 126
Vila Velha, Braz. F8 57
Vila Velha de Ródão, Port. F4 12
Vilhelmina, Swe. D11 6
Vilhena, Braz. F6 54
Vil'kickogo, Proliv, strt., Russia B14 24
Villa Ahumada, Mex. B6 62
Villa Bella, Bol. F5 54
Villablino, Spain C5 12
Villa Bruzual, Ven. C8 58
Villacañas, Spain F8 12
Villacarriedo, Spain B8 12
Villacarrillo, Spain G8 12
Villach, Aus. I13 8
Villacidro, Italy J3 14
Villa Colón (Caucete), Arg. C3 56
Villa del Rosario, Ven. I11 64
Villa de Méndez, Mex. E10 62
Villadiego, Spain C7 12
Villafranca del Bierzo, Spain C5 12
Villafranca de los Barros, Spain G5 12
Villafranca di Verona, Italy D5 14
Villa Frontera, Mex. D9 62
Villagarcía, Spain C3 12
Villa Grove, Il., U.S. D5 90
Villaguay, Arg. C5 56
Villa Hayes, Para. B5 56
Villahermosa, Mex. I13 62
Villajoyosa, Spain G11 12
Villalón de Campos, Spain C6 12
Villalonga, Arg. D4 56
Villalpando, Spain D6 12
Villa María, Arg. C4 56
Villamartín, Spain I6 12
Villa Montes, Bol. H6 54
Villanova Monteleone, Italy I3 14
Villanueva, Col. B6 58
Villanueva de Córdoba, Spain G7 12
Villanueva de la Serena, Spain G6 12
Villanueva de los Infantes, Spain G9 12
Villanueva del Río y Minas, Spain H6 12
Villanueva y Geltrú, Spain D13 12
Villa Park, Il., U.S. k8 90
Villa Pedro Montoya, Mex. G10 62
Villarcayo, Spain C8 12
Villa Rica, Ga., U.S. C2 87
Villarreal, Spain F11 12
Villarrica, Chile D2 56
Villarrobledo, Spain F9 12
Villas, N.J., U.S. E3 107
Villa San Giovanni, Italy K10 14
Villasayas, Spain D9 12
Villa Unión, Arg. B4 56
Villavicencio, Col. E6 58
Villaviciosa de Córdoba, Spain G6 12
Villedieu, Fr. D5 10
Villefort, Fr. H10 10
Villefranche, Fr. G11 10
Villefranche-de-Rouergue, Fr. H9 10
Villena, Spain G11 12
Villeneuve-de-Berg, Fr. H11 10
Villeneuve-Saint-Georges, Fr. D9 10
Villeneuve-sur-Lot, Fr. H7 10
Ville Platte, La., U.S. D3 95
Villers-Bocage, Fr. C6 10
Villers-Cotterêts, Fr. C10 10
Ville Saint-Georges, Que., Can. C7 74
Villeurbanne, Fr. G11 10
Villingen-Schwenningen, Ger. G8 8
Villisca, Ia., U.S. D3 92
Villupuram, India G5 37
Vilnius, Lith. G8 18
Vilonia, Ar., U.S. B3 81
Vilsbiburg, Ger. G12 8
Vil'uj, stm., Russia E18 24
Vil'ujsk, Russia E18 24
Vimianzo, Spain B2 12
Vimoutiers, Fr. D7 10
Vina, stm., Cam. G8 42
Viña del Mar, Chile C2 56
Vinalhaven, Me., U.S. D4 96
Vinalhaven Island, i., Me., U.S. D4 96
Vinaroz, Spain E12 12
Vincennes, In., U.S. G2 91
Vincent, Al., U.S. B3 78
Vinces, Ec. H3 58
Vindeln, Swe. D12 6
Vindhya Range, mts., India I7 38
Vine Brook, stm., Ma., U.S. g11 98
Vinegar Hill, mtn., Or., U.S. C8 114
Vine Grove, Ky., U.S. C4 94
Vineland, N.J., U.S. E2 107
Vineyard Haven, Ma., U.S. D6 98
Vineyard Sound, strt., Ma., U.S. D6 98
Vinh, Viet. E8 34
Vinhais, Port. D4 12
Vinh Long, Viet. I8 34
Vinita, Ok., U.S. A6 113
Vinkovci, Cro. D2 16
Vinnytsya, Ukr. H3 22
Vinson Massif, mtn., Ant. B4 47
Vinton, Ia., U.S. B5 92
Vinton, La., U.S. D2 95
Vinton, Va., U.S. C3 123
Vinton, co., Oh., U.S. C3 112
Viola, Il., U.S. B3 90
Violet, La., U.S. k12 95
Vipava, Slo. D8 14
Vipiteno, Italy C6 14
Virac, Phil. C7 32
Viramgām, India I5 38
Viranşehir, Tur. A6 40
Virden, Man., Can. E1 70
Virden, Il., U.S. D4 90
Vire, Fr. D6 10
Virgin, stm., U.S. G8 105
Virginia, S. Afr. G5 44
Virginia, Al., U.S. g6 78
Virginia, Il., U.S. D3 90
Virginia, Mn., U.S. C6 100
Virginia, state, U.S. C4 123
Virginia Beach, Va., U.S. D7 123
Virginia City, Nv., U.S. D2 105
Virginia Peak, mtn., Nv., U.S. D2 105
Virgin Islands, dep., N.A. E15 64
Virje, Cro. C11 14
Virkie, Scot., U.K. B11 7
Viroqua, Wi., U.S. E3 126
Virovitica, Cro. D12 14
Virtaniemi, Fin. B17 6
Virudunagar, India H4 37
Vis, Cro. F11 14
Visalia, Ca., U.S. D4 82
Visby, Swe. H12 6
Viscount Melville Sound, strt., N.W. Ter., Can. B10 66
Viseu, Port. E4 12
Vishākhapatnam, India D7 37
Vislinskij Zaliv, b., Eur. A19 8
Visnagar, India I5 38
Vista, Ca., U.S. F5 82
Vistula see Wisła, stm., Pol. A18 8
Vitarte, Peru F3 54
Vitebsk, Bela. F13 18
Viterbo, Italy G7 14
Vitigudino, Spain D5 12
Vitim, Russia F16 24
Vitim, stm., Russia F16 24
Vitória, Braz. F8 57
Vitoria, Spain C9 12
Vitória da Conquista, Braz. C8 57
Vitré, Fr. D5 10
Vitry-le-François, Fr. D11 10
Vitteaux, Fr. E11 10
Vittel, Fr. D12 10
Vittoria, Italy M9 14
Vittorio Veneto, Italy D7 14
Viver, Spain F11 12
Vivero, Spain B4 12
Vivian, La., U.S. B2 95
Viviers, Fr. H11 10
Vivonne, Fr. F7 10
Vizcachas, Meseta de las, plat., Arg. G2 56
Vizcaíno, Desierto de, des., Mex. D3 62
Vizianagaram, India C7 37
Vizille, Fr. G12 10
Vlaardingen, Neth. D4 8
Vladikavkaz, Russia I6 22
Vladimir, Russia E23 18
Vladivostok, Russia E35 128
Vlissingen (Flushing), Neth. D3 8

Name	Map Ref	Page
Vlorë, Alb.	I3	16
Vltava, stm., Czech.	F14	8
Vöcklabruck, Aus.	G13	8
Vodnjan, Cro.	E8	14
Vogelsberg, mts., Ger.	E9	8
Voghera, Italy	E4	14
Vohenstrauss, Ger.	F12	8
Vohibinany, Madag.	E9	44
Vohimarina, Madag.	D10	44
Voi, Kenya	B7	44
Voinjama, Lib.	G4	42
Voiron, Fr.	G12	10
Voitsberg, Aus.	H15	8
Volcano, Hi., U.S.	D6	88
Volchov, Russia	B15	18
Volda, Nor.	E6	6
Volga, S.D., U.S.	C9	118
Volga, stm., Russia	H7	22
Volgograd (Stalingrad), Russia	H6	22
Volkovysk, Bela.	H7	18
Voločanka, Russia	C12	24
Vologda, Russia	B22	18
Volokolamsk, Russia	E18	18
Vólos, Grc.	J6	16
Volta, Lake, res., Ghana	G5	42
Volta Blanche (White Volta), stm., Afr.	F5	42
Volta Noire (Black Volta), stm., Afr.	F6	42
Volta Redonda, Braz.	G6	57
Volterra, Italy	F5	14
Volusia, co., Fl., U.S.	C5	86
Volžskij, Russia	H6	22
Von Frank Mountain, mtn., Ak., U.S.	C9	79
Vonore, Tn., U.S.	D9	119
Voriai Sporádhes, is., Grc.	J7	16
Voronež, Russia	G5	22
Voronezh see Voronež, Russia	G5	22
Vosges, mts., Fr.	D14	10
Voskresensk, Russia	F21	18
Voss, Nor.	F6	6
Vostočno-Sibirskoje More (East Siberian Sea), Russia	C25	24
Vostočnyj Sajan, mts., Russia	G13	24
Votkinsk, Russia	F8	22
Votuporanga, Braz.	F4	57
Vouziers, Fr.	C11	10
Voyageurs National Park, Mn., U.S.	B5	100
Vraca, Bul.	F7	16
Vrangel'a, Ostrov, i., Russia	C29	24
Vranje, Yugo.	G5	16
Vrhnika, Slo.	D9	14
Vryburg, S. Afr.	G4	44
Vryheid, S. Afr.	G6	44
Vsevidof, Mount, mtn., Ak., U.S.	E6	79
Vsevoložsk, Russia	A13	18
Vukovar, Cro.	D2	16
Vulcan, Alta., Can.	D4	68
Vung Tau (Cap-St.-Jacques), Viet.	I9	34
Vuoggatjålme, Swe.	C11	6
Vuoksenniska, Fin.	F17	6
Vyborg, Russia	A11	18
Vyška, Russia	D18	18
Vyšnij Voloček, Russia	D17	18
Vysokogornyj, Russia	G21	24

W

Wa, Ghana	F5	42
Waawaa, Puu, mtn., Hi., U.S.	D6	88
Wabana (Bell Island), Newf., Can.	E5	72
Wabasca, Alta., Can.	B4	68
Wabasca, stm., Alta., Can.	f1	68
Wabash, In., U.S.	C6	91
Wabash, co., Il., U.S.	E6	90
Wabash, co., In., U.S.	C6	91
Wabash, stm., U.S.	H2	91
Wabasha, Mn., U.S.	F6	100
Wabasha, co., Mn., U.S.	F6	100
Wabasso, Fl., U.S.	E6	86
Wabasso, Mn., U.S.	F3	100
Wabaunsee, co., Ks., U.S.	D7	93
Wabeno, Wi., U.S.	C5	126
Wabowden, Man., Can.	B2	70
Wabush, Newf., Can.	h8	72
Waccamaw, stm., U.S.	D9	117
Waccamaw, Lake, l., N.C., U.S.	C4	110
Waccasassa Bay, b., Fl., U.S.	C4	86
Wachusett Mountain, mtn., Ma., U.S.	B4	98
Wachusett Reservoir, res., Ma., U.S.	B4	98
Waco, Tx., U.S.	D4	120
Waco Lake, res., Tx., U.S.	D4	120
Waconda Lake, res., Ks., U.S.	C5	93
Waconia, Mn., U.S.	F5	100
Waddeneilanden, is., Neth.	B5	8
Waddenzee, Neth.	B5	8
Waddi, Chappal, mtn., Nig.	G8	42
Waddington, Mount, mtn., B.C., Can.	D5	69
Wadena, Mn., U.S.	D3	100
Wadena, co., Mn., U.S.	D4	100
Wädenswil, Switz.	E15	10
Wadesboro, N.C., U.S.	C2	110
Wādī Ḥalfā', Sudan	D12	42
Wading, stm., N.J., U.S.	D3	107
Wadley, Ga., U.S.	D4	87
Wad Madanī, Sudan	F12	42
Wadmalaw Island, i., S.C., U.S.	F7	117
Wadsworth, Il., U.S.	h9	90
Wadsworth, Nv., U.S.	D2	105
Wadsworth, Oh., U.S.	A4	112
Wagener, S.C., U.S.	D5	117
Wageningen, Neth.	D5	8
Wager Bay, b., N.W. Ter., Can.	C15	66
Wagga Wagga, Austl.	G9	50
Wagin, Austl.	F3	50
Wagner, S.D., U.S.	D7	118
Wagoner, Ok., U.S.	B6	113
Wagoner, co., Ok., U.S.	B6	113
Wagontire Mountain, mtn., Or., U.S.	D7	114
Wągrowiec, Pol.	C17	8
Wah, Pak.	D5	38
Waha, Libya	C9	42
Wahiawa, Hi., U.S.	B3	88
Wahiawa Reservoir, res., Hi., U.S.	g9	88
Wahkiakum, co., Wa., U.S.	C2	124
Wahoo, Ne., U.S.	C9	104
Wahpeton, N.D., U.S.	C9	111
Wahweap Creek, stm., Ut., U.S.	F4	121
Waialua, Hi., U.S.	B3	88
Waialua Bay, b., Hi., U.S.	B3	88
Waianae, Hi., U.S.	B3	88
Waianae Range, mts., Hi., U.S.	f9	88
Waidhofen an der Ybbs, Aus.	H14	8
Waigeo, Pulau, i., Indon.	F9	32
Waihi, N.Z.	B5	52
Waikapu, Hi., U.S.	C5	88
Waikiki Beach, Hi., U.S.	g10	88
Wailua, Hi., U.S.	A2	88
Wailuku, Hi., U.S.	C5	88
Waimanalo, Hi., U.S.	B4	88
Waimanalo Bay, b., Hi., U.S.	g11	88
Waimea, Hi., U.S.	f9	88
Waimea, Hi., U.S.	B2	88
Wainwright, Alta., Can.	C5	68
Wainwright, Ak., U.S.	A8	79
Waipahu, Hi., U.S.	B3	88
Waipio Acres, Hi., U.S.	g9	88
Waipio Peninsula, pen., Hi., U.S.	g10	88
Waipukurau, N.Z.	D6	52
Waite Park, Mn., U.S.	E4	100
Waits, stm., Vt., U.S.	C4	122
Waitsburg, Wa., U.S.	C7	124
Wajir, Kenya	H3	46
Wakarusa, In., U.S.	A5	91
Wakarusa, stm., Ks., U.S.	D8	93
Wakasa-wan, b., Japan	G8	30
Wakatomika Creek, stm., Oh., U.S.	B3	112
Wakayama, Japan	H8	30
Wake, co., N.C., U.S.	B4	110
WaKeeney, Ks., U.S.	C4	93
Wakefield, Que., Can.	D2	74
Wakefield, Ks., U.S.	C6	93
Wakefield, Ma., U.S.	B5	98
Wakefield, Mi., U.S.	n12	99
Wakefield, Ne., U.S.	B9	104
Wakefield, R.I., U.S.	F3	116
Wakefield, Va., U.S.	D6	123
Wake Forest, N.C., U.S.	B4	110
Wake Island, dep., Oc.	E24	2
Wakema, Mya.	F3	34
Wakeman, Oh., U.S.	A3	112
Wakkanai, Japan	n19	30a
Wakulla, co., Fl., U.S.	B2	86
Walbridge, Oh., U.S.	e6	112
Wałbrzych (Waldenburg), Pol.	E16	8
Walcott, Ia., U.S.	C7	92
Walcott, Lake, res., Id., U.S.	G5	89
Walden, Ont., Can.	A3	73
Walden, Co., U.S.	A4	83
Walden, N.Y., U.S.	D6	109
Walden Ridge, mtn., Tn., U.S.	D8	119
Waldheim, Sask., Can.	E2	75
Waldo, Ar., U.S.	D2	81
Waldo, co., Me., U.S.	D3	96
Waldoboro, Me., U.S.	D3	96
Waldo Lake, l., Ma., U.S.	h11	98
Waldo Lake, l., Or., U.S.	D4	114
Waldport, Or., U.S.	C2	114
Waldron, Ar., U.S.	C1	81
Waldron, In., U.S.	F6	91
Waldshut, Ger.	H8	8
Waldwick, N.J., U.S.	A4	107
Wales, ter., U.K.	I9	7
Wales Island, i., N.W. Ter., Can.	C15	66
Waleska, Ga., U.S.	B2	87
Walgett, Austl.	E9	50
Walhalla, N.D., U.S.	A8	111
Walhalla, S.C., U.S.	B1	117
Walhonding, stm., Oh., U.S.	B3	112
Walker, Ia., U.S.	B6	92
Walker, La., U.S.	g10	95
Walker, Mi., U.S.	E5	99
Walker, Mn., U.S.	C4	100
Walker, co., Al., U.S.	B2	78
Walker, co., Ga., U.S.	B1	87
Walker, co., Tx., U.S.	D5	120
Walker, stm., Nv., U.S.	D3	105
Walker Lake, l., Nv., U.S.	E3	105
Walker River Indian Reservation, Nv., U.S.	D3	105
Walkersville, Md., U.S.	B3	97
Walkerton, Ont., Can.	C3	73
Walkerton, In., U.S.	B5	91
Walkertown, N.C., U.S.	A2	110
Walkerville, Mt., U.S.	D4	103
Wall, S.D., U.S.	D3	118
Wallace, Id., U.S.	B3	89
Wallace, N.C., U.S.	B4	110
Wallace, co., Ks., U.S.	D2	93
Wallaceburg, Ont., Can.	E2	73
Wallace Lake, res., La., U.S.	B2	95
Walla Walla, Wa., U.S.	C7	124
Walla Walla, co., Wa., U.S.	C7	124
Walla Walla, stm., U.S.	C7	124
Walled Lake, Mi., U.S.	o15	99
Wallen, In., U.S.	B7	91
Wallenpaupack, Lake, l., Pa., U.S.	D11	115
Waller, Tx., U.S.	q14	120
Waller, co., Tx., U.S.	E4	120
Wallingford, Ct., U.S.	D4	84
Wallingford, Vt., U.S.	E3	122
Wallington, N.J., U.S.	h8	107
Wallis and Futuna, dep., Oc.	G1	2
Wallkill, N.Y., U.S.	D6	109
Wallkill, stm., N.Y., U.S.	D6	109
Wall Lake, Ia., U.S.	B2	92
Wall Lake, l., Ia., U.S.	B4	92
Walloomsac, stm., U.S.	F2	122
Walloon Lake, l., Mi., U.S.	C6	99
Wallowa, Or., U.S.	B9	114
Wallowa, co., Or., U.S.	B9	114
Wallowa Mountains, mts., Or., U.S.	B9	114
Wallula, Lake, res., U.S.	C7	124
Wallum Lake, l., U.S.	A1	116
Walnut, Il., U.S.	B4	90
Walnut, Ia., U.S.	C2	92
Walnut, stm., Ks., U.S.	E6	93
Walnut Canyon National Monument, Az., U.S.	B4	80
Walnut Cove, N.C., U.S.	A2	110
Walnut Creek, Ca., U.S.	h8	82
Walnut Creek, stm., Ks., U.S.	D4	93
Walnut Grove, Al., U.S.	A3	78
Walnut Grove, Mn., U.S.	F3	100
Walnutport, Pa., U.S.	E10	115
Walnut Ridge, Ar., U.S.	A5	81
Walpole, Ma., U.S.	B5	98
Walpole, N.H., U.S.	D2	106
Walsall, Eng., U.K.	I11	7
Walsenburg, Co., U.S.	D6	83
Walsh, Co., U.S.	D8	83
Walsh, co., N.D., U.S.	A8	111
Walsrode, Ger.	C9	8
Walterboro, S.C., U.S.	F6	117
Walter F. George Dam, U.S.	D4	78
Walter F. George Lake, res., U.S.	D4	78
Walters, Ok., U.S.	C3	113
Walthall, co., Ms., U.S.	D3	101
Waltham, Ma., U.S.	B5	98
Walthill, Ne., U.S.	B9	104
Walthourville, Ga., U.S.	E5	87
Walton, In., U.S.	C5	91
Walton, Ky., U.S.	B5	94
Walton, N.Y., U.S.	C5	109
Walton, co., Fl., U.S.	u15	86
Walton, co., Ga., U.S.	C3	87
Walvis Bay, Nam.	F2	44
Walworth, Wi., U.S.	F5	126
Walworth, co., S.D., U.S.	B5	118
Walworth, co., Wi., U.S.	F5	126
Wamac, Il., U.S.	E4	90
Wamba, stm., Afr.	C3	44
Wamego, Ks., U.S.	C7	93
Wamesit, Ma., U.S.	A5	98
Wamsutter, Wy., U.S.	E5	127
Wanaka, N.Z.	F2	52
Wanamingo, Mn., U.S.	F6	100
Wanapum Dam, Wa., U.S.	C6	124
Wanapum Lake, res., Wa., U.S.	B6	124
Wanaque, N.J., U.S.	A4	107
Wanaque Reservoir, res., N.J., U.S.	A4	107
Wanatah, In., U.S.	B4	91
Wanchese, N.C., U.S.	B7	110
Wando, stm., S.C., U.S.	F8	117
Wando Woods, S.C., U.S.	k11	117
Wanganui, N.Z.	C5	52
Wanganui, stm., N.Z.	C5	52
Wangaratta, Austl.	G9	50
Wangen [im Allgäu], Ger.	H9	8
Wangpan Yang, b., China	E10	28
Wānkāner, India	I4	38
Wanxian, China	E8	26
Wapakoneta, Oh., U.S.	B1	112
Wapato, Wa., U.S.	C5	124
Wapawekka Lake, l., Sask., Can.	C3	75
Wapello, Ia., U.S.	C6	92
Wapello, co., Ia., U.S.	C5	92
Wapiti, stm., Can.	B1	68
Wappapello, Lake, res., Mo., U.S.	D7	102
Wappingers Falls, N.Y., U.S.	D7	109
Wapsipinicon, stm., Ia., U.S.	B6	92
War, W.V., U.S.	D3	125
Waramaug, Lake, l., Ct., U.S.	C2	84
Warangal, India	C5	37
Warden, Wa., U.S.	C6	124
Wardha, India	B5	37
Ward Mountain, mtn., Mt., U.S.	D2	103
Ware, Ma., U.S.	B3	98
Ware, co., Ga., U.S.	E4	87
Ware, stm., Ma., U.S.	B3	98
War Eagle Mountain, mtn., Id., U.S.	G2	89
Wareham, Ma., U.S.	C6	98
Warehouse Point, Ct., U.S.	B5	84
Waren, Ger.	B12	8
Warendorf, Ger.	D7	8
Ware Shoals, S.C., U.S.	C3	117
Warfield, B.C., Can.	E9	69
Warminster, Eng., U.K.	J10	7
Warminster, Pa., U.S.	F11	115
Warm Springs Indian Reservation, Or., U.S.	C5	114
Warm Springs Reservoir, res., Or., U.S.	D8	114
Warnemünde, Ger.	A12	8
Warner, N.H., U.S.	D3	106
Warner, Ok., U.S.	B6	113
Warner, stm., N.H., U.S.	D3	106
Warner Mountains, mts., Ca., U.S.	B3	82
Warner Peak, mtn., Or., U.S.	E7	114
Warner Robins, Ga., U.S.	D3	87
Warr Acres, Ok., U.S.	B4	113
Warren, Ar., U.S.	D3	81
Warren, Il., U.S.	A4	90
Warren, In., U.S.	C7	91
Warren, Ma., U.S.	B3	98
Warren, Mi., U.S.	F7	99
Warren, Mn., U.S.	B2	100
Warren, Oh., U.S.	A5	112
Warren, Or., U.S.	B4	114
Warren, Pa., U.S.	C3	115
Warren, R.I., U.S.	D5	116
Warren, Vt., U.S.	C3	122
Warren, co., Ga., U.S.	C4	87
Warren, co., Il., U.S.	C3	90
Warren, co., In., U.S.	D3	91
Warren, co., Ia., U.S.	C4	92
Warren, co., Ky., U.S.	C3	94
Warren, co., Ms., U.S.	C3	101
Warren, co., Mo., U.S.	C6	102
Warren, co., N.J., U.S.	B3	107
Warren, co., N.Y., U.S.	B7	109
Warren, co., N.C., U.S.	A4	110
Warren, co., Oh., U.S.	C1	112
Warren, co., Pa., U.S.	C3	115
Warren, co., Tn., U.S.	D8	119
Warren, co., Va., U.S.	B4	123
Warren, stm., U.S.	D5	116
Warren Park, In., U.S.	k10	91
Warren Peaks, mts., Wy., U.S.	B8	127
Warrensburg, Il., U.S.	D4	90
Warrensburg, Mo., U.S.	C4	102
Warrensburg, N.Y., U.S.	B7	109
Warrensville Heights, Oh., U.S.	h9	112
Warrenton, S. Afr.	G4	44
Warrenton, Ga., U.S.	C4	87
Warrenton, Mo., U.S.	C6	102
Warrenton, N.C., U.S.	A4	110
Warrenton, Or., U.S.	A3	114
Warrenton, Va., U.S.	B5	123
Warrenville, Il., U.S.	k8	90
Warrenville, S.C., U.S.	D4	117
Warri, Nig.	G7	42
Warrick, co., In., U.S.	H3	91
Warrina, Austl.	E7	50
Warrington, Eng., U.K.	H10	7
Warrington, Fl., U.S.	u14	86
Warrior, Al., U.S.	B3	78
Warrior Lake, res., Al., U.S.	C2	78
Warrnambool, Austl.	G8	50
Warroad, Mn., U.S.	B3	100
Warsaw, Il., U.S.	C2	90
Warsaw, In., U.S.	B6	91
Warsaw, Ky., U.S.	B5	94
Warsaw, Mo., U.S.	C4	102
Warsaw, N.Y., U.S.	C2	109
Warsaw, N.C., U.S.	B4	110
Warsaw, Va., U.S.	C6	123
Warsaw see Warszawa, Pol.	C21	8
Warszawa (Warsaw), Pol.	C21	8
Warta, stm., Pol.	C15	8
Wartburg, Tn., U.S.	C9	119
Warthe see Warta, stm., Pol.	C15	8
Warwick, Austl.	E10	50
Warwick, Que., Can.	D6	74
Warwick, Eng., U.K.	I11	7
Warwick, Md., U.S.	B6	97
Warwick, N.Y., U.S.	D6	109
Warwick, R.I., U.S.	D4	116
Wasaga Beach, Ont., Can.	C4	73
Wasatch, co., Ut., U.S.	C4	121
Wasco, Ca., U.S.	E4	82
Wasco, co., Or., U.S.	B5	114
Waseca, Mn., U.S.	F5	100
Waseca, co., Mn., U.S.	F5	100
Washakie, co., Wy., U.S.	C5	127
Washakie Needles, mts., Wy., U.S.	C3	127
Washburn, Il., U.S.	C4	90
Washburn, Ia., U.S.	B5	92
Washburn, Me., U.S.	B4	96
Washburn, N.D., U.S.	B5	111
Washburn, Wi., U.S.	B3	126
Washburn, co., Wi., U.S.	C2	126
Washburn, Mount, mtn., Wy., U.S.	B2	127
Washington, D.C., U.S.	C3	97
Washington, Ga., U.S.	C4	87
Washington, Il., U.S.	C4	90
Washington, In., U.S.	G3	91
Washington, Ia., U.S.	C6	92
Washington, Ks., U.S.	C6	93
Washington, Ky., U.S.	B6	94
Washington, La., U.S.	D3	95
Washington, Ms., U.S.	D2	101
Washington, Mo., U.S.	C6	102
Washington, N.J., U.S.	B3	107
Washington, N.C., U.S.	B5	110
Washington, Pa., U.S.	F1	115
Washington, Ut., U.S.	F2	121
Washington, co., Al., U.S.	D1	78
Washington, co., Ar., U.S.	A1	81
Washington, co., Co., U.S.	B7	83
Washington, co., Fl., U.S.	u16	86
Washington, co., Ga., U.S.	C4	87
Washington, co., Id., U.S.	E2	89
Washington, co., Il., U.S.	E4	90
Washington, co., In., U.S.	G5	91
Washington, co., Ia., U.S.	C6	92
Washington, co., Ks., U.S.	C6	93
Washington, co., Ky., U.S.	C4	94
Washington, co., La., U.S.	D5	95
Washington, co., Me., U.S.	D5	96
Washington, co., Md., U.S.	A2	97
Washington, co., Mn., U.S.	E6	100
Washington, co., Ms., U.S.	B3	101
Washington, co., Mo., U.S.	D7	102
Washington, co., Ne., U.S.	C9	104
Washington, co., N.Y., U.S.	B7	109
Washington, co., N.C., U.S.	B6	110
Washington, co., Oh., U.S.	C4	112
Washington, co., Ok., U.S.	A6	113
Washington, co., Or., U.S.	B3	114
Washington, co., Pa., U.S.	F1	115
Washington, co., R.I., U.S.	E2	116
Washington, co., Tn., U.S.	C11	119
Washington, co., Tx., U.S.	D4	120
Washington, co., Ut., U.S.	F2	121
Washington, co., Vt., U.S.	C3	122
Washington, co., Va., U.S.	f9	123
Washington, co., Wi., U.S.	E5	126
Washington, state, U.S.	B5	124
Washington, Lake, l., Fl., U.S.	D6	86
Washington, Lake, l., Mn., U.S.	E4	100
Washington, Lake, l., Ms., U.S.	B3	101
Washington, Lake, l., Wa., U.S.	e11	124
Washington, Mount, mtn., N.H., U.S.	B4	106
Washington Court House, Oh., U.S.	C2	112
Washington Island, i., Wi., U.S.	C7	126
Washington Park, Il., U.S.	E3	90
Washington Terrace, Ut., U.S.	B4	121
Washita, co., Ok., U.S.	B2	113
Washita, stm., Ok., U.S.	C4	113
Washoe, co., Nv., U.S.	C2	105
Washoe City, Nv., U.S.	D2	105
Washougal, Wa., U.S.	D3	124
Washow Bay, b., Man., Can.	D3	70
Washtenaw, co., Mi., U.S.	F7	99
Wasilla, Ak., U.S.	C10	79
Wasior, Indon.	F9	32
Waskom, Tx., U.S.	C5	120
Waspán, Nic.	G5	64
Wasque Point, c., Ma., U.S.	D7	98
Wassen, Switz.	F15	10
Wassookeag, Lake, l., Me., U.S.	C3	96
Wassuk Range, mts., Nv., U.S.	E3	105
Wataga, Il., U.S.	B3	90
Watauga, co., N.C., U.S.	A1	110
Watauga, stm., Tn., U.S.	C12	119
Watauga Lake, res., Tn., U.S.	C12	119
Watchaug Pond, l., R.I., U.S.	F2	116
Watch Hill Point, c., R.I., U.S.	G1	116
Watchung, N.J., U.S.	B4	107
Waterbury, Ct., U.S.	C3	84
Waterbury, Vt., U.S.	C3	122
Waterbury Center, Vt., U.S.	C3	122
Waterbury Reservoir, res., Vt., U.S.	C3	122
Wateree, stm., S.C., U.S.	D6	117
Wateree Lake, res., S.C., U.S.	C6	117
Waterford, Ire.	I5	7
Waterford, Ct., U.S.	D7	84
Waterford, N.Y., U.S.	C7	109
Waterford, Pa., U.S.	C2	115
Waterford, Wi., U.S.	F5	126
Waterhen Lake, l., Man., Can.	C2	70
Waterloo, Bel.	E4	8
Waterloo, Ont., Can.	D4	73
Waterloo, Que., Can.	D5	74
Waterloo, Il., U.S.	E3	90
Waterloo, In., U.S.	B7	91
Waterloo, Ia., U.S.	B5	92
Waterloo, N.Y., U.S.	C4	109
Waterloo, Wi., U.S.	E5	126
Waterman, Il., U.S.	B5	90
Waterman Reservoir, res., R.I., U.S.	B3	116
Waterproof, La., U.S.	C4	95
Watersmeet, Mi., U.S.	n12	99
Waterton Lakes National Park, Alta., Can.	E3	68
Watertown, Ct., U.S.	C3	84
Watertown, Ma., U.S.	g11	98
Watertown, N.Y., U.S.	B5	109
Watertown, S.D., U.S.	C8	118
Watertown, Tn., U.S.	A5	119
Watertown, Wi., U.S.	E5	126
Water Valley, Ms., U.S.	A4	101
Waterville, Ks., U.S.	C7	93
Waterville, Me., U.S.	D3	96
Waterville, Mn., U.S.	F5	100
Waterville, N.Y., U.S.	C5	109
Waterville, Oh., U.S.	A2	112
Waterville, Wa., U.S.	B5	124
Watervliet, Mi., U.S.	F4	99
Watervliet, N.Y., U.S.	C7	109
Watford, Ont., Can.	E3	73
Watford City, N.D., U.S.	B2	111
Wathena, Ks., U.S.	C9	93
Watkins, Mn., U.S.	E4	100
Watkins Glen, N.Y., U.S.	C4	109
Watkinsville, Ga., U.S.	C3	87
Watonga, Ok., U.S.	B3	113
Watonwan, co., Mn., U.S.	F4	100
Watonwan, stm., Mn., U.S.	G4	100
Watseka, Il., U.S.	C6	90
Watson Lake, Yukon, Can.	D7	66
Watsontown, Pa., U.S.	D8	115
Watsonville, Ca., U.S.	D3	82
Watts Bar Dam, Tn., U.S.	D9	119
Watts Bar Lake, res., Tn., U.S.	D9	119
Wattsville, S.C., U.S.	B4	117
Wattwil, Switz.	E16	10
Watubela, Kepulauan, is., Indon.	F9	32
Waubaushene, Ont., Can.	C5	73
Waubay, S.D., U.S.	B8	118
Waubay Lake, l., S.D., U.S.	B8	118
Wauchula, Fl., U.S.	E5	86
Wauconda, Il., U.S.	h8	90
Waugh Mountain, mtn., Id., U.S.	D4	89
Waukee, Ia., U.S.	C4	92
Waukegan, Il., U.S.	A6	90
Waukesha, Wi., U.S.	F5	126
Waukesha, co., Wi., U.S.	E5	126
Waukewan, Lake, l., N.H., U.S.	C3	106
Waukomis, Ok., U.S.	A4	113
Waukon, Ia., U.S.	A6	92
Waunakee, Wi., U.S.	E4	126
Wauneta, Ne., U.S.	D4	104
Waungumbaug Lake, l., Ct., U.S.	B6	84
Waupaca, Wi., U.S.	D4	126
Waupaca, co., Wi., U.S.	D5	126
Waupun, Wi., U.S.	E5	126
Wauregan, Ct., U.S.	C8	84
Waurika, Ok., U.S.	C4	113
Waurika Lake, res., Ok., U.S.	C3	113
Wausau, Wi., U.S.	D4	126
Wausau, Lake, res., Wi., U.S.	D4	126
Wauseon, Oh., U.S.	A1	112
Waushara, co., Wi., U.S.	D4	126
Wautoma, Wi., U.S.	D4	126
Wauwatosa, Wi., U.S.	m12	126
Wave Hill, Austl.	C6	50
Waveland, Ms., U.S.	E4	101
Waverley, N.S., Can.	E6	71
Waverly, Il., U.S.	D4	90
Waverly, Ia., U.S.	B5	92
Waverly, Ks., U.S.	D8	93
Waverly, Mn., U.S.	E5	100
Waverly, Mo., U.S.	B4	102
Waverly, Ne., U.S.	D9	104
Waverly, N.Y., U.S.	C4	109
Waverly, Oh., U.S.	C3	112
Waverly, Tn., U.S.	A4	119
Waverly, Va., U.S.	C5	123
Waverly, W.V., U.S.	B3	125
Waverly Hall, Ga., U.S.	D2	87
Wāw, Sudan	G11	42
Wawanesa, Man., Can.	E2	70
Wawasee, Lake, l., In., U.S.	B6	91
Wawayanda Lake, l., N.J., U.S.	A4	107
Wawota, Sask., Can.	H4	75
Waxahachie, Tx., U.S.	C4	120

Name — Map Ref — Page

Waxhaw, N.C., U.S. C2 110
Waycross, Ga., U.S. E4 87
Wayland, Ia., U.S. C6 92
Wayland, Ma., U.S. g10 98
Wayland, Mi., U.S. F5 99
Wayland, N.Y., U.S. C3 109
Waylyn, S.C., U.S. k12 117
Waymart, Pa., U.S. C11 115
Wayne, Mi., U.S. p15 99
Wayne, Ne., U.S. B8 104
Wayne, N.J., U.S. B4 107
Wayne, W.V., U.S. C2 125
Wayne, co., Ga., U.S. E5 87
Wayne, co., Il., U.S. E5 90
Wayne, co., In., U.S. E7 91
Wayne, co., Ia., U.S. D4 92
Wayne, co., Ky., U.S. D5 94
Wayne, co., Mi., U.S. F7 99
Wayne, co., Ms., U.S. D5 101
Wayne, co., Mo., U.S. D7 102
Wayne, co., Ne., U.S. B8 104
Wayne, co., N.Y., U.S. B3 109
Wayne, co., N.C., U.S. B4 110
Wayne, co., Oh., U.S. B4 112
Wayne, co., Pa., U.S. C11 115
Wayne, co., Tn., U.S. B4 119
Wayne, co., Ut., U.S. E4 121
Wayne, co., W.V., U.S. C2 125
Wayne City, Il., U.S. E5 90
Waynesboro, Ga., U.S. C4 87
Waynesboro, Ms., U.S. D5 101
Waynesboro, Pa., U.S. G6 115
Waynesboro, Tn., U.S. B4 119
Waynesboro, Va., U.S. B4 123
Waynesburg, Oh., U.S. B4 112
Waynesburg, Pa., U.S. G1 115
Waynesville, Mo., U.S. D5 102
Waynesville, N.C., U.S. f10 110
Waynesville, Oh., U.S. C1 112
Waynetown, In., U.S. D3 91
Waynewood, Va., U.S. g12 123
Waynoka, Ok., U.S. A3 113
Wayzata, Mn., U.S. n11 100
Wazīrābād, Pak. D6 38
Weakley, co., Tn., U.S. A3 119
Weatherford, Ok., U.S. B3 113
Weatherford, Tx., U.S. C4 120
Weatherly, Pa., U.S. E10 115
Weatogue, Ct., U.S. B4 84
Weaver, Al., U.S. B4 78
Weaver Mountains, mts., Az., U.S. C3 80
Weaverville, Ca., U.S. B2 82
Weaverville, N.C., U.S. f10 110
Webb, Al., U.S. D4 78
Webb, Ms., U.S. B3 101
Webb, co., Tx., U.S. F3 120
Webb City, Mo., U.S. D3 102
Webbers Falls, Ok., U.S. B6 113
Webberville, Mi., U.S. F6 99
Webb Lake, I., Me., U.S. D2 96
Weber, co., Ut., U.S. B4 121
Weber City, Va., U.S. f9 123
Webster, Ma., U.S. B4 98
Webster, N.Y., U.S. B3 109
Webster, Pa., U.S. F2 115
Webster, S.D., U.S. B8 118
Webster, co., Ga., U.S. D2 87
Webster, co., Ia., U.S. B3 92
Webster, co., Ky., U.S. C2 94
Webster, co., La., U.S. B2 95
Webster, co., Ms., U.S. B4 101
Webster, co., Mo., U.S. D5 102
Webster, co., Ne., U.S. D7 104
Webster, co., W.V., U.S. C4 125
Webster City, Ia., U.S. B4 92
Webster Groves, Mo., U.S. f13 102
Webster Reservoir, res., Ks., U.S. C4 93
Webster Springs, W.V., U.S. C4 125
Websterville, Vt., U.S. C4 122
Weddell Sea, Ant. B8 47
Wedgeport, N.S., Can. F4 71
Wedgewood, Mo., U.S. f13 102
Wedowee, Al., U.S. B4 78
Weed, Ca., U.S. B2 82
Weed Heights, Nv., U.S. E2 105
Weedon, Que., Can. D6 74
Weedsport, N.Y., U.S. B4 109
Weedville, Pa., U.S. D5 115
Weehawken, N.J., U.S. h8 107
Weeksbury, Ky., U.S. C7 94
Weeping Water, Ne., U.S. D9 104
Wegscheid, Ger. G13 8
Weiden in der Oberpfalz, Ger. F12 8
Weifang, China D10 26
Weihai, China D11 26
Weilburg, Ger. E8 8
Weilheim, Ger. H11 8
Weimar, Ger. E11 8
Weimar, Tx., U.S. E4 120
Weiner, Ar., U.S. B5 81
Weinheim, Ger. F8 8
Weipa, Austl. B8 50
Weippe, Id., U.S. C3 89
Weir, Ks., U.S. E9 93
Weir, Lake, I., Fl., U.S. C5 86
Weirsdale, Fl., U.S. D5 86
Weirton, W.V., U.S. A4 125
Weiser, Id., U.S. E2 89
Weiser, stm., Id., U.S. E2 89
Weishi, China A3 28
Weissenburg in Bayern, Ger. F10 8
Weissenfels, Ger. D11 8
Weiss Lake, res., U.S. A4 78
Weisswasser, Ger. D14 8
Weiz, Aus. H15 8
Wejherowo, Pol. A18 8
Welch, W.V., U.S. D3 125
Welcome, Mn., U.S. G4 100
Welcome, S.C., U.S. B3 117
Weld, co., Co., U.S. A6 83
Weldon, N.C., U.S. A5 110
Weldon Spring, Mo., U.S. f12 102
Weleetka, Ok., U.S. B5 113
Welkom, S. Afr. G5 44
Welland, Ont., Can. E5 73
Wellesley, Ont., Can. D4 73
Wellesley, Ma., U.S. B5 98
Wellesley Islands, is., Austl. C7 50
Wellford, S.C., U.S. B3 117
Wellington, Ont., Can. D7 73
Wellington, N.Z. D5 52
Wellington, Co., U.S. A5 83
Wellington, Ks., U.S. E6 93
Wellington, Mo., U.S. B4 102
Wellington, Nv., U.S. E2 105
Wellington, Oh., U.S. A3 112
Wellington, Tx., U.S. B2 120
Wellington, Ut., U.S. D5 121
Wellington, Isla, i., Chile F2 56
Wellington Channel, strt., N.W. Ter., Can. A14 66
Wellman, Ia., U.S. C6 92
Wells, Me., U.S. E2 96
Wells, Mi., U.S. C3 99
Wells, Mn., U.S. G5 100
Wells, Nv., U.S. B7 105
Wells, co., In., U.S. C7 91
Wells, co., N.D., U.S. B6 111
Wells, stm., Vt., U.S. C4 122
Wellsboro, Pa., U.S. C7 115
Wellsburg, Ia., U.S. B5 92
Wellsburg, W.V., U.S. A4 125
Wellston, Oh., U.S. C3 112
Wellston, Ok., U.S. B4 113
Wellsville, Ks., U.S. D8 93
Wellsville, Mo., U.S. B6 102
Wellsville, N.Y., U.S. C3 109
Wellsville, Oh., U.S. B5 112
Wellsville, Ut., U.S. B4 121
Wellton, Az., U.S. E1 80
Wels, Aus. G14 8
Welsh, La., U.S. D3 95
Welshpool, Wales, U.K. I9 7
Wembley, Alta., Can. B1 68
Wenatchee, Wa., U.S. B5 124
Wenatchee, stm., Wa., U.S. B5 124
Wenatchee Lake, I., Wa., U.S. B5 124
Wenatchee Mountains, mts., Wa., U.S. B5 124
Wendell, Id., U.S. G4 89
Wendell, N.C., U.S. B4 110
Wendover, Ut., U.S. C1 121
Wenham, Ma., U.S. A6 98
Wenham Lake, I., Ma., U.S. f12 98
Wenona, Il., U.S. B4 90
Wenshan, China C8 34
Wentworth, Lake, I., N.H., U.S. C4 106
Wentzville, Mo., U.S. C7 102
Wenzhou, China G9 28
Weohyakapka, Lake, I., Fl., U.S. E5 86
Wernigerode, Ger. D10 8
Wertheim, Ger. F9 8
Wesel, Ger. D6 8
Weser, stm., Ger. B8 8
Weslaco, Tx., U.S. F4 120
Wesleyville, Newf., Can. D5 72
Wesleyville, Pa., U.S. B2 115
Wessel Islands, is., Austl. B7 50
Wesserunsett Lake, I., Me., U.S. D3 96
Wessington Springs, S.D., U.S. C7 118
Wesson, Ms., U.S. D3 101
West, Tx., U.S. D4 120
West, stm., Ct., U.S. D5 84
West, stm., Ma., U.S. h9 98
West, stm., Vt., U.S. E3 122
West Acton, Ma., U.S. g10 98
West Alexandria, Oh., U.S. C1 112
West Allis, Wi., U.S. m11 126
West Alton, Mo., U.S. f13 102
West Andover, Ma., U.S. A5 98
West Baden Springs, In., U.S. G4 91
West Baton Rouge, co., La., U.S. D4 95
West Bay, b., Fl., U.S. u16 86
West Bay, b., N.C., U.S. B6 110
West Bay, b., Tx., U.S. r15 120
West Bend, Ia., U.S. B3 92
West Bend, Wi., U.S. E5 126
West Bengal, state, India I12 38
West Berlin, N.J., U.S. D3 107
West Billerica, Ma., U.S. f10 98
West Blocton, Al., U.S. B2 78
Westborough, Ma., U.S. B4 98
West Bountiful, Ut., U.S. C4 121
West Boylston, Ma., U.S. B4 98
West Branch, Ia., U.S. C6 92
West Branch, Mi., U.S. D6 99
West Branch Reservoir, res., Ct., U.S. B3 84
West Bridgewater, Ma., U.S. B5 98
Westbrook, Ct., U.S. D6 84
Westbrook, Me., U.S. E2 96
Westbrook, Mn., U.S. F3 100
West Burlington, Ia., U.S. D6 92
West Butte, mtn., Mt., U.S. B5 103
Westby, Wi., U.S. E3 126
West Cache Creek, stm., Ok., U.S. C3 113
West Caldwell, N.J., U.S. B4 107
West Canada Creek, stm., N.Y., U.S. B6 109
West Carroll, co., La., U.S. B4 95
West Carrollton, Oh., U.S. C1 112
West Carthage, N.Y., U.S. B5 109
Westchester, Il., U.S. k9 90
West Chester, Pa., U.S. G10 115
Westchester, co., N.Y., U.S. D7 109
West Chicago, Il., U.S. k8 90
West Chop, c., Ma., U.S. D6 98
West College Corner, In., U.S. E8 91
West Columbia, S.C., U.S. D5 117
West Columbia, Tx., U.S. E5 120
West Concord, Ma., U.S. B5 98
West Concord, Mn., U.S. F6 100
West Concord, N.C., U.S. B2 110
Westconnaug Reservoir, res., R.I., U.S. C2 116
West Cote Blanche Bay, b., La., U.S. E4 95
West Covina, Ca., U.S. m13 82
West Crossett, Ar., U.S. D4 81
West Cumberland, Me., U.S. E2 96
West Dennis, Ma., U.S. C7 98
West Des Moines, Ia., U.S. C4 92
West Elk Mountains, mts., Co., U.S. C3 83
West Elk Peak, mtn., Co., U.S. C3 83
Westerly, R.I., U.S. F1 116
Western Australia, state, Austl. D4 50
Western Desert see Gharbīyah, Aṣ-Ṣaḥrā' al-, des., Egypt C11 42
Western Ghāts, mts., India E3 37
Westernport, Md., U.S. m12 97
Western Sahara, dep., Afr. D3 42
Western Samoa, ctry., Oc. G1 2
Western Springs, Il., U.S. k9 90
Westerstede, Ger. B7 8
Westerville, Oh., U.S. B3 112
West Falkland, i., Falk. Is. G4 56
West Falmouth, Ma., U.S. C6 98
West Fargo, N.D., U.S. C9 111
West Feliciana, co., La., U.S. D4 95
Westfield, N.B., Can. D3 71
Westfield, In., U.S. D5 91
Westfield, Ma., U.S. B2 98
Westfield, N.J., U.S. B4 107
Westfield, N.Y., U.S. C1 109
Westfield, Pa., U.S. C6 115
Westfield, Wi., U.S. E4 126
Westfield, stm., Ma., U.S. B2 98
West Fork, Ar., U.S. B1 81
West Fork, stm., W.V., U.S. B4 125
West Frankfort, Il., U.S. F5 90
West Freehold, N.J., U.S. C4 107
West Friendship, Md., U.S. B4 97
Westgate, Fl., U.S. F6 86
West Grand Lake, I., Me., U.S. C5 96
West Grove, Pa., U.S. G10 115
West Hanover, Ma., U.S. h12 98
West Hartford, Ct., U.S. B4 84
West Haven, Ct., U.S. D4 84
West Hazleton, Pa., U.S. E9 115
West Helena, Ar., U.S. C5 81
West Hill Reservoir, res., Ma., U.S. B4 98
Westhope, N.D., U.S. A4 111
West Indies, is. E12 64
West Island, i., Ma., U.S. C6 98
West Jefferson, N.C., U.S. A1 110
West Jefferson, Oh., U.S. C2 112
West Jordan, Ut., U.S. C3 121
West Kingston, R.I., U.S. F3 116
West Lafayette, In., U.S. D4 91
West Lafayette, Oh., U.S. B4 112
Westlake, La., U.S. D2 95
Westlake, Oh., U.S. h9 112
West Lake, I., Me., U.S. C4 96
Westland, Mi., U.S. F7 99
West Laramie, Wy., U.S. E7 127
West Lawn, Pa., U.S. F10 115
West Lebanon, In., U.S. D3 91
West Liberty, Ia., U.S. C6 92
West Liberty, Ky., U.S. C6 94
West Liberty, Oh., U.S. B2 112
West Liberty, W.V., U.S. f8 125
West Linn, Or., U.S. B4 114
Westlock, Alta., Can. B4 68
West Long Branch, N.J., U.S. C4 107
West Lorne, Ont., Can. E3 73
West Marion, N.C., U.S. f10 110
West Medway, Ma., U.S. B5 98
West Memphis, Ar., U.S. B5 81
West Miami, Fl., U.S. s13 86
West Middlesex, Pa., U.S. D1 115
West Mifflin, Pa., U.S. F2 115
West Milton, Oh., U.S. C1 112
West Milwaukee, Wi., U.S. m12 126
Westminster, Ca., U.S. n12 82
Westminster, Co., U.S. B5 83
Westminster, Md., U.S. A4 97
Westminster, S.C., U.S. B1 117
West Monroe, La., U.S. B3 95
Westmont, Ca., U.S. *n12 82
Westmont, Il., U.S. k9 90
Westmont, N.J., U.S. D2 107
Westmont, Pa., U.S. F4 115
Westmoreland, Tn., U.S. A5 119
Westmoreland, co., Pa., U.S. F2 115
Westmoreland, co., Va., U.S. B6 123
Westmorland, Ca., U.S. F6 82
West Musquash Lake, I., Me., U.S. C5 96
West Mystic, Ct., U.S. D8 84
West Newton, Pa., U.S. F2 115
West New York, N.J., U.S. h8 107
West Nishnabotna, stm., Ia., U.S. C2 92
West Norriton, Pa., U.S. o20 115
Weston, Ct., U.S. E2 84
Weston, Ma., U.S. g10 98
Weston, Mo., U.S. B3 102
Weston, Oh., U.S. A2 112
Weston, Or., U.S. B8 114
Weston, W.V., U.S. B4 125
Weston, Wi., U.S. *D4 126
Weston, co., Wy., U.S. C8 127
Weston-super-Mare, Eng., U.K. J10 7
West Orange, N.J., U.S. B4 107
Westover, Md., U.S. D6 97
Westover, W.V., U.S. B5 125
Westover Air Force Base, mil., Ma., U.S. B2 98
West Palm Beach, Fl., U.S. F6 86
West Pawlet, Vt., U.S. E2 122
West Pearl, stm., La., U.S. D6 95
West Pelzer, S.C., U.S. B3 117
West Pensacola, Fl., U.S. u14 86
West Peoria, Il., U.S. C4 90
Westphalia, Mi., U.S. F6 99
West Pittsburg, Pa., U.S. E1 115
West Pittston, Pa., U.S. m17 115
West Plains, Mo., U.S. E6 102
West Point, Ca., U.S. C3 82
West Point, Ga., U.S. D1 87
West Point, Ia., U.S. D6 92
West Point, Ky., U.S. C4 94
West Point, Ms., U.S. B5 101
West Point, Ne., U.S. C9 104
West Point, N.Y., U.S. D7 109
West Point, Va., U.S. C6 123
West Point, mtn., Ak., U.S. C11 79
West Point Lake, res., U.S. C1 87
Westport, Ont., Can. C8 73
Westport, N.Z. D3 52
Westport, Ct., U.S. E2 84
Westport, In., U.S. F6 91
Westport, Wa., U.S. C1 124
West Portsmouth, Oh., U.S. D2 112
West Quoddy Head, c., Me., U.S. D6 96
Westray, i., Scot., U.K. B10 7
Westray Firth, strt., Scot., U.K. B9 7
West Reading, Pa., U.S. F10 115
West Rutland, Vt., U.S. D2 122
West Saint Paul, Mn., U.S. n12 100
West Salem, Il., U.S. E5 90
West Salem, Oh., U.S. B3 112
West Salem, Wi., U.S. E2 126
West Scarborough, Me., U.S. E2 96
West Seneca, N.Y., U.S. C2 109
West Simsbury, Ct., U.S. B4 84
West Slope, Or., U.S. g12 114
West Spanish Peak, mtn., Co., U.S. D6 83
West Springfield, Ma., U.S. B2 98
West Springfield, Va., U.S. g12 123
West Swanzey, N.H., U.S. E2 106
West Terre Haute, In., U.S. F3 91
West Thompson Lake, res., Ct., U.S. B8 84
West Union, Ia., U.S. B6 92
West Union, Oh., U.S. D2 112
West Union, W.V., U.S. B4 125
West Unity, Oh., U.S. A1 112
West University Place, Tx., U.S. r14 120
West Valley City, Ut., U.S. C4 121
West Vancouver, B.C., Can. f12 69
West Van Lear, Ky., U.S. C7 94
West View, Pa., U.S. h13 115
Westville, Il., U.S. C6 90
Westville, In., U.S. A4 91
Westville, N.H., U.S. E4 106
Westville, N.J., U.S. D2 107
Westville, Ok., U.S. A7 113
Westville Lake, res., Ma., U.S. B3 98
West Virginia, state, U.S. C4 125
West Walker, stm., U.S. E2 105
West Wareham, Ma., U.S. C6 98
West Warwick, R.I., U.S. D3 116
Westwego, La., U.S. k11 95
Westwood, Ca., U.S. B3 82
Westwood, Ks., U.S. k16 93
Westwood, Ky., U.S. B7 94
Westwood, Ma., U.S. B5 98
Westwood, N.J., U.S. B4 107
Westwood Lakes, Fl., U.S. s13 86
West Wyoming, Pa., U.S. n17 115
West Yarmouth, Ma., U.S. C7 98
West Yellowstone, Mt., U.S. F5 103
West York, Pa., U.S. G8 115
Wetar, Pulau, i., Indon. G8 32
Wetaskiwin, Alta., Can. C4 68
Wethersfield, Ct., U.S. C5 84
Wet Mountains, mts., Co., U.S. C5 83
Wetumka, Ok., U.S. B5 113
Wetumpka, Al., U.S. C3 78
Wetzel, co., W.V., U.S. B4 125
Wetzlar, Ger. E8 8
Wewahitchka, Fl., U.S. B1 86
Wewak, Pap. N. Gui. k15 50a
Wewoka, Ok., U.S. B5 113
Wexford, Ire. I6 7
Wexford, co., Mi., U.S. D5 99
Weyauwega, Wi., U.S. D5 126
Weymouth, Eng., U.K. K10 7
Weymouth, Ma., U.S. B6 98
Whaleysville, Md., U.S. D7 97
Whalsay, i., Scot., U.K. A12 7
Whangarei, N.Z. A5 52
Wharton, N.J., U.S. B3 107
Wharton, Tx., U.S. E4 120
Wharton, co., Tx., U.S. E4 120
What Cheer, Ia., U.S. C5 92
Whatcom, co., Wa., U.S. A4 124
Whatcom, Lake, I., Wa., U.S. A3 124
Wheatfield, In., U.S. B3 91
Wheatland, Ca., U.S. C3 82
Wheatland, Ia., U.S. C7 92
Wheatland, Wy., U.S. D8 127
Wheatland, co., Mt., U.S. D7 103
Wheatland Reservoir, res., Wy., U.S. E7 127
Wheatley, Ont., Can. E2 73
Wheaton, Il., U.S. B5 90
Wheaton, Md., U.S. B3 97
Wheaton, Mn., U.S. E2 100
Wheaton, Mo., U.S. E3 102
Wheat Ridge, Co., U.S. B5 83
Wheelbarrow Peak, mtn., Nv., U.S. F5 105
Wheeler, Ms., U.S. A5 101
Wheeler, Tx., U.S. B2 120
Wheeler, co., Ga., U.S. D4 87
Wheeler, co., Ne., U.S. C7 104
Wheeler, co., Or., U.S. C6 114
Wheeler, co., Tx., U.S. B2 120
Wheeler Air Force Base, mil., Hi., U.S. g9 88
Wheeler Lake, res., Al., U.S. A2 78
Wheeler Peak, mtn., Ca., U.S. C4 82
Wheeler Peak, mtn., Nv., U.S. E7 105
Wheeler Peak, mtn., N.M., U.S. A4 108
Wheelersburg, Oh., U.S. D3 112
Wheeling, Il., U.S. h9 90
Wheeling, W.V., U.S. A4 125
Wheeling Creek, stm., W.V., U.S. f8 125
Wheelwright, Ky., U.S. C7 94
Whetstone, stm., U.S. E2 100
Whidbey Island, i., Wa., U.S. A3 124
Whidbey Island Naval Air Station, mil., Wa., U.S. A3 124
Whigham, Ga., U.S. F2 87
Whiskey Peak, mtn., Wy., U.S. D5 127
Whiskeytown-Shasta-Trinity National Recreation Area, Ca., U.S. B2 82
Whistler, B.C., Can. D6 69
Whitacres, Ct., U.S. A5 84
Whitakers, N.C., U.S. A5 110
Whitbourne, Newf., Can. E5 72
Whitby, Ont., Can. D6 73
Whitchurch-Stouffville, Ont., Can. D5 73
White, co., Ar., U.S. B4 81
White, co., Ga., U.S. B3 87
White, co., Il., U.S. E5 90
White, co., In., U.S. C4 91
White, co., Tn., U.S. D8 119
White, stm., N.A. D4 66
White, stm., U.S. C4 81
White, stm., U.S. D5 118
White, stm., U.S. C7 121
White, stm., Az., U.S. D5 80
White, stm., In., U.S. H2 91
White, stm., Mi., U.S. E4 99
White, stm., Nv., U.S. E6 105
White, stm., Tx., U.S. C2 120
White, stm., Vt., U.S. D4 122
White, stm., Wa., U.S. B4 124
White, stm., Wa., U.S. B5 124
White, Lake, I., Austl. D5 50
White Bay, b., Newf., Can. D3 72
White Bear, stm., Newf., Can. E3 72
White Bear Lake, Mn., U.S. E5 100
White Bluff, Tn., U.S. A4 119
White Butte, mtn., N.D., U.S. C2 111
White Castle, La., U.S. D4 95
White Center, Wa., U.S. e11 124
White City, Or., U.S. E4 114
White Clay Creek, stm., U.S. A3 104
White Cloud, Mi., U.S. E5 99
Whitecourt, Alta., Can. B3 68
White Creek, stm., U.S. E2 122
Whiteday, stm., W.V., U.S. h10 125
White Deer, Tx., U.S. B2 120
White Earth Indian Reservation, Mn., U.S. C3 100
White Earth Lake, I., Mn., U.S. C3 100
Whiteface, stm., Mn., U.S. C6 100
Whiteface Mountain, mtn., N.Y., U.S. f11 109
Whitefield, N.H., U.S. B3 106
Whitefish, Mt., U.S. B2 103
Whitefish Bay, Wi., U.S. m12 126
Whitefish Bay, b., Mi., U.S. B6 99
Whitefish Lake, I., Mn., U.S. D4 100
Whitefish Range, mts., Mt., U.S. B2 103
Whiteford, Md., U.S. A5 97
White Hall, Al., U.S. C3 78
White Hall, Ar., U.S. C3 81
White Hall, Il., U.S. D3 90
Whitehall, Mi., U.S. E4 99
Whitehall, Mt., U.S. E4 103
Whitehall, N.Y., U.S. B7 109
Whitehall, Oh., U.S. m11 112
Whitehall, Wi., U.S. D2 126
Whitehall Reservoir, res., Ma., U.S. h9 98
Whitehaven, Eng., U.K. G9 7
White Haven, Pa., U.S. D10 115
Whitehorn, Point, c., Wa., U.S. A3 124
Whitehorse, Yukon, Can. D5 66
White Horse, N.J., U.S. C3 107
Whitehouse, Oh., U.S. A2 112
White House, Tn., U.S. A5 119
White Island Shores, Ma., U.S. C6 98
White Knob Mountains, mts., Id., U.S. F5 89
White Lake, I., La., U.S. E3 95
Whiteman Air Force Base, mil., Mo., U.S. C4 102
White Meadow Lake, N.J., U.S. *B3 107
White Mesa Natural Bridge, Az., U.S. A4 80
White Mountain Peak, mtn., Ca., U.S. D4 82
White Mountains, mts., U.S. D4 82
White Mountains, mts., N.H., U.S. B3 106
Whitemouth, stm., Man., Can. E4 70
Whitemouth Lake, I., Man., Can. E4 70
White Nile (Al-Bahr al-Abyad), stm., Sudan F12 42
White Oak, Oh., U.S. o12 112
White Oak Creek, stm., Oh., U.S. D2 112
Whiteoak Creek, stm., Tn., U.S. A4 119
White Oak Lake, res., Ar., U.S. D2 81
White Pigeon, Mi., U.S. G5 99
White Pine, Mi., U.S. m12 99
White Pine, Tn., U.S. C10 119
White Pine, co., Nv., U.S. D6 105
White Plains, Md., U.S. C4 97
White Plains, N.Y., U.S. D7 109
Whiteriver, Az., U.S. D6 80
White River Junction, Vt., U.S. D4 122
White Rock, B.C., Can. E6 69
White Russia see Belarus, ctry., Eur. G3 18
White Salmon, Wa., U.S. D4 124
White Salmon, stm., Wa., U.S. D4 124
White Sands Missile Range, mil., N.M., U.S. E3 108
White Sands National Monument, N.M., U.S. E3 108
Whitesboro, N.Y., U.S. B5 109
Whitesboro, Tx., U.S. C4 120
Whitesburg, Ga., U.S. C2 87
Whitesburg, Ky., U.S. C7 94
Whites Creek, stm., Tn., U.S. g10 119
White Sea see Beloje more, Russia D5 22
Whiteside, co., Il., U.S. B3 90
White Sulphur Springs, Mt., U.S. D6 103
White Sulphur Springs, W.V., U.S. D4 125
Whitesville, Ky., U.S. C3 94
White Swan, Wa., U.S. C5 124
White Tank Mountains, mts., Az., U.S. k7 80
Whiteville, N.C., U.S. C4 110
Whiteville, Tn., U.S. B2 119

Index

Name	Map Ref	Page
White Volta (Volta Blanche), stm., Afr.	F5	42
Whitewater, Ks., U.S.	E6	93
Whitewater, Wi., U.S.	F5	126
Whitewater, stm., U.S.	F7	91
Whitewater, stm., Ks., U.S.	E6	93
Whitewater Baldy, mtn., N.M., U.S.	D1	108
Whitewater Bay, b., Fl., U.S.	G6	86
Whitewood, S.D., U.S.	C2	118
Whitewright, Tx., U.S.	C4	120
Whitfield, co., Ga., U.S.	B2	87
Whitfield Estates, Fl., U.S.	q10	86
Whiting, In., U.S.	A3	91
Whiting, Ia., U.S.	B1	92
Whiting, Wi., U.S.	D4	126
Whiting Field Naval Air Station, mil., Fl., U.S.	u14	86
Whitinsville, Ma., U.S.	B4	98
Whitley, co., In., U.S.	B6	91
Whitley, co., Ky., U.S.	D5	94
Whitley City, Ky., U.S.	D5	94
Whitman, Ma., U.S.	B6	98
Whitman, W.V., U.S.	D2	125
Whitman, co., Wa., U.S.	B8	124
Whitman Square, N.J., U.S.	D2	107
Whitmire, S.C., U.S.	B4	117
Whitmore Lake, Mi., U.S.	p14	99
Whitmore Village, Hi., U.S.	f9	88
Whitney, S.C., U.S.	B4	117
Whitney, Tx., U.S.	D4	120
Whitney, Lake, res., Tx., U.S.	D4	120
Whitney, Mount, mtn., Ca., U.S.	D4	82
Whitney Point Lake, res., N.Y., U.S.	C5	109
Whittier, Ak., U.S.	C10	79
Whittier, Ca., U.S.	F4	82
Whitwell, Tn., U.S.	D8	119
Wholdaia Lake, l., N.W. Ter., Can.	D12	66
Whyalla, Austl.	F7	50
Wiarton, Ont., Can.	C3	73
Wibaux, Mt., U.S.	D12	103
Wibaux, co., Mt., U.S.	D12	103
Wichita, Ks., U.S.	E6	93
Wichita, co., Ks., U.S.	D2	93
Wichita, co., Tx., U.S.	B3	120
Wichita Falls, Tx., U.S.	C3	120
Wichita Mountains, mts., Ok., U.S.	C3	113
Wick, Scot., U.K.	C9	7
Wickenburg, Az., U.S.	D3	80
Wickiup Reservoir, res., Or., U.S.	E5	114
Wickliffe, Ky., U.S.	f8	94
Wickliffe, Oh., U.S.	A4	112
Wicklow, Ire.	I6	7
Wicklow Head, c., Ire.	I6	7
Wicklow Mountains, mts., Ire.	H6	7
Wicomico, co., Md., U.S.	D6	97
Wicomico, stm., Md., U.S.	D6	97
Wiconisco, Pa., U.S.	E8	115
Widefield, Co., U.S.	C6	83
Wielkopolska, reg., Pol.	D17	8
Wien (Vienna), Aus.	G16	8
Wiener Neustadt, Aus.	H16	8
Wiesbaden, Ger.	E8	8
Wiesloch, Ger.	F8	8
Wiggins, Ms., U.S.	E4	101
Wiggins Peak, mtn., Wy., U.S.	C3	127
Wikwemikong, Ont., Can.	B3	73
Wilbarger, co., Tx., U.S.	B3	120
Wilber, Ne., U.S.	D9	104
Wilberforce, Oh., U.S.	C2	112
Wilbraham, Ma., U.S.	B3	98
Wilbur, Wa., U.S.	B7	124
Wilburton, Ok., U.S.	C6	113
Wilcannia, Austl.	F8	50
Wilcox, Pa., U.S.	C4	115
Wilcox, co., Al., U.S.	D2	78
Wilcox, co., Ga., U.S.	E3	87
Wild, stm., U.S.	B4	106
Wild Ammonoosuc, stm., N.H., U.S.	B3	106
Wild Branch, stm., Vt., U.S.	B4	122
Wilder, Id., U.S.	F2	89
Wilder, Vt., U.S.	D4	122
Wilder Dam, U.S.	C2	106
Wildhorse Creek, stm., Ok., U.S.	C4	113
Wild Horse Reservoir, res., Nv., U.S.	B6	105
Wildorado, Tx., U.S.	B1	120
Wild Rice, stm., Mn., U.S.	C2	100
Wild Rice, stm., N.D., U.S.	C8	111
Wildwood, Fl., U.S.	D4	86
Wildwood, N.J., U.S.	F3	107
Wildwood Crest, N.J., U.S.	F3	107
Wilhelm, Mount, mtn., Pap. N. Gui.	m16	50a
Wilhelmina Gebergte, mts., Sur.	C7	54
Wilhelmina Peak see Trikora, Puntjak, mtn., Indon.	F10	32
Wilhelmshaven, Ger.	B8	8
Wilkes, co., Ga., U.S.	C4	87
Wilkes, co., N.C., U.S.	A1	110
Wilkes-Barre, Pa., U.S.	D10	115
Wilkesboro, N.C., U.S.	A1	110
Wilkes Land, reg., Ant.	C24	47
Wilkin, co., Mn., U.S.	D2	100
Wilkinsburg, Pa., U.S.	F2	115
Wilkinson, W.V., U.S.	D3	125
Wilkinson, co., Ga., U.S.	D3	87
Wilkinson, co., Ms., U.S.	D2	101
Will, co., Il., U.S.	B6	90
Willacoochee, Ga., U.S.	E3	87
Willacy, co., Tx., U.S.	F4	120
Willamette, stm., Or., U.S.	C3	114
Willamette Pass, Or., U.S.	D4	114
Willamina, Or., U.S.	B3	114
Willapa Bay, b., Wa., U.S.	C1	124
Willard, Mo., U.S.	D4	102
Willard, Oh., U.S.	A3	112
Willard, Ut., U.S.	B3	121
Willard Bay, b., Ut., U.S.	B3	121
Willards, Md., U.S.	D7	97
Willard Stream, stm., Vt., U.S.	B5	122
Willcox, Az., U.S.	E6	80
Willcox Playa, l., Az., U.S.	E5	80
Willemstad, Neth. Ant.	H13	64
William Bill Dannelly Reservoir, res., Al., U.S.	C2	78
Williams, Az., U.S.	B3	80
Williams, Ca., U.S.	C2	82
Williams, co., N.D., U.S.	A2	111
Williams, co., Oh., U.S.	A1	112
Williams, stm., Vt., U.S.	E3	122
Williams, stm., W.V., U.S.	C4	125
Williams Air Force Base, mil., Az., U.S.	D4	80
Williams Bay, Wi., U.S.	F5	126
Williamsburg, In., U.S.	E8	91
Williamsburg, Ia., U.S.	C5	92
Williamsburg, Ky., U.S.	D5	94
Williamsburg, Oh., U.S.	C1	112
Williamsburg, Pa., U.S.	F5	115
Williamsburg, Va., U.S.	C6	123
Williamsburg, co., S.C., U.S.	D8	117
Williams Fork, stm., Co., U.S.	A3	83
Williams Lake, B.C., Can.	C6	69
Williamson, N.Y., U.S.	B3	109
Williamson, W.V., U.S.	D2	125
Williamson, co., Il., U.S.	F4	90
Williamson, co., Tn., U.S.	B5	119
Williamson, co., Tx., U.S.	D4	120
Williamsport, In., U.S.	D3	91
Williamsport, Md., U.S.	A2	97
Williamsport, Pa., U.S.	D7	115
Williamston, Mi., U.S.	F6	99
Williamston, N.C., U.S.	B5	110
Williamston, S.C., U.S.	B3	117
Williamstown, Ky., U.S.	B5	94
Williamstown, Ma., U.S.	A1	98
Williamstown, N.J., U.S.	D3	107
Williamstown, Pa., U.S.	E8	115
Williamstown, Vt., U.S.	C3	122
Williamstown, W.V., U.S.	B3	125
Williamsville, Il., U.S.	D4	90
Williamsville, N.Y., U.S.	C2	109
Willimantic, Ct., U.S.	C7	84
Willimantic, stm., Ct., U.S.	B6	84
Willimantic Reservoir, res., Ct., U.S.	C7	84
Willingboro, N.J., U.S.	C3	107
Willis, Tx., U.S.	D5	120
Willis Islets, is., Austl.	C9	50
Williston, Fl., U.S.	C4	86
Williston, N.D., U.S.	A2	111
Williston, S.C., U.S.	E5	117
Williston Lake, res., B.C., Can.	B6	69
Willits, Ca., U.S.	C2	82
Willmar, Mn., U.S.	E3	100
Willoughby, Oh., U.S.	A4	112
Willoughby, Lake, l., Vt., U.S.	B4	122
Willoughby Hills, Oh., U.S.	A4	112
Willow, Ak., U.S.	g17	79
Willow Creek, stm., Nv., U.S.	E5	105
Willow Creek, stm., Ut., U.S.	D6	121
Willow Creek, stm., Wy., U.S.	C6	127
Willow Grove Naval Air Station, mil., Pa., U.S.	F11	115
Willowick, Oh., U.S.	A4	112
Willowmore, S. Afr.	H4	44
Willow Reservoir, res., Wi., U.S.	C3	126
Willow Run, De., U.S.	i7	85
Willow Run, Mi., U.S.	p14	99
Willows, Ca., U.S.	C2	82
Willow Springs, Il., U.S.	k9	90
Willow Springs, Mo., U.S.	E6	102
Willston, Va., U.S.	*B5	123
Wilmar, Ar., U.S.	D4	81
Wilmerding, Pa., U.S.	k14	115
Wilmette, Il., U.S.	A6	90
Wilmington, De., U.S.	B3	85
Wilmington, Il., U.S.	B5	90
Wilmington, Ma., U.S.	A5	98
Wilmington, N.C., U.S.	C5	110
Wilmington, Oh., U.S.	C2	112
Wilmington, Vt., U.S.	F3	122
Wilmington Manor, De., U.S.	i7	85
Wilmore, Ky., U.S.	C5	94
Wilmot, Ar., U.S.	D4	81
Wilson, Ar., U.S.	B5	81
Wilson, Ks., U.S.	D5	93
Wilson, La., U.S.	D4	95
Wilson, N.C., U.S.	B5	110
Wilson, Ok., U.S.	C4	113
Wilson, Pa., U.S.	E11	115
Wilson, Wy., U.S.	C2	127
Wilson, co., Ks., U.S.	E8	93
Wilson, co., N.C., U.S.	B5	110
Wilson, co., Tn., U.S.	A5	119
Wilson, co., Tx., U.S.	E3	120
Wilson, Cape, c., N.W. Ter., Can.	C16	66
Wilson, Mount, mtn., Az., U.S.	B1	80
Wilson, Mount, mtn., Ca., U.S.	m12	82
Wilson, Mount, mtn., Co., U.S.	D2	83
Wilson, Mount, mtn., Nv., U.S.	E7	105
Wilson, Mount, mtn., Or., U.S.	B5	114
Wilson Creek, stm., Wa., U.S.	B6	124
Wilson Creek, stm., Wa., U.S.	B5	124
Wilson Lake, res., Al., U.S.	A2	78
Wilson Lake, res., Ks., U.S.	D4	93
Wilsons Beach, N.B., Can.	E3	71
Wilsonville, Al., U.S.	B3	78
Wilsonville, Or., U.S.	h12	114
Wilton, Al., U.S.	B3	78
Wilton, Ct., U.S.	E2	84
Wilton, Ia., U.S.	C6	92
Wilton, Me., U.S.	D2	96
Wilton, N.H., U.S.	E3	106
Wilton, N.D., U.S.	B5	111
Wiluna, Austl.	E4	50
Wimauma, Fl., U.S.	E4	86
Wimico, Lake, l., Fl., U.S.	C1	86
Winamac, In., U.S.	B4	91
Wincheck Pond, l., R.I., U.S.	E1	116
Winchendon, Ma., U.S.	A3	98
Winchester, Ont., Can.	B9	73
Winchester, Eng., U.K.	J11	7
Winchester, Il., U.S.	D3	90
Winchester, In., U.S.	D8	91
Winchester, Ks., U.S.	k15	93
Winchester, Ky., U.S.	C5	94
Winchester, Ma., U.S.	g11	98
Winchester, Nv., U.S.	G6	105
Winchester, N.H., U.S.	E2	106
Winchester, Oh., U.S.	D2	112
Winchester, Tn., U.S.	B5	119
Winchester, Va., U.S.	A4	123
Winchester Bay, Or., U.S.	D2	114
Wind, stm., Wa., U.S.	D4	124
Wind, stm., Wy., U.S.	C4	127
Windber, Pa., U.S.	F4	115
Wind Cave National Park, S.D., U.S.	D2	118
Winder, Ga., U.S.	C3	87
Windermere, Eng., U.K.	G10	7
Windfall, In., U.S.	D6	91
Windgap, Pa., U.S.	E11	115
Windham, Ct., U.S.	C7	84
Windham, Oh., U.S.	A4	112
Windham, co., Ct., U.S.	B7	84
Windham, co., Vt., U.S.	F3	122
Windhoek, Nmb.	F3	44
Wind Lake, Wi., U.S.	F5	126
Wind Lake, l., Wi., U.S.	n11	126
Windmill Point, c., Va., U.S.	C6	123
Windom, Mn., U.S.	G3	100
Windom Peak, mtn., Co., U.S.	D3	83
Windorah, Austl.	E8	50
Window Rock, Az., U.S.	B6	80
Wind Point, Wi., U.S.	n12	126
Wind River Indian Reservation, Wy., U.S.	C4	127
Wind River Peak, mtn., Wy., U.S.	D3	127
Wind River Range, mts., Wy., U.S.	C3	127
Windsor (part of Grand Falls-Windsor), Newf., Can.	D4	72
Windsor, Ont., Can.	E1	73
Windsor, Que., Can.	D5	74
Windsor, Eng., U.K.	J12	7
Windsor, Co., U.S.	A6	83
Windsor, Ct., U.S.	B5	84
Windsor, Il., U.S.	D5	90
Windsor, Mo., U.S.	C4	102
Windsor, N.C., U.S.	A6	110
Windsor, Pa., U.S.	G8	115
Windsor, Vt., U.S.	E4	122
Windsor, Va., U.S.	D6	123
Windsor, co., Vt., U.S.	D3	122
Windsor Heights, Ia., U.S.	e8	92
Windsor Locks, Ct., U.S.	B5	84
Windward Islands, is., N.A.	H17	64
Windward Passage, strt., N.A.	E10	64
Windy Hill, S.C., U.S.	C8	117
Windy Peak, mtn., Wa., U.S.	A6	124
Winefred Lake, l., Alta., Can.	B5	68
Winfield, Al., U.S.	B2	78
Winfield, Ia., U.S.	C6	92
Winfield, Ks., U.S.	E7	93
Winfield, Mo., U.S.	C7	102
Winfield, W.V., U.S.	C3	125
Wing, stm., Mn., U.S.	D3	100
Wingate, N.C., U.S.	C2	110
Wingham, Ont., Can.	D3	73
Winifrede, W.V., U.S.	m12	125
Winisk, stm., Ont., Can.	n18	73
Winisk Lake, l., Ont., Can.	F15	66
Wink, Tx., U.S.	D1	120
Winkelman, Az., U.S.	E5	80
Winkler, Man., Can.	E3	70
Winkler, co., Tx., U.S.	D1	120
Winlock, Wa., U.S.	C3	124
Winn, co., La., U.S.	C3	95
Winnebago, Il., U.S.	A4	90
Winnebago, Mn., U.S.	G4	100
Winnebago, Ne., U.S.	B9	104
Winnebago, Wi., U.S.	h8	126
Winnebago, co., Il., U.S.	A4	90
Winnebago, co., Ia., U.S.	A4	92
Winnebago, co., Wi., U.S.	D5	126
Winnebago, stm., Ia., U.S.	A4	92
Winnebago, Lake, l., Wi., U.S.	E5	126
Winnebago Indian Reservation, Ne., U.S.	B9	104
Winneconne, Wi., U.S.	D5	126
Winnemucca, Nv., U.S.	C4	105
Winnemucca Lake, l., Nv., U.S.	C2	105
Winner, S.D., U.S.	D6	118
Winneshiek, co., Ia., U.S.	A6	92
Winnetka, Il., U.S.	A6	90
Winnfield, La., U.S.	C3	95
Winnibigoshish, Lake, l., Mn., U.S.	C4	100
Winnipeg, Man., Can.	E3	70
Winnipeg, stm., Can.	D4	70
Winnipeg, Lake, l., Man., Can.	C3	70
Winnipeg Beach, Man., Can.	D3	70
Winnipegosis, Man., Can.	D2	70
Winnipegosis, Lake, l., Man., Can.	C2	70
Winnipesaukee, Lake, l., N.H., U.S.	C4	106
Winnisquam, N.H., U.S.	C3	106
Winnisquam Lake, l., N.H., U.S.	C3	106
Winnsboro, La., U.S.	B4	95
Winnsboro, S.C., U.S.	C5	117
Winnsboro, Tx., U.S.	C5	120
Winnsboro Mills, S.C., U.S.	C5	117
Winona, Mn., U.S.	F7	100
Winona, Ms., U.S.	B4	101
Winona, Mo., U.S.	D6	102
Winona, co., Mn., U.S.	F7	100
Winona Lake, In., U.S.	B6	91
Winona Lake, l., Vt., U.S.	C2	122
Winooski, Vt., U.S.	C2	122
Winooski, stm., Vt., U.S.	C3	122
Winslow, Az., U.S.	C5	80
Winslow, In., U.S.	H3	91
Winslow, Me., U.S.	D3	96
Winsted, Ct., U.S.	B3	84
Winsted, Mn., U.S.	F4	100
Winston, Fl., U.S.	D4	86
Winston, Or., U.S.	D3	114
Winston, co., Al., U.S.	A2	78
Winston, co., Ms., U.S.	B4	101
Winston-Salem, N.C., U.S.	A2	110
Winter Garden, Fl., U.S.	D5	86
Winter Harbor, Me., U.S.	D4	96
Winter Haven, Fl., U.S.	D5	86
Winter Park, Fl., U.S.	D5	86
Winter Park, N.C., U.S.	C5	110
Winterport, Me., U.S.	D4	96
Winter Ridge, mtn., Or., U.S.	E6	114
Winters, Ca., U.S.	C2	82
Winters, Tx., U.S.	D3	120
Winterset, Ia., U.S.	C4	92
Wintersville, Oh., U.S.	B5	112
Winterswijk, Neth.	D6	8
Winterthur, Switz.	E15	10
Winterton, Newf., Can.	E5	72
Winterville, Ga., U.S.	C3	87
Winterville, N.C., U.S.	B5	110
Winthrop, Ia., U.S.	B6	92
Winthrop, Me., U.S.	D3	96
Winthrop, Ma., U.S.	B6	98
Winthrop, Mn., U.S.	F4	100
Winthrop, Lake, l., Ma., U.S.	h10	98
Winthrop Harbor, Il., U.S.	A6	90
Winton, Austl.	D8	50
Winton, N.C., U.S.	A6	110
Winton Lake, res., Oh., U.S.	o12	113
Winyah Bay, b., S.C., U.S.	E9	117
Wirt, co., W.V., U.S.	B3	125
Wiscasset, Me., U.S.	D3	96
Wisconsin, state, U.S.	D4	126
Wisconsin, stm., Wi., U.S.	E3	126
Wisconsin, Lake, res., Wi., U.S.	E4	126
Wisconsin Dells, Wi., U.S.	E4	126
Wisconsin Rapids, Wi., U.S.	D4	126
Wise, Va., U.S.	f9	123
Wise, co., Tx., U.S.	C4	120
Wise, co., Va., U.S.	e9	123
Wishek, N.D., U.S.	C6	111
Wishram, Wa., U.S.	D4	124
Wisła, stm., Pol.	A18	8
Wismar, Ger.	B11	8
Wisner, La., U.S.	C4	95
Wisner, Ne., U.S.	C9	104
Wissota, Lake, res., Wi., U.S.	D2	126
Wister, Ok., U.S.	C7	113
Wister Lake, res., Ok., U.S.	C7	113
Witbank, S. Afr.	G5	44
Withamsville, Oh., U.S.	C1	112
Witherspoon, Mount, mtn., Ak., U.S.	g18	79
Withlacoochee, stm., U.S.	B3	86
Withlacoochee, stm., Fl., U.S.	C4	86
Witless Bay, Newf., Can.	E5	72
Witt, Il., U.S.	D4	90
Wittenberg, Ger.	D12	8
Wittenberg, Wi., U.S.	D4	126
Wittenberge, Ger.	B11	8
Wittlich, Ger.	F6	8
Wittman, Md., U.S.	C5	97
Wittmann, Az., U.S.	D3	80
Wittstock, Ger.	B12	8
Wixom, Mi., U.S.	o14	99
Wixom Lake, res., Mi., U.S.	E6	99
Włocławek, Pol.	C19	8
Woburn, Ma., U.S.	B5	98
Wokam, Pulau, i., Indon.	G9	32
Woking, Eng., U.K.	J12	7
Wolcott, Ct., U.S.	C4	84
Wolcott, In., U.S.	C3	91
Wolcottville, In., U.S.	A7	91
Wolf, stm., Ms., U.S.	E4	101
Wolf, stm., Tn., U.S.	e9	119
Wolf, stm., Wi., U.S.	C5	126
Wolf Creek, Or., U.S.	E3	114
Wolf Creek, stm., U.S.	A2	113
Wolf Creek, stm., W.V., U.S.	m13	125
Wolf Creek Pass, Co., U.S.	D3	83
Wolfe, co., Ky., U.S.	C6	94
Wolfeboro, N.H., U.S.	C4	106
Wolfeboro Falls, N.H., U.S.	C4	106
Wolfe City, Tx., U.S.	C4	120
Wolfen, Ger.	D12	8
Wolfenbüttel, Ger.	C10	8
Wolf Lake, Mi., U.S.	E4	99
Wolf Lake, l., Il., U.S.	k9	90
Wolf Mountain, mtn., Ak., U.S.	B9	79
Wolf Point, Mt., U.S.	B11	103
Wolfsberg, Aus.	I14	8
Wolfsburg, Ger.	C10	8
Wolf Swamp, sw., N.C., U.S.	C5	110
Wolgast, Ger.	A13	8
Wollaston, Cape, c., N.W. Ter., Can.	B9	66
Wollaston, Islas, is., Chile	H3	56
Wollaston Lake, l., Sask., Can.	m8	75
Wollaston Peninsula, pen., N.W. Ter., Can.	C10	66
Wollongong, Austl.	F10	50
Wolverhampton, Eng., U.K.	I10	7
Woman Lake, l., Mn., U.S.	D4	100
Womelsdorf, Pa., U.S.	F9	115
Wonder Lake, Il., U.S.	A5	90
Wonewoc, Wi., U.S.	E3	126
Wŏnsan, N. Kor.	D12	26
Wood, co., Oh., U.S.	A2	112
Wood, co., Tx., U.S.	C5	120
Wood, co., W.V., U.S.	B3	125
Wood, co., Wi., U.S.	D3	126
Wood, stm., Sask., Can.	H2	75
Wood, stm., R.I., U.S.	F2	116
Wood, stm., Wy., U.S.	C3	127
Wood, Mount, mtn., Mt., U.S.	E7	103
Woodall Mountain, mtn., Ms., U.S.	A5	101
Woodbine, Ga., U.S.	F5	87
Woodbine, Ia., U.S.	C2	92
Woodbine, Ky., U.S.	D5	94
Woodbine, N.J., U.S.	E3	107
Woodbridge, Ct., U.S.	D3	84
Woodbridge, Va., U.S.	B5	123
Woodbridge [Township], N.J., U.S.	B4	107
Woodburn, In., U.S.	B8	91
Woodburn, Or., U.S.	B4	114
Woodbury, Ct., U.S.	C3	84
Woodbury, Ga., U.S.	D2	87
Woodbury, Mn., U.S.	F6	100
Woodbury, N.J., U.S.	D2	107
Woodbury, Tn., U.S.	B5	119
Woodbury, co., Ia., U.S.	B1	92
Woodcliff Lake, N.J., U.S.	g8	107
Woodcliff Lake, l., N.J., U.S.	g8	107
Wood Dale, Il., U.S.	k9	90
Wood End, spit, Ma., U.S.	B7	98
Woodfield, S.C., U.S.	C6	117
Woodford, co., Il., U.S.	C4	90
Woodford, co., Ky., U.S.	B5	94
Woodhull, Il., U.S.	B3	90
Woodlake, Ca., U.S.	D4	82
Woodland, Ca., U.S.	C3	82
Woodland, Me., U.S.	C5	96
Woodland, N.C., U.S.	A5	110
Woodland, Wa., U.S.	D3	124
Woodland Acres, Co., U.S.	D6	83
Woodland Park, Co., U.S.	C5	83
Woodlark Island, i., Pap. N. Gui.	A10	50
Woodlawn, Ky., U.S.	e9	94
Woodlawn, Md., U.S.	g10	97
Woodlawn, Oh., U.S.	n13	112
Woodlawn, Va., U.S.	D2	123
Woodmont, Ct., U.S.	E4	84
Woodmoor, Md., U.S.	B4	97
Woodridge, Il., U.S.	k8	90
Wood-Ridge, N.J., U.S.	h8	107
Wood River, Il., U.S.	E3	90
Wood River, Ne., U.S.	D7	104
Woodroffe, Mount, mtn., Austl.	E6	50
Woodruff, S.C., U.S.	B3	117
Woodruff, Wi., U.S.	C4	126
Woodruff, co., Ar., U.S.	B4	81
Woods, co., Ok., U.S.	A3	113
Woods, Lake, res., Tn., U.S.	B5	119
Woods, Lake of the, l., N.A.	G14	66
Woodsboro, Tx., U.S.	E4	120
Woods Cross, Ut., U.S.	C4	121
Woodsfield, Oh., U.S.	C4	112
Woods Hole, Ma., U.S.	C6	98
Woodson, Ar., U.S.	C3	81
Woodson, co., Ks., U.S.	E8	93
Woodstock, N.B., Can.	C2	71
Woodstock, Ont., Can.	D4	73
Woodstock, Ga., U.S.	B2	87
Woodstock, Il., U.S.	A5	90
Woodstock, Md., U.S.	B4	97
Woodstock, N.Y., U.S.	C6	109
Woodstock, Vt., U.S.	D3	122
Woodstock, Va., U.S.	B4	123
Woodstown, N.J., U.S.	D2	107
Woodsville, N.H., U.S.	B2	106
Woodville, N.Z.	D5	52
Woodville, Fl., U.S.	B2	86
Woodville, Ms., U.S.	D2	101
Woodville, Oh., U.S.	A2	112
Woodville, Tx., U.S.	D5	120
Woodville, Wi., U.S.	D1	126
Woodward, Ia., U.S.	C4	92
Woodward, Ok., U.S.	A2	113
Woodward, co., Ok., U.S.	A2	113
Woodworth, La., U.S.	C3	95
Woolmarket, Ms., U.S.	E5	101
Woolrich, Pa., U.S.	D7	115
Woolsey Peak, mtn., Az., U.S.	D3	80
Woomera, Austl.	F7	50
Woonsocket, R.I., U.S.	A3	116
Woonsocket, S.D., U.S.	C7	118
Woonsocket Reservoir Number Three, res., R.I., U.S.	B3	116
Wooramel, Austl.	E2	50
Wooster, Oh., U.S.	B4	112
Worcester, S. Afr.	H3	44
Worcester, Eng., U.K.	I10	7
Worcester, Ma., U.S.	B4	98
Worcester, co., Md., U.S.	D7	97
Worcester, co., Ma., U.S.	A3	98
Worden, Il., U.S.	E4	90
Worden Pond, l., R.I., U.S.	F3	116
Workington, Eng., U.K.	G9	7
Worland, Wy., U.S.	B5	127
Worms, Ger.	F8	8
Worth, Il., U.S.	k9	90
Worth, co., Ga., U.S.	E3	87
Worth, co., Ia., U.S.	A4	92
Worth, co., Mo., U.S.	A3	102
Worthing, Eng., U.K.	K12	7
Worthington, In., U.S.	F4	91
Worthington, Ky., U.S.	B7	94
Worthington, Mn., U.S.	G3	100
Worthington, Oh., U.S.	B2	112
Worthington Peak, mtn., Nv., U.S.	F6	105
Wowoni, Pulau, i., Indon.	F7	32
Wrangell, Ak., U.S.	D13	79
Wrangell, Cape, Ak., U.S.	E2	79
Wrangell, Mount, mtn., Ak., U.S.	f19	79
Wrangell Island, i., Ak., U.S.	m24	79
Wrangell Mountains, mts., Ak., U.S.	C11	79
Wrangell-Saint Elias National Park, Ak., U.S.	C11	79
Wrath, Cape, c., Scot., U.K.	C7	7
Wray, Co., U.S.	A8	83
Wreck Reefs, rf., Austl.	D11	50
Wrens, Ga., U.S.	C4	87
Wrentham, Ma., U.S.	B5	98
Wrexham, Wales, U.K.	H9	7
Wright, co., Ia., U.S.	B4	92
Wright, co., Mn., U.S.	E4	100
Wright, co., Mo., U.S.	D5	102
Wright, Mount, mtn., Mt., U.S.	C4	103
Wright Brothers National Memorial, hist., N.C., U.S.	A7	110
Wright City, Mo., U.S.	C8	102
Wright City, Ok., U.S.	C6	113
Wright-Patterson Air Force Base, mil., Oh., U.S.	C1	112
Wrightson, Mount, mtn., Az., U.S.	F5	80
Wrightstown, N.J., U.S.	C3	107
Wrightstown, Wi., U.S.	D5	126
Wrightsville, Ar., U.S.	C3	81
Wrightsville, Ga., U.S.	D4	87
Wrightsville, Pa., U.S.	F8	115
Wrightsville Beach, N.C., U.S.	C5	110
Wrightsville Reservoir, res., Vt., U.S.	C3	122
Wrigley, N.W. Ter., Can.	D8	66
Wrocław (Breslau), Pol.	D17	8

Name	Map Ref	Page
Wuchuan, China	D11	34
Wudu, China	E7	26
Wugang, China	F9	26
Wuhan, China	E3	28
Wuhu, China	D7	28
Wunstorf, Ger.	C9	8
Wupatki National Monument, Az., U.S.	B4	80
Wuppertal, Ger.	D7	8
Wurtsmith Air Force Base, mil., Mi., U.S.	D7	99
Würzburg, Ger.	F9	8
Wurzen, Ger.	D12	8
Wushan, China	E8	26
Wushenqi, China	D8	26
Wusong, China	D10	28
Wutongqiao, China	F7	26
Wuwei, China	D7	26
Wuwei, China	D6	28
Wuxi (Wuhsi), China	D9	28
Wuyi Shan, mts., China	I5	28
Wuyuan, China	C8	26
Wuzhong, China	D8	26
Wuzhou (Wuchow), China	C11	34
Wyaconda, stm., Mo., U.S.	A6	102
Wyandot, co., Oh., U.S.	B2	112
Wyandotte, Mi., U.S.	F7	99
Wyandotte, co., Ks., U.S.	C9	93
Wyanet, Il., U.S.	B4	90
Wyk, Ger.	A8	8
Wylie, Lake, res., U.S.	A5	117
Wyman Lake, res., Me., U.S.	C3	96
Wymore, Ne., U.S.	D9	104
Wyndham, Austl.	C5	50
Wynndel, B.C., Can.	E9	69
Wynne, Ar., U.S.	B5	81
Wynnewood, Ok., U.S.	C4	113
Wynoochee, stm., Wa., U.S.	B2	124
Wyoming, Ont., Can.	E2	73
Wyoming, De., U.S.	D3	85
Wyoming, Il., U.S.	B4	90
Wyoming, Ia., U.S.	B6	92
Wyoming, Mi., U.S.	F5	99
Wyoming, Mn., U.S.	E6	100
Wyoming, Oh., U.S.	o13	112
Wyoming, Pa., U.S.	n17	115
Wyoming, R.I., U.S.	E2	116
Wyoming, co., N.Y., U.S.	C2	109
Wyoming, co., Pa., U.S.	D9	115
Wyoming, co., W.V., U.S.	D3	125
Wyoming, state, U.S.	C5	127
Wyoming Peak, mtn., Wy., U.S.	D2	127
Wyoming Range, mts., Wy., U.S.	D2	127
Wyomissing, Pa., U.S.	F10	115
Wysocking Bay, b., N.C., U.S.	B7	110
Wythe, co., Va., U.S.	D1	123
Wytheville, Va., U.S.	D1	123

X

Name	Map Ref	Page
Xai-Xai, Moz.	G6	44
Xangongo, Ang.	E3	44
Xánthi, Grc.	H8	16
Xapuri, Braz.	F5	54
Xenia, Oh., U.S.	C2	112
Xertigny, Fr.	D13	10
Xi, stm., China	G9	26
Xiaguan, China	E9	26
Xiahe, China	D7	26
Xiamen (Amoy), China	K7	28
Xi'an (Sian), China	E8	26
Xiangcheng, China	B2	28
Xiangfan, China	E9	26
Xiangkhoang, Laos	E7	34
Xiangride, China	D6	26
Xiangtan, China	H1	28
Xianyou, China	J7	28
Xiaogan, China	E2	28
Xiaolan, China	M2	28
Xiashi, China	E9	28
Xichang, China	F7	26
Xiegeer, China	F12	38
Xigazê, China	F13	38
Xihua, China	B3	28
Xilinhaote, China	C10	26
Xinavane, Moz.	G6	44
Xingtai, China	D9	26
Xingu, stm., Braz.	D8	54
Xingyi, China	B8	34
Xinhui, China	M2	28
Xining, China	D7	26
Xinjiang Uygur Zizhiqu, prov., China	B9	38
Xinxiang, China	D9	26
Xinyang, China	C3	28
Xiping, China	B3	28
Xique-Xique, Braz.	F10	54
Xizang Zizhiqu, prov., China	D12	38
Xuancheng, China	E7	28
Xuanhua, China	C10	26
Xuchang, China	A2	28
Xuwen, China	D11	34
Xuyong, China	F8	26
Xuzhou (Süchow), China	A6	28

Y

Name	Map Ref	Page
Yaan, China	E7	26
Yacolt, Wa., U.S.	D3	124
Yacuiba, Bol.	H6	54
Yādgīr, India	D4	37
Yadkin, co., N.C., U.S.	A2	110
Yadkin, stm., N.C., U.S.	B2	110
Yadkinville, N.C., U.S.	A2	110
Yainax Butte, mtn., Or., U.S.	E5	114
Yaizu, Japan	H11	30
Yakima, Wa., U.S.	C5	124
Yakima, co., Wa., U.S.	C4	124
Yakima, stm., Wa., U.S.	C6	124
Yakima Indian Reservation, Wa., U.S.	C5	124
Yakobi Island, i., Ak., U.S.	m21	79
Yakumo, Japan	q18	30a
Yaku-shima, i., Japan	u30	31b
Yakutat, Ak., U.S.	D12	79
Yakutat Bay, b., Ak., U.S.	D11	79
Yala, Thai.	K6	34
Yale, Mi., U.S.	E8	99
Yale, Ok., U.S.	A5	113
Yale, Mount, mtn., Co., U.S.	C5	83
Yale Lake, res., Wa., U.S.	D3	124
Yalobusha, co., Ms., U.S.	A4	101
Yalobusha, stm., Ms., U.S.	B4	101
Yalta, Ukr.	I4	22
Yalu (Amnok-kang), stm., Asia	C12	26
Yamachiche, Que., Can.	C5	74
Yamagata, Japan	D13	30
Yamaguchi, Japan	H4	30
Yamato-takada, Japan	H8	30
Yambio, Sudan	H11	42
Yamdena, Pulau, i., Indon.	G9	32
Yamethin, Mya.	D4	34
Yamhill, Or., U.S.	h11	114
Yamhill, co., Or., U.S.	B3	114
Yamoussoukro, C. Iv.	G4	42
Yampa, stm., Co., U.S.	A2	83
Yamsay Mountain, mtn., Or., U.S.	E5	114
Yamuna, stm., India	H9	38
Yanbu', Sau. Ar.	D2	46
Yancey, co., N.C., U.S.	f10	110
Yanceyville, N.C., U.S.	A3	110
Yanchang, China	D9	26
Yancheng, China	B9	28
Yandoon, Mya.	F3	34
Yangjiang, China	G9	26
Yangon (Rangoon), Mya.	B2	32
Yangquan, China	D9	26
Yangtze see Chang, stm., China	E10	26
Yangzhou, China	C8	28
Yanji, China	C12	26
Yankton, S.D., U.S.	E8	118
Yankton, co., S.D., U.S.	D8	118
Yanqi, China	C4	26
Yantai (Chefoo), China	D11	26
Yantic, stm., Ct., U.S.	C7	84
Yaoundé, Cam.	H8	42
Yapen, Pulau, i., Indon.	F10	32
Yaqui, stm., Mex.	C5	62
Yaraka, Austl.	D8	50
Yardley, Pa., U.S.	F12	115
Yardville, N.J., U.S.	C3	107
Yaritagua, Ven.	B8	58
Yarmouth, Me., U.S.	E2	96
Yarnell, Az., U.S.	C3	80
Yarumal, Col.	D5	58
Yashiro-jima, i., Japan	I5	30
Yates, co., N.Y., U.S.	C3	109
Yates Center, Ks., U.S.	E8	93
Yates City, Il., U.S.	C3	90
Yathkyed Lake, l., N.W. Ter., Can.	D13	66
Yatsushiro, Japan	J3	30
Yatta Plateau, plat., Kenya	B7	44
Yaupi, Ec.	I4	58
Yavapai, co., Az., U.S.	C3	80
Yavari (Javari), stm., S.A.	D4	54
Yavatmāl, India	B5	37
Yaví, Cerro, mtn., Ven.	E10	58
Yaviza, Pan.	J9	64
Yawatahama, Japan	I5	30
Yawgoog Pond, l., R.I., U.S.	E1	116
Yaxian, China	E10	34
Yazd, Iran	B5	46
Yazoo, co., Ms., U.S.	C3	101
Yazoo, stm., Ms., U.S.	C3	101
Yazoo City, Ms., U.S.	C3	101
Ye, Mya.	G4	34
Yeadon, Pa., U.S.	p21	115
Yeagertown, Pa., U.S.	E6	115
Yecheng, China	B7	38
Yecla, Spain	G10	12
Yei, stm., Sudan	G12	42
Yekaterinburg see Jekaterinburg, Russia	F10	22
Yell, co., Ar., U.S.	B2	81
Yell, i., Scot., U.K.	A11	7
Yellow, stm., U.S.	u15	86
Yellow, stm., In., U.S.	B4	91
Yellow, stm., Wi., U.S.	D3	126
Yellow, stm., Wi., U.S.	C3	126
Yellow Creek, stm., Tn., U.S.	A4	119
Yellowhead Pass, Can.	C1	68
Yellow see Huang, stm., China	D10	26
Yellowjacket Mountains, mts., Id., U.S.	D4	89
Yellowknife, N.W. Ter., Can.	D10	66
Yellow Lake, l., Wi., U.S.	C1	126
Yellow Medicine, co., Mn., U.S.	F2	100
Yellow Sea, Asia	D11	26
Yellow Springs, Oh., U.S.	C2	112
Yellowstone, co., Mt., U.S.	D8	103
Yellowstone, stm., U.S.	D10	103
Yellowstone Lake, l., Wy., U.S.	B2	127
Yellowstone National Park, co., Mt., U.S.	E6	103
Yellowstone National Park, U.S.	B2	127
Yellville, Ar., U.S.	A3	81
Yelm, Wa., U.S.	C3	124
Yemassee, S.C., U.S.	F6	117
Yemen, ctry., Asia	E4	46
Yenangyaung, Mya.	D3	34
Yen Bai, Viet.	D8	34
Yendéré, Burkina	F5	42
Yendi, Ghana	G5	42
Yenisey see Jenisej, stm., Russia	D11	24
Yenshui, Tai.	L9	28
Yentna, stm., Ak., U.S.	f16	79
Yeovil, Eng., U.K.	K10	7
Yerevan see Jerevan, Arm.	I6	22
Yerington, Nv., U.S.	E2	105
Yerington Indian Reservation, Nv., U.S.	D2	105
Yermasóyia, Cyp.	B3	40
Yermo, Ca., U.S.	E5	82
Yerupajá, Nevado, mtn., Peru	F3	54
Yerushalayim (Jerusalem), Isr.	D4	40
Yeste, Spain	G9	12
Yevpatoriya, Ukr.	H4	22
Yexian, China	B2	28
Yiannitsá, Grc.	I6	16
Yibin, China	F7	26
Yichang, China	E9	26
Yichun, China	B12	26
Yichun, China	H3	28
Yilan, China	B12	26
Yiliang, China	B7	34
Yinchuan, China	D8	26
Yingde, China	K2	28
Yingkou, China	C11	26
Yining, China	C3	26
Yirga Alem, Eth.	G2	46
Yishan, China	B10	34
Yíthion, Grc.	M6	16
Yituliho, China	A11	26
Yiyang, China	F9	26
Ylivieska, Fin.	D15	6
Ynykčanskij, Russia	E21	24
Yoakum, Tx., U.S.	E4	120
Yoakum, co., Tx., U.S.	C1	120
Yockanookany, stm., Ms., U.S.	C4	101
Yocona, stm., Ms., U.S.	A4	101
Yogyakarta, Indon.	m15	32
Yoho National Park, B.C., Can.	D9	69
Yokkaichi, Japan	H9	30
Yokohama, Japan	G12	30
Yokosuka, Japan	G12	30
Yokote, Japan	C13	30
Yola, Nig.	G8	42
Yolo, co., Ca., U.S.	C2	82
Yolombó, Col.	D5	58
Yomba Indian Reservation, Nv., U.S.	D4	105
Yonago, Japan	G6	30
Yoncalla, Or., U.S.	D3	114
Yonezawa, Japan	E13	30
Yongdeng, China	D7	26
Yongdingzhen, China	A6	34
Yongfeng, China	H4	28
Yonkers, N.Y., U.S.	E7	109
Yopal, Col.	E6	58
York, Ont., Can.	D5	73
York, Eng., U.K.	H11	7
York, Al., U.S.	C1	78
York, Me., U.S.	E2	96
York, Ne., U.S.	D8	104
York, Pa., U.S.	G8	115
York, S.C., U.S.	B5	117
York, co., Me., U.S.	E2	96
York, co., Ne., U.S.	D8	104
York, co., Pa., U.S.	G8	115
York, co., S.C., U.S.	A5	117
York, co., Va., U.S.	C6	123
York, stm., Ont., Can.	B7	73
York, stm., Va., U.S.	C6	123
York, Cape, c., Austl.	B8	50
York Beach, Me., U.S.	E2	96
York Harbor, Me., U.S.	E2	96
Yorklyn, De., U.S.	A3	85
Yorktown, In., U.S.	D7	91
Yorktown, Tx., U.S.	E4	120
Yorktown, Va., U.S.	C6	123
Yorktown Manor, R.I., U.S.	E4	116
Yorkville, Il., U.S.	B5	90
Yorkville, N.Y., U.S.	B5	109
Yorkville, Oh., U.S.	B5	112
Yoro, Hond.	G4	64
Yoron-jima, i., Japan	x28	31b
Yosemite National Park, Ca., U.S.	D4	82
Yŏsu, S. Kor.	E12	26
Youbou, B.C., Can.	g11	69
Youghal, Ire.	J5	7
Youghiogheny, stm., U.S.	F2	115
Youghiogheny River Lake, res., U.S.	G3	115
Young, Az., U.S.	C5	80
Young, co., Tx., U.S.	C3	120
Young Harris, Ga., U.S.	B3	87
Youngs, Lake, l., Wa., U.S.	f11	124
Youngstown, N.Y., U.S.	B1	109
Youngstown, Oh., U.S.	A5	112
Youngsville, La., U.S.	D3	95
Youngsville, Pa., U.S.	C3	115
Youngtown, Az., U.S.	k8	80
Youngwood, Pa., U.S.	F2	115
Youyang, China	F8	26
Ypres see Ieper, Bel.	E2	8
Ypsilanti, Mi., U.S.	F7	99
Yreka, Ca., U.S.	B2	82
Yssingeaux, Fr.	G11	10
Ystad, Swe.	I9	6
Yu, stm., China	C10	34
Yuanling, China	F9	26
Yuba, co., Ca., U.S.	C3	82
Yuba, stm., Ca., U.S.	C3	82
Yuba City, Ca., U.S.	C3	82
Yūbari, Japan	p19	30a
Yucatan Channel, strt., N.A.	C4	64
Yucatan Peninsula, pen., N.A.	H15	62
Yucca Lake, l., Nv., U.S.	F5	105
Yucca Mountain, mtn., Nv., U.S.	G5	105
Yuci, China	D9	26
Yueyang, China	F2	28
Yugoslavia, ctry., Eur.	G11	4
Yukon, Ok., U.S.	B4	113
Yukon, prov., Can.	D6	66
Yukon, stm., N.A.	m19	76a
Yukuhashi, Japan	I3	30
Yulee, Fl., U.S.	B5	86
Yulin, China	D8	26
Yulin, China	C11	34
Yuma, Az., U.S.	E1	80
Yuma, Co., U.S.	A8	83
Yuma, co., Az., U.S.	E1	80
Yuma, co., Co., U.S.	A8	83
Yuma Marine Corps Air Station, mil., Az., U.S.	E1	80
Yumen, China	D6	26
Yuncheng, China	D9	26
Yunnan, prov., China	F7	26
Yurimaguas, Peru	E3	54
Yuriria, Mex.	G9	62
Yü Shan, mtn., Tai.	L9	28
Yushu, China	E6	26
Yutan, Ne., U.S.	C9	104
Yutian, China	B9	38
Yuty, Para.	B5	56
Yuxian, China	A2	28
Yuyao, China	E10	28
Yverdon, Switz.	F13	10
Yvetot, Fr.	C7	10

Z

Name	Map Ref	Page
Zaandam, Neth.	C4	8
Zabīd, Yemen	F3	46
Zabrze, Pol.	E18	8
Zacapa, Guat.	G3	64
Zacapu, Mex.	H9	62
Zacatecas, Mex.	F8	62
Zachary, La., U.S.	D4	95
Zacualtipán, Mex.	G10	62
Zadar, Cro.	E10	14
Zadetkyi Kyun, i., Mya.	J5	34
Zafer Burnu, c., N. Cyp.	B4	40
Zafra, Spain	G5	12
Zagreb, Cro.	D10	14
Zāgros, Kūhhā-ye, mts., Iran	B5	46
Zāhedān, Iran	C7	46
Zahlah, Leb.	C4	40
Zaire, ctry., Afr.	B4	44
Zajsan, Kaz.	H10	24
Zajsan, Ozero, l., Kaz.	H10	24
Zákinthos, i., Grc.	L4	16
Zakopane, Pol.	F19	8
Zalaegerszeg, Hung.	I16	8
Zambezi (Zambeze), stm., Afr.	E6	44
Zambia, ctry., Afr.	D5	44
Zamboanga, Phil.	D7	32
Zamfara, stm., Nig.	F7	42
Zamora, Ec.	J3	58
Zamora, Spain	D6	12
Zamora de Hidalgo, Mex.	H8	62
Zamość, Pol.	E23	8
Zanesville, Oh., U.S.	C4	112
Zanjān, Iran	J7	22
Zanzibar, Tan.	C7	44
Zanzibar, i., Tan.	C7	44
Zaouia el Kahla, Alg.	C7	42
Zaouiet el Mgaïz, Tun.	M5	14
Zaoz'ornyj, Russia	F12	24
Zapadnyj Sajan, mts., Russia	G12	24
Zapala, Arg.	D2	56
Zapata, Tx., U.S.	F3	120
Zapata, co., Tx., U.S.	F3	120
Zapata, Península de, pen., Cuba	C7	64
Zaporizhzhya, Ukr.	H5	22
Zaragoza, Spain	D11	12
Zarajsk, Russia	G21	18
Zárate, Arg.	C5	56
Zaraza, Ven.	C10	58
Zard Kūh, mtn., Iran	B5	46
Zarembo Island, i., Ak., U.S.	m23	79
Zarghūn Shahr, Afg.	D3	38
Zaria, Nig.	F7	42
Żary (Sorau), Pol.	D15	8
Zarzal, Col.	E4	58
Zāskār, stm., India	D7	38
Zāskār Mountains, mts., Asia	C4	36
Zavala, co., Tx., U.S.	E3	120
Zavolžje, Russia	E26	18
Zavolžsk, Russia	D25	18
Zawiercie, Pol.	E19	8
Zduńska Wola, Pol.	D18	8
Zearing, Ia., U.S.	B4	92
Zebulon, Ga., U.S.	C2	87
Zebulon, N.C., U.S.	B4	110
Zeehan, Austl.	H9	50
Zeeland, Mi., U.S.	F5	99
Zeerust, S. Afr.	G5	44
Zehdenick, Ger.	C13	8
Zeigler, Il., U.S.	F4	90
Zeila, Som.	F3	46
Zeitz, Ger.	D12	8
Zeja, Russia	G19	24
Zeja, stm., Russia	G19	24
Železnogorsk-Ilimskij, Russia	F14	24
Zelienople, Pa., U.S.	E1	115
Zelina, Cro.	D11	14
Zell, Ger.	E7	8
Zell am See, Aus.	H12	8
Zemio, Cen. Afr. Rep.	G11	42
Zenica, Bos.	E12	14
Zenith, Wa., U.S.	f11	124
Zenobia Peak, mtn., Co., U.S.	A2	83
Zephyr Cove, Nv., U.S.	E2	105
Zephyrhills, Fl., U.S.	D4	86
Zerbst, Ger.	D12	8
Zereh, Gowd-e, l., Afg.	D1	36
Zermatt, Switz.	F14	10
Zeytindağ, Tur.	K11	16
Zgierz, Pol.	D19	8
Zhalutegi, China	C11	26
Zhangjiakou (Kalgan), China	C9	26
Zhangzhou (Longxi), China	K6	28
Zhanjiang, China	D11	34
Zhaoan, China	L6	28
Zhaotong, China	F7	26
Zhaxigang, China	D8	38
Zhejiang, prov., China	F10	26
Zhengzhou, China	E9	26
Zhenjiang, China	C8	28
Zhenyuan, China	F8	26
Zhob, stm., Pak.	E3	38
Zhongba, China	F10	38
Zhongshan, China	M2	28
Zhoushan Dao, i., China	E11	28
Zhoushan Qundao, is., China	E10	28
Zhujiangkou, stm., Asia	M2	28
Zhumadian, China	C3	28
Zhungeerqi, China	D9	26
Zhuoxian, China	D10	26
Zhuzhou, China	H2	28
Zhytomyr, Ukr.	G3	22
Zia Indian Reservation, N.M., U.S.	h7	108
Zibo, China	D10	26
Ziebach, co., S.D., U.S.	C4	118
Ziel, Mount, mtn., Austl.	D6	50
Zielona Góra (Grünberg), Pol.	D15	8
Žigalovo, Russia	G15	24
Žigansk, Russia	D18	24
Zigong, China	F7	26
Ziguinchor, Sen.	F2	42
Zihuatanejo, Mex.	I9	62
Žilina, Slov.	F18	8
Zillah, Wa., U.S.	C5	124
Zillertaler Alpen, mts., Eur.	B6	14
Zilwaukee, Mi., U.S.	E7	99
Zima, Russia	G14	24
Zimbabwe, ctry., Afr.	E5	44
Zimmerman, Mn., U.S.	E5	100
Zinder, Niger	F7	42
Zion, Il., U.S.	A6	90
Zion National Park, Ut., U.S.	F3	121
Zion Reservoir, res., Az., U.S.	C6	80
Zionsville, In., U.S.	E5	91
Zipaquirá, Col.	E5	58
Zirkel, Mount, mtn., Co., U.S.	A4	83
Ziro, India	G15	38
Zitácuaro, Mex.	H9	62
Zittau, Ger.	E14	8
Ziway, Lake, l., Eth.	G2	46
Žižickoje, Ozero, l., Russia	E14	18
Zlarin, Cro.	F10	14
Zlín, Czech.	F17	8
Žlobin, Bela.	I13	18
Zmeinogorsk, Russia	G10	24
Znojmo, Czech.	G16	8
Zolfo Springs, Fl., U.S.	E5	86
Zomba, Mwi.	E7	44
Zonguldak, Tur.	G14	4
Zorita, Spain	F6	12
Zouar, Chad	D9	42
Zrenjanin, Yugo.	D4	16
Zuckerhütl, mtn., Aus.	I11	8
Zudañez, Bol.	G6	54
Zuera, Spain	D11	12
Zug, Switz.	E15	10
Zugspitze, mtn., Eur.	H10	8
Zuiderzee see IJsselmeer, Neth.	C5	8
Zumba, Ec.	J3	58
Zumbo, Moz.	E6	44
Zumbro, stm., Mn., U.S.	F6	100
Zumbrota, Mn., U.S.	F6	100
Zuni (Zuni Pueblo), N.M., U.S.	B1	108
Zuni, stm., U.S.	C6	80
Zuni Indian Reservation, N.M., U.S.	B1	108
Zuni Mountains, mts., N.M., U.S.	B1	108
Zunyi, China	F8	26
Zuqar, Jazīrat, i., Yemen	F3	46
Zurich, Ont., Can.	D3	73
Zürich, Switz.	E15	10
Zürichsee, l., Switz.	E15	10
Zutphen, Neth.	C6	8
Zvishavane, Zimb.	F6	44
Zvolen, Slov.	G19	8
Zwettl, Aus.	G15	8
Zwickau, Ger.	E12	8
Zwolle, Neth.	C6	8
Zwolle, La., U.S.	C2	95
Zyr'anka, Russia	D24	24
Żyrardów, Pol.	C20	8